P9-DGJ-959

A HISTORY OF
TECHNOLOGY

A HISTORY OF
TECHNOLOGY

EDITED BY

CHARLES SINGER · E. J. HOLMYARD
and A. R. HALL

ASSISTED BY

E. JAFFÉ · R. H. G. THOMSON
and J. M. DONALDSON

VOLUME I

FROM EARLY TIMES
TO FALL OF
ANCIENT EMPIRES

1954

OXFORD UNIVERSITY PRESS
NEW YORK and LONDON

Oxford University Press, Amen House, London E.C.4
GLASGOW NEW YORK TORONTO MELBOURNE WELLINGTON
BOMBAY CALCUTTA MADRAS KARACHI CAPE TOWN IBADAN
Geoffrey Cumberlege, Publisher to the University

THE LIBRARY OF SCIENCE EDITION FIRST PUBLISHED OCTOBER, 1957
REPRINTED BY ARRANGEMENT WITH OXFORD UNIVERSITY PRESS
MANUFACTURED IN THE UNITED STATES

PREFACE

For the endowment that has made possible the preparation of *A History of Technology* the editors are indebted to Imperial Chemical Industries Limited. The Chairman and Directors intend this volume and the four that will follow primarily as a contribution to technical education. The editors hope that their feelings towards this great corporation for its enlightened patronage will be shared by their readers.

The main object of this work is to provide students of technology and applied science with some humane and historical background for their studies. They may thus be helped to realize that the subjects of their special training are parts of a very ancient process and are rooted in many civilizations. These volumes will not treat of such recent history of applied science and technology as must normally find some place in a technical education. They aim rather at providing a longer perspective of the ways in which the immensely complex technical knowledge of our civilization has come into being.

In planning this work the editors have had in mind the needs of those who have little acquaintance with either the history of science or that of man. They are convinced of the human value, in our technological civilization, of an understanding of the methods and skills by which man has attained a gradual easing of his earthly lot through mastery of his natural environment. They have not, however, sought to provide, even in outline, a history of material civilization as a whole, but have felt justified in concentrating upon one of its aspects—a history of how things have been done or made. They hope therefore that their work may also prove useful as an auxiliary to the more specialist studies of historians, archaeologists, and other scholars.

This first volume opens with the humblest beginnings of the making and use of tools, the most important of which is that most characteristically human tool called 'language'. Thus it starts more than half a million years ago, as man is becoming man. It ends long before the Christian era, but when human dexterity had already so marvellously developed that it has never since been excelled. Long before there was anything that we can recognize as self-conscious science, long before steel or even iron had come into general use, long before there existed any conception of an inhabited world as a whole, long before any fuel was available other than wood and charcoal or any roads but tracks, men had produced such masterpieces of dexterity as the Gebel-el-Arak knife of flint and ivory of about 3800 B.C. (figure 458), such triumphs of portraiture as that of Sargon I of about 2250 B.C. (figure 424), and a work of such unsurpassed technical skill as the inner coffin of Tutankhamen of about 1350 B.C. (frontispiece). No one who has in mind the amount of training, experience, and technical skill necessary to produce these results can dismiss the history of early technology as wholly without bearing on the state of our own society or disregard the attainments of the men who made these things.

This work is intended for continuous reading, being designed as a course of study. In dealing with an enormous field of knowledge the editors have thought it best to omit consideration of subjects adequately treated elsewhere in accessible works. They have excluded from their survey, for example, the development of medicine, of architecture, and of certain other arts. Moreover, the technological records of further Asia have been almost entirely omitted, both for lack of authors with sufficient knowledge and also because the more ancient civilizations in that area have had relatively little direct influence on Western cultures. Aspects of their indirect influence will be considered in later volumes.

The text of this volume, after opening with man as everywhere a hunter, concentrates on the formation of the earliest settled societies. It then considers those of the Near East which produced there the first 'civilizations'. Subsequent volumes will show how the technology of the Near East spread to the Mediterranean and diffused to the north and west of Europe. It may be thought that the editors have chosen too narrow a field, but they feel that the time is not yet ripe, their space is not adequate, and the authors are not yet available to tell the history of technology on a global scale. They are well aware that their attempt is incomplete and to be regarded as merely a tentative effort.

These volumes will not provide full bibliographies, but many of the chapters provide short reading lists. Anything beyond this seems superfluous because our colleague and contributor Professor R. J. Forbes, of Amsterdam, has been producing since 1942 regular numbers of his '*Bibliographia Antiqua*' which contains many thousands of references to writings on the history of technology, arranged under headings not dissimilar to those of our chapters. Other very full bibliographies are accessible in the 'Transactions of the Newcomen Society for the Study of the History of Engineering & Technology', now in its 25th volume, and in 'Isis, an International Review of the History of Science & Civilization', now in its 45th volume.

The discussion of a few points as to the range of our work may help some readers. A preliminary question that may be asked is 'What is Technology?' It would hardly be useful to consider elaborately a term the range of which it is the purpose of the work itself to indicate. Etymologically 'technology' should mean the systematic treatment of any thing or subject. In English it is a modern (seventeenth-century) artificial formation invented to designate systematic discourse about the (useful) arts. Not until the nineteenth century did the term acquire a scientific content and come ultimately to be regarded as almost synonymous with 'applied science'. Professor V. Gordon Childe has given some attention to the scope of technology (p 38). The editors have treated it as covering the field of how things are commonly done or made, extending it somewhat to describe what things are done or made. Obviously in an account of the happenings during many thousands of years, only a minute proportion of the kinds of these things can be included. The choice has been determined partly by space but even more by the imperfect state of present knowledge on many topics. The history of technology is a newly organized subject; much may be hoped from further research. Ours is, we believe, the first attempt to set out the subject in English, though the 'Transactions of the Newcomen Society' began to appear in 1922 under the editorship of the late Dr H. W. Dickinson.

Technology is an aspect of history and specially of social history. It might have been well, though it proved impracticable, to preface this volume by another giving an outline of social history for the period covered. The place of such a preliminary volume has been partly filled by the chronological tables that have been drawn up by Professor F. E. Zeuner on pp xlviii–lv, to which the reader will have constantly to refer. For those untrained in history we would suggest the amplification of these, as time permits, by such a work as J. H. Breasted's 'Ancient Times' or Professor Ralph Turner's 'The Great Society'. Conversely we believe that the reading of 'A History of Technology' will help him in the study and understanding of such works.

It is necessary, in the interests of intelligibility, to relate the development of any human activity to the leading events of political and economic history, that is, to 'history' in the ordinary sense. But the progress of technology does not altogether fit this familiar pattern. It has its own chronology, its own critical phases. The reader must constantly bear this in mind, for he will find that some techniques were most highly developed by peoples who played a relatively modest role in the great historical drama and made but short entries therein. Examples in this first volume are the tiny and divided states of Phoenicia which gave the alphabet to the world (pp 763–4) and were the great workers of ivory (ch 24) in antiquity. Another example is the short-lived polity of the Etruscans, who produced marvels of deftness in gold work (pp 657–8), but whose culture was early overwhelmed and absorbed by the growing might of Rome. A third and striking example is provided by certain Neolithic barbarians of Britain who reared Stonehenge under the influence or guidance of an expiring Aegean culture (pp 490–4).

Many problems have been presented by technical terms. These the editors have sought to reduce to a minimum and to ensure that none beyond the range of a normal scientific education should be admitted without definition. They found, however, that neither all topics nor all contributors are equally amenable to the elimination of technical terms.

Much of the bibliographical work has been done by Miss Judith Moore, and friendly assistance has been given us by the officials of many libraries, including those of the British Museum, the Institute of Archaeology of the University of London, the London Library, the Patent Office, the Royal Anthropological Institute, and the Warburg Institute.

For this volume the editors have had much help. They should acknowledge specially that of Dr C. J. T. Cronshaw and Dr F. A. Freeth, both lately of I.C.I., to whom first occurred the idea that this history embodies. Sir Wallace Akers, formerly Research Director of I.C.I., has read all the proofs of this volume in galley and has given much useful help. Professor V. Gordon Childe, Dr O. G. S. Crawford, and Professor R. J. Forbes have not only made many suggestions but also helped in the design of the work. Mr W. J. Worboys, a Director of I.C.I., has throughout taken much sympathetic interest in the progress of the work. Special care has been taken with illustrations. The source of the figures is acknowledged in the list of illustrations, and in their preparation we have had the valuable services of Mr D. E. Woodall, and, in special cases, also those of Mrs Nina de Garis Davies, Mr Thomas A. Greeves, and Mr Maurice Wilson, as well as Mr Desmond Wyeth and the late Mr R. J. Beeching of the Kynoch Press, Birmingham. The Indexes have been made by Mr P. G. Burbidge. Much technical help has been most generously and freely given by the staff of 'Endeavour' and notably by Dr Trevor I. Williams, Miss E. G. Farmer, and Miss Y. Shute.

Lastly, though the late H. W. Dickinson was too old and ill to contribute directly to these volumes, no one who knew him or knows his work will have difficulty in tracing his influence here. His advice and help were fundamental for the first planning of 'A History of Technology'.

CHARLES SINGER
E. J. HOLMYARD
A. R. HALL

CONTENTS

LIST OF ILLUSTRATIONS, TABLES, AND MAPS xiii

LIST OF ABBREVIATIONS xli

CHRONOLOGICAL TABLES by F. E. ZEUNER, Professor of Environmental Archaeology in the University of London xlviii

MAPS lvii

PART I

BASIC SOCIAL FACTORS

1. SKILL AS A HUMAN POSSESSION by KENNETH P. OAKLEY, Senior Principal Scientific Officer, British Museum (Natural History) 1

2. EARLY FORMS OF SOCIETY by V. GORDON CHILDE, Professor of Prehistoric European Archaeology in the University of London 38

3. DISCOVERY, INVENTION, AND DIFFUSION by H. S. HARRISON 58

4. SPEECH AND LANGUAGE by A. SOMMERFELT, Professor of General Philology in the University of Oslo 85

5. PRIMITIVE TIME-RECKONING by E. R. LEACH, Lecturer in Anthropology in the University of Cambridge 110

PART II

FOOD-COLLECTING STAGE

6. WORKING STONE, BONE, AND WOOD by L. S. B. LEAKEY, Curator of the Coryndon Memorial Museum, Nairobi, Kenya 128

7. GRAPHIC AND PLASTIC ARTS by L. S. B. LEAKEY 144

8. FORAGING, HUNTING, AND FISHING by DARYLL FORDE, Professor of Anthropology in the University of London; Director, International African Institute, London 154

PART III

DOMESTIC ACTIVITIES

9. ROTARY MOTION by V. GORDON CHILDE 187

10. FIRE-MAKING, FUEL, AND LIGHTING by H. S. HARRISON 216

11. CHEMICAL, CULINARY, AND COSMETIC ARTS by R. J. FORBES, Professor of Pure and Applied Sciences in Antiquity, University of Amsterdam 238

12. BUILDING IN WATTLE, WOOD, AND TURF by JOHN BRADFORD, Lecturer in Ethnology, University of Oxford 299

PART IV

SPECIALIZING INDUSTRIES

13. DOMESTICATION OF ANIMALS by F. E. ZEUNER 327

14. CULTIVATION OF PLANTS by F. E. ZEUNER 353

15. POTTERY by the late SIR LINDSAY SCOTT, K.B.E., D.S.C. 376

16. TEXTILES, BASKETRY, AND MATS by GRACE M. CROWFOOT, Munro Lecturer (Primitive Weaving) at the University of Edinburgh 1951 413

with *A Note on the Materials of Ancient Textiles and Baskets* by JULIUS GRANT, Analytical and Consulting Chemist,

and *Rope-Making* by K. R. GILBERT, Assistant Keeper in the Science Museum, London

17. BUILDING IN BRICK AND STONE by SETON LLOYD, O.B.E., Director, British Institute of Archaeology, Ankara 456

with *A Note on Stonehenge* by R. H. G. THOMSON, Editorial Staff, History of Technology

18. DIFFERENTIATION OF NON-METALLIC TOOLS by S. M. COLE, Author of *The Prehistory of East Africa* 495

19. WATER-SUPPLY, IRRIGATION, AND AGRICULTURE by M. S. DROWER, M.B.E., Lecturer in Ancient History, University of London 520

PART V

UTILIZATION OF METALS

20. MINING AND QUARRYING by the late C. N. BROMEHEAD, District Geologist for South-Eastern England on the staff of the Geological Survey and Museum, London 558

21. EXTRACTING, SMELTING, AND ALLOYING by R. J. FORBES 572

22. METAL IMPLEMENTS AND WEAPONS by H. H. COGHLAN, Curator, Newbury Museum, Berks. 600

23. FINE METAL-WORK by HERBERT MARYON, Research Laboratory Attaché, British Museum, and H. J. PLENDERLEITH, M.C., Keeper, Research Laboratory, British Museum 623

24. FINE IVORY-WORK by R. D. BARNETT, Deputy Keeper in the Department of Egyptian and Assyrian Antiquities, British Museum 663

25. FINE WOOD-WORK by CYRIL ALDRED, Assistant Keeper in the Royal Scottish Museum, Edinburgh 684

PART VI

TRANSPORT

26. LAND TRANSPORT WITHOUT WHEELS. ROADS AND BRIDGES by S. M. COLE 704

27. WHEELED VEHICLES by V. GORDON CHILDE 716

28. BOATS AND SHIPS by ADRIAN DIGBY, Keeper of Ethnography, British Museum 730

PART VII

THE PREPARATION FOR SCIENCE

29. RECORDING AND WRITING by S. H. HOOKE, Professor Emeritus of Old Testament Studies, University of London 744

30. MEASURES AND WEIGHTS by F. G. SKINNER, O.B.E., Deputy Keeper, Science Museum, London 774

31. ANCIENT MATHEMATICS AND ASTRONOMY by O. NEUGEBAUER, Professor of the History of Mathematics, Brown University, Rhode Island, U.S.A. 785

INDEXES 805

PLATES *at end*

ILLUSTRATIONS, TABLES, AND MAPS

Part of the lid of the third and inmost coffin of Tutankhamen, last king of the Eighteenth Dynasty. c *1350* B.C.
Painting by Nina de Garis Davies FRONTISPIECE

TEXT-FIGURES*

I. SKILL AS A HUMAN POSSESSION *by* K. P. OAKLEY

1 *Burrowing Wasp* Ammophila. Drawing by M. Wilson 2

2 *One of the Darwin Finches.* Drawing by M. Wilson based on D. L. LACK. 'Darwin's Finches', fig. 10. Cambridge, University Press, 1947 3

3 *Greater Spotted Woodpecker.* Drawing by M. Wilson based on a sketch by Margaret Tracy 4

4 *Southern Sea-otter.* Drawing by M. Wilson based on E. FISHER. *J. Mammal.* **20,** 30, fig. 16, 1939. Baltimore, American Society of Mammalogists 5

5 (A) *Tree-shrew.* (B) *Spectral tarsier.* After W. E. LE GROS CLARK. 'History of the Primates', Frontis. London, British Museum (Nat. Hist.), 1950. (C) *Baboon.* London, British Museum (Nat. Hist.). Drawing by M. Wilson 8

6 *Reconstruction of* Proconsul. London, British Museum (Nat. Hist.). Drawing by M. Wilson 9

7 *Brachiating ape.* London, British Museum (Nat. Hist.). Drawing by M. Wilson 10

8 *Modification of pelvic girdle.* Drawing by M. Wilson 11

9 *Chimpanzee making a tool.* Drawing by M. Wilson based on W. KÖHLER. 'The Mentality of Apes', Pl. III. London, Routledge & Kegan Paul, 1927 15

10 *The human brain.* London, British Museum (Nat. Hist.). Drawing by M. Wilson 17

11 *Dentition of* (A) *gorilla and* (B) *modern man.* From M. BOULE. 'Les Hommes Fossiles' (3rd ed.), fig. 39. Paris, Masson, 1921 21

12 *Tools of Pekin man.* From K. P. OAKLEY. 'Man the Tool-Maker' (2nd ed.), figs. 32 a, c; 6 b. London, British Museum (Nat. Hist.), 1950 24

13 *Quartzite pebble-tool.* Bulawayo, National Museum. After N. JONES. 'The Prehistory of Southern Rhodesia.' Nat. Mus. Southern Rhodesia Mem. 2, fig. 11. Cambridge, University Press, 1949. D. Wyeth 25

14 (A) *Acheulian hand-axe.* By courtesy of Pitt Rivers Museum, Oxford. (B) *Late Palaeolithic miniature burin.* By courtesy of British Museum (Nat. Hist.), London 26

15 *Acheulian cleaver.* London, British Museum (Nat. Hist.). From K. P. OAKLEY. 'Man the Tool-Maker' (2nd ed.), fig. 19 c. London, British Museum (Nat. Hist.), 1950 27

16 *Clactonian artifacts.* (A) *Core.* (B) *Flake-tool.* London, British Museum (Nat. Hist.). From K. P. OAKLEY. *Ibid.*, figs. 21 a, c 28

17 *East Asiatic chopper-tool.* From K. P. OAKLEY. *Ibid.*, fig. 20 d 29

18 *Wooden spear and flint 'spoke-shave'.* London, British Museum (Nat. Hist.). From K. P. OAKLEY. *Ibid.*, fig. 5 30

19 *Mousterian artifacts.* (A) *Flake point.* (B) *Side-scraper.* (C) *Bone compressor.* London, British Museum (Nat. Hist.). From K. P. OAKLEY. *Ibid.*, figs. 23 d, b; 9 d 31

20 *Upper Palaeolithic blade tools.* (A) *Solutrean piercer.* (B) *Magdalenian concave end-scraper.* (C) *Gravettian knife-point.* (D) *Magdalenian burin.* (E) *End-scraper.* London, British Museum (Nat. Hist.). From K. P. OAKLEY. *Ibid.*, figs. 24 k, o, b, g, j 32

21 *Upper Palaeolithic hafted weapon-tips.* (A) *Aurignacian split-base bone point.* (B) *Solutrean shouldered 'willow-leaf' point.* (C) *Aterian arrowhead.* (B) and (C) London, British Museum (Nat. Hist.). From K. P. OAKLEY. *Ibid.*, figs. 27 f; 26 b, f 33

22 *Upper Palaeolithic carving in ivory of a female figure.* From A. P. OKLADNIKOV. *Kratkie Soobshcheniya o Dokladakh i Polevykh Issledovaniyakh Instituta Istorii Material'noi Kultury.* Akademiya Nauk USSR, **5,** 60, fig. 10, 1940. (Short communications about papers and field investigations.) 34

* The names at the end of entries are those of the artists who drew the illustrations.

23 *Fine engraving on the incisor of a horse.* After L. PÉRICARD and S. LWOFF. *Bull. Soc. préhist. franç.* **37**, no. 21, 172, fig. 8, 1940. Paris, Société préhistorique française. D. Wyeth 34

TAILPIECES: *Distribution of Lower and Upper Palaeolithic industries* 36–7

2. EARLY FORMS OF SOCIETY *by* V. GORDON CHILDE

24 *Eskimo engravings.* (A) *Drying fish.* (B) *Reindeer-hunting.* From W. J. HOFFMANN. *Rep. Smithson. Instn* for 1895, Pl. LX, line 5; Pl. LXVII, line 4, 1897 41

25 *Predynastic corn-store.* After G. CATON-THOMPSON and E. W. GARDNER. 'The Desert Fayum', Pl. XXV, Silo 12. London, Royal Anthropological Institute, 1934. D. E. Woodall 42

26 *Storing the harvest.* From P. E. NEWBERRY. 'Beni Hasan', Part 1, Pl. XXIX. London, Egypt Exploration Society, 1893 43

27 *Diagrammatic section through a* tell *at Erech.* Based upon E. HEINRICH. 'Achter vorläufiger Bericht über die . . . Uruk-Warka Ausgrabungen.' *Abh. preuss. Akad. Wiss., phil.-hist. Kl.* 1936, no. 13, p. 28, fig. 1. Berlin, de Gruyter for Preussische Akademie. D. Wyeth 48

28 *The union of the Upper and Lower Nile.* Berlin, Staatl. Museen. After H. SCHÄFER and W. ANDRAE. 'Die Kunst des Alten Orients' (Propyläen-Kunstgeschichte Vol. 2), p. 285. Berlin, Propyläen Verlag, 1925. D. E. Woodall 49

29 *Macehead of the 'Scorpion King'.* Oxford, Ashmolean Museum, Department of Antiquities, No. E. 3632. D. E. Woodall 51

30 *Citadel of Harappa.* Plan based on R. E. M. WHEELER. *Ancient India*, no. 3, Pl. XV, 1947. Delhi, Archaeological Survey of India. T. A. Greeves. (Below) *an isometric diagram of a corn-store.* After M. S. VATS. 'Excavations at Harappā', Pl. VI. New Delhi, 1940. Copyright, Department of Archaeology, Govt. of India. D. E. Woodall 52

31 *'Clerks' of Tiglath-pileser III.* London, British Museum, No. 11882. After 'Assyrian Sculptures in the British Museum', Pl. XI b. London, 1938. By courtesy of the Trustees. D. E. Woodall 54

32 *Ships of Queen Hatshepsut's fleet.* After E. NAVILLE. 'The Temple of Deir el Bahari', Part 3, Pl. XXIV. London, Egypt Exploration Society, 1898. D. E. Woodall 55

TAILPIECE. *Barter in an Old Kingdom market.* After G. STEINDORFF. 'Das Grab des Ti', Pl. CXXXIII. Leipzig, Hinrichs, 1913. D. E. Woodall 57

3. DISCOVERY, INVENTION, AND DIFFUSION *by* H. S. HARRISON

33 *Wooden digging-stick with weight.* From W. J. SOLLAS. 'Ancient Hunters', fig. 254. London, Macmillan, 1924 59

34 *Andaman Islander stringing bow.* From 'Handbook to the Ethnographical Collections of the British Museum' (2nd ed.), fig. 67. London, British Museum, 1925. By courtesy of the Trustees 61

35 (A)–(C) *Wooden clubs.* (D)–(F) *Eskimo bone snow-knife, antler club, and blubber-hook.* (G), (H) *Iron knives.* From *ibid.*, figs. 145; 113; 249 d, b, e; 222 a; 224 c 63

36 *Pygmy pounding bark-cloth.* After P. SCHEBESTA. 'Revisiting my Pygmy Hosts', fig. facing p. 81. London, Hutchinson, 1936. T. A. Greeves 64

37 (A) *Flint hand-axe.* (B) *Flint ovate.* London, British Museum (Nat. Hist.). Drawn from original. D. E. Woodall 68

38 *Stone-bladed knives.* (A) *Obsidian.* (B) *Jasper.* From T. WILSON. *Rep. Smithson. Instn* for 1888, Pl. CVI, 78, 75, 1890 69

39 *Peasants threshing.* London, British Museum, Add. MS. 42130. After the Luttrell Psalter. Facs. edition by E. G. MILLAR, Pl. XXIII c. London, British Museum, 1932. By courtesy of the Trustees. D. E. Woodall 70

40 *Methods of hafting.* (A) *Axe, Neolithic.* After G. and A. DE MORTILLET. 'Musée Préhistorique' (2nd ed.), Pl. LII, 559. Paris, Costes, 1903. D. Wyeth. (B) *Axe, North Australia.* After W. B. SPENCER and F. J. GILLEN. 'The Northern Tribes of Central Australia', figs. 203, 203 a. London, Macmillan, 1904. D. E. Woodall. (C) *Adze, New Caledonia.* After 'Handbook to the Ethnographical Collections of the British Museum' (2nd ed.), fig. 106. London, British Museum, 1925. By courtesy of the Trustees. D. E. Woodall. (D) *Adze, New Guinea.* From J. EDGE-PARTINGTON. 'An Album of the Weapons, Tools, etc. of the Natives of the Pacific Islands', series 3, Pl. LXXXIV. Manchester. 1898 71

41 *Rotary quern in use.* Drawing by D. E. Woodall 72

42 *Early stage in the evolution of the wheel.* After J. R. HILDEBRAND. *Nat. geogr. Mag.* **54**, 544, 1928. Washington. By courtesy of National Geographic Society. D. E. Woodall 72

43 *Ploughing and hoeing in Egypt.* From P. E. NEWBERRY. 'Beni Hasan', Part I, Pl. XXIX. London, Egypt Exploration Society, 1893 73

TAILPIECE. *A spinning-wheel in Cyprus.* After M. O. WILLIAMS. *Nat. geogr. Mag.* **54**, 41, 1928. Washington. By courtesy of National Geographic Society. D. E. Woodall 84

4. SPEECH AND LANGUAGE *by* A. SOMMERFELT

TAILPIECE. *Building the Tower of Babel.* From A. M. HIND. 'An Introduction to a History of Woodcut', Vol. 2, p. 457, fig. 217. London, Constable, 1935 109

5. PRIMITIVE TIME-RECKONING *by* E. R. LEACH

44 *Egyptian shadow-clock.* Berlin, Staatl. Museen, No. 19743. After R. W. SLOLEY. *J. Egypt. Archaeol.* **17**, Pl. XVI, 5, 1931. London, Egypt Exploration Society. D. E. Woodall 112

45 *Modern Egyptian shadow-clock.* London, Science Museum, South Kensington. By courtesy of the Director. D. E. Woodall 113

46 *Primitive gnomon.* After C. HOSE and W. MCDOUGALL. 'The Pagan Tribes of Borneo', Vol. I, Pl. LX. London, Macmillan, 1912. T. A. Greeves 117

47 *Slit palm-leaf* (merkhet). Berlin, Staatl. Museen, No. 14085. After L. BORCHARDT. 'Altaegyptische Zeitmessung' in E. VON BASSERMANN-JORDAN. 'Die Geschichte der Zeitmessung und Uhren', Vol. I B, Pl. XVI. Berlin, Leipzig, Vereinigung wissenschaftlicher Verleger, 1920. D. E. Woodall. *Plumb-line.* London, Science Museum, South Kensington. By courtesy of the Director. D. E. Woodall 122

48 *Egyptian water-clock.* Cairo, Egyptian Museum. After R. W. SLOLEY. *J. Egypt. Archaeol.* **17**, Pl. XIX, 1931. London, Egypt Exploration Society. D. E. Woodall 122

49A *Ceiling of Senmut's tomb.* 49B *Northern panel of Senmut's ceiling.* After A. POGO. *Isis* **14**, Pls. XIX, XX, XII, 1930. Cambridge, Mass., History of Science Society. D. E. Woodall 122, 124

50 *Maya glyph.* London, British Museum, Copan D. After J. E. S. THOMPSON. 'Maya Hieroglyphic Writing', fig. 60. Washington, Carnegie Institution, 1950. D. E. Woodall 125

6. WORKING STONE, BONE, AND WOOD *by* L. S. B. LEAKEY

51 *Cones of percussion.* (A), (B) *Diagrams of cones.* (C) *An actual cone.* From L. S. B. LEAKEY. 'Adam's Ancestors', p. 53, fig. 2 a, b; p. 55, fig. 3 b. London, Methuen, 1934 129

52 *Direct percussion with hammer stone.* From K. P. OAKLEY. 'Man the Tool-Maker' (2nd ed.), fig. 11 a. London, British Museum (Nat. Hist.), 1950 130

53 *A Chellean* (*Abbevillian*) *hand-axe.* London, British Museum (Nat. Hist.). From K. P. OAKLEY. *Ibid.*, fig. 17 c 131

54 *An Acheulian handaxe.* From L. S. B. LEAKEY. 'Stone Age Africa', fig. 2. London, Methuen, 1936 132

55 *Levalloisian artifacts.* (A) *Tortoise-core.* (B) *Three views of a flake.* London, British Museum (Nat. Hist.). From K. P. OAKLEY. 'Man the Tool-Maker' (2nd ed.), figs. 22 a″, b. London, British Museum (Nat. Hist.), 1950 133

56 *Blade flake technique.* From (W. WATSON). 'Flint Implements', figs. 12 a, b, d. London, British Museum, 1950. By courtesy of the Trustees 134

57 *Preparing a core.* From L. PFEIFFER. 'Die steinzeitliche Technik und ihre Beziehungen zur Gegenwart' in 'Festschrift zur XLIII. allgemeinen Versammlung der deutschen Anthropologischen Gesellschaft', Heft I, p. 17, fig. 11. Jena, Fischer, 1912 135

58 *Flint core with blades replaced.* From J. EVANS. 'The Ancient Stone Implements, etc.', fig. 2. London, Longmans Green, 1872 135

59 *Technique for making burins.* Drawing by M. Wilson. *Magdalenian graver.* From K. P. OAKLEY. 'Man the Tool-Maker' (2nd ed.), fig. 24 g. London, British Museum (Nat. Hist.), 1950 136

60 *An Upper Palaeolithic backed blade.* Drawing by Mary Leakey 137

61 *Diagram of pressure flaking.* Based on W. H. HOLMES. 'Handbook of Aboriginal American Antiquities', *Bull. Bur. Amer. Ethnol.* **60**, i, fig. 174 b, 1919. Washington, Smithsonian Institution. D. Wyeth 138

62 *A* lame écaillée. Drawing by Mary Leakey 138

63 *Diagram of the double notch technique.* After W. F. RANKINE. *Res. Pap. Surrey Archaeol. Soc.* no. 2, p. 19, fig. 6, 1950. Guildford. D. Wyeth 138

64 *Grooving an antler.* After photograph by courtesy of Douglas Fisher. D. E. Woodall 140

7. GRAPHIC AND PLASTIC ARTS *by* L. S. B. LEAKEY

65 *Part of a ceiling at Pech-Merle.* From A. LEMOZI. 'La grotte-temple du Pech-Merle', Pl. XLIX. Paris, Picard, 1929 145

66 *Pestle in mammoth ivory.* After K. ABSOLON. *Ill. London News,* 21 March 1936, p. 502, fig. 10. D. E. Woodall 147

67 *Broken chalk mortar.* From L. CAPITAN *et al. Rev. Mens. Éc. Anthrop.* **18**, fig. 77, 1908. Paris, École d'Anthropologie 147

68 *Stag painted with the finger-tip.* From H. BREUIL and H. OBERMAIER. 'La Pileta a Benoajan (Malaga)', Pl. III. Monaco, Institut de Paléontologie Humaine (Paris), 1915 148

69 *Galloping reindeer engraved.* Saint-Germain-en-Laye, Musée des Antiquités Nationales. From E. CARTAILHAC and H. BREUIL. 'La caverne d'Altamira', p. 133, fig. 110. Monaco, Institut de Paléontologie Humaine (Paris), 1906–8 149

70 *Pecked engraving. Gjeithus, Norway.* After J. G. D. CLARK. *Antiquity* **11**, Pl. IV, foll. p. 64, 1937. Newbury, Edwards. D. Wyeth 150

71 *Polished rock drawing. Valle, Sweden.* After L. FROBENIUS and D. C. FOX. 'Prehistoric Rock Pictures in Europe and Africa', Pl. [II]. New York, Museum of Modern Art, 1937. By courtesy of the Frobenius Institut, Frankfurt a. M. D. Wyeth 150

72 *Sorcerer from the cave Trois-Frères.* From J. G. D. CLARK. 'From Savagery to Civilisation', p. 50, fig. 14. London, Cobbett Press, 1946 151

73 *Bisons from the cave Tuc d'Audoubert.* After H. BÉGOUEN. *Anthropologie, Paris* **23**, fig. 2 facing p. 660, 1912. Masson. D. E. Woodall 152

74 *Female figures from* (A) *Věstonice*; (B) *Laussel*; (C) *Willendorf.* (A), (C) From J. G. D. CLARK. 'From Savagery to Civilisation', figs. 15 c, b. London, Cobbett Press, 1946. (B) After G. LALANNE. *Anthropologie, Paris* **23**, 129–49, fig. 1, 1912. Masson. D. E. Woodall 152

TAILPIECE. *Ivory horse from Espélugues.* From E. PIETTE. *Anthropologie, Paris* **17**, 51, fig. 28, 1906. Masson 153

8. FORAGING, HUNTING, AND FISHING *by* DARYLL FORDE

75 (A) *Paviotso seed-collecting basket.* New York, American Museum of Natural History, No. 50, 1–7924. After R. H. LOWIE. *Anthrop. Pap. Amer. Mus.* **20**, iii, fig. 15, 1924. D. E. Woodall. (B) *Pomo seed-beater.* After S. A. BARRETT. 'Pomo Indians Basketry.' Univ. Calif. Publ. Amer. Archaeol. Ethn. Vol. 7, no. 3, Pl. XXIV, facing p. 296, fig. 1. Berkeley, University of California, 1908. D. E. Woodall 155

76 *Australian throwing-sticks.* After W. B. SPENCER. 'Guide to the Australian Ethnological Collection in the National Museum of Victoria' (2nd ed.), Pl. III. Melbourne. 1915. By courtesy of the Trustees. D. E. Woodall 155

77 *Arunta boy with throwing-stick.* After H. BASEDOW. 'The Australian Aboriginal', Pl. XIV, 1. Adelaide, Preece, 1925. D. E. Woodall 155

78 *Fowling with throwing-sticks.* From NORMAN DE G. DAVIES. 'Robb de Peyster Tytus Memorial Series I, The Tomb of Nakht at Thebes', Pl. XXII. New York, Metropolitan Museum of Art, 1917 156

79 *Mesolithic wooden throwing-sticks.* From J. G. D. CLARK. 'The Mesolithic Settlement of Northern Europe', fig. 54, nos. 1, 3. Cambridge, University Press, 1936 156

80 *Egyptian sling.* After W. M. F. PETRIE. 'Tools and Weapons', Pl. LI, V 14. London, British School of Egyptian Archaeology, 1917. D. E. Woodall 156

81 *Eskimo bird javelin.* After T. MATHIASSEN. 'Material Culture of the Iglulik Eskimos.' Danish Expedition to Arctic North America of K. Rasmussen, vol. 6, no. 1, fig. 34. Copenhagen, Gyldendal, 1928. T. A. Greeves 156

82 *Magdalenian spear-thrower.* From J. CABRÉ AGUILÓ. 'El arte rupestre en España.' Instituto nacional de ciencias físico-naturales, Comisión de investigaciones paleontológicas y prehistóricas, no. 1, p. 18, fig. 11. Madrid. 1915. *Spear-thrower in use.* From K. P. OAKLEY. 'Man the Tool-Maker' (2nd ed.), fig. 27 i. London, British Museum (Nat. Hist.), 1950 157

83 *Eskimo spear-thrower.* From F. BOAS. 'The Central Eskimo.' Rep. Bur. Amer. Ethnol. Vol. 6, fig. 434 a. Washington. 1888 159

84 *Eskimo seal-skin floats and drogue.* From F. BOAS. *Ibid.*, fig. 437 159

85 *Yahgan javelin.* After J. H. STEWARD. 'Handbook of South American Indians.' *Bull. Bur. Amer. Ethnol.* no. 143, i, 160, Pl. XXXVI, 1946. Washington, Smithsonian Institution. D. E. Woodall Inset from S. K. LOTHROP. 'The Indians of Tierra del Fuego.' Heye Foundation Vol. 10, fig. 80. New York, Museum of the American Indian, Heye Foundation, 1928 159

86 *Yahgan proto-harpoon.* From S. K. LOTHROP. *Ibid.*, fig. 82 159

87 *Nootka sealing harpoon.* From P. DRUCKER. 'The Northern and Central Nootkan Tribes.' *Bull. Bur. Amer. Ethnol.* no. 144, 27, fig. 8, 1951. Washington, Smithsonian Institution 160

88 *Late Magdalenian harpoon-heads.* From J. G. D. CLARK. 'Prehistoric Europe', fig. 8. After BREUIL. London, Methuen, 1952 160

89 *Upper Palaeolithic cave painting.* From H. OBERMAIER. 'Fossil Man in Spain', Pl. XIV. New Haven, Yale University Press (for the Hispanic Society of America), 1924 161

90 *Mesolithic bow-stave.* Copenhagen, Nationalmuseet. After J. G. D. CLARK. 'Prehistoric Europe', Pl. I, f. London, Methuen, 1952. D. E. Woodall 162

91 *Compound-composite Eskimo bow.* From F. BOAS. 'The Central Eskimo.' Rep. Bur. Amer. Ethnol. Vol. 6, fig. 440. Washington. 1888 162

92 *Bashkirian composite bow.* Leipzig, Stadtgeschichtl. Museum. (A) From G. BUSCHAN (Ed.). 'Illustrierte Völkerkunde', Vol. 2, ii (2nd ed.), p. 884, fig. 542. Stuttgart, Strecker und Schroeder, 1926. (B), (C) Diagrams. T. A. Greeves 163

93 *The 'Turkish' horseman's bow. Sassanian silver dish.* Leningrad, Hermitage State Museum. After K. ERDMANN. *Jb. preuss. Kunstsamml.* **57**, 201, fig. 4, 1936. Berlin, Grotesche Verlagsbuchhandlung. D. E. Woodall 163

94 *Blow-gun and dart.* After W. W. SKEAT and C. O. BLAGDEN. 'Pagan Races of the Malay Peninsula', Vol. I, fig. facing p. 282, nos. 3, 5, 7. London, Macmillan, 1906. T. A. Greeves 164

95 *Sakai with blow-guns.* After W. W. SKEAT and C. O. BLAGDEN. *Ibid.*, figs. facing pp. 299, 377, 305. T. A. Greeves 164

96 *Yahgan bird snare.* From J. H. STEWARD. 'Handbook of South American Indians.' *Bull. Bur. Amer. Ethnol.* no. 143 i, 85, fig. 11 d, 1946. Washington, Smithsonian Institution 165

97 *Bolas.* Berlin, Völkerkunde Museum. From G. BUSCHAN (Ed.). 'Illustrierte Völkerkunde', Vol. I (3rd ed.), fig. 124. Stuttgart, Strecker und Schroeder, 1922 165

98 *Hunting scenes on a stone palette.* London, British Museum, No. 20790. After *J. R. anthrop. Inst.* **30,** Pl. B, 1900. London. D. E. Woodall 165

99 *Bas-relief showing Assyrians hunting.* London, British Museum, No. 124871. After H. SCHÄFER and W. ANDRAE. 'Die Kunst des Alten Orients' (Propyläen-Kunstgeschichte Vol. 2), p. 535. Berlin, Propyläen Verlag, 1925. D. E. Woodall 167

100 *Mesolithic and Neolithic fish-hooks.* (A) *Maglemosian.* From J. G. D. CLARK. 'Prehistoric Europe', fig. 17. London, Methuen, 1952. (B) *Natufian.* (C) *Tasian.* From V. G. CHILDE. 'New Light on the Most Ancient East' (4th ed.), figs. 7, nos. 1, 2; 9. London, Routledge & Kegan Paul, 1952 167

101 *Mesolithic basketry trap.* Copenhagen, Nationalmuseet. After J. G. D. CLARK. 'Prehistoric Europe', Pl. II, c. London, Methuen, 1952. D. E. Woodall 167

102 *Yokuts leaching acorn meal.* After W. H. HOLMES. *Rep. Smithson. Instn* for 1900, Pls. X, a; XIV, b, 1902. Washington, Smithsonian Institution. T. A. Greeves 174

103 *Plan of Nootka whaling canoe.* From P. DRUCKER. 'The Northern and Central Nootkan Tribes.' *Bull. Bur. Amer. Ethnol.* no. 144, 50, fig. 12, 1951. Washington, Smithsonian Institution 176

104 *Kuakiutl salmon-trap.* From F. BOAS. 'The Kuakiutl of Vancouver Island.' *Memoirs, American Museum of Natural History*, Vol. 8, pt. 2, fig. 137, 1909. New York, American Museum of Natural History 177

105 *Diagram of Nootka deer-deadfall.* From P. DRUCKER. 'The Northern and Central Nootkan Tribes.' *Bull. Bur. Amer. Ethnol.* no. 144, 33, fig. 11, 1951. Washington, Smithsonian Institution 177

106 *Haida village.* After J. R. SWANTON. 'Contributions to the Ethnology of the Haida.' Jesup North Pacific Expedition Vol. V, 1, Pls. IX, X. New York, American Museum of Natural History, 1905. D. E. Woodall 178

107 *Eskimo snow-knife.* By courtesy of Wellcome Historical Medical Museum, London. Drawn from original. D. E. Woodall 180

108 *Eskimo harpooning seal.* From K. RASMUSSEN. 'The Netsilik Eskimos', p. 152. Copenhagen, Gyldendal, 1931 181

109 *Eskimo heavy thrusting harpoon.* After F. BOAS. 'The Central Eskimo.' Rep. Bur. Amer. Ethnol. Vol. 6, figs. 417, 420, 423. Washington. 1888. T. A. Greeves 182

9. ROTARY MOTION *by* V. GORDON CHILDE

110 *Magdalenian* bâton de commandement. From J. CABRÉ AGUILÓ. 'El arte rupestre en España.' Instituto nacional de ciencias físico-naturales, Comisión de investigaciones paleontológicas y prehistóricas, no. 1, fig. 21. Madrid. 1915 188

111 (A) *Flint borer.* London, Archaeological Institute, University of London. Drawn from original by courtesy of the Director. T. A. Greeves. (B) *Antler awl.* London, British Museum (Nat. Hist.). From K. P. OAKLEY. 'Man the Tool-Maker' (2nd ed.), fig. 6 c. London, British Museum (Nat. Hist.), 1950 188

112 *Egyptian carpenters and beadmakers.* From P. E. NEWBERRY. 'The Life of Rekhmara', Pl. XVIII. London, Constable, 1900 189

113 *Bow-drill.* After J. D. MCGUIRE. *Rep. Smithson. Instn* for 1894, p. 721, fig. 149, 1896. D. Wyeth 190

114 *Pump-drill.* After J. D. MCGUIRE. *Ibid.*, p. 735, fig. 173. D. Wyeth 191

115 *Tubular drill.* After J. D. MCGUIRE. *Ibid.*, p. 691, fig. 95. D. Wyeth 191

116 *Bore-core.* London, Archaeological Institute, University of London. Drawn from original by courtesy of the Director. T. A. Greeves 192

117 (A) *Detail of relief showing the grinding of a vase.* Cairo, Egyptian Museum. After M. G. MASPERO. 'Le Musée égyptien', Vol. 3, Pl. XXII. Cairo, Service des Antiquités Égyptiennes, 1915. D. E. Woodall (B) *Two protodynastic flint bits.* After photograph by courtesy of Miss G. Caton-Thompson. D. E. Woodall. (C) *Hieroglyph representing the drill.* From M. A. MURRAY. 'Saqqara Mastabas', Part 1, Pl. XXXIX, no. 65. London, British School of Egyptian Archaeology, 1905 193

118 *Stone socket.* London, British Museum, No. 90849. By courtesy of the Trustees. D. E. Woodall 194

119 *Turntable and base used by Gelib potters.* By courtesy of Powell Cotton Museum, Birchington, East Kent. T. A. Greeves 196

120 *Japanese potter's wheel.* Based upon B. LEACH. 'A Potter's Book' (2nd ed.), p. 65. London, Faber & Faber, 1945. D. Wyeth 197

121 *Madrasi potter's wheel.* From E. HOLDER. *J. Indian Art* **7**, Pl. LXVII, 1897 198

122 (A) *Upper face of a Mesopotamian potter's wheel.* After E. HEINRICH. 'Sechster vorläufiger Bericht über die . . . Uruk-Warka Ausgrabungen.' *Abh. preuss. Akad. Wiss., phil.-hist. Kl.* 1935, no. 2, Pl. XV a. Berlin, de Gruyter for Preussische Akademie. D. E. Woodall. (B) *Minoan socketed clay disk.* Candia (Crete) Museum. After S. XANTHOUDIDES in 'Essays in Aegaean Archaeology' presented to Sir Arthur Evans, Pl. XVIII, facing p. 128. Oxford, Clarendon Press, 1927. T. A. Greeves 199

123 *Egyptian pivoted disk.* From P. E. NEWBERRY. 'El Berscheh I.' Egypt Explor. Fund Special Publ., Pl. XXV. London. n.d. Egypt Exploration Society 200

124 *Potter's wheel-bearing.* London, Archaeological Institute, University of London. Drawn from original by courtesy of the Director. T. A. Greeves 201

125 (A) *Cart . . . vase painting.* From V. G. CHILDE. *Proc. prehist. Soc.* new series **17**, 178, fig. **2**, 1951. Cambridge, Prehistoric Society. (B) *Limestone relief.* After E. MACKAY. *Antiq. J.* **9**, Pl. II, fig. 1, 1929. Society of Antiquaries of London; and C. L. WOOLLEY. 'The Royal Cemetery.' Ur Excavations. Rep. Vol. 2, Pl. CLXXXI a. London, British Museum, 1934. By courtesy of the Trustees. D. E. Woodall 205

126 *Pictographs from Erech.* From V. G. CHILDE. *Proc. prehist. Soc.* new series **17**, 178, fig. 1, 1951. Cambridge, Prehistoric Society 205

127 *Toy model.* From V. G. CHILDE. 'New Light on the Most Ancient East' (4th ed.), p. 215, fig. 109. London, Routledge & Kegan Paul, 1952 205

128 *Remains of a hearse.* After S. H. LANGDON and L. C. WATELIN. 'Excavations at Kish', Vol. 4, Pl. XXIII, 1. Paris, Geuthner, 1934. D. E. Woodall 206

129 *Copper model.* Stockholm, Stat. Hist. Museum, No. 14305. After S. PRZEWORSKI. *Eurasia Septentrionalis Antiqua* **10**, 87, fig. 14, 1936. Helsinki, Archaeological Society of Finland. D. E. Woodall 207

130 *Nail-studded wheel.* From V. G. CHILDE. *Proc. prehist. Soc.* new series **17**, 180, fig. 36, 1951. Cambridge, Prehistoric Society 208

131 *Representation of a copper tyre.* From V. G. CHILDE. *Ibid.*, 181, fig. 4, no. 6 208

132 *Wooden hub of a chariot wheel.* Oxford, Ashmolean Museum, Department of Antiquities. Drawn from original. Mrs. M. E. Cox 211

133 (A) *Cretan pictograph.* (B) *Late Minoan bead seal.* From A. J. EVANS. 'The Palace of Minos', Vol. 4, ii, figs. 800 b, 799. London, Macmillan, 1935 212

134 *Egyptian wheel-wrights.* From NORMAN and NINA DE G. DAVIES. 'The Tombs of Menkheperrasonb, Amenmose etc.' The Theban Tomb series mem. 5, Pl. XII. London, Egypt Exploration Society, 1933 213

135 *Wheel from Mercurago.* From R. MUNRO. 'The Lake Dwellings of Europe', fig. 59. London, Cassell, 1890 214

TAILPIECE. *Anatomical drawings by Leonardo.* After LEONARDO DA VINCI. 'I manoscritti . . . della R. Biblioteca di Windsor. Dell' Anatomia, Fogli A.' Ed. by T. SABACHNIKOFF and G. PUIMATI. Fol. 1 verso. Paris, Rouveyre, 1898. D. Wyeth 215

10. FIRE-MAKING, FUEL, AND LIGHTING *by* H. S. HARRISON

136 *The taming of fire.* From VITRUVIUS. 'De Architectura.' French trans. fol. 15. Paris. 1547 217

137 *Percussion method.* (A) *Flint and nodule of iron pyrites.* After E. BIDWELL. 'The History of Fire Making.' Cat. Exhib. E. Bidwell Collection, Exhibit 12. London, Janson, 1912. D. Wyeth. (B) *Flint, tinder, and steel.* After 'Handbook to the Ethnographical Collection of the British Museum' (2nd ed.), fig. 9 b. London, British Museum, 1925. By courtesy of the Trustees. D. Wyeth 218

138 *Fire-saw.* After *ibid.*, fig. 9 g. D. Wyeth 221

139 *Sawing-thong.* After *ibid.*, fig. 9 c. D. Wyeth 221

140 *Fire-plough.* After *ibid.*, fig. 9 f. D. Wyeth 222

141 *Fire-drill.* From *ibid.*, fig. 9 d. *Two Egyptian hieroglyphs.* From P. E. NEWBERRY and F. L. GRIFFITH. 'Beni Hasan', Part 3, Pl. V, 64, 68. London, Egypt Exploration Society, 1896 223

142 *Fire-driller.* After photograph in the Bryant and May Museum of Fire-Making Appliances, Science Museum, South Kensington, London. By courtesy of the Director. D. E. Woodall 223

143 *Fire-drill from a Mexican MS.* Oxford, Bodleian Library. After A. AGLIO. 'Antiquities of Mexico', Vol. 1, p. (10). London. 1830. D. Wyeth 224

144 *Eskimo thong-drill.* From H. ELLIS. 'A Voyage to Hudson's Bay', fig. facing p. 132. London. 1748 225

145 *Eskimo fire-making bow-drill.* From 'Handbook to the Ethnographical Collection of the British Museum' (2nd ed.), fig. 9 e. London, British Museum, 1925. By courtesy of the Trustees 225

146 *Ancient Egyptian bow-drill.* After W. M. F. PETRIE. 'Ten Years Digging in Egypt', fig. 91. London, Lutterworth Press, 1893. D. Wyeth 225

147 *The pump-drill (diagrammatic).* Based on sketch in the Bryant and May Museum of Fire-Making Appliances, Science Museum, South Kensington, London. By courtesy of the Director. D. Wyeth 226

148 *Fire-piston.* From 'Handbook to the Ethnographical Collection of the British Museum' (2nd ed.), fig. 9 h. London, British Museum, 1925. By courtesy of the Trustees 227

149 (A) *Candle and tapers*; (B) *portable candle.* From NORMAN DE G. DAVIES. *J. Egypt. Archaeol.* **10**, Pl. VII, fig. 14; Pl. V, fig. 4, 1924. London, Egypt Exploration Society. (C) *Socketed candlestick.* After A. J. EVANS. 'The Palace of Minos', Vol. 1, p. 578, fig. 422. London, Macmillan, 1921. D. E. Woodal. (D) *Reconstructed chalcolithic stone brazier.* Institute of Archaeology, University of London. From a drawing by courtesy of the Director 232

150 *Palaeolithic stone lamp.* After E. RIVIÈRE. *Bull. Soc. Anthrop. Paris*, 1899, 558, fig. 1. D. E. Woodall 235

151 *Lamps from Ur.* (A) *Shell*; (B) *gold*; (C) *calcite.* (A), (B) Baghdad, Iraq Museum; (C) London, British Museum. After C. L. WOOLLEY. 'The Royal Cemetery.' Ur Excavations. Rep. Vol. 2, Pls. CI; CLXIII a; CLXXXII b. London, British Museum, 1934. By courtesy of the Trustees. D. E. Woodall 236

152 *Saucer-shaped pottery lamps.* (A) *Phoenician*; (B) *Carthaginian.* After F. W. ROBINS. 'The Story of the Lamp and the Candle', Pl. IX, 1; 7. London, Oxford University Press, 1939. D. E. Woodall 236

153 *Graeco-Roman lamps.* (A) *Stone lamp*; (B) *earthenware lamp.* London, British Museum. From H. B. WALTERS. 'Catalogue of the Greek and Roman Lamps in the British Museum', Nos. 128, 386; p. 23, fig. 22; p. 54, fig. 62. London, British Museum 1914. By courtesy of the Trustees 237

11. CHEMICAL, CULINARY, AND COSMETIC ARTS *by* R. J. FORBES

154 *Painter's palette.* New York, Metropolitan Museum of Art. By courtesy of the Director. D. E. Woodall 239

155 *Painters and sculptors.* From P. E. NEWBERRY. 'Beni Hasan', Part 2, Pl. IV. London, Egypt Exploration Society, 1893 241

156 *The studio of the 'chief sculptor Anta'.* From NORMAN DE G. DAVIES. 'Rocktombs of el-Amarna III.' Archaeol. Survey Egypt Mem. 15, Pl. XVIII. London, Egypt Exploration Society, 1905 242

157 *Painter's equipment.* After NORMAN DE G. DAVIES. 'Five Theban Tombs.' Archaeol. Survey Egypt Mem. 21, Pl. XVII. London, Egypt Exploration Society, 1913. T. A. Greeves 242

158 *Pestle and mortar.* New York, Metropolitan Museum of Art. By courtesy of the Director. D. E. Woodall 244

159 Map: *Bituminous surface deposits.* After R. J. FORBES. 'Bitumen', fig. 1. Leiden, E. J. Brill, 1936 251

160 *Bitumen in building. Sections of* (A) *a Neo-Babylonian bathroom;* (B) *a processional road.* From R. J. FORBES. *Ibid.*, figs. 27 a, 31 255

161 *Bowl carved from rock asphalt.* Paris, Louvre. By courtesy of the Director. D. E. Woodall 256

162 *A scribe checks the storing of raisins.* From P. E. NEWBERRY. 'Beni Hasan', Part 1, Pl. XII. London, Egypt Exploration Society, 1893 263

163 *Cutting up an ox.* From NORMAN DE G. DAVIES and A. H. GARDINER. 'The Tomb of Antefoker.' The Theban Tomb series mem. 2, Pl. IX. London, Egypt Exploration Society, 1920 264

164 *Gutted fish hung to dry.* After WILKINSON MS. II, 19. By courtesy of Griffith Institute, Ashmolean Museum, Oxford. Nina de G. Davies 264

165 *Netting and curing sea-fish.* From R. LEPSIUS. 'Denkmäler aus Aegypten und Aethiopien', Part II, Vol. 3, Pl. XLVI. Berlin. 1849–58 265

166 *Netting Nile-fish and fowl.* After HAY MS. No. 29813, 37. By courtesy of the Trustees of the British Museum, London. Nina de G. Davies 265

167 *Bandaging mummies.* From J. F. CHAMPOLLION. 'Monuments de l'Égypte et de la Nubie', Vol. 4, Pl. CDXV. Paris. 1845 266

168 *An embalmer's table.* From H. E. WINLOCK. *Ann. Serv. Antiq. Égypte* **30**, 103, 1930. Cairo 266

169 *A predynastic Egyptian burial.* After R. A. MARTIN. 'Mummies.' Nat. Hist. Mus. Anthrop. Leaflet no. 36, Pl. III. Chicago, Natural History Museum, 1945. D. E. Woodall 267

170 *Bags of natron and chaff.* After H. E. WINLOCK. 'Materials used at the Embalming of Tut-ankh-amun.' Metr. Mus. Occas. Pap. no. 10, Pl. III. New York, Metropolitan Museum of Art, 1941. D. E. Woodall 269

171 *Head of Yuaa.* Cairo, Egyptian Museum, No. 51190. After J. E. QUIBELL. 'The Tomb of Yuaa and Thuiu.' Catal. gén. antiq. égypt. Mus. Caire, Vol. 49, Pl. LVIII. Cairo, Service des Antiquités Égyptiennes, 1908. D. E. Woodall 270

172 *Preparing a joint of meat.* From R. LEPSIUS. 'Denkmäler aus Aegypten und Aethiopien', Part 2, Vol. 3, Pl. LII. Berlin. 1849–58 272

173 *Early Egyptian confectioners.* After G. STEINDORFF. 'Das Grab des Ti', Pl. LXXXVI. Leipzig, Hinrichs, 1913. D. E. Woodall 273

174 *Baking 'pancakes'.* From NORMAN DE G. DAVIES and A. H. GARDINER. 'The Tomb of Antefoker.' The Theban Tomb series mem. 2, Pl. IX. London, Egypt Exploration Society, 1920 273

175 *Making spiced bread.* From NORMAN DE G. DAVIES and A. H. GARDINER. *Ibid.*, Pls. XI, XII 274

176 *An early form of saddle-quern.* Berlin, Staatl. Museen. After H. SCHÄFER and W. ANDRAE. 'Die Kunst des Alten Orients' (Propyläen-Kunstgeschichte Vol. 2), p. 231. Berlin, Propyläen Verlag, 1925. D. E. Woodall 274

177 *Upper Palaeolithic honey-collector.* From H. OBERMAIER. 'Fossil Man in Spain', p. 251, fig. 116. New Haven, Yale University Press, 1924 275

178 *Pottery model of woman in fermenting-vat.* Berlin, Staatl. Museen. After H. SCHÄFER and W. ANDRAE. 'Die Kunst des Alten Orients' (Propyläen-Kunstgeschichte Vol. 2), p. 172. Berlin, Propyläen Verlag, 1925. D. E. Woodall 276

179 *Making date-wine.* From NORMAN DE G. DAVIES and A. H. GARDINER. 'The Tomb of Antefoker.' The Theban Tomb series mem. 2, Pls. XI, XII. London, Egypt Exploration Society, 1920 277

180 *Egyptian bakers and brewers.* After W. WRESZINSKI. 'Atlas zur altaegyptischen Kulturgeschichte', Vol. 1, fig. 301. Leipzig, Hinrichs, 1923. D. E. Woodall 278

181 *Sumerian pictographs representing the pointed brewer's vat* 280

182 *Drinking beer. From a Syrian seal.* Berlin, Staatl. Museen. From L. F. HARTMAN and A. L. OPPENHEIM. *J. Amer. orient. Soc.*, Suppl. no. 10, Pl. II, no. 8, 1950. Baltimore 280

183 (A) *The Egyptian hieroglyph for a brewer.* (B) *Hieroglyph of a workman in a fermenting-vat* 281

184 *Pottery wine jar.* Cairo, Egyptian Museum. After photograph in the Griffith Institute, Ashmolean Museum, Oxford. D. E. Woodall 283

185 *Collecting and treading grapes.* From NORMAN DE G. DAVIES. 'Robb de Peyster Tytus Memorial Series I, The Tomb of Nakht at Thebes', Pl. XXII. New York, Metropolitan Museum of Art, 1917 290

186 *Working an early Egyptian bag-press.* After NORMAN DE G. DAVIES. 'The Mastaba of Ptahhetep and Akhetep at Saqqareh.' Archaeol. Survey Egypt Mem. 8, Pl. XXIII. London, Egypt Exploration Society, 1900. D. E. Woodall 291

187 *An improved bag-press.* From P. E. NEWBERRY. 'Beni Hasan' Part 2, Pl. VI. London, Egypt Exploration Society, 1893 291

188 *Merchants mixing oils.* After F. W. VON BISSING and A. E. WEIGALL. 'Die Mastaba des Gemni-Kai', Vol. I, Pl. XXIII. Berlin, Glaue, 1905. D. E. Woodall 291

189 *Gathering lilies, and expressing the oil.* Reliefs. Paris, Louvre. After G. BÉNÉDITE. *Monum. Piot* **25**, Pls. IV, VI, 1921–22. Paris, Académie des Inscriptions et Belles-Lettres de l'Institut National de France. D. E. Woodall 292

190 *An ointment-compounder's workshop.* After W. WRESZINSKI. 'Atlas zur altaegyptischen Kulturgeschichte', Vol. I, ii, Pl. CCCLVI. Leipzig, Hinrichs, 1923. D. E. Woodall 292

TAILPIECE. *An Egyptian incense-burner.* After P. E. NEWBERRY and F. L. GRIFFITH. 'Beni Hasan', Part 4, Pl. XVII. London, Egypt Exploration Society, 1900. D. E. Woodall 298

12. BUILDING IN WATTLE, WOOD, AND TURF *by* JOHN BRADFORD

191 *Magdalenian paintings.* From L. CAPITAN *et al.* 'La caverne de Font-de-Gaume', figs. 215, 216, 220. Monaco, 1910. (Institut de Paléontologie Humaine, Paris) 300

192 *Plan of a Gravettian settlement.* From V. G. CHILDE. *Antiquity* **24**, 8, fig. 3, 1950. Newbury, Edwards 301

193 *Predynastic pottery model of a house.* After V. G. CHILDE. 'New Light from the Most Ancient East' (4th ed.), Pl. X c. London, Routledge & Kegan Paul, 1952. T. A. Greeves 304

194 *Predynastic representation of a reed hut.* From E. B. SMITH. 'Egyptian Architecture as Cultural Expression', Pl. I, no. 6. New York, Appleton-Century-Crofts, 1938 305

195 *Egyptian plank construction.* From W. M. F. PETRIE. 'Egyptian Architecture', Pl. VII, Nos. 27, 28 A, 28 B, 29. London, British School of Egyptian Archaeology, 1938 305

196 *Neolithic model of a hut.* From V. G. CHILDE. 'The Dawn of European Civilisation' (5th ed. rev.), p. 139, fig. 71 (a). London, Routledge & Kegan Paul, 1950 307

197 *A reconstruction of the village at Köln-Lindenthal.* From W. BUTTLER and W. HABEREY. 'Die Bandkeramische Ansiedlung bei Köln-Lindenthal.' Römisch-Germanische Forschungen Vol. 11, Frontis. (text vol.). Berlin, Leipzig, de Gruyter, 1936 308

198 *Ground plan and reconstruction of a typical long house.* From O. PARET. *Germania* **26**, 91, fig. 1, 1942. Frankfurt a. M., Deutsches Archäologisches Institut: Römisch-Germanische Kommission 309

199 *Plan of the substructure of a house at Aichbühl.* From V. G. CHILDE. *Proc. prehist. Soc.* new series **15**, 80, fig. 2, 1949. Cambridge, Prehistoric Society 310

200 *Reconstructed framework of a house on the Goldberg.* From G. BERSU. *Germania* **20**, Pl. XLVIII, 1, 1936. Frankfurt a. M., Deutsches Archäologisches Institut: Römisch-Germanische Kommission 311

201 *Reconstruction of a palisade-barrow.* From A. E. VAN GIFFEN. *Proc. prehist. Soc.* new series **4**, 270, fig. 7, 1938. Cambridge, Prehistoric Society 314

202 *Plan of Woodhenge.* From S. PIGGOTT. *Archaeol. J.* **96**, 208, fig. 7, 1940. London, Royal Archaeological Institute 314

203 *A suggested reconstruction of Woodhenge.* From S. PIGGOTT. *Ibid.*, 211, fig. 9 315

204 *Farmstead at Buchau.* From H. REINERTH, 'Das Federseemoor als Siedlungsland des Vorzeitmenschen', p. 137, fig. 54. Filser, Augsburg, 1929 316

205 *General view of the Little Woodbury farm-house.* After J. J. HAWKES. *Antiquity* **20**, Pl. [v] foll. p. 84, 1946. Newbury, Edwards. T. A. Greeves 317

206 *Section through a mound (LVI) at Glastonbury.* From A. BULLEID and H. ST. G. GRAY. 'The Glastonbury Lake Village', Vol. 1, p. 134, fig. 31. Glastonbury. 1911. Glastonbury Antiquarian Society and Mr. H. St. George Gray 319

207 *Diagram of a timber fragment.* From A. BULLEID and H. ST. G. GRAY. *Ibid.*, p. 57, fig. 9 320

208 *Diagram of a grooved oak plank.* From A. BULLEID and H. ST. G. GRAY. *Ibid.*, p. 121, fig. 25 320

209 *The outer face of a protective rampart.* After R. E. M. WHEELER. 'Maiden Castle, Dorset.' Rep. Res. Comm. Soc. Antiq. no. 12, Pl. XCI A. Society of Antiquaries of London. 1943. D. E. Woodall 321

210 *Plan of a circular hut.* From R. E. M. WHEELER. *Ibid.*, p. 95, fig. 18 321

211 *Reconstruction of village at Biskupin.* After H. G. RICHARDS. *Archaeology* **3**, 170, fig. 1, 1950. Archaeological Institute of America. T. A. Greeves 323

212 *Cinerary urn.* Rome, Museo Preistorico ed Etnografico. By courtesy of the Director. D. E. Woodall 324

213 *The burial mound of a Scythian chieftain.* From E. H. MINNS. *Proc. Brit. Acad.* **28**, 51, fig. 1, 1942 325

13. DOMESTICATION OF ANIMALS *by* F. E. ZEUNER

214 *The domesticated cat in Egypt.* After NINA DE G. DAVIES. 'Ancient Egyptian Paintings', Vol. 2, Pl. XCV. Chicago, Oriental Institute, University of Chicago, 1936. Nina de G. Davies 329

215 *Australian dingo.* After W. HOWCHIN. 'The Building of Australia and the Succession of Life', Part 3, p. 540, fig. 224. Adelaide, 1925–30. By courtesy of the South Australian Museum. D. E. Woodall 330

216 *Greyhound.* After P. E. NEWBERRY and F. L. GRIFFITH, 'Beni Hasan', Part 4, Pl. II. London, Egypt Exploration Society, 1900. D. E. Woodall 330

217 *Mongrel dog.* After P. E. NEWBERRY and F. L. GRIFFITH. *Ibid.*, Pl. IV. D. E. Woodall 331

218 *Reindeer-hunting by decoy.* From W. J. HOFFMANN. *Rep. Smithson. Instn* for 1895, Pl. LXVII, 4, 5, 1897 336

219 *Onager on a rein-ring.* London, British Museum, No. 121348. After C. L. WOOLLEY. 'The Royal Cemetery.' Ur Excavations. Rep. Vol. 2, Pl. CLXVI. London, British Museum, 1934. By courtesy of the Trustees. D. E. Woodall 340

220 *Domestication of animals.* After P. DUELL. 'The Mastaba of Mereruka', Part 2. Univ. Chicago, Orient. Inst. Publ. Vol. 39, Pl. CLIII. Chicago. 1938. D. E. Woodall 341

221 *Asses threshing.* After G. STEINDORFF. 'Das Grab des Ti', Pl. CXXII. Leipzig, Hinrichs, 1913. D. E. Woodall 343

222 (Left) *Egyptian relief of a ram.* Cairo, Egyptian Museum. After M. HILZHEIMER. *Antiquity* **10**, 195, Pl. II, 1936. Newbury, Edwards. D. E. Woodall. (Right) *Sheep from Soay.* After photograph by courtesy of O. G. S. Crawford. D. E. Woodall 344

223 *Head of a horse in ivory.* After E. PIETTE. *Anthropologie, Paris* **15**, 142, fig. 16, 1904. Masson. D. E. Woodall 347

TAILPIECE. *Panel from an ivory toilet-box of Tutankhamen.* Cairo, Egyptian Museum. After photograph in the Griffith Institute, Ashmolean Museum, Oxford. D. E. Woodall 352

14. CULTIVATION OF PLANTS *by* F. E. ZEUNER

224 *Diagram: head of wheat.* From H. HELBAEK. *Lond. Univ. Inst. Arch. Annu. Rep.* **9**, 45, fig. 1, 1953 363

TAILPIECE. *Preparing the soil for agriculture: hoeing.* After G. STEINDORFF. 'Das Grab des Ti', Pl. CXI. Leipzig, Hinrichs, 1913. D. E. Woodall 375

15. POTTERY *by* SIR LINDSAY SCOTT

225 Raku *tea bowl.* After B. LEACH. 'A Potter's Book', fig. 13. London, Faber & Faber, 1940. D. E. Woodall 384

226 *Uganda potter.* After photograph by courtesy of H. J. Braunholtz; and K. TYLER. 'Pottery Without a Wheel', Pl. II, fig. 4. Leicester, Dryad Press, 1952. T. A. Greeves 384

227 *Building-stages.* From R. B. K. STEVENSON. *Proc. Soc. Antiq. Scotld* **73**, 235, fig. 4, nos. 1, 2, 3, 4, 9, 10, 11, 13, 15, 1939. Edinburgh 385

228 *Sindh potter and his tools.* After E. J. M. MACKAY. *J. R. anthrop. Inst.* **60**, Pl. I, 3; p. 131, figs. 1, 2, 1930. London. D. E. Woodall 386

229 *Bull* rhyton. After H. B. HAWES. 'Gournia. . . . Crete', Pl. I (i). Philadelphia, University Museum, 1903. D. E. Woodall 387

230 *Diagram of a bow-rim.* From I. BEN-DOR. *Ann. Archaeol. Anthrop.* **23,** Pl. XXXII, 21, 1936. School of Archaeology and Oriental Studies, University of Liverpool 387

231 *Neolithic rectangular trough.* After A. J. EVANS. 'The Palace of Minos', Vol. 1, fig. 11 a. London, Macmillan, 1921. D. E. Woodall 388

232 *An Egyptian pottery in the Middle Kingdom.* From P. E. NEWBERRY. 'Beni Hasan', Part I, Pl. XI. London, Egypt Exploration Society, 1893 388

233 *A peasant potter's wheel.* After L. FRANCHET. 'Céramique primitive', p. 58, fig. 7. Paris, Geuthner, 1911. D. E. Woodall 389

234 *New Kingdom Egyptian pottery.* After W. WRESZINSKI. 'Atlas zur altaegyptischen Kulturgeschichte', Vol. 1, Pl. CCCI. Leipzig, Hinrichs, 1923. D. E. Woodall 389

235 (A) *Shells and pebbles for burnishing, sherds, and bone point.* After C. H. INGE. *Palest. Explor. Quart.* 1938, Pl. XXV, 3. British School of Archaeology, Jerusalem. D. E. Woodall. (B) *Burnisher.* After original owned by the author. T. A. Greeves 390

236 (A) *Knob,* (B) *pierced lug, and* (C) *handle.* From I. BEN-DOR. *Ann. Archaeol. Anthrop.* **23,** Pl. XXX, nos. 10, 3, 5, 1936. School of Archaeology and Oriental Studies, University of Liverpool 391

237 *Nigerian women piling pots for firing.* After B. LEACH. 'A Potter's Book', fig. 72. London, Faber & Faber, 1940. D. E. Woodall 391

238 *Diagram of a primitive vertical kiln.* From B. LEACH. *Ibid.*, fig. p. 180 392

239 *Primitive Greek vertical kiln.* From O. RAYET. *Gaz. Archéol.* **6**, 106, 1880 392

240 *Horizontal kiln.* From B. LEACH. 'A Potter's Book', fig. p. 183. London, Faber & Faber, 1940 393

241 *Romano-British kilns:* (A) *from Farnham, Surrey;* (B) *Holt, Denbighshire.* (A) from and (B) based on W. F. GRIMES. *Cymmrodor* **41**, fig. 31, nos. VII, VI, 1930. London, The Honourable Society of Cymmrodorion. (B) T. A. Greeves 394

242 *Two Egyptian potters: model.* After J. E. QUIBELL. 'Excavations at Saqqara 1907–08', Pl. XVII, 3. Cairo, Service des Antiquités Egyptiennes, 1909. D. E. Woodall 395

243 *An Egyptian pottery of Dynasty V.* After G. STEINDORFF. 'Das Grab des Ti', Pls. LXXXIV, LXXXV. Leipzig, Hinrichs, 1913. D. E. Woodall 395

244 *Diagram of a vertical kiln at Susa.* From R. DE MECQUENEM. *Mém. Délég. Perse* **25,** 203, fig. 42, 1934. Presses Universitaires de France, Paris 396

245 *Reconstruction of a vertical kiln at Sialk.* From R. GHIRSHMAN. 'Fouilles de Sialk.' Louvre, Dép. Antiq. Orient., Sér. archéol. Vol. 4, fig. 5. Paris, Presses Universitaires de France, 1938 396

246 *Sketch plan of kiln 2 at Eilean an Tighe* by the author 397

247 *Chalice from Knossos.* After A. J. EVANS. 'The Palace of Minos', Vol. 1, fig. 19 A, E. London, Macmillan, 1921. D. E. Woodall 398

248 (A) *Tasian beaker.* From G. BRUNTON. 'Mostagedda and the Tasian Culture', Pl. XII, no. 54. London, Quaritch, 1937. By courtesy of Mrs. Guy Brunton; (B) *Modern African basket.* After C. SCHUCHHARDT. *Prähist. Z.* **1,** 41, fig. 1, 1909. Berlin, de Gruyter. D. E. Woodall 398

249 (A) *Western Neolithic pots.* Karlsruhe, Badisches Landesmuseum. After C. SCHUCHHARDT. *Prähist. Z.* **2,** 147, fig. 2 b, e, 1910. Berlin, de Gruyter. D. E. Woodall. (B) *Polychrome imitation.* After A. J. EVANS. 'The Palace of Minos', Vol. 1, fig. 127 g. London, Macmillan, 1921. D. E. Woodall 399

250 *Imitation of rivets.* From A. J. EVANS. *Ibid.*, fig. 47 a 399

251 *Fragment of an earthenware goblet.* From A. J. EVANS. *Ibid.*, fig. 183 b (1) 400

252 (A) *Knotted and corded jars.* After A. J. EVANS. *Ibid.*, fig. 175. D. E. Woodall. (B) *Corded urn.* After J. ABERCROMBY. 'Bronze Age Pottery of Great Britain and Ireland', Vol. 2, Pl. CIII, no. 557. Oxford, Clarendon Press, 1912. D. E. Woodall 400

253 *Corded bell beaker.* Edinburgh, Nat. Mus. of Antiquities of Scotland. After V. G. CHILDE. 'Prehistoric Communities of the British Isles' (3rd ed.), Pl. VII, 1. London, Edinburgh, Chambers, 1949. D. E. Woodall 402

254 *Face urn.* From C. W. BLEGEN *et al.* 'Troy', Vol. 2, Pl. XLV b, no. G. 30. Princeton, University of Cincinnati, 1951 402

255 *Bowl decorated with doves.* After P. DIKAIOS. 'The Excavations of Vounous-Bellapais in Cyprus 1931–2.' *Archaeologia* **88,** Pl. XV a, 1940. Society of Antiquaries of London. D. E. Woodall 403

256 *Vessels from Glastonbury Lake Village.* From A. BULLEID and H. ST. G. GRAY. 'Glastonbury Lake Village', Vol. 2, Pls. LXXV, fig. 1; LXXVI, fig. XX. Glastonbury, 1917. Glastonbury Antiquarian Society and Mr. H. St. George Gray 404

257 *Woman painting a pot. From an Athenian vase.* Rome, Collection Scaretti. From G. JATTA. *Ann. Ist. Corres. archaeol.* **48**, Pl. DE, 1876 408

16. TEXTILES, BASKETRY, AND MATS *by* GRACE M. CROWFOOT

258 *Coiled basketry.* Diagrams by Elisabeth Crowfoot 416

259 *Twined and wrapped basketry.* Diagrams by Elisabeth Crowfoot 417

260 *Matting.* Diagrams by Elisabeth Crowfoot 417

261 *Plaited basketry.* Diagram by Elisabeth Crowfoot 418

262 *Stake-frame basketry.* Diagrams by Elisabeth Crowfoot 418

263 *Basket from Gurob.* After G. BRUNTON and R. ENGELBACH. 'Gurob', Pl. VIII, 3. London, British School of Egyptian Archaeology, 1927. D. E. Woodall 419

264 *Rush matting.* After W. M. F. PETRIE *et al.* 'Tarkhan I and Memphis V', Pl. X, nos. 10, 11. London, British School of Egyptian Archaeology, 1913. Elisabeth Crowfoot 420

265 *Bed-matting.* After W. M. F. PETRIE *et al. Ibid.* Pl. VIII, no. 7. D. E. Woodall 420

266 *Chequerwork.* Diagram by Elisabeth Crowfoot 422

267 *Twined bag.* Cairo, Egyptian Museum. By courtesy of the Metropolitan Museum of Art, New York. D. E. Woodall 423

268 *Twist and spindle.* Diagrams by Elisabeth Crowfoot 424

269 *Looms.* Diagrams by Elisabeth Crowfoot 426

270 PLAIN WEAVES etc. Diagrams by Elisabeth Crowfoot 428

271 (A) *Twined weave.* (B) *Gauze weave.* (C) *Wrapped or Soumak weave.* Diagrams by Elisabeth Crowfoot. (D), (E) *Wrapped weave, varieties.* After E. VOGT. 'Geflechte und Gewebe der Steinzeit', figs. 144, 120. Basle, E. Birkhäuser, 1937. Elisabeth Crowfoot 430

272 *A horizontal loom depicted on a dish from Badari.* By courtesy of the University College, London. Drawn from original. T. A. Greeves 432

273 SPINDLE WHORLS. (A) *Stone.* After A. MALLON *et al.* 'Teleilāt Ghassūl', fig. 28, no. 8. Rome, Scripta Pontificii Instituti Biblici, 1934. (B) *Limestone.* After W. M. F. PETRIE. 'Prehistoric Egypt', Pl. XXVI, no. 68. London, British School of Egyptian Archaeology, 1921. (C), (E), (F) *Clay.* After C. W. BLEGEN *et al.* 'Troy', Vol. 1, p. 222, fig. 35–103; p. 366, fig. 36–276; p. 367, fig. 37–607. Princeton, University of Cincinnati, 1950. (D) *Bone.* After P. L. O. GUY and M. ENGBERG. 'Megiddo Tombs', Pl. LXXXIV, 9; fig. 175, 9. Chicago, Oriental Institute, University of Chicago, 1938. NEEDLESHUTTLE. (G) *Bone.* After A. MALLON *et al.* 'Teleilāt Ghassūl', fig. 31, no. 14. Rome, Scripta Pontificii Instituti Biblici, 1934. SPINDLES. (H), (K) *Wood.* After W. M. F. PETRIE. 'Tools and Weapons', Pl. LXV, N, nos. 140, 141. London, British School of Egyptian Archaeology, 1917. (I) *Bone.* After P. L. O. GUY and M. ENGBERG. 'Megiddo Tombs', fig. 175, 6. Chicago, Oriental Institute, University of Chicago, 1938. (J) *Pottery model.* After E. STEWART and J. STEWART. 'Vounous, 1937–38.' Skr. Svensk. Inst. Rom. XIV. Pl. C, fig. d. Lund, Gleerup, 1950. (L) *Wood.* London, British Museum, No. 55078. Drawn from original. Elisabeth Crowfoot. LOOM WEIGHTS. (M), (O) *Clay.* After C. W. BLEGEN *et al.* 'Troy', Vol. 1, p. 221, fig. 36–365; p. 369, fig. (a) 36–296. Princeton, University of Cincinnati, 1950. (N) *Clay with seal impression.* After G. LOUD. 'Megiddo', Vol. 2, Pl. CLXIX, no. 11, Pl. CLXIV, no. 4. Chicago, Oriental Institute, University of Chicago, 1948. (A)–(O) Elisabeth Crowfoot 433

274 *Starting border and selvedge.* After E. VOGT. 'Geflechte und Gewebe der Steinzeit', fig. 82. Basle, E. Birkhäuser, 1937. Elisabeth Crowfoot 436

275 (A) *Linen loom.* After F. CAILLIAUD. 'Recherches sur les arts et métiers de l'Égypte etc.', Pl. XVII. Paris. 1831. D. E. Woodall. (B) *Mat loom.* From J. F. CHAMPOLLION. 'Monuments de l'Égypte et de la Nubie', Vol. 4, Pl. CCCLXVI, fig. 2 b. Paris, 1845 437

276 *Spinners.* After F. CAILLIAUD. 'Recherches sur les arts et métiers de l'Égypte etc.', Pl. XVII. Paris. 1831. D. E. Woodall 438

277 *Vertical looms.* After H. L. ROTH. 'Ancient Egyptian and Greek Looms.' Bankfield Mus. Notes, second series no. 2, fig. 9. Halifax. 1913. Elisabeth Crowfoot 439

278 *Diagram of the two weaves in the girdle of Rameses III.* City of Liverpool Public Museums. After G. M. CROWFOOT and H. L. ROTH. *Ann. Archaeol. Anthrop.* **10,** ii, fig. 2, 1923. School of Archaeology and Oriental Studies, University of Liverpool. Elisabeth Crowfoot 441

279 *Weave of the Gerumsberg cloak.* After L. VON POST *et al.* 'Bronsåldersmanteln från Gerumsberget i Västergötland.' K. Vitterhets Hist. Antik. Akad. Monogr. no. 15, Pl. v. Stockholm. 1925. Elisabeth Crowfoot 442

280 *Urn decorated with spinner and weavers. Oedenburg.* Vienna, Naturhistorisches Museum. After M. HOERNES. 'Urgeschichte der bildenden Kunst in Europa', Pl. XXIX. Vienna, Holzhausen. 1898; and S. GALLUS. *Archaeologia Hungarica* **13,** Pl. XII, no. 1, 1934. Budapest, Magyar Nemzeti Museum. D. E. Woodall 443

281 *Spinners and weavers on a Greek vase.* New York, Metropolitan Museum of Art. After G. M. A. RICHTER. *Bull. Metr. Mus.* December 1931, 293, fig. 5; and original photograph. D. E. Woodall 444

282 *Fragments of a Mesolithic fishing net.* After J. G. D. CLARK. 'The Mesolithic Settlement of Northern Europe', Pl. IV. Cambridge, University Press, 1936. D. E. Woodall 452

283 *Transport of a bull colossus. Relief.* London, British Museum, Niniveh Gallery Nos. 124822–3. After H. R. H. HALL. 'Babylonian and Assyrian Sculpture in the British Museum', Pl. XXX. Paris, Van Oest, 1928. D. E. Woodall 452, 453

284 *Leather-rope makers.* From NORMAN DE G. DAVIES. 'The Tomb of Rekh-mi-rē at Thebes', Vol. 2, Pl. LII. New York, Metropolitan Museum of Art, 1943 454

285 *Rope-laying.* After E. J. H. MACKAY. *J. Egypt. Archaeol.* **3,** Pl. XV, 1916. London, Egypt Exploration Society. D. E. Woodall. *Detail.* After sketch by K. R. Gilbert 454

TAILPIECE. *Child's basket.* Photograph by courtesy of the Metropolitan Museum of Art, New York. Elisabeth Crowfoot 455

17. BUILDING IN BRICK AND STONE *by* SETON LLOYD

286 *The ruins of Babylon.* After R. KOLDEWEY. 'Das Ischtar-Tor in Babylon.' Wiss. Veröff. dtsch. Orientges. no. 32, Pl. XXIII. Leipzig, Hinrichs, 1918. D. E. Woodall 457

287 *The Hypostyle Hall. Karnak.* After K. LANGE. 'Aegyptische Kunst', Pl. XCVII. Zürich, Atlantis Verlag, 1939. T. A. Greeves 458

288 *Reconstruction of a 'farm-house', and sketch of its remains. Hassuna.* From S. LLOYD and F. SAFAR. *J. Near East. Stud.* **4,** fig. 36, 1945. University of Chicago 459

289 *Reconstruction of three temples at Tepe Gawra.* After painting by H. M. HERGET in E. A. SPEISER. *Nat. geogr. Mag.* **99,** 60, 1951. Washington. By courtesy of National Geographic Society. T. A. Greeves 460

290 *Fragments of cone mosaic at Erech.* After J. JORDAN. 'Zweiter vorläufiger Bericht über die . . . Uruk Ausgrabungen.' *Abh. preuss. Akad. Wiss., phil.-hist. Kl.*, no. 4, p. 31, fig. 17, 1930. Berlin, de Gruyter for Preussische Akademie. D. E. Woodall 462

291 *The 'Sublime Porte' at Erech.* After J. JORDAN. 'Dritter vorläufiger Bericht über die . . . Uruk Ausgrabungen.' *Abh. preuss. Akad. Wiss., phil.-hist. Kl.*, no. 6, Pl. VIII, 1932. Berlin, de Gruyter for Preussische Akademie. D. E. Woodall 463

292 *Reconstruction of a temple at Eridu* by Seton Lloyd. Redrawn from photograph. D. E. Woodall 464

293 *One variety of the 'herringbone' brick-patterns. Mesopotamia.* From P. DELOUGAZ. 'Plano-convex Bricks and the Method of their Employment.' Univ. Chicago, Orient. Inst.: Stud. ancient orient. Civiliz. no. 7, p. 21, fig. 19 e, 1934 465

294 *Section of a tomb at Ur.* From C. L. WOOLLEY. 'The Royal Cemetery.' Ur Excavations. Rep. Vol. 2, Text, fig. 16. London, British Museum, 1934. By courtesy of the Trustees 465

295 *Main sewer of the palace at Eshnunna.* After H. FRANKFORT. 'Tell Asmar, the Akkadian Palace.' Univ. Chicago, Orient. Inst.: Commun. no. 17, fig. 24, 1934. D. E. Woodall 466

296 *Brick-covered drain at Mohenjo-Daro.* After E. J. H. MACKAY. 'Early Indus Civilization' (2nd ed.), Pl. X, 1. London, Luzac, 1948. D. E. Woodall 466

297 *Closet in the palace at Eshnunna.* After H. FRANKFORT. 'Tell Asmar, the Akkadian Palace.' Univ. Chicago, Orient. Inst.: Commun. no. 17, fig. 23, 1934. D. E. Woodall 467

298 *Reconstruction of* ziggurat *at Ur.* From C. L. WOOLLEY. 'The Ziggurat and its Surroundings.' Ur Excavations. Rep. Vol. 5, Pl. LXXXVI. London, British Museum, 1939. By courtesy of the Trustees 467

299 *The structure of the Cassite* ziggurat *at Aqar Quf.* After T. BAQIR. *Iraq*, 1944, Suppl., Pl. v. London. By courtesy of the Directorate-General of Antiquities, Iraq Government. D. E. Woodall 468

300 *Restoration of a private house at Ur.* After C. L. WOOLLEY. 'The Sumerians', Pl. XXVII. Oxford, Clarendon Press, 1928. D. E. Woodall 469

301 *Partly excavated bull-colossus at Khorsabad.* After G. LOUD. 'Khorsabad', Part 2. Univ. Chicago, Orient. Inst.: Publ. no. 40, Pl. XLVI, 1, 1938. D. E. Woodall 470

302 *An Assyrian relief depicting palace windows.* From G. PERROT and C. CHIPIEZ. 'Histoire de l'art dans l'antiquité', Vol. 2. 'Chaldée et Assyrie', fig. 76. Paris, Hachette, 1884 471

303 *A terracotta window grille.* After H. FRANKFORT. 'Tell Asmar, the Akkadian Palace.' Univ. Chicago, Orient. Inst.: Commun. no. 17, fig. 9, 1934. D. E. Woodall 472

304 *Brick-vaulted culvert at Khorsabad.* From G. PERROT and C. CHIPIEZ. 'Histoire de l'art dans l'antiquité', Vol. 2. 'Chaldée et Assyrie', fig. 93, Paris, Hachette, 1884 472

305 *Reconstructed section of a private house at El-Amarna.* After S. LLOYD. *Architect, Lond.* 3 January 1930, p. 23. By courtesy of Egypt Exploration Society. D. E. Woodall 474

306 *Fluted three-quarter columns at Saqqara.* After S. CLARK and R. ENGELBACH. 'Ancient Egyptian Masonry', fig. 2. London, Oxford University Press, 1930. D. E. Woodall 475

307 *Pilaster imitating papyrus. Saqqara.* After S. CLARK and R. ENGELBACH. *Ibid.*, fig. 7. D. E. Woodall 476

308 *Head of a pilaster. Saqqara.* After S. CLARK and R. ENGELBACH. *Ibid.*, fig. 8. D. E. Woodall 477

309 (A) *Method of extracting blocks in a quarry, Egypt.* (B) *Plan of small block-masonry at Saqqara.* From S. CLARK and R. ENGELBACH. *Ibid.*, figs. 12, 94. (C) *Polishing and dressing.* After P. E. NEWBERRY. 'The Life of Rhekmara', Pl. XX. London, Constable, 1900. D. E. Woodall 478

310 *Foundations of a column in the Hypostyle Hall.* After S. CLARK and R. ENGELBACH. 'Ancient Egyptian Masonry', fig. 65. London, Oxford University Press, 1930. D. E. Woodall 479

311 *Variation in the height of courses . . . Karnak.* After S. CLARK and R. ENGELBACH. *Ibid.*, fig. 103. D. E. Woodall 480

312 *Model illustrating probable method of dressing.* After S. CLARK and R. ENGELBACH. *Ibid.*, fig. 109. D. E. Woodall 480

313 *Workmen dressing a stone block.* After NORMAN DE G. DAVIES. 'The Tomb of Rekh-mi-rē at Thebes', Vol. 2, Pl. LXII. New York, Metropolitan Museum of Art, 1943. Reconstructed drawing. Nina de G. Davies 481

314 *Mason's mallet* etc. After S. CLARK and R. ENGELBACH. 'Ancient Egyptian Masonry', fig. 264. London, Oxford University Press, 1930. D. E. Woodall 481

315 *North-south section through the pyramid of Sahure.* From I. E. S. EDWARDS. 'The Pyramids of Egypt', fig. 34. Harmondsworth, Penguin Books, 1949 482

316 *The general Egyptian method of jointing three architraves.* From S. CLARK and R. ENGELBACH. 'Ancient Egyptian Masonry', fig. 171. London, Oxford University Press, 1930 483

317 *The 'Town Mosaic'. Knossos.* From A. J. EVANS. 'The Palace of Minos', Vol. 1, fig. 226. London, Macmillan, 1921 485

318 *Plan and sections of the 'Tomb of Agamemnon'.* From W. J. ANDERSON and R. P. SPIERS. 'The Architecture of Ancient Greece', rev. and rewritten by R. W. DINSMOOR, fig. 11. London, Batsford, 1950 486

319 *Restored view of a wing of the Palace of Minos.* From A. J. EVANS. 'The Palace of Minos', Vol. 2, ii, fig. 532. London, Macmillan, 1928 487

320 *Layout of Stonehenge.* Diagram by T. A. Greeves 491

321 *Reconstruction of Stonehenge II.* London, Geological Museum. By courtesy of the Controller of H.M. Stationery Office. T. A. Greeves 492

322 *A fallen lintel.* After E. H. STONE. 'The Stones of Stonehenge', Pl. XXI, fig. 2. London, Robert Scott, 1924. T. A. Greeves 492

323 *Possible methods of erection.* Diagrams based on E. H. STONE. *Ibid.*, Ch. 6. T. A. Greeves 493

TAILPIECE. *Stonehenge today.* Based on photograph by F. Frith & Co., Reigate. T. A. Greeves 494

18. DIFFERENTIATION OF NON-METALLIC TOOLS *by* S. M. COLE

324 (A)–(C) *Three types of microlith.* From J. G. D. CLARK. 'The Mesolithic Age in Britain', Pls. XXIII, XIX. Cambridge, University Press, 1932. (D) *A transverse or chisel-ended arrow-head.* (E) *A transverse arrow-head hafted.* From J. G. D. CLARK. 'The Mesolithic Settlement of Northern Europe', figs. 50, 8; 51, 1. Cambridge, University Press, 1936 496

325 (A) *Bone arrow-point*. After O. MONTELIUS. 'Temps préhistoriques en Suède', fig. 24. Paris, Presses Universitaires de France, 1895. T. A. Greeves. (B), (C) *Perforated antler sleeves*. From J. G. D. CLARK. 'The Mesolithic Settlement of Northern Europe', fig. 40, nos. 3, 4. Cambridge, University Press, 1936. (D) *A 'Thames pick'*. London, British Museum. From (W. WATSON.) 'Flint Implements', Pl. VIII, 2. London, British Museum, 1950. By courtesy of the Trustees 497

326 *Antler axe, adze, and haft*. From J. G. D. CLARK. 'The Mesolithic Settlement of Northern Europe', fig. 27, 1–3. Cambridge, University Press, 1936 497

327 (A) *A pair of barbed bone points*. (B) *Bone points*. From J. G. D. CLARK. *Ibid.*, fig. 46, 1–3 498

328 *Flaked stone 'hoe-blade'*. From V. G. CHILDE. 'New Light on the Most Ancient East' (4th ed.), fig. 36. London, Routledge & Kegan Paul, 1952 502

329 (A) *Natufian bone sickle*. (B) *Crescentic flint sickle-blade*. From K. P. OAKLEY. 'Man the Tool-Maker' (2nd ed.), fig. 40, a, c. London, British Museum (Nat. Hist.), 1950 503

330 *Polished flint gouge and polishing stone*. After O. MONTELIUS. 'Temps préhistoriques en Suède', figs. 9, 3. Paris, Presses Universitaires de France, 1895. T. A. Greeves 508

331 *Stone adze blade with wooden handle and antler sleeve*. From K. P. OAKLEY. 'Man the Tool-Maker' (2nd ed.), fig. 40 e. London, British Museum (Nat. Hist.), 1950 508

332 (A) *Flint core, and* (B) *blade*. From J. G. D. CLARK. 'Prehistoric Europe', fig. 104. After DE MORGAN. London, Methuen, 1952. 509

333 (A) *Comma-shaped flint knife*. (B) *Scimitar-shaped flint knife*. From V. G. CHILDE. 'New Light on the Most Ancient East' (4th ed.), fig. 32. London, Routledge & Kegan Paul, 1952 509

334 *Chalcolithic flint dagger*. London, British Museum. From (W. WATSON.) 'Flint Implements', Pl. IV, 18. London, British Museum, 1950. By courtesy of the Trustees 510

335 *Some of the types of arrow-heads of the Neolithic and Bronze Ages*. (A) *Yorkshire*. London, British Museum. From (W. WATSON.) *Ibid.*, Pl. VI, 13. (B) *Suffolk*. London, British Museum (Nat. Hist.), No. E. 2363. Drawn from original. D. E. Woodall. (C) *Fayum*, (D) *Cambridge*, (E) *Fayum*. London, British Museum. From (W. WATSON.) 'Flint Implements', Pl. VI, 18, 21, 17. London, British Museum, 1950. By courtesy of the Trustees 511

336 *Battle-axe*. London, British Museum. From (W. WATSON.) *Ibid.*, Pl. IX, 2 512

337 *Stone battle-axe*. After O. MONTELIUS. 'Temps préhistoriques en Suede', fig. 130. Paris, Presses Universitaires de France, 1895. T. A. Greeves 513

338 *Antler comb*. From J. G. D. CLARK. 'Prehistoric Europe', fig. 120. London, Methuen, 1952 515

339 *Stages in the making of shell fish-hooks*. After A. J. ARKELL. *Sudan Notes* **30**, ii, Pl. VII, 1949. Sudan Government. T. A. Greeves 515

340 *Bone axe-head*. From A. J. ARKELL. 'Esh Shaheinab', fig. 21. Oxford, Oxford University Press, 1953 516

341 *Reconstruction of a wood-worker's bench*. Unteruhldingen am Bodensee, Freilichtmuseum. After photograph by H. Reinerth. D. E. Woodall 517

342 *Wooden 'boomerang'*. From V. G. CHILDE. 'New Light on the Most Ancient East' (4th ed.), fig. 15. London, Routledge & Kegan Paul, 1952 518

TAILPIECE. *Making flint implements*. After F. L. GRIFFITH. 'Beni Hasan', Part 3. Archaeol. Survey Egypt Mem. 5, Pl. VII. London, Egypt Exploration Society, 1896. D. E. Woodall 519

19. WATER-SUPPLY, IRRIGATION, AND AGRICULTURE *by* M. S. DROWER

343 *Drawing water in pots*. After NINA DE G. DAVIES. 'Paintings from the Tomb of Rekh-mi-rē', Pl. XIV. New York, Metropolitan Museum of Art, 1935. Restored drawing. Nina de G. Davies 522

344 *Irrigation by shaduf*. From NORMAN DE G. DAVIES. 'The Tomb of Nefer-Hotep at Thebes', Vol. 1, Pl. XLVI. New York, Metropolitan Museum of Art, 1933 523

345 *Watering an Egyptian garden*. From NORMAN DE G. DAVIES. 'Robb de Peyster Tytus Memorial Series V, Two Ramesside Tombs at Thebes', Pl. XXVIII. New York, Metropolitan Museum of Art, 1927 523

346 *An early shaduf. From a cylinder seal*. Paris, Louvre. After L. DELAPORTE. 'Catalogue des cylindres . . . de style oriental du Musée du Louvre', Vol. 2, Pl. LXXII, no. 12 (A. 156). Paris, Musée du Louvre, 1923. D. E. Woodall 524

347A *Assyrians raising water*. After A. PATERSON. 'Assyrian Sculptures. Palace of Sinacherib', Pl. XXXII f. The Hague, Martin Nijhoff, 1912. D. E. Woodall 524

347B *Assyrian dam.* After R. CAMPBELL THOMPSON and R. W. HUTCHINSON. *Archaeologia* **79**, Pl. LVIII, fig. 2, 1929. Society of Antiquaries of London. D. E. Woodall 529

348A, B *A modern* qanaat. After J. DE MORGAN. 'Mission scientifique en Perse', Vol. 1, p. 301, figs. 166, 167. Paris, Presses Universitaires de France, 1894. D. Wyeth 533

349 *Pottery water-pipes. Knossos.* After A. J. EVANS. *Ill. Lond. News*, 29 June 1935, p. 1164, fig. 2. T. A. Greeves 535

350 (Above) *A primitive Egyptian hoe, and* (below) *a more developed form.* London, University College, Egyptian Collection. After W. M. F. PETRIE. 'Tools and Weapons', Pl. LXVIII, Nos. 57, 62. London, British School of Egyptian Archaeology, 1917. T. A. Greeves 539

351 *Land reclamation in ancient Egypt.* From NORMAN DE G. DAVIES. 'Robb de Peyster Tytus Memorial Series I, The Tomb of Nakht at Thebes' Pl. XVIII. New York, Metropolitan Museum of Art, 1917 540

352 *Pulling flax.* Berlin, Staatl. Museen, No. 15421. After L. KLEBS. 'Die Reliefs des Alten Reiches.' *Abh. heidelberg. Akad. Wiss., phil.-hist. Kl.* No. 3, fig. 40, 1915. Heidelberg, Carl Winters Universitätsbuchhandlung. D. E. Woodall 540

353 *Treading in the seed.* After G. STEINDORFF. 'Das Grab des Ti', Pl. CXI. Leipzig, Hinrichs, 1913. D. E. Woodall 541

354 *Surveyors measuring a field.* Restored drawing by Nina de G. Davies 541

355 *Taking the oath on a boundary stone.* London, British Museum, No. 37982. After NINA DE G. DAVIES. 'Ancient Egyptian Paintings', Vol. 2, Pl. LXVIII. Chicago, Oriental Institute, University of Chicago, 1936. Nina de G. Davies 542

356 *Egyptian sickles.* (A) *Neolithic.* From G. CATON-THOMPSON and E. W. GARDINER. 'The Desert Fayum', Pl. XXX. London, Royal Anthropological Institute, 1934. (B) *Dynasty I.* Cairo, Egyptian Museum. After original photograph lent by Prof. W. B. Emery. D. E. Woodall. (C) *Dynasty XII.* London, University College, Egyptian Collection. After W. M. F. PETRIE. 'Tools and Weapons', Pl. LV, no. 7. London, British School of Egyptian Archaeology, 1917. T. A. Greeves 542

357 *Reaping corn.* From NORMAN DE G. DAVIES. 'Robb de Peyster Tytus Memorial Series I, The Tomb of Nakht at Thebes', Pl. XVIII. New York, Metropolitan Museum of Art, 1917 543

358 *Winnowing and measuring the grain.* From NORMAN DE G. DAVIES. *Ibid.*, Pl. XVIII 543

359 *Harvesting corn.* Relief. Paris, Louvre. After 'Encyclopédie photographique de l'art. Le Musée du Louvre', Vol. 1, Pls. XXV, XXVI. Paris, Tel, 1936. D. E. Woodall 543

360 *A garden of root vegetables.* After F. CAILLIAUD. 'Recherches sur les arts et métiers de l'Égypte', Pl. XXXIII A. Paris. 1831. D. E. Woodall 544

361 *A formal Egyptian garden.* After NINA DE G. DAVIES. 'Paintings from the Tomb of Rekh-mi-rē', Pl. XX. New York, Metropolitan Museum of Art, 1935. Restored drawing. Nina de G. Davies 544

362 *Picking figs.* After NINA DE G. DAVIES. 'Ancient Egyptian Paintings', Vol. 1, Pl. VII. Chicago, Oriental Institute, University of Chicago, 1936. Restored drawing. Nina de G. Davies 545

363 *An early botanical collection.* From C. SINGER. 'From Magic to Science', fig. 70. London, Benn, 1928 545

364 *Map of fields and canals near Nippur. From a cuneiform tablet.* Diagram based on an original photograph by courtesy of the University of Pennsylvania Museum, Philadelphia. D. Wyeth 549

365 *Babylonian plough. From a Cassite seal.* Philadelphia, Univ. Pennsylvania Museum. From C. W. BISHOP. *Antiquity* **10**, 270, fig. 5, 1936. Newbury, Edwards 550

366 *An Assyrian garden. From a relief.* London, British Museum, No. 11894. After H. R. H. HALL. 'Babylonian and Assyrian Sculpture in the British Museum', Pl. LV. Paris, Van Oest, 1928. D. E. Woodall 551

367 *An Assyrian park. From a relief.* London, British Museum. After H. R. H. HALL. *Ibid.*, Pl. XLIII. D. E. Woodall 553

TAILPIECE. *Assyrian seed-plough and fig-tree.* After G. PERROT and C. CHIPIEZ. 'Histoire de l'art dans l'antiquité', Vol. 2. 'Chaldée et Assyrie', Pl. XV. Paris, Hachette, 1884. D. E. Woodall 557

20. MINING AND QUARRYING *by* C. N. BROMEHEAD

368 *Section through pit.* Adapted from J. G. D. CLARK. 'Prehistoric England', p. 59. London, Methuen, 1940 559

369 *Galleries radiating from pit.* Adapted from J. G. D. CLARK. *Ibid.*, p. 58 559

370 *Diagrammatic section through flint mines.* Based on J. ANDREE. 'Bergbau in der Vorzeit' in H. HAHNE. 'Vorzeit', Vol. 2, p. 4, fig. 4. Leipzig, Barth, 1922. D. Wyeth 560

371 *Deer antler pick.* After A. L. ARMSTRONG. *Proc. prehist. Soc.* **5**, 110, 1927. Cambridge, Prehistoric Society. D. E. Woodall 560

372 *Antler rake, and shovel.* From J. G. D. CLARK. 'Prehistoric Europe', fig. 102. After CURWEN. London, Methuen, 1952 561

373 *Skeleton of a flint-miner. Obourg.* After original photograph by courtesy of the Institut Royal des Sciences Naturelles de Belgique, Brussels. D. E. Woodall 561

374 MAP: *European flint mines.* Adapted from J. G. D. CLARK and S. PIGGOTT. *Antiquity* **7**, 167, fig. 1, 1933. Newbury, Edwards 562

375 *Reconstruction of a copper-mine.* Adapted from J. ANDREE. 'Bergbau in der Vorzeit' in H. HAHNE. 'Vorzeit', Vol. 2, p. 29, fig. 20. Leipzig, Barth, 1922 566

376 *Mining tools and a rucksack.* Vienna, Naturhist. Museum. After A. MAHR. 'Das vorgeschichtliche Hallstatt.' Führer durch die Hallstattsammlungen des naturhistorischen Museums in Wien, p. 64, fig. 8; p. 65, fig. 9. Vienna, Schroll, 1925. D. E. Woodall 567

377 *The unfinished obelisk at Aswan.* After R. ENGELBACH. 'The Aswan Obelisk', Pl. II, 2. Cairo, Service des Antiquités Égyptiennes, 1922. T. A. Greeves 568

TAILPIECE. *Wooden water-trough.* Salzburg, Städt. Museum Carolino-Augusteum, No. 1511. After O. KLOSE. 'Die prähistorischen Funde vom Mitterberge.' Österreichische Kunsttopographie, Vol. 17, p. 6, fig. 6. Vienna, Schroll, 1918. D. E. Woodall 571

21. EXTRACTING, SMELTING, AND ALLOYING *by* R. J. FORBES

378 *A time-sequence showing the spread of metal technology.* By the author 573

379 *An oak sample-case.* Stettin, Museum. After L. FRANZ. 'Jäger, Bauern, Händler', fig. 20. Brünn, Rohrer, 1939. D. E. Woodall 576

380 MAP: *Ore bearing regions.* By the author 576

381 *Egyptian chisels and crucible.* After W. M. F. PETRIE. 'Researches in Sinai', figs. 160, 161. London, John Murray, 1906. D. E. Woodall 577

382 *Modern primitive bellows.* After T. C. CRAWHALL. *Man* **33**, article 48, Pl. C, 2, 1933. London, Royal Anthropological Institute. D. E. Woodall 578

383 *Casting a bronze door.* From P. E. NEWBERRY. 'The Life of Rekhmara', Pl. XVIII. London, Constable, 1900 578

384 *Egyptian gold workers.* After G. STEINDORFF. 'Das Grab des Ti', Pl. CXXXIV. Leipzig, Hinrichs, 1913. D. E. Woodall 579

385 *Egyptian map of gold mines.* Turin, Museo Egizio. After J. BALL. 'Egypt in the Classical Geographers', Pl. VII. Cairo. 1942. By courtesy of the Survey Department, Ministry of Finance, Egypt. D. Wyeth 580

386 *Casting a copper axe-head.* After photograph by courtesy of Central Office of Information. Crown copyright. D. E. Woodall 588

387 *A typical Bronze Age hoard of metal objects.* Mainz, Röm.-German. Zentralmuseum. After L. FRANZ. 'Jäger, Bauern, Händler', fig. 18. Brünn, Rohrer, 1939. D. E. Woodall 591

388 *Diagram of a primitive bloomery hearth.* After E. STRAKER. 'Wealden Iron', p. 18. London, Bell, 1931. T. A. Greeves 593

TAILPIECE. *Double mould of a Syrian goldsmith.* After C. F. A. SCHAEFFER. *Ill. Lond. News*, 20 February 1937, p. 296, fig. 14. D. E. Woodall 599

22. METAL IMPLEMENTS AND WEAPONS *by* H. H. COGHLAN

389 (A) *Neolithic polished stone celt.* After J. EVANS. 'The Ancient Stone Implements, etc.', fig. 53. London, Longmans Green, 1872. D. E. Woodall. (B) *Copper celt.* After photograph by courtesy of the Pitt Rivers Museum, Oxford (No. P.R. 1440). D. E. Woodall 601

390 *Copper axes and adze-axes.* From V. G. CHILDE. 'The Dawn of European Civilization' (4th ed.), fig. 53. London, Routledge & Kegan Paul, 1947 602

391 *Predynastic Egyptian copper chisels.* After W. M. F. PETRIE. 'Tools and Weapons', Pl. XXI, nos. 1–3. London, British School of Egyptian Archaeology, 1917. D. Wyeth 603

392 (A) *Flint saw.* Oxford, Pitt Rivers Museum. From H. M. COGHLAN. 'Notes on the Prehistoric Metallurgy of Copper and Bronze in the Old World.' Occ. Pap. Tech. Pitt Rivers Mus. No. 4, fig. 16. Oxford, Oxford University Press, 1951. (B) *Egyptian bronze saw.* From V. G. CHILDE. 'The Story of Tools', fig. 34. London, Cobbett Press, 1944 603

393 *Predynastic Egyptian flint daggers.* From V. G. CHILDE. 'New Light on the Most Ancient East', p. 75, fig. 23, nos. 1, 2. London, Routledge & Kegan Paul, 1934 604

394 (A) *Triangular copper dagger.* (B) *Dagger.* From J. EVANS. 'The Ancient Bronze Implements, etc.', figs. 298, 287. London, Longmans Green, 1881 605

395 '*West European*' *tanged dagger.* London, British Museum, No. 1938, 3-411. Drawn from original. T. A. Greeves 605

396 *Middle Minoan copper spear.* From V. G. CHILDE. 'The Dawn of European Civilisation' (4th ed.), fig. 15. London, Routledge & Kegan Paul, 1947 606

Two copper arrow-heads. From W. LAMB. 'Excavations at Thermi in Lesbos', Pl. XLVII, nos. 32.60; 32.20. Cambridge, University Press, 1936 606

397 *Stone moulds.* From J. EVANS. 'The Ancient Bronze Implements, etc.', figs. 516, 522. London, Longmans Green, 1881 606

398 *Casting a socketed celt.* From H. M. COGHLAN. 'Notes on the Prehistoric Metallurgy of Copper and Bronze in the Old World.' Occ. Pap. Tech. Pitt Rivers Mus. No. 4, fig. 1. Oxford, Oxford University Press, 1951 607

399 *One half of a bronze mould.* From J. EVANS. 'The Ancient Bronze Implements, etc.', fig. 527. London, Longmans Green, 1881 608

400 *Predynastic crucibles.* From W. GOWLAND. *J. R. anthrop. Inst.* **42**, Pl. XXVI, nos. 8, 10, 1912. London, Royal Anthropological Institute 608

401 (A) *Neolithic perforated stone hammer.* From J. EVANS. 'The Ancient Stone Implements, etc.', fig. 155. London, Longmans Green, 1872. (B) *Perforated bronze sledge-hammer.* Salzburg, Städt. Museum Carolino-Augusteum, No. 1600. After O. KLOSE. 'Die prähistorischen Funde vom Mitterberge.' Österreichische Kunsttopographie, Vol. 17, p. 21, fig. 31. Vienna, Schroll, 1918. T. A. Greeves 609

402 *Bronze socketed hammer.* From J. EVANS. 'The Ancient Bronze Implements, etc.', fig. 211. London, Longmans Green, 1881 610

403 *Bronze anvil.* Dijon Museum. From L. COUTIL. *Homme préhist.*, 1912, no. 4, p. 99, fig. 17. Paris, Gamber 610

404 *Shaft-hole chopper-axe.* From C. F. A. SCHAEFFER. 'Stratigraphie comparée et chronologie de l'Asie occidentale', Vol. 1, fig. 82, no. 16. Oxford, Oxford University Press, 1948 611

405 (A) *Bronze shaft-hole axe.* After V. G. CHILDE. 'The Story of Tools', fig. 18. London, Cobbett Press, 1944. T. A. Greeves. (B) *Sumerian transverse axe.* From V. G. CHILDE. 'New Light on the Most Ancient East', p. 189, fig. 67. London, Routledge & Kegan Paul, 1934 612

406 *Tanged and socketed Bronze Age chisels.* From J. EVANS. 'The Ancient Bronze Implements, etc.', figs. 190, 196, 192*, 200, 205. London, Longmans Green, 1881 612

407 *Hallstatt bronze file.* From W. M. F. PETRIE. 'Tools and Weapons', Pl. L, no. 48. London, British School of Egyptian Archaeology, 1917 613

408 *Bronze Age daggers.* From V. G. CHILDE. 'The Bronze Age', p. 77, fig. 7. Cambridge, University Press, 1930 614

409 *Halberd.* From J. EVANS. 'The Ancient Bronze Implements, etc.', fig. 329. London, Longmans Green, 1881 614

410 (A) *Evolution of the dirk.* (B) *Bronze rapiers.* From H. PEAKE. 'Early Steps in Human Progress', Pl. LXX, a, b. London, Sampson Low, Marston, 1933 615

411 *Bronze swords.* From H. PEAKE. *Ibid.*, Pl. LXXI b 615

412 *Bronze spearheads.* (A) *Early Bronze Age.* London, British Museum. From BRITISH MUSEUM. 'A Guide to the Antiquities of the Bronze Age' (2nd ed.), p. 35, fig. 17. London, British Museum, 1920. By courtesy of the Trustees; (B) *Early Middle Bronze Age.* From W. GREENWELL and W. P. BREWIS. *Archaeologia* **61**, Pl. LX, fig. 8, foll. p. 472, 1909. Society of Antiquaries of London; (C) *Middle Bronze Age.* London, British Museum. From BRITISH MUSEUM. 'A Guide to the Antiquities of the Bronze Age' (2nd ed.), p. 34, fig. 15. London, British Museum, 1920. By courtesy of the Trustees 616

413 *Hungarian battle-axes.* From V. G. CHILDE. 'The Danube in Prehistory', fig. 148. Oxford, Clarendon Press, 1929 616

414 *Luristan battle-axes.* From C. F. A. SCHAEFFER. 'Stratigraphie comparée et chronologie de l'Asie occidentale', Vol. I, fig. 266, nos. 2–4. Oxford, Oxford University Press, 1948 617

415 *Bronze antennae swords.* From H. PEAKE and H. J. FLEURE. 'The Law and the Prophets', p. 139, fig. 40. Oxford, Clarendon Press, 1936 618

416 *Iron sword.* Vienna, Naturhist. Museum. After F. MORTON. 'Hallstatt und die Hallstattzeit', Pl. XIV. Innsbruck, Musealverein. 1953. D. E. Woodall 618

417 *Iron dagger.* Cairo, Egyptian Museum. After photograph in the Griffith Institute, Ashmolean Museum, Oxford. D. E. Woodall 619

418 *Battle-axe.* After C. F. A. SCHAEFFER. 'Mission de Ras Shamra', Vol. 3, Pl. XXII. Paris, Geuthner, 1939. D. E. Woodall 619

419 *Iron axe.* From V. G. CHILDE. 'The Prehistory of Scotland', fig. 78. London, Routledge & Kegan Paul, 1935 620

420 *Fragment of the blade of an iron saw.* Speyer, Historisches Museum der Pfalz. After RÖM.-GERMAN. ZENTRALMUSEUM, MAINZ. 'Die Altertümer unserer heidnischen Vorzeit', Vol. 5, Pl. XLVI, no. 804. Mainz. 1911. T. A. Greeves 620

TAILPIECE. *Phalanx of Sumerian soldiers with spears. Relief on a stele.* Paris, Louvre. After E. DE SARZEC and L. HEUZEY. 'Découvertes en Chaldée', Vol. 2, Pl. III, bis. Paris, Presses Universitaires de France, 1912. D. E. Woodall 622

23. FINE METAL-WORK *by* HERBERT MARYON and H. J. PLENDERLEITH

421 *Silver bowl with inlays.* Cyprus, Antiquities Department. After C. F. A. SCHAEFFER. *Ill. Lond. News*, 24 May 1952, p. II foll. p. 884. D. E. Woodall 624

422 *Bronze chair-foot with iron collar.* London, British Museum. Diagram by H. Maryon 624

423 *Silver bull on a rein-ring.* Baghdad, Iraq Museum. After C. L. WOOLLEY. 'The Royal Cemetery.' Ur Excavations. Rep. Vol. 2, Pl. CLXVII a. London, British Museum, 1934. By courtesy of the Trustees. D. E. Woodall 626

424 *Bronze head of Sargon.* Baghdad, Iraq Museum. After M. E. L. MALLOWAN. *Iraq* 3, Pl. V, 1936. London. By courtesy of the Directorate-General of Antiquities, Iraq Government. D. E. Woodall 627

425 *Piece-moulding a Chinese* Tsun. Diagram by H. Maryon 628

426 *Bronze lion-gryphon.* London, British Museum. After O. M. DALTON. 'The Treasure of the Oxus' (2nd ed.), Pl. XXV. London, British Museum, 1926. By courtesy of the Trustees. D. E. Woodall 631

427 *Raising a bowl.* Diagram by H. Maryon 637

428 *Copper bull.* London, British Museum. After H. R. H. HALL. 'Al 'Ubaid.' Ur Excavations. Rep. Vol. I, Pl. XXVIII. London, British Museum, 1927. By courtesy of the Trustees. D. E. Woodall 638

429 *Life-size copper statue of Pepi I.* Cairo, Egyptian Museum. After J. E. QUIBELL and F. W. GREEN. 'Hierakonpolis', Part 2, Pl. L, I. London, British School of Egyptian Archaeology, 1902. D. E. Woodall 639

430 *Detail of the statue of Pepi.* After J. E. QUIBELL and F. W. GREEN. *Ibid.*, Pl. LII. D. E. Woodall 640

431 *Copper panel of Im-Dugud.* London, British Museum, No. 114308. After H. R. H. HALL. 'Al 'Ubaid.' Ur Excavations. Rep. Vol. I, Pl. VI. London, British Museum, 1927. By courtesy of the Trustees. D. E. Woodall 640

432 *Gold hawk's head.* Cairo, Egyptian Museum. After E. VERNIER. 'Bijoux et orfèvreries.' Catal. gén. antiq. égypt. Mus. Caire, Pl. LIX. Cairo, Service des Antiquités égyptiennes, 1927. D. E. Woodall 641

433 *Use of the graver and tracer.* Diagram by H. Maryon 642

434 *Gold figurines.* After C. L. WOOLLEY. 'The Royal Cemetery.' Ur Excavations. Rep. Vol. 2, Pls. CXLI, CXLII. London, British Museum, 1934. By courtesy of the Trustees. D. E. Woodall 643

435 *Gold and lapis calf's head.* London, British Museum, No. 121198. *Electrum helmet.* Baghdad, Iraq Museum. After C. L. WOOLLEY. *Ibid.*, Pl. CX; Frontis. D. E. Woodall 644

436 (Above) *Repoussé decorations on two gold cups from Vaphio.* (Below) *Cup.* National Museum, Athens. After A. J. EVANS. 'The Palace of Minos', Vol. 3, p. 184, fig. 127; facing p. 178, fig. 123 A, B. London, Macmillan, 1930. D. E. Woodall 645

437 *Bronze doors.* London, British Museum. After L. W. KING. 'The Gates of Shalmaneser', Pl. LXXIII. London, British Museum, 1915. By courtesy of the Trustees. D. E. Woodall 646

438 *Scythian gold deer.* Leningrad, Hermitage State Museum. After photograph of a cast in the Victoria and Albert Museum, London. Crown copyright. D. E. Woodall 647

(H) *Large axe.* London, British Museum. (B), (D), (E), (G), and (H) by courtesy of the Trustees. D. E. Woodall 688

488 *Furniture-makers at work.* From NORMAN DE G. DAVIES. 'The Tomb of Rekh-mi-rē at Thebes', Vol. 2, Pl. LII, detail. New York, Metropolitan Museum of Art, 1943 689

489 *Joiners at work.* After G. STEINDORFF. 'Das Grab des Ti', Pl. CXXXIII, detail. Leipzig, Hinrichs, 1913. D. E. Woodall 689

490 *Back of an ivory casket of Tutankhamen.* Cairo, Egyptian Museum. After original photograph in the Griffith Institute, Ashmolean Museum, Oxford. D. E. Woodall 691

491 *Joints from Egyptian coffins.* After W. M. F. PETRIE and E. J. H. MACKAY. 'Heliopolis, Kafr Ammar and Shurafa', Pl. XXV. London, British School of Egyptian Archaeology, 1915. Diagram by the author 691

492 *Some methods of joining members.* From P. LACAU. 'Sarcophages antérieurs au nouvel empire', Vol. 2, p. 64, fig. 2; Vol. 1, p. 200, fig. 5; p. 74, fig. 2. Catal. gén. antiq. égypt. Mus. Caire, Vols. 12, 11. Cairo, Service des Antiquités Égyptiennes, 1906, 1904 692

493 *Details of a bed.* Cairo, Egyptian Museum. After W. B. EMERY. 'Great Tombs of the First Dynasty', p. 57, fig. 28. Cairo, Service des Antiquités Égyptiennes, 1949. T. A. Greeves 693

494 *Marquetry casket of Tutankhamen.* Cairo, Egyptian Museum. After original photograph in the Griffith Institute, Ashmolean Museum, Oxford. D. E. Woodall 693

495 *Toilet casket from Thebes.* Carnarvon Collection, Metropolitan Museum of Art, New York. (A) *Box.* After H. CARTER and G. E. S. M. HERBERT. 'Five Years of Explorations at Thebes', Pl. XLVIII, i. London, Oxford University Press, 1912. T. A. Greeves. (B) *Access to the upper tray.* After H. E. WINLOCK. 'The Treasure of El-Lahun', p. 16, fig. 25. New York, Metropolitan Museum of Art, 1934. Diagram by the author. (C) *Securing lid.* After J. G. WILKINSON. 'The Manners and Customs of the Ancient Egyptians' (new ed., rev.), p. 18. London. 1878. Diagram by the author 694

496 (A) *Trinket box from Sedment.* By courtesy of Royal Scottish Museum, Edinburgh (Inv. No. 1921. 1647). Sketch by the author. (B) *Automatic fastening.* Diagram by the author 695

497 *Back of the linen chest of Tutankhamen.* Cairo, Egyptian Museum. After original photograph in the Griffith Institute, Ashmolean Museum, Oxford. D. E. Woodall 696

498 *Furniture represented in the tomb of Hesi-Re.* Cairo, Egyptian Museum. After J. E. QUIBELL. 'Excavations at Saqqara 1911–12, The Tomb of Hesy', Pl. XVII, no. 28; Pl. XVIII, nos. 35, 36, 38, 39, 40. Cairo, Service des Antiquités Égyptiennes, 1913. D. E. Woodall 697

499 *An armchair of Queen Kawit depicted on her sarcophagus.* Cairo, Egyptian Museum. After E. D. ROSS. 'The Art of Egypt through the Ages', Pl. CXLII, i. London, Studio, 1931. D. E. Woodall 698

500 *Corn-measure represented in the tomb of Hesi-Re.* Cairo, Egyptian Museum. After J. E. QUIBELL. 'Excavations at Saqqara 1911–12, The Tomb of Hesy', Pl. XIII, detail. Cairo, Service des Antiquités Égyptiennes, 1913. D. E. Woodall 698

501 *Palanquin of Queen Hetep-heres.* Cairo, Egyptian Museum. After G. REISNER. *Bull. Boston Mus.* **26**, 85, top fig., 1928. Boston, Museum of Fine Arts. T. A. Greeves 699

502 *Bedroom furniture.* Cairo, Egyptian Museum. After photograph in the Museum of Fine Arts, Boston. By courtesy of the Director. T. A. Greeves 700

503 *Jointing of the canopy shown in figure 502.* After photograph in the Museum of Fine Arts, Boston. By courtesy of the Director. T. A. Greeves 701

504 *Ointment spoon.* Paris, Louvre. After H. FECHHEIMER. 'Die Kleinplastik der Aegypter', p. 148. Berlin, Cassirer, 1921. D. E. Woodall 702

26. LAND TRANSPORT WITHOUT WHEELS. ROADS AND BRIDGES *by* S. M. COLE

505 *Load-carrying.* After C. L. WOOLLEY. 'The Royal Cemetery.' Ur Excavations. Rep. Vol. 2, Pls. XCII, CLXXXI, details. London, British Museum, 1934. By courtesy of the Trustees. D. E. Woodall 705

506 *Model of a palanquin.* From A. J. EVANS. 'The Palace of Minos', Vol. 2, i, fig. 80. London, Macmillan, 1928 705

507 *Pack asses.* From P. E. NEWBERRY. 'Beni Hasan', Part 1, Pl. XXXI. London, Egypt Exploration Society, 1893 706

508 *Runner with reconstructed sledge.* From J. G. D. CLARK. 'Prehistoric Europe', fig. 162. After ITKONEN. London, Methuen, 1952 707

509 *'Arctic' ski and stick.* From J. G. D. CLARK. *Ibid.*, fig. 165, nos. 2, 3. After BERG. 708

510 *Reconstruction of sledge-chariot.* After C. L. WOOLLEY. 'The Royal Cemetery.' Ur Excavations. Rep. Vol. 2, Pl. CXXII. London, British Museum, 1934. By courtesy of the Trustees. T. A. Greeves 709

511 *Transport of the statue of Ti.* After G. STEINDORFF. 'Das Grab des Ti', Pls. LXVIII, LXVII. Leipzig, Hinrichs, 1913. D. E. Woodall 710

512 *Primitive draught vehicles.* From A. J. H. GOODWIN. 'Communication Has Been Established', p. 74, fig. VI. London, Methuen, 1937. (Adapted from G. BERG. 'Sledges and Wheeled Vehicles'. Copenhagen, Levin and Munksgaard, 1935, and A. C. HADDON. 'The Study of Man'. London, Bliss, Sands, 1898) 710

513 *Dog travois.* From G. L. WILSON. 'The Horse and the Dog in Hidatsa Culture.' *Anthrop. Pap. Amer. Mus.* **15,** ii, 282, fig. III, 1924. New York, American Museum of Natural History 711

514 *Ancient cart tracks.* After T. ZAMMIT. *Antiquity* **1,** Pl. I, facing p. 18, 1928. Newbury, Edwards. T. A. Greeves 712

27. WHEELED VEHICLES *by* V. GORDON CHILDE

515 *Carts with paired draught.* (A) *Early Chinese pictograph.* From F. H. CHALFANT. 'Early Chinese Writing', Mem. Carneg. Mus. Vol. 4, No. 1, Pl. XV, no. 206, detail. Pittsburgh, Carnegie Museum, 1906. (B) *Clay model.* After I. V. SINITSYN. *Sovetsk. Arkheol.* **10,** 150, fig. 14, 1948. Moscow, Academy of Science, U.S.S.R. D. E. Woodall 717

516 *Clay model of a cart.* After V. G. CHILDE. *Proc. prehist. Soc.* new series **17,** ii, Pl. IX b, c, facing p. 179, 1951. Cambridge, Prehistoric Society. D. E. Woodall 717

517 *Four-wheeled war-chariots from the mosaic 'standard'.* London, British Museum, No. 121201. After C. L. WOOLLEY. 'The Royal Cemetery.' Ur Excavations. Rep. Vol. 2, Pl. XCII, detail. London, British Museum, 1934. By courtesy of the Trustees. D. E. Woodall 718

518 (A) *Model wagon.* From A. J. EVANS. 'The Palace of Minos', Vol. 2, i, fig. 78. London, Macmillan, 1928. (B) *Copper model of a cart.* After E. J. H. MACKAY. 'Chanhu-daro Excavations 1935–36', Pl. LVIII, 2. New Haven, American Oriental Society, 1943. D. E. Woodall 719

519 *Copper model of a chariot.* Baghdad, Iraq Museum. From photograph by courtesy of the Oriental Institute, University of Chicago 720

520 *Bit.* From J. G. D. CLARK. 'Prehistoric Europe', fig. 171. London, Methuen, 1952 722

521 (A) *Bronze bit,* (B) *cheek-piece.* From W. M. F. PETRIE. 'Ancient Gaza', Vol. 4, Pl. XXXV, nos. 558, 555. London, British School of Egyptian Archaeology, 1934 722

522 *Jointed Egyptian bit.* Berlin, Staatl. Museen, No. 17326. After H. A. POTRATZ. *Arch. Orientforsch.* **14,** fig. 5, 1941–4. Graz, Veldner. D. E. Woodall 723

523 *Relief showing Assyrian bit.* London, British Museum. After H. A. POTRATZ. *Ibid.*, fig. 1. D. E. Woodall 723

524 *Engraving depicting a chariot.* After V. G. CHILDE. 'Prehistoric Migration in Europe', fig. 154. Oslo, Instituttet Sammenlignende Kulturforskning, 1950. D. E. Woodall 726

525 *Egyptian chariot.* Museo Archeologico, Florence, Inv. No. 2678 a. By courtesy of the Soprintendenza alle antichità d'Etruria, Florence. T. A. Greeves 726

526 *The Assyrian hunting chariot. Relief.* London, British Museum, Nimrud Gallery no. 4 A. After H. R. H. HALL. 'Babylonian and Assyrian Sculpture in the British Museum', Pl. XVIII (B). Paris, Van Oest, 1928. D. E. Woodall 727

527 *Chariot of Thotmes IV.* Cairo, Egyptian Museum. After H. CARTER and P. E. NEWBERRY. 'The Tomb of Thutmosis IV.' Catal. gén. antiq. égypt. Mus. Caire, Nos. 46001–46529, Pl. X. London, Constable, 1904 727

528 *Fragment of a clay toy.* After A. J. B. WACE. *Ill. Lond. News*, 1 November 1952, p. 719, fig. 20 and *Annu. Brit. Sch. Athens* **48,** p. 85, fig. 47. D. E. Woodall 728

TAILPIECE. *Cretan chariot.* From A. J. EVANS. 'The Palace of Minos', Vol. 4, ii, fig. 803. London, Macmillan, 1935 729

28. BOATS AND SHIPS *by* ADRIAN DIGBY

529 *Coracle.* Cambridge, University Museum of Archaeology and Ethnology, No. 46.396. By courtesy of the Curator. D. E. Woodall 731

530 *Pottery vase made in the form of a boat.* London, British Museum, No. 1939 Am. 152. D. E. Woodall 731

531 *Boat made of ambatch reeds.* After J. HORNELL. 'Water Transport', Pl. VII A. Cambridge, University Press, 1946. D. E. Woodall 732

532 *Egyptian papyrus canoe.* After J. HORNELL. *Ibid.*, Pl. VI B. D. E. Woodall 732

533 *Reed sailing boat.* After NORMAN DE G. DAVIES. 'The Rock Tombs of Deir-el-Gebrâwi', Vol. 2, Pl. XIX. Archaeol. Survey Egypt, Mem. No. 12. London, Egypt Exploration Society, 1902. D. E. Woodall 733

534 *Egyptian river boat.* From P. E. NEWBERRY. 'Beni Hasan', Part 1, Pl. XXIX, detail. London, Egypt Exploration Society, 1893 734

535 *Model of a ship of Dynasty V.* After R. O. FAULKNER. *J. Egypt. Archaeol.* **26**, Pl. II, 1940. London, Egypt Exploration Society. D. E. Woodall 734

536 *Model of a ship of the time of Queen Hatshepsut.* After R. O. FAULKNER. *Ibid.*, Pl. IV. D. E. Woodall 735

537 *Modern* quffas *on the Tigris.* After E. A. T. W. BUDGE. 'By Nile and Tigris', Vol. 1, Pl. facing p. 182. London, John Murray, 1920. D. E. Woodall 737

538 *Dug-out canoe.* London, British Museum. From BRITISH MUSEUM. 'A Guide to the Antiquities of the Bronze Age' (2nd ed.), p. 115, fig. 123. London, British Museum, 1920. By courtesy of the Trustees 738

539 *Plank-built boat.* From E. V. WRIGHT and C. W. WRIGHT. *Proc. prehist. Soc.*, new series **13**, p. 124, fig. 7; p. 125, fig. 8, 1947. Cambridge, Prehistoric Society 738

540 *Diagrammatic sections illustrating the development of the keel.* Diagrams by the author 739

541 *Model of an outrigger.* London, British Museum. D. E. Woodall 740

542 *Singhalese* yathra dhoni. From J. HORNELL. 'Water Transport', p. 257, fig. 60. Cambridge, University Press, 1946 740

543 *War galley.* London, British Museum, No. 124772. After 'Assyrian Sculpture in the British Museum', Pl. XL. London, British Museum, 1938. By courtesy of the Trustees. D. E. Woodall 741

TAILPIECE. *Reed boat.* After J. HORNELL. 'Water Transport', Pl. V A. Cambridge, University Press, 1946. By courtesy of Mr. H. C. Gilson. D. E. Woodall 743

29. RECORDING AND WRITING *by* S. H. HOOKE

544 *Rhinoceros, buffalo, and hunter.* After ALAN HOUGHTON BRODRICK. 'Lascaux', Pl. XLIV. London, Benn, 1949. D. E. Woodall 745

545 *Pictographic tablet from Erech.* Berlin, Staatl. Museen. After S. H. HOOKE. *Antiquity* **11**, Pl. V foll. p. 272, 1937. Newbury, Edwards. D. E. Woodall 746

546 *Reconstruction of stylus.* (A) *Early form.* From A. FALKENSTEIN. 'Archaische Texte aus Uruk', p. 6, fig. 1, no. 1. Leipzig, Harrassowitz, 1936. (B) *Possible shapes of the later stylus.* From G. R. DRIVER. 'Semitic Writing.' The Schweich Lectures, British Academy, 1944, p. 24, fig. 5. London, Oxford University Press, 1948 750

547 *Development of the sign SAG.* From S. H. HOOKE. *Antiquity* **11**, 275, fig. 1, 1937. Newbury, Edwards 751

548 *Diagram showing change of position of the tablet.* From S. H. HOOKE. *Ibid.*, p. 276, fig. 2 751

549 *Early Persian syllabary.* From G. R. DRIVER. 'Semitic Writing.' The Schweich Lectures, British Academy, 1944, p. 132, fig. 79. London, Oxford University Press, 1948 752

550 *The same passage in hieroglyphic and hieratic scripts.* From S. H. HOOKE. *Antiquity* **11**, 269, 1937. Newbury, Edwards 754

551 *King Narmer's palette.* Cairo, Egyptian Museum. From S. H. HOOKE. *Ibid.*, Pl. I facing p. 272 755

552 *Collecting and preparing the papyrus plant.* From NORMAN DE G. DAVIES and H. R. HOPGOOD. 'Robb de Peyster Tytus Memorial Series II, The Tomb of Puyemre, Thebes', Pl. XV. New York, Metropolitan Museum of Art, 1922 756

553 *Hittite hieroglyphs.* From D. G. HOGARTH *et al.* 'Carchemish', Part 1, Pl. A, 3a*. London, British Museum, 1914. By courtesy of the Trustees 758

554 (A) *Linear Minoan Script B.* From J. J. M. DE MORGAN. 'La Préhistoire orientale', Vol. 3, p. 355, fig. 371. Paris, Geuthner, 1927. (B) *One side of the Phaistos disk.* From A. J. EVANS. 'Scripta Minoa', Vol. 1, p. 23, fig. 11 a. Oxford, Clarendon Press, 1909 759

555 *Pictographic seal impressions.* After J. MARSHALL. 'Mohenjo-Daro and the Indus Civilisation', Vol. 3, Pl. CIV, no. 38; Pl. CXI, no. 337. London, Probsthain, 1931. D. E. Woodall 760

556 *Sinaitic script.* From M. J. LEIBOVITCH. *Bull. Inst. égypt.* **16,** 180, fig. 2, 1933–4. Cairo, Institut d'Égypte 762

557 *A farmer's calendar from Gezer.* After D. DIRINGER. 'Le Iscrizioni antico-ebraiche palestinesi.' Pubbl. R. Univ. Firenze, Facc. lett. filos. series 3, Vol. 2, Pl. II, 2. Florence. 1934. And after M. LIDZBARSKI. *Palest. Explor. Quart.* 1909, Pl. facing p. 28, fig. 1. London, Palestine Exploration Society. D. E. Woodall 764

558 *Moabitic inscription on the stele of King Mesha.* From M. LIDZBARSKI. 'Handbuch der nord-semitischen Epigraphik', Vol. 2, Pl. 1. Weimar, Felber, 1898 765

559 *Hebrew inscription in the Siloam tunnel.* Adapted from W. GESENIUS. 'Hebrew Grammar' (ed. by E. KAUTZSCH, 2nd Engl. ed.), unnumbered Pl. Oxford, Clarendon Press, 1946 765

560 *Inscribed sherd from Lachish.* From H. TORCZYNER *et al.* 'Lachish I', p. 36, letter II. London, Oxford University Press, 1938. Copyright: by permission of the Trustees of the late Sir Henry S. Wellcome 766

561 *Nabataean inscription.* After G. A. COOKE. 'A Text-book of North Semitic Inscriptions', Pl. VII. Oxford, Clarendon Press, 1903. D. E. Woodall 766

562 *The earliest extant written Arabic.* From D. DIRINGER. 'The Alphabet', p. 271, fig. 133. London, Hutchinson, 1948 767

563 *Earliest treaty known in the Greek language.* From D. DIRINGER. *Ibid.*, p. 452, fig. 198, 2 767

564 *The* cippus *of Perugia.* After G. BUONAMICI. 'Epigrafia etrusca', Pl. XLIV, A. Florence. Rinascimento del Libro (for Istituto di Studi etruschi), 1932. D. E. Woodall 769

565 *The 'fibula' of Praeneste.* From H. DEGERING. 'Lettering', Pl. VIII. London, Benn, 1929 770

TAILPIECE. *Impression of a pictographic seal.* After J. MARSHALL. 'Mohenjo-Daro and the Indus Civilization.' Vol. 1, Pl. XII, no. 17. London, Probsthain, 1931. D. E. Woodall 773

30. MEASURES AND WEIGHTS *by* F. G. SKINNER

566 *Egyptian royal cubits of Amenhetep I* (Turin, Museo Egizio), *and of his vizier* (Paris, Louvre). From print lent by the author 776

567 *Statue of Gudea, bearing a tablet with a graduated rule.* Paris, Louvre. After photograph by Vizzavona. D. E. Woodall 780

568 *Babylonian 'sleeping duck' weights.* London, British Museum, Nos. 91438, 113897, 91433. By courtesy of the Trustees. D. E. Woodall 780

569 *Egyptian wooden balance, with animal and bird weights.* London, Science Museum, South Kensington. By courtesy of the Director. D. E. Woodall 783

570 *Egyptian copper capacity measure.* London, Science Museum, South Kensington. By courtesy of the Director. D. E. Woodall 784

TAILPIECE. *A jeweller's balance.* From NORMAN DE G. DAVIES. 'Robb de Peyster Tytus Memorial Series IV, The Tomb of Two Sculptors at Thebes', Pl. XI, detail. New York, Metropolitan Museum of Art, 1925 784

PLATES

1 *Flint-working techniques.* Photographs by courtesy of L. S. B. Leakey

2 *Late Palaeolithic representations of animals.* (A) *Bison from Altamira.* From E. CARTAILHAC and H. BREUIL. 'La caverne d'Altamira', Pl. XIX. Monaco, 1906–8. (Institut de Paléontologie Humaine, Paris). (B) *Horse from the Covalanas cave, Spain.* From H. ALCALDE DEL RIO *et al.* 'Les Cavernes de la Région Cantabrique', Pl. XII. Monaco, 1911. (Institut de Paléontologie Humaine, Paris)

3A *Cosmetic jar.* Cairo, Egyptian Museum. Photograph by courtesy of the Griffith Institute, Ashmolean Museum, Oxford

3B *Canopic jars.* London, British Museum, Nos. 59197–59200. By courtesy of the Trustees

4 *Worked oak timbers and wattle-work, Glastonbury lake-village.* Photograph by courtesy of H. St. George Gray and Glastonbury Antiquarian Society

5A *Italian Neolithic impressions of wattle-work.* Photograph by courtesy of John Bradford

5B *One of a pair of Iron Age fire-dogs.* Cambridge, Museum of Archaeology and Ethnology. By courtesy of the Curator

6A *Deer-shooting with a decoy. From a mosaic.* Rouen, Musée des Beaux Arts. Photograph by M. B. Lefebvre

6B *Head of an Iron Age man preserved in a peat bog near Tollund.* Photograph by Lennart Larsen, Danish National Museum, for the Royal Danish Ministry for Foreign Affairs

7 *Ears of wheat.* Photograph by courtesy of Institute of Archaeology, University of London

8 *Some Western Neolithic pottery types.* (A) 'Unstan' *bowl. From Eilean an Tighe.* Photograph by courtesy of Sir Lindsay Scott. (B) *Bell-beaker.* Oxford, Ashmolean Museum, Department of Antiquities. Photograph by courtesy of the Keeper. (C) *Jar. From Eilean an Tighe.* (D) *Bowl. From Eilean an Tighe.* Photographs by courtesy of Sir Lindsay Scott

9 *Basket-work.* (A) *Egyptian Neolithic basket.* London, University College. Photograph by courtesy of Miss G. Caton-Thompson. (B) *Hamper coffin.* Photograph by courtesy of the Manchester Museum. (C) *Basket of woven esparto-grass.* Photograph by courtesy of the Museo Arqueológico Nacional, Madrid. (D) *Impression of a rush mat.* Schaffhausen, Museum zu Allerheiligen. Photograph by courtesy of the Schweiz. Landesmuseum, Zürich

10 *Basket-work.* (A) *Oval basket.* Photographs by courtesy of the Metropolitan Museum of Art, New York. (B) *Basket-work bottle, and round basket.* Cairo, Egyptian Museum. Photograph by courtesy of the Griffith Institute, Ashmolean Museum, Oxford

11 *Early Egyptian textiles.* (A) *Fragment of linen from Fayum A.* Photograph by courtesy of Miss G. Caton-Thompson. (B) *Selvedge fringe from Tarkhan.* Bristol, City Museum. By courtesy of the Director

12A *Part of a towel from Deir el-Bahri.* Photograph by courtesy of the Metropolitan Museum of Art, New York

12B *Part of a reconstruction of a fabric from Irgenhausen.* Photograph by courtesy of the Schweiz. Landesmuseum, Zürich

13A *Model of a spinning- and weaving-room.* Photograph by courtesy of the Metropolitan Museum of Art, New York

13B *Braid on a linen saddle-cloth.* Photograph by courtesy of the Metropolitan Museum of Art, New York

14A *Detail of a tapestry with* 'ka-name' *of Thotmes III.* Cairo, Egyptian Museum

14B *Front of one end of the girdle of Rameses III.* Photograph by courtesy of the City of Liverpool Public Museums

15A *Part of another tapestry with the name of Amenhetep II.* By courtesy of the Director of the Egyptian Museum, Cairo. From a slide in the Victoria and Albert Museum, London

15B *Back of the girdle of Rameses III.* Photograph by courtesy of the City of Liverpool Public Museums

16 *Embroidered linen tunic of Tutankhamen.* Cairo, Egyptian Museum. Photograph by courtesy of the Griffith Institute, Ashmolean Museum, Oxford

17A *Girl's dress.* Copenhagen, Nationalmuseet. Photograph by courtesy of the Director

17B *Drawings of textile fibres.* By courtesy of the British Cotton Industry Research Association

18 *Reconstruction of Babylon.* Photograph by courtesy of the Oriental Institute, University of Chicago

19 *Reconstruction of an entrance colonnade.* From J. P. LAUER. 'Fouilles à Saqqarah, la Pyramide à degrés', Vol. 2, Pl. XLV. Cairo, Service des Antiquités Égyptiennes, 1936

20A *Reconstruction of Sennacherib's aqueduct.* Water-colour by Seton Lloyd. Photograph by courtesy of the Oriental Institute, University of Chicago

20B *Egypt: the Nile in flood.* Photograph by Exclusive News Agency, London

21A *Marks of dressing on a trilithon at Stonehenge.* Photograph by courtesy of O. G. S. Crawford

21B *Map of fields and irrigation canals near Nippur.* Photograph by courtesy of the University of Pennsylvania Museum, Philadelphia

22 *The gold inner coffin of Tutankhamen.* Cairo, Egyptian Museum. Photograph by courtesy of the Griffith Institute, Ashmolean Museum, Oxford

23 *Carved and stained panel of ivory.* Cairo, Egyptian Museum. Photograph by courtesy of the Griffith Institute, Ashmolean Museum, Oxford

24 *Furniture from Tutankhamen's tomb.* (A) *Ivory head-rest.* (B) *Ebony bed.* Cairo, Egyptian Museum. Photographs by courtesy of the Griffith Institute, Ashmolean Museum, Oxford

25 *Furniture from Tutankhamen's tomb.* (A) *Chair of state.* (B) *Stool.* Cairo, Egyptian Museum. Photographs by courtesy of the Griffith Institute, Ashmolean Museum, Oxford

26 (A) *Stile in the form of the god Bes.* Photograph by courtesy of the Royal Scottish Museum, Edinburgh. (B) *Detail of one of the panels of Hesi-Re.* Cairo, Egyptian Museum. From J. E. QUIBELL. 'Excavations at Saqqara 1911–12, The Tomb of Hesy', Pl. XXXII. Cairo, Service des Antiquités Égyptiennes, 1913

27 *A Maori war-canoe.* From J. HAWKESWORTH. 'Captain Cook's First Voyage', Vol. 3, Pl. XVI. London. 1773

28 *Inscription of Darius on the Rock of Behistun.* Photograph by courtesy of George G. Cameron, University of Michigan

29A *Detail of the Rock of Behistun.* Photograph in the British Museum, London. By courtesy of the Trustees

29B *Babylonian syllabary.* London, British Museum, No. 92693. Photograph by courtesy of the Trustees

30A *Method of writing on a clay tablet.* From photograph by the Oriental Institute, University of Chicago

30B *Tablet from Ugarit.* Paris, Louvre, No. AO 17321. From C. VIROLLEAUD. 'La Légende phénicienne de Danel', Pl. XVII. Paris, Geuthner, 1936

31A *Inscription from the tomb of Ahiram.* From R. DUSSAUD. 'Les Inscriptions phéniciennes du tombeau d'Ahiram', Pl. XI b. Paris, Geuthner, 1924

31B *Prehistoric Egyptian balance and weights.* London, Science Museum, South Kensington. By courtesy of the Director

32 *Writing outfit from the tomb of Tutankhamen.* Cairo, Egyptian Museum. Photograph by courtesy of the Griffith Institute, Ashmolean Museum, Oxford

33 *Old Babylonian mathematical text.* Photograph by courtesy of Yale University, (No. YBC 46 68)

34 *Late Babylonian table for the motions of the planet Jupiter.* London, British Museum, No. 45707. Photograph by courtesy of the Trustees

35 *Transcription of plate 34*

36 *Papyrus Carlsberg 9.* Photograph by courtesy of Ny Carlsberg Glyptothek, Copenhagen

TABLES

A. *Chronology of the Earth* xlix
B. *Chronology of Life and the Geological Periods* l
C. *Evolution of Man* li
D. *Chronology of the Old Stone Age or Palaeolithic* lii
E. *Chronology of the Mesolithic, Neolithic, and Metal Ages* liii
F. *Late Prehistoric and Historic Chronology* liv

I *Vegetable Oils of the Near East* 288
II *Natural Perfumes and Flavours of the Ancient Near East* 288
III *Outline of the Evolution of Mining* 574
IV *Chronological Chart of Early Metallurgy* 575

MAPS
(*pp* lvii–lxiv)

All maps prepared for *A History of Technology*, Maps I A and 2 by S. M. Cole, Map I B by N. J. G. Pounds, and Maps 3–8 by R. H. G. Thomson

IA *Distribution of Mousterian industries and of remains of Neanderthal Man*
IB *The 'Fertile Crescent'*
2 *Type sites of Palaeolithic industries in France*
3 *Some sites in the lake-dwelling district*
4 *Greece and Asia Minor*
5 *Persia and the Indus Valley*
6 *The Nile Valley*
7 *Mesopotamia*
8 *Palestine and Syria*

ABBREVIATIONS OF PERIODICAL TITLES

(AS SUGGESTED BY THE WORLD LIST OF SCIENTIFIC PERIODICALS)

Abbreviation	Title
Abh. heidelberg. Akad. Wiss., phil.-hist. Kl.	Abhandlungen der Heidelberger Akademie der Wissenschaften, philosophisch-historische Klasse. Heidelberg
Abh. preuss. Akad. Wiss., phil.-hist. Kl.	Abhandlungen der Preussischen Akademie der Wissenschaften, philosophisch-historische Klasse. Berlin
Acta Orientalia	Societates Orientales Batava, Danica, Norvegica. E. J. Brill, Leiden
Advanc. Sci., Lond.	Advancement of Science. British Association for the Advancement of Science. London
Ambix	Journal of the Society for the Study of Alchemy and Early Chemistry. London
Amer. Anthrop.	American Anthropologist. American Anthropological Association. Washington
Amer. Antiq.	American Antiquity. Society for American Archaeology. Menasha, Wis.
Amer. J. Archaeol.	American Journal of Archaeology. Archaeological Institute of America. Cambridge, Mass.
Amer. J. Semitic Lang. and Lit.	American Journal of Semitic Languages and Literatures. University of Chicago, Department of Oriental Languages and Literatures. Chicago, Ill. [Continued as *Journal of Near Eastern Studies*, q.v.]
Analyst	Society of Public Analysts and other Analytical Chemists. London
Ancient Egypt	Ancient Egypt and the East. London School of Archaeology in Egypt. London
Ann. Archaeol. Anthrop.	Annals of Archaeology and Anthropology. University of Liverpool, School of Archaeology and Oriental Studies. Liverpool
Ann. Ist. Corres. Archeol.	Annali dell' Istituto di Correspondenza Archeologica. Rome
Ann. Serv. Antiq. Égypte	Annales du Service des Antiquités de l'Égypte. Cairo. (Presses Universitaires de France, Paris)
Annu. Amer. Sch. orient. Res.	Annual of the American Schools of Oriental Research. New Haven, Conn.
Annu. Brit. Sch. Athens	Annual of the British School in Athens. London
Anthrop. Pap. Amer. Mus.	Anthropological Papers of the American Museum of Natural History. New York
Anthropos	Internationale Zeitschrift für Völker- und Sprachenkunde. Anthropos-Institut. Vienna
Antiq. J.	Antiquaries' Journal. The Journal of the Society of Antiquaries of London. London

Antiquity	Edwards, Newbury, Berks.
Arch. Orientforsch.	Archiv für Orientforschung. Internationale Zeitschrift für die Wissenschaft vom Vorderen Orient. Graz
Arch. vergl. Phonetik	Archiv für vergleichende Phonetik. (Deutsches Sprach-archiv.) Gesellschaft für Phonetik. Berlin
Archaeol. J.	Archaeological Journal. Royal Archaeological Institute of Great Britain and Ireland. London
Archaeologia	Archaeologia or Miscellaneous Tracts relating to Antiquity. Society of Antiquaries. London
Archaeologia Austriaca	Beiträge zur Paläanthropologie, Ur- und Frühgeschichte Österreichs. Universität Wien, Anthropologisches Institut. Vienna
Archaeologia Cambrensis	Journal of the Cambrian Archaeological Association. Cardiff
Archaeologia Hungarica	Magyar Nemzeti Muzeum. Budapest
Archeologické Rozhledy	Státní Archeologický Ústav. [Archaeological News, State Institute of Archaeology.] Prague
Bankfield Mus. Notes	Bankfield Museum Notes. Halifax
Biol. Skr.	Biologiske Skrifter. Kongelige Dansk Videnskabernes Selskab. Copenhagen
Bitumen	Arbeitsgemeinschaft der Bitumenindustrie. Berlin
Bull. Anim. Behav.	Bulletin of Animal Behaviour. Association for the Study of Animal Behaviour. London
Bull appl. Bot. Pl.-Breed.	Bulletin of Applied Botany and Plant Breeding. Federate Institute of Applied Botany and New Culture. Leningrad. Труды по Прикладной Ботанике и Селекции. Есесоюзный Институт Прикладной Ботанике и Новых Культур. Ленинград
Bull. Boston Mus.	Museum of Fine Arts Bulletin. Boston, Mass.
Bull. Brooklyn Mus.	Brooklyn Museum Bulletin. New York
Bull. Bur. Amer. Ethnol.	Bulletin of the Bureau of American Ethnology. Smithsonian Institution. Washington
Bull. Corr. Hell.	Bulletin de Correspondance Hellénique. École Française d'Athènes. Athens, Paris
Bull. Étud. orient.	Bulletin d'Études orientales. Institut Français de Damas. Cairo. (Presses Universitaires de France, Paris)
Bull. Fac. Sci. Egypt. Univ.	Bulletin of the Faculty of Science. Egyptian University. Cairo
Bull. geol. Surv. China	Bulletin of the Geological Survey of China. Peking
Bull. Inst. égypt.	Bulletin de l'Institut égyptien (d'Égypte). Cairo
Bull. Metr. Mus.	Bulletin of the Metropolitan Museum of Art. New York
Bull. Soc. Anthrop. Paris	Bulletin et mémoires de la Société d'anthropologie de Paris
Bull. Soc. préhist. franç.	Bulletin de la Société préhistorique française. Paris

Catal. gén. antiq. égypt. Mus. Caire	Services des Antiquités de l'Égypte. Catalogue Général des Antiquités Égyptiennes du Musée du Caire. (Various publishers and places)
Chem. & Ind. (Rev.)	Chemistry and Industry (Review). The Society of Chemical Industry. London
Ciba-Rdsch.	Ciba Rundschau. Society of Chemical Industry. Basle
Ciba Rev.	Ciba Review. Society of Chemical Industry. Basle
Cymmrodor	Cymmrodor. Hon. Society of Cymmrodorion. London
Denkschr. Schweiz. naturf. Ges.	Denkschriften der Schweizerischen Naturforschenden Gesellschaft. Zürich
Dtsch. Essigindust.	Deutsche Essigindustrie. Berlin
Egypt. Res. Acc. and Brit. Sch. Archaeol. Egypt	Egyptian Research Account and British School of Egyptian Archaeology. London
Ergebn. Biol.	Ergebnisse der Biologie. Berlin
Ex Oriente Lux, Jaarber.	Jaarbericht. Vooraziatisch-Egyptisch Genootschap 'Ex Oriente Lux'. Leiden
Forsch. Fortschr. dtsch. Wiss.	Forschungen und Fortschritte. Korrespondenzblatt der Deutschen Wissenschaft und Technik. Berlin
Gaz. Archéol.	Gazette Archéologique. Paris
Geogr. J.	Geographical Journal. Royal Geographical Society. London
Germania	Korrespondenzblatt der Römisch-Germanischen Kommission. Archäologisches Institut des Deutschen Reiches. Berlin, Frankfurt a. M.
Homme préhist.	Homme préhistorique. Paris
Ibis	A quarterly journal of ornithology. London
Ill. Lond. News	Illustrated London News. London
Int. Arch. Ethnogr.	Internationales Archiv für Ethnographie. E. J. Brill, Leiden
Iraq	British School of Archaeology in Iraq. London
J. acoust. Soc. Amer.	Journal of the Acoustical Society of America. Menasha, Wis.
J. Amer. diet. Ass.	Journal of the American Dietetic Association. Baltimore, Md.
J. Amer. orient. Soc.	Journal of the American Oriental Society. Baltimore, Md.
J. Egypt. Archaeol.	Journal of Egyptian Archaeology. Egypt Exploration Society. London
J. Hell. Stud.	Journal of Hellenic Studies. Society for the Promotion of Hellenic Studies. London
J. Indian Art	Journal of Indian Art. London
J. Instn Petrol. Tech.	Journal of the Institution of Petroleum Technologists. London. [Continued as *Journal of the Institute of Petroleum*]
J. Iron St. Inst.	Journal of the Iron and Steel Institute. London
J. Mammal.	Journal of Mammalogy. American Society of Mammalogists. Baltimore, Md.

J. Near East. Stud.	Journal of Near Eastern Studies. University of Chicago, Department of Oriental Languages and Literatures. Chicago, Ill. [Continuation of *American Journal of Semitic Languages and Literatures*, q.v.]
J. R. anthrop. Inst.	Journal of the Royal Anthropological Institute of Great Britain and Ireland. London
J. R. Asiat. Soc.	Journal of the Royal Asiatic Society. London
J. Walters Art Gallery	Journal of the Walters Art Gallery. Baltimore, Md.
Jb. preuss. Kunstsamml.	Jahrbuch der Preussischen Kunstsammlungen. Grote, Berlin
K. Vitterhets Hist. Antik. Akad. Monogr.	Kongliga Vitterhets Historie- och Antikvitets-Akademien Monograf-Serien. Stockholm
Kali	Kali und verwandte Salze. Deutscher Kaliverein. Halle
Lond. Univ. Inst. Archaeol. Annu. Rep.	Annual Report of the Archaeological Institute of the University of London. London
Louvre, Dép. Antiq. Orient., Sér. archéol.	Départment des Antiquités Orientales, Série archéologique. Musée du Louvre. Paris
Man	Royal Anthropological Institute. London
Man in India	A quarterly Record of Anthropological Science with special reference to India. Ranchi
Matér. hist. homme	Matériaux pour l'histoire primitive et naturelle de l'homme. Paris
Melliand's Textilber.	Melliand's Textilberichte. Mannheim. [Continued as *Melliand Textilberichte*. Heidelberg]
Mem. Amer. philos. Soc.	Memoirs of the American Philosophical Society. Philadelphia, Pa.
Mem. Carneg. Mus.	Memoirs of the Carnegie Museum, Pittsburgh, Pa.
Mém. Délég. Perse	Mémoires de la Délégation en Perse du Ministère de l'Instruction publique et des Beaux-Arts. Paris. [Continued as *Mémoires de la Mission Archéologique de Perse*]
Mém. Inst. colon. belge Sci. morales 8°	Mémoires de l'Institut royal colonial belge. Section des Sciences morales et politiques. Collection in octavo. Brussels
Mém. Inst. égypt.	Mémoires presentés à l'Institut égyptien (d'Égypte). Cairo
Mém. Inst. franç. Archéol. orient. Caire	Mémoires de l'Institut français d'Archéologie orientale du Caire. Cairo
Metr. Mus. Occas. Pap.	Occasional Paper of the Metropolitan Museum of Art. New York
Monum. Piot	Fondation Eugène Piot, Monuments et Mémoires. Académie des Inscriptions et Belles-Lettres. Paris
N. Denkschr. schweiz. Ges. Naturw.	Neue Denkschriften der Allgemeinen Schweizerischen Gesellschaft für die gesamten Naturwissenschaften. Zürich. [Later becomes *Denkschriften der Schweizerischen Naturforschenden Gesellschaft*, q.v.]

Nat. geogr. Mag.	The National Geographic Magazine. National Geographic Society. Washington
Nat. Hist. Mus. Anthrop. Leaflet	Anthropology Leaflet. Natural History Museum, Chicago
Nat. Mus. Southern Rhodesia Mem.	Memoir of the National Museum of Southern Rhodesia. Bulawayo
Nature	London
Nord. Mus. Handl.	Nordiska Museets Handlingar. Stockholm
Occ. Pap. Tech. Pitt Rivers Mus.	Occasional Papers on Technology. Pitt Rivers Museum. Oxford
Oceania	A journal devoted to the study of the native peoples of Australia, New Guinea and the Islands of the Pacific Ocean. Australian National Research Council. Sydney
Palest. Explor. Quart.	Palestine Exploration Quarterly embodying the Quarterly Statement of the Palestine Exploration Fund and the Bulletin of the British School of Archaeology in Jerusalem. London
Prähist. Z.	Prähistorische Zeitschrift. De Gruyter, Berlin
Preuss. Akad. Wiss., phil.-hist. Abh. nicht zur Akad. gehör. Gelehrter	Preussische Akademie der Wissenschaften, philosophisch-historische Abhandlungen nicht zur Akademie gehöriger Gelehrter. Berlin
Proc. Amer. philos. Soc.	Proceedings of the American Philosophical Society. Philadelphia, Pa.
Proc. Brit. Acad.	Proceedings of the British Academy. London
Proc. Geol. Ass., Lond.	Proceedings of the Geologists' Association. London
Proc. prehist. Soc.	Proceedings of the Prehistoric Society. Cambridge
Proc. R. Irish Acad.	Proceedings of the Royal Irish Academy. Dublin
Proc. Soc. Antiq. Scotld	Proceedings of the Society of Antiquaries in Scotland. Edinburgh
Proc. Soc. Biblical Archaeol.	Proceedings of the Society of Biblical Archaeology. London
Pubbl. R. Univ. Firenze, Facc. lett. filos.	Pubblicazzioni della Reale Università degli Studi di Firenze. Faccoltà di lettere e filosofia. Florence
Quart. Dept. Antiq. Palest.	Quarterly of the Department of Antiquities in Palestine. Government of Palestine. Oxford University Press, London
Rep. Bur. Amer. Ethnol.	Report of the Bureau of American Ethnology. Smithsonian Institution. Washington
Rep. Res. Comm. Soc. Antiq.	Report of the Research Commission of the Society of Antiquaries. London
Rep. sci. Exped. N.-W. Prov. China, Publ.	Reports from the Scientific Expedition to the North-Western Provinces of China. Publications of the Sino-Swedish Expedition. Thule, Stockholm
Rep. Smithson. Instn	Report of the Board of Regents of the Smithsonian Institution. Washington

Res. Pap. Surrey Archaeol. Soc.	Research Papers of the Surrey Archaeological Society. Guildford
Rev. archéol.	Revue archéologique fondée en 1844. Presses Universitaires de France, Paris
Rev. Arts Asiatiques	Revue des Arts Asiatiques. Annales du Musée Guimet. Paris
Rev. d'Assyriologie	Revue d'Assyriologie et d'Archéologie orientale. Presses Universitaires de France, Paris
Rev. mens. Éc. anthrop.	Revue mensuelle de l'École d'anthropologie de Paris
Römisch-Germanische Forschungen	Publication of Römisch-Germanische Kommission, Archäologisches Institut des Deutschen Reiches. De Gruyter, Berlin and Leipzig
S.B. Akad. Wiss. Wien phil.-hist. Kl.	Sitzungsberichte der Akademie der Wissenschaften in Wien, philosophisch-historische Klasse. Vienna
Schlachthofwesen	Schlachthofwesen und Lebensmittelüberwachung. Supplement of *Deutsche Tierärztliche Wochenschrift*. Tierärztliche Hochschule. Hanover
Sci. News, Harmondsworth	Science News. Penguin Books, Harmondsworth
Skr. humanist. VetenskSamf.	Skrifter utgivna av Kungliga humanistiska Vetenskapssamfundet i Lund. (Acta Societatis Humaniorum Litterarum Lundensis.) Lund
Skr. svensk. Inst. Rom	Skrifter utgivna av Svenska Institutet i Rom. (Lund.)
Soc. Prom. Hell. Stud. Suppl. Paper	Society for the Promotion of Hellenic Studies, Supplementary Paper. London
Sovetsk. Arkheol.	(Soviet Archaeology. Academy of Sciences of the U.S.S.R. Institute of Anthropology, Archaeology and Ethnography. Moscow, Leningrad.) Советская Археология. Академия Наук СССР Институт Антропологии, Археологии и Этнографии. Москва, Ленинград
Sudan Notes	Sudan Notes and Records. Proceedings of the Philosophical Society of the Sudan. Khartoum
Sumer	A Journal of Archaeology in Iraq. Iraq Ministry of Education, Department of Antiquities. Baghdad
Syria	Revue d'art oriental et d'archéologie. Institut français d'archéologie de Beyrouth. Paris
Tech. Stud. fine Arts	Technical Studies in the Field of Fine Arts. Harvard University. Fogg Art Museum. Cambridge, Mass.
Trans. Leics. archaeol. Soc.	Transactions of the Leicestershire Archaeological Society. Leicester
Trans. R. geol. Soc. Cornwall	Transactions of the Royal Geological Society of Cornwall. Penzance
Univ. Calif. Publ. Amer. Archaeol. Ethn.	University of California Publications in American Archaeology and Ethnology. Berkeley, Cal.

Univ. Chicago, Orient. Inst.: Commun.	Oriental Institute of the University of Chicago. Communications. Chicago
Univ. Chicago, Orient. Inst.: Publ.	Oriental Institute of the University of Chicago. Publications. Chicago
Univ. Chicago, Orient. Inst.: Stud. ancient orient. Civiliz.	Oriental Institute of the University of Chicago. Studies in ancient oriental Civilization. Chicago
Uppsala Univ. Årsskr.	Uppsala Universitets Årsskrift. Uppsala
Ur Excavations. Rep.	Ur Excavations. Reports. Publications of the Joint Expedition of the British Museum and of the Museum of the University of Pennsylvania to Mesopotamia. London
Verh. Akad. Wet. Amst., Afd. Letterkunde	Verhandelingen der Koninklijke Nederlandsche Akademie van Wetenschappen. Afdeeling Letterkunde. Amsterdam
Veröff. Völkermus. Frankfurt	Veröffentlichungen aus dem Städtischen Völkermuseum. Frankfurt a. M.
Vjschr. naturf. Ges. Zürich	Vierteljahrsschrift der Naturforschenden Gesellschaft in Zürich
Wiss. Veröff. dtsch. Orientges.	Wissenschaftliche Veröffentlichungen der Deutschen Orientgesellschaft. Leipzig
Z. Aegypt. Sprache	Zeitschrift für Aegyptische Sprache und Altertumskunde. Leipzig

CHRONOLOGICAL TABLES

F. E. ZEUNER

It is essential for the proper understanding of the History of Technology to have approximate time-scales. Six tables are given here to provide the chronological setting. They give also some guidance concerning the chronological relations of the development of the areas most important for the subject, and the dates of a few significant monarchs. It must not be assumed that the time-scales used are final. They represent temporary solutions to the problem of chronology which their author regards as the most likely. In many cases alternative chronologies have been put forward; in fact chronology is always in the melting-pot.

Table A, a chronology of the Earth, and Table B, a chronology of living forms, together illustrate the extreme slowness of organic evolution as a whole. In Table B a few important steps in the evolution of human ancestors are indicated, as well as sample dates for several other important groups of animals and plants.

Table C takes up the evolution of man in greater detail, beginning with the first simians that can be regarded as ancestral to him. The first three tables illustrate how late man appeared on earth in the long history of life there.

Table D summarizes the development of Old Stone Age (Palaeolithic) cultures to the end of the Ice Age. Table E takes up the story at the end of the Ice Age and leads through the Mesolithic to the Neolithic and Metal Ages. The first evidence for agriculture is here indicated.

Table F gives a few important historical dates from about 3000 B.C. onwards. Even here there are many uncertainties, especially in the earlier periods, where dates are liable to err up to as much as 200 years.

These tables as a whole demonstrate the acceleration of technological evolution characteristic of man. Through long periods of the earlier past there was little change in the technological level. Man's ancestors had hands free for use, and the necessary brain capacity, for a very long period of time before tools were shaped. When these appeared, the particular shapes used remained the same for hundreds of thousands of years. Only within the last 150 000 years or so has the tempo of change appreciably increased. It increased more when, about 100 000 years ago *Homo sapiens*, modern man, appeared on the scene, but even the Upper Palaeolithic cultures, the work of this new creature, are measured in tens of thousands of years. The great acceleration came with the beginning of the Neolithic, when man adopted the practice of food-production and added it to or substituted it for mere food-gathering. This great revolution freed his hands and mind from the preoccupation of acquiring foodstuffs, which could be delegated to a small number of experts in the community. From this time onwards technology has evolved at an ever-increasing rate.

The main authorities upon whom the tables rely are: R. J. Braidwood, S. L. Caiger, V. G. Childe, H. Frankfort, C. F. C. Hawkes, D. E. McCown, Sidney Smith and, in addition, the author's own work on the earlier periods.

A. Chronology of the Earth in Million Years

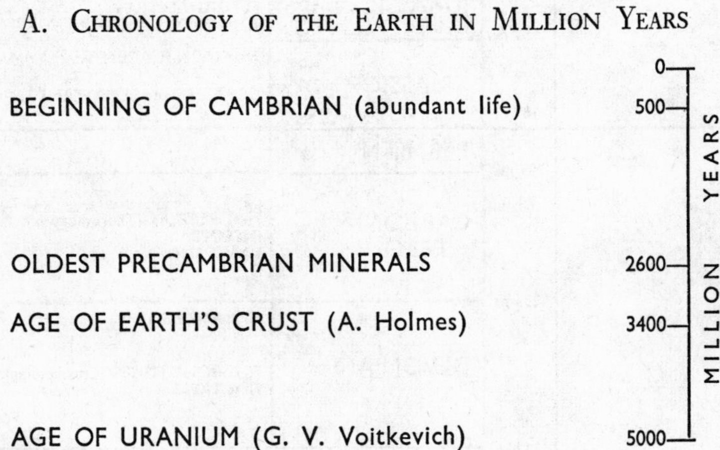

B. Chronology of Life and the Geological Periods

Groups related to the ancestry of man in italics

ERA OR GROUP	YEARS	PERIOD or SYSTEM	FAUNA
	1 m		QUATERNARY with *MAN*
CAINOZOIC	30 m 58 m	TERTIARY	First *APES* First *LEMURS* First *PLACENTALS* MAMMALS BECOMING ABUNDANT
MESOZOIC	127 m	CRETACEOUS	ANGIOSPERMS becoming frequent LARGE DINOSAURS
	152 m	JURASSIC	First BIRDS FLYING REPTILES AMMONITES
	182 m	TRIASSIC	First NON-PLACENTAL MAMMALS CONIFERS and SEED FERNS
	203 m	PERMIAN	
	255 m	CARBONIFEROUS	First *REPTILES* (Theromorpha) INSECTS LAND SPIDERS
	313 m	DEVONIAN	First *AMPHIBIA* First BONY FISHES (*Crossopterygians*) First TREES
	350 m	SILURIAN	SCORPIONS TRILOBITES First LAND PLANTS
PALAEOZOIC	430 m	ORDOVICIAN	First *JAWLESS FISHES* CORALS SEA-URCHINS
	500 m	CAMBRIAN	FORAMINIFERA, STARFISHES, BRACHIOPODS, CRUSTACEA, MARINE 'SPIDERS' (Merostomata)
PROTEROZOIC			First *WORMS*

C. Evolution of Man and Subdivisions of the Pleistocene
Time Column not true to Scale

TENTATIVE TIME-SCALE IN YEARS	PERIOD	CLIMATIC PHASE	MAN AND HIS ANCESTORS
15 000	HOLOCENE	POSTGLACIAL	*Homo sapiens*
100 000	UPPER PLEISTOCENE	LAST GLACIATION	Neanderthal Man
150 000		LAST INTERGLACIAL	Fontéchevade Man
	MIDDLE PLEISTOCENE	PENULTIMATE GLACIATION	
250 000		GREAT INTERGLACIAL	Swanscombe Man
	LOWER PLEISTOCENE	ANTEPENULTIMATE GLACIATION	Heidelberg Man
500 000		ANTEPENULTIMATE INTERGLACIAL	Pithecanthropus Sinanthropus
		EARLY GLACIATION	
600 000		VILLAFRANCHIAN	*Australopithecus* (age conjectural) *Dryopithecus*
c 12 million	PLIOCENE		
c 25 million	MIOCENE		*Proconsul, Dryopithecus*

D. The Chronology of the Old Stone Age or Palaeolithic

TIME-SCALE	CLIMATIC CHRONOLOGY	CHRONOLOGY OF THE ALPS	HUMAN CULTURES IN EUROPE
	POSTGLACIAL		MESOLITHIC and later
100 000–	LAST GLACIATION	WÜRM$_3$ WÜRM$_2$ WÜRM$_1$	UPPER PALAEOLITHIC: AURIGNACIAN, SOLUTRIAN, MAGDALENIAN MOUSTERIAN
	LAST INTERGLACIAL		MOUSTERIAN
200 000–	PENULTIMATE GLACIATION	RISS$_2$ RISS$_1$	ACHEULIAN LEVALLOISIAN
300 000– 400 000–	PENULTIMATE INTERGLACIAL	GREAT INTERGLACIAL	ACHEULIAN LEVALLOISIAN CLACTONIAN
	ANTE-PENULTIMATE GLACIATION	MINDEL$_2$ MINDEL$_1$	CLACTONIAN
500 000–	ANTE-PENULTIMATE INTERGLACIAL		ABBEVILLIAN or CHELLEAN CLACTONIAN
600 000	EARLY GLACIATION	GÜNZ$_2$ GÜNZ$_1$	PRE-ABBEVILLIAN
	VILLAFRANCHIAN		PRE-ABBEVILLIAN

E. Chronology of the Mesolithic, Neolithic, and Metal Ages, Floral Subdivisions of the Postglacial, and the Development of the Baltic Sea

TIME-SCALE	SEA-LEVELS OF THE BALTIC	CLIMATE AND VEGETATION	NORTH EUROPE ARCHAEOLOGY AND ECONOMY	THE EAST	TIME-SCALE
		SUBATLANTIC	IRON AGE		
1000	MYA SEA		Viking		1000
A.D. 0 B.C.	LIMNAEA SEA		Migration Period Roman La Tène Hallstatt	ALEXANDER	A.D. 0 B.C.
1000		SUBBOREAL	BRONZE AGE BRONZE AGE FOOD-PRODUCERS (Farmers) Food gatherers continuing in remote places		1000
2000	LITORINA SEA WITH SEVERAL TRANSGRESSIONS		Stone cists Single graves Passage Graves Dolmen (Dysser) First Neolithic NEOLITHIC	HAMMURABI	2000
3000				UR, ROYAL TOMBS JEMDET NASR URUK III *EGYPT*:	3000
4000		ATLANTIC	ERTEBØLLE CULTURE GUDENAA INLAND CULTURE	GERZEAN AMRATIAN BADARIAN URUK-WARKA EL-UBAID TEPE GAWRA TELL HALAF	4000
5000				TASIAN FAYUM-A HASSUNA JARMO (Earliest Agricultural Village)	5000
6000				KARIM SHAHIR (? PROTO-NEOLITHIC) ? NATUFIAN	6000
7000	ANCYLUS LAKE	BOREAL	Mullerup (Maglemose) MESOLITHIC		7000
8000	YOLDIA SEA	YOUNGER DRYAS TIME	Lyngby Ahrensburg		8000
9000	BALTIC ICE-LAKE	ALLERØD OSCILLATION	Bromme		9000
10 000		OLDER DRYAS TIME		PALE GAWRA. EPI-PALAEOLITHIC	10 000
11 000					11 000
12 000			? Hamburgian PALAEOLITHIC FOOD-GATHERERS (HUNTERS—FISHERMEN—COLLECTORS)		12 000

F. Late Prehistoric and Historic Chronology from *c* 3000 B.C. to the Birth of Christ

TIME-SCALE	VARIOUS EASTERN COUNTRIES	MESOPOTAMIA Periods	MESOPOTAMIA	PALESTINE Periods	PALESTINE	EGYPT King-doms	EGYPT Dyna-sties	EGYPT Kings	GREECE AND THE AEGEAN	TIME-SCALE
0								ROMAN PROVINCE CLEOPATRA		0
100					SELEUCIDS IN SYRIA			PTOLEMIES IN EGYPT	CORINTH DESTROYED BY ROMANS	-100
200										-200
300			Destruction of Persian Empire by Alexander				31–28	ALEXANDER the GREAT	ARISTOTLE	-300
400			XERXES I				27		PERSIAN WARS	-400
500			CYRUS conquers BABYLON NEBUCHADREZZAR	IRON AGE	TEMPLE rebuilt The RETURN Fall of JERUSALEM	LATE PERIOD	26		CORINTHIAN WARE	-500
600			NINEVEH destroyed ASHUR-BANI-PAL SENNACHERIB				25			-600
700			SARGON II TIGLATHPILESER III ASHUR-NASIR-PAL II		Fall of SAMARIA		24 23		(ROME FOUNDED)	-700
800			SHALMANESER III		JEHU Battle of KARKAR AHAB OMRI		22		GEOMETRIC	-800
900										-900
1000					SOLOMON DAVID		21		PROTO-GEOMETRIC	-1000
100			TIGLATH-PILESER I		GIDEON		20		SUBMYCENAEAN	-100
200			CASSITE PERIOD	LATE BRONZE AGE		NEW KINGDOM			LATE MIN. III or	-200
300							19	RAMESES II RAMESES I	LATE H. III MYCENAEAN	-300
400					JOSHUA takes JERICHO The EXODUS		18	TUTANKHAMEN EL-AMARNA TABLETS AMENHETEP III		-400
500			SAMSIDITANA		MOSES			THOTHMES III HATSHEPSUT THOTHMES I	LATE MIN. I+II or LATE HELL. I+II	-500

B.C.										B.C.
600	INDUS VALLEY CIVILIZATION					2ND INTER-MEDIATE PERIOD	17	AMENHETEP I		600
700			FIRST BABYLONIAN DYNASTY				16 15 14	HYKSOS	MIDDLE MINOAN or MIDDLE HELLADIC	700
800				HAMMURABI	MIDDLE BRONZE AGE	ABRAHAM?	13	AMENEMHET IV		800
900				SUMULAILUM		MIDDLE KINGDOM	12			900
2000			UR THIRD DYN.	NAPLANUM of LARSA SUMERIAN REVIVAL at UR			11	AMENEMHET I	E. MINOAN III or LATE E. H. II+III	2000
100				GUDEA of LAGASH		ABRAHAM?	1ST INTER-MEDIATE PERIOD	10–7		100
200	ANAU III	S.T. II A		SARGON I					EARLY MINOAN II	200
300		SHAH TEPE II B	EARLY DYNASTIC AGADE	Kings with Semitic Names		OLD KINGDOM	6	PEPI I	or	300
400				FIRST DYNASTY: ROYAL TOMBS of UR			5		EARLY HELLADIC II	400
500					EARLY BRONZE AGE			SAHURE		500
600							4	CHEOPS SENEFERU	EARLY MINOAN I or EARLY HELLADIC I	600
700						PROTODYNASTIC OR ARCHAIC PERIOD	3	ZOSER		700
800							2			800
900										900
3000	ANAU II	SHAH TEPE III		JEMDET NASR | URUK III		CHALCOLITHIC ↓	1			3000
100								NARMER KING SCORPION		100
200						PRE-DYNASTIC				200
300										300

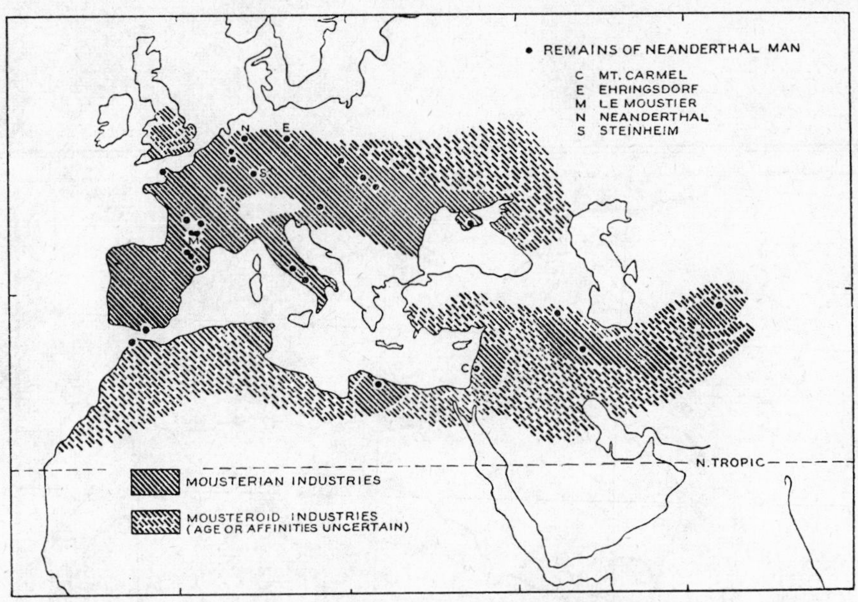

A. *Distribution of Mousterian industries and of remains of Neanderthal man*

(For other distribution maps of Palaeolithic industries see tail-pieces to chapter I)

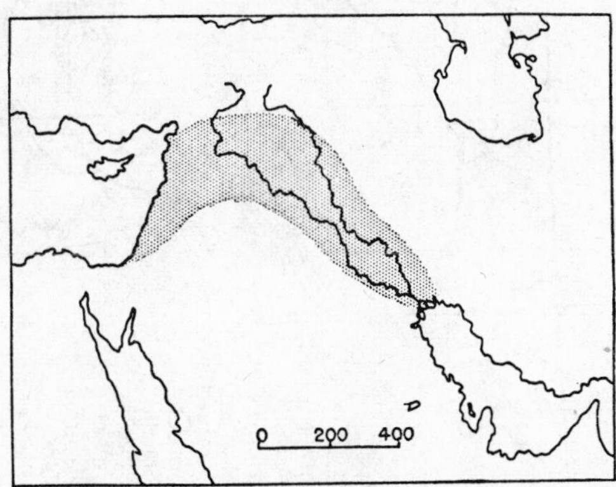

B. *The 'Fertile Crescent' which covers Palestine, Syria, and Mesopotamia*

MAP 2

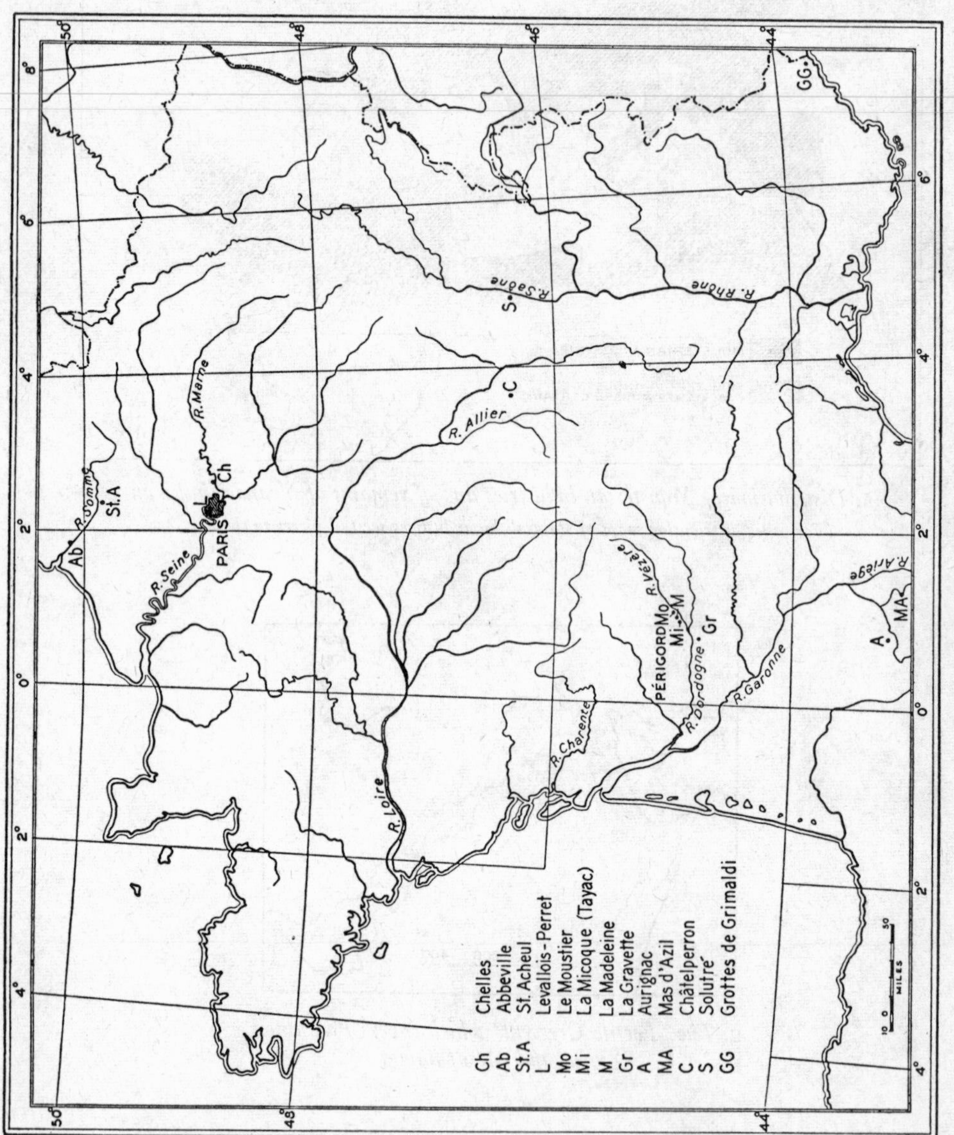

Type sites of Palaeolithic industries in France

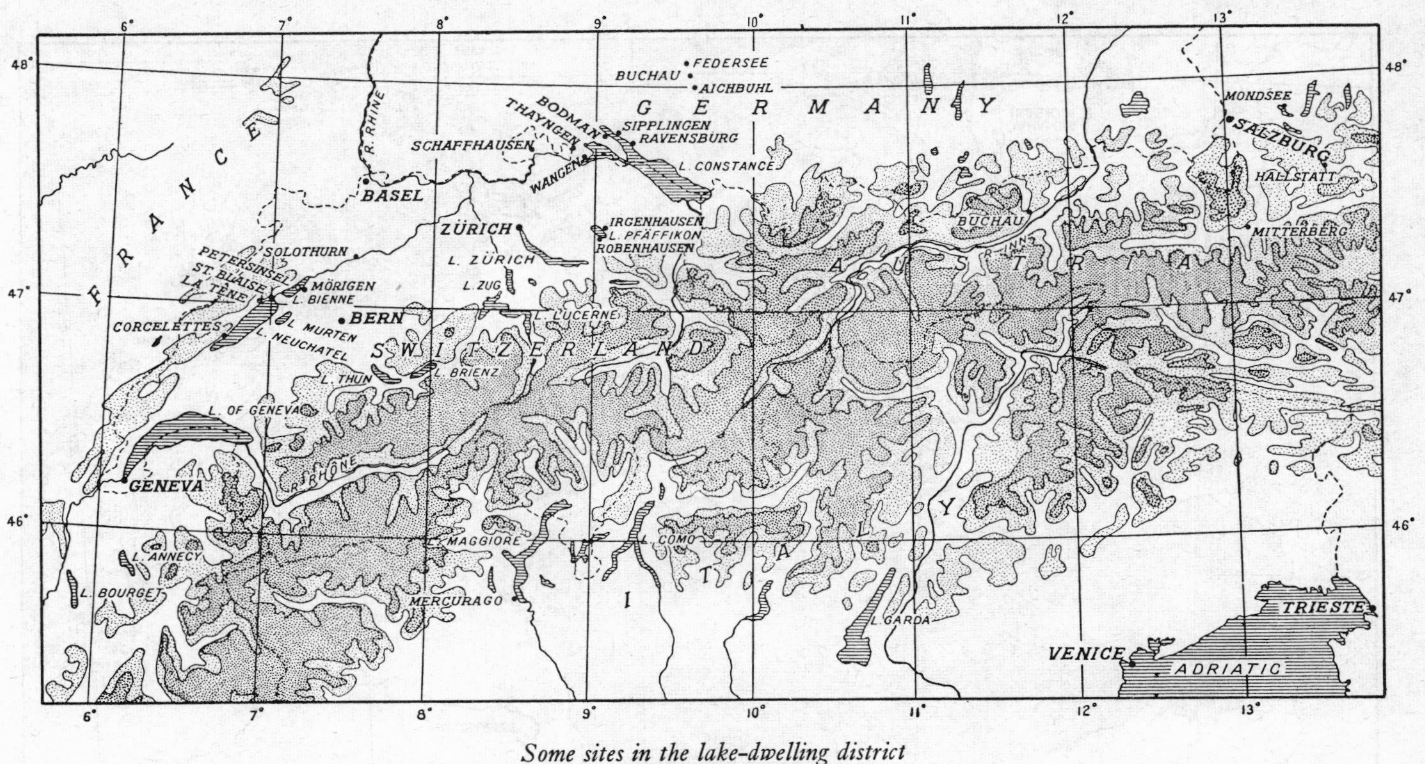

Some sites in the lake-dwelling district

Contour lines at 1000 m and 2000 m

MAP 4

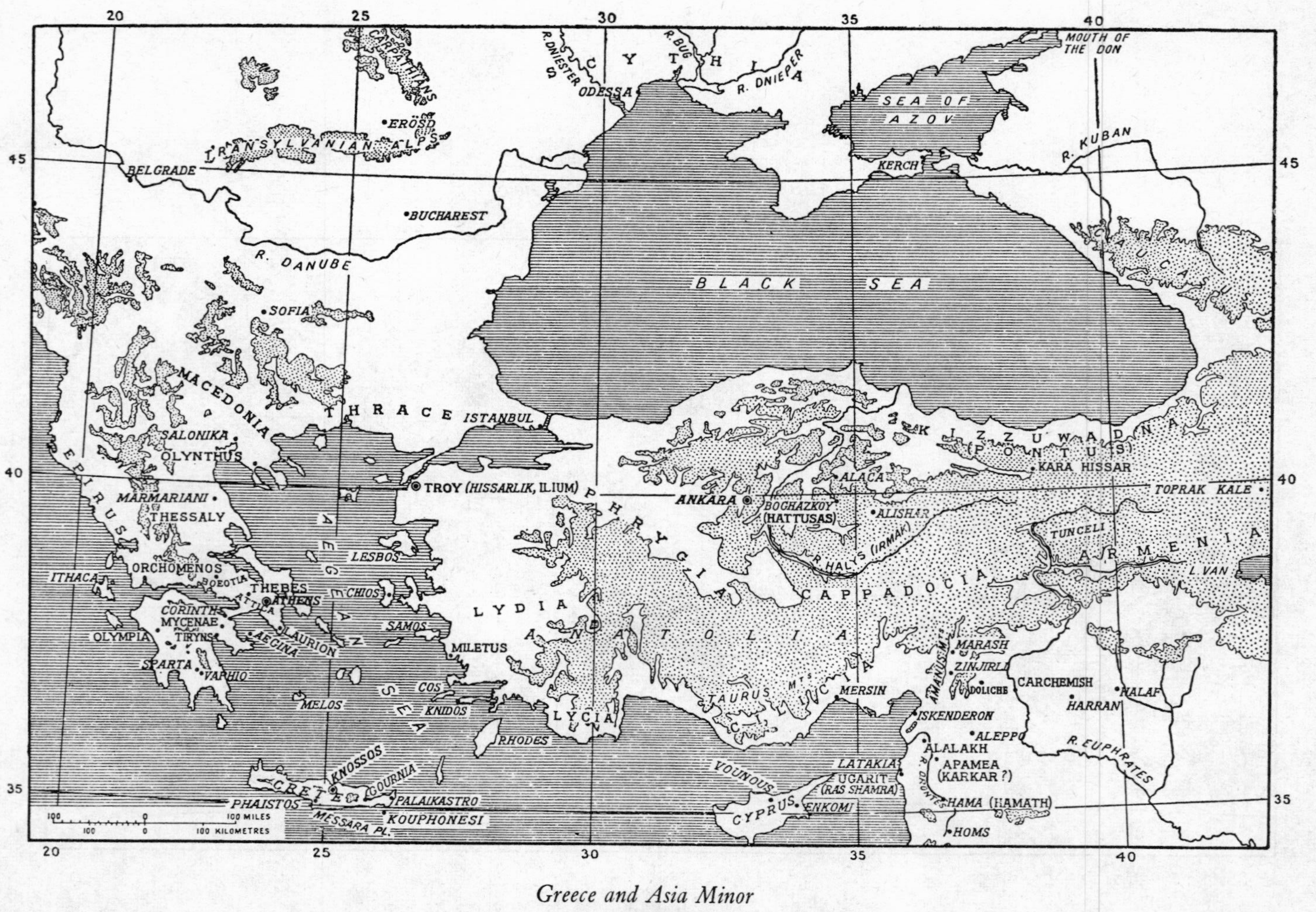

Greece and Asia Minor

Contour lines at 1000 m

Old names in roman, present-day names in italic

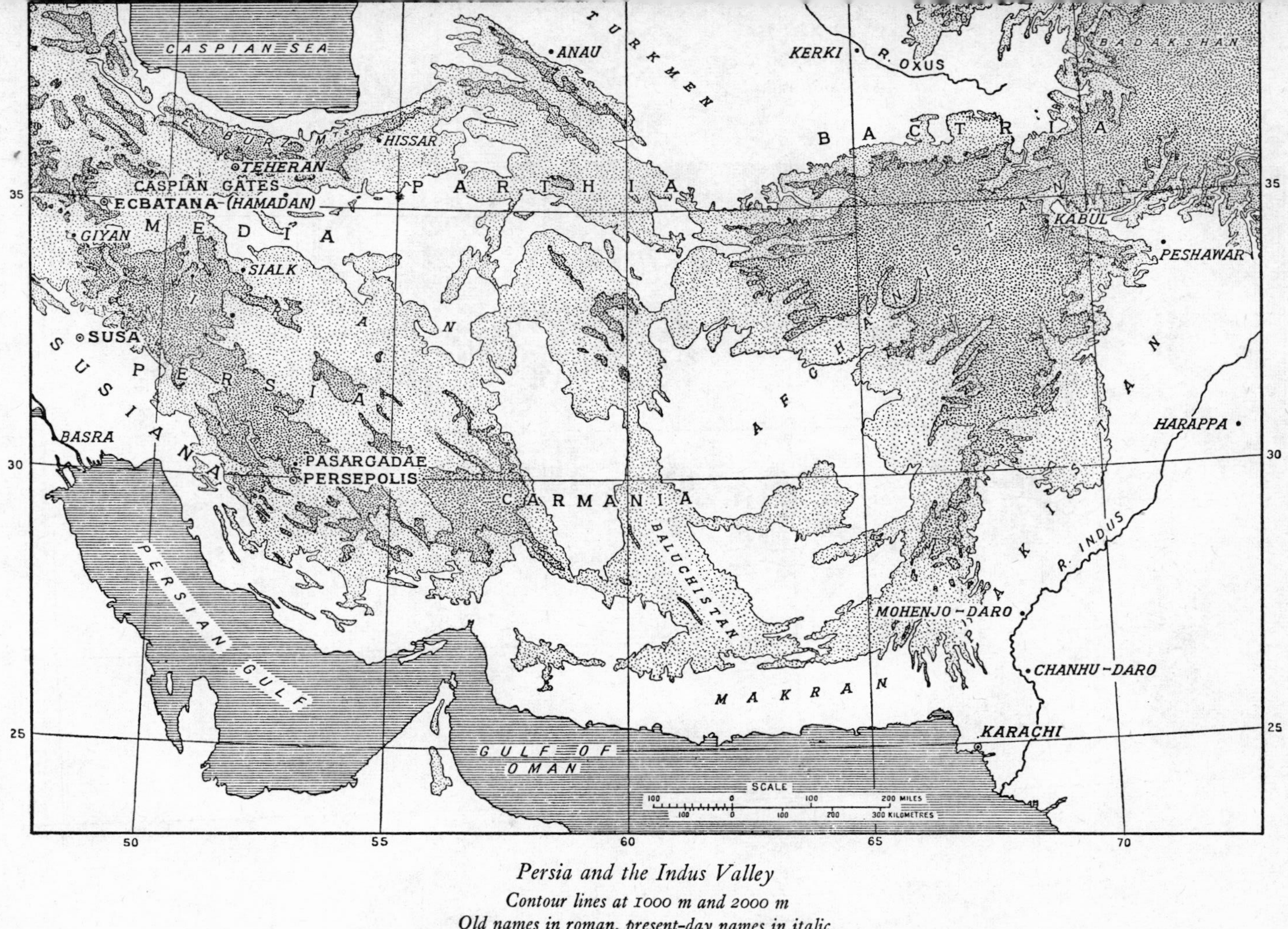

Persia and the Indus Valley

Contour lines at 1000 m and 2000 m

Old names in roman, present-day names in italic

MAP 6

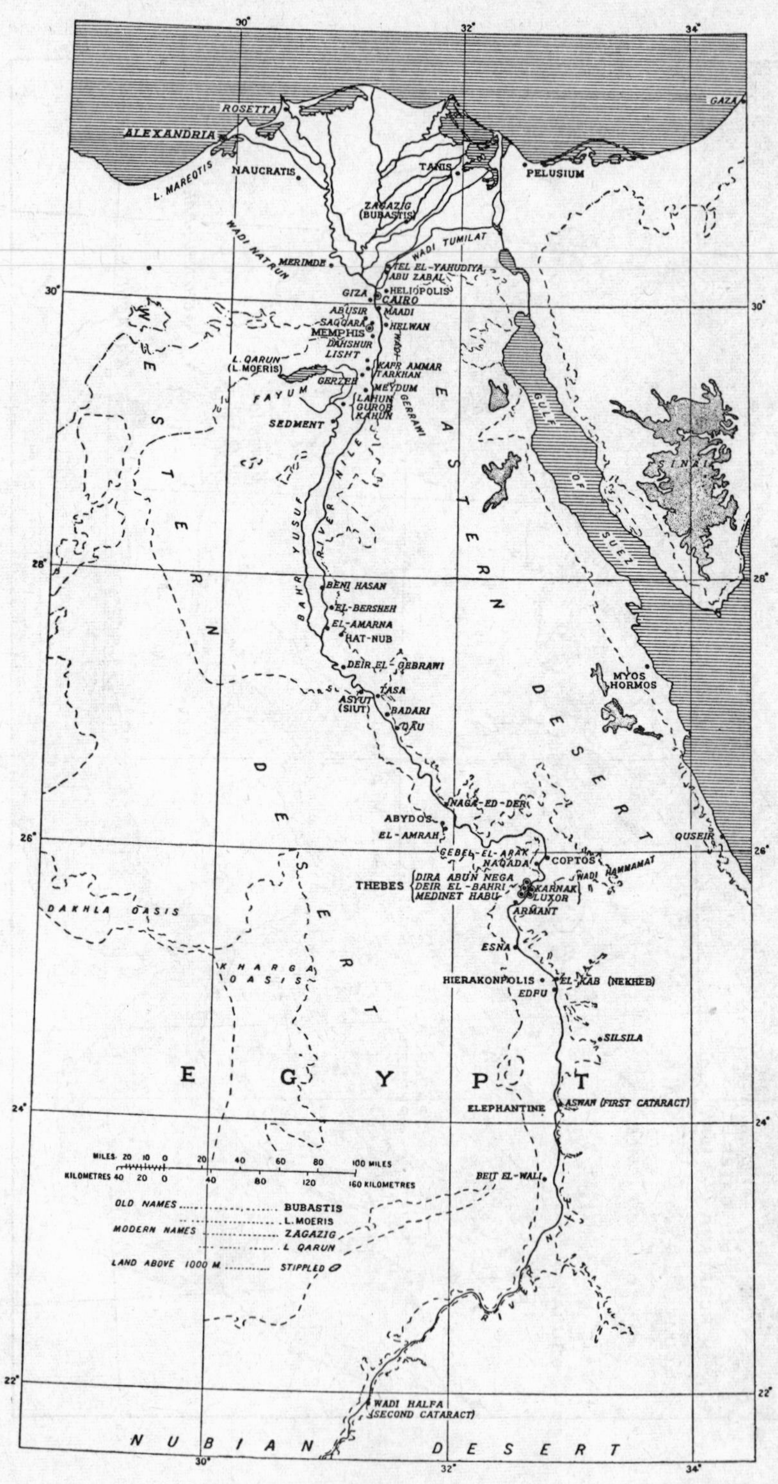

The Nile Valley

Contour lines at 200 m and 1000 m

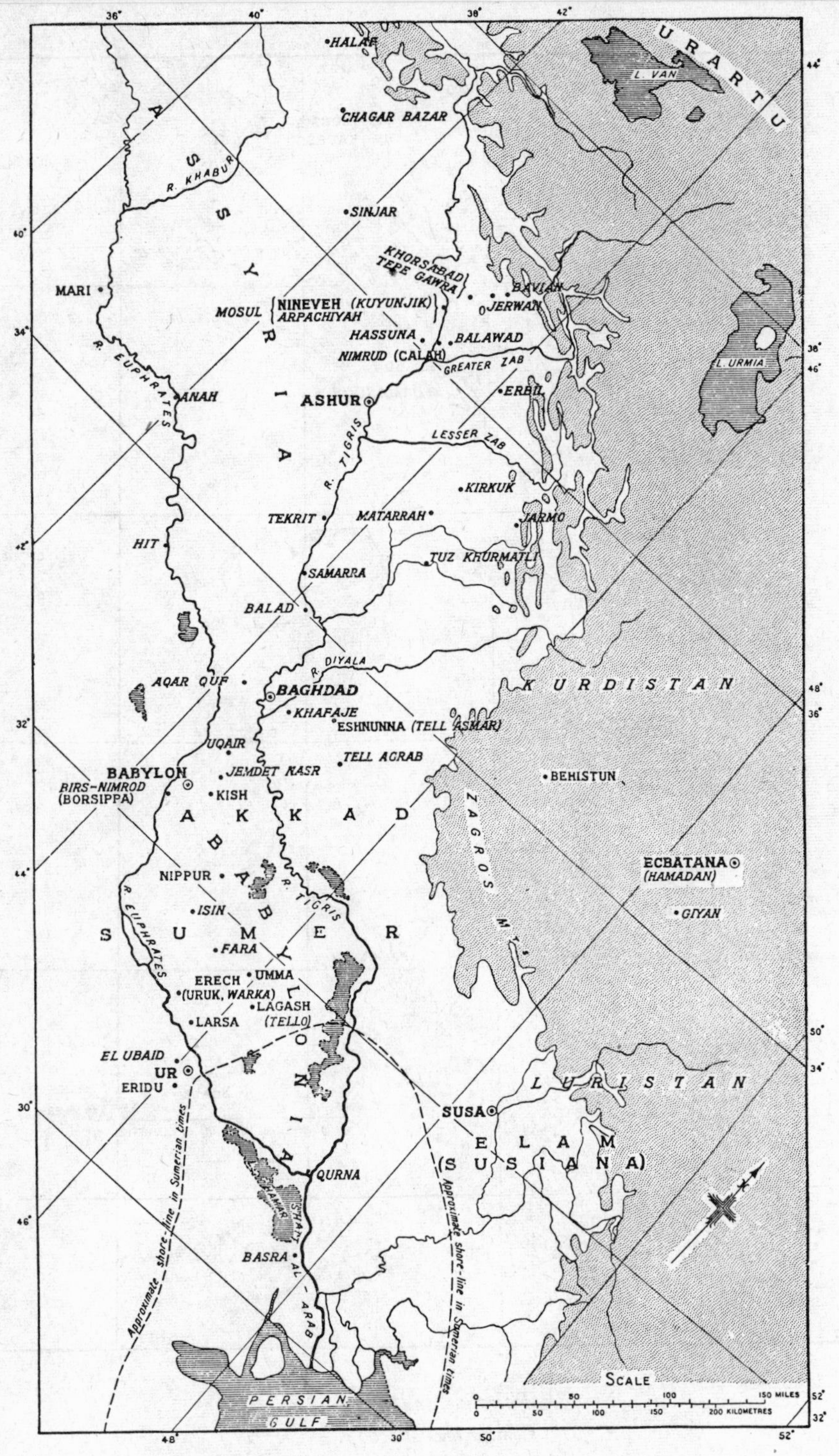

Mesopotamia

Contour lines at 1000 m

Old names in roman, present-day names in italic

MAP 8

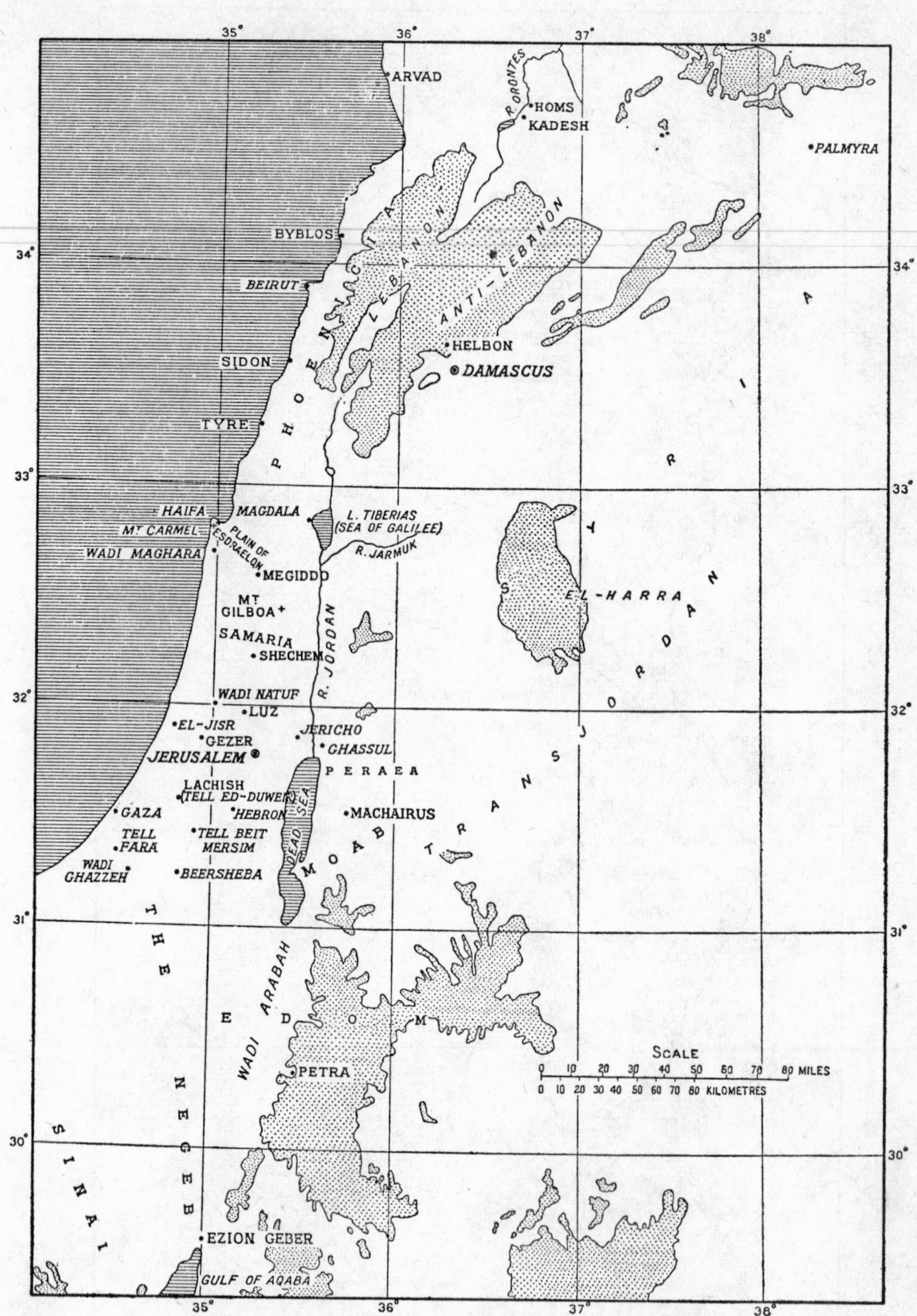

Palestine and Syria

Contour lines at 1000 m

Old names in roman, present-day names in italic

I

SKILL AS A HUMAN POSSESSION

KENNETH P. OAKLEY

I. USE OF TOOLS BY LOWER ANIMALS

In a history of technology some consideration must be given to the uniqueness of human skill. 'Man is a tool-making animal', said Benjamin Franklin (1778). To appreciate the significance of this and all that stems from it, it is useful to consider other animals which use tools but which, unlike man, do not make them.

Among animals without backbones (invertebrates), most striking is the occasional use of a pebble as a hammer by a North American solitary burrowing wasp (*Ammophila*). When the female is due to lay eggs she excavates an oblique tunnel in the soil, then seeks and paralyses a caterpillar, places it in the burrow, lays an egg on it, and temporarily closes the nest with stones. As soon as another caterpillar is found, the nest is reopened and the process repeated. When the nest is fully stocked, she removes every sign that the earth has been disturbed. The manner of this camouflage varies somewhat with the individual. One wasp, after filling the neck of the burrow with earth, was seen to bring a quantity of sand-grains to the spot and, seizing a pebble in its mandibles, use it as a hammer in pounding them down, to make the spot as hard and firm as the surrounding surface (figure 1). The process was repeated until all trace of the nest was obliterated. An individual of another species of the same genus has been known to use a pebble in the same way.

Is such action intelligent, that is, does it imply learning by experience? Most activities of insects clearly do not. They are instinctive, performed as part of an inherited pattern of behaviour. Yet all animals have some power of learning by experience, for were this not so, the evolution of instincts would be incomprehensible. When an instinct is sufficiently strongly established, there appears to be little room for adaptation of behaviour. Thus, if a caterpillar has constructed half its cocoon, and then that half is removed, it will continue unperturbed to build the second half. On the other hand, in fields of activity where instinct does not compel particular action, behaviour is more flexible.

Early theories of instinct over-stressed either its inflexibility or its adaptability, which was usually interpreted in anthropocentric terms. The more objective modern approach allows for both aspects.

A living organism possesses a certain amount of pent-up energy available for reactions suited to its existence and its reproduction. During millions of generations, behaviour appropriate to these ends has been evolved, and has taken the form of instinctive acts. These are usually performed only when circumstances are suitable, that is, when the sense-organs receive a certain pattern of stimuli which releases the pent-up energy. So long as the energy for an instinctive act is unreleased, the animal moves about aimlessly or in a seeking mood. It is during this appetitive phase, as animal psychologists call it, that behaviour is most adaptable.

FIGURE 1—*Burrowing Wasp* Ammophila *using a small pebble as a hammer to pound down the soil over its nest of eggs.*

In insects, the releasing stimuli are mainly patterns aroused by sight and smell. Some instinctive acts are complex and divisible into phases. The burrowing wasp is stimulated to a changed course of action by the sight of the fully stocked nest. It then fills the mouth of the nest with soil. So long as the ground at that spot shows signs that it has been disturbed, the wasp instinctively seeks to obliterate those signs; but there is some room for individual flexibility in the choice of means. Thus it may be only occasionally, and in a particular environment, that *Ammophila* uses a pebble as a hammer.

The behaviour of birds is largely instinctive, though in some directions it certainly may be modified to fit circumstances. Thus, birds deprived of the material normally used to build the nest will use other suitable material. Birds do not carry out instinctive acts on first performance with the same perfection as insects. For example, they will automatically peck at small objects and have to learn by trial and error which of them are noxious.

Behaviour which depends on learning by trial and error is influenced by the development of the individual in the company of its kind. In some species, innate behaviour patterns are more firmly established than in others. The South African weaverbird builds a complicated nest of sticks, with a knotted strand of horsehair as foundation. A pair was isolated and bred for five generations under canaries, out of sight of their fellows and without their usual nest-building materials. In the sixth generation, still in captivity but with access to the right materials, they built a nest perfect even to the knot of horse-hair. However, in many other birds trial and error play an important part in acquiring skilled behaviour in nest-building. Among young birds, as among mammals (including human beings), play has an important function in the improvement of some skills, e.g. flying.

A remarkable fact about birds is that, despite the smallness of the cerebrum (forebrain), they can, in a simple mechanical way, appreciate symbols. Thus the gaping reaction in a young thrush is released by the sight of a model consisting of a smaller and a larger ball placed in a similar relation to one another as the head to the body of the parent, irrespective of the actual sizes of the balls. It has also been shown that some birds are capable of unnamed counting; that they can learn to recognize 'one-ness', 'two-ness', 'three-ness' as qualities.

FIGURE 2—*One of the Darwin Finches, a* Cactospiza, *using a cactus spine to pick out insects from crevices in a tree-trunk.*

With these things in mind, it is less surprising to find birds using instruments. Such habits presumably originated in particular individuals during appetitive phases of behaviour, through an advanced form of trial-and-error-learning bordering on insight-learning. The habits probably became fixed as a behaviour-character of the species by a process which, for want of a better word, may be called tradition. After tits at several localities in England learnt to open the tops of milk-bottles, the habit spread throughout almost the whole of the British Isles—an example of 'tradition'.

The male satin-bird of Australia in the breeding season paints the stems of its bower with the bluish-brown pulp of certain deeply coloured fruits. Again, *Cactospiza*, one of Darwin's finches in the Galapagos Islands, which feeds on insects embedded in the branches or trunks of trees, uses a cactus spine or a twig held lengthwise in its beak to poke them out (figure 2). As soon as an insect is extracted, the finch drops the spine and seizes its prize. In dry districts *Cactospiza* chooses the spine of a prickly pear, but in humid regions, where cactuses do not grow, it breaks off small twigs from trees. It will reject too short or too flexible a twig.

The greater spotted woodpecker, a native of Britain, is another tool-user, in the broadest sense. It regularly constructs a vice by pecking a cleft in a tree-trunk and pushing pine-cones into it, to hold them firm while pulling out the seeds (figure 3). The cleft is V-shaped, widest above and undercut at the sides, so that a cone of any size is held rigidly when pushed down. Nat Tracy, to whom the author is indebted for this information, has observed several interesting modifications of the habit. Thus in the breeding season the birds use the same clefts for fixing 'oak-apples', which they tear in pieces to extract small insects for their young.

FIGURE 3—*Greater Spotted Woodpecker pulling seeds from a pine-cone which it has wedged in an artificial slot in a tree-trunk.*

Mammals exhibit a very wide range of intelligence, but some show less ability to learn by experience than birds. All mammals inherit instinctive tendencies to avoid pain, to obtain suitable food and drink, to mate, and even to explore—but in the higher mammals, at least, the means to attain these ends are in greater or less degree learnt by experience, including play and parental training. The hunting skill of a cat, for example, is largely developed through its play as a kitten. The remarkable achievements of the Canadian beaver, however, are generally ascribed to instinct. Young beavers on the river banks instinctively gnaw trunks of trees, and these may fall and produce dams, but full elaboration of the behaviour characteristic of the species develops only within a large colony. Not only do these colonies construct island lodges in ponds of their own making, and control the level of the water in them, but they make canals along which they convey the felled timber, stock-piling it for the food which the bark provides. These feats of engineering must involve individual learning by trial and error. It has been reported that young beavers which do not readily work for the common good are driven out of the colony and, instead of making proper lodges, revert to living in simple burrows. When, as a result of protection, the rare European beavers in the Rhône valley increased in numbers, they began to build dams like the Canadian variety.

The southern sea-otter breaks hard shells on a stone anvil which it carries in the water. This habit also perhaps arose through insight-learning, and was then perpetuated through tradition. A herd of these creatures off the coast of California has been studied by Edna Fisher. They feed mainly on a shell-fish (*Haliotis*) which they detach from the rocky sea-floor and bring to the surface.

FIGURE 4—*Southern Sea-otter striking a hard-shelled mollusc on a stone slab which it has brought from the sea-floor with the shell.*

Floating on its back, an otter holds the mollusc on its chest, which serves as a table, and scoops out the flesh with its teeth. Occasionally an otter finds a much smaller shell-fish which it regards as a special delicacy, but which has a stone-hard shell. It brings this to the surface together with a slab of rock, 15 or 20 cm in diameter, collected from the sea-floor. Turning on its back, the otter places the slab on its chest, and holding the small shell in both paws repeatedly strikes it on to the stone with full swings of its forelegs (figure 4).

Among mammals, the line of evolutionary advance that is most significant for our purpose is an increase of behaviour dependent on learning. The South African naturalist Eugéne Marais reared an otter-pup far from water, and a baboon-child far from its troop. He fed both on substances foreign to their normal way of life. When they were fully grown, he returned them to their native environment. The otter immediately began diving after fish, but the baboon was helpless, terrified by grubs and scorpions—the staple diet of its species—and began eating poisonous berries which no normal adult baboon would touch. Members of the primates, the order which includes monkeys, apes, and man, have instinctive tendencies or 'drives' like other animals, but, proportionately, many more of their patterns of behaviour are learned. It is broadly true of a species that the more slowly the offspring matures, the greater the intelligence of the adult. In the evolution of man there has clearly been a progressive delay in the onset of stultifying adult characteristics. This is important for our subject, for, basically, skills are learned and perfected during childhood and adolescence.

Evolution of skill depends on four main factors: (*a*) powers of sensory perception; (*b*) ability to co-ordinate sensory impressions, present and past; (*c*) physical capacities of the organism; (*d*) demands of the environment. All four are interrelated. The use of tools is one means by which an organism adapts itself to a particular situation (the environment); it originates through trial-and-error-learning or insight-learning, which are reflections of the degree of organization of the nervous system and require acute sensory perception; it is possible only if the organism has a suitable organ of prehension, such as a hand, a paw, or a trunk.

There is an important connexion between visual acuity and skilled behaviour, even where that behaviour has an instinctive basis, as in birds. In mammals, the evolution of intelligence is closely linked with the visual faculty. The ability of mammals to learn or profit by experience resides in a specialized layer of nerve-cells forming the cortex of the cerebrum. There the impulses from the organs of sight, touch, and hearing are received and sorted, and from there the 'voluntary' movements are controlled. Improvement in visual discrimination appears to have contributed particularly to the development of intelligence, not only in primates but in other mammals. Cats have highly developed vision, and are more intelligent than dogs which, with their poor vision, are guided mainly by the more primitive sense of smell. Manipulative skill is correlated with the power of visual scrutiny, which is greatly enhanced by the possession of a specially sensitive spot on the retina (*macula lutea*). This structure is found in the eyes of carnivores, primates, and birds, but not in those of hoofed animals which—if one excludes the elephants—have very little ability or need to manipulate objects.

II. EVOLUTION OF SKILL IN PRIMATES

To trace the origin and development of skilled behaviour in man, it is necessary to consider the history of the primates. The earliest were the *Prosimii.* These evolved from tiny insectivores similar to those found in Cretaceous rocks in Mongolia. By the middle Eocene, when sub-tropical conditions were widespread, there were prosimians in almost all parts of the world. In many ways they resembled their modern survivors, the tree-shrews, lemurs, and tarsier (figure 5 A and B). Like them, they probably lived mainly on insects and fruit. In common with other primitive mammals they had five movable digits on each limb. These were well adapted to climbing trees and grasping branches. Among the more advanced types the first digit acquired unusual mobility, so that it could be opposed to the others. This both enhanced grasping power and facilitated the catching of small insects and the plucking of fruits with the forelimbs. Thus the forelimbs began to assume many functions which in four-footed animals are usually performed by jaws and teeth. In other words, hands were being born out of habit.

Ground-dwelling mammals explore their environment and test the objects they encounter by smell; but as soon as any of them leave the ground and take to climbing, flying, or swimming other senses become more important. Being small and defenceless, the ancestors of the primates probably took to an arboreal life for security and for new sources of food. But life in the trees made its own demands; it put a premium on increased acuity of sight, touch, and hearing—particularly sight, which rapidly displaced smell as the master sense. Many early prosimians were probably, like the tarsier, nocturnal feeders: a habit dependent on special powers of vision.

In very primitive prosimians, the eyes are at the side of the head, divided by a snout (figure 5 A). In due course the eyes shifted to a forward-facing position, so that both could be focused on the same near point; the brain thus perceived a stereoscopic picture, that is, one having depth and solidity. The spectral tarsier (*Tarsius*), surviving in the Indo-Malay archipelago, is a 'living fossil' representing this stage in the evolution of the higher primates. Its eyes are enormous, and their field of vision is not divided by a snout (figure 5 B).

Certain Eocene prosimians were ancestral to the higher primates (monkeys, apes, and men). They exhibited an increase in size, more particularly in brain-size. The portion of the brain associated with co-ordination of impressions of the senses other than smell—namely, the greater part of the cortex of the cerebrum—is relatively much more extensive and also more highly organized in structure in monkeys than in the prosimians. In the evolution of apes and men the cerebral cortex continued to increase in size, with the result that it became infolded, forming a complex pattern of convolutions and fissures.

Comparing the exploratory behaviour of a typically terrestrial animal with that of a monkey, the enormous difference in their powers of sensory appreciation becomes obvious. A dog or an earth-bound insectivore, such as a hedgehog, tests an unusual object by sniffing it; a monkey fingers it while examining it visually. As a primary result of adaptation to life in the trees, the hand in the higher primates became not only a grasping organ but an important sense-organ. The development of close cerebral co-ordination between touch and sight made possible the skilled manual activities of man.

FIGURE 5—(A) *Tree-shrew.* (B) *Spectral Tarsier.* (C) *Baboon, a ground-dwelling monkey.*

Among early primates, concomitance of acute vision and prehensile powers gave a scope for intelligence, which was, however, limited in relation to manipulative skill by the restrictions of arboreal life. There is no reason to suppose that forest monkeys of today are any more intelligent than their Oligocene ancestors of 40 million years ago. The only further openings for development of intelligence were through abandonment of arboreal habits and adaptation to life on the ground, with retention of the nimbly prehensile hands of arboreal creatures. Prosimians at the end of the Oligocene evolved in three directions. One line, the New World monkeys, acquired extreme agility in the trees by developing prehensile tails. A second line, the Old World monkeys, mostly restricted to forests, retained the tail but only as a balancer—or even lost it. A few species became ground-dwellers, but were limited by undue specialization of the feet (figure 5 C).

The third line included the ancestors of apes and men. The early members were probably not very different from *Proconsul*, which lived in East Africa early in the Miocene (figure 6). They were unspecialized, monkey-like creatures, no doubt capable of tree-life and occasionally of swinging by their arms from bough to bough (brachiation), but also able to run along the ground, and even to rear

FIGURE 6—*Reconstruction of* Proconsul, *an early Miocene ape in East Africa.*

up and scuttle on two legs. Subsequent evolution in this group proceeded along two divergent lines. In one line, leading to the specialized forest-bound apes of today, brachiation became firmly established as the main mode of locomotion. The arms lengthened, and the hands were specialized for hooking on branches (figure 7). The other line, leading to man, had the advantage of remaining relatively unspecialized. Our monkey-like ancestors were probably used to tree-life, but in regions where woodland was interspersed by grassland they had to move in the open, and they acquired the habit of walking on two legs. This set the hands free to carry young and to collect food. These early *Hominidae*, which were probably clearly differentiated from the apes or *Pongidae* before the end of the Miocene, developed two interrelated specializations: first, the pelvic girdle was modified for the upright gait, and secondly, the foot lost prehensile power and became a rigid supporting organ (figure 8). The legs now outgrew the arms in length. The hand retained its primitive simplicity and prehensile power but, freed from its locomotive functions, became progressively more skilled as a manipulative organ.

FIGURE 7—*Brachiating ape* (*Orang Utan*).

III. MAN AS THE TOOL-MAKING PRIMATE

Differentiation between anthropoid apes on the one hand and fully evolved men on the other is readily made on the basis of comparative anatomy, but the question of how to distinguish 'men' from their immediate forerunners, which would have been smaller-brained and rather ape-like, is still open to discussion. There was an evolutionary tendency among most primates to increase in body-size, and for their brains to increase at least in proportion. In the later stages of the evolution of man there was enlargement of the brain unrelated to any increase in body-size. Yet, even so, brain-size is an unreliable criterion of humanity, and it is now recognized that a functional criterion, as, for example, ability to make tools, is at least equally valid. We may consider some of the chief factors which led to man's becoming a tool-maker.

It has been said that 'Man's place in nature is largely writ upon the hand' (Wood Jones). Any evidence bearing on the evolution of the human hand would be extremely interesting. Unfortunately the fossil evidence on this point is very meagre, but it is not probable that the origin of tool-making was related to any advancement in the functional anatomy of the hand. Regarded anatomically, the prehensile hands of the less specialized monkeys would be capable of making tools if directed by an adequate brain. In many ways our own hands are more primitive than those of the anthropoid apes, our closest living relatives. The reason is plain: the hands of the apes are specialized for brachiation, but our forerunners, while developing specialized feet, retained the pliant generalized hands

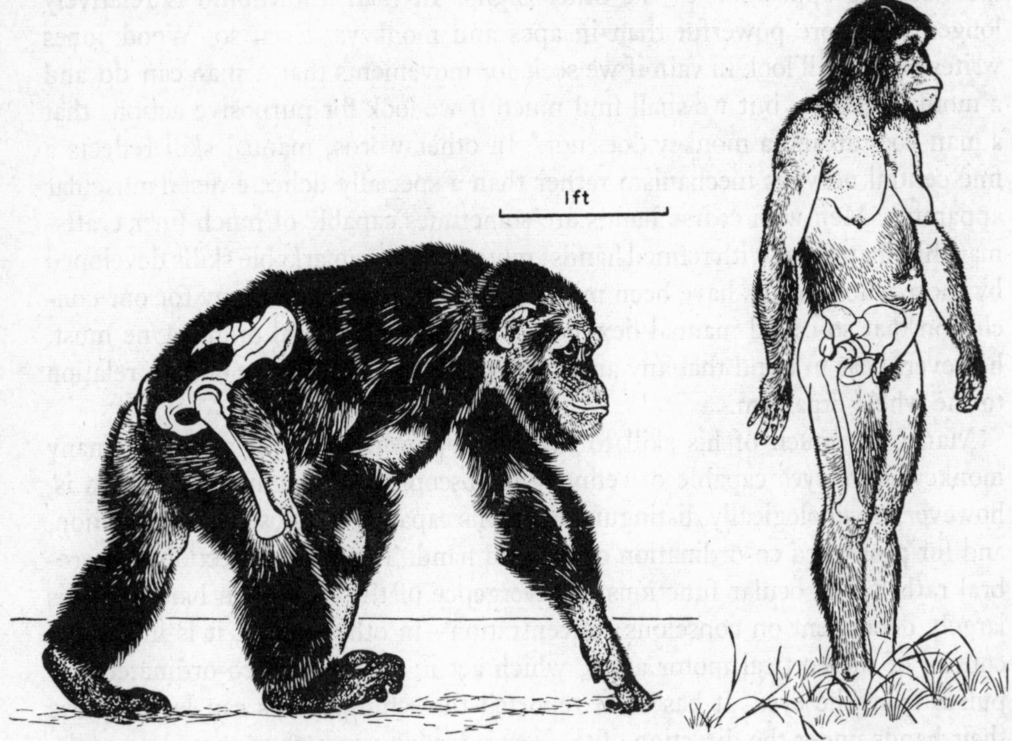

FIGURE 8—*Modification of pelvic girdle for upright gait. Chimpanzee and reconstruction of an Australopithecine.*

characteristic of the small tree-dwelling creatures, the distant ancestors of apes and men (p 7). In fact, the pentadactyl or five-fingered hand of man is so generalized that one would have to seek among the first mammals, or even go back to the reptiles from which they were derived, to find such primitive simplicity.

In its musculature, the hand of man is in fact closer to that of an Old World monkey than to that of any of the great apes. No ape can extend all its fingers flat on the ground and at the same time extend its wrist, for if the wrist is extended flexion of the fingers is inevitable. Consequently, when apes walk on all fours they support themselves on their knuckles, but men and monkeys can walk on their palms (figures 8, 5C). There is no sign in the hand of man of any of the muscular specializations connected with brachiation, but there is evidence that our ancestors were climbers.

It is a common fallacy to suppose that monkeys cannot oppose the thumb to the other digits. Most Old World monkeys do this in catching insects. It is true that apes and men have developed a greater power of rotating the thumb, which facilitates its opposition to the other digits. In man, the thumb is relatively longer and more powerful than in apes and monkeys. Even so, Wood Jones writes: 'We shall look in vain if we seek for movements that a man can do and a monkey cannot, but we shall find much if we look for purposive actions that a man does do and a monkey does not.' In other words, manual skill reflects a fine central nervous mechanism rather than a specially delicate distal muscular apparatus. Men with coarse hands are sometimes capable of much finer craftsmanship than those with refined hands; moreover the remarkable skills developed by those whose hands have been maimed, or even lost, is testimony for our conclusion that so-called manual dexterity is mainly of cerebral origin. One must, however, bear in mind that any anatomical structure can evolve only in relation to the whole organism.

Man owes much of his skill to his visual powers, and yet apes and many monkeys have eyes capable of refined stereoscopic and colour vision. Man is, however, psychologically distinguished by his capacity for close visual attention, and for prolonged co-ordination of eye and hand. These are reflections of cerebral rather than ocular functions. Convergence of the eyes upon hand-work is largely dependent on conscious concentration—in other words, it is under the control of the cortical motor areas, which act in response to co-ordinated impulses from the eyes. It has been reported that chimpanzees can learn to use their hands under the direction of their eyes for long enough to thread a needle, but in general the attention that an ape can give to manipulating an object is very fleeting. Furthermore, the erect posture of man, and the fact that his skull is poised above the top of the spine instead of being slung in a forwardly projecting manner as in apes, make it easier for him to pay close attention to any point over a wide field of vision.

There is evidence suggesting that some early *Hominidae*, beginning to walk upright on open ground but possessing brains no larger than typical apes, may have been anatomically well enough equipped to use tools. What is in doubt is when and why in their evolutionary career the *Hominidae* became tool-makers. It is probable that at first they were, like many of the lower creatures that we have discussed, occasional users of ready-to-hand tools and weapons.

Tools (including weapons) may be regarded as detachable additions to the body, supplementing mainly the functions of hands and teeth. So long as our early Tertiary ancestors led an arboreal life, their prehensile hands were fully occupied in climbing and feeding. They had neither need nor opportunity to use external objects as functional extensions of the limbs. But when they began to walk or sit on open ground, their hands were free to handle objects, first perhaps out of idle curiosity, later to some purpose. Baboons, which are ground-dwellers, sometimes use pebbles to kill scorpions—a favourite food—and if followed they will sometimes scamper up a hillside and dislodge stones or roll boulders down the slope to deter their pursuers. Observations on captive anthropoid apes have shown that emancipation from arboreal life offers wider scope for their latent intelligence. Chimpanzees make use of sticks for various purposes when captivity forces them to spend most of their time on the ground.

Though they have less concentration in solving problems, some monkeys are as quick-witted as apes. From the results of one intelligence test, a capuchin monkey was rated as high as a chimpanzee. This is probably exceptional, but it is worth bearing in mind as we attempt to trace the origins of human behaviour, because the evidence of fossils and of a study of comparative anatomy both suggest that the *Hominidae* arose from monkey-like ancestors. If they were like monkeys of today, they would have been intensely active in body and mind, restlessly inquisitive, and quick in perception and plan. Judging by the experimental tendencies in the behaviour of monkeys, the early *Hominidae* may well have begun to leave the forests out of sheer restless activity and curiosity. Recent behaviour tests showed that even in rats the instinct to explore exists as a measurable urge.

The earliest *Hominidae* are believed to have existed in Miocene times. In so far as they were adapted to life on the ground, they would have been capable of using improvised tools and weapons, as do baboons and chimpanzees when circumstances demand. Such a need would arise more often in the open, where life was more precarious than in the forest. All this would have reacted favourably on the evolution of the brain, for those individuals with a well co-ordinated cortex were obviously most likely to survive. The *Hominidae* may have remained for millions of years at the stage of occasional tool-using.

As we have seen, the mere use of tools is not confined to primates, but their planned manufacture requires mental activity of a different order. Systematic making of weapons and tools could not follow until the cortex of the brain had attained a sufficient complexity of organization. Even then it is unlikely to have become a regular practice until new habits of life were demanded by some drastic change of environment.

The qualitative difference between tool-using and tool-making is worth considering in some detail. Chimpanzees are the only apes reliably reported to make tools. Sultan, a male chimpanzee observed at the anthropoid station in Tenerife (1913–17), fitted a small bamboo cane into a larger one so as to make a stick long enough to secure a bunch of bananas which could not be reached with either rod singly (figure 9). On one occasion he attained this result by fitting into a cane a piece of wood which he pointed for the purpose with his teeth. Apes can thus evidently make tools. It is, however, important to note that all the improvisations effected by Sultan were carried out with visible reward as incentive. There is no indication that apes can conceive the usefulness of shaping an object for use in an imagined eventuality. 'The time in which the chimpanzee lives is limited in past and future. . . . It is in the extremely narrow limits in *this* direction that the chief difference is to be found between anthropoids and the most primitive human beings. The lack of an invaluable technical aid (speech) and a great limitation of those very important components of thought, so-called "images", . . . prevent the chimpanzee from attaining even the smallest beginnings of cultural development' (W. Köhler).

Thus apes are very restricted in visualizing and thinking about the relationships between objects not in sight. The power of abstraction—conceptual thought—is basic to the regular manufacture of tools. In apes it is no more than nascent. Mme Kohts in Moscow found that her chimpanzee could select from a collection of objects of extremely varied form those of the same shade of colour. This mental isolation of a single feature from a varied field of observation represents the first dawn of conceptual thought; but she found also that such ideas rapidly faded in the ape's mind.

Certain observations illustrate yet more clearly the difference between the mental capacity of ape and man. When embarrassed by lack of a stick, a chimpanzee will pull a loose board from an old box and use it as a substitute. If the boards are nailed together so as to present an unbroken surface, the chimpanzee, though strong enough to break up the box, will not perceive a series of possible sticks in it—even if his need of one be urgent. Men, on the other hand, seeking to make a tool of a shape suited to a particular purpose, will visualize it in a formless lump of stone and chip it until that which was imagined is actualized. In other words, man is basically an artist in the sense of Aristotle's definition of art, which 'consists in the conception of the result to be produced before its realization in the material' (*De partibus animalium*, 640).

There is, of course, the possibility of gradation between these two extremes, perceptual thought in apes, conceptual thought in man. Nevertheless, it is well to stress the contrast, because there is a tendency to be so impressed by the occasional manufacture of tools by apes that the difference in level of mentality implied between these and the earliest efforts of man may be overlooked. Even the crudest Palaeolithic artifacts indicate considerable forethought. The range of types of tool in the earliest Stone Age industries shows that almost at the dawn of culture

FIGURE 9—*Chimpanzee making a tool.*

tools were being made to make other tools. Using a hammerstone to make a hand-axe, and striking a stone flake to use in shaping a wooden spear, are activities which epitomize the mental characteristics of man—as most logically defined.

The capacity for foresight in man arises from efficient utilization of the records of the individual's past experience; that is, it reflects an improvement in cortical function. This is worth considering further. The nerve-cells in the cerebral cortex have been compared to the valves of an electronic computor. They are organized to receive information from the sense-organs and, by a process compared to the calculating mechanisms of a computor, to solve problems and direct suitable bodily activity through the motor cells and nerves controlling muscles. The calculations made by the cortical cells are based not only on information received in the present, but on the patterns of activity left by past experience, that is to say on memory. The co-ordination of past and present information, leading to reasoning and voluntary action, is largely the function of the so-called 'association areas' of the cortex.

The difference in size between the brains of ape and man is mainly due to the expansion in the human brain of those cortical parts concerned with the integration through which conceptual thought becomes possible. The most distinctive anatomical feature in the human brain is the large size of the frontal and temporal lobes (figure 10). There is reason to suppose that these are particularly connected with the higher mental faculties. The human brain is also distinguished by an increase in the importance of the area containing motor cells. These are concentrated in a band extending from the top or crown to half-way down the side of each cerebral hemisphere, thus including the hind part of the frontal lobe, adjacent to the front margin of the parietal lobe which receives sensations of touch.

In many lower vertebrates, co-ordinated movements, such as the motions of flight in birds, continue to take place even after the removal of the brain, for they depend mainly on patterns of nervous activity—reflexes—in the spinal cord. In the evolution of mammals, the brain entirely took over the function of co-ordination. In the lower mammals, such as rabbits, the power of initiating movements resides chiefly in the lower part of the brain, and if the motor area of the cortex be removed the animal still continues to move about in much the normal way. In the evolution of the higher mammals, the motor area came to control movements to an increasing extent, working in conjunction with the adjacent association areas. This most important development is linked with the process by which the animal becomes more conscious of all its movements, thereby acquiring greater capacity for education in skilled behaviour, and for drawing on past experience.

In man and other higher primates, movements that are purposive, that is, primarily conscious, are entirely initiated in the motor area. A large part of this area is responsible for movements of the hands, which indicates the highly significant connexion between the development of manual skill and the evolution of the brain. Injury to the motor area of the brain results in paralysis of the relevant motor apparatus. With sufficient lapse of time there may be some recovery of function, if the motor area is not completely destroyed, but the movements of the hands return more slowly and less completely than those of the feet.

However skilled behaviour in man be viewed, the conclusion that it is dependent on a large and efficiently organized cerebrum is unavoidable. Even those movements which have been so deeply impressed by training or practice as to be habitual, such as walking or knitting, are impaired or lost if one side of the motor area becomes damaged, as by cerebral haemorrhage. Acts based on reflexes in the lower part of the brain or spinal cord, like the movements of flight in birds, or the discharge of urine in man, are unaffected by such damage.

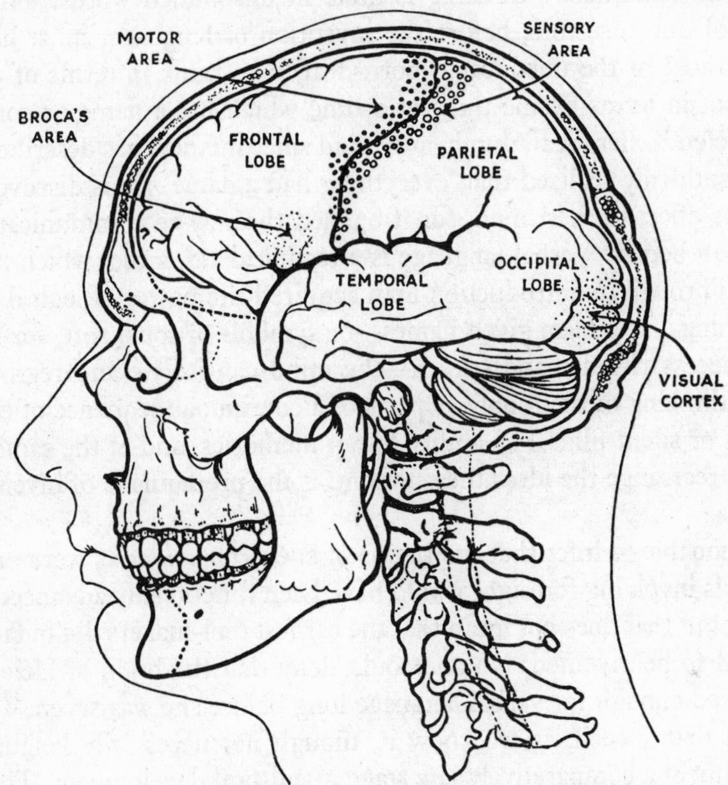

FIGURE 10—*The human brain.*

It is evident that the powers of conceptual thought on the one hand, and of skilled behaviour on the other, are closely related. Owing to the interconnexions between the motor area and the higher association areas, the movements initiated in the human brain are those which the individual can see and feel himself doing. In the association areas some patterns of past activity are stored and, on being revived as memory, serve as the origin of ideas, and therefore of consciously planned conduct.

Since the skills of man depend so much on education, it is evident that language (ch 4) has greatly facilitated such activities as systematic tool-making.

Oral tradition, in effect a new kind of inheritance, is sometimes regarded as more distinctive of man than tool-making. Apes have a language of the emotions, but the trick of giving names to things as well as to feelings implies conceptual thought. Moreover, it is extraordinarily difficult, if not impossible, to think effectively, to plan, or to invent, without the use of words or equivalent symbols. Most of our constructive thinking is done in unsounded words. The mental processes of our ancestors, before the invention of language, must have been similar to those of the uneducated born-deaf, who think in terms of events as a whole, not in terms of one thing at a time which has a name or comparable symbol. Helen Keller, deaf, dumb, and blind since infancy, has described how at seven she suddenly realized that 'everything had a name'. This discovery had a tremendous effect on her mind, for it opened the way to communication with other human beings. Verbal language is a technical aid, a tool which had to be invented. Through its introduction man acquired the power of logical thought.

When things have been given names—or symbols of some sort, for language does not necessarily demand speech—the mind can isolate and regroup them instead of thinking of them only as parts of a continuous sequence of events, as in a dream or silent film. The ability to tap memories, and at the same time to isolate and rearrange the ideas they present, is the prerequisite of invention and planning.

It is reasonable to infer that the brains of such *Hominidae* as were capable of making tools involving foresight would have been functionally advanced enough for speech, but that does not mean that the earliest tool-makers did in fact speak. Speech had to be invented. No one could deny that the brain of Helen Keller was advanced enough for verbal language long before she was seven. There are indications that speech, as we know it, though not necessarily language, was invented only at a comparatively late stage in cultural development. The invention was not delayed by any imperfection of the vocal apparatus; the larynges and tongue and lip muscles of apes are capable of articulating words. Chimpanzees have been taught to articulate such words as *papa*, *cup*. There is much in favour of the view that man's earliest means of communicating ideas was by gestures with the hands, and there is some evidence that these generate, in sympathy, unconscious movements of the mouth (ch 4). Sympathetic action of hand and mouth has been observed in chimpanzees and children. It has been suggested that an increasing preoccupation of the hands with the making and use of tools could have led to the change from manual to oral gesturing as a means of communicating. The earliest words to be invented probably represented actions; the naming of objects would have come later.

It is no longer thought that speech is connected with the development in man of a special centre in the cerebral cortex. Speech depends on the functioning of various cortical mechanisms which were already established in lower primates. Speech and its associated activities are disturbed by any injury within a broad zone extending along the side of the dominant (usually the left) cerebral hemisphere from just in front of the visual area, by the auditory area, to just below the motor area. If the injury is near the visual cortex, the patient will see printed words without realizing what they mean; if near the auditory area, he will hear words without understanding them; and if below the motor area the patient will suffer from aphasia or inability to articulate words. Injury at corresponding points in the opposite hemisphere rarely causes any disturbance of speech.

Owing to the fact that the nerve-fibres cross over on their way from the cortex to the stem of the brain, the left side of the brain controls movements on the right side of the body, and vice versa. The fact that, in most individuals, language-associations are built up in the part of the cortex which controls the right hand is probably connected with their being right-handed—another indication of the close connexion between manual activity and speech. Both may be considered as forms of tool-making.

IV. ORIGINS OF TOOL-MAKING

We may now return to the origins of regular tool-making. Perhaps within the Pliocene, certainly by the dawn of the Pleistocene, that is about a million years ago, the typically human level of cerebral development had been reached. Stone artifacts of standardized types have been found in Lower Pleistocene deposits in various parts of Africa, and in deposits only slightly more recent in Asia and western Europe. They show that tool-making was no longer merely occasional, but served permanent needs of these earliest men.

The apes of today are forest creatures subsisting on fruits, leaves, shoots, and insects, but all races of man include a substantial proportion of flesh in their diet. Early Palaeolithic men were hunters. Meat-eating appears to be as old as man. In so far as the early *Hominidae* were adapted to a mixed environment, partly wooded, partly open (see p 13), their diet would inevitably have been more varied than that of forest-bound primates.

It seems probable on the analogy of baboons (pp 8, 13) that any hominids living in open country like the African savannah, as some of them did, would take to flesh-eating when the struggle for existence was intensified by excessive drought. Baboons, almost the only monkeys completely adapted to life away from woodlands, prey on poultry and occasionally on lambs and other animals of similar size, using their powerful canine teeth as offensive weapons. This habit becomes more prevalent when conditions of existence are hard. A recent report on the habits of baboons in Zululand states that they often join in organized hunts. Usually, led by a veteran of the troop, they surround a small antelope or other victim and, at a given signal, close in on it and tear it to pieces. After the affair is over only the skull and limb-bones are left.

In men, the canine teeth are much smaller than in baboons or in the apes, and are level with the other teeth (figure 11 A, B). It has been suggested that reduction of these teeth in the evolution of man occurred as and when their functions were taken over by the hands, and by weapons and tools. In the fossil *Australopithecinae* of South Africa, probably slightly modified descendants of our Pliocene ancestors, the canines are small and level with the other teeth, even in the earliest stages of wear, and even in males. These hominids may have been tool-users, but there is no evidence that they were tool-makers. Thus it appears that the canine teeth were already reduced in the *Hominidae* at an evolutionary stage below that of tool-making. The Australopithecines lived in open country, probably hiding in caves and rock-crannies for protection. Whether the smallness of their canines was related to the use of hand weapons or not, the Australopithecines and the proto-men of Pliocene times would have needed means to defend themselves when foraging in the open. Walking on two legs with hands free, they may well have used stones as missiles, and sticks or animal long-bones as clubs.

In times of drought, then, our precursors would readily have taken to eating flesh. Although they lacked teeth suited to carnivorous habits, they were no doubt at least as ingenious as baboons in killing small animals. Life in the open set a premium not only on cunning but on co-operation. In view of the mentality and social life of other primates it is likely that the proto-men hunted in hordes, and killed medium-sized mammals by cornering them and using improvised hand-weapons.

Direct evidence of the Pliocene *Hominidae* and their habits is still lacking, but there is reason to suppose that they were not very different from the Australopithecines, now regarded as a side-branch of the family which survived locally into Early Pleistocene times. There are indications that some at least were carnivorous. The scattered fragments of animal bones, egg shells, and crab shells found with *Australopithecus* in the cave deposits at Taungs, Bechuanaland, had all the appearance of food refuse. In the *Australopithecus* level in one of the Makapan caves, Transvaal, quantities of antelope limb-bones were found, some apparently smashed as if to extract the marrow, but there were no undoubted tools.

By the time that the *Hominidae* had evolved into tool-makers they were evidently largely carnivorous; quantities of meat-bones were associated with the remains of Pekin man (*Pithecanthropus pekinensis*). It is easy to see how tool-making might arise out of the adoption of carnivorous habits. Though they may have killed game easily enough, the proto-men must often have had difficulty in removing skin and fur, and in dividing the flesh. Without strong canines, sharp pieces of stone would provide the solution. Here surely was the origin of the tradition of tool-making. Where no naturally sharp pieces of stone lay ready to hand, more intelligent individuals saw that the solution was to break pebbles and produce fresh sharp edges. Perhaps accidental breakages in using pebbles as

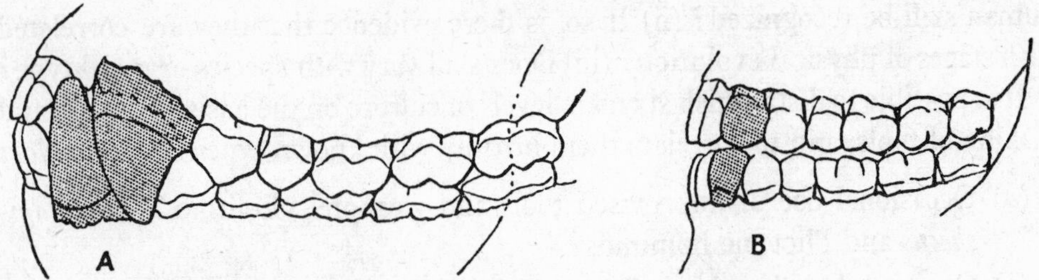

FIGURE 11—*Dentition of* (A) *gorilla and* (B) *modern man. Canine teeth shaded.*

missiles had been observed. Once this tradition had begun, the manifold uses of chipped stones became obvious (ch 6).

Dentally, and from the alimentary point of view, we should be vegetarians. We lack the teeth of true carnivores, and we have the long gut associated with herbivorous diet. Furthermore, our nearest living relations, the anthropoid apes, are herbivores, and consume only small quantities of animal protein. Man's change of habit from herbivore to semi-carnivore gave a new potential. To store a given amount of energy, a carnivore needs a smaller quantity of food than a herbivore. Its way of life is accordingly very different, from the point of view of the economy of energy. Instead of eating almost continuously, like their fruit- and plant-eating ancestors, the earliest men must have spent most of their day-time in hunting. This activity increased interdependence and encouraged social grouping. New skills and aptitudes were thus developed, through which man was able not only to survive climatic changes, but even to create his own environment. The evolution of new bodily equipment in response to environmental change normally requires hundreds of thousands, if not millions, of years; but by inventing extra-bodily equipment—such as tools, weapons, shelter, clothing—which could be discarded or changed as circumstances dictated, man became the most adaptable of all creatures.

With fire, weather-proof shelters, and skins or other clothing at his command, man became free to spread into every climatic zone. These cultural activities depended on tool-making, but were made possible through man's power, not only of conceptual thought, but of communicating inventive ideas and thus of building traditions. Where tradition is limited, culture ceases to evolve and may degenerate. Of this there are many examples.

V. EVOLUTION OF HUMAN SKILL

Having inquired into the factors of the origin and development of human skills, we find three questions to be considered: (i) Can stages in the evolution of human skill be recognized? (ii) If so, is there evidence that they are correlated with stages of physical evolution? (iii) Does skill vary with species or racial type?

It is possible to distinguish six main levels of culture on the basis of the use and making of tools, and to correlate them broadly with known types of *Hominidae*:

(*a*) Occasional use of improvised tools and weapons. 'Eolithic.' *Australopithecus* and Pliocene hominids?

(*b*) Occasional tool-making. Dawn of Early or Lower Palaeolithic. Earliest species of *Pithecanthropus*? and of *Homo*?

(*c*) Regular tool-making, but little or no standardization. Lower Palaeolithic. *Pithecanthropus* (e.g. of Pekin), and some early precursors of *Homo sapiens* (e.g. of Fontéchevade in the Charente).

(*d*) Regular tool-making, with marked standardization, but little specialization. Lower Palaeolithic. Early precursors of *Homo sapiens* (e.g. of Kanam in Kenya, and Swanscombe, Kent).

(*e*) Manufacture of specialized tools and weapons:

(1) Elementary. Middle Palaeolithic. *Homo neanderthalensis* and some early *Homo sapiens.*

(2) Composite. Upper or Late Palaeolithic and Mesolithic. *Homo sapiens* (e.g. Cro-Magnons).

(*f*) Use of mechanical principles (machine tools). Modern *Homo sapiens.* Characteristic of Neolithic and Metal Ages, but foreshadowed in some Upper Palaeolithic and Mesolithic practices.

Though man's Pliocene ancestors were not tool-makers, they were tool-users. Direct proof is difficult to obtain, but it is supported by evidence from the Australopithecine sites in South Africa. None has yielded any undoubted tools or weapons, but at Taungs there were baboon skulls which seemed to have been artificially pierced. It is also suggested that occasional river pebbles in the dolomite fissure deposit at Sterkfontein, containing remains of an Australopithecine, had been carried to the site by that creature.

Even when tool-making became widespread among the first men, it was probably for long only an occasional practice, since improvised implements and weapons often served well enough. Improvisation has played an important part in human culture at all periods. Some modern Australian aborigines carve wooden implements with naturally sharp pieces of stone. Thus a man of the Pitjendadjara tribe will take an unflaked piece of stone to chop a slab of wood from a tree-trunk, and with another unflaked stone deftly work the wood into a highly finished spear-thrower. This example of primitive craftsmanship may remind us that we cannot estimate exactly the skill of the earliest men from the crude stone tools which are almost the only evidence of their culture, for much of their equipment may have been of wood and other perishable materials. Identification of the first stone tools is almost impossible, for not only were they usually pieces of naturally fractured stone, but man's first attempts to improve their shape would have been indistinguishable from the accidental chippings produced by natural agencies. For this reason, none of the so-called eoliths can be accepted unreservedly as human work. Except for their occurrence in a cave deposit with hearths and human remains, few of the stone artifacts of Pekin man would have been recognized as human work.

There were no recognizable tools with the remains of the oldest known fossil man, the species *Pithecanthropus robustus* found in lake-clays at Sangiran in Java; or with the later *P. erectus* from river gravel at Trinil, Java; or with the species of *Homo* in river sands at Mauer near Heidelberg. This is not surprising when one considers that their dwelling-sites are unknown, and that in any case some human groups may have long remained at the stage of occasional tool-making.

Though not the oldest industry, that in the cave deposits at Choukoutien in China, with remains of *Pithecanthropus pekinensis*, is among the most primitive known. Thousands of artificially broken pieces of stone, of kinds foreign to the site, were found in all the occupation layers. Few are recognizable implements. It appears that Pekin man collected stones from a nearby river-bed and from neighbouring cliffs, and brought them to the cave in order to work them into implements when required. He broke up the lumps by using a stone slab or large bone as an anvil and striking them with a hammerstone. Usually he found it most convenient to use the resulting flakes, though sometimes the residual cores proved more useful (figure 12 A, B). Occasionally, flakes were crudely trimmed into points or scrapers. Rough choppers were made by removing a few flakes from the surfaces of oval boulders. The rarity of definable tools in the Choukoutien deposits indicates that though Pekin man was a regular and systematic tool-maker, he made little attempt at standardization; in fact many of his implements were evidently of the occasional type.

For some purposes he used broken bones as implements (figure 12 C). The crudity of his industry is partly accounted for by the poor quality of vein-

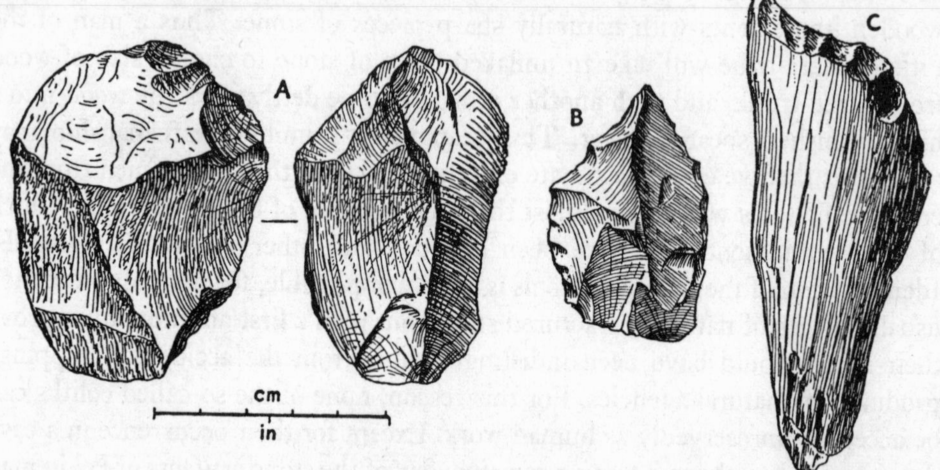

FIGURE 12—*Tools of Pekin man.* (A) *Quartz chopper tool.* (B) *Pointed flake of quartz.* (C) *Broken animal bone chipped for use as tool.*

quartz, the only raw material easily available to him, but this is not the whole explanation, for the precursors of *Homo sapiens* in Africa made shapely hand-axes from equally intractable stone. In the higher occupation layers at Choukoutien there was a noticeable increase in the percentage of tools chipped in more readily flaked stone (chert). Therefore the later stages of the industry appear more highly evolved, not through any advance in manual dexterity, but because of greater care in securing suitable raw material. Chert was already known to Pekin man at the time of his first occupation of the caves, but was presumably less accessible. Its more frequent use in the upper layers seems to indicate the development of a tradition leading to increased persistence and forethought.

All we know of the hand of Pekin man is a wrist-bone. It shows no feature which distinguishes it from that of modern man. An analysis of the better-defined tools from Choukoutien has shown that the majority were chipped by right-handed persons. Monkeys and some other animals show individual preference for the use of one hand or paw, but the acquisition of greater skill in the one hand is a human trait linked with the dominance of one side of the brain, and doubtless connected with the habitual use of tools. Ninety-five per cent. of modern adult human beings are right-handed, but left-handedness was commoner in early times, as it still is among untrained infants. Our word dexterity is from the Latin root *dexter* (Greek *dexios*), which means 'on the right (hand)'.

Pekin man had considerable skill as a hunter, for his own remains are associated with quantities of bones of butchered animals, chiefly deer, but also bison, horse, rhinoceros, elephant, bear, hyaena, and tiger. The killing of some of these must have involved the use of pits or traps. Throughout the long period of their occupation of the caves—probably seasonal—the Choukoutien hunters regularly used fire. The discovery of how to make fire was man's greatest step forward in gaining freedom from the dominance of environment (ch 10).

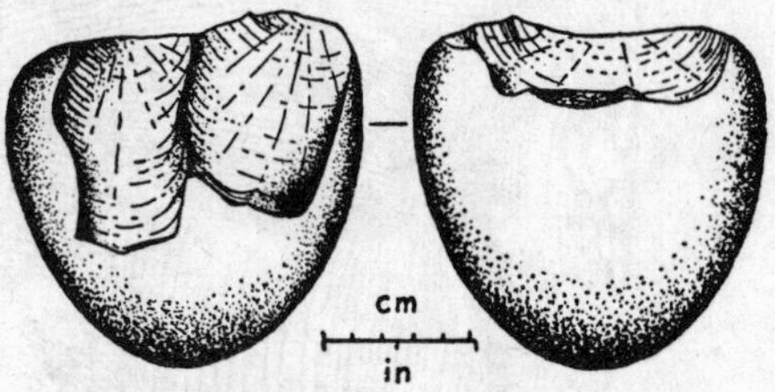

FIGURE 13—*Quartzite pebble-tool from southern Rhodesia. Lower Palaeolithic.*

The earliest known Stone Age industries in Africa are probably older than those of Choukoutien. They are represented chiefly by pebbles flaked to produce a cutting or chopping edge. These pebble-tools approach a standard form (figure 13), and are usually accompanied by rough flakes which may themselves have been occasionally used as tools. At Kanam, in Kenya, they were found in association with a heavily mineralized fragment of a human jaw of almost modern type. Thus the makers of these pebble-tools evidently included early precursors of *Homo sapiens.*

At Olduvai, in Tanganyika, it has been shown that pebble-tool culture evolved into the Chelleo-Acheulian culture, which was distinguished by the hand-axes widespread throughout Africa and parts of west Europe and south Asia during much of the Pleistocene. Hand-axes (figure 14 A) were made by flaking a pebble or stone slab round the edges from both sides, so as to produce a pointed tongue-shaped tool with a sharp margin. These were the first standardized implements; they served a great variety of purposes. They were not hafted, nor (apart from the forms known as cleavers—see figure 15) were they axes in the true sense. They were probably used mainly as hunters' knives, but may have served also for cutting wood or for digging up grubs and roots. Acheulian peoples used flake-tools to some extent, but the hand-axe was the predominant tool of a cultural tradition which not only spread over nearly one-fifth of the land-area of the globe, but persisted for more than a hundred thousand years. The hand-axe peoples lived mainly in open country, ranging from the hot

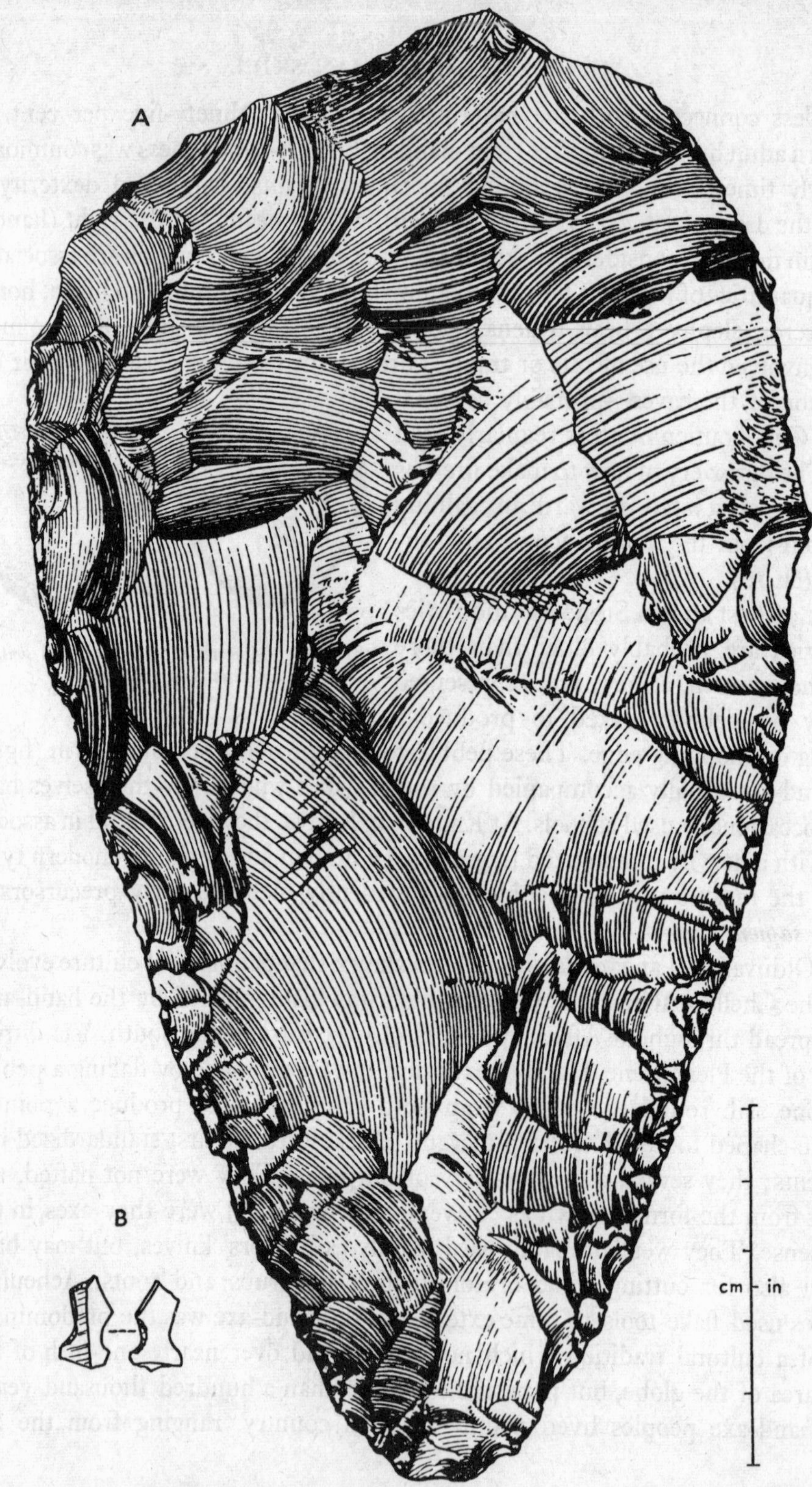

FIGURE 14—(A) *Acheulian flint hand-axe from Wolvercote, Oxfordshire.* (B) *Late Palaeolithic miniature flint burin from Les Eyzies, Dordogne.*

African deserts to the cool grasslands and open wooded valleys of north-west Europe.

Chellean and Acheulian implements collected from successively younger deposits in any one region show on the whole a gradual refinement of workmanship, but the comparative uniformity of industries of this group over so vast an area is most remarkable. Many Acheulian hand-axes from the Cape, Kenya, Madras, and London are indistinguishable from each other as regards form, whether made of flint, sandstone, quartz, or lava.

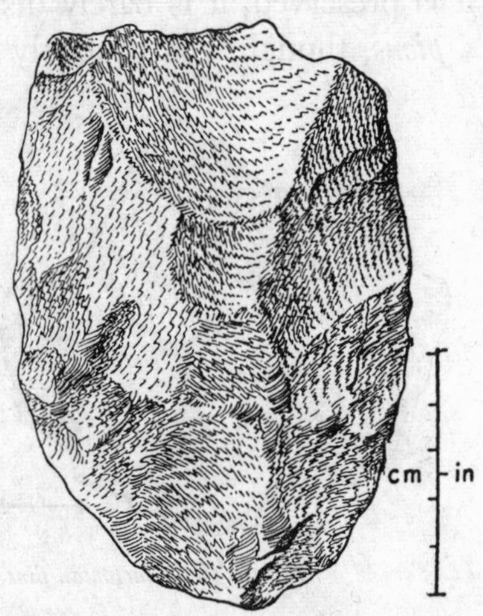

FIGURE 15—*Acheulian cleaver in quartzite. Madras, India.*

Men who made tools of standard type must have formed in their minds images of the ends to which they laboured. Human culture (and by culture we mean here all that a society practises and produces) is the outcome of this capacity for conceptual thought. The leading factors in its development are tradition coupled with invention (ch 3). The primitive hunter made an implement in a particular fashion largely because as a child he had watched another at work. The standard hand-axe was not conceived by any one individual *ab initio*, but was the end-product of exceptional individuals in successive generations, not only copying but occasionally improving on the products of their predecessors. As a result of co-operative hunting, migrations, and trade, the traditions of different groups of Palaeolithic hunters sometimes became blended.

The development of speech must have greatly facilitated these processes. The extreme slowness of cultural evolution during the Lower Palaeolithic may have been related to the rudimentary form of language. It has been suggested that the hand-axe people were still communicating by gesture and gabble, and had not yet achieved true word-making (ch 4).

We have no reason to infer that all Early Palaeolithic men had brains qualitatively inferior to those of the average man of today. The simplicity of their culture can be accounted for by the extreme sparseness of the population and their lack of accumulated knowledge. A supposed hall-mark of the mind of *Homo sapiens* is the artistic impulse—but archaeological evidence suggests that this trait manifested itself almost at the dawn of tool-making. Crystals of quartz were collected by Pekin man many miles from his home, and one may presume that, partly at least, this was because their shape and appearance appealed to him. Some of the finer Acheulian hand-axes are masterpieces of artistic craftsmanship, displaying perfection which exceeds bare technical necessity (figure 14 A).

The only undoubted skull of an Acheulian hand-axe maker is that found in gravel at Swanscombe, near Dartford in Kent, England, in 1935–6. In so far as it is preserved, it is barely distinguishable from some skulls of modern *Homo sapiens*, though it is probably more than 100000 years old. Human skulls of

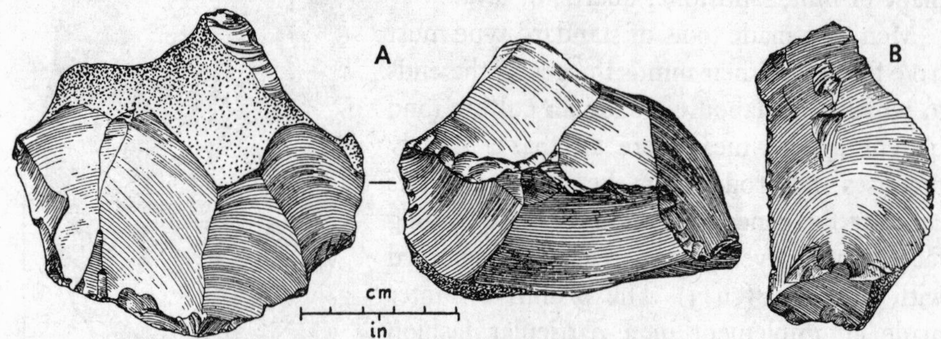

FIGURE 16—*Clactonian flint artifacts.* (A) *Core.* (B) *Flake-tool. Swanscombe, Kent.*

modern type were also found with Acheulian hand-axes at Kanjera in Kenya, though their contemporaneity is more open to doubt.

Like their more brutish contemporaries in China (p 23), the hand-axe people were well advanced in hunting skill. Lake-side dwelling sites of Acheulian man, in both Kenya and Spain, revealed quantities of broken bones of fast-moving animals such as gazelle and zebra, as well as of elephant and other big game. There is evidence of the use of fire by Acheulian hunters at only a few localities, in the Transvaal (Makapan), Spain, and Palestine.

Early stone industries are sometimes classified according to whether most of the tools were made by trimming a block of stone to the required shape (core-tool), or by detaching a flake from the pebble or block and using that (flake-tool) (ch 6). Acheulian hand-axes are classed as core-tools. Probably, however, in the basic stone-working tradition both cores and flakes were used with little discrimination. The Choukoutien industry was not far removed from that stage, and in parts of Africa and Europe there were groups of people who for long retained or reverted to it. The Clactonian of Europe (figure 16), and the industries of the type of that of Hope Fountain in southern Africa, are examples of such primitive Palaeolithic cultures, which existed alongside the more advanced Chelleo-Acheulian. Skulls of Late Clactonian man recently found at Fontéchevade, in the Charente, appear to be similar to the Swanscombe type (primitive *Homo sapiens*).

The evidence indicates that man originated in Africa but spread fairly rapidly into Asia and Europe, carrying a basic stone-working tradition out of which various specialized cultures evolved. In Africa the core hand-axe culture developed; in eastern Asia another core-culture, distinguished by standardized chopping tools (figure 17); and in western Asia and Europe, flake-cultures. There was considerable overlapping of these traditions, with consequent hybridization of cultures in some regions.

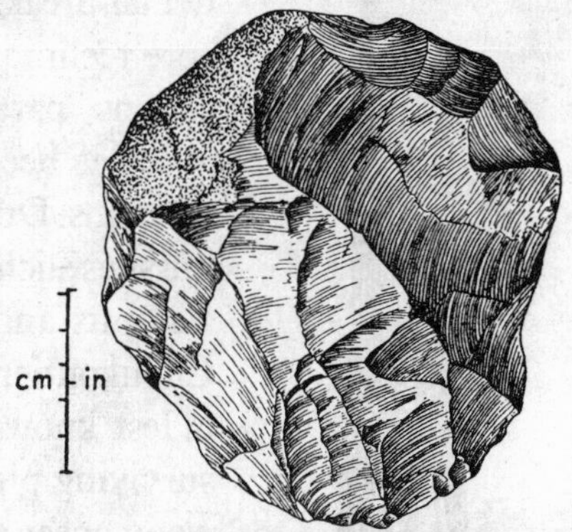

FIGURE 17—*East Asiatic chopper-tool in silicified tuff. Java. Lower Palaeolithic.*

It would be wrong to give the impression that there was no specialization of tools in Lower Palaeolithic times. The hammerstone or anvil for flaking, the flake for cutting skins, the crude chopping-tool for splitting bones or wood, were primary specializations in the most primitive known industries. But the use of a single standardized tool-type for a variety of different purposes was a leading feature of Lower Palaeolithic culture. The pointed hand-axe is an extreme example of an all-purpose tool, for it served equally well for piercing, cutting, and scraping. With the advent of what is generally known as the Middle Palaeolithic stage of culture, specialized types of tool were devised to perform each of these functions, and specialization then became a conspicuous feature of culture. For example, it became the fashion among some later hand-axe people, and also among some of the flake-tool people, to prepare blocks of stone in such a way that a flake of accurately determined form could be struck. The preparatory flaking aimed at so shaping the block that the flake eventually detached was immediately serviceable as an implement, without further trimming (figure 55). This was the specialized tortoise-core technique used by many different groups of hunters in Africa, Asia, and Europe, including the Neanderthalers. Cultures in which this technique was extensively employed are generally termed Levalloisian.

The typical Levallois tool struck from a tortoise-core combines the plano-convex form of some hand-axes with the straight cutting-edge of the ordinary flake, and was thus very well suited for use as a skinning-knife. The tortoise-core technique is interesting for the evolution of skill, because its manufacture implies much more forethought than that of any of the tools characteristic of Lower Palaeolithic culture. An unstruck tortoise-core so closely resembles a high domed plano-convex hand-axe that one way in which the technique was discovered might have been through the accidental breaking of such a tool. The Levalloisian or tortoise-core technique long continued in use with various modifications, particularly in Africa.

It has been convenient to use the term 'tool' to include weapons. During Lower Palaeolithic times these were simple missiles such as pebbles or all-wood spears, and presumably also pits and traps. The frontal bone of a hyaena skull at Choukoutien had been smashed by a missile boulder. The oldest known actual weapon (and, incidentally, the oldest surviving piece of woodwork) is the pointed end of a yew-wood spear associated with the typical Clactonian industry in the water-logged Elephant Bed at Clacton-on-Sea in Essex, England (figure 18). It has been shaped by the use of flint flakes. Judging from the practice of modern Australian aborigines, many of the so-called scrapers from Lower Palaeolithic sites were probably used for working wood rather than for dressing skins as was formerly supposed. A complete spear of yew-wood, with fire-hardened tip, within the skeleton of an elephant and associated with a Levalloisian flint industry, was found at Lehringen, about 30 kilometres south-east of Bremen, Germany.

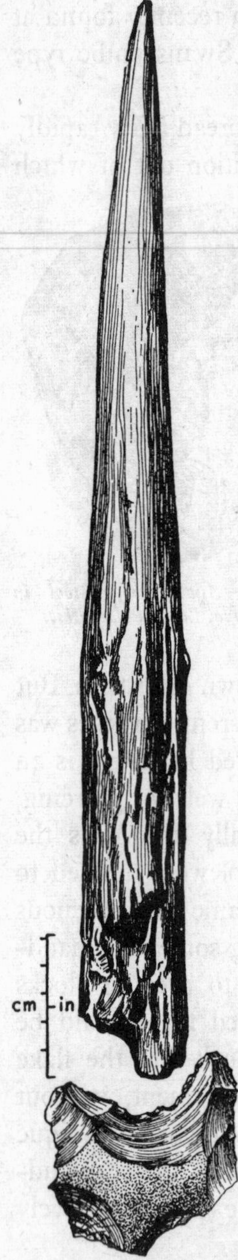

FIGURE 18—*Wooden spear and flint 'spoke-shave' from a Lower Palaeolithic deposit, Clacton-on-Sea, Essex.*

The typical Neanderthalers, or *Homo neanderthalensis*, formed a specialized offshoot of mankind, the earliest members of which (for instance at Ehringsdorf, Germany) were barely distinguishable from the precursors of *Homo sapiens*. They were essentially a European and west Asian group. Their culture, known as Mousterian, had Clactonian roots and followed a flake-tool tradition, but was locally influenced by the Acheulian. The early Neanderthalers lived under the warm conditions that prevailed in Europe during the third interglacial period, and their mode of life was similar to that of the Acheulians (p 25 ff). The later or typical Mousterian culture developed under the wet or tundra conditions associated with the fourth glaciation. The Neanderthalers adapted themselves to the severe climate by using caves as dwellings wherever possible, and probably by wearing animal pelts as rough cloaks in severe weather, as do the modern inhabitants of Tierra del Fuego.

In material equipment the Neanderthalers showed little more inventiveness than the Lower Palaeolithic peoples. They do not appear to have mastered the craft of working bone, but like Pekin man they sometimes used broken long bones of animals as tools. They selected dense bones for chopping-blocks and pressure-flakers (figure 19 C), and broke fibulae of bear for use as skin-sleekers. Mousterian industries consist principally of stone flake-tools, struck either in the simple Clactonian fashion, or by the Levalloisian technique, but with edges finely retouched by pressure-flaking (p 137) to make them more durable. They include three main standard types, (*a*) triangular points with both edges retouched (figure 19 A); (*b*) D-shaped side-scrapers (figure 19 B); (*c*) small heart-shaped hand-axes. The flake-tools were predominant. The Neanderthalers used spears of wood. A Neanderthal skeleton at Mount Carmel had a clean-cut hole, extending through the head of one thigh bone into the pelvis, which was the work of a wooden spear point. Some of the more advanced Neanderthalers appear to have used hafted narrow flint points as detachable spear-heads. Occasionally they applied the principle of hafting to scrapers. Thus their equipment was more specialized than that of their predecessors, though still very elementary. They were fearless and proficient hunters, for they slew mammoth, rhinoceros, and bear. Their weapons included missile stones, but it is doubtful if they were slung or used in the form of a bolas. The abundance of limb-bones of game animals, and the rarity of ribs and vertebrae, in the Neanderthal cave-dwellings shows that they did not drag whole carcasses to the cave, but cut them up and carried away portions. They made extensive use of fire, and cooked their meat.

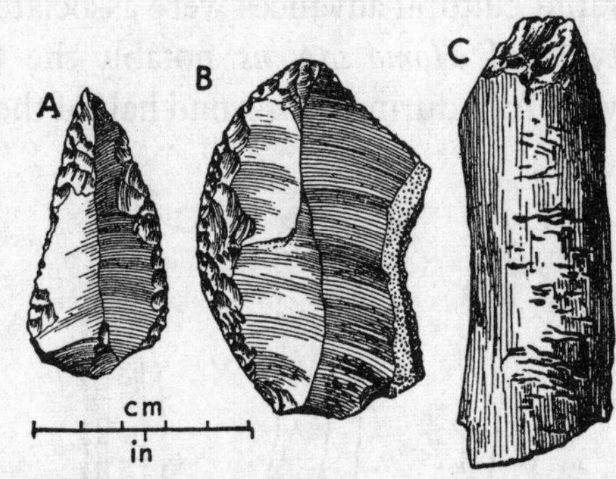

FIGURE 19—*Mousterian artifacts.* (A) *Flake point and* (B) *side-scraper in flint, from Le Moustier, Dordogne.* (C) *Bone compressor from La Quina, Charente.*

Judging from the few arm and hand bones known, Neanderthal men were usually right-handed. Their fingers were relatively shorter and thicker than those of modern man, but the joints allowed easy movement. Their implements, although simple, were often exquisitely finished, particularly in the Upper

Mousterian, indicating considerable dexterity, and pride in exercise of skill. At Sergeac, in the Dordogne, they made a few tools in rock-crystal of gem-stone quality, indicating some artistic sense.

In most parts of Europe, Middle Palaeolithic culture gave place with almost dramatic suddenness to the Upper Palaeolithic, distinguished by a wide range of new specialized tools and weapons, and by various new techniques. These rapid cultural advances were associated with the emergence of highly successful types of *Homo sapiens*, notably the Cro-Magnons. They spread from south-west Asia during the second half of the last glacial period, and entirely supplanted

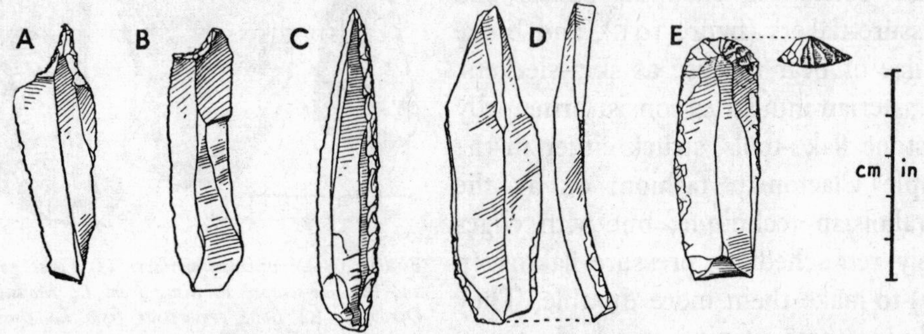

FIGURE 20—*Upper Palaeolithic blade tools in flint.* (A) *Solutrean piercer or 'hand-drill', Dordogne.* (B) *Magdalenian concave end-scraper or 'spoke-shave', Dordogne.* (C) *Gravettian knife-point, Dordogne.* (D) *Magdalenian burin, Dordogne.* (E) *End-scraper, Vale of Clwyd, Wales.*

the Neanderthalers, whose disappearance may be likened to the reduction in the number of aborigines in contact with European culture. The Cro-Magnons and related groups were not only much more inventive than their predecessors, but exhibited remarkable aesthetic sense and displayed artistic skills scarcely excelled in any later period. This rapid evolution of culture may have been due to the invention of a system of verbal symbolism.

Upper Palaeolithic industries show an increased mastery over materials. New techniques had been evolved for working flint and similar stone, such as the production of narrow blades with parallel sides by means of punch and hammer, and the surfacing as well as the edge-trimming of flakes by indirect percussion or pressure (e.g. Solutrean spearheads). Artifacts of complicated form were wrought in bone, antler, and ivory by a combination of sawing, splitting, grinding, and polishing. By now, tools were not only used to make implements in the sense of end-products, such as meat knives or spears, but many tools were made which were tool-making tools. This is good evidence that the hunter-craftsman was showing considerably greater foresight, and no longer worked merely to satisfy immediate ends. Thus, numerous specialized types of flint chiselling-tools (burins) were devised mainly for working bone, antler, ivory, and probably wood into other tools (figures 14 B, 20 A–E).

It may be noted that many of the tools and weapons of the Upper Palaeolithic peoples were composite (figure 21 A–C). Missile and thrusting spears were regularly provided with hafted heads of bone, antler, or flint, and some of the flint blade-tools were set in bone or wooden handles. One important factor in the efficiency of a tool or weapon is the means of giving its working edge or point the desired motion through the material to be worked or penetrated. Originally all tools were grasped in the hand; the first step towards a mechanical device was hafting. In Upper Palaeolithic times, men were beginning to apply mechanical principles to the movement of tools and weapons. Spears were launched with throwers which, working on the lever principle, increase the effective propelling power of a man's arm. The bow was invented late in this period, probably in north Africa. It was the first means of concentrating muscular energy for the propulsion of an arrow, but it was soon discovered that it also provided a means of twirling a stick, and this led to the invention of the rotary drill (ch 9).

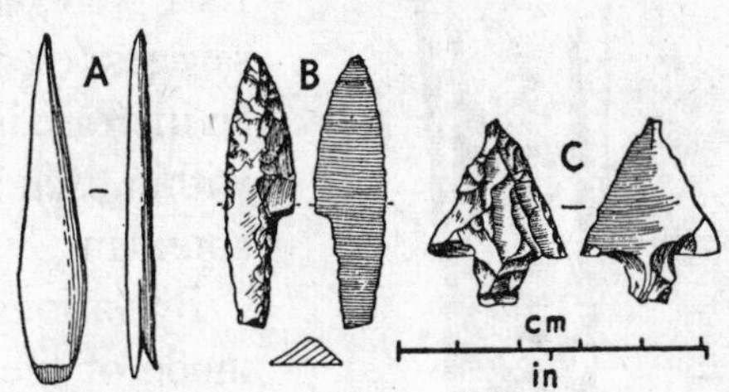

FIGURE 21—*Upper Palaeolithic hafted weapon-tips.* (A) *Aurignacian split-base bone point, Dordogne.* (B) *Solutrean shouldered 'willow-leaf' point showing pressure-flaking, Dordogne.* (C) *Aterian arrowhead, Morocco.*

Bone and ivory bodkins, bone needles with eyes, belt-fasteners, and, rarely, even buttons have been found in Upper Palaeolithic sites. Carved representations of clothed figures (figure 22) show that these hunters wore sewn skin garments with fitting sleeves and trousers. These greatly increased their efficiency in the very cold winters that they had to endure.

Thus men were making their own environments in various ways. In the limestone hills of western Europe, the Upper Palaeolithic tribes made their winter homes in shallow caves or rock-shelters. They were principally hunters of reindeer and horse. In the summer, they followed the migrating herds and used tents or huts as dwellings. In eastern Europe, they specialized in hunting mammoth, and adapted themselves to life on the open steppe by constructing permanent communal huts deeply sunk in the ground. The cave-art of the western tribes shows that some of these hunters had remarkable powers of observation and visual memory (ch 7). Most of the drawings and paintings were done in the dark innermost recesses of caverns, usually by the light of open

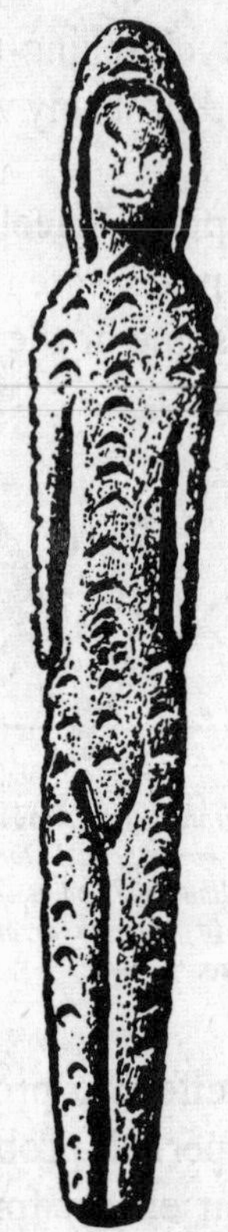

FIGURE 22—*Upper Palaeolithic carving in ivory of a female figure with tailored clothing. Siberia. (Slightly enlarged.)*

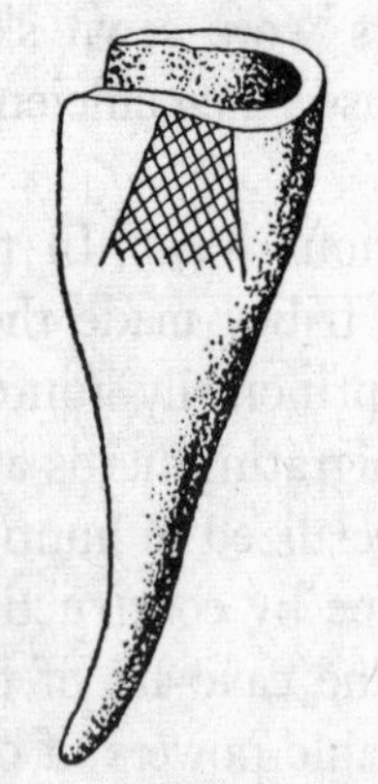

FIGURE 23—*Fine engraving on the incisor of a horse. Vienne, France. Magdalenian.*

stone lamps (figure 150). The acuity of vision and co-ordination of hand and eye which late Palaeolithic tribal artists possessed is illustrated by the fineness of some of their tools and engravings (figures 14 B, 23).

In spite of their artistic and other skilled achievements, the Upper Palaeolithic people of Europe and Asia were economically no more than food-collecting savages (ch 2). Their varied culture, probably reflecting an increase in population and a certain amount of leisure within each group, was possible only because game was abundant.

By various inventions, men now came to adapt their mode of life to the new environments consequent on the climatic changes which brought the last glaciation to an end. In this Mesolithic phase, life remained at the level of bare subsistence until certain groups in the Middle East began the revolutionary practice of cultivating plants and domesticating animals as sources of food and raw materials. With food-production, man passed from the hunting stage and was on the way to civilization (p 42). He ceased to be a rare species. Larger, settled communities could be supported, and it was no longer necessary for all their members to be occupied in gathering or producing food, with the consequence that a great variety of new skilled crafts could develop.

VI. CULTURE AND PHYSICAL TYPE

There seems to have been little correlation between physical type and culture once the human status had been attained in the evolution of the *Hominidae*. Thus, the industry of the Fontéchevade men, with brain-cases of modern type and a cranial capacity of about 1420 cc, was as crude as that of the beetle-browed Pekin cavemen with brains known to vary from 850 cc to 1300 cc in volume. Swanscombe man had a brain-case of essentially modern form (1320 cc), and was a skilful artificer in flint; yet he was the exponent of a cultural tradition which remained almost static for more than 100000 years. The Neanderthalers had brains which on the average (1450 cc) were larger than those of modern men (average 1350 cc), yet their simple culture adapted to Ice Age conditions stood no comparison with that of the inventive Cro-Magnons who succeeded them.

Two reasons for this lack of correlation may be suggested. First, neither the size nor the morphology of the brain-case gives any detailed information as to the efficiency of the cortex of the contained brain. Weidenreich summed up the modern anatomical opinion on this point when he said that the interpretation in detail of the markings on the cast of the interior of a brain-case was 'no more reliable than any other form of phrenology'. Secondly, it has to be remembered that much in any culture is based on communicated ideas, i.e. tradition, and bears little relationship to the mental calibre of the particular individuals who practise it. The Levalloisian technique was used by several species of man (e.g. *Homo neanderthalensis*, *H. rhodesiensis*, and *H. sapiens*), but it must remain uncertain whether it was invented independently by all those different groups, or whether the ideas that are involved were diffused from a single source.

The primates have always shown a tendency to break up into species and communities of relatively few individuals, and it appears that before civilization man was no exception. However, the innate mental differences between the different groups of early men may well have been much less than the physical.

Owing to the close relationship between the mental processes of any individual and the type of society in which he has grown up, it is extremely difficult to make valid comparison between the intelligence and innate abilities of different racial groups. Such tests as have been carried out indicate that while in average intelligence certain primitive racial groups rank lower than civilized peoples, individuals in all groups stand out as more able than the average of any civilized people. Among existing types of men, neither differences in brain-weight nor those in brain-size appear to be reflected in their mental capacities. It has been claimed that in cortical pattern the brains of Australian aborigines appear under-developed in comparison with the brains of, for example, the Chinese; but it is doubtful if the more highly developed aboriginal brains are any different from many normal Chinese brains. The density of nerve-cells in the cortex of the average European brain is said to be greater than in the brains of some East African natives, but both the reliability and the significance of this observation are doubtful. Tests to measure the acuteness of the senses show only small differences between primitive and civilized peoples.

The senses of vision and hearing appear more acute in primitive people, but this may be due to early training in observation, so vital to their mode of life. On the other hand, hereditary influences appear to be more important than environmental in determining some skills. It is found, for example, that the Chinese and the Japanese are more commonly short-sighted than the Anglo-Saxons, while optical errors are as frequent among Arabs living in the desert as among the members of industrial communities in Europe. Dark-eyed people have higher resolving power under intense glare than those whose eyes are lightly pigmented. The pigmentation of the retina is partly an anti-glare mechanism. The survival of hunters depends so much on ability to distinguish game at great distances that in the hunting stage dark-eyed people have always been at a considerable advantage in deserts. However, in moonlight and twilight the resolving power of unpigmented eyes is equally good.

In building sky-scrapers, the Iroquois Indians have proved particularly skilful workmen, for their sense of balance at great heights is well above the average. In deducing the origin of such skills it is difficult to disentangle the physiological from the psychological and social determinants.

To what extent there really are racial or ethnic differences in physical skill or in the acuity of the special senses, which might be reflected in aptitudes for particular types of employment, are questions that have scarcely been scientifically studied. We can but await the results of further research.

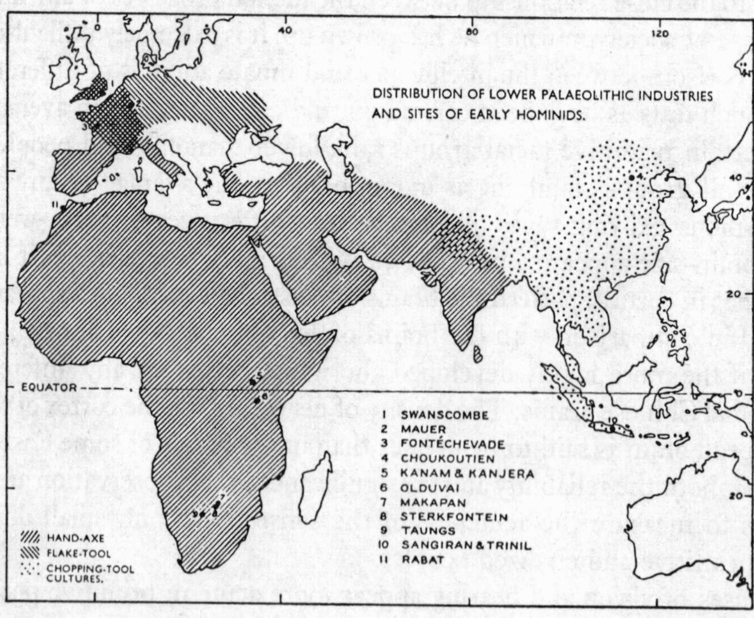

BIBLIOGRAPHY

CLARK, W. E. LE GROS. "The Scope and Limitations of Physical Anthropology." *Advanc. Sci. Lond.*, **1**, 52, 1939.

Idem. 'Fitting Man to his Environment.' Thirty-First Earl Grey Memorial Lecture. Armstrong College, Newcastle-on-Tyne. 1949.

Idem. 'History of the Primates' (2nd ed., revised). British Museum (Natural History), London. 1952.

FIRTH, R. 'Human Types.' Nelson, London. 1938.

FISHER, E. M. "Habits of the Southern Sea Otter." *J. Mammal.*, **20**, 21, 1939.

GRINDLEY, G. C. 'The Intelligence of Animals.' Methuen, London. 1937.

HOOTON, E. A. 'Up from the Apes.' Macmillan, New York. 1946.

JONES, F. WOOD. 'The Principles of Anatomy as seen in the Hand' (2nd ed.). Baillière, Tindall and Cox, London. 1944.

KOEHLER, O. "The Ability of Birds to 'count'." *Bull. Anim. Behav.*, no. 9, 41, 1951.

KÖHLER, WOLFGANG. 'The Mentality of Apes' (2nd ed.). Kegan Paul, London. 1927.

LACK, D. 'Darwin's Finches.' Cambridge University Press, London. 1947.

OAKLEY, K. P. 'Man the Tool-Maker' (2nd ed., revised). British Museum (Natural History), London. 1952.

PAGET, SIR RICHARD A. S. "The Origin of Language." *Sci. News, Harmondsworth*, no. 20, 82, 1951.

Idem. 'Human Speech.' Kegan Paul, London. 1930.

PECKHAM, G. W. and PECKHAM, E. G. 'Wasps, Social and Solitary.' Constable, London. 1905.

THORPE, W. H. 'Physiological Mechanisms in Animal Behaviour.' Cambridge University Press, London. 1950.

Idem. "The Learning Abilities of Birds." *Ibis*, **93**, i, ii, 1951.

TINBERGEN, N. 'The Study of Instinct.' Clarendon Press, Oxford. 1951.

WALLACE, A. F. C. 'Some Psychological Determinants of Culture Change in an Iroquoian Community.' *Bull. Bur. Amer. Ethnol.*, **149**, 1951.

YERKES, R. M. and YERKES, A. W. 'The Great Apes.' Yale University Press, New Haven. 1929.

ZUCKERMAN, S. 'Functional Affinities of Man, Monkeys and Apes.' Kegan Paul, London. 1933.

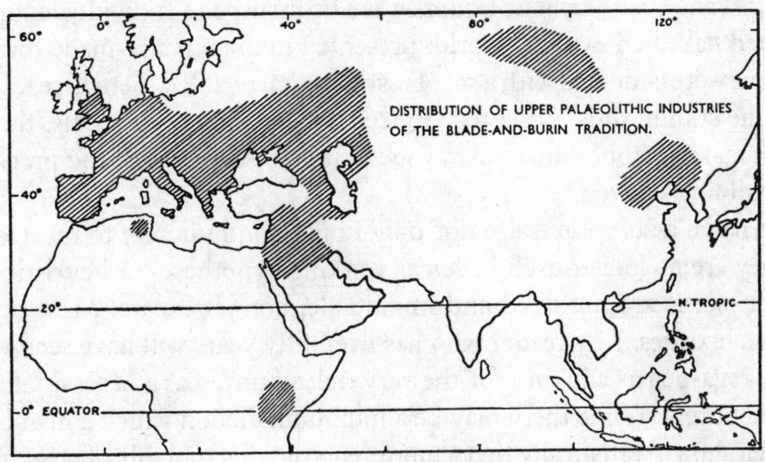

2

EARLY FORMS OF SOCIETY

V. GORDON CHILDE

I. INDIVIDUAL, SOCIETY, AND TECHNIQUE

TECHNOLOGY should mean the study of those activities, directed to the satisfaction of human needs, which produce alterations in the material world. In the present work the meaning of the term is extended to include the results of those activities. Any technology in this sense, like human life itself, involves the regular and habitual co-operation of members of a human group, of a society. The character of the co-operating group is profoundly affected at any time by its size, by the needs that are socially recognized, and by the relations between its members (social organization).

We have inherited from the eighteenth century and earlier a conception of humanity as composed of individuals all sharing certain natural needs—food, drink, reproduction, warmth, shelter, clothing, and so on. These drives to action were regarded as fixed and rigid. In the nineteenth century it was supposed that there were fixed amounts of food and so forth that would satisfy these needs and thus allow the individuals concerned to keep alive and reproduce their kind. These satisfactions were called necessities: everything else was a luxury. There was at least a tendency to regard activities and articles directed to the satisfaction of these basic needs as alone economic; the status of golf-clubs, tombstones, poems, battleships, and even alcoholic liquors was a little suspect. Individuals supposedly confronted naked an external world, presented to them ready-made through the senses, but were endowed with a set of instincts that enabled them to react successfully to the stimuli thus presented. Indeed, given suitable materials, they would set about making stone axes or skin robes with the same automatic precision as a spider building its web.

These naïve assumptions are not only in flat contradiction to most observed facts: they are no longer useful even as working hypotheses or heuristic devices.

Human needs are not fixed and immutable, nor yet innate. Most necessities were once luxuries. Any reader who has lived fifty years will have seen what was formerly regarded as a luxury for the very rich admitted as a necessity for unemployed labourers. While there may be a minimum diet on which a man can exist, it has been shown statistically that a more generous diet, notably of meat, increases the average stature and physical efficiency of human bodies. It may be that finer diet leads to refinement in thinking, but no-one has tried to devise ways of testing this statistically.

The means that enhance physical efficiency can be condemned as economic luxuries only by short-sighted apologists for the *status quo*. Men certainly have no innate taste for intoxicants or narcotics, no spontaneous desire for cinemas, religious celebrations, or battleships, but the provision of these is the object of much of modern technology and plays a decisive role in contemporary economics. The production of cricket bats, liturgies, whisky, and armaments represents activities that economists can ignore no more than the manufacture of cloth or the cultivation of wheat. Only profound prejudices against war or against religion could lead economists to ignore the economic roles of warfare, religion, and magic, and induce historians to minimize the importance of the technical devices elaborated in furtherance of these activities.

The so-called instincts—in human beings at least—turn out to be merely blind urges. Apart from a few purely bodily reflexes, like blinking, breathing, shivering, or scratching, they lead to no effective changes in the external world until given form and direction by training. The human infant does not automatically make the correct response to any external stimulus; it has to learn even such things as personal hygiene from the accumulated experience of its society, transmitted immediately by parents and elders. Still less would it discover unaided how to produce even the simplest tool. Every tool embodies the collective experience of countless generations. Form and material, methods of manufacture and of use, have been preserved by social tradition, and are imparted by precept and example to each new initiate into that tradition.

II. TECHNOLOGIES AS SOCIAL PRODUCTS

The external world on which rational beings act rationally is not, then, the world of individual personal experience. Sensation alone gives no world at all, but only a chaos of fleeting impressions. These are reduced to order with the aid of the conventional symbols of language, the use of which has to be learned. They are given a place in an orderly world far transcending the limits of individual experience. Most of our world is known not by individual sensory experience, but by hearsay and reading, for it is the product of the pooled experience of all the members of the society, both past and present. Knowledge of his world is acquired by everyone through the spoken and written words of his fellows, elders, and forerunners.

To put it briefly, an individual apart from society would not be human. In particular, without society rational human action would be unthinkable, and most of all the sort of action which technology studies. Technologies are produced by groups of men; they are the co-operative activities of societies. A study of techniques accordingly presupposes some knowledge of the sorts of groups which practise or apply them. On the other hand, modern ethnography presents not only a bewildering variety of technologies, but a still greater variety of forms of social organization, of beliefs, and of standards of living. Archaeology illustrates, for the past, an equal variety of techniques and, as supplemented by written history, of polities and economies.

In a history of technology it is manifestly impossible to describe all the varieties of economy and polity that exist today, or to trace the development of concrete societies or nations from the dawn of writing to our own time. Fortunately no such universal history is necessary or relevant. For the purposes of this work, all human societies can be divided into a few very abstract types, and these then arranged in a hierarchy that is also, in some degree, a chronological sequence. The productivity of any technology depends in the long run on the raw materials available and the number of persons engaged. The former factor can be taken as virtually a constant, but the size of the co-operating group is limited at least by the food-supply.

Let us hasten to add that it would, for reasons already indicated, be a mistake to expect the same sort of relation to hold between human populations and their environment as for a population of fruit-flies in the laboratory. An experiment on fruit-flies can determine a measurable quantity that will in fact guarantee the maintenance of the population at constant density. Experiments of the same sort might determine quite as accurately what weights of protein, fat, and carbohy drate are needed to keep an individual alive, but the quantity actually needed to maintain a human population at a constant density is incalculable.

It remains true, however, that there is a dietary scale below which a human population cannot be maintained, though there is no sort of guarantee that it will in fact continue to reproduce itself if brought down to that minimum scale. But the supply of food available to support a human population is determined not only by the fertility of the environment but by the techniques for extracting food and, further, by the system of distributing the product. The latter factors provide bases for classifying societies into groups which are also stages in a temporal sequence. Let us term the way in which a society secures its food 'the basic economy'.

III. FOOD-GATHERERS AND FOOD-PRODUCERS

Within the 500000 years or so of human existence there have been two opposed, but not exclusive, basic economies, if we ignore a purely hypothetic prehuman stage in which each subhuman individual, like a plant or a microbe, just drew from the environment such sustenance as it could appropriate. The simplest basic economy consists in collecting or catching available wild food. It will be termed in the sequel 'savagery'—here used as a convenient equivalent for food-gathering or wild-food economy. 'Savages' here means food-gatherers, without pejorative implication.

This food-gathering is in fact normally conducted in a deliberate, planned, and systematic manner, and usually by organized co-operation of groups; but the foresight, prevision, and co-operation involved differ in degree rather than in

FIGURE 24—*Eskimo engravings on ivory.* (A) *Drying fish. The cone-shaped objects are winter quarters; between them pieces of fish hang from poles; the second structure from the right includes a store reached by steps.* (B) *Reindeer-hunting with the bow. On the left the hides hang drying.*

kind from those which are exhibited by animals that hunt in packs. Human food-gatherers are just as much parasitic on the animals or vegetables they catch or collect as are subhuman organisms. They are almost as dependent on the external environment as are other animals, and the human population is almost as strictly limited by the natural food-supply.

Almost, but not quite—for one thing because, since the discovery of how to preserve, produce, and control fire, men have been able to utilize as food a wider range of nutritive substances than has any other living creature. Nevertheless, in general, food-gathering societies are faced with a constant threat of starvation, and are often short of food. Normally, every able-bodied member of the group is fully occupied with the urgent task of getting food. In other words, only if every able-bodied member of the group is fully employed in collecting, hunting, trapping, or fishing is sufficient food obtained to keep the group alive; therefore the total production tends to equal the total consumption. There is nothing left when the minimum needs of the group have been satisfied.

Some food-gatherers, placed in an exceptionally favourable environment, may, of course, for a time enjoy such an abundance of food as to have a surplus. If they have devised means of preserving food—for example, pemmican among pre-Columbian hunters in America, or dried fish among Arctic fishers—there is a possibility of accumulating what we shall call a social surplus. By this term is meant a regular and reliable supply of food over and above what is consumed by the actual productive members of a group, together, of course, with infants and a very few people too old to get their own food. Such prosperous food-gatherers have been represented in recent times by various fishing tribes on the Pacific coasts of Canada and by the buffalo hunters of the prairies—after the introduction of the horse—and in the past, perhaps, by the reindeer-hunting Magdalenians of France and the mammoth-hunters of the Ukraine. Such economies are, however, unstable as well as exceptional and need not be considered here. The Australian aborigines, the South African Bushmen, and the Eskimo, may be taken as more typical of a food-gathering economy (figure 24).

FIGURE 25—*Predynastic corn-store from the Fayum, Egypt. Diameter: 110 cm.*

Of such, it is true to say that no regular and reliable surplus is produced. Hence, since every adult must be contributing directly to the food-supply, there can be no true division of labour, no full-time specialists. No one, for instance, could live by making stone tools to barter for game, fish, and fruits caught or gathered by his fellows, for there is no guarantee that the latter would be regularly so successful as to keep him supplied. We do, however, find part-time specialists among such gatherers. A skilful flint-knapper may be able to supplement and vary his diet by exchanging his products with some of the food which, from time to time, the more proficient hunters and fishers have caught above their own needs. It must not, of course, be assumed that the technology of food-gatherers or savages is necessarily very primitive, inferior, or rudimentary. On the contrary, it will appear in the sequel that, quite apart from innumerable ingenious devices for catching game or fish, savages devised many fundamental techniques, and invented such complicated instruments as the bow drill, to say nothing of knives, saws, wedges, mallets, chisels, adzes, and axes.

IV. THE NEOLITHIC ECONOMY

For at least 95 per cent. of the whole life-span of humanity all men were savages in the sense defined above. Throughout the vast period termed Pleistocene by geologists, collecting, hunting, and fishing constituted the sole sources of human food. At some point, however, in the post-Pleistocene period, called by geologists Recent, an entirely new economy began to supplement and compete with food-gathering. Men began to cultivate edible plants, i.e. plants bearing nourishing seeds or fruits, and to breed cattle, sheep, goats, and pigs for milk, blood, skins, or meat. We shall term the new economy thus initiated food-production or 'barbarism'.

Barbarism or food-production, whether by agriculture or stockbreeding or the combination of both as mixed farming, initiated the Neolithic stage. Its beginning is often called the Neolithic revolution, using the term by analogy with the industrial revolution, for there are reasons for supposing that it was followed by a somewhat comparable relative increase in population. Archaeologically, Neolithic villages and cemeteries are larger than Palaeolithic or Mesolithic. In ethnography, barbarous populations are generally substantially denser than savage groups.

FIGURE 26—*Storing the harvest. From a tomb at Beni Hasan, Egypt.* c *1900* B.C.

In theory, the same area used as pastures, and still more as cornfields or yam gardens, will provide food for more men than the same area used only for hunting and collecting. In theory again, food can be produced for an expanding population merely by extending the cultivated area and allowing herds and flocks to multiply. But these ideal conditions are seldom fulfilled. Even at the present time the Arctic will support more hunters and fishers than it would farmers—far more, indeed. By no means all land is suitable for tillage or pasture.

Yet, whatever its limitations, farming permits and indeed requires the regular production of a social surplus (figures 25, 26). A farming family—let us call it a productive unit—must harvest enough not only to support it till the next harvest, but to provide seed for that harvest. Actually it is easy to produce a much larger surplus. In 1935 one American farming family could produce enough to feed nine city families; of course, the first Neolithic farmers were far below that standard. In practice, we find that barbarian tribes are often actually hungry during the eleventh, and perhaps even the tenth, month after each harvest. They expect such a situation to arise, for it is often implied in ritual practice or in calendarial terminology. Still, it remains true that only very inefficient or unlucky farmers fail to produce more than they consume.

One result of these developments is that it now became worth while to keep prisoners as slaves instead of eating or torturing them; for, employed on the land, a slave can produce more than his keep. Moreover, even a Neolithic barbarian society normally produces a social surplus. This surplus—consisting in the first instance of food—is available to support full-time specialists who themselves grow no food. Or it can be used to barter with other communities, not only in exchange for other kinds of food—that exchange could and does happen among savages—but for other materials or products. Barbarians and even savages want more than nourishment—the best materials for tools and weapons, intoxicants or sedatives, articles of adornment, and, above all, things supposedly invested with magical properties bringing health and good luck. Such things at first may seem mere pleasant luxuries, but they are liable to become regarded as necessities.

In a hypothetical pure Neolithic economy there would be no full-time specialists. Trade, even if fairly regular, would be confined to luxuries. But intercommunal specialization did develop. Neolithic groups mined flint and quarried specially suitable rock for axes, exchanging their products over a wide area (ch 20). The women of the Amphlett Islands today make pots for export to the adjacent coast of New Guinea and neighbouring archipelagos. However, they are not full-time potters, but gardeners who make pots in their spare time. There is no reason to suppose that the Neolithic flint-miners of Grimes Graves or the Neolithic axe-quarrymen of Craig Lwyd did not also till their own corn plots, or at least graze their own cows and sheep, to feed themselves. Nor need the tribes on Salisbury Plain, who occasionally purchased axes from Craig Lwyd, have regarded them as necessities rather than luxuries. The Melanesian purchasers of Amphlett pots could presumably make home-grown gourds suffice. Theoretically at least, Neolithic barbarians are self-sufficing in that they can supply all essential needs from home-made products of local materials.

V. THE URBAN REVOLUTION

The Neolithic revolution should, then, have given rise to self-sufficing food-producing communities. The economy thus characterized is somewhat hypothetical, for it formed the basis of a third revolution resulting in a new economy. Most barbarian societies today, and the best known Neolithic communities in prehistoric Europe, already exhibit traits proper to the next stage. It is always uncertain whether these deviations from the ideal standard of self-sufficiency really denote steps towards the third revolution, or are due to repercussions of that revolution elsewhere.

The fatal limitation of the Neolithic economy was that the sole outlet for an expanding population was to annex more land for cultivation or grazing, and suitable land was not unlimited. Owing to the extravagant methods of Neolithic cultivators and herdsmen this limitation must have been felt earlier than might at first be supposed. The revolutionary solution was to intensify the exploitation of the existing land, and to use the regular surplus thereby extracted for the support of full-time specialists who did not produce their own food.

This revolution therefore did not render farming obsolete, in the way that the Neolithic revolution had superseded hunting and collecting. It should perhaps not be termed a revolution at all. The term could, however, be justified by comparing the oldest known urban areas with those of contemporary and earlier Neolithic villages. The change in magnitude is so great as to be indicative of qualitative change. Moreover, though doubtless gradual, the change was in fact very radical both in social structure and in psychology, as well as in economy. The author is inclined to doubt whether a mere multiplication of the deviations observed in Neolithic or barbarian societies would be sufficient to produce the final result. That result required a very unusual conjunction of circumstances, which occurred at most five times—in the Tigris–Euphrates delta, in the Nile valley, in the Indus basin, in Central America, and perhaps in Peru. It is, however, just possible chronologically that the Egyptian and Indus civilizations, for all their radical divergences, were in some degree dependent on the Sumerian, while the dependence of the Maya and Inca civilizations on the Old World has been repeatedly—but never very convincingly—argued.

Unfortunately, the prehistoric—and especially the Neolithic—stage of these regions is as yet very imperfectly known.[1] The conditions for, and the stages in, the revolution have to be reconstructed by inference from the results, supplemented by the data available from Mesopotamia and Egypt. Evidence from Late Neolithic communities or from ethnography is inadmissible in view of what was remarked above.

Essential elements in the transformation were (*a*) the conversion of luxuries into necessities, and (*b*) an increase, and above all a concentration, of the social surplus.

Admittedly, even Neolithic barbarians did devote some of their little surplus to the provision of luxuries, but, as long as such things were accepted as luxuries, their use did not destroy the fundamental self-sufficiency of the Neolithic group. As long as they remained luxuries, their provision would offer a very unreliable livelihood for their makers and purveyors. Few would risk becoming full-time specialists; most remained farmers or hunters or fishers who secured a more varied diet and enhanced prestige by plying a handicraft or by trading.

[1] That of the New World centres is totally unknown to the author.

VI. THE ADVENT OF METAL

It is believed that, in the Old World, copper was the first luxury to become a necessity. The superiority of copper weapons over those of stone or bone was almost as decisive as that of firearms over bows and arrows. At the same time, metal-workers were among the first full-time specialists in industrial production, though specialists in magic or religion may have become so earlier. The techniques of prospecting, mining, smelting, casting, and forging are too exacting to be successfully combined with farming or hunting. Moreover, copper ores being comparatively rare, and located generally in mountainous regions (ch 20), the metal has to be transported by persons who cannot very well tend farms at the same time.

Thus a number of men, with their families, have to be supported from the surplus produced by the farmers who ultimately benefit by their products. In the sequel, other handicrafts were gradually separated out from agriculture, but this can happen only with an expansion of the available social surplus. The more full-time specialists there are, the more food there must be available after the needs of the food-producers are satisfied. Note that the requisite increment can be achieved in two ways—which are not mutually exclusive: either each farming unit must produce more food without a proportionate increase in home consumption, or the number of units must be multiplied so that the little surpluses each of them produces can somehow be pooled to swell a total available for distribution. In practice, it was the second procedure that led to the third revolution in both the Old World and the New.

It is obviously no accident that the revolution was first achieved in sub-tropical countries. In them, under intensive cultivation, even a small area will support a large population. In particular, irrigation-farming in the valleys of the Nile, the lower Tigris–Euphrates, and the Indus with its tributaries, yields an exceptionally high return per acre, permitting a considerable density of population. The exploitation of these possibilities requires the co-operation of a substantial labour force for digging canals and embankments. At the same time, in boats or rafts on the rivers and, in Mesopotamia and the Indus valley, on sledges over the alluvial plains, foodstuffs, bulky though they be, can easily be transported to one centre from comparatively distant fields. Here then, even under a Neolithic economy, population could become relatively dense. Small though the surplus produced by each individual unit may have been, the total surplus of the large settlement might itself be relatively large, and sufficient to support full-time specialists who made or brought luxuries. In other words, such a settlement provided a potential market for services or goods.

The mere physical juxtaposition of a number of independent units, even if each produced a surplus, would not guarantee a livelihood to specialists not engaged in food-production. While any farming unit under reasonable conditions ought to be able to produce more food than it consumes, barbarian farmers do not seem inclined to work any harder than is necessary to ensure a living. It is notoriously difficult to convert a luxury into a necessity, to make a peasant so much want a more efficient agricultural machine, electric light, a bath, or air-conditioning that he will regularly work harder to get it. It was doubtless the same with copper axes in prehistoric times. At the same time, such a degree of communal life necessarily exists among subsistence farmers, as well as among most food-gatherers, that the unfortunate and inefficient are supported by their relatives. A complicated nexus of claims between kinsmen hampers the disposal of the produce of the chase, of fields, or of flocks in exchange for luxuries. Moreover, with a Neolithic equipment and rural economy the surplus that the average peasant could produce, even with the best will in the world, was minute; it would seldom be the equivalent of a copper axe—say a day's keep for the smith. For supposing the latter could produce 365 axes a year, each axe must fetch at least a day's keep for himself and his family.

To overcome these complications and make the surplus really available to support new classes of the population, it must be concentrated. This can happen in two ways.

VII. THE TEMPLE CITY

Barbarians, and even savages, are always ready to do a little extra work for one object, namely, the favour or help of imaginary supernatural forces upon which life and prosperity are genuinely believed to depend. Thus savage reindeer-hunters in Pleistocene Europe cast the first kill each season into a lake as a sort of first-fruits offering. Among farming barbarians today such offerings are universal, and they may be converted into capital. An offering thrown into a bog is wasted from the economist's standpoint—though not from the archaeologist's. First-fruits in the form of grain can, however, be stored, since the imaginary power does not in practice consume them. They may thus be used to support a priest—a full-time specialist in conciliating the imaginary powers—or indeed a whole college of priests. If sufficiently abundant, they may then be used to support full-time smiths and other specialists.

Again, in savagery the most successful hunter, or the leader in the hunt, not only brings down more game than his fellows but is usually allowed to retain a larger share of the collective product. Among barbarians, the war-chief actually takes more prisoners than the rank and file. If he keeps them as slaves he can therefore cultivate more land, and so vicariously produce more food. He is, in fact, though in a different way, concentrating the surplus of several productive units. He is clearly likely to appreciate the value of a new weapon, say a metal spear or dagger, and to devote part of the surplus which he cannot consume to its acquisition—that is, to supporting the specialists who alone can provide it.

Finally, the two roles may be combined; the leader in war may become the representative and sole recognized intermediary of the supernatural powers.

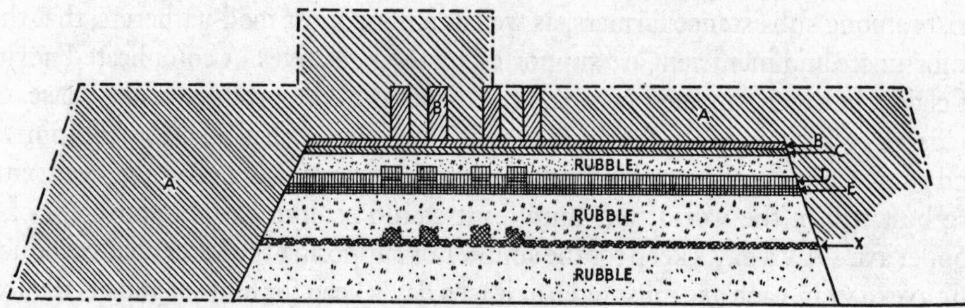

FIGURE 27—*Diagrammatic section through a* tell *at Erech, Mesopotamia. The lowest level* X *is the supposed foundation of the first temple built on this site. Levels* E *and* D *indicate foundations of two later temples.* C *shows a still more recent temple platform. At* B *are the ruins of the 'White Temple' and its walls. Later still, these were encased in the brickwork* A.

The first farmers to colonize the fertile soils of Mesopotamia everywhere built as the most substantial structure in their settlements what we can only call a shrine. They periodically reconstructed these shrines on an ever grander scale, but always on the same hallowed site. So the foundations of superimposed temples eventually constitute a mound or *tell*, the scientific excavation of which provides an archaeological record of the growth of wealth and population on the site (figure 27).

In lower Mesopotamia or Sumer (the fertile Tigris–Euphrates delta) the shrines grew into regular temples, attached to which were granaries and storehouses to hold the free-will offerings of the pious cultivators, and these temples contained written documents bearing the names of deities. It is evident from these documents that the Sumerian farmers firmly believed that they were dependent upon the favour of deities, who were regarded as in a sense the owners and creators of the soil they tilled. To secure the maintenance of the favour of the deities, they paid tribute from the produce of their labour. These revenues were used not only to provide the gods with gigantic feasts and ample supplies of beer, but to support a corporation of priests, who acted as ministers of the gods, and a variety of specialist artisans, who provided for the equipment of the temple and also for the more efficient working of the temple estates. A portion was used to pay for the importation of raw materials for the adornment of the gods' houses, the enjoyment of their ministers, and the better equipment of their tenants.

In some such way, the temple of each Sumerian city became the repository where was concentrated the really vast social surplus produced by the city lands, which were in fact the temple estates. The growth and physical size of the temples are clearly a reflection of the growth in the surrounding population.

FIGURE 28—*The union of the Upper and Lower Nile, symbolized by two female-breasted gods who tie their emblems, the papyrus and the lotus, together around the sign for 'uniting'. Throne of Senusret I.* c *1900* B.C.

The village had, in fact, grown into a city of 8000–12000 inhabitants. Though most of the citizens were themselves actively engaged in farming, stockbreeding, or fishing, the urban population did include new classes of residents, such as full-time specialist artisans, priests, administrators, and clerks. The administration of the vast revenues of the imaginary deities by a corporation of priests required the invention of a system of conventional signs comprehensible to all members of the corporation, by which the receipts and expenditure might be recorded. This invention of writing is conveniently taken as the sign of the transition from barbarism to civilization, which took place in Mesopotamia perhaps shortly after 3500 B.C.

VIII. THE CONQUERING CITY

In Egypt, soon after this date, a similar transformation took place in a rather different way. From Neolithic times, the Nile Valley below the First Cataract had been bordered with substantial villages of farmers, living by subsistence-agriculture based on natural irrigation by the river. Eventually, the war-chief of the Falcon clan, domiciled in Upper Egypt, conquered the whole Nile Valley and established a permanent kingdom over the territory, economically unified by dependence on the one river (figure 28).

By this act, the chief of the Falcon clan—who may already have been high priest of the Falcon totem as well as leader in war—became a god entitled, by his magic powers over the fertility of the land as much as by right of conquest, to receive as tribute the surplus produce of the whole valley. The conquest secured for its cultivators internal peace, protection from Bedouin marauders, and the organization of an irrigation system. One very early figured monument, of about 3200 B.C., depicts a Pharaoh probably 'cutting the first sod' of an irrigation canal (figure 29). In Egypt, too, the surplus thus concentrated by the Pharaoh was accumulated in vast granaries and storehouses, and was used to support new classes of full-time specialists: artisans, officials, and—once more—clerks; for naturally the administration of the vast revenues of the Pharaoh must be entrusted to a corporation of civil servants, who would need, even more than the priests of a Sumerian deity, a system of conventional signs to record receipts and disbursements (figure 26).

Though in Egypt cities were less prominent physically and politically than in Mesopotamia, the villages certainly grew in size, and thus settlements which housed the specialist artisans and civil servants who ministered to the needs of the Pharaoh and his deputies may fairly be called cities. In this sense it is legitimate to speak of the urban revolution in Egypt as well as in Mesopotamia.

A similar revolution took place about the same time in the Indus basin, though nothing is known of its background. Its consummation is symbolized by the growth of really gigantic cities and the construction therein, as almost the principal buildings, of enormous granaries (figure 30), and by the appearance of written documents.

IX. THE TRIBUTE STATE

Thus between 3500 and 2500 B.C. an economic revolution had been accomplished in Mesopotamia, in Egypt, and north-western India. This revolution insured the production and concentration of a surplus of foodstuffs above what was required to support the actual producing families, and the employment of some of this surplus to support new classes in the population. It must nevertheless be insisted that the enormous majority of the peoples of Egypt, Mesopotamia, and the Indus basin were still actively engaged in farming, or in producing their own food in some other way. The increase of population which indubitably occurred was due, in some large degree, to the maintenance of order and the better organization of the rural economy.

It is for our purpose irrelevant how the adequate surplus was first accumulated.

FIGURE 29—(A) *Macehead of the 'Scorpion King'* (C *3200 B.C.*). (B) *Detail showing the Scorpion King 'cutting the first sod' of an irrigation canal. Hierakonpolis, Egypt.*

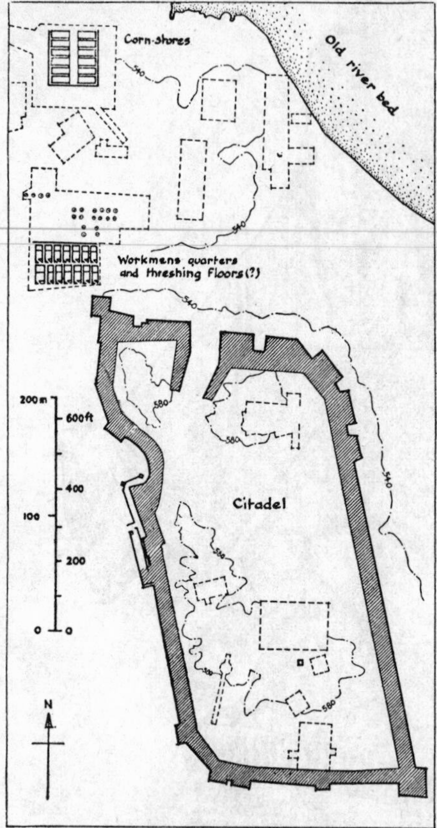

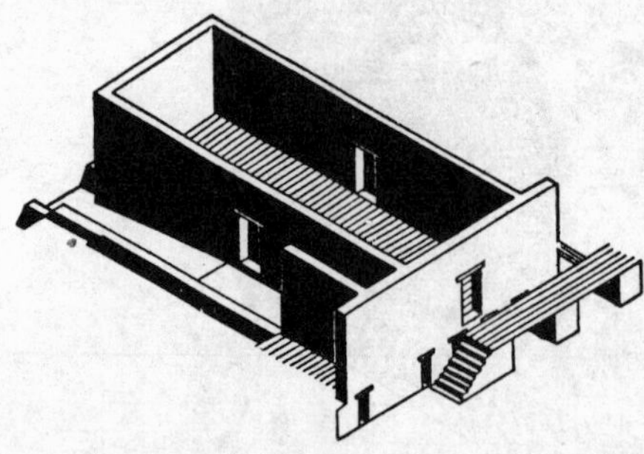

FIGURE 30—*Citadel of Harappa, Indus Valley, with (below) an isometric diagram of a single corn-store. Note the relative size of the corn-store area. Contours in feet.*

Whatever the method, the result is the same. The temple and royal granaries, or both (the existence and importance of granaries is archaeologically or textually attested in Sumer, Egypt, and the Indus valley; figures 26, 30), held vast stocks of foodstuffs available for use as capital. It was, in fact, used to support directly or indirectly a whole new class of full-time specialists who did not themselves grow their own food. They included in the first place, of course, a corporation of priests, a hierarchy of officials, and a variety of specialist craftsmen. Indirectly, it helped to support the merchants and transport workers who brought metal, precious stones, timber, spices, and aromatics to the temple and the palace, and still more indirectly, the miners or woodmen who extracted the raw materials. Even in agriculture itself, production for the market of cash-crops could begin to replace subsistence-farming. The mass of the peasantry continued on the former level, but on temple lands, and the estates of kings and nobles, specialist crops were cultivated by slaves or wage-labourers supported from the temple or royal granaries.

A further result was to start the change of Sumerian and Egyptian society from a mechanical aggregate of persons, all doing much the same things but held together by feelings of kinship or some other emotional bonds, into an organic unit whose members perform complementary functions and are united by the mutual benefits thus conferred. Actually neither Sumerian nor Egyptian society had got very far in that direction; both were held together more by dependence on the temple or the Pharaoh[1] than by common interdependence. As a corollary, however, the social unit was no longer composed of groups united by real or imaginary kinship bonds, but rather of persons who lived in the same place; a territorial unit replaced an organization based on kinship.

The organic solidarity achieved by the urban revolution was, however, imperfect. The urban revolution divided society into economic classes whose interests did not coincide and were at least superficially opposed. The whole point of the revolution was that one person—the king—or a few priests should appropriate whatever the peasant masses produced above the needs of domestic consumption. It was in the economic interests of the rulers to extort as much as they could from the peasants, while the latter might want to retain as much as they could for their own enjoyment. Again, the rulers could not, and did not, themselves consume what they thus appropriated. It was largely devoted to recompensing specialists for goods and services, but economically the rulers would aim at giving as little as possible in return, while the specialists would try to get as large a portion as they could.

In practice, the priestly hierarchy and high officials managed to secure quite a generous part of the surplus, for they became the agents of its acquisition. In Egypt, there was eventually a nobility of hereditary landholders, many descended from the children and officials of early Pharaohs, though all were far more effectively subordinated to the Pharaoh than the feudal barons of medieval Europe to the king. In Sumer, land had been communally owned, that is, owned by a god who stood for the community which formed his people. So in Sumer most of the land round each city belonged to gods, i.e. temples, but was parcelled out among the gods' people—the citizens—to be worked as individual allotments. But in the earliest decipherable documents, the higher temple officials certainly enjoyed the use of, and could probably bequeath, very much larger lots in the temple lands than the ordinary members of the divine household.

While the majority of specialist craftsmen as much as the peasantry, belonged to the lower classes economically opposed to the rulers, there was at least one class of specialist closely associated with the latter, namely, the clerks (figure 31), who might in theory aspire to rise into the ruling class. Not perhaps the least significant result of the revolution, and indeed that which archaeologists take to be the criterion of its completion, had been the invention of writing, i.e. the standardization of conventional graphic symbolism. The art of reading and writing became an accomplishment invested with considerable prestige. The initiates

1 'Pharaoh' etymologically means 'the great house', i.e. palace.

were exempted from all manual tasks and guaranteed some leisure for research. In fact, to them, or to some of them, was entrusted the task of thinking for society, that is, of formulating in logical terms the world view of society. They also were pioneers of sciences—arithmetical, geometrical, and calendarial—which ulti-

FIGURE 31—*'Clerks' of Tiglath-pileser III counting the spoils of war. Central Palace at Nimrud, Mesopotamia. c 800 B.C*

mately found applications in technology. Craftsmen, on the other hand, remained as illiterate as peasants during the period covered by this volume.

The urban revolution must have had immediate repercussions outside the society where it occurred. Internally, the concentrated surplus provided a livelihood for new classes within, and perhaps outside, the community. As soon as the revolution was completed in Mesopotamia and in Egypt, exotic materials—copper in large quantities, regular supplies of timber, precious metals, jewels, aromatics—began to arrive (figure 32). To some extent these materials were obtained by expeditions sent out by the state. For copper and turquoise, miners were periodically sent from Egypt across the desert to Sinai, accompanied by soldiers to protect them, and pack-animals with food from the royal granaries to support them while at work and on the way. More usually, perhaps, the transportation was organized by merchants, who might or might not belong to the consumers' community, while the collection or extraction was probably conducted by aborigines.

The surplus accumulated in the Sumerian temples made it worth while to organize caravans to cross the Iranian mountains and fetch lapis lazuli from

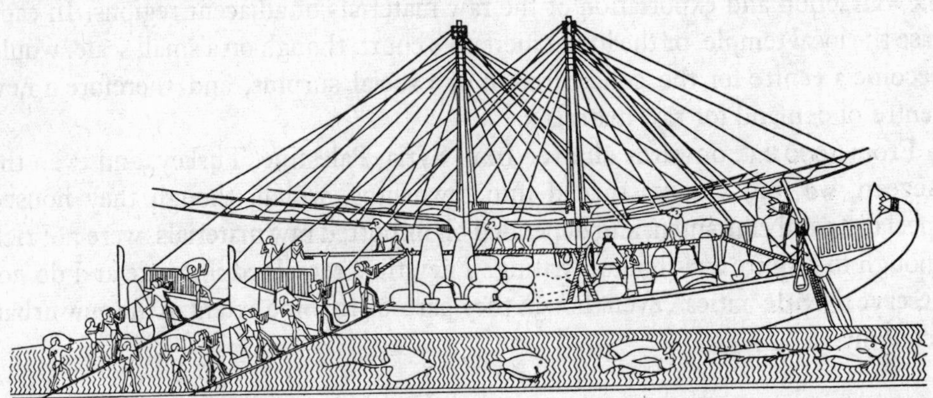

FIGURE 32—*Ships of Queen Hatshepsut's fleet loading at Punt with exotic merchandise for Egypt. From a temple at Deir el-Bahri, Egypt, c 1500 B.C. Note the tame baboons, the marine character of the fishes depicted, and the carriage and storage of growing incense plants. For a description of the type of ship see chapter 28.*

Badakhshan, or the Syrian desert and the Taurus to bring silver, copper, and tin. The Sumerian surplus must have been great enough to guarantee at least their keep to all those engaged in the transportation—and the merchants would demand a profit as well.

X. REPERCUSSIONS OF CIVILIZATION ON OUTER BARBARISM

Once the traffic was organized in reliance on this concentrated surplus or capital, all small barbarian communities on the route that could not themselves produce a sufficient surplus to support the craftsman could use what surplus they did possess to purchase materials in transit, and incidentally perhaps to supplement the merchants' profit. So, if the caravan had to pass Giyan, Rayy, and Hissar—sites of prehistoric villages on the lapis lazuli route across Iran—it might well be worth while adding to its load a few urban manufactures for the barbarians living in these villages: indeed, it might be necessary, for the merchants would probably have to bribe the barbarians to secure unmolested passage.

Now, on modern analogy the appropriate recipient of this *douceur* would be the local chief or headman, presuming such a one existed as at least a part-time specialist. He could then become a full-time specialist, no longer dependent on the freewill offerings or customary gifts of fellow tribesmen, but economically independent of them. What is true of transit zones applies even more to the producing regions—to the communities who produced lapis, silver, copper, or timber. In the Phoenician ports of the timber trade, and in the metalliferous regions of Turkey and Persia, chiefs or deities received generous gifts in return for organizing the extraction and exportation of the raw materials of adjacent regions. In each case the local temple, or the local chieftain's court, though on a small scale, would become a centre for the concentration of a social surplus, and therefore a new centre of demand for raw materials.

From 3000 B.C. onwards all over Iran, Syria, Palestine, Turkey, and even the Aegean, we find villages turned into townships, which, though they housed specialists and craftsmen, and depended on imported raw materials, were not rich enough to require a system of writing. They thus remained illiterate and do not deserve the title 'cities', even though they partook to some extent in the new urban economy.

XI. ECONOMIC IMPERIALISM

Before 2500 B.C. the temple cities of Mesopotamia had all been independent states. These states were frequently at war with one another over land and water rights. It has been suggested that, at first, the leaders in war had been elected, but in the earliest written documents the war-chief has already become a hereditary prince, sometimes also the high priest of the city god. Even so, he would remain merely the servant of the god, and therefore of the community whom the god represented. In the internecine wars between city states after 2500 B.C., it sometimes happened that the leader of a victorious city found himself ruler over the population of a hostile state. He would no longer be the servant or representative of these, but their conqueror, lord, and master, and this new relationship and new authority would react upon his relations even with the citizens of his own city. The city prince would become a king.

About 2250 B.C. Sargon of Agade conquered the remaining cities of Mesopotamia, and thus established a kingdom that lasted for over a century (figure 424). The princes of Ur, Larsa, Isin, and eventually Babylon established similar kingdoms in lower Mesopotamia. But Sargon extended his military operations beyond the boundaries of lower Mesopotamia, 'to the silver mountain and the cedar forest' (probably the Taurus and the Amanus ranges). He thus established the first, if an unstable, empire. He was imitated by the kings of Ur and Babylon, and, later still, by the Hittites and the Pharaohs of Egypt.

The very terms of Sargon's inscriptions revealed the economic motives which inspired his imperialism. One object certainly was to secure as tribute the raw materials needed for Mesopotamian industry, especially the armaments industry, and imperialism thus became a new instrument in the concentration of a still vaster social surplus. It was at the same time an instrument in the diffusion of the urban revolution itself. Not only did the conquerors found temples and governors' palaces, which as centres of concentration converted villages into cities, but resistance to imperialism or aggression also encouraged the spread of urbanization. To resist the well armed forces of civilized states the barbarian victims must organize their economy to secure regular supplies of metal, at least, and the services of competent metal-workers. At the same time, the authority of any chief who led the resistance movements would be consolidated. He could, and indeed must, become a concentrator of the social surplus and so his court would become a new centre of demand for raw materials. In these ways civilization, in the economic sense defined above, was bound to spread, and spread it did.

Barter in an Old Kingdom Egyptian market. From a tomb at Saqqara. c 2400 B.C.

3

DISCOVERY, INVENTION, AND DIFFUSION

H. S. HARRISON

I. MAN'S EARLY STEPS

THE discoveries made by most men, however intelligent and inquiring they may be, neither extend the bounds of knowledge nor foster progress in science or technology. Only the man who is exceptional, by birth or opportunity or both, treads his way into unknown territory. It is with very simple yet significant discoveries, made by such pioneers long ago, that we are primarily concerned: with yet a further limitation.

Discovery by finding—whether of an Egyptian royal tomb, of a nugget of gold, or of a comet—must be distinguished from discovery by finding out, which involves an advance in knowledge of the properties of materials, of natural laws and forces, and of methods of applying such knowledge to a purpose. Discovery by finding may be mere localization or recognition. While this is a necessary preliminary to the exploitation of materials, true discovery, from the standpoint of the student of human products and methods, goes further; it reveals new possibilities of progress. In general, the order of events is from observation, through discovery, to application—though observation is not always followed by discovery, or discovery by application. To pass from observation to discovery needs more than the casual noting of an event or a phenomenon, and still more is required before a discovery is applied to practical purposes. Early and frequent observation of forest fires probably led to the discovery that a little fire, a conflagration tamed, could be domesticated. From the observation that fire exhausted that on which it fed, arose the discovery that it could be tamed by underfeeding. The forest fire was a centrifugal force from which men fled, but the domestic fire became centripetal, holding them to hearth and home.

The same kind of thing is true of many observations that ultimately led to progress. Many vital discoveries were made before our ancestors were human (ch 1), since an acquaintance with food-materials, for example, was needful for survival; but fruits and seeds were eaten long before it was observed that plants arose from them, and still longer before it was dicovered that seeds might be sown to produce a crop (ch 14). With every hesitating forward step in man's nascent material culture, new openings were revealed. Eventually, discovery and invention could proceed along many lines instead of along very few.

The term invention has in ordinary usage no clearer meaning than has discovery. The two words are, moreover, so closely involved in their customary applications that they can scarcely be disentangled. It might seem safe to say that a simple invention is a material application of a discovery, but since some inventions (in the ordinary sense) may have been discovered only after they had in effect been made, and since inventive steps may not be due to discovery alone, or even mainly, this definition breaks down. At this stage it is not desirable to attempt to limit too closely the application of the word. It must be pointed out, however, that a discovery is a subjective event, and that in its relation to technology it acquires importance only if applied practically; only then does it, in that relation, secure objective value. The word invention, on the other hand, is in material culture already an objective term. Between these two terms a clear distinction is desirable, as well as between the subjective aspects of the words discovery and invention viewed as mental processes. The extent to which these terms can be applied to non-material products, such as social and moral formulae and codes, does not concern us here.

FIGURE 33—*Wooden digging-stick with perforated stone weight to supplement push. Bushmen of South Africa.*

Obviously, discovery has a far wider field of action than has invention, which can manifest itself only in relation to man's shaped or constructed artifacts. Discovery, on the other hand, is not only responsible for many of the steps in the morphological evolution of implements and machines, but for the initiation and development of methods and processes in which chemistry, physics, and biology, for example, play their part.

As an example of evolution in discovery and technique, we may reduce to their simplest form the stages leading to the production of the iron-bladed tools and weapons of the early Iron Age (ch 21). The initial steps arose out of the discovery of the malleable nature of native copper (p 585). This led to the production of simple types of implements by cold hammering, later assisted by some heating of the metal. Then followed casting of the molten metal in open moulds. The discovery that copper could be obtained by heating a certain kind of stone led to the smelting of its ores, some of which were, in all probability, found intermingled with an ore of tin. This association paved the way to the production of the alloy bronze, from which a greater variety of efficient tools could be cast in closed moulds (ch 22). Such metal-working no doubt fostered the idea that other metals might lie dormant in other kinds of heavy shining stones. Thus began the smelting of iron ores, probably within or adjacent to the region of western Asia in which the Neolithic revolution had its origin. The new metal was not then known to be amenable to the method of casting, and there was a reversion to forging.

Early man's knowledge of the latent possibilities of his environment necessarily developed very slowly, even in relation to materials and methods that could hardly be overlooked. Its beginnings lie so far back that we shall never be able to say that at such and such a period he began to crack nuts with a stone, dig up tubers with a stick (figure 33), or correct his friends with a club. As a speechless ape-man he may well have got as far as that, or even farther. The knowledge that we have of man's first stumbling attempts to make implements has already been discussed (ch 1), but we may pause to consider the mental background of such attempts.

II. EXTREME SLOWNESS OF PROGRESS

It is often supposed that invention may be described as the devising of means to fit the end, but this is to take a complacent view of the process, in which the end may be revealed only by a chance discovery of the means, already in existence. Man has progressed less by the pressure of his needs than by the insistence of his opportunities. Human progress has always depended largely upon opportunism—in the earliest times casual and obtuse, but later becoming intermittently persistent in certain directions, and in our own day strongly and systematically canalized towards many defined ends. We have become far less dependent upon accident than were our distant forefathers, but chance continues to play an important though sporadic part in scientific and technological progress.

To appreciate the sluggishness of discovery and invention in prehistoric or early historic times, and down to the present day in most parts of the world, it is essential to realize that our own civilized conditioning to a technological environment has made this appreciation extremely difficult. As we grow in mind and body, each of us becomes familiar with a multitude of apparently simple facts and artifacts, principles and practices, along with others far from simple, that were as remote from the conception of early man as the idea of television would have been to Queen Victoria. We leave our cradles to push a button and effect a miracle, accepting it as commonplace. It is difficult for us to realize that such apparently simple implements as the axe, the adze, and the archer's bow did not easily spring ready-made from the precocious mind and hand of some prehistoric genius (figures 34, 40). Yet the evidence shows that such inventions were quite beyond the power of early man to conceive, and remained so until he had, by prolonged preliminary stages, approached so near to them that the conclusive step could be suggested by a chance occurrence, leading to a simple discovery; or even until he had practically achieved the end before he recognized the aim.

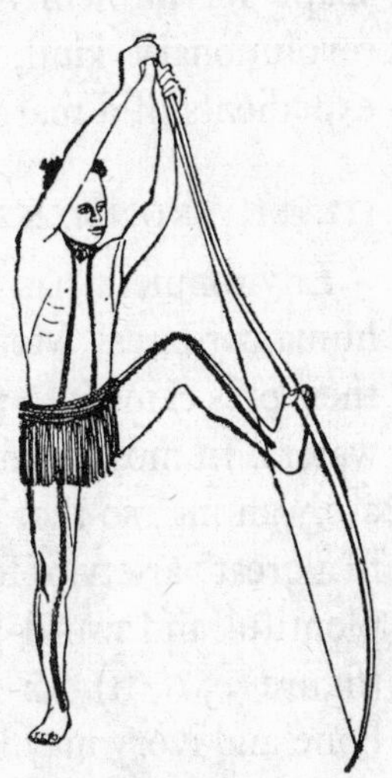

FIGURE 34—*Andaman Islander stringing bow.*

We are so accustomed to read of great modern inventions, and our ideas of their origin and nature are usually so superficial and confused, that we are apt to gain the impression that now at least there are men who can look far ahead of the knowledge of their time, and discover and invent by laboratory or workshop divination. It is not so. The greatest discoverer or inventor can build only upon the work of his predecessors, and his greatness depends on his powers of analysis, insight, and synthesis, aided by some little foresight. By experimental methods he lays traps for suggestions, and although he has an end in view, the ultimate solution of his problem may evade him or surprise him. Experiment is experience sharpened to a point—useful as a digging-stick, but not as a divining-rod.

It is sometimes assumed that the devising of means to overcome the small mechanical and other difficulties apt to occur in normal civilized life, or on occasions when greater emergencies arise, may be placed in the category of inventions. Were the reader cast ashore on a desert island, he would hasten to 'invent' means, and devise methods, of procuring food and shelter. If the conditions were not too repressive, it may be that he would make a passable job of it, though the chances would be against the average unpractical town-bred man. But what he did would be based on what he remembered of his previous experiences. He would sample different kinds of wild plants for food, and to add to his bill of fare he might make a crude fishing-line provided with gorge or hook; he might produce a knife by grinding a shell to a sharper edge, and use it for cutting up small animals that he had killed with sticks or stones. Many other things he might contrive, but all his appliances and methods would be based upon what he had learnt before, and the chances would be against his making progress beyond the range of his civilized conditioning. Early man, on the other hand, had even to discover at first hand that two stones knocked together might produce flakes or splinters that would cut or scrape or pierce; that pointed sticks had penetrating powers that could be put to use; that wood could be shaped by hacking and cutting; and much later that plants could be grown to provide food, and that some kinds of 'stone' (native copper) could be beaten into shape for implements. These were original discoveries, new knowledge of a revolutionary kind, far more difficult of conception than the second-hand expedients of a marooned civilian.

III. ENVIRONMENTAL FACTORS

Environment has obviously been a limiting as well as a furthering factor in human progress. Metal-working could be initiated only in a region where metals or their ores came into prominence; canoes would not be devised without navigable waters. In most islands of the Pacific, hard and heavy woods abound and metals are wanting, so that massive wooden clubs and wooden spears were developed in a great variety of forms (figure 35 A, B, C). In Africa, on the other hand, iron is plentiful, and sword-knives and heavy iron-bladed spears are widespread weapons (figure 35 G, H). In the Arctic regions, wood and metals alike are scarce, while bone and ivory may be obtained in quantity, and the Eskimo use these materials to an extent and with an ingenuity rarely found elsewhere (figure 35 D, E, F). The natural environment is therefore of the utmost importance, but although it provides the raw materials, as well as incentives and encouragements, it does not display signposts indicating the ways to progress in discovery and invention in evolutionary detail.

Factors in environment are both the material and the social conditions under which men live. Environmental elements are not only natural but also artificial, since, for example, steel tools and motor-cars are as much a part of our modern environment as stones or trees. In contemporary civilized life, the artificial environment overshadows and largely supersedes the natural, and discovery and invention have high-level starting-points. Under simpler conditions, man's progress has had to start at much lower levels, with restrictions in direction as well as in equipment. The harpoon could have been invented only by a people who already had the spear (figure 86), and the loom only by those who were familiar with textiles made by hand (ch 16). Bombs, torpedoes, rockets, and other complex weapons of modern warfare became possible only when explosives, metals, and other materials and devices had reached certain stages of development. Savage man limits his homicidal ingenuities to weapons the construction of which depends upon the few materials within his reach, the types that are

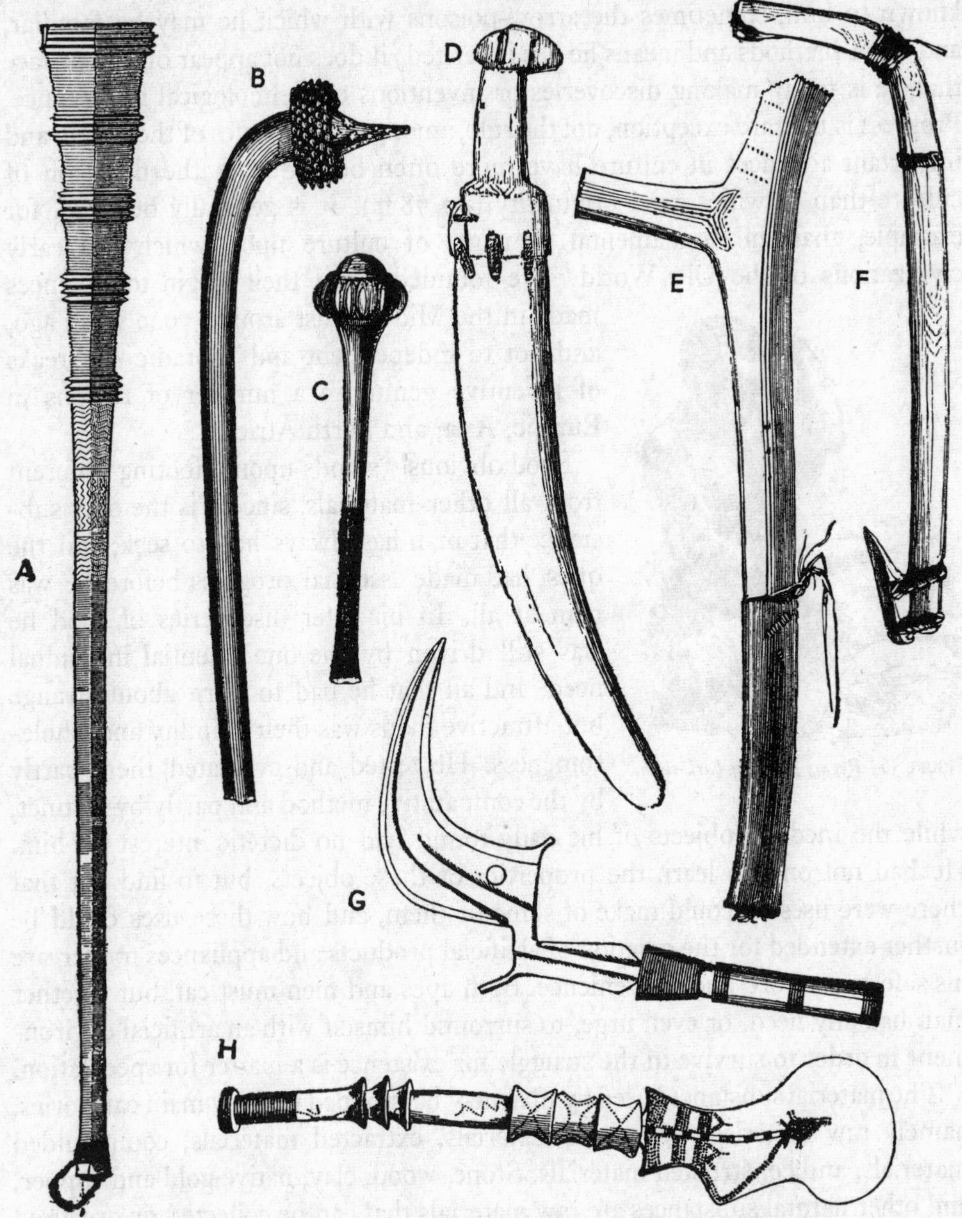

FIGURE 35—(A)–(C) *Wooden clubs from the Pacific Islands.* (D)–(F) *Eskimo bone snow-knife, antler club, and blubber-hook.* (G), (H) *Iron knives from the Belgian Congo.*

known to him, sometimes the arrow-poisons with which he may be familiar, and other methods and means he has inherited; it does not appear on the surface that he is today making discoveries or inventions of technological importance. Progress is the rare exception, not the rule, amongst the peoples of the Earth, and important advances in culture have more often been due to the diffusion of culture than to widespread originality (pp 78 ff). It is generally believed, for example, that the fundamental elements of culture upon which the early civilizations of the Old World were founded owed their origin to advances made in the Middle East around 7000 years ago, and not to independent and sporadic outbreaks of inventive genius in a number of regions in Europe, Asia, and north Africa.

FIGURE 36—*Pygmy pounding bark-cloth.*

Food obviously stands upon a footing different from all other materials, since it is the only substance that man has always had to seek, and the quest had made essential progress before he was man at all. In his later discoveries of food he was still driven by the one essential individual need, and all that he had to learn about strange but attractive foods was their edibility and wholesomeness. He tested and evaluated them partly by the comparative method and partly by instinct, while the inedible objects of his daily round had no dietetic interest for him. He had not only to learn the properties of these objects, but to find out that there were uses he could make of some of them, and how these uses could be further extended for the creation of artificial products and appliances to increase his safety, comfort, and convenience. Both apes and men must eat, but whether man had any need, or even urge, to surround himself with an artificial environment in order to survive in the struggle for existence is a matter for speculation.

The material substances used by man may be grouped in a few main categories, namely raw materials, separated materials, extracted materials, compounded materials, and constructed materials. Stone, wood, clay, native gold and copper, and other natural substances are raw materials that can be collected or procured in a state of readiness for shaping into artifacts, but they did not themselves always suggest the nature of their usefulness. Separated materials, such as vegetable fibres, bark, bone, sinew, and skin, need removal from their plant or animal context, and usually also some kind of adaptation (as shredding, beating, drying, tanning) before they are ready for use (figure 36). Extracted materials, of which tin, iron, and other metals are good examples, may be obtainable only by chemical separation under great heat, while bronze and other alloys and mixtures are compounded materials. String, basket-work, woven cloth, and other textiles may be called constructed materials, and though they may serve as components of other artifacts they must themselves be classed as artifacts.

The processes of shaping most hard and infusible substances involve the use of tools, by means of which they are subjected to the coercion of percussion and pressure (including friction), in which sharp-edged implements may play an essential part. For the shaping of metal, fire is usually required, either for softening it for forging, or melting it for casting. The points of wooden digging-sticks and spears may be hardened by charring, which may also aid in the hollowing-out of a canoe; and fire, sometimes in conjunction with water, may assist in shaping objects of wood and horn and by imparting to these materials some measure of plasticity. In the main, however, simple wooden, bone, and horn artifacts, like those of stone, result from the forcible removal by means of tools of portions of the raw material; wood-working and stone-working are thus wasteful processes, though some of the debris may be utilizable (ch 6). Reducing stone by frictional abrasion may lead to polishing, as in the evolution of many Neolithic implements.

There are few useful substances that can be shaped by the hand unaided, and potter's clay is the most important of them. Although force is required, this is more persuasive than coercive, and the form of the future pot may be reached by methods of shaping—moulding, modelling, or building—in which the hands do most of the work (ch 15). The potter's wheel is an invention which supplements and concentrates the control of the hands. The casting of metal, again, in spite of the heat required for the temporary melting of the material, is another persuasive method, contrasting with the violence of forging.

There is clearly great variety in the amount of force and energy required to shape materials to desired forms, as well as in the history of the forms and of the methods by which they are produced. The utilization of stone and metal, and of other hard materials, has been determined not only by the nature of the materials, but by the tools and appliances available for working them. The reactions and uses of ready-to-hand or easily accessible materials required only to be discovered, whereas the extracted materials, such as most metals, lay entirely outside man's conceptual environment until some chance event revealed their hidden presence and methods of smelting ores were discovered. Only then could he proceed to acquire knowledge of their properties, develop their uses, and seek for other substances that might resemble them. He had no need of metals until he had discovered them, and until then they could not exist even in his imagination. Copper and gold, found in the native state in Stone Age times, were the malleable foundation of modern metallurgy.

IV. ANALYSIS OF DISCOVERY AND INVENTION

At this stage it is convenient to consider in some detail certain analytical problems raised by the study of the evolution of human products and methods, even those of relatively simple character.

If our knowledge of the whole history of, say, the woodman's axe, were complete, we could reconstruct all the stages in its development from its beginning until the present day. But even if all the essential evolutionary stages were made available for inspection, there would still remain questions as to why and how particular changes in form and structure were made. The improvements effected by the changes might be obvious, but only by adopting the untenable view that man has always foreseen and developed the possibilities dormant in his appliances could we regard their appearance as having been determined by directional efforts towards preconceived types. Stone Age man, and even the early metal-worker, could not aim at the production of the modern woodman's axe, with a socket parallel to the blade edge, because any such implement lay entirely outside his experience—he had no model and no steel. His vision reached no further than the known, or than what would be readily suggested by what was known.

It may be said that, even if this be true, in later times there must have come a change, by which man was able to conceive ideas of form and construction that were prophetic and original. The aeroplane may be briefly considered in this connexion, since it has evolved from its precursors, the gliders, within recent memory, and we are familiar with some at least of the improvements made. Its rapid development has been the result of an intensive canalizing process of trial and error, accompanied by mathematical and engineering computations of great complexity, and sustained by the bravery and endurance of many men at the peril, and often the loss, of their lives. But it is clear that modern aeroplanes were not evolved to conform to early preconceptions of what they should be like, except with regard to some overriding features of airworthiness. In some of man's earlier dreams of flight, arising from long familiarity with the flight of birds, he confidingly endowed himself with wings to flap. He became an angel or an Icarus, with no great profit to himself, and thus to the modern inventor the flapping wings made little appeal. The requirements of two great wars led to a greatly increased urgency in aeronautical research and experiment, but there is still perhaps no general agreement as to what the perfect aeroplane should be like. It cannot be said that in jet-propulsion finality in engine design has been reached, since atomic energy lurks significantly in the background, and there still remain possibilities of new types of helicopters and other planes that can hover and alight in a small space. The modern types have left Blériot's monoplane and many others very far behind, and there are no prophets to tell us what is to come.

If we are to arrive at definite conclusions as to factors influencing early discovery and invention, we must concentrate in the first instance on those artifacts which we may assume, not without good grounds, to have been amongst the earliest human implements. The inquiry should afford at least presumptive evidence of the manner in which the mind of early man reacted to the suggestions of his environment, and of the way in which his reactions were expressed in the forms and construction of his implements.

Again, the use of pebbles for hammers or missiles (as by some modern apes) was based on discoveries of their effectiveness, and the same is true of naturally or accidentally fractured stones or sticks which gave opportunities for the discovery of the uses of the edge and the point. Discoveries of this nature were essential steps in the metamorphosis of man from a tool-user into a tool-maker, and were necessarily associated with discoveries of methods of producing the features themselves.

We may suppose that man found out by chance that if he knocked together two pieces of stone with sufficient force, he obtained sharp-edged fragments such as he had already picked up at random and utilized. From our point of view the natural knife or chopper is, however, poles apart from the artificial, which arose in the first case, we surmise, as the result of a discovery applied for the production of something that had never been made intentionally before. However comparable the two may have been in form and effectiveness, the step from one to the other was of a discontinuous character subjectively, since the tool was either shaped by intention, or it was not. We may anticipate a little by calling a definite step of this kind a mutation, and since it represented a kind of step which converted a natural object into an artifact, we may call it a primary mutation. In the case of stone, it was the opening-up of the method of shaping by percussion, since the breaking of a pebble by a single blow led naturally to a repetition of blows, either on impulse, or because the first shape obtained was not good enough. The method was of wide application, capable of giving rise to a great variety of forms, many of them having serviceable edges or points. Since the discovery was easily made, and of immediate value, it might have often been independently hit upon and utilized; or it may have been made so early that it spread with the first movements of the human stock from their centre of origin outwards. Perhaps there never was an early man—assuming that any such vaguely defined anthropoid could be distinguished from an ape—who did not break stones. Even Pekin man (p 23) seems to have got as far as this.

That such implements as the Palaeolithic hand-axes and ovates arose by gradual development out of roughly chipped stones of indeterminate forms can scarcely be doubted, though Palaeolithic man continued to make both roughly shaped and finely finished implements over a long period. The nature of the stone would have much influence on the results of flaking, but the more useful and handy forms were recognized, after they were made, as worthy of imitation, and in the Lower Palaeolithic of Europe, and in some other regions, a large measure of standardization was eventually reached. The implement halted for a time at an 'expression point' (such as the hand-axe), later to proceed by variation to another expression point (the sharp-rimmed ovate), and the two types remained in use together, along with others, over an immensely long period in several parts of the Old World (figure 37). The earliest changes in shape were based on what we may call random variation, in which there was a large element of chance, but selective variation would come into play later, leading to the production of forms which gave greater satisfaction, though not necessarily on the grounds of increased efficiency. At the same time, a process of adaptive variation would show itself, leading directly to the practical improvement of the implement.

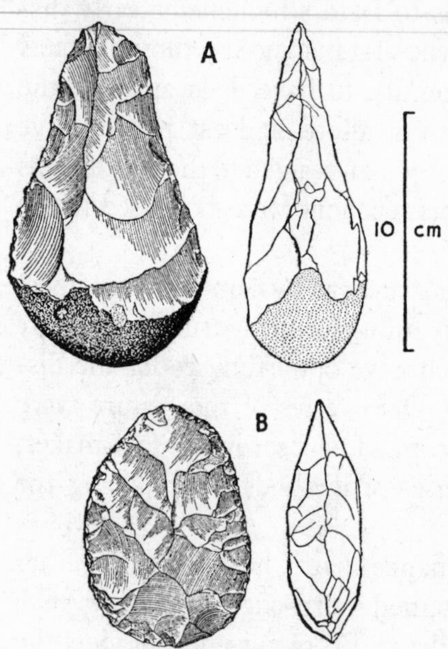

FIGURE 37—(A) *Flint hand-axe from Swanscombe, Kent.* (B) *Flint ovate from Palestine. Both Acheulian, Lower Palaeolithic.*

Variation has been especially active in changing the form and proportions of artifacts, and in some features, such as increase in size, a single change may have been relatively great; even here, however, the modification would be such as might have been produced by the summation of a number of smaller variations. No large discontinuous steps in advance have occurred by variation, though it may gradually have transformed an implement (or a component) in such a direction as to afford an opportunity for the intervention of higher factors.

Variation, unlike mutation, does not depend on discovery or invention, but it is not always an involuntary process, and it may be influenced by more or less conscious imitation.

We may draw upon methods of hafting for our first illustrations of mutations occurring in the further development of one-piece artifacts which had already acquired an individuality of their own.

It is obvious that a hand-grip of skin, or other common material, attached to a cutting or hacking tool of stone, might owe its origin to the desire to protect the hand from a sharp edge in the wrong place, a loose piece of the skin being picked up and used in emergency. The effectiveness of the casual device was the essential discovery, but the decisive step in its application was to convert the handgrip from a hasty or temporary expedient into a fixed component of the knife or chopper, as exemplified by some of the knives of the modern Eskimo, and thus to construct a composite implement, representative of the first of its kind (figure 38). We can, however, scarcely surmise with profit what came first in the long series of hafted implements. The permanent addition arose out of an appreciation of the immediate possibilities of the discovery, both in the material used for the grip and in the method of attachment. In no way could variation have led to the provision of a permanent hand-grip, which was something entirely new. The addition constituted an abrupt and discontinuous step, and for such steps the word mutation is clearly appropriate. On the assumption that the first provision of a hand-grip for a stone blade arose out of a discovery made during the use of the tool itself, and was not suggested by a feature of any other contemporary implement, we may call the step a free-mutation.

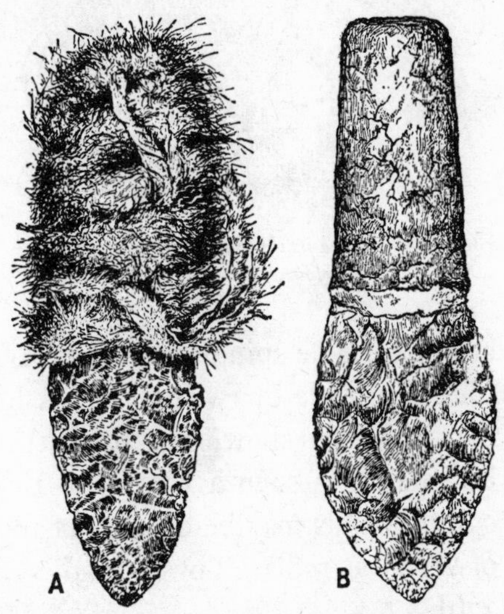

FIGURE 38—*Stone-bladed knives from California.* (A) *Obsidian, wrapped at one end with otter-skin as grip.* (B) *Jasper, wooden handle attached with bitumen.*

A few other examples may be given. Some simple wooden digging-sticks have a foot-rest, which facilitates the forcing of the implement into the soil. If the first such foot-rest was a spur, the base of a branch having been incompletely cut away when the tool was trimmed, the discovery would be easily made that the accidental feature enabled the leg to reinforce the arms in digging. The intentional provision of such a spur or foot-rest would be an evolutionary step which may be called a free-mutation. Again, if, in using a long stick for threshing corn, a breakage occurred which left a short distal segment for a time in connexion with the proximal portion, by means of a strip of tough bark, a suggestion was provided for the construction of the hinged flail (figure 39), by free-mutation. Nevertheless the evidence is that the flail was not in use for threshing corn until Roman imperial times; this apparently obvious invention was thus long delayed. The temporary seizing of a stone blade within the curve of a bent stick may have led to the free-mutation which gave rise to the first permanent axe-type with wooden haft, if conditions at the time were such as to make an implement of this kind of sufficient value to attract attention. The spindle may have arisen through the habit of winding on a stick the yarn made by twisting fibres between the hands or on the thigh. Chance may well have shown that by a little care in manipulation this spool-stick could be rotated in such a way as to twist the fibres, and so act as what we call a spindle. This may be called a change of function, but when the coil or bunch of yarn was replaced by a spindle-whorl the free-mutation was complete (figure 276).

FIGURE 39—*Peasants threshing a sheaf of corn with flails. From a fourteenth-century miniature.*

Some of the early free-mutations, like the early primary mutations, were associated in origin with simple methods capable of wide application, which rapidly became incorporated in the body of knowledge available to later inventors. The idea of lashing parts together, for example, could have originated in association with a free-mutation, but it became established as the basis of a general method by which a desired connexion between any two suitable components could be effected or reinforced. As just suggested, the idea of attaching a stone blade to a wooden haft may have arisen out of some incidental method of holding the blade temporarily in position in a bent haft, and, perhaps only at a later stage, with a lashing for security (figure 40 B). The adoption of the holder as a permanent haft constituted the free-mutation, while the method of doing it was capable of variation as well as of extension to other artifacts, thus foreshadowing, or even exemplifying, cross-mutation (see below). Similarly with other and less easily derived types of attachment, such as those effected by the intervention of sleeves, sockets, and perforations in a variety of forms and relationships: these involve structural adaptations as well as method, and, although there is close association between the two, the individuality of the completed whole lies in its visible characters. It is these, and not the methods used in construction, that may be described in terms of variation and mutation (figure 40).

It is tempting to suggest that man discovered the 'principle' of the sleeve, of

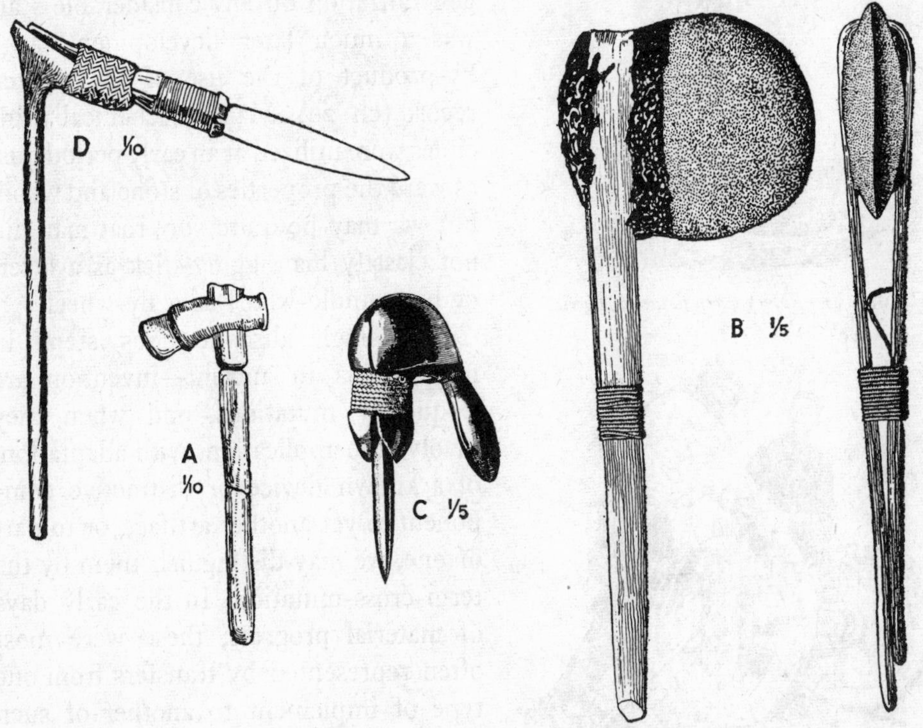

FIGURE 40—*Methods of hafting axes and adzes with stone blades.* (A) *Axe with blade inserted in a socket of deer antler, which is perforated for the haft. Neolithic France.* (B) *Axe with blade gripped in the bend of a withy, the attachment strengthened with hardened gum and a lashing. North Australia.* (C) *Adze with blade bound in a split of the shouldered haft. New Caledonia.* (D) *Adze with blade lashed in a wooden sleeve, which is attached to the shouldered haft by a band of plaited cane. New Guinea.*

the socket, and, say, of rotary motion, but what he actually discovered was that, in the case of the sleeve and the socket, these particular features of form facilitated the union of two components, and, in the case of rotary motion, that circularity in certain mechanisms had its advantages. It is not improbable that uses of rotary motion were discovered independently in the development of several types of appliances, and that there was no evolutionary relationship between, for example, the spindle (figure 276), the fire-drill (figure 141), and the rotary quern (figure 41). Relationship between the vehicular wheel (figure 42), the potter's wheel (figure 119), and the spinning wheel is, however, probable. The last is an invention of the Middle Ages (tailpiece).

The knowledge of early man was embodied in his artifacts, and he generalized less widely than we do, partly because he had far less provocation, and partly because scientific and technological generalization on any considerable scale was a much later development, as a by-product of the use of the written record (ch 29). Many mechanical principles were utilized at an early period, just as were the properties of stone and wood, but we may be quite sure that man did not classify his digging-stick as a lever, or his spindle-whorl as a fly-wheel.

FIGURE 41—*Rotary quern in use in Algeria.*

The single discontinuous steps in modern—as in ancient—invention are frequently mutations, and when they involve the application, with adaptation, of a known device or distinctive component to yet another artifact, or to part of one, we may distinguish them by the term cross-mutation. In the early days of material progress, these were most often represented by transfers from one type of implement to another of such features as sleeves, sockets, and other known means of attachment. Only much later, when mechanisms and machines were developing, was it possible to effect such a conspicuous cross-mutation as the combination of a wheel and endless cord with a simple spindle in a bearing, to produce the earliest type of spinning-wheel. The complexity of many modern artifacts, especially of machines, is such as to make evolutionary analysis impossible without overwhelming labour of research into historical technology; this would reveal the object of study as a complex resulting from numerous discoveries, variations, and mutations, often—even usually—extremely difficult or impossible to unravel in detail. In most cases, cross-mutations could be identified, and it may be noted that these are steps which involve foresight and

FIGURE 42—*Early stage in the evolution of the wheel. The axle turns with the wheels. Takla Makan desert, Sinkiang.*

not discovery, since they arise out of the recognition that one appliance may be improved by adapting to it, by a kind of hybridization, a functional feature or device already in use in one or more other artifacts. If it were necessary to attempt to define the exact nature of the inventive process, it is the cross-mutation that would appear as its typical manifestation. The free-mutation, on the other hand, was a result of observation and discovery, and presented itself almost ready-made.

Simplest of all kinds of mutation is that which effects change in the number of parts of an artifact, such as barbs on a spear, or spokes in a wheel, and this we

FIGURE 43—*Ploughing and hoeing in Egypt. From a tomb at Beni Hasan. c 1900 B.C.*

may speak of as numerical mutation. In its simpler manifestations it approaches random variation.

Substitution, or the translation of the form of implements or other artifacts into new materials, has been a frequent factor in discovery and invention, and in its ultimate results often an important one. It has occurred conspicuously in the case of pottery, where the shapes of gourds, shells, and metal and stone vessels have been copied in clay, though in the process the nature of the secondary material has compelled or induced modification in details of form (p 397). Still more important were the respective substitutions of copper for stone, bronze for copper, iron for bronze, in implements (ch 22), and of stone for wood in building. The first translations aimed at getting as near the original as possible—just as, to compare the simple with the complex, the first motor-cars were built on the lines of horse-drawn carriages—and it was only by degrees that the unforeseen capabilities of the new material revealed openings for development along new lines. This was especially the case when the new material was not only of greater immediate efficiency, but had wider potentialities. It was only after copper, and later bronze, had been substituted for stone that such a weapon as an efficient sword-blade could be produced, while iron led to still better types.

Change of function has no doubt played a part in material progress, as perhaps in the case of a digging-stick used on impulse as a stabbing weapon, with the spear and the javelin as possible derivatives. When a paddle, also, was set aside for use in steering only, and attached to the side of the stern of a canoe, it opened up the line of variations and mutations which led first to the quarter-rudder and later to the median rudder (figures 534–5). Related to change of function is change in method of use, by which the pick or hoe dragged through the surface soil may have initiated—at one step—the evolution of the plough (figure 43). Neither of these types of change is of a morphological character at the outset, but it is clear that they revealed possibilities of formal and structural modification of an adaptive nature.

To sum up the conclusions so far reached, we may say that the following factors, among others, have been active in the origin and development of human artifacts. By a *primary mutation* a natural object suffered modification in form to produce an artifact (e.g. a chipped stone, a sharpened stick); by *variation*, chipped stones developed into implements of standardized types, pointed digging-sticks broadened at the end into a blade, pots and baskets changed in shape; by *numerical mutation* similar parts were increased or diminished in number; by *substitution*, or *translation*, stone points were replaced by metal points, pots were made in the forms of gourds, textiles took the place of skins; by *free-mutation*, artifacts were given characters that were entirely new, and of such a nature that they could be reached only by a definite and original discovery that could be applied to produce a decisive modification, e.g. a hand-grip, a haft, a detachable point instead of a fixed point converting a spear into a harpoon (figure 86); by *cross-mutation*, a known device or functional feature was applied and adapted to an artifact that had developed to a certain stage without it. Early man had little opportunity of progressing by the aid of cross-mutation except in the transfer of very simple devices, such as those mentioned above (p 72). On the other hand, an original free-mutation is probably a rare occurrence at the present time, the simpler possibilities having long been more or less exhausted. Modern cross-mutation frequently involves the transfer of mutational and variational complexes. It is this factor, with a generous running contribution from discovery in supplying and improving materials and methods, that is conspicuous in modern invention, just as was free-mutation in the beginning. Mechanisms and machines comprising a number of moving parts provide the field in which cross-mutation is now predominant.

It is obvious that in attempting an analysis of discovery and invention in the manner proposed, the point of view adopted varies from objective to subjective, as the focus shifts from material objects to hypotheses concerning the factors postulated and the nature and scope of their influence. There also enters into our reconstruction a measure of dramatization and dogmatism which may be at times unjustifiable and perhaps misleading. Greater stress is laid upon the ultimate responses of the human brain and hand to the reactions of the inert materials involved, than upon the transitional mental stages that must have intervened between casual observation and discovery, and between this and its practical application; and also between the first inkling of the possibility of a practicable cross-mutation and the carrying it out to a successful issue. If any identification and classification of the factors of invention are to be attempted, however, a summary and apparently dogmatic treatment is the only one available, since we know or can deduce something of the artifacts and their evolution, but practically nothing of the mental states of which they were the outcome. Nor can we fruitfully surmise how far the steps in invention were due to the exceptional man—the born discoverer and inventor—who succeeded where others did not try. We may be sure, however, that the success of such a man would depend on the mental and material receptivity of his place and time, with posterity alone doing justice to his more precocious efforts.

Another result of the adoption of the present standpoint is the contrasting of variations with mutations—gradual changes with decisive steps—which leads to lack of agreement with a classification based on discovery and invention in the ordinary sense of these words. Thus, primary mutation and free-mutation are based on discovery, but adaptive variation, numerical mutation, and cross-mutation are dependent upon foresight in greater or less degree, though only to the last-named can the term invention in the strict sense be applied. This discrepancy does not, however, tend to any real confusion, since no precise meaning for general use can now be forced upon the words discovery and invention. The attempt to put ordinary words into scientific strait-jackets rarely, if ever, has much success.

The method of analysis may be applied not only to artifacts, but to the methods and processes by which man procures and shapes his raw materials, and by which he obtains greater control over the organic and inorganic environment in which, and by which, he lives. Here, however, we deal with sequences of applied discoveries, which cannot be divided into variations and mutations, though analogies may be identified. Among the more important of what may be called these discovery-complexes are the domestication of animals, the cultivation of plants, and the working of metals (chs 13, 14, 21).

Emphasis must be laid on the significant difference that exists between a discovery containing the potentialities of the development of an art or craft, or of a discovery-complex, and that development itself. The plasticity of clay, the malleability of copper, the growing of seeds, the floating of a hollow log, may have been observed a hundred times without significant result. Those who argue that, because such discoveries are not difficult, the development of arts and artifacts based on them may have occurred with frequency, are making the assumption that early man could see into the future as clearly as they themselves can see into the past. An easy discovery having an immediate practical value, such as that of some use for a pointed stick, a pebble, or a sharp-edged shell, may have been made and applied many times over. Another easy discovery, such as that of a young plant growing out of a familiar edible fruit or seed, could have been made equally often, but for this to form the starting-point of a system of plant-cultivation required the combined influence of many favouring factors acting over a period of time, since no immediate profit could be derived from the bare discovery. The lack of prevision, the conservatism and superstition characteristic of uncivilized peoples, and the innumerable opportunities of failure, must always have stood in the way of the exploitation of discoveries whose useful potentialities were not immediately obvious. Many beginnings must have come to an end before they got under way. Brief reference may be made here to the probable influence of the vested interests (so to speak) of efficient implements such as the socketed bronze celt or the spear-thrower, which may have hindered the adoption of better types. In this connexion also man's innate conservatism was no doubt sometimes inhibitory in its action, as it still is. It is not improbable that in the early civilizations human vested interests already made themselves felt.

Modern research in science and technology is provided with opportunities for discovery and invention immeasurably greater than those of any earlier century, and the investigator is better equipped than any of his forerunners for giving direction to his aims. Directional research, however, must have had its beginnings long ago, even before the development of agriculture had established conditions in which large aggregates of men could be fed and given opportunities to civilize themselves and their environment. The ancient Egyptian and Mesopotamian empires had their beginnings in groups of men who laid the foundations of fundamental arts and crafts such as cereal culture, the domestication of animals, pottery-making, spinning and weaving, and much else (ch 2), and we may be sure that such advances were not made without some directional concentration on aims and ends. In the fully developed civilizations of the Nile, the Two Rivers, and the Indus, directional and even experimental research in restricted fields, if only in a nascent form, must later have played a part in maintaining and expanding the high level of culture, though experience must still have been of most importance. We can scarcely doubt that the more observant and inquiring members of such advanced communities, and those who had leisure to think consecutively, would envisage and encourage the improvement of the methods and appliances commonly used in the arts and industries. But the knowledge available in these times—and for many hundreds of years later—was so limited in comparison with that of the present day that the field for directional research, and the stimulus to undertake it, may well seem to have been insignificant. Nevertheless, over expanding areas the advance continued, though the continuity was not always racial or geographical, since the diffusion of culture (see below) played an essential part. Our own country, for example, now for many years in the forefront of scientific and technological advance, was still occupied by a Stone Age people while the Old Empires flourished in their advanced and elaborate civilizations. Such civilizations, like many later, had their adventures in research, but could achieve nothing comparable with the scientific and technological excitements of our own times; these had to wait until chemistry, physics, and biology, among other sciences, had established themselves on the accepted basis of evidence elicited by controlled experiment.

Man the discoverer and inventor—even at some of his lower cultural levels—has travelled far from his starting-point, but, in spite of the ambitions and achievements of modern pioneers, he has not entirely outlived the simplicities of his early aids to progress. Opportunism is not lacking in our laboratories and workshops, nor has chance lost the power to intervene. Some spreading trees of knowledge have grown from laboratory snags, and a true discovery is still a revelation of the unpredictable, or at least the unpredicted.

The student may choose his path, broad or narrow, among the aims and ambitions of directional research, but he still must plod as a pedestrian. Yet at any time he may hit upon a discovery which seems to have no present value, but which may form the basis for a revolutionary advance of tomorrow, or of another century. Ramsay's discovery of the inert gases is a good illustration.

V. DIFFUSION

It is common knowledge that within historical times civilized and other countries have benefited by accepting or borrowing, from outside, knowledge and ideas, customs and beliefs, together with material appliances and techniques of many kinds and uses. Food and drink, also, in most parts of the civilized world, have been enormously increased in variety by this process of diffusion, which has often led to commercial importation—as, for example, in the case of the tea that we in England first obtained from China in the seventeenth century. Introduced animals and plants have often proved capable of naturalization.

They have thus been bred or cultivated, often with a production of superior strains, as with our domesticated animals, our food grains, and our potatoes. All these reached us by diffusion.

The introduction of porcelain from China into Britain eventually had an effect which illustrates an important cultural result of diffusion. The English potters of the seventeenth and eighteenth centuries were stimulated by the beauty of Chinese porcelain to attempt to rival it. This led them to the production of fine white earthenware, of salt-glazed stoneware, and later of porcelain itself, all representing noteworthy advances in the history of ceramics. Many comparable cases indicate the great value of diffusion as a stimulus, when an introduced culture-trait comes into a technological environment of progressive character. On the other hand, when such progress is sluggish or lacking, the new culture-trait may merely be accepted passively (if at all), giving rise to no further development and even itself degenerating or disappearing.

Borrowing by diffusion has often enough been involuntary and unpremeditated by the recipient, sometimes taking the form of a 'forced loan' by invasion and conquest, with a large-scale infusion or mass imposition of the culture of the conquerors, as so often in early Britain. Where there has been little difference in culture between borrower and lender, the culture-traits involved may have been rapidly absorbed into the way of life of the recipients—as were various electrical appliances, for one recent example among innumerable others, in many parts of the civilized world—and the process still continues as an accepted factor in social as well as in material development.

On the other hand, diffusion from a high culture to a low may produce different results. Bicycles are used by natives in parts of Africa, but they remain foreign objects, since the natives cannot yet make them. In some such cases, introduction has led to the deterioration of native crafts, as when petrol tins displace indigenous pottery, and European cloths compete with native textiles.

Similar effects must have been produced even in prehistoric times, though contrasts between the cultures concerned were less conspicuous than they are liable to be today. Diffusion by commerce has its roots in very ancient methods of barter, not yet extinct in backward regions.

Diffusion is thus very far from being a new feature in human progress. Even in Palaeolithic times, when hunter and food-gatherer rarely had a permanent place of habitation, there must often have been an interchange of ideas, and a comparison of weapons, between the groups which occupied adjacent hunting grounds. Moreover, the archaeological and other evidence clearly indicates that, even in very early human time, there were movements of peoples that may be called migrations. The tribal contacts established by such wanderings, as well as by less casual proximity, must have played an essential part in the multiplying, and also in the standardizing, of forms of implements of stone, bone, and other materials. Diffusion in the Neolithic stage had much greater scope and opportunities, though land transport and travel, then and for many generations, were still made on foot.

The extent to which diffusion may account for similarities in culture-traits in different regions, especially those far distant from each other and in days before recorded history, has aroused in the past controversies of great acrimony. The fundamental part played by diffusion within the Old World, in both early and later times, is now beyond question, except in relation to some individual culture-traits. We may, therefore, pass on to consider prehistoric situations in which diffusion had its first full opportunity; this took it in the course of centuries across three continents: Asia, Africa, and Europe. Let us at the same time keep in mind the potential evolutionary capacity of many culture-traits when introduced into a progressive artificial environment—a cultural forcing-house for ideas and realities. Diffusion has thus for long been an essential dynamic factor in human progress, since only by its agency could the thoughts, the discoveries, and the inventions of men develop their potential under new and often more stimulating conditions.

The centuries following the development of the initial features of Neolithic culture, during which the hunter and food-gatherer first became a farmer and stock-breeder, were the most significant in the history of human progress. Steps were taken then that were essential to the building of civilizations upon which later cultural revolutions depended. It is in the Near East, at many points in a wide area stretching between Egypt and Persia, often spoken of as the 'fertile crescent', that most of the archaeological evidence on these matters has been unearthed.

The evidence indicates that the ferment leading to the development of the new culture was in progress before 5000 B.C. Centuries, and not years only, were consumed in the processes which led to the cultivation of cereals (ch 14) and the domestication of hoofed animals—the dog had been domesticated earlier (ch 13). New opportunities and stimuli emerged that led into other fields of discovery and invention. Provided now with reliable sources of grain for winter as well as summer consumption, men were enabled, by action and reaction between the fertility of the soil and the fecundity of their own species, for the first time to live together in larger communities and in permanent homes.

With these changes came increased opportunities for social intercourse, and for the interchange of ideas and information that could lead to still further progress. New arts and crafts were evolved, especially pottery-making, spinning, and weaving (chs 15, 16). Division of labour gave rise to specialization. The potter's wheel, and the vehicular wheel itself, appeared (ch 9), while stone implements were ground, polished, and shaped for greater efficiency in hafting. As the centuries rolled on, the discoveries were made that led to metal-working. After private property and diffusion by trade had assumed importance, picture-writing began its slow conversion into a hieroglyphic system, which later begat the greatly differing systems of Mesopotamia, Egypt, and the Indus valley (ch 29).

Between 4000 and 3000 B.C. the Neolithic revolution became well established in Egypt and the fertile crescent. By 3000 B.C. there were flourishing and highly organized cities and city-states over a wide area in the three great river-valleys of the Near East. The term urban revolution has been applied by V. G. Childe to the rise of social integration, in which technology played a fundamental part.

Out of these urban communities and their surrounding areas of cultivation arose the kingdoms and the later empires. The underlying unity of these early civilizations was eventually obscured by divergent and conspicuous developments in both social and material culture. Intercommunication was not sufficiently constant and effective—in spite of wars and conquests—to neutralize the effects of differing climate, terrain, and other factors on the development of arts, industries, and social and religious beliefs and practices. The facts relating to the processes of diffusion within and outwards from these early civilizations do not form a coherent picture, but have to be pieced together like the parts of a difficult and incomplete jig-saw puzzle. However, the main outlines of much of the picture can be assembled, and more details are constantly being adduced.

VI. BRITAIN'S DEBTS TO DIFFUSION

We pass from this sketch of the foundation and progress of the agricultural civilization of the Old World to a consideration of the events leading to the establishment in Britain, over a period of centuries, of the essential features of the Neolithic revolution, as well as of some developments of later origin.

The final period of the European Stone Age is particularly well known for Britain. It was ushered in by the arrival, from across the North Sea and the English Channel, of tribes and bands of immigrants bringing with them the essential culture-traits that characterized the Neolithic revolution, and which had spread widely in Europe before reaching our shores, both losing and gaining in the process of diffusion. These invasions or intrusions were spread over the period between about 2500 and 2000 B.C., the later arrivals bringing the more advanced Neolithic acquirements. There were also differences in racial origins, and several routes were used. In the end, however, Britain received cattle, sheep, and pigs, together with seed-corn in the form of wheat, and the knowledge of simple agricultural methods. Pottery, spinning and weaving, polished stone implements, and much else came in also. The later Neolithic invaders introduced the custom of erecting large burial mounds and great stone monuments or megaliths. Many of these, though now fully exposed. were originally burial chambers within the mounds. The vast circles of Stonehenge and Avebury, the greatest of all the megaliths of Britain, were the work of the later Neolithic peoples (ch 17).

The Neolithic invaders brought their culture almost, it might be said, into a vacuum, or at least into a country the scattered inhabitants of which, the Mesolithic hunters and food-gatherers, could have offered little resistance. But the conveyance of the essentials of the Neolithic revolution, its ideas as well as its material culture, from the west of Asia to the west of Europe, must not be imagined as a steady and direct march of progress. It must often have been more like a slow-moving flow of rising water; ideas, knowledge, and artifacts passed from tribe to tribe and people to people in small instalments, becoming modified in the process, and sometimes by-passing large areas altogether. Culture-contact and culture-creep no doubt played a part, but movements and migrations were predominant factors in the advance towards and into Britain, settlements being also established in favourable environments on the way.

Two main routes were followed, one up the Danube valley, and thence overland till the western coasts of Europe were reached, and the other along the Mediterranean and its shores. Landings took place at many points on the eastern and southern shores of Britain. Narrow seas and rivers have always been conspicuous agents in diffusion, whereas great oceans were obstacles in early days, as were also ranges of lofty mountains.

Prehistoric diffusion of culture into Britain did not end in Neolithic times. Before the close of this period, soon after 2000 B.C., there began a series of intrusions by peoples having a knowledge of copper and later of bronze. The Bronze Age thus begun reached its fullness of achievement in Britain between 1000 and 500 B.C., as a result of invasions from the continent by the people called Celts, who were of mixed origin. These tribes were much more skilled in the working of bronze than their predecessors, and were able to produce much larger and finer implements, including swords, shields, socketed axe-heads, and many others. Their clothing and dwellings were of better types, and the wheeled chariot was well known to them.

By about 500 B.C., the Early Iron Age in Britain had its beginnings. More Celtic invaders introduced the metal, though at first bronze implements still predominated with the newcomers, those of iron being few in number. But iron gradually came into its own, especially for weapons, and bronze became subsidiary except as a material for ornament. The late Celtic art of this period is justly famous for its metalwork and enamelling, the artificers showing a great mastery of technique and of decorative design. The 'Ancient Britons' of this time were very unlike the woad-covered savages of early traditional histories. The Roman legions quickly realized that ornamented weapons in Celtic hands were also highly functional.

After the Romans had come and gone, leaving the mark of their practical civilization deeply impressed on a large part of Britain, there followed further invasions of continental barbarians. This is not the place to enter into detail concerning the effects of the later invasions from the Romans onward, but it is clear that, in the end, we can claim Britain of those days as a classic example of culture-change by diffusion depending largely upon immigration and conquest. The conquered had little choice, though at times some of them evaded the immediate issue by taking refuge in the mountains of the west and north, and in lowland fens. Even now it cannot be said that the British Isles are completely homogeneous in physical type or in cultural status.

VII. AMERICA AND DIFFUSION

The general acceptance of diffusion as a predominant factor in the development of human culture within the larger part of the Old World, gives place to a great divergence of opinion as to the cultural relationship between the Old World and the New, and we may outline the question as exemplifying the extent to which critical (and other) minds may differ in the interpretation of evidence which has long been available to students of the subject.

The controversy on diffusion that has been most liable to volcanic eruption relates to the source of the several high cultures of America, which are themselves generally accepted as having a common origin. The cultures in question are found in Mexico (Aztec, Toltec, and others), Central America (Maya), and Peru (Inca and others). If it be agreed that they arose independently of Old World influences and are due to large-scale independent invention, then it must be assumed that a Neolithic revolution, or perhaps rather a post-Neolithic revolution, occurred also in the New World. But there are at present available no archaeological evidences comparable to those found in western Asia of a gradual evolution of the advanced cultures.

In one or all of the American cultures there occur cereal-culture (maize) with irrigation systems, as well as the growing of many other food plants; pottery-making (without the potter's wheel, but with glazes and paints); ore-smelting and metal-working (copper, and alloys such as bronze, as well as gold and silver); spinning (with the spindle) and weaving (with the true loom); plank boats; building with large stone blocks; and elaborate stone-carving. Amongst tools there are many significant resemblances to those of the Old World in the forms of stone and metal implements, and in the provision for various methods of hafting. It is noteworthy that these peoples never invented, or borrowed by diffusion, the vehicular wheel, the potter's wheel, the spinning wheel, or the rotary quern. Finally, the Maya of Yucatan had a highly developed hieroglyphic writing system, together with paper and books. The hieroglyphs are even more pictorial than the early Egyptian and there is no question of direct transfer; but the latter is also true as regards the cuneiform characters of Babylonia and Assyria as compared with those of ancient Egypt, both based on earlier Old World picture-writing. The idea of picture-writing could have been transmitted to the New World, as within the Old, in such a way as to give rise to a variety of modes of writing, of writing-materials, and of symbols.

It may be noted here that it is agreed by most, if not all, American students of the problem that Neolithic and even later culture-traits came across to north-west America from the opposite coast of Asia, some of them (such as slat-armour) being of relatively recent date. The controversy concerns chiefly those features of the American high cultures which might, or might not, have been diffused by migrations or otherwise, chiefly from certain of the high cultures of east and south-east Asia, but in a few cases (e.g. the blow-tube) from less advanced culture. Most American students believe in the independent evolution of these features, since convincing proofs of the passage of the relevant knowledge and artifacts cannot be given. Opinions in Britain are perhaps more divided, but diffusionists can point to the absence of archaeological proofs of gradual evolution, and to the probability that evolution involving parallel and converging lines of development would make too great a demand on 'those common factors of the human mind' upon which so much stress was laid by the relevant disputants of last century. Discovery and invention before the time of directional research were incomparably slower and more uncertain processes than they have since become (p 60). It is perhaps generally agreed, also, that the independent origin that might be admitted for very simple artifacts, such as the digging-stick and the spindle, becomes less and less acceptable as the distance of a finished implement or appliance from its starting-point increases. Where a number of discoveries, variations, and mutations have been involved, a belief in independent origin in two widely separated regions may assume not merely one significant coincidence but a chain. In such discovery-complexes as the making of bronze, and casting it into implements, the chain becomes a network, thus putting a still greater strain upon coincidence.

However, the cogency of such arguments, and there are others on both sides, is not generally accepted as entirely convincing, and it may perhaps be admitted that the position taken up on either side is fortified by faith. In its most acute forms, the controversy may sometimes seem to approach a competition in credulities. On the American question a verdict of 'not proven' must therefore be accepted by all but convinced diffusionists—and their equally convinced opponents.

In conclusion, it must be emphasized that diffusion has played a major part in man's cultural progress, especially since the Neolithic revolution. A sketch such as this, which merely skims the surface of the technological aspect of diffusion, and leaves out of account the intangible evidences of languages, folk-lore, magic, religion, and much else, cannot claim to do even rough justice to a vast and fascinating subject.

A spinning-wheel in Cyprus.

4

SPEECH AND LANGUAGE

A. SOMMERFELT

I. SOME TERMS DEFINED

In what follows, the understanding of certain elementary technical terms will help the reader, and it will be best to begin by defining them. Spoken language obviously preceded written but, since we must here discuss spoken language in writing, we must explain some of the terms for the mechanism by which writing expresses speech.

English, like most European languages, uses the Latin alphabet, the origin of which is considered elsewhere (ch 29). In English, the letters are given certain sound-values which differ in greater or less degree from those given to them in other European languages. These languages, in their turn, differ from each other in comparable ways. Systems have been devised to express the sound-values in many related languages, but we are not concerned with them here.

In English, as in allied languages, there is a distinction between vowels (Old French *vouel*, from Latin *vocalis littera*, vocal letter) which can be pronounced by themselves, and con-sonants which can usually be sounded only with the help of vowels. As often, there is a half-way house. Thus in *bottle* and *fathom* the second syllables are carried by *l* and *m* which are thus semi-vocalic. Similarly, it is difficult to be dogmatic about the *y* in *yes* or the *w* in *well*. In the table below they are classed as consonants; a purist would call them semi-consonants.

The actual number of separate sounds that can be made by the human voice is very large indeed, perhaps infinite. Speech is comprehensible only because, in every language, the number of these sounds is conventionally limited, though limited differently in different languages. Let us try to classify as simply as we can.

There are five vowel-symbols in English (*a*, *e*, *i*, *o*, *u*) and one (*y*) which may designate a combination of two vowels, i.e. a diphthong, as in *by*, or a consonant as in *yes*. This is clearly not enough for accurate definition. Even if we add such combinations as *ea* and *ie* we have still not enough vowel-symbols, especially as our alphabet does not invariably distinguish between long and short vowels. Moreover, we often use the vowel-symbols that are at our disposal in a very illogical way. Thus, in *read*, *sleep*, *lever*, *deceive*, and *believe* the vowels *ea*, *ee*, *e*, *ei*, and *ie* all designate the same sound; in *though*, *rough*, *through*, *bought*, *bough* the symbol *ou* has five different pronunciations; and for some words, such as *bow*, only the context can tell us what they mean and how they should consequently be pronounced. It is strictly true that a word like *bow*, in isolation, has neither meaning nor pronunciation. Not many languages are as wildly illogical in these matters as English, yet something of the sort is found in nearly every language, even if it is difficult to parallel a monstrosity like *viz.*—the contraction for Latin *videlicet*, which is usually read as 'namely'. It is therefore safer and more scientific, in considering language problems, to think of the sounds made, rather than of the way in which they are represented on paper. In what follows, the reader must give special attention to this point.

Consonants usually show more variety than vowels. We can classify them into two main groups: *stops* and *continuants*. The terms mean what they say; stops stop, continuants continue. If you try to say a number of *p*'s very quickly the sound produced will be very much like an *f*. *F* is therefore the continuant corresponding to the stop *p*, except that the *f* produced by this process is a bi-labial, i.e. formed between the two lips, whereas the ordinary English *f* is produced between lower lip and upper teeth, and is therefore a *labio-dental*.

According to the position where we 'stop' the breath, or narrow the gap to produce a continuant, we can distinguish lip-sounds or *labials*, tooth-sounds or *dentals*, hard palate-sounds or *palatals*, and sounds pronounced with the tongue pushing up to the velum (palate) or *velars*. Sounds formed while the mouth-passage remains closed whereas the nasal passage remains open are called *nasals*. When we close the mouth at the lips we produce the nasal *m*, when we close it just behind the teeth we produce the nasal *n*. The *m* is therefore closely related to *p*, *b*, *f*, *v*, and the *n* is similarly related to *d*, *t*, *th*, etc. A peculiar sound is *l*. It is produced by putting the tip of the tongue against some part of the roof of the mouth, and then blowing the breath out on one or both sides of the tongue. A little experimenting will show that in English, in the word *lip*, the tip of the tongue rests lightly against the back of the upper teeth or the alveolar region, whereas in the word *full* the back part of the tongue is curved upwards. The English *r* is produced in a very similar way, but the top of the tongue does not touch the roof of the mouth. These two sounds, *l* and *r*, are known as *liquids*, which is not a very satisfactory term, though hallowed by usage.

The classification given here suffices for normal English, which really has no so-called *gutturals* (Latin *guttur*, throat). It is sometimes said that German has gutturals, but this is not so. No-one who has listened to the true gutturals of Arabic, for example, can ever again regard the German sounds as guttural. They are merely rather far back in the velar region.

A few further words are needed on vocalization. There are folds of lining membrane on the larynx known as the *vocal cords*. These, if taut, vibrate when a stream of air passes through them from the lungs into the mouth. The vibration is communicated to all the surrounding parts of the body. Thus is produced the quality known as *voice*. If you place the palm of your hand on top of your head and say 'ah' you will feel your skull vibrating. Whistle and you will feel no vibration at all. All vowels are normally voiced, and a consonant can be either voiced or unvoiced. Lack of voice occurs when the vocal cords are slack and there is thus no vibration.

English Simple Consonants

	Voiceless Stops	*Voiced Stops*
Palatal	k	g (good)
Dental	t	d
Labial	p	b
	Voiceless Continuants	*Voiced Continuants*
Palatal		y (yes)
Dental	th (thumb)	th (then); n, ng (sing)
	s, sh	z, zh (measure)
Labio-dental	f (fan)	v (van)
Labial		w (well); m
Liquid		l, r
Breath	h (hit)	

There are also complex consonants, such as the *ch* in *church*, in which each *ch* is voiceless, and its voiced equivalent *judge* where the *j* and the *dg* stand for exactly the same sound. The letter *x* is really *ks*, as in *axe*. Its voiced equivalent we find in *example*. A very frequent consonantal sound in English is *sh*; its voiced equivalent is found in *measure*, *pleasure* and some words of French origin as in *garage*.

All languages have characteristic rhythms, which are often more important than the correct enunciation of vowels and consonants. A foreigner speaking English who gets his rhythm right may be understood without undue difficulty, but if he gets the rhythm very wrong, as many do, his speech may become a meaningless noise. For, most of the time, we do not listen very carefully. We know the patterns—rhythms, almost tunes—of our language, and we know when to expect a certain type of speech-melody. The unaccented dips we fill in largely by ourselves. This has a bearing on the very nature of speech.

A word must be said about the theory of the *phoneme*, which has led to much theoretical discussion. A phoneme is a small bundle of sound features, serving to differentiate words and word-forms. In English, for example, *l*, *m*, *p*, *r*, *s*, *t*, *th*, and *w* are phonemes, because they serve to differentiate from one another the words *link*, *mink*, *pink*, *rink*, *sink*, *tink*, *think*, and *wink*. In some languages, e.g. Chinese, certain features such as different tones, or differences of stress, may serve to differentiate words. A phoneme is a speech-sound, and phonemes are, in theory, infinite in number, though only a limited number is used by any one language. The simplest possible system of phonetic transcription of a language would provide one symbol for each phoneme. English, like most languages, uses far more phonemes than can be provided by its alphabetic forms.

II. SIGNALS MADE BY ANIMALS

Animals have means of communication, but no language in our sense. Many higher animals, especially those with a social life, use differentiated signals. A cock utters a sharp cry when he sees a hawk in the air; quite another and lower sound when he hears rats or mice under the floor of the poultry house; a third and very different signal when he calls a hen to a worm or other titbit. Lions roar to each other, probably as a challenge. Sometimes they will put their mouths close to the ground, causing a greater reverberation [1]. Monkeys and apes chatter. Chattering is caused by rapid, rhythmical, movements of lip, jaw, and tongue. Jaws and lips quickly open and shut, while the tongue is rhythmically extruded. When the tongue movements are suppressed these activities are often referred to as smacking the lips. This often seems to signify a friendly greeting tinged with fear. The chimpanzee has a particular sound which it produces when in danger. On hearing this sound, all other chimpanzees will rush to the spot and set upon the intruder. But animals may use signals of other types than sounds. Bees communicate to their fellows at the hive the presence of pollen or nectar, its direction, and its approximate distance. They do this by performing a dance, the movements of which convey the information. If the flower has an odour, it is indicated by the scent which adheres to the body of the bee [2].

There is a fundamental difference between such sounds, signals, or gestures and human speech. The animal reaction is a whole and cannot be decomposed into words. Its field of reference is limited to particular situations and cannot be used for things. Animal signals are characteristic of the species and are mostly inborn. A German dachshund barks just like an English one, but human language varies from social group to social group, has to be learnt during childhood, and changes with time. It is true that the longer sounds, signals, or gestures of animals may consist of a succession of different parts, as with the wiggling dance of the bee, but this structure is different from linguistic structure—it can at most be called semi-syntactical [3]. Its interpretation is an inborn power which does not need to be learnt.

III. SPEECH AS A HUMAN SOCIAL PHENOMENON

In the evolution of man, step by step with the increasing use of the hand and in association with it, went the increasing use of eye, ear, and brain. Power of discrimination by sight and hearing thus advanced simultaneously with the freeing of the hand for exploring its surroundings. Man seems to have started to use some form of language at the same time as he learnt to fabricate tools. Language is correlative to the tool [4]. If man is a tool-maker he is also a word-maker. The use of tools presupposes intelligent behaviour, with the existence of at least some rudimentary concepts expressed in language. This evolution, which needs co-operation between individuals—in fact a society—was greatly facilitated by the character of the human group. Man is and has always been gregarious, as were his forbears. Group-life favoured discipline by leaders. Thus language became an instrument of the utmost importance, which, it must be stressed, was not primarily a means of expressing thoughts; its first role was more practical —to control behaviour. Thus language is one of the chief cultural forces, and in human behaviour plays a part that is unique and irreplaceable [5].

The science of linguistics distinguishes between *language* and *speech*. Language is a system of communication between individuals; it is a method of establishing co-operation and control; it is a pattern for the use of the speech organs. Speech, or spoken language, is the use made by the individuals of the linguistic pattern, method, and system. Language is the 'code'; speech is the 'message'.

This pattern we are accustomed to analyse into words. To what extent words are a reflection of our own ways of writing, and to what extent they can be said to exist in primitive speech, we need not now discuss. But the pattern of speech as we know it consists of words which are composed of a limited number of speech-sounds or phonemes.

The pattern further comprises rules for possible changes in the form of the words, and for the arrangement of the words into sentences. By the meaning of the word, we understand its power to evoke more or less identical responses in individuals of the same social group. There are no direct or natural connexions between the word and its referent. Different social groups may use quite different signs for the same referent; *house* is *maison* in French, *casa* in Italian, *dom* in Russian. Onomatopoeic or imitative words—*bow-wow* or *gee-gee*—in which the combination of certain phonemes is felt to picture a sound or another characteristic of the referent, form only an apparent or temporary exception, because the use of such a combination of phonemes is seldom strictly limited to the meaning for which it is onomatopoeic. Thus *bow-wow* is onomatopoeic only for a dog that barks, not for a kind of dog that yaps. Again, the combination of a stop with *l* and the vowels *a* or *i* in English is often felt to symbolize sounds made by different kinds of metal as in *clank* and *clink*, but such a combination is not onomatopoeic in *plank* and *plinth*.

All human groups, however simple and undeveloped their culture, possess speech. Tales of peoples who have no speech, or one so rudimentary that it can be understood only by the supplementary use of gestures, have not been verified. On the contrary, all peoples or tribes studied for the purpose are found to use a well-developed system of linguistic sounds and grammar, and to possess a vocabulary of at least several thousand different words. Moreover, even the manufacture of rude flint instruments, their trading over great distances, and their communal employment, implies some linguistic process (not necessarily articulate speech). Palaeolithic man surely had a language, as had the native Tasmanians, the only truly Palaeolithic group that survived into modern times.

Though the progressive development of speech and language presents no insoluble problems, the determining factor which initiated this revolutionary change in the evolution of man is still hidden from us. We know nothing of the origin of language, nor do we know if the languages of the world all go back to one original source or have a multiple origin. Both views have their advocates. The speech-organs differ very little among the different anthropological types. Such differences as thick or thin lips or different configurations of the hard palate are not important, as they are found among the speakers of the same language without determining any difference in pronunciation.

In spite of what has just been said, some significant differences from the rest of mankind do seem to exist in certain of the most aberrant human groups, such as Bushmen and Hottentots. These differences seem linked with the use of *clicks* (p 95). The chin of these peoples is less developed than in other anthropological types, and the configuration of the hard palate fits a slender and pointed tongue [6]. Even these differences, however, are not fundamental, and, since tools presuppose language, all human beings and not only *Homo sapiens* may be supposed to have used some sort of language.

It has been thought by some that during the Ice Age man was as yet unable to use articulate speech, since the oldest specimens of the human race had a construction of the lower jawbone which would not permit the adequate development of certain tongue muscles. Were this so, many Australian natives as well as the African pygmies would have difficulty in articulating, and such is not the case. At any rate, some sort of language may be assumed to be as old as man himself, to have developed together with the tool, and to date at least from the first phase of the Pleistocene [7]. And any child may learn any language to perfection if reared in a community where it is spoken.

Is it possible to imagine how language, or the different languages, sounded during the first part of the Palaeolithic period? Yes, within certain very wide limits, and these we shall now discuss.

The inarticulate human cries of fear, anger, or joy correspond to animal sound-signals. Such interjections may be said to occupy an intermediate position between the inarticulate cry and the linguistic sign, in so far as they often contain sounds which do not form part of the local phonemic system. Of this kind are some sounds used to direct animals, or the sounds represented in English by *whew*, *ugh*, *humph*. (These are but awkward renderings of sounds which cannot be indicated by the usual letters of the alphabet.) In fact, interjections are to a great extent conventionalized, and differ from language to language. 'That man is no Afghan, for they weep Ai, Ai. Nor is he a Hindustani, for they weep Oh, Ho. He weeps after the fashion of the white men, who say Ow, Ow', writes Kipling in one of his stories.

Human speech, then, seems to have developed out of animal sound-signals, but how did this come about? Psychologists, sociologists, and linguists have proposed several different answers [8]. Some have hoped that biological factors would furnish an explanation. But to suppose that the expressions of emotions and the signals of domination and control known among animals have developed 'naturally' into speech and language is to explain nothing. Why is man the only animal capable of this? The growth of speech in the child, from the first vocalizations onwards, sheds little light on the problem. Child-speech may exhibit features reminiscent of the character of languages spoken by the simpler peoples, but in fact the child actually learns to talk from the grown-ups. He does not develop his own language.

A popular theory derives speech from the imitation of natural sounds heard by man's ancestors, and supposes that language was at first onomatopoeic. Again why have not other animals been able to do the same? Onomatopoeic elements play no fundamental part in any known language, however primitive. Moreover the onomatopoeic or 'bow-wow' theory fails to explain how sound-imitations developed into words and concepts, so that such a development is not self-explanatory. The same may be said of the theories which try to derive language from primitive singing, whether by imitation of birds or through the urge of joyful emotions during courtship [9]. A similar criticism applies to the theory—which is really a variety of the onomatopoeic theory—that speech originated in mouth-gestures (p 94). These theories, perhaps especially the last one, may explain *how* speech developed, but not *why*.

IV. SPEECH OF CHILDREN AND APHASIACS

Study of how children acquire language has contributed to the understanding of language-development in general, though not to that of its origins. It has been shown that a child learns the different parts of the phonemic and grammatical systems by stages [10], and that the same stages occur in the reversed order when, through lesion of the brain, an aphasiac loses his power of speech [11].

Before the child acquires the first rudiments of language, it passes through the so-called babble-period, during which it can produce all sorts of sounds. It is worth note that it loses almost all these sounds when it starts to learn to articulate. In some cases, it takes a very long time to recover some of the sounds it previously used, notably the *s*, *l*, and *r* sounds. This cannot be explained by loss of motor faculties, nor is there an acoustic difficulty, for children can often understand differences which they are unable to express. This very surprising loss of power of articulation is to be correlated with the fact that during the babble-period the sounds have no meaningful relations. They are produced by movements which, like the other movements of the infant at this stage, result from the use of the machinery without any intention other than pleasure in the exercise of increasing powers. Thus they produce all the possibilities of sound of which the muscles concerned are capable [12].

Only when language-learning starts do the sounds acquire phonemic values. Then, the child must master sounds which have definite and arbitrary functions, for there is no natural link between the word (of which the phoneme forms part) and the thing or phenomenon to which the word refers. It is quite natural that the child should start modestly with phonemes which constitute simple, clear, and stable contrasts, as *mama* and *papa*, *bow-wow* and *gee-gee*, etc. It is surely significant that certain children pass through a mute period between the babbling and the language-learning periods.

Research on the way in which children acquire different languages in Europe, America, and Asia has yielded one interesting result. It has been shown that the speed with which the child learns to pronounce the different phonemes varies individually, but that the relative sequence is everywhere broadly the same. The first vowel is *a* and the first consonant *m*. The first contrast among phonemes is *p*/*m* (e.g. *papa*/*mama*); the next is between the labials *p* and *m* on the one hand and the dentals *t* and *n* on the other. Then comes the contrast between a broad vowel *a* and a narrow one, e.g. *papa/pipi/pepe* (as in English *bar*, *react*, *yet*), followed by the use of three vowel degrees, either *a*: *i*: *e* or *a*: *i*: *u* (*oo*). These contrasts correspond to the simplest vowel systems known from actual languages.

Features of a less general character appear later, but even here there is a surprising conformity between the sequence of phonemes mastered throughout a language group and that of an individual child. It is significant, in view of this sequence, that phonetic *stops*, i.e. sounds that cannot be prolonged, as *b*, *d*, *k*, are found in all languages, but that sibilants, e.g. *s*, *sh*, and fricatives, e.g. *f*, *th*, are absent in some languages, such as certain Oceanic, African, and American groups. Similarly, the child uses the *p* sound for the *f* sound of the language of the grown-ups; the *t* sound for the grown-up *s*; the *k* sound for the grown-up *sh*.

Back consonants, that is those formed in the throat, appear in the child's speech only after front consonants, formed by lips, tongue, or teeth, have been acquired. Thus the presence of the back consonant *k* presupposes an earlier capacity to use the sounds *p* and *t*; the presence of the back consonants *ch* (as in Scots *loch*) and *s* (*sh*) presupposes that of *f*, *s*, and also *k*. English, Scandinavian, and German children learn *ng* (e.g. in *sing*) after *m* and *n*. This is reflected in many languages which lack back consonants, whereas no language has back consonants without the corresponding front consonants.

The power of contrasting two vowels of the same degree of openness is not acquired by the child until a corresponding power of contrast between closer vowels is attained. French, Scandinavian, and German children cannot pronounce the vowel *ö*, as in French *peu*, until after they have made a distinction between *u* (*oo*) and *y* (*ü*), the vowel in French *loup* and in *lune*. Similarly the contrast *u* (*oo*): *o* (as in *anchor*) comes after that of *i* (as in *react*): *e* (as in *yet*).

In general, we may say that features which are rare in linguistic systems are the last to appear in child language. For example, nasal vowels, such as those of French and Polish, are infrequent among the languages of the world, and French and Polish children learn such vowels only after having mastered all the others—generally not until near their third year. On the other hand, the nasals *n* and *m* belong to the earliest; they are known from all languages and children master them early. Many languages have only one liquid (*l* or *r*), and these sounds are among the last mastered.

It has already been remarked that loss of speech by aphasiacs follows the reverse order of that of acquisition by children. The liquids are the first lost. French aphasiacs lose their nasal vowels very early; English lose *th* before *s*—just as English children acquire *th* after *s*. In an intermediate period, children and aphasiacs replace *th* by *z*, as do many foreigners, especially Germans and French, when they speak English. Aphasiacs replace fricatives by stops, e.g. *f* by *p*, *s* by *t*, *sh* by *k*. Front consonants resist aphasia longer than back, *t* lasts longer than *k*, etc. The last sounds to remain are the vowel *a* and the lip consonants. Moreover, it is highly significant that when an aphasiac regains speech he follows the order known from the child's language efforts [13].

V. SPEECH AND GESTURE

These important facts may well illustrate older stages of language, but they provide no key to its origin. Some scholars have therefore sought the origin in gesture. Many peoples possess an elaborate system of gestures. Among the Australian Arunta, when the camp is occupied only by women there will be almost perfect silence, yet conversation is all the while being conducted on their fingers, or rather with hands and arms, as many of the signs are made by putting the hands, or perhaps the elbows, in varying positions [14]. One observer lists 454 words rendered by Arunta gestures [15].

Systems of gesture are more used in so-called primitive societies than in those of higher civilization. This has led to the view that gesture language preceded articulate language, a view defended with vigour by some who believe that some form of writing or picturing has been a factor in this development. This theory involves the hypothesis that man began to picture gestures very early, when oral signals were still rare. Thus a Chinese scholar derives the oldest Chinese characters from manual gestures which, he believes, preceded the acoustic element. Others have applied similar reasoning to the literate peoples of the Near East and of Central America. Again, it has been suggested that the transition from gesture language to articulate language was direct. This view would place the rise of articulate language as late as the fourth millennium B.C. At that period, language of manual concepts was changed into language of the oral character generally recognized today [16].

Even were this hypothesis defensible, it would not explain the origin of language. The problem of how man acquired a conceptual means of communication would still remain. That gesture language has been largely used in the oldest form of Chinese and pictographic scripts is natural. Gesture language consists of signs which are simplified reproductions of actions and situations, much easier to depict than the actions or situations themselves. The peoples of China and the Near East probably used many gestures similar to those of peoples today. They certainly used pictograms early, but were at first unable to render acoustic elements by them. This is the situation today with many Eskimo, who use pictograms but have also a well-developed oral language that is not written. Psychologically, the supposition that gesture language precedes articulate language encounters serious difficulties, since the inward language of thought is linked with oral language and not with gestures. Yet it is true that gesture language is very ancient, and has probably developed together with ordinary language, but it has not gone so far or become so flexible [17].

It is obvious that there is a kind of language which is a common property of mankind and is based on imitation. By using pantomimic signs, speakers of any one language can make themselves understood, in some degree, by speakers of any other language. One theory would ascribe the origin of speech to pantomimic gestures with the mouth. The sounds that thus result, it is claimed, correspond to word-roots traceable in very different language groups. Such a theory fails to explain how a gesture, being of its nature a signal and thus signifying a situation, can pass into a word which signifies a thing or an action [18].

VI. DIFFERENCES IN PHONEMIC SYSTEMS

There are today considerable differences between the phonemic systems of the many languages. In certain parts of the world the phonemic systems are simple, as in general among the indigenous peoples of Oceania and Australia. The vowels are often few, usually *a*, *i*, *u*; the system of stops is simple, often without distinction between voiced and unvoiced; fricatives, e.g. *s*, may be absent; often only one liquid occurs, which may sound like an *r* or an *l*. Unfortunately, our knowledge of these simpler systems is frequently obscured by the failure of those who have noted them to apply the phonemic principles of distinguishing between sounds and phonemes. In a language in which there is no phonemic difference between *d* and *t*, for example—where therefore no words are distinguished through such contrasts as those between English *dug* and *tug*—the speaker will use *d* and *t* indifferently. The record of a European who notes such a language phonetically, according to what he hears, without regard to the functions of the sounds, gives a wrong impression.

Speech-sounds in European languages are pronounced by expiration, the air being pushed out from the cavity of the mouth and from the lungs. But in a group of languages in southern and eastern Africa, notably Hottentot, Bushman, and some Bantu languages such as Zulu, certain speech-sounds are formed by inspiring. Thus the glottis is closed and then opened suddenly, the air being drawn inward instead of being expelled. In Hottentot (Nama) there are twenty such *clicks* [19]. They seem to have been current in the original languages of the pygmies. Similar clicks are used by children during the babbling period. They are also found in certain interjections in many languages, as in the English exclamation commonly written *tch*. Clicks are often employed in commands to horses.

It has been suggested that the oldest types of language consisted of clicks without vowels (that is, without phonemic vowels). Vowel-like articulations would necessarily occur here and there between clicks, but they would be devoid of differentiating value. The assumption that there may have been languages without phonemic vowels has some justification. The view that clicks were once much more common is suggested also by the existence of glottalized consonants, that is, consonants accompanied by a glottal stop, which may have developed out of clicks. Clicks probably originate from the suction movements of the child at the breast of its mother. We have seen that the evolution of the phonemic systems has followed the process of development in the child, and that the aphasiac loses command of the phonemes in the inverse order. Unfortunately, the order in which these gains and losses proceed in people speaking click languages is unknown. To reveal it would be an investigation well worth the making.

VII. DIFFERENCES IN GRAMMATICAL SYSTEMS

The differences among grammatical systems are as marked as among phonemic systems. Grammatical systems used in Palaeolithic times must have been radically different from those we know. In our European languages there are well defined parts of speech, distinguished from each other by their forms, or by their relations to other parts of speech, or by both, as for example, nouns, verbs, and adjectives. Such parts of speech are not, however, universal. Many living languages are without prepositions or conjunctions. In several languages, quality is not as in European languages expressed through a special part of speech, the adjective, but through verbal forms. Such are the archaic Asiatic languages, such as that spoken by the Ainu, as well as Korean and to a large extent Japanese. One would say, for example, in such a language that a thing 'reddens', not that 'it is red'. Again, while a language may seem to distinguish between two parts of speech corresponding to ours, the usage may differ greatly. Thus the language of Indians of the State of Washington differentiates between a verb and a noun so far as form is concerned, but things which we consider nouns may be verbs in their language. The noun designates persons, animals, and man-made objects only, while words for things in Nature, such as island, lake, creek, mountain, or tree are verbs [20].

When we turn to grammatical processes, the picture becomes even more complex. Many languages involve a process by which the lexical meaning of the word and the expression of its grammatical relations in the sentence are welded together, so that the elements do not clearly stand apart. Such is the case with Latin. Some languages employ internal changes. Such is Arabic, where the lexical meaning is expressed by consonants, while different vowels, prefixes, and suffixes render the different grammatical forms and derivations, a process that is dimly seen in English strong verbs (*swim*, *swam*, *swum*), and is highly developed in Arabic and Hebrew. Finally, there is the so-called isolating system, which has no inflexions at all. The words are here invariable. Grammatical relations are expressed through small 'empty' words and word-order. The best-known of these languages is Chinese.

These different linguistic types do not seem directly dependent on the character of the civilization of which they are the vehicle. The isolating type (Chinese, etc.) is used by people who have developed highly refined cultures, and also by tribes of simple civilization; the highly inflexional types are used by the great civilizations of the Mediterranean lands but also by barbarian tribes. In the beginnings of linguistic science, it was thought that the several types of grammatical structure represented different stages of development of human expression, Chinese grammar being the original type and Latin and Greek the later highly developed type, the most perfect means of expression. More accurate knowledge of Chinese linguistic history has shown that the Chinese system, far from being original, is the end result of a long development of a language that was once inflected.

Nevertheless, that a linguistic system is not wholly independent of the culture in which it is set is obvious from the vocabulary. There is, moreover, a certain degree of demonstrable correlation between a culture and a grammatical type, but this is of a more complex and indirect character than was at first held to be the case. It can hardly be an accident that in the course of modern European civilization a simplification of the structures of its leading languages has run parallel to the great development of abstract thought.

There are other factors which may lead to grammatical simplification. This is clearly shown by the so-called *linguae francae*, rudimentary means of communication used between tribes speaking mutually incomprehensible languages. In a *lingua franca*, grammar is reduced to a minimum. A typical example is the so-called beach-la-mar, or beche-le-mar, spoken and understood all over the western Pacific, a sort of pidgin English originally used in plantations where negro slaves were gathered from different parts of Africa, whence it spread to the English Pacific colonies. In this idiom, the word has usually only one form, the lexical one, though there are a few exceptions as *man*: *men*, and *he* before verbs, with *him* in all other positions. Grammatical relations are expressed by auxiliary words or left unexpressed. If, for example, the plural is expressed, it is indicated by a prefixed *all*: *all he talk*, 'they say'. The word *belong* serves to mark the genitive: *tail belong him*, 'his tail'. There is no gender even in the pronoun; *he*, *him* means also 'she', 'her'. The verb has no tense forms. When necessary, *by and by* signifies the future: *brother belong-a-me by and by he dead*, 'my brother is dying'; and the completed action by *finish*: *me look him finish*, 'I have seen him' [21].

If a language comes to serve an increasingly large group it will tend toward simplification as does a *lingua franca*, and for comparable reasons. On the other hand, a well organized state administration may exert a conservative influence on its language. In western Europe the linguistic systems, apart from the vocabularies, have undergone little change since the consolidation of the great states. The main changes took place during the medieval period, when centrifugal forces manifested themselves more freely.

A language spoken by a highly civilized group may be taken over by a people less civilized or more powerful. Such changes of language have often happened, and are still happening. In Africa, for example, the language of ancient Egypt has been replaced by Arabic, and the pygmies now use the languages of their negro neighbours. The Lapps in Scandinavia took over a Finno-Ugric language in prehistoric times. We may therefore find peoples on quite different cultural levels using the same type of language. 'When it comes to linguistic form,' it has been said, 'Plato walks with the Macedonian swineherd, Confucius with the head-hunting savage of Assam' [22]. Yet these facts do not entirely preclude the possibility of finding some correlation between linguistic form and type of civilization.

VIII. LANGUAGES OF SOME LIVING PRIMITIVE PEOPLES

Can a linguistic system be without parts of speech? The answer is surely yes. It is probable that the first speech entities were of a holophrastic character. A holophrase is a language-element which expresses a phrase. Later, the holophrastic elements might themselves be combined to express ever more differentiated meanings. The examination of a central Australian language, Arunta, may illustrate how this took place.

In Arunta, which has been well studied by anthropologists [23], the fundamental lexical element seems to consist of a consonant, or consonant group, followed by a vowel. The consonant or consonant group may be preceded by a vowel which has no particular meaning. The fundamental elements refer to actions or states, and may be combined to express certain grammatical relations.

Take, for example, *nta* (*inta*, *anta*), which means 'to lie' and also 'stone'. It may be combined with *ka*, 'to cut off', to express that the action is finished: *nta-ka*, 'he lay down'; combined with *ma* 'to take, to give much, more', we get *nta-ma*, 'he lies down, is lying down'; with *la*, 'to go', *nta-la*, 'where', and so on [24]. These complexes may be compared with our compounds, for example 'stone-mason', where the meanings of the two elements, which exist also separately, are fused into a single, more complex one. Some of the Arunta complexes seem no longer completely analysable from the point of view of the speaker, e.g. *ninta*, 'one'. There are no formal differences between these complexes and the ordinary compounds. They can no more be classed as separate parts of speech than English 'wedlock', which has lost its compound character, for only the first element is analysable from the standpoint of current English. A similar history is involved in such words as 'Godhead' or 'maidenhood'.[1]

Societies of the Arunta type need to express action, state, and position. The difference between the Arunta language and a western European one becomes particularly striking when we examine how the notion of time is rendered (ch 5). The Arunta had no calendar and did not know our divisions into years, months, and weeks; he had words only for the hot and cold seasons. Yet he had an elaborate system for marking the different points of day and of night, which he conceived as beings walking around. Some time before sunrise was called 'the night has been standing in the west'; just before sunrise, 'the night stands in the west'; sunrise, 'many hands' (the 'hands' are the rays of the sun just over the horizon); after sunrise, 'the night has lain down'; towards evening, 'throw away the stick', the sun-woman having thrown away her stick at the end of her walk; and so on.

Similarly, the different actions or states are not made to refer to time, but to the way in which the action or state occurs; forms as *nta-ka*, 'he lay down' (quoted above), or *la-ka*, 'went', correspond in function to our preterite. They are, however, more akin to the aspects of the Russian verb which express the manner in which the action takes place. The idea of time is of a more spatial character with the Arunta type than in our society, in which time is divided mathematically and events are referred to the different points of a continuous time-sequence.

The spatial character of the Arunta notion of time is seen clearly in their ideas on the origin of the totemic groups into which the tribe was divided. The ancestors 'came out of the ground' at various places, or were made by certain superhuman beings. The period during which the ancestors wandered, and the

[1] The element 'lock' in 'wedlock' has probably nothing to do with locking, but is related to Anglo-Saxon *lac*, in the sense of a pledge or gift. Similarly, 'Godhead' has nothing to do with 'head', or 'maidenhood' with 'hood'.

ancestors themselves, were called by the same designation, *alchera* (*altjira*). But this word means 'dream', a state in which a man can see his *alchera*. The ancestors were thought still to exist, but in a part of the world ordinarily invisible [25].

Such a language[1] with no differentiated parts of speech may serve a society of a simple type. The Arunta tribe consisted of small groups of hunters and food-gatherers, with no organization based on production. They produced no food, and no objects in any considerable numbers. They had no domesticated animals, apart from the dog, and no armies. They had no need of real numerals. They had four compounds, which Europeans translate by the numbers 1 to 4, 3 and 4 consisting of combinations of 2 and 1, and 2 and 2. Etymologically, these words seem to be words for positions.

It is when a society produces food and objects in greater quantities than it can use that it begins to need numerals. Thus the Trobriand islanders produce fruit in very large quantities and possess an elaborate series of numerals [26]. It is probable that the development of parts of speech has run roughly parallel to the divisions of society caused by the division of labour, though there could be no question of a uniform development everywhere [27].

Absence of parts of speech differentiated by their form does not necessarily imply a poor language. The Arunta language is far from poor. It has a rich oral literature, prose tales, and sacred songs which contain many archaic words. It contains many combinations of the fundamental elements answering the need of expressing not only everyday work and activity, but extremely complex totem ceremonies and a highly elaborate kinship system. There are differences of vocabulary between men and women, who form groups with different functions. In some other cases, as among the Kafirs of south-east Africa, the differences are so great that the tribe is said to have a special 'woman language'.

IX. LANGUAGE IN THE STONE AGE

During the Palaeolithic and Mesolithic periods, man must have lived much as did the Australians, and the even more backward Tasmanians. When Europeans first explored Australia there were some 500 tribes with a total population of about 300 000. The membership of the tribes varied from about 100 to 1500, and averaged about 500 or 600. There were as many languages as tribes [28]. The languages of such groups could not remain uninfluenced by each other, either in Australia or in Palaeolithic and Mesolithic times. It must be remem-

[1] The above interpretation of the Arunta language has been challenged, though this does not affect the theoretical value of the examples.

bered how extremely small were the units in Palaeolithic times; thus the cave population of England in Late Palaeolithic times has been estimated as no more than a few hundreds. Words, like other cultural elements, wander—and have wandered from time immemorial. Languages have spread as the result of the growth of tribes, or through conquest, or by contacts, and many languages have died.

Some think that there were considerable advances in means of human communication in the Late Palaeolithic, with the improvement of tools and the advent of graphic art. However, it is probable that the archaic linguistic systems used through the hundreds of thousands of years of Palaeolithic time did not undergo their fundamental change of character before the Neolithic revolution, when man learnt to produce food by cultivating plants and domesticating animals (ch 2).

As with Palaeolithic times, we have no direct knowledge of the languages spoken by the peoples who went through the Neolithic revolution. Nevertheless, by comparison of the related languages of historic times, we can reconstruct, within limits, certain aspects of the language from which those languages are descended. For the Indo-European parent language, we can even provide some approximation to a date.

Though the different languages during the Late Palaeolithic and Mesolithic periods may have remained of the same type as that of the numerous Australian languages [29], there must have been differences of structure and great differences in meaning between the lexical elements. With the Neolithic revolution, though it affected a limited area, language may be supposed to have undergone changes which have led to considerable differences in linguistic type.

X. THE URBAN REVOLUTIONS AND THE ADVENT OF WRITING

The rise of urban civilization from about 3500 B.C. must have accentuated this development. Above all, script was now invented. This has been of incalculable importance both to language in general and to civilization as a whole (ch 29).

Among the Sumerians of Mesopotamia, writing came into use probably toward the end of the fourth millennium B.C. The invention was not improbably made by priests, who had to administer the great accumulation of goods belonging to the gods.

The Sumerian language may have gone through a considerable development between the fifth millennium B.C., when the Sumerian tribes came down from the hills, and the time when they began to use writing. As known in inscribed clay tablets, the sound system of the language was comparatively simple, though certain details are difficult to determine owing to the character of the script [30]. The Sumerian phonemic system may have been simpler than that of many other peoples of advanced civilization, e.g. the Semites. The fundamental lexical element of Sumerian is a 'root', the meaning of which corresponds to those of a noun, a verb, and an adjective in modern European languages. The different functions of this root are expressed through the addition of special elements. Sumerian distinguished between parts of speech, and used many elements which had acquired a purely functional character. The language had become adapted to a rich urban civilization. Weights and measures had been standardized (ch 30).

In Egypt, the urban revolution took place at about the same time as in Sumer, and with similar consequences. The sound system of Egyptian is known only for the consonants. It may have been somewhat more complicated than the Sumerian, but included most of the same types of phonemes represented, with differences in detail. Middle or classical Egyptian (*c* 2240–1740 B.C.) differs little from old Egyptian.

In Egyptian grammar we find the main parts of speech current in Sumerian [31]. The verbal forms have flexional endings, and are also marked by changes in the position and quality of the vowels, variations only to a small extent deducible from the writing. The tenses express aspects, particularly contrast between the action which develops or repeats itself and the instantaneous or completed action. As distinct from Sumerian, there are passive forms contrasted to the active. The noun has no cases; its function in the sentence is expressed through word-order and prepositions. There are adjectives which seem originally to have been verbal participles. The noun, the adjective, the pronoun, and the verb distinguish between masculine and feminine forms. Verbs, nouns, and pronouns originally distinguished between three numbers: singular, dual, and plural. The dual form is generally an archaic trait in a language, and its disappearance can be followed in the history of Greek. In Egypt as in Sumer, the invention of writing stimulated the development of science.

XI. SOME SOCIAL CONSEQUENCES OF THE ADVENT OF WRITING

The invention of writing was highly significant for the development not only of language, but of society, and favoured the progress of commerce. Writing became an element in the complex of factors that led to the expansion of city states into empires. It confirmed the power of the priests through the trained scribes, and even more the might and prestige of the ruler—witness the many inscriptions glorifying the deeds of Egyptian and Mesopotamian monarchs. It fixed historical tradition, and thus strengthened social cohesion.

The Neolithic revolution, which led to food production and to a differentiation of society, must have resulted in changes in the vocabulary. At first, these would mainly strengthen the difference between men and women who, doing different work, would tend to develop somewhat diverging technical vocabularies. In similar societies today (p 100), the women till the ground, prepare the food, spin, weave, and make pottery; the men clear plots, build houses, hunt, and make tools. With the rise of an urban mode of life, there appeared technical vocabularies characteristic of higher civilization. Commerce and building made for the standardization of weights and measures, and this again required a strict terminology.

From Mesopotamia and Egypt, higher civilization spread to other countries of the Near East, with results similar to those in the countries of origin. In such early days we thus meet with the same interplay of social and linguistic factors that can be observed later in the Mediterranean lands, and still later in Europe. The art of writing was generalized and a number of languages became literate, but many of them are undeciphered or little known. The art of writing itself, however, underwent changes which in the end made it possible also for ordinary people to become literate, especially through the medium of an alphabet (ch 29).

XII. THE INDO-EUROPEAN LINGUISTIC GROUP

Meanwhile, the Near East had received the advance guard of peoples speaking languages which in due time were to dominate the whole world. The first Indo-Europeans appear in Asia Minor toward the end of the third millennium B.C. At the beginning of the following millennium, the Hittites, who spoke Indo-European, founded a kingdom which, about 1600 B.C. and again in the fourteenth century B.C., grew into an empire that disappeared about 1192 B.C. They used cuneiform script as well as hieroglyphs. Their language underwent considerable simplification, and adopted many foreign terms through the influence of the conquered populations. Another Indo-European people, the Aryans, ruled the Mitanni in north Syria in the fifteenth century B.C. The first Indo-European speakers may have reached Greece as early as the third millennium B.C. Their language has not survived, though the country seems to have been definitely conquered by them in the first half of the second millennium B.C.

Where the original speakers of Indo-European languages came from is unknown. Of the many suggestions, the most likely seems to be somewhere in eastern Europe or western Asia. Comparison between the oldest records of the languages of these parts has made it possible to determine some of the more important features that characterized the original Indo-European language before the emigration of the different Indo-European tribes. They must have formed a fairly uniform group some time in the first half of the third millennium B.C., or even earlier, though certain dialect differences which date from the common period have been established. The sound systems comprised more phonemes than those of the languages we have examined hitherto. Rhythm was, as in ancient Greek and Latin, dependent upon the gradation between long and short syllables. Tones were used to distinguish between words and forms, as in ancient Greek and in many modern languages. The grammar was extremely complicated, for the word expressed not only the lexical meaning but its function in the sentence. Thus there were at least eight cases in the noun, and an abundance of verbal forms. Homeric Greek and Vedic Sanskrit give some idea of the original system. There were sharp distinctions between noun, pronoun, and verb. Three numbers—that is, singular, dual, plural—were expressed in each. The verb rendered a rich system of aspects and had three different moods: indicative, optative, and subjunctive [32]. Some of the original dialects, to which Greek belonged, distinguished also between categories of active and medium, the latter indicating an action undertaken in the interest of the subject, i.e. reflexive. There was no passive. There was a well differentiated series of numerals comprising the numbers up to a hundred, but no common old denomination for a thousand is known.

The first Indo-European language to develop in the service of civilization in Europe was Greek. The rise of Sanskrit in India seems to be more or less contemporary. From the Phoenicians, the Greeks took over the alphabet, some time between 1100 and 900 B.C. [33], making the very important innovation of a systematic notation of vowels. Inscriptions in the different dialects of ancient Greece exist from the first half of the eighth century B.C. onwards, and the literary language in its oldest form, the epic idiom of Homer, is—at least in its oral form—contemporary with the oldest inscriptions and probably older. (But see p 109.)

The Greeks entered as conquering barbarians into the world of Aegean civilization, by which they were strongly influenced. They adopted many terms from the languages spoken by its peoples. Words such as *elai(w)a*, 'olive'; *(w)oinos*, 'wine'; *sykon*, 'fig'; *minthe*, 'mint'; *rhodon*, 'rose', are probably of Aegean origin, and all these words survive, in some form, in modern European languages, including English. It is significant that many terms for material culture and social organization come from the same source, e.g. *asaminthos*, 'bath-tub'; *basileus*, 'king'; *(w)anax*, 'lord, master'. Non-Greek, probably Aegean, words are particularly numerous in naval terminology, e.g. *kerkuros*, 'light vessel, boat'; *lembos*, 'ship's cock-boat'; *karabos*, 'light ship'; *merinthos*, 'cord, line', etc. [34].

The importance of the Greek language in the development of European civilization can hardly be exaggerated. It has moulded our thought; Aristotle founded his logic on the categories of Greek grammar. Greek civilization, through its philosophy, science, and art, continues its influence to this day. Though Greek is usually regarded as a dead language which has been the object of study since the Renaissance, it is in reality a living language, through its vocabulary. Greek words or word-elements form the basic vocabulary of our sciences and our techniques, either in the original Greek form or in a Latinized or translated shape. Words like *cathedral*, *eclipse*, *echo*, *gastric*, for example, have come to us from Greek through Latin; *substantive*, *adjective*, *verb* are Latin translations of Greek originals; 'sleeplessness' is a translation of Latin *insomnia*, which again reproduces Greek *aupnia*. That the Greeks were the pupils of the old rulers of the Near East is certain. Herodotus says they learnt geometry from the Egyptians and arithmetic from the Phoenicians. We know that Thales of Miletus (640?–546 B.C.) had visited Egypt. The Greeks, however, were more than pupils. Whereas Mesopotamian and Egyptian scientific thought was either mythopoeic or directed solely towards the solution of purely practical problems, the Greeks gradually developed the scientific attitude, building up a body of truth by observation and experiment [35].

In modern times, the vocabulary of science has been consciously based on Greek, but what is much more significant is that the names of all the older sciences are of Greek origin. Thus mathematics is from *mathesis*, 'learning', that is, learning about forms and numbers. Arithmetic is from *arithmos*, 'number'. Geometry is from *geometria*, literally 'earth-measuring'. Physics is from *physika*, 'natural things'. *Botany* is itself the Greek for 'plant'. History is from *historia*, 'inquiry', a shortened form of which is our word 'story'. The modern sciences have been named on the model of the ancient ones, as genetics, anthropology, biology, entomology, meteorology, technology, etc.

The Greeks created also large vocabularies for the various handicrafts, arts, and trades, vocabularies which have had a similar influence on our terminology, often through Latin adaptations or translations.

XIII. CONCLUSION

The origin of language is unknown. The conditions which led to the development of the animal cry into speech have left no direct or indirect traces. It is clear, however, that language and the tool are the two factors which enabled man to be man. The character of the linguistic systems of the Palaeolithic and Mesolithic ages is also unknown, but a systematic, structural study of the language of present-day food-gatherers may throw some light on the general character of the linguistic systems in use towards the end of the period preceding the invention of food production. This invention, the domestication of animals, and the subsequent urbanization in the Near East had revolutionary effects on the linguistic system.

As far as pronunciation is concerned, it seems difficult to establish a correlation between the history of civilization, in the ancient world and in Europe, and the evolution of phonemic systems. But there is a tendency, most clear in Europe, to avoid phonemes articulated far back in the throat, to get away from glottalization, at least as an element entering into the articulation of a phoneme, and, finally, to develop fairly rich vocalic systems. In grammar, the correlation is clearer. It must have been when society was transformed through an extensive division of labour that the parts of speech characteristic of the language of the ancient world and modern Europe were framed. These parts of speech correspond to, and reflect, social necessities, and, on their part, mould the thought of the social groups who use them. The growth of social groups into large societies and the development of abstract thought tend to simplify grammar. There is a distinct correlation between the development of language and civilization in general in the Mediterranean and western Europe, but it must be kept in mind that a comparatively precise correlation is a possibility realized only when other conditions permit. On the other hand, the refinement of civilization and culture results in an enrichment of the vocabulary. Comprehensive technical vocabularies are created, each used by professional groups and at least partly unknown by other groups. Literacy leads to the greater use of certain parts of speech, such as subordinating conjunctions, and to a complicated form of exposition with extensive subordination and special styles. The existence of a literary tradition exerts a conservative influence on linguistic development. Even in the ancient world, the part played by language in society had manifested itself in such a way that very few really new features have come to light since, excepting only the conscious, systematic, linguistic nationalism of the last two centuries.

REFERENCES

[1] Huxley, J. and Koch, L. 'Animal Language', p. 46. Transatlantic, New York. 1938.

[2] Frisch, K. von. 'Aus dem Leben der Bienen' (4th ed.). Springer Verlag, Vienna. 1948.
Idem. 'Bees: Their Vision, Chemical Senses, and Language', chap. 3. Cornell University Press, New York. 1950.
Lotz, J. *J. acoust. Soc. Amer.*, **22**, 712, 1950.

[3] *Idem. Ibid.*, **22**, 715, 1950.

[4] De Laguna, Grace A. 'Speech. Its Function and Development', p. 49. Yale University Press, New Haven; Humphrey Milford, London. 1927.

[5] MALINOWSKI, B. 'Coral Gardens and their Magic.' Allen and Unwin, London. 1935.
[6] STOPA, R. *Arch. vergl. Phonetik*, **3**, 105, 1939.
[7] ZEUNER, F. E. 'Dating of the Past' (2nd ed. rev. and enl.), chap. 9. Methuen, London. 1950.
[8] RÉVÉSZ, G. 'Ursprung und Vorgeschichte der Sprache.' Francke, Bern. 1946.
[9] JESPERSEN, O. 'Language, its Nature, Development and Origin', chap. 21. Allen and Unwin, London. 1922.
[10] GRÉGOIRE, A. 'L'apprentissage du langage.' Bibliothèque de la Faculté de philosophie et lettres de l'Université de Liége, fasc. 73, 1 Libr. Droz, Paris. 1937.
[11] JAKOBSON, R. *Språkvetenskapliga Sällskap. Förh. 1941*, *Uppsala Univ. Årsskr.* **9**, 1–83, 1942.
[12] GOLDSTEIN, K. 'Language and Language Disturbances,' p. 35 ff. Grune, New York. 1948.
[13] JAKOBSON, R. See ref. [11].
[14] SPENCER, SIR W. BALDWIN and GILLEN, F. J. 'The Arunta', p. 433. Macmillan, London. 1927.
[15] STREHLOW, C. 'Die Aranda und Loritja-Stämme in Zentral-Australien', part IV, 2, pp. 54 ff. Veröff. Völkermus. Frankfurt, no. 1. 1911–15.
[16] VAN GINNEKEN, J. J. 'La reconstruction typologique des langues archaïques de l'humanité.' *Verh. Akad. Wet. Amst.*, *Afd. Letterkunde*, new series **44**, i, 99, 1939.
[17] RÉVÉSZ, G. See ref. [8], pp. 68 ff.
[18] PAGET, SIR RICHARD A. S. 'Human Speech.' Kegan Paul, London. 1930.
[19] BEACH, D. M. 'The Phonetics of the Hottentot Language', chap. 6. Heffer, Cambridge. 1938.
STOPA, R. See ref. [6].
[20] VOGT, H. 'The Kalispel Language', p. 30. Norske Videnskaps Akademi, Oslo. 1940.
[21] JESPERSEN, O. See ref. [9], chap. 12.
[22] SAPIR, E. "Language" in 'Encyclopaedia of Social Sciences', Vol. 9, p. 234. New York. 1938.
[23] SPENCER, SIR W. BALDWIN and GILLEN, F. J. See ref. [14].
STREHLOW, C. See ref. [15].
[24] SOMMERFELT, A. 'La langue et la société.' Instituttet for sammenlignende Kulturforskning, Ser. A, no. 18. Aschehoug, Oslo. 1938.
[25] SPENCER, SIR W. BALDWIN and GILLEN, F. J. See ref. [14].
STREHLOW, C. See ref. [15].
[26] MALINOWSKI, B. See ref. [5].
[27] DURKHEIM, E. 'De la division du travail social.' Alcan, Paris. 1893.
[28] ELKIN, A. P. 'The Australian Aborigines', pp. 9 ff. Angus and Robertson, Sydney and London. 1938.
[29] *Idem.* See ref. [28], p. 110.
[30] GADD, C. J. 'A Sumerian Reading-Book', p. 14. Clarendon Press, Oxford. 1924.
[31] GARDINER, SIR ALAN H. 'Egyptian Grammar' (2nd ed.). University of Oxford, Griffith Institute, London. 1950.
LEFEBVRE, G. 'Grammaire de l'égyptien classique.' Bibliothèque d'Étude, Vol. 12. Inst. franç. Archéol. orient., Cairo. 1940.
GARDINER, SIR ALAN H. *Proc. Brit. Acad.*, **23**, 81, 1937.
[32] MEILLET, A. 'Introduction à l'étude comparative des langues indo-européennes' (7th ed.), pp. 223 ff. Libr. Hachette, Paris. 1934.

[33] DIRINGER, D. 'The Alphabet' (2nd ed.), pp. 195 ff. Hutchinson's Scientific and Technical Publications, London. 1949.

FÉVRIER, J. G. 'Histoire de l'écriture', chap. 9. Payot, Paris. 1948.

[34] MEILLET, A. 'Aperçu d'une histoire de la langue grecque' (3rd ed.), pp. 52 ff. Libr. Hachette, Paris. 1930.

CHANTRAINE, P. "Le vocabulaire maritime des Grecs" in 'Étrennes de linguistique offertes . . . à Émile Benveniste', p. 1 ff. Geuthner, Paris. 1928.

[35] FRANKFORT, H. *et al.* 'Before Philosophy.' Especially chap. 8. Penguin Books, Harmondsworth. 1949.

BIBLIOGRAPHY

General Works:

BLOOMFIELD, L. 'Language.' Allen and Unwin, London. 1935.

BÜHLER, K. 'Sprachtheorie.' Fischer, Jena. 1934.

DE LAGUNA, Grace A. 'Speech. Its Function and Development.' Yale University Press, New Haven; Humphrey Milford, London. 1927.

FIRTH, J. R. 'The Tongues of Men.' Watts. London. 1937.

GARDINER, SIR ALAN H. 'Speech and Language' (2nd ed.). Clarendon Press, Oxford. 1951.

GRAFF, W. L. 'Language and Languages.' Appleton, New York, London. 1932.

GRAY, L. H. 'Foundations of Language.' Macmillan, New York. 1939.

JESPERSEN, O. 'Language. Its Nature, Development and Origin.' Allen and Unwin, London. 1922.

LEWIS, M. M. 'Language in Society.' Nelson, London. 1947.

MEILLET, A. 'Les langues dans l'Europe nouvelle' (2nd ed.). Libr. Payot, Paris. 1928.

MEILLET, A. and COHEN, M. 'Les langues du monde' (2nd ed.). Libr. Anc. Édouard Champion, Paris. 1953.

ROSETTI, A. 'Le mot. Esquisse d'une théorie générale.' Société Roumaine de Linguistique, Sér. I, Mém. 3, Bucharest. Munksgaard, Copenhagen. 1943.

SAPIR, E. 'Language.' Oxford University Press, London. 1921.

Idem. 'Selected Writings in Language, Culture and Personality' (ed. by D. G. MANDELBAUM). University of California Press, Berkeley and Los Angeles, Cambridge University Press, London. 1949.

SAUSSURE, F. DE. 'Cours de linguistique générale' (ed. by C. BALLY *et al.*). Libr. Payot, Lausanne, Paris. 1916.

SCHMIDT, W. 'Sprachfamilien und Sprachenkreise der Erde.' Winters Univ.-Buchhandlung, Heidelberg. 1926.

SOMMERFELT, A. 'La langue et la société.' Instituttet for sammenlignende Kulturforskning, Ser. A, no. 18. Aschehoug, Oslo. 1938.

VENDRYÈS, J. 'Language' (trans. from the French by P. RADIN). Kegan Paul, London. 1925.

Phonetics:

JONES, D. 'An Outline of English Phonetics' (7th ed.). Heffer, Cambridge. 1949.

Idem. 'The Phoneme.' Heffer, Cambridge. 1950.

TROUBETZKOY, N. S. 'Principes de phonologie.' Libr. Klincksieck, Paris. 1949.

Origin and Prehistory of Language:

PAGET, SIR RICHARD A. S. 'Human Speech.' Kegan Paul, London. 1930.

RÉVÉSZ, G. 'Ursprung und Vorgeschichte der Sprache.' Francke, Bern. 1946. (A French translation has been published by Payot, Paris.)

VAN GINNEKEN, J. J. 'La reconstruction typologique des langues archaïques de l'humanité.' *Verh. Akad. Wet. Amst., Afd. Letterkunde*, new series **44**, i, 1939.

Bibliography:

'Linguistic Bibliography.' UNESCO, Permanent International Committee of Linguists. Spectrum, Utrecht, Brussels. Annually, having started with the bibliography for the war years (1939–47).

Note: Since paragraph 2, on p 104, was written, an earlier form of Greek, dating from about 1400–1200 B.C. and found in the Mycenaean archives, has been deciphered. It is written in a special alphabet, the so-called Linear Script B. Cf. M. Ventris and F. Chadwick, *J. Hell. Studs.* **73**, 84, 1953.

Building the Tower of Babel (Gen. xi. 1–9), as imagined by an Italian wood-engraver of the fifteenth century.

5

PRIMITIVE TIME-RECKONING

E. R. LEACH

I. LOGIC OF DIMENSIONS

How did men come to regard that intangible experience which we call 'time' as measurable in much the same way as length—that is, as a dimension?

First, let us consider what we mean by dimension, a word the very form of which involves the idea of measurement (Latin *mensio*, *dimensio*, a measuring). When we seek to describe the dimensions of anything, we refer almost automatically to some unit of scale—feet, hours, ounces, and so on. This is natural, since we can measure a thing unknown only in terms of something known, normally of units of scale. All societies have such units, which are however not necessarily standardized. The relation between dimension and scale is not always what a twentieth-century scientific European might expect. For example, some peoples, as we shall see, measure area by volumetric scale, or time by distance scale.

This question of standardization is crucial. We take it for granted. Some use the metric system, some other systems, but any one of our standard scales is interchangeable with any other. An inch equals 2·54 cm. We cannot imagine that an inch would equal 2·54 centimetres in England and 3 elsewhere. We assume that the validity of measurement scales rests on mathematical calculation and exact observation. Nevertheless, this kind of precision is certainly not primitive. Our own ideal scale is scientifically exact, but other peoples have preferred scales easier to use.

Now if the criterion of a good scale is convenience, it may follow that what seem to us primitive ideas of dimension are, in their own social context, as good as, or better than, our own sophisticated notions. Primitive craftsmen always use natural units of length: e.g. fingerwidth, palm, span, forearm (cubit), nose to finger-tip (yard), arm-span (fathom) (ch 30). We think such measures crude compared with the standardized units of a tape-measure or a foot-rule, but, if the same expert makes all the measurements, the natural units are sufficiently exact and much quicker to use. Standardized carpenter's measures are necessary and advantageous to us largely because we subdivide technical tasks, so that products of different carpenters, working independently, may fit together. If the technical accomplishments of primitive or ancient peoples are to be properly appreciated, it is important to bear these things in mind. A few examples of pre-scientific dimensions will suffice.

(*a*) *Baskets.* In south-east Asia the cultivator usually measures the 'area' of his rice-field by the number of baskets of seed he sows in it. The quality of his land is stated in terms of the number of baskets of paddy he expects to harvest, compared with the number sown. Thus, a 3-basket field of 50-basket land will yield, in an average year, 150 baskets. This is simple and sensible, though it tells nothing of the area of the field.

(*b*) *Acres.* The word was originally applied to unenclosed land (compare Latin *ager*) and implied no measurement. It came to mean the area ploughed in a day by a yoke of oxen. On poor light soils the area of an 'acre' would exceed that on rich heavy soils, but the expected yield from the two 'acres' was roughly the same. The farmer is interested in yields, not geometry.

(*c*) *Remen.* In ancient Egypt, the principal measures of length were finger-width (digit), palm, cubit, and a measure called the remen. Some textbooks say that 'the double remen was the diagonal of a square royal cubit', then, by averaging the length of numerous cubit measuring-rods, reach the conclusion that the 'correct' length of the royal cubit was 20·62 inches. This, by our geometry, gives 29·16 inches as the 'correct' length of the double remen, a statement which suggests that the Egyptians were concerned with accuracies of 0·01 in. Believing this, one authority [1] suggested that the length of the double remen may have been calibrated against that of a natural pendulum swinging 100 000 times a day in the latitude of Memphis! This was a fantasy. We know that the ratio of the diagonal to the side of an accurately drawn square is 1·4142. The Egyptians had no means of knowing this, but by trial and error they evidently concluded that the ratio lay close to both 7/5 (that is, 1·4) and 10/7 (that is, 1·429). They may even have thought these two ratios identical. They therefore constructed measuring rods in the ratio 5 palms = 1 remen, 7 palms = 1 royal cubit, 10 palms = 1 double remen, and assumed that geometrical figures drawn either with remen as sides and royal cubit as diagonal, or with royal cubit as sides and double remen as diagonal, would both be squares. The error in a right-angle of either of these 'squares' would be only about plus or minus 1° 10′. The second 'square' has an area twice the first, with negligible error. This gave a very simple and accurate method of measuring land areas. Paradoxically, its efficiency depended upon the fact that the initial assumptions were incorrect.

(*d*) *Li.* Textbooks usually give the Chinese *li* as a measure of about a third of a mile. But in parts of west China where there are no reliable maps, the *li*-distances between important places are known, yet these *li* do not average 3 to the mile. A coolie with a standard burden is expected to cover so many *li* per day, according to the nature of the country. Such coolie-day stages are all some multiple of 10 *li*. At every tenth *li* along main routes, there is a stage-post at which the coolies always halt for a rest—roughly one rest every hour. In mountainous country, loaded coolies move more slowly, and the stage-posts are, therefore, closer together, though from the Chinese view they are still 10 *li* apart. This is logical, since for commercial purposes a distance-scale should be in time rather than length. Similar systems prevail in many mountainous regions—notably in the Alps, where guides always give distances in terms of 'hours'.

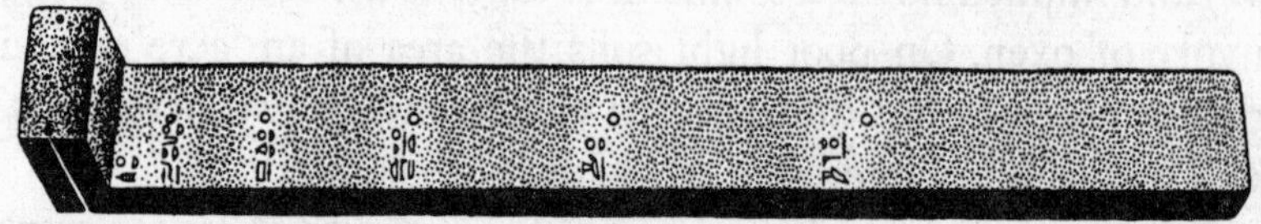

FIGURE 44—*Egyptian shadow-clock of green slate. The division on which the shadow of the end-block falls indicates the time in approximate temporal hours. The oldest example of this instrument is attributed to the reign of Thothmes III,* c *1450* B.C. *Length about 14 in.*

(*e*) *Zodiacal Hours and Degrees.* Peoples who have neither a mechanical clock nor even the idea of one do not think of time as built of an accumulation of short equal intervals such as minutes or seconds. To them, time appears as a kind of distance travelled, or else as a recurring cycle of familiar natural events. Even the Babylonian and Greek astronomers, who eventually developed notions of time similar to our own, started with a vague cyclical time-distance scale.

They early observed that the Moon completes her journey through the heavens in about 28 days (actually 27·3216 days). They began to note particular stars and constellations as marking what later came to be called by the Latins *mansiones* (from *manere*, to sojourn), corresponding to the daily movements of the Moon. Some time before 400 B.C., the movements of the Sun came to be thought of as mapped on the same lines as those of the Moon. Thus stars and constellations were used to mark the distances marched by the Sun in the course of an annual series of lunar months.

The word used by the Babylonians to describe these stages of Sun and Moon was *danna*. Of such stages, there were early held to be twelve in the day. A *danna* comprised 30 'lengths' (*us*). Eventually, the star-track of Sun and Moon came to be thought of as a geometrical circle of 360 degrees, that is of *us*. Each *danna*, defined as a particular constellation of the zodiac, then represented 30 *us* or degrees of arc. The use of these originally vague distance-terms to denote precise geometrical angles illustrates how drastic is the logical shift from an empiric to a scientific basis for time reckoning.

(*f*) *Temporal and Equinoctial hours.* In the Greco-Roman world the only mechanical time-recorders were water devices, which conveyed a notion of constant flow rather than of consecutive equal intervals. All such apparatus was, in any case, extremely inaccurate. Until the fourteenth century A.D., the only reliable way to tell the time was by reference to a sun-dial or shadow-clock. In Egypt, sun-dials were in use very early (figures 44, 45). Their scales were not constructed upon geometrical principles but divided according to simple rules involving whole numbers. The lengths of the twelve day-hours indicated were

FIGURE 45—*Modern Egyptian shadow-clock. The board, with 'hour' divisions marked, is orientated so that the shadow of the horizontal bar falls on it. Length* c *3 ft 10 in.*

consequently not all equal. Moreover, since the same scale of hours was used at all times of the year, the errors varied at different seasons [2].

In the Roman period, the most common type of sun-dial was the hemicycle, which served to divide the hours of daylight into equal intervals called temporal hours (*horae temporales*) by the Romans, and true hours (*horai kairai*) by the Greeks. By our reckoning, these hours were substantially longer in summer than in winter. This seems odd to us, but when only the hours of daylight were of much practical use, such a mode of reckoning had much to recommend it. The system was maintained in the Turkish Empire until modern times. Astronomers of course found these temporal hours inconvenient, but, until the coming of the balance-clock in the thirteenth century A.D., standard equal-interval hours, such as we know, were used in astronomical studies only. For their standard hours, the astronomers took the length of the temporal hour at the date of the spring equinox (p 115). They were therefore called equinoctial hours (*horae equinoctales*).

Incidentally, the public preference for temporal hours greatly complicated the problem of constructing a satisfactory mechanical clock. The first constant-flow water-clocks were developed about 250 B.C., supposedly by Ktesibios in Alexandria. The great complexity of these devices (which we know from descriptions by Vitruvius) is due to the need to show temporal hours [3]. A water-clock designed to show equinoctial hours is much simpler to construct.

II. DIFFERENT ASPECTS OF THE TIME DIMENSION

Some at least of the characteristics of dimensions which have been regarded as self-evident thus depend on initial assumptions. These in turn depend upon the kind of practical context in which the notion of dimension is to be used. In practice, there seem to be five principal modes of thinking about time. All five logics, either singly or in combination, have influenced the way different peoples have sought to measure and calculate time.

(*a*) *Primitive Attitude to Time*. Time can be regarded as a recurring cycle. Certain events repeat themselves in definite sequence. This sequence is a continuity without beginning or end, and thus without any clear distinction between past and present. The most important time-sequences are seasonal activities and the passage of human life. Both these cycles are conceived as of the same kind. For such thinking there is no chronology, and time is not measurable.

(*b*) *Historical Time*. Time can be thought of as history. The emphasis here is upon a sequence of completed stages which are unique and never precisely recur. Time-thinking of this kind involves listing and counting events in regular order, but the events are not necessarily of comparable time-length. Indeed, while most histories record events in correct chronological sequence, space is generally allocated between one event and another not on the basis of time-duration but on that of historical importance. Historical time, then, is not cyclic, but sequential.

(*c*) *Magical Time*. Time can be thought of as a religious or magical quality which influences events, and can in turn be controlled by suitable ritual action. Such time-reckoning is part of a wider set of magico-religious procedures thought necessary to bring the supernatural and the human orders into harmony. A kind of pseudo-science may result from such magical procedures, for, in seeking to discover the divine laws thought to be manifested in apparently haphazard events, men have been led to make observations which are equivalent to treating time as measurable. The Hebrew, Christian, and Muslim eras contain elements of this way of thinking.

(*d*) *Scientific Time*. Time can be thought of simply as duration, without regard to its economic, historical, astronomical, or magical associations. In this context, time becomes a simple dimension, analogous to length, and capable of being measured in equal intervals according to any convenient scale. This attitude is of much more recent origin than is commonly realized.

(*e*) *Political Time*. Finally, time can be treated in opportunist fashion to suit the whims and ambitions of individual leaders. In the development of our own European system of time-reckoning, this purely adventitious factor has been of considerable importance. The calendars of various revolutionary movements come at once to mind.

III. PRIMITIVE ASTRONOMICAL OBSERVATIONS

All these ways of time-reckoning involve astronomical observations, however rudimentary. To comprehend their basic nature, it is necessary to consider the definition of modern time-concepts which derive from the geometry of the celestial sphere. These are part of the apparatus of scientific time, but we are concerned with them here only as tools of description.

The technical terms and precise figures used in spherical astronomy in relation to celestial events are largely the product of a relatively modern science equipped with astrolabes, armillary spheres, and other apparatus. Certain of the time-points involved can, however, be observed without these complications. Thus, to observe the heliacal rising of a bright star or the appearance of the new moon requires no apparatus at all. To observe the culmination or time of transit across the meridian of a star requires only a fixed line of sight and a transit-staff or plumb-line. The brightest stars, and those most likely to be observed in this way, are the fixed stars Sirius and Canopus, and the planet Venus (as morning star). Another very obvious astronomical marker is the star cluster known as the Pleiades.

To observe a solstice by noting the extreme positions of sunrise or sunset requires only a fixed line of sight—though outside the tropics diffraction may cause certain difficulties. Within the tropics, an easy observation is the day when the Sun is at the latitude of the observer, i.e. at the zenith. At this date a vertical rod will cast no shadow at noon. On the other hand, to observe a sunrise or sunset equinox one must first draw a line of sight due east and west. This is not difficult, but is not likely to be attempted until some body of astronomical theory has been accumulated.

We should, therefore, expect the most primitive systems of astronomical dating to depend upon observations of heliacal risings, new moons, culminations, solstices, and zenith points in the ecliptic. Substantially, this is in fact the case.

IV. PRIMITIVE TIME

(*a*) *Seasonal Check Points.* Many primitive peoples still have no proper calendar, and make no systematic observations of stars, of the Sun, or of the Moon. Their methods of time-reckoning provide clues as to the kind of time-logic which early man must have possessed. The passage of time is most commonly experienced as a cyclical change of the seasons, and in every type of human economy these seasonal changes are crucially significant. Time-reckoning of some kind is necessary to human life because, lacking adaptive instincts, man must plan ahead to meet impending seasonal changes.

The simplest of all types of time-reckoning is that of noting direct correlations between synchronous natural events, e.g. when certain plants blossom, the rains come. Observations of this kind lead to the naming of a cycle of seasons, each name being associated with a set of natural phenomena and an associated set of social activities. These named seasons follow one another in definite order, but the units of time described have no definite length. Thus the seasonal indications of the Greek poet Hesiod [4] (*c* 800 B.C.) are typical of the maxims of many modern primitive societies:

> 'The cry of the migrating cranes shows the time of ploughing and sowing.'
>
> 'If one sows too late, the crop may yet thrive if it rains within three days of the first hearing of the cuckoo.'
>
> 'Vines should be pruned before the appearance of the swallow.'
>
> 'When the snail climbs up the plants there should be no more digging in the vineyard.'

Such signs are commonly natural events, as the appearance of birds, the blossoming of flowers, a change in the winds, and so on, but often they include also the heliacal rising of a star. Even the primitive Bushmen of South Africa take note of the heliacal rising of Sirius and Canopus, and use their later movements as an index of the passage of winter. Many primitive peoples take the heliacal rising or setting of the Pleiades as a check-point for agricultural or other economic activities.

At first sight this seems surprising, but though the term heliacal rising may suggest something abstruse, it is really a very obvious phenomenon. Primitive peoples have little artificial lighting. They sleep largely in the open, and are more familiar with the night sky than their civilized contemporaries. Nearly all have names for a few easily recognized stars or star clusters. The temporary disappearance and reappearance of such prominent stars from the night sky is readily observed. There is therefore nothing sophisticated in the use of heliacal risings as a sign of the changing seasons.

Another celestial phenomenon which may be observed without astronomical understanding is the oscillation of the Sun between the two solstices. In many types of terrain, the movement of the rising and setting points of the Sun in relation to landmarks on the horizon is very obvious. The coincidence of the Sun with a particular landmark can be, and often is, used as a seasonal check-point. Such calendars, it is true, do not readily lend themselves to very accurate predictive statements, for the north-south movement of the Sun between the solstices is very irregular in terms of days.

A third type of astronomical observation available to pre-literate peoples is the observation of shadows. If a stick is set vertically in the ground to form a gnomon, the minimum length of the shadow on any given day is easily observed (figure 46). If this point is marked, and the experiment continued for several days, the minimum (i.e. noon) shadow will be seen to grow shorter or longer on successive days, according to the phase of the Sun in the ecliptic and the latitude of the observer. In latitudes near the equator, the maximum or minimum shadow can be used as a seasonal check-point. Techniques of this kind are employed by the modern Dyaks of Borneo, and were formerly used by the sophisticated, though pre-literate, Peruvians. Astronomically, this amounts to observations of the solstices and the zenith point of the ecliptic.

FIGURE 46—*Primitive gnomon, used by Borneo tribesmen to determine the season of the year for planting rice.*

In all these cases we need to be careful not to inject into the primitive situation the bias of our advanced knowledge. The heliacal rising of a star, or the solstitial setting-point of the Sun, or the minimum noon shadow of a gnomon, will always fall on the same calendar day, but the primitive peoples who use such observations as seasonal check-points do not necessarily know this. They may not even think of the yearly cycle as having any fixed duration at all.

(*b*) *Moon-Counts.* Among primitive peoples, the notion that the year has any particular length or duration is generally lacking. The seasons recur, and there may be a word for the cycle of recurring seasons which we can translate as 'year', but it cannot be defined as a period of so many moons or days. Nevertheless the counting of moons (lunar months) is quite common, even among primitive peoples, and we must consider its implications.

The obvious function of a moon-count is to aid economic planning. That there are nine moons of pregnancy, or, say, six moons between sowing and harvest, are facts which are easily ascertained and important to know. Such reckoning is not calendarial, but merely an elaboration of the use of seasonal signs.

Moon-counts become more complicated when associated with ritual, as is often the case. A major function of any system of annual rites is to mark the different seasons of social activity. Agricultural communities commonly have a ritual feast at the time of preparing the land, another at sowing, another at harvest. Fishing communities often have open and closed seasons for particular types of fishing, each period being marked by a ritual feast. The occasion of such rites can, of course, be indicated by natural signs, but this method is often too inexact. Moon-counts permit much more definite predictions.

The resulting practice of describing the seasonal cycle as a series of moons, instead of as a series of natural events, is a step towards our kind of thinking. Yet still the year may have no definite length. Frequently a moon-count series is incomplete. The cycle starts off with a ritual feast timed for some particular new or full moon; then a series of perhaps eight or ten named moons is recognized; but the tail end of the year, being economically unimportant, is allowed to run out unnoted. The system of the ancient people of Latium—from which the Roman, and ultimately many of our own, month-names are derived—seems to have been of this kind. The year started on a new moon reckoned as the first of the month March. The cycle then ran for ten moons until the end of December (*decem*, ten); after which there was a gap of two (or sometimes three) moons until the next cycle started.

Although several such incomplete moon-cycles have been described, the descriptions are not always satisfactory. Whether or not all the moons are named, it is certain that any particular cycle must, in fact, contain either 12 or 13 lunar months, since otherwise the moon-count would not fit the seasons at all. If the primitive users of such calendars are not aware of the astronomical facts, how do they decide when to start off the new seasonal cycle? For example, it is sometimes asserted that, in the original Roman calendar, the first of March was the time of the new moon closest to the spring equinox. This, however, is unlikely to have been the primitive arrangement, since the notion of an equinox-point depends upon some degree of astronomical sophistication (ch 31).

Any seasonal cycle reckoned in moons must clearly be calibrated by some natural event which, from our point of view, appears to occur at a fixed time in the sidereal year. Accordingly, when anthropologists find primitive peoples using such check-points, they are liable to describe this as correcting the lunar cycle to fit the solar or sidereal year. It is important to realize that such corrections can be made without any awareness of the existence of a solar or sidereal year.

Two examples serve to illustrate this point. The Yami of Botel-Tobago Island near Formosa have an economy greatly influenced by the seasonal arrival of large shoals of flying-fish, which appear in these waters around March. A further seasonal fact is that, from about mid-June, typhoons are so frequent that deep-sea fishing is impracticable in the small craft of the Yami. They reckon time by moons, and all their festivals occur at a particular new or full moon. The check-point for their year is a festival in the dark phase between months nine and ten of their cycle; that is, about March. At this festival, the Yami go out to summon the flying-fish with lighted flares. Before this event, flare-fishing is taboo. Provided the flying-fish turn up to the summons, the flare-fishing continues for three moons until the end of the 12th month, and this is then deemed the end of the yearly cycle. From the beginning of the first month, flare-fishing is taboo again. If no flying-fish turn up to the summons, the Yami do not blame themselves for miscalculating the time—they blame the fish for being late for their appointment. In such years, they extend the flare-fishing season for an extra moon, and the year-cycle continues for 13 months instead of 12. In this way, over a period of years the Yami calendar will keep in step with the sidereal year, although the Yami themselves have no notion of such a year and make no astronomical observations.

The Trobriand Island practice is another example which demands a minimum of systematic knowledge, though in description it may seem complex. The Trobriand area (Northern Massim Islands, New Guinea) is divided into four districts which we may call *A*, *B*, *C*, and *D*. Each has the same cycle of ten month-names, but the series is staggered. Month 1 in district *D* is month 2 in *C*, month

Scheme representing the Trobriand Calendar

District A	*District B*	*District C*	*District D*
1			
2 Milamala	1		
3	2 Milamala	1	
4	3	2 Milamala	1
5	4	3	2 MILAMALA check-point
6	5	4	3
7	6	5	4
8	7	6	5
9	8	7	6
10	9	8	7
—	10	9	8
—	—	10	9
1 (same as 10 in D)	—	—	10
2 Milamala	1	—	—
	2 Milamala	1	—
		2 Milamala	1
			2 MILAMALA check-point

3 in *B* and month 4 in *A*. The Trobrianders know this, and the people of *A* know that their first month coincides with month 10 in *D*. The Trobrianders have no clear idea of how many moons there are in a year or of calibrating the cycle of ten moons, but they agree that the correct calendar is that of *D*, the people of which are fishermen. At the full moon, around November of our year, they go out after the palolo worm, a species of marine annelid relished as a foodstuff. Vast numbers of these creatures rise to the surface of the sea at this time. This phenomenon only occurs a few days after full moon, and if the palolo worm misses a full moon it will not appear until the next.

The palolo worm is expected to arrive in the month of Milamala of district *D*. If it turns up a month late, *D* has a second Milamala month and then carries on as before. This will put the other districts out of position, but the error is later corrected by one or other of the districts doubling its own Milamala festival season. The Trobrianders are very casual about this procedure, and the different districts can be said to keep in step at all only by averaging a period of several years.

Here then is the seeming impossibility of a moon-count calendar which recognizes only ten months to a cycle and takes no account of astronomical observations. That the system should work at all is almost a paradox; it does so only because the logic with which the natives approach calendarial time is vague in the extreme, and even inconsistent [5].

(*c*) *The Counting of Days* is much less common among primitive peoples than the counting of moons. The main reason for this is, no doubt, the difficulty of maintaining a system of tallies for the larger numbers. Some of the simpler peoples count the number of days in a month, but among modern pre-literate societies the counting of days in long cycles is almost entirely confined to tribes, such as those of Central America, which have a background of literate tradition.

V. HISTORICAL, MAGICAL, AND POLITICAL TIME

If there is any single criterion which distinguishes primitive society from that which is more advanced, it is that, in the former, all persons of one sex have the same interests and acquire the same skills, while, in the latter, technical tasks and social duties come to be carried out by specialists. It seems that historical and magical time-thinking develop out of primitive time-thinking along with specialization of labour, and reflect the special interests of the priestly and official classes. In ancient centralized states, such as Egypt and Mesopotamia, the common man was still concerned only with the present; his year was a recurring cycle of activities. The official, on the other hand, looked to the past, and was concerned with maintaining precedents and ordering activities into categories. The year and its divisions became instruments of organization. For the priest, the names and numbers associated with these divisions provided an acrostic which led ultimately to astrology.

In almost all early societies, there were priests or priest-magicians whose status and authority depended on their secret knowledge. In primitive societies these secrets are techniques of ritual and verbal spells, but, as writing develops, such formulae tend to become associated with geometrical shapes and magic numbers. Arithmetic and number theory may later be developed for their own sake without reference to practical utility. For example, the sexagesimal system of enumeration of ancient Mesopotamia and China was the invention of learned men who must have pursued complexity for the sake of complexity. For the peasant with ten fingers, there is no convenience in having 60 minutes to an hour, 24 hours to a day, and 360 degrees in a circle, but these numbers have exceptionally numerous simple factors, and so have fascination for arithmeticians interested more in magical combinations than in practical calculation. Thus, the administrative official and the priest are both interested—for different reasons—in devising time-systems which are neat, symmetrical, and arithmetically attractive. There are two ways of doing this. One is to devise and operate a pure number-system, ignoring the facts of astronomy. The other is to devise a pure number-system, but from time to time to introduce supplementary rules—also of a formal kind—which will gradually bring the number-system into relation with astronomical fact.

The ancient Egyptians, the Chinese, the Maya, and the Greeks each tackled this problem in a slightly different way. The Egyptians produced a number-system which ignored seasons. The Chinese maintained two separate official calendars, one for the peasant, which followed the seasons, and one for the scribe, which was a pure number-system. The Maya devised a pure number-system, and became obsessed by the marvellous intricacy of numbers. They took note of astronomical facts, but only to provide themselves with more and more complex number series which might be built into their magical system. The Greeks pursued a system of magical geometry, and in the process developed a true self-conscious science.

In the Egyptian calendar-system of Dynasty XVIII, say 1500 B.C., which is the earliest of which we have adequate information, three distinct elements can be detected: (*a*) a primitive seasonal calendar based on the annual rise and fall of the Nile; (*b*) a complicated system of magical rites designed to ensure that the Sun returns each day from its sojourn in the underworld, and that the fertilizing Nile floods return in due season; (*c*) a beautifully tidy calendar of festivals having no immediate astronomical reference but based simply on a system of counting days.

FIGURE 48

FIGURE 49 A

FIGURE 47

FIGURE 47—*Slit palm-leaf* (merkhet) *and plumb-line, c 600 and 525 B.C. To time a transit, the passage of the star across the plumb-line is observed through the slit in the* merkhet.

FIGURE 48—*Egyptian water-clock. An alabaster vase, decorated with symbolical figures, with an outflow at the bottom on the left. A scale of hours is marked on the inside. Thebes, Egypt.* c *1400 B.C. Depth of vase 14 in.*

FIGURE 49 A—*Ceiling of Senmut's tomb. Part of the southern panel. Thebes, Egypt.* c *1500 B.C.*

From an early period, Egyptian religion developed as a cult mainly preoccupied with resurrection from the dead. The Egyptians saw the Sun as dying each evening and being born again each morning; the Nile began to die each October and was reborn each June. Just as spells, incantations, and festivals were necessary to ensure the survival and rebirth of dead men, so also it was necessary to hold rites for the dead Sun and the dead Nile. Just as in human rites the deceased was identified with Osiris, the judge of the dead, the god who was slain and reborn, so also the Sun-god Horus and the Nile were on these occasions identified with Osiris.

The Egyptians thought of life and death, day and night, parched land and flooded land, as perpetual alternations. The Sun-god Horus represented life and light; the god Set-Apep represented death and darkness, and was symbolized by the stars of the Great Bear, which are extinguished by the light of day but which never sink below the horizon. Osiris and his sister-wife Isis were the intermediaries between life and death; they held Set-Apep at bay and guided the dead through the realms of darkness. They had many manifestations, but among others they were the heralds of rebirth. For example, Venus, the morning star, is represented as Osiris in the guise of a phoenix. The constellation Orion and the star Sirius, the appearance of which heralded the rebirth of the Nile, were identified as Osiris and Isis respectively.

The intervals of the civil calendar of 365 days were marked by religious rites. There was a major rite at the rising of Sirius, another on the first day of the year, and probably one for each of the 36 successive ten-day intervals or decans of the 12-month series. Eventually each decan festival became associated with its own star or constellation, so that the sequence of decan stars formed a consecutive series. Indeed, in late Hellenic times, the Egyptian decans were, for astrological purposes, fitted to the zodiac, with three decans for each sign. In origin, however, the decan and zodiac systems are distinct (ch 31).

The marking of the hours of day and night in Egypt followed a similar pattern to that of the decans of the year, temple rites being held at regular intervals so as to ensure the successful progress of the Sun-god Horus on his daily circuit. Crude sun-dials were used to mark the hours of daylight (figure 44); night hours were marked by the culmination of particular stars recorded with the aid of a plumb-line or simple transit staff (figure 47). Shorter intervals still could be measured by means of a water-clock consisting of a graduated bowl with a small hole in the bottom (figure 48). Such a bowl will always take the same amount of time to empty itself, even if no two bowls ever behave in exactly the same manner.

Figures 49 A, B provide a good illustration of many of these themes. They show the decoration on the roof of the tomb of Senmut (*c* 1500 B.C.). The theme of both panels is the victory of life over death. In the southern panel (figure 49 A), the four central deities are Osiris as Orion (note the three stars in line) followed by Isis as Sirius, followed by Horus as the planet Jupiter, followed by Horus

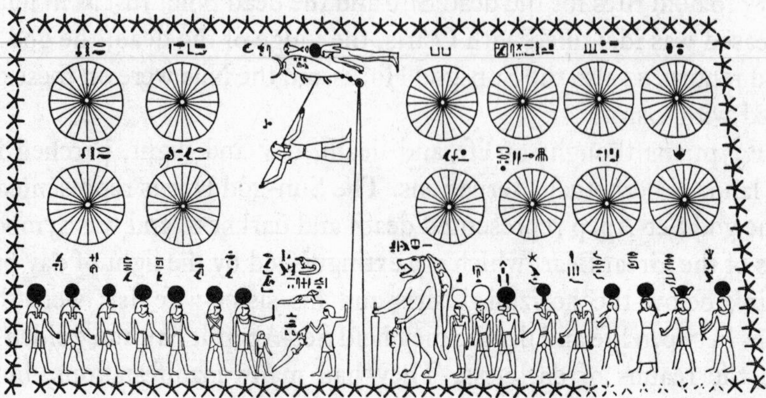

FIGURE 49 B—*Northern panel of Senmut's ceiling.*

again as the planet Saturn. The bird at the extreme left of the panel represents Osiris as a phoenix, linked with the planet Venus as morning star. Columns of writing further to the right of the panel give a catalogue of the 36 decans and their associated star deities, none of which is firmly identified. In the northern panel (figure 49 B), the 12 circles are the 12 months of the year in three seasonal groups of four, with spaces for the names of the 24 deities of the hours in each month. The central figure shows Horus spearing an ox, representing Set-Apep as our *Ursa Major*. A star in the tail of the ox is seen in culmination against a transit staff, presumably marking the hour of midnight, when Horus should enter the realm of Set and begin to come back to life. The animals at the bottom of the transit staff are thought to represent other constellations in the circumpolar groups of stars, and hence to be 'hour stars'.

The Maya of Mexico, like the Egyptians, counted days, and like them reckoned the year as 360+5 days. But where the Egyptians seem to have thought of chronological time as an ordered sequence, the Maya were far more occupied with the oddities of arithmetic. They thought of time as composed of overlapping cycles of deified numbers. They 'conceived of the divisions of time as burdens which were carried through all eternity by relays of bearers . . . these were (personifications of) the numbers by which the different periods were distinguished; each number carried the period with which he was associated over his allotted course. . . . Time was not portrayed as the journey of one bearer and his load, but of many bearers, each with his own division of time on his back' [6] (figure 50). It is impossible to give a simple account of this extraordinary system, since the Maya clearly pursued complexity because they enjoyed it. At one period, they engaged in computations corresponding to that of ascertaining on what day of the week fell the 31st December, 90000000 B.C.! Yet though Maya time-reckoning is really a kind of astrology, or magical arithmetic, we may learn from it something about the general principles that govern the transition from magical to scientific thinking.

FIGURE 50—*Maya glyphs, from the initial series of a date. This detail shows one of the lords of the night bearing his load of time. From Copan, Honduras. Date uncertain, probably eighth century A.D.*

The important dates, from the Maya point of view, were those which completed a cycle, since, in Maya theory, the good or ill fortune of a particular period could be divined from a knowledge of its date of completion. A date which completed several different cycles all at once was correspondingly more important. Thus, by analogy to our system, Saturday would be important as being the last day of a week; a Saturday falling on the 31st December would be more important; Saturday, 31st December falling on the last day of a century would be yet more important.

The Maya had 20 basic digits instead of our ten, and they developed a positional notation. Thus, a number we should write 861 (i.e. $8 \times 10 \times 10 + 6 \times 10 + 1$) was written by the Maya as 2.3.1. (i.e. $2 \times 20 \times 20 + 3 \times 20 + 1$). Each of the first 13 digits had special magical associations.

There were 20 day-names comparable to our days of the week, following on perpetually in continuous sequence. These days were, however, also numbered in series of 13, likewise in continuous sequence. Thus, each day had both a name and number. If we denote the names by capital letters down to the twentieth letter, which is T, a series might run

1A; 2B; 3C; 4D; 5E; 6F; 7G; 8H; 9I; 10J; 11K; 12L; 13M;
1N; 2O; 3P; 4Q; 5R; 6S; 7T; 8A; 9B; 10C; 11D; 12E; 13F;—

In a period of 260 days, no two days will have both the same name and the same number, but after 260 days the cycle will repeat itself.

The sequences of 13 days repeated, 20 days repeated, 260 days repeated are all *cycles* in the sense that the word is used above. They were the basic cycles of the Maya system. But the Maya also took note of many others. We cannot follow them here, because it would lead to a long and very complex discussion foreign to our objective.

The importance of the Maya system from our point of view is not in its complexity or in its accuracy, but in the fact that, on the basis of a wholly irrational body of astrological theory, the Maya arrived at genuine scientific truths. In this respect, the Greco-Babylonian mode of time-reckoning, from which most of our own time concepts are derived, bore a striking resemblance to that of the Maya. The Pythagorean theory of the harmony of the spheres insisted that, no matter what might be the appearances, all heavenly bodies must move in perfect circles and in accordance with simple arithmetical rules. This approached very closely to a deification of geometry, just as the Maya pattern did in fact become a deification of number.

If the Maya scheme was a product of magical rather than scientific thinking, how far was the Greco-Babylonian system genuinely scientific rather than magical? That subject is discussed later (ch 31).

A little introspection will reveal to any of us that, so far as his own life is concerned, time is not reckoned on any scientific or numerical basis. It is reckoned by events. Our lives as we look back on them are punctuated not by dates but by salient events in our personal history. Each of us is a legislator who establishes for himself his own era.

Since time has no self-evident manifestation, our ideas about it are greatly influenced both by the context in which we use notions of time, and by the apparatus or notation through which we represent it. Our own ideas about time are closely associated with the fact that we are familiar with pendulum clocks capable of regulation. Of the ancient peoples, the Greeks came nearer to our way of thinking than any of the others. Greek time-recording apparatus consisted, however, only of sun-dials, water-clocks, sand-clocks, and crude astronomical sighting-instruments. The time recorded from such instruments resembled the irregular flowing of a river rather than an exactly graduated measuring rod. Yet in some respects the vagueness of the time-dimension suited the Greeks very well. Greek philosophy was constructed on the assumption that geometrical knowledge is perfect knowledge. We realize nowadays that natural phenomena do not in general conform absolutely to simple geometrical rules. The Greeks not only accepted this absolute conformity, but were convinced that it had been demonstrated by their empirical observations.

In the other societies discussed, the whole basis of time-thinking was clearly far removed from our own. Though we can claim that our system is technologically superior, we cannot claim that it is sociologically superior. The efficient use of dimensions is not solely a technological problem. Different societies have found different kinds of dimensions convenient, partly because their social and religious organization called for different types of technological thinking. It is not inconceivable that our own society will outgrow the notions on these matters which we now regard as scientific.

REFERENCES

[1] Petrie, Sir (William Matthew) Flinders. 'Measures and Weights', p. 4. Methuen, London. 1934.

[2] Ward, F. A. B. 'Time Measurement. Part I' (3rd ed.), p. 16. Handbooks of the Science Museum, London. 1950.

[3] Vitruvius (*c* 30 B.C.); author of 'De Architectura Libri Decem.'

[4] Hesiod. The quotations are from his chief work 'Works and Days' as quoted by Nilsson, M. P. 'Primitive Time-Reckoning.' Skr. humanist. VetenskSamf., no. 1. Lund. 1920.

[5] A fuller account of the Yami and Trobriand systems will be found in Leach, E. R. *Oceania*, **20**, 245, 1950.

[6] Thompson, J. E. S. 'Maya Hieroglyphic Writing', Introduction. Carnegie Institution, Publ. 589. Washington. 1950.

BIBLIOGRAPHY

Boll, F. 'Sphaera.' Teubner, Leipzig. 1903.

Bouché-Leclercq, A. 'L'astrologie grecque.' Leroux, Paris. 1899.

Colson, F. H. 'The Week.' University Press, Cambridge. 1926.

Duhem, P. 'Le système du monde. Histoire des doctrines cosmologiques de Platon à Copernic.' 5 Vols. Libr. Scient. Hermann, Paris. 1913–17.

Eisler, R. 'The Royal Art of Astrology.' Joseph, London. 1946. (Bibliography.)

Gundel, W. 'Dekane und Dekansternbilder.' Studien der Bibliothek Warburg, Vol. 19. Hamburg. 1936.

Hooke, S. H. 'New Year's Day: the Story of the Calendar.' The Beginning of Things, no. 2. Howe, London. 1927.

Leach, E. R. "Primitive Calendars." *Oceania*, **20**, 245, 1950.

Mercer, S. A. B. 'The Religion of Ancient Egypt.' Luzac, London. 1949. (Bibliography.)

Neugebauer, O. "Die Bedeutungslosigkeit der Sothisperiode für die älteste ägyptische Chronologie." *Acta Orientalia*, **17**, 169, 1938.

Idem. "The Origin of the Egyptian Calendar." *J. Near East. Stud.*, **1**, 396, 1942.

Idem. "The History of Ancient Astronomy: Problems and Methods." *Ibid.*, **4**, 1, 1945. (Bibliography.)

Nilsson, M. P. 'Primitive Time-Reckoning.' Skr. humanist. VetenskSamf., no. 1. Lund. 1920. (Bibliography.)

Petrie, Sir (William Matthew) Flinders. 'Measures and Weights.' Methuen, London. 1934.

Thompson, J. E. S. 'Maya Hieroglyphic Writing', Introduction. Carnegie Institution, Publ. 589. Washington. 1950. (Bibliography.)

Ward, F. A. B. 'Time Measurement. Part I: Historical Review' (3rd ed.). Handbooks of the Science Museum, London. 1950.

Winlock, H. E. 'The Origin of the Egyptian Calendar." *Proc. Amer. philos. Soc.*, **83**, iii, 446. 1940.

6

WORKING STONE, BONE, AND WOOD

L. S. B. LEAKEY

I. MATERIALS USED BY PALAEOLITHIC MAN

THE making of weapons and implements of stone, bone, and wood doubtless goes back to the time when man first became man. One of the most widely accepted descriptive phrases to designate man as he is today is 'the tool-maker'. As more and more of the fossilized remains of the stages in human evolution come to light, it becomes increasingly difficult to draw the line between human and pre-human beings. Nevertheless, such creatures become recognizable as having human qualities when members of their stock have started to make tools as distinct from merely using natural objects as tools.

As man slowly and gradually became more and more a tool-maker he used, as his principal materials throughout the 'Stone' Age, not only stone but bone, wood, and to a lesser extent horn, antler, and ivory. Of these, the objects made of stone, by reason of their great durability, naturally survive in vastly greater numbers than those made of the other materials. Consequently we know far more of the early techniques of working stone than of those used for working any other material. Indeed, the name Stone Age is based upon this very fact. We may perhaps safely infer that wood played a very important part in man's life in those earliest days, but wooden objects of such antiquity are preserved only under very exceptional conditions. Our knowledge of the techniques employed in wood-working in the earliest days is therefore very limited. Bone is more durable than wood, but it too is far more liable to disintegration than to fossilization. Thus our knowledge of the techniques of working bone and allied substances, such as antler and ivory, is limited also.

In view of all this, we may first consider the techniques of working stone and pass thence to wood and bone, meanwhile remembering that the dominance of stone over other materials is apparent rather than real. We often think and speak of prehistoric chipped stones as crude instruments. To remove any possible misunderstanding, it is well to say at once that there are multitudes of stone implements the manufacture of which has involved technical skill of the very highest order. The attainment of that skill implies traditions extending over ages, and an accompanying high degree of inventive skill combined with endless patience. The technical achievements of primitive man are thus worthy of the greatest respect. *La distance n'y fait rien; il n'y a que le premier pas qui coûte*, said the blind, witty, and wicked Marie, Marquise de Deffand 200 years ago. The earliest achievements of men of the Stone Age must be accepted as fully comparable, in their place, time, and circumstance, to those of the greatest modern inventors and engineers.

The term 'stone' is comprehensive, covering such widely different materials as flint and obsidian on the one hand and coarse-grained granites and quartzites on the other. Naturally, early man chose, when he could, the finer-grained and more homogeneous rocks from which to make his artifacts, though there is scarcely any form of stone which he did not use at one time or another. Contrary to common belief, the nature of the stone available made very little difference to the techniques employed in working it. From the earliest period until about 3000 B.C., techniques for working stone were in effect confined to various methods of chipping and flaking. We therefore begin by discussing these techniques.

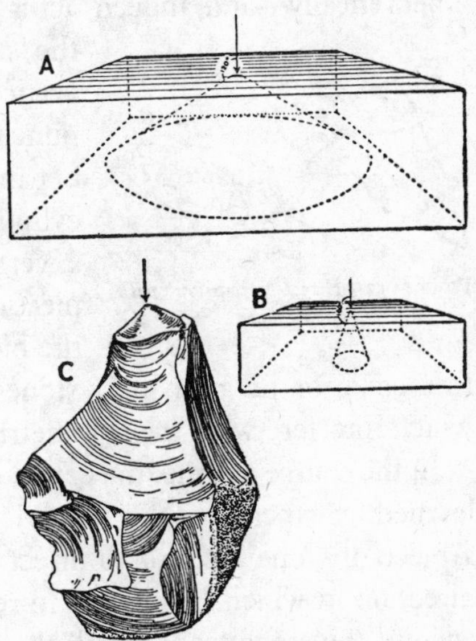

FIGURE 51—*Cones of percussion. Arrows show points of impact of hammer-stone.* (A), (B) *Diagrams of cones formed in material of high and low resistance to fracture respectively.* (C) *An actual cone of percussion in flint made by the author.*

II. HAMMERSTONE TECHNIQUE

At first, only the simplest hammerstone technique of flaking was employed. This consisted of taking a water-worn pebble of suitable size and shape, holding it in the hand, and using it as a hammer for knocking off flakes from another stone in order to shape it roughly into form. This sounds fairly easy, but in fact the worker had to master a knowledge of the correct angle at which to strike a blow before he could be certain of detaching a flake at the desired point and in the desired direction. The acquisition of such a technique was by no means easy, and there is ample evidence that it involved periods of time that are vast when measured by later standards.

When a blow is struck upon a piece of stone with the convex surface of a water-worn pebble, fracture does not take place in a continuation of the direction of the blow. As a result of stresses built up near the surface during the period of contact, the material breaks under tension round the periphery of the area of contact, and a crack spreads rapidly downwards and outwards (figure 51). Theoretically—and indeed actually, if the blow is of sufficient force, and if the struck stone is of suitable texture—a strong vertical blow on a piece of fairly flat stone will punch out a complete cone, just as a bullet hitting a pane of plate-glass forms a conical, and not a cylindrical, hole in the glass. Ordinarily, however, a vertical blow with a hammerstone on another piece of stone causes only shattering, either because the blow is not strong enough to punch out a perfect cone, or because most stones have inherent lines of weakness and faults which interfere with the symmetrical distribution of the stress.

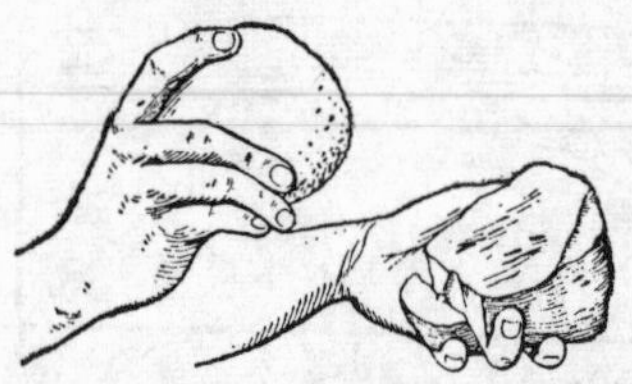

FIGURE 52—*Direct percussion with hammerstone.*

In the course of time, the extent of which cannot be estimated, Stone Age man learned by experience that, in order to detach a flake in a desired direction from a piece of stone, he had to direct his blow at an angle of roughly 120° to the direction in which he desired to remove the flake, and also at a point near the edge of the stone from which the flake was to be detached. In this way only a part of the cone of force penetrated the stone, the rest being dissipated outside. Thus a flake was detached with a clearly defined semi-cone—or bulb of percussion as it is sometimes called—marking the point of impact of the hammerstone. Once Stone Age man had mastered the hammerstone technique of detaching flakes from other stones (figure 52), he gradually and slowly used the knowledge to make new and better types of stone implements, and he also evolved certain modifications of this first technique. For example, whereas it was possible to knock off flakes weighing up to 2 or 3 lb, it was difficult to detach really large flakes using a simple hammerstone technique.

III. ANVIL TECHNIQUE

To meet this difficulty the so-called anvil technique was at some point invented. In this technique, the 'hammer' was a fixed block of stone, and the stone from which it was desired to detach a really large flake (from which a big implement could be made) was swung against this fixed anvil. Here again, the essential for success was knowledge of the correct angle at which the stone should be struck against the anvil. The angle is fundamentally the same as in the simpler hammerstone technique (plate 1 A).

A main disadvantage of the hammerstone and anvil techniques of flaking was that the scar from which the flake had been struck had a deep negative bulb of percussion at the point of impact of the original blow. Thus—since several flakes were detached in succession—the cutting edges of tools made by this technique were irregular and jagged. Massive as well as small instruments of this type with jagged cutting edges are associated with what is known as the Chellean stage of the great hand-axe culture. It is well to interpolate here the information that Stone Age cultures are generally named after the places where they were first found, or at least recognized as distinctive cultures. The name Chellean is derived from the pits in France at Chelles (near Paris); in this particular case, however, subsequent work has shown that no true Chellean stage of culture is to be found at Chelles, and this had led to some authorities substituting the term Abbevillian for Chellean. The Stone Age culture known as the hand-axe or Chelleo-Acheulian (see below) culture continued for something over 200 000 years. During the first half of this period only the hammerstone technique was employed, although naturally even with this technique there was a slow and gradual improvement in the types of tool that were made (figure 53).

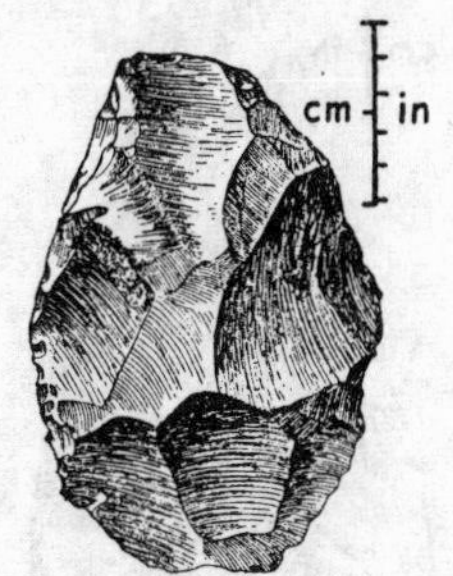

FIGURE 53—*A Chellean (Abbevillian) hand-axe made by the hammerstone technique resulting in short thick flake scars. Chelles-sur-Marne.*

IV. CYLINDER-HAMMER TECHNIQUE

Towards the second half of the period a new technique of flaking—the so-called cylinder-hammer technique—was discovered or invented, and this new development is taken to mark the beginning of the Acheulian stage (from St Acheul, near Amiens) of the hand-axe culture (figure 54). The older hammerstone technique was still used for making rough tools as well as for the initial preparation of finer tools, but the new cylinder-hammer technique was used for the finishing-off process.

The new technique consists of knocking off very thin flakes with very shallow bulbs of percussion—thus producing a nearly even surface—by means of a round-edged hammer of some comparatively soft material such as bone, hard wood, or weathered stone (plate I B). The essential factors in this technique are: (*a*) that the force of the blow is directed at the actual edge of the stone struck and not at a little distance in from the edge, and (*b*) that although one particular point of the hammer hits the stone first, the fact that the hammer is comparatively soft means that, almost instantaneously, force is applied also from other points along the rounded surface of the hammer. Thus, instead of the crack spreading from one point and giving rise to a marked bulb of percussion, it spreads from a larger area of contact through a flattened arc. This results in the removal of a flake that is very flat. A series, or rather the intersections of a series, of these flat flakes produces a nearly straight cutting edge.

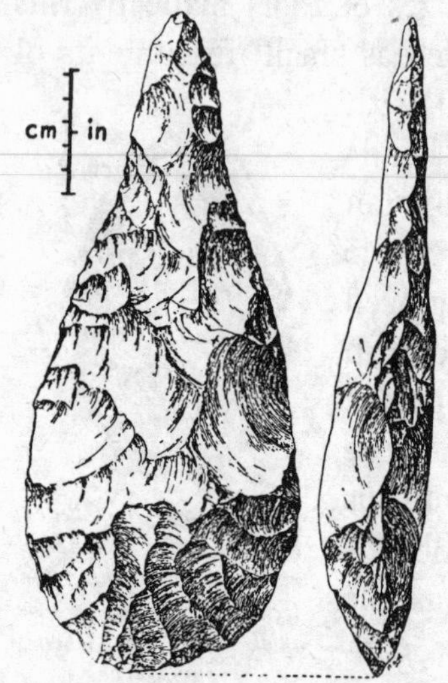

FIGURE 54—*An Acheulian hand-axe. The smooth shallow scars indicate that it has been made by the cylinder-hammer technique. Lewa, Kenya.*

It is probable, though the evidence is of an indirect character, that the commonest form of soft cylinder-hammer used by Stone Age man was a branch of wood. The evidence must be indirect, since we can hardly hope to find such perishable articles as wooden hammers on actual Stone Age sites. Experiment shows, however, that a section of a branch about 2 inches in diameter, with the bark removed (for the bark is too soft for the purpose) makes an excellent hammer for this process. No less effective materials for such hammers are jaw-bones of large ungulates, limb-bones of suitable size, and even cylindrical pebbles with a weathered surface which is not too hard. Since hammers of bone and weathered pebbles are relatively rare on sites where we know the technique was used, we must believe that a hammer of wood was most commonly used, although, as previously stated, wooden objects of such antiquity are hardly ever preserved.

V. PREPARED-CORE TECHNIQUE

At about the time that one group of Stone Age men discovered the cylinder-hammer technique for removing flat flakes, another group was evolving what is called the prepared-core technique to obtain flakes of a very special shape. This technique—sometimes called tortoise-core—differs greatly from other early Stone Age techniques in that the shape of the flake to be finally struck off, to serve as a tool with little or no subsequent retouching, was blocked out on the core or lump of stone beforehand and then removed by one blow. Previously it had been customary to take either a nodule, a pebble, a lump of stone, or a large flake already struck from a piece of stone, and strike off a series of flakes to trim the specimen into a tool.

The prepared-core technique appears in South Africa and in north-west

Europe at about the same time. It is not clear, as yet, whether it was evolved independently in these two areas or whether the idea was carried from one area to the other. The evidence suggests that it is an example of that relatively rare phenomenon, an independent invention of the same technique in two widely separated areas, for though the final stages of the technique are almost indistin-

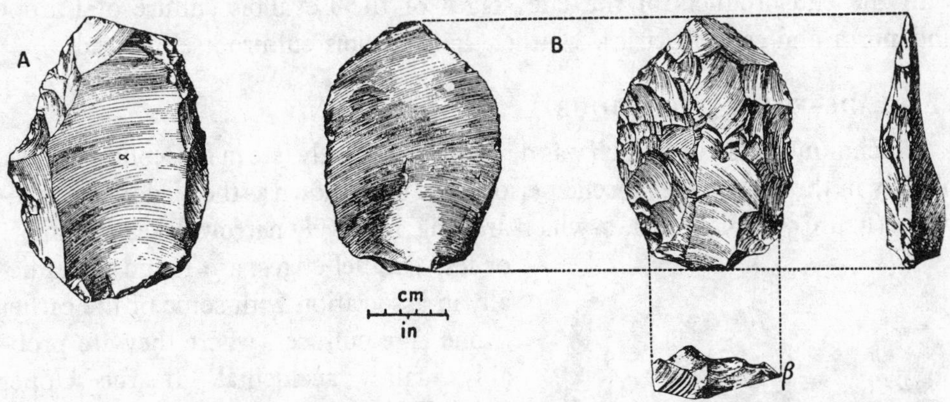

FIGURE 55—*Levalloisian artifacts.* (A) *Tortoise-core.* (B) *Three views of a flake, similar to the one struck from* (α) *of the above core, and a view of its faceted striking-platform* (β). *Northfleet, Kent.*

guishable in the two areas the earliest stages seem to differ markedly. If this is so we must regard it as a case of what is called convergent evolution (cf p 83).

In South Africa, the prepared-core technique first appears in the so-called Victoria West variant of the Chelles-Acheulian culture. The technique seems to have been evolved to facilitate the making of good hand-axes of reasonable size from large water-worn pebbles and small boulders, in an area where these were easily accessible. To make a medium-sized hand-axe from such materials by the ordinary flaking methods of knocking off flake after flake, until the block was reduced to the required size, would have been very laborious. However, it was now found that if a boulder of, say, the size of a football, were used, it was possible to trim one side fairly carefully and then detach a large flake from that side by a single blow. Such a flake was already trimmed and needed only a minimal amount of further flaking to form an excellent hand-axe. Occasionally the block or boulder was trimmed further, and a second large side flake similarly removed. In the main, however, the very characteristic cores were discarded after one side flake had been removed.

In Europe the prepared-core technique started with the Levallois (Levallois-Perret, a suburb of Paris) culture (figure 55). This was entirely distinct from the method of the Chelles-Acheulian culture. The object was not to simplify the making of hand-axes, as in South Africa, but to produce large flat symmetrical flakes which could be used without further trimming. In South Africa, however, once the technique was evolved it developed and was modified until the end-products in the so-called Middle Stone Age complex of that area are small triangular-shaped flakes with flat faceted striking platforms, in form identical with the end-products of the late stages of the Levallois culture of Europe and north and central Africa, whither the Levallois culture itself spread.

VI. BLADE-FLAKE TECHNIQUE

A technique of flaking which was developed relatively late in Palaeolithic times, namely in the Upper Pleistocene period, was that known as the blade-flake technique (figure 56). Blade-flakes, which are long, relatively narrow flakes with more or less parallel edges, are found sporadically in association with some of the earlier Stone Age cultures, where they are probably mainly accidental. In the Upper Palaeolithic cultures, however, blade-flakes became a characteristic feature, essential in making many of the very specialized types of tool of those cultures. The correct technique for obtaining blade-flakes was discovered at the dawn of the Upper Palaeolithic.

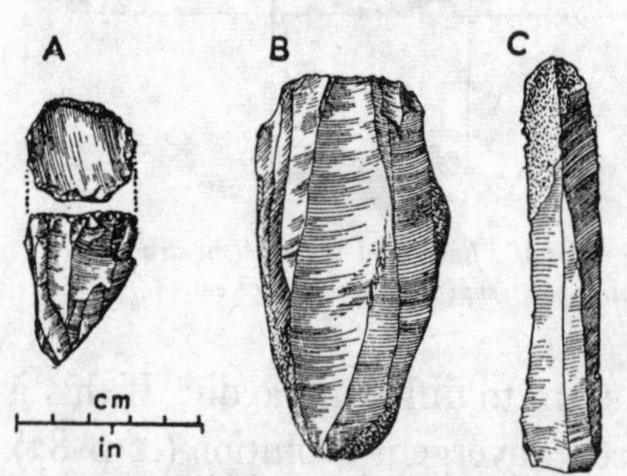

FIGURE 56—*Blade-flake technique.* (A), (B) *Blade cores.* (C) *A typical well-controlled blade, with edges down both sides.* B *and* C *are from La Madeleine, type-site of the Magdalenian culture.*

The blade-flaking technique might, on appearances, almost be included as a variant of the prepared-core technique, since it was essential to prepare a core carefully by preliminary trimming before a series of good blade-flakes could be struck from it. Actually, however, it was not a true prepared-core technique, if that term be reserved for the technique in which a more or less finished tool was blocked out on a core before being struck off. This is not the case in the blade-flake technique, in which the aim was to obtain long, narrow flakes with parallel edges. Such flakes could be converted into knives with blunt backs, chisels, end-scrapers, and so on, by various methods of secondary trimming.

The preparation of a core for producing blade-flakes involved in the first instance a mastery of the technique of quartering a nodule of flint or block of obsidian or fine-grained lava (plate 1 C, D). Quartering is a term used by modern flint-knappers at Brandon and elsewhere, but is somewhat unsuitable, since in most cases the process is to halve the block in order to have a suitable flat striking platform for a blade-flake core. For this purpose, the lump of flint or other rock has to be broken in such a way as to obtain an even-surfaced fracture, if possible without the concavity of a negative bulb of percussion. A heavy follow-through blow is struck on a suitable projection of the flint nodule, which should be massive enough to take the blow without coming away. The nodule snaps across roughly at right angles to the direction of this blow and above the point of impact.

FIGURE 57—*Preparing a core for the removal of blade flakes. Long parallel-sided flakes are removed by light tapping blows all round the edge, so that the core becomes a fluted cone.*

In quartering, the impact of the hammer working against the grip of the hand momentarily applies a very large bending moment to the nodule, so that it snaps across just as if it had been subjected to large static forces at the hand-grip and at the point of impact.

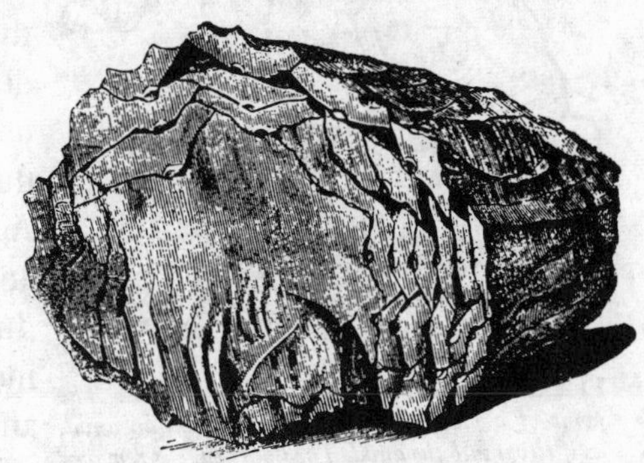

FIGURE 58—*Flint core with blades replaced. This core is from Brandon, Suffolk. The blades are afterwards divided into gun-flints.*

When a nodule of flint or other stone has been thus quartered, the process of preparing the core for the removal of blade-flakes begins (figure 57). The quartered block is held on the knee with the striking platform—that is, the quartered face—facing obliquely upwards. Light tapping blows with a small hammerstone are then struck along the edge, always just above the point where the block rests on the knee. As each blow is struck, the block is simultaneously tilted backward, altering the point of pressure against the knee, so that an effect of peeling is produced. The blows must be struck at an angle of about 45° to the surface of the striking platform, that is to say about 135° to the direction in which the flake will be removed. After each flake has been struck, the block is slightly rotated about its own axis (keeping the striking platform always facing the same way) so that successive flakes can be removed round the edge of the core. Thus irregularities on the block are removed and, since all the flakes are removed in the same direction, a fluted appearance results, due to the parallel negative flake scars.

The whole of the circumference of the core having been thus prepared, it is ready for the removal of the blade-flakes. To achieve this, it is held as for the preliminary trimming. Each blow is now, however, struck above an intersection of two earlier negative flake scars, so that the ridge formed by their intersection will form a more or less central keel on the flake knocked off (figure 58). As a variant, the blow may be struck so as to detach a wider blade-flake with two parallel keels on its upper face.

VII. SECONDARY FLAKING

All the techniques of working stone so far described have been connected with the detaching of relatively large flakes, either in the course of making large stone tools, or to make implements by further trimming of the flakes themselves. When we turn to the techniques for this further and finer secondary trimming, we find that some were the same as those already described. Small hammerstones were used for much of the secondary trimming during all stages of the various Stone Age cultures, and by slightly altering the angle of the blow it was possible to produce variations in the secondary flaking, including what are known as step-flaking and feather-flaking. A modification of the cylinder-hammer technique—which we have seen was first used during the Acheulian stage of the hand-axe culture—was also used to some extent to produce very fine flaking on lance-heads by some of the Upper Palaeolithic peoples of Africa. This modification consisted mainly in using a very much smaller piece of wood or bone, not thicker than a finger.

FIGURE 59—*Technique for making burins. The point of a blade flake is held lightly on an anvil, as if to cut into the anvil. The upper edge is removed by a sharp tap with a cylinder hammer. The blade flake is then turned over and the process repeated. Above is a Magdalenian graver made in the manner described.*

Even the anvil technique, which has been mentioned as a modification of the hammerstone technique, was used to a certain extent from quite early times for secondary flaking. During the Upper Palaeolithic it was used in a very specialized manner for the making of 'burins' or gravers. To convert a blade-flake with its thin, fine-set cutting edges into a chisel with a thick-set, narrow cutting edge, one or more flakes down the length of the blade must be detached, thus removing the side cutting edges and leaving a cutting edge at the end only. One of the principal techniques for doing this has been shown by experiment to be as follows (figure 59).

A blade-flake is taken and one end is trimmed a little on both sides, to remove part of the sharp edges and to make a rough point. Then the point is held lightly on the edge of an anvil stone with cutting edge vertical to the plane of the anvil stone. A sharp tap is now given to the edge of the flake, thereby causing the tip of the blade resting on the anvil to receive the force of the blow by ricochet. Provided that the tip is held at the correct angle on the anvil, this causes a long narrow flake to be removed from the upper edge of the blade. By turning the blade over, a similar flake can be removed from the opposite side. The intersection of these two flake scars at the tip of the flake will produce a burin of the *bec-de-flute* type. Innumerable minor variations of this technique were invented to produce different types of burin.

VIII. PRESSURE FLAKING

Apart from the technique for producing blade-flakes, and its various modifications, the major advance of the Upper Palaeolithic period was the invention of a number of different techniques which can be grouped together as pressure flaking. To transform a narrow blade-flake into a small knife-blade with a sharp cutting edge and a blunt back upon which pressure could be exerted with the forefinger while cutting, it was necessary to remove part of one side of the blade (figure 60). At first, this was probably carried out by using the old instrument—a small hammerstone—and experiment shows that this can be done. The use of a hammerstone for this purpose has at least two disadvantages: (*a*) a false blow is very liable to break the blade before the work is finished, and (*b*) knocking off small flakes with a hammerstone from a long, narrow blade held in one hand is liable to injure the fingers. Stone Age man, however, discovered that this type of secondary flaking could be more easily and accurately achieved by pressure. The pressure-fabricator was indeed one of his great inventions. This tool was not specialized in form. All that was needed was any rough flake on which there was somewhere a thick, more or less rectangular, edge.

FIGURE 60—*An Upper Palaeolithic backed blade. A blade flake transformed into a small knife blade with a sharp cutting edge and a blunt back upon which pressure could be applied with the forefinger when cutting.*

By holding the fabricator in one hand and placing its end against the edge of the blade which was to be blunted, and exerting pressure, little flakes could be pushed off very rapidly and with practically no risk of snapping the blade. When the value of this new technique had been appreciated, irregular flakes with a fabricator edge, showing signs of abrasion due to such use, became common. They are found in most Upper Palaeolithic sites.

FIGURE 61—*Diagram of pressure flaking. The flaking tool, of bone, ivory, or hard wood, is held in one hand and the specimen in the other, a direct push being effected.*

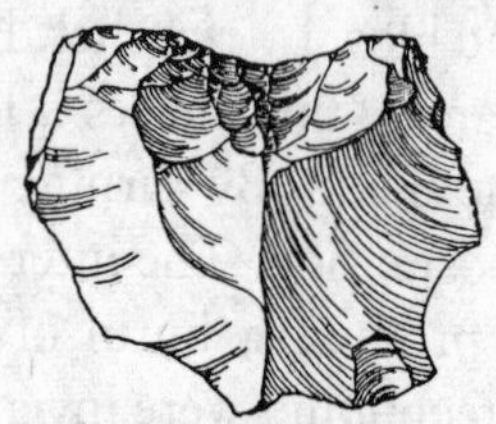

FIGURE 62—*A* lame écaillée. *This type of fabricator was used during very late Upper Palaeolithic and Mesolithic times for detaching tiny flakes from a blade flake in order to produce lunates or arrow barbs. The upper edge has been worn by use to a concave curve.*

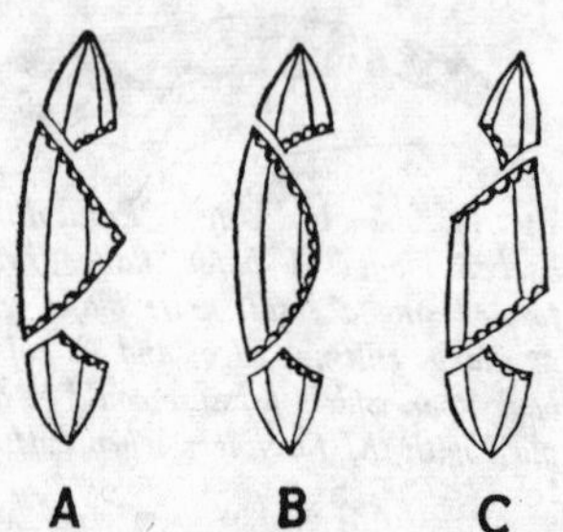

FIGURE 63—*Diagram of the double notch technique for making microliths. A notch was made at either end of the blade and the basal rejects were separated by a blow or by snapping. The microliths left in the middle represent:* (A) *a triangle;* (B) *a lunate;* (C) *a trapeze.*

In later Palaeolithic times, and continuing into the Neolithic and Bronze Age periods, another form of pressure flaking was invented. It was for removing very thin flat flakes from the surface of a blade in order to trim it into a lance-head or arrow-head. Experiment, as well as comparison with similar flaking in recent times by the American and Australian aborigines, suggests that there were several different modifications of the basic principle of flat pressure flaking. The size of the detached flakes is of the order of 3 mm across, but varies widely according to method. In this technique of flaking, the point of a special tool of bone, hard wood, or ivory, or the incisor of some large rodent such as a beaver, is placed against the edge of the stone to be pressure flaked. A sudden push is then given, detaching a small flat flake (figure 61). In the simplest method, the flaking tool is held in one hand and the specimen to be flaked in the other, a direct push being effected. A more complex method was to fasten the pressure flaking tool to a wooden shaft, the end of which was pressed lightly against the chest, while the point of the tool was placed against the edge of the flake to be trimmed, which was held in both hands. Once the correct position was achieved, a push with the chest sufficed to press off a flat flake. A disadvantage of pressure flaking is that it can be successful only with very fine-grained materials such as flint, obsidian, and chert. The most highly developed form of pressure flaking was that of predynastic times in Egypt (figure 458). Specialists in the craft had there brought it to such perfection that they could even make wrist-bangles of flint.

In very late Upper Palaeolithic times, and during the Mesolithic period, another type of pressure flaking was evolved for a specialized type of arrow barb known as a lunate. For making this, a type of fabricator was invented called a *lame écaillée* (figure 62). With but a few movements of this tool a whole series of tiny flakes could be simultaneously pushed off, thereby transforming a narrow irregular blade-flake into a lunate. This advance once made, Stone Age man began to invent other ways of speeding his work. One was the so-called microburin or notch technique. Having selected a small narrow blade-flake for transformation into a lunate, or one of its variants such as the trapeze or the triangle, two notches were made along one edge of the blade (figure 63) and the two superfluous ends of the blade removed at the centre point of each notch, either by a sharp blow or by twisting. To finish off the middle section into a lunate, trapeze, or triangle was then a very quick and easy process.

IX. POLISHING AND GRINDING

All the techniques of working stone so far described have been variations of chipping and flaking. Towards the end of the Stone Age, however, methods of polishing and grinding were invented. These resulted in the production of such tools as axes, adzes, and chisels with cutting edges far tougher than could be achieved by chipping.

In many cases the manufacture of axe-heads, etc., with ground and polished cutting edges was preceded by a preliminary shaping of the tool by one or other of the flaking techniques. In other cases, and especially with certain types of rock such as dolerite (a basaltic stone), the blocking-out of the tool was done by battering and abrading rather than by chipping. Various rocks such as sandstone and schist were used for grinding and polishing the cutting edges of axes and adzes. Sometimes the grinding-stones are in the form of portable pieces, while in other cases the grinding seems to have been done on outcrops of the living rock itself.

The technique for boring holes in stone to convert them into mace-heads, net-sinkers, weights for digging-sticks, and beads was perfected in the later Stone Age, though crude examples of holed stones do occur at the end of the Upper Palaeolithic and Mesolithic. There is at present little evidence as to the method of drilling. Some of the holes are of hour-glass form and were clearly bored from two directions; others are conical; yet others are almost perfectly cylindrical. The materials of some stone beads, such as agate and carnelian, were so hard that the drilling of fine perforations shows that prehistoric man had complete mastery of a very specialized technique, of the nature of which we have no evidence. Presumably, hand-drills and bow-drills were employed, and were used with abrasive powders for some of the harder rocks (ch 9).

The idea of using stone tools for the making of stone bowls and vases and of grindstones for corn was also developed during the later stages of the Stone Age. Chisels of very hard rock were used to block out the external shape of the object and the interior was hollowed out with rough stone gouges. Finally, both exterior and interior were finished off by a process of rubbing, abrading, and sometimes polishing. Materials used for making stone vessels included soapstone, alabaster, gypsum, and a variety of volcanic rocks such as lava and consolidated ash.

X. WORKING IN BONE

There is little, if any, evidence of the widespread use of bone and such materials until Upper Palaeolithic times. From then on they were used considerably, and special techniques were devised for their production. At first, rough splinters of limb-bones that had been broken open to extract the marrow were selected. These were sharpened and polished at one end by rubbing on a stone. Thus treated, they were used as simple bone awls. Later, it was found that with stone chisels of the burin type it was possible to cut parallel grooves in bone, antler, or ivory, and to extract from between the grooves pieces of material of pre-selected shape and size which could then be shaped into weapons, such as barbed harpoon-heads, arrow-tips, and fine needles (figure 64).

FIGURE 64—*Grooving an antler with a flint chisel.*

While burins were used in the first part of the technique, for cutting the grooves to obtain the required lengths of material, it seems likely that primitive saws of flint and similar stones were used for shaping and finishing the barbed harpoon-heads, etc. Concave scraping tools, which are almost the prototype of spoke-shaves, were also probably used in the finishing processes. It is significant that where tools and weapons of bone, antler, or ivory are found in Stone Age cultures, there usually also occur burins, saws, and concave scrapers (figures 18, 59, 392 A).

In certain areas, as for example in the Sudan, there is evidence that large pieces of bone, probably parts of the limb-bones of large animals such as the elephant and buffalo, were used to make polished and ground axe- and adze-heads in exactly the same way that stone was used for this purpose. Bone and also teeth were also extensively used for making beads. The holes were perforated by drilling. This was probably done with a drill-point of flint or similar stone, set in a wooden shaft and rotated either by hand or by a bow-drill.

The early use of massive pieces of bone for tools has been suggested. The pointed elephant bone from Piltdown has been cited in support of this, but is now known to have been shaped in recent times with a steel knife. Some of the broken animal bones in the Pekin Man cave deposit show chippings as though they had been used as occasional tools, but there is little evidence that bones were systematically worked for use as tools in earliest Stone Age times. Of much greater importance was the use, in Mesolithic and Neolithic times, of antlers as picks for mining flint from seams in the chalk (figure 371). The technique employed was simple, consisting of cutting off the superfluous tines and leaving the main stem of the antler as the handle and one selected tine as the point of the pick.

XI. WORKING IN WOOD

Although there is much indirect evidence that early man made use of wood almost from the very beginning of the Stone Age, direct evidence is very scanty, since wood is preserved over long periods only under most exceptional circumstances. There are a few records of wooden objects from the lower and middle stages of the Palaeolithic. The most notable are the wooden spear-point preserved in peaty deposits at Clacton-on-Sea (figure 18), and a similar specimen from Germany. Both are believed to be of the Middle Pleistocene period. They were associated with Stone Age cultures in which there is a great deal of indirect evidence for the utilization of wood. The deposits yielded concave stone scrapers, which were ideal tools for scraping wood. They were, in fact, an early form of spoke-shave. It is from such indirect evidence that we deduce that nearly all the early Stone Age cultures utilized wood.

Careful experiment shows that it is possible to use even untrimmed flakes—such as those knocked off in making hand-axes from a large block of stone—to sharpen and shape a sapling into a reasonably good wooden spear-head, or to shape a rough wooden club. By combining the positive evidence of the very few specimens preserved with the indirect evidence of the constant presence of hollow scrapers and flakes which show signs of use, we can be reasonably certain that in the Lower and Middle Palaeolithic periods man made fairly extensive use of wood.

When we come to the Upper Palaeolithic the evidence is greater, for by this period specialization of stone tools had been much developed (ch 18), and we have every reason to believe that some of the small stone artifacts were specifically made for hafting in wood. Thus, for example, the lunates and other forms of microliths which first appear in the Upper Palaeolithic—and continue until the end of the Stone Age—were certainly used, in part at least, as barbs for wooden arrow- and spear-points. Many Upper Palaeolithic paintings, moreover, show the use of bows, clubs, and spears, and prove that such deductions as to the use of wood are in fact correct (figure 89).

The hollow scraper or spoke-shave remains a constant feature of these Upper Palaeolithic cultures. Moreover, among the stone tools of the period are knife-blades with a blunt back and one keen edge which, even today, can be used most effectively to sharpen pieces of wood. The burins, chisels, and saws, referred to in connexion with the techniques of working bone, were also well adapted to wood-working. Nevertheless, direct evidence for wood-working, even in the Upper Palaeolithic, is exiguous. We may reasonably assume that wood was used for such purposes as arrow- and spear-points—with or without stone barbs—for clubs, arrow-shafts, bow-staves, spear- and-lance shafts, and probably for the construction of rafts and for the roofing of crude huts, as well as for many other purposes. We may also guess that the techniques of the wood-worker consisted of sawing, cutting in the direction of the grain with fine-edge knives and across the grain with burins or chisels, and scraping with concave scrapers or spoke-shaves.

Perhaps, during the more advanced stages of the Mesolithic and certainly by the dawn of the Neolithic, new techniques for the working of wood had become practicable. This was due to the invention of much better axes, adzes, and larger chisels with ground cutting edges (figures 330, 389 A). Whereas with stone tools made by the ordinary chipping and flaking techniques it was very difficult indeed to cut down a tree, let alone shape large pieces of wood symmetrically, the invention of ground and polished stone axes completely altered the position. Experiments have shown that with a polished axe of Neolithic type, and even with a chipped axe of late Mesolithic type, it is possible to cut down a sapling of about 6 inches diameter fairly quickly, while much larger trees could also be felled, given sufficient time.

It is thus natural that, from Mesolithic times onwards, evidence for a far more extensive use of wood is forthcoming. We can study the techniques employed by Late Stone Age man for wood-working. This investigation is also greatly facilitated by the fact that a proportion of the settlements of the period were so situated that many wooden objects have been preserved in peat bogs and in wet clays and muds, whereas extremely few wooden objects of the earlier peoples have survived.

The use of wood for structural purposes in Mesolithic and Neolithic times is discussed elsewhere (ch 12), but it is necessary to refer here to certain techniques connected with it. There is no evidence of the making of large saws. The only saws we know of were suitable merely for the finest work, such as making barbs to wooden points and so forth. Saws suitable for cutting branches of trees and logs were never made. Such work, it appears, was done entirely by chipping with axes and adzes.

At this period a primitive form of the tenon and mortise was invented. The tenon was laboriously cut out, and the mortise was formed by cutting with a stone chisel. Wood was also used at this time to make dug-out canoes from the boles of large trees. The external shaping of the log was done with stone axes and adzes, while, since it is manifestly easier to chip charred wood than fresh, fire was employed to speed up the hollowing-out of the interior with adzes. The technique seems to have consisted in lighting small fires to char the parts to be chipped away, and repeating the process again and again until the body of the canoe had been suitably hollowed out. In Neolithic times, too, beautifully made, and often quite small, wooden vessels were carved and hollowed out of solid wood, but there is no evidence to show how the hollowing was effected.

To summarize, we may say that throughout the period of the Stone Age, from its inception to the dawn of the use of metal, techniques for working stone into implements and tools, and later into domestic utensils, evolved slowly and gradually, and were carefully worked out to achieve the purposes for which they were designed. On the other hand, techniques for working wood and bone appear to have remained very simple, and to have been confined to cutting, chopping, adzing, scraping, and, very rarely, sawing. Great care was taken to devise speedy and efficient methods of making tools and weapons of stone, while the working of bone, ivory, and wood with these stone tools remained a slow and simple process without any major elaborations or developments of technique throughout the period.

7

GRAPHIC AND PLASTIC ARTS

L. S. B. LEAKEY

I. ORIGINS OF PALAEOLITHIC ART

HOW and why did it first occur to man to make images of parts of his world? Did plastic or graphic art come first? The answers to these and kindred questions can, at best, be no more than guesses. Nevertheless, it is certain that the mere making of an image proclaims its maker human. Such an achievement is even farther from the powers of a pre-human animal than is the shaping of a tool or articulate and purposeful speech.

One of the guesses as to how man came to picture the animals around him, or very occasionally his fellow men, is that he was aroused to do so by the mystery of the shadow. This seemed at certain times to follow and mock him, and to imitate his gestures. The painting or drawing of the figure of an animal may have seemed to place the animal so depicted in the power of the painter by, as it were, fixing its shadow (p 146). Who shall say? These are the merest conjectures. They belong rather to a mystical psychology than to a genuine science of man.

The simplest of all techniques of drawing—older than any of the other that will be discussed, yet one for which we have little positive evidence, because of its very nature—is drawing with the finger. Long before man attempted to mix colours with which to paint, or to make special tools for engraving on hard substances, he must have made rough drawings in the earth with his finger-tips, as children often do. Inevitably, such transient manifestations of art are mostly lost, but, by rare chance, a few examples have survived under somewhat surprising conditions. A part of the ceiling of the huge subterranean cavern of Pech-Merle in France (figure 65) is covered with a thin layer of clay kept perpetually damp by moisture seeping through the rock above. At several places, this damp clay ceiling carries drawings made by the finger-tips of prehistoric man in remote Upper Palaeolithic times. A few similar examples are known in other French caves, while there are also some drawings in clay on the floor of the cave of Tuc d'Audoubert, where the clay bisons are preserved. Thus, by the happy chance that artists of the later Palaeolithic occasionally used a surface which has never since been trampled on, which has never dried out, which has been sealed in for thousands of years by rock-falls, and which has remained to be rediscovered in modern times, we know that this simple technique was among those practised by Stone Age man. These few surviving examples are relatively late, but, as has been indicated, they represent what was probably the earliest technique to be employed in art.

Is it possible to say at what stage in human history the idea of artistic expression was born? Only under very exceptional circumstances do examples of early

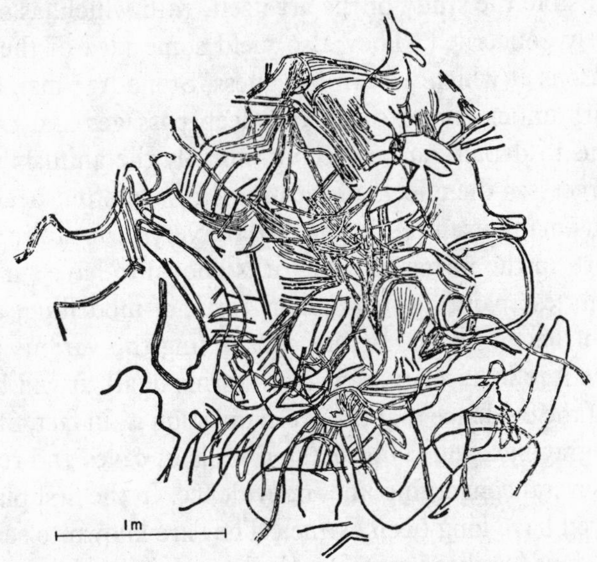

FIGURE 65—*Part of the ceiling of one of the caves at Pech-Merle, Lot, France. Representations of human and animal figures.*

prehistoric art survive for us to study, but, judging by what we know of the art of modern primitive peoples, it seems more than likely that many of the early expressions of graphic art practised by Stone Age man were executed on such perishable materials as the smooth bark of certain kinds of tree, very soft rock exposed to weathering, and similar surfaces. So too, and also by analogy with modern primitive peoples, we may assume that many early examples of plastic art and carving were made in such impermanent substances as unbaked clay and wood.

II. DATING OF PALAEOLITHIC WORKS OF ART

During the Upper Palaeolithic period in some parts of the world, more particularly in south-west Europe and in parts of Africa, man took to living in rock-shelters and in the mouths of caves. It is fortunate for our study of his powers and mentality that he often decorated the walls of these living-sites with paintings and other examples of his art. There is reason to suppose that he believed that these images tended to bring the creatures depicted within his power as hunter, and that the representations are thus exhibitions of sympathetic magic. In those cases where the walls of the caves and shelters were of particularly hard rock, or where circumstances prevented the weathering of the rock face, excellent examples of Palaeolithic drawings, paintings, and even bas-reliefs have survived. These make possible the study of the art itself, with which, as such, we are not here immediately concerned. They also yield some idea of the techniques involved. For reasons at which we can but guess, Stone Age man commonly used the walls of dark underground caves and deep passages and crevices in limestone formations to depict various scenes, notably the animals that he hunted. In the remote recesses the effects of weathering have often been slight or even negligible. Thus many examples of his art are very beautifully preserved.

Prehistoric art, in the forms in which it is known to have survived, falls into five main categories: painting, engraving, carving, modelling, and drawing in soft media with the finger-tip. Before considering the various techniques employed by Stone Age man for these various forms of art, it will be well to touch on the nature of the evidence that the art in question is, in fact, of the Stone Age.

Paintings, engravings, and sculptures on walls of caves and rock-shelters can be dated from several converging lines of evidence. In the first place, some of the animals portrayed have long been extinct. They are known to science only from the evidence of their fossilized remains. Such remains can be dated on geological and palaeontological grounds. When, for example, we find in a French cave a painting of a mammoth or a woolly rhinoceros, evidently portrayed by one familiar with the living animal, we can say with certainty that this painting cannot be younger than such and such a geological period, for after that time the creature was extinct. Even with animals that are not extinct, such as the reindeer, we can learn from geology, palaeontology, and the study of past climates when it was that these creatures last inhabited the region. We can then confidently say that this painting, clearly done from life, cannot be younger than such and such a period. Similarly, though some of the animals represented may have survived in the areas where the paintings occur long after the end of the Stone Age, we can still often date the painting by showing that it is executed in an identical style, and by the same technique, as were used for the painting or engraving of other, but extinct, animals at the same or a neighbouring or a comparable site.

Another line of evidence for dating prehistoric art is to be found when blocks of stone with paintings or engravings on them have, as is not infrequent, fallen from their original positions and become buried in the floors of the rock-shelters by cave-earth, and material from hearths, which contain Stone Age tools identifiable with some particular culture. Clearly, since the paintings are buried beneath the remains of that culture, they must belong to an earlier date.

Again, the artists who decorated the walls of caves and rock-shelters often made engravings and occasionally paintings on pieces of bone or ivory, or on small stones. These, when found in a Stone Age cultural level, link the art with the culture. By studying the styles of these engravings and so on, and comparing them with the styles of painting on the walls of caves and rock-shelters, it becomes possible to link a particular style with a particular cultural stage. In the case of paintings, it is often possible to find examples of the particular colouring materials used for the wall-paintings in a cultural level deep in the floor of a cave or rock-shelter, and thus again obtain a link between a culture and some particular paintings.

III. TECHNIQUES USED IN PALAEOLITHIC PAINTING

Some few details of the pigments used for the cave paintings of Altamira (Spain) and Lascaux (France) are known. The primary pigments were natural iron and manganese oxides, giving red and black colours, and yellow carbonates of iron. At Lascaux, a blue-black and a dark brown manganese oxide were found. White occurs quite early in certain prehistoric paintings in Africa. Carbon blacks were derived most probably from soot. The pigments were finely ground with pestle and mortar (figures 66, 67), and mixed with a suitable medium, in most cases aqueous rather than fatty. They were stored in hollow stones or bones, large shells, and even human skulls; decorated receptacles for paint have been found at Les Cottes, Vienne. Stone lamps illuminated the dark recesses of the caves (figure 150).

FIGURE 66—*Pestle in mammoth ivory from Věstonice, Moravia.*

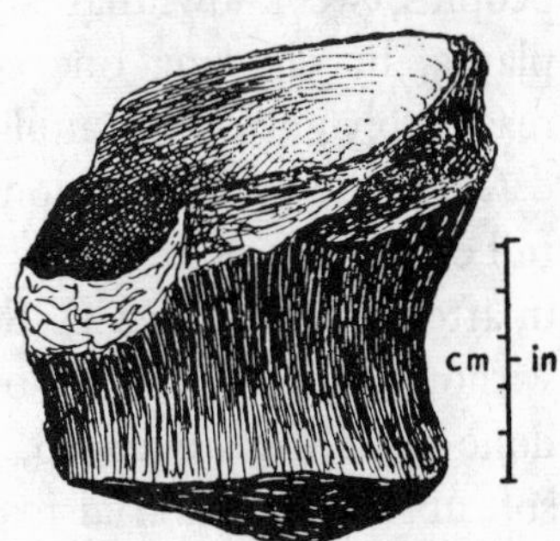

FIGURE 67—*Broken chalk mortar for grinding colours. Dordogne, France.*

Many of the well known cave paintings in Europe are, unfortunately, in such a bad state of preservation that it is difficult, if not impossible, to obtain any idea of the actual techniques employed by Stone Age man. The early use of the finger-tip dipped in paint is fairly obvious, and it is apparent that primitive brushes of various sizes were used for the finer details. The bodies of the larger animals depicted in Franco-Cantabrian art may have been filled in with a broad brush, or by daubing with pads. It is often supposed that a spray technique may have been used in some cases, but it must be admitted that daubing with a pad can lead to very similar results.

(*a*) *Painting with the Finger-tip*. This was the earliest form of 'brush' employed. Examples of prehistoric painting, particularly of outline paintings of animals in thick lines, are widespread. Close examination leaves no doubt that they were done with a finger dipped in the paint (figure 68). This technique of painting is still widespread among primitive peoples.

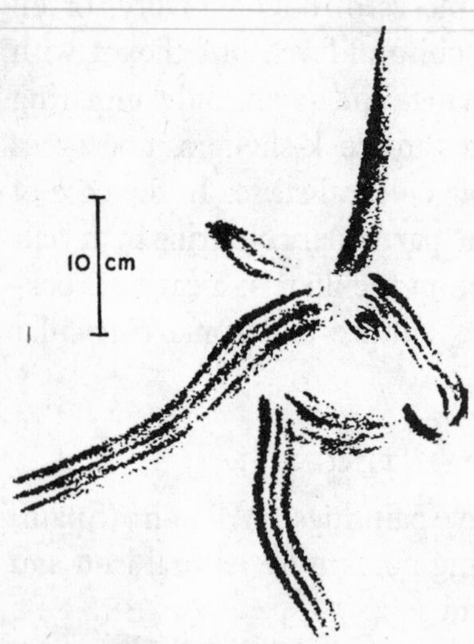

FIGURE 68—*Stag painted with the finger-tip from the cave la Pileta at Benoajan, Malaga, Spain.*

(*b*) *Painting with Brushes*. Numerous paintings have lines so thin that a different technique must have been used. An examination of these paintings suggests that some were executed with a solid point dipped in paint—perhaps a sharpened piece of wood or quill. At Altamira, the dark outline and more salient features are painted with a well-pointed brush dipped in paint of a full black or some other strong colour (plate 2 A). Others exhibit traces of what we may call brushwork, indicating the use of a primitive brush of some sort. From the study of modern primitive peoples, we know that simple brushes can be made from twigs of fibrous plants, by chewing one end until the fibres become decorticated. We may reasonably guess that similar primitive brushes were used by Stone Age artists.

(*c*) *Daubing*. In addition to paintings in outline, there are many examples in full colour. Sometimes the outline was carefully drawn first, and the body filled in afterwards (plate 2 A). Sometimes the whole painting was done by daubing, without any preliminary outline. While some of this filling-in may have been done with the finger-tip, in other examples the appearance suggests that a soft absorbent material may have been used, such as moss or animal fur, first dipped in the paint and then dabbed on the painting.

(*d*) *Spray Painting*. To present-day people the term spray-painting suggests a modern technique involving ingenious devices and machinery. Yet it is possible that this technique is of very great antiquity. Negative outlines of the human hand, with the fingers splayed, are not uncommon, and experiment has shown that this effect can be produced by placing the hand against a suitable surface and then taking a mouthful of paint and spraying it from between the lips.

Examination of some of the polychrome paintings of prehistoric times suggests that a similar method of spray-painting may have been employed to obtain the peculiar blending of colours in areas where two different colours overlap.

(*e*) *Dot Painting*. Another peculiar technique occasionally employed by prehistoric man was that whereby the entire painting of an animal, or sometimes the outline only, was carried out by dipping a stamp of some sort into the paint and applying the colour in a series of small dots (plate 2 B). This stamp was perhaps a stick, sometimes padded at the working end with fur.

(*f*) *Dry-point Techniques*. The discovery of pointed crayons made of mineral colouring materials in cultural levels of some prehistoric sites, and an examination of actual paintings, make it probable that some paintings were carried out by means of a dry crayon technique. Charcoal and other soft colouring materials were probably used in this way.

IV. PALAEOLITHIC ENGRAVING

In prehistoric times, engraved art was produced by one of two basic techniques: (*a*) by incised lines, and (*b*) by a process of pecking. There are also some examples of polished outlines.

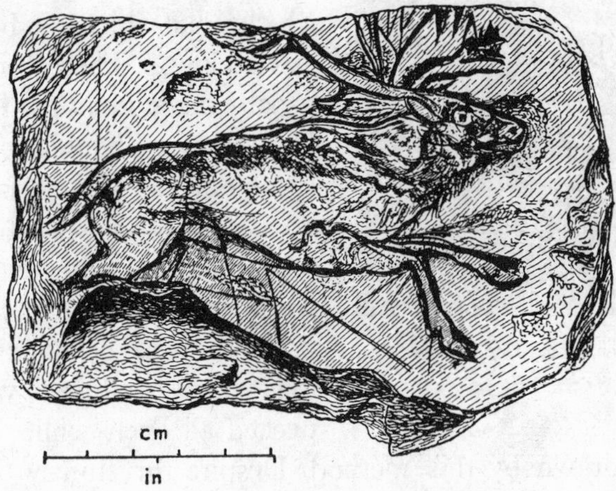

FIGURE 69—*Galloping reindeer engraved on a plaque of schist. Saint Marcel, Indre, France.*

(*a*) *Incised Engravings*. The vast majority of prehistoric engravings were made by incised lines, cut either on rock-faces or small stones, or on pieces of bone, antler, or ivory (figure 69). There is considerable evidence in Europe to show that the engraving tool was mainly a burin or graver made specially (figure 59).

This evidence is mostly indirect, and is based upon the fact that the Stone Age cultures in which engraved objects are commonly found include among their implements a high proportion of gravers of different shapes and types. There is also, but rarely, evidence in the discovery of worn flint gravers lying on ledges just below rock-faces covered with engravings made by Stone Age man.

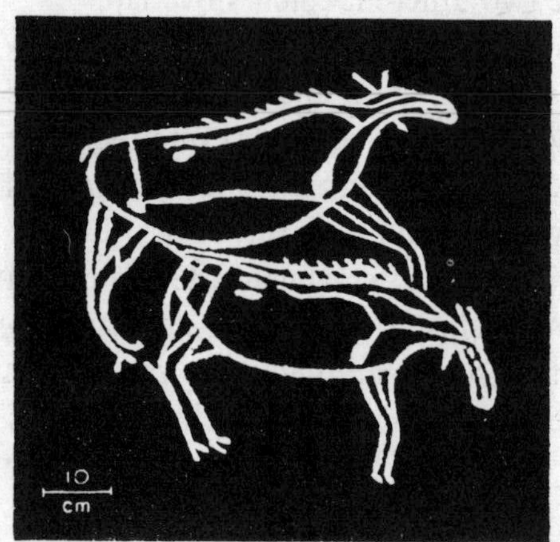

FIGURE 70—*Pecked engraving on rock of elks. Gjeithus, Norway.*

Outside Europe, there is little evidence as to what type of stone tool was used for incised engravings. Thus, in the Union of South Africa and in Libya, many prehistoric engravings are found under conditions which would seem to link them with Stone Age cultures in which the burin was either totally absent or very rare. In these places, there is nothing to indicate what type of tool was used in its place.

FIGURE 71—*Polished rock drawing of a brown bear from Valle, Sweden.*

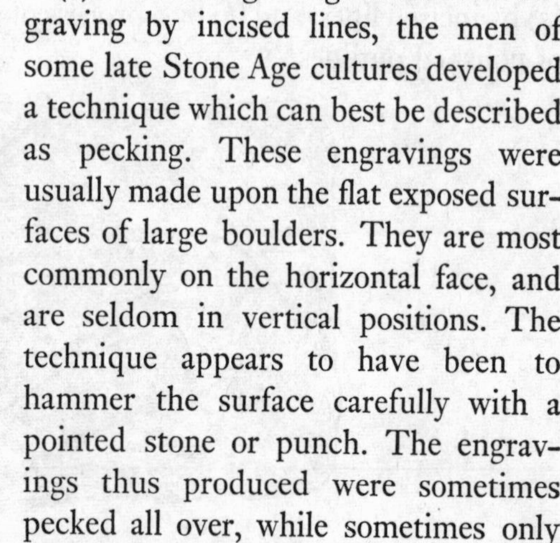

(*b*) *Pecked Engravings.* Instead of engraving by incised lines, the men of some late Stone Age cultures developed a technique which can best be described as pecking. These engravings were usually made upon the flat exposed surfaces of large boulders. They are most commonly on the horizontal face, and are seldom in vertical positions. The technique appears to have been to hammer the surface carefully with a pointed stone or punch. The engravings thus produced were sometimes pecked all over, while sometimes only the outline was drawn by this method. Despite the clumsy technique, some remarkably good results were obtained (figure 70).

(*c*) *Polished Outline.* On the coast of Norwegian Nordland are some monumental Stone Age rock pictures of animals, drawn life-size and depicted with great accuracy and beauty of line. Their contours, instead of being cut into the rock, show a smooth surface which was probably achieved by polishing the stone with wood, sand, and water. These polished outlines have resisted erosion better than the surface of the rock itself, so that they now stand out in relief (figure 71).

Before leaving prehistoric painting and engraving, it must be mentioned that there are many examples of animals portrayed by a combination of both engraving and painting. The well known 'sorcerer' from Trois-Frères (figure 72), the reindeer from Font-de-Gaume, and some of the Altamira bisons were done in this way. In these cases, the outline was usually engraved first, and the heated grease paint was brushed in, in a fairly thin form, to reinforce and supplement the engraved outline.

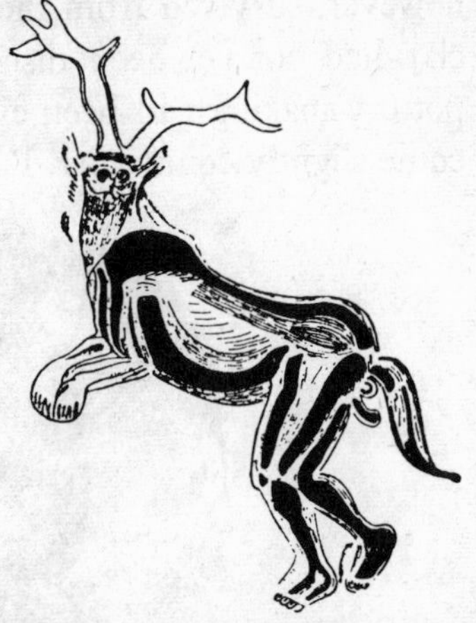

FIGURE 72—*Sorcerer portrayed by engraving and painting combined, from the cave Trois-Frères, Ariège, France. He has the horns of a stag, the face of an owl, the ears of a wolf, the fore-legs of a bear, and the tail of a horse.*

V. PALAEOLITHIC PLASTIC ART

The plastic art of the Stone Age can be divided into two major groups, neither as often preserved as are examples of painting and engraving; they are modelling in bas-relief and modelling in the round. The scarcity of examples of these forms of art among prehistoric discoveries can be accounted for by the fact that neither lends itself to preservation over a long period of time. Sculptured objects, because of their more enduring media, are commoner than modellings, though they too are rare enough.

(*a*) *Modelling in Relief.* Examples have survived only under the most exceptional circumstances. Most famous are the clay bisons of Tuc d'Audoubert, executed in exceptionally high relief (figure 73). In this type of modelling, masses of wet clay were built up against a fallen slab of rock which acted as a support on one side, the modelling being confined to the uppermost side. The result was a sort of relief statue in clay. Such statues can naturally continue to exist for long ages only in the deep recesses of caves which have remained damp but not waterlogged since the modelling was completed, and have also been cut off from access by some accident of nature, such as an earthquake. They have thus remained sealed in, until discovery and preservation by prehistorians of today. The modelling seems to have been done mostly with the bare hands, but details such as the eyes and manes were probably finished off with a pointed stick or stone.

(*b*) *Modelling in the Round.* If we may judge by comparison with modern primitive peoples, the early artists of the Stone Age probably often made models from clay and mud. Only a very few examples of this type of artistic work have, however, survived from the Upper Palaeolithic period, when the art of baking clay had not yet been discovered. Toward the end of the Stone Age, when pottery-making had been evolved, baked clay models of animals and so on become slightly commoner. Pottery vessels were moulded in the shape of animals.

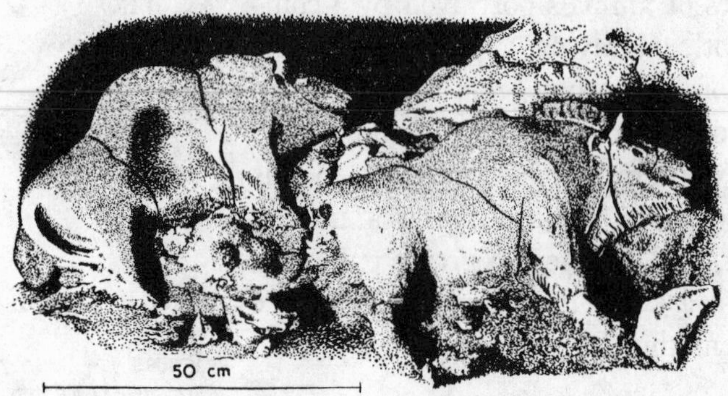

FIGURE 73—*Bisons modelled in clay from the cave Tuc d'Audoubert, Ariège, France.*

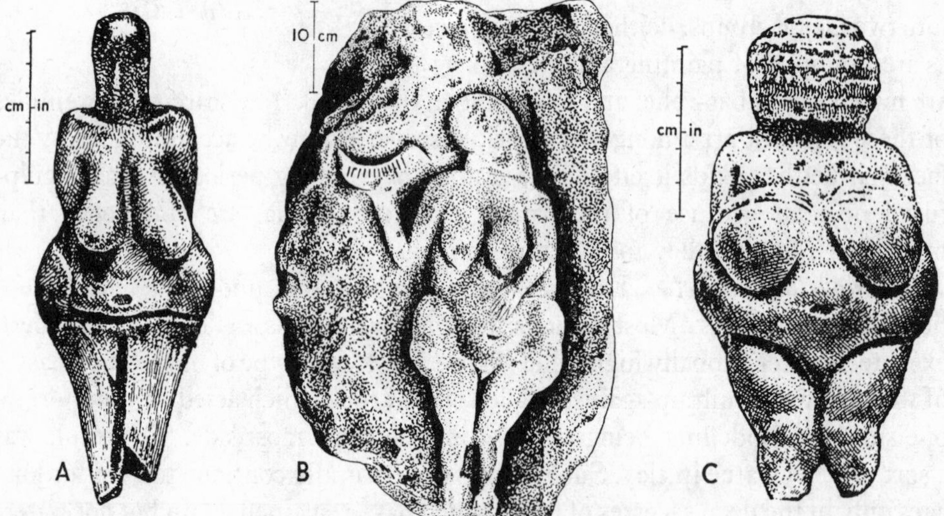

FIGURE 74—*Female figures from:* (A) *Věstonice, Moravia;* (B) *Laussel, Dordogne, France;* (C) *Willendorf, Lower Austria.*

Of early modelled art, the little figurines from Věstonice are perhaps the most worthy of note. They are made of clay mixed with pulverized mammoth-bone to provide grit, and are unbaked (figure 74 A).

At Montespan a headless bear made of clay was found, with the skull of a cave-bear lying between its paws. The Abbé Breuil considers that the head of a bear was fixed on to the neck of the clay model, the whole probably being covered with the bear's skin, for the purpose of some ceremony.

VI. SCULPTURE

Sculptured art appears from an early period of the Upper Palaeolithic and is preserved in the form of little carved objects in ivory, antler, and stone, and especially in magnificent bas-relief sculptured friezes on the walls of some rock-shelters, such as the horses at Cap-Blanc, Laussel, Dordogne. Again we must distinguish between work in bas-relief and in the round.

The carving of large and sometimes life-size bas-relief sculptures on the limestone walls of rock-shelters and caves must have been a slow and laborious process in Upper Palaeolithic times (figure 74 B). The sculptures themselves give very few clues as to the techniques employed. Whenever possible, the artist certainly made the greatest possible use of natural features in the uneven rock face. Such tool-marks as are preserved suggest that, in part at least, the work was carried out with fairly small burins.

The relatively large number of finds of small objects in ivory and the like, ranging from figurines of pregnant women to heads of animals, strongly suggests that, before the carving was carried out in these hard materials, there had been a long period of development when wood and other soft materials were used. We may safely assume that the earliest known examples are not in fact the earliest efforts at sculpture by Stone Age man.

The sculpturing of ivory and antler seems to have been executed with the aid of burins, concave scrapers, stone knives, and occasionally small saws. There is nothing to show that any very specialized technique was employed. Many examples of sculpture in hard rock have been found, such as the limestone 'Venus' of Willendorf, near Krems, Lower Austria (figure 74 C).

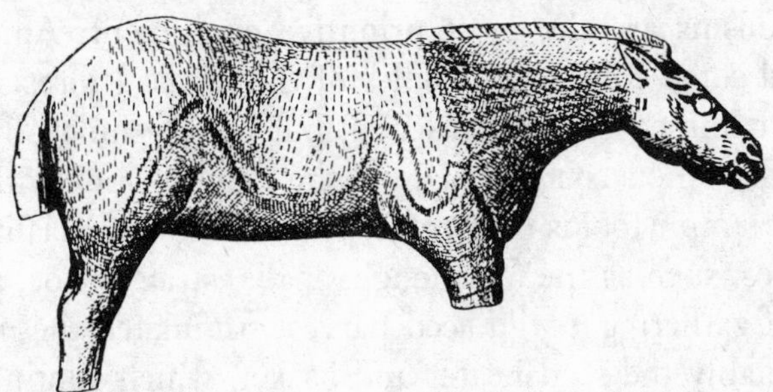

Ivory horse from the cave at Espélugues, near Lourdes. Length 7·5 cm.

8

FORAGING, HUNTING, AND FISHING

DARYLL FORDE

I. TECHNIQUES AND TYPES OF WEAPON

THE sole means whereby the human species obtained its food and raw materials for far the greater part of its history was by foraging, hunting, fishing, or trapping. These basic procedures man shares with the rest of the animal kingdom. Techniques of food collection and storage used by man correspond, to this extent, to those of his sub-human precursors [1]. For at least 95 per cent of his history he was completely dependent on food-gathering techniques (ch 2). The remoter history of these techniques is being revealed piecemeal by archaeology, but much can also be learned from peoples who are, or were till recently, food-gatherers. While such practices may often be studied among peoples who have long been occupied with agriculture or stock-breeding, the potentialities and limitations of the foraging techniques are best observed among the many small human groups which lack these later crafts. Food-gatherers survived till recently in every climatic and vegetational zone. Understanding of the various techniques that they employ is necessarily associated with some consideration of their economies.

(*a*) *Foraging Tools and Techniques.* Among the true hunting peoples, foraging for immobile or slow-moving resources may be of minor importance, though under some conditions it may provide the major food-supply, as among the aboriginal Californian gatherers of wild acorns and buck-eye nuts.

Staves, as for knocking down fruits, prizing shell-fish from rocks, and digging for buried organisms are the most primitive equipment. Among the extinct Tasmanians and some collecting peoples of the tropical forests, digging-sticks may be merely trimmed or fire-hardened, but the Bushmen, who had to deal with hard-pan near the surface, weighted the digging-stick with a bored stone (figure 33). This simple tool is the prototype of a host of specialized instruments in higher cultures, such as the footplough, spade, straight hoe, and fork.

The labour of gathering a wild seed-harvest stimulated the invention of collecting tools, notably the seed-beater and basket, which continue to play their part among many non-agricultural peoples. Thus women of the Paviotso, of the

North American Sierra Nevada, sweep a fan-shaped beater across the heads of the ripe low grasses, gathering the seeds into a deep basket which they hold at the hip (figure 75). The development of basketry seems closely associated with the collection and storage of hard seeds (ch 16).

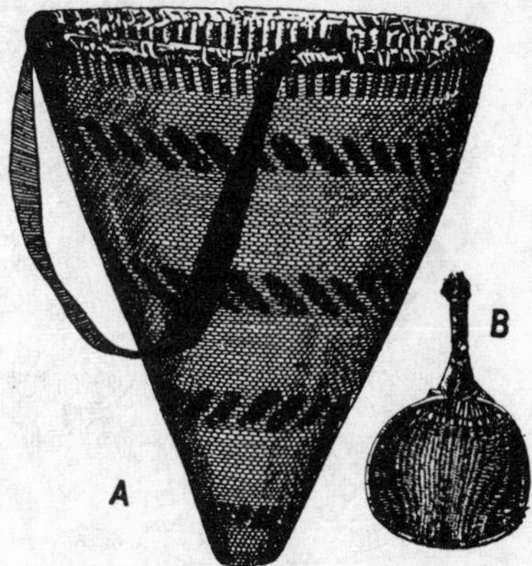

FIGURE 75—(A) *Paviotso seed-collecting basket.* (B) *Pomo seed-beater. North American Indian.*

Foraging has evoked techniques for the propagation of gathered plant products, from which agriculture developed (ch 14). Surviving peoples provide evidence of this development. Patches on which wild yams grew abundantly were protected, partially cleared, and transmitted from mother to daughter among some Australian aborigines. The seed-gathering Paviotso diverted mountain streams and dug channels to make the water from the melting snow fan out over the slopes, to increase the growth of wild grasses.

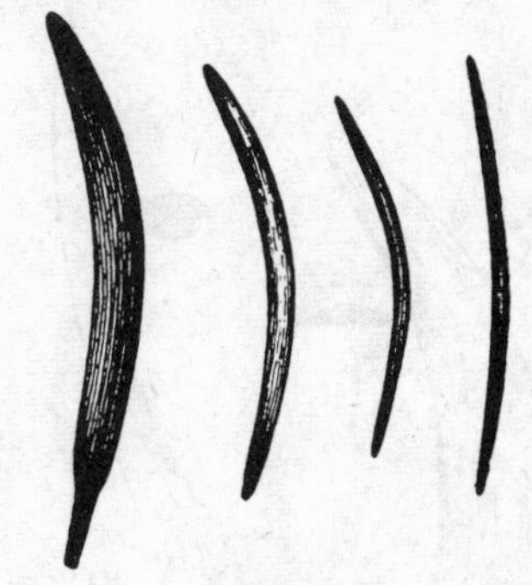
FIGURE 76—*Australian throwing-sticks ('boomerangs').*

(*b*) *Hunting and Fishing Devices* may be distinguished, according to their impact and effects as crushers—clubs, throwing-sticks, sling-stones, pellets, and dead-fall traps; as piercers—knives, spears, harpoons, arrows, blow-gun darts, concealed spikes, and fish-hooks; and as entanglers—pen-traps, spring-traps, noose-snares, lassos, bolas, and nets.

The distinction between hand, missile, and staged or untended instruments is also important. Within each of the latter categories, the several types of impact may be employed in different weapons.

FIGURE 77—*Arunta boy with throwing-stick. Australia.*

Wood billets were available before shaped instruments had been devised. To a species as vulnerable and slow as man, however, the club has limited usefulness in the chase and, like that used for stunning the impaled quarry by seal hunters and halibut fishers of the north-west American coast, is

FIGURE 78—*Fowling with throwing-sticks. From a tomb at Thebes, Egypt.* c *1400 B.C.*

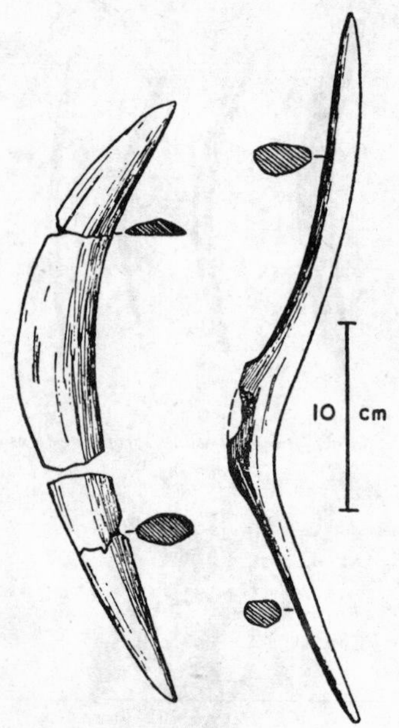

FIGURE 79—*Mesolithic wooden throwing-sticks from Jutland.*

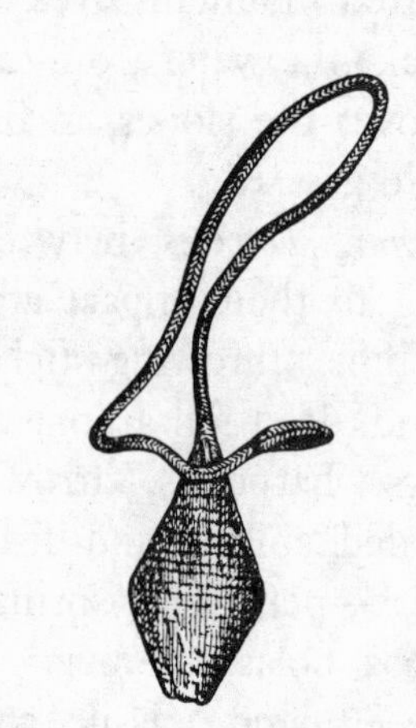

FIGURE 80—*Egyptian sling.* c *800 B.C.*

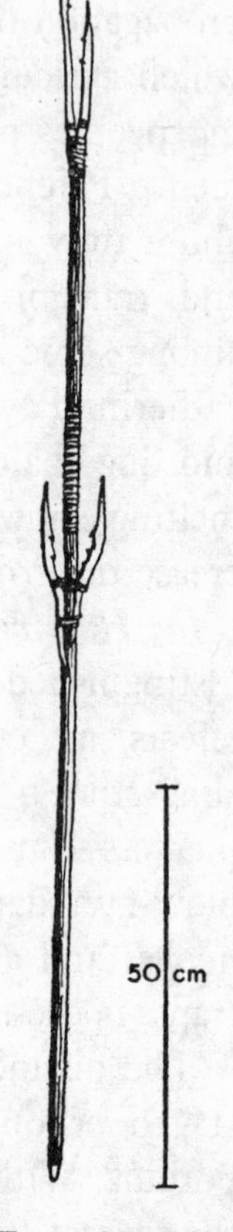

FIGURE 81—*Eskimo bird javelin.*

important only as a secondary weapon. Throwing-sticks, on the other hand, have continued in every continent as primary weapons in hunting smaller game. With the specialized form of throwing-stick, the boomerang, a very high degree of flight control can be obtained. The Australian boomerang is sickle shaped, with the arms slightly skew to one another as in a propeller (figures 76, 77). A cross-section shows one surface convex and the other plane. Boomerangs are also to be found in south India, Africa, and North America, and were used in ancient Egypt and Mesolithic Europe (figures 78, 79, 98).

Missile-stones have been used more in fighting than in hunting. To the simple techniques of hand-throwing—wherein many primitive peoples achieve great accuracy—was added the sling. This was probably a very early device, for shaped missile-stones have been found in Upper Palaeolithic sites in Europe. The sling was later figured on Mycenaean monuments, is recorded in 1 Samuel xvii and

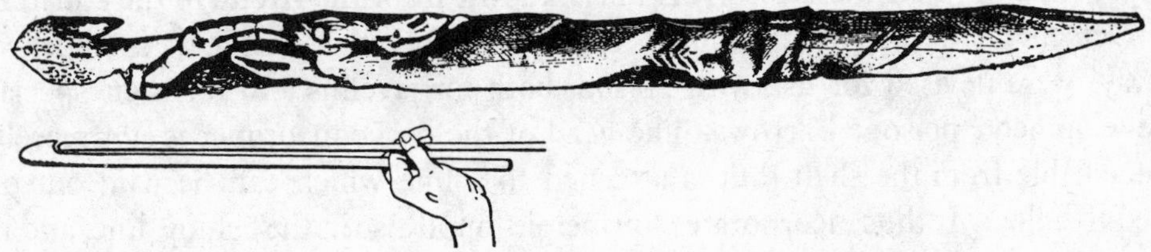

FIGURE 82—*Magdalenian (Upper Palaeolithic) spear-thrower carved in antler. Mas d'Azil, France.* Below. *Spear-thrower in use by Australian aborigine.*

other places in the Bible, was widespread in Bronze Age Europe, and is familiar to many primitive peoples in both the Old and New Worlds (figure 80). The pellet shot from bow or tube is also used for stunning small game, especially birds.

Piercers, both thrusting and missile, have been more generally effective in hunting. They have been elaborately developed from Early Palaeolithic times against fast-moving animals. The very large yield of food, skins, sinews, bone, and horn from such creatures stimulated specialization. From the simple stave, which could be used indifferently for digging, thrusting, or throwing, whole families of piercing weapons were early developed.

The spear, at first a mere stiff sapling with point sharpened by stone-trimming or burning, was early specialized and barbed into a heavy lance for thrusting, and into a missile or javelin. Even in Palaeolithic times spears were probably universal (figure 18). With technical advances in working wood, stone, bone, and metal, and the devising of bindings, they became increasingly well shaped, balanced, and fitted with heads of great variety for many different purposes. Spear-heads were shaped to penetrate deeply, and the points multiplied to increase the chance of striking elusive targets, such as birds and fish (figure 81). Barbs (figure 88) were already a device of Palaeolithic man, and detachable heads were developed to retain the spear-head in the wound. Finally, spears have been incorporated in pit, trip-line, and spring-traps.

Propulsive force and range were increased by spear-thrower and bow, both familiar to some later Palaeolithic peoples. The line-held detachable head or harpoon-point was adapted for both lance and javelin, including the bow-shot arrow. That the spear-thrower was devised earlier than the bow is suggested both by its wide distribution and by archaeological evidence. It was in use by the reindeer-hunting Magdalenians of the park-tundra in Late Glacial Europe, and in historic time among the Australian aborigines ignorant of the bow, as well as among the Eskimo of the circumpolar belt and the natives of New Guinea (figures 82, 83). In the New World it is known from the Arctic to the equator.

Detachable heads, which remain in the wound even if the shaft is knocked away, were devised for use with poison, both for javelins and for their special development, poisoned arrows. The head of the harpoon proper is not merely detachable from the shaft, but is attached to a line which can be paid out or tied to a float. It thus incorporates a principle found also in the fishing-line, and is specially associated with the hunting of aquatic animals, which can quickly dive beyond recovery. Among the central Eskimo, the line of the thrusting harpoon is attached to a float when hunting seals at sea (figure 84), or may be paid out by the hunter in ice-hole hunting (figure 108). The line in the missile harpoon may be coiled on the shaft itself, which then serves as a float.

The primitive harpoon of the Fuegians has a long barbed bone point fitted detachably into a slit in the end of the shaft, and is also tied to the shaft by a short rawhide thong. The head cannot be completely buried in the quarry, and the shaft serves only as a drag at close quarters. As the Fuegians also used a spear with a non-detachable but slit-socketed and hide-bound bone point, they appear to have preserved both the pre- and the proto-harpoon stages of this invention (figures 85, 86).

More efficient harpoons, including harpoon-arrows, are widely used in north-western America against seal and porpoise, in South America against turtle, and in Africa against the hippopotamus. They are so designed that the hollow or socket at the point of detachment is in the head, and not on the shaft, of the harpoon (figure 87). The head can thus be completely embedded in the quarry before detachment, and is held at its base on a long line.

Finally, in the most elaborate of primitive harpoons, the toggle-headed Eskimo harpoon, the line is fixed not to the base of the socketed point but mid-way (figure 109). Thus the point is turned transversely in the wound by the pull of the line, and so is more firmly held. These harpoons have also a flexible shaft. The lashed joint between the main and the fore shafts allows sufficient play to facilitate the detachment on impact of the head, which was previously held rigid by the

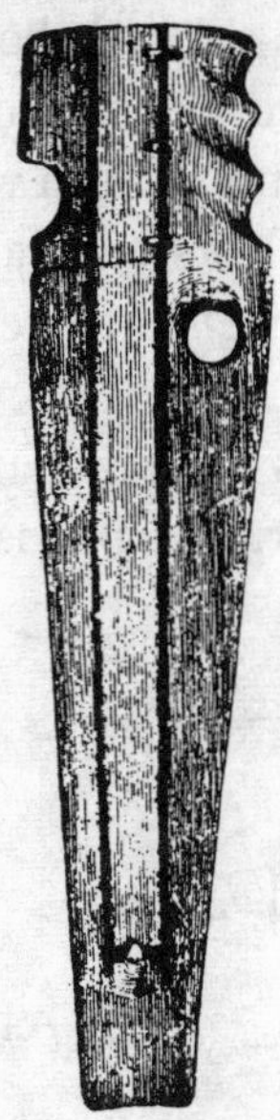

FIGURE 83—*Eskimo spear-thrower with hand grip.*

FIGURE 84—*Eskimo seal-skin floats and drogue.*

FIGURE 85—*Yahgan javelin, with slit-socketed hide-bound bone point. Tierra del Fuego. Length of blade* 10·75 *inches*

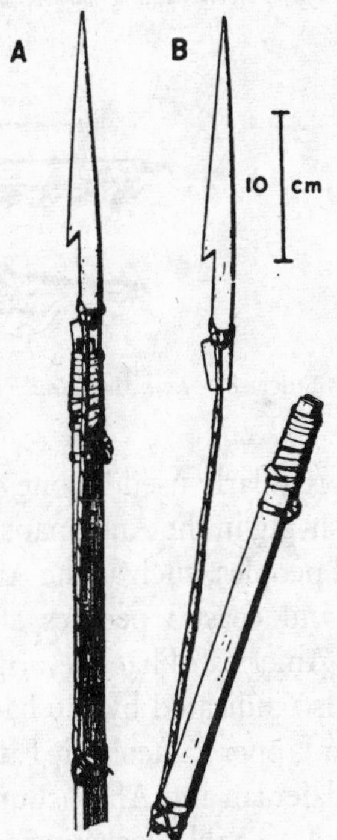

FIGURE 86—*Yahgan proto-harpoon.* (A) *Assembled for casting.* (B) *Position when dragging through the water. Tierra del Fuego.*

line connecting it to the main shaft. The Eskimo have applied these principles both to the heavy thrusting harpoon used against seal and walrus and to harpoon-arrows employed against sea-otters in Alaska. The second type, in which the line is wound round the arrow-shaft which, after impact, floats vertically to expose the feathered butt as a marker, is widely recognized as a masterpiece of primitive technique.

The spear-thrower as among the Eskimo, the bow as in Brazil, and the blow-pipe as in south India, have all been employed to discharge harpoons, which have

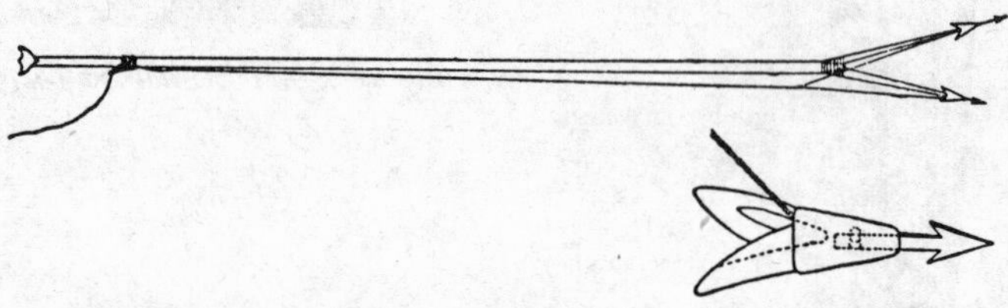

FIGURE 87—*Nootka sealing harpoon with* (below) *detail of harpoon-head. Length of shaft 12 ft. British Columbia.*

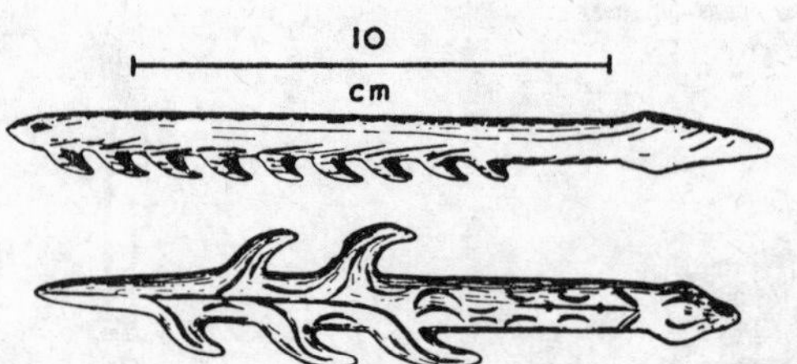

FIGURE 88—*Late Magdalenian* (*Upper Palaeolithic*) *harpoon-heads of reindeer antler.*

also been regularly used by one or another people in hunting land animals, such as the bush-pig in the Andamans. The types described above occur among widely separated peoples, such as the Andamanese, the people of Torres Strait and the Eskimo, and coastal peoples at both the northern and southern extremities of South America. That the origin of the harpoon device is of very great antiquity is also indicated by the barbed bone points of the Magdalenian reindeer-hunters in Upper Palaeolithic Europe (figure 88). The short swollen base of these late Magdalenian and Ahrensburgian harpoon-heads appears to be designed for loose and detachable socketing to the spear-shaft, but so far no complete spears have been found.

Spears with multiple points both at the tip and along the shaft have been widely used in Old World and New, to increase the chance of capturing swiftly moving animals. Such are the fish spears of marsh dwellers in Iraq, and the bird spears of the Eskimo. The same principle has been incorporated in the harpoon, e.g. the double-headed sealing harpoon used from canoes by the Nootka and other peoples of the north-west American coast (figures 81, 87).

In all these piercing weapons, as in fish-hooks, effectiveness is increased by the principle of the barb, which was known in Upper Palaeolithic Europe and widely used in the earliest Mesolithic cultures of the Nile valley. From serrations of the sides of the point have developed single and multiple backward projections or barbs. These are carved or hammered in the head itself, or formed of separately shaped attachments of stone, bone, shell, or metal.

FIGURE 89—*Upper Palaeolithic cave painting showing archers hunting stags. Cueva de los Caballos, Albocácer, Castellón, Spain.*

The bow is specially interesting as the first method of concentrating energy. Though there is clear evidence from Magdalenian art of the use of missile shafts, they were not necessarily projected from the bow; but the light, short flint-tipped projectiles of the Ahrensburgians imply a bow for their propulsion—as is confirmed by the occurrence of small-sectioned, grooved shaft-smoothers [2]. The first clear representation of the bow is from northern Africa, at a period corresponding to the middle phase of the Upper Palaeolithic in Europe, 30000–15000 B.C., when the present Sahara was largely grass and park land. It probably entered Europe by way of the Iberian peninsula, where it was used for hunting the warmer woodland fauna: deer, aurochs, and wild pig (figure 89). In both Spain and north Africa, Upper Palaeolithic sites yield tanged, barbed, and microlithic flint points suitable for arrow-heads. There is also evidence for the use of the bow in the hunting economies in south-west Asia about the same period, though whether it spread there from north Africa, and what was its early development in Asia, are uncertain. Australia and Tasmania form the only major region from which the bow has remained absent.

When, with the final retreat of the ice, tundra gave place to forest in central and western Europe, elk and, later, several species of deer and aurochs replaced the reindeer. These were hunted with bow and arrow by men of Mesolithic culture. Such was the setting of bows of elm from a peat bog at Holmegaard in Denmark (figure 90) [3]. In them, the stave is already of specialized form, being flat and expanded on either side of the round-sectioned central grip. The associated arrow-shafts had grooves near the tips, seemingly for insertion of flint barbs. Pointed, triangular, and, later, chisel-shaped flint tips for arrows long characterized Mesolithic cultures in post-glacial Europe (figure 324). Moreover, there is evidence that eagle feathers were the preferred choice, ritually transferring swiftness to Mesolithic arrows. The wide and ancient distribution of the

FIGURE 90—*Mesolithic bow-stave. Holmegaard, Denmark. Length about 145 cm.*

hunting-bow in Late Palaeolithic and Mesolithic times in the Old World makes probable its early spread to North America by way of north-eastern Asia.

The bow consists of either a single springy element of wood, horn, or antler—the simple bow—or of a number of elements. In the latter case, a distinction

FIGURE 91—*Compound-composite Eskimo bow of reindeer antler. Made of three pieces; the two side-pieces are riveted to the stout central slanting one. Strengthened by plaited sinews.*

should be made between a compound bow, that is, a number of shorter lengths which partially overlap, and a composite bow, in which, to increase elasticity, lengths of the same or another material are attached to an element which extends through the length of the bow. A bow may be at once compound and composite, as are some sinew-backed bows of the Eskimo and of certain Indians of the Plains (figure 91). In these bows, the stave is built up by glue and lashings from several shorter lengths of antler or horn or both (compound) before attaching the sinew backing which makes it composite.

The simple bow is commonly of some elastic wood, from palm and split bamboo to the yew of medieval England, but occasionally of a single length of horn or antler. It ranges in length from less than one metre, as with Kalahari Bushmen and Bronze Age Scandinavians, to over two metres among the Semang and Andamanese (figure 34). For functional reasons, a bow thins out at the ends, and has notches, perforations, or end-caps for the attachment of bowstrings. Hide, fibre, hair, sinew, and rattan-strip are among the substances used for bowstrings. The effective range of a simple bow will depend on many factors, but accurate and powerful impact, with low trajectory of several hundred feet, can be expected from the larger forms.

The compound bow is a response to the shortness of pieces of elastic material, notably in treeless regions, as with the Arctic Eskimo, who must rely on drift-wood, horn, or antler. The simplest and most widespread composite type, the sinew-backed bow, is found from south-eastern Europe, south-western, central, and northern Asia to north-western America. A band of animal sinew, corded, matted, or moulded, is glued or lashed (or both) to the outer, convex face of the stave. The added elasticity is such that the unstrung and the strung stave may curve in reverse directions. This type of bow was probably developed in high-latitude grassland, coniferous forest, or tundra, where inferior wood and horn are the only possible materials. The more complex bows, such as those of Siberian hunters and pastoralists (figure 92), usually have not only a sinew back-ing, but strips of horn attached to the inner, concave, face of the stave. In the higher civilizations of the south and west, notably in Persia and Turkey, finer craftsmanship produced light, highly elastic bows of multiple layers of wood, horn, sinew, and bone plates (figure 93). The Turkish bow, a short composite war weapon for the horseman, is said to have had a range of 500 metres, or twice that of the English long-bow, and to have been largely accountable for the extraordinary military success of the Turks in the later Middle Ages.

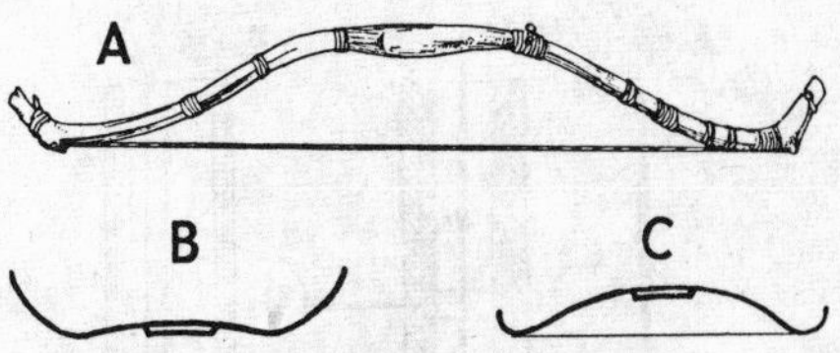

FIGURE 92—(A) *Bashkirian composite bow. The wooden stave is reinforced on the outer face with strips of sinew and on the inner with horn, and covered and bound with birch bark. The bow is shown released at* B, *strung at* C.

FIGURE 93—*The 'Turkish' horseman's bow. Represented on a Sassanian (Persian) silver dish. Fourth century A.D.*

The blow-gun is used to shoot miniature javelins by several peoples in south and east Asia, Indonesia, and tropical South America. Harnessing the propulsive force of the human thorax, its wooden darts are necessarily light, and seldom over a foot long. For killing-power they depend on poisons coating their breakable tips. The blow-gun is a tube, usually from one of the tropical reeds or giant grasses, between two and four metres long with internal diameter of 0·6 cm or less. A butt of pith with compacted down behind the dart prevents leakage of air (figures 94, 95). Simple, short reed tubes are used for fishing on the Malabar coast in India and in Amazonia, but the longer tubes needed for hunting must be of considerable strength; this involves fairly elaborate construction. One or

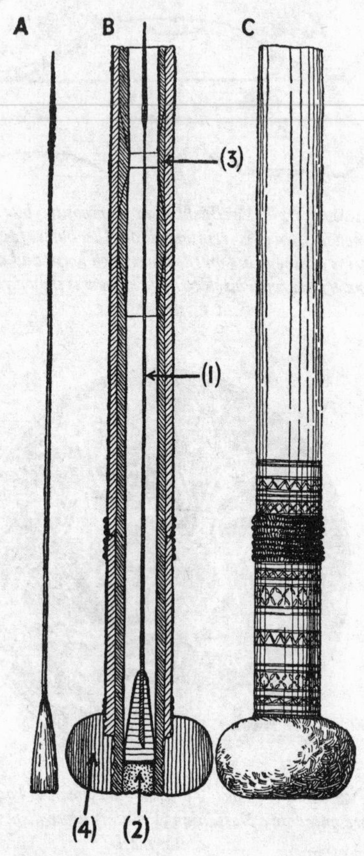

FIGURE 94—*Blow-gun and dart from the Malay Peninsula.* (A) *Dart with pith butt, coated with poison paste at the tip.* (B) *Cross-section of mouth end of gun with dart* (1) *resting on fibre wad* (2), *showing splicing of inner tube* (3), *and attachment of mouthpiece* (4). (C) *Exterior of mouth end.*

FIGURE 95—*Sakai with blow-guns. Malay Peninsula.*

more lengths of small sectioned reed or bamboo may be encased in a stouter tube. The inner tube of the blow-gun of the Sakai of the Malay peninsula, of the Punan of Borneo, and of other Indonesian peoples, is from a species of bamboo (*Bambus wrayi*) the internodes of which may be nearly two metres long. Two are fitted, end to end, inside a length of stouter bamboo the nodes of which have been punched out. Similar tube-in-tube techniques are used by the Guiana

Indians of South America. Alternative techniques in south India, Malaya, the Philippines, and Amazonia employ an outer cover formed by fitting together two artificially grooved pieces of straight wood, as of palm, to form a cylinder. The

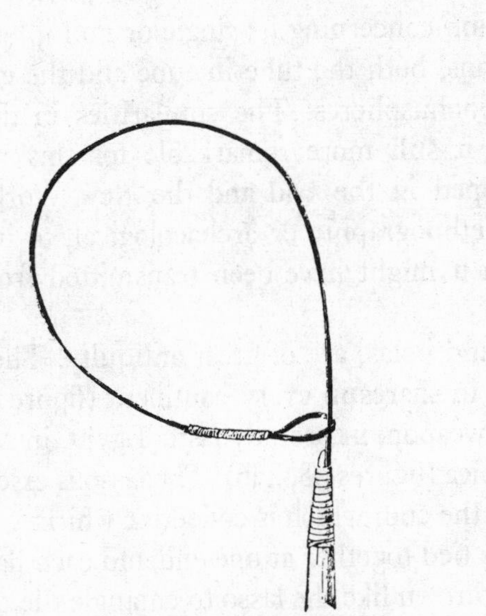

FIGURE 96—*Yahgan bird snare. Tierra del Fuego.*

FIGURE 97—*Bolas of the South American Tehuelche.*

FIGURE 98—*Hunting scenes on a stone palette from Abydos, Egypt. The lasso, throwing stick, spear, bow (with chisel-ended arrow), and club can be seen. Before 3000 B.C.*

making of a directly usable bored tube, as opposed to the covering, demands a metal chisel and is thus confined to the Old World (India and Borneo).

The blow-gun darts of the Sakai, about 20 cm long by 0·3 cm in diameter, are made from a piece of palm rib. The point, notched to break off in the wound, is smeared with upas poison, while the base is set in a blunt cone of pith which fits the tube. A fibre wad behind secures full air-pressure. Similar darts are used in Guiana and elsewhere in South America, where accurate shooting up to 50 metres is claimed. The extensive distribution of the blow-gun in two widely separated regions has raised discussion concerning its single or multiple invention. The more complex constructions, both the tube-in-tube and the grooved half-tube, are reported from both hemispheres. The similarities in the preparation of the darts would make it still more remarkable for this weapon to have been independently developed in the Old and the New World, but so far there is no direct evidence, ethnographic or archaeological, to indicate either a route or a period by which it might have been transmitted from one to the other.

Two entangling weapons, noose and bolas, are of great antiquity. The principle of the running noose is found in snares in every continent (figure 96). It was employed as the lasso, a missile weapon, in protodynastic Egypt, in Minoan Greece, and in pre-Columbian America (figures 98, 436). The lasso is essentially a long cord, with a running noose at the end, which is coiled for whirling before release. The bolas is a series of cords tied together at one end and each having a weight at the other (figure 97). It is thrown like the lasso to entangle the quarry. Used in the Americas at the extreme south, in Patagonia in hunting the guanaco and rhea, and at the extreme north in fowling by the Eskimo, and reported also in East Africa as a child's plaything, the invention may be very ancient.

Many varieties of primitive staged weapons, such as traps or pounds to which the quarry moves, have been long and widely employed. Land-nets strung in line, to which animals are driven, are widely used in forest hunting of smaller game (figure 99). Dip-nets, cast-nets, seines, and nets held vertically by floats and sinkers are widely used in rivers, estuaries, and lagoons. The main types of net, and the basic techniques of their manufacture, are so widely distributed that, like the cordage of which they are made, they must be among man's oldest inventions (p 451). There is some evidence of them in Palaeolithic art. The floated and weighted seine, handled by a boat-crew for fishing in smooth water, was in use in Mesolithic Europe, as is testified by preserved portions of nets with floats and sinkers from Finland (figure 282) and Estonia. Nets, hooks, and pronged spears were adapted for the abundant pike, which may already have been an important food-fish in Upper Palaeolithic times in the Baltic region.

The fishing-line may well be as ancient, for fish-hooks are used by primitive peoples in every region. Hooks range from the simple gorge—a centrally-tied

FIGURE 99—*Bas-relief showing Assyrians hunting with nets. Nineveh. Seventh century* B.C.

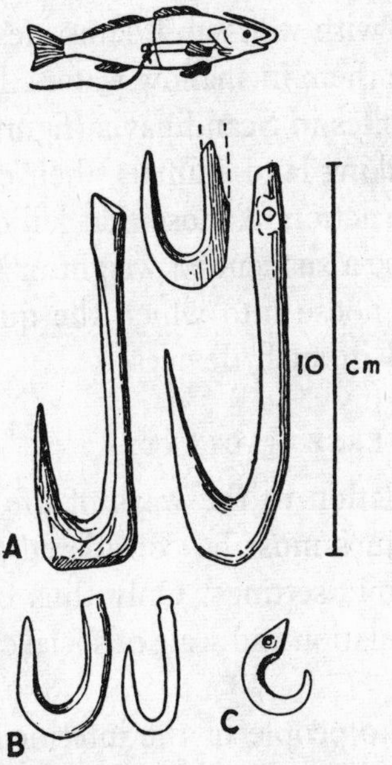

FIGURE 100—*Mesolithic and Neolithic fish-hooks.* (A) *Maglemosian; the fish shows a possible method of securing bait;* (B) *Natufian, bone;* (C) *Tasian, shell or horn.*

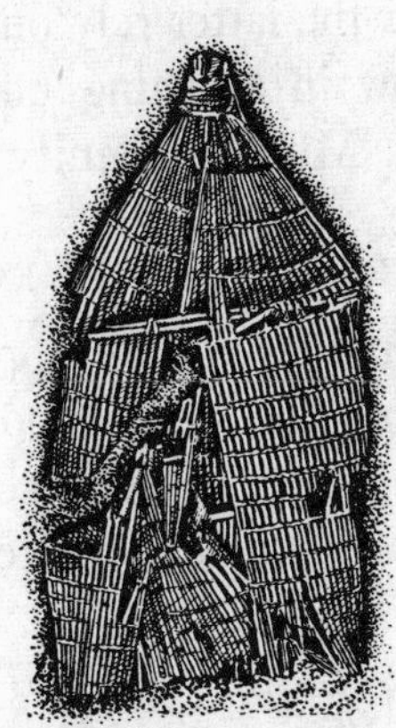

FIGURE 101—*Mesolithic basketry trap from Holbaek, Zealand. Width c 40 cm.*

pointed spike, which is attested for the Upper Palaeolithic from the Grimaldi caves—to elaborate composite forms with strong barbs, sometimes including elements of gleaming shell as lure. Fish-hooks are reported from Mesolithic sites in the Baltic [4] and Palestine [5], and are found in the most ancient predynastic Egyptian settlements (figures 100, 339). The Baltic peoples, at least, were using the later widespread practice of drilling to assist in carving the U-shaped hook from bone. V-shaped hooks did not appear until late in Mesolithic times, and in Neolithic settlements in central Europe, but were very early in Egypt. More specialized primitive fishers have designed hooks for particular fish, such as the horizontal U-shaped bentwood halibut hooks of the Nootka and Kwakiutl, which are, furthermore, set in groups on sunken wooden spreaders.

Primitive fish-traps are characteristically of the pen type, in which the entering fish, unable to turn or swim backward, is held at the narrow end, or prevented by the spiked ends of the internal opening from swimming out. Remains of funnel-entrance traps have been preserved from Mesolithic sites in Denmark. These world-wide forms are often associated with weirs and dams, designed to divert the fish into the traps or to concentrate them in shallow waters. Evidence of them is also reported [6] from Mesolithic sites in Scandinavia (figure 101).

Though pit- and cage-traps are used for taking land animals, their construction is laborious as compared with the construction of those that kill or maim. Most of the latter rely on a trip-line to release a suspended weight or spear, or an arrow in a strung bow, or to tighten a noose into which the quarry has entered. Much ingenuity has been exhibited in such devices.

II. TECHNIQUES AND ECONOMIES IN DIVERSE HABITATS

Techniques can be appreciated only in relation to the ways of life of their users, and specifically food-gathering techniques must be considered from region to region in their corresponding economic settings. Only thus can their significance for such matters as density of population and scale of social organization be assessed.

Tropical Rain-forests. The Semang, a negrito people of the interior forest of Malaya, illustrate primitive hunting and gathering techniques in exploitation of tropical rain-forest. There are here no large herds of game or continuous tracts of a plant species. Resources are fairly widespread, but scanty, so that the local group or band is necessarily small, with an upper limit of about twenty, including children. The chief supplies are vegetable foods, collected mainly by the women, who gather wild roots and tubers, and especially yams, nuts, leaves, and soft fruits. Roots and tubers, sometimes several feet deep, are obtained with a fire-pointed digging-stick. The produce is carried to the camp in rattan or bamboo baskets strapped to the back. Several of these foods, including the wild yam, contain poisonous juices, which are removed by prolonged soaking, grating, and fire-drying, or by steaming in a pulp mixed with ashes. Fruits, especially the durian (*Durio zibethinus*), are abundant at times, and provide a surplus for feasts. The fruit-trees are owned individually, though the harvest is largely shared by the camp. The Semang make no pottery, but cook food in lengths of green bamboo, which sufficiently resist charring.

Though the Semang are good bowmen and make an effective arrow-poison from the gum of the upas-tree, *Antiaris toxicaria*, their hunting is sporadic and confined to smaller game. Unlike the African pygmies, they dread and avoid the elephant. Wild pigs are their most prized game, but rats, squirrels, and birds are the more usual quarry. Their fairly powerful bow, up to two metres long, is made from a branch of langset or lanseh tree (*Lansium*), scraped down with stones and sharp slivers of bamboo. The upas poison on their wooden-tipped cane arrows will, when fresh, kill a monkey or wild pig in a few minutes. They snare game in simple noose- and spring-traps, and lime birds with the sticky sap of species of wild fig-tree. They originally had no dogs or other domestic animals. Fish are driven into narrow places where they can be speared; small fry are caught in bamboo scoops or basket fish-traps. No dams or weirs or fish poisons are used. They have no canoes, nets, or lines but improvise rafts to cross rivers.

Equipment, like food, comes mainly from vegetable sources. The bamboo is the main source of tools. Its toughness and the sharpness of its cut edges adapt it for many uses, from arrow-quivers and cooking-vessels to knives, fire-hardened slivers being used to cut the green bamboo itself. Animal bones are scraped down to make points, but stone tools are not specialized, and consist only of rough flakes picked up at need for the splitting and scraping of wood.

Each local group or band has its traditional territory of 20 square miles or so, over which its claim to occupation and the use of the more valuable resources is recognized among its neighbours; all may wander more widely in hunting and foraging. The storage of food is naturally difficult under the conditions of humid heat, and the Semang hardly attempt it. The band is not therefore closely tied to any one place by stores, dwelling, or equipment. It gathers its daily food as it moves, and has few relations with groups other than its immediate neighbours. As the major economic unit, it is organized round the spontaneous leadership of one of its older men.

The Sakai, who occupy the Malayan forests to the south of the Semang, appear to have somewhat modified their equipment by contact with Malayan cultivating peoples, from whom they may have adopted tree-houses and stockaded encampments; but their general pattern of life resembles that of the Semang. Their blow-gun, adopted from the Malays, appears to be as effective as the bow for small game at 20 to 30 metres (figure 95). Racially, the Sakai are unlike the Semang, for they are Australoid like the Vedda of Ceylon—who are, however, bow hunters. Blow-guns are used also by some negrito peoples in the Celebes, and by the Punan of central Borneo, who have an economy similar to that of the Sakai but are racially Malay. The blow-gun does not appear in Australia. It appears that there is no correlation between racial types and hunting techniques in south-east Asia.

Economies essentially similar to those of the Semang and Sakai, and based on the same hunting and foraging techniques, are found in many forest peoples in south-east Asia, among whom the Andaman Islanders are of special interest. The coastal groups have a larger and more secure food supply, including shell-fish and turtles, and this forms a basis for exchanges with the interior bands. They are also superior in equipment, using a more powerful bow, resembling a Melanesian form, and employing it with harpoons for both turtle and pig. The coastal groups have outrigger dug-out canoes. The equipment suggests influence from the more advanced peoples of the Nicobar Islands and the continental mainland.

A comparable hunting economy, based on bow and poisoned arrow, characterized areas in the Congo rain-forests, and has survived longest among certain negrito or pygmy groups. This economy is rendered more elaborate by the organization of drives for game. Nets capable of stopping and entangling deer and pig are set up across a considerable tract of forest. Several bands may co-operate in the drive into the nets, behind which bow- or spear-men are concealed.

African pygmies are also superior both in their boldness with the elephant and in constructing deadfalls and others traps equipped with poisoned spikes for large game. The Ituri forest pygmies are renowned for their intrepidity in spearing elephant. This has probably been encouraged by their dependence for vegetable food, bartered for meat and ivory, on agricultural negro village communities. The hunter, often alone, goes to a muddy pool frequented by elephant, and smears himself with mud to conceal his scent. His weapon is a short, metre-long, thrusting spear, of which a third is a razor-sharp iron head; it is provided by a headman in the negro village, who lends it. The hunter sneaks under a standing elephant, where it can neither see him nor reach him with its trunk, thrusts the spear into the belly and turns it in the wound as he slips aside and seeks cover in the forest [7].

The symbiotic relations in the Congo between pygmy hunting-groups and agricultural negro communities have resulted in the so-called silent trade. There is a tacit agreement of mutual non-interference between pygmies and cultivators, which affords the latter some security in moving along forest trails. The pygmies, after a successful hunt, are free to enter the gardens of the villages, leaving supplies of game in return for the food they collect.

Hunting-techniques essentially similar to those of the pygmies are reported from many agricultural peoples of the forested Congo–Guinea region of tropical Africa. Indeed, the indigenous economies of these areas combine hunting with hoe cultivation and small-stock rearing. Hunting-drives, on a larger scale than those among the pygmies, were formerly characteristic, greater stress being laid on the use of powerful bows with iron-tipped arrows than on stealth and poisons as employed by the pygmies.

Tropical Grassland and Scrub. Most surviving aboriginal peoples of the tropical grasslands are cultivators, but hunting economies have persisted in some areas, as in the Matto Grosso of South America, in the Kalahari in South Africa, and in tropical Australia. Such regions have marked seasonal contrasts between short summer rains and the long drought in the cooler season. Thus permanent water, and therefore dense tree-formations, are confined to the neighbourhood of larger rivers and depressions. The best known of these hunting economies is that of the South African Bushmen, though invading peoples have increasingly confined it to the more arid scrublands. The Bushman economy has been largely determined by the number and variety of large migratory herbivores. Herds of giraffe, zebra, quagga, rhinoceros, and many species of antelope moved seasonally across their territories in the wet season, when game was ubiquitous, but in the dry season the animals were forced to concentrate round permanent water sources. For both game and Bushmen, water was the key to survival. In contrast to the tropical forest hunters, there was thus greater stress on group possession of hunting territory, which had to be adequate for the long dry season.

The Bushman band consisted of a number of related families. Groups of about a hundred persons were reported, though in the drier areas of the Kalahari, to which the later Bushmen remnants were pushed, a band was often fewer than twenty. Only temporary shelters were constructed, usually dome-shaped grass huts on a frame of branches with a wide opening. Each band was autonomous. Entry into the territory of another band would be met by attack unless friendly relations, generally by intermarriage, were well established. The band dispersed in the dry season but during the wet could draw together, and adjacent bands would organize collective drives across extensive tracts. These interrelations were strengthened by barter between individuals, whereby special products were distributed through their territory. Culture and dialect were thus kept uniform over considerable areas. The major dialect groups of Bushmen were, however, in no sense political units.

The scattered character of settlement over much of the year rendered the small family groups largely independent. Each produced its own food and stored it in its own small caches, with emergency water buried in ostrich-egg shells. Women foraged, seeking roots, berries, gourds, and small animals. The weighted digging-stick and skin kaross, at once a garment and a hold-all, were their characteristic equipment. The men concentrated on hunting. Employing tracking and retrieving dogs, they went out in the dry season, usually alone or in small parties, to stalk game at the waterholes, using disguises, decoys, and imitative cries. The essential weapon was the short bow strung with sinew or barkcord, with its reed arrows tipped with a variety of vegetable, snake, and insect poisons. In such open country, traps played a smaller part than among the forest hunters, though drinking places might be poisoned with *Euphorbia* branches. For the larger drives of the wet season, brushwood fences with pitfalls in the gaps, at which hunters were concealed, were set up across miles of country.

Stress on the self-subsistent family unit in the long dry season appears in the personal rights in resources. Individuals set up their marks on caches, root patches, and bees' nests. Abundance of game and limitation of vegetable resources are reflected in the use of hides and skins for protective clothing and utensils, and of bone, shell, and sinew for implements and ornaments.

The grasslands to the east and north of the Congo–Guinea forest zone have long been occupied by agricultural and pastoral peoples, but collecting, hunting, and fishing have continued to play an important part in their economies. Some south-eastern Bantu, and the west Sudanic peoples, show skill in both collective hunting-drives and individual stalking of game. The more specialized pastoral peoples in East Africa, on the other hand, regarded game as a danger to their pastoral stock, as unfit for food, and as valuable only in supplying materials. They often relinquished hunting to dependent groups.

Continental Scrub and Desert. A food-gathering economy, comparable in basic techniques with that of the Bushmen, survived in the scrub-lands of the plateaux and basins of western North America until the late nineteenth century. Climatically, the area differs from southern Africa in that there is a long cold winter, during which the body needed greater protection and fresh vegetable food was unobtainable. Thus the northern Paiute established permanent winter settlements of bark or reed huts, containing hearths and storage pits. A Paiute band of a hundred or so exploited a common territory of some hundred square miles. This usually included tracts of valley-floor yielding grass seeds, and wooded ridges providing the most important food source, namely, pine nuts. Surpluses were dried and stored. Seed-collecting led to the development of basketry seed-beaters, with which the ripe grass heads could be gathered into open carrying baskets (see above, p 154 and figure 75). Grasses, edible bulbs, and roots were most copious where the snow-melt provided additional water-supply. This suggested a form of irrigation, which extended such areas. In spring, dams of boulders and brushwood were thrown across the beds of the hill-streams. Ditches, sometimes a mile long, were cut with sticks to divert the water across the slope, and allow it to seep over areas on which wild food-plants would become luxuriant. For the pine-nut harvest in late autumn large parties moved into the mountains.

Winter was the hunting season. Parties then went to the mountains to hunt wild sheep, others decoyed wild goats and drove rabbits. The bow was generally composite, with backing of sinew or strips of mountain sheep-horn attached with fish glue, though some were also compound, being of two sections of mountain sheep-horn spliced together. Somewhat inefficient arrow-poisons were obtained from the poison glands of snakes or the spleens of goats. Fish were stupefied by leaf-poisons in dammed pools, and taken by two-pronged spears or lines with double-barbed bone hooks. Decoys were floated out on reeds on the mountain lakes, to induce ducks to land on the lake near an ambush.

The stress the Paiute laid on collection and storage is reflected in the elaborate development of baskets. The women made a great variety by twining and coiled techniques (ch 16), for collecting and storing food. Boiling, for cooking, was effected by means of heated stones. Game was scarcer than with the Bushmen, so that the Paiute needed more co-operation to secure a substantial bag. Food-storage, completely lacking among the Semang (p 169) and little resorted to by the Bushmen (apart from emergency water-supplies), was extensively developed by the Paiute in response to the long severe winter.

Regions resembling the Mediterranean. Non-agricultural economies have persisted in some regions flanking the continental grasslands and deserts on the western side of the great land masses. Such areas in southern Australia were remarkable in that continent for their high density of aboriginal population. This was also relatively dense in areas with a similar climate in the central Chilean coastlands and in central California, where the food-gathering economies of such regions have been the most closely studied.

The central Californians, such as the Yokuts, specialized on the abundant natural harvests of acorns and buck-eye nuts. Large stores could be gathered in the extensive woodlands. Neither was edible in its native state, but a technique had been developed for extracting tannin from the one and poison from the other (figure 102). They were pounded in stone mortars, the coarse meal was set in the hollow of a mound of sand, and hot water was poured through it. A wide variety of roots, fruits, insects, waterfowl, small animals, and larger game contributed to the diet. Elk, deer, and wild goat and sheep were hunted in the winter, and fish were obtained by water-poisoning, traps, and nets.

FIGURE 102—*Yokuts leaching acorn meal with hot water on a sand bed. California.*

These conditions sustained much greater stability of habitat. The winter villages of the Yokuts, for example, consisted of several spacious, gabled structures, in each of which a dozen or so related families lived together. The total group was larger than a Paiute band, though its territory was smaller, and a characteristic group consisted of some 250 people. But the nature of the quest for food, which offered no advantage to larger scale organization, inhibited any wider political community. The winter-village group remained economically and politically autonomous, and a typical tribe consisted of some fifty villages, each proud of its distinctiveness in custom and even dialect. Closer settlement favoured social relations within and between villages, in intermarriage and ceremonial exchanges. A shell-bead currency had been adopted by some of these Californian peoples from their food-gathering northern neighbours (p 176), whereby exchanges of a wide range of goods and services were effected. The central Californians, like all the peoples of western North America, had elaborate basketry techniques, but a settled life encouraged their pottery-making, a craft that had probably reached them from farther south.

The High Latitude Grasslands occupied after the Ice Age by large herds of herbivores, including the wild horse and the aurochs in the Old World and the bison in the New, favoured hunting-economies, but the severe winter and the fleetness of the herds severely limited exploitation until the later introduction of horse-riding into such areas (p 721). We have glimpses of the development of this later phase in south-eastern European and Asiatic grasslands, through the classical accounts and from archaeological records of the Scythians, the Tatars, and their predecessors. Equestrian hunting played a major part in the economies of this area during and after the first millennium B.C., but agricultural techniques penetrated these regions as early as, if not earlier than, the domestication of the horse, so that the early grassland economies of the Old World included grain cultivation—except on the northern margins, with their long winters.

In the New World, pre-Columbian settlements were at first as few, small, and ephemeral in the continental grasslands as in the northern forests (see p 176), both in the western plains of North America and the pampas and Patagonian grasslands of South America. The introduction of the horse by the Spaniards, however, rapidly transformed the human occupation of both areas. In South America the Patagonian Indians, who had long used the bolas against fast-moving game, could now run down the herds of guanaco with their horses. In North America, with horses initially stolen from the Spaniards, mounted Indians could surround and drive the herds of bison, thus securing large surpluses of food and materials. The indigenous draught device, the travois—an open basket dragged on poles by a dog—could be greatly increased in size for horse-traction (figure 513). The conical skin-covered tent, for which longer poles could now be hauled from place to place, was greatly enlarged. Thus equipped, and with great herds of bison migrating seasonally over established routes, many agricultural peoples of the adjacent Mississippi basin were led to adopt a predominantly hunting life. In the seventeenth and eighteenth centuries, with amplified food-supply, they multiplied rapidly and combined bison-hunting with internecine warfare, stimulated by the westward pressure of European colonization which was ever narrowing their economy. With the introduction of the rifle and European control, the herds of bison were exterminated and the Indians confined to reservations. The horse had proved the ultimate ruin of its rider.

This exceptional and short-lived economy was characterized by a strong seasonal dichotomy. During the summer season of abundant grass, large groups, which might number several thousand, congregated to live in great tribal encampments, from which organized hunts were made under the authority of a tribal council. As the severe winter season approached, the tribe broke up into a number of smaller bands, carrying with them large surpluses of dried food in the form of jerked meat, pemmican, and dried roots and fruits, to engage in winter hunting on a smaller scale.

Northern Forest Lands. The deciduous and coniferous forest lands of north-west Europe, after the retreat of the ice sheet, afforded in Mesolithic and early Neolithic times a rewarding habitat for hunting and collecting peoples. The Maglemosian and other Baltic cultures (p 498) of this area from *c* 8000 B.C. illustrate the development of fishing and hunting techniques, and of the essential craft of woodworking, so valuable for providing tools, shelter, and means of transport. There is a contrast to be noted between inland activity and that of the coastal and estuarine areas where, besides the game and vegetable resources of the forests, the yields of sea and river could be exploited. A similar contrast appears at its most dramatic in North America, between the economies of the north-west coastlands from southern Alaska to northern California, with dense and wealthy populations, on the one hand, and, on the other, those of the hunting territories of the much poorer Athabaskan and Algonkin peoples of the interior. Among the hunting-devices of the latter were snow-shoes and harpoons as well as weirs and dams to trap fish, otter, and beaver. The poor reward of hunting in coniferous forest, in which herbaceous vegetation was scanty and game dispersed, kept population thinly scattered. Most groups were small autonomous tribelets scattered through the forests.

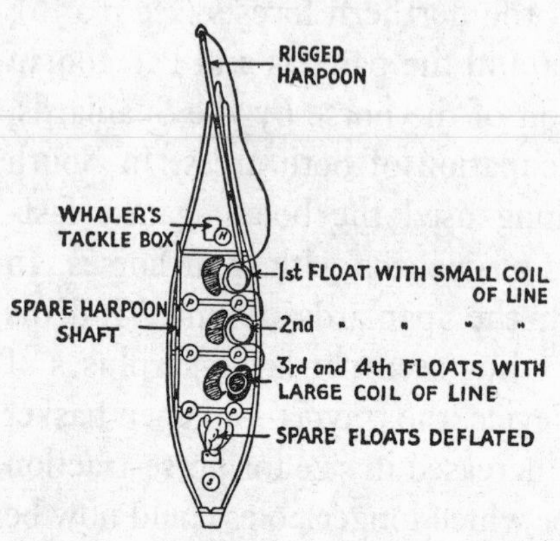

FIGURE 103—*Plan of Nootka whaling canoe.* H—*harpooner.* P—*paddlers.* S—*steersman. British Columbia.*

On the north-west coast, however, a wealth of coastal and river fish and marine mammals permitted a richer economy. The deep fjords and lower river valleys of the mainland, as well as the islands, enjoyed a mild wet climate and had dense forests sloping down to the shore. Of game—mainly deer, elk, and mountain sheep—there was sufficient in the forests, but the accessible animal wealth of the sea and rivers was far greater. Halibut, herring, and other fish were abundant, and the seal, sea-lion, sea-otter, walrus, and porpoise that preyed on them could also be hunted. Salmon and candlefish (*Thaleichthys pacificus*) swarmed up the rivers in spring and summer.

Coastal fishing from canoes, and by set lines and nets, was elaborately developed. Bone and bentwood hooks of special forms were used for different types of fish, and were often trolled behind canoes. Shoals of fish, especially herring, came inshore in spring to spawn, in masses so dense that they could often be taken from canoes with a fish-rake, a long shaft fitted with numerous bone barbs. Sea mammals were harpooned from canoes, and some tribes applied the harpoon principle in porpoise-hunting, with a two-pronged spear of which each prong had a detachable barbed head tied to a line. Harpoon-arrows were used for the swift, wary sea-otter. Sea-lions and seals were stalked and harpooned among the coastal rocks. Some peoples, including the Nootka, hunted whales from large canoes, using a heavy thrusting harpoon-spear with a triangular shell point, barbed with antler, and a long line of whale sinew to which inflated seal-skins were tied to prevent the quarry from diving and to tire it (figure 103). So many harpoons and trails of inflated skins were needed to exhaust these huge creatures, and there was such risk at every approach by canoe, that most groups contented themselves with the more occasional supplies from stranded whales.

FIGURE 104—*Kuakiutl salmon-trap for narrow streams. British Columbia.*

By far the largest single source of food was salmon, taken by line and hook from coastal canoes, or speared, netted, and trapped behind dams in tidal estuaries and rivers during the breeding-runs, which, for the various species, extended throughout the summer (figure 104). Candlefish were also taken during spring runs up the rivers. They were valued for their oil, which could be extracted by stone-boiling in huge wooden troughs, and stored without deterioration for both food and lighting. Thus in spring and summer there was intense fishing activity. In the early part, men were mainly engaged in canoe-fishing at sea, but they moved up the rivers later for salmon and candlefish runs. Women collected shellfish and edible seaweeds on the shore, and later in the season gathered harvests of roots and berries for food and nettles for fibre.

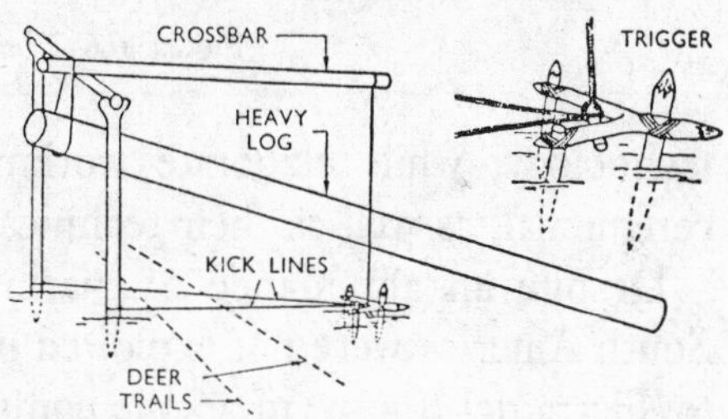

FIGURE 105—*Diagram of Nootka deer-deadfall. The kicklines are secured to the trigger; the line from the trigger holds down the crossbar.*

Forest game was sought in winter, chiefly for horn, sinew, wool, and skins, but the flesh of land animals was less valued, and some of these peoples actually disliked it. Extensive hunts were organized to drive deer (figure 105), and smaller parties went into the mountains for sheep and bear.

Large timber houses, each the dwelling of a number of related families, were established in the winter villages on or near the coast from which spring fishing was organized. Larger villages would have thirty or more houses, set in one or more rows along the waterside, for a population of several hundreds (figure 106).

The high productivity of the peoples of the north-west coast depended on a matching of rich sea and land resources by efficient and specialized techniques, including such hunting elements as an effective harpoon. Long, sinew-backed bows were used both by sea and by land. The high finish and careful adaptation of implements to their special purpose was a striking feature of these peoples' technology, while elaborate workmanship characterizes their decorative and ceremonial, as well as their technical, equipment.

FIGURE 106—*Haida village. British Columbia.*

Despite an abundance of marine resources, the south-west coastlands of South America were not exploited in comparable measure. From Chiloe Island to Tierra del Fuego, in a zone comparable in terrain and climate to that of the west coast of North America, no similar productivity was achieved. Thus, though the Yahgan of Tierra del Fuego had a detachable spear-point (figure 86) to attack sea mammals, they were ignorant of fish-hooks and traps. It is true that the abundant and voracious fish in the coastal kelp beds could be easily caught by baited lines without hooks, but bark-fibre nets made by the Chono, farther north, were far inferior to those of the north-west coastal peoples, elaborate fish-traps were unknown, and, finally, only light bark- or leaky, flat-bottomed plank-canoes were available. The huge shell middens confirm the explorers' belief that easily gathered mussels and other shell-fish were staple diet on the south-west coast of South America. The lack of refinement in the techniques of the south Chileans appears not only in their fishing equipment, but in their small ephemeral huts of thin poles covered with grass or fern, in their very limited use of the bow in hunting, and in their poor exploitation of plant-food. Food-storage, too, was limited and the settlements were small, scattered, and ephemeral.

Some techniques of the north-west coast, such as the detachable long-lined harpoon and methods of working heavy timber, probably reached the New World late and had not extended to South America, but the contrast between the British Columbians and the south Chileans points also to the importance of other cultural factors, including basic drives towards the full exploitation of available means, and the display of resulting wealth.

Arctic Hunting Economies. With the retreat of the Quaternary ice, the Arctic tundras of both the Old and the New World were colonized by man, and there developed along the coastland, mainly in the New World, a land and marine hunting economy which, by adaptations of advanced hunting techniques, made human life possible under the most extreme climatic conditions.

In Arctic Europe and western Siberia, hunting was early subordinated to pastoral techniques. Originally developed for cattle and other herds in more southern regions, these techniques were adapted to reindeer farther north, and, on the tundra of northern Europe and Siberia, primitive hunting economies remained dominant only among scattered groups of Yukaghir in the Kolyma basin. Farther east, northern Tungus and other peoples had a semi-pastoral economy, based on half-tamed herds of reindeer (ch 13).

The treeless Arctic tundra has a frost-free season of little more than two months in the year. From its marginal woodlands of pine and larch, sparse tracts of dwarf beech and Arctic willow extend northward. The basic vegetation of lichens, mosses, sedges, and a few berry-bearing shrubs supports a migrant animal population during the short summer season, but reindeer, which can survive on the tundra throughout the year, have long been the most important source both of food and of materials. Adapted to a diet of lichens, for which they forage to surprising depths beneath the snow, and with their splayed feet able to move over marshy ground, they were hunted at all seasons by the Yukaghir of north-eastern Siberia. Largely immobilized in winter, some bands of Yukaghir lived near the forest margins and moved north over the tundra as the days lengthened, with equipment packed on birchwood sleds drawn by dog teams. Others remained on the tundra throughout the year, wintering in pit-dwellings with low roofs of branches and turf. At all seasons, reindeer herds were lured and driven towards ambushed hunters, equipped with sinew-backed bows, at the ends of lanes of widely spaced stones or posts. Elk and hare were also hunted and, in the woodlands, mountain sheep, bear, and deer. From May to September there were fowling and fishing in the streams and lakes, while the women collected food-plants. Surpluses were accumulated towards the end of the summer. Fishing techniques were simple and directed mainly to catches during runs in spring and autumn, when nets were set in the streams. For line-fishing, only a bone gorge was employed.

Conical reindeer-skin tents, dug-out canoes and rafts in summer, and dog-drawn sleds in winter, facilitated extensive seasonal migration, and a return to

FIGURE 107—*Eskimo snow-knife engraved with hunting scenes: reindeer and walrus.*

winter quarters with stores of dried meat and fish to eke out the uncertain rewards of the winter hunt. The leader of each band appears to have had considerable control over the movements of the component families and the activities of its hunters. During the summer, several bands might join forces for collective hunting, and for feasts and ceremonies.

The peoples of Siberia failed to develop effective techniques for exploiting maritime resources. Among the Eskimo of the New World, on the other hand, shore-hunting of marine mammals became the main element in the economy. From the Asiatic shore of the Behring Straits, along the coasts of northern Alaska and Canada to Baffin Land and Greenland, Eskimo communities have adapted marine hunting-techniques to a very difficult region. Except in parts of Alaska, and in Greenland with its ice-covered interior, the Eskimo economy has a seasonal dichotomy of winter shore life and brief inland summer hunting, and their equipment shows a corresponding seasonal contrast (figure 107). During the long winter, the floe-ice is protected from gales in sheltered bays, to form a flat extension to the land from which marine resources can be pursued. Small Eskimo communities of half-a-dozen families collect along the shore or on the floe-ice to hunt seals, which remain inshore and maintain breathing-holes in the ice. Moving on sled over the ice, alone or in pairs, hunters regularly visit such holes, to wait until a seal comes to breathe and can be attacked by a thrusting harpoon (figure 108). Some families remain in earth-covered pit-dwellings on the land, but those on the floe-ice live in snow-block igloos. They all depend on the seal in winter, for both food and fuel, burning its blubber in flat lamps to warm and light their shelters. In spring, as the ice breaks up, the seals congregate on the surface of the floes and along the shore, where they can be stalked or approached by kayak. Surpluses of seal meat and blubber secured at this season are stored in pits.

The Eskimo move inland when the herds of caribou, the American wild reindeer, migrate northward following the summer thaw, at which season they are more easy to approach. They follow definite routes well known to the Eskimo, and are driven by large parties into narrow valleys or lanes flanked by piles of stone and brushwood. The snaring of smaller game, fishing, and fowling are also active at this season. Weirs and dams facilitate the catching of fish with bag-nets or trident spears, as they move in shoals in the rivers. Women take part in the drives and fishing, and also collect roots and berries to add to the winter stores. With the onset of winter, the Eskimo return to the coast, living mainly on stored food until the floe-ice will bear. In the sub-Arctic areas of southern Alaska, southern Greenland, and Labrador, where floe-ice is less developed and the sea is open for most of the year, land hunting is less developed in the summer season, and is largely replaced by summer walrus-hunting and whaling from large, open, skin-covered boats.

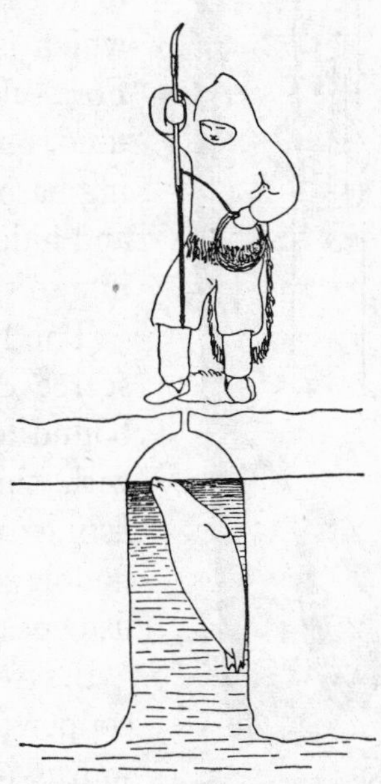

FIGURE 108—*Eskimo harpooning seal through an ice-hole.*

Eskimo hunting-equipment is remarkable for its skilled manufacture, and for its nice adjustment to the requirements of both land and sea hunting. The harpoon spear, their most elaborate weapon, differs in weight according to whether it is for thrusting or for throwing, but the essential construction is the same (figure 109). The head is superior to that used by the Indians of the north-west coast, in that the line is attached on the toggle-principle midway along the detachable point, so that, when pulled, it turns in the wound and comes away less easily. It consists of a socketed head of bone, in the top of which is fitted a point formerly made of stone, ivory, or native copper. It fits snugly on to a foreshaft of walrus-tusk, from one to three feet long according to the weight of the harpoon. The foreshaft in turn is socketed into a carved ivory head which has been rammed tightly on to the main shaft, to which it is lashed by thongs running through drill

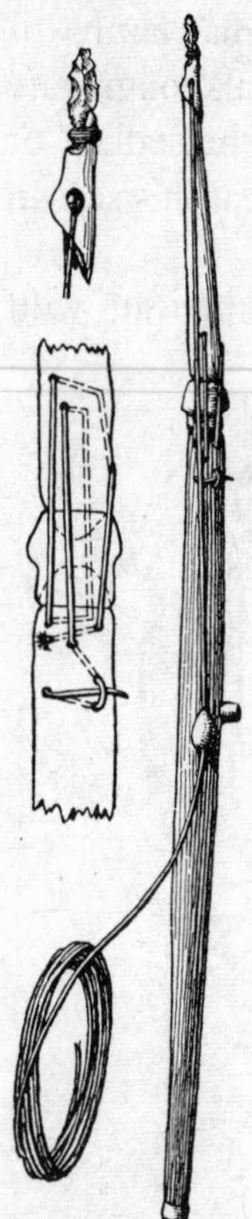

FIGURE 109—*Eskimo heavy thrusting harpoon for hunting walrus; length 2 m.*

holes in such a fashion that it can turn through a small angle in its socket. Midway along the wooden main shaft, which is about 1·5 metres long, an ivory knob is attached, round which the harpoon line, drawn tightly from the head, is looped to hold the head securely in position until the strike is made. When the point of the harpoon strikes home, the foreshaft gives enough to release it, and the quarry can then be played on the line, which is allowed to run out from a coil at the hunter's feet. For seal-hole hunting and for whaling, thrusting harpoons are used, but for shore and sea hunting from kayaks a lighter throwing harpoon is employed. In sea hunting, inflated seal bladders and hide-covered hoops are attached at intervals to the harpoon line to slow down the larger animals (figure 84).

The Eskimo bow is usually compound, of short lengths of scarce driftwood or of caribou antler, the parts riveted and bound together before the outer face of the bow is reinforced with sinew (figure 91). There are also thrusting spears for fishing and land hunting, bird lances of walrus-ivory with a double set of multiple barbs near the shaft-head (figure 81), and fish spear-points flanked by incurving barbs to retain the fish.

Before the introduction of iron, hammered points of native copper (ch 21) were riveted and bound to carved lengths of walrus-ivory and antler, thus providing effective barbs on spears, gaffs, and fish-hooks. This elaborate bone-work was made possible by the bow-drill (figure 113), whereby a point of stone, and later iron, could be rapidly rotated to drill small, deep holes in antler and walrus-ivory. Archaeological evidence, especially from Alaska, shows that Eskimo techniques have developed over a long period, and that the bow-drill, the socketed harpoon, and the double-paddled skin-covered kayak were introduced fairly late from north-east Asia.

Despite the technical ingenuity and skill of the Eskimo, the severity of the habitat prevented stable settlement: a bad winter could wipe out the entire population of a region. On the other hand, with the dog sled, the open boat, and the kayak, the Eskimo were sufficiently mobile to recolonize deserted areas. Though communities in the Arctic zone from north Alaska to Baffin Land could not reach numbers of more than a hundred or so, and though the total Eskimo population of the vast Arctic coast area was probably less than 10000, they maintained a remarkable continuity of culture. The very instability of settlement favoured intercommunication, and, in the historic period at least, there has been great freedom of movement for the individual from one band to another. In Alaska, Arctic Canada, and Greenland some essential features of Eskimo culture have existed for two millennia, but the culture has not been static. Certain Eskimo techniques were introduced or developed in the Alaskan region at successive periods, and there is evidence of impoverishment in parts of the central area where the old 'Thule' culture was more effective for the hunting of marine mammals than is that of the later central Eskimo.

III. FORAGING, HUNTING, AND FISHING TECHNIQUES SURVEYED

Food-gatherers display great diversity, both in the combination of techniques and in the degree of specialization on particular means and resources. There is often a marked concentration on one natural resource. Thus the acorn among the central Californians affected supplementary techniques such as food preparation, basketry, and storage, and patterns of settlement. On the other hand, concentration on large land-game, or on marine resources, may lead to highly specialized hunting procedures, while contrasts in diet between one people and another may be extreme, some, like the Indians of the Plains and the Eskimo, living almost entirely on meat, and others, like the peoples of the north-west coast of North America and the lower Amure river in eastern Siberia, living on fish.

Food- and collecting-techniques are, however, never completely specialized, and nothing suggests that men have ever entirely neglected subsidiary food sources. Man is by nature omnivorous and we shall seek in vain for pure gleaners, pure hunters, or pure fishers. The Tasmanians, with the most meagre equipment of all recent peoples, were collectors of wild roots, fruits, and shore molluscs, but they also organized small drives for game. The Arctic Eskimo, specialized as hunters and fishers, also gather vegetable foods in summer. The collecting of auxiliary foods tends to be left to women, but where there is no great specialization, as among the Semang (p 168) and the Paiute (p 172), though hunting is a male prerogative men also help to gather the vegetable food.

Peoples with greater specialization on particular techniques tend to develop more elaborate appliances and more marked social specialization. A specialized technique for the exploitation of an abundant resource naturally permits a food-gathering economy to reach higher levels of production, and it may then support a denser population than does primitive agriculture under difficult conditions. The degree to which the Alaskan Eskimo, the peoples of the north-west coast of North America, and, with the aid of an exotic domestic animal, those of the North American plains and the South American pampas excelled the Semang, the

Paiute, and the Australians in population-density, settlement-stability, and scale of social organization, indicates the significance of adaptation to particular abundant resources. The denser and more stable populations of food-gatherers are particularly prominent in the temperate latitudes of the New World, similar habitats in the Old World having long been occupied by agriculturists.

It is to be stressed, furthermore, that food-gathering may remain of major importance among primitive cultivators. Thus many peoples of the forests and savannah of Africa, despite their agriculture and stock-raising, depended largely on hunting for meat, skins, and other animal products.

Food-gathering peoples differ in their basic techniques and corresponding economic reward, not according to broad differences of terrain in climate and vegetation, but rather with regard to the specific resources of the particular environment and the adjustment of their techniques in relation thereto. Areas of general geographic similarity may differ widely in available resources, and still more in the efficiency of the techniques applied to them. The Tasmanians, the Fuegians, and the peoples of the British Columbian coast occupied marine forest environments generally similar in climate and vegetation, but they ranged from a very low level to the highest technical elaboration, economic security, and density of population achieved by non-agricultural peoples.

The fact that their resources are widely available, cannot be closely controlled, and do not require continuous attention does not imply that food-gathering peoples are freely nomadic. Even the most poorly equipped, who live in the smallest groups, seek to remain in occupation of delimited territory occupied by successive generations. Indeed, such claims are more stressed by such peoples as the Semang, Bushmen, and Australian natives than they were by the bison-hunting Indians of the Plains. Among the latter, despite large-scale tribal organization, there was considerable long-term movement in pursuit of migratory herds, as there is among the Eskimo with their highly specialized hunting economy. Fixity of habitat appears as a function not so much of specialization of technique as of fixity and scarcity of particular resources, such as the dry-season water-holes of the Bushmen and the Australian Aranda, and also of the need to establish a permanent base for food-storage, as among the seed- and nut-gathering Paiute and the Arctic Eskimo. Food-storage is itself a response to seasonal variations in food-supplies and possibilities of preservation, the latter depending on differences in the perishability of the food-supply and the development of techniques, such as the jerking of meat, for preserving it. Where, as among the peoples of the British Columbian coast and the central Californians, large supplies of preserved food can be accumulated, permanent villages and defined group-territories are occupied for generations. In the North and South American grasslands, on the other hand, success in hunting depended on following wandering herds. This resulted in instability of settlements and simplification of dwellings. Eskimo hunting by sea and land similarly imposed seasonal migrations, but the Arctic climate facilitated pit-storage and permanent winter shore settlements—a neat example of adaptation of settlement to variation in location of food supplies.

The wealth of natural resources affects the stability, size, and elaboration of settlements only in so far as techniques have been developed for their exploitation. The natural resources for permanent dwellings were probably as good among the Tasmanians and Fuegians as among the British Columbians, but the former had not developed techniques for either storage or building. Thus the ranking of food-gathering peoples results essentially from differing combinations in the development and adaptation of techniques in relation to specific opportunities.

Reference to group or band territories must not be taken to imply that food-gathering economies are characterized by a complete communism of resources. Although among all such peoples there are customs of food distribution, whereby the individual hunter or collector has obligations to a larger group of kin or neighbours, there remains a considerable field of personal or family control of supplies. On the other hand, where supplies are meagre, uncertain, or perishable, the need for mutual aid continually reinforces the obligation to distribute the products of hunting, fishing, and foraging.

Where resources and techniques afford a considerable surplus, opportunity arises for social display, as with the British Columbian coast peoples. Among them, food-gatherers though they are, the control of production and supplies by individuals of high status makes its appearance. This is hardly private property in our sense, since its possession entails the obligation to disburse it in socially approved ways which redound to the prestige of the producing group.

The techniques of food-gathering peoples are not to be interpreted as merely automatic responses to local resources. Discovery, invention, and the spread of knowledge have been fundamental in the cultural adaptation of human societies from their beginning. The Tasmanians, early isolated, remained ignorant of bow and even spear-thrower and canoe. The Eskimo, on the other hand, expanded into far more difficult territory with an equipment almost certainly derived from the Old World, but, later on, further elaborated with their own devices.

Nor do their particular techniques rigidly define the social institutions of food-gathering peoples. They merely set limits, which vary according to the resultant productivity, to the potential scale and differentiation of social organization. Among the majority of such peoples, past and present, the population that can concentrate for any length of time in one place is small, and can rarely rise above one or two to the square mile. The social unit also is small, and inter-connected groups, allied by marriage and direct exchange, rarely exceed a hundred or two each. Further, low productivity requires the absorption of all in the collection of supplies, so that, apart from differences of age and sex, there can be little specialization. Leadership is correspondingly limited either to organization of temporary co-operative tasks, such as hunting drives, or to situations where experience, reputation, or knowledge of custom are significant to the maintenance of harmony. The political organization of food-gathering peoples is thus as a rule less specialized than that of cultivators, but since the relationship is to the intensity of production, the stability of habitat, and the accumulation of wealth more specialized institutions are found where the organization and intensity of production are relatively high.

REFERENCES

[1] GARROD, D. A. E. *et al. Archaeol. J.*, **58,** 111, 1928.
[2] CLARK, J. G. D. 'Prehistoric Europe', p. 30 f. Methuen, London. 1952.
[3] *Idem. Ibid.*, p. 35.
[4] *Idem. Antiq. J.*, **28,** 52, 1948.
[5] TURVILLE-PETRE, F. *Archaeol. J.*, **62,** 272 and Pl. XXVIII, 1932.
[6] CLARK, J. G. D. 'Prehistoric Europe', p. 44. Methuen, London. 1952.
[7] JANMART, J. *Amer. Anthrop.*, **54,** 146, 1952.
SCHEBESTA, P. 'Les Pygmées du Congo Belge,' pp. 137 ff. *Mém. Inst. colon. belge Sci. morales* 8°, **26,** ii, 1952.

BIBLIOGRAPHY

Techniques in general:

BOAS, F. (Ed.). 'General Anthropology', chap. 6: "Invention", by F. BOAS, and chap. 7: "Subsistence", by R. LOWIE. Heath, Boston. 1938.

CHAPPLE, E. and COON, C. 'Principles of Anthropology', chap. 6: "Techniques of Manufacturing". Holt, Cape. 1942.

SAYCE, R. U. 'Primitive Arts and Crafts.' University Press, Cambridge. 1933.

Palaeolithic and Mesolithic techniques:

CLARK, J. G. D. 'Prehistoric Europe.' Methuen, London. 1952.

Weapons:

BRITISH MUSEUM. 'Handbook to the Ethnographical Collections' (2nd ed.). London. 1925. (Consult index and list of illustrations.)

[HARRISON, H. S.] 'War and the Chase: Handbook to the Collection of Weapons . . . of The Horniman Museum.' P. S. King for L.C.C. 1929.

Economic significance of techniques:

FORDE, C. D. 'Habitat, Economy and Society' (especially Part I and Conclusion). Methuen, London. 1945.

Most of the above contain bibliographies or guides to further reading in which more detailed information on particular topics can be found.

9

ROTARY MOTION

V. GORDON CHILDE

I. NATURE OF ROTARY MOTION

ROTATING machines for performing repetitive operations, driven by water, by thermal power, or by electrical energy, were the most decisive factors of the industrial revolution; and, from the first steamship till the invention of the jet plane, it is the application of rotary motion to transport that has revolutionized communications. The use of rotary machines, as of any other human tools, has been cumulative and progressive. The inventors of the eighteenth and nineteenth centuries were merely extending the applications of rotary motion that had been devised in previous generations, reaching back thousands of years into the prehistoric past. Hence a special section is devoted in this work to the initial and early stages of its use.

Rotary motion, in the form we know it in machines and vehicles, was a comparatively recent addition to man's equipment—recent, that is, as measured against the geological time-scale of prehistorians. The potter's wheel and the wheeled vehicle are a bare 6000 years old, the spindle has not been used for more (and perhaps much less) than 2000 years longer (chs 15, 16, 27). Men have been making tools, however, for perhaps some 500 000 years, and some of the tools employed in that vast period were probably already in a sense rotated or partially rotated. It is, therefore, convenient to introduce a distinction between continuous or true and complete rotary motion, and partial or discontinuous rotary motion.

For true rotary motion, the revolving part of the instrument must be free to turn in the same direction indefinitely. There are, however, a number of processes which involve a partial turn of the instrument; such are boring and drilling by hand. There are even machines like the bow-drill (p 189) or the pole-lathe, which allow a number, but only a limited number, of complete revolutions of the revolving part. Partial rotary motion of this sort has been used by man much longer than true rotary motion. Indeed, it began among his pre-human ancestors.

II. PARTIAL ROTARY MOTION

(*a*) *Boring.* It is a feature of the anatomy of the primates that the bony structure and the musculature of the forelimbs permit the execution of twisting movements. These depend on a partial rotation of the lower end of the radius around the fixed lower end of the ulna (see tailpiece). As soon as some subhuman primate began to supplement his powers by manipulating bits of stone or wood, he could turn these in a boring movement. It was after *homo faber* had begun to modify such ready-made tools into artifacts more suited to his needs that he must have begun to shape them to serve for boring and other purposes.

The earliest recognizable standardized tool, the hand-axe (figure 14 A), is an all-purposes tool. It could be used for boring—although there is no evidence that it was so used, nor in fact how it was used at all—but if employed for digging up roots and grubs it could hardly fail to be given a twist in the process. Among the Lower Palaeolithic flake-tools of the Clactonian industry, standardized tools cannot be recognized, but there are flakes which would serve very well for boring holes in wood or hides, though no products thus perforated survive or indeed would have been likely to survive (figure 111 A).

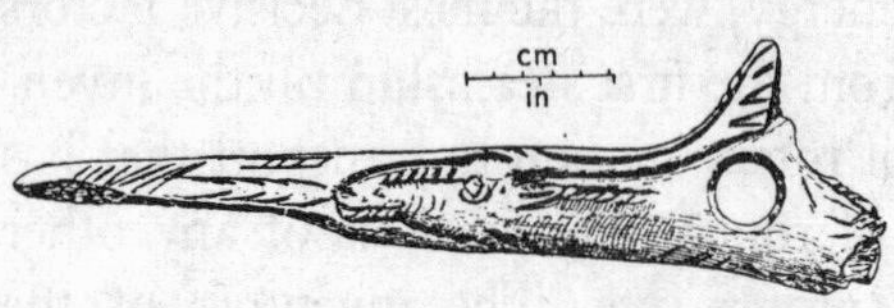

FIGURE 110—*Magdalenian* bâton de commandement. *Dordogne, France. Upper Palaeolithic.*

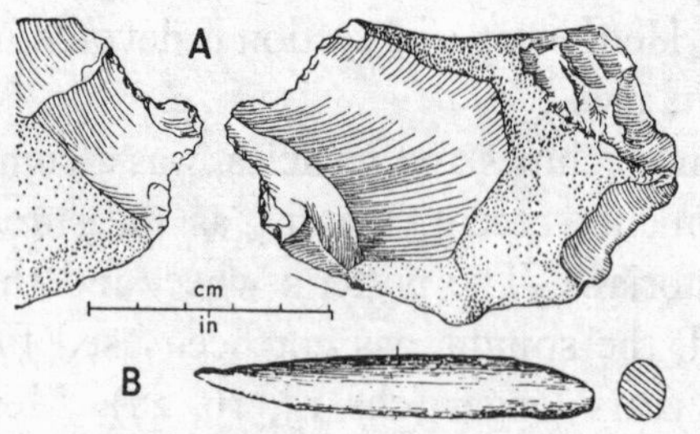

FIGURE 111—(A) *Flint borer from Clacton-on-Sea; Lower Palaeolithic.* (B) *Antler awl from Torquay; Upper Palaeolithic.*

The first perforated objects of antler, bone, ivory, and shell that survive are from the Upper Palaeolithic phase, which also yields perforated stone objects. Stone may have been perforated by percussion, but the antler has certainly been bored, while small holes in bones, shells, or teeth were quite probably drilled. From the Aurignacian, we have already sections of reindeer antler pierced with holes about 2 cm in diameter. The use of these so called *bâtons de commandement* (figure 110) is disputed, but that the holes were pierced by boring through the antler is generally agreed. In fact, stout flint tools trimmed to a point survive from this period, and are probably correctly termed tap-borers.

For finer perforations, a new implement not at first involving the use of other muscles was developed. Awls for piercing leather and similar materials were probably first made from splinters of bone or antler (figure 111 B). They may have been utilized as early as Lower Palaeolithic times, but only in the Upper Palaeolithic phases did men invent techniques for working bone by grinding and polishing. They were thus able to make sharp but relatively tough pointed implements. Such piercers must have been worked like borers, by twisting from the wrist. For perforating harder materials, such as shell, bone, and ivory, bone was unsuitable, and flint blades, trimmed by bi-lateral flaking to a sharp point, were manufactured. Very probably, these were soon mounted at the end of a wooden shaft, and in this state they can perhaps be more accurately described as drill-bits (figure 117 B).

(*b*) *Hand-drill.* A smooth cylindrical stick armed at one end with a flint point can be set in motion by a different set of muscular movements. It can be made

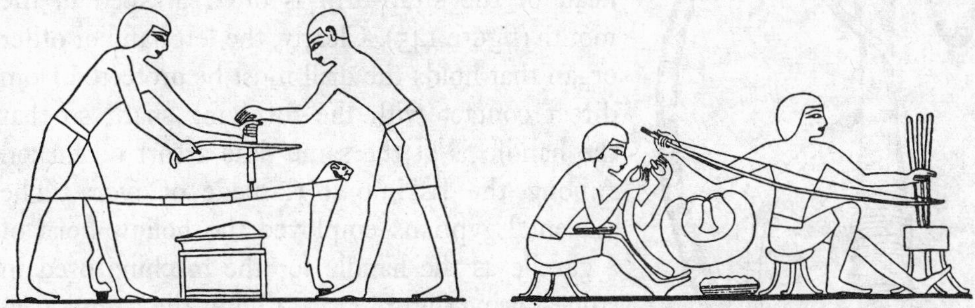

FIGURE 112—*Egyptian carpenters and beadmakers.* (*The bead-driller uses a triple drill; behind him the beads are threaded, and beneath his right arm a finished necklace is outlined.*) *From a tomb at Thebes.* c *1450* B.C.

to revolve by rubbing between the palms. This motion is used even today by savage and barbarous tribes to actuate the simplest drills, and is and was used for other purposes than making holes. The ancient Maya and many other peoples used the simplest form of drill, rotated between the palms, for making fire (figures 141–3).

There are living or recent peoples of a low cultural level who use indirectly operated drills which deserve the name of machines and, in effect, convert to-and-fro horizontal motion into rotary motion. These drills are still driven by human muscle-power, but the driver pulls, or pushes and pulls, with the forearm instead of twisting with his wrist. Thus in the strap-drill the spindle is rotated by pulling backwards and forwards a sinew or thong twisted round it. This device is very widely distributed today, and must be very old, though little direct evidence of its former use is likely to have survived (figure 144).

(*c*) *Bow-drill.* This may be regarded as an improvement on the strap-drill (figures 112, 113). In it, the ends of the cord, sinew, or strap are attached to the extremities of a bow, and the spindle is made to rotate by moving the bow back and forth. The bow-drill is very widely distributed, and was used even in Europe for most drilling operations until supplemented by the brace in the Middle Ages.

It is still occasionally used in Turkey. It is represented in Egypt from 2500 B.C. onwards, and is probably as old as the bow and goes back to Palaeolithic times; but as the first Upper Palaeolithic populations in Europe, the Aurignacians and Gravettians, are not definitely known to have used the bow, we cannot confidently attribute the bow-drill to them (p 33). Both strap-drill and bow-drill require a handle in which the spindle can rotate freely, for the driller must hold the head of the instrument and press it into the work. In point of fact, the head of the strap-drill is often grasped in the mouth (figure 145). Clearly, the left hand or other organ that holds the drill must be protected from direct contact with the revolving shaft, so that the handle is at the same time a sort of socket. Among the Eskimo it is made of ivory. The ancient Egyptians employed the hollow horn of a gazelle as the handle for the machine used in stone-boring (figure 117 A, C), but the commonest form of socket is probably a knob of hard stone 2·5–6 cm in diameter. The revolving butt of the drill will gradually wear a convenient socket in the underside of such a stone knob.

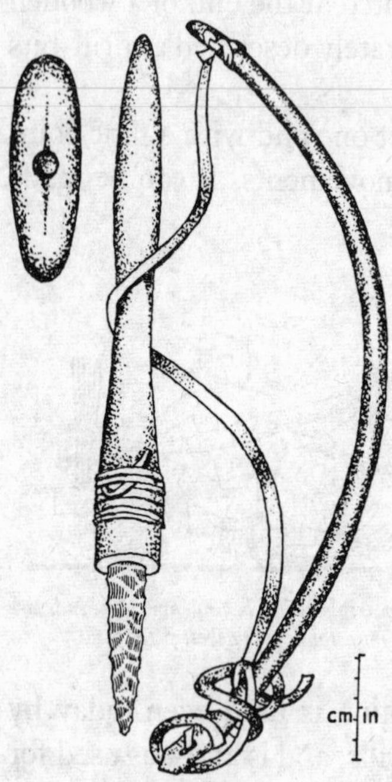

FIGURE 113—*Bow-drill from Alaska with flint bit, and socket for upper end of shaft.*

(*d*) *Pump-drill.* The pump-drill may conveniently be mentioned here, though there is no evidence for its use before Roman times. It is a more complicated machine than any of the foregoing. Though still driven by human muscle-power, it involves, at least in its perfected form, the use of a fly-wheel to preserve the momentum imparted to the spindle by the human driving-force. It will be noticed that the cross-piece introduces a second type of bearing, serving to steady the spindle (figure 114).

Perforated shells, teeth, stone beads, and even bone needles adequately attest the use of some sort of drill throughout Upper Palaeolithic times. An exuberant use of drilling—even for ornamenting bone implements—among the Maglemoseans of northern Europe may perhaps be taken as evidence that the bow-drill was already in use, at least by Mesolithic times.

Among the peasant societies of the New Stone Age and the succeeding Palaeometallic or Bronze Age, many improvements in drilling and boring are attested by their results, without having any demonstrable bearing on the development of rotary motion. Thick blocks of hard stone were perforated with shaft-holes to serve as mace-heads, axes, or hammers (figures 29 A, 336, 401 A). Of course, in this and similar operations the actual perforating agent was an abrasive, usually sand, for no hard steel bits were available. At first, the abrasive was moved by a solid bit, and the maker had laboriously to grind to powder a whole cylinder of hard stone exactly equal in volume to the perforation desired. Generally, when the hole had been driven half-way through the block, this was turned over and grinding begun at the opposite end. The result is a very characteristic bi-conical hole (figure 115). In most cases, the accuracy is so astonishing that some centring device is usually postulated, and elaborate drilling machines have been imagined, providing both centring and downward pressure on the spindle.

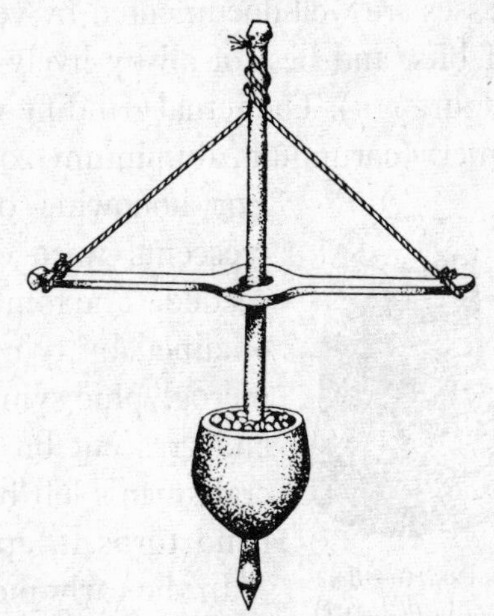

FIGURE 114—*Pump-drill from Nias, Indonesia, with a stone-filled coconut as fly-wheel.*

Such reconstructions, though frequently illustrated and logically plausible, are completely imaginary. One labour-saving device is, however, well attested—the hollow borer (drill). In this tool, the bit is tubular, and only a thin tube of the stone need actually be ground to powder. As soon as the tube has pierced the block, out drops the bore-core—a little cylinder of solid stone equivalent to at least two-thirds of what would have been completely pulverized under the older system (figure 116). The best bits for hollow boring are, of course, metallic tubes, such as the tubes of folded copper sheet used by pre-Columbian tribes in America (figure 115), but even these would grind only with the aid of an abrasive. In practice, a hollow reed or bone will work quite well, though the operator will have to keep changing his bit, and must provide himself with a stock of reeds of equal diameter before starting any big operation. Even using the tubular drill, it was the normal practice to turn the block over, if it was at all thick, and continue on the opposite side.

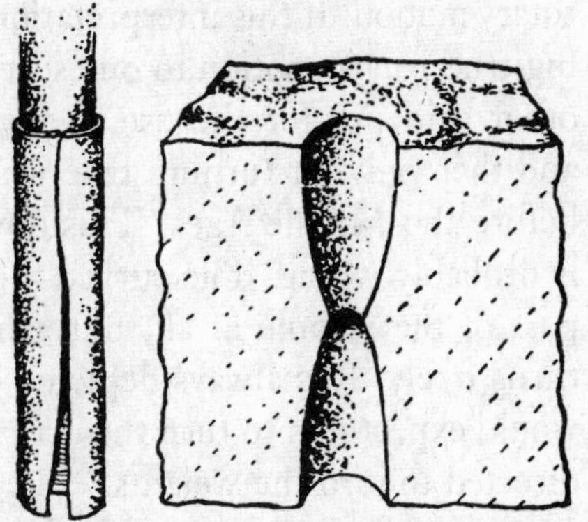

FIGURE 115—*Tubular drill of copper, and bi-conical bore-hole.*

The most relevant of the boring operations is that involved in the manufacture of the stone vases which were used extensively in the Near East from the Neolithic stage onwards. No doubt at first hollowed merely by percussion, by early metallic times these vases were drilled out. From Egypt in particular, the processes are well documented by vessels in all stages of manufacture, by a variety of bits, and best of all by lively pictures from Old Kingdom and later tombs (figure 117). The actual grinding was still done by an abrasive—sand or sometimes emery (corundum, aluminium oxide). The bits were of flint fixed into cleft sticks. For hollowing out globular vessels, a series of graded flint crescents were employed successively as the operation proceeded. The tomb pictures show that the requisite pressure was obtained by tying a pair of heavy stones to the spindle. The hieroglyphic symbol is a picture of this device with its weights and crescent bit fixed in the forked stick (figure 117 C). The craftsman's left hand grasps the top of the stick while the right hand turns it, apparently by pushing on the weights.

FIGURE 116—*Bore-core (actual size). Danish Neolithic.*

In the early pictures the upper end of the stick seems curved, and this has suggested that it was used as a sort of crank handle. The swing of the arms to and fro would then be converted into rotary motion. If this interpretation is correct, the ancient Egyptians were applying true rotary motion to one sort of drilling before 2500 B.C. There seems no other evidence for the use of anything like a crank for nearly two millennia, and then only for turning true wheels. As for the brace, it is nowhere attested before the Middle Ages. This obvious interpretation of the Egyptian pictures is probably wrong. The curved piece at the top of the spindle is very likely not part of the spindle at all, but a handle of hollow horn in which the spindle turns freely. It is always depicted grasped in the operator's left hand, while one would expect him to turn the drill with his right. This hand is, however, shown directed toward the weights.

(*e*) *The Earliest Form of Lathe.* There is a set of machines which in practice provided discontinuous rotary motion, though in principle they were as capable of revolving in one direction as the Egyptian vase-borer. The lathe works on the same essential principles as the drill, but differs from it in two respects. In the lathe, the work, and not the cutting tool, is rotated, and the spindle is horizontal, not vertical. The horizontal arrangement of the spindle almost inevitably involves the use of a second bearing or support, in addition to the socket in which the butt may turn. Moreover, the simplest sort of lathe, the so-called pole-lathe, generally operates by some force independent of the operator though originally generated by his own exertions. It is, in fact, driven by a belt or strap wrapped round the spindle, one end of which is attached to a weight raised by the operator, or to a supple piece of wood which the operator has bent. It is the fall of the weight by gravity, or the recoil of the strained timber, that turns the spindle, which undergoes two or more, but a limited number of, complete revolutions. While this device is geographically fairly widespread, there is no direct evidence

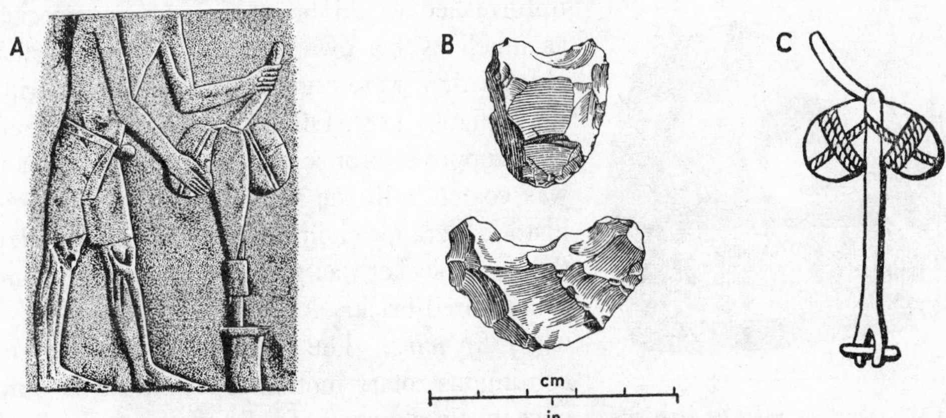

FIGURE 117—(A) *Detail of an Egyptian relief showing the grinding of a vase, from a tomb at Saqqara.* c 2500 B.C. (B) *Two protodynastic examples of the flint bits thus used.* (C) *Hieroglyph representing the drill.*

for its use till classical times.[1] Its employment is in any case later than that of the potter's wheel, which provides continuous rotary motion.

(*f*) *Door-sockets.* Before discussing wheels, which are essential constituents of all machines producing true rotary motion, and which imply bearings, it is necessary to refer to another device, with no direct relation to rotary motion but one which, together with the drill-handle, may have played a part in inspiring the earliest bearings.

Until metal hinges came into use, doors were swung on poles projecting slightly above and below the margins of the door-frame. The upper end hung freely in a loop of hide fixed to the door-post, the lower stood in a hollow in the threshold, or in a stone embedded in the floor at the foot of the door-post. Wooden thresholds equipped with such sockets have been found in Neolithic houses preserved in peat bogs in central Europe. In a slightly more advanced technological stage, but in an earlier period of time, stone door-sockets were used in Hither Asia. As early as the protochalcolithic village of Hassuna in Assyria, that is, by 4500 B.C., we find the characteristic socket stone—a block of stone fixed in the floor of the

[1] I believe, but cannot definitely prove, that it was in use in the Bronze Age in Mesopotamia and the Indus valley.

doorway, with a cup-like depression in the upper surface. At a later date, similar door-sockets were very widely used. They are attested quite early throughout Hither Asia and the Aegean, and before the beginning of our era we find socket stones of the familiar form in Scottish structures that are still 'prehistoric'.

In Mesopotamia, where stone was scarce, door-sockets were always valuable articles. They were not regarded as part of a house; the tenant renting a dwelling unfurnished would bring his own door-socket as much as his own couch. In temples and palaces they were regular vehicles for inscriptions (figure 118). Often the socket was lined with copper or bronze, and the pivot of the gate was coated with the same metal. In the prehistoric Harappa civilization of the Indus valley the stone socket was generally replaced by one of kiln-fired brick.

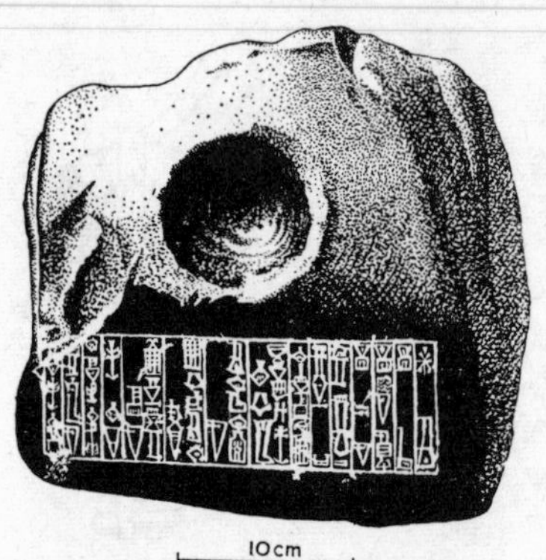

FIGURE 118—*Stone socket for lower pivot of door. The inscription records the restoration of a temple by Gudea, prince of Lagash, Sumer.* c *2500 B.C.*

(*g*) *Spinning.* The earliest application of continuous rotary motion to an industrial purpose involves the use of a different set of human muscles from those employed in boring and drilling—twirling between finger and thumb. Spinning was practised almost from the beginning of the Neolithic revolution. Thus it is substantially older than the more complicated machines for partial rotary motion that have just been discussed.

All Neolithic societies seem to have woven fabrics from spun threads, either of flax, wool, or, in some cases, cotton. In spinning, the threads are wound on a rotating spindle as they are drawn out. The spindle is just a straight stick held vertically between finger and thumb at the upper end. A perforated disk of stone or pottery, termed a whorl, is generally attached to act as a fly-wheel and to maintain the momentum of the spin (figure 273). The spin is started by twirling with the finger and thumb, and this motion must be constantly repeated. As the winding is always in one direction, spinning must rank as true rotary motion, but, from its invention in Neolithic times throughout antiquity and well into the Middle Ages, the spindle was always operated by finger and thumb and worked without bearings.

III. TRUE OR CONTINUOUS ROTARY MOTION

(*a*) *Wheels.* All effective industrial applications of rotary motion have developed from some sort of wheel—ideally a disk equipped with bearings to allow it to spin freely. The manufacture of a disk requires in itself the performance of another rotary motion, namely, tracing a circle. This can be accurately executed only with an appropriate instrument. A true circle can be traced by a length of string, one end of which is fixed, or by a forked stick or bone (a wish-bone for example), one prong of which is rotated on the other as a fixed point. Neither device is likely to survive in the archaeological record, or to be recognized if it did. Yet it is certain that illiterate barbarians in Britain and Ireland, long before 1000 B.C., were accurately marking out large ceremonial circles over 50 metres in diameter, like Grange (Limerick), and Stonehenge. This must have been done with some sort of rope pegged at the centre. Contemporary artists incised smaller but truer circles on stone or metal. These must have been described with a sort of compass, which after all is but a forked stick.

Save for a minute instrument, adjustable in the manner of a beam-compass, from a Bronze Age site in central Italy, no compass survives from earlier than classical times, but hard-pointed, if not necessarily hinged, compasses can be inferred reliably from circles precisely inscribed on bone or clay before 3000 B.C. Most conclusive are some pot-sherds and bricks from the Harappan cities of the Indus basin. On these, soon after 2500 B.C., the impressions of points, almost certainly metallic, can be discerned both at the centre and on the circumference. Slight discrepancies between the diameters of intersecting circles show that the arms of the instrument were movable.

Disks revolving freely on a fixed axis, or with an axle free to turn in a bearing, were in use in both the ceramic and the transport industries between 3500 and 3000 B.C. The earliest reliably dated evidence comes from Sumer and Susiana. Wheels and their essential appurtenances were at first of wood, and consequently can only exceptionally survive. In this respect, however, the potter's wheel is slightly better placed than the vehicular, for it may leave on the pot characteristic striations which an expert can recognize even on a fragment. Though pots are easily broken, pottery is practically indestructible. As a result, the first evidence for potter's wheels seems a little earlier than that for wheeled vehicles, and their distribution can be plotted much more accurately. This apparent priority of the potter's wheel may be adventitious.

(*b*) *The Potter's Wheel: Definitions and Ethnographic Data.* In pottery manufacture the function of the wheel is to supply centrifugal force to a lump of still plastic clay accurately 'thrown' on its centre. Such a well centred lump when spinning fast—100 revolutions per minute at least are required—needs only light guiding-pressure from the potter's hand to rise and assume any sectionally circular form he may wish to impose upon it. Instead of expending his own muscular energy in pressing, moulding, or coiling the clay, he merely directs energy imparted to it. Till the machine age, however, that energy was supplied by human effort and was no more derived from a non-human source of power than that of the bow or the pole-lathe.

Potters' wheels, ancient and modern, are made almost entirely of wood. No ancient ones have survived complete. The striations on wheel-made vases tell hardly anything of the machine that was used in making them, and even the few surviving stone bearings and pottery disks supply at best ambiguous testimony. To get some idea of the first potters' wheels we must examine the folk-industries of the less highly mechanized peoples. Among them we encounter two kinds of machine capable of imparting the requisite spin to the well centred clay. Both are correctly termed wheels, but they are described in French by distinct terms, *tournette* and *tour* respectively. The former name is also applied to another device, the turn-table, that cannot fulfil the distinctive function of a wheel as just defined, though in theory it may be the precursor of the wheel.

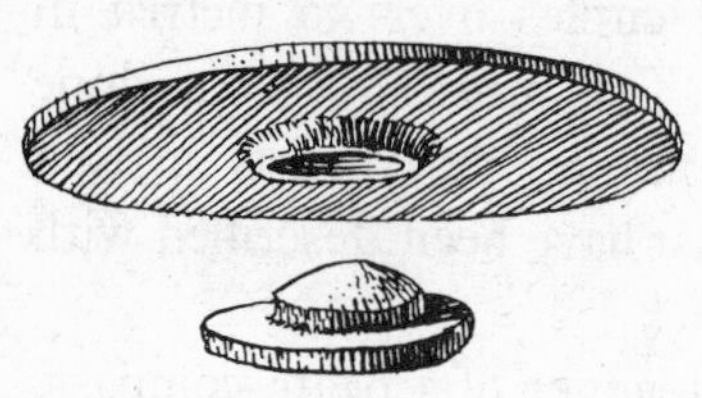

FIGURE 119—*Turn-table and base used by Gelib potters. Diameter 30 cm. Somaliland.*

In building up a large pot by hand, many barbarian potters set the vessel on a movable base—a mat, a stone slab, a sherd—which can be turned as required, to bring the several segments of the pot within convenient reach of the hand. To facilitate turning, the base is occasionally pivoted. The result will be called a turn-table here, and is that described by some French writers as a *tournette*. For example, the Gelib potters in Italian Somaliland use a stout wooden disk, planted firmly on the ground, from the upper surface of which projects a boss. On the boss, a second wooden disk is poised at the centre, and the pot is built up on its upper face (figure 119). Its underside is generally slightly hollowed out at the centre, but not always enough to deserve the name of socket, while the boss is domed, not pointed. Pots are built up on this machine by coiling, the upper disk being slowly turned round by the foot, as the process advances, but never set spinning. It doubtless could be made to spin, though the disk is not heavy enough to maintain its momentum. The true wheel might have developed out of some such device, but there is no evidence for the priority of turn-tables; indeed, no turn-table is known until a time when the wheel had been long in use.

Undocumented speculations as to how wheels might have developed having no place in a history, the turn-table might have been left without further reference. Unfortunately, English archaeological literature has been bedevilled by the translation of the French *tournette* by the self-contradictory term 'slow-wheel'. The term *tournette* should properly be restricted to turn-tables on which the pot is built, not thrown, by the potter. Both the simplest and more complex forms of the potter's wheel are wheels which may be made to spin fast enough to impart centrifugal force to a centred lump of clay. The distinction concerns not the speed, but the source, of the motion. The simple wheel is normally set spinning by the thrower himself, but keeps spinning by its own momentum, like a top. In contrast, the compound wheel consists of two wheels, fixed one above the other on a common axle, so that the thrower can move the lower wheel with his foot, leaving both his hands free to manipulate the clay, which is centred on the upper wheel or head. The compound wheel is, therefore, often called the foot-wheel.

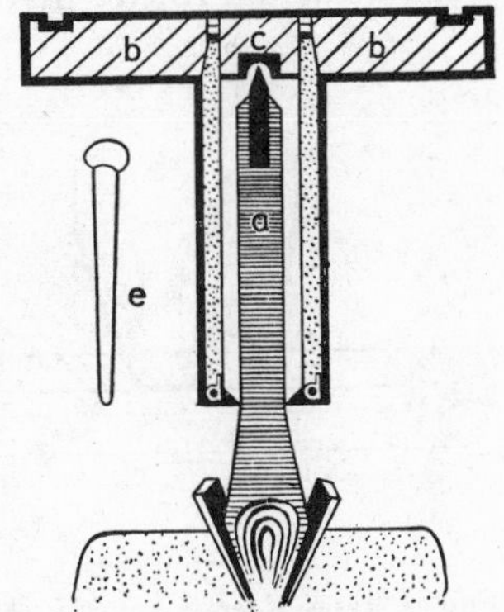

FIGURE 120—*Japanese potter's wheel with socketed disk.* (a) *A hardwood pivot, firmly wedged into a stone or concrete base;* (b) *a hardwood wheel with a porcelain cup as bearing at* (c). *A hollow cylinder extends down the pivot to provide an annular bearing at* (d) *which steadies the wheel;* (e) *is the turning-stick.*

(*c*) *The Simple Wheel.* The simple wheel is essentially a centrally pivoted disk of wood, stone, or clay on a wooden frame. The wheel must be heavy enough to retain its momentum when set spinning. It may be started with the bare hand of the thrower or an assistant, by a jerk with a stick that engages in a notch or hollow near the rim of the disk, or by pulling a strap wound round the rim of the disk or its axle, as in the strap-drill. Once started, even by a jerk from a stick, such a wheel will spin long enough for the thrower to complete a small pot, though for larger pots he may have to use the stick again.

There are two varieties of the simple wheel, which may be termed respectively the socketed and the pivoted disk. In the first, the wheel revolves freely on a fixed pivot which fits into the socket on the underside of the disk (figure 120) Alternatively, the pivot projects from the underside of the disk or is mortised firmly into it, but turns in a fixed socket—generally a stone hollowed out like a door-socket and embedded in the ground (figure 121). In the second type, the pivot, when not in one piece with the disk, may be elongated to become an axle, but then an additional bearing is required above the socket, to support the axle yet allow it to revolve. The socketed disk is used today in south-east Asia—India outside the Indus basin, China, and Japan—and has been reported from the Congo. The pivoted disk, on the other hand, is still used by village potters in Crete, but only to supplement the foot-wheel and mainly as a turn-table in the manufacture of large jars. Finally, the foot-wheel is employed today in Sindh and the Punjab (where it is termed the Pathan wheel), in Iraq, Palestine, Crete, and in the less industrialized countries of continental Europe. It can obviously be regarded as an improvement on the pivoted disk in which a second wheel has been attached to the pivot after it had been elongated into an axle. The survival of the two types side by side, as in the Cretan industry, lends some support to this theory of genetic connexion. Both require a support to steady the axle, which in the foot-wheel comes between the two wheels. All these machines impose severe strain on the bearings, which must support the weight of a disk heavy enough to maintain its momentum for from five to seven minutes.

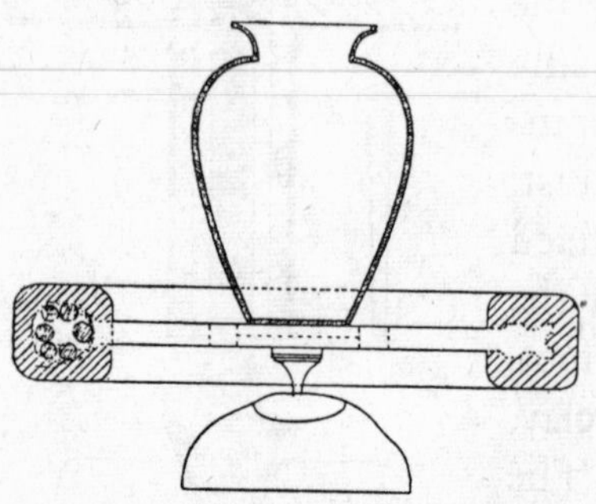

FIGURE 121—*Madrasi potter's wheel with pivoted disk. The rim is made of bent bamboos covered with bonded clay; the spokes and centre are of wood. The pivot is of hardwood or steel. The base is a mass of clay in which is embedded a piece of hardwood or stone with one or two depressions to take the pivot. The wheel is revolved by hand or with a bamboo turning-stick. Diameter about 1 m.*

The fire-drill (p 190), if it helped to suggest the idea of a fixed socket, would have given the first wheelwrights an obvious warning of the friction generated by rapid rotary motion. Ideally, the pivot or spindle should be of metal, or at least cased in metal at its tip, but in practice hard wood is still used both in India and in China. The socket, too, should be metal-lined, like the sockets of temple doors in Babylonia, but no metal linings have been reported. In China, a hard porcelain cup is used as a lining, while in India a flint pebble, concave on one face, is inserted in the underside of the disk. The support needed to steady the axle of the foot-wheel, or of the simple wheel with elongated pivot, is most readily furnished by a horizontal plank perforated with a hole through which the axle passes, but further friction will arise between its edges and the revolving shaft. On the other hand, the socketed disk and the short-pivoted disk will require some support while at rest. When in full spin, each would doubtless remain horizontal, but friction with the support is liable to retard starting-up. At these points lubricants—fats, vegetable oils, or bitumen—might be helpful.

(*d*) *Ancient Potters' Wheels: the Archaeological Evidence.* In so far as they were made of wood, these machines have left no trace. Luckily, however, the heavy disks were often made of clay or stone, and these may survive; a few have actually been recognized by excavators, and a score adequately described. The bearings of one type of wheel consisted of pivoted and socketed stones in pairs.

Since 1908, such pairs have been turning up in Palestine and were described as grinders (figure 124). Their connexion with potters' wheels was not suspected till 1939, but by 1951 several had been disinterred. Flint bearings, such as are described in India, have doubtless survived too, but have been consigned, unrecognized, to the excavation dumps. Finally, Egyptian tomb-paintings from 2600 B.C. contain lively, but painfully ambiguous, pictures of potters at work using a simple wheel—or a turn-table (p 200).

The oldest surviving portion of a potter's wheel can be dated 3250±250 B.C. At Ur, in 1930, Woolley found in a layer now described as of the Uruk period,

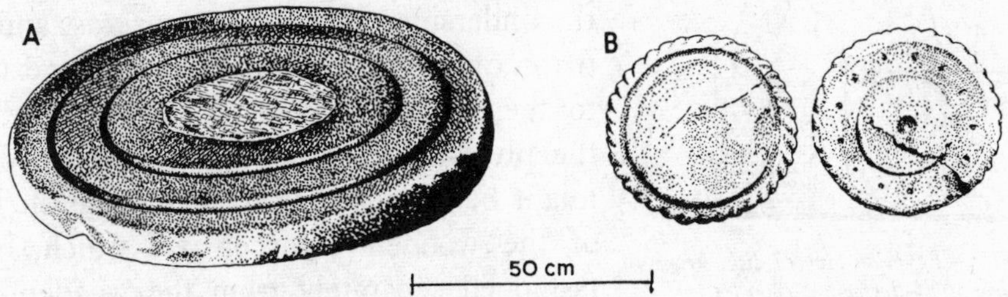

FIGURE 122—(A) *Upper face of a Mesopotamian potter's wheel in clay, from Erech.* c 2000 *B.C.* (B) *Minoan socketed clay disk.*

among the debris of many potters' kilns, part of 'a thick disk of clay with its pivot hole smeared with bitumen and a series of small holes near its circumference'. A complete clay disk, 90 cm in diameter and 8 cm thick, had been buried with its owner at Erech (in Sumer) about 2000 B.C. (figure 122 A). In this case a round patch of bitumen was used to support the clay on the upper face of the disk, on which there were three concentric rings in relief; but the socket-hole on the underside is explicitly mentioned. Over a score of similar disks of varying sizes have been dug up from towns and palace-workshops in Minoan Crete (figure 122 B), while further examples were subsequently found in Middle Helladic strata on Aegina and in mainland Greece. All these disks admittedly belong to genuine wheels, but it is by no means certain how the wheels themselves should be classified.

The excavator of the Minoan disks, Xanthudides, compared them to those now used by the island potters and placed by them upon their wheels, which are of wood. The smaller Minoan disks, 24 to 25 cm in diameter, and two stone disks of 21 and 22 cm in diameter, he compared to those now set upon the head of the foot-wheel. Larger clay disks, 29 to 40 cm across and 5 cm thick, he regards as equivalent to those used by contemporary potters in making large storage jars on a simple wheel of the pivoted-disk group, used principally as a turn-table.

Holes on the surface of the disks would then be designed to make them adhere better to the surface of the wooden disk, which is still smeared with wet clay. On this interpretation, the clay disks would be evidence for the use of the pivoted disk and of the foot-wheel in Minoan Crete and in mainland Greece from 1800 B.C.

Woolley, on the contrary, clearly regarded the disk from Ur as part of a socketed disk, as did other excavators in describing the specimen from Erech; the series of holes near the rim would be used in starting up the wheel, as are the notches in which the Chinese potter engages his stick. Now the Cretan disks, too, have central depressions on the underside, three to five cm across and one to three cm deep. On the theory of their excavator these central hollows, and presumably even the pivot-holes on the Mesopotamian disks, might be supposed to accommodate the head of the wooden pivot or axle which, being fashioned separately from the wooden disk, might conceivably project through it. But are they not really the sockets into which fitted, with or without the interposition of some lining or bearing, the wooden pivot upon which the wheel turned? In that case, the clay disks would establish the existence in the Aegean and Hither Asia, during the Bronze Age, of wheels of the socketed disk group to which the south-east Asian wheels belong.

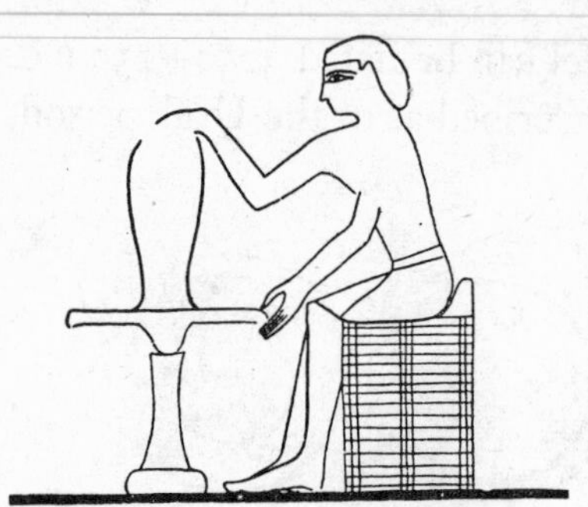

FIGURE 123—*Egyptian pivoted disk. From a tomb at El-Bersheh.* c *1800* B.C.

The pivoted disk seems, however, to be explicitly represented in the Egyptian tomb pictures which begin shortly before 2500 B.C. In a painting of *c* 1800 B.C. the disk, coloured red as if of wood or baked clay, has on the lower face a dome-shaped pivot of the same material, which rests on a fixed base of grey stone (figure 123). The potter is shaping a tall lump of (white) clay centred on the disk with his right hand, while the left is extended towards the disk. After 1500 B.C., however, the disk, equally simple, seems to be moved with the feet (figure 234). It must be admitted that in most of such pictures the potters look as if they were operating turn-tables rather than spinning wheels, but no other wheels are depicted, while wheel-marks are reported on most Egyptian vases after 2750 B.C.

No foot-wheel could be expected to survive 3000 years, and none is depicted before 1000 B.C. There is, however, some indirect or inferential evidence for the use of such wheels in the Near East well before 2000 B.C. Firstly the paired 'grinders' from Palestine are most likely bearings for foot-wheels (figure 124). The plane faces show a high polish, with concentric striae produced by rotary motion. The polished surface of the socketed member is often surrounded by a low collar, inside which the other member fits. Mentioned first in 1908, the connexion of these stones with a potter's wheel was not established until 1939. Another pair was found at Lachish, in a cave which served about 1200 B.C. as a potter's workshop and contained stores of prepared clay, pigments, and other distinctive utensils of the craft. In the floor had been hollowed a pit suitable to accommodate a foot-wheel, with a stone seat near its edge.

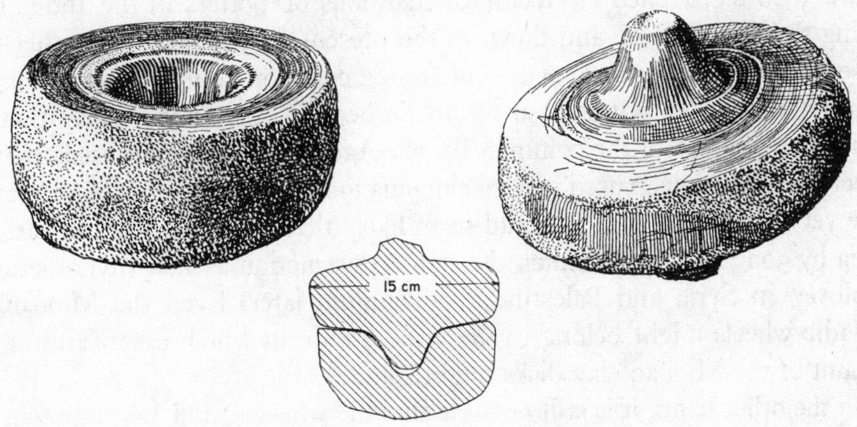

FIGURE 124—*Potter's wheel-bearing from Jericho.*

Arab potters in Palestine still use precisely similar pairs of stones as bearings for their foot-wheel. The socketed member is firmly embedded in the bottom of the pit. The pivoted stone fits into it, tenon downwards, while to its reverse is attached the large wooden disk which the potter actuates with his foot, and a stout wooden axle, the upper end of which supports the smaller wheel or head upon which the pot is thrown. The axle is steadied by a looped iron rod set across the pit, but is not exactly vertical. It must be assumed that this modern device is directly descended from the Bronze Age, the sole modification being the replacement of a perforated plank by an iron support for the axle. In that case, the Bronze Age paired stones must be accepted as bearings for foot-wheels.

They have been found at Megiddo, Gezer, Jericho, Lachish, and other sites in Palestine, at Ugarit on the north Syrian coast, Hama on the Orontes, and Halaf on the Khabur in northern Mesopotamia. At least at Hama, some specimens are securely dated before 2000 B.C. Hence, on the above assumption, the foot-wheel was extensively used over a wide area of Hither Asia before 2000 B.C. There are indirect arguments in favour of extending its domain in space and time.

As we have seen, the foot-wheel is today common to Syria-Palestine, Iraq, and western India, but is unknown in the rest of the Indian peninsula or farther east. But the technical traditions of village potters in Sindh and the Punjab, and their more durable tools, are identical with those applied and employed by the prehistoric potters of Harappa and Mohenjo-Daro as early as 2500 B.C. At the same time, the techniques and durable tools of the Harappa potters are just as closely allied to those current among Sumerian potters in Mesopotamia even before 3000 B.C. Hence the technical traditions of potters in the Indus basin during the Bronze Age, and down to the present day, are derived either from those of Bronze Age Mesopotamia or from a common source. As the contemporary Indus valley potters use the foot-wheel, it seems most likely that this device too was part of the common Bronze Age heritage. In that case, the foot-wheel would have been used in Mesopotamia too by 3000 B.C. While no bearings have yet been recognized, it would seem likely that the wheel used in Mesopotamia by 3000 B.C. was of much the same construction as that (hypothetically) employed in Syria and Palestine a millennium later. Even the Minoan and Helladic wheels might belong to the same group, in which case Xanthudides' account of the Minoan clay disks might stand.

On the other hand, it is still possible that the wheel shared by Sumerian and Indus potters by 2500 B.C. was a simple wheel of the socketed disk group, which would have been transmitted to the rest of India and to China from the Indus basin. If so, the foot-wheel would have been developed after 2500 B.C. from some undocumented type of pivoted disk common to Egypt and Syria-Palestine about 2750 B.C. The foot-wheel would then have spread to western India with the rotary quern in Hellenistic times. This second reconstruction of the course of events looks rather less plausible than that given in the previous paragraph.

(*e*) *Origin and Diffusion of the Potter's Wheel.* The deficiencies of the archaeological record forbid any attempt to define precisely what sort of wheel was used in any given province at any given time, but sherds of wheel-made vases give more or less exact dates for the appearance of potters' wheels in any province. These dates, as far as they go, lend support to the thesis that the idea of making pots on a fast-spinning wheel was diffused, and they furnish some clues as to the original focus.

The earliest evidence of this kind comes from Mesopotamia. This is largely, but not exclusively, because written history, beginning earlier there, affords a higher *terminus ante quem* for prehistoric chronology than is available elsewhere, save in Egypt. We should be going beyond our evidence if we claimed that the use of the wheel in Sumer before 3000 B.C. is absolutely the oldest, for a potter's wheel was certainly used in India before 2500 B.C. and presumably just as early in Iran. The archaeological record from Persia and India is, however, still so incomplete, and a continuous written tradition begins there so late (only after 600 B.C.), that priority for Iran can be neither proved nor disproved. It can merely be stated that the potter's wheel was used in Sumer or Iran, or both, earlier than in China or Egypt or Syria or Crete.

As far as the west is concerned, we can add that the farther we move from the Persian Gulf and the Tigris, the later is the first appearance of wheel-made vases. Some likely approximate dates are: Sumer 3250±250; Mediterranean coast of Syria and Palestine 3000; Egypt 2750; Crete 2000; mainland Greece 1800; south Italy 750; upper Danube—upper Rhine basins 400; southern England 50 B.C.; Scotland 400 A.D.; the Americas 1550 A.D. If then we plotted isochrons—contour lines representing the first appearance of wheel-made pots—at 400-year intervals, we should find the 'anticyclone' round the head of the Persian Gulf. If this be accepted as proof of diffusion, it is not of course diffusion of the wheel. We have encountered at least three machines that could leave the evidential marks on our pots. It was the utilization of the centrifugal force imparted to a fast-spinning lump of clay, rather than any particular device for making the lump spin, that was diffused.

Admitting diffusion, the date of adoption of the idea at any given place would not be a simple function of its distance from the hypothetical centre of invention. Potters' wheels are not toys, but machines for the rapid production of fragile pots, and they are operated by full-time specialists. Whereas the housewife built up by hand the pots needed for domestic use, just as she made the family clothes, full-time specialists manufactured vases on the wheel for sale, and got their living by selling them. In other words, a precondition for the use of the wheel is a social surplus sufficient to support the potter and his family—that is, an effective market for his wares. Pots, being fragile and bulky, cannot normally be exported under primitive conditions of transport over any considerable distances. The market must be local. With the low productivity of primitive farming, it would not pay to set up a wheel in a village of less than a couple of hundred households. That may seem a modest enough figure to us, but in Europe, north of the Alps, no settlement unit approached that magnitude before 500 B.C. From Neolithic times, population remained scattered in hamlets of from ten to fifty houses. It was in the Near East and in the great river valleys that the requisite density of population was soonest reached.

It does not take a very large social surplus to support a potter; the raw materials for his wares as well as for his equipment are generally available locally. A potter is much less expensive than a smith. Yet even in the Near East few villages would need, or could afford, more than one potter. Hence if they were to follow the family profession, a potter's younger sons would have to emigrate and seek a growing village in want of a potter. That necessity provides a mechanism whereby the wheel could have been diffused. At the same time, the professional who came to a new village would have to adapt his shapes and designs to conservative local tastes. The first wheel-made pots generally reproduce the forms and decorative style in vogue locally for hand-made vessels. Technical agreements with other countries may, however, betray the foreign origin of professional potters. On Aegina, the first professional potters not only used the Minoan form of clay wheel-disks, but tried to reproduce Minoan styles in the local clay, thereby disclosing their Cretan origin to modern archaeologists.

The potter's wheel might seem the pioneer of those machines that turn out cheap consumption goods by the application of rotary motion. This is not quite accurate. Admittedly, thanks to the wheel, a professional can shape in ten minutes a vessel that might take a housewife ten hours to build by hand. This acceleration, however, is achieved not by simply speeding up the manipulations, but by a change in the forces employed. The energy required to shape a pot by hand is entirely supplied by the potter; in throwing, it is the momentum of the spinning wheel which the potter has merely to guide without appreciable expenditure of bodily force. This holds good whether the wheel is spun by the potter's hand or foot, by an assistant, or by a steam-engine. Thus regarded, the potter's wheel has contributed less directly to the general development of rotating machines than the quern. To the invention of this latter device for grinding grain the potter's wheel, or at least the stone bearings of the Syro-Palestinian type, doubtless contributed, but the result will emerge only in the period dealt with in the next volume of this work.

(*f*) *Wheeled Vehicles: Carts and Wagons with Tripartite 'Solid' Wheels and Paired Draught.* Transport was revolutionized by the application of the wheel idea very soon after, if not at about the same time as, the transformation of the ceramic industry by the potter's wheel. The early evidence for the wheel in transport is sparser though more complete. Wheeled vehicles can be made even more completely of wood and other perishable materials than potters' wheels, and rarely leave such imperishable traces as the latter. On the other hand, owing to the prestige soon acquired by wheeled vehicles, they were often buried in royal tombs, where a few have survived intact or have left very complete impressions in the soil; or they were deposited as votive offerings in bogs which have

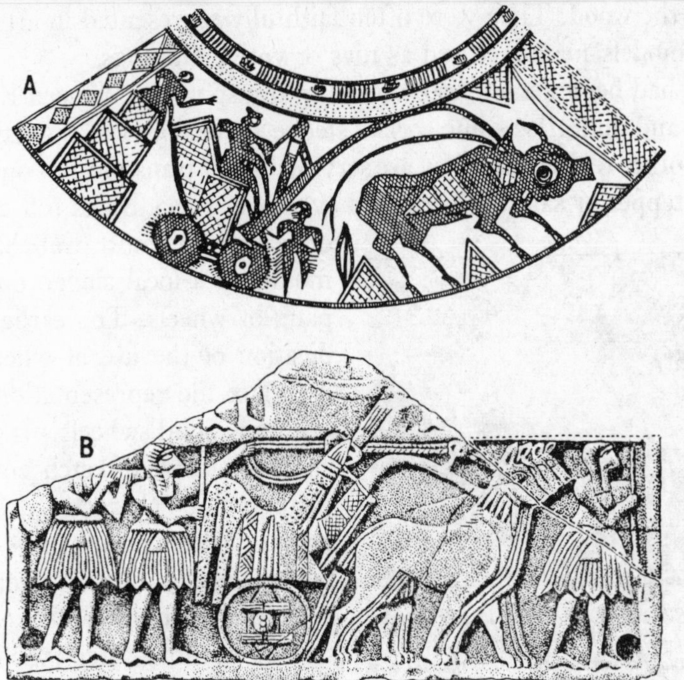

FIGURE 125—(A) *Cart on a scarlet ware vase from Susa, Iran.* (B) *Limestone relief from Ur, reconstructed at upper right from a similar relief found at Khafaje, Mesopotamia. Both before 2500 B.C.*

FIGURE 126—*Pictographs from Erech, Mesopotamia, representing sledge and cart. c 3500 B.C.*

FIGURE 127—*Toy model of a covered wagon from Tepe Gawra, Assyria. Third millennium B.C.*

preserved the wood. They were often faithfully represented in art (figure 125), or in clay models manufactured as toys or votive offerings.

Sledges had been demonstrably used in transport in northern Europe before 5000 B.C., and doubtless some sort of sledge or travois was similarly used just as early in other regions; for they are serviceable for transport not only over snow, but over steppes or sandy deserts and even over rocky tracts (ch 26). The cart or wagon was most probably created by mounting a local sledge on one or two pairs of wheels. The earliest extant indication of the use of wheeled vehicles is in fact the representation of a sledge on four solid wheels. It is a rather conventionalized sketch employed as a pictographic character in the oldest extant written documents—the account tablets of the Inanna temple at Erech in lower Mesopotamia (Sumer), inscribed not long after 3500 B.C. Another character in the same tablets depicts the sledge, which is just the wagon without the wheels (figure 126). Nearly a thousand years later, in the famous royal cemetery at Ur, we still find sledges as well as carts and wagons used as hearses at royal funerals.

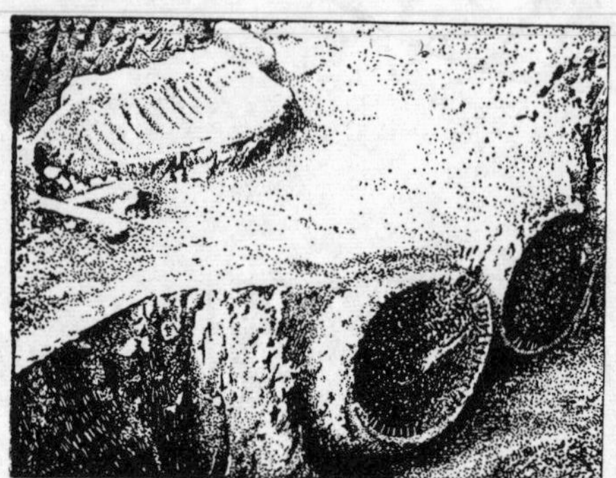

FIGURE 128—*Remains of the hearse in a royal tomb at Kish, Mesopotamia. Third millennium* B.C. *The metal studs round the rims and, behind, the ribs of a draught animal can be seen.*

Several royal tombs at Kish, Susa, and Ur, of between 3000 and 2000 B.C., contain actual vehicles (figure 128), while numerous works of art (figures 125, 517) from these and other Mesopotamian cities, and clay models (figures 127, 516), found not only in Mesopotamia but in Assyria, north Syria, the Indus valley, and even Turkmenia, provide relatively detailed information on the structure of carts and wagons as well as evidence for their use. At later periods, royal tombs, votive deposits in bogs, models, or pictures illustrate the use of similar types in Georgia, south Russia, upper Italy, and Denmark. Indeed, in the ethnographic record, the archaic vehicles known from the archaeological record before 2000 B.C. in Mesopotamia and the Indus basin can be paralleled in China, Sindh, the Balkans, Sardinia, Spain, Scandinavia, and the British Isles.

Two peculiarities distinguish all the oldest vehicles known to archaeologists and the types most widespread in non-industrialized countries today—solid wheels and paired draught. Solid wheels are distinguished not only by the absence of spokes but by another feature. Most wheels anterior to 2000 B.C., and the most widely distributed type today, are tripartite disks. They consist of three wooden planks carved to fit segments of a circle and clamped together by a pair of transverse wooden struts, while a swelling left in the middle of the central plank forms a raised hub round the axle hole. The axle was fashioned independently and projected beyond the hub, but neither archaeological nor ethnographic data suffice to decide whether the wheels revolved freely on the axle or turned with it. In the ancient royal tombs, at most only a thin film of actual wood survives, the woodwork being represented otherwise by replacement soil, distinguishable from the surrounding earth only by its darker colour, so that two excavators have given contrary answers to the question. Copper models from Babylonia and Syria respectively are equally ambiguous (figures 519, 129). However, the axle holes are always circular in models and pictures, and allegedly in the royal hearses too. In the Sumerian pictures, a wooden peg is shown fixed through the axle as if to prevent the wheel from coming off. In a rather later tomb at Susa (about 2000 B.C.), the peg is replaced by a copper bolt with decorative head, precisely like the linch-pins familiar in later periods. These features seem most appropriate to free-turning wheels. On the other hand, in the village carts in modern Sindh, which preserve the main outlines of the ancient Harappan vehicles, the wheels turn in one piece with the axle, as do those of many other recent carts with solid wheels (figure 42).

FIGURE 129—*Copper model of a wagon from north Syria.*

The tripartite disk is demonstrably the oldest as well as the most widespread form of simple wheel, but it is by no means the only conceivable form, or theoretically the simplest. The wide distribution of this particular form accordingly constitutes a very cogent argument for the diffusion of the device. It is also an argument against the popular theory of the derivation of vehicular wheels from rollers—a theory unsupported by any direct archaeological evidence. One reason for the complex tripartite structure might be the absence of trees large enough to yield solid planks of adequate width in the region where the wheeled vehicle was invented. In Denmark, a well wooded country, we do find wheels carved from a single wide plank side by side with tripartite disks. Again, it is difficult to imagine how wheels of any kind could be fashioned without saws and, therefore, since saws for cutting timber must be made of metal, without a supply of copper sufficient for the manufacture of large metal tools. It may be significant that at

Kish, in the hearse graves, but in no others, metal saws were actually found. Both these considerations favour Mesopotamia as a centre of invention.

While the features described above are almost universal concomitants of the tripartite disk, the early Mesopotamian and Elamite specimens already exhibit refinements not so universally attested. In an exceptionally well preserved wheel from Susa, datable soon after 2500 B.C., the three planks were encircled by a felloe, also apparently of wood, 4·5 cm high (figure 130). It was impossible to

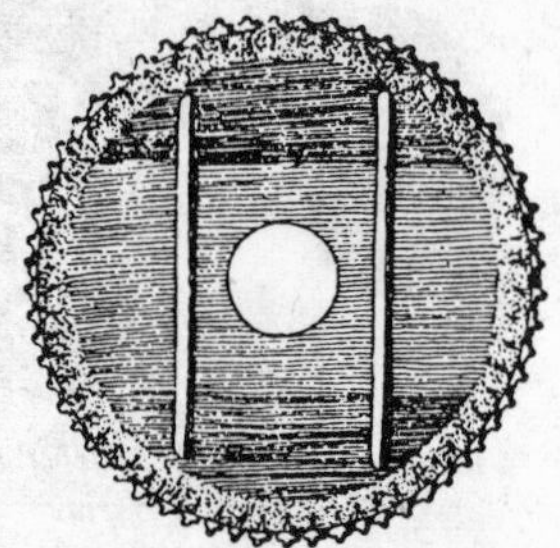

FIGURE 130—*Nail-studded wheel from Susa (Apadana). c 2500 B.C. Diameter 0·75 m.*

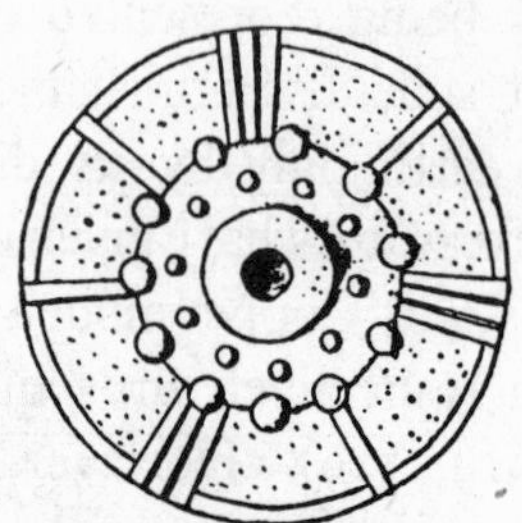

FIGURE 131—*Representation of a copper tire on a model wheel from Susa.*

determine whether the felloe was formed of several segments mortised together, or of a single strip bent by heat. The rim of this wheel, like those of contemporary wheels from Ur and of earlier wheels from Kish, was studded with small copper nails, and similar nails are faithfully represented, projecting like cogs from the circumferences of the wheels, in pictures and models from 3000 B.C. The primary function of these nails was to protect the rims from wear. The device was retained even after metal tires had come into use—for instance, among the Assyrians and Achaemenid Persians.

The copper studs round the wheels at Ur may also have served to fasten leather tires to the wooden disks. There have been observed ambiguous traces of such tires, which would help to keep the three planks together. In modern Ulster, the transverse clamps are removed as soon as the iron tires are fitted, since the latter suffice to hold the three planks in position. Copper tires were in fact attached to chariot wheels at Susa about 2000 B.C. They consisted of four or six concave copper bands, forming segments of a circle. They fitted over the rims of the tripartite disks, to which they were clamped with the aid of pairs of tongues projecting radially towards the hub from both ends of each tire-segment (figure 131). These wheels at least were remarkably thin, the tread of the tire being only 3 cm wide.

Most early wheels are comparatively small. Typical diameters are:

Site	Date B.C.	Diameters (metres)	
		Front wheels	*Rear wheels*
Kish	2750	0·50	0·50
Ur.	2500	0·60	0·80
	,,	1·00	1·00
Susa	,,	0·66	0·83
	2000	1·05	chariot
Trialeti (Georgia)	1500	1·15	1·15
Yelista (S. Russia)	? 1200	0·70	cart
Mercurago (N. Italy)	? 1000	..	..
Dystrup Mose (Denmark). . . .	200	? 0·54	..
Tapper (N. Germany)	,,	0·92	..

(*g*) *Uses and Origin of Wheeled Vehicles.* The most obvious use for carts and wagons would be to convey bulky foodstuffs from the fields to the settlements, and to carry farmyard manure in the opposite direction. By thus allowing a larger population to be fed at a single centre, the invention of the wheeled vehicle must have contributed to the urban revolution. That it was used for long-distance commerce is less likely, since roads and bridges would be available only within the narrow territories of small states. Nevertheless, as early as 1200 B.C. migrating hordes from the north did convey their families and chattels across Palestine to the frontiers of Egypt, in ox-carts with solid wheels which Egyptian artists, after the repulse of the invasion, duly depicted on the north wall of Rameses' temple at Medinet Habu. While wheeled vehicles were doubtless often employed for such rational purposes, their earliest uses, and those best attested in the archaeological record, were as engines of war and as hearses to convey royal corpses to their tombs.

The earliest actual vehicles that survive are the hearses buried with draught animals and human attendants in the royal tombs at Kish, Susa, and Ur. Before 2500 B.C., burial with a hearse had become a prerogative of kings in Mesopotamia. Significantly enough, the first wheeled vehicles to survive in Georgia, south Russia, Bohemia, and Bavaria are also hearses, buried in the tombs of barbarian kings or chiefs. It looks as if the association of wheeled vehicles and kingship had been diffused with the wheel itself.

Yet even before 3000 B.C. the wheeled vehicle was being used also as a military engine. Chariotry was undoubtedly a decisive arm in Sumerian warfare before and after 2500 B.C. By 2000 B.C. it was playing a similar role in north Syria. Considering the relatively small total resources available to early urban societies, the war chariot is fairly comparable to the tank of today; it was an engine which only a rich civilized state could produce and maintain, and against which no barbarian tribe or rebellious peasantry could compete. Improvements in vehicular transport may well have been developed for war-chariots, much as advances in aeronautics have been first associated with military planes. Of the improvements to be considered in this volume, the spoked wheel, appearing in the archaeological and literary record just after 2000 B.C., is the most significant. Before examining that innovation further, the origin and diffusion of wheeled vehicles in general should be briefly discussed.

The peculiarities of the oldest and most widely distributed type of wheel, the tripartite disk, have already been cited as indicative that the device was diffused; for it is *a priori* most improbable that people at several different centres should independently have hit upon just this kind of wheel. Paired draught points in the same way, since sledges and carts can be, and are, pulled by beasts harnessed to traces or between shafts, while the yoke is now hardly used except for harnessing oxen. The yoke was surely designed originally to fit the shoulders of oxen, and only secondarily transferred to onagers, horses, and asses—to their great discomfort. Oxen had been yoked to ploughs in many regions long before they or any other draught animals began locally pulling carts or wagons. Since evidence for ploughs is usually still harder to come by than that for wheels, this statement cannot be proved for Mesopotamia or the Indus valley, but it is demonstrably true of Egypt, Cyprus, Poland, and Denmark. Moreover, paired draught is virtually imposed by what we have come to think of as the natural form of the plough.

We have seen that the oldest wheeled vehicle in Sumer was a sledge on wheels. Can we not go on to say that it was a sledge on wheels attached in place of share and beam to the pole of an ox-drawn plough? On the other hand, when that combination was first conceived the sledge had already been in use for at least 2000 years. That gave time for it to develop into divergent local forms. The earliest wheeled vehicles in the several localities have been found to differ in chassis-construction and body-build, despite uniformity in type of wheel and method of traction. This diversity would be at once intelligible if different local types of sledge had been mounted on a common type of wheel. All that was diffused would then be the idea of the wheel—the tripartite wheel, of course—and of paired draught for it.

The theory that so much at least was in fact diffused can be further supported by plotting the distribution of the first wheeled vehicles on isochrons. The conditions governing the diffusion of wheeled vehicles differ from those found to hold good for potters' wheels. For practical purposes, carts and wagons are not much better than sledges in heavily wooded or mountainous country, and cannot compete with water-transport in a narrow river valley like Egypt. On the other hand, as an arm in war and a weapon of prestige the chariot would become essential for the preservation of tribal independence. Nor did their acquisition require any particular density of population, though it did presuppose a social surplus adequate to maintain and keep supplied at least one full-time coppersmith.

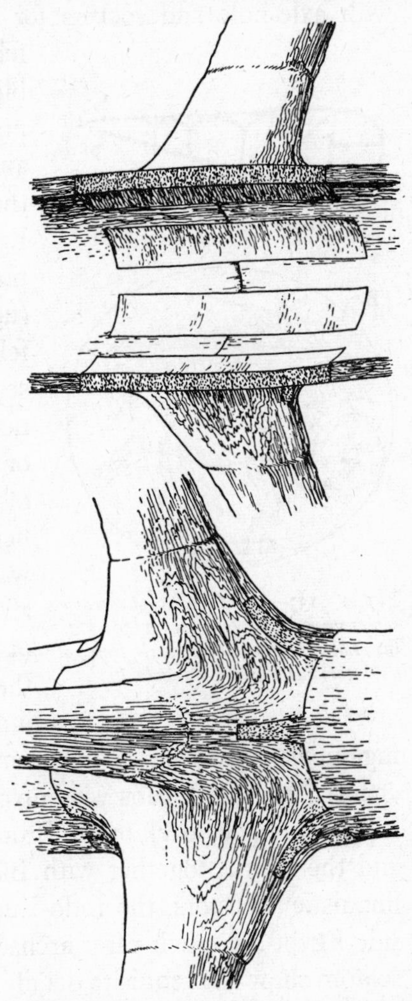

FIGURE 132—*Wooden hub of a chariot wheel from an Egyptian tomb, section and view.* c *1350* B.C. *Internal diameter 6–6·3 cm.*

We find, then, wheeled vehicles in use in Sumer soon after 3500 B.C.; in Elam and probably as far up the Tigris as Assyria about 3000; on the steppes of central Asia and in the Indus valley soon after 2500; on the upper Euphrates just before or after 2250; on the Orontes, in south Russia, and in Crete about 2000 (these all solid wheeled); in central Anatolia about 1800; in Egypt and Palestine about 1600; in mainland Greece and Georgia about 1500; in China by 1300; in north Italy before 1000; in central and northern Europe a little after that date; and in Britain about 500 B.C. This pattern, as far as it goes, accords well with previously cited indications pointing to a cradle in lower Mesopotamia, but the earliest wheeled vehicles actually represented in the archaeological record, both on the Greek mainland and north of the Alps, already have spoked wheels.

(*h*) *Spoked Wheels in War and Peace.* Solid wheels are strong and perfectly efficient for the transport of goods, hence their long survival; but where speed and manoeuvrability are required they are heavy and clumsy. In the spoked wheel these defects are reduced to a minimum, so they rapidly replaced solid wheels on war-chariots, for which pace and easy control are crucial. On the other hand, spoked wheels must be even more costly than tripartite disks, for they demand more labour and higher skill. A spoked wheel must consist of at least the following parts, each of which has to be fashioned separately: a hub with axle-hole and sockets for the spokes; four to eight spokes; a felloe or felloes. The hub is usually carved out of a single block of wood, but in ancient Egypt was composite. Each spoke must be of the same length, and trimmed at both ends to fit exactly into the dowel holes on the hub and felloe; ancient Egyptian wheel-wrights made their spokes of two pieces of wood glued together longitudinally (figure 132). The Egyptians normally made their felloes ot several segments of wood, carved separately to fit on the same circle and then connected by mortise and tenon joints. But in one or two Egyptian wheels the greater part at least of the felloe consists of a single strip of wood, bent by heat (figure 525). And by 500 B.C. Celtic wainwrights in Bohemia and the Rhineland were already shaping the felloe from a single length of timber, bent into a circular form with heat; the ends were bevelled and overlapped, and the junction was held by a metal swathe. This ingenious technique is apparently referred to in one of the Vedic hymns, chanted by the Aryans who invaded India between 2000 and 1000 B.C. Thus it probably goes back to the Bronze Age, and was diffused between the Ganges and the Rhine, together with Indo-European languages, by our half-mythical linguistic ancestors, the Indo-Europeans. But, since actual spoked wheels outside Egypt are much rarer archaeologically than tripartite disks, while pictures seldom show the requisite detail, the distribution of these two methods of felloe construction cannot be more closely defined.

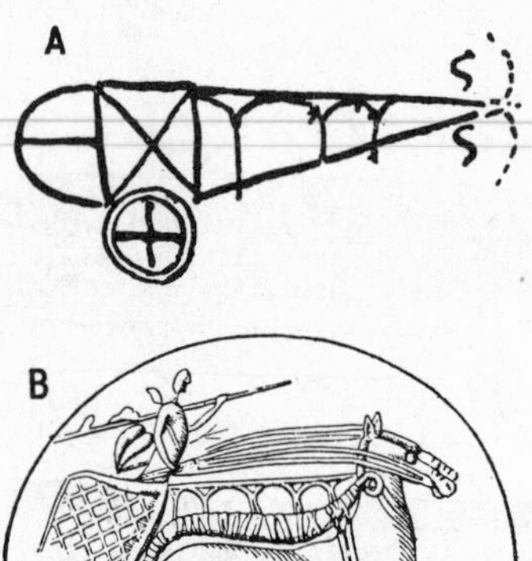

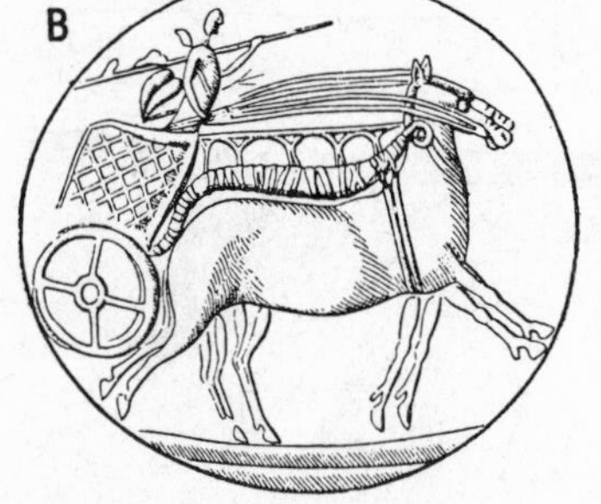

FIGURE 133—(A) *Cretan pictograph representing a chariot.* c *1500 B.C.* (B) *Late Minoan bead seal from a tomb at Vaphio.* c *1400 B.C.*

Spoked wheels are first represented in the archaeological record just after 2000 B.C., by painted clay models from Chagar Bazar on the Khabur in northern Mesopotamia, on seals from Cappadocia (central Turkey), and on an imported seal found at Hissar in north-eastern Persia. They were soon in use throughout Hither Asia—how soon is uncertain owing to a curious lacuna in the record of several centuries. They were adopted in Egypt soon after 1600 B.C. (figure 134), are repeatedly depicted on clay tablets from Knossos in Crete about 1500 B.C.

(figure 133 A), and were figured on grave stelae from Mycenae by 1500 B.C. In China, spoked wheels are fitted to the war-chariots of the Shang dynasts who established the first historical empire about 1300 B.C., while in northern Europe a four-spoked wheel is represented on a chariot carved in a chieftain's tomb at Kivik in south-eastern Sweden somewhere about 1000 B.C. In central Europe,

FIGURE 134—*Egyptian wheel-wrights. From a tomb at Thebes. c 1475 B.C.*

their use is attested a little earlier by so-called wheeled cauldrons of bronze, used to contain the ashes of cremated chieftains in both Bohemia and Denmark, while a gold sun-disk mounted on four-spoked wheels from Trundholm in Denmark may be still older.

Four-spoked wheels are characteristic of the vehicles on Cappadocian seals, of Egyptian chariots before 1400 B.C. (figures 134, 525), of all Minoan and Mycenaean chariots in the Aegean area (figure 133 A, B), of the Kivik chariot (figure 524), and of the central European bronze vessels. A larger number of spokes is, however, attested quite early: eight or more on a model wheel from Chagar Bazar about 1900 B.C., and six regularly on Hittite and Syrian chariots by 1400 B.C.

It is generally believed that the spoked wheel developed out of the solid wheel by multiplication of openings carved in the wooden planks. It is true that a pair of crescentic slits round the hub has been carved in some solid wheels from upper Italy and Denmark, and is still so carved on the wheels of Sindh carts, but these examples are quite late and, in any case, crescentic openings bear no relation to the radial spaces between spokes. There is no real archaeological evidence for this theory of the origin of spokes. The only wheel which looks in the least like a transitional form is from the lake-dwelling of Mercurago in upper Italy (figure 135). In it, a single plank has been carved to form the hub and two spokes, one on each side. Into the edges of these spokes, two pairs of 'spokes' have been mortised, not into the hub. Finally, segments of wood, carved to fit a single circle, have been fitted on to the six free ends. This odd object is probably not much older than 1000 B.C., and is certainly more recent than the perfectly regular spoked wheels on the grave stelae from Mycenae and the tablets from Knossos, to say nothing of the still earlier Asiatic specimens. It looks more like the product of a wheelwright who had seen a spoked wheel without being initiated into the mysteries of its construction, than a stage in its development from the tripartite disk.

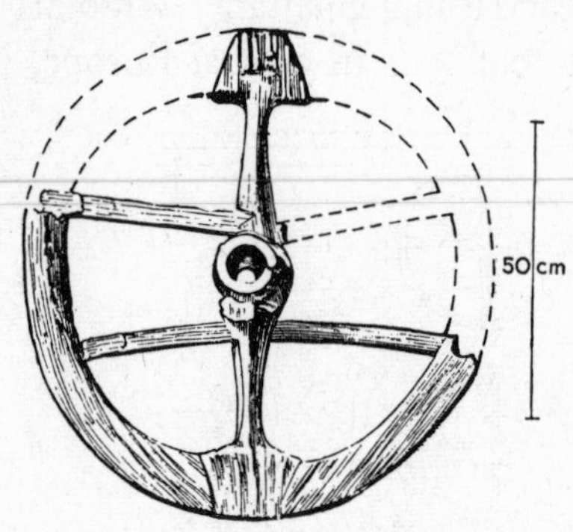

FIGURE 135—*Wheel from Mercurago, northern Italy. Late Bronze Age.*

Though naturally an expression of the wheel idea, the spoked wheel was a new invention rather than a modification of the tripartite disk. Other new applications of rotary motion, such as the windlass, may have been invented shortly before or after 1000 B.C. They cannot be given more than mere mention here. The archaeological evidence is still too scanty to determine even the date of invention, to say nothing of the structure of what was invented. The next great extensions of the domain of rotary motion—the olive-press, the quern, the donkey-mill, the water-wheel, the capstan, and the screw—were achievements of the classical period.

BIBLIOGRAPHY

Drilling and Boring:

BISSING, F. W. VON. 'Steingefässe.' Catal. gén. antiq. égypt. Mus. Caire. Holzhausen, Vienna. 1904.

CATON-THOMPSON, G. 'The Desert Fayum.' R. Anthrop. Inst. Publ., London. 1934.

MCGUIRE, J. D. "A Study of the Primitive Method of Drilling." *Rep. Smithson. Instn for 1894*, pp. 623–756. Washington. 1896.

OAKLEY, K. P. 'Man the Tool Maker' (2nd ed.). British Museum, Natural History, London. 1950.

PETRIE, SIR (WILLIAM MATTHEW) FLINDERS. 'Tools and Weapons.' Egypt. Res. Acc. and Brit. Sch. Archaeol. Egypt, Publ. 30. London. 1917.

Potters' Wheels and Wheelbearings:

WOOLLEY, SIR (CHARLES) LEONARD. "Excavations at Ur." *Antiq. J.*, **10**, 332, 1930.

HEINRICH, E. 'Sechster vorläufiger Bericht über die in Uruk-Warka unternommenen Ausgrabungen', p. 25, Pl. XV *a. Abh. preuss. Akad. Wiss., phil.-hist. Kl.*, no. 2. 1935.

XANTHUDIDES, S. "Some Minoan Potter's-wheel Discs" in 'Essays in Aegean Archaeology presented to Sir Arthur Evans', (ed. by S. CASSON), p. 111, Pl. XVIII. Clarendon Press, Oxford. 1927.

SCHUMACHER, G. 'Tell el-Mutesellim', Vol. 1, p. 65. Hinrichs, Leipzig. 1908.

MACALISTER, R. A. S. 'The Excavation of Gezer', Vol. 2, p. 36, and fig. 228. Palest. Explor. Fund. Murray, London. 1912.

GARSTANG, J. "Jericho: City and Necropolis. Fourth Report." *Ann. Archaeol. Anthrop.* **21,** Pl. XIX, 2, 1934.

KLEBS, L. 'Die Reliefs des Alten Reiches', p. 90. *Abh. heidelberg. Akad. Wiss., phil.-hist. Kl.*, no. 3, 1915.

Idem. 'Die Reliefs und Malereien des Mittleren Reiches', pp. 116 ff. *Abh. heidelberg. Akad. Wiss., phil.-hist. Kl.*, no. 6, 1922.

Idem. 'Die Reliefs und Malereien des Neuen Reiches', p. 159. *Abh. heidelberg. Akad. Wiss., phil.-hist. Kl.*, no. 9, 1934.

GHURYE, G. S. "A note on the Indian Potter's Wheel." *Man in India*, **16,** 68, 1936.

MACKAY, E. J. H. "Painted Pottery in Modern Sind: a Survival of an Ancient Industry." *J.R. Anthrop. Inst.*, **60,** Pl. 1, 2, 1930.

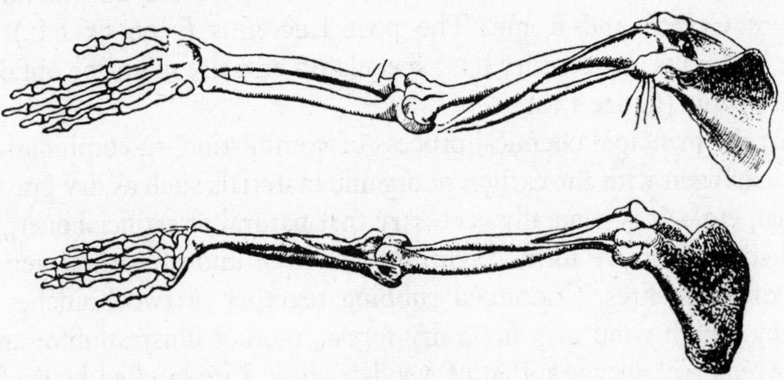

Anatomical drawings by Leonardo da Vinci, showing rotation of the hand.

10

FIRE-MAKING, FUEL, AND LIGHTING

H. S. HARRISON

I. FIRE AS MAN'S SERVANT

In the ancient legend, the giant Prometheus first brought fire to man. Thus he earned the enmity of the gods, to whose level men could now raise themselves. The taming of fire is a topic that touched the imagination of the thinkers of Greece and Rome. The poet Lucretius (*c* 96–55 B.C.) and the architect Vitruvius (1st century B.C.) speculated how fire might be obtained by a primitive people (figure 136).

To start the principal chemical process of combustion—a combination of atmospheric oxygen with the carbon of organic materials such as dry grass, leaves, wood, coal, etc.—it is generally necessary that natural or artificial energy should be supplied in effective form. Lightning is a well known natural generator of fire and of forest fires. Continued rubbing together of two branches of trees agitated by a high wind may fire a dry forest, another illustration of an ancient method which still survives, that of wood-friction. Fire kindled by such means, or by the contact of combustibles with molten matter of volcanic origin, may have been utilized by man before he learned how to make fire for himself, but from the time he became human he had ample opportunities of exercising his dawning intelligence in learning how he could use the properties of what was at first a dreaded foe, to be shunned or circumvented.

Whether early man made his first fires out of curiosity, or mischief, or for warmth or protection may never be determined, but we can be sure that he was dependent for his earliest camp-fires upon larger conflagrations for which he was not responsible. It is certain that he did not begin by regarding fire as a means of making his food more palatable, though it is obvious that this use of fire may have been hit upon in early days. A roast pig was good to eat, as Charles Lamb long ago observed, whatever the size of the conflagration that did the cooking, provided the process stopped short of incineration.

All modern peoples use fire. Practically all have means and methods of making it, though primitive tribes are usually careful not to be at the considerable pains that this may involve more often than is necessary. They keep their home fires burning and, when travelling, may carry with them a smouldering brand or log, a slow match, or other source of fire. The Andamanese, alone amongst modern peoples, have apparently no method of making fire, and are hence dependent on

FIGURE 136—*The taming of fire as imagined by Vitruvius, pictured in an edition of his works printed in Paris in 1547. In the left background animals and men are in flight from the burning forest. In the foreground others have overcome their fear and are gathering round and feeding a fire that they have isolated.*

the maintenance of continuity. Yet it is much more probable that they have lost the art than that they have never known it.

There is ample evidence that fire was used by Palaeolithic men in Europe and Asia, and that it was produced by Neolithic and probably by Late Palaeolithic men by the percussion method (figure 137). Material evidence of the means employed, even in much later times, is, however, very meagre. The earliest evidence of man's use of fire comes from caves occupied by Pekin man (*Pithecanthropus pekinensis*), who is structurally nearer to the apes than Palaeolithic man in Europe, and is of earlier date. It is uncertain whether he was able to make fire himself.

II. FIRE BY PERCUSSION

Familiarity with flying incandescent particles, and with their power of starting a blaze, must have been gained long before such sparks were intentionally produced by percussion. The way was thus paved for utilization of minerals which

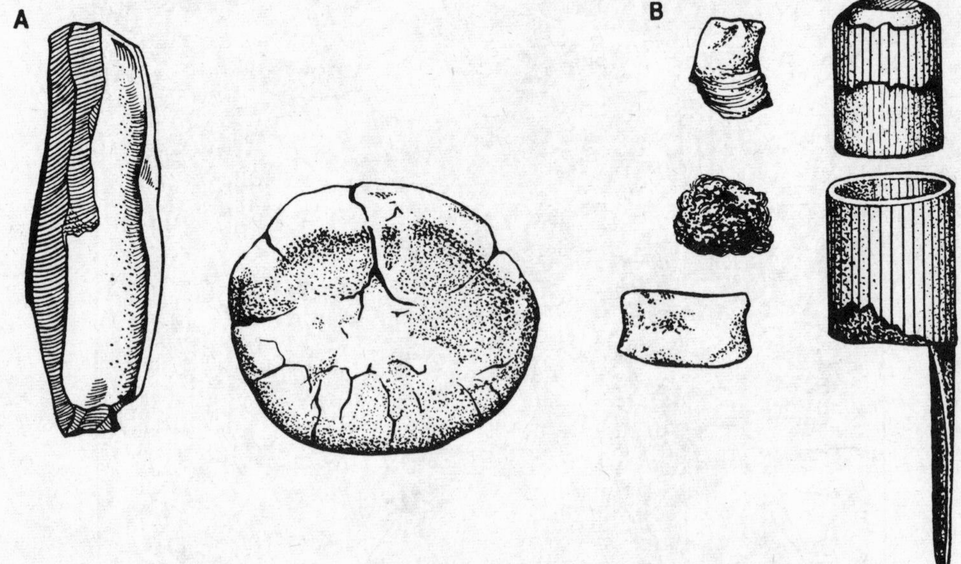

FIGURE 137—*Percussion method.* (A) *Flint and nodule of iron pyrites from a Neolithic barrow at Rudstone, Yorkshire.* (B) *Flint, tinder, and steel, with bamboo container, from Burma.*

gave rise to sparks as a result of sharp impact. Iron pyrites, being of common occurrence, often as small nodules, presented itself as a convenient fire-making material, when once the discovery had been made that two pieces, fortuitously thrown or knocked together, were liable to yield sparks. The percussion of two such nodules for fire-production was a simple application of an easy discovery.

When one of the nodules was replaced by a piece of flint, chert, quartz, chalcedony, or other siliceous stone, the change was of course merely one of substitution. The chief importance of this substitution lies in the fact that, at a much later time, it was found that flint together with iron was a still better combination, the iron, and in the sequel steel, yielding hotter sparks than the pyrites nodules, which were discarded (figure 137B). In this connexion, however, it is interesting to note that the snaphaunce gun of the sixteenth century, the successor of the matchlock and the forerunner of the flintlock, was dependent on the combination of iron or steel and pyrites. In the early history of fire-making by percussion, material played a more conspicuous part than form or method.

Evidence as to how fire was made in Palaeolithic times is scanty, but points to the very early use of flint and pyrites. There is, however, tangible archaeological evidence that pyrites was used in the Neolithic and Bronze Ages (figure 137A). The employment of two pyrites nodules survived amongst some American Indian tribes until recently, and even in England the method was occasionally used until as late as 1827, the year in which friction matches were first made. The use of pyrites and flint is recorded also amongst the Eskimo, some North American Indians, and the South American Fuegians. To obtain fire from sparks, and especially from the ephemeral sparks of the percussion method, it is necessary that they should fall on some material that is readily enkindled. Early man had to discover the best materials for this purpose. Thus were established the many recognized forms of tinder, such as dried moss or (especially) fungus, the down or floss of seeds, and dry and rotten wood.

There is no satisfactory evidence that the substitution of iron for pyrites was due to a prompt discovery of an unexpected use to which the metal might be put. The wrought iron of the early Iron Age was, indeed, not well adapted for producing sparks. Steel was made only by chance even in later times, and then in small quantities and as a surface layer (ch 21). The Romans may sometimes have used a steely iron with flint for fire-making, but tangible evidence of the use of flint and steel is not forthcoming until well into the Christian era.

Once established in Europe and Asia, flint and steel held their place for personal and domestic use until the days of the friction match. Mention may, however, be made of the use of iron (not steel) and quartzite by some Scandinavian peoples of the first millennium A.D., since it appears to be an independent discovery, not of a method, but of materials that could be employed—again a mere matter of substitution. It seems more surprising that sparks can be struck from the surface of bamboo—a variety having a rough skin— with a fragment of porcelain. This method of making fire has been recorded from south-east Asia—for example, in the Malay Peninsula and the Philippines.

The use of iron pyrites, or of pyrites and flint, for fire-making is such a simple process that it might have been discovered by more than one people, but if it came into vogue at a very early period, as seems probable, it may well owe its wide distribution to an early spread of man of the physical type to which all existing peoples belong. With the (later) knowledge of iron, and given an acquaintance with the percussion method of getting sparks, the use of flint and iron presents no difficulties, except those which might arise from lack of a reliable supply of hardened iron or steel, as, for example, over a large part of Africa, where the wood-friction method held its own.

III. FIRE BY WOOD-FRICTION

There are three chief methods of producing fire by wood-friction, and one or other has been employed in all parts of the world. Even in Britain there are records of a survival of the method as late as the last century, for the production of 'need-fire', through which cattle were driven with the idea that it saved them from pestilence. In some other parts of the world, where wood-friction has been superseded by more efficient methods, ceremonial or sacred fire is still sometimes obtained by the earlier process, as by Brahmins in India, who obtain sacrificial fire by means of a thong-drill (p 224). Old fashions may be ridiculed, but some of them acquire an odour of sanctity.

In all the methods in which wood is used, the essential feature is that wood-dust is produced by the friction of one piece of wood on another. In this process so much heat is developed that the little heap of dust begins to smoulder and can be blown into a glowing mass. This will set fire to tinder, which is often so placed that the dust falls upon it as produced. The time taken in getting fire may range from under a minute to several minutes, according to the method, the skill of the operator, the wood employed, and other conditions. One of the pieces of wood, held at rest on the ground, is called the 'hearth', the other is the 'saw', the 'plough', or the 'drill', according to its form and manner of use. The three methods are distinguished by the direction of working of the active component in relation to the grain of the wood of the hearth—sawing across the grain, ploughing along it, or drilling into it at right angles. The last-named method is the most widely distributed, and it is often worked by means of mechanical aids which cannot be utilized for the other two.

The fire-saw is especially characteristic of south-east Asia and its islands, occurring also in India, Australia, and formerly in Europe. In the typical case, both saw and hearth are short lengths of split bamboo, the edge of the saw being worked in a transverse slit cut across the hearth, which is held down with the convex face uppermost, so that the wood-dust can fall through the slit on to tinder placed below; sometimes there is a longitudinal slit as well. In Australia, the wood used is not bamboo, and sometimes the saw is a spear-thrower and the hearth a small shield (figure 138). In other cases in Australia, the hearth may be split at the end at which the sawing is done, the two sides of the slit—between which the tinder is placed—being kept apart by a wedge.

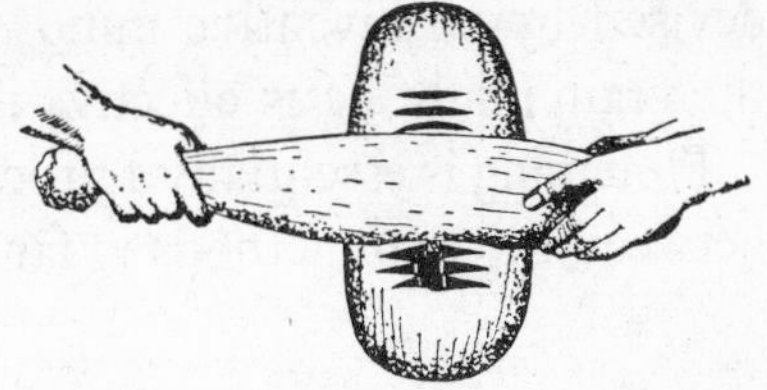

FIGURE 138—*Fire-saw: the hearth is a shield and the saw a spear-thrower. Australia.*

A similar splitting and wedging of the hearth is very typical of the sawing-thong variant of the fire-saw, in which the saw takes the form of a narrow flexible band of cane or rattan, the hearth being usually of wood other than bamboo. The hearth is held firmly down on the ground under the feet, the thong is passed under it, and, by pulling up and down with the two hands alternately, the necessary friction is effected (figure 139). The distribution of the sawing-thong method coincides very largely with that of the ordinary fire-saw, occurring from Assam sporadically through Indonesia to Melanesia (New Guinea). It has been employed in modern times even in Europe, and there is some evidence for its use in West Africa.

The concentration of the typical fire-saw in the region of distribution of the bamboo, and the very general utilization of strips of bamboo for the appliance, suggests that the initial steps were associated with this material. It is not unlikely that attempts to cut bamboo with bamboo may have led to discovery of the heated by-product. The use of a thong in place of a rigid saw is probably a case of substitution. As regards the use of the sawing-thong in Europe, the view has been suggested that it may have been due to independent discovery arising out of misuse, rather than use, of a type of thong-drill worked by a pliant strip of wood, which, instead of twirling the drill effectively, gave rise to an overheated bearing.

The fire-plough (figure 140) has a wide distribution, though only in Polynesia is it used to the exclusion of other kinds of fire-sticks. It is probable that it arose in the East Indies, from which the Polynesians are usually believed to have set forth to colonize the Pacific. It occurs in Australia, Melanesia, and in one or two parts of Africa. The active component is pushed along in a groove of the hearth, which is of a softer wood than the plough. The heated dust accumulates at the end of the groove. It is the simplest and least variable of the wood-friction methods, but it sometimes takes bizarre forms, which may be of a ritual or ceremonial nature. It is probable that the fire-plough arose from the fire-saw. It was

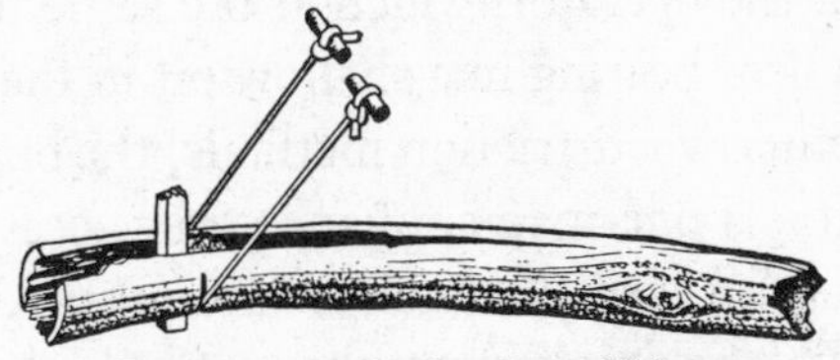

FIGURE 139—*Sawing-thong. Malaya.*

devised by an inventive mind with the insight to realize that rubbing along the grain might be as effective in producing fire as rubbing or sawing across it.

Ploughing is essentially a process of sawing along the grain, and the difference between the two methods is far less than that between either and the fire-drill. Emphasis must be laid on the fact that exact form counts for little, for both fire-saw and fire-plough are but means of applying friction to two pieces of wood. This fact overshadows any importance that attaches to the pieces of wood regarded as artifacts. In grinding stone by friction, the object of the method is to remove particles of the stone, to shape it. The stone-dust and the heat are here both waste products, but there is eventually a ground or polished implement to reward the labour. In the grinding of the wood of a fire-saw or a fire-plough, on the other hand, it is the heat and the wood-dust that are needed, and the effects produced on the fire-sticks themselves are purely incidental. Fire-making, by whatever method, is an operation which in its aims is as unlike any other performed by primitive man as fire itself is unlike any other of the phenomena of nature.

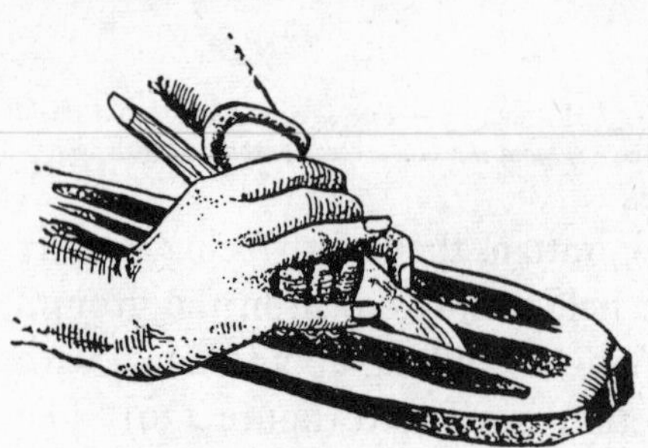

FIGURE 140—*Fire-plough. Oceania.*

The fire-drill is, or has been, used in nearly all parts of the world, Polynesia being the only region from which it is entirely absent. In Europe, it probably dates from Neolithic times, with survivals into the nineteenth century and even later. In Asia, it is no doubt of greater antiquity, and is not yet obsolete. It was used by the ancient Egyptians, who represented it in their hieroglyphs (figure 141). It was the prevailing method in most parts of Africa down to recent times (figure 141). The same may be said of Australia, Melanesia, and Tasmania, as well as of America from the extreme north to the far south, in ancient times (figure 143) as in modern (figure 142).

In the simple two-stick apparatus, the cylindrical or tapering drill held vertically is given a reciprocating movement of rotation between the two hands of the operator, which at the same time press downwards so as to give the stick a firm bearing in a shallow pit in the stationary hearth (figures 141–2). As in the other wood-friction methods, the burning wood-dust is used to set fire to tinder. It is a one-man appliance, but occasionally two or more men co-operate (figure 143). Usually a notch is cut in the side of the pit for the escape of the wood-dust. The Eskimo frequently cut along the hearth a ledge so placed that the dust may fall on a surface that does not chill it. Often the hearth, which usually has several pits, is of softer wood than the drill, and sometimes grains of sand are placed in the pit to increase the friction. It is worth noting that in boring stone or other hard material with a plain stick-drill worked by hand, sand is employed, along with water, to give the wood abrasive power (p 191).

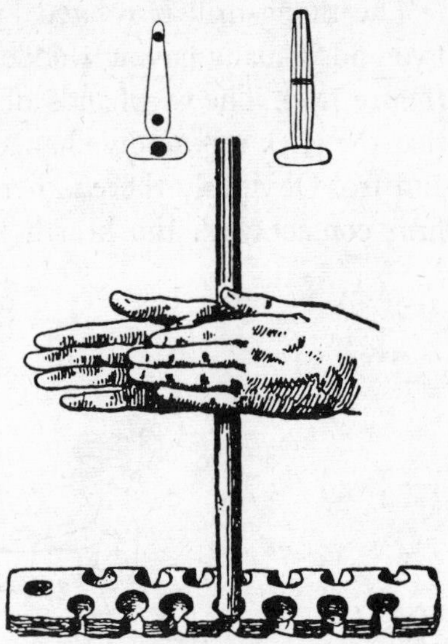

FIGURE 141—*The fire-drill as commonly used in Africa. Above are two Egyptian hieroglyphs representing fire-drills.*

The most interesting feature of the fire-drill is the nature of the mechanical means adopted by some peoples for rotating the stick, and it is noteworthy that for each type of fire-drill there is a boring drill (ch 9) with the same mechanism. Compared with the fire-saw and the fire-plough, the fire-drill has a greater range of type, and indeed the two former are at a low level in respect of the constancy of form of their components, which are of any convenient size and shape, and may even be artifacts made for other purposes (figure 138). The drill of the fire-drill, on the other hand, must at least be straight, and circular in section. The three mechanically worked types of drill are the thong-drill, the bow-drill, and the pump-drill, the last named being very rarely used for making fire.

FIGURE 142—*Fire-driller. Bolivia.*

The thong-drill is rotated by a cord passed round it in a simple loop, the two ends usually having wooden or bone handles for convenience of working (figure 144). The two hands of the operator pull on the thong in such a way that the stick repeatedly changes its direction of rotation as the hands move to and fro. Obviously there is here a necessity for the drill to be held upright in firm contact with the hearth by pressure from above, and a small socketed

FIGURE 143—*Fire-drill depicted by a native artist in a sixteenth-century Mexican manuscript. Two men steady the hearth, while a third works the drill. Highly dramatized.*

holder of wood, bone, or stone, or even the cut end of a coconut shell, is provided for the purpose. This socket-piece may be held down on the top of the drill by an assistant (figure 144), or if its shape is suitable, as it usually is in the Eskimo appliance, it may be gripped in the mouth of the fire-maker (figure 145). The thong-drill is used especially by the Eskimo, but is found also in northern Asia, and here and there in India and Indonesia.

The bow-drill is essentially similar in its working to the thong-drill. The two ends of the thong, instead of being attached to separate handles, are tied to the extremities of a short stave, often curved, with the result that a small bow with loose thong is produced (figure 145). The thong (or thick bowstring) must be loose enough to go round the drill in a simple loop, as with the thong-drill. Unlike this, however, the rotation of the bow-drill is effected by one hand only, alternately pulling and pushing with the bowstave, and the other hand is therefore free to hold the socket-piece. As a fire-drill, the bow-drill is less widely distributed than the tool of the same type (which persists in Europe, Asia, and north Africa), but it is much used by the Eskimo, as well as by some Siberian and North American Indian tribes. It was also employed by the ancient Egyptians (figure 146), and an excellent example, with all the parts complete, was found in Tutankhamen's tomb. This example had probably symbolic significance, and possesses an unusual feature found in other ancient Egyptian examples. The lower end of the drill-stick has a socket for a short detachable working 'bit' of wood (figure 146), thus suggesting close relationship with the boring-drill having an exchangeable working point or bit.

FIGURE 144—*Eskimo thong-drill in use in the Hudson Bay area. From an illustration published in 1748.*

For making fire, the pump-drill (figure 147) has been relatively little used, though it occurs amongst the Chuckchi of Siberia, some Iroquois Indians, and in one or two Indonesian islands. As in all other fire-drills, there is a reciprocating movement of rotation, but here the movement is produced by an up and down pumping action of the hand, pressure of the bearing between drill and hearth being increased by a weight attached to the lower part of the drill, which serves chiefly as a fly-wheel. The cord or thong is in two lengths, one end of each being attached to the top of the drill, while the other ends are tied to the opposite extremities of a wooden cross-piece, which either hangs loosely against the side of the drill or is perforated to receive it. The action begins with a slight twisting of the drill with the fingers, the cross-piece being held in one hand; the two cords are thus given a spiral twist round the upper part of the drill. When the cross-piece, held horizontally, is sharply depressed, the spiral is unwound,

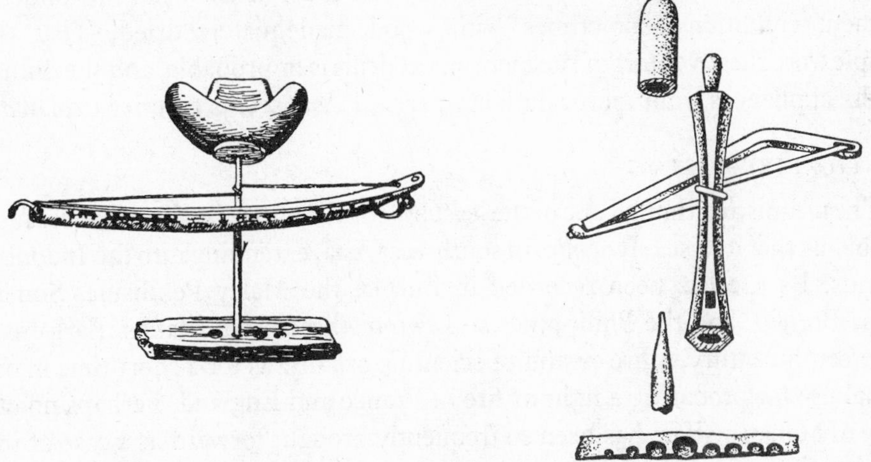

FIGURE 145 (*left*)—*Eskimo fire-making bow-drill with mouthpiece.*

FIGURE 146 (*right*)—*Ancient Egyptian bow-drill for making fire. The bit is a detachable plug of wood, shown separately. The drill turns in a loose hollow handle, shown above, by which pressure can be exerted on the hearth.*

the drill being rotated in the process. At its lowest point, pressure on the cross-piece is relaxed, and the momentum of the drill, reinforced by the fly-wheel, is sufficient to wind up the cord in a spiral again, reversed in relation to the first one. By an alternate pumping up and down with the cross-piece the drill is kept in almost constant rotation, but the appliance is not mechanically so efficient for the purpose of fire-making as are the thong-drill and the bow-drill.

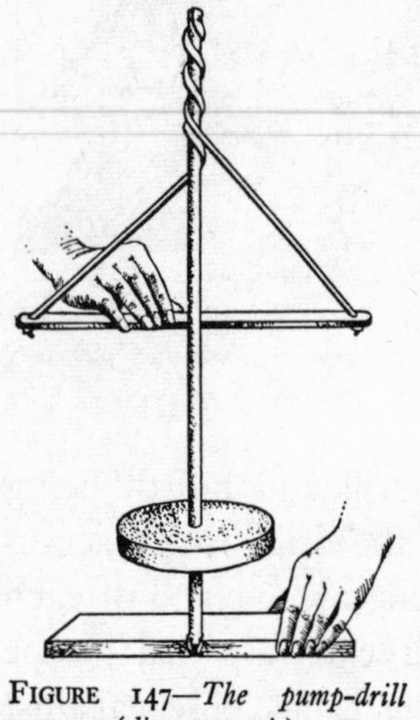

FIGURE 147—*The pump-drill (diagrammatic).*

The wide distribution of the two-stick fire-drill suggests an early origin, and it would appear probable that it was a derivative of the boring-drill of wood worked with sand and water. For no other purpose does it seem likely that rotary friction of such a kind would have been carried on so persistently as to produce sufficient heat to attract attention to the phenomenon, as a possible means of obtaining fire. On this assumption, the fire-drill arose out of an existing appliance by a change of function. As regards the mechanical fire-drills, they may be regarded as of later origin than the single-stick boring-drill.

It is worth noting that the use of the mechanical fire-drills, by means of which heat may be much more quickly and certainly developed than with the simple drill-stick, is especially characteristic of peoples, such as the Eskimo of the Arctic and some tribes of northern Asia, who must often make fire under inclement conditions, sometimes with wood inadequately dried. That these people were the inventors of the mechanical drills is improbable, and the diffusion of the appliances from more southerly parts of Asia seems a better explanation.

IV. THE FIRE-PISTON

The fire-piston, though one of the least practical devices, is of interest because of problems that it raises. It occurs in south-east Asia, extending into the Indonesian islands. Its use has been recorded in Burma, the Malay Peninsula, Sumatra, Java, Borneo, and the Philippines and two or three other islands. Early in the nineteenth century, a fire-piston of scientific origin was for a short time in occasional use for procuring a light or fire in France and England. Perhaps no other type of human artifact has been so frequently brought forward as a case of independent invention.

The fire-making power of the fire-piston depends upon the fact that if a body of gas (in this case air) in a confined space be abruptly compressed, heat is developed, which may under arranged conditions serve to set fire to tinder. The phenomenon is as simple a one as the sparking of flint with steel; but it is clearly one which is far less likely to be fortuitously produced or observed. Furthermore, the opportunism involved in making use of it for fire-making is more enlightened than would be expected to occur amongst uncivilized peoples.

The fire-piston of south-eastern Asia consists of a short and narrow hollow cylinder of bamboo, wood, horn, or (in Borneo) lead, closed at one end, with a closely fitting piston of wood or horn, the total length ranging from about 4 to 6 inches (figure 148). The lower end of the piston is often wrapped with thread or fibre, to make it fit more accurately, and it has a shallow depression on its face, for the reception of a small quantity of efficient tinder. The piston, drawn out to the top of the cylinder, is struck smartly on the terminal knob and is forced rapidly to the bottom of the chamber. On withdrawal, if the attempt is successful, the tinder is found to be alight. It is essential that the piston should fit closely, or air will escape and the pressure in the cylinder will not be sufficiently raised. At the same time the piston must work easily enough for a single blow to force it to the bottom. The instrument is therefore one that demands far greater precision of design and workmanship than any fire-stick or simple flint and steel.

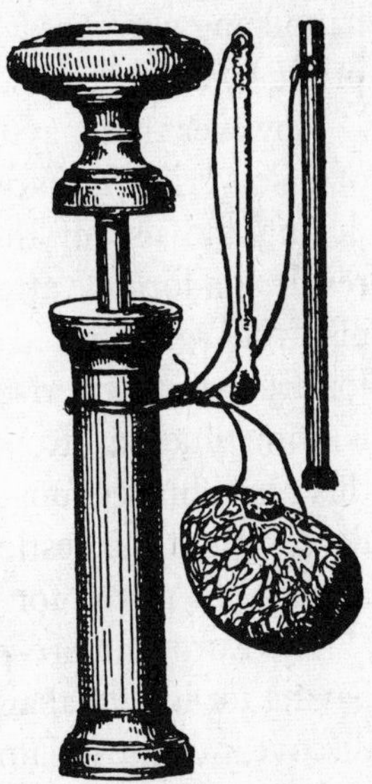

FIGURE 148—*Fire-piston from Borneo with ball of tinder and accessories.*

The fire-piston is exceptional among human artifacts in being less complex than it appears to be. Only one discovery and its appreciation were necessary, though the prerequisite conditions cannot have been common among primitive people. Furthermore, it is very rare for such people to possess a distinctive invention that is not already well known in civilization. Perhaps the fire-piston is the best example—assuming that it was known in Asia first. It seems very probable that this was in fact a case of independent invention, and we may discuss the problem under the provisional assumption that there was no relationship between the European and Asiatic instruments.

The invention of the fire-piston in south-east Asia must have been a happy chance, simple in itself, but remarkable in the fact that it was ever made and utilized. It could have arisen only through the use of a hollow cylinder with a closely fitting potential piston-rod. Surmise has connected it with such appliances as the tube-bellows, the blow-tube, the pestle and mortar for areca-nut (betel-nut), and with small brass cannon, all of which occur in various parts of the region of distribution of the fire-piston. In any case, we may obviously assume that the discovery was the result of experience with an appliance in common use and not of experiment with any kind of scientific apparatus, or even with instruments of real precision. One is tempted to suggest that it was a case in which a very unusual happening was observed by an individual who was sufficiently alert to repeat and profit by a single observation.

However that may be, the fire-piston as such does not lie at the end of a chain of discoveries, mutations, and variations. The discovery may have been made during the use of the appliance, whatever it was, or it may have been the result of a forcible attempt to remove an obstruction in a blocked tube by means of a rod which fitted closely. The suggestion that the small pestle and mortar for areca-nut gave rise to the fire-piston is largely based on the fact that there is sometimes a strong superficial resemblance between the two appliances; this resemblance must be allowed some weight, though it may be secondary. In the fitting of the pestle in its mortar there is, indeed, little resemblance to that of an efficient piston for the compression of air.

The European fire-piston most likely arose out of the use of refined apparatus, having for its actual aim the compression of air, though not for fire-making. The discovery of the inflammatory possibilities was bound to have been made sooner or later, even if it were not deduced from theoretical considerations arising out of growing scientific knowledge of the rise of temperature produced by the act of compression. That the discovery led to the origin of a practical fire-making device, as well as of a lecture experiment, was no doubt mainly due to the fact that there was at the time a hue-and-cry after new methods of fire-making, some of the chemical methods dating from before 1800, and some from after that year, with the friction match coming in at the finish (1827) to supersede them all.

The fire-piston of Asia is an astonishing invention. Though by no means complex, to the man who made the first discovery it must have seemed a miracle worth repeating. The European fire-piston, on the other hand, may be said to have been inevitable, but if the discovery had been made after matches became common it would probably never have emerged from the laboratory or the lecture-room.

V. FUEL

Much of man's cultural development has been dependent upon the fuels he could obtain. Evidences of those used in very early days are scarce indeed, but we need not hesitate to accept the practices of modern backward peoples as indicating the general nature of the fuels used in prehistoric and protohistoric times. To learn what would burn and what would not was an easy step, once man had his own fires on which to make his tests.

There were many other things man had to find out about the fuels he adopted—whether they ignited quickly and burnt brightly, or were slow to kindle and gave much smoke; whether they needed careful tending, or could be relied upon to burn steadily and long; and whether the heat they gave was fierce or feeble. By experience and trials he learnt the combustible qualities of different woods, which were certainly the first fuel used. From the beginning, man could procure brushwood, undergrowth, roots, and fallen branches. Until he had tools with which he could cut up large branches, relatively small ones would mainly have been used for burning.

Charcoal has had a long history of usefulness as a fuel in its own right. At first a by-product of the wood fire, discovery of its usefulness led to its intentional production by partially burning wood under reducing conditions. As a fuel, it has the convenient property of burning without smoke, and the inconvenient one of yielding the dangerous gas carbon monoxide. Regarded simply as a fuel, charcoal is still one of the best and most efficient. Spontaneous fires in outcrops of coal and lignite, and of dry peat, have been recorded, and may have led to the use of these substances as fuels in a few cases, but evidence of such use in early days is inconclusive.

In Old World caves occupied in Late Palaeolithic times, and even earlier, there are clear traces of fires in the blackened hearths that now lie buried at varying depths below the present cave-floor. Burnt clay, charred wood, and carbonized bones are found on such sites. It is probable that the value of bones for occasional use as a fuel was known to these Palaeolithic men, as it is to some modern backward peoples among whom animal bones are at times abundant while wood is scarce.

Those who lived when the European climate was arctic may well have employed, for heating and lighting, oil fuels similar to those of the modern Eskimo, such as the blubber and fat of seals, walruses, and certain birds.

An animal product that has served as a fuel over wide regions is dried dung. In parts of India, where wood is scarce, the dung of cattle is so important as fuel that its value as manure is neglected, and the yield of cultivated land is correspondingly reduced. The use of such fuel from sheep, camel, yak, bison, and other animals, wild or domesticated, has been recorded. We may surmise that the Early Neolithic farmers discovered the value of this incidental fuel.

Starting a new fire from an existing one saves both fuel and labour. When the new fire is to be near the old, a smouldering or flaming brand, or a small quantity of hot embers, may serve, but for a journey of hours or days a more enduring carrier is needed. Decaying wood, dried fungus, and fibrous material from bark or wood, chosen from experience of their smouldering properties when deprived of a free supply of air, have all been widely used. The wood of some coniferous trees, such as cedars, is notably efficient for the purpose. Such a fire-carrier is perhaps intended in the Biblical picture of a gentle character: 'A bruised reed shall he not break, and the smoking flax shall he not quench' (Isa. XLII. 3).

Tinder (from the OE *tyndre*, kindle) is the term that has long been applied to combustible materials that have played a part in the initial stages of lighting a fire or getting a light. It is of such a nature that it will ignite and smoulder when sparks fall on it, or it may inflame when a small flame is applied to it. The heated wood-dust of frictional fire-making becomes tinder when it is blown to produce a flame, but a second kind of tinder, in larger quantity, must be ignited for kindling the fire. The tinder-boxes which were essential articles of domestic use down to the time of development of the friction match contained flint and steel, tinder, and sulphur-tipped splints of wood which could easily be inflamed by smouldering tinder. This was usually charred linen, decayed wood (touchwood), dried moss, or amadou—the last a piece of dried fungus (*Polyporus* sp) made more effective by soaking in a hot solution of saltpetre (potassium nitrate). Tinder has always been an essential aid in procuring fire and light by the simple methods described in this chapter.

A method of transporting a fire, as distinct from transferring it, is found amongst the Tierra del Fuegians of South America. They cover a part of the floor of their canoes with clay upon which, as on a hearth, they maintain a fire indefinitely. Similar methods have been recorded elsewhere.

VI. HEATING

Man's first fires may have been objects of curiosity and experiment; of the uses to which they could be put, those of warming the body and giving light during the hours of darkness were the most obtrusive. Fire-worship may be regarded as man's testimony not only to the mysterious and sometimes terrifying aspect of a common phenomenon, but to the privileges conferred upon him through its agency. The sun-god was a powerful and personified benefactor, but more aloof.

We are not concerned here with methods of using fire in cooking (ch 11), pottery-making (ch 15), and metal-working (ch 21), but with those for warming the individual and the dwelling. Man's early fires were no doubt of the nature of camp-fires, each forming a focus of assembly for the family group. Such fires would sooner or later be found to afford some protection against wild beasts —beasts wilder and more persistently carnivorous than early man himself. A smoky fire, also, would serve then as now to discourage stinging and blood-sucking insects. How long it was before man began to cook his food is past finding out, but that he did so by Palaeolithic times is certain (ch 11).

Early man, we may be sure, did not sit over the fire to do his daily work, and his nights were mainly spent in sleep, or sometimes in the communal ceremonies and festivities so often found among modern backward communities. His women also had outdoor occupation during the day. Similar conditions would apply to the early farmers and stock-breeders of the Neolithic revolution (ch 2), before the establishment of large villages and towns. In the latter, better housing and division of labour gave rise to new problems of domestic heating, especially in the cooler climates. It was under such conditions of family and communal life that fire became finally domesticated, as distinct from tamed.

When the camp-fire first began to go under cover in a tent or a hut, its simplicity was little affected. The indoor hearth was just a shallow depression lined with stones or clay, or the flattened top of a low heap of stones. Several large stones were sometimes placed round the fire to keep it in place, and, at a certain stage, to support cooking pots. Cooking has had a predominant influence in the development of the various kinds of grate, and on the accessories that ultimately enclosed and tended the fire itself. With indoor fires in a tent or hut, the disposal of the smoke was imperfectly effected by a hole in the roof, and owing to the inflammable nature of the walls the grate was normally relegated to the centre.

In the absence of more adequate provision for the escape of smoke, and in conditions where continuity of heating was not required, charcoal was often burnt in open pans of earthenware or in stone braziers (figure 149D). The present use of metal braziers in Mediterranean countries suggests continuity with practices in similar climates in the ancient civilizations. Bronze vessels of this class have been found on early sites in Mesopotamia. They have pierced sides, and legs to raise them a few inches above the ground. Braziers for heating large rooms were sometimes of considerable size, and a particularly large Roman example, with a heating-surface of 7 ft 8 in by 2 ft 8 in was found at Pompeii. From the portable fire-vessels arose closed-in iron stoves, with an aperture for stoking and, later, a flue for draught and the passage of smoke. These are first known from smaller, portable, usually metallic containers for charcoal or hot water, designed as body-warmers and bed-warmers. The period of their origin cannot be determined. When buildings were of brick or stone, the central fireplace was no longer a necessity, though it did not disappear from the great halls of our castles and other buildings till the twelfth century or later. Fires near the walls were provided with a flue leading to the exterior; the true chimney in and above the wall developed later. The chimney may have been foreshadowed in quite early days, in connexion with the need for a strong draught in pottery-kilns, or in

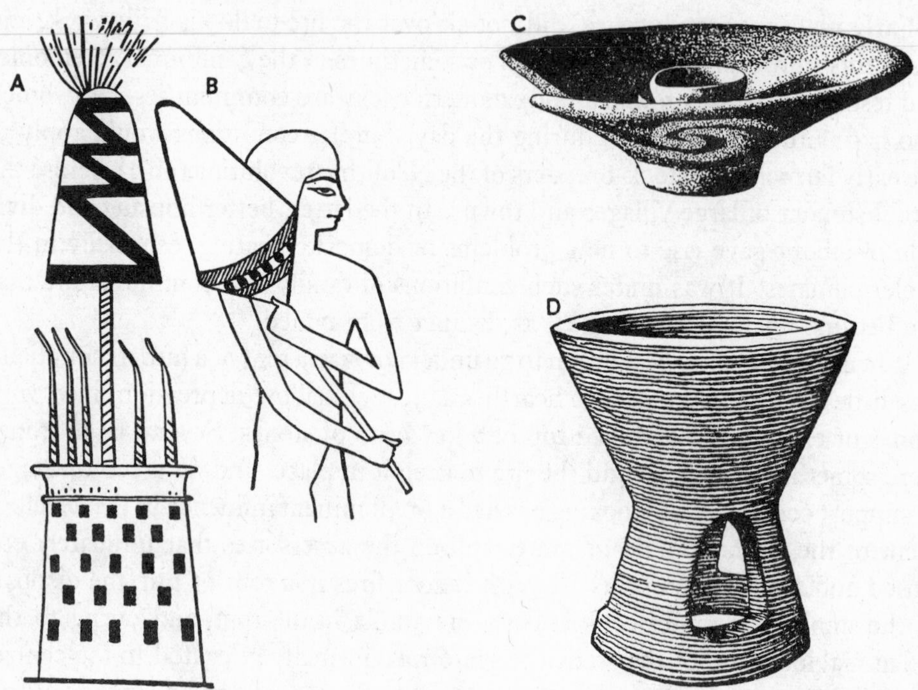

FIGURE 149—(A) *Candle and tapers*; (B) *portable candle. From a tomb at Thebes, Egypt.* c *1300* B.C. (C) *Socketed candlestick from the Palace of Minos, Crete. Before 1600* B.C. *Diameter* c *7 in.* (D) *Reconstructed Chalcolithic stone brazier from Wadi Ghazzeh, near Gaza, Palestine. Height* c *10 in.*

furnaces for smelting metal ores. In the same way, early types of braziers and cressets (p 234) with latticed metal sides may have suggested the idea of fire-grates similarly constructed.

Andirons or fire-dogs also played a part in the origin of the grate. It is a known practice of recent times to encourage draught through a fire by placing large stones in such a position that fuel can be supported away from the hearth. These serve also to support cooking-vessels, and their early use may have foreshadowed the development of such metal andirons as were already in use in the early Iron Age of Europe. A fine pair made of wrought iron was discovered in Cambridgeshire, dating from this period (plate 5 B). It may be that such andirons were used not only to raise the ends of logs, but had horizontal bars of iron across them to support cooking-pots. By fixing such bars to the horizontals of the andirons, and adding others to the vertical front legs, a grate would be produced needing little adaptation to convert it into a fixed receptacle for the fire itself.

VII. HEARTH ACCESSORIES

Several types of implements were early devised for use in connexion with fires, hearths, and fire-grates. Some may have originated before metal was available. Of them, the poker is surely the most ancient. Tongs required a little more ingenuity. We may suggest two origins, one the use of two separate sticks to grasp an ember, foreshadowing the hinged metal type, and the other a flexible stick bent in the middle, acting like the modern spring tongs.

Simple types of bellows, such as are in use today in Asia and Africa, were more probably invented in connexion with metal-working than for use in the home. The human lungs were the original bellows by which a reluctant fire was encouraged. The addition of a mouth-tube to concentrate the draught was a simple matter, especially in regions where bamboos grow. The translation of a bamboo tube into metal would be straightforward. The next steps toward the modern bellows was the attachment of a bag or two bags to a tube adapted for the purpose and perhaps provided with an earthenware nozzle. This type is known from ancient Egypt, and is still used in various parts of Africa (figures 382–4).

In one well known type of bellows used in south-eastern Asia, the air-chambers are two bamboo cylinders, with plungers wrapped with birds' down which acts as a valve. Other types are used in Asia. It is clear that the bellows had an early development in the ancient civilizations, and that it was in no way dependent on the use of metal in its structure and composition, though its main use was probably in metallurgical operations (ch 21).

VIII. LIGHTING

In the domestic life of early man, as of his backward modern representatives, there was no need for lighting in huts or villages. In so far as he did not sleep through the hours of darkness, the camp-fires gave all the illumination he needed; the night in any case was no time for work. If for any special purpose he needed a portable light he could be sure of a brand from the fire, and so the torch began its still unfinished career. Torches that would remain alight longer had to be prepared in advance, and wood was still an obvious choice. Resinous wood, such as that of cedars and some other conifers, sometimes as splints bound together, was found to burn well and not too quickly. Lumps or fragments of various kinds of tree-resin, tied up in a quantity in palm-leaf, are still widely used in Malaya and elsewhere. Torches were commonly used by the ancient Egyptians, by the Greeks and Romans, and in all parts of Europe in medieval times. They tended to become processional accessories, sometimes carried in socketed holders or mounted on poles or brackets.

Of similar application, though different in structure, were the bowls or open-work metal buckets or cressets, containing fuel carried or fixed at a height above the ground. Cressets were in general use in ancient Egypt, Syria, and Persia, and in much later times elsewhere. Between the torch or cresset and the candle may be placed the Polynesian lighter of candle-nuts strung in single file on a bamboo strip. Burning continues in orderly fashion from top to bottom of the series. Before passing to a consideration of candles and oil-lamps, we may note that certain complete animals are used for fuel and lighting. Examples are the stormy petrel and the candlefish, which, being rich in fat, burn without a wick. Fire-flies—in reality beetles of the *Elateridae* and *Lampyridae* families—may also be mentioned here, though they have no relationship with any other source of illumination used by man. The two species most used have their distribution in the western and eastern hemispheres respectively. The light emitted by a single insect may enable print to be read, or fine work to be done, and when a number are brought together—as in some American Indian and Japanese festivities—the illumination is surprisingly brilliant.

The candle is later in origin than the torch, and its structure less based on direct observation. The ancient Egyptians made tapers and candles. The tapers were slender, and apparently consisted of fibrous materials impregnated with tallow or wax. It seems highly probable that the candles—which might be called specialized torches—had wicks, but this is not certain. The early form was a lump of tallow, with one end pointed for ignition, and the body pressed round a stick for support. This type was improved by supporting the conical lump of tallow or wax on a flat or cup-shaped base attached to the top of the stick. To prevent the cone from collapsing as it burnt and melted at the top, narrow bands, probably of combustible material, were wrapped round it. Such torches or candles could be either carried, or stuck in the ground or in tubs of earth (figure 149 A, B). It was in association with funeral rites that they had their importance, and their use may have been to fumigate as well as to illuminate. The use of a wick coated with tallow or wax, could arise only as a result of preliminary steps that suggested possibilities previously unrecognized. Capillarity is not an obtrusive property, and the candle is entirely absent from lower cultures.

Cylindrical candles were first made by dipping the wick into melted wax, and much later by pouring the wax into moulds each containing a wick. The Romans had candles both of tallow and of wax. Waxes are obtainable from other insects besides bees, and also from some trees. The taper has a wick coated with tallow or wax. The old rush-light of our country was a taper rather than a candle.

Pricket-candlesticks may be as ancient as the more usual socketed types, but the latter, with the convenience of saving the drippings from the wax or tallow, goes back to the third millennium B.C. Examples suggestive of modern types have been found in Crete and elsewhere (figure 149 C).

Archaeological evidence of the early use of candles, as well as of torches, is very unsatisfactory, partly because the essential materials are not suited to long preservation, and partly because such holders or sockets as there may have been are not easily identified.

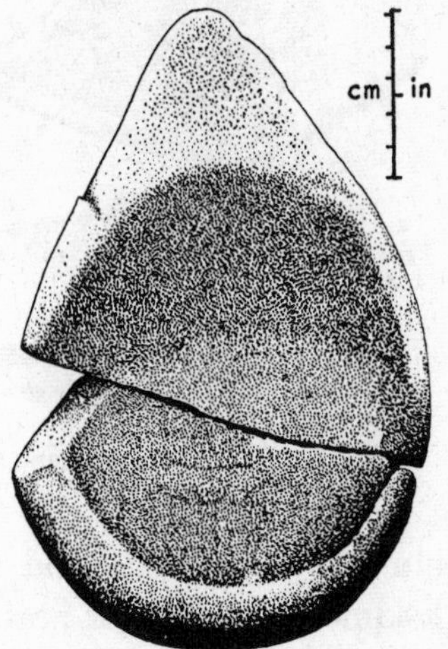

FIGURE 150—*Palaeolithic stone lamp from La Mouthe, Dordogne, France.*

IX. OIL-LAMPS

Unlike torches and candles, oil-lamps cannot exist without a container, and thus more archaeological evidence is available concerning ancient types. On the other hand, the great simplicity of the early oil-lamps often makes it difficult to determine with certainty whether a small and shallow cup-shaped or saucer-shaped object of earthenware or metal may not have had some other use. Traces of blackening during use may aid in identification.

The earliest lamps known are those of the Palaeolithic cave-dwellers of western Europe. Painting the inner walls of caves (ch 7) demanded artificial light. The lamps used were simple cups of stone, made to hold a small quantity of oil and a wick (figure 150). Much later are the equally simple forms made of a small lump of chalk, with a hollow for oil and wick, used by the Neolithic flint-miners at Grimes Graves, East Anglia (ch 20), and dating from around 2000 B.C. Both the men of the Old Stone Age in the caves, and the New Stone Age men in the pits, working for very different ends, would have been helpless without their lamps. It is not improbable that these lamps were the result of two independent inventions, and it may be that invention was again independently at work in the case of other simple lamps still to be considered.

Comparable with the Stone Age lamps are those of the modern Eskimo. These are, however, of larger size and hold more oil. Sometimes the stone is a hard beach pebble with a hollow, natural or artificially produced, and sometimes a stone such as quartzite or soapstone, worked to the shape and size required. Earthenware lamps of similar type are also made, and, though in all cases the oil is freely exposed, there may be a shelf to support the wick. The oil is derived from the

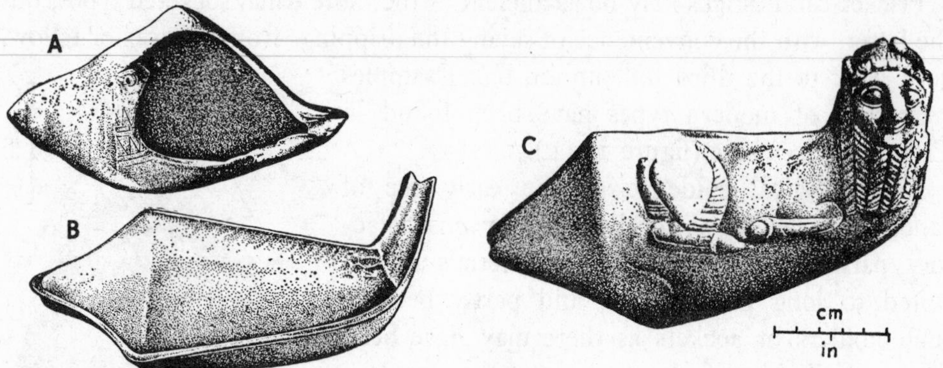

FIGURE 151—*Lamps from the royal cemetery at Ur, Mesopotamia.* c *2500 B.C.* (A) *Shell;* (B) *gold;* (C) *calcite.*

blubber of walruses and seals, and the wick may be of twisted moss. The Eskimo use lamps for heating and cooking as well as for lighting.

Lamps of an early date, before 3000 B.C. as well as after, have been found at Ur, many in the excavations of the royal cemetery. Shells of marine molluscs, modified if necessary or desirable by cutting away portions of the shell, were used as containers for the lamp-oil and wick. Conch shells and shells of the large bivalve *Tridacna* were chosen for the purpose, the oil being fully exposed, while the natural shape of the shells provided one or more open grooves for the burning end of the wick (figure 151 A). Such shell-lamps were closely copied at Ur in alabaster, gold, silver, and copper. In other cases, however, the shape was so far modified that the shell origin was obscured (figure 151 B), and some were elaborately carved in the round with a figure of a man-bull (figure 151 C), but as lamps they still remained of the open type, as did others from various Mesopotamian and other sites.

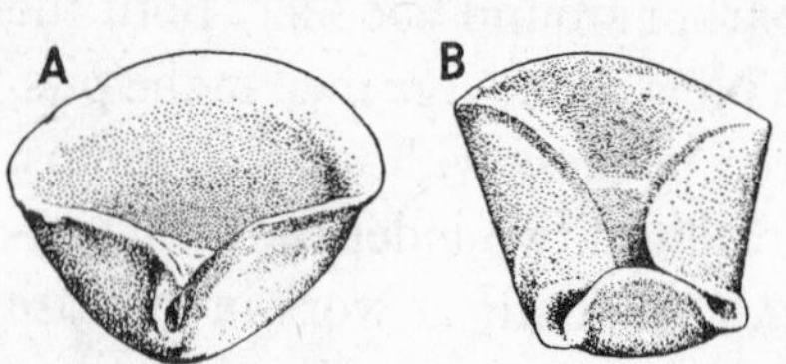

FIGURE 152—*Saucer-shaped pottery lamps.* (A) *Phoenician;* (B) *Carthaginian.*

In Palestine, at a rather later period, lamps of shell-form were made in pottery, some in imitation of scallop-shells. Such saucer-lamps became widely distributed in the eastern Mediterranean region, some with a groove or grooves for the wick, others without (figure 152). There is a clear evolutionary continuity of these lamps with the Greek and Roman forms that followed them. These later forms came to develop features of functional importance as well as of artistic merit. They remained, however, small in size, and made no use of gravity to aid capillarity in keeping up the oil-pressure in the wick. They were often covered in, a small hole being left in the lid for replenishing the supply of oil (figure 153).

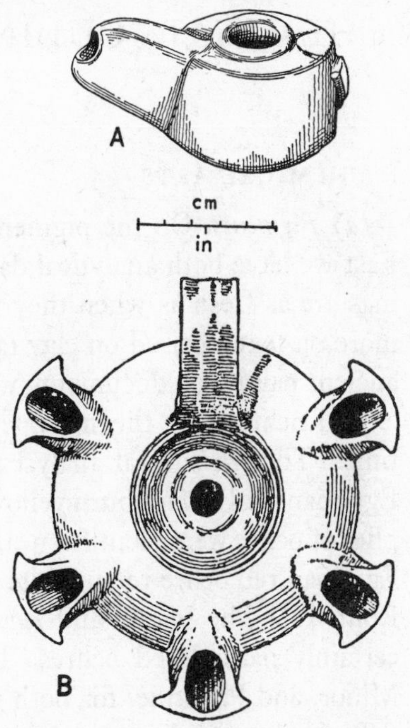

FIGURE 153—*Graeco-Roman lamps.* (A) *Stone lamp from Tel El-Yahudiya, Egypt;* (B) *earthenware lamp with handle from Knidos, Asia Minor.*

There is some obscurity as to the kinds of lamp used in ancient Egypt, partly because most of the scenes of life and industry are representative of daylight occupations, and partly because some forms of lamp are not so readily identified as those that can be traced back to shell-forms. The earliest Egyptian lamps appear to have been open pottery saucers or small bowls, containing tallow or castor-oil, with a wick of twisted grass or the like. Similar lamps are described by Herodotus as 'small vases filled with salt and olive-oil, on which the wick floated and burnt during the whole night'. The vases may have been of earthenware or perhaps of glass. There are several Egyptian hieroglyphs that are interpreted as having a relation to means of lighting, and some of them were evidently derived from lamps.

Information as to the nature and origin of the fats and oils of early days is scanty. Animals were the first source to be widely utilized. In the northerly regions, the blubber or fat of fishes, birds, whales, and seals continued to predominate, whereas vegetable oils became general in the Mediterranean region. The Romans, for example, used olive, castor, linseed, and rapeseed oils for their lamps. The mineral oil petroleum is believed to have been used in Babylon, as it was in later times in Persia (ch 11).

II

CHEMICAL, CULINARY, AND COSMETIC ARTS

R. J. FORBES

I. CHEMICAL ARTS

(*a*) *Pigments*. On the pigments used by the civilizations of the ancient Near East we have both analytical data and documents. In Egypt, many tomb paintings are as fresh as when they were painted. In Mesopotamia, we have to rely more on texts incised on clay tablets, for the humidity has destroyed almost all ancient paintings, documents written on papyrus or parchment, and textiles.

Red ochre[1] was the most widely used mineral pigment from predynastic times. Though several analyses report burnt ochre it is doubtful whether the Egyptians did in fact burn yellow ochre to obtain their red pigment. Natural supplies of ochre were plentiful near Aswan, and in the oases of the Western Desert. Egyptian red ochre retained its good reputation with the authors of Greece and Rome [1]. The *sinopis* and *rubrica* mentioned by Pliny (A.D. 23–79) are almost certainly natural red ochres. They were used as well in Mesopotamia, Asia Minor, and Palestine, for both pottery and wall-paintings.

Red ochreous clays, haematite, and other natural iron oxides, were also used. These pigments are often referred to by classical Greek authors as *sandyx* or *serikon*. They were employed as a basis for rouge. The use of cinnabar as a pigment during the early period is doubtful. Red lead was known in ancient Mesopotamia, and was prepared by heating lead, lead dross, and white lead (a basic lead carbonate) in an oven to form litharge (a lead oxide); this was then ground and heated. It was probably used in ancient Palestine to paint timber. Its introduction into Egypt was later, and was due to the Romans. The Egyptian term then applied to red lead is much older, and seems first to have indicated a certain bole (a form of ochre) occurring near Elephantine. Pink colours in the Near East were usually prepared by mixing red and white pigments or other substances—often powdered sea-shells.

The yellow pigments of the Egyptians were mostly ochres. Small cakes of yellow limonite or goethite, a hydrated ferric oxide, were found in a grave at

[1] The term *ochre* refers to a large class of natural pigments with colours varying from red to yellow, consisting essentially of hydrated iron oxides, often diluted with clay. Burnt ochres are natural ochres which have been calcined.

Gezer, while there was orpiment (a natural arsenic sulphide) in a bag in Tutankhamen's tomb, and in the pigment of wall-paintings of the Theban necropolis of Dynasty XVIII. It was fairly generally used from then onwards. As the mineral does not occur in Egypt it must have been imported from Persia, Armenia, or Asia Minor. Its use in Mesopotamia is beyond doubt, for cakes of it were found in the palace of Sargon II.

Orange pigments were obtained in Egypt by mixing red and yellow ochres, but the colour was not frequently used. Massicot, or yellow lead monoxide, was used in Egypt from predynastic times, and it has been found on a painter's palette of 400 B.C. A basic lead antimonate (now called 'Naples yellow') was an important pigment in Babylonian glazes, but has not been found in Egypt.

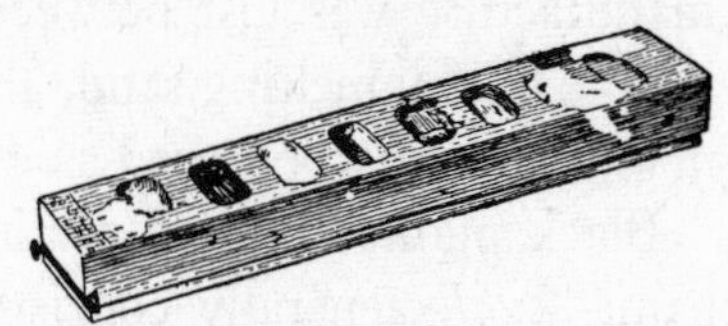

FIGURE 154—*Painter's palette for eight colours. Egypt.* c *1500 B.C.*

Brown colours were produced in Egypt from other natural ochres, such as occur in the Dakhla oasis. The brown paint on a box of Dynasty XVIII is a mixture of ochre and gypsum. Red over black pigments were sometimes used to obtain brown. Other combinations were haematite over black, or yellow ochre over haematite (figure 154).

The choice of green pigments was rather limited. In both Egypt and the Near East there was early use of powdered malachite (a native form of basic copper carbonate) or chrysocolla (natural hydrated copper silicate). In the technology of Egypt and Mesopotamia, an artificial frit was developed by melting sand, alkali, and copper minerals, and when powdered it could be used as a green pigment. This frit occurs in Egypt from Dynasty VI onwards. Sometimes mixtures of the artificial blue frit mentioned below and a yellow ochre were used (in tombs of Dynasties XII and XVIII). The manufacture and use of verdigris, though unknown in ancient Egypt, is well attested for ancient Mesopotamia.

The choice of good blue pigments was similarly limited. Powdered lapis lazuli and turquoise are often suggested, but both yield poor pigments when merely ground, though they cannot be entirely ruled out. Cobalt compounds have been found in Mesopotamian glazes and glass, but were probably due to a contamination. They were certainly unknown in Egypt, where the earliest blue pigments are of imported lapis lazuli. This was also used in ancient Mesopotamia, where a special type of pestle and mortar was employed to obtain a finely powdered pigment.

A substitute for lapis lazuli was found in Egypt in Dynasty IV. It was known by the same name as the genuine article, and was prepared by heating silica, malachite, calcium carbonate, and natron (native sodium carbonate, *trona*). The minimum temperature for the formation of the blue compound is 830° C [2]. There are remains of such a frit-factory at El-Amarna in Egypt. This blue frit is no doubt the *caeruleum* of Vitruvius and Pliny, and possibly the *kyanos* mentioned by Theophrastus (*c* 300 B.C.) in his 'History of Stones' [3]. Its manufacture was known to the ancient Assyrians about 1500 B.C., and it was much admired by them. It was used, as in Egypt, as a substitute for the expensive lapis lazuli in paints, glass, and glazes. Small objects were even shaped from it. The secret of its manufacture was lost between A.D. 200 and 700. The Assyrians could make a purple frit by melting sand, alkali, and copper salts, but it is not known whether it was ground to be used as a pigment.

Black pigments were available in considerable variety. Black Egyptian eye-paint, *kuhl*, generally consisted of galena. The use of pyrolusite (manganese dioxide) is very doubtful.[1] Most of the black pigments hitherto analysed contain carbon in some form, generally a finely divided soot (lamp-black, bone-black), but in some cases powdered charcoal. The use of bitumen as a paint was restricted to Mesopotamia. A black iron oxide may sometimes have been used. Greys were obtained in Egypt by mixing gypsum or a pale yellowish earth (ochre?) with lamp-black or charcoal.

White pigments in Egypt from predynastic times onwards are some form of either calcium carbonate (chalk) or calcium sulphate (gypsum); both occur in many places in that country. The Sumerians prepared their gypsum for pigment and plaster by calcining with cow-dung the calcareous gypsum so plentiful in their country, and crushing the mass thus obtained in mortars. They also had at their disposal white lead, which they prepared by the action of vinegar on lead as described by Theophrastus and Pliny [4], and *terra melia* (a form of kaolin) was used in certain cases. Tin oxide was a component of some Assyrian glazes, but it has not been identified as a pigment in the few traces of ancient wall-paintings in Mesopotamia. Metallic mercury, termed sublimate of cinnabar, was occasionally applied to the surface of little metal figurines.

(*b*) *Painting Grounds*. Painting was early connected with pottery in the ancient Near East, as can be shown by an analysis of the words used in the craft. Colours had names taken from nature, but acquired an important religious and magical significance.

We have hardly any information on the painter's craft from Mesopotamia. In very early Egypt, most of the craftsmen seem to have done their own painting. We find the sculptor painting or gilding his own statues. Yet there are examples

[1] For green eye-paint, see p 293.

of individual painters, and even of easel-painting and its products [5], as far back as 2600 B.C. We know that they made decorated screens (figure 155). By 1500 B.C., however, painters had become fully independent craftsmen, and names of individual artists are recorded (figure 156). Reliefs also show the painting of pillars, woodwork, and other objects (figure 155), but we never find any picture of the painting of reliefs on tomb walls, probably on account of religious taboos. Preliminary sketches have been found, as well as a picture of an artist's

FIGURE 155—*Painters and sculptors at work. From a tomb at Beni Hasan, Egypt. c 1900 B.C.*

workshop of the Amarna period. The painting grounds of the ancients were pottery, plaster, stone, wood, canvas, papyrus, ivory, metal, and semi-precious stones. The decoration of pottery dates from prehistoric times. In Egypt white slips, or red ochre, blue frit, black iron oxide, or carbon paints were applied to pottery. In Mesopotamia, incised lines were filled with black, white, or red pigments; and glazes were made using bone-ash, black manganese oxide, blue and green copper compounds, or yellow lead antimonate as pigments (p 398).

Wall-plastering started very early in the history of architecture. Materials such as clay, lime, or gypsum were mixed with water and left to set on the wall. Sometimes inert material (sand, crushed bricks, stone) or binders (hair, straw, jute) were added.

In Egypt, lime was introduced only in the Graeco-Roman age, but clay plaster was made from predynastic times; later it went out of fashion for more important buildings except during the brief Amarna period (ch 17). It consisted of the ordinary Nile alluvium mixed with straw. Better quality plaster was obtained by adding a finishing coat of somewhat finer clay, the most suitable being a natural mixture with limestone found in hollows and pockets at the foot of certain hills. In Mesopotamia also, clay plaster filled with chopped reeds or straw was very common. Clay plaster does not, however, make a good ground for paintings, and mural paintings were usually on gypsum plaster. In Egypt, this was prepared by heating crude gypsum at about 130° C, and powdering and slaking the product. The very pure gypsum employed in the tombs of Giza and Saqqara was from quarries in the Fayum. In the early period, great care was taken to select good quality gypsum, and often a second layer of gypsum with up to 85 per cent of powdered limestone was applied to obtain a smooth painting ground.

Gypsum plaster was also employed in Mesopotamia, but it was more usual to prepare a lime mortar. The knowledge of lime-burning was very old in that country, and there is a lime-kiln at Khafaje of at latest 2500 B.C. The white lime mortar was sometimes mixed with ashes and applied in layers about 4 mm thick. In later periods there was a tendency to add coarse powdered brick to the lime mortar.

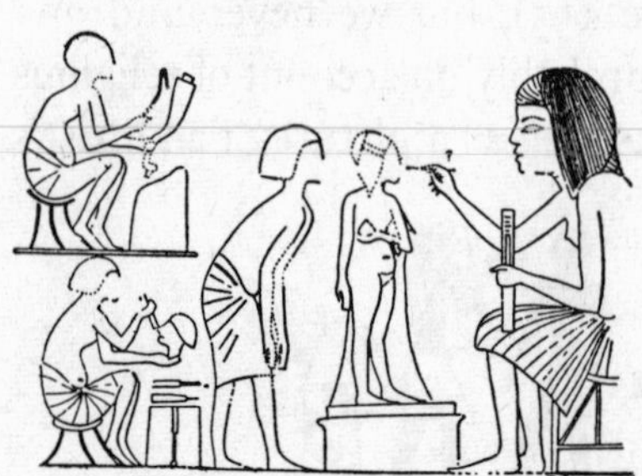

FIGURE 156—*The studio of the 'chief sculptor Anta'. From a tomb at El-Amarna, Egypt.* c *1500 B.C.*

The same coarsening of the quality of plaster can be observed in Egypt. The Egyptians originally applied on brick walls a thin coat about 1·5 to 3 mm thick. As time passed this was made less fine, until in Ptolemaic times it became a mere daub. The finishing coat was a priming to which glue had been added; it can therefore be called gesso, a term derived from 'gypsum' but later denoting any aqueous white priming coat.

For painting on stone, such a gypsum or lime plaster was in many cases first applied. This priming coat is, however, often missing, and, in both Egypt and Mesopotamia, we find that paint has been applied directly to the stone surface of statues. In Mesopotamia, where brick architecture is more prominent, brick walls were sometimes painted directly in white, black, purple, blue, and orange, and in a few cases even silvered or gilded. It was, however, more common to paint on stuccoed brick walls.

Painting direct on wood was avoided in ancient Egypt. Coffins, boxes, stelae, and even the wooden panels of the easel painters were primed with a layer of gypsum or whitening, unless a single colour was used. It should be remembered that the Egyptians never practised fresco painting—that is, they never painted on a wet surface made caustic with lime. Nor did the inhabitants of ancient Mesopotamia know this art, as far as we can tell from the few fragments of mural paintings that survive there. The home of the real *buon fresco* paintings was Crete, where, from 2500 B.C., mural paintings were executed on wet, pure lime plaster. In later periods, this lime

FIGURE 157—*Painter's equipment from Thebes.* c *1400 B.C. The brushes are lengths of wood with the fibres separated at one end, and were clogged with paint when found. The rope, which was covered with a red pigment, was used for ruling lines.*

plaster coat became thinner, and overlay a thicker gypsum backing. Frit of various colours—red, white, black, yellow, deep red, orange, green, and blue—was applied directly to the wet lime coatings (the green and blue frits were imported from Egypt). In Egypt, canvas or cloth paintings have been found dating back to about 1500 B.C. In Graeco-Roman times, painting on linen shrouds, and portrait-painting on linen or wood, had become quite common. Both in Egypt and in Mesopotamia, leather was dyed white, green, yellow, black, and red as early as predynastic times, but we have no details of the methods used. Nor do we know how ivory was coloured, though some of our museum ivory pieces show traces of blue and red paints and dyes (p 677).

The artificial staining of metals was practised in ancient times. Coloured metals were highly valued. The variety of colours of native metals and alloys was increased both by preparing artificial alloys and by treating the metallic surface. Thus the Egyptians produced a pink-coloured gold surface by heating gold which contained a trace of iron. This art, and that of staining semi-precious stones, contributed to the rise of alchemy and, in due course, chemistry.

Mesopotamia seems to be the country where the art of colouring semi-precious stones was discovered. Not only were small blackened shells—which may represent Pliny's 'cochlides of Arabia' [6]—discovered at Nineveh, but Mesopotamian texts inform us of artificially stained stones [7]. One stone seal may be coloured with green vitriol. Other examples remind us of Pliny's artificially stained Indian beryls [6].

The remains of the Assyrian mural paintings are too imperfect for any inferences as to the medium used. But the Samaritan woman Ohola saw 'men figured on the wall, the images of the Chaldeans figured in vermilion' (Ezek. XXIII. 14). It seems that neither there nor in Egypt were oil paints known. Linseed and other drying oils were probably known at an early date, but they were used only for medicinal, culinary, or cosmetic purposes. Again, such thinners as oil of turpentine were not known until the days of early Greece, and even then were not employed in painting. All Egyptian paintings were in tempera, that is, some adhesive was used in their production, such as size (gelatine, glue), gum, or albumen (white of egg). This conclusion from analyses agrees with Pliny's statements.

(*c*) *Painting Media, Varnishes, and Inks.* Casein, prepared from curd of milk, forms a strong glue, and was used for centuries in Egyptian woodwork. Hebrew texts also speak of the use of curd for house-painting and decoration. Gum arabic (from the bark of *Acacia arabica*) was imported into Egypt from Punt and southern Arabia, and was also known in Mesopotamia. Starch prepared from grain was used in Egypt. Gelatine and gum tragacanth (from the bark of *Astragalus* spp) were available. Lac, the resin prepared in India from the lac insect, is not mentioned in ancient times. White of egg was used, but the eggs were those of geese and ducks, for domestic fowls were not kept in early Egypt. Ws also know that honey was sometimes added to such water-soluble media as gum arabic or size, because it retains some water and thus prevents the gum from becoming too brittle.

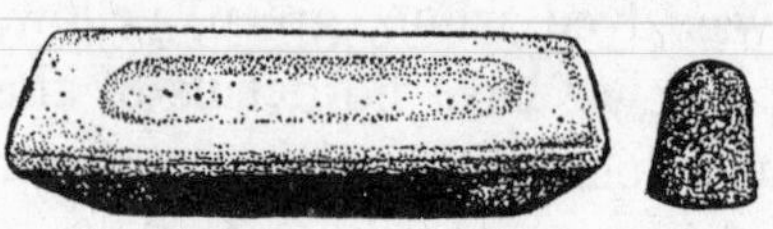

FIGURE 158—*Pestle and mortar for grinding pigments. Egypt. c 1900 B.C.*

The many mortars, pestles, and palettes show that pigments were mixed in advance (figure 158). They were made into cakes or kept in small bags. They were then rubbed down on a rubbing-stone, and mixed with the medium and water. The cakes found on palettes were often made by drying the mixture of pigments and gum-water. A Dynasty XVIII palette contained no fewer than 3 yellows, 3 browns, 2 reds, 2 blues, 2 greens, and one cake each of white and black.

In the reigns of Amenhetep I and II, beeswax was used in tombs as a fixative and as a varnish; its application seems to have improved the brilliance of certain pigments [8]. As suitable solvents were still unknown, it must have been applied hot. Sometimes the varnish was applied to the whole surface, sometimes only to some specific colour. In the latter case, we suspect that it was intimately mixed with the pigment and that this was the first experiment in the encaustic painting [9] so dear to the Egyptians of the Roman era. The earlier experiments with beeswax were soon discontinued.

The composition of the varnish applied to other Egyptian mural paintings is still a mystery. Like the varnish found on wooden objects, it is now often brown, red, or yellow, but originally it must presumably have been colourless. A varnish made of acacia gum was not applied until after 1000 B.C. The earlier varnishes must have been natural semi-liquid oleo-resins applied hot with a brush (figure 157), since solvents for resins had not yet been discovered. The gum arabic from the Red Sea coasts was satisfactory for varnishing wood, and for making gummed layers of linen for mummy cases. The gum produced from *Acacia nilotica* [10] was used in making papyrus. Neither of these gums, however, has the properties of the unknown paint varnish, which possesses certain qualities in common with shellac. It disappeared in Ptolemaic and Roman times, as if supplies were cut off by war. Its source may have been Persia, from which country the inhabitants of Mesopotamia also imported a varnish the composition of which is unknown, though its name seems related to the gum produced from *Acacia nilotica* in Egypt and exported in large quantitites.

From about 1500 B.C., the Egyptians used a natural black varnish that forms a black lustrous surface. It may be related to, or identical with, the black dammar resin produced from *Canarium strictum* in western and southern India. However, the whole subject of the Egyptian varnishes is still unsettled.

Though in Mesopotamia most of the perishable writing materials have disappeared, we know that, in Egypt, bone, clay, ivory, leather, linen, metal, papyrus, parchment, vellum, pottery, reed, stone, wax, and wood were used as writing surfaces. Pens were made from rushes (*Juncus maritimus*). The pigment was mixed with a gum-solution and ground. For this operation there were small pestles or stone spatulas and rectangular stone mortars, with a depression in the middle and with raised sides. The mix was finally formed into cakes and dried.

Scribes and painters, and even noblemen, had beautiful palettes of ivory, wood, alabaster, sandstone, schist, or serpentine (plate 32). Scribes usually kept to a wooden palette with a sliding lid, oval or circular hollows for the cakes of ink, and grooves for pens. Their pens were originally frayed out into a kind of brush, but in Hellenistic days were cut like quill pens. Though they had many pigments at their disposal, papyrus scrolls demanded black ink only, except for initials or titles, where red was often used. The scribe, frequently depicted with his brushes behind his ear, dipped them into a water-pot and rubbed them on the cake of ink like a modern water-colour artist.

Common ink was made from lamp-black and gum-solution. Various kinds of carbon-black are mentioned in medical papyri. Ink was certainly invented in Egypt, but perhaps independently outside Egypt too. Marking-inks used on linen and the like are usually found to be of iron oxide [11].

(*d*) *Organic Dyes.* The ancient texts mention many dyes, only a few of which have been precisely identified. The dye known today as cochineal (carminic acid), chemically a derivative of anthraquinone, is obtained from the Mexican *Coccus cacti*, a scale-insect parasitic on a species of cactus (*Opuntia coccinellifera*), and was originally imported from the New World. There is, however, a wide range of cochineal insects, many members of which contain either identical or closely related red dyes. Some of these were known in antiquity; in particular the varieties obtained from insects living on the kermes oak (*Quercus coccifera*), and on certain grasses growing in the Ararat valley. Preparation of these dyes was simple, since it merely involved collecting, drying, and crushing the insects. The product was most likely sold in grains (the dried bodies of the insects) or cakes [12].

The kermes oak was introduced into Assyria by Tiglath-pileser I about 1100 B.C., and its Akkadian name seems to indicate its use as a breeding place for the insect. Among the booty accruing to Sargon II from his invasion of Urartu (Ararat), in 714 B.C., were included 'red stuffs of Ararat and Kerki'. It is likely that this class of dye was produced in Persia and the Indus valley, for the Greek Ctesias (fifth century B.C.) mentions imports of kermes from India in his day. The scarlet that held such an important part in Jewish religious ceremonies (Exod. XXVI. 1, 31; XXXVI. 8, 35; Lev. XIV. 4) may have been obtained from a variety of cochineal insect. The best variety is said in the Old Testament to have come from the mountains—that is, the Armenian region. Finally, of the two brilliant red dyes which the Egyptians knew and compared with blood, one is definitely stated to have been imported from Syria in the form of grains, and made from a tree (kermes oak?), and therefore probably belongs to the above class. The other is mentioned explicitly as a dye for linen and leather and is probably archil, a poorer quality dye derived from lichens (*Roccella* and *Lecanora*).

The next important red dye is madder, known to Strabo as *rhiza*, the root [13]. No trace of it has been found in Mesopotamia, though samples of cotton from Mohenjo-Daro (Indus valley), dating back to the third millennium B.C., are said to have been dyed with it. The madder plant (*Rubia tinctorum*) occurs in nature in Syria, Palestine, Egypt, and many other regions; in Egypt it was certainly known in antiquity.

There are two more red dyes for staining the hands and other parts of the body. In Egypt, Palestine, and Syria henna was produced from the conifer *Lawsonia inermis*, which was sometimes cultivated. According to Pliny, the best plants were found in Egypt [14]. It is often supposed to have been introduced into Egypt about 1500 B.C., but indications of its application to an Old Kingdom statue prove that it was in use at least a thousand years earlier. Though early Mesopotamian stone pots were found to contain henna, the ladies of that country usually resorted to decoctions of asafoetida instead.

A great variety of yellow dyes was known, notably safflower, saffron, and turmeric. Safflower, obtained from *Carthamus tinctorius*, has been discovered in early stone pots in Mesopotamia. The seeds of this plant, which have been found stored in Theban tombs of *c* 2000 B.C., were used for the production of a vegetable oil. Its use as a dye (ranging from pale red to golden) in ancient Egypt has been confirmed by chemical analyses of sheets of yellow linen in which mummies were wrapped. Its name in classical antiquity is derived from an oriental root meaning yellow. Saffron, a beautiful orange-yellow dye from *Crocus sativus*, was produced in Syria, Crete, Egypt, and Cilicia, but not in Palestine. The dye was made from the dried stigmas of the flowers, and was highly appreciated in ancient Crete, where it was well known. Scenes showing the picking of the flowers survive. The Phoenicians dyed stuffs with saffron and delivered them to the Assyrian king Ashur-nasir-pal. The meadow saffron (*Colchicum autumnale*) was familiar to the Assyrians, but they are not known to have extracted a dye from it. Turmeric was from a species of *Curcuma* growing in southern Arabia, India, and Mesopotamia. Sumac, obtained from the dried leaves and twigs of various shrubs of the *Rhus* order, was known in Mesopotamia as the 'drug for marking a hide', and was used in tanning and dyeing leather. Finally a yellow dye, made by grinding the rinds of pomegranates and extracting them with water, was used in ancient Mesopotamia from the Ur III period. In Egypt, it is found in tombs from 1500 B.C. In Palestine, it was used for dyes and inks.

The range of good blue dyes was practically limited to woad and indigo. It is certain that the ancient Egyptians early knew indigo which, as its name may imply, is of Indian origin. It has been found on cloth of Dynasty V (about 2500 B.C.) and on later mummy wrappings, though it did not become common until about 300 B.C. The indigo plant, *Indigofera tinctoria*, was then cultivated in Egypt and Syria, but not in Palestine. Classical authors like Dioscorides and Pliny [15] believed indigo to be a mineral pigment. They knew, however, that it originally came from India [16]. Woad, from *Isatis tinctoria*, was well known by 300 B.C. both in Egypt and in Mesopotamia, though real cultivation began only then. In Mesopotamia it had long been used for dyeing, and the dye gave its name to a certain type of blue cloth. The blue colouring-matter of woad is chemically identical with that of indigo (indigotin).

The most highly prized dye of antiquity was that extracted from the molluscs *Purpura* and *Murex* on the coast of the eastern Mediterranean between Tyre and Haifa. The heyday of Tyrian purple, the 'imperial' dye, was in classical times, but there is no doubt now that it was known much earlier. A tablet from Ras Shamra on the Syrian coast [17] refers to the local dyeing of wool in the ancient town of Ugarit about 1500 B.C. The wool dyed black-purple and red-violet with it was sold by weight, in lots of at least 200 shekels. Most of the names of the dealers are of west Semitic (north Syrian) origin. In the tribute paid by a king of Carchemish to Ashur-nasir-pal the same two shades of dyed wool appear. In ancient Crete also, Tyrian purple was highly valued. A mass of murex shells were found with Minoan pottery on the island of Kouphonisi, and near Palaikastro on the main island. Herodotus [18] mentions Cretan dealers in purple of his own time, and the molluscs have been well described by classical authors [19]. The streets of Tyre had a reputation for bad smells, and as it was the main centre for the production of murex purple this is not surprising. The smell was probably due to the decomposing bodies of the molluscs, for only a small part of the animal was used. The dye was prepared by macerating the essential tissue, and boiling it with a 1 per cent. salt solution for three days, during which the liquid was reduced to one-sixth of its original volume.

The art of obtaining these dyes was a secret of the inhabitants of Tyre (2 Chron. II. 14): 'the workers in purple, crimson and blue' for the 'veil of the Temple' (2 Chron. III. 14). Some displacement of text makes Tyre buy 'purple and blue' from the West (Ezek. XXVII. 7) and the Far East (Ezek. XXVII. 16), but the phrase probably implies a centralization of the production of these dyes from molluscs bought from far countries. Judas Maccabaeus took 'blue silk (*hyakinthos*) and purple (*porphyra*) of the sea' (1 Macc. IV. 23) from the Syrians. The secret of obtaining the right shade by mixing the two dyes was carefully kept. Its testing with a decoction of fenugreek (the seeds of *Trigonella*), or with sour barley-dough, is also mentioned.

Black dyes were obtained from oak galls and the myrtle. The former came later to be used in Egypt for ink in place of suspensions of carbon-black (p 245). Both were used universally for dyeing the hair black in the ancient Near East. The Mesopotamians relied on the natural colour of wool to achieve white, black, or brown colours. Grey wool was prepared by 'spinning black and white wool together with the spindle to a double thread'.

(*e*) *The Dyers' Craft*. The ancients revelled in brightly coloured garments. The relation between fashions and availability of dyes is an important factor. Early Egyptian pictures show red, yellow, and green cloth. By 1500 B.C. striped red, deep blue, and yellow cloth became fashionable; striped edges had been introduced some 560 years earlier. From that time, wool fabrics were imported from Babylonia. Later, brown, salmon, and bright blue colours began to appear.

Mesopotamia and northern Syria were the centres of the woollen industry, and Egypt produced linen of excellent quality. As early as 2000 B.C., the dyeing of linen and leather was not only an individual craft but a temple industry. In the temple workshops, the sacred vestments of gods and priests were given the correct colours and patterns. In Hellenistic times dyeing became a state monopoly, but private dyeing continued because dyeing licences could be bought.

In Palestine, as in Syria, the dyers were concentrated in certain towns. There was 'Magdala of the dyers' on the river Jarmuk. Kirjath Sepher was another centre for dyeing wool. A house in Palestine identified as a dyers' workshop [20] contained two stone vats and stone weights, but it is more likely that they were oil presses—as were probably the so-called dyers' vats at Gezer. However,

Gezer was an important dyers' centre in Hellenistic times, and probably earlier, as was the 'town of Byssos', Beth-Asbea (1 Chron. IV. 21; Vulg. I, Par. IV, 21), and the centre for blue stuffs, Luz near Shechem (Gen. XXVIII. 19).

There are only scattered data of the actual dyeing operations. We know that the Egyptian dyers had books of recipes, though the oldest extant examples are as late as the third century A.D. They contain the notes of an alchemist from ancient recipe books describing the dyeing of cloth with alkanet, safflower, saffron, kermes, madder, and woad. Some of these refer to originals of at latest 300 B.C., and probably much earlier. A study of these and kindred documents shows that by Hellenistic times vat-dyeing of wool with indigo was a commonplace [21]. As detergents in dyeing there were used the roots of *Saponaria officinalis*, soapwort, which was well known in pre-classical antiquity. Natron and the root of asphodel were also used (see p 260 for general detergents).

Most ancient dyes needed a mordant to fix them to the fibres. Alum and many copper and iron salts, earths, and organic materials were used for this purpose. *Convolvulus scammonia*, several species of cucumber, and other plants give acid decoctions necessary for the dissolution of some dyes. Indigo, however, requires no mordant, and is probably the oldest dye to have been used for wool. It occurs in *Indigofera tinctoria* and certain other plants as a glycoside of indoxyl. In the preparation of indigo, the indoxyl is first freed by fermentation. As it is formed and comes into contact with air it is oxidized to indigo. The action of dilute acids has the same effect as fermentation, and the above process was preceded in time by an older one which involved dissolving the dye in urine. The use of the urine-vat for dyeing wool with indigo is attested in a papyrus of *c* 2000 B.C. which describes the sorry lot of a dyer as compared with that of a scribe: 'His hands stink, they have the odour of rotten fish, and he abhorreth the sight of all cloth.' The urine-vat is nowadays restricted to a few localities, but the fermentation method is still quite common in the East.

Wool was often first dyed blue with indigo and then dyed again with some other dye like madder; the result yielded a purplish colour. A recipe for this re-dyeing with madder can be found in the earliest alchemical papyrus. Ashes are scattered over the indigo-dyed wool, and trodden in with the feet. The wool is then rinsed in water and clay (or fuller's earth) and pickled in alum. Finally the madder is dissolved, together with some flour of beans (to make the water softer), and the treated wool dyed for the second time.

We know from other papyri that by the use of different mordants the shade could be varied. Thus, for a red shade, madder was used with an alum mordant; for a deep black shade, the mordant was an iron or copper salt. The 'workers in purple' tested the strength of their dye with washed wool to discover the best concentration. Then the wool was dyed for five hours in stages of alternate immersion and removal, until the correct shade was obtained. The classical authors report many combinations of such processes. We know little about the Egyptian processes for dyeing linen, but the instruments of pre-classical antiquity are still in use in the dyeing operations of primitive peoples. The craftsmen of ancient Mesopotamia had several tools that derived their name from kermes-dyeing processes.

In ancient Palestine the dyer's was a respected craft. His vat of dye solution was checked for strength with small test pieces of material, and he wore special gloves to protect his hands. Wool was dyed before being woven. After immersion in the dye, the wool or other material was laid out on a bench for inspection, and the surplus liquid was expressed; there was a special mat for final drying. A decoction of bran was sometimes specified as a mordant. Wool dyed purple was stored in leather bags or wrapped in skins. The re-dyeing of indigo-dyed wool was common also in Palestine; this process was clearly connected with the saying 'colour attracts the dye'. Dyes were expensive: indeed, the Hebrew term for spices—a notoriously costly commodity—included dyes.

(*f*) *Bitumen.* In antiquity, particularly in Mesopotamia, bitumen was used as a building material and, to a smaller extent, as a paint. It adheres firmly to porous bricks of the kind then used, and forms an excellent waterproof coating. There was a flourishing bitumen industry in Mesopotamia, which died a natural death when building methods changed with the coming of the Greeks and the Romans. In the Roman world, the smaller demand for bitumen was met by supplies of wood-tar and pitch. In consequence, the ancient knowledge of bituminous materials, such as those found in the surface deposits of Mesopotamia, was forgotten [22].

Several members of the petroleum family were known to the ancient inhabitants of Palestine, Syria, and Egypt. The Palestinians and Syrians did not exploit or use them to any extent until, in Hellenistic days, the bitumen of the Dead Sea —*pix judaicum*—became an object of trade [23]. In ancient Egypt bitumen was not produced, neither was crude oil collected from the seepages on the coast of the Red Sea. Bitumen was not used in mummification until the Ptolemaic period, and for long afterwards its use remained uncommon. Although there were many natural sources of crude oil and bitumen in the Near East, we shall confine our attention to ancient Mesopotamia, where for centuries the important bitumen trade was centred. Both excavations and philological evidence show that the Mesopotamians knew many varieties of petroleum, though their knowledge was limited to those that appeared on the earth's surface. The deposits shown on the map (figure 159) are confined to natural gases, crude oil, and the different forms of bitumen. The use of all these has been confirmed by literary evidence.

Natural gas played some part in ancient omen-literature, and its appearances and fluctuations foretold evil or happy events. However, it had no importance in technology. Its oracular importance, as it escaped from the gypsum strata seamed with bitumen and sulphur deposits, is demonstrated

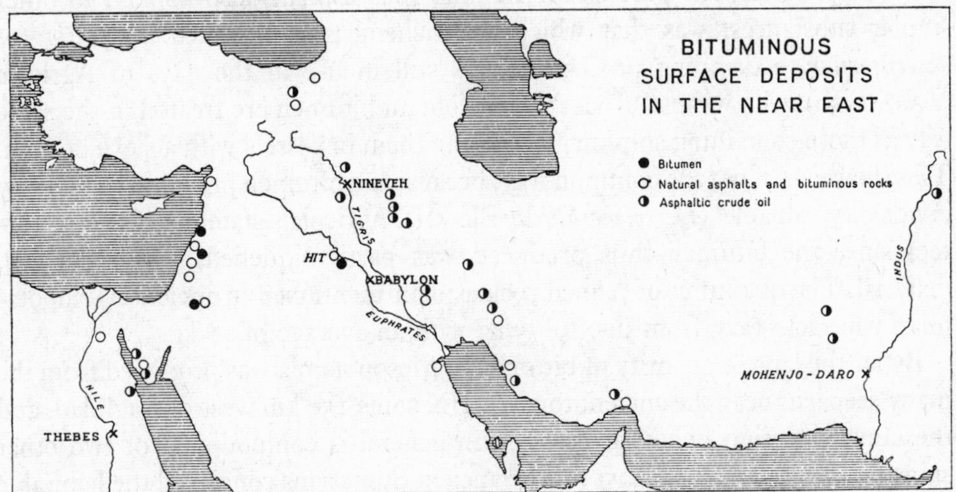

FIGURE 159.

by the passage in King Tukulti Ninurta's annals (889–884 B.C.): 'Opposite Id (Hit), close to the sources of bitumen, I camped at the place where the voice of the gods issueth from the Ušmeta rocks.' The noises, caused by the passage of gases through fissures in the earth's surface, were associated with the voices of the gods in the underworld. Crude oil was not used in remoter antiquity, but Pliny refers to it as naphtha. 'Some authorities', he says, 'include among the bitumens, naphtha, a substance which we have already mentioned. . . . ; but the inflammable nature which it possesses, and its susceptibility to igniting, render it quite unfit for use' (*Nat. Hist.* XXXV, LI, 179). The Greek word *naphtha* goes back to an old Babylonian *naptu*, used, as early as 2000 B.C., in texts describing methods of prophesying from the appearance of oil-seepages and the figures formed by oil poured on water. This Babylonian *naptu* is from a verb meaning 'to flare up, to blaze', an apt description of crude oils containing low flash-point fractions.

The heavy petroleum products such as bitumen were those on which the ancients concentrated: indeed, it is claimed that the use of bitumen is characteristic of Mesopotamian antiquity. It was produced partly in the form of rock asphalt from the mountains, as the Sumerian term first indicates. The 'steward of the gods', Gudea, king of Lagash (*c* 2400 B.C.), obtained his supplies from the mountains of Magda, a quantity equivalent to 110 000 kg being mentioned in one of the documents. About 2000 B.C. we read of quantities varying from 840 to 7200 kg, and of one consignment of 56 000 kg.

The typical ancient process for refining rock asphalt, also applied to other similar substances, was that which the alchemists later called *distillatio per descensorium*, a dripping process. It was still in use in the days of Agricola (*c* A.D. 1550), who writes: 'Rocks which contain bitumen are treated in the same way as those containing sulphur, by heating them in vessels with a sieve bottom. This, however, is not the common way, because the bitumen prepared in this way is not very valuable' (*De re metallica*, Bk. XII). Agricola's statement is quite correct since the bitumen thus produced was partly liquefied, partly cracked, material. The quantities of refined rock asphalt mentioned in ancient Mesopotamian contracts vary from five to 75 kg with an average of 40 kg.

By far the largest quantity of bitumen in Mesopotamia was produced from the many seepages near the ancient town of Hit, some 150 km west of Baghdad, and the cuneiform sign denoting bitumen in general is compounded of two other signs denoting 'well' and 'abyss'. The ancient Sumerians conceived the habitable earth as floating on a large lake, the domain of gods, from which rivers and wells received their water. It is only natural that bitumen, oozing with water and gas from the seepages, should have been thought of as a typical product of the underworld. Furthermore, it was believed to be the symbol of the powerful evil spirits whence it came, rising to harm mankind. We may read something of the sort in many contemporary magical incantations. This belief was perhaps the origin of the Biblical idea of the 'lake of pitch which is Hell'. The town of Hit was originally called Duddul by the Sumerians, a name meaning 'wells along the river'. Its later Accadian title became the name of its chief product, bitumen. It is mentioned by classical authors under the name of Is. Strabo says (XVI, C 743):

> Babylonia produces great quantities of asphalt, concerning which Eratosthenes states that the liquid kind, called naphtha, is found in Susis (Iran), but the dry kind, which can be solidified, in Babylonia. There is a fountain of this latter asphalt near the Euphrates [at Hit]; and when this river is at its flood at the time of the melting of the snows, the fountain of asphalt is also filled and overflows into the river; and that there large clods of asphalt are formed which are suitable for buildings of baked bricks. Other

writers say that the liquid kind also is found in Babylonia. Now writers state in particular the great usefulness of the dry kind in the construction of buildings, but they say also that boats are woven with reeds and, when plastered with asphalt, are impervious to water.

We know that all this is true both of the ancient Mesopotamian buildings and of the boats (ch 17 and 28).

The bitumen from seepages was free of mineral matter. The water in it was easily removed by expression and subsequent heating. For use as a mastic (see p 254) it was mixed with suitable fillers. Its quality was equal to that of the modern asphaltic bitumen produced as a residue from the distillation of crude oils. Many economic texts inform us of the extent of its production. It was sold by volume or weight in quantities varying from 1100 to 8500 litres, or 20 to 5000 kg. The price was about 3·5 shekels of silver per 1000 kg. Taking the index figure based on the prices of corn and cattle for the same period, we get a price in our modern currency roughly equal to that of our refinery bitumen. A huge tribute of 290 000 kg was paid by the town of Girsu (Lagash) to the king of Ur to be used 'for the house of the grand vizier'. Another text mentions five shiploads of bitumen as being dispatched to Ur. We can therefore speak of a real industrial exploitation of these seepages.

In the days of the great Sargon of Akkad, the town of Hit had already become so important that he came there to worship the fish-god Dagan, the Dagon of the Old Testament. Records show that the production of bitumen went on locally at Hit even when the industry had lost its national importance, and Arab and European travellers alike testify to a continuous production, on a smaller scale, up to the present century. The extraction of bitumen from these seepages was simple. Tacitus, who refers to the later industry on the banks of the Dead Sea, writes:

> Those in charge of collecting bitumen, which art they have learnt from experience, seize it and draw it on to the deck of the boat whence it flows by itself and fills [the boat], until it is severed. It cannot be cut with bronze or iron. . . . Thus say the ancient authors, but those familiar with the place relate that the floating mass of bitumen is driven, and pulled by hand, to the shore, and that, soon dried up by the exhalation of the earth and the strength of the sun, it can be cut by axes and chisels like timber or rock. (*Hist.* v. 6.)

Excess water could be driven off by heating, but, owing to the high cost of fuel, it is doubtful whether this method was often used. The mass, if properly worked, could be sufficiently dried in the sun. We do not know whether the ancients practised the fluxing or cutting-back with olive-oil, mentioned by classical authors (Pliny, Strabo) for pitch [24], to produce a product of constant hardness.

The bitumen was used in the form of mastic, that is, it was melted and mixed with sand, fillers, and fibrous materials. This bituminous mastic must of course not be confused with the resin, gum mastic. Many contracts mention mastic—no fewer than 77 for the Ur III period alone—for amounts ranging from a few kilograms to 3500 kg and an average of 450 kg. Curiously enough, the amounts are usually expressed in volumes. The liquid mastic was shaped by baskets or moulds into cakes of standard volume. A sample from ancient Ur still clearly bears the impression of the basket. As might be expected, the price of mastic was considerably higher than that of unfilled bitumen, owing to the cost of the fuel consumed. In very early days, it was 21 shekels per 1000 kg, but it soon fell to 18 shekels, the usual price found in most contracts. Hence mastic was dearer than barley or dates. Comparing prices and average lots of the bitumen and mastic produced in these centuries, it is clear that most of the mastic was made on the spot and used before it cooled. Since it had to be applied hot in any case, this involved only one heating operation instead of two.

Several terms are used for this mastic, each denoting a specific application. The quantities mentioned above refer to a house-asphalt, or mastic for masonry, floors, and walls. There was also a composition called irrigation-bitumen, which seems to have been used to coat irrigation machinery and to caulk ships, as was the plough-bitumen mentioned in other texts. These compositions were sold in lots of five to 300 kg, but no price is mentioned.

The fillers used to compound the mastic were loam and lime (from Neo-Babylonian times onwards); in some cases limestone (quarry dust) may have been used. Many of the ancient mastics contain fibrous vegetable matter in the form of chopped reeds, rushes, or straw. These can be identified under the microscope, and thus form a valuable addition to our knowledge of the flora of ancient Mesopotamia at the times of the buildings from which the samples of mastic have been taken.

The mastics and mortars found in ancient buildings contain from 25 to 35 per cent. of bitumen. Modern engineers, who use as a rule from 12 to 16 per cent, would consider this a high proportion. However, the addition of fibrous material compensated for the overdose of bitumen, and prevented mastic applied to vertical faces from flowing in the heat of the sun. The quantity of vegetable matter in ancient mastics varies from five to 15 per cent by weight, and had been adjusted to the proportion of bitumen. Pots covered on the inside with bitumen, found on several sites, may have been the vessels in which the mastic was prepared.

Two types of mastic were usually made up; one, with about 35 per cent of bitumen, was mortar for brickwork. The other, with about 25 per cent of bitumen, was for floors, walls, and thresholds. One of the best illustrations of their widespread use is a mathematical table in which one can read the quantity of bitumen needed to compound a mastic with 25 per cent of bitumen for any

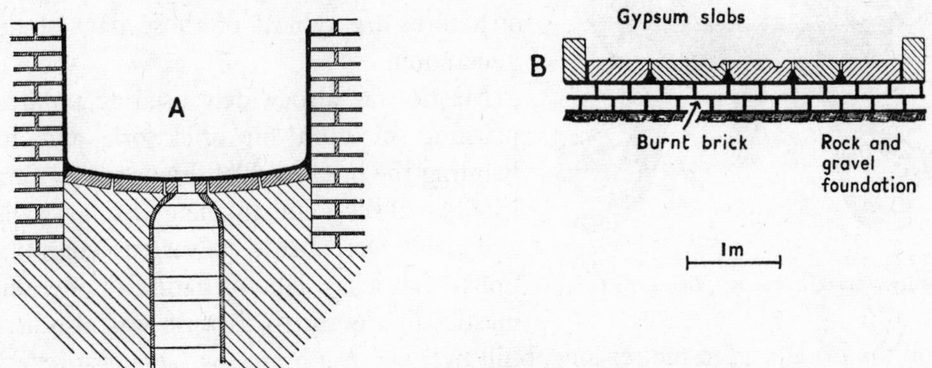

FIGURE 160—*Bitumen in building. Sections of* (A) *a Neo-Babylonian bathroom, with mastic water-proof layer, and drain made of pottery rings, and* (B) *a processional road of the third millennium* B.C. *at Ashur, Assyria.*

given floorspace, assuming that a 2 cm layer is applied [25]. The composition of mastics remained almost unchanged up to the Neo-Babylonian period, when nearly pure bitumen was often used as a mortar. In Persian times, gypsum and lime mortar took the place of bitumen, which was thereafter used only for caulking ships.

The application of the mastic was simple. After heating, it was trowelled or poured on to the surface to be covered. Being expensive, it was very seldom used for walls of sun-dried bricks (which were usually laid in mud), except to make the walls and floors of such buildings impervious to water, especially in bathrooms and toilets (figure 160 A). It was, however, widely used in baked-brick buildings [26]. These, again because of the cost of fuel, were expensive, and were normally used only for palaces, temples, and other official buildings. The low firing-temperature of the bricks (550-600° C) resulted in a high porosity; thus the mastic was freely absorbed, and gave 'such strength that the walls made of it are stronger than rock and any kind of iron' [27]. Modern excavators have found that it is virtually impossible to separate brick from mortar in these buildings.

Strangely enough, the Neo-Babylonian architects adopted another method in the extensive reconstruction projects of Nabopalassar and Nebuchadrezzar. No fibrous material was incorporated in the mastic. Each course of bricks, after being painted with mastic, was covered with a layer of the same mastic. To this, a thin coat of loam was applied, which carried the next course of bricks, leaving joints 1–1½ cm wide. Every fifth joint was provided with a layer of bands of reeds beaten and plaited into mats, evidently intended as reinforcement of the whole structure. We have no indication why the architects departed from the older and sounder techniques, but cheap showy structures are typical of those days of degeneration.

FIGURE 161—*Bowl carved from rock asphalt. Mesopotamia.* c *2500* B.C. *Diameter 28 cm.*

Mastic was also widely used as a waterproofing medium on brickwork, and for painting the brickwork of drains and sewers. Floors, dykes, embankments, quay-walls, and roads were made in various combinations of bricks, slabs of natural stone, and mastic (figure 160 B). Mastic was also used for the bridge, 1130 metres long, built over the Euphrates by Nebuchadrezzar.

Of the use of mastic as paint, Strabo writes: 'On account of the scarcity of timber their buildings are finished with beams and pillars of palm wood. They wind ropes of twisted reed around the pillars; and then they plaster them and paint them with colours, though they coat the doors with asphalt' (XVI, C 739). Other palmwood pillars were overlaid with mosaic in red-veined stone and mother-of-pearl set in mastic. Bitumen was also extensively used as a cement or adhesive. The typical wickerwork coracle, or *quffa*, of ancient Mesopotamia was coated inside and out with layers of mastic (figures 283, 537). The Code of Hammurabi commands that every *sar* (35·3 m^2) of a house shall cost a maximum of 2 shekels of silver, that is, the same as the cost of caulking a *quffa* of 7½ m^3 capacity. Mastic cores were used to model sheets of metal, and rock asphalt itself was carved into vessels and statues of great beauty (figure 161).

II. PRESERVATION

(*a*) *Preservative Substances*. Discussion of the salts known to pre-classical antiquity must be confined to those produced on a fairly large scale. Such are common salt, natron, natural alkalis, and alum. Saltpetre and sal ammoniac will be included, since they are often wrongly identified in translated texts owing to the complications of ancient nomenclature.

Common Salt. Salt (sodium chloride) was always a leading economic necessity, and the quest for it from the earliest times is reflected in the salt-routes. These, with the trade-routes for amber, flint, and other valuable merchandise formed a network over Europe and the Mediterranean basin, stretching beyond the Near East into Asia. Of the prehistoric production of salt little is known. Cakes of salt have been found along some of the trade-routes; such cakes were used as money and often served to pay imposts, as was customary in Abyssinia till quite recent times.

Both rock-salt deposits and salines were worked. On the Atlantic and North Sea coasts, as well as inland, places were well known where salt was obtained by evaporation of sea-water or of saline springs. These are sometimes traceable by place-names. In German the words *hall* or *halle* and in Anglo-Saxon *wich* often signify a boiling-house for evaporating brine. Thus German town-names such as Hall, Halle, Hallstatt, Reichenhall, and English town-names such as Droitwich, Nantwich, Northwich, tell of ancient saltworks, often contemporary with the beginning of iron metallurgy. Now and then passages in classical writings enlighten us further. Thus Strabo (*c* 62 B.C.–A.D. 24) reveals that rock-salt deposits in the foothills of the Sierra Nevada in Spain had been worked long before the fifth century B.C. [28]. The salt, together with that from salterns near Cadiz, was used for curing provisions shipped thence to Greece and other Mediterranean countries. German tribes are reported to have quenched burning logs with sea-water to obtain ashes enriched with salt. Deposits in the Libyan desert played an important part in the ancient salt trade. The very important desert-trade between Syria and Mesopotamia from the Palmyrene salt-oases became possible only after the introduction of the camel for transport in the third (?) century B.C.

Natron (p 259) had in Egypt the religious and magical significance attached to sodium chloride in Mesopotamia. In both areas, the more important mineral was designated by a variety of terms specifying quality and source, while the less important was considered unworthy of more than a general term. The salt-production of ancient Egypt was fairly large, but we have little information on it. There are several salt deposits in the Western Desert, though the evidence of Herodotus (fifth century B.C.) that 'the ground there is coated with salt, so that the very pyramids are wasted thereby' is not to be taken too literally [29]. We get the impression that salt was mainly produced from sea-water in the lakes of the Delta. Pliny (A.D. 23–79) mentions among them a 'lake near Memphis' and, like Herodotus, the 'salt pans of Pelusium' [30]. Pelusium was in Ptolemaic times the centre of the royal salt monopoly, which later shifted to Lake Mareotis, in the north-west corner of the Delta. These salterns ensured an abundant supply of salt, the main application of which was in the seasoning of food and the preservation of fish. Smaller quantities were needed for gold-refining, glazes, and medical recipes. A curious custom was to add salt to the oil for lamps [31]. It would colour the flame yellow and may have given a better or pleasanter light thereby; perhaps it also made the wick last longer. To obtain castor-oil the Egyptians mixed the seeds of the plant with salt before expressing them.

Salt was marketed in ancient Egypt in lumps or bricks, of which many have been found. Two of about 1500 B.C. measured 20×11×6 cm and 19×9×4 cm. Even the oldest that has been analysed (Dynasty VI, *c* 2200 B.C.) proved to be very pure. This indicates saline springs as the source of supply.

In the Semitic world salt played a much larger part than in the Egyptian. If Egypt be the land of natron, the land of salt is Mesopotamia, though natron was known there too. Many different types of rock-salt were recognized, e.g. mountain-salt, *sal gemma*, and red *sal gemma* (the *andarānī* of India). Large deposits and brine-springs were numerous in Mesopotamia, Persia, and Phrygia but they are hardly mentioned in the documents. The well known bitumen seepages of Hit (p 252) produce large quantities of saline water. However, the table-salt for everyday use was impure river-salt obtained by simple evaporation, a mixture of crude sodium chloride and magnesium salts often referred to as 'the salt that broadens the tongue', 'salt from the river midst', and 'salt of mankind'. This and the purer desert salt were sold in rough lumps. The existence of crude salt mixed with earthy impurities explains the famous phrase of St Matthew (v. 13): 'If the salt have lost its savour, wherewith shall it be salted? It is good for nothing but to be cast out.' If such salt be allowed to become wet, it loses first its soluble ingredients, including sodium chloride, and thus its characteristic taste. It must be added, however, that the Biblical phrase may be a mistranslation, and that the passage may actually refer to the use of lumps of salt in bakery-ovens. The salt appears to catalyse the combustion of the poor fuel—typically camel-dung—and gradually acquires impurities in doing so. After some years, the impurities have accumulated to such an extent as to make the salt useless; it is then thrown into the street and replaced.

The desert-salt, being of the best quality, was used in the service of the gods, for the offerings had always to be seasoned with salt. 'Thou art salt, produced in a pure place and destined to [the high god] Enlil for eating by the great gods. Without thee no meal is taken in the temple', says the Assyrian text. In Leviticus (II. 13) we find the command: 'With all thy offerings shalt thou offer salt.' It seems that this first-quality salt was refined by crystallization. Medically it was in frequent use, e.g. as an emetic. It figures in recipes for glass and glazes. The magical purifying power that was ascribed to it was indeed of practical use, since it preserved food.

As early as the Agade period (2300–2100 B.C.) we hear of fish and salt dispatched together, which suggests that the fish was salted, or pickled in brine. Later texts mention that 'fish in salt thou shalt preserve unto sunrise', and that 'meat has been brought thee in salt'. In chemical texts and recipes, salt sometimes occurs under the pseudonym 'stone of the blood'.

Cooking-salt became a necessity as soon as meat was eaten other than raw or roasted. Boiled meat, fish, and vegetables need salt and spices, and these commodities were therefore in demand in all settled civilizations. In Mesopotamia, as in Palestine, salt was needed for baking bread. To eat somebody's salt was like partaking of his bread. Salt was indeed considered one of the 'principal things for the whole use of a man's life' (Ecclus. XXXIX. 26) among the ancient Hebrews. Fish was cooked and eaten with salt. 'Cook fish in its brother [salt], put it in its father [water], eat it with its son [juice], and drink with it its father [water].'

In ancient Palestine salt had a definite religious meaning, often referred to in the Bible. Not only was there a 'covenant of salt' (2 Chron. XIII. 5), but there are references to the use of salt in offerings (Lev. II. 13; Mark IX. 49), even when the sacrifice consists of a slaughtered animal (Ezek. XLIII. 24). This salt was mainly rock-salt from the neighbourhood of Sodom near the Dead Sea, a fact which recalls the story of Lot's wife (Gen. XIX. 26). The salt from the pans near Ostrakina on the coast not far from Pelusium was considered inferior. In Hellenistic times, salt for the curing of fish seems also to have been produced at Magdala from the water of Lake Tiberias [32]. The temple in Jerusalem had store-houses for salt, supervised by a special official (Ezra VI. 9; VII. 22). It was probably sold in lumps or cakes, for we read that it was crushed in wooden mortars. Apart from the seasoning of food and the curing of fish, salt was used in oil lamps, as in Egypt.

Natron. This naturally occurring form of sodium carbonate played only a small part in ancient Mesopotamia. A substance called 'dust of the wall' was an impure sodium carbonate obtained from an efflorescence often found on walls. It was collected and used in dyeing with turmeric. The purer *nitiru* is mentioned in some dyers' recipes, but never in texts on glass manufacture. The shores of Lake Capauta (Urmia) were said to yield an efflorescence of soda [33].

In Egypt the use of natron, the *nitron* or *litron* of classical authors, eclipsed that of common salt, even as a preservative. Egyptian natron is a natural mixture consisting largely of sodium carbonate and sodium bicarbonate, approximating to sodium sesquicarbonate, with varying percentages of sodium chloride and sodium sulphate. The absence of potassium compounds is typical, and can be used as a test as to whether or not plant-ash—which always contains potassium carbonate—has been added.

There were three centres of natron production, all mentioned by Strabo and Pliny [34]. The most important was the oasis in the Western Desert still called Wadi Natrun. Water from the Nile seeps into this wadi in the flood season, forming small lakes which dry up as the Nile retires. The formation of crusts and layers of natron from this seepage is not yet fully understood. The second centre was near the ancient merchant port of Naucratis in the Delta. The third was a group of some five localities near El-Kab in Upper Egypt. The natron of all these is known to have been an important state monopoly in Ptolemaic times (from *c* 320 B.C.).

The numerous forms and varied composition of natron yielded many Egyptian terms. The crude product is often said to be red, and the term for it and for its production came to mean 'purify oneself'. The purified product, ready for use, bore the name *ntrj*, the source of the Greek term *nitron*. The Egyptian word may be connected with the words *ntr* ('god', viz. 'the pure one') and *sntr* ('incense') for, in the Egyptian mind, natron and incense were both associated with ritual purity of men and buildings.[1] Incense was burned to please the gods and was often mixed with natron. This may have also been the case in Palestine, where perfume and incense were 'a confection after the art of the apothecary' (Exod. XXX. 35; Eccles. XLIX. 1). Natron was used by the worshipper to purify his mouth, either by chewing, or by rinsing with a solution. Both natron in solution and solid natron were used in mummification (p 266). Like aromatic resins and incense, natron was often granulated. It was sold both in that form and in lumps.

Apart from religious functions, which absorbed large quantities, natron was employed in Egypt in the manufacture of glass, glazes, and the blue and green frits used as pigments. It occurs frequently in medical recipes and was used in cooking vegetables and bleaching linen. Natron, perhaps mixed with clay, was probably used instead of soap, just as the fullers of Palestine used *nether* (Prov. XXV. 20; Jer. II. 22) imported from Egypt.

Natural Alkali, Soap, Detergents. Alkali, apart from natron, was available in plant-ash, though the analyses of Egyptian glazes or glass fail to reveal any vegetable alkali of high potash content. Neither did the Egyptians use natural

[1] It has also been suggested that 'natron' is derived from the Hebrew *natara*, to bubble, with reference to the effervescence caused when vinegar is added to soda.

alkali to make soap, the functions of which were performed by mixtures of natron and clay, as mentioned above.

In the Semitic world, on the other hand, the ashes of certain plants rich in alkali were widely used. The fullers of Palestine obtained *borith* or *kali* by burning the soda plant (*Salsola kali*) The fuller's soap mentioned by Malachi (III. 2) may have been 'cinders of borith'. Ancient texts from Mesopotamia mention ashes from two common species of glasswort (*Chenopodiaceae*), which abound in soda, as the alkaline component in many glass-recipes. In some cases there is added to their name in the text the adjective *kalâti* (= burnt) which is the ultimate root of our term *alkali*; the immediate derivation is from the Arabic *al-qālī*, the (plant) ash. Curiously enough the glass-recipes give the weight of the raw dried plant to be used but not of the ashes.

The problem of soap in pre-classical antiquity demands a few words. Despite the frequent ritual ablutions and washings of the ancient Egyptian priests there is no real sign that soap was known to them. Hieroglyphic, demotic, and Coptic terms generally taken to mean 'soap' are all doubtful. The common Egyptian detergents were natron, fuller's earth, and perhaps pounded lupins; the last is still used. Some detergents used in dyeing operations are mentioned on p 249. Certain medical recipes indicate the boiling of oils and fats with large quantities of alkaline substances, but the soap thus formed is never mentioned. Nor was soap known in ancient Palestine, where *nether* and soda as well as the vegetable alkali *borith* were used for washing. These were sometimes combined with urine, fuller's ashes, and other ingredients. The Hittites cleansed their hands with plant-ashes dissolved in water.

In Mesopotamia, however, some kind of soap was certainly manufactured by the early Sumerians of Ur. They made it by boiling oil with alkali. Various recipes mention the use of palm-oil, castor-oil, potash, soda, resin, and salt to form soap. Nevertheless, the soap was neither separated from the mixture nor given a special name. For washing wool, the use of beech-ash was recommended. Textiles in general are known to have been washed with soda, vegetable alkali, and alum.

Nitre and Sal Ammoniac. The false identification of the ancient natron with nitre has been very frequent. The substance that we call nitre (potassium nitrate) had no practical importance in pre-classical antiquity. Sodium nitrate occurs as an efflorescence in large areas of Upper Egypt, where it is now used as a fertilizer, but neither potassium nor sodium nitrate seems to have been known in Egypt or Palestine, though the former was known in Mesopotamia. Potassium nitrate occurs in the deposits of Elburz and Azerbaijan in Iran, and was mined there, but it does not seem to have been imported into Mesopotamia [35]. There, as in modern India, the substance is obtained from an efflorescence of the soil in certain localities. This mixture of salt and nitre was 'washed', that is, separated by fractional crystallization. It was dissolved in boiling water, and the solution was strained and boiled down for a day, after which crystals of nitre separated from the lye. The Akkadians distinguished different kinds of this salt as white, black, male, female, washed, and unwashed. All are mentioned in the glass-making texts and in some medical recipes.

Early technology did not employ ammonium chloride, though the Akkadian medical recipes used it in the form of a substance known as sublimate of scrapings. Another name, equivalent to 'soot from dung fires', probably indicates the same substance, though this term sometimes loosely denotes any efflorescence.

Alum. Though alum was produced in large quantities in Roman Egypt, we have less evidence for its earlier production. Pliny claims Egyptian alum as the best, and refers to its use as a mordant for dyers and as an ingredient in medicines [36]. It was produced in the oases of Dakhla and Kharga, west of the Nile valley; both are honeycombed with ancient workings. Surface sherds at Kharga indicate very active production in Roman times, and Greek papyri point to the same for the Hellenistic period [37]. Herodotus recounts that after the destruction of the temple of Delphi (584 B.C.) the Egyptian king Amasis II gave the people of Delphi 1000 talents (about 17 tons) of alum and the Greek settlers (in Egypt) 20 minae (about 25 lb) [38]. Late Assyrian texts mention imports of Egyptian alum into Mesopotamia. Furthermore, modern exploration of Egyptian oases has revealed that miles of the outlying foothills are riddled with shallow workings. Thus we can safely assume that alum was mined there centuries before Pliny.

Alum was used by dyers and leather workers. It is denoted by two Egyptian terms, which may be identical; that alum is meant is shown by their inclusion in medical texts where astringent qualities are indicated. Alum is also mentioned in magical incantations.

For Mesopotamia, we find a substance identifiable as alum in some glass-recipes. If not imported from Egypt, it was won from the deposits near Kara Hissar on the river Lycus, some 90 km from the southern shores of the Black Sea; or from Tuz Khurmatli in Mesopotamia or Hamairan on the Persian Gulf. Alunite or alum-stone is a hard substance that was used for seals. Alum was derived from it by roasting and then boiling in water, as related in some medical recipes. The different Akkadian terms for alum indicate that it was refined by recrystallization, and that various qualities were recognized. Its pseudonym, used as in alchemy to prevent identification by the uninitiated, was 'lichen from the tamarisk'.

In late pre-classical times Cyprus seems to have produced 'plumous' alum (= aluminium sulphate?) for export to the Near East. In Palestine, alum was known and produced from deposits near the Dead Sea, while an inferior quality came from the town of Machairus in Peraea.

(*b*) *Preservation of Foods.* The practice of preserving foodstuffs against times of shortage began in the food-collecting stage. It became even more important when transport and storage followed definite trade-routes. With an increasing population it became a major social activity, and developed its own technology.

FIGURE 162—*A scribe checks the storing of raisins. From a tomb at Beni Hasan, Egypt.* c *1900* B.C.

The processes at first available were few. There was no knowledge of the causes of decomposition, and for many millennia preservation remained purely empirical. Drying, smoking, curing, salting with dry granular salt, pickling in brine, or combinations of these methods, were applied to foodstuffs. Pickling in vinegar was of course possible, but we have no evidence of its use. Herodotus is alone in referring to honey for preservation.

All the known methods of preservation were based on desiccation—nature's own way. Natural products, such as nuts, which contain less than about 10 per cent. of water, keep more or less indefinitely. Smoking, still used for fish and meat, was certainly known to the prehistoric inhabitants of Europe. It was used by the Romans in historic times and even by the German tribes. Pope Zacharias (eighth century A.D.) warned Boniface, the English 'apostle to the Germans', to stick to boiled or smoked bacon and pork during his travels amongst the heathen tribes. In the ancient Near East, however, smoking is not known to have been practised: the lack of cheap fuel always limited technological processes there.

Sometimes resort was had to drying by the artificial application of heat, as for certain drugs and plants; thus the hieroglyphic notation of the Egyptian verb meaning 'to dry drugs' includes the brazier sign. The preparation of a few other ingredients for medical recipes also seems to have involved a combined drying and roasting process. The Egyptian words for 'to dry cereals' and 'to dry dates, grain, or bread' are both connected with the term for the blaze of a fire. The custom of slightly roasting cereals to aid separation of chaff in threshing, and to improve storage quality, was practised in prehistoric times only in Europe and the Mediterranean world. Storage pits for dried corn are known from all three of the ancient valley civilizations (figure 25).

FIGURE 163—*Cutting up an ox carcass and hanging the meat to dry. From a tomb at Thebes, Egypt.* c *1900* B.C.

Drying on a large scale generally meant relying on sun and wind. This was the common procedure for dates, figs, and grapes. We have one representation of the storing of raisins (figure 162). Dried figs and raisins (1 Sam. XXV. 18; XXX. 12; 2 Sam. XVI. 1; 1 Chron. XII. 40) were known in ancient Palestine and Mesopotamia. In Egypt, medicinal plants and drugs were also preserved by simple drying. Meat, which was not yet consumed on a large scale, was generally dried (figure 163). The monuments show the store-rooms of the rich as containing a fair muster of pieces of dried meat, but not until the first millennium B.C. do we find terms for smoked and pickled beef.

In Mesopotamia, meat was rather more frequently salted than dried. In certain cases, even human bodies were preserved by putting them into salt—a custom common also among some Spanish tribes, according to Valerius Maximus. An Assyrian king ordered the corpse of the slain king of the Elamites, 'preserved in salt', to be sent to him, probably as a check on battle reports.

Fish and various birds were consumed in great quantities in Mesopotamia. Drying was often combined with salting. Herodotus says of the Egyptians: 'Many kind of fish they eat raw, either salted or dried in the sun. Quails also, and ducks and small birds, they eat uncooked, merely salting them first. All other birds and fishes, excepting those set apart as sacred, are eaten either roasted or boiled.' The popularity of birds as a food can be gauged from the remark of Hipparchus (*fl* 130 B.C.): 'Nor did I care for the life that the Egyptians lead, forever plucking quails and slimy magpies' [39].

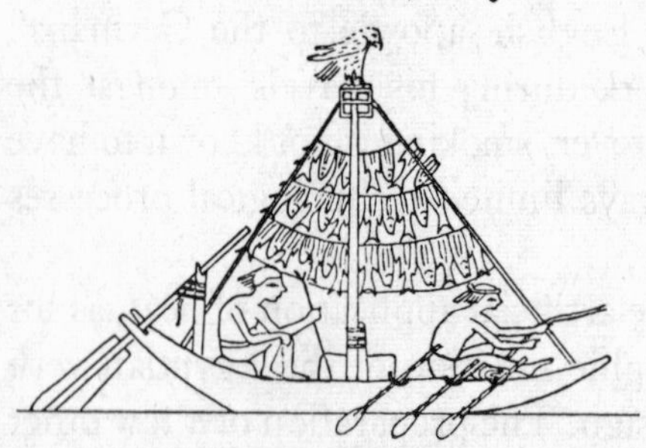

FIGURE 164—*Gutted fish hung to dry from a mast. Egypt.* c *1900* B.C.

Salting is basically a process of desiccation. An old way of producing dried salted fish, still common in the East, is

FIGURE 165—*Netting and curing sea-fish. Saqqara, Egypt.* c *2500* B.C.

probably that by which the salt fish exported from Egypt to Syria and Palestine was produced. The modern Egyptians do it by gutting fish on a cemented slope, washing with water, and rubbing in coarse salt. Alternate layers of salt and fish are covered by dry matting. After standing from three to five days the pile is turned over, and left again for a similar period. Thus the body-fluids drain, salt in solution penetrates the tissues, and the fish are by now firm and hard. This process is depicted in ancient Egyptian reliefs. Fish were cut in half and suspended on ropes to dry in the sun, the wind hastening the process. Sometimes the body was simply laid open with a knife from head to tail (figures 164–6). The roe was collected and stored in pots as a special delicacy.

FIGURE 166—*Netting Nile-fish and fowl; curing fish. From a tomb at Beni Hasan, Egypt.* c *1900* B.C.

In Palestine and Mesopotamia similar methods of preparing fish were common, though pickling was also used, at least in the first millennium B.C. The large stores shown in pictures of ancient houses, and the records of exports of cured fish to Syria, suggest that the process was efficient.

We must note the intimate relation between salt-production and food-preservation. Availability of salt on the coast is the operative factor in the extensive prehistoric salt-trade. The ashes of salt-bearing plants such as *Salicornia* might form a substitute for salt, as in ancient Palestine and Mesopotamia, but they could never be obtained in sufficient quantities to meet the demand for any large trade in preserved fish.

(*c*) *Mummification.* The intimate connexion between the methods for curing fish and those for preserving the human body is well illustrated in the classical authors. Herodotus and Diodorus Siculus use the same Greek word *taricheuō* for both, as does Athenaeus (*c* A.D. 200) in his passage on fish in ancient Egypt. This word means embalming, pickling, salting, preserving. It emphasizes that mummification was consciously associated with curing fish. A discussion of the religious background to mummification in Egypt is beyond our scope, but in no other country were there such extensive and persistent attempts to preserve the body after death. The striking evolution of the process was followed by a general decline in technique.

FIGURE 167—*Bandaging mummies. From a New Kingdom tomb at Thebes.*

We must bear in mind that mummification was a magico-religious act. Its object was to prepare the body as a fit receptacle for the returning soul. Every act was minutely regulated by the ritual of embalming, from the moment the body was placed on the embalming table to the final ceremony of 'opening the mouth'. Certain papyri describe the prescribed ritual and incantations, and give minute instructions on the swathing of head, back, hands, legs, etc. (figure 167).

In early days, the embalmer's chamber was a temporary affair—a booth set up for the seventy days necessary for the process. It had the aura of a shrine, and was called the 'beautiful house', 'house of purification', or 'tent of the god'. This last expression referred not only to its temporary character, but to the hall wherein Anubis embalmed Osiris; thus the dead man was linked to the god Osiris, whose band he hoped to join. Sometimes it was called simply 'embalming tent' or 'bandaging place'. Only in the first millennium B.C. (during Dynasties XXI and XXII) did the embalmer's hall become more permanent and its title indicate a definite building in the necropolis.

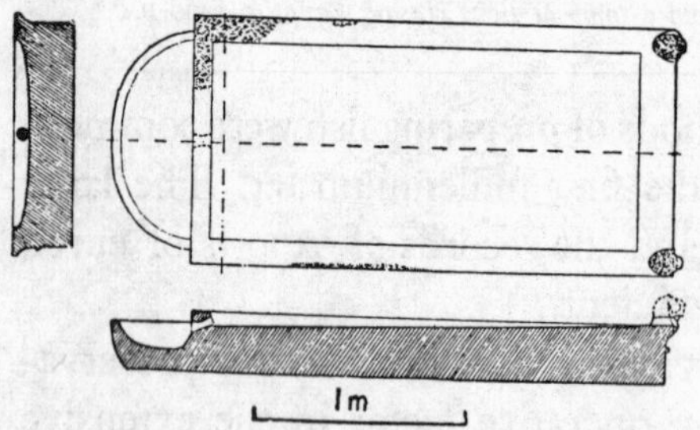

FIGURE 168—*An embalmer's table of Dynasty XXVI, c 600 B.C. The slope of the surface allows liquids to drain to a basin at the end of the table.*

In prehistoric times the Egyptians buried their dead in a contracted position which has been compared to that of the child in its mother's womb. They were wrapped loosely in animal skins or folds of linen in shallow desert graves (figure 169). The sun's heat and the sterile porous sand provided conditions that desiccated and mummified the bodies. The custom is echoed in the oldest portions of the Pyramid Texts, where limbs and flesh are summoned 'to shake off the desert sand'. After the union of Upper and Lower Egypt by King Menes, deeper pits lined with sun-dried bricks were dug into the desert sand for burial of kings and nobles. The method of close-wrapping the body was evolved in the first three dynasties. Finally, each limb was separately swathed, and the whole body covered by a second bandage.

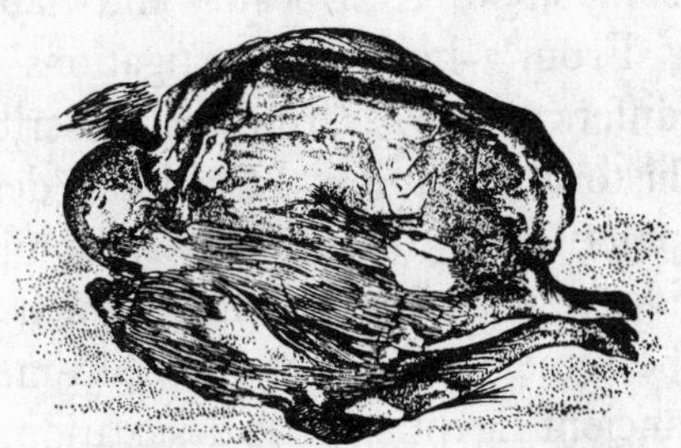

FIGURE 169—*A predynastic Egyptian burial. The knees have been drawn up to the head, and the body is loosely wrapped. Before 3000* B.C.

The ancient Egyptians were perfectly aware of what would happen if decomposition of the fleshy parts were not stopped. Religious tenets demanded that the body be preserved as a receptacle to house the soul, should it wish to enter again the world of the living. For this it was imperative that the exterior forms of the body be preserved. Thus arose the whole elaborate technique of embalming, a tireless effort to avert decomposition. The ritual was performed by skilled craftsmen, headed by the chief embalmer, a man of priestly rank equal to that of the ceremonial priest. He was assisted by another, who personified the god Anubis, patron of embalmers. Between them they recited the incantations appropriate to each stage.

Our information on details of the process is based on careful and minute examination of actual mummies, begun early in the nineteenth century. Conclusions are supplemented by the reports of classical authors. A fairly good description is given by Herodotus, who visited Egypt in 449 B.C., and certain details can be added from the account of Diodorus some four hundred years later.

In the time of Herodotus there were three classes or grades of mummification. The most costly and elaborate involved: (*a*) removal of brain and of abdominal and thoracic viscera, except heart and kidneys; (*b*) cleaning the viscera with palm-wine and spices; (*c*) filling the body-cavities with myrrh, cassia, and other aromatic substances, and sewing up the embalming incision; (*d*) treating the body with natron and washing it; and finally (*e*) anointing it with cedar-oil and other ointments, rubbing it with fragrant materials, and wrapping it in bandages.

A second and cheaper method was to substitute an injection *per anum* of cedar-oil for the operations (*a*) and (*b*), the rest of the treatment being as described. The third and cheapest method also removed the viscera by solution, but the expensive cedar-oil was replaced by some cheaper, less efficient oil. We have no descriptions of the dissolving action of these injected oils, nor have we early details of the fate of viscera removed, though at a later date they were preserved in the so-called canopic jars. Numbers of these jars have survived and some are of great beauty and elaboration (plate 3 B).

From a host of investigations we can picture this intricate process, which differs somewhat from that described by Herodotus, and we have learned of its historic evolution. Herodotus describes merely the phase of mummification practised during the Persian domination of Egypt. Mummification is not really identical with embalming (which literally means 'to place in balsam'). It must be remembered that the only means of preserving the body available to the ancient Egyptians was desiccation, and this was difficult since 75 per cent. of the human body is water. Drying in the sun would be too slow and insecure. Artificial heat was never used. Quicklime was not available before the Ptolemaic period, though limestone was abundant. The dehydrating agents were salt and natron. It was the sacred nature of natron that determined its choice in place of the cheaper salt.

After treatment with natron, the body is so well desiccated that no further drying is needed. There is no evidence that soaking in a bath of natron solution played any part in mummification, though certain mummies appear to have been damp when wrapped. On analogy with the methods of curing fish and fowl, the desiccation is most likely to have been effected by treating with dry granular natron. The use of the same word for both embalmers and the curers of fish and fowl in Greek literature on Egypt supports this view. Dehydrating the body with dry natron in wooden boxes or mats was clearly the basic operation in mummification.

During the Old Kingdom (*c* 2200 B.C.) the Egyptians could not preserve the body adequately, and we may regard this as the experimental period. They had certainly learned to remove the intestines, for an alabaster box has been found with four compartments containing the viscera of Queen Hetep-heres (*c* 2650 B.C.), mother of Cheops. They were immersed in a 3 per cent. natron solution after having been wrapped in linen bandages. This was the first phase of viscera preservation.

In later Old Kingdom graves the viscera were divided between the four canopic jars, placed at the four corners of the sarcophagus. The abdomen and other body cavities were stuffed with linen. To preserve the features of the dead and to counteract their distortion by decomposition, linen soaked in resinous materials was moulded on the shrunken body, and resins were sometimes applied in paste form. The resinous linen under the outer bandages of Old Kingdom mummies has been found to mould limbs and external features with accuracy. Dynasty II mummies already show signs of careful bandaging. From Dynasty VI onwards the heart was treated separately; it was removed, and a stone substitute was placed in the body. Bodies that had been disturbed by tomb-robbers were carefully re-wrapped and re-buried.

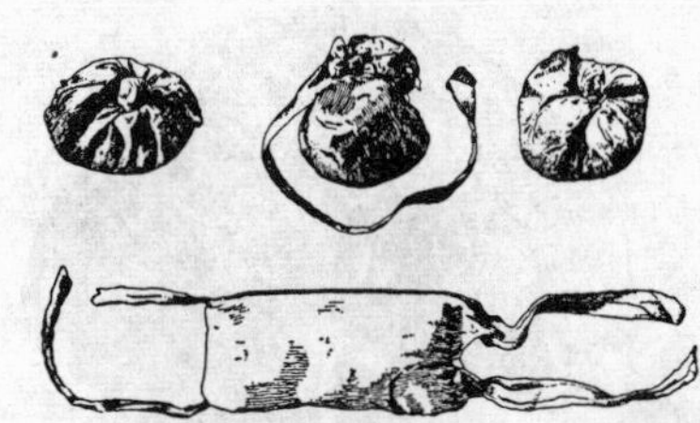

FIGURE 170—*Bags of natron and chaff used in the embalming of Tutankhamen.* c *1350* B.C. *Scale* c *1/10.*

Some mummies of Dynasty XI (*c* 2050–2000 B.C.) have all the organs still present, and no attempt had been made to open the abdomen. Work was concentrated on the surface of the body, which was still soft when bandaged. In general, no incision was found, but in some cases attempts were made to remove the viscera through vagina and rectum by introducing some dissolving agent. After desiccation with natron, the body was swathed in linen followed by a layer of linen soaked in a resinous aromatic mixture, though this layer was sometimes applied direct to the body. In some cases the bodies of soldiers or other attendants must have been buried temporarily in desert graves before mummification and burial with their chief.

During Dynasty XII (*c* 2000–1780 B.C.) treatment was elaborated. The incision in the flank grew more common, and viscera were generally removed throughout. Liver, lungs, stomach, and intestines were preserved in the four canopic jars. The heart was removed, washed and bandaged, and then put back in the body with the 'heart amulet' in the form of a scarabaeus. The body-cavities were stuffed with bandages soaked in resinous mixtures.

In the New Kingdom to Dynasty XXI (*c* 1580–1090 B.C.) we find a new state of affairs. Solid natron became commonly used to stop decomposition on the surface. Brain and viscera were extracted, and the heart was returned to the body after treatment; the heart-amulet was wrapped into the outer bandages of the mummy. Abdominal and chest cavities were filled with linen sometimes impregnated with resins, and hot resinous compositions were poured into them. Mummies were occasionally covered with a layer of beeswax before swathing. In some cases the cavities between skin and bones were filled with chaff or other materials, to replace the shrunken muscles (figures 170, 171). Here again, members of a family must have been buried first in desert graves until the last member died, when the whole family was embalmed, to be buried ritually.

Dynasty XXI (1090–945 B.C.) saw a further change. The body-cavity was filled with bags of linen full of natron, or with chaff, lichen, or sawdust impregnated with natron. In this mass the organs were placed after washing and swathing, together with images of the 'canopic deities'. Canopic jars disappeared. Mud and sand were now regularly used to pack the skin, and mixtures of butter and natron wrapped in linen were inserted in mouth and cheeks. The brain was extracted, and the cavity was filled with resin; the body was then washed and swathed.

FIGURE 171—*Head of Yuaa, an official of Dynasty XVIII. The modelling of the face results in a striking expression of dignity and repose. Egypt. c 1500 B.C.*

As the dynasties roll by, embalming practices degenerate. Ritualistic intricacy replaces methods of preservation. Elaborate series of bandages often cover nothing but a body encased only in pitchlike material with no further treatment; sometimes the skeleton is moulded into a human form with pitch and resins. A mummy is often a mere jumbled collection of swathed bones enclosed in a *cartonnage* case, on which a portrait and decorations form a substitute for the preserved body of earlier generations.

The materials used by embalmers of different dynasties are further revealed by several caches of their surplus materials which, being sacred, were carefully wrapped up and buried after the ceremony. Both the process and its details vary through the dynasties, the changes being prompted by developments of religious thought. The darker side of the craft is well illustrated by a passage from a papyrus (Sallier no. 2): 'The embalmer's fingers are foul, for the odour thereof is that of corpses. His eyes burn from the greatness of the heat. He is too weak to stand up against his own daughter. He spends the day cutting up old rags, so that clothing is an abomination to him.'

III. CULINARY ARTS

(*a*) *Preparation of Food.* The kitchen is the birthplace of many technical operations and apparatus. To it we owe furnaces and ovens, apparatus for grinding and crushing, the use of alcoholic fermentation, methods of preservation, and the extraction of liquids by pressure from seeds and fruit. The methods of preparation of food have undergone an evolutionary development since the Palaeolithic age, when the only process to which they were subjected was roasting. Boiling became possible when suitable receptacles were invented. This stage can still be studied among such people as the Eskimo [40], who eat most of their animal food raw but resort also to roasting and boiling. Besides flesh, Palaeolithic man used many plant-foods that are no longer eaten (ch 14). Up to Neolithic times and beyond, food materials were often steeped in water which was heated indirectly by the immersion of hot stones [41] (p 173).

In the Neolithic stage, with the advent of the cultivation of cereals, stockbreeding, and pottery, cooking developed a new importance. Cereals were dried for storage and grinding. Boiling was carried out in containers heated by direct contact with fire. A kind of porridge was made by heating cereals in boiling water, and towards the end of the Neolithic period biscuits and flat unleavened cakes were prepared. Wild animals were still the main source of the meat-supply, which, with fish, was an important part of the diet. The first alcoholic beverages probably date also from this cultural stage.

Shortly before the rise of the first urban civilizations, the introduction of the plough, and the cultivation with it of larger tracts of drained and irrigated land, started a new dietary revolution. Grain was now crushed, ground, and sieved. Loaves of bread with added spices and condiments were baked, and fermentation was used in the process. Improvement in cereal cultivation introduced a wider variety of farinaceous foods. Meat was now mainly obtained from domesticated animals; the chase tended to become the pastime of the rich, though fishing still supplied food for the masses. With the coming of writing, we can supplement the data from excavations, for climates generally do not allow the survival of foods.

In Egypt, cereals formed a substantial proportion of the diet. The Papyrus Harris (Dynasty XX, *c* 1200 B.C.) mentions over thirty different forms of bread and cakes. Beans, peas, and lentils were eaten, though subject to certain taboos. Water-melons, artichokes, cucumbers, lettuces, endive, and radishes, as well as the fruit of the lotus-tree (perhaps *Zizyphus lotus*), joined the more common vegetables (ch 14). Onions, garlic, and leeks were common condiments. Fruits were mainly dates, figs, nuts of the doum palm (*Hyphaene thebaica*; Arabic *daum*, Theban palm), and pomegranates. There was considerable variety of vegetable oils and animal fats. Milk and cheese were consumed, as was butter, mainly as butter-fat like the Indian ghee or *ghī*.

In Palestine, famous for its wine and oil, the diet was much as in Egypt,

FIGURE 172—*Preparing a joint of meat; roasting a goose (note the fan in left hand); boiling; and plucking. Giza, Egypt.* c *2500* B.C.

whence many foodstuffs were imported in exchange for these products. In Hebrew, 'bread' and 'food' are synonymous. As elsewhere in the ancient East, grain in Palestine was consumed fresh or parched. Mixtures of flour, honey, and oil were common, and thin flat cakes of dough were still baked on hot stones, on embers, or on fires of dried dung. The principal vegetable oil was that of the olive, though nut-oil, fish-oil, and colocynth-oil were known. As in Egypt, salt and other forms of seasoning were much appreciated. Sweets were made with honey, and milk and butter were used. Though camels and swine were familiar, the only meat consumed was that of cattle, goats, and sheep. Pickled and salted fish formed a major constituent of the food of the poor. Geese and ducks, often eaten in Egypt, appeared seldom on the tables of ancient Palestine.

In Mesopotamia, beef was part of the diet of the rich, but in Persia it was a principal food of all classes. The Mesopotamians consumed milk and cheese from the earliest historical period. Many vegetable oils were available, that of sesame being the commonest. Efforts failed to introduce production of olives which, though known, formed only a minor part of the diet. There was a large variety of fruit, and most of the kinds with which we are now familiar were introduced into Europe from this region by way of Greece. Cereals remained the staple plant food and were roasted, parched, or bruised, and prepared either as a kind of porridge with milk, honey, or oil, or baked into cakes.

In early historic times many kinds of cooking were already known, and suitable utensils had been developed. The oldest form, roasting, was applied to beef and the flesh of wild animals. In Egypt, representations of cooking geese and ducks are numerous in all periods; after plucking, the birds were skewered and roasted over a fire (figure 172). After 1500 B.C. the roasting of beef was more commonly depicted, though this may not necessarily mean a change in food habits. Meat was often beaten before cooking.

The development of ovens can be studied in ancient bakeries. In Egypt, the simplest and earliest form was made of horizontal stones laid flat on two or three vertical stones, between which the fire was lighted and raked by an attendant,

FIGURE 173—*Early Egyptian confectioners. The fire on the left is used to heat pots which are probably inverted over it in a single layer—by an artistic convention they appear to be piled high. Ingredients are poured into the hot pots (centre), stirred, and covered (right). Note the characteristic attitude of the attendant at the fire who shades her eyes from the heat (see also figure 175). From a tomb at Saqqara, Egypt.* c *2500* B.C.

who is often shown guarding his eyes from the glow with his left hand. About 2000 B.C. there appeared a clay oven with a grate, on which was a tray for cakes or loaves. By the time the pyramids were built, the kitchens of the larger estates contained brick furnaces, braziers with special pans for frying, and other kinds of cooking apparatus [42] (figures 173–5).

In Mesopotamia, where large bakeries formed part of the ancient Sumerian temple-economy, there were furnaces for mass-production even earlier. The temple kitchens of Ur had large clay beehive bread-ovens and clay cooking-ranges with flat tops and circular flues. At the same time, the more primitive braziers and stone hearths for cooking-pots were also in use. In Palestine, the simple arrangement of heated stones, embers, or dung fires served for baking bread [43]. At a later date beehive furnaces were introduced. Fires were lit inside these ovens, and when they had become sufficiently hot the fires were raked out, leaving the ovens ready for baking. This method originated in the use of pots which had been previously heated in the fire. It remained the standard form in the Near East until recent times.

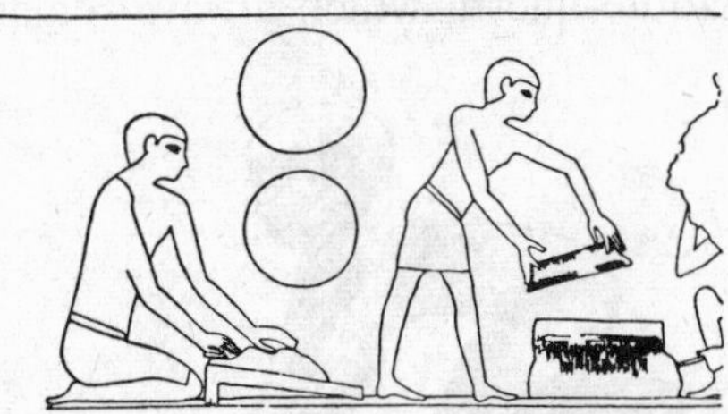

FIGURE 174—*Baking very thin unleavened 'pancakes'—depicted as circles—on a hot surface. The dough is kneaded on the left, and the man on the right probably holds a cover to be placed over the cake on the stone over the fire. From a tomb at Thebes, Egypt.* c *1900* B.C.

To the kitchen we owe the development of grinding and crushing apparatus. Pestle and mortar were the general tools for crushing and pounding (figure 175); they differed little in form from those of today. In Mesopotamia, they were probably preferred to the saddle-quern for making flour in the earlier period, for the miller took his name from the operation of pounding. In Egypt, pounding appears to have been limited to removing the husk of grain, though herbs and the like were disintegrated in mortars.

The early history of grinding is still obscure. Flour-making in Egypt was the task of the housewife, who ground the cereals on a saddle-quern from the earliest

FIGURE 175—*Making spiced bread which might be subsequently further baked for eating, or alternatively soaked in water and fermented to make beer. From the right: the grain is dehusked in mortars, sieved, and ground on a quern. The group of women on the left then form it into cones of dough which are baked on the fire in the centre. The woman on the extreme left is colouring a cone of dough with a red pigment. From a tomb at Thebes, Egypt.* c *1900 B.C.*

historic times (figure 176). Not till about 1500 B.C. do we hear of a miller handling corn in large quantities. He had to kneel to grind his corn, and soon a new form of saddle-quern was developed. As far back as the Pyramid age the saddle-quern was raised on a base inclining slightly away from the miller, thus enabling him to grind more energetically. The millstone carried on its farther side a cup in which the flour collected (figure 175). There is no trace of rotary querns in Egypt before Hellenistic times.

In Mesopotamia, several forms of handmills were known besides the old saddle-quern, which always remained popular in the household and had three different forms, adapted respectively to the grinding of corn, sesame, and dates. We do not know whether the earlier handmills mentioned in the texts were of the rotary type (figure 41), which they certainly were after 1000 B.C. Larger mills driven by donkeys were of the roller-mill type. The date of introduction of these rotary mills has still to be more closely studied on the basis of excavated material. In Palestine, the rotary mill was introduced in Hellenistic times; till then, only the mortar and saddle-quern had been used. A rotary mill has been found at Gezer with no peg or handle to the upper stone, which suggests movement to and fro—discontinuous rotary motion [44].[1]

FIGURE 176—*An early form of saddle-quern. Egypt.* c *2500 B.C.*

[1] The early history of rotary motion is discussed in ch 9. A different interpretation of these archaeological finds is suggested by Professor Childe, p 200.

Another important operation derived from the kitchen was sieving. Both in Egypt and in Mesopotamia sieves were made of reeds, rushes, or papyrus, in different sizes of mesh (figures 175, 179). In bread-making, the husks were removed and the grain was crushed, but usually only the better quality flour was sieved; ordinary bread was always contaminated with grit. The Egyptians from the earliest times made sieves in the form of very shallow baskets. In Hellenistic times a deep basket was used, the bottom of which held the sieve, by now generally made of metal. The Mesopotamian terms for sieves clearly show their manufacture from reeds and rushes and their use for flour. The term 'sieved' was aptly used by the Egyptians to denote the scintillating of little particles of dust in the sunlight.

FIGURE 177. *Upper Palaeolithic honey-collector. Rock painting, Cueva de la Araña, Bicorp, Valencia.*

(*b*) *Fermentation techniques.* These have always been closely connected with baking. When leaven, that is, a mass of yeast, is added to dough, the organisms multiply and fermentation takes place. The gas (carbon dioxide) evolved in the process causes the dough to rise and to change its texture. By the time of the end of the ancient empires this principle became generally used, but it did not altogether displace the baking of various unleavened forms of bread, cakes, and biscuits. The biblical story of the origin of the Passover—the feast of unleavened bread—admirably illustrates this point.

Alcoholic fermentation was carried out in pots, of which simple forms were known by the end of the Upper Palaeolithic. Few of the plants first collected gave infusions suitable for alcoholic fermentation, as they were mostly too poor in appropriate carbohydrates. Even the wild species of grapes and other fruit would hardly be of much use. The techniques of fermentation came in Neolithic times with organized agriculture, and a more regular production of suitable cereals. The only material the fermentation of which may go back beyond Neolithic times is honey [45]. Nectar, mythical drink of the gods, was probably mead with a moderate content of alcohol, made by fermenting honey; this may be even older than agriculture. The collection of wild honey in the forests (figure 177) near the clearings of the earliest prehistoric European farmers was soon followed by the domestication of bees, the hives of which were made from the straw harvested on the fields.

The alcoholic fermentation of sugary fruit-juices or honey was known to the ancient Egyptians when history began (figure 178). They were aware that the first (alcoholic) fermentation, usually over in 3 or 4 days at the high temperatures of their country, was later followed by a second fermentation, forming mainly acetic acid. Consequently beer eventually turned sour, and from the earliest period the Egyptians prevented the second fermentation by stoppering their beer jars; they were thus excluding the air necessary for the growth of the acetic organisms (*Mycoderma aceti*).

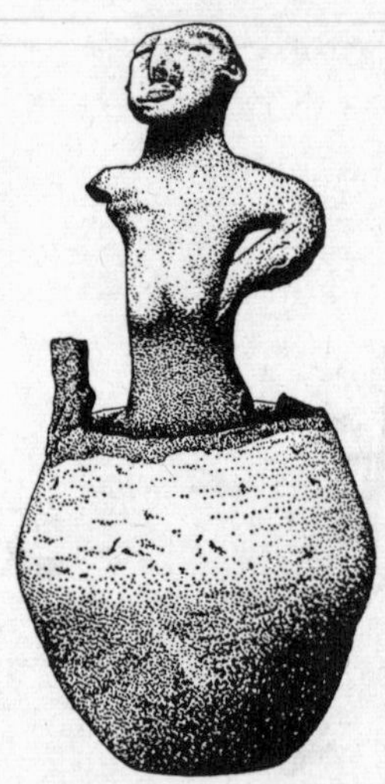

FIGURE 178—*Pottery model of a woman treading the mash in a fermenting-vat (the right arm from shoulder to elbow is missing). From a predynastic Egyptian tomb.*

Lactic acid fermentation was practised in Europe in early times, but came to be neglected when alcoholic beverages were made from the modern grains. Nevertheless, the Slavs still have their *koumyss* and other drinks based on this type of fermentation. Traces of records of lactic acid fermentation occur in the Pyramid age in Egypt, where too it later passed into neglect.

Date-wine was probably the most popular of fermented fruit juices. In Egypt it seems to have been first prepared by pressing the liquid from soaked dates, and leaving the juice to be fermented by the wild yeasts introduced with the date skins. This process is depicted on wall paintings of about 2000 B.C. (figure 179). After fermentation the liquid was poured off, the dregs were pressed, and the wine was filtered into jars, which were carefully stoppered and stored. Date-juice has a high content of sugar—indeed, it was used like honey for sweetening. Honey was often added to the date-juice before fermentation, and the resulting alcohol-content must have been high. This strongest drink of pre-classical antiquity was especially popular in Mesopotamia; between the Cassite period and the beginning of the Neo-Babylonian it replaced beer as the popular drink. Dates here formed a major foodstuff, the yield per palm per annum being as high as 121 litres of fruit in some regions. The juice pressed from the dates was used in part to concoct sherbets (non-alcoholic drinks made from fruit-juices), of which there were many kinds, and partly to prepare the fermented intoxicating drink often mentioned in the texts and denoted later by the same terms as beer, which it outran in popularity. The dregs were used as cattle-fodder, and the stones were dried for fuel.

The Greeks found this date-wine 'a pleasant drink causing headache' [46]. Special brands were made by adding herbs, cassia leaves, and oils such as sesame, and the secrets of their manufacture were as well kept as those of modern liqueurs. We thus have different names for date-wines prepared from exactly the same

FIGURE 179—*Making date-wine. From the right: the mixture is prepared, and crushed through a sieve into the fermenting-vat. The fifth figure from the right decants the liquid into a jar which will be sealed and stored with those on the left. From a tomb at Thebes, Egypt.* c *1900* B.C.

dates, dried figs, and raisins, but of widely differing tastes. The high alcohol-content made subsequent fermentation impossible, hence such a beverage could be stored for a year or so. There was no knowledge of distillation in antiquity.

The intoxicating drink of ancient Palestine bears a name that seems closely related to that of the Mesopotamian date-wine. It is often cited in the Bible along with grape-wine, and some have supposed that it was just old strong wine, but the storage of wine over a long period is most unlikely at this period [47]. In Palestine, strong drinks were made not only from dates, but from pomegranates, apples, and even from barley. There was an Egyptian strong drink described as 'brewed in the orchard'; its nature is uncertain. It was certainly not ordinary pomegranate or date-wine, but may have been one of these with the addition of herbs and honey.

Palm-wine is mentioned as early as the Pyramid texts, and was used in mummification [48]. The sap is obtained by making an incision in the heart of the tree (*Raphia vinifera*) immediately below the base of the upper branches. Palm-wine cannot have been popular, since a date-palm treated in this way seldom survives.

(*c*) *Beer*. There are in the ancient texts many terms for beer, an alcoholic preparation from barley and other cereals. The old Sumerian texts mention eight types derived from barley, eight from emmer or amelcorn (a variety of wheat), and three mixed beers. The Egyptian nomenclature is no less complicated, and it is not always possible to distinguish between types of beer and proprietary brands[1] [49].

The preparation of malt was—as it still is—the all-important process. When farinaceous grains germinate, an enzyme, diastase, converts part of the starch into the sugar maltose or malt-sugar. Malting is the reproduction of this natural process under controlled conditions. The maltose is an important factor in the specific sweet taste of the beer. Malting was not invented for brewing, and is older than the baking of loaves of bread: it was intended to make cereals and other seeds or fruits more palatable. Such foodstuffs can be made pleasanter and more digestible by the germination induced on prolonged soaking in water, to which salt or lye may be added, without the use of fire. The nutritional value of farinaceous grains thus germinated is greatly improved. The product could be preserved after drying, ground into groats or flour, and subsequently made into dough for baking (figure 180). Germination could also be effected by sprinkling the grain with water and leaving it to stand, protected from direct sunlight. The cakes made in this way are a kind of 'durable bread', which was anciently used among other travel-provisions such as groats and dried bread. Malted products were often given as wages in kind to workmen of the temple administrations in Mesopotamia, but with the rise of Dynasty III of Ur they disappeared as a food. This diversion of malted cereals from food to a basic material for brewers may have been caused by a change of popular dietary preference.

FIGURE 180—*Egyptian bakers and brewers of Dynasty XVIII. The operations of baking in a circular oven (top right; cf pottery kiln, figure 242), grinding on a quern, kneading dough (second row left and right), and straining into a fermenting-vat (bottom right) can be recognized. From a tomb at Thebes.* c *1500 B.C.*

The cakes made from malted cereals now became beer-bread, to which could be added herbs, spices, dates, and other ingredients. To make beer, the beer-bread was mixed with cereals, soaked in water, and subjected to fermentation. The solid matter was sometimes removed after soaking and before fermentation, by filtration and pressing (figure 180). For a controlled fermentation yeast is required, the enzymes in which convert malt-sugar into dextrose and then into alcohol and carbon dioxide. The fermentation processes available to the ancient

[1] Descriptions tend to be lyrical rather than factual: the plentiful, the joy-bringer, the addition to the meal, the heavenly, the beautiful-good.

brewer were less controlled, for he necessarily depended on such other micro-organisms as were casually available in the air or on the skins and husks of fruits and cereals [50]. These organisms can often survive the baking temperature of the beer-bread (50–55° C); this would kill all yeast cells, hardly any of which have been found in the remains of ancient beer-jars. It was the custom for early brewers to carry their containers round with them, and these vessels would convey suitable organisms in their cracks and crevices. In later times, the dregs of a previous fermentation were added to the mash of beer-bread. For Egypt, there is evidence that a pure, or almost pure, yeast was available by 1500 B.C. There is no direct evidence for Mesopotamia, but leavening was known about the same time all over the Middle East.

The type of fermentation is influenced by many factors, such as time of storage, character of the climate, and temperature of the brewing process. If the beer-bread after soaking was heated for a short time at about 50° C, the starch would be quickly broken down and the later rapid fermentation to alcohol would be ensured. Those beer-breads with a high proportion of spices and dates may have developed directly from the making of palm-wine. The complexity of the mixtures obscures analysis of ancient fermentation techniques.

Even at this early period we find a complex terminology for alcoholic beverages, varying according to period and region. Many recipes mention odoriferous plants added to give the beer special tastes. There are also recipes for varying the strength of the product by mixing types of beer or by adding water; beers were strengthened by adding honey. The brewer is always depicted straining the mash through a sieve into a vat (figures 180, 183 A). In Mesopotamia, malting and practical fermentation were well understood as early as the third millennium B.C. The mash was stirred in the fermentation vat and left for 3 or 4 days, covered with mats at night to prevent undue cooling. It was next transferred to clarifying vats so that the sediment could settle, and the liquid was then filtered and poured into pottery jars containing from two to five litres if for transport, but more if for storage. That in Mesopotamia about 40 per cent of the cereal production was used for brewing indicates the economic importance of these operations. Early in the third millennium, 60 per cent of the total cereal was barley and the rest emmer (one of the earliest of the wheats). Later, there was a tendency to use less and less emmer for beer production, and emmer-beers always contained a percentage of barley. The use of emmer and of white, red, and brown types of barley and their mixtures produced differently coloured and flavoured beers. In the Sumerian temple-economy a workman had a ration of about a litre of beer a day, officials of low grade obtained double, higher officials (including the ladies of the court) treble, and the highest functionaries as much as five litres. Brewing employed numerous workers, for the accounts show that up to 60 per cent of the cost of beer went into wages.

There were several considerable changes in Sumerian and Assyrian brewing methods [51]. Beer was originally written in cuneiform by inserting the symbol for bread in the sign of the pointed brewer's vat. A change in the type of vat used in the sign occurs between the reign of Urukagina and the kings of Agade (figure 181). This probably indicates that the druggist had taken over the preparation of alcoholic beverages of a novel taste, or that the addition of spiced ingredients and a better control of temperature were playing an important part. The situation was further complicated by the brewing of cereals from which the husks had not been removed. This type of beer was drunk through tubes or reeds, mainly in north-western Mesopotamia, Asia Minor, and Syria (figure 182).

FIGURE 181—*Sumerian pictographs representing the pointed brewer's vat. That on the right is a later form and seems to indicate the addition of some form of heating apparatus.*

A further change in the brewing trade during the Old Babylonian period was social and economic. The trade had two patron goddesses, and in early times brewing was largely in the hands of women, who sold the home-brew in their houses. These small beer-shops acquired a bad name for disreputable amusement. Hammurabi ruled that they should not sell beer of too low a strength or at too high a price, and also threatened with death those who ran them if political conspiracies were plotted on the premises. With the semitization of the country, and with the advent of mass-production of beer, the female brewer made place for her male counterpart, as she did in practically all other countries.

Finally, between the end of the Cassite era and the beginning of the Neo-Babylonian, the use of cereals was more and more restricted to bread and other foodstuffs, and beer came to be brewed mainly of dates and aromatic ingredients.

Mesopotamian beer was regarded by the Greeks as slightly sour to the taste, while Egyptian beer, in the opinion of Diodorus Siculus (first century B.C.), had an aroma and sweetness that made it 'very little inferior to wine'. Emmer and different varieties of barley were used also in Egypt, to compound beer-bread, though the Egyptians had a much smaller range of recipes. There are many pictures and models of Middle Kingdom breweries, and we have a fairly clear description by the alchemist Zosimos (fourth century A.D.) of their traditional

FIGURE 182—*Drinking beer through tubes. From a Syrian seal.*

methods of malting. In Palestine, an Egyptian-type beer was occasionally brewed, in which safflower and salt were added for flavour, but it was never popular in a country that devoted much attention to vine-growing. Special brands of beer flavoured with extracts of lupin, skirret, rue, mandrake, etc., were used by Egyptian physicians. As in Mesopotamia, the first brewers were the women of the household; later, operations on a larger scale were conducted by men. It has been claimed that brewing came to Egypt from Mesopotamia with the introduction of barley and other improved types of grain. Grain was always pounded and freed from husk (often by hand), sieved, and made into a dough to which malt and aromatic substances were added. The dough was lightly baked into a beer-bread. This, either crushed hot from the oven or taken from storage and broken, was soaked; salt was added, and the mash was mixed in the fermenting vat. In this great vessel workmen trod the mash with their feet (figure 183 B). After some fermentation the liquid was transferred to a second vat where fermentation continued. Sieves were used to separate solid and liquid. Sometimes a poorer quality beer was made by kneading the solid matter with more water and expressing the liquid for fermentation as before; the remaining dregs were used as food or fodder. Finally, the liquid was filtered into jars. In some cases fuller's earth seems to have been used to clear the beer. The jars were prepared in some way beforehand, for men are depicted with their arms inside them. They may be merely cleaning them, or perhaps applying a layer of resin to the interior, since Egyptian pottery was rather porous. The jars were closed with clay stoppers, sealed, and stored.

FIGURE 183—(A) *The Egyptian hieroglyph for a brewer, showing him in the characteristic attitude of straining mash into a fermenting-vat.* (B) *Hieroglyph representing a workman treading the mash in a large fermenting-vat.*

This method of brewing is still practised by the Egyptian fellahin in making their *būzah* from wheat (or millet), part of which is malted and part baked into beer-bread cakes. This beer contains 6–8 per cent of alcohol. With the ancient brewing methods, the manufacture of stronger beers was possible. The fermentation process at 40–45° C with wild yeasts (much less susceptible to the concentration of alcohol than our cultivated yeast) allowed the ancient brewer to attain an alcohol-content of about 12 per cent. especially if he added substances rich in sugar. As early as the Pyramid age there were five types of beer, several of which were said to be 'strong', that is in comparison with the ordinary *būzah* type.

(*d*) *Wine.* A species of vine, *Vitis silvestris* Gmel., formerly grew wild over much of Europe. *V. vinifera* L., the modern vine, may have been a cultivated scion of this older species in the Caucasian region. At any rate, wine was known as early as the prehistoric Jemdet Nasr period in Mesopotamia, and was brought to protodynastic Egypt before 3000 B.C. In Greek tradition, Dionysos, god of wine, fled from Mesopotamia in disgust because its inhabitants were addicted to beer. This reflects a truth, for beer was always the popular drink in Mesopotamia while wine was an expensive commodity. Though Urukagina (*c* 2400 B.C.) knew the vine and drank wine, we have the first definite data on viticulture from the reign of Gudea (*c* 2110 B.C.), who built for his vines irrigated terraces protected by trees. At a later period we have reports of vineyards in Singara in north-west Mesopotamia with 2400 vines, and in the neighbourhood of Harran, also in this area, others with 15 000 and even 29 000 vines are mentioned. The Assyrian kings in particular were most interested in the 'wine from the mountains', which could not be grown in the plains. Ashur-nasir-pal (884–859 B.C.) had vineyards near his residence at Kalah, while Sennacherib (705–681 B.C.) tried to acclimatize exotic kinds of vines. Many good wines were imported by Nebuchadrezzar (604–561 B.C.), and by Sargon II (722–705 B.C.), who had large wine-cellars in his palaces and gave preference to the wine from the region of Lake Van (p 554). Nabonidus (sixth century B.C.) had from 50 to 100 bunches of grapes on his vines.

A wine list in the library of Ashur-bani-pal (668–626 B.C.) enumerates the ten best types. It is headed by the 'pure wine from Izalla', followed by the wine from Helbon (near Damascus), which was well known to the prophet Ezekiel (XXVII. 18); the wine of the royal vineyard is placed third. In Mesopotamia, as in other countries, spices and aromatic ingredients were often added to wine. The inhabitants of ancient Palestine knew such spiced wines; they had a honey-wine, and a 'vermouth' which was spiced with the herb *Artemisia absinthia* L. Many names of ancient wines may be proprietary designations, others are poetical descriptions of their excellent qualities.[1] The officials declare in their reports that certain wines were 'cellared in their presence': almost the equivalent of the modern 'château bottled'. Libations of wine were poured to the gods on many ceremonial occasions, such as the laying of the foundation stones of important new buildings.

There was no essential difference between the ways in which wine was made in Mesopotamia and in Egypt. In both countries wild yeasts that occur on the skin of grapes converted the grape-sugar into alcohol. The operations of pressing, fermentation, filtration, filling, storage, and transport, are best illustrated from Egyptian texts, which give much fuller information on these matters than do Mesopotamian.

[1] The virtues of wines, like beers, were extolled on their labels: 'the divine liquid', 'the unguent of the heart'.

Seals and clay stoppers from Dynasty I tell of royal vineyards. In a Dynasty I tomb the body was buried with a layer of grapes to accompany it on its journey to the 'western country'. Originally, the vineyards were mostly in the Delta and in the surroundings of the capital Memphis, but gradually they spread southward to the first cataract and even to the western oases and the Fayum. The acreage devoted to viticulture was necessarily restricted in a country so densely populated. Vineyards were mostly situated in the higher parts of the Nile valley, which had to be irrigated artificially. They were not quite vineyards in our sense of the term, for vines were grown in gardens where vegetables and fruits, oil- and date-palms, figs, melons, and cucumbers were cultivated by irrigation and manuring. These gardens were often adorned with a pond with lotus flowers growing in the middle (figure 361). The nobleman Methen made such a garden under King Seneferu (Dynasty III), and later built a vineyard of 2600 square metres. King Perabsen (Dynasty II) had his vineyard 'Prince of the Boats' laid out in the form of a ship. King Zoser founded the famous vineyards 'Praise of Horus, First in Heaven' and 'Soul of Egypt' in the Delta; both of them survived many generations. The kings of the New Kingdom (after 1580 B.C.) took particular pride in the vineyards they laid out for themselves and for the temples of the gods. Amenhetep III (*c* 1400 B.C.) gave one to the temple of Luxor; its production of 'wine was more plentiful than the water of the Nile at its highest mark'. Private vineyards became common in Egypt only from Hellenistic times, for wine in very early times was used exclusively for temple ritual; it was only later that the rich began to drink it. The Greeks introduced wine-drinking to all classes, and vineyards of about 5000 to 15 000 square metres (but sometimes as large as 550 000) were now exploited by private wine-growers.

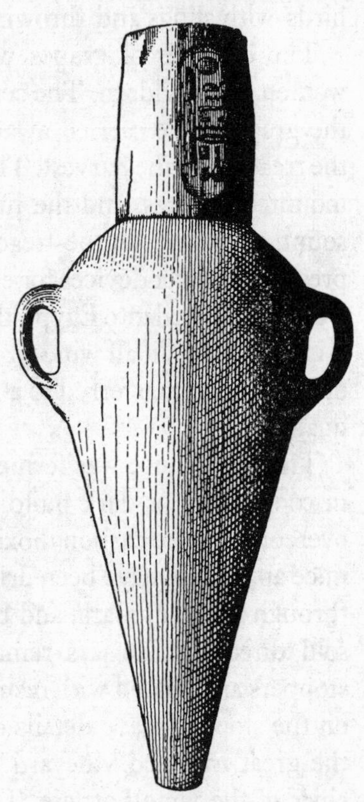

FIGURE 184—*Pottery wine-jar from the tomb of Tutankhamen with an inscription on the seal. Egypt.* c *1350 B.C.*

The ponds in the vineyards were used for irrigation of the vines. The colours in tomb pictures show that the Egyptians had white, green, pink, red, deep blue, and violet grapes. In Palestine and Mesopotamia the vines wound their way up trees or sticks. In Egypt, however, pergolas were constructed and the bunches of grapes could ripen in the shadow (figure 185), while boys chased away the birds with slings and throwing-sticks.

The bunches of grapes were harvested with sickle-shaped knives by men, women, and children. The ceremony was accompanied by singing and music, and the grapes were carried away in baskets covered with vine-leaves. Then came the treading of the harvest. The grapes were thrown into a wooden vat, sometimes mounted on legs, and the juice was expressed by treading (figure 185) to the sound of music. Grape-treading was the first stage in the evolution of the wine-press. Even after devices for expressing liquids, such as the bag-press (figure 186), were introduced into Egypt, the best quality wine was still obtained by treading, as it is to this day in all wine-producing countries. After treading, the solid residue, or marc, was transferred to a press for the extraction of more liquid of an inferior quality.

The grape-juice was fermented, as far as our information goes, in vats placed in cool cellars or dark buildings. There are pictures of workmen creeping out, overcome by the carbon dioxide evolved. In early times the unfiltered fermented juice appears to have been drunk through tubes, but in general it was first filtered through linen into jars, and the lees were used for fodder. Most of the wine was sold directly. The jars remaining in storage were carefully sealed with clay stoppers and coated with resin to prevent further oxidation (figure 184). The seals on the stoppers gave details of the vintage such as 'In the year I. Good wine of the great irrigated vineyard of the temple of Rameses (II) at Per-Amen. The chief of the wine-bottlers, Tothmes.' Tax inspectors—'inspectors of the wine-tasting'—assessed quality, and many wine-bottlers adopted poetic titles such as 'Weramen, prophet of the wine-cellar of the House of Amen'. The pointed jars stood in sand or rings of straw in the cellar: 'The place where the wine product is [stored]. One is glad there and the heart of those who leave it is in rapture.' The different qualities and brands of wines often carried fancy titles, in which the name of the god Horus was prominent. When taken out of the cellars to be used at dinner parties, the wine-jars were put on stands and decorated with garlands of flowers, kept wet so that the wine might be cooled by evaporation. Wines were tapped from the jars with siphons, and mixed to taste. It was the universal custom in antiquity to dilute the wine with water. Other products of the grape known to the Egyptian were the unfermented juice and raisins.

The classical authors did not consider the Egyptian wines worth drinking: Martial declared that vinegar tasted better. According to Strabo, Libyan wine tastes well if mixed with seawater, does not cause headache, and helps digestion; other wines are considered passable.

The Egyptians imported wines from Palestine and Syria, and even tried to obtain their vines for cultivation. In Palestine, the culture of the grape was second only to that of the olive and the fig. According to Jewish tradition the tree of life, planted in Paradise by the evil spirit, Sammael, was the vine, which was afterwards saved from the Flood by Noah. Vines play a considerable part in Jewish history. The must, called the blood of the grapes, was expressed by treading. Raisins were produced by drying the grapes. Jewish lore tells that the wine-cellar contained two vats, the upper for fermenting the must, and the lower for storage. These vats of stone, wood, or pottery were coated with resin. Sometimes there were special vats for the deposition of sediment. Many Palestinian wine-vats and jars have been excavated, a high proportion of them burst by the pressure of the gases developed by subsequent fermentation. From the texts we learn that wine could be stored for a period of up to three years; it was well known that the taste of wine improved on storage, but reached a maximum after a certain period and then deteriorated.

Vinegar was important, as being the strongest acid known in antiquity, but we have very few details of its manufacture. It was known that fermentation, if not stopped at the proper moment, ended by converting the wine into vinegar (through the oxidation of alcohol to acetic acid). Vinegar was, therefore, most commonly prepared by leaving date- or grape-wine to turn sour. In Mesopotamia a medicinal vinegar was produced by fermenting an infusion of the root of *Cyperus papyrus* L. It was used 'to remove poison from the body'. The texts also mention an 'inspissated acid vinegar' prepared from the juice of the sweet flag (*Acorus calamus* L). Vinegar was often used as a solvent for drugs and herbs.

In ancient Palestine and Egypt vinegar was prepared from dates, grapes, and lees of wine. Though taboo to the Nazarites, it was used as a dressing for salads, cabbage, and turnips. It was rarely drunk in the undiluted state, but sometimes bread was dipped in dilute vinegar (Ruth II. 14). It was applied medicinally in certain cases, and was in general used in the ancient East to preserve vegetables and meat. Stronger vinegar was produced from the fermented liquid by inspissation, herbs being sometimes added. The distillation of sour wine was not introduced until well into the Christian era.

IV. COSMETIC ARTS

(*a*) *Nature of Ancient Cosmetics.* A special obstacle makes it difficult to trace early stages in the manufacture of cosmetics and perfumes. It is that the determination of the composition of ointments and oils presents great analytical difficulties even with fresh products, and, with the passage of time, chemical action inevitably alters the constitution of ancient preparations.

In the West, cosmetics could hardly be regarded among the necessities of life, but in the ancient Near East they were in universal demand for protection against the blistering heat of summer; their use was an essential part of general hygiene.

The ancient Egyptians were a cleanly race, bathed frequently, and accepted as an obvious fact that ointments and aromatic oils were necessary for all classes. 'Oil is the remedy for the body', say the texts. We read of an 'apportioner of ointment' under King Amenhetep III (1411–1375 B.C.). The Harris papyrus, of the same period, states that 'no future vizier shall make any requisition upon any priest of these temples for ointment', implying that the priests should be left to distribute it themselves. King Seti I (1313–1292 B.C.) increased the army's rations of ointment. Labourers even went on strike for cosmetics; thus during the reign of King Rameses III (1198–1167 B.C.) the workers in the Theban necropolis refused to work because food was bad and 'we have no ointment'.

The demand for ointments and perfumed oils stimulated the manufacture of the beautiful stone vases and bottles which adorn our museums (plate 3 A). The woman who anointed the feet of Christ had an 'alabaster box of very precious ointment' (Matt. XXVI. 7)—not an uncommon possession for a woman of the people. The demand must also have proved a factor in the rise in production of the less costly glass bottles, made at first from rods moulded on a clay core and heated to fusion. These closely imitated their predecessors of stone.

It is doubtful whether such hygienic needs prompted the use of ointments in ancient Israel. Though 'ointment and perfume rejoice the heart' (Prov. XXVII. 9) the prophet curses the son of the sorceress: 'thou wentest to the King with ointment, and didst increase thy perfumes, and didst debase thyself even unto hell' (Isa. LVII. 9). All the peoples of the Fertile Crescent—Assyrians, Babylonians, Sumerians, Hebrews, and Syrians—did, in fact, use cosmetics and perfumes profusely. They seem to have been less given to bathing than the Egyptians, for such things as bath-tubs were confined to the rich, and the Mesopotamians appear to have washed the entire body only on festal occasions. Purity in all the ancient religions was a spiritual concept, though its physical symbol, baptism—or its equivalent, anointing—certainly had hygienic associations. Cosmetics admittedly contained the 'oil of life which makes the joints of man more supple', as we learn from a Sumerian text, but their religous and magical aspects were more significant. In the New Testament, unguents are carried to the tomb of Christ to anoint his dead body (Luke XXIII. 56, XXIV. 1; John XIX. 40). The election of a king or a leader was confirmed by the ceremony of anointing him with holy oil (1 Sam. XVI. 13).

Philological evidence reveals the direct or indirect magical element in the use of cosmetics, a powerful factor which goes far to explain the variety and cost of the customary ingredients for ointments. The ancient Egyptian language contains two general terms for cosmetics. One is related to a root which means 'agreeable', 'pleasant'. The other is derived from the name of the little vases in which perfumes and cosmetics were stored. There are, however, many more terms connected with cosmetics, some of which have a definite medical application. One which gave rise to the word for 'oil for the massage of the scalp' is not inappropriately used for glazing pottery. A second term is perhaps from the name of the part of Egypt adjoining Nubia whence came aromatic incense. This word was also used for embalming. A third term suggests balm for wounds. A fourth, also with medical associations, came to have the connotation of rubbing. As the centuries pass, more terms appear denoting the everyday use of cosmetics. Thus there are special terms for personal anointing before festivities and dinners, for unguent-makers, and for filling lamps—which is called 'anointing' them. Again, there is a Ptolemaic term for an unguent-kitchen which is clearly derived from a word meaning adornment, thus stressing the cosmetic side.

We can trace a gradual secularization of cosmetics that were of religious, magical, or medical origin. This is also obvious in the terminology of the many types of unguents and cosmetics in Egyptian texts. Of the 35 specifically named unguents, 22 are mentioned in texts of the Middle Kingdom or earlier, that is, before 1600 B.C. No fewer than ten of these are pharmaceutical and occur in medical texts only. Most of the others have a ritual function. Of the 13 later terms we find only one definitely pharmaceutical, the others having mainly a cosmetic application.

In Mesopotamia there is the same relation between religion, magic, and medicine on the one side, and unguents and incense on the other. All aromatic herbs are called by a term which comes to imply also substances oozing from plants, hence gums or resins. The Egyptian term for this was *kemait*. This gave rise to the Greek work *kommi*. Hence Low Latin *gomma*, French *gomme*, and English 'gum', which is thus ultimately a word of Egyptian origin.

(*b*) *Preparation of Cosmetics*. Many of the terms for the ingredients used by the ancients to compound their cosmetics remain unidentified, and chemical analyses of remains of unguents in cemeteries and temples yield hardly any useful data. We tabulate, however, the oils more commonly mentioned by later Greek and Latin authors in discussing medical and pharmaceutical practices of

TABLE I

Vegetable Oils of the Near East

Oil	*Obtained from*	*Oil*	*Obtained from*
Almond	*Prunus amygdalus* Stokes, *v. sativa*	Lettuce	*Lactuca sativa* L.
Balanos	*Balanites aegyptica* Delile	Linseed	*Linum usitatissimum* L.
Ben	*Moringa oleifera* Lam.	Olive	*Olea europaea* L.
Castor	*Ricinus communis* L.	Radish	*Raphanus sativus* L.
Colocynth	*Citrullus colocynthis* Schrad.	Safflower	*Carthamus tinctorius* L.
Malabathrum	*Cinnamomum malabathrum* Batka	Sesame	*Sesamum orientale* and *indicum* DC.

their predecessors, and give their identification when possible (table I, above). Olive-oil and castor-oil were those typically used by the poor. Ben (*Moringa*)[1] -oil, radish-oil, colocynth-oil, and sesame-oil were also very common. The cosmetic use of linseed-oil is doubtful. Mesopotamia was the main source of sesame-oil. According to Herodotus, the seeds of the plant were pressed by special crafts-

TABLE II

Natural Perfumes and Flavours of the Ancient Near East

Perfume or Flavour	*Obtained from*	*Parts Used*
Bitter almond	*Prunus amygdalus* Stokes, *v. amara*	Seeds
Aniseed	*Pimpinella anisum* L.	Seeds
Calamus	*Acorus calamus* L.	Rhizomes
Cassia	*Cassia tora* L.	Flowers & bark
Cedar	*Cedrus libanotica* Link. and	Wood
	Abies cilicica Ant. *et* Ky.	Wood
Cinnamon	*Laurus cinnamomum* Andr.	Bark
Citron	*Citrus medica* L.	Fruit
Ginger	*Zingiber officinale* Roscoe	Rhizome
Heliotrope	*Heliotropaeum europaeum* L.	Flowers
Mimosa	*Acacia nilotica* Nees	Flowers
Peppermint	*Mentha piperita* L.	Flowers & leaves
Rose	*Rosa sancta* A. Rich.	Flowers
Rosemary	*Rosmarinus officinalis* L.	Flowers & leaves
Rushes	*Cyperus rotundus* L. and	Flowers
	Cyperus esculentus L.	Flowers
Sandalwood	*Santalum album* L.	Wood
Gingergrass	*Cymbopogon schoenanthus* Spreng.	Roots

men, who obtained a yield of oil of nearly one-third of the weight of the seeds. Herodotus, Diodorus, Strabo, and Pliny discuss the pre-classical production of these oils and their quality. Their use for cookery and unguents is, in most

[1] Arabic *bān*, the ben tree.

cases, clear from the recipes. The use of olive-oil in ointments was forbidden in Israel (Deut. XXVIII. 40). Both Egyptians and Mesopotamians had a general term for vegetable oil or fat.

The fats at the disposal of the ancient perfumer were all animal. Though the Egyptians had a pharmaceutical term which denoted equally fat from plant or animal, we hear almost nothing of plant-fats. Butter-fat and cheese are unsuitable for cosmetics, but ox-fat, sheep-fat, and goose-fat are mentioned in very early texts, and there are special medical terms for the fat of sacrificial animals. Fish-oil, known both in Egypt and in Mesopotamia, can hardly have been used cosmetically. Many oils of ancient texts seem to have been naturally perfumed compounds, especially the seven (or ten) holy oils so frequent in Egyptian religious texts. It would then seem that the oils tabulated in table I, together with animal fats, were almost all those available to the ancient perfumer.

When we consider what perfumes were available to the ancient compounder of unguents, we can exclude musk, ambergris, civet, and beaver, for they are from animals inaccessible to the ancient Near East. The possible vegetable perfumes of that region are too numerous to detail, but many of those still in use can be identified in Egyptian or Mesopotamian texts, or both (table II). Apart from these, the Greek and Latin authors mention many others, such as henna flowers, the root of the iris, honey, wine, and many other ingredients no longer commonly used in perfumery.

The ancient Egyptian word for a smell when referring to perfume was always combined in a form equivalent to 'fragrance of the gods'. This suggests that the basic use of perfume was religious. There was a special term for the offering of perfume, a special priest who surveyed the offering of incense and the like, and a special word for the fragrance of incense. The later general term for fragrance is connected with the word for nostril, while another term for fragrance seems related to the smell of the fruits of the carob-tree (St. John's bread-tree, *Ceratonia siliqua*). In Mesopotamia also, perfumes and incense had primarily the aspect of purification and ritual cleansing. Their purpose was to render the worshipper acceptable to the gods, to whom the perfumes were agreeable. The prophet Jeremiah (VI. 20) asks in derision of the heathen and his false gods 'To what purpose cometh there to me incense from Sheba, and the sweet cane from a far country?'

Documents that show or describe the manufacture of incense are few, and often represent the artist's impressions rather than technical details. No form of distillation was used. The only three processes available for producing perfumes from flowers, fruit, and seeds were *enfleurage*, maceration, and expression.

In *enfleurage*, the flower petals are spread on a layer of animal fat. When their perfume has been absorbed, they are replaced by fresh flowers, until the fat has become fully charged with perfume. The resulting pomades were popular with the ancients. Balls or cones of them can be seen on the heads of the gaily decorated merry-makers at festivities, and they form part of the regular make-up of an Egyptian lady. 'Let thy head lack no ointment', says the preacher (Eccles. IX. 8). The Psalmist speaks of 'the precious ointment upon the head, that ran down

FIGURE 185—*Collecting and treading grapes. From a tomb at Thebes, Egypt.* c *1500 B.C.*

upon the beard, even Aaron's beard: that went down to the skirts of his garments' (Ps. CXXXIII. 2).

In maceration, flowers are dipped into fat or oil at about 65° C. This treatment is often found in recipes for ointments. The perfumer is told to heat his herbs in oil and strain the mixture while hot. This was quite feasible, since in the Near East, from the earliest times, the apparatus for it was to be found in the kitchen. Indeed, the pharmacists and perfumers drew heavily on kitchen utensils and operations, and developed them to react on cooking, to influence the worker in metals, and ultimately to determine the laboratory equipment and terms of the first alchemists.

For expressing the liquid from flowers or seeds, the manufacturers of essential oils and perfumes used presses of the type already developed for making wines and oils. Though but few Egyptian reliefs show the extraction of perfumes by this process, we have ample knowledge of the development of the oil and wine press. The oldest form was the tub in which grapes or olives were trodden (figure 185). The first true press, also known at the beginning of history in Egypt, consisted of a linen cloth filled with grapes or other ingredients, then folded together in such a way as to leave a loop at both ends. The bag was compressed by pushing a stick into each loop and turning them in opposite directions.

The operation is often depicted in distorted perspective (figure 186). The man stretched from one stick to the other is evidently pressing them apart for the final twist. As early as Dynasty III (*c* 2670–2600 B.C.) an improvement was made. One of the sticks was replaced by a noose attached to one of the two uprights between which the bag-press was now suspended. The other end of the bag still held a stick to be twisted by workmen (figure 187). This was the last stage of mechanization of the press before the introduction of the beam-press and screw-press in the Graeco-Roman world, after an interval of more than 2500 years.

FIGURE 186—*Working an early Egyptian bag-press. From a tomb at Saqqara, Egypt.* c 2500 B.C.

Essential oils were naturally not prepared in large quantities. In the recipes for cosmetics and other preparations the aromatic ingredients are usually incorporated into the oil or fat by maceration or *enfleurage*. The ingredients used were often those from which we now prepare perfumes, and aromatic gums and oleo-resins, such as were used for incense, were frequently added. Some of the ingredients of the perfumed oils and unguents may have been fixatives, to prevent the more volatile essential oils from evaporating too readily.

FIGURE 187—*An improved bag-press in which the ends are held apart by a frame. An inspector tests the cloth for holes. From a tomb at Beni Hasan, Egypt.* c 1500 B.C.

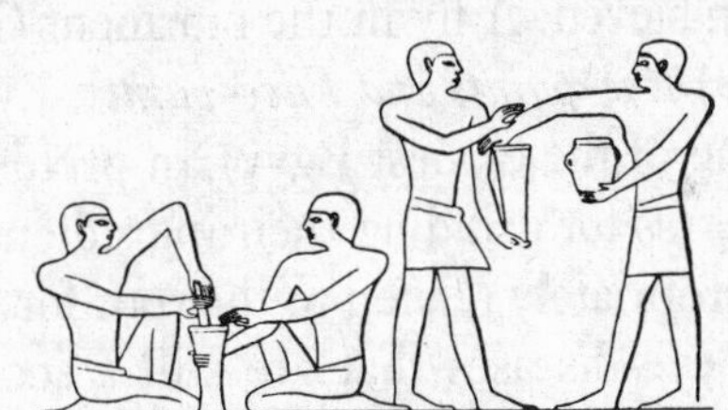

FIGURE 188—*Merchants mixing oils. From a tomb at Saqqara, Egypt.* c 2400 B.C.

The preparation of cosmetics required only simple operations, most of which were first used in the preparation of food. Illustrations of the ointment-compounder's craft are not infrequent in Egyptian art. The oil-merchants are seen carrying their products—described as clear, fresh, yellowish-red, etc.—in animal skins. Some carry funnels and are shown mixing different oils (figure 188). In one scene women are expressing oil from a kind of lily, the heraldic flower of Upper Egypt, the essential oil of which may have had some extra magical importance (figure 189). It would then be mixed with odourless oils and fats, but pictures of such processes are rare. There is a fairly complete picture of an ointment-compounder's workshop (figure 190). The workmen wear curious collars, unknown elsewhere. The unguent, if solid on cooling, was shaped into different forms, mostly balls or cones. The instrument for this operation is crescent-shaped, the inner rim being formed by two small semi-circles }). The method of its application is unknown.

FIGURE 189—*Gathering lilies for their perfume, and expressing the oil. Egypt. c 400 B.C.*

The Old Testament mentions both male and female ointment-compounders (1 Sam. viii. 13). They had formed a guild of apothecaries by the time of Nehemiah (Neh. iii. 8), and lived in a special alley in Jerusalem. Roots and herbs were cooked in water, and oil was poured into the mixture to be decanted subsequently; alternatively, the ingredients were crushed in oil or hot fats and then sieved. A fly in the ointment (Eccles. x. 1) might spoil the results.

(*c*) *Eye-paints and Face-paints.* Eye-paints were used very far back in time. In some of the earliest Egyptian prehistoric graves are beautifully decorated stone palettes for grinding their ingredients (figure 98). The name for these palettes is appropriately related to the root for 'protect', since eye-paints were used to avert the eye-diseases that are still a scourge of the Near East. Eye-paints or their

FIGURE 190—*An ointment-compounder's workshop. Three assistants (1, 2, 3) crush dried herbs or olives with pestle and mortar. The man crouching (4) is possibly grinding further ingredients on a quern. The mixture is added to the bowl of molten fat and stirred (5). On cooling, it is shaped into balls (6). The seven jars, decorated with flowers, probably contain spiced wine, a useful solvent because of its alcohol-content. An assistant (7) is siphoning wine out of one of them and filtering it into a bowl. The man on the extreme left (8), shaping a piece of wood with an adze, is perhaps the overseer. A bowl heaped with the unguents that have been made rests on a table above the crouching figure. From a tomb at Thebes, Egypt. c 1500 B.C.*

ingredients were offered to the gods, their statues were painted with them, and they are often mentioned in connexion with the Eye of Horus, which the god Seth tore from him and which plays an important part in religious texts. The images of the Pharaohs often have the eyelids carefully painted.

The mineral ingredients for eye-paint were carried in small linen or leather bags, shells, or hollow reeds, or wrapped in leaves. Such containers are often found in graves. Though a word meaning liquid is sometimes used as a general term for eye-paint, we more often find other terms, derived from its mineral constituents. A common term is that of which the hieroglyphic form gives rise to the Coptic *stem*, whence Greek *stimmi*, Latin *stibium*. Though in later periods this term denotes stibnite (antimony trisulphide), and in some cases (when statuettes of the god are made from it) antimony, it originally meant galena (lead sulphide), a fact well supported by archaeological finds. Galena was used not only for eye-diseases, but occurs on the list of offerings with the green eye-paint discussed below. Until the later stages of Egyptian history the custom persisted of painting the upper eyelid black with galena, and the lower one green with malachite (basic copper carbonate). Malachite had other uses, as a source of copper, as a pigment, and as an ingredient of medicines. It has been found in graves dating from the remote prehistoric period (fifth millennium B.C.) to Dynasty XIX (*c* 1300 B.C.). The earliest finds of galena are slightly more recent (Badarian, early fourth millennium B.C.), but they continue right into the Coptic period, that is until the Middle Ages in the west. Both ingredients were obtainable locally, though we sometimes read of imports from 'the Asiatics', or again from Punt (see p 583).

The Mesopotamian name for eye-paint, *guẖlu*, usually translated as stibium powder, appears from both archaeological finds and records of the original mines to have denoted either stibnite or galena. The word *guẖlu* passed into Arabic as *kuhl*, and later gradually changed its meaning from a definite black eye-paint into a finely divided powder, then to a subtle spirit, and finally (in the hands of Paracelsus) gave birth to our word alcohol, an extraordinary evolution of meaning.

We can follow the progressive change of eye-paint from a real defence against flies and infection into one of the many beauty preparations. The older double or quadruple tubes in which eye-paint was stored bore the labels 'good for the sight' or 'to stop bleeding'. Later, such expressions as 'to put on the lids and lashes' become more frequent. At the same time, the insect-repelling properties of the ingredients become of smaller, and the colour of greater, importance. Hence burnt almond-shells, soot, or manganese dioxide came to be used instead of galena and malachite. Today, soot is practically always used. Malachite was in its turn replaced by a green resin from conifers, which was also a component both of unguents and of incense.

The manufacture of eye-paint was very simple. The mineral ingredient was finely ground on a palette or on a small flat stone, and made into a paste with water or a solution of a water-soluble gum. This paste was applied to the eyelid with the finger or the end of the kohl (*kuhl*)-stick—a bone, wooden, or ivory rod often found in tombs. The instrument is depicted in a curious sign meaning 'make-up artist', which shows an eye-paint rod in a small spherical bowl. The use of some kind of small knife or scalpel is suggested by the later hieroglyphs for eye-paint.

In Egypt, lips and cheeks were coloured with red ochre. A red pigment often applied to palms, soles, nails, and hair was derived from henna, obtained from the root and leaves of *Lawsonia inermis*. The inhabitants of Mesopotamia used red ochre, asafoetida, and henna, but the Sumerians seem to have preferred yellow ochre for colouring the cheeks. It is referred to as gold clay or face-bloom. We know practically nothing about the dental, shaving, or toilet preparations of the ancients, but the 'barber's stone' used in Mesopotamia to remove superfluous hairs was pumice.

(*d*) *Incense*. Gum-resins and oleo-resins were used not only as vehicles for perfumes, but for incense. In Egypt, the use of incense goes back to the Pyramid age, from which incense-burners have been recovered. These were jars, but spoon-shaped incense-burners with long handles are depicted on the reliefs of worshippers (see tailpiece, p 298). The Egyptian word for incense is equivalent to festival-perfume. The identification of all the aromatic substances and oleo-resins used in the ancient Near East would be very difficult. Remains of incense in Egypt date back to Dynasty XVIII (1580–1350 B.C.), but the nomenclature of their ingredients changed during the centuries.

There are many terms for the burning of incense, the most common implying either smoking or purification. One word, originally signifying merely fruit, was also used for incense in the form 'fruit of the gods'. Another and later term for incense may be connected with an Egyptian word for peace or happiness. In some cases, imported incense was called by a name derived from a foreign original, such as *kedret*, corresponding to the Hebrew *ketoreth*, the usual word for incense and perfume in the Old Testament.

In the case of certain semi-liquid gums or oleo-resins the fragrant liquid components seem to have been obtained by expression, as with myrrh, the liquid part of which, the *stakte* of the Greeks, was added to cosmetics. The dry forms of incense seem to have been submitted to some kind of heat-treatment before compression into the forms desired; for not only does incense appear in the texts and reliefs as small balls or grains, but the reliefs show disks and cakes of incense. The 'shaper of incense' was a special craftsman, and stress was laid on the degree of compression, for which there was a special scale, measured apparently by the ratio of bulk to weight. In this way the incense was often shaped into other special forms, such as the high cones illustrated on the temple-walls and in the graves, which are called by words equivalent to 'white bread'. On the walls of the temple of Deir el-Bahri there are reliefs showing the Egyptians bringing incense trees from Punt so as to grow them in their own country and thus become independent of the long and dangerous expeditions down the Red Sea (figure 32). This experiment seems to have failed. They also traded for such products with the coastal range of the Lebanon, Asia Minor in general, Palestine, Syria, and Nubia. Incense was imported in the form of heaps of small grains, such as the dry myrrh of the texts, or as semi-liquid plastic resins, e.g. the 'fragrant liquid myrrh'.

The Ptolemaic period was the zenith of the use of incense in great variety. During the early Christian centuries, the more costly imported types of incense became rare and were replaced by resin from coniferous trees, or from those plants which probably provided the original incense before the Pyramid age.

REFERENCES

[1] DIOSCORIDES V, 112.
VITRUVIUS VII, vii, 2. (Loeb ed. Vol. 2, p. 112, 1934.)
PLINY XXXV, xiii, 31–xv, 35. (Loeb ed. Vol. 9, pp. 284 ff., 1952.)

[2] JOPE, E. M. and HUSE, G. *Nature*, **146**, 26, 1940.

[3] VITRUVIUS VII, xi, 1. (Loeb ed. Vol. 2, p. 122, 1934.)
PLINY XXXIII, lvii, 161 ff. (Loeb ed. Vol. 9, p. 118 ff., 1952.)
THEOPHRASTUS on Stones VIII, 55. *Opera omnia* ed. F. WIMMER. Paris. 1931.

[4] THEOPHRASTUS on Stones VIII, 56. *Ibid.*
PLINY on *psimythium*: XXXIV, liv, 175 f. (Loeb ed. Vol. 9, pp. 252 ff., 1952.)

[5] DUELL, P. *Tech. Stud. Fine Arts*, **8**, 175, 1939–40.

[6] PLINY XXXVII, xii, 74; v, 20.

[7] HARPER, R. F. 'Assyrian and Babylonian Letters', part 6, no. 570. Luzac, London; University of Chicago Press, Chicago, 1902.

[8] MACKAY, E. J. H. *Ancient Egypt*, 35, 1920.

[9] PLINY XXXV, xxxi, 49; xxxix, 122; xli, 149 (Loeb ed. Vol. 9, pp. 296, 350, 370, 1952.)

[10] HERODOTUS on *akanthos* II. 96. (Loeb ed. Vol. 1, p. 382, 1920.)

[11] MITCHELL, C. A. *Analyst*, **65**, 100, 1940; **52**, 27, 1927.

[12] KURDIAN, H. *J. Amer. orient. Soc.*, **61**, 105, 1941.
DALMAN, G. 'Arbeit und Sitte in Palästina', Vol. 5: 'Webstoff, Spinnen, Weben, Kleidung', p. 84. Schr. des Deutschen Palästina-Inst., Vol. 8. Bertelsmann, Gütersloh. 1937.

[13] STRABO XIV, C. 630. (Loeb ed. Vol. 6, p. 188, 1929.)
[14] PLINY XII, li, 109. (Loeb ed. Vol. 4, p. 78, 1945).
[15] DIOSCORIDES V, 107.
PLINY XXXIII, lvii, 163. (Loeb ed. Vol. 9, p. 120, 1952.)
[16] PLINY XXXV, xxvii, 46. (Loeb ed. Vol. 9, pp. 294 ff., 1952.)
[17] THUREAU-DANGIN, F. *Syria*, **15**, 137, 1934.
THOMPSON, R. CAMPBELL. *J. R. Asiat. Soc.*, 781, 1934.
[18] HERODOTUS IV, 151. (Loeb ed. Vol. 2, p. 352, 1921).
[19] PLINY IX, xli, 80; lii, 102–3. (Loeb ed. Vol. 3, pp. 216, 230 ff., 1940.)
VITRUVIUS VII, xiii. (Loeb. ed. Vol. 2, p. 126, 1934.)
[20] ALBRIGHT, W. F. 'The Archaeology of Palestine', p. 140 and Pl. 22. Penguin Books, Harmondsworth. 1949.
[21] REINKING, K. *Melliand's Textilber.*, **6**, 349, 1925; **20**, 445, 1939.
[22] FORBES, R. J. 'Bitumen and Petroleum in Antiquity.' Brill, Leiden. 1936.
Idem. J. Instn. Petrol. Tech., **22**, 180, 1936.
Idem. Ambix, **2**, 68, 1938.
Idem. Bitumen, Berl., **8**, 128, 161, 1938.
[23] VITRUVIUS VIII, iii, 9. (Loeb ed. Vol. 2, p. 158, 1934.)
PLINY XXXV, li, 178. (Loeb ed. Vol. 9, p. 392, 1952.)
DIODORUS II, 48, 6. (Loeb ed. Vol. 2, p. 42, 1935.) XIX, 98, 2.
STRABO XVI, C. 763. (Loeb ed. Vol. 7, p. 292, 1930.)
DIOSCORIDES I, 99.
[24] PLINY XXXV, lvi, 194. (Loeb ed. Vol. 9, pp. 402 b., 1952.)
STRABO VII, C. 316. (Loeb ed. Vol. 3, p. 266, 1924.)
[25] THUREAU-DANGIN, F. *Rev. d'Assyriologie*, **33**, 79, 1936.
[26] DIODORUS II, 10, 5; 12, 1. (Loeb ed. Vol. 1, pp. 384, 388, 1933.)
HERODOTUS I, 179. (Loeb ed. Vol. 1, p. 222, 1920.)
[27] DIO CASSIUS LXVIII, 27. (Loeb ed. Vol. 8, p. 412, 1925.)
HERODOTUS I, 186. (Loeb ed. Vol. 1, pp. 232 b., 1920.)
[28] STRABO III, C. 144. (Loeb ed. Vol. 2, p. 32, 1923.)
[29] HERODOTUS II, 12. (Loeb ed. Vol. 1, p. 286, 1920.)
[30] PLINY, XXXI, xxxix, 74, 78.
[31] HERODOTUS II, 62. (Loeb ed. Vol. 1, p. 348, 1920.)
[32] STRABO XVI C. 764. (Loeb ed. Vol. 7, p. 296, 1930.)
[33] STRABO XI, C. 523, 529. (Loeb ed. Vol. 5, pp. 302, 326, 1928.)
[34] STRABO XVII, C. 803. (Loeb ed. Vol. 8, pp. 70 ff., 1932.)
PLINY XXXI, xlvi, 106 ff.
[35] PLINY XXXI, xlvi, 106 ff.
[36] PLINY XXXV, lii, 184. (Loeb ed. Vol. 9, pp. 396 ff., 1952.)
[37] e.g. *Oxyrrhynchus Papyri* XVII, no. 2116.
[38] HERODOTUS II, 180. (Loeb ed. Vol. 1, p. 494, 1920.)
[39] ATHENAEUS *Deipnosophistae*, IX, 393. (Loeb ed. Vol. 4, p. 279, 1930.)
[40] STEFANSSON, V. *J. Amer. diet. Ass.*, **13**, 102, 1937.
[41] MAURIZIO, A. 'Histoire de l'alimentation végétale' (Transl. by F. GIDON), p. 53. Payot, Paris. 1932.
[42] WRESZINSKY, W. *Z. Ägypt. Sprache*, **61**, 130, 1926.

[43] HROZNÝ, B. 'Das Getreide im alten Babylonien'. *S.B. Akad. Wiss. Wien, phil.-hist. Kl.*, **173**, no. 1, 1913.

[44] MACALISTER, S. 'The Excavation of Gezer', Vol. 1, pp. 96, 369, 392; Vol. 2, p. 36 and fig. 228. Murray, London. 1912.

SELLIN, E. and WATZINGER, C. 'Jericho, Ergebnisse der Ausgrabungen.' Deutsche Orientgesellschaft, Wissenschaftl. Veröffentlichungen no. 22, p. 153, fig. 41. Hinrichs, Leipzig. 1913.

SCHUMACHER, G. 'Tell el-Mutesellim.' Vol. 1, p. 62 and fig. 82. Hinrichs, Leipzig. 1908.

[45] MAURIZIO, A. 'Geschichte der gegorenen Getränke', p. 30. Parey, Berlin. 1933.

GARDINER, SIR ALAN H. 'Ancient Egyptian Onomastica.' Vol. 2, pp. 233–7. Oxford University Press, London. 1947.

[46] XENOPHON *Anabasis*, II, iii, 14–16. (Loeb ed., p. 368, 1921.)

[47] DALMAN, G. 'Arbeit und Sitte in Palästina', Vol. 4: 'Brot, Öl und Wein', pp. 291–437. Schriften des Deutschen Palästina-Inst., Vol. 7. Bertelsmann, Gütersloh. 1935.

[48] HERODOTUS II, 86. (Loeb ed. Vol. 1, p. 370, 1920.) DIODORUS I, 91, 5. (Loeb ed. Vol. 1, p. 310, 1933).

[49] HUBER, E. "Bier und Bierbereitung bei den Babyloniern", p. 18; "Bier und Bierbereitung bei den Ägyptern", pp. 37, 47, in 'Bier und Bierbereitung bei den Völkern der Urzeit'. Ges. für die Geschichte und Bibliographie des Brauwesens, Publ. 1. Berlin. 1926.

LUTZ, H. L. F. 'Viticulture and Brewing in the Ancient Orient', pp. 77, 86. Hinrichs, Leipzig. 1922.

[50] GRÜSS, J. *Forsch. Fortschr. dtsch. Wiss.*, **12**, 110, 1935/6.

LINDNER, P. *Dtsch. Essigindust.*, **38**, 413, 1934.

[51] HARTMANN, L. F., and OPPENHEIM, A. L. *J. Amer. orient. Soc.*, Suppl. no. 10, 1950.

BIBLIOGRAPHY

Preservatives:

KOLLER, R. "Die Pökelung im Altertum." *Schlachthofwesen*, no. 17, 549, 1939.

FREYDANK, H. "Das Salz und seine Gewinnung in der Kulturgeschichte." *Kali*, **23**, 145–51; 161–8; 177–81, 1929.

LÖW, I. "Das Salz" in 'Jewish Studies in Memory of G. A. Kohut', pp. 429–62. The Alexander Kohut Memorial Foundation, New York. 1935.

ENGELBACH, R. and DERRY, D. E. 'Mummification." *Ann. Serv. Antiq. Égypte*, **41**, 233, 1942.

WINLOCK, H. E. 'Materials used at the Embalming of King Tut-Ankh-Amun.' Metropolitan Museum, Paper no. 10, New York. 1941.

LUCAS, A. "The Use of Natron in Mummification." *J. Egypt. Archaeol.*, **18**, 125, 1932.

Cosmetics:

PLINY *Nat. Hist.* XIII, ii, 4 ff.; XV, vii, 24 ff. (Loeb ed. Vol. 4, pp. 100 ff., 304 ff., 1945.)

ATHENAEUS *Deipnosophistae*, II, 66; I, 24; XII, 553. (Loeb ed. Vol. 1, pp. 290 ff., 107, 1927; Vol. 5, pp. 510 ff., 1933.)

THEOPHRASTUS, Conc. Odours, VI, 27–31; IX, 38–41; X, 42–47; XI, 51 ff. (Loeb ed., 'Enquiry into Plants and Minor Works', Vol. 2, pp. 350 ff., 360 ff., 364 ff., 372 ff., 1916.)

STEUER, R. 'Myrrhe und Stakte.' Schriften der Arbeitsgemeinschaft der Ägyptologen und Afrikanisten in Wien. Wien. 1933.

Idem. "Stacte in Egyptian Antiquity." *J. Amer. orient. Soc.*, **63,** 279, 1943.

EBBELL, B. "Die ägyptischen aromatischen Harze." *Acta Orientalia*, **17,** 89, 1939.

DALMAN, R. 'Arbeit und Sitte in Palästina', Vol. 4: 'Brot, Öl und Wein', pp. 260–8. Schriften des Deutschen Palästina-Inst., Vol. 7. Bertelsmann, Gütersloh. 1935.

Other works mentioned in FORBES, R. J. 'Bibliographia Antiqua, Philosophia Naturalis' on *preservatives*: chapters IX. F. 3 and IX. J, and on *cosmetics*: chapters IX. I., IX. H., and IX. D. 4. Nederlandsch Instituut voor het nabije Oosten, Leiden. 1940–50.

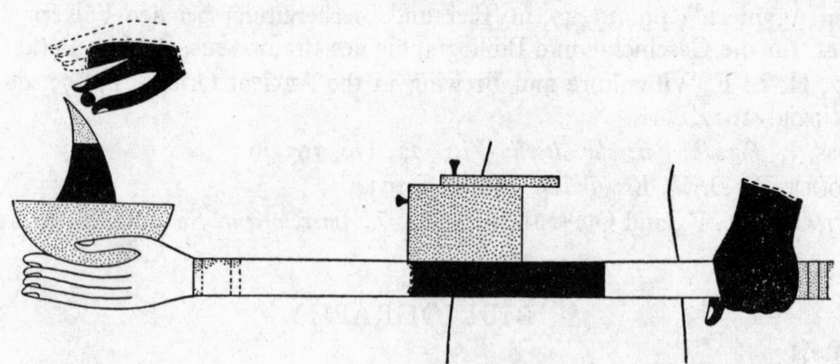

An Egyptian incense-burner from a tomb at Beni Hasan. c 1900 B.C.

12

BUILDING IN WATTLE, WOOD, AND TURF

JOHN BRADFORD

I. PALAEOLITHIC AND MESOLITHIC BEGINNINGS

It is no paradox that even primitive dwellings may be complex, for they are the product of many techniques worked out by practice long customary. The archaeological evidence for the evolution of early building is, however, very unevenly spread in space and time. Occasionally it provides adequate remains for reconstructions of a widely distributed series of house-types; more often the gaps are only too obvious. Moreover, a building, even of such simple materials as wattle, wood, or turf, is usually a complex entity in detail and in the choice and treatment of these materials. Complete plans of prehistoric European houses—to say nothing of whole settlements—are not easy to find or to excavate when found, and the traces left by perishable organic building materials are often very slight.

Technological skill, and the tools available, were prime determinants of structure-type. Other significant factors were those of environment. Thus, heavy rainfall makes some form of pitched roof necessary; cold in mountain heights calls for protection as the first essential; and the rate of decay in the tropics determines the temporary character of building. The nature of local materials is also fundamental. In North America and north and central Europe, timber, turf, and grass are abundant, but in dry zones and highlands adobe and mud-brick or stone are more easily available. Further, communal habits always have a large share in determining the form of dwelling. Nomadic or settled, in families, tribes, or hordes—all these ways of life affect ways of buildings. Moreover, opportunity to imitate dwellings of more advanced cultures is an important factor. Lastly, whim and will must be allowed for. The effects of the other determinants are calculable, but these factors of personal choice must never be forgotten.

Among settled primitive societies, dwellings are not thought of only as structures or places to eat and sleep in, but have something approaching a spirit of their own. Their very orientation, and the position of the hearth or door, may be traditional or express some belief. Technological aspects cannot be appreciated without some reference to social and natural setting.

In studying primitive ground-plans, it must be remembered that much of the household furniture, e.g. beds, benches, bins, and ovens, were often integral features. Nor must neat individual hut-plans suggest a vacuum round them: the many subsidiary buildings of a modern farm are as essential as the farm-house itself. In many buildings of primitive cultivators, small and sometimes simple structures for storage or cooking, or for drying corn and grass, as well as such things as loom-frames, may be fundamental to the whole complex. The tendency to assume close parallels between prehistoric and modern tribal communities has its dangers, for the practices of many modern primitive peoples are less survivals, or archaic forms of prehistoric culture, than independent cultures of a simple form. Nevertheless, prehistory has gained much from the judicious use of such comparisons. Ethnographical parallels at least enable us to touch and to see the kinds of building that can be constructed with a stone adze and chisel, to watch these tools in use, to study the social and sexual division of labour in building, the role of the expert builder, the customary places for persons and possessions within the house, and the features of ceremonial buildings. Not least instructive is the attitude to the disposal of rubbish, for on such remains much of the interpretation of archaeological sites may depend.

FIGURE 191—*Magdalenian paintings in the Font-de-Gaume cave, Dordogne, which may represent summer huts. Upper Palaeolithic.*

A simple classification of modern primitive dwellings into four loose categories can usefully be applied to prehistoric equivalents: (i) open windbreaks; (ii) pole-construction, of spaced saplings, etc., in light open-work; (iii) frame-construction, of close-set posts, etc.; (iv) solid construction, of planks, turf, mud, adobe, or stone.

In the remote past of the Upper Palaeolithic, small hunting and food-collecting groups essayed crude, artificial dwellings in regions where natural caves were absent. For western Europe the evidence for the existence of these dwellings is slight, though traces of surface structures have been claimed for two or three sites. However, some Magdalenian paintings on the walls of the Font-de-Gaume cave, and elsewhere in the Dordogne, exhibit designs regarded by some as representing light, temporary summer huts. These tectiform (tent-shaped) structures may have been like the summer huts of spaced saplings still built by the Paiute Indians of Nevada (p 172), or those of the Alacaluf of Tierra del Fuego. Others have regarded the paintings as representing staked pit-traps (figure 191).

The most striking evidence of more substantial Upper Palaeolithic dwellings is from Russia. Unfortunately the accounts of these are poorly reported and inadequately illustrated, especially in view of the fact that the recognition and recovery of the plans of such flimsy structures demand great technical skill. It can be said, however, that the remains, whatever they are, are widely distributed, and

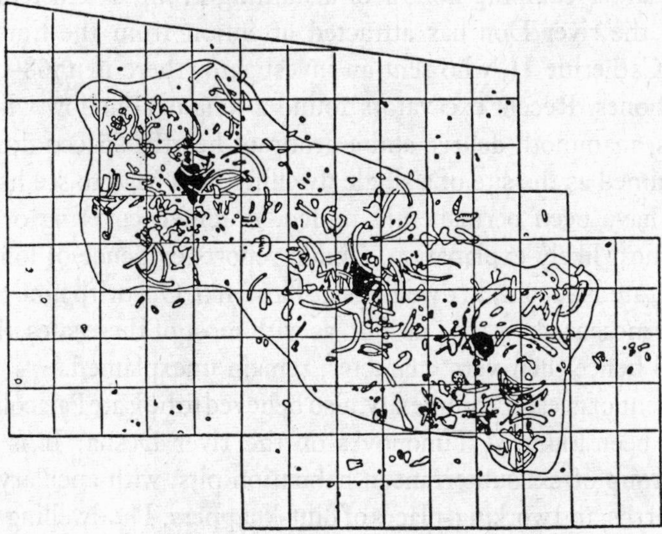

FIGURE 192—*Plan of a Gravettian (Upper Palaeolithic) settlement at Pushkari, Ukraine. One metre squares.*

such occupation layers are often literally stuffed with stone implements and the debris of the activity of hunters.

In the loess (black earth) belt of south Russia, where caves are lacking, small groups of hunters built themselves winter quarters. At Gagarino on the river Don was found the floor of a roughly oval dwelling (*c* 4·5 to 5·5 m in diameter), dug out to half a metre below the old ground level. There were no post-holes, but slabs of stone and mammoth tusks lay round the sides of the hollow, perhaps weights for a stretched covering [1]. There are somewhat similar dwellings in Siberia, also inhabited by mammoth-hunters, near the west end of Lake Baikal, and at Buryet. At the last site, it is suggested, the phalangeal bones of mammoth round the edge of the floor 'helped to support the roof, not as pillars so much as struts upon the tops of which would have been supported inward-slanting poles, the lower ends of which would have rested on the ground where the stone slabs stood along the margin of the depression' [2], but the reconstruction is questionable.

Besides these sub-oval huts, there are traces of other semi-subterranean dwellings with roughly rectangular outlines. Thus at Pushkari, on the river Desna near Chernigov, a roughly rectangular hollow of 4 × 12 m had three hearths in a row down its length. Associated with it were mammoth bones. The manner of roofing is unknown. A scatter of some thirty holes (*c* 10 cm across and 10 cm deep) in the floor may have held thin uprights (figure 192).

A much larger camping-hollow of a hunting group at Kostenki (i.e. 'bone-village') on the river Don has attracted attention from the time of Peter the Great and Catherine II, who sent an investigator there in 1768–9 to report on mammoth bones. Recent excavators found a long oval hollow which contained implements, mammoth debris, and a group of hearths spaced down its length. Though claimed as the site of a single dwelling, it is hard to see how so large an area could have been permanently roofed. A tented covering or row of tents seems the most likely explanation. Childe reports evidence of long rectangular hollows of Late Palaeolithic dwellings at Kostenki. One with nine hearths strung out in a line measured 5·5 × 34 m, but, as with most of these sites, the problem of roofing, and hence their very character, remain unexplained.

A settlement of greater complexity, also believed to be Late Palaeolithic (Magdalenian), has been found at Timonovka on the river Desna. It is claimed that there is a group of six subterranean habitation pits, with ancillary storage pits, open-air hearths, and working-places of flint-knappers. The dwelling pits were long rectangles, varying in length between 11·5 and 12 m, and in width between 3 and 3·5 m. Hearths were seen in two of them. Over one hearth, it is said that there had been a conical chimney of clay-covered bark. Apparently the entrance was down a narrow sloping ramp about 1 m wide. The floors had been much more deeply excavated, to as much as 2·5 or 3 m, and there were traces of timber revetment to the vertical walls [3]. Were this confirmed, we might suppose that the roofing was of logs laid horizontally and heaped over with earth. Such a building would then resemble a burrow or artificial cave, much like the earth-houses of the circumpolar Eskimo. Perhaps, indeed, such earth-houses, originally invented as warm winter dwellings in the cold zone bordering on the north European ice-sheet, withdrew to circumpolar regions with the retreat of the ice [4].

There is, then, evidence for two types of artificially constructed dwelling in Upper Palaeolithic Europe—tent-like and subterranean.[1]

In the succeeding Mesolithic era we find again dwellings adapted to a seasonal mode of life. In summer camping-places in Denmark, tents may well have been

[1] Important details have recently arrived of newly excavated huts of mammoth-hunters in Czechoslovakia. They resemble those described above, but give the clearest known picture of the techniques of building the oldest types of human dwelling in Europe. See *Antiquity*, **28**, 4, 1954.

used, since the high standard of preservation of perishable materials at several of the bog sites would have yielded at least traces of wooden structures had such existed. In England, small summer shelters covered with birch branches and twigs can be safely inferred from excavated sites in the Pennine Hills. To withstand the cold of the boreal winters of the caveless south-east of England, however, the small groups of Mesolithic hunters needed stouter dwellings. There is a set of hut sites at Farnham, Surrey [5], where floors were scooped out of the gravel [6]. One contained some 15 000 worked flints, and must therefore have remained in use for a considerable time. Such dwellings, 'when banked around with soil from the original excavation and roofed with branches and possibly turves . . . must have been quite snug in their time. There is no evidence in the form of post-holes to suggest that our Mesolithic people understood the principles of frame-construction; the nearest approach was the placing of a post at the entrance of one of the Farnham dwellings, presumably to give head-clearance' [7].

Mesolithic sites show a marked preference for the lighter sandy soils that carried less vegetation. The social unit seems normally to have been very small—hardly more than individual family groups—but on the edge of the Federseemoor in Württemberg was a settlement of 38 slightly sunken oval huts of *c* 3·5 × 2 m. Well preserved traces of a framework of branches, probably covered with reeds, were found. As the occupation may have been seasonal, the group at any one time may have been smaller than the number of huts suggests. Indications of wattle and daub construction are reported from a Belgian Mesolithic site [5], and floors of birch bark from several sites in northern Europe.

In general, in Mesolithic times semi-sunken dwellings, generally close to a river or stream, continued to be built to meet the winter cold, though in some sites the floors were now only slightly below the ground-level. As an exception, the Ertebølle fishing-people of Denmark (p 495), with their coastal midden-settlements, managed to maintain their occupation all the year round, thanks to the exceptional fortune of an assured food supply. One Mesolithic hut, at Bockum, Hanover, stood entirely above ground. It had a pebble hearth and a framework of close-set saplings, five to ten cm in diameter, perhaps brought together at the top.

A Mesolithic working-site of great technological interest was recently found near Seamer, Scarborough, Yorkshire [8]. A flooring of birch brushwood, wonderfully preserved in levels now waterlogged, had been built close to the edge of what was then a lake. Quite substantial trees were felled, for the greater part of two birches, one 35 cm thick, had been chopped through with a crude adze. This work had been done evenly, and at a very inclined angle all round, so that the bottom looked like a sharpened pencil. On the whole, Mesolithic hunters seem to have developed their dwellings comparatively little beyond the types adopted in the Upper Palaeolithic, apart from a limited response to the modifications of climate and environment in the transition from glacial to temperate conditions.

II. FIRST BUILDINGS IN THE NEAR EAST

From Egypt, evidence of the earliest buildings of wood, reeds, or wattle is slight. The first positive traces come from Neolithic settlements like that in the western delta of the Nile at Merimde. Occupation there was spread over an area of *c* 550×350 m. Post-holes suggest saplings supporting mud huts, though perhaps the rows of poles were for mere windscreens of matting. In Upper Egypt, at Badari, a dwelling assigned to the fourth millennium B.C. seems to have been a mere shelter, perhaps of skins or matting stretched over wooden frames. 'Stumps of poles' have been noticed occasionally in other 'villages' of this culture [9]. In Badarian graves there is sometimes a kind of hamper of sticks and matting, which may be an imitation of the dead man's hut. In the Neolithic settlements along the edge of the former Fayum Lake there are no traces of post-holes, even for wind-screens, but there are many sunk hearths—fire-holes cut into the rock—mostly 30 to 90 cm across and 15 to 30 cm deep. No structures or social groupings could be deduced from their scattered distribution [10], though a considerable society is suggested by the numerous basketry-lined grain-storage pits (figure 25).

FIGURE 193—*Predynastic pottery model of a house. El-Amrah, Egypt.*

Incoming peoples in the early predynastic period introduced round huts with floors partly excavated. By mid-predynastic times, with a fresh influx, more highly developed forms of building appeared, at the same time as the first metal tools became diffused more effectively (ch 22). Of this period comes, from El-Amrah, a clay model of a house, perhaps that of a member of the upper class. It represents a rectangular building with walls of wattle and daub or mud, and a timber-framed doorway (figure 193). The size of the house of which this is a model might be estimated at *c* 8×5 m [11]. Such rigid structures mark a development beyond the round huts, and required more tool-work. It is not a long step further to the first mud-brick buildings that followed in the early dynastic period.

The history of the house in Egypt in these early periods is still obscure because, since soil conditions are difficult, excavation technique has not yet been able to record the many details of the more perishable structural remains, and also because insufficient attention has been spared from obviously impressive temple and mortuary architecture. Nevertheless, Petrie, E. Baldwin Smith, and others have collected the scanty evidence for early building in wood, from sarcophagi in the form of houses, from house-timber re-used in roofing graves, and from the persistence of primitive forms in religious architecture and the like.

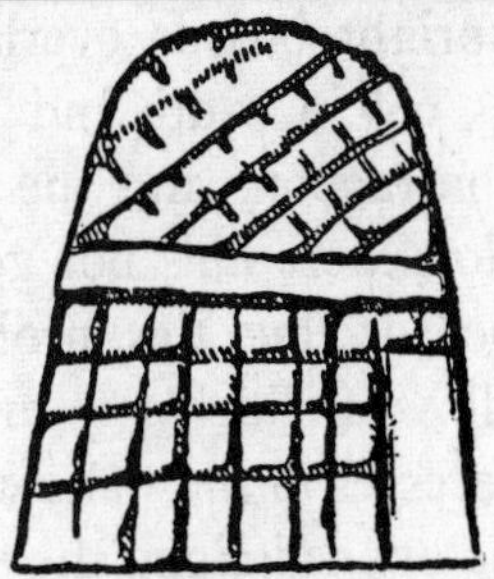

FIGURE 194.—*Predynastic representation of a reed hut. Egypt.*

By predynastic and early dynastic times the limited local supply of timber was becoming exhausted, and importation of wood had begun. It was much used in the royal tombs of Dynasty I. The largest were roofed with timbers of up to six m span, and those still remaining in the floor are 28 × 18 cm in section. The walls were faced with vertical wooden planks seven to ten cm thick. In later periods, ornamental wooden panelling was used in important buildings, and fine natural graining was highly esteemed.

Wood had important alternatives available in reed and palm, which have continued in use from the earliest times to the present. A carved ivory of Dynasty I, from Abydos, shows a hut apparently with a frame of the ribs of palm-branches (figure 194). On a predynastic mace from Hierakonpolis there is a king in a reed or tent shelter. In these reed huts, the walls form a screen on three sides, and the open part is shaded by carrying the reed stems of the roof forward, supporting them on two columns of bundled reeds. Daub adds rigidity; the binding material would be palm-fibre. The tops of vertical papyrus stalks, used for walls and fencing, were tied in a distinctive manner which later became an architectural motif in dynastic palace-buildings (p 476). Indeed, these early constructional methods in wood, reed, and palm greatly influenced stone and brickwork.

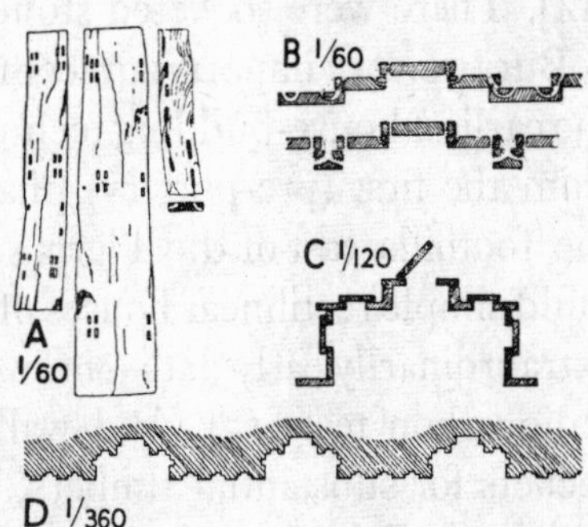

FIGURE 195—*Egyptian plank construction.* (A) *Planks with slots to carry lashings for overlap joins.* (B) *Method of joining planks for the wall of a house.* (C) *Bay made of overlapped planks with movable plank for entrance or ventilation.* (D) *Part of the front of a Dynasty I mastaba (burial structure of mud-brick) imitating the style of* (C).

Plank construction, too, was much imitated in other materials. Figure 195 shows the favourite and highly specialized Egyptian method of planking. Houses were framed with upright boards overlapping one another at the edges and averaging 30 to 35 cm in width and 1·8 to 2·5 m in height. This allowed for expansion and contraction, and the action of wind and sand. 'To hold the boards together slots were cut, not going through, but returning in the face or edge of the board; thus ties, probably of hide, could lash the boards one on another and allow a slide of $\frac{1}{4}$ in for contraction', giving a permanently tight joint. The recesses in the walls were sleeping-places for retainers. A house thus built could be opened along the sides to let the air blow through, and could easily be dismantled and re-erected in the desert during the annual inundation. The most comprehensive evidence of work in wood in later Egyptian architecture is from El-Amarna, the city of Akhenaten (*c* 1350 B.C.); here were painted wooden columns, ceiling beams, bonding for walls, supports of stairs, and inlay work.

From Mesopotamia, the evidence from the earliest known peasant cultures is in many ways similar to that from Egypt. Particularly on the swampy lower reaches, timber as well as stone would have had to be imported. Huts or tents may be inferred at Hassuna, near Mosul in north Iraq, from the specially made hearths in the bottom Neolithic levels, dating perhaps from the sixth millennium B.C. [12]. At Sialk, on the western edge of the Persian desert, where seventeen layers of mud-walled houses had accumulated by 3000 B.C., traces of wattle and daub huts were found in the very bottom levels [13]. When the swamps of the lower Tigris and Euphrates became habitable, the earliest settlements were reed huts, built on reed platforms. At El-Ubaid, near Ur, the huts had clearly been of post-and-mat, mud-plastered like those used by Arabs of the neighbourhood today [14]. There were socketed stones for door pivots (figure 118).

But two very important recent discoveries warn us to keep an open mind about the earliest house-building techniques in the Near East, for we now have evidence from the first (pre-pottery) phase of the Neolithic. Thus at the Jarmo *tell* on the foothills east of the Tigris such pioneer food-producers were already able to build simple rectilinear houses of compacted clay walls, with floors of reeds, at an extraordinarily early date—between 5270 and 4630 B.C. according to a provisional radiocarbon test [15]. And walls of mud-brick, including one with a series of sockets for substantial timbers, have lately been found in the earliest strata at Jericho in Palestine, also of pre-pottery Neolithic culture [16].

III. DEVELOPMENT OF HOUSE-TYPES IN NEOLITHIC EUROPE

For the forested area of Neolithic Europe, the evidence of timber house construction is now fairly ample. Wood was normally the most abundant and convenient material for domestic architecture. On wind-swept treeless spots like

Orkney, stone would be more practicable; in the south Balkans and, perhaps, in the Ukraine, mud-brick was used, but these are exceptions among Neolithic cultures. Given a rainfall, soil, and climate that ensure abundance of timber, a sloping roof was necessary, and the simplest way of securing the run-off is a ridge-pole from which the eaves slope down direct. The easiest, but by no means the only, way to support it is a line of posts. Other posts would be needed to support walls of wattle or split saplings plastered with dung or clay. Such is the construction found north of the Balkans. Log-cabins did not come in until the Late Bronze Age, when cheap metal tools facilitated carpentry [17]. There are many points of resemblance throughout these Neolithic groups and their buildings. Indications can be given only of the major regional variations and evolutions in form.[1]

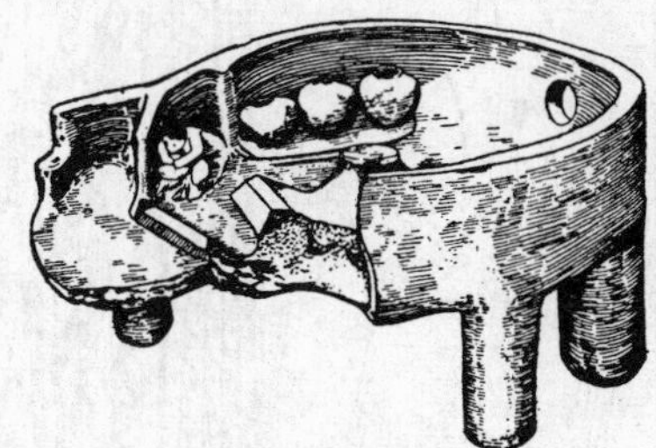

FIGURE 196—*Neolithic model of a hut from Popudnia, Ukraine.*

Neolithic Europe with its damp climate and continuous woodland was naturally the site of the first substantial timber houses. The beginnings of a food-producing peasantry, even though the cultivation was largely shifting, made for settlements of much greater permanence than hunters had needed. With this settlement went the immense increase in skill at carpentry made possible by the superiority of polished stone tools over merely flaked ones. The emphasis on the woodworker's craft throughout the Balkans is made manifest by the widespread distribution of his chief tool—the ground and polished stone adze-blade hafted to a long handle. The most common form is still often described by the old and unsatisfactory term of shoe-last celt (p 507).

The earliest Neolithic peasantries on the forested lower Danube were accustomed to work in wood. Even their pots were modelled on the forms of wooden vessels. We find here, from the first, substantial rectangular houses, walled with split tree-trunks filled in with wattle and daub, and equipped with a central fireplace and a front porch. These houses, in fact, have already achieved one simple version of the *megaron* type of house-plan, which was to become of such importance in the later Greek world (p 485).

North-eastward, in the loess zone of south Russia—the home of one of the richest of earliest peasant cultures—house-sites are common. Long timber houses

[1] In Greece and Macedonia, building in stone or mud-brick attained primary importance even from Neolithic times (though with the use of timber uprights for roofing supports, etc.). It is also noteworthy that, in the Mediterranean, rectangular houses seem to have predominated over round houses from the first.

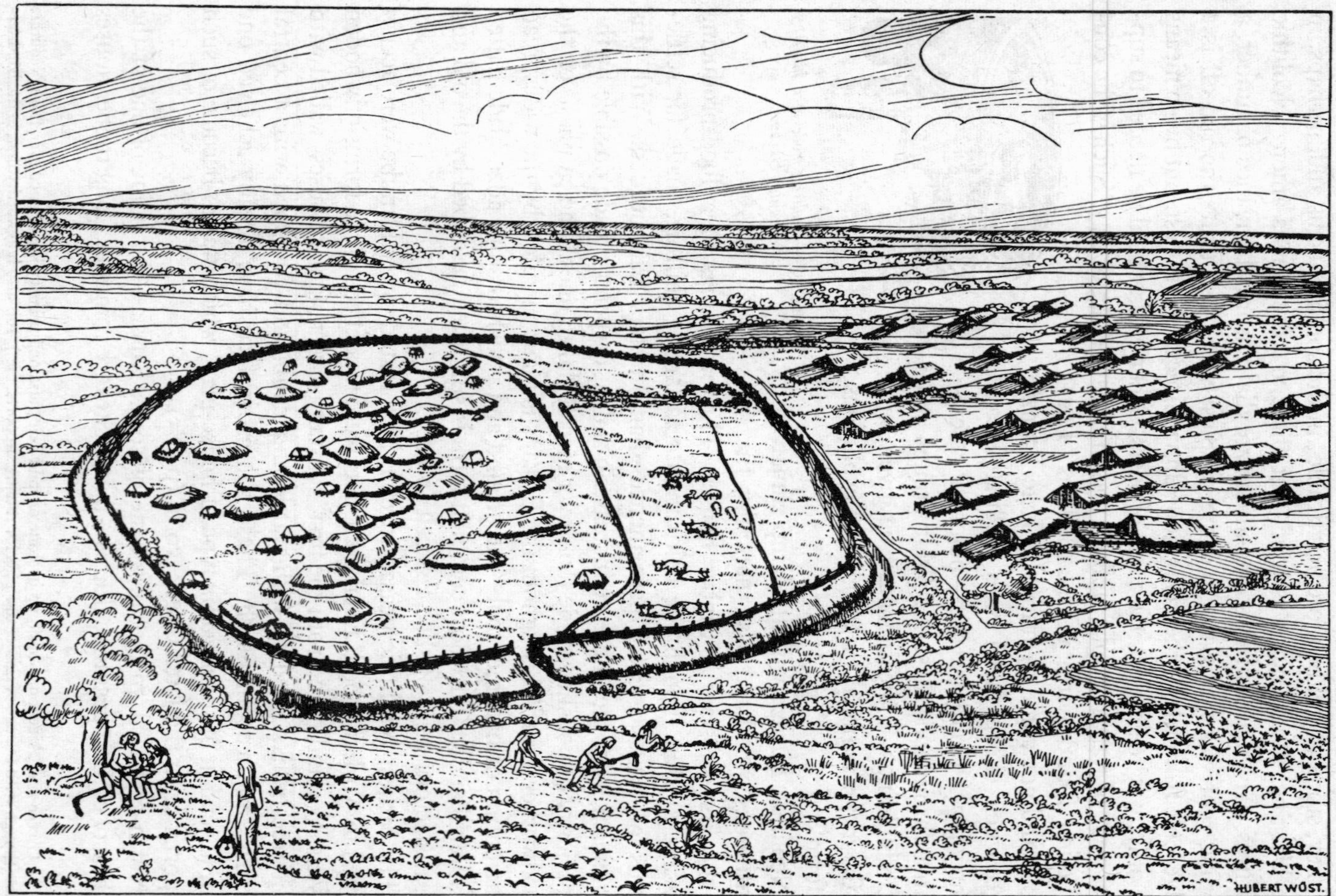

FIGURE 197—*A reconstruction of the Neolithic village of Köln-Lindenthal in its last stage. The typical long dwelling-houses are on the right. Inside the palisade are, firstly, small granaries on posts, and secondly, large irregular structures now interpreted as fenced hollows used as communal working-places. A roofing for the latter is hypothetical.*

were grouped in villages, but many details of construction are still vague. Excavation, however, has confirmed the pattern shown by small model clay houses made throughout this area. A model hut from Popudnia in the Bug basin shows the interior of one of these houses with its porch, oven, storage jars, and even the housewife at work with her saddle-quern (figure 196). Contemporary Neolithic houses at Erösd, within the Carpathian girdle, had roof-finials with elaborate spiral-shaped mouldings of clay.

On and round the fertile loess of central Europe, in the Neolithic Danubian cultures, there can be distinguished three basic types of house, which usually

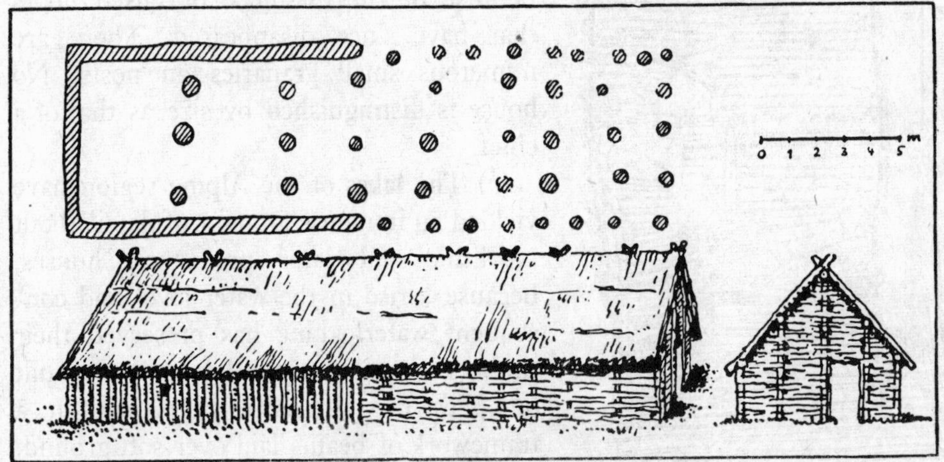

FIGURE 198—*Ground-plan and reconstruction of a typical long house at Köln-Lindenthal.*

succeeded each other chronologically. The earliest (*a*) is an impressive, roughly rectangular, timber building up to 32 m long. The second (*b*) favoured a smaller two-roomed house akin to the *megaron* type. The third (*c*) shows dwellings smaller still, usually with a single chamber.

(*a*) The best examples of the 'long houses' of the first phase are at Köln-Lindenthal in the Rhineland [18] (figure 197). In its developed state it was a palisaded settlement, and it is estimated that it took 3000 man-days to dig the defensive ditch. This involved the same type of organized co-operation as in the laying of the corduroy (log) road in the Neolithic villages on the Alpine moors (p 713). The excavators thought that the peasants of Köln-Lindenthal occupied semi-subterranean dwellings of irregular shape, encased by a light wattle and daub superstructure; but the belief is now that the long rectangular buildings (figure 198), formerly interpreted as barns, were the true dwellings of this village in the First Danubian culture. This divergence shows how radically explanations of archaeological facts have sometimes to be modified. These 'long houses' of 10 to 35 m are most imposing when compared with any earlier European dwelling. They were divided into two parts, one apparently with a raised floor. The ridge-pole must have been supported by posts set at intervals in three parallel rows. The sides were partly of split timbers set upright in the subsoil, and partly of wattle and daub. No traces of hearths or ovens were observed in the houses, possibly because of the existence of raised floors that have since disappeared. There are numerous small granaries on posts. No house is distinguished by size as that of a chief.

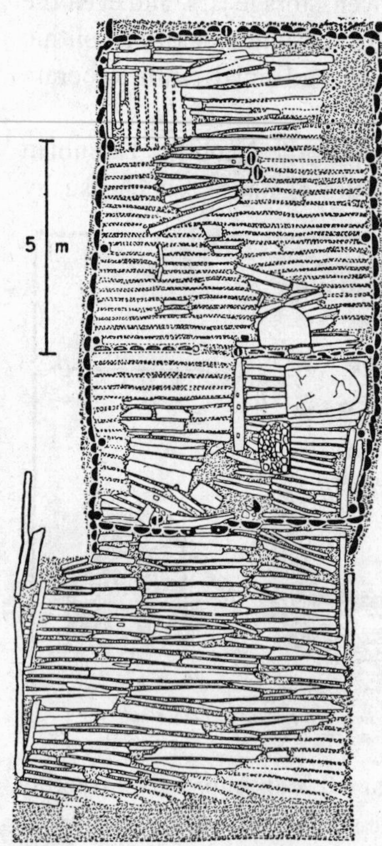

FIGURE 199—*Plan of the substructure of a Neolithic house with forecourt at Aichbühl on the ancient Federsee, Württemberg.*

(*b*) The lakes of the Alpine region have yielded an immense amount of detail about Neolithic and later prehistoric houses, because a rise in the water-level and consequent waterlogging has preserved their timbers. Sometimes the houses were built on piles or, alternatively, placed on a framework of beams laid over soft ground. Those at Aichbühl on the Federsee were of the latter form. They may form a representative village, and also well illustrate the second type of central European Neolithic house. The house whose plan is shown in figure 199 was rectangular and had two rooms—an ante-room and an inner chamber. The roof was gabled, and the walls were of split saplings and wattle. In the ante-room, a beam with mortise holes for two uprights lay before the open hearth; it was probably part of a drying-frame. In the inner room, in the right-hand corner, were supports for a raised couch or bench, and a hearth lay against the partition. It is thought that food and materials were prepared in the outer room, where there was normally a clay oven, doubtless for bread-making. The positions of the clay hearths and baking-ovens had evidently become standardized. In front of each house was a planked forecourt, presumably a place for working and sitting.

Remains of houses of the Second Danubian Neolithic culture have been demonstrated also on the Goldberg in Württemberg, from post-holes alone. One house in the chalk soil of the Goldberg had four post-holes down the length, indicating a gabled roof (figure 200). Internally, the house was divided into a small ante-room and a big back-room, as at Aichbühl. At Erösd in Transylvania another village of this period displayed the same kind of plan and internal arrangements, indicating a small community well set in its ways.

(*c*) In the Late Neolithic (Third Danubian) phase in central Europe, houses were much simpler. This suggests less prosperity, but may also be explained by more emphasis on pastoralism than on cultivation, or by new settlers with more primitive technical traditions. At the Goldberg, huts of this period were one-roomed and only $4\frac{1}{2}$ m square, with a large central pit (? storage silo) and adjacent hearth in the sunken floor. A line of thin saplings formed the walls, and perhaps came together at the top in tent-like fashion. There are other varieties of Neolithic house-plan, such as that of a pair of important timber houses, each with a rounded apse-shaped end, perched on a crag overlooking the Danube at the settlement of a special ('Baden') culture at Vučedol (Yugoslavia) [19]. One was a large dwelling, with the apsidal end partitioned as a separate room; the other was apparently the cook-house, workshop, and store-place. Such specialization is remarkable at this period, shortly before the Early Bronze Age.

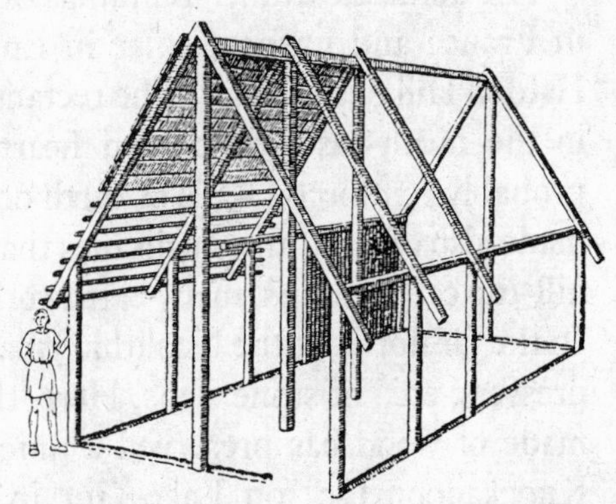

FIGURE 200—*Reconstructed framework of a house of the Second Danubian culture on the Goldberg, Neresheim, Württemberg.*

Many major problems remain. One concerns those houses of the Swiss lake-villages that were raised on piles. Their great excavator, Vouga, has argued convincingly that the Neolithic pile-structures were primarily built on the shore and not over the water, and that they were raised up solely as a protection against floods. However, a strong body of opinion holds that many were built well out into the lakes.

Birch was extensively used throughout the Neolithic period. Pitch and glue were doubtless made from the bark, while strips of bark placed side by side were used as floor-coverings, as is seen in a south German site. The achievements of Neolithic carpenters and house-builders, with stone tools, are nowhere better seen than in the village at Trøldebjerg in Denmark. A remarkable structure here was a continuous row of rectangular buildings totalling 70 m in length. Two were certainly houses, each *c* 30 m long and apparently having one end for the owners and one for the beasts. The gabled roof, *c* 3 m high, sloped down to the ground on one side, the other resting on a wall *c* 2 m high. They housed the social unit—perhaps a family clan. The dead were interred in elaborate collective sepulchres—'passage graves'. The plans of two other oblong ranges of buildings at Barkaer in Denmark suggested that one held 50 to 60 families, thus resembling the huge communal houses on the coast of British Columbia, where a stone-using technique survived into the nineteenth century.

The domestic timber-buildings of the Neolithic groups are virtually unknown in France and unspectacular in England. The best-preserved plan is that on Haldon Hill near Exeter. The rectangular hut was only *c* 6 m long, with entrance in the north-east corner and hearth in the south-east. The slender uprights probably reinforced walls of earth or turf with stone footings. Mention must be made also of the timber palisades that supplemented the ditches round Neolithic hill-top cattle camps, many earthworks of which survive in the south of England. In the far north, at the Neolithic village at Skara Brae, in the Orkneys, were beds, dressers, etc., of stone slabs. Here 'the translation into stone of articles normally made of wood has preserved a unique record' of hut furniture. In Ireland, at Knockadoon [20] on Lake Gur in Limerick, one Neolithic house measured 9·5×*c* 5 m. 'The walls, possibly of turf, were defined by a stone footing and a double row of post-holes, in which were set the uprights of the wooden frame; the hearth was central and two rows of posts dividing the house into aisles presumably helped to support the roof.' It seems that there were also round Neolithic houses on the same site.

IV. RITUAL BUILDINGS IN LATE NEOLITHIC AND EARLIER BRONZE AGE EUROPE

There are considerable gaps in our knowledge of domestic timber-buildings in the Bronze Age. In Lowland Britain, the evidence for more than 1000 years until the Late Bronze Age is particularly meagre, though it can be eked out from dry-stone building in the Highland zone. Climatic changes or social disturbances are the probable explanations of this lack of settlement on the downlands, so favoured in previous and subsequent periods. Evidence from Early Bronze Age domestic buildings in central Europe is more abundant. We may note here the device used in Swiss lake-settlements of pile-shoes—small transverse timbers under the uprights to minimize sinking.

For evidence in England, we have to rely mainly on craftsmanship in ritual and burial structures, which goes only a little way to fill the gap. Direct evidence of Bronze Age carpentry technique can be seen, for example, in the ritual timber canoes preserved under the great cairn at Loose Howe, Yorkshire, in oak coffins from Yorkshire, Sussex, etc., and in mortised beams of the Early Bronze Age from the submerged surface of the Essex coast. Indirect, but reliable, evidence is provided by post-holes of timber structures, as, for example, by the small ritual mortuary house on Beaulieu Heath, Hampshire [21]. It is *c* 1·5 m square, with the sides formed of fifty-seven thin stakes, represented by post-holes, standing on the bottom of a ritual pit, underneath the burial mound or 'barrow'. Such structures are associated with groups of a specific Battle-axe culture which extended north-west from the Black Sea right across Europe. As the result of modern excavation methods, the traces of more timber work have been found in barrows than they were formerly believed to contain. When Pitt-Rivers (1827–1900), a father of scientific archaeology, stripped the huge Wor Barrow (Dorset) down to the chalk, he found traces of a palisaded wooden enclosure, about 9 m across. Within this, the burial rites were probably conducted before the mound was raised over it. In a barrow at White Leaf Hill, Buckinghamshire, there are similar indications of a wooden chamber of horizontally laid tree-trunks, opening into a forecourt, besides traces of other massive timbers. Particularly elaborate timber work is indicated by post-holes in the Giant's Hill long barrow at Skendleby, Lincolnshire [22]. There had been palisading along the sides, heavy revetment of the forecourt at the upper end, and hurdle-work down the main axis of the mound. The prominent posts at the lower end were of exactly the same number as the burials in the barrow. If they symbolized the dead, they may well have been decorated.

The most remarkable application of timber to burial structures in Britain at this period is at Bleasdale, Lancashire [23]. Here a circle 11 m in diameter, of stout oak posts, enclosed two cremations in Middle Bronze Age urns. Surrounding this again was a horseshoe-shaped ditch lined with birch poles, entered by a causeway between two timber gate-posts. This complex lay inside a great circular palisade, 46 m in diameter, of poles closely set between substantial oak posts. Many of the stumps were preserved by waterlogging.

In addition to timber, turf was much used in England in the construction of barrows, both as core and in revetment work. There are kerbs of piled turves round some types of long barrow. Later, in Iron Age hill-forts, turf revetment of the ramparts was still used to retain the materials of the core (e.g. St Catherine's Hill, Winchester). Its appearance in the soil as a dark compact mass is usually distinctive.

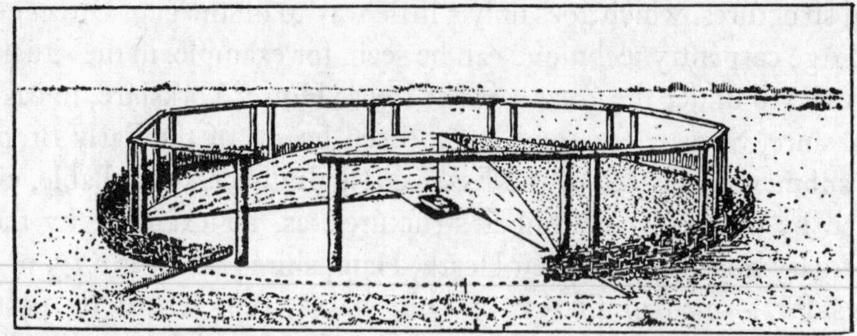

FIGURE 201—*Reconstruction of a Bronze Age palisade-barrow near Hooge Mierde, Holland. Diameter c 12 m. The height of the posts is an estimation.*

On the European continent, timber structures within barrows take many forms. In a tumulus of the central German Bronze Age at Leubingen (Saxony), an old man and a young girl were buried under an inverted V-shaped structure of thick oak beams.

Specially favourable conditions in waterlogged soil in south Jutland and Schleswig have preserved oak coffins. In some English barrows there are circles of posts. Similar finds have been made in Holland (figure 201) and Denmark. The connexion between the continental structures[1] and henge-type monuments in wood in England (see below) is noteworthy. Common ties of religion and culture are exemplified by architecture, in prehistory as they are today.

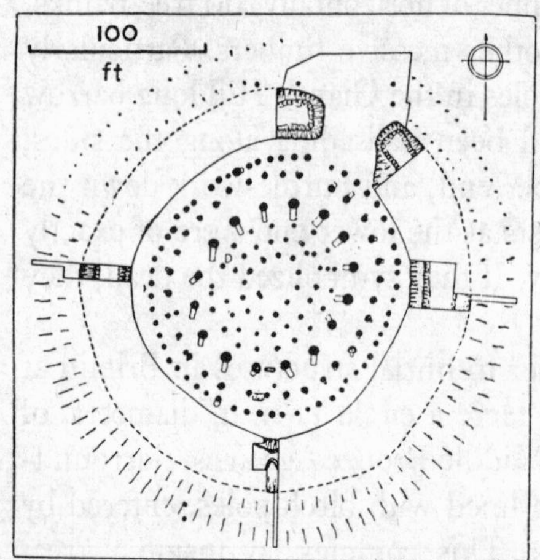

FIGURE 202—*Plan of Woodhenge, showing the position of ramps to post-holes, and parts of the surrounding ditch excavated.*

Two famous 'woodhenge' ritual sites were detected from the air by crop-markings over them. At Arminghall, near Norwich, there was a monument of eight great oak uprights set in a horse-shoe plan, surrounded by two concentric ditches [24]. The socket-holes of two of these were over 2 m deep. The base of a post that remained was slightly pointed and heavily charred. It had been stripped of its bark before erection, conceivably for carving or painting. The diameter of

[1] One group is associated with Neolithic pottery, another has produced beaker pottery; but classification is again in the melting-pot, and beakers, previously classified as typical of the Early Bronze Age are now (it is urged) to be called Late Neolithic. The idea of henge-type monuments, however, does seem to survive well down through the Bronze Age.

the post, *c* 90 cm, indicated a substantial tree about 100 years old. Clearly, it was a ritual site of great importance.

Woodhenge is the modern name given to a site, in south Wiltshire, of six concentric and roughly circular rings of post-holes for timber uprights (figure 202). It is considered by some as akin to Stonehenge, and to have been an open-air temple. It has even been suggested [25] that the posts formed the uprights of a circular roofed building (figure 203), and a similar interpretation has been given

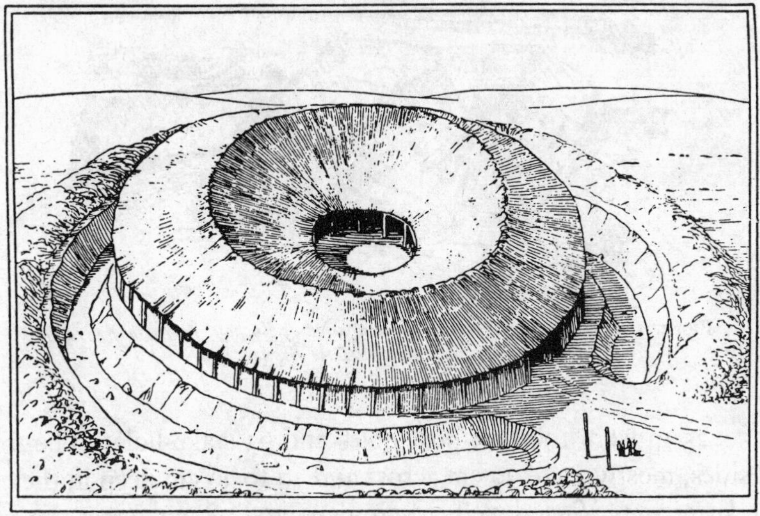

FIGURE 203—*A suggested reconstruction of Woodhenge. Isometric drawing.*

to the concentric timber and stone circles excavated at the Sanctuary, near Avebury! The period was one of extraordinary individuality and invention in religious architecture.

The use of mortise and tenon joints in securing the cross-pieces of the inner trilithons at Stonehenge is both laborious and unnatural as a means of jointing stone. It is a method effective only with wood, and must have been taken over from carpentry. Further, the lintels of the outer circle at Stonehenge are secured by another technique appropriate only to wood, inasmuch as their ends are fish-tail jointed each to the next [26] (figure 321). Evidence now shows that these techniques were not copied from structures of 'Woodhenge' type, but in this case were introduced from overseas.

V. BUILDINGS IN LATER BRONZE AGE EUROPE

In the Late Bronze Age there was again great variety of house-building techniques in wood and wattle. In Holderness, Yorkshire, there are marsh settlements on foundation platforms of brushwood laid on logs, with piles driven down for strength. On uplands in Sussex, round timber huts, *c* 6 m across, with a central post for a conical roof, are associated with new settlers from continental Europe. One of the best groups is that at Thorny Down, Winterbourne Gunner, Wiltshire [27]. A low bank enclosed a small downland family farm, and in an

FIGURE 204—*Farmstead of the second occupation at Buchau, Württemberg, restored from surviving timbers. Late Bronze Age.*

area *c* 35×25 m were 199 true post-holes and 63 stake-holes. The former had vertical sides, mostly 20 to 30 cm across and 13 to 30 cm deep in the chalk subsoil; the latter were V-sectioned, 15 cm deep and 18 cm across the top. There were a circular hut 6 m across, another sub-rectangular, and a third, perhaps a cook-house, besides structures suggesting small storage sheds on posts. The walls were apparently of horizontal logs. Some estimates of the duration of such settlements can be made from the rates of rotting for various kinds of hard- and softwood posts, in conjunction with the evidence of renewal of posts.

The most spectacular evidence for this period comes from the waterlogged sites of central Europe, e.g. that of the Wasserburg Buchau, on a former island in the ancient Federsee. The first occupation, from *c* 1100 B.C. was of thirty-eight small rectangular one-roomed buildings; the second, from *c* 900 B.C., when bronze tools were fairly plentiful, had nine large farm-houses, each built round three sides of a yard and constructed on the log-cabin method with interlocking timbers (figure 204). 'An outer palisade, consisting of some 15,000 pine stakes stuck in the lake mud and probably projecting several feet above the water, served at the same time as a breakwater and an outer defence. Traces of defensive platforms were met with at several points on the inner edge of the palisade and each was connected by a small bridge with the island' [28].

Favourable soil conditions have preserved much timber in the so-called terramare settlements in the Po valley.[1] These were often as extensive as 15 000 to 75 000 sq m, or about 4 to 18 acres, and remained in use in the Middle and Late Bronze Ages and into the Iron Age. They are small equivalents of the *tells* of the Near East, built up by successive occupation levels [29]. On some sites, there survive indeed regular forests of posts, but attempts to disentangle details of timber structures and technology from the published plans and photographs are disappointing.

VI. IRON AGE METHODS IN BRITAIN

Here we discuss timber and turf construction of farms, villages, and hill-forts. The most fully excavated Iron Age farm in Britain is at Little Woodbury, Wiltshire, where a roughly oval ditch enclosed an area 140 m across [30]. Many details of the internal features were first revealed by crop-marks on air-photographs, which also showed a larger and similar site about 450 m away. Little Woodbury was probably typical of many other Iron Age farms in lowland England. The chief structural features were two substantial circular timber houses, and the circular pattern predominates for the dwellings of Iron Age Britain. The larger and earlier house consisted of two outer rings of post-holes for timbers,

FIGURE 205—*General view of the Little Woodbury Iron Age farm-house and surroundings as reconstructed. Near Salisbury.*

[1] The remains of these settlements consist of low mounds of occupation debris, and are found chiefly on the south side of the lower Po.

with a prominent solidly built porch, which may have had some ornamental superstructure. At the centre stood four posts in a square. During its occupation, all the posts had at various times been renewed, or reinforced by others. The house seems to have been fitted with a drain later. The length of occupation was perhaps two centuries. The size, shape, and filling of the post-holes of the outer ring suggest that it was of rectangular uprights about 20×40 cm, that the inner ring was of round posts with diameters of 30 to 40 cm, and that those of the square were massive round trunks of 50 to 55 cm diameter. These trunks were set 1·2 m deep in the ground, and those of the entrance porch were little inferior in strength. There was no trace of wattle and daub for the walls, and horizontal planking was suggested. Several reconstructions of the roof are possible, fundamentally affecting the appearance of the building (figure 205). The present writer's preference is for one with cross-beams connecting the tops of the four central uprights, possibly carrying a small 'lantern' structure as in the medieval hall. Bad lighting, however, does not disturb modern tribal peoples, as the massive Maori and British Columbian plank-built houses show. The excavator has since changed his original opinion about the external appearance of this Woodbury house.

Another house at Woodbury was circular, but of simpler plan and possibly unfinished. Other structures of interest included numerous pairs of post-holes, very probably for drying-frames for corn or the like, comparable with those used by the Maori. Groups of four post-holes set in a square of *c* 2·1 m side are interpreted, here and on other Iron Age sites, as supporting small granaries similar to those used today in British Columbia for storing food. Many deep single post-holes may have held tall posts like those on which a quantity of hay is now hung to dry in many parts of Europe. There are also deep pits, perhaps with wooden lids, for storing roasted grain, shallower pits for wooden water-tubs, etc., and small domed ovens of cob—a mixture of chalk, clay, and straw—for roasting grain to prevent germination. There were post-holes of a probable gate-tower at the entrance to the palisade.

Village life in Iron Age Britain has been well displayed by the very complete investigations in Somerset at the Glastonbury lake-village [31] and at Meare, where the wonderful preservation of usually perishable objects in the peat has provided uniquely valuable data on tools and craftsmanship in timber in the closing stage of British prehistory. The Glastonbury village was built in a swampy lake, about 120 m out from what was formerly the margin. The Meare pool was still 1·5 to 2 sq km (400 to 500 acres) in extent as late as A.D. 1500, though all this area is now farming land. Such sites were real villages, not mere refuges or short-lived trading stations. That at Glastonbury was originally selected because it provided an area of peat firmer than other parts of the swamp, and near navigable water. This was the surface level when the settlers arrived and cleared the trees and scrub—leaving for the excavators chips of wood as clean and white as when cut. At ground level, the site consisted of 90 low mounds barely visible in tall grass; about 70 contained traces of buildings. The village measured approximately 90 × 120 m. An irregular area of about 8800 sq m was enclosed by

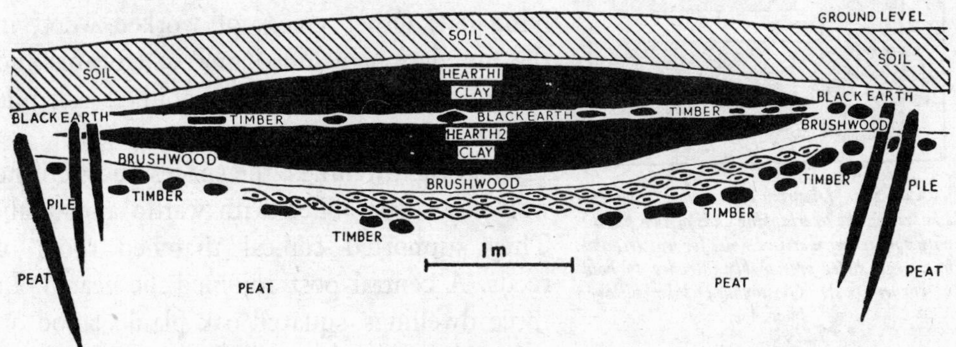

FIGURE 206—*Section through a mound (LVI) at Glastonbury, showing the position of the wattle hurdles illustrated on plate 4.*

a closely set timber palisade, which both kept the village's foundations in position and formed a defensive stockade. The posts of alder, birch, oak, etc., were occasionally in single line, but most often two to four abreast, being 1·5 to 4·3 m long—as at present existing—and 8 to 23 cm in diameter. Many had slanted outwards, displaced by pressure from within. The ends were sharpened, and, on removal from the peat, the axe and bill-hook marks were fresh and sharply defined. Within the palisade, a substantial foundation-layer of brushwood, logs, and so forth had been placed all over the peat, especially on the sites for dwellings. These consisted of circular clay floors 5·5 to 8·5 m across, superimposed on one another as they tended to sink (figure 206). Round the floor was a close-set circle of wall-posts, 8 to 23 cm in diameter and 15 to 38 cm apart, driven down into the foundation-layer.

One house had ten successive floors, but the great majority had from 1 to 4. Split-wood flooring boards were observed in eight mounds, and in two cases the boards were supported by joists. Piles were driven in round the sides of the buildings to prevent sinkage; they, like those round the village, needed constant additions. One mound, with 5 clay floors and 11 hearths, rested on a very elaborate foundation of 35 alder trunks about 2 to 4 m long. Another mound, adjoining the palisading, had a specially reinforced arrangement of beams and piles under the entrance. The third of its eight floors was encircled by fine wattle work. Massive radiating timbers lay between floors three and four. Outside the wall-posts were two large oak piles, 1·5 m long, with sugar-loaf-shaped knobs. In yet another mound, under the lower and earlier floor was a layer of brushwood on a layer of compressed leaves. Below this again were three hurdles of wattle lying flat. Other pieces of worked wood in the foundation included mortised beams and planks of oak, and a large knobbed oak pile (figure 206 and plate 4).

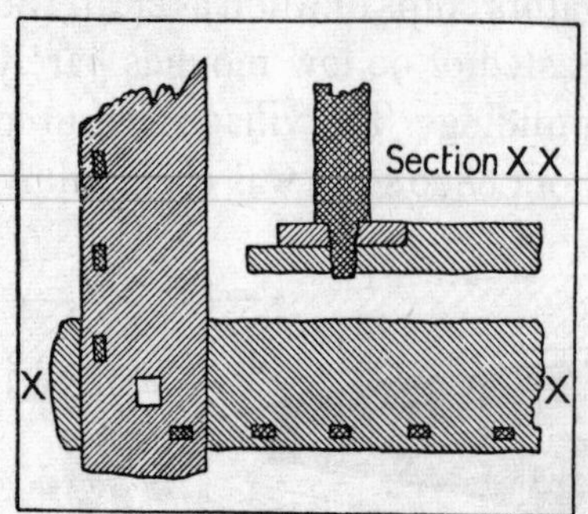

FIGURE 207—*Diagram of a timber fragment comprising the overlapping ends of two planks with square cut mortised holes for wattles, and one larger hole, presumably intended to hold a corner post. Glastonbury lake village. Iron Age.*

In all the dwellings, the spaces between the wall-posts were filled with wattle and daub. They supported conical thatched roofs of reeds. A central post adjoined the hearth. In three dwellings, squared oak planks stood on each side of the doorway. Doorways were 1·2 to 2·1 m wide; a pivoted door of a solid slab of oak, 104×44 cm, was presumably half of a double swing-door. Timber door-sills sometimes lay across the threshold.

Under these round houses were worked timbers from earlier rectangular structures, apparently flung down for re-use as a rough foundation layer. They included oak beams with lines of regular mortised holes for wattle hurdles found with them (figure 207). There were traces of similar structures at Meare. Some of the clay floors with hearths in that village lacked traces of posts. In such cases, this absence may indicate light structures easily renewed—perhaps tents. Dome-shaped clay ovens were also found.

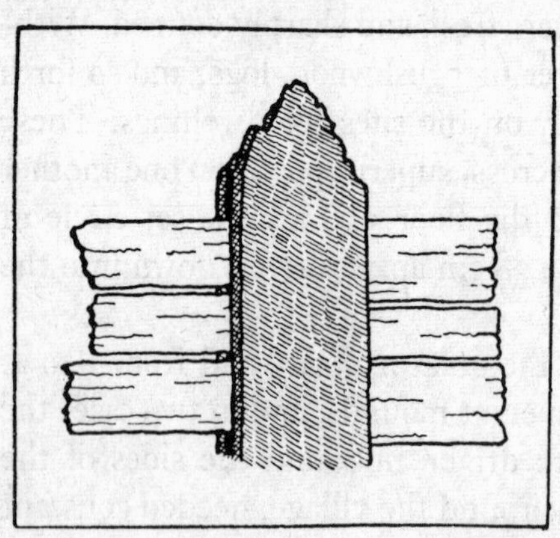

FIGURE 208—*Diagram of a grooved oak plank from the causeway, Glastonbury, with boards in position.*

At Glastonbury, the village was approached by a narrow causeway of timber, clay, and stone 48 m long. At the further end was a landing stage, and at the entrance to the village was a gap presumably bridged by movable planks. The edge of the causeway was largely supported by thick vertical oak planks, sharpened at

FIGURE 209—*The outer face of the protective rampart in front of the eastern entrance, Maiden Castle, Dorset. Two empty sockets for posts can be seen on the left, and on the right a rough repatching after the decay of a post and the collapse of part of the wall. Iron Age. Scale rod in 10 cm divisions.*

the lower end, finely finished and squared by an adze. These planks were grooved down each side to receive the ends of horizontal split oak boards, about 20 cm wide (figure 208). All the clay and most of the timber had to be brought to the site. One dwelling alone contained 150 tons of clay in its floors. The immense task of moving this material was done with primitive dug-out canoes and very simple tools. Iron tools found on the site include saws, adzes, files, awls, gouges, and knives, which had all been originally in wooden handles. Some form of lathe was known, and many wooden objects were turned on it; a wooden ladder was also found. Only 109 articles of iron were recovered. All the metal tools could have been made in the village, for there were remains of furnaces, crucibles, clay bellows-nozzles, slag, and unfinished metal articles. Implements of flint were relatively few and unimportant.

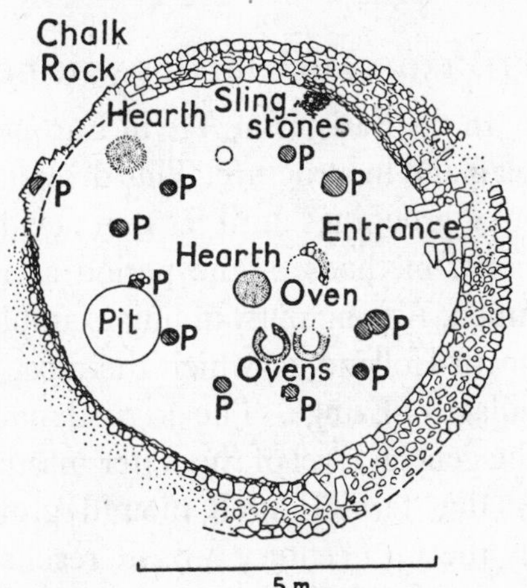

FIGURE 210—*Plan of a circular hut of the later Iron Age, Maiden Castle. Within a low wall of chalk rubble is a ring of post-holes for uprights to support the roof. The three little domed clay ovens were covered by a later floor with a central hearth.* P = *post-hole.*

Of the hill-forts of the Iron Age in Britain, the most detailed picture of the complex and extensive use of timber revetment and palisading is that at Maiden Castle, Dorset [32] (figure 209). Inside were several varieties of hut-plans, to add to the picture of the highly specialized constructional methods in the lake-villages (p 318). A rectangular setting of post-holes of 4·5×6·5 m has been claimed as a hut of the Early Iron Age, though rectangular buildings were then unusual in England. Parallels are huts of similar plan and date on the Goldberg. The huts of the later Iron Age cultures at Maiden Castle were, by contrast, circular or polygonal. The most elaborate was in occupation at the end of the first century B.C. (figure 210).

Finds of iron tools on most British Iron Age sites are infrequent. In the extensive Maiden Castle excavations, apart from knives only two chisels and two fragmentary saws were found. They were of the first quarter of the first century B.C. Such rarity indicates that iron was carefully husbanded, for it is evident that a great amount was required for woodworking. When iron was actually smelted in quantity close to the source of supply, as at Hunsbury hill-fort in Northamptonshire, tools are much more numerous, and we see from them that the same kinds—adzes, axes, saws, chisels, etc.—were used for building hill-forts as also were used in such villages as Glastonbury.

Mention must be made of the elaborate use of reinforcing timber beams and ties in the stone walls round the so-called 'Gallic Wall' hill-forts of the later Iron Age in Scotland. It was estimated by Childe (1946) that construction of the fort at Finavon 'involved the quarrying of more than 200,000 cubic feet of stone, while at least half as much timber must have been felled and cut up to provide the lacings'. Yet the evidence suggests that the iron tools made in that region were produced only at the expense of incredible labour.

VII. IRON AGE METHODS IN CONTINENTAL EUROPE

In the Early Iron Age in Europe there was a great variety in building, both in plan and in structure. This diversity can, however, hardly be used to define cultural groupings until far more evidence is available. Nevertheless, the constructional methods of the period as revealed by large-scale excavation have told much. Among outstanding examples are the settlement-mounds on the coast of north Holland, of which the most famous is that partly covered by the present village of Ezinge. 'The original mound only attained a height of 1·2 metres above the general level of the water meadow and did not exceed 35 metres in diameter. As the "terp" [Dutch, mound] grew it covered a progressively bigger area, until, by the 13th century A.D., it reached a height of 5·5 metres and a diameter of 450 metres.' This site revealed six periods of occupation from the Early Iron Age into the Middle Ages. In the middle of the Iron Age, the main building consisted of a long rectangular frame-building of posts, wattle, and daub, with steeply pitched thatched roofs carried over the walls to rest on rows of small external posts. Inside, pairs of uprights carried the rafters. This traditional plan was maintained for centuries. Some of the buildings had a broader roof-span to make room for cattle-stalls down the aisles, each partitioned off by wicker-work [33].

A second type of site in which soil-conditions have preserved building-plans is represented by the Iron Age Biskupin, a Polish lake-village north-east of Poznan. The site, chosen for defence and sited on a promontory in a former peat-

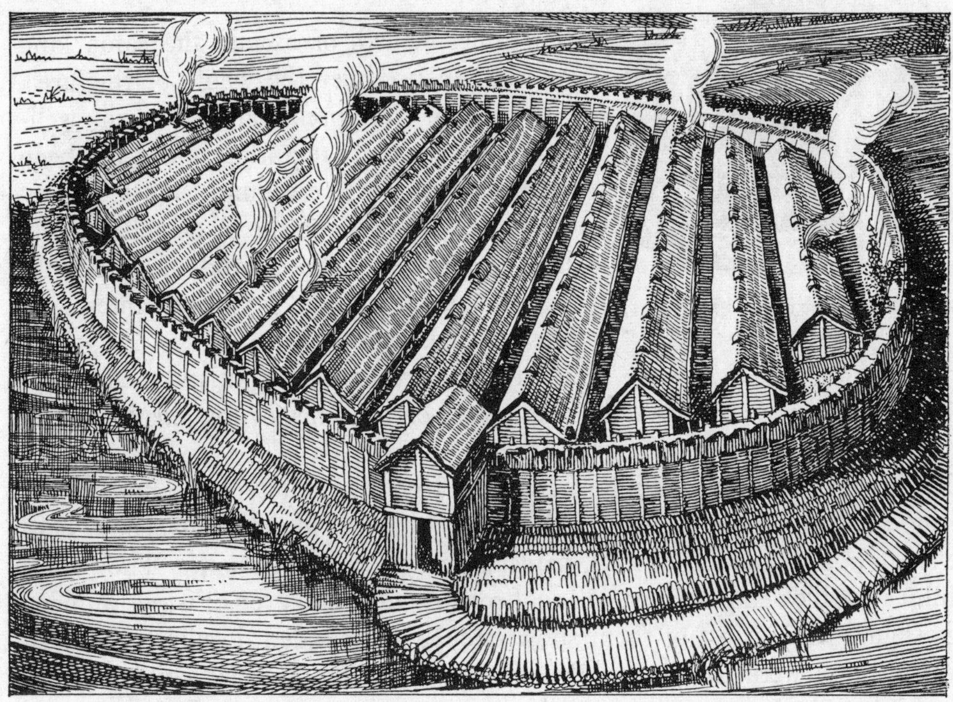

FIGURE 211—*Reconstruction of the Iron Age village at Biskupin, Poland.*

bog, was occupied between 700 and 400 B.C. It was inundated and covered with sand and mud, so that the timbers are well-preserved (figure 211). The village consisted of 80 to 100 huts, built on a layer of birch brushwood resting on peat. Round it ran a rampart of stout timber facings filled with earth between. This was rebuilt three times. At the foot, piles were driven in as a breakwater. A single fortified gateway, perhaps of two storeys, was the only entrance. Unlike that of the Glastonbury lake-village, the internal plan was laid out with mechanical precision. A road ran round the inside of the palisade. Parallel lanes of the same corduroy construction of thick oak logs were flanked by rows of uniform wooden huts standing end to end, frequently with a common end-wall. They were built of stout pine posts, either round or rectangular, and grooved to receive horizontal plank walls, a skilled method still used in Poland. The huts, each about 9 m square, usually had a main room with hearth and vestibule. The doors, always facing south, were up to 2·3 m wide. The floors were of wooden beams, with foundation of crossed or interwoven birch branches. The walls seem to have been about 3 m high. The tools included socketed iron celts [34].

FIGURE 212—*Cinerary urn in the shape of a hut. Central Italy. Iron Age. Height 10 in.*

Timber houses of exactly the same kind are still in use over the whole of this area. Sociological interpretations of such well-preserved plans are tempting, and it has been claimed that such dwellings 'must be regarded as belonging to the matriarchal family in its later stages—the period of its zenith, just before dissolution' [35]. Such inferences are very hypothetical.

In Iron Age houses in Jutland a considerable use was made of turf walls, somewhat on the lines of the existing black houses of the Hebrides.

An interesting source of information on Iron Age hut types in north Italy during the first half of the first millennium B.C. is provided by hut-urns. These are small pottery models of huts, made to contain cremated bones. They often exhibit valuable details of post and roof construction, and even of window openings (figure 212). Most of them show circular or rounded dwellings, perhaps because these were easier to make in clay, but there are also square model huts [36].

An important example of timber construction for specialized purposes is the great burial mound of the mid-sixth century B.C. at Kostromskaya Stanitsa, on a tributary of the Kuban in south Russia. This tomb of a Scythian chieftain was surrounded with bodies of horses. It contained magnificent gold trappings and a model house or tent of pole construction, decked out with the weapons of the warrior, who lay in a safe cache below (figure 213). In south Russia, timber-lined grave cists and shafts go far back into the Bronze Age. Nor must we forget the ancient buildings deeper in the Asiatic steppes, whether in oases, garrisons, or caravan cities. Craftsmanship in wood is sometimes preserved with extraordinary perfection by extreme dryness and other factors. Gaunt lines of lofty wooden house-posts have endured above ground from as early as the last century or two B.C.

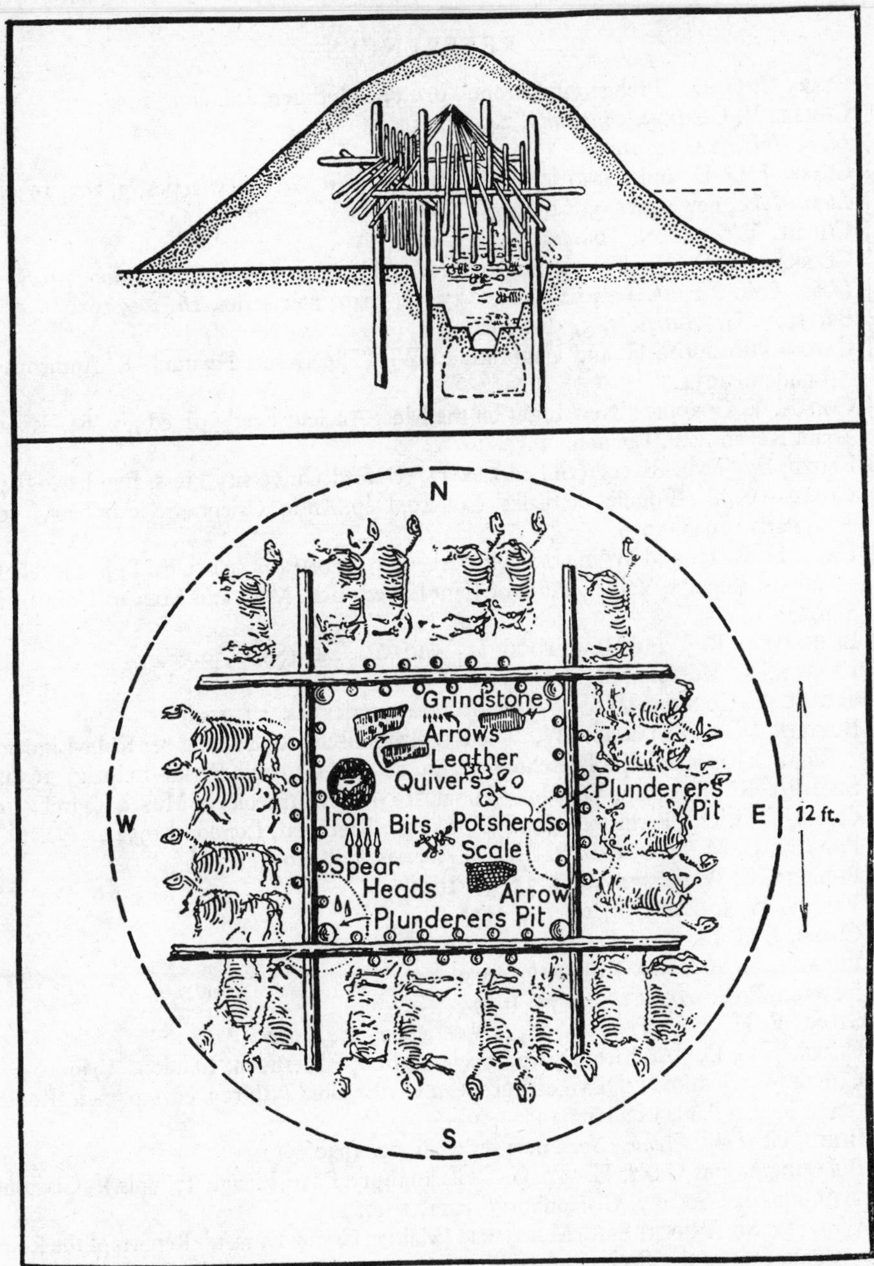

FIGURE 213—*The burial mound of a Scythian chieftain at Kostromskaya, south Russia. Sixth century* B.C.

REFERENCES

[1] CLARK, J. G. D. 'Prehistoric Europe', p. 133. Methuen, London. 1952.
[2] CHILDE, V. GORDON. *Antiquity*, **24**, 6, 1950.
[3] *Idem. Ibid.*, **24**, 10, 1950.
[4] CLARK, J. G. D. and RANKINE, W. F. *Proc. Prehist. Soc.*, new series, **5**, 103, 1939.
[5] *Idem. Ibid.*, new series, **5**, 61, 1939.
[6] CHILDE, V. GORDON. *Antiquity*, **24**, 7, 1950.
[7] CLARK, J. G. D. 'Prehistoric England' (4th ed.), p. 29. Batsford, London. 1948.
[8] *Idem. Proc. Prehist. Soc.*, new series, **15**, 52, 1949; new series, **16**, 109, 1950.
[9] BRUNTON, G. *Antiquity*, **3**, 462, 1929.
[10] CATON-THOMPSON, G. and GARDNER, E. W. 'The Desert Fayum.' R. Anthrop. Inst., London. 1934.
[11] CHILDE, V. GORDON. 'New Light on the Most Ancient East' (4th ed.), p. 64. Routledge and Kegan Paul, London. 1952.
[12] LLOYD, S. 'Twin Rivers' (2nd ed.), p. 11. Oxford University Press, Bombay. 1947.
[13] GHIRSHMAN, R. 'Fouilles de Sialk.' Louvre, Dép. Antiq. Orient., Série archéol., Vols. 4, 5. Paris. 1938, 1939.
[14] HALL, H. R. H. and WOOLLEY, SIR (CHARLES) LEONARD. 'Al-'Ubaid', p. 57. Ur Excavations. Reports, Vol. 1. Publ. of Joint Exped. Brit. Mus. and Mus. of Univ. of Penn. 1927.
[15] BRAIDWOOD, R. J. and BRAIDWOOD, L. *Antiquity*, **24**, 189, 1950.
[16] KENYON, K. M. *Ibid.*, **26**, 116, 1952.
[17] CHILDE, V. GORDON. *Proc. Prehist. Soc.*, new series, **14**, 77, 1949.
[18] BUTTLER, W. and HABEREY, W. 'Die Bandkeramische Ansiedlung bei Köln-Lindenthal.' Römisch-Germanische Forschungen, no. 11. De Gruyter, Berlin–Leipzig. 1936.
[19] SCHMIDT, R. 'Die Burg Vučedol.' Hrvatski Državni Arheoložki Muzei, Zagreb. 1945.
[20] CLARK, J. G. D. 'Prehistoric Europe', p. 151. Methuen, London. 1952.
[21] PIGGOTT, C. M. *Proc. Prehist. Soc.*, new series, **9**, 8, 1943.
[22] PHILLIPS, C. W. *Archaeologia*, **35**, 37, 1935.
[23] VARLEY, W. J. *Antiq. J.*, **18**, 154, 1938.
[24] CLARK, J. G. D. *Proc. Prehist. Soc.*, new series, **2**, 1, 1936.
[25] PIGGOTT, S. *Archaeol. J.*, **95**, 193, 1939.
[26] NEWALL, R. S. *Antiquity*, **3**, 75, 1929.
[27] STONE, E. H. *Proc. Prehist. Soc.*, new series, **7**, 114, 1941.
[28] CLARK, J. G. D. 'Archaeology and Society', p. 67. Methuen, London. 1939.
[29] CHILDE, V. GORDON. 'Dawn of European Civilization' (5th rev. ed.), p. 242. Routledge and Kegan Paul, London. 1950.
[30] BERSU, G. *Proc. Prehist. Soc.*, new series, **6**, 30, 1940.
[31] BULLEID, A. and GRAY, H. ST. G. 'Glastonbury Lake Village' (2 Vols.). Glastonbury Antiquarian Society, Glastonbury. 1911, 1917.
[32] WHEELER, SIR (ROBERT ERIC) MORTIMER. 'Maiden Castle, Dorset.' Reports of the Research Committee of the Society of Antiquaries, no. 12. London. 1943.
[33] CLARK, J. G. D. 'Archaeology and Society.' Methuen, London. 1939.
[34] KOSTREWSKI, J. *Antiquity*, **12**, 311, 1938.
[35] TOLSTOV, S. P. *Ibid.*, **20**, 94, 1946.
[36] PATRONI, G. "Architettura Preistorica." 'Storia dell' Architettura', ed. by U. OJETTI and M. PIACENTINI, Vol. 1. Istituto ital. d'arti grafiche, Bergamo. 1941.

13

DOMESTICATION OF ANIMALS

F. E. ZEUNER

I. THEORIES OF DOMESTICATION

THERE is no evidence that man had acquired the habit of keeping animals in captivity or domestication before he reached the stage of living in social units of some size. The first animal to pass under his sway was the dog. The hoofed animals that followed were at a certain stage systematically used only as sources of food. Increased security and food supply gave Neolithic man more time, and therefore more opportunity, to improve certain domestic products. Thus domestication is not only a technique introduced by early man but, as so often with the arts, is important for the advancement of other arts.

As to the origin of domestication there are many theories, nearly all based on the conception of purposeful procedure. Man, it was thought, needed certain animals and therefore contrived to tame them. This view includes the theory of a religious origin—the animals being for use as sacrifices—and the theory that domestication was invented to satisfy economic needs for meat and skins. Such views ignore the fact that in Mesolithic times, when domestication began, it would have been far easier to obtain the necessary supplies by the ancient methods of hunting and trapping than to embark on extensive experiments in taming, which could bring their reward only after generations.

It is much more fruitful to consider man as an integral part of his physico-biological environment. It then becomes apparent that both his habits and those of certain animal species make domestication almost inevitable. For the social relation of domestication is not restricted to man and his animal subordinates. He has applied the same practice to his own species, though it is then commonly called slavery. Nor is man the only species to practise domestication. So many species have domesticated others that only a few examples can be given. These are relevant, since they indicate the way taken by man on reaching that crucial stage of his social development which led to the appearance of slavery.

Domestication presupposes a social medium. A species must have reached a certain level of social evolution before domestication becomes possible. This applies both to domesticator and domesticated.[1] Animals which have social relations with members of their own species are more ready to form the same with other species. Mixed herds of zebra with gnu, waterbuck, and other antelopes are commonly seen in Africa. It is therefore not surprising that the vast majority of species domesticated by man belong to the gregarious hoofed animals. Actual domestication of one animal species by another, however, occurs almost exclusively among the social insects, especially the ants.

II. SYMBIOSIS AND ITS GRADES

It is necessary to clarify certain kinds of social relationship. These relationships are linked by many intermediate cases, for absolutely clear-cut divisions hardly exist.

Symbiosis includes all conditions of the living-together of two different species, provided both derive advantages therefrom. Cases in which both partners benefit equally are rare. Two non-social species which enter frequently into such relationship are a species of hermit-crab, and its rider, a species of sea-anemone. The crab is protected by the tentacles of the anemone, while the latter obtains food-morsels scattered by the crab's untidy eating-habits. The crab is careful not to lose the anemone, and transplants it when changing into a larger whelk-shell. The anemone, however, is a passive partner and, if regarded as subject to the crab, its case might be classified as one of domestication.

A case of apparent equality is that between two species of ants, the small *Crematogaster parabiotica* and the large *Camponotus femoratus*. They live together in a ball-shaped nest, the small species in the superficial, the large in the central part. The galleries made by the two species open into one another, and the workers of both forage together. When the nest is slightly disturbed, only the small ants emerge to defend it, but a severe shaking brings forth also the large pugnacious *Camponotus*. There is mutual advantage here, for the large species need not attend to minor disturbances, while the small enjoys protection by the large when matters become serious.

Many cases are known of unequal partnership which, however, is not so unequal that it must be regarded as social parasitism. *Myrmica canadensis*, for example, is a large ant of the northern parts of America, the nest of which is sometimes intertwined with that of a small ant, *Leptothorax emersoni*. The small species can enter the galleries of the other through openings so minute as to be inaccessible to the larger ants. Far from being hostile to their little neigh-

[1] The wild pig forms merely associations of individuals which forage together. Dogs, wolves, etc., hunt in packs, though they are quite capable of leading a solitary life. All other ancestors of domesticated animals (except, notably, the cat) live in herds, which often have a leader.

bours, the *Myrmica* welcome the *Leptothorax* with tolerant indifference, treating them much as dogs are treated by those who neither like nor dislike them. The *Leptothorax* lick the *Myrmica* and beg food from them, and are indeed readily supplied with regurgitated drops of food-juice. It cannot be said that the invaded

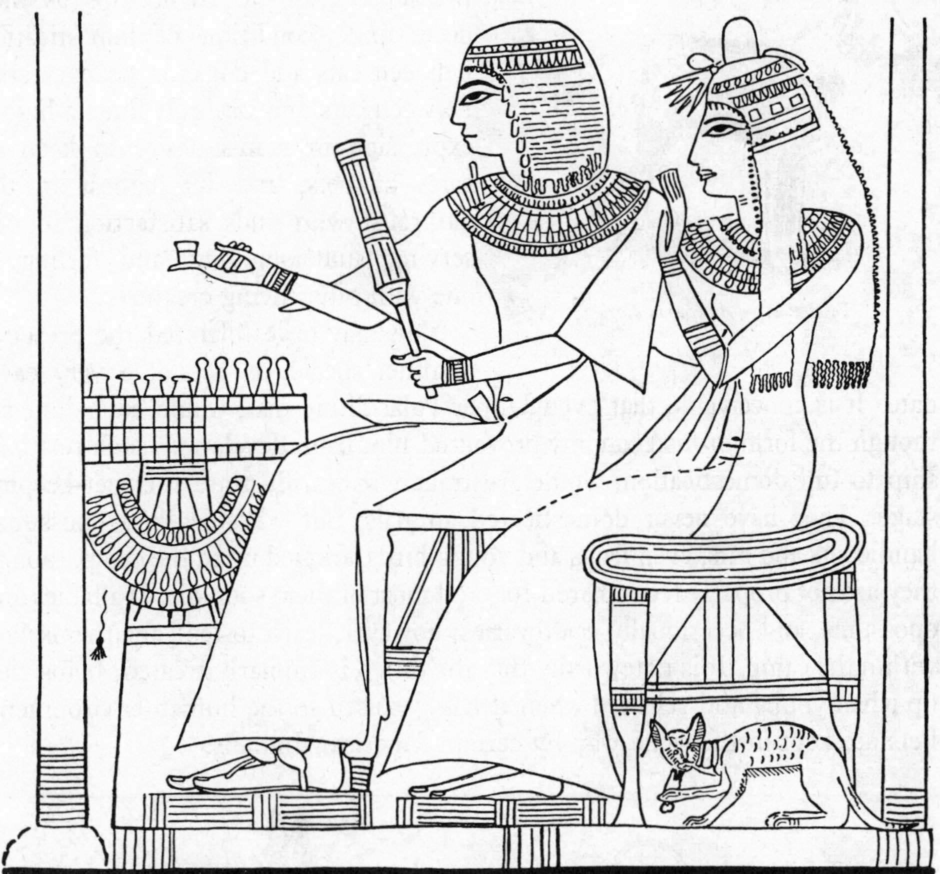

FIGURE 214—*The domesticated cat in Egypt. From a tomb at Thebes. c 1300 B.C.*

colony suffers from the invasions of the smaller ants, though it is doubtful whether they bring any advantage. Nevertheless, the behaviour of the *Leptothorax* almost makes them social parasites. They live entirely by begging while the going is good, though when need arises they can fend for themselves.

This case is instructive from the human point of view, for it shows one form of life supporting another which is intrusive but not an open enemy. Similarly in pre-Mesolithic times, long before the realization that dogs can be an economic asset, there may well have been (as there still is) a stage of throwing morsels to wild dogs invading the camps. Such acts are elementary manifestations of the solidarity of life, especially of related life. This solidarity is characteristic of most higher animals which have developed a social medium of some sort, and which are not enemies. It finds a simple expression in animal friendships as they occur under conditions of domestication between cats and dogs, or stranger still, between cats and birds. It finds a higher expression in man's desire to keep all sorts of pets, and its highest in the naturalist who finds satisfaction in observing, understanding, and feeling at one with other living creatures.

FIGURE 215—*Australian dingo.*

Man may have tolerated the presence of other species as pets at a very early date. It is conceivable that even Upper Palaeolithic man would have done so, though the form of his economy prevented him from developing such relationship to full domestication. Some Australian tribes illustrate this pet-keeping stage. They have never domesticated animals, but wallabies and opossums, bandicoots and rats, even frogs and young birds, are tied up in the camp, though they are not properly fed or cared for, and most of them soon die. Wallabies and opossums, and occasionally cassowaries, however, learn to fend for themselves within the camp. It is noteworthy that the dingo is similarly treated, being tied up when young and released when it has got used to the human environment. Pets are kept in the same way by certain American Indians.

FIGURE 216—*Greyhound. From a tomb at Beni Hasan, Egypt. c 1900 B.C.*

In view of such facts, it is not surprising that the belief has arisen that the habit of keeping young animals as pets is at the root of domestication in general. This is certainly an overstatement, but it is probable that pet-keeping provided one basis for domestication on an economic scale. The mothering instinct of women may have played a part. Pet-keeping is particularly likely to have been a factor in the domestication of the dog. The scavenging habits of

FIGURE 217—*Mongrel dog. Beni Hasan.* c *1900 B.C.*

wild dogs brought them into contact with the human social medium (figures 215–17), and the pups may have been adopted. One of the camp-fire stories of the Africans of Calabar, in southern Nigeria, tells how a boy grew fond of a wild pup and brought it up in the village in spite of attempts of the pup's mother to rescue it. When fully grown, the dog induced a bitch to join him, and their litter became used to camp conditions. They went out on hunting-expeditions with their human friends. Of course this folk-tale is not an ancient tradition, but it does describe the views of a people who are still in close contact with their natural environment.

There is another theory of how domestication arose under conditions of amicable relations. It assumes that totem animals, the killing of which is often taboo, would become tame. There is, however, a great difference between the taming of a totem animal (in any case an unusual event) and its economic exploitation under conditions of complete domestication. Moreover, animals which are now domesticated do not appear to have been often chosen as totems. Though totemism is perhaps as old as the Upper Palaeolithic, as witnessed by the bison hunter of Lascaux (figure 544), it is very improbable that it ever led to domestication, which is based on the motive of exploitation of the properties and abilities of the animals.

Symbioses are not always voluntary. A certain amount of coercion, i.e. transplantation into the social medium of the more intelligent species, or extension of the latter into the social medium of the weaker species, is common. Yet both parties derive certain advantages; thus the animal obtains personal security, while his human master secures an easier and more ample food-supply.

III. ANIMAL SCAVENGERS

Food-supply appears to have played an important part in the establishment of close associations of animals and man. This is most obvious with the scavengers. Some species enter into a relationship in which one lives regularly on the food-debris or other waste products of the other. If the removal of the waste products is an advantage to the producer, scavenging might closely approach a true symbiosis. But scavengers often have the habit of preying on the host, and especially on its progeny, as opportunity arises. Scavenging thus grades into social parasitism.

Most scavengers are, moreover, not closely host-specific. Thus the jackal can live perfectly well without man, but, where human settlements are available, he will enter into a loose and impermanent, though nevertheless quite regular, relationship with him. The mutual advantage is obvious enough. In other associations of the scavenging type, the relations are permanent. The loose associations of the wild dogs with human society are of great interest, since they illustrate one of the ways in which domestication is likely to have begun. The two social media, that of the dog and that of the man, overlap because man produces offal which dogs will eat. There is no cause for enmity in this, unless one of the species interferes with the habits of the other. This is indeed so in the case of hyenas, for example, which are prone to steal man's food-reserves and are too fierce for the establishment of friendly relations. The smaller species of wild dogs are in a different category. Not only do they fear man, but their association in packs with a recognized leader affords the possibility of transfer of allegiance to man, once he is appreciated as a being of superior strength and cunning.

It is obvious enough that not every scavenger of the dog tribe is a prospective candidate for domestication. The jackals head the list in so far as they are unlikely to attack man. Their social level, however, is lower than that of those wild dog-like creatures which practise active hunting, and which for this reason would be more ready to form with man groups that can be regarded as mixed packs. The smaller races of wolves found in southern countries, which scavenge as well as hunt, would therefore appear to be the most amenable to domestication, but they also tend to regard human settlements as legitimate hunting-grounds, from which, as in India today, they frequently steal goats, domestic dogs, and even children. These propensities are most strongly developed in the large northern races of wolves, and these wolves are thus the least likely to have provided the initial stock from which the domestic dog emerged.

The combination of scavenging and robbing is of course exceedingly common in nature. It has often provided the conditions for the evolution of regular pests and even parasites. Thus, while scavenging in its pure form is symbiosis, it grades imperceptibly into exploitation of the host by the scavenger. On the other hand, where conditions favour domestication the scavenging species can in due course be exploited by the host.

The pig is another scavenger that has been domesticated. Since its social level is low, its relations have rarely developed beyond that of an exploited captive. But scavenging thus exhibits more clearly than any other social relationship the possibilities of further developments, either in the direction of pests and parasites (the guests exploiting the hosts), or in the direction of domestication (the hosts exploiting the guests).

The various possibilities inherent in the guest–host relationship are, somewhat inadequately, summarized thus:

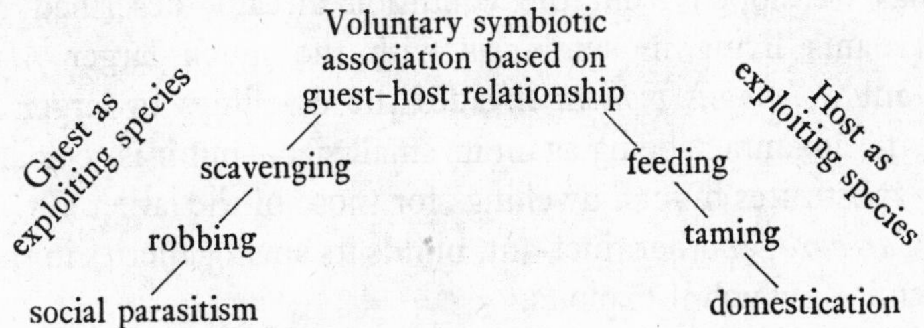

IV. FROM SCAVENGER TO SOCIAL PARASITE

The examples of scavenging and related guest–host relationships which have been given so far were drawn from the social medium of man. There are many others, especially among social insects like termites, bees, wasps, and ants, which show that similar conditions develop wherever social media overlap, and one at least may usefully be quoted here to illustrate the point.

Pure scavengers are as rare among insects as in the human social medium. Most are more or less predacious, though some enter into friendly relations with their hosts, as they offer them exudates which have a pleasant taste. Since such substances are unlikely to have a significant food-value, they have produced in many insect societies biologically unhealthy conditions which may be compared to selling the child for a tin of tobacco—for some scavengers which have become adopted by ant colonies feed on the larvae of their hosts, who nevertheless suffer their presence since they enjoy the flavour of their exudates. This perversion has arisen independently many times over, for the ants are used to licking the exudates of their own larvae. Such a condition of scavenging and robbing combined with the offer of a reward has no parallel in the social relations of man and beast; there are, however, many examples of straightforward scavenging in ants' nests, the scavengers receiving no attention from the ants. A case is that of a white woodlouse, *Platyarthrus*, which feeds on the small pellets of waste food-material which the ants disgorge from the pockets inside their mouths. Another true scavenger is the beetle *Antherophagus*. Its larvae feed on refuse in the nests of bumble-bees, its adults on flowers. From these and many similar cases a series of more and more intimate relations with the host leads to extreme conditions in which the scavenger becomes a robber, but is not recognized as such by the host.

Scavengers of the robber kind may be regarded as parasites of the social medium on which they depend, but the ant-world has produced cases of social parasitism on a grand scale, which parallel certain man–animal relationships and have innumerable counterparts in the interconnexions of human social groups. The condition of social parasitism, in which one organized community exploits another, has developed from the condition already described of the small *Leptothorax* ants living in symbiosis with the much larger *Myrmica*. The American ant *Solenopsis molesta* invades the dwellings of larger ants—which it pillages, the advantage being again its small size—but it is so adaptable that it frequently substitutes human dwellings for those of the larger ant. In much the same way *Carebara*, another thief-ant, builds its small galleries in the mounds of African termites, which it exploits.

In these cases, the females of the social parasite breed in their own quarters, which are inaccessible to the host-community. There are more extreme cases, however, in which even the breeding is transferred to the premises of the host-community, which feeds and rears the progeny of the social parasite. Young queens of *Strongylognathus testaceus* enter the nests of *Tetramorium caespitum*, another ant, and are accepted by the workers, which feed them and tend their eggs and larvae. Only a small proportion of the colony consists of the invading parasite species. This condition finds many a parallel in the history of mankind, wherever numerically small invading races have imposed themselves upon the more numerous natives.

V. PARASITISM A QUESTION OF VIEWPOINT

Whenever man has made himself a social parasite on an animal species, it has been by succeeding in domesticating the host. In insect societies the opposite is more common, namely that the host succeeds in domesticating the invading parasite. These cases are of interest as they show how initially similar social relationships may continue to evolve along very different lines.

A particularly interesting example is a beetle, *Lomechusa strumosa*, which lives in the nest of a European slave-making ant, *Formica sanguinea*. The segments of its abdomen secrete an exudate which is eagerly licked by the ants. These beetles are literally reared by ants, much to the detriment of the colony. Sociologically, they are domesticated animals producing a secretion for the delectation of the ants. From the beetle's point of view, the situation represents a case of social parasitism. *Lomechusa* lays its eggs in the ant nests. These eggs (or the young larvae) are collected by the ants and placed in their own brood-chambers beside their own larvae—and are treated better, for the beetle-larvae regale the ants with an exudate which the ants prefer to that of their own larvae. Hence the *Lomechusa* larvae are regularly fed by the ants with regurgitated food. In addition, however, the beetle-larvae eat many of the ant-larvae. When the beetle-larvae are mature, the ants cover them with earth, as they do their own larvae, so as to enable them to spin a cocoon. But from now on the beetles suffer greatly from the care lavished on them, for the ants expose the cocoons to the sun, a practice which is deadly for the beetle. Thus survival of the beetle colony depends mainly on some of their cocoons being overlooked by the ants. In heavily infested *Formica* nests the beetles so tax the ant brood that the colony may die out. The later stages of this process may almost be regarded as a case of successful domestication of the ants by the beetles, though the process is liable to lead to a complete destruction of the domesticated stock.

The case of *Lomechusa* and *Formica* is exceptionally instructive because it shows that there are two points of view to every case of domestication. The social relationship may appear advantageous from both points of view, but its biological effects are usually decidedly in favour of one of the species; which of them it will be cannot be predicted on theoretical grounds in any of nature's experiments. In the case of man, we believe that it is our own species which invariably maintains the upper hand and gains the advantages.

It is impossible to sort the various possibilities of social relationships between different species into hard and fast categories. The classification here adopted is arbitrary in several respects. On the whole, the examples so far discussed belong to cases in which the host-species remains in control of the environment. Nevertheless, the balance occasionally shifts so much to the advantage of the guest (reindeer, *Lomechusa*) that the host is ruled by the guest. True domestication seems to have arisen more than once in this manner.

VI. THE CASE OF THE REINDEER

There is one example of domestication of an animal by man which may be regarded as social parasitism. It is that of the reindeer. Both the domesticators and the domesticated have here remained in the state of nomadism. Nevertheless, the activities of man in relation to the reindeer can only be described as those of a social parasite. Like so many guests of ants and termites, the human guest-species has even supplied a delicacy which the animal host-species is eager to obtain. In so far, however, as the exploiting species gains the upper hand in this

FIGURE 218—*Reindeer-hunting by decoy. Eskimo engraving on walrus-ivory.*

process and the exploited species degenerates, the case of reindeer and man might equally well be discussed under the head of true domestication; but since it appears to have begun as ordinary social parasitism, it is more usefully treated here.

Of the several theories concerning the domestication of the reindeer, that which derives it from the practice of decoy-hunting is the best founded. There are numerous records of reindeer-hunting with decoy animals. Three methods may be quoted. According to Pallas (an eighteenth-century traveller), the Samoyed hunter, in his time, would select four or five tame hinds and fawns. Under their cover, holding them by ropes, he would approach the herd of wild reindeer against the wind, until near enough to shoot his arrow. A second method now practised by the Tungus is to leave a few tame hinds, during the rutting season, on a feeding-ground of the wild deer. The wild stags associate with the hinds, and are killed when the hunter approaches the herd in a day or two. A third method is adopted by both Tungus and Samoyed. Ropes or thongs are tied around the antlers of a strong, tame, rutting stag. It is set free when a wild herd with a stag is in sight. The tame stag begins to fight the wild one (figure 218). Their antlers become entangled and give the hunter the chance to approach.

Tame reindeer which have proved their worth would naturally be cared for by the hunter. Since tame hinds will mate with wild stags, any hunter owning decoy reindeer would almost unintentionally become a reindeer-breeder. The ease with which domestication of reindeer can be effected is due largely to the similarity of the social state of man and of deer. Both are nomads, and domestication compels neither to adopt any profound change of habit. To this day, reindeer, both wild and domesticated, remain nomadic as do the tribes who follow the herds, preying on the wild and controlling and exploiting the tame. In doing so, man takes his toll of the species much as wolves do, and the only advantage that accrues to the domesticated reindeer is protection from these and other predators. The reindeer, as a community, have to pay heavily for this protection since, instead of being devoured by wolves and bears, they are eaten by man. Man's numerical inferiority to the reindeer and his adaptation of himself to their habits make him their social parasite. Despite their domestication, hunting of wild reindeer continues. The more elaborate forms of exploitation of the domesticated deer, as for draught or riding, or as a source of milk, are all comparatively modern.

At the outset of the process of domestication, man appears to have availed himself of the eagerness of reindeer for salty matter, notably for human urine. This substance attracts and binds reindeer to human camps. The craving arises from lack of salt in the available water which is derived from melting snow. Even today the human nomads take full advantage of this weakness of the reindeer, so that the supply of a delicacy provides the meeting-ground on which the social media of the two species overlap. This is a most remarkable parallel to the conditions under which societies of social insects are invaded. The reindeer is not the only animal domesticated through salt-licks. Another example is the mithan of Assam, a cross of the gaur with domesticated humped cattle (p 348). The gaur is a large wild bovine, not closely related to cattle; it is attracted by salt-licks placed in suitable localities.

VII. DECOY-HUNTING AND DOMESTICATION

It should be noted that deer in general are readily tamed when young. It is relatively easy to obtain fawns of any species. Young red deer were tamed as decoys in Germany until the Middle Ages, so that the method of transforming fawns into decoys has been practised in widely distant areas (plate 6 A). Nor is decoy-hunting with tamed young animals restricted to deer. Apart from birds, with which we are not concerned here, both aurochs and bison were stalked in this way, as shown by the ancient Frankish, Alamannic, and Langobardian laws. It is perfectly conceivable, therefore, that the use of tamed oxen as decoys was a feature characteristic of the initial stages of the domestication of cattle (figure 436).

Despite this possibility, difficulties arise if the decoy method is regarded as the only way in which the aurochs was subjected to domestication. It is one proposition to tame specimens and quite another to train them for special tasks.

The circus-director succeeds in doing the latter with animals very unpromising for domestication, but to cause such creatures to breed freely in captivity and to make them indifferent to personal freedom, so that they stay with man without cage, fence, or chain, is a very different matter.

Other domesticated species which may have gone the way of the reindeer and subsequently been compelled even to renounce their migratory habits, are the sheep, the goat, and the horse. In the case of sheep and goat, this suggestion is based on their natural habits; they are shy and fond of mountainous country, and far less likely to invade fields than, for instance, pigs or wild cattle. As to the horse, a highly nomadic species, it was domesticated by nomadic peoples, although at a comparatively late period.

The invention of agriculture brought in its train fresh opportunities for developing the guest–host relation, since cultivated lands are excellent feeding-grounds for several herbivorous and gregarious animals. So long as the land lay fallow, this state of affairs would not differ radically from other cases of scavenging. But when the crop was growing, the same practice of the animals constituted an act of robbery, though it afforded social contacts which may well have led to the domestication of the aurochs and related large bovines, and perhaps of other species.

VIII. TAMING

In many cases there is, in the strict sense, no guest–host relationship, but one species, whose social medium overlaps another's, proceeds to limit the freedom of movement of the latter. This is conspicuously so in many cases of domestication by man. The meeting-ground of the social media of two species is a common geographical area. The absence of the guest–host relationship presupposes systematic and compulsory incorporation in the social medium of the domesticator. This condition is characteristic of man, but it is not exclusively his, for it is common among social insects. In both men and insects this relationship is far from primitive, for it appears only in the more highly developed societies.

Ants of the genus *Polyergus* are keepers of slaves, to whose presence in their colonies their entire economy is adjusted. Hence slave-making is a necessity for them. Thus the species *P. rufescens* makes raids on the nests of *Formica fusca* with great precision. A powerful excitement pervades the raiding army, which avails itself of the element of surprise in attacking a *Formica* nest. Resisting *Formica* workers are killed, and the young, especially pupae, are immediately carried off to the raiders' nest. There the victims are handed over to slaves already present, who rear them as faithful servants of the colony. *Polyergus* has become so dependent on slaves that the whole domestic work of the mixed colony, even to nest-building, is done by them. The slave-holders themselves restrict their activities to war.

Many other examples of many varieties of slavery among social insects could be quoted. It will be noticed that the closest parallels exist between these conditions among insects and conditions of human slavery. All the insect cases are, however, interspecific, while man's slave-making is intraspecific, a type with which we are not directly concerned. Man's interspecific activities, in which he tames another species, fall under the heading of true domestication.

Just as the ant communities of the *Polyergus* type have passed through stages of more primitive conditions of slave-holding, it is more than likely that the taming of animal species which would not voluntarily enter into a guest–host relationship with man can have occurred only after man had already gained experience in the keeping of domesticated animals. They are, therefore, to be regarded as a higher level of domestication. The guest–host relationships discussed earlier represent a more primitive and possibly more ancient condition. Once man was familiar with the practice of keeping animals like the dog or sheep, he might have conceived the idea of trying to keep other species which he was in the habit of hunting. This can hardly have happened before the beginnings of agriculture, because the initial social contact between man and the animal species in question can only have been an unfriendly one. Elephants, for example, are used as slaves of man on the *Polyergus* principle. Sociologically independent (wild) specimens are caught and compelled to work for man. The process of taming is simplified by the presence of previously tamed elephants, a remarkable parallel to the conditions under which *Formica* slaves enter into the social medium of the *Polyergus*. Nevertheless, the domestication of elephants has never proceeded clearly beyond the stage of taming, for they are generally allowed to breed in freedom and only captured from time to time. The reason is surely the large size of the animal.

Domestication of the large bovines probably proceeded along similar lines. This does not mean that bovines were originally caught in order to perform definite jobs for man, as are elephants today, but first contacts of settled communities with large bovines must have raised the thought of the possibilities of domestication already familiar from the dog and sheep. Then, as now, herds of wild animals robbed the cultivated patches, a habit of cattle as much as of elephants. Attempts to tame young individuals may have been made early in the Neolithic. There is likely to have existed for some time a condition intermediate between taming and true domestication, the tamed animals being allowed to interbreed with the wild. One example is the reindeer (in some areas), another the mithan of Assam. In the latter case, interbreeding regularly with the wild gaur is regarded as necessary for maintaining the qualities of the domesticated stock.

A serious obstacle to incorporating large animals into the human social medium is their fierceness and intractability. Here man gradually derives advantage from keeping animals even under unfavourable conditions. The sole interest of the Neolithic husbandman was to keep the animals subjugated. To give them good living conditions and to provide them with the most suitable provender were ideas that could not enter the minds of men whose own requirements of food and shelter were so elementary. Animals kept in captivity must inevitably have deteriorated. Their progeny would tend to be smaller, weaker, and more docile than their wild ancestors, being selected, consciously or unconsciously, for precisely those qualities. It may well be that the so-called *Bos longifrons* type of cattle was the outcome of such a process. Only cattle of small size and great docility could have been managed under Early Neolithic conditions; they were obtained, without any knowledge of the principles of heredity, from those individuals which alone could be retained near the Neolithic encampment. Once, however, the domestication of the species had been thoroughly effected, the idea of increasing the body-size is likely to have been regarded as useful, in order to increase either the meat-supply or the working strength of the animals. Under primitive conditions, interbreeding with wild specimens was an easy matter.

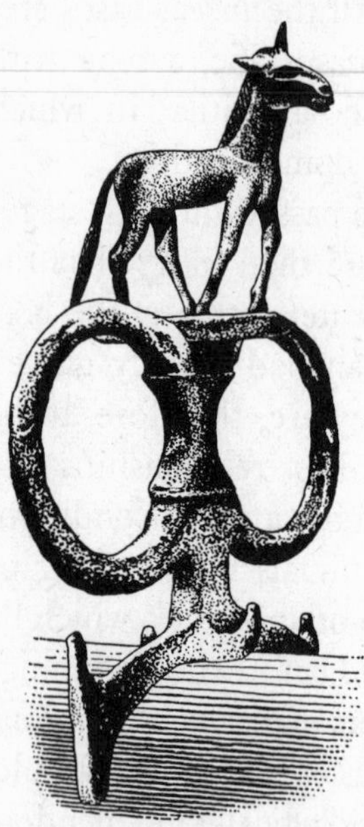

FIGURE 219—*Onager on Queen Shub-ad's rein-ring. Ur, Mesopotamia. Third millennium* B.C.

With increasing experience in keeping domesticated stock, it would also have occurred to prehistoric man from time to time to restart the entire process from fresh wild stock, which process, as well as that of allowing cattle to interbreed with wild individuals, is likely to have played a decisive part in the appearance of the so-called *primigenius* breeds of domesticated cattle.

IX. SYSTEMATIC DOMESTICATION

Domesticated animals proved their worth and played their part in the Neolithic economic revolution. In the urban revolution which followed there were many experiments in domestication (figure 219), notably in Egypt in Old Kingdom times. Pictorial representations, such as those in the grave of Mereruka at Saqqara, show animals like gazelles, ibex, and addax antelopes with collars round their necks, not to mention monkeys and even carnivores like hyenas. Hyenas appear to have been kept and stuffed like geese (figure 220). These attempts to tame or fully to domesticate animals, other than the well known standard stock beasts, were abandoned sooner or later.

FIGURE 220—*Domestication of animals in the Old Kingdom. In the bottom row hyenas are being stuffed. From a tomb at Saqqara, Egypt.* c *2500* B.C.

There are two species regarding which it is difficult to construct a case of overlap of social media leading to domestication. These are the domestic fowl and the rabbit. Both are suspected of having been domesticated by peoples already familiar with the possibilities of domestication. The male bird may originally have attracted man by his fighting habits rather than as an economic proposition. Jungle-fowl are shy birds, and would hardly associate themselves voluntarily with man.

X. SOME GENERALIZATIONS

In any particular case of domestication of a species there must have been an initial stage when it had but loose ties with the human social medium. Interbreeding with the wild forms must have remained common, holding the species morphologically close to the wild ancestor. A second stage completed the process of subjugation, and made the species dependent on the human social medium.

This was a period of relatively strict captivity, during which the domesticated beasts can have had no opportunity of interbreeding with wild stock. The outcome was a stock with distinct characters of domestication, such as reduction of body-size and of horns, and the appearance of a frontal eminence in certain breeds of cattle, a reduction of the chewing apparatus in dogs and cats, and many other characters. It was with domesticated stock which had passed this second stage that Neolithic man settled in Europe. He came with small and distinctive breeds of sheep, cattle, and pigs. Similarly, it appears that in Mesolithic times the domesticated dog was brought into Europe as a ready-made race.

A third stage begins with intentional development of certain characters in the stock. Large size was now an economic advantage, provided that the animals could be maintained and did not revert to the fierceness of their ancestors. For this reason, one may suspect that Neolithic and Bronze Age man from time to time interbred their domestic stock with wild. This applies specifically to cattle, but it also provided a means of developing more aggressive races of dogs from Maglemosian time onwards.

The fourth stage arose imperceptibly from the third, and sometimes directly from the second, when man began to pay increasing attention to the qualities of the beast, both economic (as yields of milk, meat, and wool), and morphological (as horn-shapes, drooping ears, colour). In the Middle East this fourth stage had been entered long before 3000 B.C. Well-marked breeds of sheep, goats, and cattle were in existence even at this early date. In this fourth stage domesticated stock becomes standardized, and so different from the ancestral type that interbreeding would spoil the qualities laboriously obtained. The wild species would now have become an enemy and be persecuted. There are many medieval reports of the extermination of wild cattle, and the tarpan, the wild horse of south-east Europe, was exterminated by the local peasants partly because the tame mares were apt to elope with wild stallions.

As the wild form became rarer, its last survivors would be absorbed into the domesticated stock. Thus the last wild horses in the great game-park at Zwierzyniec, near Bilgoraj, Poland, were caught and given to the peasants in 1812. Similarly, the Przewalski horse of Mongolia appears to have been absorbed into the domesticated stock of the nomads of the country. At an earlier date, this must have happened to the dromedary of Arabia and the two-humped camel of central Asia. The process of the extermination of wild forms has been much accelerated by the destruction of their natural environment, e.g. by deforestation or the spread of cultivation.

XI. MORPHOLOGICAL EFFECTS OF DOMESTICATION

Size. More often than not, the size of domesticated animals is less than that of their wild relations. This is seen with dogs, cats, cattle, sheep, goats, and pigs. In prehistoric deposits where wild and domesticated forms occur together, small size is diagnostic. The camels of the Old World and their congeners of the New (llama, guanaco, vicuna) are about the same size as their wild ancestors. The domesticated rabbit and domesticated birds tend to be larger than the wild forms. In all domesticated species, however, the total range of variation of body-

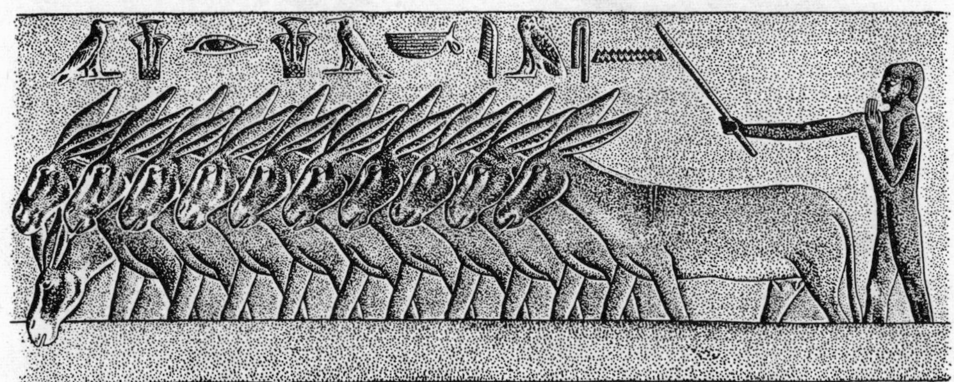

FIGURE 221—*Asses threshing. The dark stripe can be seen on the shoulder of the right-hand ass. From a tomb at Saqqara, Egypt.* c *2500 B.C.*

size is greater than under natural conditions. Giant as well as dwarf forms have often been selected and developed into races by man. Even goats and sheep, which show comparatively little variation in size, have such races. In cattle, horse, and most of all in the dog, this tendency is even more conspicuous. Apart from the variations in over-all size, there are dwarfs and giants due to the modification of body-proportions; these are most conspicuous among dogs.

Colour. Domesticated animals are often conspicuously coloured. Though in the dromedary and the two-humped camel the wild colour is the commonest, very dark and very light specimens are highly valued. Among elephants, the colour of the skin is often patchy, being marbled with white; this phenomenon in extreme cases results in the rare white elephant, but such variability is hardly due to domestication, for elephants are not normally bred under controlled conditions. The ass also, in most individuals, has retained the wild coloration—grey with a dark stripe on the back (figure 221)—though black races are regularly bred in certain areas, and white individuals occasionally occur.

In other domesticated animals, wild coloration is the exception. It is usually preserved in particular races, in which it is regarded as a desirable character. The Alsatian among dogs, the 'Belgian hare' among rabbits, and the striped tabby among cats are examples. Among the horses, wild colours are exceptional, but they are found in the yellow dun of the Mongolian wild horse and the mouse-grey of the tarpan. The reddish-brown shade for horses has always been popular and selected for preference. In cattle, the wild colour is preserved in some breeds of south-west Europe and north-west Africa, such as the

FIGURE 222—(Left) *Egyptian relief of a ram represented with four horns.* (Right) *Sheep from Soay, Hebrides.*

Camargue race of the Rhône delta and certain Spanish breeds. The common domestic cattle of Morocco show clearly how some of the characteristic domestic coloration arises from the wild. The bulls are usually blackish with a cream-coloured stripe on the back and on the forehead. The cows are not so dark, but often more reddish, and the lighter colour develops from the light line on the back, assuming the shape of a saddle. The plain red or reddish-brown common among cattle is a retention of juvenile coloration, but other colours like black, plain white, and piebald seem due to mutations (tailpiece).

The colours discussed are not in themselves products of domestication, since black, white, and red pigments are present in the hair of the wild racial ancestors of all domestic animals. The mutations, therefore, are characterized rather by the absence, local or general, of one or more pigments. Piebaldness, a matter of the distribution of the pigments on the body, is very common in domesticated breeds but very rare in nature. Only one wild piebald species is known to the writer, viz. the hyena-dog, *Lycaon pictus*. Piebaldness of the animals depicted by early man, therefore, is an indication of domestication.

Sheep and goats have, on the whole, been less ready to discard their wild colour-scheme, until intensive breeding began in comparatively recent times. There are even today many hairy stocks of sheep with the moufflon coloration—

brown with a white patch on the side of the rump—for instance, in the Fezzan race in north-west Africa. Domination of the woolly undercoat over the hair tends to make sheep single-coloured, but, as suggested by the Soay (Hebrides) sheep, this is likely to have appeared on the body long before it spread to the legs, neck, and head (figure 222). It is extremely unlikely that Neolithic farmers were in possession of white-wool sheep.

Skull changes. Very noticeable under domestication, skull changes are important because they are easily recognizable in material from ancient dwelling-sites. With certain exceptions, the facial part of the skull tends to shorten relative to the cranial, as is evident in man himself. It is virtually absent in horses, asses, and camels, but very conspicuous in the pig. A similar condition becomes extreme in some breeds of dogs, e.g. the bulldog, boxer, and pekinese. The process is less conspicuous in cattle, sheep, and goats, but is fairly marked in the cat. This tendency of domestication is occasionally replaced by its opposite, a lengthening, which has become a fashion with some modern dog-breeders. Many races, such as sheep-dogs, terriers, and dachshunds, have changed their appearance in recent years owing to intensive selection of long-faced specimens, but even the most long-faced domesticated dog has a shorter face than the larger wolves, the effect of extreme lengthening being produced mainly by the narrowing of the skull across the zygomatic arches, and by the straightening of the concavity between nose and forehead. The dentition is inevitably affected by changes in skull-proportions. At a very early stage of domestication the teeth became smaller; thus in dogs the fourth pre-molar of the upper jaw and the first molar of the lower, which together form the characteristic bone-cutting pincers of carnivores, are always smaller than in wolves. With progressive facial shortening, teeth which are in the state of reduction may disappear. With extreme shortening, the position of the teeth in a single row may be replaced by an overlapping oblique arrangement, as in bulldogs and some kinds of pig.

On the whole, domestication tends to reduce the size of horns, though there are some conspicuous exceptions. Neolithic cattle of the *brachyceros* (= *longifrons*) race, and sheep and goats of Neolithic lake-dwellings, have small horns. Hornless cattle are known from the Iron Age onwards. Domesticated buffalo have smaller horns than wild. On the other hand, man has often delighted in producing races with abnormally shaped horns, regardless of their economic value. Four-horned sheep have been bred, and the shape of horns of cattle, sheep, and goat vary astonishingly. Hungarian steppe-cattle, those of the Watussi of East Africa, the Bechuana breed of South Africa, and the Texan longhorns have huge horns with an outward curve not present in wild species. In sheep and goats the shape of the horns varies even more. The horns may be rolled into a close spiral, or drawn out into an open one, or even assume the form of a straight rod that has been twisted (figure 222). Great variability is present in the wild races and species of this group of ruminants. In modern breeds, economic considerations being paramount, the oddly shaped horns are fast disappearing.

Changes in skeleton of body and limbs. It was once held that the bones of the body and limbs of domesticated animals were distinguishable from those of wild forms. Further investigation has shown that single bones of dogs, cats, horses, and camels cannot usually be recognized as domesticated or wild. Such recognition is normally impossible even for sheep and goats, except where mere size provides evidence. In the bones of domesticated cattle, however, weak muscle-ridges and poorly defined facets of the joints are fairly diagnostic, while in domesticated pigs the failure of the end-pieces of the long bones to fuse with the shaft until long after maturity, and the persistence of the sutures of the skull, make them easy of recognition. In the tail, the number of vertebrae may be reduced, as in the Manx cat and certain dogs, or increased, as in certain sheep. Twisting of the tail, due to irregular growth or oblique fusion of the vertebrae, or both, occurs in some domestic forms, as in the pig and the remarkable angular or knotty tails of certain bulldogs and cats. The spiral tail of some dogs, notably of the ancient Egyptian greyhound (figure 216), is probably also due to structural modification of the caudal vertebrae. In the sheep, increase in the number of tail-vertebrae beyond thirteen is a sign of domestication, present in practically all domesticated races; the number may rise to as many as twenty-five.

The bones of the limbs vary considerably in domesticated races. They may be longer, but are usually shorter than in the wild form. They are frequently less nearly straight, and are sometimes even curved in a manner which must be regarded as pathological.

Changes in soft parts. The most striking are those in the skin, and in the length and texture of the hair. In the hair of cattle there are no very obvious modifications. The sleek coats of the common breeds are inherited from the wild forms. Other types, such as the thin coat of some southern races, and the curly coat of certain park-cattle, are easily interpreted as characters of southern and of northern geographical races. In the horses, mane and tail-hair have become longer. The falling mane of domesticated, as distinct from the upright mane of wild, horses is usually regarded as a good diagnostic feature, but it is said that the mane of the Przewalski horse in its winter coat is not upright. Since this creature has long shaggy body-hair in winter, the statement is possibly true. On the other hand, the crossing with domesticated horses may easily have introduced this character into some members of the Przewalski stock. A shaggy winter coat was depicted by Upper Palaeolithic artists on European wild horses, and the pattern of streaks on the ivory-carving from Mas d'Azil provides confirmation (figure 223). Among the asses, shaggy coats occur occasionally, as in the Poitou breed. Long hair has further appeared in cats and dogs. While in some cases domesticated breeds have been developed with hair longer than in the wild forms, the opposite, namely

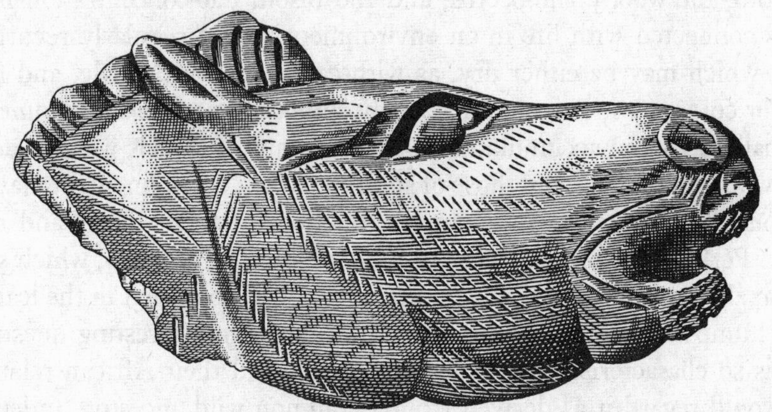

FIGURE 223—*Head of a horse carved in ivory. From Mas d'Azil, Ariège, France. Upper Palaeolithic.*

hairlessness, has sometimes been favoured; obvious examples are the pig and the hairless Chinese dog.

The profoundest changes have, however, been produced in the woolly undercoat, especially in species which have much wool in the wild forms. In most cases, the connexion between wool-bearing domesticated animals and the production of human garments is evident. It would be worth investigating the connexion between the making of felt and woollen cloth and the keeping of wool-producing animals. On the borderlands of the western Asiatic mountains, wool-producing sheep appear early, but they are absent from Egypt until the Middle Kingdom. Though the sheep is a wool-producer *par excellence*, hair-producing sheep, with large manes in the males, have also been developed. Similarly, goats have been bred for hair, e.g. the Mamber goat, while wool is obtained from the Angora and Kashmir races. The woolly undercoat is heavily developed in the domesticated races of the yak, while camels are good natural wool-producers.

The skin itself is frequently modified as the result of domestication. Dewlaps and skin-folds, which are normally characteristic of young animals only, are retained by the adults in certain breeds of dogs and cattle.

The character of the skin, which, as pelt or leather, is one of the most important products of the animal world, is intimately connected with the development of subcutaneous fat. Apart from its deposition under the skin, fat is often concentrated in certain parts in a way that affects the shape of the animal. Obvious cases are camels, humped cattle, and fat-tailed sheep. Several species which were never domesticated show or have shown the same character; such are the mammoth, the woolly rhinoceros, and the bison. Fat-concentration in certain parts is connected with life in an environment with a regularly recurring lean season, which may be either dry, as with camel, humped cattle, and fat-tailed sheep, or cold, as with mammoth, woolly rhinoceros, and bison. Domestication has usually favoured accumulations of fat. Humps of camels which lead a more or less wild life are small, but those of specimens kept in confinement may become enormous. The differences are simply functions of food-supply and muscular activity. Perhaps the bronze image of a camel found at Khurab, which shows no hump at all, depicts the normal condition of a wild specimen in the lean season.

The hump of the zebu or humped cattle raises an interesting question. The hump is so characteristic of the Indian breeds and their African relatives that some would regard it as derived from a common wild ancestor. Indeed, it has been claimed that these cattle have some gaur blood. The hump of the gaur, however, is supported by enlarged dorsal spines of the vertebrae, and this is not so in the humped cattle. Such humped animals are, moreover, of considerable age, since the Indus civilization of about 2500 B.C. was familiar with them, and distinguished them sharply from the *primigenius* type of cattle (figure 555). It is conceivable, therefore, that there was another race of wild cattle in the drier parts of India, which was in possession of the hump and is now extinct.

A very peculiar fat-storage system appears in some sheep, namely in the tail. This is strange, since the wild sheep shows no tendency to increase the fat-content of the tail. Lacking evidence to the contrary, fat-tailed sheep must be regarded as a pure product of domestication. In some races, the tail is so long and heavy that it has to be supported by rollers.

The brain is affected by domestication, and in dogs becomes smaller in proportion to the body. The parts of the brain are not all equally affected; it is mainly those associated with sensual perception which suffer, while those carrying the centres of the complex psychic processes are little, if at all, affected. It would be instructive to study the brain of breeds of dogs which have become specialized in using their noses, e.g. bloodhounds, in contrast with that of types which depend mainly on sight, e.g. greyhounds.

Many domesticated races have been bred to excel their wild relations in physical powers. This applies among horses to the racing breeds, which have much stronger shoulder muscles than the wild horses, and to the heavy draught-horses; it also applies to many breeds of dogs (tailpiece). Reduction of musculature is equally common. Thus the chewing muscles of domesticated carnivores are inferior to those of their wild relations, so that the shape and size of the muscular ridges on the skull, and even the shape of the lower jaw, are affected.

Examples of modifications of the soft parts resulting from domestication may easily be multiplied. One more may be mentioned, namely the length of the digestive tract, which has increased in domesticated carnivores. This applies not only to the dog and the cat, but even to the otherwise little-modified ferret. The length of the gut is connected with the change from a pure flesh diet to one which includes quantities of vegetable matter.

Some general considerations. In spite of the great variety of modifications under domestication, some general rules emerge. New characters are not usually produced, but existing ones are selected and modified, or advantage is taken of sports. Pathological characters are often favoured. The withdrawal of animals from natural selection makes it possible to establish such characters, especially when the breeding communities are small. Under natural conditions, large populations make it difficult for recessive genes to establish themselves, and natural selection eliminates pathological types. Hence domesticated animals which have become feral tend to revert to standard forms resembling their wild ancestors. Many characters of domestication are in reality juvenile characters persisting to the adult stage.

Another important rule is that domestication affects relative growth-rates. Many modifications are due to changes in physiological equilibrium, and in the balance of internal glandular secretion.

Man has mainly followed economic considerations in the selection of types, though little or no deliberate selection was made in the earliest stages of domestication. Geographical races particularly suited to withstand certain environmental conditions would naturally soon be preferred, but standards of beauty must also have appeared early. Early man was wont to adorn himself and to conform to a certain standard of outward appearance, and he would also have taken an interest in the appearance of his stock. Thus bizarre forms of no economic significance may have been favoured.

It is now widely held that the domestication of animals is closely linked with agriculture; this view is in part based on archaeological evidence from very early Neolithic sites. A view previously held, that nomadic herding of animals preceded the agricultural stage, is not supported by available archaeological evidence, yet it almost certainly contains elements of truth since it is certain that pre-agricultural man had begun to domesticate at least one species, the dog. Remains of dogs from the Maglemosian and Natufian are recognizable as those of domesticated specimens. Archaeology owes a debt to dogs for developing domesticated characters so rapidly, for, had they not done so, we should hardly have hesitated to regard the specimens in question as coming from wild wolves and jackals respectively, and might even have constructed a theory that these species were hunted.

The first step toward domestication may actually have occurred in Upper Palaeolithic times. The beginnings are bound to have been slow, and taken after considerable intervals. The suggestion that the reindeer-hunting economy of Magdalenian and related cultures was perhaps supported by some primitive domestication has occasionally been put forward, but has usually been rejected. We should be clear in our minds, however, that the absence of evidence does not mean that the idea is wrong. While hunting was still the dominant practice, it was after all not above the mental level of Upper Palaeolithic man, as we know him from other activities, to keep reindeer as decoy animals. It is in fact a small step from stalking in the disguise of a deer whose horns and skin were worn by the hunter, to approaching the quarry hidden behind some live animals. Thus the question whether Magdalenian man had taken the first step towards domestication by keeping decoy animals must not be regarded as closed. In any event, agriculture is not a prerequisite of domestication as such, and the domestication of certain species may well date far back into pre-Neolithic times. On the other hand, there are species which, for biological reasons, are not likely to have come into the orbit of man before agricultural operations had begun; chief among them are cattle. The Neolithic revolution was a change that placed an enormous economic premium on animal domestication, which therefore became established as a universal practice.

It is a curious fact that out of an enormous number of available kinds of mammal only very few have been domesticated. Others were tried by the Egyptians, and probably similar experiments were made at earlier periods. The lake-dwellers of Switzerland domesticated foxes. But as soon as man adopted the settled Neolithic mode of life, restrictions of movement, space, and climate made it increasingly difficult to try out new species. Moreover, once a sufficient number of species had been domesticated to satisfy the needs of human life, providing him with food and raw material, little was to be gained from the difficult task of reducing additional species to a state of domestication. Economic considerations as a rule, therefore, prevented further experiment.

XII. SEQUENCE OF DOMESTICATION

From the preceding considerations it is possible to deduce an order in which domesticated animals are likely to have appeared. The scavengers were domesticated first. This would have been possible even at a Palaeolithic level. The second group are the nomadic animals, i.e. those which carry out seasonal migrations. For them, a fully fledged Neolithic economy with agriculture would not have been a suitable medium. It is suggested, therefore, that this group was domesticated earlier than the true Neolithic, and at the latest in the Late Mesolithic. These animals enabled man to obtain food by slaughtering in addition to hunting, so that human habitation could be more permanent. If this view be right, the domestication of goat and sheep would have preceded agriculture. The third group includes those animals for the maintenance of which settled life is a prerequisite, at least in the early stages. The main members of this category are cattle. Finally, a fourth category comprises animals which were domesticated primarily as a means of transport, i.e. as beasts of burden, for riding, or for traction. The origin of this group is obscure, though it seems more recent than the third group. Its most curious feature is that its members are not normally slaughtered for food. This suggests that religious inhibitions applied to it that did not exist in the case of other groups (except perhaps the dog). The use of animals for transport was probably developed mainly with cattle. Thus we reach a tentative grouping of some of the early domesticated animals: (i) dog, fox; (ii) reindeer, goat, sheep; (iii) pig (?), cattle; (iv) horse, ass, onager.

This theoretical sequence is to some extent confirmed by the evidence from the Belt cave on the Persian coast of the Caspian Sea. Domestication seems to have begun there in late Mesolithic times, when the cave was occupied by hunters whose chief game consisted of gazelle, wild cattle, sheep, and goat. The proportion of mature to immature specimens suggests that slaughtering of goats was practised already, but, the number of usable specimens being as low as 13, further evidence will be required. In the Early Neolithic level, both goat and sheep are believed to have been domesticated. Again we must await larger numbers of specimens, but it is noteworthy that the same horizon has also yielded domestic fowl.

The later Neolithic, characterized by pottery, weaving, stone axes, and cultivation of cereals, has provided more definite evidence of domestication. Among the goats and sheep the number of immature specimens exceeds that of the mature. Ox and pig may have been domesticated at this time, or a little later. If the tentative view put forward above should be borne out by further evidence, domestication of the sheep and goat would have been practised as early as 6000 B.C. as based on radiocarbon dating; domestication of the goat may well have begun even earlier.

BIBLIOGRAPHY

AMSCHLER, J. W. 'Tierreste der Ausgrabungen von dem "Grossen Königshügel" Shah Tepé, in Nord-Iran.' Rep. sci. Exped. N-W. Prov. China, Publ. 9, pp. 35–149. Thule, Stockholm. 1940.

Idem. "Ur- and Frühgeschichtliche Haustierfunde aus Österreich." *Archaeologia Austriaca*, Heft 3, 1949.

ANTONIUS, O. 'Stammesgeschichte der Haustiere.' Fischer, Jena. 1922.

DUERST, J. U. 'Animal Remains from the Excavations in Anau, and the Horse of Anau in its Relation to the Races of Domestic Horses.' Carnegie Institution Publ. 73, pp. 339–442. Washington. 1908.

HAHN, E. 'Die Haustiere und ihre Beziehungen zur Wirtschaft des Menschen.' Duncker and Humblot, Leipzig. 1896.

HESCHELER, K. and KUHN, E. "Die Tierwelt der prähistorischen Siedelungen der Schweiz", in TSCHUMI, O. 'Urgeschichte der Schweiz', Vol. 1. Huber, Frauenfeld. 1949.

HILZHEIMER, M. 'Natürliche Rassengeschichte der Haustierwelt.' De Gruyter, Berlin. 1926.

Idem. 'Animal Remains from Tell Asmar.' Univ. of Chicago, Orient. Inst.: Stud. ancient orient. Civiliz., no. 20. Chicago. 1941.

KELLER, O. 'Die Antike Tierwelt', Vol. 1. Engelmann, Leipzig. 1909.

RÜTIMEYER, L. 'Die Fauna der Pfahlbauten der Schweiz.' *N. Denkschr. schweiz. Ges. Naturw.*, **19**, 1862.

THÉVENIN, R. 'Origine des animaux domestiques.' Presses Universitaires de France, Paris. 1947.

Panel from an ivory toilet-box, engraved and stained with hunting-scenes. The bull is piebald. From the tomb of Tutankhamen, Thebes. c *1350 B.C.*

14

CULTIVATION OF PLANTS

F. E. ZEUNER

I. ORIGINS OF CULTIVATION

THE cultivation of plants implies intentional sowing or planting for the production of a crop. This is not possible under purely nomadic conditions.[1] On the other hand, by ensuring permanent food-supply, the cultivation of plants makes permanent settlement possible. This interrelationship provided the basis for the Neolithic revolution. Though later than the domestication of animals, that of plants was more fundamental and more revolutionary.

The art of cultivating plants is likely to have been discovered several times. Nuts, grass-seeds, and the pips of fruit, brought in by food-gatherers, must have often germinated near camp-sites. Similarly, edible roots or root-fragments must have frequently been observed to sprout. The great step was when it occurred to man to make use of these things to his advantage.

The idea of cultivation, once conceived, would have been applied to many kinds of plants. The rapid growers must have received special attention at the start. Among them are the cereals, many common vegetables, pulses, and a few roots, most of which will yield a crop within a year. Shrubs and trees are in a very different category, for several years may elapse before the first crop is obtained, and their products must have long continued to be gathered, as many are still. The cultivation of blackberries and raspberries (*Rubus*) is very recent, and even more so is that of the bilberry (*Vaccinium*), which is practised only in North America, but these are still regularly collected from wild plants wherever they occur. The first stages in the cultivation of fruit trees and bushes may well have been due to the accidental scattering near settlements of seeds from gathered fruits. Evidence for prehistoric horticulture is, however, extremely scanty. It appears that the first apples showing evidence of improvement under cultivation came from the Late Neolithic (p 357).

Apart from food, early man was interested in some plants as providing useful raw materials such as wood for building; leaves, bark, and fibre for clothing; as

[1] This does not apply to the secondary nomads of the present day who have tribal areas and carry with them a supply of seed. I have seen nomads in north Africa sowing, after exceptional rainfall, in the hope of obtaining a crop. This practice is evidently widespread, especially where winter rain occurs regularly.

well as resin and pitch, dyestuffs, and material from which useful articles can be made by carving or shaping. It is thus not surprising that industrial plants are found on early prehistoric sites. Flax, for instance, is known from the fourth millennium in Egypt (Neolithic Fayum) and from the beginning of the third millennium B.C. onwards from many parts of the world, such as Mesopotamia (Khafaje), as well as the lake-dwellings of Switzerland and the Danubian I period in the loess lands of central Europe (p 373).

In discussing cultivated plants a necessarily arbitrary economic classification is here adopted for the species in use in pre-classical times. The actual treatment of these species for culinary, industrial, and other purposes is considered elsewhere (ch 11, 16).

FOOD PLANTS[1]

(a) *Green vegetables*: cabbage, lettuce, spinach, nettle, cress, immature beans and peas.
(b) *Roots*: carrot, radish.
(c) *Fruit*: apple, pear, plum, cherry.
(d) *Nuts and oil-seeds*: walnut, linseed, poppy-seed, *Camelina*, rape, olive.
(e) *Pulses*: beans, peas, lentils.
(f) *Cereals*: wheat, barley, rye, oats, millet, rice, weed-seeds.
(g) *Condiments*: mustard, cane sugar.

INDUSTRIAL PLANTS

(h) *Construction materials*: palm-trunks, reeds, etc.
(i) *Vessels*: gourds.
(j) *Fibre-plants*: flax, hemp, cotton.
(k) *Dyestuffs*: madder, saffron, woad, indigo, etc.

II. FOOD PLANTS

(a) *Green vegetables* are intrinsically likely to have been cultivated early, though archaeological evidence for such perishable substances is necessarily unsatisfactory. The records are mainly based on the occasional presence of seeds that would not normally have reached dwelling-places.

The cabbage tribe (*Brassica*) includes many plants of great economic importance. Some are dual-purpose plants, for both leaves and seeds, and sometimes the roots, can be used. Most seem derived from varieties or species of wild

[1] This list contains mainly plants important in the food economy of prehistoric Europe. Others, which entered the European orbit in the classical period and later, will be discussed in the second volume.

cabbage (*Brassica oleracea*), native from the western coasts of Britain and France to the Mediterranean. From somewhere in this area, presumably from the Mediterranean region, cabbage cultivation early penetrated into the remainder of Europe. There are numerous Celtic names for the cabbage group, suggesting establishment by the Celtic period. Early evidence of seeds and impressions, perhaps of the ordinary head-forming cabbage, comes from the Late Bronze Age lake-dwelling of the Alpenquai on Lake Zürich. The Iron Age man of Tollund in Denmark (plate 6 B) had eaten seeds of a kind of *Brassica*. In the medieval period, red cabbage and kohlrabi were also known. Broccoli, cauliflower, and savoy were unknown until the sixteenth century, while Brussels sprouts were first described by de Candolle in 1821. The great variety of cabbage-tops is thus recent. Before the Middle Ages, cultivated cabbages were probably of the kale type, that is, with a stem and separate leaves.

Cultivation of the lettuce (*Lactuca sativa*) is very old. Its wild progenitor (*L. serriola*) occurs in many parts of Europe, north Africa, central Asia, and the Himalayas. It was known to the ancient Egyptians, who regarded it as one of their chief vegetables, and to the Greeks and Romans. Theophrastus (died *c* 287 B.C.) described several varieties. All ancient lettuces belonged to the long-leaved form, and would be classified as cos. Head-forming (cabbage) lettuce is a late, possibly medieval, development. Lettuce cultivation did not spread north of the Alps before the Middle Ages.

Spinach proper (*Spinacia oleracea*) was introduced into Europe by the Arabs who received it from Turkistan, Persia, or Afghanistan, where a wild plant closely resembling it is still collected. Several species of the related goosefoot family were, however, eaten in Europe long before the introduction of true spinach. Of these, *Atriplex hortensis* was the predecessor of spinach in the Middle Ages. Seeds which may be of this species were found in the Late Neolithic lake-dwelling of Sipplingen (Lake Constance). Should this identification be confirmed, *Atriplex* would be a true prehistoric vegetable. It was well known to the Greeks and Romans. Another prehistoric European 'spinach' was the white goosefoot (*Chenopodium album*), a common weed in present-day fields and waste-land. It is first found in the Danubian phase of the Neolithic at Öhringen and Böckingen in western Germany, in Late Neolithic sites in the Federsee Bog and Lake Constance, in Late Bronze Age sites like Buchau (Federsee), and from the Iron Age and Roman times. An interesting Iron Age find of this plant comes from the stomach-contents of Tollund man (Denmark) (p 370).

The nettle (*Urtica dioica* and *U. urens*) has played an important part as a fibre-plant. Nettlecloth was still made in Europe in the first world war. It was used in earlier centuries as a substitute for flax or hemp and probably more extensively than is realized, for it is difficult to identify its fibres under the microscope. It was eaten, but its ubiquity as a weed makes it difficult to prove its prehistoric use.

Cress comprises many cruciferous plants with a peppery taste. The garden cress (*Lepidium sativum*), eaten mainly when immature, has been found both in ancient Egyptian graves and in the Viking funeral boat of Oseberg, near Oslo (A.D. 850). It is quoted by Theophrastus as *cardamom*, while the Romans, according to Pliny, knew it as *nasturtium*. It is possible that it spread to Europe as a weed in linseed fields.

(*b*) *Root vegetables* must have been gathered on a large scale long before the Neolithic. The wild ancestors of modern root vegetables like carrots and swedes were not juicy, but early man would not have despised them for this reason. The wild stock from which modern garden races were developed was certainly known to man at the beginning of the Neolithic.

What little is known about this group from the archaeological point of view is largely due to finds of seeds and to literary sources. There is, for instance, no prehistoric evidence for the use of the beet, though it is certain to have been cultivated at an early date.

The carrot is the hybrid of two wild species, *Daucus carota* and *D. maxima*. Its origin is, therefore, where these overlap, namely in the Mediterranean region. It reached northern Europe early, for its seeds are known from Neolithic layers of the Schussenthal near Ravensburg and the Late Neolithic lake-dwellings at Sipplingen (Lake Constance), Robenhausen (Lake Pfäffikon), and Utoquai (Zürich). It occurs in Late Bronze Age, Celtic, and Roman sites in Switzerland.

The radish of our gardens is probably not derived from the European wild radish (*Raphanus rhaphanistrum*), but is the hybrid of *R. maritimus* and *R. rostratus*, and presumably originated in Greece or Asia Minor. The Greeks and the Romans knew it well, but it existed long before their time in the gardens of Egypt. The workmen erecting the pyramid of Cheops were supplied with radishes in addition to onions (figure 360) and garlic (p 271). Pliny says that radish cultivation brought more money to Egypt than cereal export, but he refers probably to a kind of radish from the seeds of which oil was obtained. In the north, finds of radish are extremely few. In Roman times radishes were exported from the Rhineland to Italy. Pliny relates that they grew as large as children's heads! The small, usually red, radish, much eaten today, is a product of the sixteenth century.

(*c*) *Fruit* plays a large part in the diet of apes and monkeys, and in the food-collecting stage of human economy. Primitive horticulture did not quickly produce characters distinguishing the cultivated fruit from the wild, so that the first phase of the cultivation of fruit remains uncertain.

The apples eaten by the Danubians of Germany (Böckingen near Heilbronn), were of so small a kind that they are assigned to the 'apple of Paradise' (*Malus paradisiaca*), a crab-apple found wild from southern Germany to Siberia. In the Late Neolithic Swiss and German lake-dwellings, apples are often found cut in halves for drying. They exceed the paradise apple in size and agree well with the fruit of the wild crab-apple of temperate Europe (*M. sylvestris* = *M. acerba*). In this Late Neolithic period it begins to show signs of being cultivated. In several lake-dwelling sites, such as Wangen, Bodman, and Mondsee, apples are found that are larger than the crab, and it is agreed that they do not represent a wild type. The Mondsee type, moreover, was found to contain an anthocyanin present in cultivated apples only.

The pear has a prehistory very similar to that of the apple, though its remains are less common. It is derived from the wild *Pyrus communis*, and many botanists believe that this was crossed with related species, especially the Mediterranean *P. amygdaliformis*. But the first cultivated pears of the Late Neolithic of Wangen, Robenhausen, St Blaise (Lake Neuchâtel), Ruhestetten (Hohenzollern), and from the lake-dwellings of Baradello (Lake Como) were not hybrids.

The common cultivated plum has been shown, on genetic grounds, to be a hybrid between the cherry plum (*Prunus cerasifera*), a native of Russia, central Asia, Persia, Caucasus, and the Balkans, and the sloe (*P. spinosa*). This can hardly be the whole story, for many small-fruited plums have the same 32 chromosomes as the sloe, while greengages have only 16 like the cherry plum. Moreover, in temperate Europe, there is another plum, *P. insititia*, regarded by some as a genuine wild species, which is hexaploid (48 chromosomes) like the cultivated plum, and therefore possibly a primitive form of the hybrid of *P. spinosa* and *P. cerasifera*. The damson is considered to be a variety of *P. insititia*. Since the only indubitably wild species of temperate Europe, *P. spinosa*, on the evidence of its chromosome number (32), must have been crossed with a foreign form, plum cultivation was almost certainly introduced into northern Europe from abroad. Prehistoric plum stones are not rare. Many are very small, but in Late Neolithic Sipplingen (Lake Constance) three sizes occur, the largest of which is suggestive of a cultivated form. Other Neolithic sites have yielded tiny plum stones, some perhaps nothing but stones of the cherry plum. It is likely, though not yet proved, that the Danubians brought the cherry plum to central Europe, where it hybridized with the sloe and thus produced, presumably accidentally, the cultivated plum.

Cherries are of two kinds, sweet and sour, descended from two closely related wild species. The wild cherry (*Prunus avium*, 2n = 16 chromosomes) is native to the British Isles, Scandinavia, west and central Europe, south-west Russia, western Asia, and north Africa. The cultivated sweet cherries are derived from it. Though stones referable to it are known from the Mesolithic onwards, and though its stones are common in Swiss lake-dwellings, its cultivation has not been proved before Celtic times. The sour cherry comes from *P. cerasus* (2n = 32 chromosomes). Its origin is uncertain. Some believe that it is truly wild between the Caspian Sea and the Bosphorus, where it may have originated as a natural tetraploid of *P. avium*. The sour cherry is unknown from sites earlier than Celtic or Roman.

(*d*) *Nuts and oil-seeds* are valuable both for food and in industry. Many vegetable oils are used in medicine. Some oil-plants serve yet other purposes, such as flax and cotton which yield fibres, or rape, the roots of which are eaten as swedes and the green parts used as fodder. The larger kinds of nuts especially were collected from early times. The hazel-nut was an important and regular food in many Mesolithic communities. This plant has still hardly emerged from its wild state. In most parts it is regularly collected and eaten but in few deliberately planted.

The walnut (*Juglans regia*) is a forest tree of Greece, Asia Minor, Persia, the Himalayas, and China. It was perhaps indigenous in southern France but in Italy was regarded as a foreigner by Pliny. Walnuts were found at the Mesolithic site of Mas d'Azil in south France, where they were presumably collected from wild trees. Walnuts have also been found in certain Neolithic lake-dwellings of Switzerland and south Germany, such as Wangen in Baden. Since the tree is not indigenous north of the Alps these nuts are evidence either of Neolithic trade or of cultivation of the imported tree. Cultivation on a large scale began in Greece, where Theophrastus distinguished wild and cultivated types, but the extension to many parts of Europe was due to the Romans.

Linseed is the seed of flax (*Linum usitatissimum*) which has played so eminent a part in the development of weaving (ch 16). The ancient Assyrians used linseed for poultices, and its oil for other medical purposes.

The opium poppy (*Papaver somniferum*) is a cultivated plant of considerable antiquity. Its natural home appears to be the Middle East and possibly Greece, but it is not certain whether any existing plants are uninfluenced by cultivation. It was presumably first collected for its oily seeds, which are wholesome and have a pleasant taste and are still much used in baking and cooking in eastern Europe. The narcotic properties of the juice from the unripe capsules may have been discovered early, for the Assyrians had innumerable prescriptions involving it. By Late Neolithic times it was cultivated in Spain (near Granada), Italy (Lagonza), Switzerland (Robenhausen, etc.), and southern Germany (Sipplingen, Federsee, etc.). For the Bronze Age, Austria (Mistelbach), and Savoy (Le Bourget-du-Lac) may be added. There is no evidence that the plant was cultivated in Europe north of these areas.

Camelina, known as 'gold of pleasure', found today as a weed in cornfields, commonly in association with flax, was once widely cultivated for the oil from its seeds, which was esteemed as highly as olive-oil. It grows well on sandy soil which is not otherwise useful. There is reason to believe that its cultivation arose from its occurrence as a weed in flax-fields. Seeds were found in the Danubian site of Aggtelek in western Hungary, but these may belong to a weed-race. Cultivated remains are known from the Late Bronze Age at Erfurt (Thuringia). It also occurs in Iron Age sites in Silesia, Lusatia, and central Germany. The former area of cultivation extended to Scotland and Ireland, and it formed a fair proportion of the stomach contents of the Iron Age body found at Tollund, Denmark (plate 6 B). Today it is almost extinct in cultivation.

The olive-tree (*Olea europaea*) is important to the economy of south Europe. Its origin is obscure. The Mediterranean cultivated olive is accompanied by a form called oleaster, an unproductive plant that is either a wild and possibly ancestral type, or feral. A wild olive with yellow or ferruginous undersides of the leaves (*O. chrysophylla*) occurs south of the Sahara and in Afghanistan, Baluchistan, and western India, and is regarded by some as the ancestor of the cultivated form.

The earliest reliable archaeological evidence for the olive is the importation of its oil into Egypt during Dynasty IV, from Palestine and Syria. There was a sacred olive-tree at Heliopolis in Dynasties V and VI. The olive never played a conspicuous part in Egypt, except in the Fayum, and after 2000 B.C. is rarely mentioned. In the eastern Mediterranean it was much cultivated, apparently first on the Asiatic side. In Greece, legends, such as that of the dove from Phoenicia carrying a branch to the temple of Zeus in Epirus, point to an Asiatic origin. In Crete it is known from the Early Minoan, and its kernels were found at Mycenae and Tiryns in the Late Helladic period. In Sicily, it was found in a cemetery of very late Mycenaean age (*c* 1200 B.C.). The Bible mentions the cultivated olive frequently from Exodus onwards. Several passages refer to the practice of beating the olives from the trees (Exod. XXVII. 20; XXIX. 40; Deut. XXIV. 20). It was, however, either rare or absent in ancient Mesopotamia, where the common oil was sesame.[1]

Rape (*Brassica napus*) is one of the many Cruciferae the seeds of which yield oil. Many are agricultural weeds, and it is likely, therefore, that they were used by man since the earliest agriculture. Several are dual- or multi-purpose plants, their leaves, thickened stems, and roots serving as food. The seeds themselves, e.g. of mustard, can serve as condiment, and have medicinal uses, such as the mustard plaster and many others known to the Assyrians. Evidence for cultivation of Cruciferae is scanty by reason of the perishable nature of the plants and the difficulty of distinguishing seeds of wild from those of cultivated kinds. One of the parental species is evidently the wild cabbage (p 355), the chromosomes of which are ranged in sets with the unit $n = 9$. Another wild species is the turnip (*Brassica rapa*, $n = 10$), with a range largely coincidental with the cabbage, but extending as far east as China. Its seeds were found in the Late Bronze Age lake-dwellings of the Alpenquai (Zürich). *B. napus* ($n = 19$) is believed to be a hybrid of the turnip and the wild cabbage. In addition many polyploids exist among the cultivated races of cabbage, turnip, and rape (or swede).

That the use of cruciferous seeds for oil-production was common in antiquity is further indicated by the cultivation of radishes in ancient Egypt (p 356). The availability of oil-producing Cruciferae safeguarded the oil- and fat-supply. Though many other plants are preferred where they can be grown, such as olive in the Mediterranean, sesame and castor-oil plant in Egypt and Mesopotamia, and linseed which was obtainable wherever flax was grown for linen, it was possible to fall back on the seeds of *Brassica* and related genera. The cultivation of oil-producing plants can make men independent of the relatively small amount of animal fats available even under conditions of domestication. Oils and fats are needed for eating, lighting, anointing, and medicines, as bases for perfumes, and for innumerable industrial products. The discovery of oil-producing plants was thus one of the most important made by Neolithic man.

(*e*) *Pulses* are the seeds of leguminous plants. They have always been important foods, especially in the warmer countries. The importance of pulses rests on such properties as large size of seeds, ease of storage, wide distribution, and high protein content. Moreover, the green pods are often eaten, and some species provide edible tubers. The size of the seeds must have made the pulses important for the collector's food-bag. Wild beans, peas, lentils, vetches, etc. are easily obtained and appear on the list of agricultural plants from early times. Merimde (*c* 4400 B.C.), for instance, possessed the pea. Many of the smaller leguminous

[1] Sesame (*Sesamum indicum*) was cultivated in the Indus valley at Harappa (*c* 2500–1500 B.C.).

plants thrive as weeds in fields, so that some at least may have thus passed into cultivation. In no group of crop-plants is the number of species so great, and in none do the species differ so much among themselves. In this they are the very opposite of the cereals, of which a small number of species have spread to all suitable parts of the world. But easy storage is a feature that pulses have in common with cereals. They can also be converted into flour, and take the place of cereals where the latter are not grown.

The high protein-content of pulses has enabled civilization to persist where animal food is scarce, or for religious or other reasons unobtainable. Whole populations in the East are mainly or wholly vegetarian and obtain their protein largely from pulses, such as the soya bean (*Glycine max*) of China and Japan and the grams of India (*Phaseolus mungo*, the black gram, and *P. aureus*, the golden gram). The vernacular classification of pulses is based merely on the shape of the seeds, the oblong being called beans, the globular peas, and those that are flat and circular lentils. Since many ancient records are not precise it is useful to retain these rough categories.

Of beans, the most popular in present-day Europe are of South American origin. Such are the runner-beans and French beans (*P. vulgaris*), which do not concern us here. There are some Old World beans belonging to this genus, such as the Indian grams.

The bean of ancient Europe was the broad bean (*Vicia faba*). It appears to be a descendant of a north African wild species, *V. pliniana*, known to Pliny (died A.D. 79) but not rediscovered until 1911. This bean had reached Spain in the Neolithic, and thence spread rapidly to the Channel Isles, and Lake Bourget in Savoy. A second species, *V. narbonensis*, is wild in the Mediterranean region, Asia Minor, and Persia, and is found perhaps in the Bronze Age dwellings of Lakes Neuchâtel, Bienne, and Zug. The bulk of the cultivated beans appear to belong to the *V. faba* group.

Apart from the movement into Europe by the western route, *V. faba* arrived with stage I of the Danubian culture from the south-east. At that time, therefore, it was already a part of the early farmer's regular food. By Bronze Age times it was used over much of Europe and western Asia. It occurs in Troy II and in Crete at Knossos and elsewhere, in Dynasty XII in Egypt, and somewhat later in numerous lake-dwellings in Switzerland and in the terramare settlements of Italy (p 317). From then on it has been cultivated very widely, reaching its climax as a staple food in the Middle Ages.

Of peas there are two cultivated kinds, *Pisum sativum*, the garden pea, with white flowers and *P. arvense*, the field pea, with coloured flowers. It is generally held that the garden pea is a mutation of the field pea, which is descended from *P. elatius*, a wild species with a Mediterranean distribution, that penetrated from the Balkans into Hungary and extends wild through Asia Minor to India and Tibet. The wild pea, like the vetches of today, appears to have been a common agricultural weed. It is known from Merimde in Lower Egypt, where a few were found among the grain. Their size suggests that they came from the wild plant, which still occurs in Egypt, though the pea appears never to have played an important part in the ancient Egyptian diet.

The pea was cultivated in Europe by the beginning of the Neolithic. The Danubians brought it to central Europe. In the Late Neolithic it was known in Switzerland and upper Austria also. About the same time Troy II had it. Bronze Age localities widen the area of the pea still further. It occurred in Crete as well as in Spain. In the Hallstatt period a northward extension of the pea is noticeable. In the course of the Iron Age it reached Öster-Götland (south Sweden).

Lentils in their cultivated form (*Lens esculenta*) are derived from *Lens nigricans*, the black lentil of the Mediterranean area, south-east Russia, and countries east of the Himalayas. They appear to have been in cultivation very early, and are still much grown in oriental countries. The earliest record is from Khafaje in southern Iraq (*c* 3000 B.C.). They were well known in Mesopotamia during the Assyrian period. They also occur in literary records, and specimens of the seventh century B.C. were found at Ashur. Troy II had the lentil, as did Minoan Crete. Egypt had adopted it at least by Dynasty XI, and classical writers emphasize that it had been the mainstay of the poorer classes in Egypt since the earliest times. It was brought to Europe by the Danubians, with whom it reached the eastern tributaries of the Rhine. From the Late Neolithic it occurs in several Balkan countries and in south-west Germany. In the lake-dwellings of Switzerland it appears in the Bronze Age. The Romans appear to have cultivated it extensively, and the name of the plant in many European languages is derived from the Latin.

Vetches are of several cultivated species of the genera *Vicia* and *Lathyrus*. Many have today become mere fodder crops, but they played an important part in the past. An interesting plant is the ervil or French lentil (*Vicia ervilia*), a Mediterranean species known from the Middle Kingdom site of Abu Ghalep, near Merimde in Egypt, from Ashur (seventh century B.C.), and from Troy. Many other vetches are occasionally found in prehistoric sites, but their identification is difficult.

(*f*) *Cereals* have become the most important of plants. Their cultivation marks the beginning of the Neolithic, and it—not the domestication of animals—made settled life finally possible. It has repeatedly been claimed that cereals were cultivated earlier than the Neolithic, or at least collected by pre-Neolithic peoples. The latter alternative is certainly true, especially for the Mesolithic, and there is evidence from the Near and Middle East and from India of sickles and grinding-stones, illustrating the stage of gathering of wild grasses. This is very different from the untenable claim that agriculture, including ploughing, began in the early Mesolithic, or that sowing was first practised in the Palaeolithic.

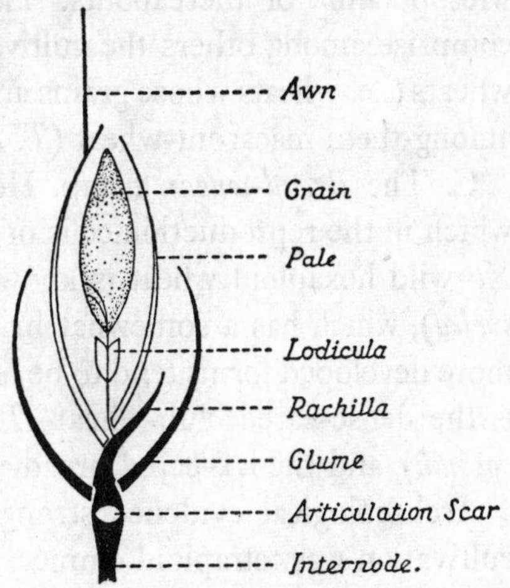

Wheat is the most important extra-tropical cereal. Its history has been studied in the morphological, genetic, and archaeological aspects by many workers. The multiplicity of its forms, and the many names involved, make it difficult to review its history. The outline here provided is greatly simplified (plate 7). Three major groups of wheat are distinguished according to chromosome numbers:

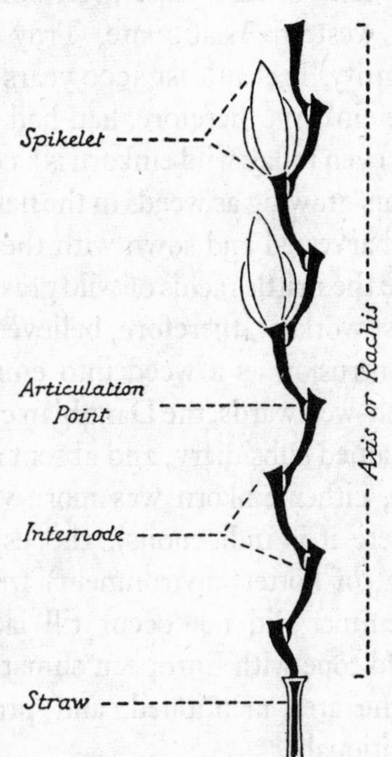

FIGURE 224—*Diagram: head of wheat.*

A. The *Einkorn* group. Diploid (i.e. with 2 sets of 7 chromosomes). Wild einkorn occurs in two geographical races, *Triticum boeoticum* or *aegilopoides* in the Balkans and western Asia Minor, and *T. thaoudar* from Lycia, Phrygia, Pontus, Galatia, Cataonia, Syria, Mesopotamia, and west Persia. The spikelets (figure 224) of the former are usually single-grained and each grain has a single awn (= beard), while in the latter the second flower of the spikelet is commonly fertile, so that it is double-awned and double-grained. The cultivated einkorn is known as *T. monococcum.*

B. The *Emmer* group. Tetraploid (i.e. with 4 sets of 7 chromosomes, which in the reproduction cells of the plants divide into two equal series of 14). Wild emmer, *Triticum dicoccoides*, occurs in Palestine, Jordan, Syria, Mesopotamia, Armenia, and Persia. Archaeological evidence points to an origin in northern Mesopotamia or thereabouts. The cultivated members of the emmer group comprise among others the cultivated emmer (*T. dicoccum*), and several naked wheats (i.e. wheats whose grains are easily detached from the chaff by threshing), among them macaroni-wheat (*T. durum*) and rivet-wheat (*T. turgidum*).

C. The *Bread-wheat* group. Hexaploid (i.e. with 6 sets of 7 chromosomes, which in the reproduction cells of the plants divide into two equal series of 21). No wild hexaploid wheat is known. The basic form of this group is spelt (*T. spelta*), which has a somewhat brittle axis and other primitive characters. The more developed forms tend to be half-awned or awnless and naked. Among them is the dense-eared club-wheat (*T. compactum*), the Indian wheat (*T. sphaerococcum*), and the lax-eared bread-wheat (*T. vulgare* or *T. aestivum*).

Archaeological evidence strongly suggests that the first wheat taken into cultivation was tetraploid emmer, and not as one might expect diploid einkorn. The sites of early date invariably contain far more emmer than einkorn. Only one western Asiatic site, Troy II (2300–2200 B.C.), has provided einkorn in quantity. It is at least 3000 years later than the beginning of emmer cultivation. The einkorn, therefore, had had plenty of time to pass through the weed stage, and even today wild einkorn is a common weed in Anatolian wheat fields. Einkorn plants growing as weeds in the fields have a comparatively tough rachis, and hence are harvested and sown with the crop. But plants growing away from the fields have the brittle rachis of wild grasses, being the ordinary form of the wild einkorn. Most workers, therefore, believe that einkorn became a crop cereal as a result of its intrusion as a weed into emmer fields. Yet, curiously enough, from Troy north-westwards, the Danubian culture carried mainly the einkorn, while emmer remained subsidiary, and absent altogether in many sites of Danubian I. Therefore, either einkorn was more viable in western Asia Minor and the Balkans (where it is indigenous), and especially on the high plateaux where emmer (a plant of hotter environment) would be handicapped, or the successful spread of emmer did not occur till later, when it had been proved that the plant could cope with European climates. In any event einkorn was cultivated as such in the area mentioned, and preferred to emmer for some reason—perhaps traditional.

Even before the time of Troy II, einkorn was known in the Balkans, for it occurs in Danubian I sites in Thessaly and Hungary and it spread mainly over the loess lands of central Europe as far as Belgium. At Dümmer in Oldenburg (Megalithic) it was the main cereal, and it reached Denmark (Jutland Dolmen period) about 2000 B.C. and is found in early, middle, and late passage-graves. It thus appeared with the first Neolithic occupation of that country. Since then its area of cultivation has progressively dwindled. It is now restricted to a few remote areas of mountainous districts.

The einkorn thus played a temporary part in the conquest of the world by the wheats. Perhaps it paved the way into Europe for the polyploid wheats, and could do so on account of its modest climatic requirements. By the time emmer had become adapted to cooler conditions, einkorn had to give way. If this view is correct, however, Troy II must be an exception. It may be that einkorn developed as a cereal on the high plateaux of Anatolia, or came in from elsewhere, for the climate of Troy is too mild to be detrimental to emmer.

The history of the einkorn is remarkable, because one would expect the wheat with the lowest chromosome number to be the ancestor of all cultivated wheats. But since the existence of a true wild emmer is established, the tetraploidy of that wheat is evidently older than its cultivation by man. In Danubian III times (Baden culture, 1800–1700 B.C.) einkorn was still in use, but emmer had become more conspicuous in the fields, and it continued into the Bronze Age with a more restricted distribution than during the Late Neolithic.

Emmer (together with two-row barley, p 367) is the oldest cultivated cereal known at present. It has been found at Jarmo in the foothills of north-eastern Iraq in a Neolithic deposit dated by the radiocarbon method at about 5000 B.C. Some einkorn occurs there also, presumably as a weed. The Jarmo emmer is more primitive than any other cultivated form. Its spikelets are variable, some being large and coarse, others delicate and like those of cultivated emmer. There is little evidence that selection had been carried far.

In the third millennium B.C., emmer and barley were the most widely used cereals. In Mesopotamia, emmer has been found at Arpachiyah (precincts of Nineveh) and Halaf, and in Egypt it occurs in many predynastic sites such as Merimde, at Maadi in Lower Egypt, in the Tasian and Badarian cultures of Upper Egypt, and in the Fayum with its storage-pits (figure 25). It flourished in the Old Empire and was still grown in Greco-Roman times. It then became rare, though in the Coptic translation of the Old Testament the word for emmer was still used.

It has been pointed out (p 364) that emmer spread into Europe with the einkorn and was carried by the Danubians. But at the beginning it was not everywhere conspicuous and is indeed absent from many sites, though it reached Scandinavia and Britain. It was most widely cultivated in the Late Neolithic, from which period a very large number of localities are known covering the whole of Europe.

In the Bronze Age, a slight decline of the emmer is noticeable; it was caused, at least in the British Isles, by an increase in barley.

The hexaploid bread-wheats did not become economically important until the Iron Age. In small quantities, however, a hexaploid wheat occurs from the European Neolithic onwards. Whenever glumes or internodes make determination possible, it was club-wheat, a climatically resistant, short, and dense-eared plant, which found a refuge in some high valleys of the Alps and other mountain ranges. It is known from El-Omari (near Helwan, Egypt, Neolithic, *c* 3500 B.C.) and from Harappa (Indus valley, *c* 2500–1500 B.C.). Apart from chalcolithic finds in Asia Minor, there are several in south-east Europe and as far north-west as Württemberg, all belonging to the Danubian culture. In the Late Neolithic of Switzerland, however, club-wheat became an important cereal. In the Bronze Age it is found, somewhat sporadically, in most parts of Europe, and as far west as Spain. In the Iron Age, when emmer was being abandoned, it gained correspondingly in importance.

The origin of club-wheat is still obscure. Its hexaploidy and sporadic occurrence (originally with einkorn and emmer) would suggest that it was the hybrid of these two species. Experiments have shown that diploid and tetraploid wheats can be crossed, though with difficulty and provided polyploidy occurs.

In a wheat-field with millions of plants belonging to the two parental forms, the chances of hybridization are perhaps less remote than one would expect. While the hybrid origin of hexaploids is not disputed, the chief objections against the cross *monococcum* × *dicoccum* are that the former is genetically somewhat isolated from the other wheats, and that the hexaploids are believed to contain chromosomes derived from goat-face grass (*Aegilops cylindrica* or *Ae. squarrosa*). Archaeological evidence, however, favours this hypothesis rather than one which would derive the hexaploids from a hybridization with *Aegilops*.

Spelt is a hexaploid wheat with primitive characters, morphologically resembling einkorn and emmer, and therefore might be regarded as the earliest hexaploid. Chronologically, however, the club-wheat appears to be older. Spelt first appears in the Bronze Age of Switzerland, where around Lake Zürich it became the main crop. It reached England in the late Bronze Age. Its main area of distribution was centred around the Rhine, where it was abundant in the Iron Age. It was an essentially Germanic, almost an Alamannic, cereal. The phylogenetic interpretation of spelt is difficult. Morphologically and cytologically much is to be said for its origin as a hybrid between a tetraploid wheat (perhaps emmer) and a species of goat-face grass. These are eastern species, and they may have contributed to the club-wheat and the bread-wheat, but not directly to spelt. An alternative is to suppose a cross between emmer and club-wheat, both of which occurred in the Rhine area. A third view postulates mutation of chromosomes of the club-wheat and reappearance of primitive characters.

Bread-wheat is closely related to club-wheat, the chief difference being its longer rachis. Its first established occurrence is in the Hallstatt period (Karhof Cave, Westphalia). This form, which is extremely variable, is now the most widely distributed, and its dispersal must have been very rapid if it originated as late as in the Hallstatt period. Since, however, cytological research suggests that it contains chromosomes derived from *Aegilops*, an eastern origin has to be considered. The difficulty of distinguishing grains of naked wheats makes it impossible to recognize bread-wheat unless portions of ears are found. Moreover, statements of Roman writers about naked wheats may equally apply to tetraploid forms like macaroni- or rivet-wheat. The hypothesis that bread-wheat is a hybrid of spelt with club-wheat is therefore tenable, but it would place its origin in the restricted central European area of the spelt. Being so closely related to club-wheat, however, a slight mutation may have put the bread-wheat on the map, and this could have happened anywhere in the club-wheat area.

Barley occurs in two major types, the two-row (*Hordeum distichum*) and six-row (*H. polystichum*) (plate 7). The latter is divisible into a dense-eared type (*H. hexastichum*), with six grains of two opposed spikelets giving the ear a hexagonal cross-section, and a lax-eared type (*H. tetrastichum*), in which the six grains give the ear a rectangular cross-section (so-called four-row barley). In two-row barley, only the middle grains of the spikelets are fully developed, but the lateral are not altogether lost. All these forms occur either with hulled or with naked grains. For long, only a two-row wild barley was known, *H. spontaneum* of Palestine, Arabia, Asia Minor, Transcaucasia, Persia, and Afghanistan. More recently, a six-row wild barley, *H. agriocrithon*, was described from eastern Tibet.

Barley as a crop is as old as emmer. Both occur together at the earliest known agricultural site, Jarmo, the barley of which shows that *H. spontaneum* is the direct ancestor of the cultivated two-row form. That cultivated two-row barley is of great age had been known previously, for it occurred at Anau in Turkestan and Halaf in Mesopotamia. It also occurs at Matarrah, a site of the Hassuna period, and in the Fayum Neolithic. In the Late Neolithic it had reached Switzerland (Wangen). This barley, therefore, had spread together with the emmer and from the same area of origin. It did not, however, extend eastwards. Although essentially a western cereal, it remained very rare until modern times.

Curiously enough, the bulk of the early barley of the West belongs to

H. polystichum. Four-row barley is known from the prehistoric Fayum, from the Badarian sites of Qau and Mostagedda (near Tasa), from Maadi in Lower Egypt, and from Dynasty III Saqqara, as well as later sites. In the Late Neolithic it is present in the Swiss lake-dwellings, though rare. Six-row barley is evidently the common form of Late Neolithic and Bronze Age Europe. Its earliest occurrence, apparently, is in the Fayum Neolithic (with both hulled and naked forms); other early sites are Maadi and the Dahshur pyramid. Unfortunately, loose grains, so frequently found, rarely allow of precise identification. In Egypt as well as in Europe, hulled and naked barleys occur side by side even in the early sites. Nakedness of the grain appears to have arisen early, and perhaps independently in different areas.

That six-row barley arrived in Europe with the Danubians, and together with the two-row and four-row types, is very likely. But while this route is reasonable for the two-row form, the other types appear to have originated farther east than Iraq, Persia, and Afghanistan. The distribution of the wild six-row barley, *H. agriocrithon*, is not yet fully known, but there is a great centre of evolution of six-row cultivated barleys in China and adjacent countries. Hence it would appear that six-row barley had not yet entered the Middle East region at the time of Jarmo, and that about 1500 years later it was well on its way to conquer the West.

Barley thus comes from two centres, the two-row types from western Asia, the six-row types from eastern Asia. Both reached Europe with the wheats. At Jarmo (*c* 5000 B.C.), six-row barley is still absent, while not much later it had spread at least to Egypt. Does this suggest that six-row barleys were cultivated farther east at the time of Jarmo? Does it suggest that there was an eastern centre of cultivation at least as old as that of the Fertile Crescent of western Asia?

Rye (*Secale cereale*) is the best example of a 'secondary cultivated plant', i.e. of a weed that has become the main crop. Its original form is *S. ancestrale*, found in Lydia, Persia, and Afghanistan. It has a brittle rachis like other wild grasses but, like the cultivated rye, it is an annual.

Vavilov was the first to claim that rye became a cereal by unintentional selection in rough climates. His observation that in western Asia wheat-fields gradually pass into rye-fields as one ascends the hills has since been confirmed many times. Experiments in Brandenburg (which lies outside the wheat belt) have shown that a 1:1 mixed crop of wheat and rye changes into a pure rye crop within three years. It is evident that where climatic conditions become difficult for the wheat, the more resistant rye spreads at its expense. The Turkish peasant believes that wheat changes into rye, and in parts of Turkestan a portion of the wheat-field is reserved for seed production, and is not harvested until the rye in it has been destroyed. Even so, rye invades the field again from the edges within a few years. Thus, as a regular weed in wheat-fields, rye was equipped to become a substitute for wheat when at the end of the Bronze Age the deterioration of the climate pushed south the northern limit of wheat cultivation.

Oats are essentially a European cereal. Two wild species have contributed, *Avena fatua* of eastern Europe, western Asia, and north Africa, a plant adapted to a steppe environment, and the black or bristle-pointed oat (*A. strigosa*), a species found from Armenia through the Mediterranean area to Portugal, Spain, western France, and Britain. The black oat appears to have been taken into cultivation by Neolithic man in western Europe, where he encountered the plant. It did not become popular but has been identified from at least three lake-dwelling sites, namely Montélier on Lake Murten, Petersinsel on Lake Bienne, and Le Bourget on Lake Annecy, Savoy. The other wild oat, *A. fatua*, passed through the weed stage in wheat and barley fields. It entered Europe together with the main crop, where it existed together with many other weeds. In Iron Age finds from Bornholm and Götland in the Baltic, wheat and barley contain up to 2 per cent of *A. fatua*. The wild plant is similarly known from Bronze Age sites in Denmark, the lake-dwellings of Alpenquai and Mörigen, the Sirgenstein cave in Württemberg, the Hallstatt fort of Lengyel in Hungary, and elsewhere. No finds, however, are older than the Bronze Age, which appears to be the period when it reached Europe.

The cultivated derivative of *A. fatua*, *A. sativa*, is essentially an Iron Age product and almost certainly gained ascendancy in the fields owing to the deterioration of the climate after the Bronze Age. It is known from many La Tène sites, extending from north Europe to the eastern Alps and north Italy.

Millets are cereal grasses with more or less round grains belonging to several distinct genera. The African millets (*Sorghum*), the pearl millet (*Pennisetum*), the German millet (*Setaria*, one of the fox-tailed grasses), Deccan-grass (*Echinochloa*), and true millet or panic-grass (*Panicum*) are examples of this group. They are still important in tropical countries where wheat does not thrive. In temperate lands they have been pushed into the background by wheat and barley.

Panic-grass, of which the most important is the common or panic millet (*Panicum miliaceum*), has been cultivated in central Asia and north India since early times, and spread thence to Europe, where it played a not unimportant part in Neolithic economy. The plant has in its migrations preferred loessic soils and, on the whole, the plains. It never crossed the western Asiatic mountains in sufficient quantity to become economically important. Europe received the panic millet presumably by way of the Danubian culture which brought it to the foothills of the Alps, where it occurred in Neolithic lake-dwellings. Its route is indicated by finds at Tripolye in the Ukraine, Ripac in Bosnia, and Aggtelek in western Hungary. It spread to central Germany and westwards to the Savoy. During the Bronze Age it extended its area to the Baltic and to Pomerania. Bronze Age localities are known from the terramare settlements of the Parma area of Italy.

Weed-seeds. Attention must be drawn to the fact that weed-seeds made up a considerable proportion of the cereal grain obtained in prehistoric times, and that several of these are of great food value. Occasionally one or the other became a main crop, as for instance rye, oats, and *Camelina.* As an example of the composition of the porridge of a primitive European, the stomach contents of Tollund Man (Iron Age, Denmark) may be listed: four-row barley, oats, *Setaria pumila* (a millet), *Rumex acetosella* spp (docks), *Polygonum lapathifolium* (pale persicaria), *P. convolvulus* (black bindweed), *Chenopodium album* (goosefoot), *Spergula arvensis* (spurry), *Stellaria media* (chickweed), *Camelina linicola* (gold of pleasure), *Thlaspi arvense* (penny-cress), *Capsella bursa-pastoris* (shepherd's purse), *Erysimum cheiranthoides* (treacle mustard), *Brassica* cf *campestris* (cabbage), linseed, *Viola arvensis* (field pansy), *Galeopsis* sp (hemp-nettle), *Plantago lanceolata* (plantain), and *Sphagnum* moss. Some of these, such as pale persicaria and other 'weeds', were cultivated in the Iron Age. Perhaps, too, there was a system of crop rotation and these mixed seeds were harvested in the year when the fields lay fallow, to serve as food for the poorer population. In any case, men of the past did not object to admixtures of this kind, and possibly regarded them as tastier than pure grain porridge. Moreover, the combination of cereal and oil-seeds makes such meals very nourishing.

Condiments. Of the numerous plants used to give taste to food, two may be mentioned, mustard and sugar.

Of mustard at least three species have been cultivated, black mustard (*Sinapis nigra*), field mustard (*S. arvensis*), and white mustard (*S. alba*). Field mustard is known from several archaeological sites, such as the Dynasty XII grave of Dira Abu'n-Nega near Thebes, Egypt, the Bronze Age lake-dwelling of Mörigen (Lake Bienne), the Mycenaean site of Marmariani (Greece), and various Hallstatt and Iron Age localities north of the Alps. That the plant was cultivated for its seeds is evident at Marmariani, where they were contained in a bag. Apart from serving as a condiment, mustard was cultivated for its oil.

The sugar-cane (*Saccharum officinarum*) is not known in the wild state. It is probable, however, that it originated in India, where it is mentioned in Hindu mythology; moreover, the name *Saccharum* appears to come from the Sanskrit word *karkara*. The European invaders accompanying Alexander the Great (*c* 325 B.C.) were the first to see the sugar-cane. Nearchos, who was on the campaign, described it as a grass which produced honey without the help of bees. Sugar was known to Greek and Roman authors as 'honey which comes from bamboos' (Theophrastus) and as 'Indian salt' (Paulus Egineta, late seventh century A.D.). As it requires tropical conditions to succeed, its westward spread was slow. In ancient Mesopotamia, it appears to have been unknown. When Egypt became linked with the south-east as a result of the Arab conquest, sugar-cane cultivation developed into an important industry in that country.

INDUSTRIAL PLANTS

III. CONSTRUCTIONAL MATERIALS

Wood has been one of the most important raw materials from the Lower Palaeolithic onwards, both for building and for the manufacture of weapons, vessels, and furniture. However, planned cultivation of trees for timber is recent. On the other hand, trees were grown for such products as resins, turpentine, and galls, and their wood is bound to have been used when the tree was spent. Some care of the woods by destroying undesirable plants cannot be ruled out in highly civilized countries like Assyria. In the reign of Sargon, the district of Harran was a centre for the oak, mainly in connexion with the production of galls. Since an Assyrian record lists the number of trees as 49300, these woods must have been sufficiently tended for the tax-collector to be able to count them.

The date-palm (*Phoenix dactylifera*) (figure 344) necessitates cultivation, since the female flowers have to be fertilized. The wood of spent trees was undoubtedly used, and it is known that the logs, sawn in half, served for roofing as early as Dynasty III in Egypt. In Dynasty XX the sycamore-fig (*Ficus sycomorus*) was planted in gardens, and about the same time its wood used in the construction of boats. The wood of other fruit-trees will not have been wasted either. Compared with the need for wood, however, such incidental use of horticultural wood was an exception to the rule that in respect to this raw material man remained a collector, and with devastating results. Whole countries have been deprived of their trees and the desert invited in. Entire civilizations have been destroyed by the resulting soil erosion, especially in western Asia.

Among the constructional materials collected since earliest times, the growth of which has in places been encouraged, are the reeds, especially the Mediterranean giant reed, *Arundo donax*. It is used for huts and shelters in north Africa today, and it was so used in Egypt 5000 years ago (figure 194). The plant itself and its numerous substitutes hardly reached the stage of actual cultivation, though it was and is cared for and controlled to some extent, and occasionally planted. In the tropics, bamboos play a similar role.

The leaves of cultivated palms, date, coconut (*Cocos nucifera*), and wine-palm (*Caryota urens*) are frequently employed for roofing, walling, and mat-making (p 450) in warmer countries, a practice likely to date from prehistoric times.

IV. VESSELS

The bottle-gourd (*Lagenaria siceraria*) has the distinction of being the only plant exclusively cultivated for the production of vessels. A native of the tropics of the Old World, it had recommended itself to man almost certainly at a time when he was still a collector. When pottery had been invented, many clay vessels were made in imitation of the gourd, and several peculiar forms of bottle, which persisted into the classical period, are derived from a gourd prototype. The gourd-shaped vessel was popular in western Asia where *Lagenaria* was known to the Assyrians, and it reached eastern Europe with the Danubian invasion. Its presence in Danubian I in Hungary, where the plant cannot grow, is evidence of an Anatolian provenance of the invading culture. It would be worth making a detailed study of gourd-shaped vessels in early pottery sites, since the original home of the plant may perhaps thus be detected. It is so easily cultivated by sowing in the neighbourhood of habitations that Neolithic non-pottery-making cultures could persist in climatically suitable regions.

Another cultivated fruit that provided vessels to early man is the pomegranate (*Punica granatum*). Its hard shell, cut open and dried, was used in Middle Bronze Age Palestine (*c* 1650 B.C.) as a small box or cup. Specimens of this kind were found in Jericho by Dr Kathleen Kenyon. But in addition to the genuine article, imitations in wood occur (figure 484). This again suggests survival of an early material whose shape was traditional and was therefore copied, though there was no longer any technical reason for continued use of the particular shape.

Many other plants provide containers, but the materials were mostly collected from wild plants. Among these the birch should be mentioned, the bark of which was sewn into vessels by the Neolithic lake-dwellers of Switzerland.

V. FIBRE PLANTS are considered elsewhere (p 447), but something may be said of the cultivation of certain of them.

Flax (*Linum usitatissimum*) was taken into cultivation in early times, primarily for its oil-bearing seed. Early records are from Khafaje in Babylonia (*c* 3000

B.C.) and Alishar (central Anatolia) of about the same time. In Egypt it is known from the Fayum Neolithic onwards, which is probably earlier than Khafaje. The Badarians knew it, and on the tomb paintings of the early dynastic periods are pictures of flax-reaping, of the treatment of the stems to obtain the best fibres (figure 352), and of the gadgets for spinning and weaving (figures 275–6). It is, therefore, reasonable to assume that by 3000 B.C. flax was well established, both in Mesopotamia and in the Nile Valley.

Although several species of wild *Linum* exist in Europe, among them the presumed ancestor of the cultivated form, *L. bienne*, the latter entered northern Europe with the early Danubians. It is known from Danubian I sites of south-east Europe (*c* 3500 B.C.) and the Cortaillod culture of the Swiss lake-dwellings (*c* 2200 B.C.), and appears subsequently in the Danish passage-graves. Its spread to northern Europe is thus clearly indicated. The plant was important in the Late Neolithic of Switzerland, where the transition to a cultivated form (with beaked seeds and closed capsules) is evident.

Hemp (*Cannabis sativa*) is another fibre-plant with oil-seeds. Moreover, it produces a secretion with narcotic properties used in the preparation of hashish. Nevertheless hemp has been adopted less generally than other cultivated plants, perhaps because male and female flowers occur on different plants, the former dying earlier than the latter. The fibre obtained is therefore liable to be unequal in quality. In spite of this, hemp was the first fibre-plant of the Chinese, and before the arrival of cotton was used for clothing almost exclusively. In the fifth century B.C. it is mentioned in Chinese writings and by Herodotus. The Scythians and the Thracians, who had received it from the Dnieper area, wove clothing-materials of hemp, while in Greece the plant was still unknown. In Europe and the Mediterranean world, where beer and wine were available, the narcotic properties of hemp were perhaps less appreciated, especially since flax provided fibres and an oil of at least equal quality. In temperate regions the plant is used only for the manufacture of rope and strong tissues.

The prehistory of hemp is still obscure. In the Orient there is the difficulty that several fibre-plants are called 'hemp'. Hempen fabrics are known in Egypt from Badarian, predynastic, and early dynastic sites, but Lucas suspected that they were of Deccan hemp (*Hibiscus cannabinus*), a member of the hollyhock family.

Cotton. The early history of cotton (*Gossypium* spp) is riddled with problems, the most serious being the presence of cotton species of apparently Old World origin in prehistoric America. Cotton did not enter the Mediterranean world until the fifth century B.C., when it appeared in the Nile valley. Somewhat before this it was known to the Assyrians as a kind of tree-wool. The Babylonian and Greek names point to an Indian origin, and this is confirmed by finds in Mohenjo-Daro (2500–1500 B.C.). Yet the wild relatives of this ancient Indus valley cotton are not to be found among the Indian species, but in a group confined to Africa and Arabia. Was cotton first grown in southern Arabia and thence taken to the Indus valley long before 2500 B.C.? The Mohenjo-Daro cotton was in no way primitive but had all the measurable characteristics of modern Indian cotton. Its evolution from the wild plant must thus have occurred very early.

Dyestuffs are considered elsewhere (ch 11).

VI. CONCLUSION

In surveying the several histories of the cultivated plants, certain points of general interest emerge. At first, cultivation was simply a method of increasing the food-supply. In this, man was eminently successful, though many improvements in the crops were due to natural processes of selection, that is, to luck rather than design. The first attempts to improve production did not aim at improving existing crops, but at a widening of the field of application. Numerous plants were tried out and sooner or later found wanting, so that at the present day man is equipped with a reduced number of crop-plants of high quality.

The effects of cultivation on man's manner of life have been pointed out by Childe (ch 2) and others, so that a few aspects only remain to be stressed. First, it had an immediate effect on animal husbandry, mass-produced fodder becoming available. This, together with settled life, made it possible to domesticate species, such as cattle, beyond the orbit of nomadic man. Furthermore, agriculture necessitated the development of new tools, such as hoes, ploughs, harrows, and the invention of storage devices. Technology thus received a great impetus.

It became possible to take technological advantage of vegetable products that were waste from the nutritional point of view. Linseed provided fibres, grain produced straw. The development of new industries was thus initiated. Man must soon have noticed that it is worth while to cultivate plants primarily for their industrial use, and the industrial plant was thus developed, a group which has increased vastly during the ages.

Finally, agriculture intensified trade, and that not only in vegetable products. For the first time, man was faced with the problem of bulk transport, and the development of the cart and other vehicles can be considered as a result of his adoption of cultivating, instead of collecting, vegetable foods. A simple idea, that of sowing the seeds of some food plants, thus became one of the major landmarks of technological evolution.

BIBLIOGRAPHY

BERTSCH, K. and BERTSCH, F. 'Geschichte unserer Kulturpflanzen.' Wissenschaftl. Verlagsgesellschaft, Stuttgart. 1947.

HELBAEK, H. "Archaeology and Agricultural Botany." *Lond. Univ. Inst. Archaeol. Annu. Rep.*, **9**, 1953.

JESSEN, K. and HELBAEK, H. 'Cereals in Great Britain and Ireland in Prehistoric and Early Times.' *Biol. Skr.* **3**, ii, 1944.

LUCAS, A. 'Ancient Egyptian Materials and Industries' (3rd ed.). Arnold, London. 1948.

NEUWEILER, E. 'Die prähistorischen Pflanzenreste Mitteleuropas.' Exkursionen, botan. u. pflanzengeogr. Studien in der Schweiz, ed. by C. SCHRÖTER, Heft 6. Raustein, Zürich. 1905.

Idem. "Nachträge urgeschichtlicher Pflanzen." *Vjschr. naturf. Ges. Zürich*, **80**, 98, 1935.

PERCIVAL, J. 'The Wheat Plant.' Duckworth, London. 1921.

SCHIEMANN, E. 'Weizen, Roggen, Gerste: Systematik, Geschichte und Verwendung.' Engelmann, Leipzig. 1946. Fischer, Jena. 1948.

Idem. "Entstehung der Kulturpflanzen." *Ergebn. Biol.*, **19**, 409, 1943.

TÄCKHOLM, V. and TÄCKHOLM, G. 'Flora of Egypt I.' *Bull. Fac. Sci. Egypt. Univ.*, **17**, 1941.

THOMPSON, R. CAMPBELL. 'A Dictionary of Assyrian Botany.' British Academy, London. 1949.

VAVILOV, N. I. 'Studies on the Origin of Cultivated Plants.' *Bull. appl. Bot. Pl.-Breed.*, **16**, ii, 1926.

Preparing the soil for agriculture: hoeing in early dynastic Egypt. From the tomb of Ti at Saqqara. c *2400 B.C.*

15

POTTERY

SIR LINDSAY SCOTT

I. THE QUESTION OF ORIGINS

POTTERY had no single origin. Children make mud pies, and from the earliest levels of culture savages have made images of men and animals for magical purposes. The hardening of clay by fire was known at least equally early, since it occurs unintentionally when a patch of clay is chosen for a hearth. Indeed, the mammoth-hunters of Věstonice, in Moravia, during the last Ice Age, even constructed a hearth at which they deliberately hardened clay images of animals [1]. The evidence for the independent development of pottery in America is hardly needed to show the manifold origins of the use of fired clay.

Some light is thrown on origins by sites at which there has been continuous occupation into a period when pottery was introduced. At Jericho, the Middle Neolithic level yields pottery believed to be the earliest made in Palestine, while the Lower Neolithic levels have no pottery but figurines in unbaked clay [2]. At Jarmo, in the Kurdish foothills, possibly the earliest Neolithic hamlet known (p 306), clay-lined basins scooped in the floors had been hardened by fires lit in them. At a later stage in the history of this settlement, pottery-making was developed [3]. These intentionally hardened basins may provide a link between the fortuitous hardening of a clay hearth and the firing of clay vessels.

Basket-making has been suggested as the antecedent of pottery-making. There is no archaeological evidence for this suggestion. The oldest surviving baskets were used to store grain in the Neolithic settlements of Merimde and the Fayum in Egypt, and these settlements already had pottery (p 418). In the pre-ceramic cultures of Peru there are various forms of basketry but no pottery, and in some cultures, as with the Pueblo people of the south-western United States, baskets caulked with clay preceded clay vessels; and there are living savages who make no pottery but make baskets [4]. This suggests no more than that pottery could have originated from basket-making. The reinforcement of clay by wicker-work is a specialized development, of value only where a large fireproof surface is required; for nearly all purposes fired clay does not need such reinforcement. Thus in the Hebrides, in the eighteenth century, a wicker-work barrel daubed on both sides with clay was stood on the hearth and used for drying corn. But in this case a large surface was required which, if made in unreinforced clay, would have been inconveniently heavy [5]. While basket-work affected the development of pottery, it was only one of many influences.

Pottery is indeed of its very nature a substitute material, and has itself no characteristic form. The shapes which we think of as characteristic of pottery are the product, not of clay as a material, but of a particular method of working clay—by spinning on the potter's wheel. Trays of wood or basket-work, leather bags and bottles, cups of hollowed stone or whalebone, natural containers such as gourds (p 372), ostrich eggs, and sections of bamboos, have all been imitated in pottery at low levels of culture. In more advanced societies, pottery frequently has been, and still is, a substitute for metal. The history of pottery is accordingly largely moulded by the histories of other materials.

The main factors controlling the adoption of pottery have been economic, and the strange and insufficiently recognized vicissitudes to which it has been subject reflect the unequal advantages which it has offered at different times and places. It is a commonplace of the history of industry that exploitation of a new material or process follows, not the first discovery of it, but the first occasion on which it offers a sufficient economic advantage to attract capital and to overcome the inertia of custom. Because of its fragility, pottery could offer no economic advantage to pure nomads. In our own time, gipsies and soldiers use vessels of metal. It was when settled life began that the economy of raw materials and labour offered by pottery enabled it to oust more permanent materials.

Since the cost of pottery is immensely reduced by capital equipment and production in quantity, its development followed the growth of urban civilization. Pottery did not, however, originate in such civilizations, for it occurs in the Neolithic settlements, such as those of the Fayum, which preceded any urban culture in Egypt.[1] Nevertheless, its large-scale development awaited the introduction of town life in the early centres of civilization. In remoter areas, such as north-west Europe, its introduction was seldom, if ever, an independent local development, but was the work of settlers and colonists influenced directly or indirectly by the urban centres.

The range of fluctuation in the use of pottery is obscured by the reliance that archaeologists put upon it as an index of a culture. Periods in which pottery fails tend correspondingly to disappear from the archaeological record. For example, a product of the settlements, of ultimate Mediterranean origin, in Britain in the second millennium B.C. was an ample and excellent pottery. During the

[1] Sir Lindsay Scott died before the recent excavations at Jericho. (Editorial note.)

following millennium, this was reduced, over a large part of the island, to a successively degenerating series of cinerary urns. This situation might reflect a decline in settled agriculture, and a larger reliance on cattle-breeding, inevitably partly nomadic: such an economy as Caesar attributed to the interior of the island in the first century B.C. [6]. However that may be, the decline in the use of pottery is a fact—and a fact to be explained. A similar problem is posed by the virtual absence of pottery from the forts and crannogs of Ireland in the Dark Ages. In Britain, the revival of the use of pottery occurred in the areas settled by Gaulish tribes which had been influenced by Roman culture, and above all in the area urbanized by the Roman occupation.

If, however, a reversion to less settled rural conditions, and *a fortiori* a collapse of town life, is one cause of the disappearance of pottery, it is not the only possible cause. The introduction of wood-turning, and the development on a commercial scale of the metal industry, may provide serious rivals to pottery in respect of both efficiency and cost. The effect of these developments in Britain in the immediately pre-Roman period had been offset by the simultaneous development, under indirect and then direct Roman influence, of an efficient pottery industry using the wheel and firing its production in kilns. Upon the decline of that industry, which did not occur until the seventeenth century, wood, iron, and pewter had the opportunity to oust pottery from a large field of culinary and table uses. Some of these uses it has never recovered.

The decline of pottery may also be caused by migration to an area where the raw materials are not available. This happened to the Polynesians, who must have had pottery in their Asiatic home-lands. Their acceptance of this deprivation, which many of the islands could have remedied—though at high cost—by import, argues that pottery is not the essential of life which we are apt to think it, especially in an environment where natural vessels are abundant.

Thus the history of pottery is anything but one of steady expansion and progress. Frequent set-backs have been accentuated by a lack of development in the industry itself, for the techniques used up to recent times had in the main survived from remote antiquity. The one radical invention before the modern industrial period was the shaping of a wide range of pots by throwing, that is, by spinning on a rapidly rotating wheel, the hands guiding the shaping instead of directly effecting it. This method, which Childe believes to have been introduced in Mesopotamia in the Uruk period before 3000 B.C. (p 199), achieved a large saving in the time spent in making a pot. Only in the last century was it displaced by liquid moulding—a technique known (though little used) in antiquity—and the dust-pressing, plastic-pressing, extrusion, and so on of the present industry. For the rest, the many improvements introduced in the preparation of the clay, and in the temperature reached by enclosed firing in kilns, are hardly fundamental. Recent times apart, the pottery industry therefore exhibits few technical advances by comparison with rival industries. Its periods of large expansion have mainly followed the establishment of urban communities, with consequent economies in marketing and wider opportunities for large-scale production.

II. THE BASIC PROCESSES

The clays that most commonly occur in nature are plastic if mixed with an appropriate quantity of water. They can then be modelled into a great variety of shapes, which they will retain during subsequent drying in the air. When this drying has reached a stage at which the clay is 'leather-hard' and the water content reduced to some 8–15 per cent., the vessel can be further worked by scraping, cutting, and turning. After this stage, it is further dried in the air to a 'white-hard' state, in which the uncombined water content is reduced to some 3 per cent. The clay is then fired. At a temperature varying from 450° C upward, the clay substance decomposes with the loss of its chemically combined water, becomes incapable of further chemical combination with water, and is then similar to moderately hard stone. If the firing is continued to higher temperatures, the clay substance, according to its composition, will become denser and less porous and will ultimately vitrify and fuse. These latter stages were rarely reached in early pottery, the range of firing-temperatures seldom exceeding 1000° C and frequently being much less.

Clay, the raw material of pottery, is formed by the decomposition of other rock-forming minerals, notably the feldspars. This very important group of minerals composes the larger part of granite and gneiss, rocks which form three-fourths of the known surface of the earth. The resulting clay minerals are hydrated aluminium silicates with subordinate amounts of alkalis, alkaline earths, iron oxides, etc. Chemical decay of feldspar is due to the action of carbon dioxide and water on rock surfaces from which air is excluded, particularly in marshes or bogs. Of the primary clays thus formed, the principal are the kaolins, or china-clays, of which extensive deposits occur in Devon and Cornwall, in Brittany, the Pyrenees, and near Limoges, in Saxony, Czechoslovakia, and the Ukraine, and, outside Europe, in China and the southern United States.

The vast majority of clays are however, secondary clays, that is, they have been transported by water, wind, or ice from their primary source and have acquired additional impurities in the process. Of these secondary clays, much the commonest and most important is red clay, which, suitably fired, becomes a rich red owing to contained iron compounds. The secondary clays are found, broadly speaking, over all the Earth's surface, save in sandy deserts and coral islands. They form, for example, the flat lands of north Europe and the muds of the Mississippi valley. In upland country, they occur in lakes and rivers. The local distribution of good and easily worked clays, a principal determinant of the siting of pottery industries, is naturally sporadic.

Secondary clays, because of the shape and minute size of their crystals, which are very small flat plates, become exceptionally plastic when mixed with water. When the wet clay is air-dried, the water evaporates and the crystals come into direct contact with one another. This evaporation causes contraction, the variable extent of which constitutes a practical difficulty, particularly when parts of a pot have to be joined together. A further smaller contraction occurs in firing, when the water chemically combined with the clay is driven off.

The primary clays have very little plasticity, and when kaolin is used in pottery-making the addition of a more plastic secondary clay (ball clay) is necessary to make it workable. Secondary clays as found in nature, and in particular red clay, are usually adequately plastic owing to their smaller particle-size, though their plasticity may be improved by weathering, that is, by exposing the material to sun, air, and rain for mechanical disintegration. Ice-borne boulder-clays, however, are not very plastic, and are therefore usually less suitable for pottery-making. Natural red clay is often too plastic for working—too sticky or, in technical language, too rich—and has to be tempered with non-plastic materials, of which those most commonly used are ground and finely divided quartz, flint, sand, limestone, shell, or old sherds ('grog'), and even chopped grass and other vegetable matter. These additions to the natural clay have a varying, but generally beneficial, effect in improving its porosity, and therefore reduce its tendency to warp and crack in drying and subsequent firing. The mixing of water with the clay, and any tempering used, has at many periods been effectively done by treading with the wet feet, a practice at least as old as a Dynasty XII tomb (figure 232); this secures both the even distribution of water and the removal of air bubbles.

The preparation of the clay is a principal part of the potter's art. It is therefore unfortunate that we know so little of the processes actually employed in early times. The type of tempering used has been fairly widely noted, but it has very rarely been ascertained what the source of the tempering was, though this is frequently determinable by mineral analysis and may be of major importance as evidence of trade in pottery. Nor have the sherds from excavations been systematically examined by a practical potter, though an exception is provided by the excavation of Tell Beit Mirsim, in Palestine. The report on this work, published in 1943, contained the first detailed technical analysis of the potting-methods used on any ancient site [7]. We can thus do no more than surmise that the preparation of the clay was commonly achieved by washing and settling in a chain of vats dug on a slope. This was the method employed in medieval times, when pits some 5 ft square and 3 ft deep are known to have been used. The lowest vat would contain the finest clay, which might be further refined by straining through a cloth. We know, however, that some modern primitive potters, such as those of Sindh, who still retain much of the technique used soon after 3000 B.C. at Mohenjo-Daro, are content merely to beat the clay dry, and to strain it through a cane sieve [8]. Experience shows that a useful pottery can be made by taking a suitable dry clay, picking out the coarser rock fragments, and kneading it with water. This was the normal practice of Hebridean potters until a century ago [9]. Since the perennial merit of pottery is not its refinement of texture or of form, but its cheap efficiency, it is likely that such elementary methods of preparation have been used at all periods, outside the factories producing in quantity for urban markets.

Drying and Burnishing. When the prepared clay has been modelled it is air-dried. This demands that, to avoid cracking, drying shall proceed at a steady temperature, and uniformly throughout the pot. When the clay has reached the leather-hard stage, burnishing is commonly undertaken to reduce porosity. This process consists in the application of mechanical friction to the surface with the aid of a smooth pebble or other hard implement, to close the surface pores of the clay. Since the efficiency of burnishing depends on the fineness of the clay burnished, it is economical to give the pot a finer surface by dipping it in, or painting it with, a slip of the finest portion of the clays used in building it. The slip is the product of the final washing of the clay, the coarser material having been used for the body of the pot. Slips of a separate clay can be used, but only if that clay is adjusted in composition (e.g. by the addition of non-plastic materials) so that its contraction in drying is the same as that of the clay body of the pot, otherwise the slip will peel off.

The elimination of porosity by burnishing is never complete, but it commonly sufficed to enable the pot to hold liquids, since the solids in milk, oil, and the like assist in filling up the tiny pores. The Hebridean potters who made craggans (rough domestic earthenware vessels) till late in the nineteenth century cured their porosity, even without burnishing, by pouring milk into them while still hot, and doubtless such elementary expedients have been adopted in all ages.

Firing. The chemical changes effected in clay by firing are of extreme complexity, and depend on the composition of the clay, the temperature of firing, the rate at which that temperature is achieved, and the gases in contact with the pot at all stages in the firing. Firing can be effected in kilns or in open fires, and with all sorts of fuel. Kiln-firing allows of a higher temperature and also of better control of the atmosphere around the pots. The quantity of fuel used, normally billets of wood, is very great and, even with kilns using coal, its weight may many times exceed that of the pottery fired. Open firing is quite effective up to about 750° or 800° C, though the heating of the different pots is necessarily uneven and many are spoiled. The fuel for open firing is commonly such as will burn rapidly, e.g. brushwood, supplemented by grass and dung thrown on the pile of pots to conserve the heat as the flames die down.

As the fuel for firing accounts for much of the cost of potting, and as good wood for burning frequently became more or less inaccessible, resort to low quality fuels was often necessary. Thus in Orkney, in the second millennium B.C., wood was so scarce as to compel the use of peat for firing, as has been inferred from the softness of the wares. Even today, in the hill country between Assam and Tibet, potters sell their product unfired, having no fuel and expecting the purchasers to fire the pots in the first patch of forest they reach on their journey home. Thus a governing consideration in the siting of a pottery must have been proximity or easy access to a good fuel-supply. A Hebridean pottery which made a ware similar to the Orkney ware, but kiln-fired with wood, was on the edge of a lake fringed with birch and willow.

The minimum firing-temperature of a pot is such as will drive off the combined water in the clay. This varies from 450° to 700° C. At this temperature, the clay particles are still unfused, but useful pots result and, considering the cost in fuel of firing to higher temperatures, it is not surprising that great numbers of prehistoric pots appear not to have been fired further. If firing is continued, a further shrinkage of the clay occurs, owing to change in crystal structure, with increase in mechanical strength and decrease in porosity. Ultimately, the clay substance becomes quite soft, the pores are completely filled, and the body becomes vitrified (p 379), but this stage could not be reached by the pottery industry at the cultural levels treated in this volume.

In general, we do not know the firing-temperature of ancient pottery, though in isolated cases it has been inferred from some special circumstance. Thus an Iron Age sherd from Leicestershire was shown to have been fired to less than 500° C from the fact that an included fragment of oyster shell remained incompletely calcined [10]. The only extensive series of tests of firing-temperature known to the writer is that made on the ware from Tell Beit Mirsim (p 381). This ware covers a long period of the late second and early first millennium, the items most fully studied technically being those of the end of the period in the seventh century B.C. The tests show that no ware was fired to 1030° C, and little to 970°. Most of the pottery was probably fired to less than 890°, and a considerable proportion to less than 800°. An imported Mycenaean stirrup-vase had, however, been fired to 1030° and, though this figure was exceptional, the imported ware was generally fired to a higher temperature than the native. This may mean no more than that common wares were not imported, and the standard of native potting was judged by the excavation to fall very little short of the best Greek standard [11].

It is impracticable to deal here with the many changes that occur during firing to the very varied substances mingled with the pure clay. It may be noted, however, that the organic matter in clays, which tends to have a brown to black colour before firing, should be fully burnt out before baking is completed; in the event this frequently did not happen, and the core of the ware remains grey or black, either because the surfaces became fused before the carbon had been fully oxidized, or because too little oxygen was available. Further, iron compounds, when present in sufficient quantity, may produce a red colour in the pot if fired to a high temperature with ample free oxygen, and a grey to black if fired with a deficiency of oxygen. The former effect is well seen when the pot was covered with a red ochre slip containing a high percentage of ferric oxide, but generally there are too many factors determining colour to allow of conclusions being drawn without technical examination. Thus black ware may result from the reduction of ferric oxide in firing; but it may also be produced by soaking the pot in oil and heating it to a low temperature to carbonize the oil; or by depositing particles of carbon throughout the fabric by throwing vegetable matter into the kiln at the end of the firing; or by placing the pot, while still hot from the kiln, in vegetable matter such as chaff [12].

In the painting of pots after firing, either organic or inorganic colours could be used. For painting before firing organic colours are useless, since they would be burnt out, but such natural earths as the siennas, umbers, and ochres could be used. By mixtures of these, with or without clay, and by treatment in firing, a considerable colour-range can be achieved. The great difficulty must have been to forecast closely the tints assumed by the pigments on firing. Considerable skill was also required to secure uniform absorption in applying the paint on the porous clay surface. The brush can never be lifted when working, and a defective line cannot be retouched, since this produces a blot where the correction is made.

Except in twice-fired pottery, painting is done when the pot is dried white-hard, before firing [13].

III. THE BUILDING OF POTTERY

The instinctive, and presumptively earliest, method of shaping a pot is to hollow a ball of clay by pressing in the thumbs and then thinning the walls between thumb and finger in a spiral movement. A thick bowl some three inches across and high results, and this can be thinned, and thus enlarged, by starting again at the bottom and repeating the pressure. The pressure must be evenly exerted to achieve a uniform thickness of wall and a smooth surface. In simple shapes and small sizes, pots of high technical merit can be made by this method, exemplified in prehistoric times by the earliest pottery of Britain and north-west Europe, and in recent centuries by the *Raku* tea bowls of Japan (figure 225) [14]. The former ware, Western Neolithic, was spread from Languedoc westward to Spain, Brittany, and Britain, and northward up the Rhône to the Swiss lakes; it is to its earlier stage that the simple bowls mainly belong (plate 8 C, D).

FIGURE 225—Raku *tea bowl. Japan. Diameter* c *10 cm.*

FIGURE 226—*Uganda potter building up a pot with strips of clay. A new length has just been attached.*

Another method of shaping a pot, familiar from American Indian practice, is by coiling. The clay is rolled into the form of a sausage, $\frac{1}{4}$ to 2 inches thick, which is built into the pot spirally, each coil being pressed and smeared into that below. Normally the pot is stood on an old sherd or mat and rotated, the potter standing still, though, if the pot is large, he may walk round it backwards with his rope of clay coiled on his arm. When one rope of clay is used up, another is joined to its end, and the work proceeds. If the pot is tall, it may be bound with string to support its weight as it grows. It seems more likely that early potters employed what is termed the strip method, in which each circuit of the pot is formed of a separate length of clay (figure 226) [14]. It is of course difficult to be sure from sherds whether the strip or the coil method has been employed, but examples of one or other method can be drawn from the whole range of British prehistoric pottery, and from the Neolithic wares of northern Eurasia from the North Sea to the Behring Straits. Various methods were used of jointing the successive coils so as to secure a firm joint (figure 227).

These methods of shaping leave the surface more or less rough, and various ways of smoothing are adopted [15]. Modern Chinese and Japanese potters, who build large jars by hand, follow a practice going back to prehistoric times in China, and beat the surface smooth with a wooden bat, supporting the vessel inside with another piece of wood held in the left hand. The same method is used by modern potters in Sindh, who still follow the practices of the Indus civilization of the third millennium B.C. (figure 228). Convex disks so used have survived from Harappa, and also from Baluchistan sites [16]. The final smoothing might be done with wet cloths, a method adopted in Britain, as shown by striations resulting from its careless use. When a pot is dried to, or near, the leather-hard stage, it can be further shaped by scraping with a sherd or knife; sherds survive from a potter's workshop of the late Bronze Age at Lachish in Palestine (figure 235) [17].

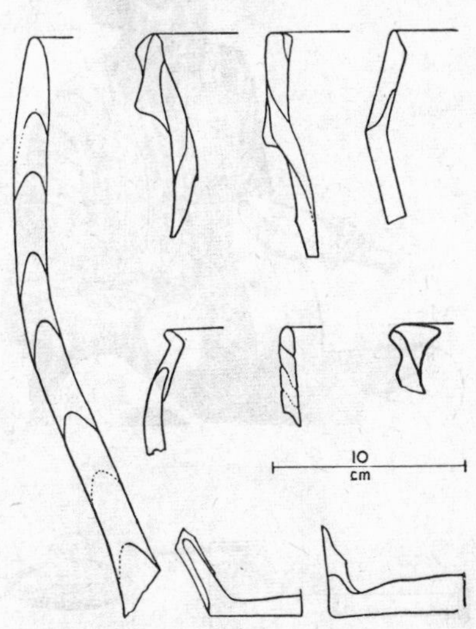

FIGURE 227—*Building-stages: Variations on the jointing of successive coils or strips, from prehistoric Britain.*

The two methods of shaping a pot are sometimes combined. Thus Western Neolithic storage jars, too large to be modelled from a lump of clay, might have their round bases so modelled while their walls were built up from the base in coils or strips [18]. The base of the pot may also be made by a third method. If the base is rounded it is shaped by pressing the clay into a mould of the desired shape; commonly an old sherd was used and was absorbent enough to take up water from the wet clay, which thus contracted and came away cleanly from the mould. Great thinness could be attained in this way, and the finest bowls in Western Neolithic ware may have bases no more than one-tenth of an inch thick. (plate 8 A). If, as in the great bulk of British prehistoric pottery, the base is flat, it may be formed by pressing the clay into a flat disk on a stone slab. The joint between this disk and the built upper part is commonly effected by pressing up the edge with the fingers. The result is that the centre of the base is thicker than the periphery. Alternatively, the body of the pot may be pressed inward on the disk, giving the vessel a splayed foot. In some fine jars of the Iron Age ware which extended in western Britain from the Somerset marshes to the Orkneys, neither of these effects is seen, the base being a uniformly thin disk joining, both internally and externally, in a smooth curve into the equally thin lower wall of the pot.

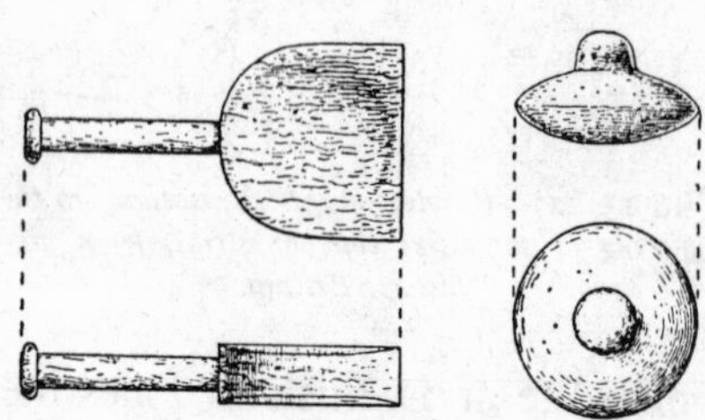

FIGURE 228—*Sindh potter smoothing a pot. His tools: beater and convex disk.*

Moulding is capable of great elaboration, both in the shaping of complete vases and in the impressing on them of patterns cut in the surface of the mould, as well as in the forming of vases imitating animal forms, such as the bull's head *rhyton* (figure 229). In the main these developments, and particularly the use of moulding for mass-production, lie beyond the limit of this volume. In contrast to modern practice, which uses moulds of plaster, the moulds used by Greek potters were of fired clay, which, as has been said, is absorbent enough to allow the clay to shrink away from the mould in drying, while large wine jars might be moulded on a wooden core. The standard modern practice of liquid moulding, or slip casting, does not appear to have been identified in Greek work [19], but a few examples have been observed in Palestinian Iron Age pottery [20].

At all but the earliest stages of pottery technique, pots have been made in two or more parts, luted together with slip after a measure of drying. The need for this procedure arises with large pots from their tendency to sag under their own weight before they are dried to sufficient rigidity, and with narrow-necked pots since the worker cannot get his arm inside. The difficulty of making a pot in two or more rings is not merely that considerable accuracy is needed to secure a fit, but that allowance has to be made for the shrinkage of each part as it dries. The risk of a ridge at the joint is mitigated if the walls of the two parts of the pot are designed to join at an angle. Such carinations or keels are characteristic of early pots in the west which are known to have the neck made separately from the body (plate 8 A, D). Throughout the west, carinated bowls occur in the second stage of Western Neolithic ware. The same development is seen at Jericho in the Late Neolithic ware which succeeded what is believed to be the earliest pottery made in Palestine [21]. In the bow-rim jars from Jericho, and in Western Neolithic bowls made in the north of England and of Ireland, the junction between neck and body is exaggerated into a deliberate overlap, doubtless concealing errors in fit (figure 230).

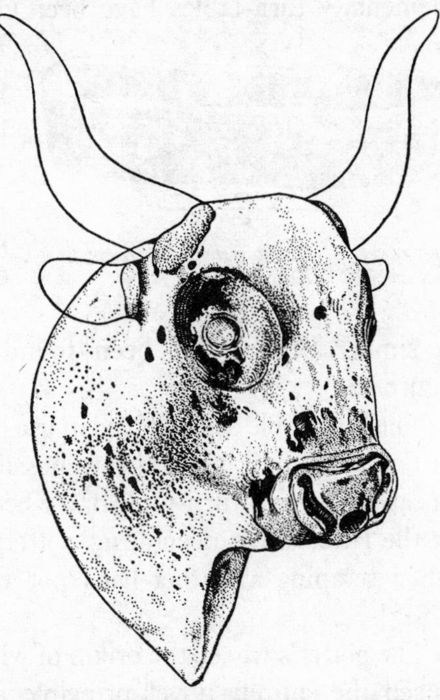

FIGURE 229—*Bull* rhyton (*libation-vase in the form of an animal's head) in grey clay, from Gournia, Crete. Covered with a shining white slip in imitation of silver. Horns and ears missing.* c *1500 B.C. Scale approx. 1/3.*

It will be noted that, whether a pot is modelled from a lump of clay or built up, it is necessary to rotate the vessel as it is shaped. This method of manufacture may explain the very curious fact that, even before the advent of the wheel, pots are with few exceptions circular in section. Nothing in the nature of the material requires this shape. True, sharp angles involve some risk of cracking, but that difficulty was overcome very early, when pots were given flat bases. It may be significant that, to the extent that pots not of circular section occur in prehistoric pottery, they are mostly of the earliest stages of development, when the convention of making vessels round may be supposed to have been less firmly established. Examples from the earliest cultures of Egypt are found in rectangular dishes from Tasa and the Fayum, and oval bowls from Badari (figure 272); from the Neolithic wares of Crete in the rectangular troughs divided into partitions discovered below Knossos (figure 231); and from the earliest Danubian pottery in square-mouthed vessels which extended from Transylvania to the Rhine and into north Italy.

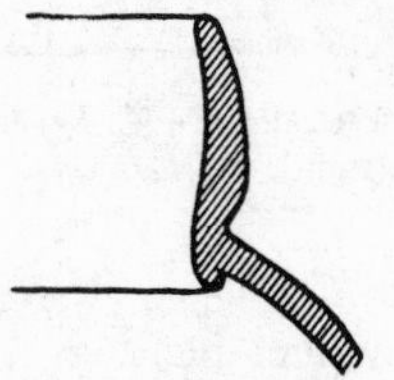

FIGURE 230—*Diagram of neck and upper part of the body of a bow-rim jar. Jericho. Late Neolithic.*

The rotary motion required in pottery-making is facilitated if the clay is placed on a flat pebble or sherd. To judge by modern primitive potters, such elementary turn-tables have been in use from the earliest stages of the craft. Efficiency is increased at no great expense of mechanical skill if the turn-table is pivoted, for example with a wooden pin, working in a socket of wood or stone. A stone pivot from the Late Bronze Age potter's workshop at Lachish may be part of such a turn-table, though it is possible that it belonged rather to a potter's wheel. A similar bearing has been found at Jericho [22]. (Cf above, p 200 and figure 124).

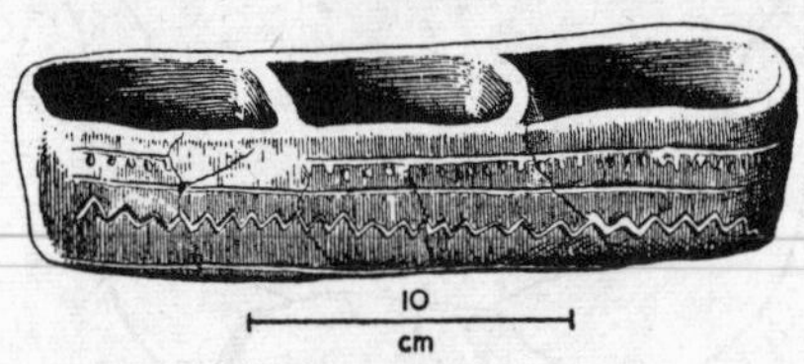

FIGURE 231—*Neolithic rectangular trough from Knossos, Crete.*

The turn-table has survived in use into our own time, as among peasant potters in Brittany, but it is not always possible to decide whether a machine employed in early times is a turn-table or a wheel (figure 232). The former is as serviceable as the latter when decorating pottery, and it can also be used as a slow lathe when scraping a leather-hard pot with a knife or sherd to shape or smooth it [23].

The potter's wheel, the origin of which has been discussed (pp 195-204), introduced the entirely novel principle of 'throwing' pottery, i.e. of shaping the plastic clay by spinning, the energy being derived from the rapidly rotating

FIGURE 232—*An Egyptian pottery in the Middle Kingdom. Pots are shaped by hand* (left), *and on a turntable or wheel* (right). *Workers knead clay with hands or feet. The narrow vertical kiln is characteristic of the period. From a tomb at Beni Hasan.* c *1900* B.C.

wheel-head and not from the potter's fingers. Essentially, the wheel consists of a vertical rotating spindle; a head, commonly a small disk, on which the clay is placed; and a heavy fly-wheel, which stores momentum and allows the spindle to rotate uniformly. The fly-wheel may be set at the head of the spindle and thus itself serve as a wheel-head, but this greatly limits its size if the potter is to get adequately over his work. The potter, or an assistant, spins the wheel with his hand, or with a pole which he fits into notches in it, or by kicking it with his foot; or it may be turned by the assistant with a band, in which case the fly-wheel is not essential (figures 233–4).

The wheel presents mechanical problems not easily solved without the resources of a fairly advanced metallurgy. On the one hand, the spindle must run in bearings which are true and tight enough to prevent rocking. On the other hand, it must support a heavy fly-wheel and yet run with so little friction as to remain in rotation long enough to throw a small pot. The former condition may be satisfied by a rigid frame and bearings of hardwood; the latter has been satisfied in recent times by a cup-bearing of porcelain in China and Japan (figure 120) and of flint in India [24]. Though none such have been found, it is difficult to believe that bearings of equivalent hardness were not used in the best potteries in antiquity. We must reconcile ourselves to the fact that, in the absence of archaeological finds, we can learn little of the construction and operation of ancient potters' wheels. We can only judge the economy resulting from the rapid throwing of vessels on the wheel from the elaboration of shapes in the pottery, and from the quantity produced. The methods of throwing in antiquity were, so far as we can judge from the product, the same as those now used. The thrown pot,

FIGURE 233—*A peasant potter's wheel in Brittany.*

FIGURE 234—*New Kingdom Egyptian pottery. The wheel is moved by foot. One man is kneading clay with his feet. The kiln is of the same type as in figure 243. From a tomb at Thebes. c 1450 B.C.*

like the hand-built one, was relatively rough, and required scraping and smoothing. This is particularly the case at the lower part of the wall, which throwing tends to leave too thick, and at the base, where the pot is cut away from the clay on the wheel-head with a string.

For the further shaping of a thrown pot the wheel can be used as a lathe in the same way as the turn-table, and with the additional advantage that, even without an assistant, the potter has both hands free. By lathe-turning, it is possible to cut grooves, under-cuttings, and mouldings at the lip and foot of the vase with cleanness and precision; lids may be made to fit neatly on their ledges; and parts left too thick by the thrower can be pared away. The extent to which lathe-turning was used in antiquity has seldom been expertly studied, but it is known that the method was adopted in Palestine, and with utmost perfection, in Middle Bronze Age wares [25]. Turning was the regular practice with the finer Greek wares, though it was not commonly used before the sixth century B.C. [26]. The metal lathe-tools used for fine work are known to us only from a site at Arezzo. Sherds, such as have already been mentioned as in use for scraping on a turn-table, were doubtless used equally with the wheel.

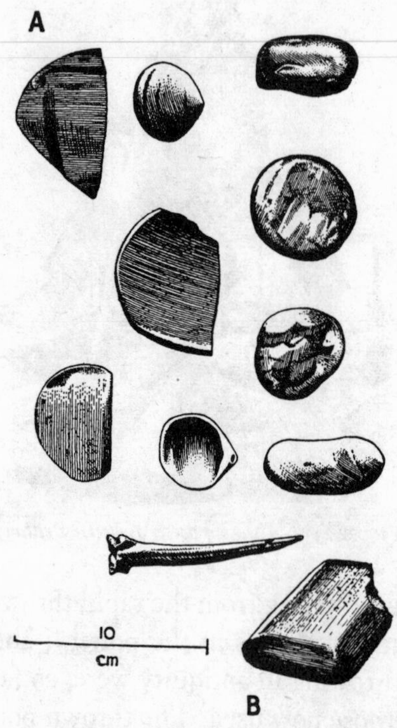

FIGURE 235—(A) *Shells and pebbles for burnishing, sherds for smoothing on the wheel, and a bone point, from Tell ed-Duweir, Palestine. Late Bronze Age.* (B) *Burnisher from Eilean an Tighe, North Uist. Second millennium B.C.*

Tools for the smoothing of pottery have ranged from the bunch of grass with which the outside of the earliest Palestinian pottery was wiped [27] to the sand-paper and sponges now employed to give the last touch to fine ware. The tools have seldom survived or been recognized, but we have from the Hebridean pottery workshop described below a collection of pumice rubbed into various shapes in smoothing Western Neolithic pottery. The same site produces a fine burnisher (figure 235 B), while burnishers of pebble and shell are known from Tell ed-Duweir (Lachish) (figure 235 A).

The provision of means for hanging pots over the fire, lifting them out of the ashes, or carrying them about was a problem to the earliest potters. Handles luted on to the pot require a finely washed slip if they are to stick securely; and eversion of the lip as in the bell beakers (plate 8 B), to prevent a suspensory string from slipping off, entails risk of the thinned edge cracking in drying or firing. Accordingly, the straight-sided pots of the earliest Neolithic pottery in the west were provided with knobs or lugs which could be pinched up out of the wall in the soft state. These sufficed to retain a string, but the improvement of piercing the lugs to allow the string to pass through them was early adopted. As the lugs became enlarged they needed to be luted on, but their extensive bearing-surface made this easier than the attachment of loop handles, though the latter quickly developed. These three stages are all seen in the earliest Neolithic pottery of Jericho, though the loop handles are very elementary (figure 236). The introduction of enlarged and elaborated handles belongs to the Late Neolithic level [28].

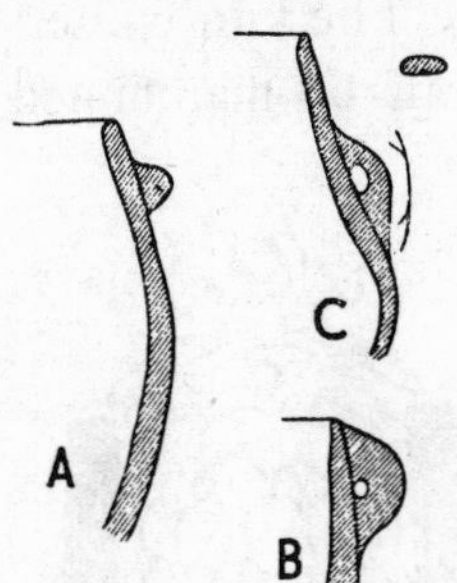

FIGURE 236—(A) *Knob*, (B) *pierced lug, and* (C) *handle. Jericho. Middle Neolithic.*

IV. FIRING

The oldest, and in early times the commonest, way of firing was in unenclosed fires. Such hearths have occasionally been recognized, as at the site of La Terrière (Charente-Inférieure), where Neolithic pottery was fired [29]; since nothing more can survive, the methods used can only be surmised from modern primitive practices. The most elementary of these is firing on the domestic hearth, as with the potters of Barvas in Lewis as late as 1863. The pots were filled with hot peat-ash and piled round with burning peats [30]. The general primitive practice is,

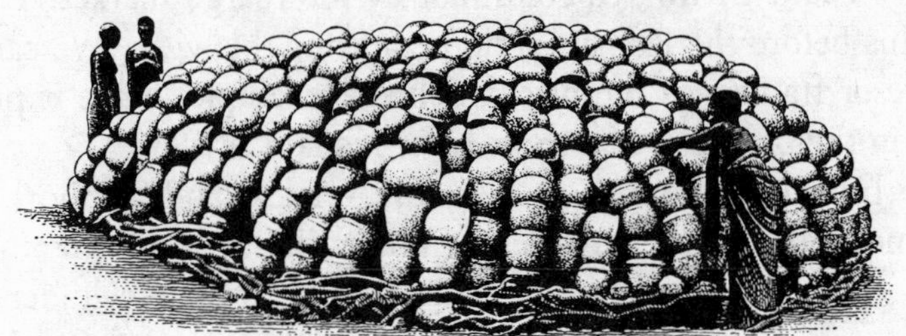

FIGURE 237—*Nigerian women piling pots for firing in the open.*

however, to fire the pots in quantity, piled on the ground or in a dug hollow, with fuel below, among, and above them (figure 237). Such firings with a hot fire of brushwood may last as little as an hour, but the uneven heating, as in all open firing, may cause a heavy wastage. The more developed practice resembles charcoal-burning, the fire being damped and, as far as possible, enclosed by piling vegetable matter, earth, or dung on the burning heap. Such firing may last for as much as three days, the potters constantly watching the pile to cover any hole through which heat may escape. The fuels used may be brushwood, grass, straw, reeds, or cattle-dung, whichever is the cheapest and most easily available. It is said that a temperature of 750° to 800° C can be attained. The cooling may need to be as long as seven days, to minimize the risk of breakage.

The kiln conserves heat better than the open fire, and higher temperatures can be maintained. Furthermore, improved draught-control results in more uniform quality and permits adjustment for colour and other desired effects. In early times, however, the advantages of the kiln in terms of high output were much more doubtful. Those of which remains have been found have a far smaller capacity than the known open-firings (cf figures 237 and 244). Moreover, kiln-firing demands as fuel either wood in billets or charcoal, both of which are always more expensive than the fuels that can be used for open-firing, and are often unobtainable. Finally, the kiln involves a capital expenditure which would be uneconomic for a peasant-potter working for his own village. It is thus unlikely that kiln-firing would oust open-firing except in the larger urban communities, where pottery could be worked continuously for a large market. The rarity of surviving kilns before the Roman period confirms this view. We cannot ignore the economic or traditional motives which, for example, made it preferable to fire pottery on the domestic hearth in Lewis as late as 1863.

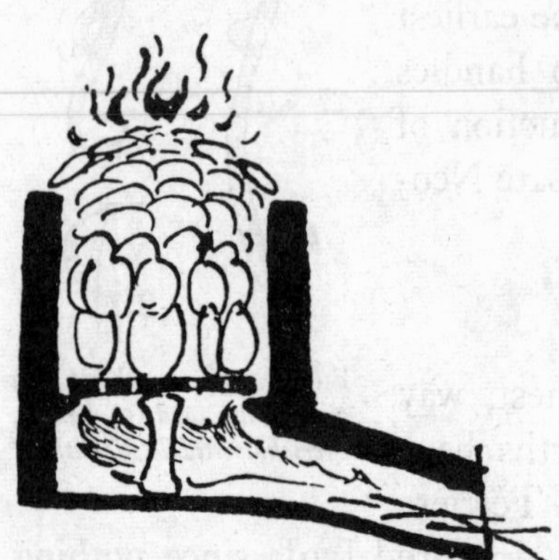

FIGURE 238—*Diagram of a primitive vertical kiln.*

There are broadly two types of kiln, the vertical and the horizontal. The former, the more elementary, has been dominant in the west until modern times. Essentially, it is a cylinder which encloses the hot gases from the hearth at its base, and leads them upwards into a dome, whence they escape through an aperture or chimney. In its simplest form (figure 238), the dome may be merely temporary, and may even consist of layers of sherds resting on the pots being fired; the kiln can then be packed and emptied from the top. If the dome is permanent, there must be a door in the side of the kiln which is sealed with

FIGURE 239—*Primitive Greek vertical kiln with side-door, represented on a black-figured clay plaque from Corinth. Sixth century* B.C.

clay at each firing. To protect the pots from direct contact with the flames, it is desirable that they be raised on a perforated floor of clay, and for adequate strength this requires solid supports. The difficulty of providing the floor and its supports without unduly restricting the space left as a flame-way tends to limit the practicable diameter of vertical kilns [31]. The vertical kiln should be of brick, stone structures being unduly clumsy and insufficiently refractory to high temperatures. It is noticeable that the vertical kiln developed mainly in brick-using countries [32]. It is possible, however, to build wholly in clay, and kilns in the Congo were so made with wall and dome of an average thickness of 10 in, and an internal diameter of up to about 2 ft 6 in [33].

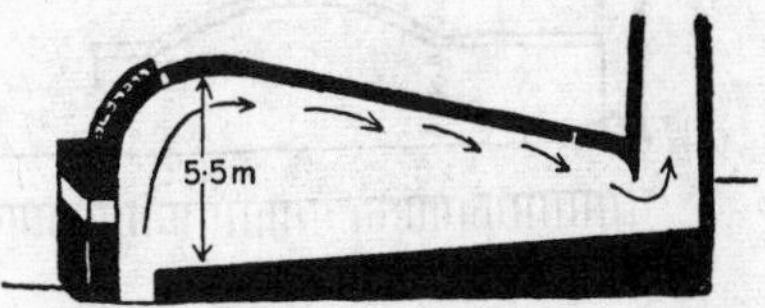

FIGURE 240—*Horizontal kiln built of fire-hardened clay and some brick. The single firing pit is stepped below the chamber. China.* c *A.D. 100.*

The main weakness of the vertical kiln is in the regulation of draught. The hot gases tend to roar upwards, and it is difficult, even under modern conditions, so to baffle the kiln as to equalize temperature and atmosphere between the top and bottom of the chamber. The Greeks apparently had the same difficulty (figure 239). The horizontal kiln solves this problem by directing the hot gases out through a horizontal flue leading from the bottom of the kiln to the chimney. Such kilns have been widely adopted in the west in modern times, and were in use, though not widely, in Roman Britain. In the modern horizontal brick kiln, the heated gases are thrown down from the dome and led off through a grating in the floor along a horizontal flue to the chimney. The principle has long been followed in China (figure 240), as shown in kilns of the later Han Dynasty (first two centuries A.D.) recently excavated at Chiu Chen, site of a Chinese colony in what is now (1954) French Indo-China [34]. In the interpretation of the exiguous remains of the kilns of pre-Roman times we must be guided by the relatively well preserved examples of the Roman Empire. Romano-British kilns were of both vertical and horizontal type, the former much commoner (figure 241) [35].

For the kilns of the Aegean and the Near East we have to rely on pictures, on scanty remains, and on a few models from Egypt showing kilns of a very simple type. In the classical period, the Greeks used vertical kilns of moderate size with a permanent dome and a door at the side. An enclosed hearth stood out some 2 ft from the structure, and the chimney, if it existed, was very short. From the hearth, the hot gases were drawn into the body of the kiln, probably, though not certainly, through a perforated clay floor supported on piers or arches. Since these internal arrangements are not shown in the pictures [36], and there have been no excavations, we can only deduce them by analogy with Roman vertical kilns. Pictures of Egyptian kilns, the earliest of which dates to the mid-third millennium B.C., show much narrower structures capable of taking only relatively small pots, but the general arrangement seems the same, save that the kilns had no permanent domes and were packed and unpacked from the top (figures 232, 234, 242–3).

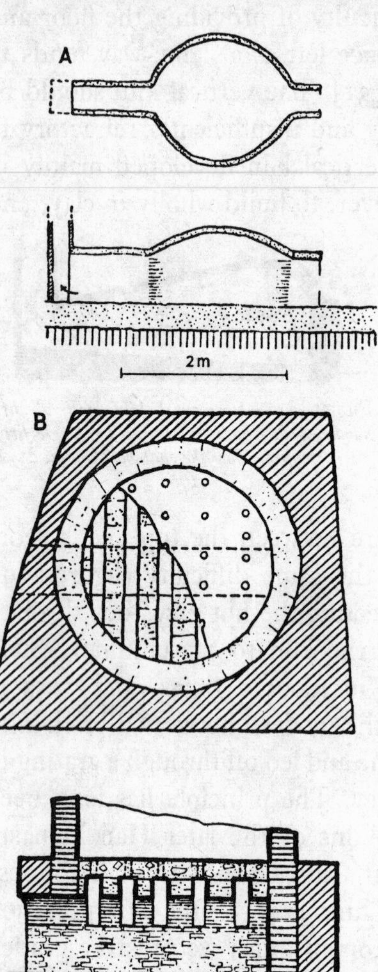

FIGURE 241—*Romano-British kilns.* (A) *Ground plan and vertical section of a horizontal kiln from Farnham, Surrey.* (B) *Round vertical kiln:* (above) *plan of baking chamber, the floor partly uncovered to disclose flues underneath;* (below) *vertical section. Holt, Denbighshire.*

Of the fragmentary kilns of similar type known from excavation, an example may be taken from Susa (figure 244). Though it belongs to the earliest stratum, which goes back into the fourth millennium, it is larger than the Egyptian kilns as represented in pictures and models. Of the baking-chamber, nothing survives except the perforated floor, nearly 6 ft across; beneath this is a solid sub-structure, arched from a central pillar and nearly 3 ft high. Here, it is suggested, the fire was made, the fuel being fed in through the circular aperture in the side, which could be closed with brick. A large circular opening into the baking-chamber served as a chimney. The practical working of this construction is uncertain [37].

A concave and perforated floor discovered at Sialk in the third level (Sialk III) is probably another type of vertical kiln (figure 245). Under the floor a series of ducts, leading to three apertures, is apparently designed to admit air, the fuel being burned in the combustion-chamber with the pots to be fired [38]. The combustion-chamber has been reconstructed with a flat dome springing, not from the head of a wall, but immediately from the floor, and on this basis would be only some 3 ft in diameter and 18 inches high. If the reconstruction is correct, and if the firing was as described, the structure was rather an oven than a kiln.

A kiln of the Neolithic settlement at Olynthus in Macedonia, of the early third millennium, resembles the Sialk oven in having air-ducts, but it has also a shallow hearth beneath its baked clay floor extending as an apron in front of it [39]. The small clearance between hearth and floor must have made firing difficult, even with charcoal, but with the aid of the air-ducts, which could be regulated by closing any one of them with a sherd, a fair amount of heat was doubtless led up into the baking-chamber through the single hole in the floor. As the superstructure was not preserved, we do not know whether it was a shallow, oven-like dome, as reconstructed, or built up with a vertical wall.

FIGURE 242—*Two Egyptian potters. One kneads the clay while the other builds up pots on a turn-table. On the left is their kiln. Model from a tomb at Saqqara.* c 1900 B.C.

A fourth type, sometimes claimed as a pottery-kiln, cannot be satisfactorily distinguished from the domed cooking-oven [40]; the latter, being designed for a cooking-temperature of some 200° C, could hardly be heated to temperatures as high as those attainable by open-firing. More business-like kilns at Carchemish, on the upper Euphrates, which are perhaps as early as the fourth millennium, may when more adequately known be regarded as a fifth type, since some at least of them were provided with external firing-pits. The floors of the baking-chambers measured as much as 6 ft across, and the superstructures, as far as can be gathered, were solidly walled with mud-brick. Air-ducts led under the wall to control the firing. Unfortunately, the manner in which the firing-pits led into the baking-chambers has not been ascertained [41].

FIGURE 243—*An Egyptian pottery of Dynasty V. The small kiln appears to be closed at the top with a layer of vegetable matter. A turn-table is used. The jars are finished by smoothing inside and outside.* c 2500 B.C.

The sparsity of information on the pottery-kilns of the Near East is not fully explained by inadequate excavations, the small size of most of those which have

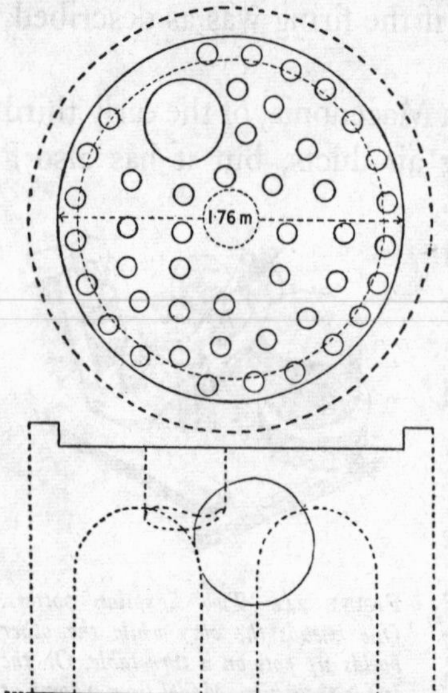

FIGURE 244—*Diagram of a vertical kiln at Susa.* (Above) *The perforated floor.* (Below) *Side view of the firing-chamber (perforations omitted). Fourth millennium* B.C.

been found suggests that kiln-firing was of only a limited use [42]. Woolley considers that much of the Carchemish pottery was open-fired, probably in shallow holes found on the kiln site. It is a fallacy to suppose that, after the invention of the kiln, open-firing was ousted. Brushwood, reeds, and dung used for open-firing were cheap, and it is probable that much of the pottery, both painted and unpainted, was so fired. The practice of the Sindh potters today shows that this can be done.

Different conditions prevailed in the west. It was formerly believed that in these backward areas the kiln was not introduced until a very late date, but horizontal-type kilns have now been found on the sea-route by which certain aspects of Mediterranean culture reached western Britain, and as far north as North Uist. They yielded Western Neolithic pottery of high quality in the mid-second millennium B.C. They were built of stone blocks, packed with turf to make them gas-tight, and roofed, when in use, with stone slabs. The gases were drawn from a flat hearth into a low and broad baking-chamber, which had a central stone block to support the slabs of the roof; baffle-slabs protected the pots

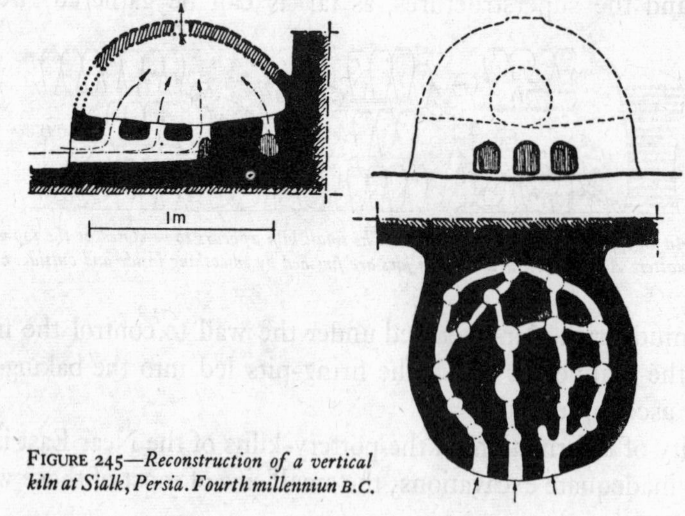

FIGURE 245—*Reconstruction of a vertical kiln at Sialk, Persia. Fourth millenniun* B.C.

from direct contact with the flames. From this chamber the gases were drawn off through a short and narrow flue. The chimneys have not survived, but were probably of wood, like many house chimneys in the Hebrides today. The kiln illustrated (figure 246) was strictly horizontal, and used a vertical rock face to provide one side of its flue; another kiln had a step up from the hearth to the combustion-chamber, like the Chinese horizontal kilns already described. The fuel was wood.

The horizontal kiln is not recorded again in the west until Roman times, when examples in southern Britain (figure 241 A) resemble fairly closely those at Eilean an Tighe on North Uist. There is reason to believe that a horizontal corn-drying kiln was in use [43]. The pottery-kilns which were gradually introduced into central Europe in the course of the first millennium B.C.—though not, so far as is known, into Britain—were of the vertical type.

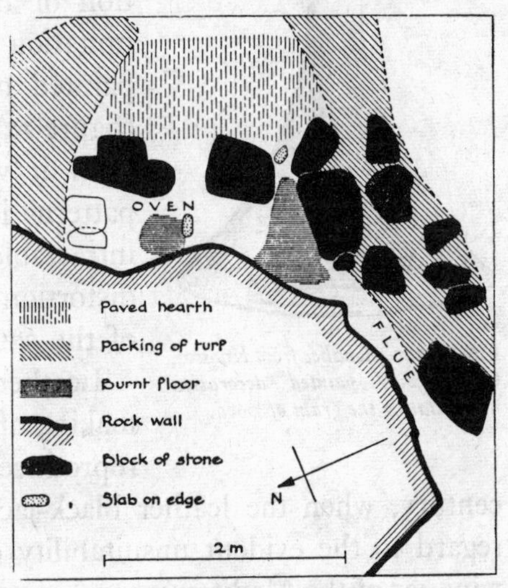

FIGURE 246—*Sketch-plan of kiln 2 at Eilean an Tighe, North Uist. Second millennium B.C.*

V. SHAPES AND DECORATION

Attention has already been drawn to shallow oval dishes and rectangular troughs which imitate vessels made, in a pre-pottery age, of wood or basket-work (p 387). Since these vessels go back to the beginnings of pottery, their makers may well have directly and consciously imitated the pre-pottery prototype. The process of imitation has, however, gone on continuously into our own age, shapes developed in other materials being reproduced as nearly as possible in clay. Side by side with these first imitations, the older ones have continued to be made, with the variations resulting from the successive reproduction of a shape of which the origin was long ago forgotten.

Thus, in Early Minoan Crete, wooden chalices—which have not survived—were reproduced in pottery with a painted imitation of the grain of the wood (figure 247). In Bronze Age Britain, staved wooden mugs, then probably an innovation, can be identified in some of the vessels known as handled beakers, which reproduce not only the shape of the mugs but, in the decoration of the underside of their bases, the method by which the wooden mugs were made.

FIGURE 247—*Chalice from Knossos, Crete, with painted decoration imitating the grain of wood.*

Basket-work has been suggested as the origin of the shapes of some pottery, and still more often of its decoration. To take one of the earliest examples, the Neolithic Tasian beakers from Egypt are decorated with zoned patterns in incised lines emphasized with a white paste filling, and baskets similar in shape and ornament are made in Africa today (figure 248) [44]. A similar case has been advanced for the later Spanish beakers, thought to imitate the decoration of baskets of esparto grass. A more subtle imitation is shown in the human and animal forms painted on the early pottery from Susa in Elam (figure 125 A). These were interpreted as abstract art until it was shown that they copied basket-work patterns in which the figures were distorted by the intractable character of that material [45]. A similar distortion has been observed in figures on the pottery of the south-western United States.

Leather is not a substance which lends itself to the making of vessels, but its inconveniences have been reproduced in pottery even as late as the sixteenth century, when the leather black-jack was faithfully imitated in clay without regard to the evident unsuitability of the product. In antiquity, the familiar wine-jar of the Mediterranean—very tall and narrow and with a pointed base—imitates wine-skins of leather [46]. Its traditional shape no doubt found obstinate defenders, who argued its convenience for carrying by donkey, or stacking in the fore-part of a boat. At Troy, a pitcher for drawing water persisted close to the leather form through successive cities. It has been suggested that the developed types of Western Neolithic pottery, with their carinated necks (p 386), imitate leather vessels stiffened with hoops at the carination and the rim, and that the diagonal strokes which sometimes decorate these parts reproduce the sewing by which the hoops were kept in place (figure 249 A) [47].

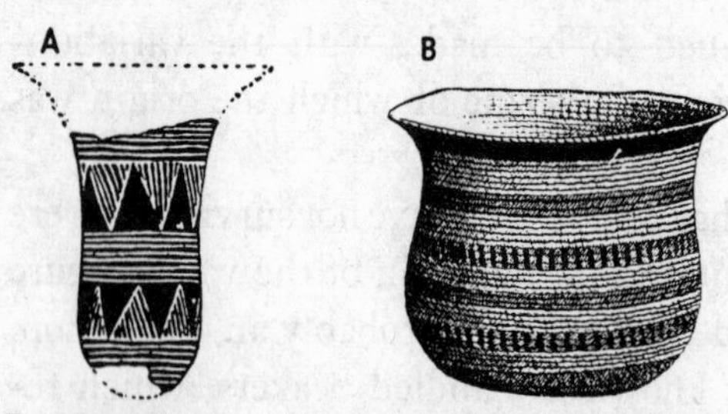

FIGURE 248—(A) *Tasian beaker imitating basketry patterns; Egyptian Neolithic.* (B) *Modern African basket. Compare also figure 253.*

The making of stone vessels goes

back in Egypt to Neolithic times. In the predynastic period they were beautifully fabricated in decorative stones. Cheaper reproductions in pottery of these fine vessels imitate not the shapes only, but, by painted decoration, the mottled appearance of the stone. The art of working decorative stones

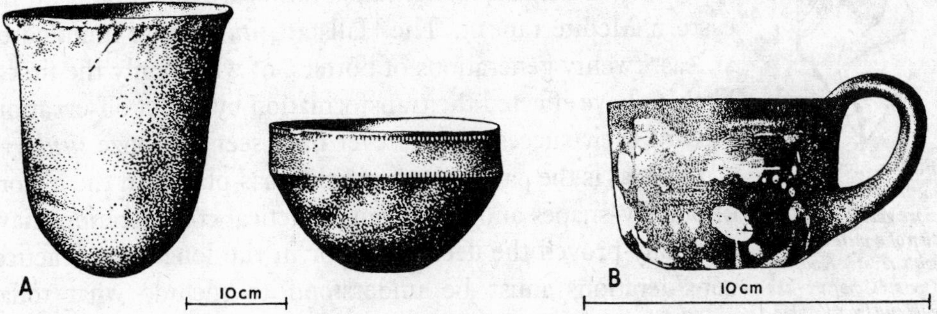

FIGURE 249—(A) *Western Neolithic pots imitating leather bags in shape and decoration; Michelsberg, south Germany.* (B) *Polychrome imitation of stone in a Cretan pottery cup.*

passed to Crete in Early Minoan times, and the imitations of such vessels in clay (figure 249 B) provided a main impulse in the development of polychrome designs on the pottery of the succeeding Middle Minoan period [48].

It was, however, the development of metallurgy to the stage at which vessels could be made of sheet-metal which most radically transformed the shapes of pottery vessels. The imitation extended to the reproduction of shapes for which clay is ill fitted, and of details, such as rivets, which were functionless (figure 250). The design of handles was revolutionized, and the flamboyant and often elegant forms which are readily made in metal were reproduced with great endeavour, but inevitably clumsily, in clay (figures 251, 436). It was not only in fine vessels that the influence was felt; the Hallstatt bronze *situla* or bucket was long dominant, in increasingly degenerate form, in the pottery of the west, and even the copper cooking-pot, which came to be part of the equipment of the Roman army, was the prototype of a popular Iron Age ware widespread in Gaul and western Britain.

FIGURE 250—*Imitation of rivets on an Early Minoan jug.*

While the imitation of vessels originally made in other materials has been a dominant factor in the development of pottery-shapes and decoration, it is a mistake to suppose that the origination of a type in any area can always, or even frequently, be explained by pointing to its pre-pottery prototype. The imitation has commonly been indirect, and we can seldom show that the new type links on without intermediaries to the pre-pottery vessel. It is most unlikely that the Western Neolithic carinated bowls made in Britain were shaped through the potter's direct observation of a leather original. Nor is this much more likely in the western Mediterranean, whence the type reached Britain, for carinated bowls are much older in the eastern Mediterranean. The Hallstatt *situlae* were imitated by at least twenty generations of potters, of which only the first is likely to have effected the transformation by direct observation. Few of their successors can ever have seen a bronze *situla*.

FIGURE 251—*Fragment of an earthenware goblet in imitation of a metal handle with rivets. Knossos, Crete. Compare the gold cup from Vaphio, figure 436.*

Large as is the part which imitation has played in the history of pottery-shapes and decoration, practical considerations have naturally proved the decisive factor in the long run. Practical considerations must be understood to include what today would be described as the magical and ritual, for we are concerned with the mentality of the potter, who regarded magic and ritual as normal and effective means of achieving his purposes. Indeed, an attempt to distinguish between these—to us—different motives will generally fail, as may be seen from the common storage-jar with rope decoration, and its derivatives, which spread in the early second millennium B.C. from the Aegean to Macedonia in the north, to the Pyrenees in the west, and beyond. This was probably a result of a trade in wine or oil up the Rhône to north-east France, and by the Aude-Garonne route to north-west France and Britain. As seen in Crete these jars are elaborately corded, though only in imitation, no doubt to give added strength and to provide slings to secure their many handles. It is

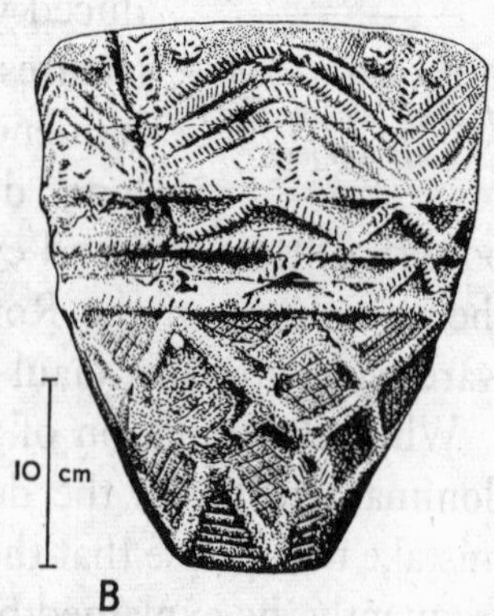

FIGURE 252—(A) *Knotted and corded jars from Knossos, Crete.* c *1800 B.C.* (B) *Corded urn from Co. Down, Ireland.*

idle to ask how far the thick clay cordons were believed by the potter and his customers to give real mechanical strength, and how far to coerce the heavy object to hold together by mimetic magic. Still less is it useful to analyse the expectations of remote potters in the Pyrenees or Ulster in providing their smaller storage jars with like slings and cordons. We can be sure only that they were not merely gratifying an aesthetic fancy, and that their aim was practical, whether it was to be reached by mechanical or by magical means (figure 252).

The adaptation of shapes to utility is best displayed where a community, as it rises from barbarism, develops also a wide variety of types each designed to meet a separate need. There are few communities of which this can be shown, owing to the too frequent absorption of archaeologists in the aesthetic merits of their pots, but excellent examples are provided by the classical periods of Greece and China. The organized industries of such cities as Athens and Corinth, with their highly valuable export trade, created a range of standard types designed to meet both home and export demands. Perhaps in part as a response to the requirements of salesmanship, these types were regularly linked with names, which compelled a consideration of each type's purpose. In the classical period of China (before 200 B.C.) pots were named, and their uses specified, in the books of ritual; the names referred to bronze vessels, but were applied to the pottery vessels which were made in imitation. The association between name and shape naturally grew vaguer with the years, and in A.D. 1125 a standardization was effected in an illustrated catalogue. The names are still in current use, and enable us to identify the uses of pots from prehistoric sites.

In the west our knowledge is less, and the speculative terminology of early antiquaries—drinking-cups, food-vessels, cinerary urns—has not stimulated a study of the practical use of the equipment of our early settlement sites. With the attention now being given to these sites, it is possible tentatively to identify the employment of fine beakers as cooking-pots, of the shallow Western Neolithic bowls for curd- or cheese-making, and of the large jars of the latter ware, as also the collared and other 'cinerary' urns, for food-storage.[1] We can thus begin to observe the diversification of the pottery-types in Britain in response to the demands of the developing community.

It is easier to distinguish decorative characteristics of pottery which appear to be derived from magical beliefs than such as arise out of rationally practical requirements. Among the latter, however, may be included the roughening of beakers by all-over rustic decoration to prevent slipping in the wet hands.

[1] As elsewhere, for example in Minoan Crete, the storage-jars of the settlements came to be turned to funerary uses.

Over wide stretches of the coast of the west Mediterranean the early, if not the earliest, pottery is erratically impressed all over its surface with the finger-nail, the point of a stick, or the edge of a shell, and this impressed decoration has been regarded as a distinctive style, spread by diffusion [49]. In its more elaborated forms it may in fact be so, but the variety of the dates of its first appearance in the different areas, and its much earlier advent in parts of west Asia, make it more likely that its initial purpose was not decorative, but merely the roughening of the pot. The same utilitarian purpose may lie behind the rippling and finger-tip fluting of Western Neolithic bowls (plate 8 D), and of Neolithic wares in Egypt and Crete, pleasing as the effects thus produced often are.

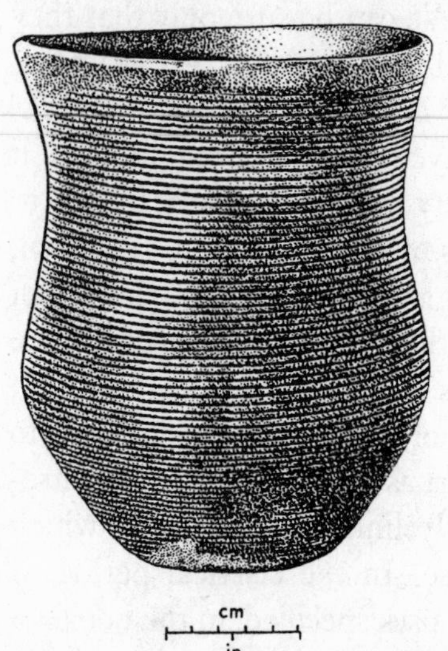

FIGURE 253—*Corded bell beaker. Midlothian. Early second millennium B.C.*

What appears as decoration may sometimes be merely an incidental effect of the method of manufacture of the pot. The burnishing of vessels has often been attributed to an aesthetic motive, but it is a method of making pottery non-porous, and it is likely that this was usually the potter's purpose. String wrappings, whether used to support the lower part of a heavy vessel while building its upper part, or, more elaborately, in methods of string-moulding used by pre-historic Chinese potters, leave impressions which appear decorative to us; that they were not so intended is shown by examples in which they have been smoothed out, but not quite successfully [50]. The string-wrapped corded beakers of Atlantic Europe may reflect such a process (figure 253). Again, the use of a wooden beater in shaping a pot by hand produces an effect of pattern, and when, as in ancient China, the beater is wound with string to prevent it from sticking to the clay, the effect may easily be mistaken for decoration. Water-jars are, however, still made in China by the ancient method and, for shaping the lip, a special beater is used carved with a raised design, thus making what is specifically a band of pattern [51].

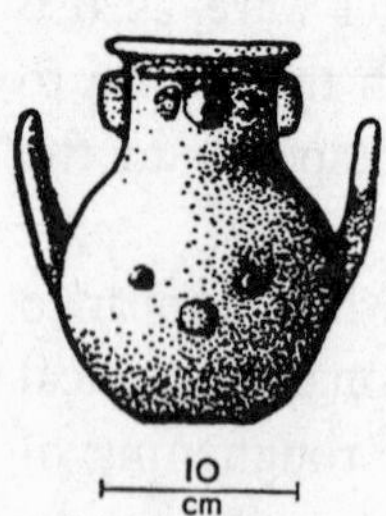

FIGURE 254—*Face urn from Troy. Early Bronze Age.*

Among decorative motives which, though they strike us as aesthetic, served a magical purpose, significant examples are found in jugs and mugs with a moulded human face.

These first appear in the second city of Troy, whence they migrated up the Danube as far as Germany (figure 254). They may have been supposed to protect the drinker from evil—the purpose of the eyes incised on bowls found from Spain to Scandinavia, and painted on the bows of Mediterranean fishing-boats even today.

Vessels of special shapes and decoration have been very widely made and used for ritual purposes; a few may be quoted from Cyprus, Crete, and Greece. Most come from sanctuaries, but some from tombs, though the dead are commonly served with the types of pot they used when living. Some votive vessels are mere miniatures of normal pottery; such occur in Cretan shrines in the palaces of Phaistos and Knossos, and in the hill-top sanctuary of Petsofa near Palaikastro [52]. More common are pots embodying animal forms, particularly the bull, the dove, and the serpent. The bull is familiar in the bull's-head *rhyton*, a Middle Minoan libation vessel of a type still in use in Greece in classical times (figure 229) [53]. Bowls with moulded bulls'-heads and snakes, and pottery bulls'-horns, occur in the Vounous cemetery of rock-cut tombs of the late third millennium B.C. in Cyprus [54]. In the same tombs, vessels have been found with doves moulded in the round perching on their rims (figure 255), sometimes in association with bulls or snakes. In Crete, dove figurines go back to Neolithic times; a Middle Minoan bowl has one fixed on its bottom, and a ritual vessel of the same period is moulded in the shape of a dove [55]. In Greece, in the third shaft-grave at Mycenae, doves modelled in gold perch on a female figure. In contrast to these ritual objects, it is significant to notice that in the great cemetery of rock-cut tombs at Mycenae, in which the citizens were buried, the vessels laid with the dead are entirely such as were used by the living. The only pottery objects peculiar to the tombs and belonging specifically to the ritual of interment were incense-burners and charcoal-scoops [56].

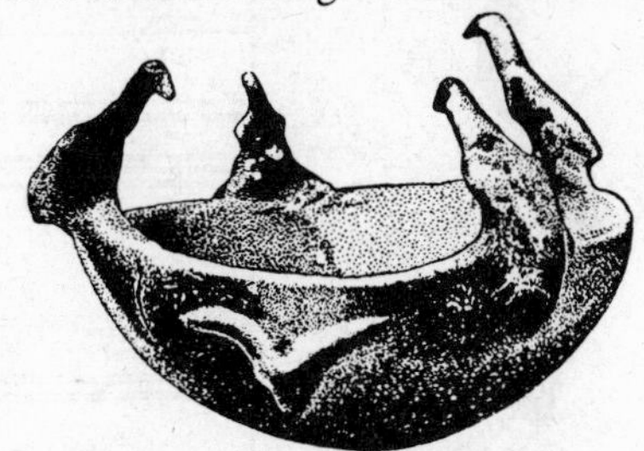

FIGURE 255—*Bowl decorated with doves. Cyprus.* c *2500* B.C. *Scale 1/5.*

A factor which has naturally influenced shapes and decoration has been the development of technique, and that not merely negatively. For example, the making of pots with narrow necks necessarily awaited the discovery that vessels could be made in two tiers which could then be luted together (p 386). At first, decoration tended to spread all over pots, unenclosed in a framework, but quite early appears a formal arrangement in zones, frequently outlined by horizontal lines. In Western Neolithic pottery this type of decoration occurs in the course of the second stage of its development (plate 8 C); it is characteristic also of the bell and zoned beakers (plate 8 B). The change may be ascribed to the introduction of the pivoted turn-table, which made it easy to draw horizontal lines.

A much more potent influence was the introduction of the wheel. Though its main effect was to speed production of existing shapes, it created a strong tendency to elaboration. There are indeed few shapes which, given skill, patience, and a turn-table, cannot be built up by hand, but the exhilaration of spinning,

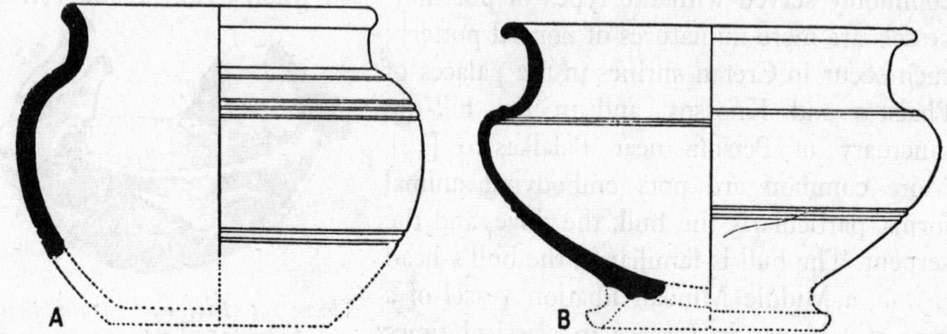

FIGURE 256—*Vessels from Glastonbury Lake Village. The gently everted rim of the hand-made pot* (A) *changes to the curled-over lip of the wheel-made pot* (B). *The hands of decoration are replaced by refined, but formal, cordons and grooves. Maximum external diameters:* (A) c $9\frac{1}{4}$ *in.* (B) c *8 in. Iron Age.*

and the aesthetic sense that came with ease and speed, gave the potter a taste for form. Mouldings, groovings, and such refinements as heavily under-cut and extravagantly curled lips characterize the new technique.

An exact demonstration of all this development is hampered by lack of precision in dating the introduction of the wheel in different areas. Yet broad comparison of, say, Middle Minoan and Middle Helladic work with the more robust pots of an earlier age illustrates the change. The classical age in Greece displays the fullest flowering of the cult of elegance. In making the comparison, flamboyant handles and spouts should be discounted, since these were always made by hand or in moulds, and appear early in the Near East. Perhaps the clearest view of the change is provided by Britain, where the wheel was introduced from Gaul at a known date, namely in the century before the Roman conquest (figure 256).

Why were ages in which decoration was common repeatedly succeeded by others in which pattern was largely banished, or reduced to a stylized remnant of former exuberance? Figure 256 of ware from Glastonbury suggests at least a practical answer, for the new interest in form, brought by the wheel, could well make potters unwilling to allow form to be confused by irrelevant pattern. At any rate, the change at Glastonbury has a parallel three millennia earlier in Mesopotamia, in the disappearance of decoration as the wheel came into general use [57]. An analogous development, that of fine glazes, may have contributed to the virtual disappearance of pattern from Chinese pottery. Pottery of the Han period (ending *c* A.D. 200) has elaborate stamped, incised, and relief decoration, but when, after a period of obscurity, pottery again becomes known in the T'ang period, fine glazes have been introduced and the ware is devoid of ornament, though decoration continues on unglazed pottery. The magnificent glazed wares of the succeeding Sung period are either entirely plain, or permit only highly reserved patterns incised under the glaze, as in celadon ware. Not till the fifteenth century did decoration again become dominant in the blue-and-white and other elaborately patterned styles of the Ming dynasty.

It must not be supposed, however, that the changing shapes and decoration of pottery in its long history are to be wholly explained by the influences enumerated above. The indeterminable element is personal taste. Human individuality is the factor which archaeology has been the least ready to recognize. Thus, in conclusion, it is well to bear in mind certain recorded facts regarding design in the pottery of the Pueblo villages of the south-western United States. While they have much in common, the styles of decoration are distinct from village to village, and some are known to have persisted over long periods. It also happens that a potter of individuality may evolve a new style of decoration, which is adopted by all the potters of the village to the exclusion of the designs previously used [58]. The frequency of such changes may have become greater under the stimulus of European contacts, but there is no reason to doubt that, there and elsewhere, and in the remote as in the immediate past, novelty is the fruit of the originality of the individual craftsman and must evade the systems of the classifier.

VI. THE POTTERY INDUSTRY

The writer of the ancient *Geoponica* says: 'It is most necessary for every reason to have potters [on a farm], since we are convinced that it is possible to find potter's clay on any land' [59]. It may be questioned whether this is more than one of those pious adjurations to revive folk-industries to which industrialized ages are prone, and we should not infer that any significant amount of Greek pottery was made on the farms. Nor is this situation confined to Greece. Even at a low level of culture there has been a strong tendency towards specialization in pottery; first because of the economic advantages of skilled workmanship and specialized tools, and secondly because, despite *Geoponica*, potter's clay is not to be found 'on any land'. Even in the plentifully supplied lands of Greece, good clay was not ubiquitous, and the success of the industry of Athens, as of Corinth, was attributed to the excellence of its raw material.

We may illustrate from modern evidence the tendency of the pottery industry to develop a measure of organization even at low cultural levels. In Melanesia, the people of the Amphlett Islands, who export pots to the neighbouring islands, organize expeditions to Ferguson Island, a day's journey distant, to obtain a six months' supply of raw material. The expedition digs the clay, dries it, and carries back some two tons in each canoe [60]. Clay is traded between the various islands of the Nicobar group in the Indian Ocean. The Pueblo potters of Zuni in the south-western United States make an expedition to the top of a mountain to obtain their clay, which is brought back to the accompaniment of religious rites [61].

More commonly, the manufacture is sited where clay and fuel are both available, and the products are distributed among surrounding villages. This is the case in Sindh, where in the village of Balreji (within a few miles of Mohenjo-Daro) three families make pottery, substantially, it is believed, in the same manner as in the third millennium B.C. [62]. The clay is brought from the fields by donkeys, and the pots are sold in the neighbouring villages. In the Naga territory pottery is made at two hill-villages which have a monopoly of the trade in the area, since they are near the only suitable beds of clay. The Nagas of the foothills are supplied from places in the Manipur valley which also have sources of clay, and carry on potting in the dry winter months [63]. In the elementary Hebridean industry already mentioned (p 396), which survived into the nineteenth century, clay was abundant and the fuel used was peat, but each pottery supplied a whole township [64].

A third method of organization is illustrated by the peripatetic potters of modern Crete. There the potters of the village of Thrapsanos tour the island for some three months in the summer, in parties of ten or twelve, and set up their simple gear wherever clay, fuel, and water are available and there is sufficient population to provide a market. Each party arrives with its donkey carrying the gear, and, on leaving, the pots, including wine jars 3 ft high, are also loaded on the donkey and carried round the district until sold. Each member of the party has his task; the master-potter and wine-jar-maker; the second potter who uses the wheel; the kiln-stoker; the clay-digger; the wood-cutter; and so on. When the wanderings are over, the party returns to Thrapsanos and spends the rest of the year in agriculture, though always ready to make a pot when required [65].

The three methods of organization illustrated above probably cover most of prehistoric pottery-making, of which we have no direct knowledge other than the factory industry of the larger urban centres. This excepted, the potters were probably part-craftsmen, part-agriculturists, as are the Cretan and Naga potters —and as indeed country craftsmen have commonly been in less advanced areas until very recent times [66]. No doubt there were isolated prehistoric farms and homesteads on which pottery was made solely for home use, but the economic and geographic conditions of success in the industry must always have tended to eliminate the purely domestic potter.

It has been generally considered that potting is a women's industry at the primitive level—that is, before the introduction of the wheel. This matter cannot, however, be regarded as entirely clear. It is true that women make the fire-pots in Nigeria, and in Africa generally; that women conduct the Pueblo and other native American industries; and that the Melanesian industry in the Amphlett Islands employs women, though not to get the clay or sell the product. On the other hand, only men are employed among the Nagas, but both men and women among the Manipuris. Except at a very low standard of culture, the exclusive employment of women in prehistoric potteries is to be inferred from modern practice only with caution. A like caution is to be adopted towards such direct evidence as the supposed recognition of the prints of women's fingers on prehistoric pots [67]. After the introduction of the wheel, pottery seems to have become an exclusively masculine industry, as in India, China, Crete, and Brittany; but women potters worked in the Hebrides.

Apart from analogy with modern potteries, we can judge of the organization of prehistoric potteries only from the slight remains of them of which we have knowledge. We may take as an example the Hebridean site already described (p 396), where Western Neolithic pottery was manufactured about the middle of the second millennium B.C. The birch and willow timber used by the potters as fuel, and doubtless the clay, had to be fetched by dug-out. Tempering for the clay was provided by the coarse grit of the loch shore; this was ground down before use, and heavy stone pounders were found on the site. All these are tasks that must have been done by men. The pottery was made by hand, but with the use of a turn-table, since the later wares were decorated in zones outlined by accurately and firmly drawn horizontal grooves (plate 8 A). Smoothing and burnishing, for which the tools survive, may have been done by women. The firing involved men's work in lifting the slabs which covered the kiln, as did distribution of the product, which must have been by sea round the islands. The extent of the trade can only be vaguely guessed from the rubbish-heap.

Considerable quantities of potsherds survive, and much has been washed away by the raising of the loch level to serve a mill. Mineralogical tests on a few sherds have shown that Orkney pottery of similar design was not imported but made locally, and it is probable enough that a pottery of this size found an adequate market for its wares in the Outer Hebrides, if not in Uist itself.

For the nature of urban potteries we may study the industry of Athens, for which we have literary evidence. Though this represents a very high level of organization, it provides a more reliable guide than the Near Eastern sites of which we have knowledge from excavation. At Athens, industry was in the hands of aliens not eligible for citizenship, who controlled the trade of the city and enjoyed a recognized status in it. Potters were grouped with other craftsmen in this middle class, and that the painters of pots were no differently regarded appears from a reference of Isocrates (436–338 B.C.) to the 'insolence' of saying 'that Zeuxis and Parrhasius [two famous contemporary painters] had plied the same trade as the painters of *pinakes*'.

FIGURE 257—*Woman painting a pot. Detail from an Athenian vase. Fifth century B.C.*

Pottery in Athens was made in factories which might employ, under the master-potter, as many as seventy men. The painters constituted a separate trade, and a large factory might employ two. Women were sometimes employed as painters (figure 257), but this was exceptional. From the pictures—there have been no excavations—it appears that the plant of a pottery consisted of wheels, probably handspun, whether by potter or assistant [68]; turn-tables for finishing and painting pots; and kilns (p 393). Since the kilns were relatively small, firing must have been frequent. We have no information on the preparation of the clay, which was presumably carried out in the factory. Presumably also it was the factory hands who dug it in the *kerameiskos*; this was the potters' field in the low ground on the border of the city, which, by the quality of its red clay, *keramos*, had provided the basis for the fame of the city's pottery-industry and its name 'ceramic'. Red ochre, used as a slip to give the bright red colour for which Athenian pottery was valued, was imported into Attica. The city protected its industry against competitors by trade agreements with the states supplying ochre, securing exclusive right to buy it [69].

In the fifth century, first place in the export trade in pottery, which had been held by Corinth, passed to Athens, which then paid for its great imports of corn partly with pottery. The trade was predominantly a luxury one in fine wares which, by their high value in relation to weight, best repaid the cost of transport: before the advent of modern ships even sea-transport was very expensive. In addition, large numbers of pottery containers were incidentally exported in the course of other trades, most notably that in oil. This overseas trade, and not local demand, explains the rise of the factories. It is not to be expected that a comparable large-scale organization of the industry will be found in other urban centres of antiquity such as those of Mesopotamia, where trade was confined to a river traffic and to such commodities as might be expensively distributed by pack-animal transport. Since the exports of Athens were largely carried in her own ships [70], and financed by her own bankers, and since their geographical range extended from the Black Sea to Spain, it is probable that the pottery industry rose to a higher economic importance in Attica than in any state before or since.

BIBLIOGRAPHICAL NOTE

The best technical discussion of ancient pottery making is still: L. FRANCHET, 'Céramique primitive' (Geuthner, Paris. 1911). Earlier archaeological criticism on technique had not been based on practical experience or scientific study, and it was this consideration which led Dr GISELA M. A. RICHTER to go to a pottery school and afterwards to write her valuable 'Craft of Athenian Pottery' (Metropolitan Museum of Art, Yale University Press, New Haven. 1923). A brief scientific study of Egyptian pottery is in A. LUCAS, 'Ancient Egyptian Materials and Industries' ((3rd ed.). Arnold, London. 1948). For discussion of the making of Chinese wares see G. P. WU, 'Prehistoric Pottery in China' (University of London, Courtauld Institute of Art, Kegan Paul, London. 1938).

The first full and expert study of technique was made by J. L. KELSO and J. P. THORLEY, (*Annu. Amer. Sch. orient. Res.*, **21–22**, 85, 1943). They give a general account of the ancient technical processes with particular reference to the Palestinian wares at Tell Beit Mirsim. The collaboration of expert potters in the examination of archaeological finds constitutes a new departure, and, within its field, this study is the best yet available.

Knowledge of ancient pottery is necessarily based on the techniques used by modern potters. For these, the most useful book is B. LEACH's 'A Potter's Book' (Faber and Faber, London. 2nd ed. 1945). It includes data on Far Eastern methods. The latest account of the chemical processes, and of modern factory technique, is in E. ROSENTHAL's 'Pottery and Ceramics' (Penguin Books, Harmondsworth. 1949). The data about modern primitive technique are scattered. Some of them are quoted in the references.

REFERENCES

[1] KLIMA, B. *Archeologické Rozhledy*, **4**, 193, 1952.
[2] GARSTANG, J. *Ann. Archaeol. Anthrop.*, **23**, 70, 1936.
[3] KENYON, K. M. *Antiquity*, **24**, 196, 1950.
"Archaeol. News", *Amer. J. Archaeol.*, **53**, 50, 1949.

[4] VAILLANT, G. C. 'The Aztecs of Mexico', p. 31. Penguin Books, Harmondsworth. 1950.

[5] BOSWELL, J. G. 'A Tour of the Hebrides with Samuel Johnson', published from the original manuscript by F. A. POTTLE and C. H. BENNETT, p. 138. Viking Press, New York; Heinemann, London. 1936.

[6] *De Bello Gallico*, v, 14 (Loeb ed. p. 252, 1937). There is no ground for questioning Caesar's description as applying to the large areas of the island which were as yet untouched by the settlements which took place from Gaul in the late first millennium.

[7] KELSO, J. L. and THORLEY, J. P. *Annu. Amer. Sch. orient. Res.*, **21–22,** 86, 1943.

[8] MACKAY, E. J. H. *J. R. Anthrop. Inst.*, **60,** 127, 1930.

[9] MITCHELL, SIR ARTHUR. 'The Past in the Present', p. 26. Rhind Lectures on Archaeology, 1876, 1878. Douglas, Edinburgh. 1880.

[10] KENYON, K. M. *Trans. Leics. Archaeol. Soc.*, **26,** 46, 1950.

[11] In TOBLER, A. J. 'Excavations at Tepe Gawra' (Vol. 2, pp. 159–62. Joint Exped. of the Baghdad School, the University Museum and Dropsie College to Mesopotamia, University Press, Philadelphia. 1950) a few determinations of firing temperature are recorded, including one of about 1200° C. So high a temperature is not elsewhere recorded except in China (WU, G. D. 'Prehistoric Pottery in China', p. 52. University of London, Courtauld Institute of Art, Kegan Paul, London. 1938).

[12] This question concerning ancient pottery technique has been the subject of extensive expert discussion, mainly in connexion with the early black and black-topped wares of Egypt: see LUCAS, A. 'Ancient Egyptian Materials and Industries' (3rd ed.), pp. 425 ff. Arnold, London. 1948, and references there given. For subsequent discussion and experiments see CHILDE, V. GORDON. *Man*, **37,** art. 55, 1937; and KELSO, J. L. and THORLEY, J. P. *Annu. Amer. Sch. orient. Res.*, **21–22,** 90, 1943.

[13] It is probable that painted pottery, except perhaps glazed ware, was not twice fired, but the point has been disputed; for discussion see RICHTER, G. M. A. 'The Craft of Athenian Pottery' (p. 37. Metropolitan Museum of Art, Yale University Press, New Haven. 1923) and references there given. Dr Richter concludes that even glazed ware was not twice fired at Athens.

[14] LEACH, B. 'A Potter's Book' (2nd ed.), p. 63. Faber and Faber, London. 1945. STEVENSON, R. B. K. *Proc. Soc. Antiq. Scotld.*, **73,** 233, 1939. The latter deals with British wares; the building of continental prehistoric wares is still largely unstudied. A primitive community in southern India, the Urali Kurumbars of Wynad, shape the outside of their pots from a ball of clay and then scoop out the inside with a bamboo blade (AIYAPPAN, A. *Man*, **47,** art. 54, 1947).

[15] WU, G. D. See ref. [11], p. 132.

[16] MACKAY, E. J. H. *J. R. Anthrop. Inst.*, **60,** 127, 1930.

[17] INGE, C. H. *Palest. Explor. Quart.*, **70,** 249 and Pl. XXV, fig. 1, 1938.

[18] Noted by Mr. Basil Megaw in storage jars from Glencrutchery and other sites in the Isle of Man (information from Mr. Megaw).

[19] RICHTER, G. M. A. See ref. [13], p. 29.

[20] KELSO, J. L. and THORLEY, J. P. *Annu. Amer. Sch. orient. Res.*, **21–22,** 102, 3, 1943.

[21] BEN-DOR, I. *Ann. Archaeol. Anthrop.*, **23,** 77, 1936.

[22] Kick-wheels used by modern Gaza potters are reported to have similar bearings.

[23] The turn-table is sometimes called a 'tournette' and sometimes a 'slow-wheel'. The use of turn-tables, and the means of determining whether a prehistoric pot has been made with a turn-table or a wheel, are valuably discussed by Dr WU. See ref. [11], pp. 39, 47, 52, and 134 ff.

[24] LEACH, B. See ref. [14], p. 69.
FRANCHET, L. 'Céramique primitive', p. 60. Geuthner, Paris. 1911.
[25] KELSO, J. L. and THORLEY, J. P. *Annu. Amer. Sch. orient. Res.*, **21–22,** 96, 101, 1943.
[26] RICHTER, G. M. A. See ref. [13], p. 11.
[27] At Jericho. BEN-DOR, I. *Ann. Archaeol. Anthrop.*, **23,** 78, 1936.
[28] *Idem. Ibid.*, **23,** Pls. XXX and XXXII, 1936.
[29] BURGAUD, P. and BURGAUD, P. *Bull. Soc. préhist. franç.*, **36,** 202, 1939.
[30] MITCHELL, SIR ARTHUR. See ref. [9], p. 27.
[31] For an adequate draught the flame-way must not be smaller in section than the chimney; the latter should be in diameter a quarter to a fifth of the kiln diameter. (LEACH, B. See ref. [14], p. 191.)
[32] For a description of modern Cretan kilns built of fire-resisting sandstone or volcanic rock in a hole dug in a bank see XANTHUDIDES, S. in 'Essays in Aegean Archaeology presented to Sir Arthur Evans' (ed. by S. CASSON), p. 126. Clarendon Press, Oxford. 1927. Even the floor of the combustion chamber was of stone, supported on a pillar and arches, which must have occupied much space.
[33] FRANCHET, L. See ref. [24], p. 127.
[34] JANSE, O. 'Archaeological Research in Indo-China', Vol. 1, p. 60 and Pls. CXXXVIII–CLIX. Harvard-Yenching Institute, Monograph Series Vol. 7. Harvard University Press, Cambridge, Mass. 1947.
[35] GRIMES, W. F. *Cymmrodor*, **41,** 53, 1930, from which the illustrations are taken.
[36] Except perhaps in RICHTER, G. M. A. See ref. [13], figure 80, which might suggest horizontal heat inlets into the combustion chamber, but can hardly be interpreted with any safety.
[37] MECQUENEM, R. DE. *Mém. Délég. Perse*, **25,** 204, and fig. 42, 1934.
[38] GHIRSHMAN, R. 'Fouilles de Sialk près de Kashan', Vol. 1, p. 36 and fig. 5. Louvre, Dép. Antiq. Orient., Sér. archéol., Vol. 4. Paris. 1938.
[39] MYLONAS, G. E. 'Excavations at Olynthus', Vol. 1, p. 12. Johns Hopkins Univ. Stud. in Archaeol., no. 6. Johns Hopkins Press, Baltimore. 1929.
[40] Though the Erösd example illustrated in CHILDE, V. GORDON. 'The Dawn of European Civilization' ((5th ed. enl.) fig. 67. Routledge and Kegan Paul, London. 1950) is said to have had pots in it when excavated.
[41] WOOLLEY, SIR (CHARLES) LEONARD. *Iraq*, **1,** 147, 1934.
[42] Larger kilns were built, but for brick-making: for instance at Khafaje near Baghdad (FRANKFORT, H. *et al.* 'Tell Asmar and Khafaje', p. 76. Univ. of Chicago, Orient Inst.: Commun. no. 13, Chicago. 1932); at Nuzi near Kirkuk (STARR, R. F. S. 'Nuzi', Vol. 1, p. 238, Vol. 2, plan 25. Harvard University Press, Cambridge, Mass. 1937); also, probably, at Gaza (PETRIE, SIR (WILLIAM MATTHEW) FLINDERS. 'Ancient Gaza I', Pl. LII. Egypt. Res. Acc. and Brit. Sch. Archaeol. Egypt, Publ. 52. London. 1931). A large kiln at Nippur resembles Roman kilns so closely as to throw doubt on its alleged date. (FISHER, C. S. 'Excavations at Nippur', p. 40, plan 3, Pl. III, 2. Babylonian Expedition of the University of Pennsylvania, Univ. of Penn. Dept. of Archaeol. and Palaeon., Philadelphia. 1905.)
[43] SCOTT, SIR (WARWICK) LINDSAY. *Proc. Soc. Antiq. Sctld*, **85** (1950–1) 1, 1953.
Idem. Antiquity, **25,** 196, 1951.
[44] CHILDE, V. GORDON. 'New Light on the Most Ancient East' (4th ed.), p. 34. Routledge and Kegan Paul, London. 1952.
SCHUCHHARDT, C. *Prähist. Z.*, **1,** 41 f., 1909.

[45] CHILDE, V. GORDON. See ref. [44], p. 138.

[46] Though the pointed base might derive from water jars designed for lowering into a well; in north China well-buckets have pointed bases today (WU, G. D. See ref. [11], p. 51).

[47] By Professor S. PIGGOTT (*Archaeol. J.*, **88,** 80, 1931) developing a suggestion made by C. SCHUCHHARDT.

[48] EVANS, SIR ARTHUR J. 'The Palace of Minos', Vol. 1, p. 177. Macmillan, London. 1929.

[49] BREA, L. BERNABÒ. *Riv. Studi Liguri*, **16,** 1, 1950.

[50] WU, G. D. See ref. [11], pp. 62, 72.

[51] *Idem. Ibid.*, pp. 37, 105.
HOMMEL, R. P. 'China at Work', p. 351. Bucks County Hist. Soc., Doylestown. [1937].

[52] EVANS, SIR ARTHUR J. See ref. [48], pp. 153, 219, 252.

[53] *Idem. Ibid.*, p. 237.

[54] For ritual pottery in that cemetery see DIKAIOS, P. 'The Excavations at Vounous-Bellapais in Cyprus 1931–2'. *Archaeologia*, **88,** 118, 1938 (1940).

[55] EVANS, SIR ARTHUR J. See ref. [48], pp. 180 and 223–5.

[56] WACE, A. J. B. 'Chamber Tombs at Mycenae.' *Archaeologia*, **82,** 142, 1932.

[57] CHILDE, V. GORDON. See ref. [44], p. 124.

[58] BUNZEL, RUTH L. 'The Pueblo Potter', pp. 83 ff. Columbia University Contribution to Anthropology no. 8, New York. 1929.

[59] *Geoponica*, II, 4913. This work was put together in the tenth century from a compilation of the sixth century itself taken from much more ancient sources.

[60] MALINOWSKI, B. 'Argonauts of the Western Pacific', pp. 283 ff. Robert Mond Expedition to Guinea, Stud. in Econ. and Polit. Sci. no. 65, London. 1922.

[61] BUNZEL, RUTH L. See ref. [58], p. 6.

[62] MACKAY, E. J. H. *J. R. Anthrop. Inst.*, **60,** 127, 1930.

[63] BETTS, F. N. *Man*, **50,** art. 197, 1950.

[64] MITCHELL, SIR ARTHUR. See ref. [9], p. 28.

[65] XANTHUDIDES, S. See ref. [32], p. 118.

[66] For instance, the craftsmen on a Highland farm in the eighteenth century were also tenants of a piece of land, or cotters. (GRANT, I. F. 'Every-day Life on an Old Highland Farm 1769–82', p. 151. Longmans, London. 1924.) Hebridean crofters are in the same position today.

[67] See ВОЕВОДСКИЙ, М. В. *Советск. Археол.*, **2,** 51, 1936 (VOYEVODSKIĬ, M. V. *Sovetsk. Arkheol.*). The impressions of string necklaces, supposedly female, have been seen in patterns on pottery by ROSENBERG, G. 'Kulturströmungen in Europa zur Steinzeit', p. 24. Høst, Copenhagen. 1931.

[68] DR RICHTER points out that there are references to, and pictures of, the spinning of the wheel by hand, but that the use of the kick-wheel in the Athenian potteries is not evidenced. (See ref. [13], pp. 90 ff.)

[69] For decrees made by the Ioulietai and the Koresians in implementation of such treaties, see *Corpus Inscriptionum Graecarum*, Vol. 2, i, no. 546. Kgl. Akad. Wiss., Berlin. 1877. DR RICHTER discussed at length the method of use of red ochre in the Athenian potteries (see ref. [13], pp. 53 ff.); it is clear from KELSO, J. L. and THORLEY, J. P. (*Annu. Amer. Sch. orient. Res.*, **21–22,** 90, 1943) that its effectiveness as a slip in giving a bright red surface on firing derived from its high ferric oxide content (some 17 %).

[70] DUNBABIN, T. J. ('The Western Greeks', pp. 241 ff. Clarendon Press, Oxford. 1948) thinks that, by agreement with Corinth, the movement of Attic ware westwards of the Isthmus may have been in Corinthian ships.

16

TEXTILES, BASKETRY, AND MATS

GRACE M. CROWFOOT

I. ORIGINS

A TEXTILE is a woven (Latin *textilis*) fabric. The word is generally applied to fabrics formed by twisted or spun threads, but there are exceptions in both primitive and modern practice. Baskets and mats are made from strands either twisted or not twisted, more commonly not. It is probable that basketry and mats were made earlier than textiles, but there is no direct evidence on this point, and there are textiles as ancient as any datable remains of baskets or mats yet found. The earliest definite evidence of both weaving and basketry comes from the Neolithic cultures of *c* 5000 B.C. Nevertheless, knowledge of how men lived before that date gives some idea of yet more primitive techniques from which they may have derived.

In the icy cold of the Upper Palaeolithic age in Europe clothing was doubtless made of skins. A statuette from Mal'ta in Siberia seems clad in a trousered suit of fur, such as Eskimo wear (figure 22) [1]. The garments were probably sewn with fine leather thongs or strands of sinew. Sinew-dressing has been classed as a textile art, and in Lapland twisted threads are produced as delicate as fine yarn.

In southern Europe, where the climate was more genial, the Palaeolithic bone needles were exceedingly fine, and plant fibres may have been used for sewing as well as for bowstrings and lashing flint weapon-heads. If so, the secret of spinning, the trick of twisting fibres into a thread, may have been discovered in a Palaeolithic cultural stage.

From the Mesolithic stage, after the ice had melted in Europe, we have at last an example of interlacing threads, the remains of a fishing-net made of twined threads of plant bast from Korpilahti in Finland (figure 282) [2]. No doubt it was from nets like this one that the carrying-net developed, of such value to nomadic peoples. Wandering hunters and fishers, however, leave few traces.

The Neolithic revolution is so startling in its rapid cultural development, linked as it is with the beginnings of agriculture, that it has been likened to the industrial revolution. As food-production replaced food-gathering, communities settled in villages. The women then had time to develop crafts of which they had already acquired some elements in the hunting stage. Paralleling advances in agriculture and pottery, they began to apply their knowledge of the making and interlacing of threads to basketry and weaving.

Basketry and mats are commonly distinguished from weaving, but it is often difficult to know where to make the division. Baskets are vessels made by hand by interlacing two or more sets of strands in different ways, and these ways are sometimes closely similar to weaving. Mats may be made in a similar manner to basketry, but are often true weaves. In weaving, one set of threads, the warp, is stretched, while another set, the weft or woof, is passed through it at right angles, in such a way that the two sets of threads are regularly held by each other. The warp may be stretched in many different ways, and any apparatus used for this can be called a loom.

Baskets, serving simple needs, have changed little through the ages, but textiles, with their decorative value and their many uses, have developed unceasingly. Anciently, however, the two techniques were much closer to each other than they are now. Strands of threads were interlaced by hand, whether for mat, basket, or textile. Only with the fuller development of the loom did the techniques draw apart.

The evolutionary story of these techniques is still full of gaps. Natural fibres of all sorts are extremely perishable, and survive only under very special circumstances. Dry desert sands give the best condition for conservation. The most important examples are from Egypt, where textiles of all periods, from Neolithic to medieval, have been found in profusion. The arid sites of Peru have yielded a great quantity for some periods. There is also an exceptionally dry cave in Spain where important finds have been made. There are moreover certain wet conditions that make for preservation of fibres. These are present in the peat-bogs and lake-dwellings of Scandinavia and Switzerland. Much material from these sites is carbonized, the reason for which is still obscure.

One other circumstance preserves fragments of textiles. Contact with metal may save a scrap of fabric from perishing. Bronze ornaments and weapons have here been the most helpful, as oxidation products of copper are good preservers of fabrics. Iron oxide commonly works too strongly, sometimes entirely replacing the original fibres, though the character of the weave may still be ascertained. Much, too, can be learnt from impressions on pottery. Textiles have also been found preserved for long periods in salt mines, but the absence of stratification makes their dating almost impossible. Radiocarbon-dating may prove useful here.

In considering gaps in the knowledge of textile history, it must be remembered that there are vast areas where little archaeological study has been undertaken.

China, for example, is poorly represented, though silken textiles were certainly produced there for centuries before the Christian era. Moreover, in earlier excavations the record is sometimes very incomplete. Surviving pieces of rag were often rejected as without interest, though there is still much material in museums which would repay examination. Determination of the exact botanical origin of the fibres used in basketry and weaving has only quite recently been recognized as of archaeological importance.

As with other cultural products, the technical advances in weaving proceeded at very different rates in different areas. Here the methods of basket-making or weaving are described first, and then the more important or interesting finds, arranged in roughly chronological order. This method brings out the constant recurrence of primitive types, as different civilizations arise in different parts of the world. Thus, contemporary with the finest pattern-weaves of Egypt, there are cultures in northern Europe still in the Neolithic stage, and the earliest types of both weaving and basketry are in constant use even today, though the more complicated primitive pattern-techniques have disappeared with the development of modern looms.

II. TYPES OF BASKETRY AND MATTING

A stage in which basketry is present but weaving unknown has not yet been discovered. By about 5000 B.C., basketry and weaving have already been developed in distinct directions. The material of basketry is generally unspun vegetable fibres, though hand-twisted cords are found in some types of baskets, especially for handles and bases, and are sometimes used in matting. Obviously, the fibres used depend on the local vegetation, but even when they have been preserved they are often difficult to identify. Moreover, many of the early records are not of the fibres themselves but of their impressions on pottery—though, even from these, species of reeds and grasses may sometimes be distinguished.

Most of the earliest evidence comes from three areas, namely the Near East, including Egypt, Mesopotamia, and Palestine; Peru; and Europe, including Switzerland, the Balkans, Spain, and the British Isles. Before discussing these finds it is necessary to describe in some detail the main techniques in use.

(*a*) *Coiled Basketry*. This earliest, and by far the most important, form has been continued to the present day in most parts of the world. Unlike other basketry techniques, it has no obvious affinities with any sort of weaving. Coiled work requires two elements, the coil or core, and the wrapping or sewing-strip. The core, usually consisting of a bundle of grass, rushes, or fibres, is coiled spirally in the shape required, the different layers being fastened together by a sewing-strip of similar material. The holes through which the sewing-strip is passed were probably pierced with pointed bones or sticks, the equivalent of the modern awl. The work always begins at the base, and there are three chief varieties of centre found: a simple coil or snail; a rosette, with radiating stitches; and the four-cross, with centre of four pieces of palm or reed laid crosswise, with the free ends split and drawn into the coil (figure 258 E-G). In early work, four variations in the method of wrapping are distinguishable:

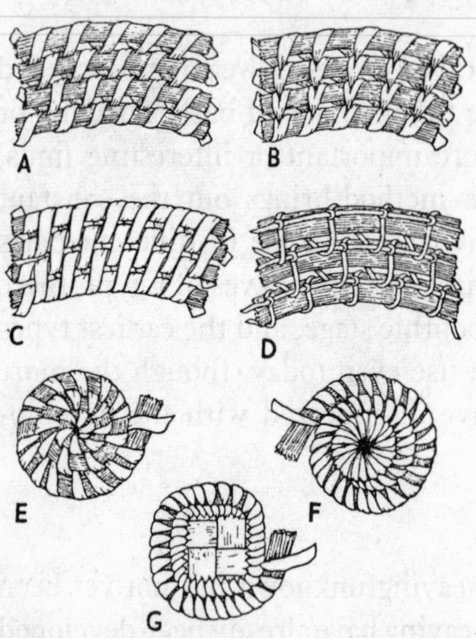

FIGURE 258—*Coiled basketry.* (A) *Strip piercing coil, type 1.* (B) *Strip piercing preceding stitch, type 2.* (C) *Strip wrapping coil between stitches, type 3.* (D) *Strip knotted through itself, type 4.* (E) *Snail centre.* (F) *Rosette centre.* (G) *Four-cross centre.*

Type 1. The strip passes round the latest coil, piercing the edge of the one below already in place (figure 258 A).

Type 2. The strip passes in the same way but, in addition to piercing the coil, it pierces also the stitch immediately below it (figure 258 B).

Type 3. After each stitch, one or more wraps are made round the latest coil before the next stitch through the coil below. In the example shown, the strip passes round the coil below instead of piercing it (figure 258 C).

Type 4. The strip passes round the coil and knots through itself, as in a button-hole-stitch; the strip on the following coil passes through the strip on the first coil, and does not pierce or pass round this coil (figure 258 D).

(*b*) *Twined Work.* This technique, sometimes called twined plait or twined weave, is half-way between a plait and a weave. It was most commonly used for matting. Single rushes, or bundles of rushes or flax, are laid side by side and interlaced by two threads which twine between each reed or bundle. There are several varieties:

Type 1. Simple twine, with rows of twining widely spaced showing the flax or rushes (figure 259 A).

Type 2. Simple twine, with the rows so closely pressed as to hide the other element completely (figure 259 B).

Type 3. Simple twine; half of each bundle of grasses or reeds is caught with half of the following one, leaving a series of triangular spaces (figure 259 E).

Type 4. Tufts of flax fibre are held by rows of simple twining to give a pile effect (figure 259 C).

Type 5. One twining thread pierces through each reed, the other passes round it, so that no twine is visible on one side (figure 259 D).

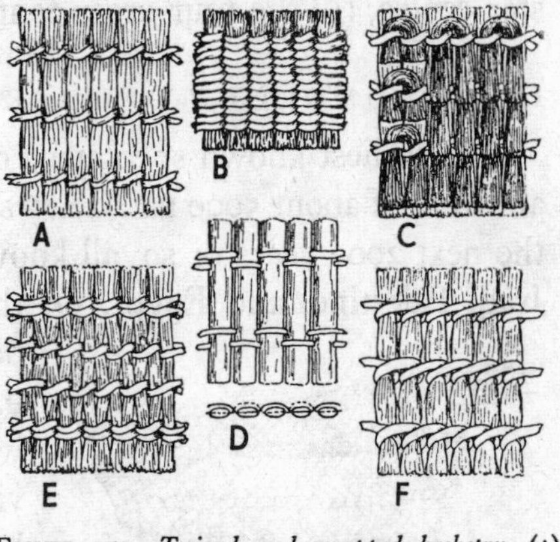

FIGURE 259—*Twined and wrapped basketry.* (A) *Simple twined basketry, open, type 1.* (B) *Simple twine, close, type 2.* (C) *Twine with pile, type 4.* (D) *Twine with pierced reeds, type 5.* (E) *Ornamental twine, type 3.* (F) *Wrapped matting.*

(*c*) *Wrapped Work.* This is usually classed as weaving, though it is always done with the fingers. In the only type present in matting here, the wrapping strand passes round bundles of reeds, passing over two and under one (figure 259 F).

(*d*) *Matting Work.* These techniques are much akin to weaving. In some cases, they must have been made as on a loom, with one series of strings or rushes stretched (a warp) and another (a weft) woven through, as in a plain or twill weave (see below, figure 270 A, J). In this technique we have what may have been the beginning of spinning, the cords of strands being twisted together, as in a two-plyed thread (p 425).

Type 1. Rushes woven through a cord or string warp, as if darned (figure 260 D).

Type 2. Rushes interlaced at right-angles, as in darning or a plain weave (figure 260 E).

Type 3. Rushes interlaced as in a twill weave (p 430). (Figure 260 A–C, F.)

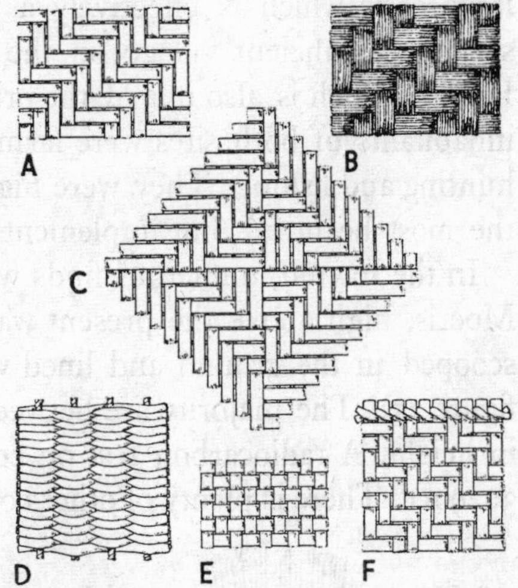

FIGURE 260—*Matting.* (A) *Twill, single reeds, 3×3, type 3.* (B) *Twill, bunches of grasses, 2×2, type 3.* (C) *Twill, ornamental centre, type 3.* (D) *Plain weave, reeds on cord warp, type 1.* (E) *Plain weave, single reeds, type 2.* (F) *Twill, 2×2, type 3, with twined edge.*

(*e*) *Plaited Work.* Plaits can be made separately, and then sewn into the required shape. In the only example known from the period here discussed, the plaits are laced together with a palm cord in such a way that this does not show (figure 261).

(*f*) *Wickerwork or Stake-frame Basketry.* Baskets of strands, woven in and out of a stake-frame—'randed', in modern basketry phraseology—have been found in a very few examples (figure 262). Three centres are shown: (B) the usual star centre, (C) the four-cross centre, and (D) an adaptation for oval baskets.

III. CHRONOLOGY OF BASKETRY AND MATTING

The earliest known specimens of basketry are from Neolithic sites in Egypt and Iraq of about 5000 B.C. They show a technique already fully developed. For the next 2000 years or so, all known examples come from village sites in Iran, Iraq, Palestine, and Egypt. Of these, possibly the earliest is Jarmo in Iraq, dated (by a radiocarbon test) to 5270–4630 B.C. [3]. Here, only mud impressions of plain-weave mats (see matting types 1 and 2) survive. There are, however, actual examples of basketry and textiles preserved in the dry desert sand of both Upper and Lower Egypt from not long after 5000 B.C.

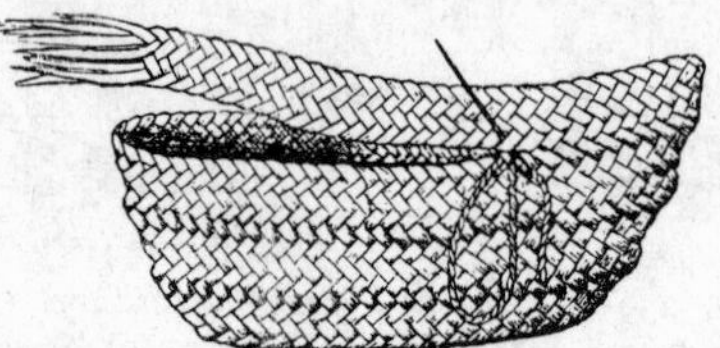

FIGURE 261—*Plaited basketry, sewn.*

The two most productive Egyptian sites are, first, Fayum A, a site in the large oasis which is effectively a westward extension of Lower Egypt, and second, an ancient village on the east bank of the Nile near the town of Badari, which is also one of the principal sources of predynastic remains. The inhabitants of both sites were farmers, but must still have largely depended on hunting and fishing. They were highly skilled peoples, and makers of some of the most beautiful flint implements known.

In the Fayum, numerous finds were made on the shores of the ancient Lake Moeris, high above the present water-line [4]. The granaries there are holes scooped in the ground and lined with coiled basketry of corn-straw (type 1: figure 25). The majority are between 3 and 4 feet in diameter and 1 and 2 feet in height. A radiocarbon test on corn from the granaries gave the date 4784–3929 B.C. There is plenty of other coiled basket-work of the same type, some with snail centre (figure 258 E). There are large circular mats in loose straw; flat platters or lids of grass up to 19 inches in diameter; a miniature basket 3 inches high; and a very fine boat-shaped basket with foundation coil of grass and wrapping-strand of bast probably from flax, with three coloured vertical strands interwoven in the side (plate 9 A).

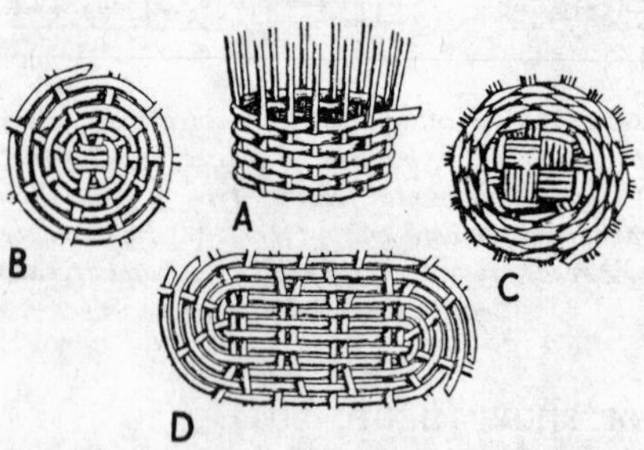

FIGURE 262—*Stake-frame basketry.* (A) *'Randing'.* (B) *Wickerwork round centre.* (C) *Four-cross centre in rushes.* (D) *Oval centre.*

The finds at Badari are more varied [5].

There are fragments of coiled basketry, again of type 1, of reed-coil with reed-wrapping, and of round lids for pots. Mats were used for wrapping bodies in the cemetery, and there are remains of a possible hamper coffin. The reed-mats are of two styles, one of bundles twined with thin reed-fibre strands (twined type 1), and an example, unique at this period, of the same material in wrapped work (figure 259 F).

Later predynastic yields from Badari are baskets again in coil but now of three types (1, 2, and 3, p 416). Among materials, palm has been added to grass and

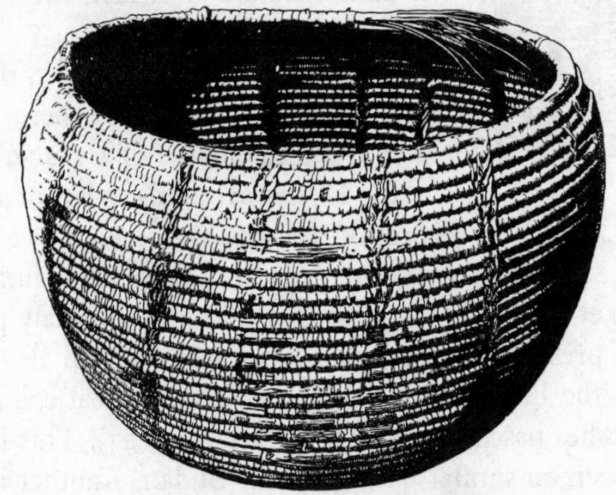

FIGURE 263—*Basket from Gurob in the Fayum, Egypt.* c *3400* B.C.

flax. From now on, it becomes the commonest basketry material in Egypt. From this period we have also reed matting, including a unique fragment of twined work (type 5, figure 259 D) and two of matting on a cord warp (matting type 2), one with an edge formed by interlacing the warp cords (see figure 264 for a later example of this edging).

For the next period we have only impressions on pottery. Such mouldings on the base or sides of hand-made pots may occur accidentally or intentionally. If a round-bottomed pot is made on a mat, impressions, sometimes confused, may be left all over its lower part. This is the case in a late Neolithic Chinese culture-site (Yang Shao) of about 3000 B.C. [6]. There, hand-made pottery appears to have been made upon a bed of cloth, matting, or basket-work, the impressions of which are still visible, though it is difficult to tell what type they represent. If, however, the pot is set to dry on a mat, a common practice, a clear impression of the mat is often left on the base.

From three Palestinian sites, Jericho, Ghassul (20 miles to the east), and

Wadi Ghazzeh in southern Palestine, there are impressions on pottery bases, all probably of the fourth millennium B.C. [7]. They reveal the existence of coiled baskets (coiled type 1), one with a rosette centre (figure 258 F), and reed- and rush-mattings in various designs of type 3 (figure 260 A–C). The impressions are mostly so clear that the actual species of reeds and rushes are identifiable—*Typha angustata* B. *et* Ch., *Juncus acutus* L., *Scirpus lacustris* L., and *S. littoralis* Schrad. From the Early Bronze Age site of Vounous in Cyprus, perhaps a little later, there is one impression on a sherd of a very fine basket, coiled or twined—it is difficult to say which [8].

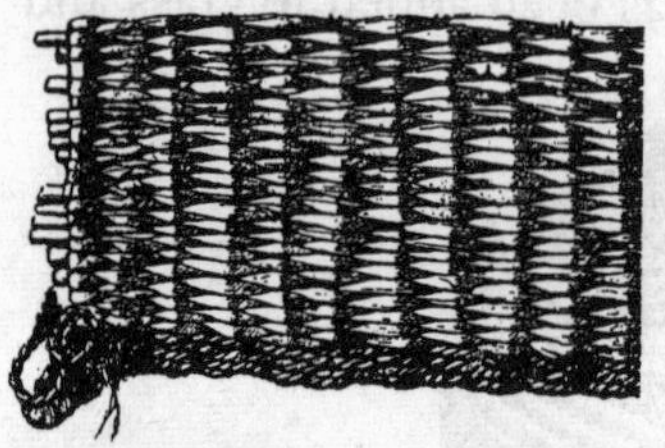

FIGURE 264—*Rush matting type 1 from Tarkhan, Egypt.* c *3400 B.C.*

From Mohenjo-Daro, also, in the Indus basin, a site of about 3000 B.C., there comes the impression on a pot-base of a coarse coiled mat.

Early Dynastic burials in Egypt at Tarkhan near Cairo, of perhaps 3400 B.C., show coiled basketry persisting [9]. Here there is the first appearance of a large round basket with a lid, a shape that became extremely popular in later periods. It is here present in both coiled types 1 and 2, and also from the same date at Gurob, in the Fayum [10], in type 2, with vertical coloured lines with split feathered stitches passing over two coils (figure 263). This form of decoration may still be seen on similar baskets in the Sudan. Another development of coiled basketry from Tarkhan, the hamper coffin in type 4, is of rushes with a thin twisted wrapping-strand (plate 9 B). Coffins are also made in twined basketry (twined type 1) of rushes twined with cords. Matting is present in several forms, including the rush matting on a cord warp (matting type 1) with a corded edge (figure 264) as at Badari (p 419). Here are also the first examples of a type of bed which still persists in the northern Sudan with matting made on the bed-frame. Among varieties known are one of rush matting in plain weave type 2, and another in two-plyed palm-fibre strands with a herring-bone 3×3 twill pattern (type 3) (figure 265).

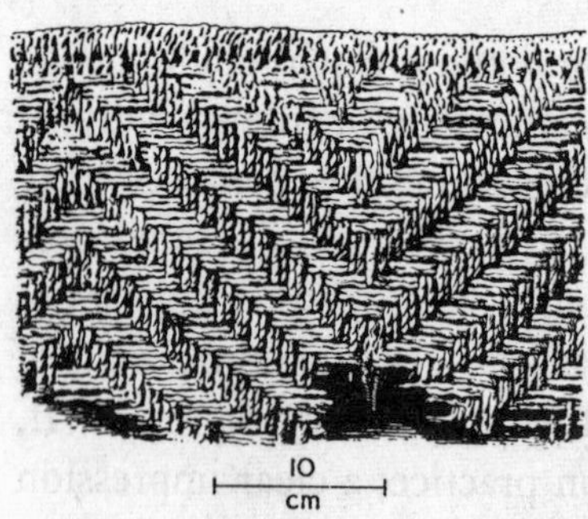

FIGURE 265—*Bed-matting, 3×3 herring-bone twill, from Tarkhan, Egypt.* c *3400 B.C.*

The first European evidence appears about 2500 B.C. It is from the Swiss lake-villages [11]. The people, though still in the Neolithic state, were highly skilled in making baskets, matting, and textiles. Their settlements have yielded a collection of primitive techniques, some missing from the more developed Egyptian sites. They include knotless netting and netting with a simple knot, a great variety of twined work, and some coiled basketry. The remains are carbonized, but the material, where determinable, is usually flax, though bast and rushes were also used. The Swiss material is very fragmentary, but from a dry cave in Spain (Cueva de los Murciélagos, Andalusia), we have a collection of complete bags and baskets of esparto grass (*Stipa tenacissima* L., now confined to north Africa), which makes some of the Swiss fragments more intelligible.

The Swiss coiled basketry was of both types 1 and 2. The twined work seems to have come mostly from flat bags (in twined type 2 and perhaps 1), worked spirally (see plate 9 C, a Spanish example). One very interesting development of the simple twining is the introduction of a nap or pile of fibrous flax, which gives a fleecy effect (twined type 4). Some of these pieces are thought to have come from cloaks, covers, or mats. There were also some padded fragments in spiral twine with very thick pile, which may have come from cushions. Besides the twined mats, there is an impression on a baking plate of an unfinished rush mat in plain weave (matting type 2, plate 9 D).

From Late Neolithic sites in Hungary and the Balkans there are a number of impressions on pot bases in 2×2 twills (matting type 3). One of these, from Aradac in Yugoslavia, of single reeds, shows the edge of the mat, cut and finished with a row of simple twining (figure 260 F). Examples of stake-frame basketry, made like English willow baskets today, come from the Late Bronze pile-dwellings at Zürich [12]. One has an oval centre (figure 262 D).

There are a few examples, probably of around 2000 B.C., of an Early Bronze culture from the British Isles [13]. An impression of coarse coiled basketry on a pot base, and two fragments of twined sedge-matting (twined type 1) come from the Orkneys. The sedge used here is the same as in one of the Palestinian chalcolithic examples (*Scirpus lacustris* L., pp 420, 450), a favourite basket-sedge. A very recent discovery of pot impressions on the bases of urns from a Late Bronze site in the Scilly Isles again reveals both coiled and twined work, the latter showing attempts at more elaborate patterns (twined type 3, figure 259 E).

Conditions in the dry valleys of Peru are as perfect for the preservation of textiles as in the deserts of Egypt. A wealth of this material, starting with the preceramic period, which begins about 2500 B.C., has been discovered [14] [15]. The farmers of the Chicama valley were then living in very similar circumstances to those of the Fayum and Badari (p 418), supplementing agriculture with fishing and bird-snaring. They lacked pottery and hunting-weapons, but their baskets and matting were highly developed. Sedges, reeds, and leaf-bast were used. In one interesting type of basket the sides are closely twined (twined type 2) but the base is made in stake-frame technique, with four-cross centre (figure 262 C). Reed-matting is sometimes twined, sometimes woven on a corded warp (matting type 1). In this early Peruvian culture it is extremely difficult to draw the line between matting and weaving; both employed twining and plain weave. The twining and matting techniques, already highly developed, seem here to be actually passing into true weaving.

For the rest of the period we are discussing, almost all the material is from Egypt. Throughout the Middle Kingdom the same techniques in twined mats and coiled basketry continued in use. The only new developments come from Kerma in Nubia [16]. There the basketry is coiled (types 1 and 2), and includes bowls, trays, and lids in split straw and reed. Besides the usual snail centre a new centre, the four-cross, is introduced (figure 258 G); it is generally regarded as a labour-saving device. A most interesting new form is the round basket with pointed lid, often imitated in painted pottery. The shape persists in this district to the present day, along with the four-cross centre, and is still decorated with brilliant geometric patterns of the very kind painted on the pottery.

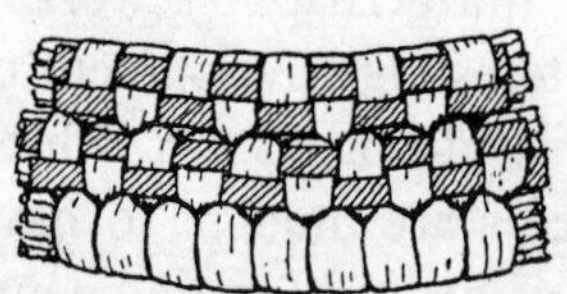

FIGURE 266—*Chequerwork. Coloured strands darned under wrapping-strand on coiled basketry, type 1.*

In Dynasty XVIII (1580–1350 B.C.), as we should expect in a period of such elaborate artistic development, Egyptian basketry is extremely accomplished. Twining and matting are still much in use. There are the usual reed-mats in graves, but there are also sandals in reed on a cord warp (matting type 1), flat bag-baskets of corded palm-fibre in which the twining runs vertically, miniature sieves such as those from a foundation deposit of Queen Hatshepsut (*c* 1500 B.C.) at Deir el-Bahri, with edge coiled and centre twined [17]; and examples, from El-Amarna, of a basket of palm-leaf plaits sewn together with two handles, exactly like the *maktaf* used today for carrying soil on excavations (figure 261) [18].

Fine coiled basketry was used for every purpose. It is often decorated with coloured patterns in the coil. Thus an oval basket from the tomb of Meryet-Amen (*c* 1440 B.C.) has a design of rows of ostriches on the lid and the sides (plate 10 A). In some examples from other sites—Sedment [19], El-Amarna, and Gurob—there are coloured patterns in the coil; in others, coloured threads are darned over and under the wrapping strand, giving a chequered effect which still survives in Nubia (figure 266) [20].

That such baskets were valued is proved by the number deposited in the tomb of Tutankhamen (*c* 1350 B.C.) [21]. In the larger baskets, the coils are of the fruit-bearing stalks of the date-palm, and the wrapping-strand is of fronds of doum-palm (*Hyphaene thebaica* Mart.). The smaller baskets were of a grass, probably halfa (esparto, *Lygeum spartum* L.) with a high polished surface, often dyed. Colours used for pattern work include purple, red, and blue-green. The coiling was of types 1, 2, and 3, with snail and rosette centres. The commonest shape (plate 10 B) is a round basket with raised lid. The design of checks on the specimen illustrated is a very favourite ornament. This basket has, just below the rim, a tiny basketry ledge to support the lid. Earlier lids of this shape sometimes just sit on the rim. Other shapes were a large round basket with a flat lid and a rather irregular pattern of occasional split stitches in the coil; an oval basket with lid of almost exactly the same shape as that found at Fayum A; and three basket-work bottles, two of which contained grapes. One of these (plate 10 B) has patterns on the side suggesting the props of a vineyard, and lines of chequer-work.

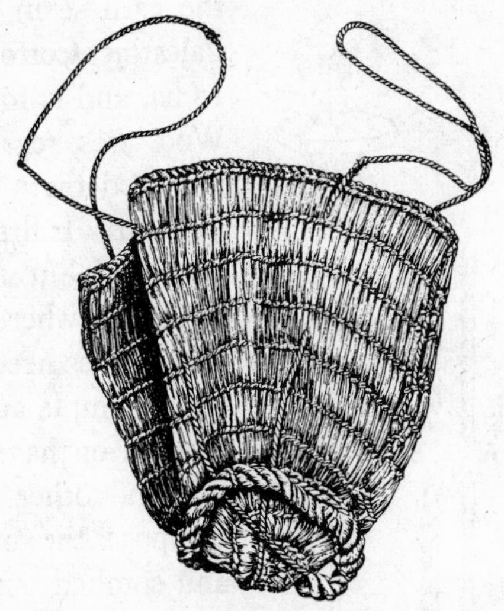

FIGURE 267—*Twined bag from Deir el-Bahri, Egypt.* c *900 B.C.*

From the following centuries two examples from Deir el-Bahri are worth mentioning [17]. One, of about 900 B.C., is a bag-shaped basket, twined horizontally at wide intervals, with two cord handles and a heavily corded base (figure 267). The other, of Dynasty XXV, is a child's basket of coiled work with a lid (type 3), showing a striking use of colour work on the edges (tailpiece p 455).

A group of pot impressions from Phylakopi, on the island of Melos in the Aegean, is specially interesting [22], because there the primitive practice of setting a pot to dry on a mat was in use even for highly ornamented geometric vases. The mats here were circular, in a wickerwork technique but probably made of rushes, and so large that often the impression shows that the vase was set down far from the centre of the mat. There were also rush mats in plain weave (type 2).

It will be seen that basketry is a craft in which it is easy to understand the work of past ages because the same techniques are in use to this day, even to details of ornamentation, favourite colours, and local variations. The fine basketry of 5000 B.C. is still being reproduced in the Fayum, while the individual four-cross centre, invented in Nubia about 2000 B.C., has still not been accepted in Lower Egypt.

IV. SPINNING [23] [24]

All the chief natural fibre groups—bast, cotton, silk, and wool—are represented in early archaeological textile remains. Of these, the vegetable fibres, bast and cotton, appear earlier than wool or silk. Vegetable basts, particularly flax, are the earliest in use throughout Egypt, Mesopotamia, and Palestine. Cotton makes its first appearance about 3000 B.C. in India, and is found later in Peru, together with leaf-basts. Wool was regarded as unclean in Egypt, and has been recorded there in only a few instances, mostly of doubtful antiquity. It first appears in profusion in Scandinavia about 1000 B.C., but it is extremely perishable and may have been in use elsewhere and long before.

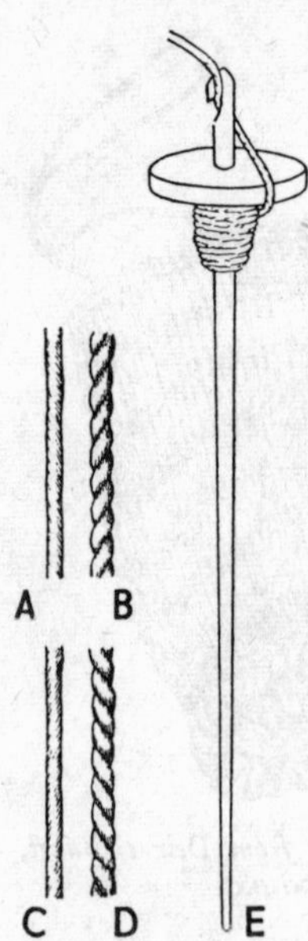

FIGURE 268—*Twist and spindle.* (A) *S-spun.* (B) *Z-doubled.* (C) *Z-spun.* (D) *S-doubled.* (E) *Spindle with thread in position.*

All fibres need some preparation for spinning. Sometimes this is simple and sometimes elaborate. For example, wool and cotton have only to be cleansed and teased out, while flax and other vegetable fibres have to be soaked to decompose the outside layer (retted), beaten and scraped, and combed out (hackled). Primitive people no doubt were content with the minimum preparation.

Spinning is the forming of threads by drawing out and twisting fibres. The thread has also to be wound, but this is always a separate process, while drawing and twisting are sometimes separate and sometimes simultaneous. Drawing consists in pulling out the fibres lengthwise, which arranges them in a more or less parallel order. Twisting is the important factor in spinning. All fibres have irregularities visible under the microscope, and it is by these that they adhere to each other when pressed by twisting (plate 17 B). It is the twisting that gives elasticity and strength to the spun yarn. The twist may be in either direction, to the right (Z) or to the left (S) (figure 268 A, C).

(*a*) *Spinning without Implements.* Among many primitive peoples spinning is done entirely by hand, without any implement. The thread can be made by rolling the fibres between the palms of the hands, or between the hand and another part of the body, usually the cheek or thigh. This is no doubt how spinning began.

(*b*) *Spindle-spinning*. The need of winding up the spun thread on something must have been felt very early, and a stick was used for the purpose. From a simple stick there derived the spindle. This is a slender stick, tapering at one end or both, usually weighted with a whorl, which may be at either end. The stem above the whorl may have a hook or groove in it. The spindle is generally of wood, but may be of bone, ivory, or metal, with whorls of wood, stone, pottery, bone, or glass (figure 273). A distaff is a larger stick, plain or ornamented, sometimes used to hold prepared fibres from which the thread is spun. There are three different ways in which the spindle is known to have been used during the early periods (figure 276):

1. *Suspended Spindle*. A length of fibres is drawn out, twisted by hand, and fastened to the spindle, and then caught under the hook or round the stick (figure 268 E). The fibres are then paid out regularly while the spindle is rotated by hand, dropped, and allowed to swing. The whorl acts as a weight to maintain the spin. In this way a very fine even thread is produced.
2. *Grasped Spindle*. A rove, that is, a thread drawn out but only very slightly twisted, is passed through a ring or over a forked stick or other support, and is then spun on a large spindle grasped and rotated in both hands. This produces a coarse uneven yarn.
3. *Spindle rolled on the Thigh*. This is a most primitive method, but it is easy to see how it could have developed into the suspended-spindle method. The spinner draws the fibres between her hands, and then rolls the spindle on the thigh to twist it.

In primitive life, either because the spun thread is weak, or because a very strong cloth is required, e.g. for tents, the thread used is frequently doubled. This can be done by hand or on a spindle. The yarns are usually doubled (two-plyed) in the opposite direction to that in which they are spun (figure 268 B, D).

There is no evidence for any more advanced spinning-machinery than the spindle throughout our period.

V. LOOMS [25] [26]

A loom has been defined as any apparatus for stretching a warp. In primitive practice, this stretching can be done in many ways—for example, between a tree and the weaver's waist, or round two bars tied to trees or roof-beams or pegged out on the ground. These looms are sometimes described as frameless, and the earliest loom of which evidence is found is in this category. This is the horizontal ground-loom, which first appears in predynastic Egypt, *c* 3000 B.C., and is

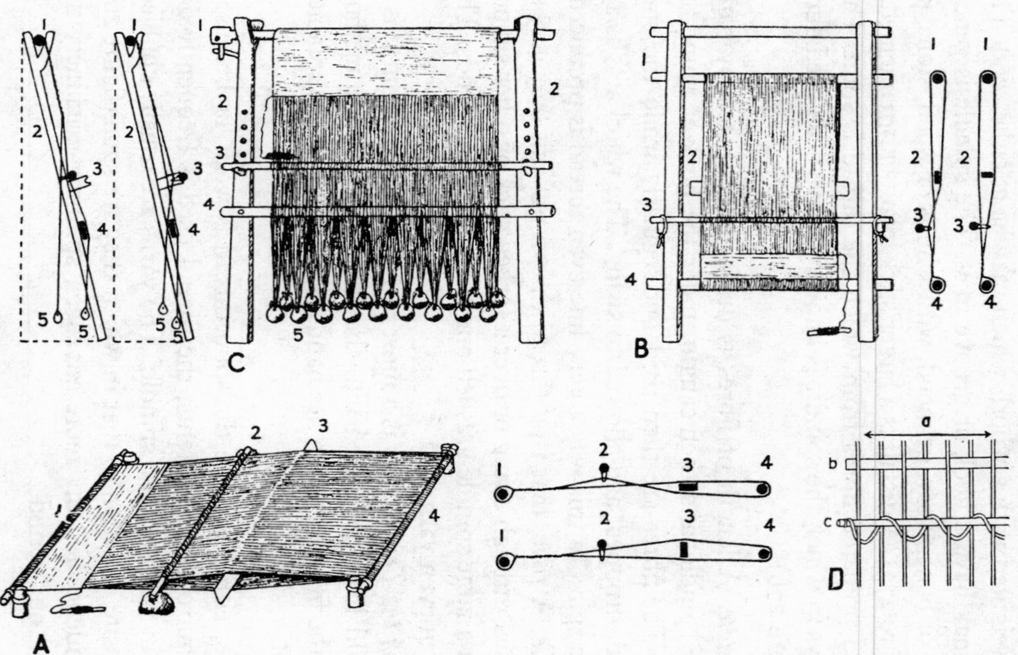

FIGURE 269—*Looms.* (A) *Horizontal ground-loom and shedding diagram:* (1) *breast-beam,* (2) *rod-heddle supported on stones,* (3) *shed-rod,* (4) *warp-beam.* (B) *Vertical two-beamed loom and shedding diagram:* (1) *warp-beam,* (2) *shed-rod,* (3) *rod-heddle,* (4) *breast-beam.* (C) *Warp-weighted loom and shedding diagram:* (1) *warp-beam (revolving) held by a spoke,* (2) *side-beams,* (3) *rod-heddle,* (4) *shed-rod,* (5) *warp-weights.* (D) *Diagram to show* (a) *warp threads,* (b) *shed-rod, and* (c) *rod-heddle with continuous spiral lashing.*

of a type still used by nomadic people, e.g. the Bedouin, throughout the Near East. The vertical framed loom with two beams was in use in Egypt by 1400 B.C., and also persists to the present day. The earliest evidence for the use of both these looms comes from pictorial representations, but for the third loom, the warp-weighted loom, we have in addition well-preserved loom-weights, the oldest dating from Troy *c* 2500 B.C. or, probably, earlier. This loom was in use from Palestine and Greece to the far north, but unlike the other two types has now died out.

(*a*) *The Horizontal Ground-loom* (figure 269 A). The warp is stretched between two beams fastened to four pegs driven into the ground. It may be put on directly over the warp-beams, in a figure of eight, or wound over pegs and transferred to the loom later (p 437 and plate 13 A). The warp threads are divided into two layers, of which half, the odd threads, are lashed to a stick tied above the warp, the 'rod-heddle' (figure 269 D). When this is raised it makes a space, the 'shed', through which the weft can be passed. To obtain the 'countershed', for the next passage of weft, the even threads have to be raised. This is done with the 'shed-rod', a flat piece of wood turned on edge, as can be seen in the shedding diagram.

This is the developed loom as found today, but there were no doubt two earlier stages, both of which are still in use; first, a stage in which there is no division of the warp, and the weave is darned by hand, as in the mat-looms of Cairo; and second, a stage in which a shed-rod gives one shed, but the other is darned, as among the Hadendoa on the Red Sea coast.

On this loom, two tools are used to beat up the weft, a flat wooden sword, the 'sword-beater', and a pointed stick or gazelle horn. The weft may be passed in a ball, or wound on a stick spool.

(*b*) *The Vertical Two-beamed Loom* (figure 269 B) [27]. The warp is stretched between two beams fastened in a rectangular wooden frame. In the modern survival of this type, in Palestine, Syria, and Greece, the same arrangement of rod-heddle and shed-rod is in use as in the horizontal ground loom. The weaver sits, and the work is at the bottom of the loom.

In modern use, three tools are used for beating up on this loom, the sword-beater, the pin, and a comb.

(*c*) *The Warp-weighted Loom* (figure 269 C) [28]. An upper beam is supported on two posts. The warp is stretched between it and a series of weights. No doubt in this loom there were also earlier stages, but from the evidence of one of the last survivals, in Iceland less than a century ago, the rod-heddle and shed-rod were used in exactly the same way, though of course their position was transposed, as the weaving is done at the top of the loom. The weights were made of stone or pottery, pierced with holes, and each was tied to a bunch of warp threads. The tools used were the same, a flat beater, in the north often a bone, and a pointed stick or bone, with a stick spool for the weft.

On all these types of looms, varieties of pattern can be obtained by multiplying heddles or shed-rods, and other devices to raise or lower a certain number of

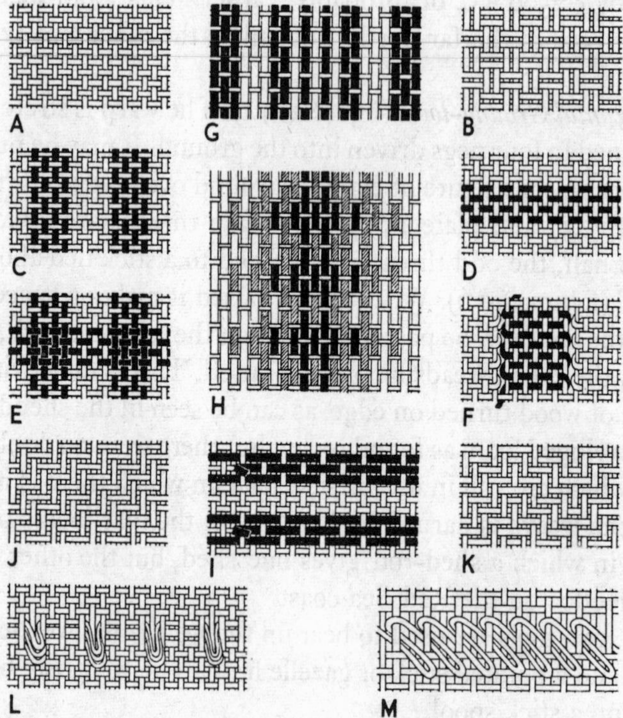

FIGURE 270—PLAIN WEAVES. (A) *Linen weave, type 1.* (B) *Canvas weave, type 2.* PATTERN WEAVES. (C) *Warp stripes, type 1. i.* (D) *Weft stripes, type 1. ii.* (E) *Checks, type 1. iii.* (F) *Tapestry weave, type 2.* (G) *Warp-face weave, simple, type 3.* (H) *Warp-face weave with threads floating at back, type 4.* (I) *Pattern weave with weft floats.* TWILL WEAVES. (J) 2×2 *Twill, type 1.* (K) *Waved twill, type 2.* WEAVES WITH PILE. (L) *Simple loops, type 1.* (M) *Sehna loops, type 2.*

threads, causing warp or weft 'floats'. There are pictorial indications that little hand-frames may have been used (figure 280) for weaving, embroidery, or for the technique known as 'sprang' (p 442).

VI. TYPES OF WEAVING

Weaving, as mentioned above, appears together with basketry at *c* 5000 B.C., already well developed. Again our evidence comes from the same areas, with the addition of Scandinavia. It is necessary to describe the main techniques in use during the period before discussing the finds.

(*a*) *Plain or 'Tabby' Weave*. This type was the earliest to appear, and is common in all countries to the present day. A series of wefts passes over and under a series of warps alternately, as in darning. Two types appear:

Type 1. Single wefts over single warps. When the number of warps and wefts is equal, this is termed linen-weave (figure 270 A). If the warps predominate so as completely to cover the wefts it is a warp-face weave. If the wefts predominate completely to cover the warps it is a tapestry-weave. There are of course many intermediate gradations.

Type 2. Two or more wefts over two or more warps, generally known as canvas weave (figure 270 B).

(*b*) *Pattern Weaves*. These simple pattern weaves are all based on the use of colour or texture in a plain weave technique.

Type 1. Lines or bands in equal plain weave in colour, or made by threads of a different texture (self-stripes), either in warp or weft.

(i) Coloured threads set up in warp (figure 270 C).

(ii) Coloured threads thrown in weft (figure 270 D).

(iii) When (i) and (ii) are combined at regular intervals checks can be formed (figure 270 E).

Type 2. Tapestry-weave (wefts predominating). Patterns are made by covering small areas with different colours. Vertical slits or openings are left where two colours meet (figure 270 F).

Type 3. Warp-face weave, simple. Coloured threads are set up in the warp to form simple stripes and checks (figure 270 G).

Type 4. Warp-face weave. Coloured threads are set up in the warp; those not needed in any particular line of the pattern float at the back (figure 270 H; cf p 440).

(*c*) *Pattern Weaves with Floats*. The pattern is made by allowing certain threads to pass over more than one thread, i.e. 'floating', either in warp or weft. In the weft this is often called 'brocading'. In the example illustrated, coloured threads pass as if darned over three warps and under one, practically invisible on the reverse side. One of these floats is an extra weft, passing directly over the ground weft (figure 270 I).

(*d*) *Double Weave*. The only double weave known in this period is a warp-face double weave with pattern on both sides. Here there are two sets of coloured warps arranged one above the other, but only one weft is necessary. The two sets are of different colours. To make the pattern, certain of the back warps are raised to replace front warps which are lowered; colours are exchanged and ties formed between otherwise separate portions of the fabric. (For diagram of the unique example of this weave see figure 278.)

(*e*) *Weaves with Pile.*

Type 1. Several threads are thrown together in the weft, passing at intervals round a stick to form a loop (figure 270 L). This can also be done with single threads. The loops can make patterns, as in Turkish towelling (plate 12 A).

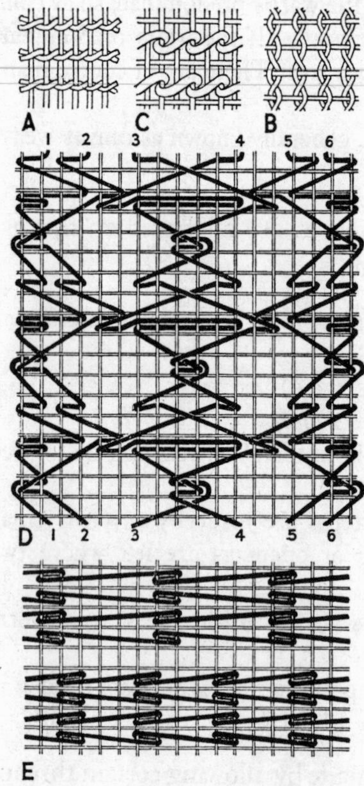

FIGURE 271—(A) *Twined weave.* (B) *Gauze weave.* (C) *Wrapped or Soumak weave.* (D), (E) *Wrapped weave, varieties.*

Type 2. The weft passes round each alternate warp, over a stick or cord to form a long loop, and then under the same warp again before passing round the next alternate one. This gives a row of long loops. Usually there are rows of plain weave between the pile ones (figure 270 M). This type of looping has been named Sehna loops.

Type 3. Bunches of thread encircle two or more warps, the ends hanging down to make rows of pile between a number of rows of plain weave.

(*f*) *Twill Weaves.* There is again a single set of warps and wefts, but instead of passing alternately over and under adjoining threads, as in plain weave, the weft passes over two or more warps and under one or more. In the second row, the under-pass is moved one thread to the right or left, forming a diagonal line. The simplest twill requires at least three heddles on the loom, and for those shown here four heddles are needed; each heddle carries the warp threads to be raised for one throw of weft.

Type 1. The weft passes over and under a constant number of threads, as 2×2 (figure 270 J).

Type 2. By changing the direction of the weave, i.e. reversing, waves (figure 270 K), herring-bones, and diamonds (figure 279) can be produced.

(*g*) *Twined Weave.* The warps are interlaced with two weft threads which twine round one or more warp threads, exactly as in twined mats and basketry (figure 271 A).

(*h*) *Gauze Weave.* The warps are manipulated to form crosses, and these are secured by a passage of the weft (figure 271 B).

(*i*) *Wrapped or Soumak Weave*. The weft thread wraps round the warps. There is usually a row of plain weave on either side of each row of pattern-wrapping. The wrapping has always to be done with the fingers.

Type 1. The commonest variety, over two warps and under one, is as in the rush matting (figure 259 F); another is over three and under one (figure 271 C).

Type 2. There are many complicated varieties, with wraps passing over and under different numbers of warp threads. Two of these are shown (figure 271 D, E).

VII. CHRONOLOGY OF ANCIENT TEXTILES

The earliest textiles preserved come from the same Egyptian sites, Fayum and Badari, as the earliest basketry, that is, probably from soon after 5000 B.C. They are in plain weave, as indeed is all the fine linen of Egypt and the East until *c* 2500 B.C.

The one fragment of textile from Fayum A (plate 11 A) [4], found in a pot in a granary, has been determined as linen. Seeds of flax, *Linum usitatissimum* L., were also found in the lowest deposit. The weave is fairly even, with a count of 20–25 × 25–30 threads per inch. (Here, and in all figures of counts, the first figure always refers to the warp threads, the second to the weft.) The piece is torn on all sides. The thread is 2-plyed S, both in warp and weft, and so lightly spun that it is difficult to see a twist, but where distinguishable it is Z.

Many fragments were found in graves at Badari [5]. In those examined, the fibre resembles coarse flax, but cross-sections made in 1928 indicate an unidentifiable plant fibre. The weave in all pieces is very regular and open. Counts vary from 34 × 22 to 20 × 20 per inch. On one fragment there is a true selvedge, that is, a side edge with the weft returning. This proves that already the weft was a spun yarn of considerable length, passing normally backwards and forwards. The thread again is 2-plyed S, strongly twisted, with a very faint Z-twist occasionally visible in the single thread. The same description applies to nearly all the Badarian textiles found at the near-by Mostagedda, where also the thread is 2-plyed and the plant-fibre undetermined.

Predynastic textiles from Badari, *c* 3000 B.C., are mostly flax. The weaves are often finer and closer, with a finest count of 88 × 50 per in. On one piece both selvedges are present, giving a total width of 5·1 in. The threads are crowded towards the selvedge. The yarns often appear to be S-doubled, but this may be due to splitting. In predynastic cloths from Matmar (near Tasa) also, some threads were fine and evenly spun and others doubled.

A few other fragments of this period, in a very rotten condition, were found at Gerzeh, of a fibre determined as ramie (*Boehmeria nivea* L.), a plant now found chiefly in the Far East. They were very fine, open and lace-like, with a count of 72×6 per inch [29].

The earliest representation of a loom comes from a pottery dish of this period found in a woman's tomb at Badari (figure 272) [5]. The design, in pale yellow on red, clearly shows a ground-loom with warp stretched between two beams with four pegs at the corners. Three lines cross the centre, which may indicate rods placed to keep the crossing, that is, the division between the odd and even threads. The three lines at the right no doubt indicate three throws of weft. By the loom lies an unknown implement, perhaps a comb. Above, two men are hanging strands over a pole. All the textiles so far discovered could easily have been woven on this simple loom, the ideal loom of nomadic people. The pegs can be pulled out and the weaving rolled up on the beams to carry away.

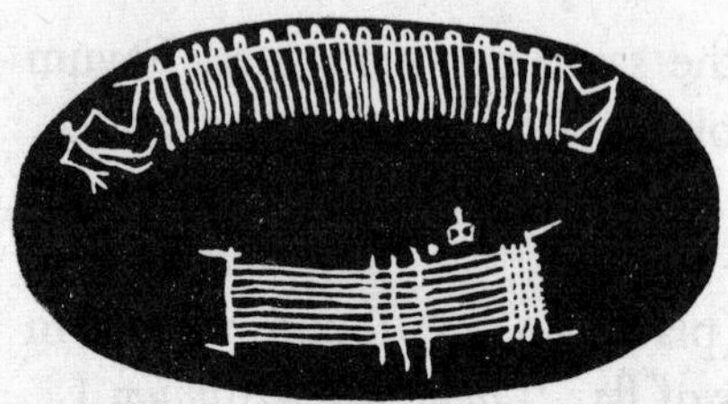

FIGURE 272—*A horizontal loom depicted on the inside of a predynastic dish from Badari, Egypt. c 4400 B.C.*

A few other fragments have been found from this period from other sites in the Near East and India. The earliest are from Susa I in Mesopotamia [30], linen, preserved on copper axe-heads, S-spun in warp and weft, quite regular, with a possible attempt at an ornamental band made by inserting several rows of very coarse weft. The fibre of a fragment from Sialk in Iran [31], again preserved on copper, has not been determined, but some Z-plyed threads can be distinguished.

Two scraps of textile were found at Mohenjo-Daro [32] [33], in India, from *c* 3000 B.C., preserved on a silver vase and a copper razor. Both, as well as some pieces of string, are cotton, with a fibre unlike that in use today, but similar to that of an indigenous Indian variety, *Gossypium arboreum* L., still occasionally cultivated. The first piece, 1/10×1/3 in, is very fine, with widely spaced threads and a count of 60×20 per in. The other, a close weave, has a count of 44×43 per in.

From Ghassul, in Palestine, several fragments of about the same period were recovered [34]. Unfortunately they are completely carbonized and the plant-fibre is unidentifiable. The weave is loose and open, with counts of 30–32×32–35 per in, and the thread 2-plyed S. The spinning direction is not clear. On this site there were interesting weaving tools, including the needle-shuttle (figure 273 G), a double-purpose tool having a fine bone blade with a point at one end and a hole at the other, a possible warp-spacer in bone, and a number of rather clumsy

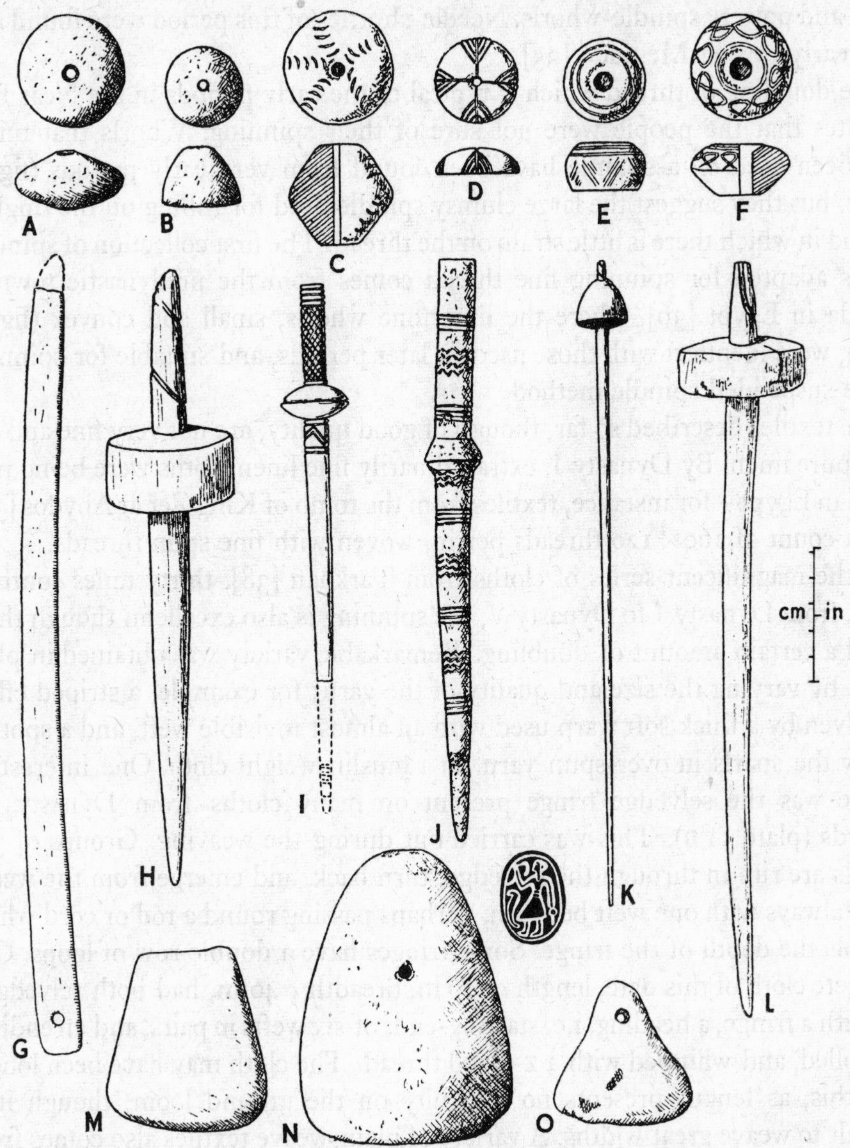

FIGURE 273—SPINDLE-WHORLS. (A) *Stone from Ghassul, Palestine.* c *3000* B.C. (B) *Limestone from Naqada, Egypt.* c *3000* B.C. (C) *Clay with fingernail decoration from the First Settlement at Troy.* c *3000* B.C. (D) *Bone from Megiddo, Palestine. Late Bronze Age,* c *1500* B.C. (E), (F) *Clay with incised decoration white-filled, from the Second Settlement at Troy.* c *2500* B.C. NEEDLE SHUTTLE. (G) *Bone from Ghassul.* c *3000* B.C. SPINDLES. (H) *Wood from Kahun, Egypt.* c *1900* B.C. (I) *Bone from Megiddo. Late Bronze Age.* (J) *Pottery model from Vounous, Cyprus. Bronze Age.* (K) *Wood from Gurob, Egypt.* c *1500* B.C. (L) *Wood from El-Amarna, Egypt.* c *1500* B.C. LOOM WEIGHTS. (M) *Clay, from the First Settlement at Troy.* (N) *Clay with seal impression (seal 3/4 nat. size), from Megiddo. Middle Bronze Age,* c *2000* B.C. (O) *Clay, from the Second Settlement at Troy.*

stone and pottery spindle-whorls. Needle-shuttles of this period were found also in an early cave at Megiddo [35].

The doubling of thread which is typical of the early periods in the Near East indicates that the people were not sure of their spinning. Whorls that might have been used on a spindle have been found from very early periods (figure 273 A), but they suggest the large clumsy spindle used for rolling on the thigh, a method in which there is little strain on the thread. The first collection of spindle-whorls adapted for spinning fine thread comes from the predynastic town of Naqada in Egypt [36], where the limestone whorls, small and convex (figure 273 B), were identical with those used in later periods, and suitable for spinning by the suspended spindle method.

The textiles described so far, though of good quality, are not very fine and not all of pure linen. By Dynasty I, extraordinarily fine linen cloths were being produced in Egypt—for instance, textiles from the tomb of King Zer at Abydos [37], with a count of 160× 120 threads per in, woven with fine spun threads.

In the magnificent series of cloths from Tarkhan [38], thirty miles south of Cairo, from Dynasty I to Dynasty V, the spinning is also excellent, though there is still a certain amount of doubling. Remarkable variety was obtained in plain weave by varying the size and quality of the yarn; for example, a striped effect was given by a thick soft warp used with an almost invisible weft, and a spotted one by the snarls in over-spun yarn on a muslin-weight cloth. One interesting feature was the selvedge fringe present on many cloths from Dynasty III onwards (plate 11 B). This was carried out during the weaving. Groups of 3–5 threads are run in through the selvedge, turn back, and emerge from the weave again, always with one weft between, perhaps passing round a rod or cord which controls the depth of the fringe. Some fringes have a double row of loops. One complete cloth of this date, length *c* 126 in, breadth *c* 40 in, had both selvedges, one with a fringe, a heading, i.e. starting-end, of six wefts in pairs, and an ending, cut, rolled, and whipped with a Z-plyed thread. The cloth may have been longer than this, as length presents no difficulty on the ground loom, though it is difficult to weave great widths. A variety of plain-weave textiles also comes from sites such as Meydum and Kafr Ammar, including the canvas weave (plain weave, type 2, figure 270 B).

Two pieces of textile have been found showing decorative features which became popular later: a piece with blue stripes in the warp (pattern type 1) [37] from the pyramid of King Unas, *c* 2600 B.C.; and the first instance of the pleating so often figured in tomb-paintings, a horizontally pleated shirt of fine linen from a tomb at Naga-ed-Der.

In Dynasty XI, *c* 2160 B.C., there are the first examples of looped techniques in some towels from Deir el-Bahri, similar in appearance to modern Turkish towels [17]. One, measuring 20 × 18 in, has a pattern of alternate straight and zigzag bands (plate 12 A), and others, from the tomb of Neb-Hepet-Re's soldiers, are covered with uniformly spaced looped spots (weaves with pile, type 1). Rugs from Kerma, in Nubia, a little later [16] have a pile (type 3), in some cases of bunches of long fibre threads on a canvas weave, and in others of ostrich-feather barbs, inserted in the same way but closer together.

Not a solitary rag survives from Troy, but the evidence for spinning and weaving is remarkable. Eight thousand spindle-whorls were found in the earliest excavations, and many later, some with incised decoration filled with white clay (figure 273 E, F). The emplacement of what must have been a warp-weighted loom of the Second Settlement, which began *c* 2500 B.C., has been recently discovered [39]. Two holes indicate the existence of posts to which the warp-beam must have been fixed, the other end being fastened to the wall, 43 in away. Between these points the warp-weights lie in orderly rows, just as they fell on the collapse of the roof when the town was sacked and burnt. The weights are flattened lumps of clay, roughly pear-shaped, with holes pierced through, and partly baked by the fire. Many other loom-weights were found on the site, some from the First Settlement, beginning *c* 3000 B.C. (figure 273 M, O).

At Vounous, in Cyprus, Early Bronze Age tombs contained also many spindle-whorls [8] of polished pottery with incised decoration white-filled, and one model spindle of pottery, decorated in the same way (figure 273 J).

Another site from which weaving implements but no textiles remain is Megiddo, in Palestine [35]. There are clumsy stone whorls and loom-weights from the period from 3000 B.C. onwards, and from the Middle and Late Bronze Age cultures, beginning *c* 1750 B.C., there are beautifully decorated whorls of bone and ivory, several complete bone spindles, and loom-weights with impressions of seals (figure 273 D, I, N.)

The first European evidence comes again from the Swiss lake-village cultures, beginning *c* 2500 B.C. [11]. Some of the linen twined work described under basketry (twined types 1, 2, and 3) could as justly be called textile, and may have come from cloaks or covers. There are also plain weaves. The thread is always 2-ply, generally S. As in the Near East, this constant doubling must have been done to strengthen a weak, poorly spun thread, and stone spindle-whorls are rare in this culture. The weaves are very even, rather loose. Counts taken on two samples were 30 × 30 and 48 × 35–37 threads per in. Many pieces have starting-borders. It is suggested that these were woven separately on a small loom, as in

Lapland today. The warp is stretched, and the weft put through, leaving long loops. When finished, the border is tied to the beam of the larger loom, the long weft loops becoming the warps. In the Swiss examples, the threads are held firm by crossing these warps before the main weave (figure 274). These borders serve to space the warps evenly, and are considered to indicate the use of the warp-weighted loom.

There are also thick selvedge borders and end borders, some with fringes and some in repp technique, i.e. alternate thick and thin lines of weft giving a ribbed effect, which is also used for narrow bands or ribbons. There are three fragments with weft stripes (pattern weave with floats, figure 270 I), and one famous unique piece from Irgenhausen in a Soumak weave (wrapped type 2). This is now completely black, but is believed to have been worked in two colours, as shown in the reconstruction (plate 12 B). Six different varieties of wrapping were used (see figure 271 D, E for two of these). This piece probably dates from after 2000 B.C.

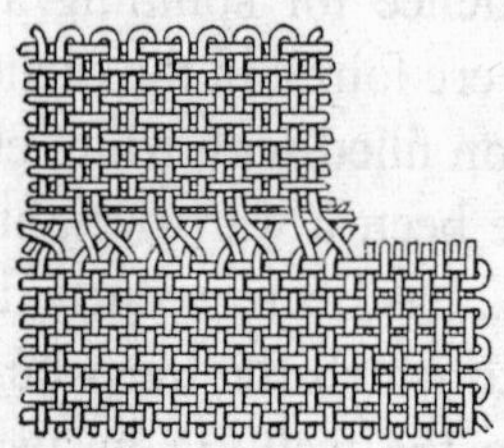

FIGURE 274—*Starting border and selvedge (corner missing). Swiss lake-village. c 2500 B.C.*

In the Spanish Cueva de los Murciélagos, of about the same date, bodies were found still clothed in the remains of esparto-grass tunics, made in twined and plaited techniques akin to those of their basketry.

Almost at the same time on the other side of the world, in the preceramic culture of the Chicama valley in Peru, there is a mixture of twining and weaving in both basketry and textiles [15]. The textiles are of cotton, but sometimes a plant bast is blended or plyed with it. The cotton is almost entirely S-spun, the bast largely Z. Plain weave alone is rare. Most pieces have some twining, sometimes in compact rows at the warp ends, sometimes in large areas, or as one or two rows twined across a plain weave. There are also simple patterns formed by warp floats. Pieces are all small, the largest found being 8×16 in. In twined textiles, the wefts are all short lengths, crossing the weave once and returning to be tied at the selvedge, and this sometimes also occurs in plain weave. A blue dye was occasionally used. There are no spindle-whorls, and to this day natives in the district spin with a small unweighted stick.

Returning to Egypt, we find that no patterned textiles have survived from the Middle Kingdom. Though there is much plain linen of the finest quality, some still shows the primitive peculiarity of very lightly twisted threads paired, doubled, or even trebled. But at last the tomb-paintings and models of Dynasties XII and XIII (*c* 2000–1700 B.C.) give definite evidence of the looms, and of the methods of spinning and warping, in use. Judging from these pictures, the Egyptians continued to wear pure white linen, while the foreigners are represented in patterned garments.

The linen-loom in the tomb of Khnemhetep at Beni Hasan (figure 275 A) is drawn as if vertical, while the mat-loom in the tomb of Khety (figure 275 B) is obviously horizontal, but models found at Deir el-Bahri [17] and Beni Hasan make it clear that both were horizontal. The Beni Hasan model shows a spinner and a loom [25], but the other model (plate 13 A) a weaving-room, where all the stages in weaving are shown. Three women, sitting, prepare the flax. Each has

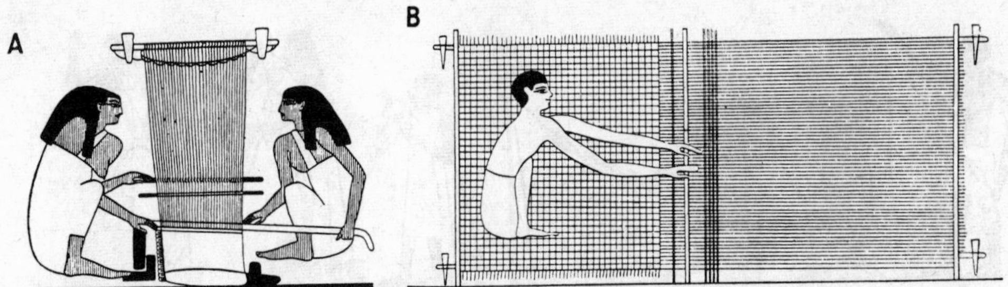

FIGURE 275—(A) *Linen loom, horizontal, tomb of Khnemhetep.* (B) *Mat loom, tomb of Khety. Both from Beni Hasan, Egypt.* c *1900 B.C.*

before her a semicircular platform with a rounded top, on which she forms flax into a rove (p 425) and winds it into a ball ready for the spinners. These hold two spindles each, and appear to be spinning or doubling threads drawn from a pot or basket. Two women make warps on pegs on the wall from a spindle held in the hand, winding one thread at a time in a figure of eight. There are two ground-looms fastened to pegs in the floor, with rod-heddle and shed-rods, and sword-beaters. Small wooden implements by the side of the looms may have been used to raise the heddle.

All these details, and more, are present in tomb pictures. The scene of preparation is shown in tombs at Beni Hasan and El-Bersheh. In the tomb of Daga at Thebes there seems to be an earlier stage, equivalent to combing or hackling the flax. The spinners must have been extremely skilful. Beside the ordinary spinning with one suspended spindle, there are spinners who spin with two spindles (tombs of Baqt and Daga), and double four threads simultaneously on two spindles (tomb of Khety, figure 276), as in the model. Not only the suspended spindle method was in use: all three methods described above (p 425) are shown in the tombs of Khety and Baqt—suspended spindle, spindle rolled on the thigh, and grasped spindle with the rove running over a support (figure 276). Spindles in all these pictures are spun whorl uppermost, no doubt twirled in the hand, and also given a roll on the thigh, a method still used in the northern Sudan to get a strong twist. Warping methods again feature in many scenes. One in the tomb of Baqt suggests a very primitive way of laying the warp directly on the loom-beams, as done by Bedouin today. The method used in the weaving-shed model appears in the tomb of Tehutihetep, as well as a much more advanced method, namely twelve threads at a time drawn off twelve bobbins held in a frame. A third method, warping round three posts set in the ground, is shown in the tomb of Daga. Reference has already been made to the mat-loom in the tomb of Khety, where the drawing suggests a simple darning of reeds, and the linen-loom in

FIGURE 276—*Spinners. Left to right, men spinning with suspended spindle, spindle rolled on thigh, grasped spindle, and two spindles; women doubling and spinning with two spindles. Tomb of Khety, Beni Hasan, Egypt.* c *1900* B.C.

the tomb of Khnemhetep, which is clearly a horizontal loom of the same type as those in the model, with rod-heddle and shed-rod. A row of loops at one side of the weaving may indicate a selvedge fringe like those on the Tarkhan cloths.

In the paintings of the New Kingdom, from *c* 1580 B.C., a new type of loom appears, the vertical 2-beamed loom in a rectangular wooden frame, seen in three tombs at Thebes (figure 277). All these paintings are much damaged, but it is probable that the loom had a rod-heddle and shed-rod, and the sword-beater is much in evidence. On this loom, for the first time, the weavers are almost all men. An ancient song laments their lot: 'The weaver within doors is worse off there than a woman; squatting, his knees against his chest, he does not breathe.'

The spindle used throughout Egyptian history is a very simple type. Few complete examples have been found, and they are of wood with wooden whorls. The older type, Middle Kingdom (figure 273 H) [23], has a cylindrical whorl with a deep spiral groove round the shaft above it. The later type, New Kingdom (figure 273 K, L), has a flat or convex whorl and a hook cut close to the top of the shaft. Whorls found without spindles are generally wood or stone, particularly limestone.

The vertical two-beamed loom is still that preferred for tapestry-weaving, and it is interesting that the paintings of it should coincide with the appearance of the magnificent series of pattern-weaves that begins with Dynasty XVIII (1580–1350 B.C.), a change of fashion perhaps due to Syrian influence. The

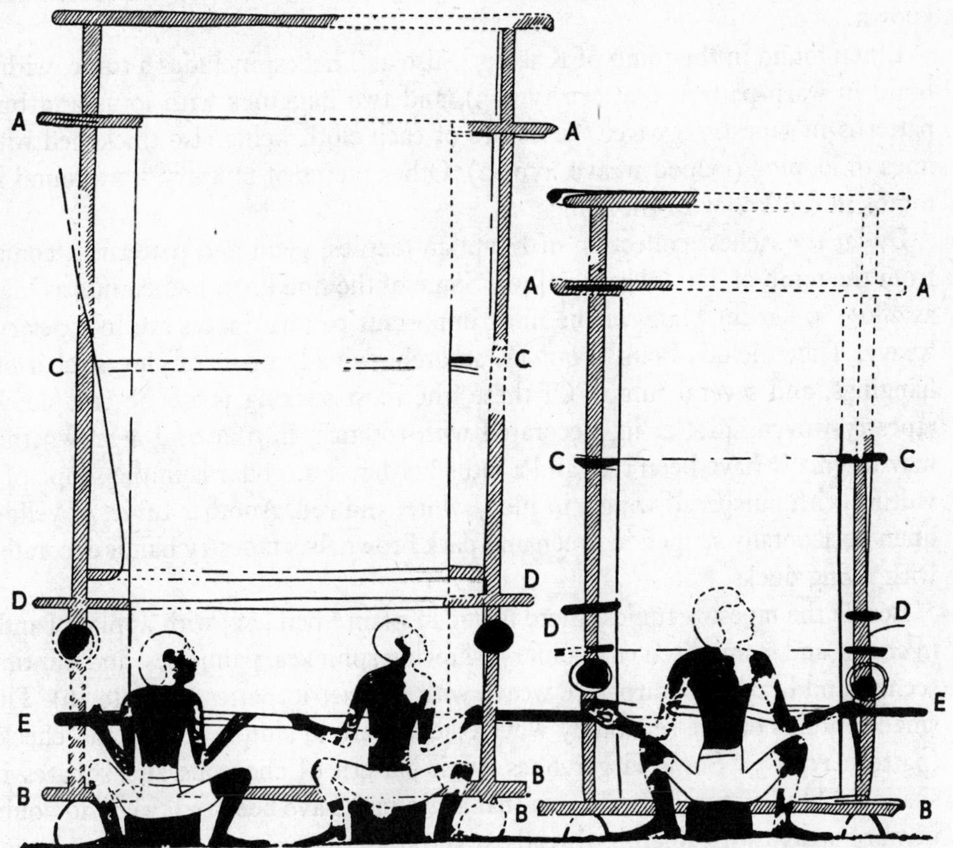

FIGURE 277—*Vertical looms in the New Kingdom.* (A) *Warp beam,* (B) *breast beam,* (C) *laze rods* (?), (D) *beams—possibly rod-heddle and shed-rod,* (E) *sword-beater. From tomb of Thotnefer at Thebes, Egypt.* c 1500 B.C.

first tapestries are those from the tomb of Thothmes IV at Thebes, *c* 1405 B.C. [37]. One (plate 14 A) has the '*ka*-name' of Thothmes III, his grandfather, and may be an heirloom and the earliest piece known. The hieroglyphs are squeezed into the weave, and gores of extra threads run into the ground-weave to even it up. The warp is vertical, the designs woven as seen. Another piece is part of a robe ornamented with rows of lotus flowers in blue and red, alternating with papyrus in red, blue, yellow, and brown, outlined in black (plate 15 A). To the left, hieroglyphs give the name of Amenhetep II, father of Thothmes IV. A third fragment, also with hieroglyphs, has the figures woven sideways, a feature often seen in later tapestry work, where it is done to avoid long vertical slits. A piece of plain weave has pink warp stripes (figure 270 C) ornamented with rosettes of pink and green in tapestry-stitch, probably the earliest Egyptian embroidery known.

Linen found in the tomb of Kha [37], also at Thebes, includes a tunic, with a braid in warp-pattern (pattern type 3), and two hangings with lotus and bud patterns in tapestry weave, the centre of each cloth being also thickened with lines of looping (looped weave, type 2). Other pieces of tapestry were found in tombs in the Valley of the Kings.

By far the richest collection of Egyptian textiles, plain and patterned, comes from the tomb of Tutankhamen [40]. Some of the fine linen had counts as high as 280×80 per in. Many of the most important pattern pieces are in tapestry-weave. They include belts, a quiver, an archer's pad, a pair of gloves, chariot-hangings, and several tunics. Of these, the most striking is a robe completely tapestry-woven, 48×32 in, decorated with rosettes, in blue and a brown that may originally have been red, and a lotus border. The collar is in the shape of a vulture with outspread wings, in blue, white, and red. Another tunic, of yellow linen horizontally striped in green and dark brown, has tapestry bands decorated with flying ducks.

Beside the tapestry tunics, there is one in plain linen [41] with applied bands in chain- and stem-stitch embroidery, showing sphinxes, palmettes, and hunting scenes, and braids in warp-face weave with geometric patterns (plate 16). The smaller braids on the separately woven sleeves are in simple stripes and checks (pattern type 3). Some larger ones, with pattern of chevrons and squares in shades of blue, natural, and brown that again may have been red, were no doubt in warp weave with floating threads at the back (pattern type 4). These braids were fastened to the tunic, but the floating threads could be seen on portions torn and turned over. The same weave was also used for a separate piece of rather similar design. This had so many threads that it would have required at least seven heddles, and the side-braids on the tunic not less than ten: very difficult to manage on any of the Egyptian looms. It could be woven, however, by the simple procedure used for warp-patterns on the ground-loom by Bedouin. Here warp-threads of two colours are set up in pairs together; only the ones needed for the pattern are used, the others float at the back until required. In these more complicated patterns three threads of different colours can be set up. The threads needed for the pattern are selected by hand. The simpler cloth of this type, of Dynasty XVIII [40] (of which the three-colour pattern is shown in figure 270 H), could have been woven after this fashion, or on two rod-heddles and a shed-rod. Another famous braid that must be in a similar kind of weave (plate 13 B) is that from the saddlecloth of Senmut's favourite horse [37], *c* 1500 B.C., but it cannot be studied as again it is sewn down.

There is an extraordinary resemblance between the technique and designs on these braids and those of the famous girdle of Rameses III, *c* 1170 B.C. (plates 14 B, 15 B) [42] [43], though here the weave is double, with a similar pattern on the back.

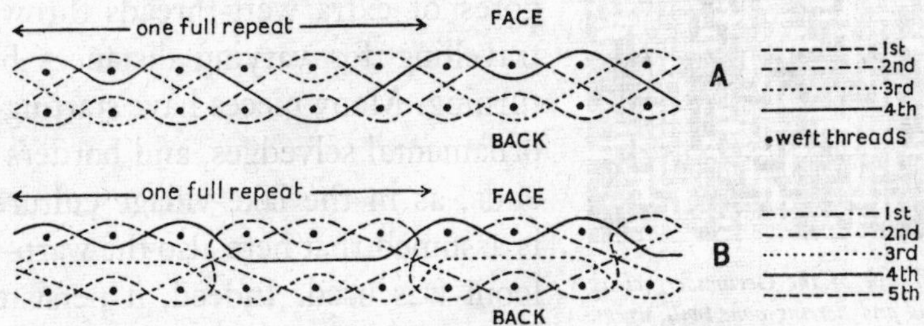

FIGURE 278—*Diagram of the two weaves in the girdle of Rameses III.* (A) *Design on four warp threads.* (B) *Design on five warp threads.*

The floating threads are all inside. There are two different qualities of weave in the girdle, one of which requires four threads for each one shown on the face, while the other cannot be woven with less than five threads. A reproduction of part of the girdle was woven by the draft shown in figure 278, on a primitive loom using only rod-heddles. It has been suggested that this girdle might have been more easily woven in a double-weave tablet-technique, using four and six threads, but there is no evidence for tablet-weaving till a much later date, and, so far, examination has nowhere revealed more than five threads. The colours used are red, blue, natural, and a little yellow and green. The thread is 3-plyed, and the count of threads showing on the face of the weave is $68 \times 30\frac{1}{2}$ per in. As the cloth is double, this means that in some parts the count is 272×61, and in others 340×61, per in.

All these textiles are still of linen, and the difficulties experienced in dyeing it account for the limited range of colours. Among dyes determined are indigo, madder, henna, and the flower of *Carthamus tinctorius* L. (safflower) [40]. Patterns are plentiful only in this limited period of Dynasties XVIII–XX (1580–1090 B.C.). Although no doubt the Egyptians continued using pattern-weaves after this, few have been discovered, and indeed records of any textiles are scanty until the early centuries after Christ.

There is a striking contrast when we turn from the high civilization of Egypt, with its perfect weaving techniques, to the Bronze Age cultures of Scandinavia, beginning *c* 1150 B.C. [44]. Again complete garments are preserved, but here they are all of wool taken from sheep of a primitive race, the wool of which contains long coarse hairs. The textiles are coarse plain weaves, with counts varying from 13×10 to 7×6 per in. The warp is S-spun, the weft usually Z. Garments are made from pieces direct from the loom, with as little cutting as possible. An oval cloak was shaped during the weaving by gores of extra weft-threads thrown in and travelling for varying distances before returning. Many pieces have starting-borders, ornamental selvedges, and borders of warp-ends, as in the lake-village cultures, and it is assumed that here also the warp-weighted loom was used. Indeed, it persisted in the Faeroe Islands within living memory.

FIGURE 279—*Weave of the Gerumsberg cloak. Checked diamond and herring-bone twill, irregular. Sweden. Late Bronze Age.*

There were some fine belts and tassels. One from Borum Eshoj in Denmark was in warp stripes (pattern type 1) of two shades of brown, the stripes being accentuated by using different spinning directions for the two colours. A woman's cap and a hairnet in 'sprang' were found. This technique is intermediate between plaiting and weaving. A warp is stretched on a frame, and a fabric, often resembling lace, is formed by crossing or twining the warps; small sticks are used as temporary wefts, taken out and reinserted as required. Some kind of fastening has to be made when the work, which appears simultaneously at each end of the warp, meets in the middle. There were a few other decorative details, but these were mostly sewn. Pile fabrics were used for caps and cloaks, but the pile tufts were run in with a needle after the weaving. Some embroidery was done on a woman's jacket from Skrydstrup in Denmark—ribbed decoration in button-hole stitch, and a neck-filling of knotless netting with corded rows sewn afterwards.

With similar jackets a corded skirt was worn (plate 17 A). The only complete example, found at Egtved in Denmark, was made by a continuous thread passing up and down over a large cord at the top. The loops were held at the top below the cord by rows of plain weave, over and under four threads. Each set of four threads was then corded together as in the ancient Egyptian fringe-cording, in which two pairs of two threads each are twisted together in one direction, and then all four are twisted together in the opposite direction. At the bottom, the loops were tied into metal rings or tubes and lashed by a row of twining. The rings were then oversewn with woollen thread. In graves where the skirt has perished, the metal tubes or rings have been found in position just above the knees. The garment was no doubt suited to the hot dry climate of Denmark at that period.

One interesting piece comes from the Late Bronze Age, a mantle, oval in shape, length 100 in, from Gerumsberg in Sweden [45]. The fabric, which is checked light and dark, is in irregular herring-bone twill, reversing in some parts to make diamonds (figure 279). There are so many irregularities that it has been suggested the weavers were still experimenting in fancy twills. The cloak is dated by pollen

FIGURE 280—*Urn decorated with spinner and weavers. Oedenburg (Sopron), Hungary. Late Bronze Age. Height* c *40 cm.*

analysis, and has some fairly close parallels among the twills of the early Danish Iron Age.

Twill weaves, so characteristic of the Iron Age in Europe, were obviously just coming into popularity. There are a few fragments from Solothurn and Schaffhausen [12], *c* 700–600 B.C., fine 2×2 twills (type 1, figure 270 J), and others from La Motte d'Apremont, Haute Saône, France [46], possibly of the same date, again 2×2. All these are preserved on metal. Pieces of twills, plain and pattern weaves, found in the salt mines of the Durnberg, Austria, may be as old or older, but the dating is very uncertain.

There is actually a representation of the loom on which these twills must have been woven on an urn of the Hallstatt culture from Oedenburg in Hungary [47] (figure 280). The loom, with woven cloth at the top, has two rows of warp-weights hanging. Three sticks across the warp indicate that somehow the crossing was being kept. To the left a woman is spinning with suspended spindle; to the right is one with a little hand-loom or embroidery frame, and another expresses her admiration.

There are better contemporary pictures of this loom in Greek vase paintings from 600 B.C. onwards. The best and earliest of them forms part of a scene showing stages in the making of textiles (figure 281) [28]. To the left of the loom are two women; one spins with suspended spindle, whorl downwards, and a distaff, and the other prepares a rove and coils it into a basket. The top beam of

FIGURE 281—*Spinners and weavers on a Greek vase. c 560 B.C.*

the loom is clearly lashed to the side-beams, which are planted in the ground. The weaving is at the top of the loom, some rolled round the beam. The pyramidal weights have rings into which bunches of warps are tied. As in all Greek pictures of looms, there are two rods across the middle of the warps, indicating that the crossing was kept, though whether by shed-rods or rod-heddle cannot be proved. The wide spacing of the warps suggests a tapestry-weave, in which much of the work is done by hand. Two women are working at the loom, the left-hand one beating up the weft, the right-hand one preparing to open the shed for the next throw. The yarn is wound on a stick spool. On the right, women are weighing the wool on scales and folding finished pieces of cloth.

It has been calculated that this loom was about 65 inches wide and a little higher. The breadth of the loom also appears from references in the 'Odyssey' to the weaving of Penelope's voluminous robe, and to Circe, singing as she walked to and fro at her great loom. There are other vases with paintings, and many spindle-whorls and loom-weights, but the beautiful robes and hangings so frequently mentioned in Greek literature have disappeared. One fragment of plain linen, on a Late Minoan sword, is all that remains from Crete.

Other lands have been more fortunate. In Peru there was a sudden appearance of higher weaving techniques with the beginning of the cultist period about 800 B.C. [15]. Larger pieces, proper selvedges, more plain weave and less twining, warp and weft stripes, sometimes combined in checks, occasional tapestry, and gauze-weaves (p 430 and figure 271 B), sometimes with pattern areas, all suggest the development of a proper loom with a heddle. Though there is no definite evidence till a later period, it seems likely that this was the backstrap loom, a two-beamed loom with a similar set-up to the horizontal loom, but attached at one end to a post and at the other to the weaver's belt.

On this loom, as on the other types discussed and figured—horizontal, vertical, two-beamed, or warp-weighted—the weaving is done in the same way by means of rod-heddles and shed-rods. All is hand-work. Yet, as we have seen, a variety of weaves in pattern was made, some indeed so complicated that they would be difficult or even impossible to reproduce on a modern loom: for example, the fine linen Soumak patterned cloth of the Swiss lake-villages, the warp pattern weaves of ancient Egypt, and the gauze weaves with design areas of ancient Peru.

Perhaps before the close of this period a more developed loom was evolving in China. Some tiny fragments of textiles in true silkworm silk, preserved on bronzes of the Yin period, *c* 1000 B.C., show traces of twill damasks in pattern [48], suggesting a weaving knowledge beyond any yet seen. This is our first glimpse of modern techniques, but it was centuries before such knowledge was diffused. The old techniques sufficed elsewhere till the birth of Christ, and persist in many places to the present day.

REFERENCES

[1] CHILDE, V. GORDON. 'What happened in History.' Penguin Books, Harmondsworth. 1950.

[2] CLARK, J. G. D. 'The Mesolithic Settlement of Northern Europe.' University Press, Cambridge. 1936.

[3] BRAIDWOOD, R. J. and BRAIDWOOD, L. *Antiquity*, **24,** 196–200, 1950.

[4] CATON-THOMPSON, G. and GARDNER, E. W. 'The Desert Fayum.' Royal Anthropological Institute, London. 1934.

[5] BRUNTON, G. and CATON-THOMPSON, G. 'The Badarian Civilisation.' Egypt. Res. Acc. and Brit. Sch. Archaeol. Egypt, Publ. 46. London. 1928.

[6] ANDERSSON, J. G. *Bull. geol. Surv.*, no. 5, i, 1–68, 1923.

[7] CROWFOOT, GRACE M. *Ann. Archaeol. Anthrop.*, **25,** 3–11, 1938.

[8] STEWART, E. and STEWART, J. 'Vounous, 1937–38.' Skr. svensk. Inst. Rom, Vol. 14. Lund. 1950.

[9] PETRIE, SIR (WILLIAM MATTHEW) FLINDERS, WAINWRIGHT, G. A., and GARDINER, SIR ALAN H. 'Tarkhan I and Memphis V.' Egypt. Res. Acc. and Brit. Sch. Archaeol. Egypt, Publ. 23. London. 1913.
[10] BRUNTON, G. and ENGELBACH, R. 'Gurob.' Egypt. Res. Acc. and Brit. Sch. Archaeol. Egypt, Publ. 41. London. 1927.
[11] VOGT, E. 'Geflechte und Gewebe der Steinzeit.' Birkhäuser, Basel. 1937.
[12] *Idem. Ciba Rev.*, **54**, 1938–70, 1947.
[13] HENSHALL, A. S. *Proc. Prehist. Soc.*, new series **16**, 130–62, 1950.
[14] BENNETT, WENDELL C. 'A Reappraisal of Peruvian Archaeology.' *Amer. Antiq.*, **13**, no. 4, ii. April, 1948. (Supplement.)
[15] BENNETT, WENDELL C. and BIRD, J. 'Andean Culture History.' American Museum of Natural History, Handbook Series no. 15. New York. 1949.
BIRD, J. and MAHLER, JOY. *American Fabrics*, no. 20, p. 73, Winter 1951–52.
[16] REISNER, G. A. 'Excavations at Kerma.' Harvard African Studies, Vol. 6. Cambridge, Mass. 1923.
[17] WINLOCK, H. E. 'Excavations at Deir el Bahri.' Macmillan, New York. 1942.
[18] PEET, T. E. and WOOLLEY, SIR (CHARLES) LEONARD. 'Tel El-Amarna, The City of Akhenaten.' Egypt Explor. Soc., Memoir 38. London. 1923.
[19] PETRIE, SIR (WILLIAM MATTHEW) FLINDERS and BRUNTON, G. 'Sedment II.' Egypt. Res. Acc. and Brit. Sch. Archaeol. Egypt, Publ. 35. London. 1924.
[20] SCHMIDL, M. "Altägyptische Techniken an Afrikanischen Spiralwulstkörben" in 'Festschr. P. W. Schmidt', pp. 645–54. Mechitharisten-Congreg.-Buchdruckerei, Wien. 1928.
[21] From notes in the Howard Carter Collection, by kind permission of the Ashmolean Museum, Oxford.
[22] EDGAR, C. C. in ATKINSON, T. D. 'Excavations at Phylakopi in Melos.' Soc. Prom. Hell. Stud. Suppl. Paper 4, p. 80. London. 1904.
[23] CROWFOOT, GRACE M. 'Methods of Hand Spinning in Egypt and the Sudan.' Bankfield Museum Notes, second series no. 12. Halifax. 1931.
[24] HORWITZ, H. TH. *Ciba Rdsch.*, **49**, 1782–1808, 1941.
[25] ROTH, H. LING. 'Ancient Egyptian and Greek Looms.' Bankfield Museum Notes, second series no. 2. Halifax. 1913.
[26] JOHL, C. H. 'Altägyptische Webstühle und Brettchenweberei in Altägypten.' Untersuchungen zur Geschichte und Altertumskunde Ägyptens Vol. 8. Hinrichs, Leipzig. 1924.
[27] CROWFOOT, GRACE M. *Palest. Explor. Quart.*, **73**, 141–51, 1941.
[28] *Idem. Annu. Brit. Sch. Athens*, **37**, 36–47. Session 1936–37. 1940.
[29] PETRIE, SIR (WILLIAM MATTHEW) FLINDERS, WAINWRIGHT, G. A., and MACKAY, E. J. H. 'The Labyrinth Gerzeh and Mazghuneh.' Egypt. Res. Acc. and Brit. Sch. Archaeol. Egypt, Publ. 21. London. 1912.
[30] MORGAN, J. J. M. DE. 'La Préhistoire orientale', Vol. 2. Geuthner, Paris. 1926.
[31] GHIRSHMAN, R. 'Fouilles de Sialk, près de Kashan.' Louvre, Dép. Antiq. Orient. Sér. archéol. Vols. 4, 5. Paris, 1938, 1939.
[32] MACKAY, E. J. H. in MARSHALL, SIR JOHN H. (Ed.). 'Mohenjo-Daro and the Indus Civilisation', Vol. 2, p. 585. Probsthain, London. 1931.
[33] GULATI, A. N. and TURNER, A. J. *Bull. of the Indian Central Cotton Committee*, Technical series B, no. 3. October, 1928.
[34] MALLON, A., KOEPPEL, R., and NEUVILLE, R. 'Teleilāt Ghassūl.' Scripta Pontificii Instituti Biblici, Rome. 1934.

[35] LOUD, G. 'Megiddo', Vol. 2. Univ. of Chicago, Orient. Inst.: Publ. 62. Chicago. 1948.
[36] PETRIE, SIR (WILLIAM MATTHEW) FLINDERS. 'Prehistoric Egypt.' Egypt. Res. Acc. and Brit. Sch. Archaeol. Egypt, Publ. 31. London. 1921.
[37] RIEFSTAHL, E. 'Patterned Textiles of the Pharaonic Period.' Brooklyn Mus. Inst. of Art and Science, Brooklyn. 1944.
[38] PETRIE, SIR (WILLIAM MATTHEW) FLINDERS and MACKAY, E. J. H. 'Heliopolis, Kafr Ammar and Shurafa.' Egypt. Res. Acc. and Brit. Sch. Archaeol. Egypt, Publ. 24. London. 1915.
[39] BLEGEN, C. W. *et al.* 'Troy', Vol. I. University of Cincinnati Publication. University Press, Princeton. 1950.
[40] PFISTER, R. *Rev. Arts Asiatiques*, **11**, 207–18, 1937.
[41] CROWFOOT, GRACE M. and DAVIES, NORMAN DE G. *J. Egypt. Archaeol.*, **26**, 113–30, 1941.
[42] LEE, T. D. *Ann. Archaeol. Anthrop.*, **5**, 84–96, 1913.
[43] CROWFOOT, GRACE. M. and ROTH, H. LING. *Ibid.*, **10**, 7–20, 1923.
[44] BROHOLM, H. C. and HALD, M. 'Costumes of the Bronze Age in Denmark.' Nyt Nordisk Forlag, Copenhagen. 1940.
[45] POST, L. VON. 'Bronsåldersmanteln från Gerumsberget i Västergötland.' K. Vitterhets Historie och Antikvitets Akademien, Monografi-Serien no. 15. Stockholm. 1925.
[46] PERRON, E. *Matér. hist. homme*, 2éme série, **11**, 337–59, 1880.
[47] GALLUS, S. 'Die figuralverzierten Urnen vom Soproner Burgstall.' Pest Magyar Nemzeti Muzeum: Archaeologia Hungarica, Vol. 13. Budapest. 1934.
[48] SYLWAN, V. 'Investigation of Silk from Edsen-Gol and Lop-nor.' Rep. sci. Exped. N.-W. Prov. China Publ. 32. Thule, Stockholm. 1949.

BIBLIOGRAPHY

Basketry

BOBART, H. H. 'Basketwork through the Ages.' Oxford University Press, London. 1936.
MASON, OTIS T. 'Aboriginal American Basketry. Indian Basketry.' *Smiths. annu. rep. 1902*, pp. 171–548, 1904.
OKEY, T. 'An Introduction to the Art of Basket-making.' Pitman's Handwork Series. Pitman, London. 1912.

Weaving

BÜHLER-OPPENHEIM, K. and BÜHLER-OPPENHEIM, A. 'Die Textiliensammlung Fritz Iklé-Huber im Museum für Völkerkunde und Schweizerischen Museum für Volkskunde, Basel. *Denkschr. schweiz. naturf. Ges.*, 78, ii. 1948.
KISSELL, L. 'Yarn and Cloth Making.' Macmillan, New York. 1918.

A NOTE ON THE MATERIALS OF ANCIENT TEXTILES AND BASKETS

JULIUS GRANT

It is by no means always possible to link with certainty a vegetable material used in ancient times with a definite living species or variety. This applies particularly to grasses, rushes, sedges, and palms. Perfect specimens of plant-tissue from ancient fabrics are rare, since they are almost inevitably damaged by the processes to which they have been submitted. Moreover, the difficulty of identifying one of a number of varieties of a species or species of a genus is sometimes increased by their extinction, their rarity, or their remoteness. Further, the relationship between fibre-structure and its use has to be considered; a species or variety was often chosen because it was readily available rather than because it was the most suitable.

Much of the structure of a plant is built up from small, simple, more or less cylindrical fibres, the tracheids, set in the direction of the stem or leaf. These consist essentially of cellulose, and are strengthened by other materials such as pectins, gums, and lignin. They are mainly responsible for the strength and pliability of stem and leaf. Such fibres may be grouped closely or in isolated bundles, or again may be scattered throughout the section of the stem or leaf. In trees they are arranged in concentric rings, and in those plants which have a fibrous bast, there is a closed ring of bast-fibres just below the surface. In a few plants, cotton for instance, fibres of a different kind are found on the seeds. If fibres are isolated from the surrounding cementing material and subjected to mechanical treatment, they may often be split longitudinally into smaller fibres or fibrillae. The extent to which this can be done varies with the plant, but it is particularly marked in flax, where the fibres are of the type known as elongated sclerenchyma. Hence the fineness of linen. If these small fibres are split yet further and examined under the ultramicroscope, they are found to consist of micelles, which X-ray evidence indicates are elongated bundles of actual cellulose molecules, probably crystalline in character. As the cellulose molecule itself has the form of a chain, the general fibrous structure of the plant is reproduced in its ultimate constituent, which is less than one ten-millionth of a centimetre long. On this basis, a micelle, comprising say 100 molecules, may be regarded as the unit from which the plant is built. The characteristic appearances under the microscope of the fibres of flax, cotton, and wool are shown in plate 17B.

Flax and Linen. The flax plant (*Linum usitatissimum*) belongs to the natural order Linaceae. It has been known from very early times, but only in the cultivated state. However, unworked bundles of a flax, probably the wild perennial *L. angustifolium*, were found in the Neolithic Swiss lake-dwellings. Linen has been in use in the Near East from Neolithic times. It is mentioned in the Book of Exodus (XXXIX. 28, etc.), and occurs frequently in Egyptian mummy-wrappings. That from the tomb of Tutankhamen (*c* 1350 B.C.) is still in first-class condition. Seeds of *L. usitatissimum* were also found in the lowest deposits of the Neolithic Fayum sites, which are of about 5000 B.C. These may be contemporary with Badarian linen, in which warp and weft are both two-ply, a state very rare in pre-dynastic specimens (p 431).

The stem of the flax plant, as distinct from its fibres, was used for basketry because of its great strength and suppleness. The plant, however, was and is usually grown both for the seed, linseed, a source of oil and of cattle-food, and for the fibres, which have good spinning properties. The latter are the bast-fibres; the rest of the stem is mostly non-fibrous and of no commercial value. To obtain linen fibres, the leaves and seeds are removed and the stems soaked in water, in bundles. A fermentative rot (retting) ensues, and in a few days the structure of the stem is loosened. The bundles of bast-fibres, which form only about 5 per cent of the original stem, can then be separated mechanically from the unwanted material.

Characteristics of linen fibres are their great strength and the ease with which they split into fibrillae, especially at their ends, thus giving a brush-like effect. The inter-meshing of fibrillae between fibre and fibre supplements the strength of the fibre, and produces the strongest of textiles.

Cotton. Cotton, genus *Gossypium*, belongs to the order Bombacaceae. It has been used for spinning thread from very early times. Doubtless wild cottons, such as those known in India by 3000 B.C. and mentioned in a Hindu hymn of the Rig-Veda of about 1000 B.C., were first used. Cultivated varieties of cotton certainly existed in India by 1000 B.C. Nor was it only in the Old World that cotton was known. Cotton wrappings of perhaps earlier than 2000 B.C. have been found in Peru. There is a theory, based on genetic evidence, that Asiatic cotton found its way to the Americas, where it was early hybridized with an indigenous American species and ultimately gave rise to those American varieties that we know today. Cotton from India is mentioned in the writings of Herodotus (*c* 484–425 B.C.) and of Pliny (A.D. 23–79). It was certainly used in Egypt many centuries earlier.

Some fifty existing species of *Gossypium* are known, but few are of commercial importance. Of these, *G. herbaceum*, cultivated in Asia and formerly in southern Europe, and *G. barbadense*, cultivated in the West Indies and Egypt, are probably the most important in the present connexion. Cotton plants are shrub-like, grow usually as perennials, need much water and heat, and are 3–10 ft tall. They have lobed leaves and white, yellow, or red flowers somewhat resembling those of the hollyhock. Around the flowers are three or four heart-shaped green bracts, which remain after the flowers have fallen, and contract to hold the seed pods (bolls) of the actual cotton (seed-hair) which encloses all the seeds. The latter must be removed by ginning before the raw cotton is processed into thread for spinning, but the traces of them which remain, especially with a primitive technique, often provide a guide to identification.

The most important feature of raw cotton fibres is the number of times they are twisted—usually 200 to 300 per in. This accounts for the spinning-qualities of the fibres (plate 17 B).

Ramie. Ramie, known also as China grass, is obtained from the bast of two varieties of plant of the order Urticaceae (nettle family), viz. *Boehmeria nivea* and *B. nivea tenacissima.* The early history of this fibre is obscure, but there is evidence that it was used in predynastic Egypt, probably as a substitute for flax. Its fibres are long, fine, and strong, but it has not the felting quality of flax. It is said to impart to textiles warmth-retaining properties similar to those of wool, and this may have influenced its early use in districts where wool was not available.

Reeds, Rushes, Sedges, and Grasses are large groups of plants of great importance in early basketry. Their members are difficult to characterize or identify, partly because there are so very many and widespread species and varieties, and partly because they belong to groups the structures of which are remarkably uniform. There is also a scarcity of authentic material which might form the basis of type comparisons.

'Reed' is the common name for several tall grasses (Gramineae) which grow in marshy areas, and for certain other plants of similar habit. The common reed, *Phragmites communis*, is a true grass; it attains 5 to 10 ft and has large, spreading, branched, dull purple panicles. The common reed-mace is an example of a British member of a different order, namely Typhaceae. It is sometimes known as a bulrush, but this name is also given to a sedge (below).

Rushes belong to the family Juncaceae; they are grass-like herbs which also flourish in marshy areas. There are many British species or varieties, e.g. *Juncus conglomeratus.* Such forms have been used for mat-making, and probably basketry, from very early times.

Sedges are perennials of the order Cyperaceae; they belong mostly to the genus *Scirpus. S. lacustris* has long been, and still is, used for mats and basketry. It is the most familiar British bulrush. Sedges, like reeds and rushes, flourish in marshy areas especially in temperate zones. The European sedges (*Carex* spp) have many Asiatic relatives (e.g. *C. baccans*), long used for basketry.

The palms (Palmaceae) form a group of about 130 genera and some 1100 species. They are monocotyledonous trees, and flourish in the tropics and semi-tropics. Certain of them are well suited to basketry. The fronds of the doum palm (*Hyphaene thebaica*) have for countless years been used for the wrapping-strands of baskets. This particular palm is the only member of its tribe having dichotomous branched leaves and a branched cylindrical stem. It provides very suitable material for mats, tent-covers, cordage, and similar objects.

The date palm (*Phoenix dactylifera*) was also used for basketry in ancient times. It grows in arid regions throughout the Near East, and is distinguished by the great height (90 to 100 ft) to which some specimens grow.

Esparto-grass (*Stipa tenacissima* and *Lygeum spartum*) is known also as halfa, the latter being an Arabic name adopted in France. In Egypt, halfa implies *L. spartum*, not *S. tenacissima.* It is a tall, hardy, slender, wiry grass growing in Mediterranean lands and especially in the sandy soils of the south of Spain and north Africa. Though its most important present use is for paper, it has for many centuries been used for baskets and mats, for which it is eminently suitable. There is evidence of its use for basketry from the finds in the Murciélagos cave in Spain. There were also esparto-grass baskets in the tomb of Tutankhamen.

Straw from cereals is one of the most familiar of basket-making materials. Almost all cultivated cereals and many wild kinds have been used for this purpose, but most of the straw of ancient basketry, in Egypt at any rate, was probably wheat-straw. The arrangement of the straw fibres in separate bundles embedded in the mass of non-fibrous cellular tissue accounts for its suitability for basketry. Cereal-straw fibres are easily identified as a class, but it is extremely difficult to distinguish the different types.

Jute (*Corchorus*, of the family Tiliaceae) has been cultivated for making coarse textiles for many centuries. It is derived from the inner barks of the *C. capsularis* and *C. olitorius*; the latter is the smaller and was thought (probably wrongly) by Celsius and Sprengel to be identical with the 'mallow' mentioned in the Book of Job. They flourish in loamy soil under hot moist conditions, notably in Bengal, and are sown in March to May and cut in July to October, when the plant is 10 to 12 ft high and flowering. The fibre is separated by retting (p 448). The finer kinds are pale yellow and silky, and are used in textiles; the coarser grades serve for mats, rope, and paper.

Wool was used in the Danish Bronze Age, in the lake-dwellings of central Europe, and notably at Hallstatt, perhaps as early as about 1000 B.C. It has not been found in previous cultures, but the possibility of its earlier use cannot be excluded. The Scandinavian wool appears to have come from a primitive race of sheep with long coarse hairs.

Wool is microscopically distinct from hair and is more elastic. It is similar in chemical composition to horn, but contains some 40 per cent of natural grease. The principal microscopic feature of wool fibres, which distinguishes them from hair, is their scaly surface-structure, which accounts for their felting properties (plate 17B).

A wool fibre consists of three parts: (*a*) the central medulla, usually best seen near the root, and, in the fine grades, only there; (*b*) the cuticular tissue, which forms the bulk of the fibre; and (*c*) the outer layer of highly characteristic flat, horny, tubular cells forming overlapping scales.

We are accustomed to think of wool as essentially a product of the sheep, but there are many other ungulates which grow wool, usually under a coat of hair. The sheep of certain domestic breeds are perhaps unique in carrying wool alone, but there are wild and domesticated breeds of sheep that carry both wool and hair. It is said that there are sheep which, like their kindred goats, carry only hair. At any rate, sheep have been kept for their wool since Neolithic times.

BIBLIOGRAPHY

BUSHNELL, G. H. S. *Antiquity*, **25**, 145, 1951.
GARNER, W. 'Industrial Microscopy.' Pitman, London. 1932.
GRANT, J. 'Books and Documents: Dating, Permanence and Preservation' (2nd ed.). Grafton, London. In preparation.
Idem. 'Laboratory Handbook of Pulp and Paper Manufacture.' Arnold, London. 1942.

ROPE-MAKING

K. R. GILBERT

THE making of cord and rope by plaiting or twisting fibres, hair, and strips of hide presumably began in Palaeolithic times, since Stone Age man needed cordage for fishing-equipment (figure 282) and for the construction of traps. Indeed, a cave-painting in eastern Spain of Late Palaeolithic or Mesolithic date [1] depicts a person using what appear to be ropes to climb down the face of a cliff, in order to collect wild honey (figure 177).

In ancient Egypt, the earliest specimens of rope, which are of reed, are of the Badarian period (*c* 4000 B.C.). Fibre from the date-palm was commonly used in Egypt for rope-

FIGURE 282—*Fragments of a Mesolithic fishing net from Finland.*

making, but examples have also been found of rope made from flax, grass, halfa, papyrus, and camel-hair [2].

The manufacture of ropes was of the greatest importance in the ancient empires, for man was the chief source of motive power, and it was only by means of ropes that the gangs of slaves could apply their combined strength to move the huge stones used in the construction of the pyramids and other great monuments. A bas-relief in the British Museum from the palace of Sennacherib (706–681 B.C.) at Nineveh shows the transport of a colossus, which rests on a sledge on rollers (figure 283). The ropes by which the men are hauling appear to be as thick as a man's wrist. A similar scene in an Egyptian tomb of Dynasty XII shows a statue estimated to weigh

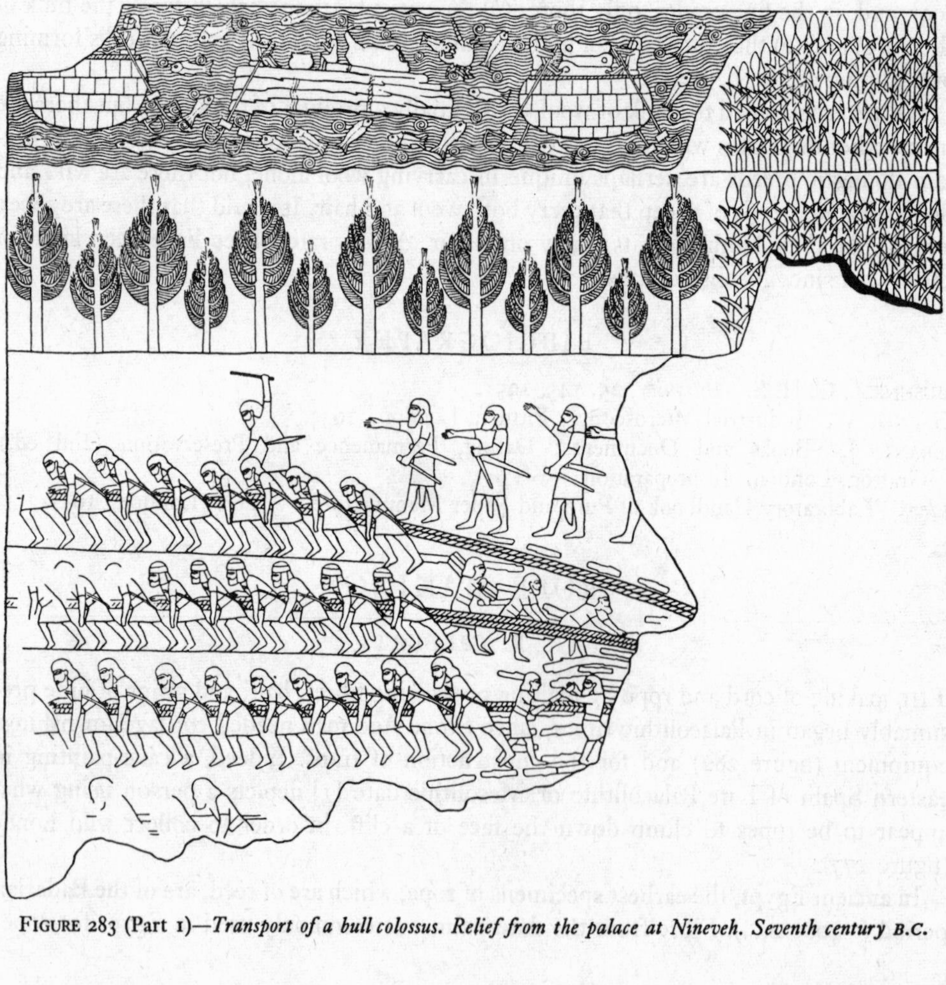

FIGURE 283 (Part 1)—*Transport of a bull colossus. Relief from the palace at Nineveh. Seventh century B.C.*

60 tons being hauled by 172 men pulling on four long ropes [3]. In one of the Tura caves, where blocks of limestone were quarried, ropes 2½ inches in diameter have been found. They are of papyrus and have three strands. Each strand consists of about forty yarns, and each yarn of about seven fibres [2]. Large quantities of rope must also have been required for the rigging of ships.

The first stage in the manufacture of rope from suitably prepared fibre is spinning the yarn. The earliest representation of this process is in a Dynasty V tomb at Thebes [4]; it has the inscription 'twisting the ropes for boat-building'. The painting in the Dynasty XVIII tomb of Rekhmire (fifteenth century B.C.), however, illustrates the process more clearly (figure 284) [5]. In this instance, a rope is being made by twisting together strips of leather which have been cut for the purpose; the same method would be used for palm or papyrus fibres. The man, who is seated, feeds the fibres at a steady rate into the rotating yarn, which is attached to the whirling-tool. This tool has a projecting handle, to which is bound a stone to give it momentum. The man who is turning the tool walks backwards as the yarn is formed. This procedure is reversed in the modern method of spinning, in which it is the spinner with a bundle of fibres who backs away from his assistant.

FIGURE 283 (Continuation).

The yarns are then stretched to an even tension. The final process is to lay or form the yarns into strands and the strands into rope, the sense of the twist being reversed at each stage to ensure the stability of the final product. When two or more strands are combined by twisting them together, they must each at the same time be separately twisted in the

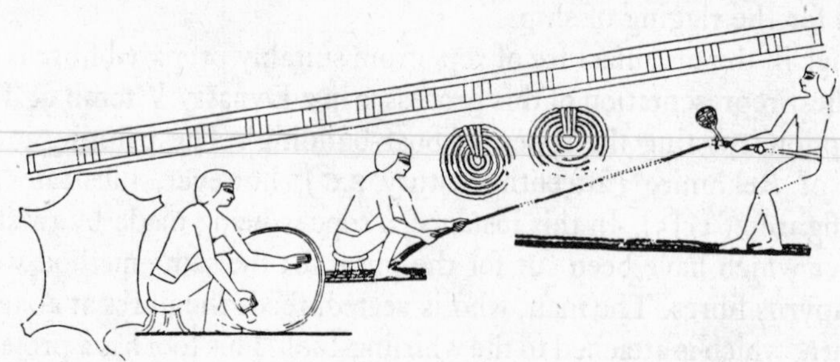

FIGURE 284—*Leather-rope makers. From a tomb at Thebes, Egypt.* c *1450 B.C.*

FIGURE 285—(Left) *Rope-laying. From a tomb at Thebes.* c *1500 B.C.* (Right) *Detail showing how the man in the centre controls the closing of the two strands.*

opposite sense, so that they do not untwist when they are released. An alternative way of describing the process is to say that the strands are twisted separately at one end and allowed to untwist around each other at the other end.

Rope-laying in ancient Egypt is depicted in a scene from a Dynasty XVIII tomb (figure 285) [6]. The man on the right is separately twisting the two strands, which are attached to whirling-tools, in the clockwise sense and slowly walking forwards. Meanwhile, the man on the left is closing the strands by twisting the tool, to which both strands are attached, in the anti-clockwise sense and walking backwards as the rope is formed. The man in the middle, who is seated, holds a marlinspike between the strands and other spikes are shown stuck into the ground. His role is to control the forming of the rope by ensuring that the strands are laid tightly together. Although the painting is somewhat defaced, the explanation given is supported by the fact that the Egyptian fellahin of today make rope of palm-fibre and halfa in the same way. The painting also shows papyrus plants, a bundle of cut reeds, and four coils of rope. There is also a group of the tools used in rope-making, including a knife for cutting the papyrus stems, a mallet for beating them, two whirling-tools, and two marlinspikes.

REFERENCES

[1] OAKLEY, K. P. 'Man the tool-maker' (2nd ed.), p. 66. British Museum (Natural History), London. 1950.

[2] LUCAS, A. 'Ancient Egyptian Materials and Industries' (3rd ed.), pp. 160–1. Arnold, London. 1948.

[3] NEWBERRY, P. E. 'El Bersheh' Part I, p. 19, Pl. xv. Egypt Explor. Fund: Special Publication, London. No year.

[4] DAVIES, NORMAN DE G. 'The Mastaba of Ptahhetep and Akhethetep at Saqqarah'; Vol. I, Pl. xxv. Archaeol. Survey of Egypt. Memoir no. 8. Egypt Explor. Fund, London. 1900.

[5] *Idem*. 'The Tomb of Rekh-mi-Rē at Thebes', p. 50, Pl. LII. Metropolitan Museum of Art, Egyptian Expedition. Publications, Vol. 11, New York. 1943.

[6] MACKAY, E. J. H. *J. Egypt. Archaeol.*, 3, 125, Pl. xv, 1916.

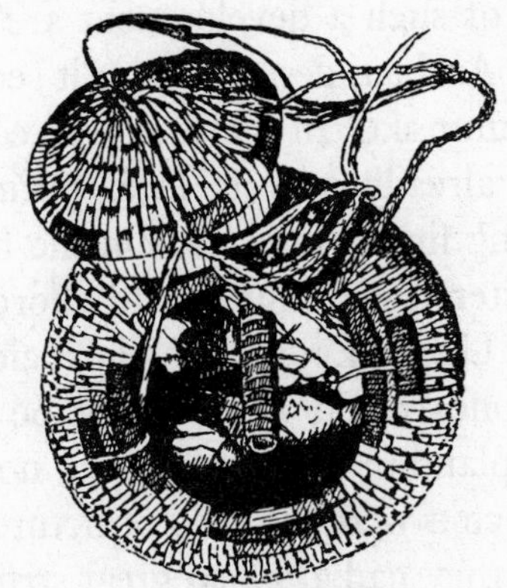

Child's basket from Deir el-Bahri, Egypt. Seventh century B.C.

17

BUILDING IN BRICK AND STONE

SETON LLOYD

I. EVOLUTION OF REGIONAL PATTERNS

SETTLED communities first came into being as a necessary result of the transition from a food-gathering to a food-producing economy, and the impulse to build resulted from the absence of shelter in the most productive areas. The earliest traces of such a development are in the crescent of fertile countries surrounding the Arabian desert, where it seems to have begun before or during the fifth millennium B.C. In each of these countries, the earliest form of shelter to be devised already reflects local peculiarities of environment, earlier nomadic forms being finally rejected. On the banks and in the deltas of the great rivers, reeds plastered with mud could afford protection from the sun and wind, as at Badari in Upper Egypt and El-Ubaid in south Iraq. Beside a torrent-bed in Cilicia, stones could more easily be piled to make a shelter (Mersin), while a loamy upland in Assyria afforded no better material than clay (Hassuna). First to be rejected were the reed structures, though in the marshes of southern Mesopotamia they had attained great structural complexity. These were everywhere replaced by more solid walls of rammed clay (*pisé*), and later by sun-dried brick. Once it was discovered that such bricks only required baking in a kiln to fit them for more exacting and permanent functions, and that stone could be shaped into blocks and structural features, the elements were already present which could promote mere building to the dignity of architecture.

The profound influence of geological environment on the evolution of building technique continues to be in evidence throughout the early history of the eastern countries. It is responsible for sharp distinctions between the archaeological remains of cultures which, in other respects, developed on broadly similar lines. The greater part of Iraq is a flat alluvial plain, where no stone is to be found, and wood only with difficulty. Accordingly, bricks of clay have there continued to be the universal building-material for more than six millennia, and brick vaults have always been preferred to flat ceilings. The Nile valley, on the other hand, is richly supplied with fine building-stone; yet at an early date the quarrying and use of stone for structural purposes became a state monopoly, and mud-brick was employed for the less pretentious buildings of the secular community. The Anatolian plateau seems hardly to have been occupied before the beginning of the third millennium B.C. The first settlers there found an ample supply both of wood and of stone. With technological skill doubtless acquired in a previous

FIGURE 286—*The ruins of Babylon with the foundations of the Ishtar gate in the foreground. (For a reconstruction see plate 18.)*

environment, they built structures of mud-brick reinforced with wooden beams on a stone foundation. Cretan builders, with their own forests available, followed suit, until their technique was superseded by the all-stone architecture of the Greek mainland. Thus, both the initial appearance and the durability of buildings were affected by the materials available, and these in turn depended on factors of geology and vegetation. Their diversity is symbolized today by the aspect of the surviving ruins, e.g. by the contrast between Babylon and Karnak, (figures 286–7) and between Boghazköy and the citadel at Tiryns.

In discussing the development of building methods from the earliest times, it would therefore clearly be impracticable to treat the ancient world as a single unit. It would be equally vain to expect much evidence of stylistic cross-

FIGURE 287—*The Hypostyle Hall in the great temple of Amen-Re, Karnak. Fourteenth to twelfth centuries* B.C.

influences, or of the diffusion of techniques among the principal centres of culture.[1]

The two greatest centres, the Nile valley and Mesopotamia, show a regional conservatism in technology which was impervious to political or military upheavals. In Egypt, this characteristic was emphasized by geographical isolation, and building methods were stereotyped there over a period of nearly three thousand years. In Mesopotamia, the incorporation of an exotic architectural feature of Hittite origin in an Assyrian palace was an innovation worth recording in a monumental inscription. It is true that the architecture of, for instance, the Aegean during the supremacy of Mycenae owed much to the genius of the Minoans. Yet it is in the diversity of approach to building problems that the major interest lies. It may accordingly perhaps be accepted that, throughout the period of pre-Greek civilization, the science of building and its collateral crafts evolved according to purely regional patterns, and that these patterns should here be considered separately and in succession.

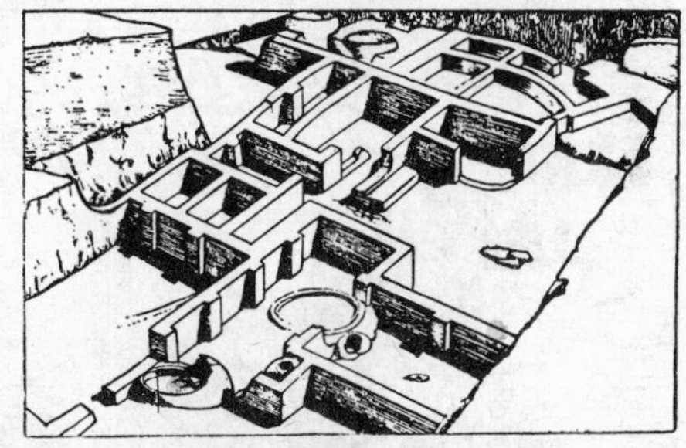

FIGURE 288—*Reconstruction of a 'farm-house', and sketch of its remains as found. Hassuna, Mesopotamia. Probably fifth millennium* B.C.

II. PRELITERATE AND PROTOLITERATE MESOPOTAMIA

In Iraq, the history of the two millennia before the invention of writing and the beginnings of written history are commonly thought of as divisible into six somewhat ill defined phases, named after the sites at which traces of the corresponding cultures were originally found.

The first phase covers the beginnings and improvement of clay buildings from the abandonment of nomadism to the invention of the mould-made brick. The process is well illustrated at the type-site, Hassuna, a small stratified mound 36 km due south of Nineveh [1]. The earliest clay huts here, overlying the emplacements of nomadic tents or shelters (recognizable by the domestic implements

[1] For a possible exception see H. FRANKFORT, 'The Birth of Civilization in the Near East', pp. 103 ff. London, 1951.

round open hearths), had walls of coarse rammed or kneaded clay. They showed no signs of deliberate planning. The levels above exhibit the evolution of a standard so-called farm-house, with a main unit of several chambers and dependencies grouped around an open courtyard (figure 288). The buildings were generally rectangular, and suggest a pitched roof. Frequent buttresses

FIGURE 289—*Reconstruction of three temples at Tepe Gawra, Mesopotamia. Fourth millennium B.C.*

strengthened the walls, and the *pisé* was composed of lumps or slabs of clay. The size and shape of these lumps are hard to distinguish, for though the clay was tempered with fine straw or pounded scrub, the lumps had not been dusted with it, nor were they dried before use, and so became merged into each other. Underground grain-bins showed the technical refinement of a protective coating of bitumen and a lining of gypsum plaster.

In the second period, named after Halaf, a site on the Khabur, prismatic bricks of clay were first used. Some later variations in shape and method of manufacture will be discussed presently (p 464), but the normal preparation of the *pisé* was with a rectangular wooden mould, open at top and bottom. This was ubiquitous in antiquity, and continues today throughout the Near East. Almost any soil can be used as a basis of the mixture, though one with a greater content of clay gives better results. Some form of tempering is necessary in all cases, owing to the tendency to warp and crack, and chopped straw or dung is most often used for this purpose. A puddle is formed by adding water to the soil, and the tempering is trodden into it. The brickmaker works on a prepared piece of ground, with the mixture stacked on a mat beside him. The mould, which often consists of two brick-sized compartments, is filled, and the surplus mud is smoothed off with the hand. The mould is then removed by handles projecting on either side, and the bricks are left in place to dry, for a period which varies according to the heat of the sun. They are then turned over or tilted together for a further period. A more liquid form of the same mixture is used as mortar, and as plastering for both internal and external wall-faces.

By the third or Ubaid period (*c* 3500 B.C.) this simple material could be used for buildings of considerable architectural pretensions, as exemplified in a group of prehistoric temples at Tepe Gawra, where the recessed ornament of the wall-faces may be seen (figure 289). This façade treatment occurs also in the earliest brick temples at Eridu in south Iraq; it must have given the building an exaggerated impression of height, though in both cases the walls are so thin that it is hard to imagine what form of roof they could support. It established a precedent which was to determine the appearance of Mesopotamian public buildings for three thousand years. There has been much speculation as to its origin. Most authorities consider it derived from a form of reed-construction used in domestic buildings of the same period at Eridu, and surviving today among the Marsh Arabs of the neighbouring Hamar Lake. A temple of this period at Eridu was distinguished by another feature, which later became characteristic of Mesopotamian religious architecture. It was raised on an artificial platform of solid mud-brick, approached by a ramp or stairway, thus originating the principle which culminated in the great *ziggurats* of later times.

The first half of the fourth or Uruk period[1] showed little advance in building methods. Its second half has more recently been combined with the fifth period, the succeeding Jemdet Nasr phase (*c* 3200–2800 B.C.) [2], under the broader designation 'protoliterate'. It was during this period that the first great strides were made in the adornment and, so to speak, dramatization of religious buildings. A remarkable access of technical ingenuity, which has been considered to indicate some foreign invasion, produced a whole range of changes in the use of brick and terracotta. Substantially coincident with these changes were the first experiments in fresco-painting, the invention of the cylinder-seal, and the introduction of pictographic writing—a very significant series of associations.

Mud-bricks up to this time had usually been large and flat, with average dimen-

[1] Named after the ancient city Uruk or Erech, excavated at Warka.

sions of about 20×40×3–4 cm. Those of the protoliterate period were of the more modern and smaller proportions, which permit of two or more being handled at a time. For special purposes they were now baked in a kiln. Even smaller, place-made bricks were used for circular columns and other architectural features. Occasionally, bricks of cement were preferred to those of baked clay. Stone hardly ever occurs, except as small decorative elements. Only in rare instances[1] were blocks of undressed limestone used as a foundation, the walls usually resting on beds or platforms of solid mud-brick.

FIGURE 290—*Fragments of cone mosaic at Erech, Mesopotamia. Fourth millennium B.C.*

Perhaps the most remarkable advance during this period was in the decoration of wall-faces. For surfaces likely to be exposed to the weather, an ornamental mosaic was obtained by thrusting long, pointed cones of terracotta into the soft mud-plaster (figure 290). It is just possible that these originated at an earlier period, in mosaics composed of similar cones chipped out of coloured stone [3]. If so, these were now imitated by dipping the ends of the terracotta cones in red, yellow, or black paint before inserting them in the walls. Patterns thus contrived often recall the woven reeds of more primitive buildings. The cones for this finer surface-decoration are usually 7–8 cm long; but examples up to 30 cm are often found in positions at some distance from the ground, or where they serve to emphasize an important 'string-course'. Their ends are then usually dipped in bitumen, or hollowed to give a deeper shadow. Cones of this size at Eridu were of gypsum, with ends encased in thin copper-plating fastened on with bitumen. Others were carved out of black or mottled stone. Large mosaic elements, ornamenting the platform of the White Temple at Warka (the ancient Erech), are described as 'pottery beakers'. More elaborate forms of decoration, such as pieces of coloured stone cut to ornamental shapes, were pierced behind and attached by copper wire to the heads of terracotta cones.

Traces of crude wall-paintings of as early as the Halaf period have been found at Tepe Gawra. The first appearance of fresco-painting as part of a formal architectural *décor* is in the protoliterate Painted Temple at Uqair [4]. Above a dado of plain colour, the internal wall-faces were panelled with bands of trellis

[1] e.g. the limestone temple at Warka. Cf. V. G. CHILDE, 'New Light on the Most Ancient East', p 125. London, 1952.

and other geometrical patterns, in a variety of colours but excluding blue or green. In the panels, human and animal figures were grouped in formal scenes. The designs and figures were painted in mineral colours on a white ground, which, in its turn, was applied directly to the mud-plaster.

It is specially from the Painted Temple at Uqair that the appearance of such buildings can be reconstructed. It occupied part of a platform, 5 m high, of irregular shape, approached in two stages by three flights of mud-brick steps. Like those of an earlier period at Eridu, they were flanked by a rain-water channel

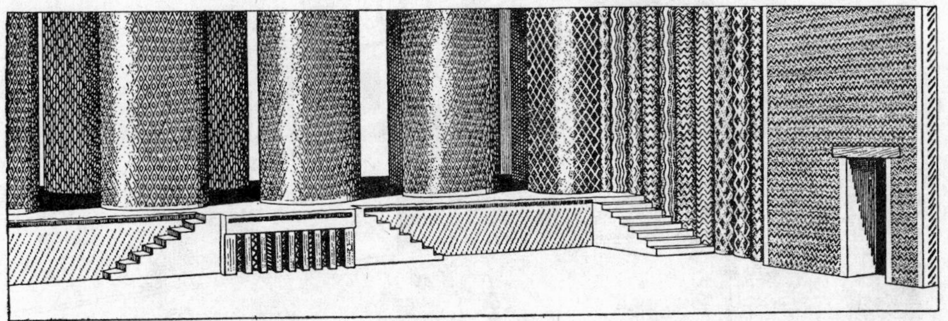

FIGURE 291—*The 'Sublime Porte' in the Red Temple complex at Erech (Uruk), Mesopotamia. The colonnade stands on a raised terrace at the approach to a sanctuary. It is composed of four pairs of cylindrical brick columns each about 1·5 m in diameter. The side walls are relieved by projecting half-columns. All these features, including the face of the terrace, are completely encrusted in cone mosaics, their painted heads forming a rich variety of patterns. Fourth millennium* B.C.

to prevent their erosion in bad weather. The faces of the platform, formed of alternate shallow buttresses and recesses, terminated in a deep band of 20-cm mosaic cones set in bitumen, in which their hollow ends also were dipped. The walls of the temple itself were ornamented with doubly recessed vertical grooves which, judging by a painted representation of such a building inside the temple, must also have terminated at cornice-height in a band of mosaic ornament. It seems that the roof was flat, and that the wide central hall, flanked on either side by smaller chambers, received clerestory lighting. The upper flight of a mud-brick staircase was supported on wooden beams. Doorways, to judge by almost contemporary buildings at Eridu, must have had lintels similarly supported.

Another building serves to emphasize the theatrical quality already present in architecture of this very early period. This was the 'Sublime Porte' in the Red Temple complex at Erech (figure 291). The Red Temple itself appears to have had interior wall-faces decorated with bas-reliefs in mud-plaster [5].

Equally dramatic qualities may be attributed to a contemporary building at Eridu (Temple I), the character of which can be guessed only from the evidence of its surviving platform [6]. Eridu was unique among Sumerian cities in that its situation on the outer fringe of the alluvium made several varieties of stone easily available. In the protoliterate period, the whole mound had been surrounded by a retaining-wall of undressed white limestone, to make an emplacement for a new sacred *temenos*. Above this, the temple-platform rose at a sharp

FIGURE 292—*Reconstruction of a temple at Eridu, Mesopotamia. Fourth millennium* B.C.

angle, its face constructed of pale pink limestone in small stepped courses. At a point some 15 m above the surrounding plain, this stepped face gave way to a vertical façade, consisting of successive semicircular bastions, apparently framing an open loggia, supported on columns. With its bronze-headed mosaic cones and inlay of brightly coloured marbles, this structure must have presented a remarkable picture (figure 292).

III. PERIOD OF SUMERIAN AND AKKADIAN SUPREMACY

Sumerian history begins with the rise of the Early Dynasties (*c* 2800–2300 B.C.). This epoch is marked by a notable change in the shape and method of laying bricks. For a brief, transitional period, the wooden mould appears to have been completely discarded, and the brick shaped merely by slapping the sides and ends on to a flat surface. The proportion generally preferred was a double cube about 20 cm long. This method, however, was almost immediately superseded, and there emerged a new mould-made shape—the criterion of Early

Dynastic buildings for several centuries—usually referred to as plano-convex. This shape was obtained by piling the mud well above the top of the mould, and then rounding it off with the hands. The curved upper face of the loaf-shaped form thus obtained was then indented by prodding with the fingers. In laying these bricks to make a wall, a special convention was evolved, and then used invariably. The bricks were laid on edge, in rows, leaning sideways against each other like books on a shelf; successive rows were arranged to lean in opposite directions, giving a herring-bone effect, occasionally interrupted by a few courses laid flat to improve the bond (figure 293). At the corners, and in the jambs of doors and windows, where special stability was needed, a more normal bonding was adopted. It is possible that this method of building was derived from a stone original [7]. Plano-convex bricks continued as the standard building material of southern Mesopotamia till the Akkadian supremacy, and, for many years after that, kiln-baked bricks at least retained traces of the same asymmetrical shape.

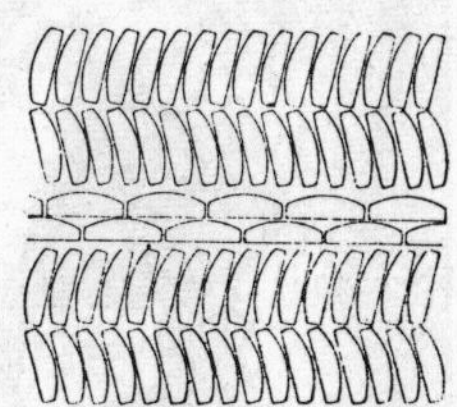

FIGURE 293—*One variety of the 'herringbone' patterns found in walls built of plano-convex bricks. Mesopotamia. Third millennium* B.C.

Apart from this new brick-laying technique, building methods in the Early Dynastic period show only minor improvements on those of protoliterate times. The use of kiln-baked bricks increased, especially for pavements and in situations where protection against rain was needed. Architectural ornament was considerably elaborated, as at the temple at El-Ubaid. This building, again, stood upon a brick platform approached by a flight of stone steps between brick retaining-walls. Though almost completely demolished, it was possible to reconstruct from its remains an open portico, with wooden columns overlaid with copper, or with a mosaic in mother-of-pearl, black shale, and red limestone set in bitumen. The entrance was flanked by life-size heads of lions, worked in copper with inlaid eyes and teeth, while above the door was a great copper relief. Elsewhere, the walls were ornamented with copper bulls, modelled in high relief over a bitumen base (p 638), and with friezes of figures inlaid in white stone or shell set against a background of black shale. Rosettes of coloured stone were attached by copper wire to terracotta cones thrust into the wall-face.

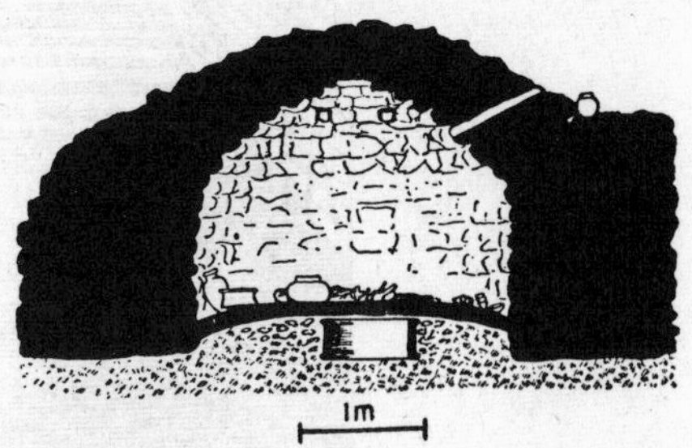

FIGURE 294—*Section of a tomb at Ur with a corbelled dome. Mesopotamia. Third millennium* B.C.

True arches appear for the first time in this period, and there are both vaults and

FIGURE 295—*Main sewer of the Akkadian palace at Eshnunna, Mesopotamia. Third millennium B.C.*

domes in the burial-chambers of the royal tombs at Ur. These are modest structures (figure 294) built of limestone rubble, and the vaulting is contrived by corbelling (cf also figure 318).

During the Akkadian supremacy in southern Mesopotamia, the drainage systems were improved and elaborated. That found beneath an Akkadian palace at Eshnunna strongly suggests comparison with contemporary buildings at Mohenjo-Daro in the Indus valley, where very similar methods disposed of both domestic waste and rain-water during the monsoons (figures 295–6). At Eshnunna, all bathrooms and closets are ranged along the outer side of the building, so that their drains discharge directly into a vaulted main sewer, running the length of the street beyond. They are of baked brick, jointed and lined with bitumen, with open inspection chambers at their principal junctions. Elsewhere there are inspection 'eyes', through which a rod could be inserted for cleaning. The bathrooms have a pavement and surrounding revetment of bitumen-covered brick, and the closets a raised pedestal with the occasional refinement of a shaped bitumen seat (figure 297) [8].

FIGURE 296—*Brick-covered drain at Mohenjo-Daro, Indus valley. Third millennium B.C.*

FIGURE 297—*Closet in the Akkadian palace at Eshnunna, Mesopotamia. Third millennium B.C.*

With the Sumerian revival under Dynasty III of Ur (*c* 2100–1950 B.C.), the peculiarly Mesopotamian craft of large-scale building in brick reached its zenith. Its most spectacular accomplishments are the *ziggurats* or staged-towers which adorned the religious centres of all the greater cities. In the Early Dynastic period such structures had already progressed beyond the stage of mere temple-platforms, but they were now rebuilt on a colossal scale, usually with several receding storeys and approached by a multiple stairway. The reconstruction of the Ur-nammu *ziggurat* is a good example (figure 298). It measured 72 × 54 metres, and its original height was about 26 m. The façades, consisting of a revetment 2·5 m thick made of kiln-baked brick set in bitumen, are relieved by broad, shallow buttresses and lean inwards with a pronounced batter, to give an appearance of strength. Horizontally, they are even given a deliberate convexity to correct the illusion of perspective. The dangers of shrinkage and uneven settle-

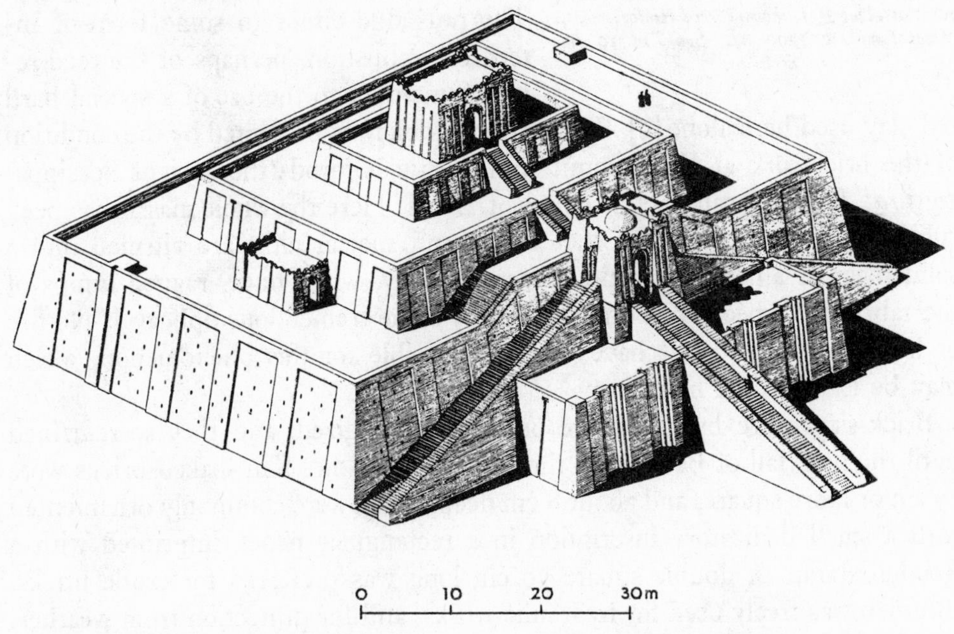

FIGURE 298—*Reconstruction of Ur-nammu's* ziggurat *at Ur, Mesopotamia.* c *2000 B.C. (Isometric projection.)*

ment of the bulk of the solid internal mud-brickwork presented a special engineering problem. The use of reeds as a binding material for buildings had long been known, as we learn from the account by Herodotus of Babylonian building methods (Herodotus, i. 179). A good example of this ingenious technique has been revealed in a recent examination of the Cassite *ziggurat* at Aqar Quf. Here the fabric of the mud-brick is interrupted at intervals of five courses by a deep layer of reed-matting, while the whole structure is tied together by heavy, multiple cables of tough reeds, running right across it from face to face in alternating directions (figure 299).

FIGURE 299—*The structure of the Cassite* ziggurat *at Aqar Quf, showing reed reinforcement. Mesopotamia.* c *1200* B.C. *Scale in 10 cm divisions.*

The internal fabrics of two famous *ziggurats* show peculiar phenomena, which have not been adequately explained. One is the tower already mentioned at Ur (figure 298). There the internal brickwork with mortar, now exposed by the denudation of the building, has acquired a deep red colour and a hardened consistency, distinguishing it from any other building in the city. This was due either to some form of internal combustion, perhaps of the reed reinforcement, or to the use of a special hard red clay used here alone [9]. The second problem is presented by the condition of the brickwork at the summit of the Birs-Nimrod (the ancient Borsippa) *ziggurat*, known locally as the Tower of Babel. Here the whole massif has been subjected to so great a heat that bricks and mortar alike are vitrified into a solid mass of almost porcelain-like consistency, while huge, ragged lumps of the fabric have been torn out of place by some tremendous upheaval. No fire or human agency could have been responsible for this phenomenon, which may be the effect of lightning.

Brick-sizes were by now more or less standardized, and they so remained until the final fall of Babylon in the sixth century B.C. Kiln-baked bricks were 30 cm or more square, and about 8 cm deep. They were commonly ornamented with a small dedicatory inscription in a rectangular panel, imprinted with a wooden stamp. A double square 30 cm long was preferred for crude bricks. Bitumen was freely used for hydraulic works, and for protection from weather. Large spans were covered by corbelled vaulting (Dynasty III tombs at Ur), timber being employed sparingly on account of its scarcity. Woolley reconstructs private houses of a few centuries later, at Ur, with wooden balconies around the central court, but these could have been supported on palm-trunks (figure 300).

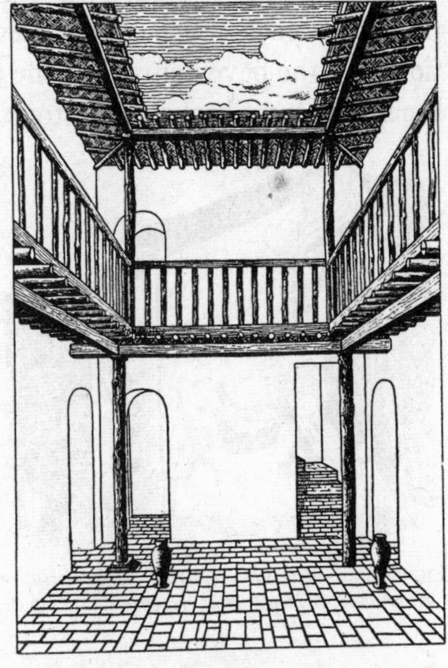

FIGURE 300—*Restoration of a private house at Ur, Mesopotamia.* c *1800* B.C.

IV. PERIOD OF ASSYRIAN SUPREMACY

Assyrian architecture departs hardly at all from the Mesopotamian tradition of the south, and building methods show little innovation, though there is a considerably increased use of stone. This was available in northern Iraq, and particularly easily quarried in the district of Nineveh. Qualities vary from a fine, chalky limestone to a dark grey-brown gypsum capable of receiving quite a high polish. Gypsum, which is used for the majority of Assyrian sculptures, is easy to carve but very susceptible to weathering, on account of its solubility.

In the palace-platform at Khorsabad (Sargon II, 722–705 B.C.), which, like the *ziggurats* of the south, is constructed of solid mud-brick, a facing of finely trimmed, square-hewn masonry is used. The blocks, which measure 2 × 2 × 2·75 m, each weigh about 23 000 kg and are laid as headers, while an occasional stretcher projects into the crude brick behind, to form a bond. Sennacherib (705–681 B.C.), son of Sargon II, constructed a stone canal, at some points over 20 m wide, to bring fresh water to Nineveh from Bavian in the northern foothills, a distance of more than 80 km. At a place where the canal was compelled to cross a wide valley, a stone aqueduct was constructed; this structure has been excavated and recorded in great detail (plate 20 A). In its construction, something over two million blocks were used. Each measured approximately 50 × 50 × 65 cm, and in the centre five pointed arches, formed by corbelling, spanned the bed of a wide stream. The treatment of the façades of this great structure was curiously haphazard. Groups of closely dressed square blocks alternated with others heavily rusticated but having a carefully drafted margin. A heavy deposit of stone chips along the base showed that the faces had been dressed *in situ* [10].

The waterproofing of the canal-bed here showed considerable technical sophistication. A 40-cm bed of excellent concrete was floated in bitumen to a depth of about 3 cm, and upon this a stone pavement was laid, accurately jointed and laid to a fall of 1/80. The bitumen was turned up along the inner faces of the parapets, and a tilting-course prevented water from accumulating at their junction with the pavement when the canal was empty. The concrete is a mixture of lime, sand, and broken limestone in the proportion 1 : $1\frac{1}{2}$–2 : 4. The grading of the canal pavement, which was made with far greater accuracy than necessary for assuring a regular flow of water, appeared to be connected with the process of quarrying and transporting the stone. The quarry (where the stone may still be seen, lying in conveniently regular natural laminations, corresponding in depth to that of the courses used by the builders) adjoins the head of the canal at Bavian. There can be little doubt that, as one section after another was completed, the finished water-bed was used to transport the blocks on wheels or rollers.

FIGURE 301—*Partly excavated bull-colossus at Khorsabad, Mesopotamia. Seventh century* B.C.

In the later Assyrian capitals, Nimrud, Nineveh, and Khorsabad, stone was used for the great hybrid colossi which now guarded the gates of royal palaces, and for the slabs, sculptured in relief, which adorned the lower faces of the walls in their principal chambers. An average-sized bull-colossus from Khorsabad weighed over 20 000 kg. It measured 4·4 m square and had a thickness of 45–60 cm (figure 301). Masons' debris around the bases of these figures showed that they were carved for the most part *in situ*. A sculptured relief depicting a colossus in transit confirms that the blocks were only rough-hewn to the required shape in the quarry (figure 283). In another relief, the colossus is being brought to land from a Tigris raft, and, though the location of the quarries used by the Assyrian kings is by no means certain, there can be little doubt that water-transport was most often used for these huge masses of stone. The picture also shows ropes, levers, and pulleys used in moving the great wheel-less sledge on which the figure was mounted.

The sculptured wall-slabs of the late Assyrian period often stood to a height of 2·5 or 3 m. Surviving reliefs from Khorsabad show that colour was sometimes applied to certain parts of the figures: a reddish tint to the naked flesh and black to hair and beards. The plastered wall-faces above them were often covered with formal frescoes in colours of great brilliance [11]. Another form of architectural decoration which began to be extensively used in late Assyrian times was glazed ornament in colour on the face of kiln-baked bricks. This was used in formal bands to take the place of a cornice at the summit of external façades, and in certain other standard situations. Arched doorways with guardian colossi were often decorated with a glazed archivolt framing the brick key-piece, and friezes of mythical figures in the same technique enriched the faces of low platforms at the bases of the flanking towers. Preliminary drawings of these designs were scratched on large panels of clay, which were subsequently cut with wire into bricks of a standard size. The bricks were then separately painted and the glaze fired. It is probable that standard cartoons were used both to trace the original drawing on the damp clay, and afterwards to set the finished bricks in their correct order. The adhesive used was bitumen.

FIGURE 302—*An Assyrian relief depicting a palace with small square openings as windows.*

A large-scale use of glazed bricks, with figures modelled in relief beneath the glaze, characterized the final efflorescence of Babylonian architecture after the fall of Nineveh (612–539 B.C.). The famous Ishtar Gate (figure 286, plate 18), and the walls of the Procession Street leading to the centre of Babylon, were thus ornamented. Here again, each figure was moulded or modelled in a single panel of wet clay, and the panel was afterwards divided into bricks for separate glazing and firing. A peculiarity of this architectural group is that both gate- and street-walls are carried down to the equivalent of their full height beneath the ground. Here, where their façades would never be visible to the human eye, the many tiers of mythical figures in relief were exactly repeated, though the coloured glaze was replaced by a protective coat of mud-plaster.

Much that remains to be said of Mesopotamian constructional methods applies to the buildings of both Babylonia and Assyria. In both countries, crude brick walls of public buildings acquired an almost exaggerated solidity, even those between chambers often having a thickness of several metres. Yet it is rare to find any kind of prepared foundation. Where they were not built directly upon a solid brick platform, their lower courses usually rested upon the levelled ruins of earlier buildings. Only a city wall, such as that at Nineveh, with a thickness of more than 20 m, would occasionally be provided with a foundation of limestone rubble. Doorways, from Sumerian times onwards, were spanned by brick arches with accurately radiating key-pieces. Wooden doors, sometimes plated with bronze, pivoted on a large round stone sunk beneath the pavement (figure 118), and were secured above by a staple of stone or metal built into the jamb. The pivot itself was often protected by a metal cap. Of windows, there is little evidence—or need in a country where the sun is to be excluded, and sufficient light comes through open doorways. Yet there are small square openings recognizable in buildings depicted in Assyrian reliefs (figure 302). Even in Sumerian private houses such openings were to be found, fitted with pierced terracotta panels (figure 303). Sculptured column-bases occasionally appear in Assyrian palaces. In the absence of shafts or capitals, these must be presumed to have been of wood; their form and treatment may be reconstructed from representations in sculptured reliefs.

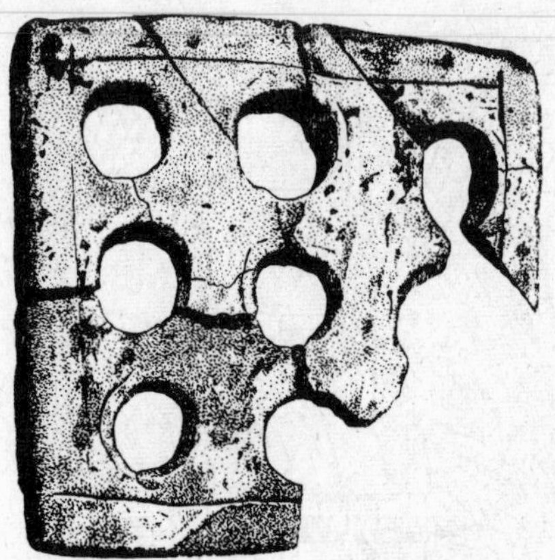

FIGURE 303—*A terracotta window grille. Mesopotamia. Third millennium* B.C. *Width* c *450 cm.*

Methods of roofing the larger Mesopotamian public buildings have been a subject of controversy. Shortage of wood, and the preference for long, narrow chambers, suggested the use of vaulting, though there is little to confirm this view. Few indisputable traces of fallen vaulting have been found, but there is much evidence compatible with timber ceilings. Nevertheless, underground structures such as sewers show that, in Babylonian and Assyrian times, the principle of brick vaulting was already well known. It continued in general use for wide spans down to Arab times in Persia and

FIGURE 304—*Brick-vaulted culvert at Khorsabad, Mesopotamia.*

Mesopotamia. By this method, the vault is constructed of vertical rings, each lying back at a slight angle upon the previous one, and the need for temporary centring is thus avoided (figure 304).

V. BUILDING IN BRICK IN EGYPT

A Greek historian of the first century B.C., Diodorus Siculus, wrote: 'They say the Egyptians in ancient times . . . made their houses of reeds, of which there are some marks among the shepherds at this day, who care for no other houses, but such like, which they say serve their turn well enough.' Traces of such shelters have in fact been found in the predynastic settlement at Badari in Upper Egypt [12]. Yet these appear to have represented a temporary retrogression, since settlers of an earlier phase elsewhere, as at Merimde on the edge of the Delta, had already learnt to build dome-shaped huts of rammed clay. Sun-dried bricks appear for the first time before the end of the predynastic period, and remain the standard material for buildings other than temples, palaces, and tombs for the remainder of Egyptian history [13].

The popular conception of Egyptian architecture is so permanently associated with fine masonry that it is no longer easy to imagine its familiar monuments against a drab background of interminable mud-brick houses. Archaeology has done little to emphasize this particular circumstance. The mud-brick mastaba tombs of the very early kings, with their panelled walls and rubble filling, have indeed been examined with great interest, particularly in relation to the great pyramid-forms of later times, which were derived from them.[1] From Dynasty IV onwards, the superior claims of stone buildings asserted themselves, and in Egyptian cities little attention has been paid to the decaying remains of the residential quarters. This neglect might have been less pronounced had the Egyptians ever adopted the practice of baking their bricks, but brick-kilns were unknown in Egypt down to classical times.

An exception to this generalization is the Dynasty XVIII city of El-Amarna. There, many brick houses, including some of considerable pretensions, have been excavated (figure 305). The typical Amarna house had main structural walls of mud-brick nearly 1 m thick. The principal rooms were paved with similar bricks, laid on edge and plastered. The rooms were grouped around a square central hall, which received clerestory lighting and, like the other principal living-rooms, had columns supporting the flat roof. Certain parts of the latter

[1] Cf. I. E. S. EDWARDS, 'The Pyramids of Egypt', pp. 37 ff. Penguin Books, Harmondsworth. 1952. For their possible association with contemporary buildings in Mesopotamia *vide* H. FRANKFORT, 'The Birth of Civilization in the Near East', pp. 103 ff. London, 1951.

were again covered in, to form rooms or verandas at first-floor level. The columns, which stood on circular stone bases, were of wood, painted to resemble the stone forms of Egyptian temples. They carried the main beams of an open timber roof, which in their turn supported minor joists. All beams seem to have been circular in section, and the larger scantlings may well have been palm-trunks. They were carefully squared up with an encasement of mud-plaster tempered with straw, and the panels between them were floated smooth.

FIGURE 305—*Reconstructed section of a brick-built private house at El-Amarna, Egypt.* c *1300* B.C.

The clerestory windows in the central hall, which occurred directly beneath the ceiling, were square openings in the wall provided with pierced grilles. These grilles were ingeniously contrived entirely from mud-plaster on a skeleton of reeds, the edges of the bars being so finely trimmed that the whole might have been carved from a single panel of wood. So strong was the architect's feeling for formal symmetry that, where the existence of rooms at first-floor level made light unobtainable, blind windows were introduced to match the real ones. In one subsidiary hall, where similar windows occurred in the outside wall only, another device has been used: the uppermost part of the wall was ornamented with a continuous frieze of vertical plaster bars, matching and incorporating those of the windows.

A corresponding formality was applied to the placing of doorways, for where symmetry required such a feature at an inconvenient point in the plan, a blind niche was introduced, framing a plaster panel painted to resemble a wooden door. All these features, including the beam-casings, were ornamented with formal frescoes in bright colours on a white ground. Column-bases and the thresholds of doors were the only features in these houses for which stone was used. An exception is found in a single instance of a sculptured stone lintel over a central doorway, lintels elsewhere being of wood.

The gardens or estates surrounding the houses were often enclosed by a high girdle-wall. Since such walls were designed merely for privacy, their thickness could at times be reduced to a half-brick, the line of the wall being undulating to improve stability. By contrast, the huge mud-brick enclosure-walls, common in the New Kingdom, were divided up into comparatively short sections, one section being laid on a bed concave to the horizon, and the adjoining sections on convex or level beds—an arrangement the purpose of which is obscure.

FIGURE 306—*Fluted three-quarter columns at Saqqara, Egypt. c 2600 B.C. Height of foreground column from foundation block 1·15 m.*

The sizes of Egyptian mud-bricks are [14]:

Private houses generally: 23×11×8 cm, approximately.

Public buildings:

Nubian fortress (Middle Kingdom)—30×15×7·5 cm.
El-Kab (New Kingdom)—38×19×17 cm.
Karnak " " —40×20×15 cm; 35×17·5×13 cm.
Armant—35×17·5×11·5 cm; 30×15×9·5 cm.

VI. BUILDING IN STONE IN EGYPT

From Dynasty III, when the possibilities of stone for permanent buildings began to be realized, its quarrying and employment became and remained the prerogative of royalty. The circumstances, however, under which the mason's craft was first born and came so early to be perfected are a mystery. The earliest known group of substantial stone buildings, the step-pyramid of Zoser at Saqqara with its extraordinary dependencies, exhibits a high technical skill applied with manifest confidence. Whether material evidence survives of a more tentative stage, time alone can decide.

The Zoser complex stands by itself in another sense. It represents an extremely ephemeral phase in the evolution of masonry technique, which, once superseded, was largely forgotten. Its small-block masonry, so-called because stones were preferred of a size which could be handled without mechanical devices, gave way early in Dynasty IV to the Cyclopean conception more normally associated in our minds with ancient Egyptian masonry. And since, from that time onwards, every process connected with the use of stone in building became stereotyped into a conventional pattern, destined to remain unchanged for two millennia, the Dynasty III complex at Saqqara should receive individual treatment as a prelude.

FIGURE 307—*Pilaster imitating the head and stalk of papyrus. From the chapel of a princess at Saqqara, Egypt.* c *2600 B.C.*

The Zoser masonry shows an extraordinary refinement of detail, and, to our eyes, good taste. Perhaps its most surprising feature is the general use, not of pilasters (as they are occasionally described), but of three-quarter columns, attached sometimes to the main wall-faces and sometimes to the ends of fly-walls projecting from them (figure 306). There can be no doubt that the contemporary builder was alive to the possibility of using a detached column, yet, perhaps on account of some structural inadequacy in his past experience, he preferred this method of ensuring stability for his roof-supports. The details of the columns still bore traces of their derivation from more primitive materials such as reed-bundles or palm-trunks, and were correspondingly organic in character. The shafts, tapering from the bottom upwards, were often ornamented with vertical reeding. A common alternative was vertical fluting, and this form has received disproportionate attention in relation to possible connexion with the Doric order of later times. There is even more organic realism in the triangular pilaster, imitating the stalk and head of a papyrus plant (figure 307), and in the attractive treatment of a capital with two fluted leaves pendent on either side (figure 308). Stone ceilings of this period are also still retrospective. Roof-blocks were laid on edge, giving them a depth equal to more than twice their thickness, and their lower edge was rounded to give the appearance of tree-trunks (plate 19).

The apparent technical perfection of all this Dynasty III masonry is unfortunately largely illusory, permanence and structural soundness being everywhere sacrificed to external appearance. The blocks were dressed so that they met accurately only to a depth of a few centimetres from the face. Thereafter the spaces between them rapidly widened, so that an appearance of fine jointing was obtained only at the cost of solidity (figure 309 B).

Stone of very good quality, and of many varieties, is obtainable from the cliffs which separate the Nile valley from the high desert on either side, and from the escarpments surrounding the Delta. Limestone rocks of many different qualities are to be found from Cairo to a little beyond Esna; Beni Hasan and Qau are noted for particularly fine-grained varieties. South of Esna, sandstone deposits range intermittently as far as Wadi Halfa; the finest quarries are at Silsila. Aswan was the chief ancient source of granite though there are other old quarries near Wadi Hammamat. Alabaster was worked at Hat-Nub, near El-Amarna, and the ancient supply of basalt was probably obtained from the Fayum [15].

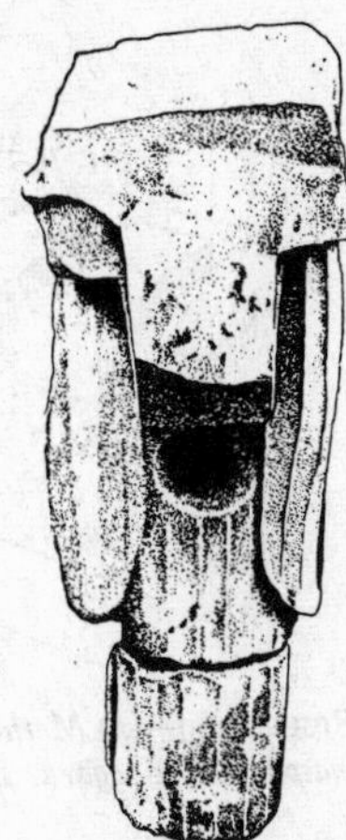

FIGURE 308—*Head of a pilaster. Masonry of King Zoser, Saqqara. c 2600 B.C.*

Of these materials, limestone was in general use until Dynasty XI. Granite had been employed for wider spans, and also for such purposes as statues and sarcophagi. Basalt was used in the Old Kingdom for pavements, and for revetments of limestone buildings. Silsila sandstone largely superseded limestone since, when used as beam-blocks, it could span much wider openings.

Many ancient quarries worked by the Egyptian state monopoly have been located, and a good deal is now known about the technique used. This of course varied according to whether the quarry was open-cast or underground, and the rock hard or soft. When the best beds were at some depth, tunnels several hundred metres long were cut to reach the required stratum, and, if they could be directed upwards from some cliff face, the removal of the stone was greatly facilitated. Inside, the process of removing the blocks is made clear by marks on the quarry-face at certain points where the process has been, for one reason or another, left incomplete. By cutting to waste, a deep recess was formed in the vertical face just beneath the ceiling, high enough for a man to work in, in a crouching position. In the floor of this recess, the blocks were outlined and separated by channels 11 cm wide, cut to the depth of a course. The blocks were then split from the rock by a line of wedges driven into the outer face (figure 309 A). As working-space above increased, the recess could be extended to a depth of three or more blocks, and the quarrying could then proceed in stepped formation. It seems doubtful whether a chisel was used for cutting the vertical channels; such a pre-Roman implement 48 cm long has been found, but the marks left on the quarry-face correspond more closely to a mason's pick such as is commonly used today, with a 2·5 kg head and 45 cm haft.

Occasionally, as at the Silsila sandstone quarries—where an architrave stone measuring 6 × 0·8 × 1·5 m remains in place, shaped but not separated from the

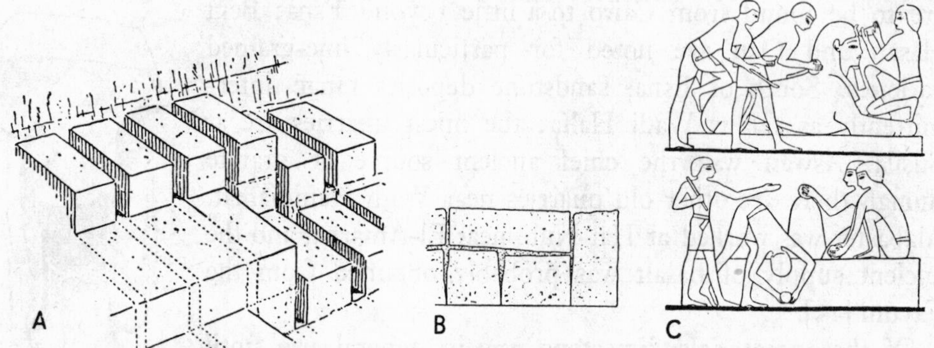

FIGURE 309—(A) *Method of extracting blocks in a quarry, Egypt.* (B) *Plan of an example of King Zoser's small-block masonry at Saqqara, Egypt (slightly exaggerated).* c *2600 B.C.* (C) *Polishing and dressing with stone implements; Thebes, Egypt.* c *1500 B.C.*

rock—some part of the work of quarrying had been avoided by taking advantage of regular vertical faults. The final separation of such a block, as indeed the splitting of stones for all purposes, was accomplished with wooden wedges swollen by wetting. The Egyptians, however, are suspected of having occasionally used hard metal wedges between 'feathers' of a softer material.

Any consideration of the process by which the hard rocks, such as the pink and gray granites from Aswan, were quarried involves the much wider problem as to how these stones came to be worked at all with the limited technical means available. Suggestions that the Egyptians had discovered the use of steel may be dismissed (ch 21). Hardened copper has also been suggested but, however effective, its expenditure in carving granite would be prohibitive. On the other hand, numerous balls and hammers of dolerite found at these sites make it certain that pounding took a great part in the working of hard stone. The balls, weighing up to 5·5 kg, were held in both hands, as may be seen from sculptured reliefs (figure 309 C). It is also certain that granite was both drilled and sawn with the help of some abrasive, and that much shaping could be done with a heavy, somewhat blunt instrument, resembling a mason's pick or a quarryman's jumping-iron, a tool requiring an exactly moderated blow.

Occasionally, there is a larger block in the quarries which, having overturned or otherwise behaved eccentrically during extraction, has been abandoned and left where it fell. This reflects a deficiency in knowledge of the most elementary dynamics, so that any departure from a fixed routine of removal and transport was shunned. The use, for example, of capstan or pulley was unknown, and there is no evidence of wheeled vehicles before the New Kingdom. The only devices generally available were levers, operating on bosses left in the face of the stone; sledges, which, in a certain form, could be used as rockers for raising blocks vertically; rollers, which being made of a perishable material have left no traces; and the so-called Spanish windlass, a device for exerting tension by twisting a multiple rope. Considering these limitations, the feats of engineering regularly accomplished in moving stones of great weight over long distances appear the more remarkable; they must be attributed to such factors as the exploitation of the Nile as a water-way, the use of draft-animals, and the skilled co-ordination of human labour.

FIGURE 310—*Foundations of a column in the Hypostyle Hall, Karnak.* c *1300 B.C. See figure 287.*

Since Egyptian ingenuity could transport a block of stone weighing a million kilograms from a distant quarry to a building site, it is disconcerting to find certain elementary structural inadequacies in the buildings themselves. Thus one would expect that, since their foundations were often built on comparatively soft alluvial soil, their stability would receive special consideration—but at Karnak, for example, 45 cm of sand in the bottom of a trench is the basis of some of the largest walls. As a result of flooding, eleven of the great columns in the Hypostyle Hall fell flat in November, 1899. It was then found that their foundations consisted of friable little blocks carelessly placed in a hole (figure 310). Such architectural lack of foresight continued until as late as Dynasty XXV, when important buildings came at last to be placed upon a platform of masonry several metres deep. Again, in the dressing and laying of the blocks, there are eccentric elements which would puzzle a modern mason, with his standards based on the use of scaffolding, tackle, water-levels, and other apparently simple devices. His ancient Egyptian predecessor never seems to have acquired the

FIGURE 311—*Variation in the height of courses, and oblique rising joints. Wall of Thothmes III, Karnak, Egypt. c 1400 B.C.*

idea of squaring his stones before building, or to have conceived that geometrically prismatic blocks would be an advantage. His attention, too, was so concentrated on the bedding and rising joints of the façade that he almost completely ignored problems of internal bonding. Most surprising of all, the rising joints themselves are often set obliquely to the line of the bed or to the line of the façade, and stones in the same bed are sometimes of varying heights (figure 311).

Any attempt to explain these things must involve a careful consideration of the contemporary method of procedure. First, then, instead of scaffolding, earth ramps were built, up which the blocks could be rolled or drawn toward the bed. As the wall rose, the correct horizontal and vertical alignment of the façade was fixed at the joints only, the remainder of the blocks being left in the rough. The final dressing of the whole face was eventually completed from the top downwards, as the ramp was gradually removed. Initial levelling was corrected by a water-channel banked up with clay. Vertical checks were made by means of open shafts left at intervals in the embankment.

Since the geometrical peculiarity of contemporary jointing could hardly have been contrived deliberately, several theories have been advanced to explain it. Of these, the most simple is that the stone arrived from the quarry in irregular shapes, and that by adapting the angle of the block-faces accordingly, some saving could be made in the expenditure of labour and material. This would especially apply to hard stones which could be dressed only by pounding. Nevertheless, it is obvious that by using stones with irregular angles and of unequal sizes, the builder involved himself in a very complicated task, the normal practice of which has been ingeniously reconstructed from the evidence available.

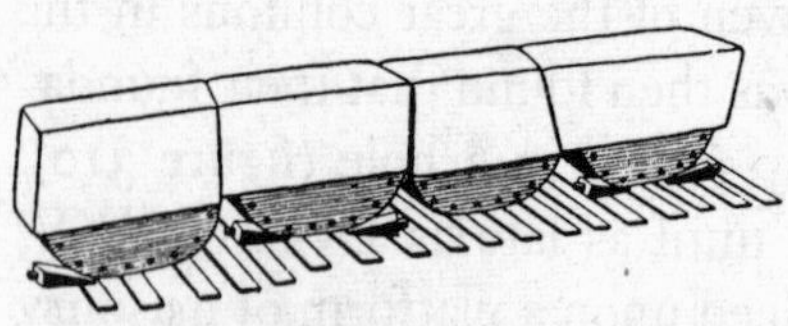

FIGURE 312—*Model illustrating the probable method of dressing resulting in oblique rising joints. Pairs of faces have been cut parallel and brought into contact on rockers. The top faces have then been dressed level to form the bedding joint. Egypt.*

To begin with, it is clear that the rising joints between blocks were not adjusted *in situ*, that is, when one was already in place.

Before being brought to the wall, they were lined up, probably each on its own wooden rocker, and their ends brought together, so that approximately parallel faces could then be cut where the joint was to occur, and final adjustments made by varying the tilt of the rocker. The tops of the whole row of blocks were then accurately trimmed to a single flat face which, when the stones were inverted, would eventually form the bedding-joint. Only what were finally the bottom edges of the blocks were thus trimmed beforehand to the line of the bedding-joint, the upper edges being afterwards cut *in situ* to fit the eccentricities of the course above (figure 312). This was necessitated by the occasional use of blocks of uneven height in the same course. Tools and other devices used in this process of dressing the blocks are depicted in scenes in contemporary wall-paintings (figure 313). Thus a chisel is shown in use with an ordinary sculptor's mallet; it was afterwards held in the fist to give a final trim. Boning-rods are seen employed to adjust the face of the block to an exact plane, and have been found in a contemporary setting. The mason's square and plumb-bob are also known to have been used (figure 314).

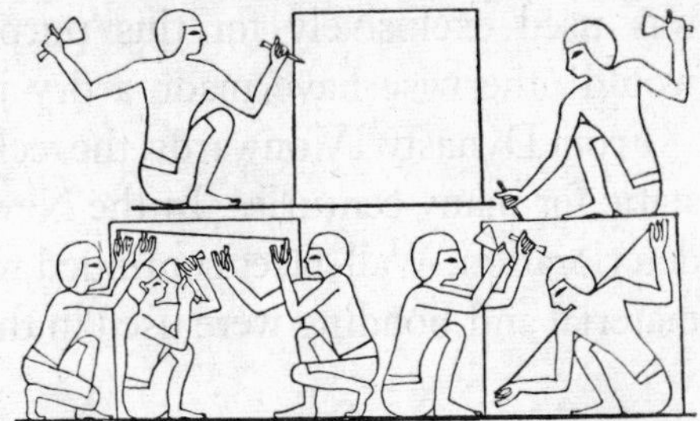

FIGURE 313—*Workmen dressing a stone block. Below, on the left, men are dressing the surface by means of boning-rods, while on the right the last touches are being given, and the flatness is tested by holding a thread against the face. From a tomb at Thebes.* c *1450 B.C.*

It is not impossible that the colossal blocks used, for example, in the facing of the pyramids could likewise have been adapted one to the other by the method described above, while still mounted on the great wooden sleds known to have been made to carry them. The process, however, of placing each block on its appropriate bed in the wall, and of bringing its prepared face into contact with that of its neighbour, without the use of pulley or tackle, is one which must have taxed Egyptian ingenuity to its utmost. In this case we have a clue only to the culminating stage, the final sliding of the block into position against its neighbours. Where the friction of stone upon stone would have made this operation virtually impossible, it was accomplished with comparative ease by floating on a thin bed of viscid mortar. It is in fact assumed that the mortar

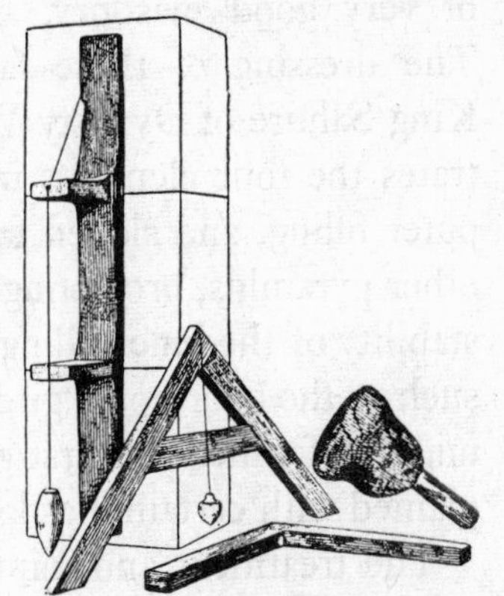

FIGURE 314—*Mason's mallet from Saqqara,* c *2600 B.C. Square, level, and plumb-rule from Thebes, Egypt.* c *1100 B.C.*

was used exclusively for this purpose, since the fine dressing of the faces would otherwise have made a dry joint perfectly practicable.[1]

From Dynasty IV onwards, the technique of stone-building in Egypt remained static for many centuries. In the New Kingdom there are unmistakable signs of deterioration. Wall-faces continued to be carefully jointed, but increasingly poor material and bonding were used in the filling. In the great pylons of the temples this became mere rubble, and internal cross-walls had to be constructed dividing them into cells to keep it in place.

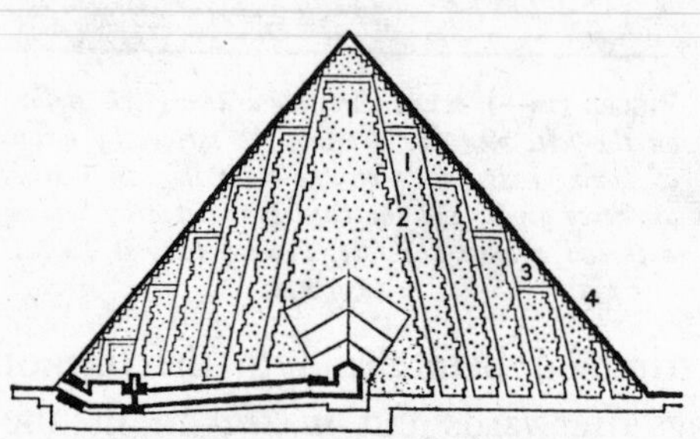

FIGURE 315—*North-south section through the pyramid of Sahure, Abusir, Egypt.* (1) *Core masonry.* (2) *Internal casing of fine limestone.* (3) *Packing-blocks of stone.* (4) *Smooth outer casing of limestone.* c 2400 B.C.

Pyramid construction had its special problems, detailed discussion of which would involve us in the tangle of retrospective speculation which has persisted since Herodotus; a mere outline must suffice here. The earliest stage of the development from a mastaba form is represented by the step-pyramid of Zoser at Saqqara. This oblong structure consists of successive skins of masonry, each with its own properly dressed accretion-face. The latter, like the face of a mastaba, has a batter of 1 : 4. Next comes the Meydum pyramid, built for King Seneferu of Dynasty IV. This is a true square, and its proportions are those of a fully developed pyramid (i.e. the height corresponds to the radius of a circle equal to the perimeter of the base, giving an angle of 51° 51′ to the façade.) It is covered with a facing of very good masonry, but the accretion-faces are still at mastaba angle. The dressing of these faces was afterwards discontinued. The pyramid of King Sahure of Dynasty V at Abusir takes the same form, and admirably illustrates the four elements in construction, namely inner filling, accretion-faces, outer filling, and sloped facing (figure 315). The relieving devices, in this and other pyramids, protecting the internal chambers show lack of confidence in the stability of the inner filling, which was never adequately bonded. Other devices, such as the enormous 'girdle-stones' in the Great Pyramid at Giza, through the middle of which the first gallery passes at intervals of 5·2 m, can never be explained with certainty as long as the monument remains intact.

The treatment and jointing of the more important architectural elements in

[1] Lime was unknown as a component of mortar until Hellenistic times. The ancient Egyptian builders used gypsum (hydrated calcium sulphate, $CaSO_4$, $2H_2O$). The hemihydrated form, plaster of Paris, $2CaSO_4$, H_2O, can be made by heating natural gypsum to about 100° C. On recombination with water it sets very hard in its original form. If the gypsum is heated too strongly ('dead burnt') it loses all its water, and will not set with water afterwards.

Egyptian temples need consideration. Pavements are usually composed of blocks laid to their full depth in an almost random patchwork, their top faces being trimmed *in situ*. Column-bases are found, either penetrating the pavement to rest on a foundation of small blocks beneath, or placed directly upon it. Occasionally they rest upon a shallow circular boss, reserved during the dressing of the pavement blocks. Columns are either monolithic or composite, and their forms show two main sources of derivation. One is the kind of organic origin already foreshadowed in the Dynasty III buildings at Saqqara. The other reflects more closely the solid vertical shafts left to support the ceiling in quarries, and afterwards treated more decoratively in rock-cut tombs. The vegetable originals of the former are the papyrus, the lotus, and the palm. The first of these types is used in situations of maximum importance, such as the Hypostyle Hall at Karnak, where the scale is so colossal that the capital alone is built up of several separate blocks (figure 287). The second type is used to support the lower ceilings in the same building, and elsewhere varies from the slim elegance of early examples to the gouty monstrosities of Dynasty XIX, whose shafts are covered with inscriptions. The palm column is used indiscriminately from Dynasty V onwards. Columns in the non-organic category develop towards a polygonal shape from an original chamfering of a square shaft. Later, the vertical facets become flutes, and a form is reached which has again been inevitably associated with the origin of the Doric Order. A good example is the charming treatment of the shaft in a rock-hewn temple of Amenhetep III at Beit el-Wali.

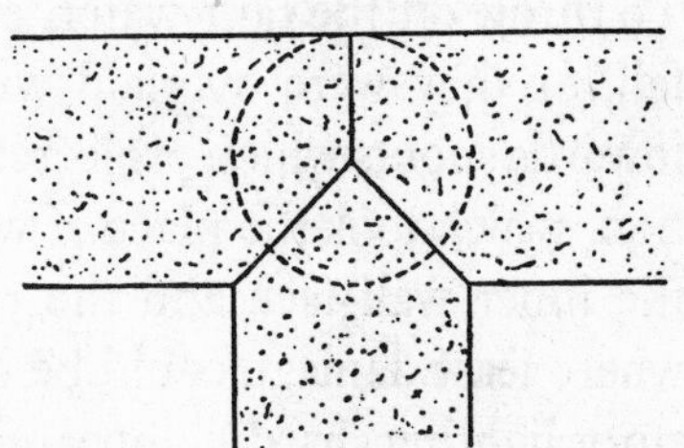

FIGURE 316—*The general Egyptian method of jointing three architraves on a column. Plan view.*

Columns, like facing-blocks, received their final dressing and carving *in situ*, the underside only of each drum being trimmed to form a bedding-face before being placed in position. Their alignment was fixed by a string stretched tangentially to the whole row of corresponding drums. The points of contact were marked with small dressed areas, which would afterwards provide a datum for the facing surface. Their spacing was at first dictated by the maximum distance which could safely be spanned by a limestone block used as a beam. Since this never exceeded 3 m, the later introduction of Silsila sandstone, which could span up to three times that distance, proved a great advantage. One factor which proved detrimental to the stability of these architrave beams was the absence of sufficient bearing-space, where two or more met over a column.

To meet this difficulty, several ingenious forms of mitre were contrived (figure 316).

From Dynasty IV onwards, roofing-slabs themselves were laid flat. The greatest care had then to be taken to waterproof the joints between them to protect the paintings inside the building from damp. From the Middle Kingdom, carefully fitted stone fillets between the raised edges of the slabs were used for this purpose. To throw off the rain-water, either the slabs themselves were dressed to a slight fall, or they were overlaid with a mosaic of smaller blocks, leading the water towards spouts which projected from the parapets. Apertures for light and ventilation, which took the place of windows, usually occurred at the junctions between the inner wall-face and the ceiling. These were presumably located at points where least damage could be done by the weather. True windows, giving clerestory lighting, hardly appeared until the New Kingdom. They were then cut in the form of gratings from a single block (figure 287).

One point about the general appearance presented by an Egyptian temple which has not often been considered is that, owing to the frequent rebuilding of the shorter-lived structures around it, the level of occupation outside tended in time to rise, until the neighbouring houses even reached the summit of the temenos-wall.[1] The temple itself would thus eventually come to occupy a deep depression, in which the disposal of rain- or flood-water must have presented something of a problem.

VII. CRETE AND THE AEGEAN

In the eastern Mediterranean, during the second and third millennia B.C., the evolution of building methods, like other forms of technical progress, followed two distinctive courses dictated by the main ethnic divisions of the area. This is primarily to be seen in the dissimilar forms acquired by the ordinary dwelling-house, first among the Mediterranean people of Crete and the Aegean islands, and secondly among the Greek-speaking inhabitants of the mainland, who later spread to the islands and Asia Minor.

In Crete, a few Early Minoan tholos tombs[2] in the Messara and elsewhere are the only possible indications of any recollection which the islanders may have had of circular nomadic huts. For the rest, their houses are from the beginning rectangular, shallow, and wide, with a terraced flat roof; they develop in plan from a simple two-compartment affair, with a single entrance, described by the

[1] Cf. the description of Bubastis (Zagazig) in HERODOTUS II, 138 (Loeb ed. Vol. I, pp. 443 ff., 1920).

[2] These tombs are discussed by J. D. S. PENDLEBURY in 'The Archaeology of Crete', pp. 63 ff. London, 1939, and by M. E. L. MALLOWAN, in relation to the prehistoric Mesopotamian tholoi at Arpachiyah, in *Iraq*, 2, 28, 1935. Tholos tombs are circular and bee-hive shaped, and are approached by a horizontal passage in the side of a hill.

Scottish colloquialism 'but-and-ben'. Early in the second millennium B.C. plans become more complex, with rooms grouped around central courts and light-wells. The famous 'town mosaic', a group of faience plaques of about 1700 B.C., shows the façades of houses with two or even three storeys, lighted with windows furnished with glazing-bars (figure 317). It is known that, in such houses, wooden columns were used to increase the size of the rooms, and that when rooms occurred at first-floor level they were supported on stone piers in the basement room beneath. The most usual form of wall-construction, common to both the Aegean and Asia Minor, has the lower part of stone-rubble

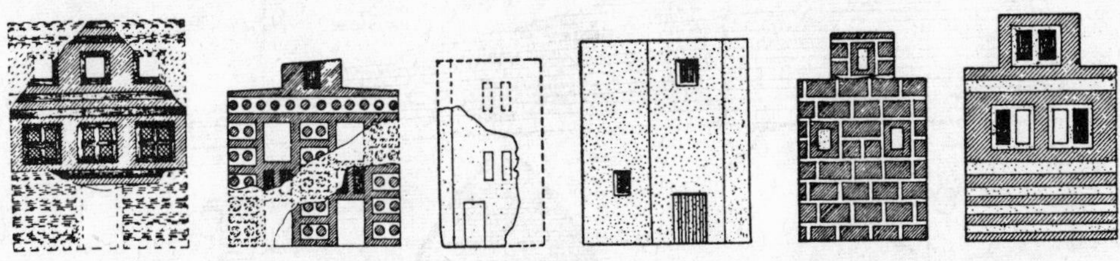

FIGURE 317—*The 'town mosaic'. Six of the many faience tablets representing towers and houses found a Knossos, Crete.*

and the upper of sun-dried brick framed in timber beams, linked horizontally and vertically.

On the Greek mainland, the circular nomadic hut formed the basic element from which the house-plan evolved. From a simple circular structure with conical pitched roof developed a horse-shoe form. This passed into a straight-sided affair, with the entrance on the long axis at one end and a semicircular apse at the other. The apse was soon partitioned off as a sleeping-chamber (*thalamus*), and the area immediately inside the entrance as a porch (*prodomos*), thus creating a three-compartment unit with a rectangular living-room in the centre. The pitched roof had meanwhile acquired a central ridge. Next, the apse was squared, and the entire plan became rectangular. The living-room, its potential size increased by the introduction of columns, was now furnished with a permanent hearth, thus introducing the European conception of the fireside as focus of domestic life. When the porch-entrance was spanned by a beam resting on the thickened ends of the lateral walls (*antae*), and widened by the addition of columns here also, all the elements of the classical *megaron* were already present.

Palaces developed logically from an elaboration of the contemporary house-plan, but there are fundamental differences of arrangement and construction between those of Crete and those of Mycenae. In Crete, there is the vast, labyrinthine complex at Knossos, and another at Phaistos on the south side of the island. These buildings had no fortifications, since military security depended upon sea-power, but their own walls were sturdy enough. Up to a certain height, they were built of ashlar masonry with a layer of clay between courses and a backing of rubble. Above this was a superstructure of sun-dried brick or

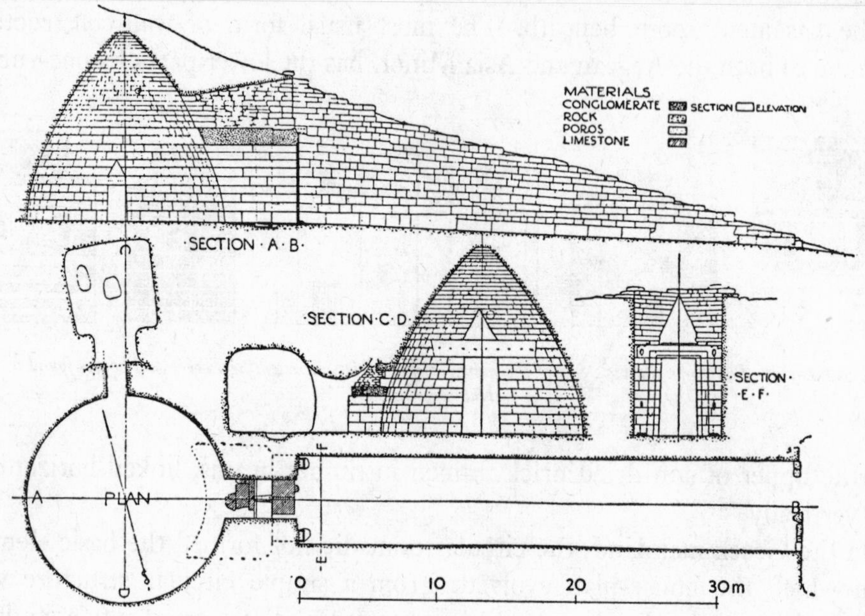

FIGURE 318—*Plan and sections of the 'Tomb of Agamemnon' at Mycenae. c 1450 B.C.*

stone rubble, held rigid by a framework of timber beams. These upper wall-faces were plastered over, and painted with elaborate decorative frescoes or sometimes in imitation of their internal construction. From the third Middle Minoan period onwards, ashlar masonry was used within the timber framework and the faces were left exposed.

At Knossos, the Cretan preference for flat roofs and terraces proved easily adaptable to the steep slope of the site chosen for the Palace of Minos (figure 319). Its plan also to some extent reflects the extremes of temperature to be expected from the Cretan climate. The main living-rooms have a minimum of outside exposure, being grouped for the most part around rectangular light-wells, from which the sun was reflected through columned peristyles. The main halls were approached through ranges of doorways with deep reveals, into which the doors could be folded back in the summer. Whether by chance or otherwise, a similar arrangement was adopted by the Hittites [16]. Terracing, and the choice of an upper storey as a *piano nobile*, laid some emphasis on staircases, which now for the first time in history received attention as domestic architectural features. That in the 'King's Suite' is 1·8 m wide with a central newel-post 90 cm square. Its 45-cm

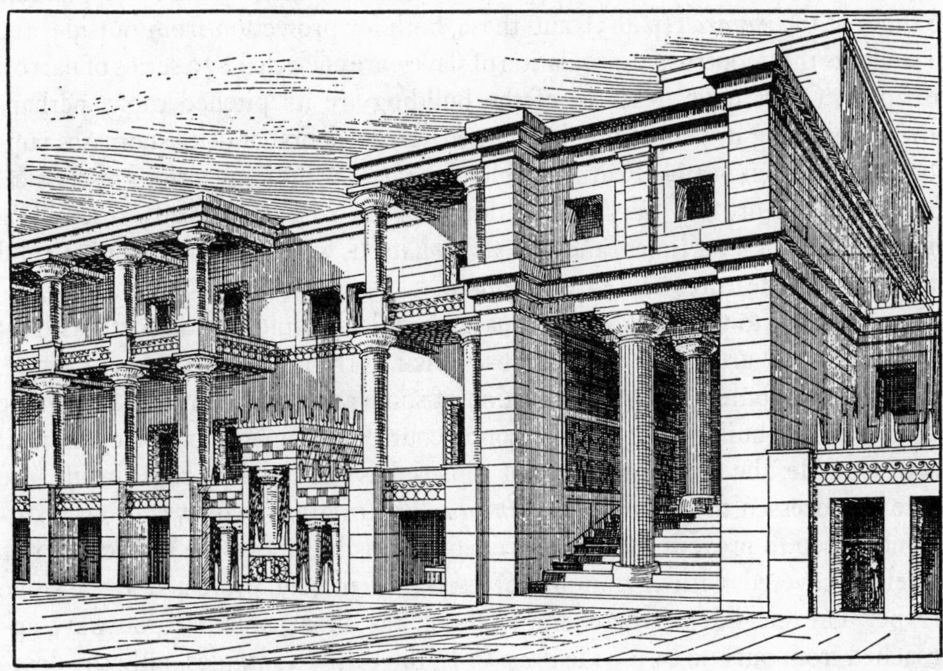

FIGURE 319—*Restored view of a wing of the Palace of Minos, Knossos, Crete.*

treads are each cut from a single slab of gypsum, built 18 cm into the wall on either side and dressed on the underside, to form a stone ceiling to the flight below.

The development of Cretan architecture introduced a completely new element into the realm of column-design. For the first time the pillars, which are of cypress wood, taper sharply from the top downwards.[1] Their stone bases were at first tall in proportion, and were made of variegated stone. In the Late Minoan period flat disks of limestone were preferred.

Of the Mycenaean palaces on the Greek mainland the best preserved and

[1] The ingenuity of some scholars has clearly been overstrained in the attempt to find a practical explanation of this irregularity (e.g. PENDLEBURY, op. cit., p. 153). If rigid wooden supports be considered in terms of furniture no explanation would appear necessary.

most characteristic is that at Tiryns. Like other mainland centres, such as Troy, it was surrounded by a fortress-wall, enclosing sufficient space for the dependent population of the settlement to take refuge in time of war. In the palace itself, in contrast to that at Knossos, all the important rooms are on one floor. There are no light-wells, the whole building being sufficiently low to admit adequate light through high windows. The nucleus of the plan consists of units corresponding to those of the *megaron* (p 485), and these, both for protection from outside, and to facilitate the unobtrusive circulation of slaves, are encircled by a series of narrow corridors. Other novel features of the building are its pitched roofs, perhaps now terminating in pediments, its painted stucco floors, and its staircases supported on wooden beams. Features which foreshadow the conventions of classical Greek architecture are the free-standing *porticos in antis*, already resembling the propylaea of later times, and the *megaron* itself, with its columns *in antis* and other standard features of a Greek temple.

No reference to the work of Mycenaean builders would be complete without mention of the great 'beehive' tombs. Their form, like the tholoi in Crete, probably contributed to the preservation of some ancestral memory. They were pointed domes, built of stone in horizontal courses, at the bottom of a cylindrical shaft. Outside, the filling of earth was replaced as the building rose; inside, the stone was dressed to a smooth face *in situ*. The original shaft was often insufficiently deep to prevent its summit remaining visible above the surface. It was therefore covered with a tumulus of earth, or merely protected by a stone parapet. On one side of the chamber there was an ornamental doorway, approached from outside by a wide *dromos*. In the earlier examples, only the doorway and façades of the *dromos* are of ashlar masonry, the remainder being rubble, but towards the end of the period the whole structure was faced with sawn breccia blocks. Among the later tombs, the so-called 'Treasury of Atreus' or 'Tomb of Agamemnon' (*c* 1450 B.C.) is the largest and best preserved (figure 318). It incorporates a number of features that may be considered characteristically Mycenaean. The inner face of the dome was decorated at intervals with bronze rosettes and other metallic ornaments. The doorway is flanked outside by engaged three-quarter columns of the Cretan type. These are of green alabaster, enriched with an elaborate ornament of chevrons and spirals, perhaps to imitate a metal sheathing over wood. The door has an architrave ornamented with receding fascias, which for the first time return across the flat lintel; the lintel itself is surmounted by a triangular relieving-space like that above the equally famous 'Lion Gate', also at Mycenae, which is filled with a heraldic-religious relief.

Having passed in review a sequence of technological discoveries, and the varying structural patterns contrived from them in the great primary centres of pre-classical civilization, we might expect peripheral cultures to be of interest in relation to their solution of problems arising from special circumstances. Yet in fact—among the Hittite ruins of Boghazköy, for example—there are few structural features to be found which have not already been discussed in relation to their occurrence elsewhere. The palace-builders of Susa may be seen to have added some technical refinements to processes originally adopted from the Babylonians, yet they boast of few authentic innovations. The architecture of the Indus valley in the mid-third millennium B.C. differs from that of Akkadian Mesopotamia hardly more than in the preponderant use of kiln-baked brick and a preference for sloping façades. A detailed appreciation of the supplementary contribution of such minor centres to the fabric of architectural knowledge and accomplishment would involve a far more lengthy study.

REFERENCES

[1] LLOYD, S. and SAFAR, F. *J. Near East. Stud.*, **4**, iv, 255, 1945.

[2] DELOUGAZ, P., LLOYD, S. *et al.* 'Pre-Sargonid Temples in the Diyala Region', p. 8 footnote, p. 134 diagram. Univ. of Chicago, Orient. Inst.: Publ. 58. Chicago. 1942.

[3] GORDON, D. H. and GORDON, M. E. *Iraq*, **7**, 8, 1940.

[4] LLOYD, S. and SAFAR, F. *J. Near East. Stud.*, **2**, ii, 139, 1943.

[5] JORDAN, J. 'Zweiter vorläufiger Bericht über die . . . in Uruk unternommenen Ausgrabungen.' *Abh. preuss. Akad. Wiss., phil.-hist. Kl.*, no. 4, 1930.

[6] SAFAR, F. *Sumer*, **3**, ii, 100 and Pl. II, 1947.

[7] DELOUGAZ, P. 'Plano-Convex Bricks and the Method of their Employment', pp. 1–38. Univ. of Chicago, Orient. Inst.: Stud. ancient Orient. Civiliz. no. 7. Chicago. 1934.

[8] FRANKFORT, H. *et al.* 'Iraq Excavations of the Oriental Institute. Third preliminary Report', pp. 23 ff. Univ. of Chicago, Orient. Inst.: Commun. no. 17. Chicago. 1934.

[9] WOOLLEY, SIR (CHARLES) LEONARD. 'The Ziggurat and its Surroundings.' 'Ur Excavations'. Reports Vol. 5. Publ. of Joint Exped. Brit. Mus. and Mus. of Univ. of Pennsylvania. 1939.

[10] JACOBSEN, TH. and LLOYD, S. 'Sennacherib's Aqueduct at Jerwan.' Univ. of Chicago, Orient. Inst.: Publ. 24. Chicago. 1935.

[11] LOUD, G. 'Khorsabad', Part I, fig. 83. Univ. of Chicago, Orient. Inst.: Publ. 38. Chicago. 1936.

[12] BRUNTON, G. and CATON-THOMPSON, G. 'The Badarian Civilisation', pp. 82–3. Egypt. Res. Acc. and Brit. Sch. Archaeol. Egypt. Publ. 46. London. 1928.

[13] PETRIE, SIR (WILLIAM MATTHEW) FLINDERS and QUIBELL, J. M. 'Naqada and Ballas', p. 54. Quaritch, London. 1896.

[14] CLARKE, S. and ENGELBACH, R. 'Ancient Egyptian Masonry', p. 209. Oxford University Press, London. 1930.

[15] GLANVILLE, S. R. K. (Ed.) 'The Legacy of Egypt', p. 143. Clarendon Press, Oxford. 1941.

[16] BITTEL, K. 'Die Ruinen von Bogazköy der Hauptstadt des Hethiterreichs', fig. 38. De Gruyter, Berlin and Leipzig. 1937.

BIBLIOGRAPHY

General:

FRANKFORT, H. 'The Birth of Civilization in the Near East.' Williams and Norgate, London. 1951.

CHILDE, V. GORDON. 'New Light on the Most Ancient East' (4th ed.). Routledge and Kegan Paul, London. 1952.

Mesopotamia:

SPEISER, E. A. "Ancient Mesopotamia." Reconstructions by H. M. Herget. *Nat. geogr. Mag.*, **99**, i, 41–105, 1951.

WOOLLEY, SIR (CHARLES) LEONARD. 'The Sumerians.' Clarendon Press, Oxford. 1928.

PERROT, G., and CHIPIEZ, C. 'Histoire de l'art dans l'Antiquité', Vol. 2: 'Chaldée et Assyrie.' Librairie Hachette, Paris. 1884.

Egypt:

LUCAS, A. 'Ancient Egyptian Materials and Industries' (3rd ed.). Arnold, London. 1948.

EDWARDS, I. E. S. 'The Pyramids of Egypt.' Penguin Books, Harmondsworth. 1952.

CLARK, S. and ENGELBACH, R. 'Ancient Egyptian Masonry.' Oxford University Press, London. 1930.

PERROT, G. and CHIPIEZ, C. 'Histoire de l'art dans l'Antiquité.' Vol. 1: 'L'Égypte.' Librairie Hachette, Paris. 1882.

GLANVILLE, S. R. K. (Ed.). 'The Legacy of Egypt.' Clarendon Press, Oxford. 1941.

Crete and the Aegean:

PENDLEBURY, J. D. S. 'The Archaeology of Crete.' Methuen's Handbooks of Archaeology, London. 1939.

ANDERSON, W. J. and SPIERS, R. P. 'The Architecture of Ancient Greece.' Rev. and rewritten by DINSMOOR, B. W. Batsford, London. 1950.

Hittite:

DELAPORTE, L. 'Les Hittites.' La Renaissance du Livre, Paris. 1936.

BITTEL, K. 'Die Ruinen von Bogazköy der Hauptstadt des Hethiterreichs.' Archaeologisches Institut des Deutschen Reiches, Abteilung Istambul. De Gruyter, Berlin and Leipzig. 1937.

Indus Valley:

MACKAY, E. J. H. 'Early Indus Civilizations' (2nd ed. of 'The Indus Civilization', rev. and enl. ed. by D. MACKAY). Luzac, London. 1948.

A NOTE ON STONEHENGE

R. H. G. THOMSON

THE very name of Stonehenge conjures up those remote vistas with which this volume is concerned, and the study of its construction raises again some of the technological problems that have been discussed. It may therefore be useful to summarize the state of our knowledge of this unique megalithic monument.

Stonehenge is on the chalk plateau of Salisbury Plain, about 7 miles north of Salisbury. It is essentially a series of circular works arranged almost concentrically, and is approached from the north-east by a banked trackway known as the Avenue. Stonehenge is orientated towards sunrise at the summer solstice, but the adjustment is no more exact and its achievement is no greater than might be expected from peoples sufficiently organized to construct works of this magnitude. It now appears that there are only two main constructional periods (figure 320), of which Stonehenge II comprises the famous stone monument.

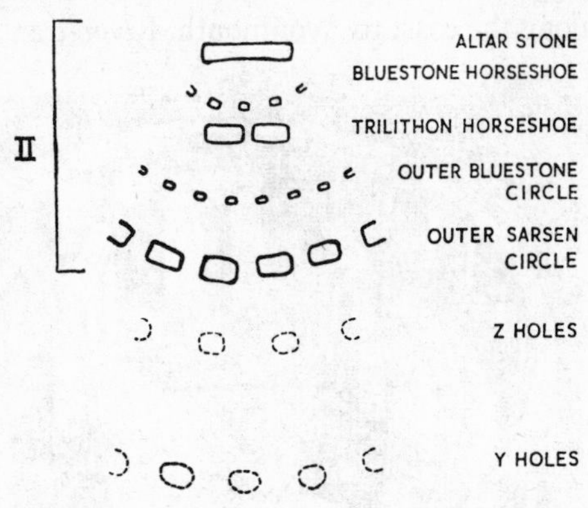

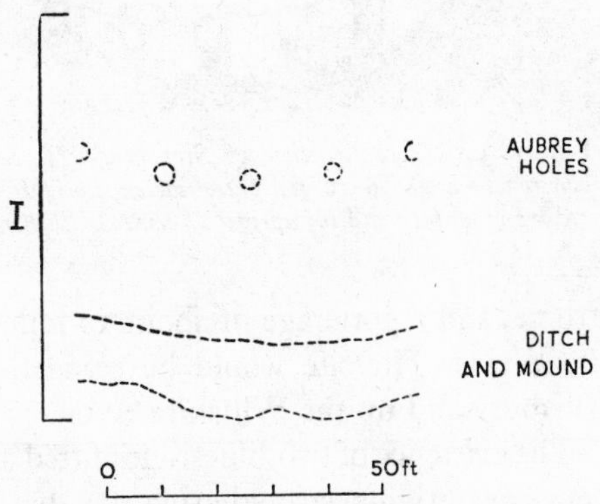

FIGURE 320—*Layout of Stonehenge, showing constructional periods I and II.*

Stonehenge I consists of a circular ditch and bank of irregular construction, surrounding a circle of holes, 56 in number, known as the Aubrey holes, and a cremation-cemetery lying mainly in the eastern quadrant. The primary function of the holes is uncertain, though many of them contain cremations. The evidence suggests that they did not contain stone or timber uprights. There are settings of similar 'ritual' pits at Dorchester, and at Cairnpapple, West Lothian.

The carbonized fragments from an Aubrey hole have been dated by the radiocarbon method as of between 2200 B.C. and 1600 B.C. This is consistent with the evidence from finds such as sherds, flint fabricators, and bone pins, which places Stonehenge I in the Late Neolithic period.

Two kinds of stone were used in the building of Stonehenge II: sarsen, a hard sandstone from the neighbourhood of Avebury in north Wiltshire (the Marlborough Downs) 18 miles away, and a class known as bluestones which can only have come from the Preselly mountains in Pembrokeshire, 150 miles away. The outer circle and the horseshoe of large trilithons are of sarsen, while the smaller upright stones are bluestones. Originally, Stonehenge II must have consisted of a continuous ring of sarsen uprights supporting lintels, enclosing the arrangement of free-standing bluestones and sarsen trilithons shown in figure 321.

Because the final dressing of stones was carried out on the site, chips of sarsen and bluestone were scattered over the whole area. The level of these chips in relation to the filling of the ditch and Aubrey holes allows us to deduce that Stonehenge II was built while Stonehenge I was still in ritual use.

The average weight of the outer sarsen uprights is about 26 tons, while the uprights of the central trilithons may weigh as much as 40 tons. Although these figures probably preclude water-transport, the conveyance of dressed sarsens from their quarry in the Marlborough Downs by rollers and levers is feasible. The bluestones are smaller, and Piggott has suggested a land-sea route from the Preselly hills to Milford Haven, then along the coast to Avonmouth. River-transport up the Bristol Avon and its tributary the

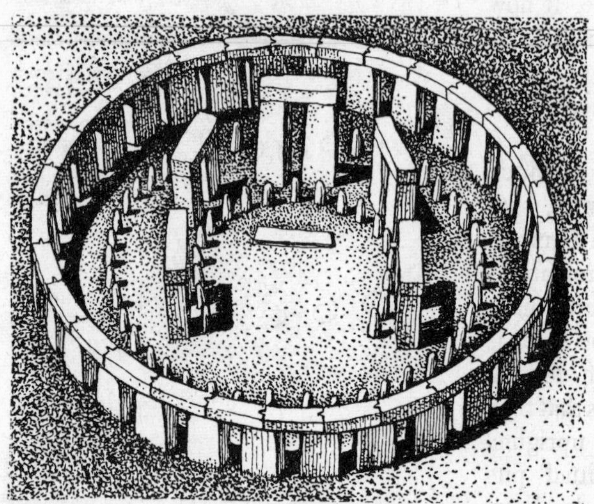

FIGURE 321—*Reconstruction of Stonehenge II. Some dimensions: bluestones—height 6–10 ft; outer sarsen uprights—average height above ground 13 ft 6 in; upright of central trilithon—height 22 ft.*

FIGURE 322—*A fallen lintel with its two mortise holes. The tenon on top of the upright can also be seen.*

Frome, and a porterage of about 10 miles, would bring the stones to the headwaters of the Wylye. The site would be reached after a final stage of river-transport through Salisbury and up the Wiltshire Avon.

The existence of two bluestones fitted as lintels with mortise holes, but used in Stonehenge as uprights, strongly suggests that the bluestones originally formed another stone circle, either in Pembrokeshire, where there are copious remains of similar monuments, or quite close to Stonehenge near an earthwork enclosure known as the Cursus. The latter site has been suggested by the recent recognition there of bluestone fragments.

Outside the outer sarsen circle are two rather irregular circles of pits known as the Y and Z holes, usually regarded as of Early Iron Age date. Recent (1953) excavations, however, have shown that these holes were dug at an early date and allowed to silt naturally; by inference they may date to the general period of Stonehenge II, though subsequent to the setting-up of the sarsens, and it is suggested that they were intended to hold the bluestones in a scheme never carried out.

All the sarsens have been carefully dressed, the lintels for instance being cut on the curve, while there is some attempt at entasis in the uprights, that is, a convexity introduced to correct the illusion of concavity. The technique adopted for dressing was almost unique in Britain, though paralleled in Ireland and the Near East. Grooves were worked across the stone using heavy stone hammers, the intervening ridges being later flattened by further hammer-work (plate 21 A). Each of the lintels has a mortise hole under

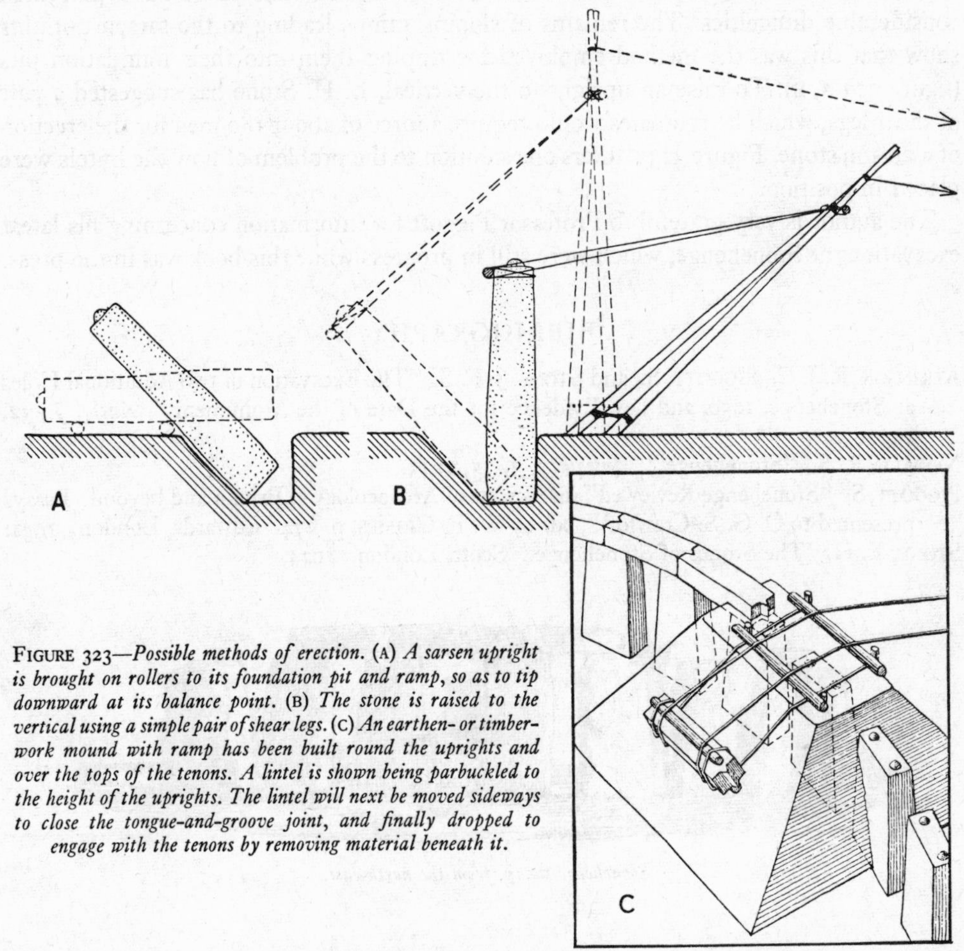

FIGURE 323—*Possible methods of erection.* (A) *A sarsen upright is brought on rollers to its foundation pit and ramp, so as to tip downward at its balance point.* (B) *The stone is raised to the vertical using a simple pair of shear legs.* (C) *An earthen- or timber-work mound with ramp has been built round the uprights and over the tops of the tenons. A lintel is shown being parbuckled to the height of the uprights. The lintel will next be moved sideways to close the tongue-and-groove joint, and finally dropped to engage with the tenons by removing material beneath it.*

either end which fits a corresponding tenon at the head of the upright on which it rests (figure 322). Each upright of the outer circle has, therefore, two tenons. The lintels are further secured by their ends being tongue-and-groove jointed to each other. Such a design was early recognized as having originated in wooden architecture, and accounts for the general opinion that Stonehenge is a copy in stone of a wooden structure such as that excavated at Woodhenge a short distance away.

One of the uprights of the sarsen trilithons bears carvings of a bronze dagger and axe-heads; another stone has further carvings of similar axes. The objects have been depicted by a pecking technique over their whole surface to a depth of up to half an inch.

The axe-heads are of British Middle Bronze Age types, but the dagger finds its closest parallels in Mycenaean Greece, *c* 1500 B.C. This agrees with other archaeological evidence of trade contacts between Britain and the Aegean at that time.

The erection of a monument on this unprecedented scale must have presented considerable difficulties. The remains of sloping ramps leading to the sarsen uprights show that this was the method employed for tipping them into their foundation pits (figure 323 A, B). To raise an upright to the vertical, E. H. Stone has suggested a pair of shear legs, which he estimates would require a force of about 180 men for the erection of a 26-ton stone. Figure 323 C offers one solution to the problem of how the lintels were placed in position.

The author is very grateful to Professor Piggott for information concerning his latest excavations at Stonehenge, which were still in progress while this book was in the press.

BIBLIOGRAPHY

ATKINSON, R. J. C., PIGGOTT, S., and STONE, J. F. S. "The Excavation of two Additional Holes at Stonehenge, 1950, and new Evidence for the Date of the Monument." *Antiq. J.*, **32**, 14, 1952.

NEWALL, R. S. "Stonehenge." *Antiquity*, **3**, 75, 1943.

PIGGOTT, S. "Stonehenge Reviewed" in 'Aspects of Archaeology in Britain and beyond. Essays presented to O. G. S. Crawford', ed. by W. F. GRIMES, p. 274. Edwards, London. 1951.

STONE, E. H. 'The Stones of Stonehenge.' Scott, London. 1924.

Stonehenge today, from the north-east.

18

DIFFERENTIATION OF NON-METALLIC TOOLS

S. M. COLE

I. MESOLITHIC TECHNIQUES

SOME tools and implements will be discussed here that have not been mentioned, or have been only lightly treated, in previous chapters. For this purpose it is necessary to dip back into the Late Palaeolithic, and forward into the ages of Bronze and even Iron. This volume as a whole is centred on the Near East, where food-production first began, where men first settled as farmers, where they first learned how to mine, extract, and use metals, and where the first civilizations arose. In this chapter, however, more attention is paid to Europe, where special cultures developed beyond the periphery of the ancient civilizations.

With the onset of the milder climate of post-glacial times in Europe, about 8000 B.C., dense forests, coniferous in the north, mixed farther south, spread over areas formerly occupied by Arctic and sub-Arctic tundra and steppe. The mammoth, the hairy rhinoceros, and their like, which had been hunted by Upper Palaeolithic men, now became extinct, while other forms, such as the reindeer and wild horse, sought open land farther north, and were superseded first by scrub-living and then by true forest types. This situation had arisen by about 7000 B.C.

The food-gatherers who adapted themselves to the new conditions developed cultures known collectively as Mesolithic. Compared with their Upper Palaeolithic forerunners, they were very poorly equipped. They seldom invented new weapons or made technological improvements, though they did develop axes and adzes, tools which were to be of the utmost importance for the Neolithic farming peoples who spread through Europe from about 4000 B.C. Meanwhile, the area that could be occupied by peoples of Mesolithic cultures had been narrowed by the rise of sea-level which flooded the land-bridge between Sweden and Denmark, joined the Baltic lake to the North Sea and, about 6000 B.C., separated England from France. Increasing humidity and growth of forests further reduced the scope of hunting. Some of the survivors lived on or near the shore, subsisting largely on a diet of shell-fish, and their expiring culture left huge mounds of refuse or kitchen-middens, known by the site-name of Ertebølle in Denmark. In these mounds are found many tools, together with sherds of coarse pottery foreshadowing the ensuing Neolithic age.

It is worth considering certain Mesolithic traditions, first in relation to microliths, secondly for their characteristic *tranchet* technique, and thirdly for the working of bone, antler, and wood, by which they are continuous with both preceding and subsequent cultures.

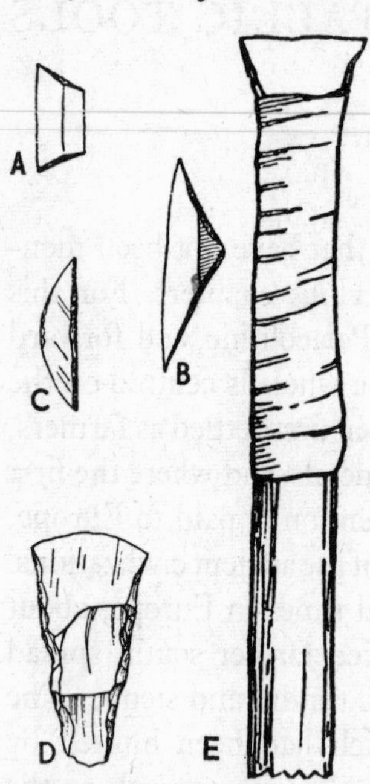

FIGURE 324—(A)–(C) *Three types of microlith: trapeze, triangle, and lunate respectively.* (D) *A transverse or chisel-end·d arrow-head* (petit tranchet) *from Ertebølle, Denmark.* (E) *A transverse arrow-head hafted, from Jutland, Denmark.*

A microlith is a 'narrow flake, blunted on one or both edges by steep secondary chipping, but devoid of any secondary work on either face' [1]. Microliths are generally diminutive, and later specimens usually conform to geometric shapes (figures 63, 324 A–C). The trapeze is especially characteristic of the later Mesolithic. Microliths were mounted with pitch in shafts of wood or bone, to form composite tools such as arrow-heads (figure 325 A); the bow-and-arrow had become the favourite weapon in Mesolithic times.

All over Europe, as the Mesolithic advanced, there was a significant change from pointed to chisel-ended arrow-heads (figure 324 D, E). These are typical of the Danish kitchen-middens, and persist into the Western Neolithic. Similar arrows are well known from predynastic sites in Egypt, where they were commonly used for shooting birds (figure 98). The wider surface presented by this type of arrow-head would produce more shock and less bleeding than a pointed form. Chisel-ended arrows are also depicted in the scene of a lion-hunt on a basalt stele from Erech in Sumer.

The Mesolithic Natufians of Palestine (*c* 5500 B.C.), and the Helwanians of Egypt of about the same time, used microliths of crescentic, triangular, and trapeziform shape. Microliths have a wide distribution in Africa, and may have spread thence to Europe during the Upper Palaeolithic. Capsian invaders from north Africa may have introduced microliths into Spain, while a southward movement of this tradition from East Africa is probably responsible for the microlithic element in South Africa. From Kurdistan, microlithic industries spread northwards to Russia and the Caucasus, while they reached Australia from southern India or Ceylon.

The *tranchet* technique is typical of the Mesolithic, and was used in the making of core- and flake-axes, picks, and chisel-ended arrow-heads. In this technique, the cutting edge of the tool was produced by the intersection of two or more flake surfaces.[1] This is well seen in the *grand tranchet* flake-axes of the Danish kitchen-middens and the Campignian culture, transitional between the Mesolithic and Neolithic. The advantage of this type of edge is that it is easily resharpened by taking off another transverse flake (figure 325 D).

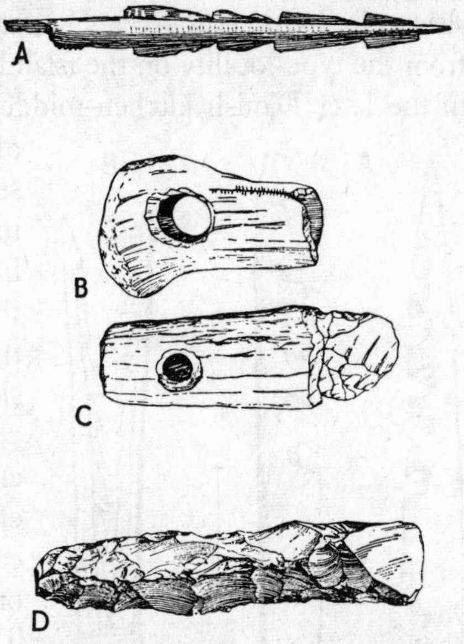

FIGURE 325—(A) *Bone arrow-point, with flints inserted in the sides, from Skåne, Sweden.* (B), (C) *Perforated antler sleeves of the Maglemosian culture,* (C) *with an adze blade inserted.* (D) *A 'Thames pick' from Farnham, Surrey; the cutting edge was obtained by removing a transverse flake by the* tranchet *technique. Scale 1/4.*

Another important technique invented in Mesolithic times was the grinding and pecking of the edges of stone celts. This technique was much developed in Neolithic times and is discussed below (p 506).

The working of bone, antler, and horn into tools is known from Palaeolithic times among the Aurignacians, and was extensively used among the Magdalenian reindeer-hunters. Antler was generally preferred to bone as a material for tools, since it is easier to work. Parallel grooves were cut through the hard outer wall by flint gravers (figure 64). By working a pronged flint in these grooves, the spongy interior was cut away, so that the intervening splinter could be prised off. From splinters thus obtained, European Mesolithic peoples shaped the heads of their harpoons and arrows. In the earliest antler axes and adzes the handles consisted of the stems of the antlers, and the blades were the brow-tines, cut according to the type of instrument needed (figure 326).

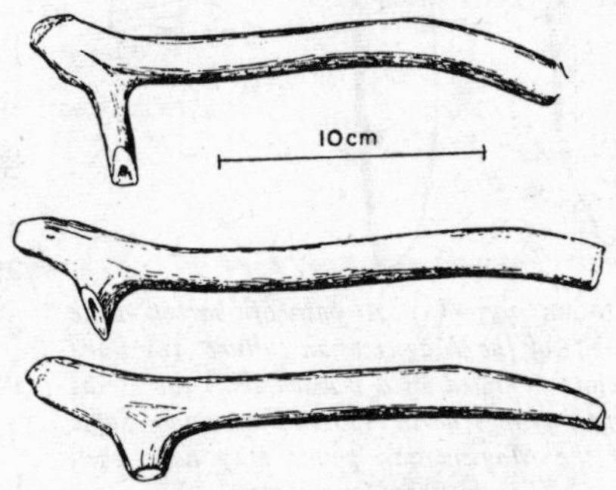

FIGURE 326—*Antler axe, adze, and haft of the 'Lyngby' Mesolithic culture.* c *8000 B.C.*

Perforated antler adzes were common during the middle northern Mesolithic, but axes were rare, while during the later Mesolithic the reverse was true. Antler

[1] In the case of core-tools the edge was obtained by a special blow struck at one corner of the extremity.

sleeves for hafting (figure 325 B, C) are often found in Maglemosian sites (named from the type-locality on the island of Zealand), though such sleeves are absent in the later Danish kitchen-middens. In an antler sleeve from Denmark, part of the wooden handle was sufficiently preserved to show the simple method of preventing it from working loose. One end of the handle was left considerably thicker than the perforation in the sleeve, the slim part of the handle was pushed through it, and the sleeve was wedged tightly.

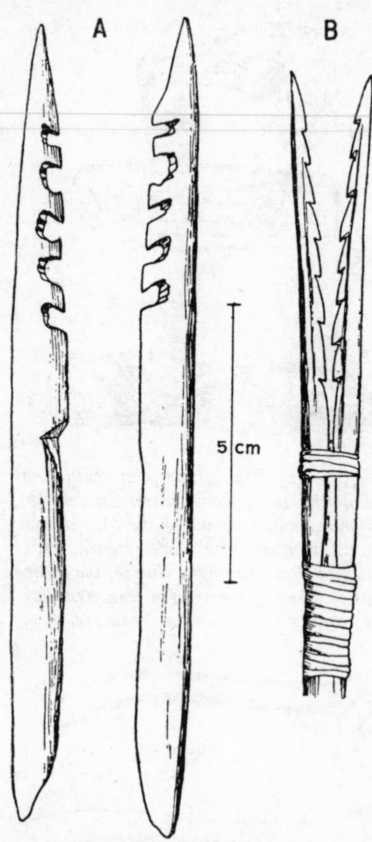

FIGURE 327—(A) *A pair of barbed bone points of the Maglemosian culture.* (B) *Bone points mounted on a wooden shaft for use as leister prongs, north Hudson Bay region. Some of the Maglemosian points may have been mounted in this way.*

Antler adzes and axes, though not strong enough for chopping wood, could be used effectively for cutting off the meat from carcases, and as mattocks for grubbing up roots or making holes in the ground for setting traps. Throughout the Neolithic and even the Bronze Age in some parts of Europe, axe- and adze-heads of antler continued to be made, with little or no change from the Mesolithic form.

The highly specialized equipment of bone evolved by the Maglemosians included slotted points armed with flints, fish-hooks, netting-needles, and bodkins. These people evolved a great variety of bone points, some used singly as harpoons, others in groups of two or three as pronged fish-spears or leisters (figure 327), and others in bunches as bird-catchers. The Maglemosian culture extended to the British Isles over the North Sea area, then dry land. A Maglemosian harpoon was actually dredged by a trawler off the Norfolk coast.

The fish-hook is well known in predynastic Egyptian cultures. In Europe it began to supplement the fish-spear and gorge in Mesolithic times. The earliest hooks were without barbs; those of the European Mesolithic peoples were sometimes secured to the line by a swelling at the top of the shank, by a perforation, or by an indentation in the shank (figure 100 A). The drill was employed to separate the point of the hook from the shank; by the end of the Mesolithic and during the Early Neolithic, V-shaped hooks were made by sawing or cutting. Another tool adopted by Late Mesolithic people (Maglemosians), and carried on from them, was a leather-polisher made from the metapodial bones of ungulates. The amount of preparation needed for skins, and the long period over which they were used for clothing (cf figure 22), explain the ubiquity of flint scrapers and their persistence with little change from the Upper Palaeolithic to the Early Iron Age, but bone tools for this purpose are by no means rare.

The hunting and fishing equipment of the Maglemosians was relatively so efficient that it persisted on the forested plains of northern Europe and Siberia, with few modifications, long after food-production had been established in central Europe. But with the marine transgression which ushered in the Atlantic climatic phase, from about 6000 B.C., certain communities settled along the coasts of southern Sweden and Denmark, practising sea-fishing and sealing, and collecting shell-fish. These kitchen-midden (Ertebølle) people were sufficiently sedentary to make rough pottery and to grind stone celts, both arts perhaps learned from the advancing Neolithic farmers. While antler axes were still made, flint was now increasingly used for making large tools. Where bone as a tool-making material is found to the exclusion of flint, the same tradition was sometimes supplemented by the use of slate.

Flint knives and scrapers, together with awls and adzes, were capable of producing a variety of wooden equipment needed for hunting and domestic life. This equipment included handles for axes and adzes, arrow-shafts, and—a most important weapon in Mesolithic times—the bow. The bow is already represented in the cave-art of eastern Spain, some of which is probably of Upper Palaeolithic date, though some is almost certainly later. Two elm-wood bows with very well shaped hand-grips were found at the Maglemosian site of Holmegaard in Zealand (figures 89, 90).

Probably to avoid damage to the skin, the Maglemosians used blunt-ended wooden arrow-heads or conical bone points for shooting birds and small game. At Holmegaard rods were found, their ends pointed and hardened by fire, which probably served as pikes. There were also club-like weapons which may have been used as throwing-sticks. A willow paddle-rudder was recovered from the same site; it and a specimen from Star Carr (Yorkshire) are probably the oldest in the world.

II. NEOLITHIC TRADITIONS

The change from a hunting economy to one of food-production was more gradual in Europe than in the Near East:[1]

[1] Hunting and fishing continued to supplement the primitive farmers' diet, and provided such raw materials as skins, bone, and antler. Nor did farming enforce an immediate modification of stone-working methods.

'Practically every form and every technique [of stone-working] available to neolithic man had already been anticipated or even perfected by craftsmen at a food-gathering stage of subsistence . . . the polishing of the flint blades . . . itself represents no more than the transference of a technique applied since upper palaeolithic times to bone and antler and already extended by mesolithic hunter-fishers to the shaping of stone blades. The technique of shaping stone by pecking was applied by mesolithic, as well as by neolithic man, to the production of axes from coarse-grained rocks. The cutting of fine-grained rock by means of saws, either of sandstone or of wood or bone used with an abrasive, to form flat axes and chisels, marks another extension of a technique applied much earlier to antler and bone. . . . Some advance can be noted in the direct perforation of stone axes by means of a tubular drill, since mesolithic man perforated sandstone and quartzite by the clumsy method of sinking hollows from opposed faces resulting in holes of hour-glass form; on the other hand the method of direct perforation was commonly applied to bone and antler axes and adzes in mesolithic times. Two of the most characteristic elements in the equipment of European farmers up to well into the Bronze Age, the flint bladed reaping knife and the sickle, incorporate the mesolithic innovation of insetting flint blades into slots to form a sharp edge . . . the neolithic farmers of Europe made no fundamental advances in the technology of flint and stone, though . . . they extended the application of certain techniques . . . to new materials, and to new uses' [2].

While food production to a certain extent freed man-power for specialist activities leading to technical improvements, the most important discoveries of Neolithic man were pottery and weaving. Improvements in the sphere of stone-working consisted mainly of the increased use made of polishing and grinding, and the perfection of pressure-flaking which had already been finely executed by the Solutreans of the Upper Palaeolithic. Often, however, these achievements were aesthetically satisfying rather than of real practical use.

There is necessarily a close relationship between the properties of raw materials available and the suitability of techniques for working them, but the choice of raw materials was often determined by cultural traditions, and the effective distribution of such materials became increasingly modified by trade. Many Neolithic communities must have obtained supplies of bone and antler by barter with neighbouring Mesolithic tribes. The earliest farmers in Egypt and Mesopotamia lacked timber, which had to be imported from long distances. The Neolithic community at Skara Brae overcame the timber shortage by substituting stone or bone for wood, and it is for this reason that their dwellings and furniture, things generally not preserved if of wood, are known to us today.

While Neolithic communities were essentially self-sufficient, the high quality of certain flints was recognized, and regions where good supplies were obtainable became important centres of trade. One of the most important was Grand

Pressigny in France, but in this case the yellow colour of the flint (suggesting copper) rather than its quality probably accounts for its popularity. The trade in this flint, while lasting a long time, was particularly extensive during the Beaker period. Flint-mining was carried out also in England, Belgium, Sweden, Poland, Portugal, Sicily, and Egypt (ch 20).

The same tools appear over and over again in Neolithic sites—polished stone celts, scrapers for leather-dressing, arrow-heads, and sickles. Implements which required no special skill to make, and for which local materials were adequate, such as scrapers, awls, and blades, were made by all households, to judge by the widespread debris of flint-knapping. The fine polished stone celts and beautifully flaked stone knives and daggers were probably the work of specialists, traded for farm produce and skins.

Criteria of the Neolithic

The essential criteria of Neolithic cultures have always been held to be the domestication of stock (ch 13), the cultivation of cereals (ch 14), the making of pottery (ch 15), and the manufacture of polished stone celts. Some of these achievements had been foreshadowed already in Mesolithic times. The forest-dwellers of northern Europe had domesticated the dog, ground the edges of their axes, and made pottery, though they practised no agriculture. Pottery, or at any rate the baked-clay lining of baskets, is already known in the Upper Palaeolithic Kenya Capsian culture, but there is evidence that at Jericho it was preceded by stone town walls. It is uncertain whether the Mesolithic Natufians of Palestine sowed seed to supplement the wild grasses which they gleaned with their sickles.

It sometimes happens that not all four criteria are present within a Neolithic community. At Anau in Turkestan, for example, though pottery is plentiful there were no stone axes. Of the five Neolithic cultures known in Kenya, only one had polished axes. At Mesolithic Khartoum, possibly before 4000 B.C., and at Neolithic Shaheinab, also in the Sudan, there are pottery, polished celts, and signs of the domestication of animals, but there is no evidence of agriculture. It seems doubtful whether a culture should be termed Neolithic on the basis of pottery and polished celts alone: definite evidence of agriculture and the domestication of sheep and cattle are more reliable criteria of a true Neolithic economy.

In Egypt, mixed farming started about 5000 B.C. The primitive farmers continued to hunt and to fish; bows and arrows were their favourite weapons, while throwing-sticks and sling-stones indicate fowling. Fish were caught in the Nile by hook and line, and on the Fayum lake by spearing. Many of the agricultural implements used were of earlier origin: the digging-stick, weighted with pierced stones, served to break up the soil, and stone pestles and mortars, now used for grinding grain, had already been employed by Upper Palaeolithic artists for pulverizing their pigments.

At Jarmo in Kurdistan agriculture of comparable antiquity is attested by saddle-querns, sickle-teeth, and weighted digging-sticks. Axe- and adze-blades were sharpened by grinding, but no weapons have been recovered except microlithic blades which might have armed arrows. Perhaps slightly later than at Jarmo were the farmers of Hassuna in Iraq. Heavy flaked implements of quartzite may have been used as hoe-blades, mounted with the aid of bitumen (figure 328). Curved sickles had overlapping teeth, also held by bitumen. Clay pellets served as ammunition for slings, and points of imported obsidian may have armed reed-darts. Similar finds were made at the Neolithic site at Matarrah, not far away.

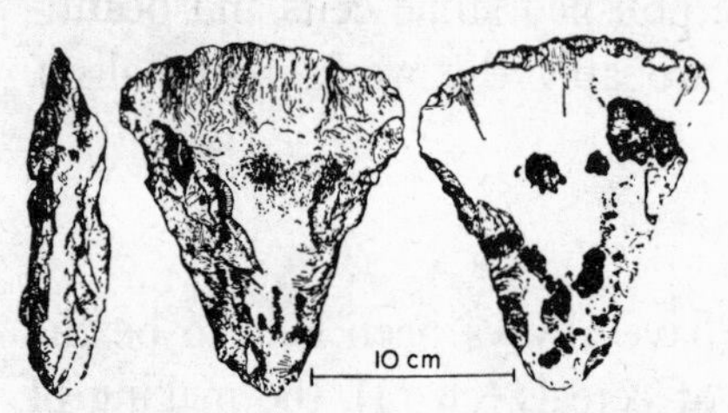

FIGURE 328—*Flaked stone 'hoe-blade' from Hassuna, Mesopotamia. Fifth millennium B.C.*

In the Levant, particularly at Mersin, the long sequence of layers points to a very protracted Neolithic occupation, which may rival in antiquity anything known in the Nile valley or in Mesopotamia. It is possible that the first food-producing settlement at Jericho may be earlier still, for here there was no evidence of pottery.

At an industrial level comparable to that of the Badarians in Egypt (*c* 4000 B.C.), there were farmers at Anau in Turkestan and at Sialk in Iran. The equipment from the earliest levels in both sites is very similar, and is essentially the same as in Egypt. Evidence of hoes and digging-sticks weighted with perforated stones are found, together with sickles resembling those of the Natufians. The handles of sickles from Sialk were carved with animals' heads, as in Palestine (figure 329 A). Hunting equipment is less important, but includes stone mace-heads and clubs. Stone celts are polished and perforated, though there were no axes at Anau.

Hoe cultivation was introduced into Europe, possibly from Egypt, and spread along the Danube valley on fertile loess lands. Agricultural implements from Danubian villages include hoes, sickles, and querns, but hunting equipment is very rare. Axes and adzes follow the same traditional pattern throughout the whole area. While the Danubians relied largely on adzes, the westerners of Switzerland, France, Belgium, and Britain preferred axes. The individual tools of the westerners show some difference from those of the Danubians, but their equipment in general was much the same, and again hunting seems to have been unimportant.

III. BRONZE AGE DEVELOPMENTS

Since many of the tools used in Neolithic times continued with little change into the metal ages, it is more convenient to consider the actual implements of the two periods together, after a brief account of the impact of metallurgy. It is

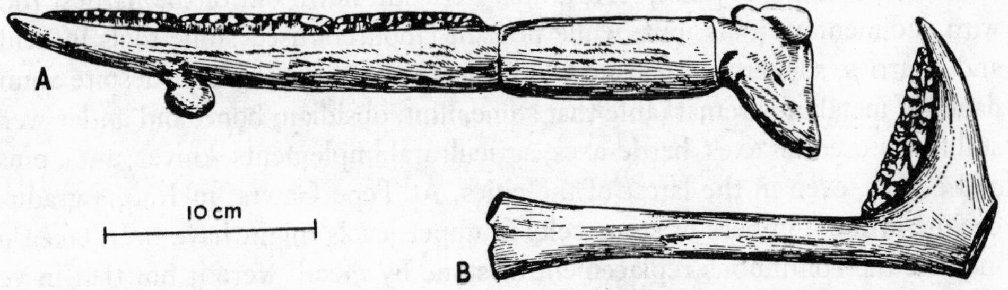

FIGURE 329—(A) *Natufian bone sickle with animal's head handle and flint teeth (restored). Mount Carmel, Palestine.* c *6000* B.C. (B) *Crescentic flint sickle-blade with haft reconstructed. Chalcolithic. Denmark.* c 2000 B.C.

difficult to give a short and satisfactory definition of a Bronze Age. A chalcolithic period may arise merely through the influx of metal objects by trade; a true Bronze Age, on the other hand, implies some real knowledge of metallurgy by the inhabitants of the region concerned. The necessary prerequisites for the spread of metallurgy were a more stable food-supply, the possibility of larger social groups, and greater subdivision of labour. The special geographical environment of an alluvial plain, where suitable stone was rare, was required to drive home the value of the new material, and to create a general demand for it.

The advantages of metal should not, however, be exaggerated. For hoeing the soil, cutting up carcases, reaping grain, or trimming leather, stone tools serve very well. Small trees can be felled, posts shaped, and canoes hewn out with stone axes and adzes, if the edges are finely ground, almost as neatly and quickly as with bronze. When worn out, or broken, new tools can be made fairly rapidly where flint is available. For weapons of war, however, metal has the obvious advantage that it is less likely to break at a critical moment.

Metallurgy must have been practised widely in the Near and Middle East soon after 4000 B.C., but metal ousted stone there very slowly—and still more slowly elsewhere. Even in Assyria, polished stone celts were not largely superseded by bronze implements until about 3000 B.C., in Egypt not till 2000 B.C., and in the Aegean not till 1500 B.C., while in barbaric Europe they continued to be used after the end of the Bronze Age. Syria and Assyria were populous long before 3000 B.C.: they preserved their independence because they were content with stone tools and weapons and did not have to rely on imports. Stone weapons, however, were in the end found to be no match for the bronze armament of the Babylonians, and the Syrians and Assyrians were forced to adopt metal for arms.

In Egypt during Dynasty III, tombs were still hewn out of the hardest rock with rudimentary tools, but, while peasant labourers used stone tools in fields and quarries, soldiers were armed with metal weapons. At Troy, despite abundance of metal, it is remarkable that stone, flint, obsidian, bone, and antler were still freely used for axes, battle-axes, agricultural implements, knives, awls, pins, and combs, even in the latest of the cities. At Tepe Gawra, in Iraq, a gradual decline in the numbers of stone celts in upper levels might have been taken to indicate the continuous replacement of stone by metal, were it not that in yet later levels the number of stone implements rises again.

It is not surprising that early metal tools should have been copied from stone, as with the earliest flat celts of copper, hafted like those of stone (figure 389). On the other hand, the makers of some of the finest flint work were at much pains to copy bronze tools as closely as possible, as in daggers and knives from Denmark and Egypt. Stone rather than metal was often used for ceremonial purposes; this was, in many cases at least, a matter not of economy but of ritual conservatism. Certain African tribes in the present century have refused to use metal ploughs or mattocks, since they believed that iron would be harmful to the crops. Indeed, the use of iron and of other metals is subject to a multitude of taboos and superstitions.

Metal tools meant much progress in the working of stone, inevitably a laborious process when only stone tools with abrasives were used. Metal gouges, awls, chisels, and so forth brought mastery in the shaping of stone vessels, finer relief sculpture and carvings in the round, and the shaping, drilling, and engraving of cylinder-seals. For dressing large blocks of stone, the Egyptians ran saw-cuts to a depth of about half an inch on all sides; the surface was then hammer-dressed, nearly down to the plane of the cuts. For dressing the faces of stones, the Egyptians from the time of the pyramids onwards used metal adzes.

A more advanced metallurgy spread in the Mediterranean zone of Europe than into the country farther north. Bronze implements were traded to central and northern Europe among communities at a Neolithic stage of culture. During much of the European Bronze Age, flint and stone tools continued to play an important part, though metal was used increasingly for ornaments and weapons. The prestige and high cost of metal objects, by stimulating the production of analogous forms in cheaper materials, led to local advances in flint-flaking, as with the flint daggers of the Grand Pressigny factories, of the Stone Cist period in Denmark, of the 'A' Beaker culture in Britain, and of the Remedello culture in Italy. As native metallurgy established itself, however, flint axes probably declined in standing, though they continued to be made.

Owing to the labour involved in mining metal, the transport difficulties in obtaining exotic natural supplies, and the complicated processes to be mastered in smelting ores, metal tools were presumably at first confined to specialist craftsmen. When metal became available for tools in substantial quantities, towards the end of the Bronze Age and particularly during the Early Iron Age, flint-working at last began to decline, and survived only at a domestic level.

IV. IMPLEMENTS OF THE NEOLITHIC AND BRONZE AGES

Although it would seem convenient to place tools and weapons in categories such as agricultural implements, hunting weapons, war weapons, domestic tools, and so on, in practice such a classification leads to ambiguities. In some cases, this may be due to our ignorance of the true purpose of the tools concerned, but there was much overlapping in usage, so that classification becomes difficult. Weapons for hunting and for war are particularly hard to distinguish. The ground axe, though primarily for clearing forests, was put to numerous other uses, and the adze could be used for tilling the soil, to hew out canoes, or to construct wheels.

Polished stone celts must have had great significance for Neolithic man. They are found in numbers in almost all Neolithic sites, and their makers took great pains to secure the most suitable material for them, whether by trading stone of particular toughness and tractability, or by mining the most perfect flint available. Moreover, the celts themselves were often made with great care and skill, and their manufacture must have consumed much time and labour. The Early Neolithic farmers had to embark on large-scale forest clearance in Europe in order to practise agriculture, and this would have been impossible without tools with ground edges. Pollen analysis confirms that heath and grass-lands began to replace forest after Neolithic man had started on his immense task.

An axe has the edge parallel to the handle, an adze across it; other differences between the tools arise out of their different uses. The axe is mounted into a handle, or *vice versa*, while the adze is in general bound on to a handle. The axe is equal-faced and symmetrically edged; the adze has one face longer or flatter, and is usually ground on one side. The axe is used to drive into wood and to split it; the adze to take a thin slip off a larger mass. The axe usually had a short blade and a means of pulling it back, or twisting it loose, from the grip of the cloven wood; the adze had a long blade and only a weak attachment to the handle, as it was never driven in deeply. The axe was thick to carry weight and bear shock; the adze was thinner as its momentum was less important. These differences were not all fully developed at first.

The typical polished stone celt was first shaped by percussion-flaking, and the cutting-edge or the whole surface was then pecked or ground down by rubbing on a slab of wetted sandstone or other rock, using an abrasive. Polishing-stones, with hollows to fit the shapes of the celts, have been found at many Neolithic sites in France and elsewhere. The finer-grained rocks, like basalt or epidiorite, lend themselves to grinding and polishing more readily than flint, and it seems probable that the technique was first adopted in regions where such materials were used.

The head of the axe was commonly hafted into the end of a wooden or antler handle. Occasionally in Mesolithic times, and commonly during the Neolithic and Bronze Ages, certain types of stone axe-heads, hammers, and mace-heads were perforated to take the shaft. The earliest shaft-holes are hour-glass shaped, made by pecking or drilling from alternate sides (figure 401 A). The cylindrical shaft-holes of the Late Neolithic and the Bronze Ages were evidently made with a rotary, and in some cases a tubular, drill, presumably operated with a bow. The attachment of the head of the weapon to the handle was often assisted by insertion into a short sleeve of antler.

After the earliest known axe-heads with ground edges made by the Ertebølle people in Scandinavia from about 6000 B.C., ground celts are again found in the first Neolithic levels of Egypt and the Near and Middle East of about 5000 B.C., or possibly somewhat earlier. As the types are essentially the same in all sites, only the more unusual ones will be described here.

In Egypt, the making of polished stone celts was abandoned in predynastic times, for with increasing aridity there were few trees to cut. Metal tools for carpentry were adopted about 3000 B.C. As the Fayum lake shrank, the culture degenerated; axes ceased to be polished, and when worn were resharpened by flaking. Associated with the Neolithic 'gouge culture' of Shaheinab, in the Sudan, were bone celts with polished edges, perhaps for hacking hippopotamus and elephant flesh, but, for wood-working, axe-heads and gouges of rhyolite (the lava form of granite) were made, with edges sharpened by grinding. Very fine polished axes of haematite have been found in the northern parts of the Belgian Congo.

The earliest cultivators at Hassuna used adzes of flaked stone, and also ground stone celts as hoe-blades. At Sialk, an important Neolithic site in the western highlands of Iran, polished flint hoes were used—evidently without handles, as the lustre caused by handling can still be seen on them.

In Europe, the first Danubian period is characterized by shoe-last celts, flat on one side and arched on the other. Hoards of such celts found on the northern borders of the Danubian province were probably the stocks of specialized travelling merchants. Shoe-last celts, when mounted on knee-shafts, served as hoe-blades and, if perforated, as axes, while larger ones were probably ploughshares. Perforated celts were not normally used south of the Danube, but adzes might be mounted in antler sleeves, and antlers themselves were sometimes perforated for use as axes or picks.

During the second Danubian period, greenstone axes, hollow-bored axe-hammers, and antler axes were made, as well as the shoe-last celts. During the third period, shoe-last celts were imitated by the bronze flat-axes of Hungary, though, in the north of the province, trade was not sufficiently developed for this to happen. In the loess belt east of the Carpathians, adzes were commoner than axes, as in the Danubian province.

The Neolithic Age in northern Europe is divided into four periods, based on the most characteristic tools:

I. Pointed-butt axes.
II. Thin-butt axes.
III. Thick-butt axes.
IV. Daggers.

In its essentials, this classification still holds good, despite some overlapping. The pointed-butt axe of period I is the final derivative of the Mesolithic axe, but it is not ancestral to the thin-butt axe, which is contemporary or even anterior. The thin-butt axes of period II have polished edges and a rectangular cross-section, recalling copper originals, while axes of fine-grained rock, polished all over, are sometimes splayed at the blade in imitation of metal castings. Core- and flake-axes of Mesolithic type continued to be used throughout the northern Neolithic, but they lacked the fine blade-technique characteristic of the Ertebølle tradition.

Period III is the period of 'passage graves' in Denmark, during which communities of flint-miners were producing specialized tools such as carpenters' gouges and chisels. Polished grindstones, worn away in the middle by grinding down gouges and chisels, have been found (figure 330). Although the passage-grave builders obtained some metal tools, supplies were insufficient to allow metal to compete with stone. Axes were also used as weapons during this period.

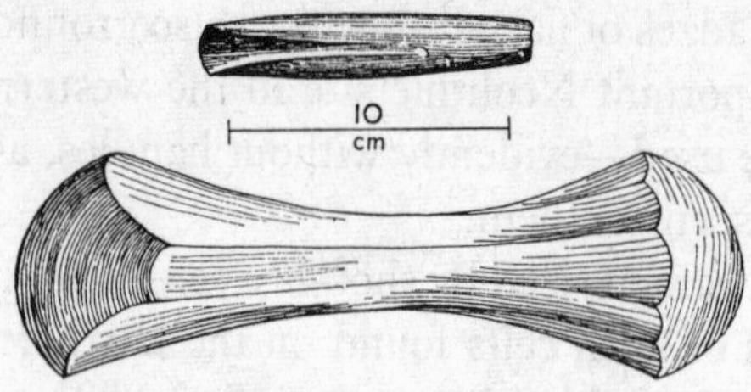

FIGURE 330—*Polished flint gouge, and well worn polishing stone. Sweden.*

Thick-butt axes similar to those of Scandinavia have been found in Wessex, dating from the Middle Bronze Age.

During period IV, the northern Stone Cist period, flint axes imitated metal models, but were seldom polished; indeed polished axes of period III were often re-flaked all over and used during period IV, as had happened in the Fayum.

The axes and adzes of the Swiss and Italian lake-villages were commonly mounted in antler sleeves (figure 331). At Remedello, they were perforated with square-cut holes for the shaft, and the stone blades had notched butts, evidently imitating copper models. At Cortaillod, axes and adzes were made from pebbles or sawn-out blocks of fine-grained rock, mounted in tapering antler sleeves fitted with straight wooden shafts. After flooding by the rising lake, many of the old sites on Lake Neuchâtel were reoccupied and, in the period which followed, local flint replaced imported metal axes, while unbored western celts were mounted as axes in perforated or heeled antler sleeves, or as adzes in socketed ones. New types of sleeve were introduced during the Late Neolithic.

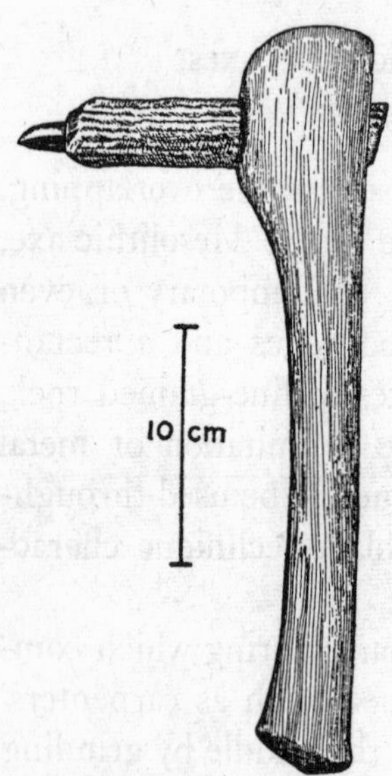

FIGURE 331—*Stone adze blade mounted in a wooden handle with an antler sleeve. Neolithic lake-dwellings, Switzerland.*

In north-west France, round the Gulf of Morbihan, large, thin, superbly polished axes, often of jadeite, were obviously used for ceremonial purposes; some have expanding blades in imitation of metal. They were exported to Portugal and England. Celts with a knob at the butt-end seem to copy Egyptian adzes, while double stone axes imitated the Minoan metal form or the ingot axes of Vogtland. The earliest copper axes of Cyprus, Italy, Spain, and Sweden imitate the pillowy, rounded outlines of stone types.

Blades, knives, and daggers. The blade is essentially characteristic of the Upper Palaeolithic, though naturally this useful tool continued throughout the Neolithic and Bronze Ages. Only one or two uncommon types need be mentioned. Upper Palaeolithic types of blade continue with little change into later stages, though occasionally new types appear. This was the case, for example, in East Africa, where obsidian blades with blunted backs, characteristic of the Upper Kenya Capsian, were replaced during a Mesolithic culture (derived directly from the earlier industry) by long, two-edged blades, often with the bulbs of percussion trimmed away to facilitate hafting. Obsidian is well suited to making knives and blades, as it will take an extremely sharp edge, though it is easily broken. It was widely used in the Mediterranean region, and there was considerable long distance trade in it. The side-blow flake of the Fayum was detached from the core by a blow at right-angles to its length, and then retouched on both sides. At Merimde (*c* 4000 B.C.), blades were retouched along both edges, but were sometimes polished on the face as well. During the Gerzean period (*c* 3250 B.C.) blades struck from true prismatic cores came into general use, without superseding bifacially trimmed flakes and cores, and pressure-flaking reached a new summit of excellence.

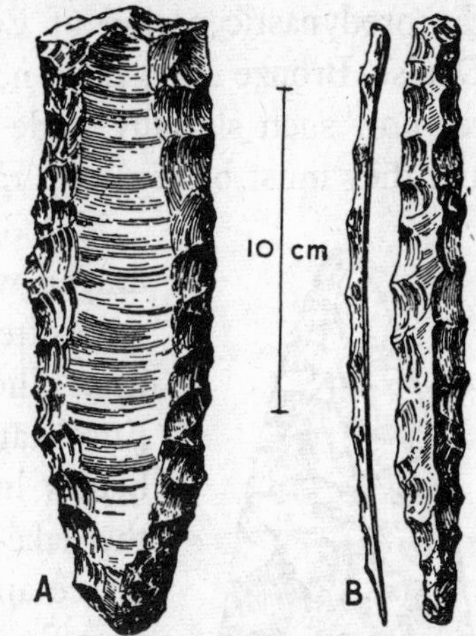

FIGURE 332—(A) *Flint core, and* (B) *blade. Grand Pressigny, France.*

Perhaps the best-known blades are those of Grand Pressigny, which continued to be exported throughout most of the Bronze Age. At this site, abandoned cores from which the blades were struck are found in thousands. The cores are longish pieces of flint with large chips flaked off from every side, one of which alone was prepared for the splitting-off of blades (figure 332).

The distinction between blades and knives is somewhat arbitrary, though a knife may be more complex, as, for example, the comma-shaped knives of Amratian times (*c* 3500 B.C.) in Egypt (figure 333 A). These were replaced during the Gerzean period (*c* 3250 B.C.) by scimitar-shaped forms, some showing beautiful serial flaking (figure 333 B). To make such knives, flakes were first ground down, and long parallel scars were then removed by pressure-flaking, possibly by the indirect percussion method using a wooden or bone punch combined with a hammer or mallet. In dynastic times, flat double-edged knives of copper were copied from flint models.

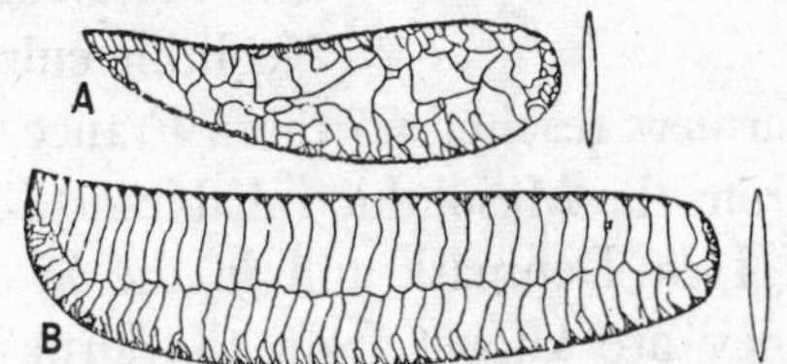

FIGURE 333—(A) *Comma-shaped flint knife of Amratian times, Egypt.* (B) *Scimitar-shaped flint knife, with serial flaking, of Gerzean times, Egypt. Fourth millennium* B.C. *Scale* c *1/4.*

Some of the finest craftsmanship in the making of stone tools is seen in the delicate pressure-flaking of daggers and lance-heads; the daggers from Mersin in Cilicia, those of the predynastic period of Egypt, and the fish-tailed and other forms of the Danish Bronze Age, have never been surpassed (figure 334). It is difficult to see how such skilfully made objects could have served any utilitarian purpose, and they must be regarded rather as artistic *tours de force*.

The distinctive weapon of the Beaker folk is the flat-tanged west European dagger of bronze, but flint copies were often made as substitutes, for funerary and ceremonial use. The hollow-based hilt, regularly attached to west European daggers, was already used for flint and copper blades in Egypt in predynastic times. Similarly, among the lake-dwellers of Switzerland and Italy, metal was scarce and the tanged, riveted, and kite-shaped unriveted west European daggers were copied locally in flint.

FIGURE 334—*Chalcolithic flint dagger, from Denmark. The shape is influenced by contemporary metal types imported from the south. Scale 1/2.*

Hunting weapons. Bows and arrows were primarily for hunting game, and sling-stones for fowling and killing small animals, but mace-heads could be used both as weapons of war and for dispatching wounded game, while other so-called mace-heads were probably weights for digging-sticks.

The Upper Palaeolithic Aterians of north Africa are generally credited with the invention of the tanged stone arrow-head (figure 21 C). From north Africa, the bow and arrow probably spread to Spain, and became the favourite weapon of Mesolithic times. During the Neolithic Age, and continuing into the Bronze Age, a great variety of arrow-heads was made. Some of the more important of these are detailed below:

(i) The transverse or chisel-ended arrow-head (figure 324 D, E), characteristic of the later Mesolithic, continued into the Neolithic in many areas. It occurs in the earliest Neolithic culture in southern France and, when Neolithic farmers reached northern France, they also adopted the transverse arrow-head from the Mesolithic inhabitants. Transverse arrow-heads survived into period III in Denmark and in the lake-dwellings of Remedello. In Mesopotamia they are known from the Uruk period, and they were extensively used in Egypt.

(ii) The leaf-shaped arrow-head (figure 335 A) is characteristic of the Windmill Hill culture, the oldest Neolithic of Britain. It is found in megalithic burial-chambers in southern France and elsewhere, at Badari in Egypt, and, finely trimmed in chert, at Susa.

(iii) The triangular arrow-head, a primitive type, is found in the latest Natufian layers (*c* 5000 B.C.), notched near the base for hafting; it continued into the Neolithic in many areas (figure 335 B).

(iv) The tanged arrow-head (figure 335 C), already known in the Late Palaeolithic Aterian of north Africa (a unique development in a cultural stage of this time), is common in the Fayum, all over the Sahara, and at Remedello.

(v) Tanged-and-barbed arrow-heads are common in the Neolithic of western Europe, and are characteristic of the Beaker cultures. Square tangs and barbs (figure 335 D) occur in the Wessex culture of the Middle Bronze Age in Britain, and beautifully made arrows with square tangs and barbs are found in the Early Bronze Age tombs of Brittany.

(vi) The most pleasing to the eye are the hollow-based arrow-heads (figure 335 E), which were especially perfected in Egypt—in the Fayum, and at Merimde and Badari. Within one village in the Fayum, Caton-Thompson distinguished four varieties of hollow-based arrow-head: a narrow, straight-sided type with a shallow notch; a type with an exaggeratedly deep notch and long, curving wings; an ogival form; and a broad, convex-sided form. Similar arrows are found in megalithic Spain, where they were often superbly worked. At Los Millares, in Almeria, 68 per cent were hollow-based, 17 per cent tanged-and-barbed, and 7 per cent leaf-shaped; there were also transverse arrow-heads. Hollow-based arrow-heads of Iberian type, as at Alcalá, are found in megalithic Ireland, and are known from the northern Stone Cist period in Scandinavia.

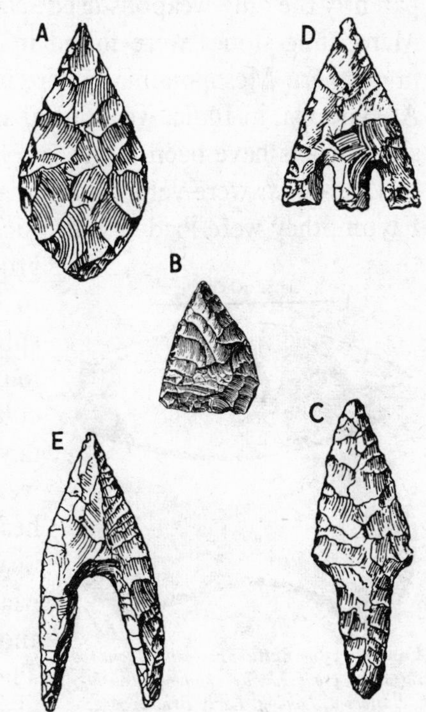

FIGURE 335—*Some of the types of arrow-heads made during the Neolithic and Bronze Ages.* (A) *Leaf-shaped, Northdale, Yorkshire.* (B) *Triangular, Suffolk.* (C) *Tanged, Fayum, Egypt.* (D) *Square tanged-and-barbed, Cambridge.* (E) *Hollow-based, Fayum. Scale 2/3.*

Arrow-heads were also sometimes made of cylindrical bone points, as in the Capsian of north Africa, the Natufian, and the Maglemosian cultures. During the Neolithic, they are found at Fayum, and at Cortaillod in period I of the Swiss lake-dwellings.

Sling-stones have been found at sites in many parts of the world. At Hassuna (*c* 4500 B.C.), clay pellets were baked as ammunition for slings, which were apparently the only weapons used; clay sling-pellets are also very common in Iran. Many sling-stones were found in Phoenicia, and at Tepe Gawra (*c* 3500 B.C.) in northern Mesopotamia, where maces and slings were the favourite weapons. At Harappa, in India, weapons of any kind were uncommon, but round or ovoid sling-pellets have been found.

Mace-heads were very common and varied in Egypt and western Asia. In the Fayum, they were loaded with thick disks of perforated stone, and with pebbles grooved to take the thong which bound them to the shaft. At Merimde, mace-heads were spheroid or pyriform, as is common in Babylonia, and the same type appears in the Gerzean culture. During the Uruk period in Mesopotamia, pyriform mace-heads were used as weapons of war. A double-edged stone mace-head from Gawra XI in Assyria is very like the boat-axes of Denmark and Sweden (below). Mace-heads were also used for commemorative and votive carvings in Egypt and Mesopotamia. The technique of hammer-dressing was employed to shape mace-heads and battle-axes with concave surfaces (figure 336).

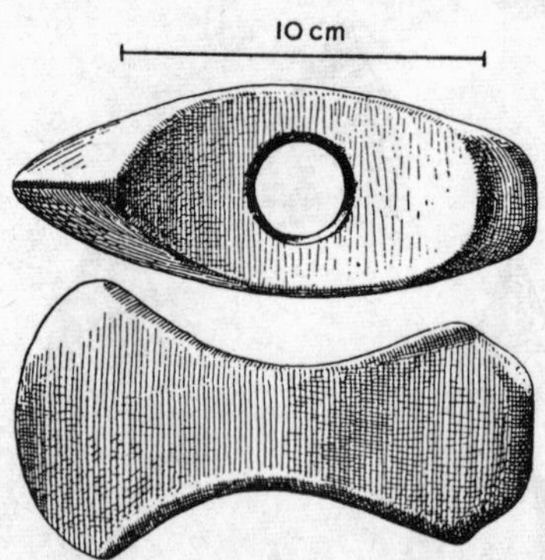

FIGURE 336—*Battle-axe with concave surfaces produced by hammer-dressing. Battersea, London. Early Bronze Age.*

Battle-axes. The early farmers with boundless land were peaceful folk fully occupied in cultivating the soil and tending their stock. In time, however, the number of war-like weapons on sites shows a marked increase. This was doubtless due to a struggle for good land arising from the wasteful methods and migratory habits of cultivators. The battle-axe became very widespread in Europe during the Bronze Age. Battle-axes, whether of antler, stone, or copper, were buried regularly with the dead throughout the large area occupied by the people of the distinctive 'battle-axe' culture.

The term battle-axe is used to denote a celt of which the butt-end is elongated and carefully shaped. The first known specimens are clay models of the Ubaid period (*c* 3500 B.C.) in Mesopotamia. In Europe, the weapons displayed wide local divergences in shape, only one form being represented in most groups. This form has a rounded body, expanded blade, and knobbed butt (figure 337).

The rounded body and knobbed butt may have been copied from antler axes of Mesolithic ancestry, but the expanded blade and longitudinal groove or ridge obviously reproduce the seam of casting in metal types. Concerning the origin of the weapon, Childe writes that it was derived from antler axes of Mesolithic origin 'not so much directly as through metal translations. Food-production and metal were alike introduced in most of the battle-axe provinces. But introduction need not imply migration, but only diffusion. In a word, the battle-axe culture would result when certain food-gatherers adopt food-production and acquire some metal weapons' [3].

Between 2300 B.C. and 1900 B.C., battle-axe warriors swept from the Black Sea to the Baltic, and from the Urals to the Alps. During Danubian period III, weapons of various kinds, especially battle-axes, appear in ever-increasing quantities, doubtless owing to the competition for land. In Hungary at this time there were no stone battle-axes, but there were copper types imitated directly from antler axes.

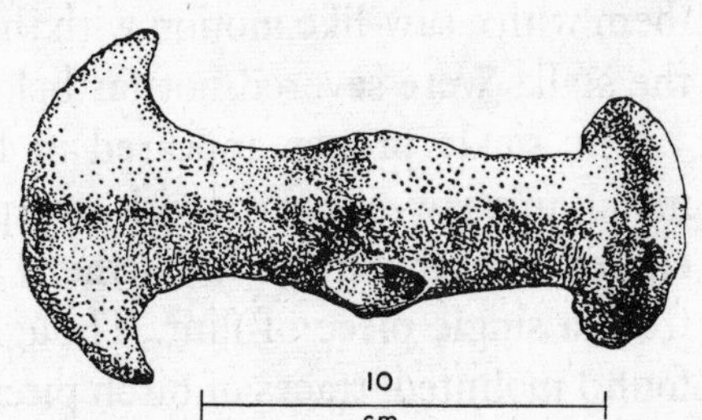

FIGURE 337—*Stone battle-axe copied from a metallic model. Dalsland, Sweden.*

In the North Sea area, polygonal battle-axes are common; they indicate southern inspiration, while expanded blades indicate a metal prototype. The earliest graves contain the finest specimens, often very metallic-looking, but in the upper graves the forms degenerate. The 'boat-axes' of Denmark and Sweden, so called because of their shape, are always provided with a shaft-tube. The concave surfaces of the early battle-axes were probably produced by using flint as a rubbing-stone, together with sand as an abrasive.

The faceted battle-axe is distinctive of the 'corded ware' cultures of Saxo-Thuringia. Its peculiar form may show some influence from the spiked club-heads of Mesolithic ancestry, but stray copper battle-axes exhibit much the same form. Other weapons associated with this culture include antler axes, asymmetrical stone axes, almond-shaped celts mounted as adzes, and occasional spheroid mace-heads and rough flint daggers.

Farming implements. Reaping-knives, with cutting edges formed by small flakes inset into straight grooved handles, are known first among the Mesolithic Natufians (*c* 5500 B.C.). They were presumably used for gathering wild grasses. The handles were sometimes carved at one end to represent an animal's head (figure 329 A). Similar blades are known from Mersin in Cilicia, probably dating from before 5000 B.C. The same type of sickle was adopted by the earliest farmers, from Egypt to Iran. At Merimde (*c* 4000 B.C.) sickles were more numerous than weapons, but few were found at Badari (*c* 4000 B.C.). In the Fayum, sickle-teeth of serrated flint flakes were set into straight wooden shafts (figure 356 A). In Mesopotamia, where flint and metal were scarce, there were sickles of baked clay; these were displaced in Early Dynastic times by angled sickles of wood with flint teeth.

In Europe, the most primitive sickles had antler handles, grooved for overlapping flint flakes. In western Bulgaria, such sickles are associated with painted pottery. Sickles from north Italy were provided with ear-hooks, for holding a bunch of stalks in preparation for grasping them in the left hand and severing them with a saw-like motion with the right. Judging by Egyptian tomb-paintings, the stalks were severed not far below the heads.

The sickle proper appeared in Europe, about the same time as the use of metal, in a jaw-like form with a reaping-edge of flint teeth (figure 329 B). By the end of Neolithic times in northern and central Europe, sickle blades were made from a single piece of flint. Though none of these crescentic blades have been found mounted, traces of birch pitch are still visible on some Swedish examples, evidence that they were set in slots cut into the inner arc of wooden handles, curved in imitation of metal types.

The treatment of the butt-ends of certain single-piece flint sickle-blades from Britain suggests that they were hafted at right-angles to straight handles. The handle of a sickle from Stenild in Jutland shows signs of having been shaped by a metal tool, and it is likely that sickles of this type were substitutes for those of bronze. Surviving wooden handles of unbalanced bronze or iron sickles show careful workmanship to give a good grip. The idea of bending the blade rearwards from the handle, to produce a balanced sickle, was apparently not developed until the Iron Age. This device made possible a simpler handle and a longer blade, and in time gave rise to the scythe.

For grinding grain, the most primitive contrivance is the pestle and mortar, which, like the reaping-knife, was inherited from Mesolithic sources or from the Upper Palaeolithic, where it was used for grinding pigments. This device continued in use in remote places, such as the Shetlands, until the present century. As a rule, Neolithic farmers used saddle querns; rotary querns first appear in Europe with the Iron Age La Tène culture.

Antler, bone, and ivory. The extensive use made of these materials by Mesolithic peoples was continued during the Neolithic. The use of antler for making bows is discussed elsewhere (p 163). An important use of antler was for the picks of flint-miners, from Grimes Graves and other centres, which 'could hardly have been used to hew the chalk with a swinging blow as one might wield a metal pick. . . . The most satisfactory explanation is that . . . the brow tines were hammered at intervals into natural lines of fracture in the chalk and that intervening slabs were then levered out by pressure on the handles of one or more picks at a time. In an uncompleted operation of this kind . . . seven picks appear to have been used. This helps to account for the very large numbers' [4]. Other antler tools found in flint-mines include two-pronged rakes, hammers or mallets, wedges made from single tines, and perforated axe-hammers. Shovels were made from shoulder blades of oxen (figures 371–2).

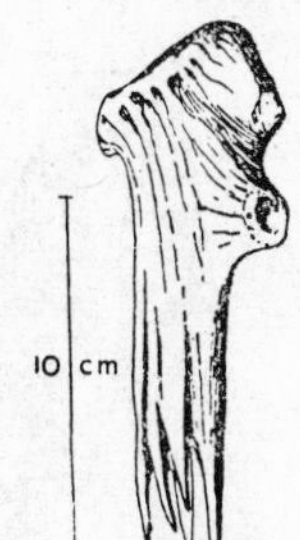

FIGURE 338—*Antler comb. Windmill Hill, Wiltshire. c 2500 B.C.*

Antler axes and adzes, invented by Mesolithic hunters, continued to be used in many parts of Europe during Neolithic times. The antler sleeves for hafting celts to their handles, found in Swiss lake-villages, resemble Mesolithic prototypes, but in this case the sleeve was inserted into, not perforated by, the handle.

Antler tines were often used for pressure-flaking flint implements during the Neolithic and Bronze Ages. Antler and bone combs (figure 338) are common in Neolithic sites. They were probably used for the hair, in connexion with weaving, and for leather-working, since some are very similar to Eskimo combs for removing hair from skins. They are specially characteristic of the causewayed camps of south England, Belgium, and Schleswig-Holstein.

Fish-hooks and harpoons of bone continued to be used as in Mesolithic times.

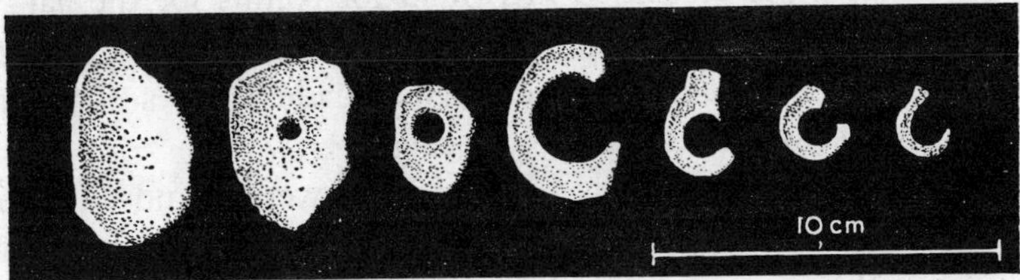

FIGURE 339—*Stages in the making of shell fish-hooks. Shaheinab, Sudan. c 3900 B.C.*

The oldest known fish-hooks are probably those of the Natufians of Palestine (? sixth millennium B.C.) and the Tasians of Egypt (figure 100 B, C) of the fifth millennium B.C. Barbed hooks appear in the Neolithic of Denmark and southern Sweden, and somewhat later in central Europe. Composite hooks were used in the circumpolar zone from western Norway to Russia; the shank and point of bone (or sometimes of slate) were made as separate members lashed together at the base. Metal hooks did not appear in the north until the Late Bronze Age and Early Iron Age, though they were known at a very early date in predynastic Egypt. Sea-fishing flourished off the coast of Gotland in Neolithic times, and hooks were made either of bone or of boar's-tusk enamel. Many were very large, like the modern cod-hook, and most were barbed. Fish-hooks made of shell were found at Shaheinab, Sudan, and from unfinished specimens the technique of making them can be well seen (figure 339).

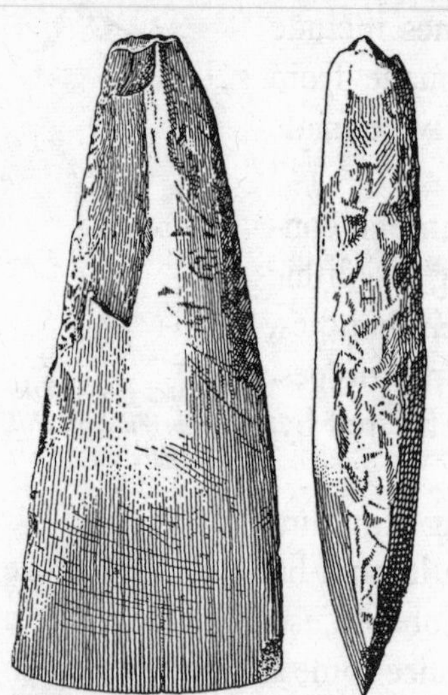

FIGURE 340—*Bone axe-head. Shaheinab, Sudan. Scale* c 2/3.

Slender harpoons with barbs projecting from a cylindrical stem, very similar to those of the Natufians, were used by the Fayumis. The coarse harpoons of Neolithic Switzerland reveal an unusual technique: they were shaped while still attached to the antler from which they were made.

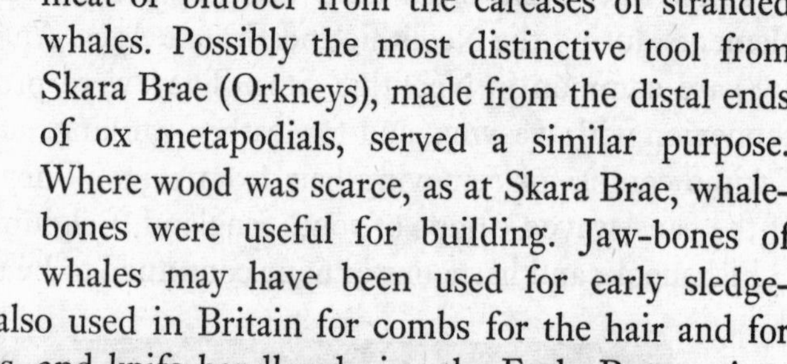

Clark has suggested that perforated antler axe-blades could well have been used for removing meat or blubber from the carcases of stranded whales. Possibly the most distinctive tool from Skara Brae (Orkneys), made from the distal ends of ox metapodials, served a similar purpose. Where wood was scarce, as at Skara Brae, whale-bones were useful for building. Jaw-bones of whales may have been used for early sledge-runners. Whale-bone was also used in Britain for combs for the hair and for weaving, harness ornaments, and knife-handles during the Early Bronze Age. Seal-bone was used for harpoon-heads. Awls made from seal-fibulae were probably used to perforate sealskin for sewing.

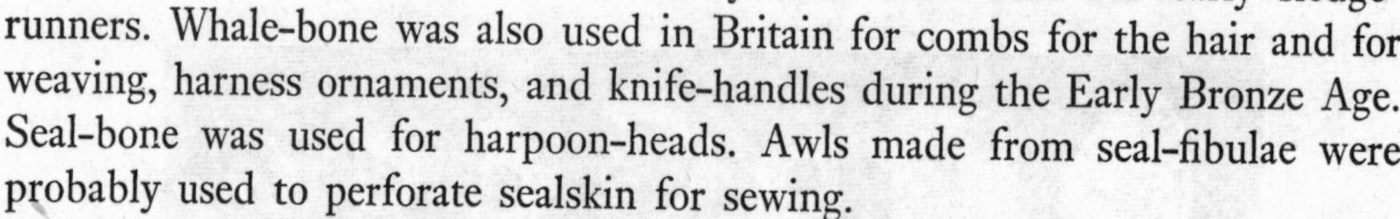

Some very interesting axe-heads made of bone were found with the Neolithic culture of Shaheinab, which may be roughly contemporary with the Fayum Neolithic (figure 340).

Among the many other tools made from bone, the commonest include needles, bodkins, pins, and chisel-ended smoothing-tools found, for example, at Merimde, where they were similar to Natufian models. At Badari, there were carved ivory handles and ivory combs ornamented with carved birds. In Gerzean times (early fourth millennium B.C.) the former long-toothed combs are replaced by short-toothed scratching-combs. There are also beautifully carved ivory handles for knives. A famous handle is that from Gebel-el-Arak depicting a naval battle. Its execution is purely Egyptian, but the theme is of Asiatic inspiration (figure 458).

Craftsmanship in the making of bone implements was little improved by the introduction of metal tools. The domestication of animals did, however, increase the supply of raw material, more than compensating for the decrease in hunting. Bone and antler, now more readily accessible, were made to serve many new purposes as economic life developed after the coming of metallurgy. The use of bone and antler as substitutes for new metal devices of the Bronze Age, such as cheek-pieces for harness, was fairly frequent. Other tools which continued to be made during this period include leather-polishers, weaving-combs, bobbins, and handles for metal tools.

FIGURE 341—*Reconstruction of a wood-worker's bench, with examples of his work, in a Neolithic lake-village on Lake Constance.* c *2200* B.C.

Wood-working was naturally improved greatly with the advent of efficient carpenters' tools during the Neolithic, and still more with Bronze Age metal tools. With polished stone adzes, gouges, chisels, and awls, Neolithic man produced a variety of well made wooden implements. Bronze Age craftsmen became sufficiently skilled to make such complex structures as the spoked wheel (p 211), an achievement impossible without metal saws. Splitting by wedges along the grain of the wood, and smoothing by abrasion, were simple techniques involved in the production of such objects as the long-toothed combs of Swiss lake-dwellers. A variety of wooden objects has been found in Switzerland, including adzes, mallets, ladles, and wooden bowls (figure 341). Throwing-sticks and boomerangs (figure 342) were other wooden objects made in Neolithic times. Wooden vessels were cut out of the solid with the adze. This is proved by an unfinished lugged bowl from Utoquai (Zürich), but, as a rule, all traces of workmanship are removed by polishing. Work of this kind continued throughout the Bronze Age, though gradually the method of cutting grooves with metal gouges and making wooden containers with inserted bases was adopted. Wooden vessels were often the sources of ceramic forms, for example, the straight-handled beakers of the Cambridge region, copied from wooden tankards at the dawn of the Bronze Age. Wood-carving, too, was often imitated by incisions on pottery, notably at Alishar, in Anatolia, where wood-carving was particularly fine (cf p 397).

The lathe spread from the Mediterranean to northern Europe; possibly it was used in Greece as early as the middle of the second millennium B.C., judging by a shallow dish of cypress-wood from a shaft-grave at Mycenae. The lathe was not in common use, however, until iron cutting-tools were available. The oldest known vessels turned on a rotary lathe came from an Etruscan warrior's tomb at Corneto, perhaps of *c* 700 B.C. Perhaps the Etruscans brought the lathe with them when they colonized Italy from Asia, and from Italy it spread into south-west Germany during the late stage of the Hallstatt (first Iron Age) culture.

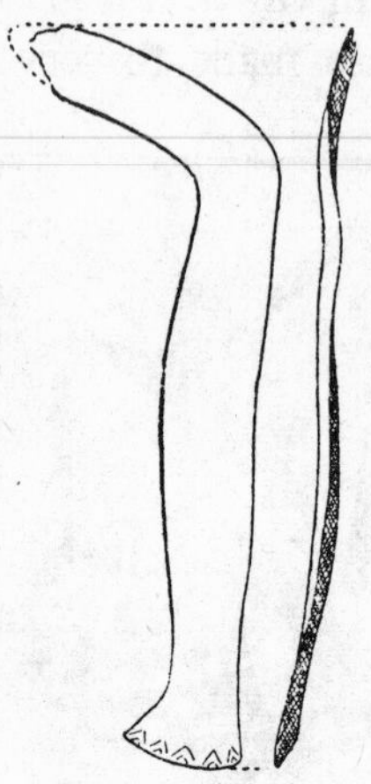

FIGURE 342 — *Wooden 'boomerang'. Badari.* c *4000 B.C. Scale 1/5.*

The tread-trap appeared during the late Bronze Age of Europe. Heavy wooden frames, 2–4 ft long and tapering slightly at the squared ends, were used for the traps. In the middle they had either a single oblong aperture fitted with a wooden flap, or a pair of them. The flaps were held in a closed position by wooden springs set in grooves cut in the frame and held down by cross-pegs. As a rule, the frames were made of oak, though one from Jutland was of willow. For the springs, a more pliable wood was favoured, most often hazel but sometimes willow or beech. The finds are widely distributed in the temperate forest zone and it is thought that the traps were used to catch red deer.

Lastly, one more material, bark, deserves mention. It was much used for containers, and as floats for fishing-nets. Birch-bark containers are common in the northern Bronze Age, and a lime-bark box sewn with bast was found in the Early Bronze Age coffin-burial of Egtved in Denmark. Containers for fluids with wooden bases and bark walls are known, and the lake-dwellers of Switzerland used spools of birch-bark as tapers or torches, of which charred stumps have been recovered.

REFERENCES

[1] CLARK, J. G. D. 'The Mesolithic Age in Britain', p. xx. University Press, Cambridge. 1932.
[2] *Idem.* 'Prehistoric Europe', pp. 172 f. Methuen, London. 1952.
[3] CHILDE, V. GORDON. 'The Dawn of European Civilization' (5th ed. rev.), pp. 174 f. Routledge and Kegan Paul, London. 1950.
[4] CLARK, J. G. D. 'Prehistoric Europe', pp. 175–7. Methuen, London. 1952.

BIBLIOGRAPHY

ARKELL, A. J. "Esh Shaheinab." *Sudan Notes*, **30**, ii, 212, 1949.

CATON-THOMPSON, G. and GARDNER, E. W. 'The Desert Fayum.' R. Anthropological Institute, London. 1934.

CHILDE, V. GORDON. 'The Dawn of European Civilization' (5th ed. rev.). Routledge and Kegan Paul, London. 1950.

Idem. 'Man Makes Himself.' Watts, London. 1951.

Idem. 'New Light on the Most Ancient East' (4th ed.). Routledge and Kegan Paul, London. 1952.

CLARK, J. G. D. 'The Mesolithic Age in Britain.' University Press, Cambridge. 1932.

Idem. 'The Mesolithic Settlement of Northern Europe.' University Press, Cambridge. 1936.

Idem. 'Prehistoric Europe.' Methuen, London. 1952.

OAKLEY, K. P. 'Man the Tool-maker' (2nd ed. rev.). British Museum (Natural History), London. 1952.

PETRIE, SIR (WILLIAM MATTHEW) FLINDERS. 'Tools and Weapons.' Egypt. Res. Acc. and Brit. Sch. Archaeol. Egypt, Publ. 30. London. 1917.

Making flint implements. From a tomb at Beni Hasan, Egypt. *c 1900 B.C.*

19

WATER-SUPPLY, IRRIGATION, AND AGRICULTURE

M. S. DROWER

I. BEGINNINGS OF IRRIGATION AND DRAINAGE

THE most vital need of early man in regions of scanty rainfall such as the Near East is water. In these regions the origin of irrigation is inseparable from that of agriculture. With both of them is bound up the emergence of Neolithic man as a being of corporate life, with settled habits, living in villages, cultivating plants, often making a crude pottery, and domesticating animals.

Some form of rudimentary agriculture without irrigation may have been practised in the Near East even before Neolithic times. There are regions of copious spring rainfall in Palestine, Syria, and the Caucasus where today barley and emmer (*Triticum dicoccum*) grow wild. There a group might sow a little grain in the moistened earth, and gather the crop when ripe. At the very end of the Palaeolithic period, the cave-dwelling Natufians of Mount Carmel reaped grain with a primitive sickle, a grooved bone-haft set with flint teeth (figure 329 A)—probably the earliest agricultural implement known [1]. It is possible that in Palestine, as well perhaps as in the highlands of Kurdistan, where Late Palaeolithic settlements have also been found, the small grass-like ears of these wild cereals, springing up after vernal rain, were gathered and eaten by a people who cannot yet be said to have practised agriculture—they were still food-collectors rather than food-growers.

Such wild harvests are known to be augmented by a very simple form of irrigation by peoples still in the food-gathering stage (p 173). Food-gatherers know that wild grasses grow more luxuriantly near streams, by springs, and in the dry beds of water-courses. They have been seen to erect a rough dam of stones to retain the water, and to scratch runnels to lead the water towards the valley's edge. Even the soaking of ground around a spring by splashing may be used to encourage the growth of wild food-plants. Whichever method came first, deliberate watering of the ground and preservation of seed from season to season must soon have gone hand-in-hand.

Irrigation, the artificial supplying of water to crops where the rainfall is insufficient, is inseparable from drainage, the removal of surplus water from land. This association leads us to consider also the general question of water-supply for other purposes, such as drinking, since wells and cisterns, canals and aqueducts may be used both for irrigation and for providing drinking-water for man and beast. In Arabia today there is usually a trough for watering animals beside a well, and a channel by which water may be run off to the neighbouring fields. So also conduits and aqueducts which supplied ancient cities with their domestic water filled on the way innumerable irrigation channels.

Many ancient springs and wells survive, some underground channels have been excavated, and the remains of former canals and aqueducts are still to be seen. The age of many such survivals, however, is in doubt, though some of the channels used in classical, medieval, and even modern times are of very great antiquity. For our knowledge of the irrigation and cultivation of the great river-valleys of the Near East in ancient times we depend largely on textual evidence which is far from complete. The digging of an important new canal is sometimes recorded, but seldom the maintenance of the numerous canals already in use; as a matter of agricultural routine, it was taken for granted. Certain laws which survive deal with water-claims and obligations of 'rivals'. That very word in Roman law denoted those who shared the water of a *rivus*, or irrigation channel; it thus implies jealously guarded rights and frequent quarrels. But we possess no complete ancient code of laws dealing with agrarian property, and age-old custom must always have dictated local usage.

Though we have a far greater body of private documents from Mesopotamia containing such records as the yield of land under cultivation—themselves evidence of an efficient control of irrigation—we are better informed on agricultural methods in Egypt. There the farmer's cycle of ploughing, sowing, and reaping was a favourite theme of the artists who drew the lively scenes of daily life that adorn the tombs. In the great alluvial valleys, and on the upland slopes of more northerly countries of the Near East, with their terraced hillsides and well watered valleys, methods of cultivation have probably changed little in five millennia or more.

Two other great valley civilizations go back to remote times—those of the Indus and the Hwang-Ho. Their general geographical conditions are similar to those of the Nile and Euphrates: rainfall is scanty and summer temperatures high; the rise of the river is comparable in height though the volume of water brought down, and silt deposited, by the Hwang-Ho far exceeds that of the other rivers. Both valleys resembled Mesopotamia rather than Egypt in enjoying a system of perennial irrigation. Yet we know little of the early irrigation of either region. Primitive water-lifting apparatus is used in both areas today, and the same methods may have persisted through the ages, though we have little evidence to support this view. Excavations in the great cities of the Indus valley of the late third millennium B.C. reveal extraordinary technical skill in designing domestic and municipal drains, and embankments to retain flood-water, but tell hardly anything of agricultural or irrigation methods (figure 296). We do know, however, that barley, wheat, sesame, and cotton were grown [2], as well as melons, dates, and other fruits. Few agricultural implements have been found; perhaps they were generally of wood and have perished. No ancient canals have been revealed by air survey. It has been supposed that the rainfall of Sind and the Punjab was formerly heavier than it is today—but, if so, how are we to explain the absence of any evidence of attempts to control flood-waters which must then, even more than now, have turned the countryside in summer into a lake?

FIGURE 343—*Drawing water in pots from a lily pond. From a tomb at Thebes, Egypt. c 1450 B.C.*

We must thus confine our study of the early history of irrigation to the Near East. Each region had its own typical methods, determined by geological formation and hydrography, by the nature of its soil, climate, and flora and, not least, by social conditions—though the latter arose from the need for organized irrigation as much as they determined its form. This chapter falls naturally into two: (*a*) a general survey of ancient methods of obtaining water from springs, wells, cisterns, underground conduits, aqueducts, and the like (sections II–V), and (*b*) discussion of the irrigation systems of the two great river-valleys, and the social and economic conditions in which they developed and which they in part created (sections VI–IX). The Nile valley provides the classic example of basin irrigation; and in the valley of the Tigris and the Euphrates perennial irrigation was practised.

II. WATER-LIFTING DEVICES

The simplest device for raising water is the hollow of the hand. The amount does not suffice for storage purposes, for domestic animals, or for the simplest form of irrigation. Leather bags, wooden scoops, or clay vessels were more satisfactory (figure 343), and a rope of wool, thongs, or twisted fibres increased the length of the lift. A plank over the mouth of a well, or a platform over a river or stream, enabled the drawer to obtain a vertical pull. His labour could be lightened by passing the rope over a horizontal pole supported on two uprights, so that he could stand at the margin of well or river and haul downwards instead of drawing upwards. The simplest wells today have tackle of this construction, though the invention of the pulley, which seems to have been made well before 1500 B.C.,[1] greatly simplified the drawer's task. In Arabia today a second man often stands on a plank over the well to steady the rope, or may descend into the well to fill the bucket and guide its ascent, in order to avoid injuring the well-coping or spilling the water.[2]

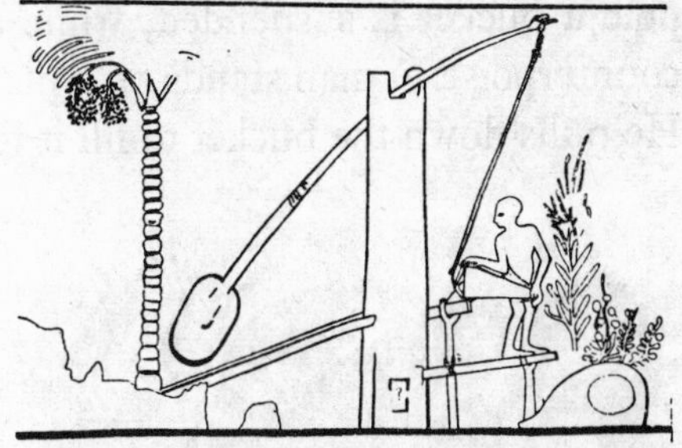

FIGURE 344—*Irrigation of a palm garden by shaduf in Egypt. The gardener stands on a plank platform. He has dipped his bucket into a pool surrounded by marsh plants, and the clay counterpoise has raised it to the level of the sloping funnel into which he is pouring the water, to fill the mud basin at the foot of the tree. From a tomb at Thebes.* c *1500 B.C.*

FIGURE 345—*Watering an Egyptian garden. In the centre stands a house or pavilion with steps leading down to the water. From the pools on either side gardeners are watering fig and olive trees and flowering plants by means of a row of shadufs. Lotus grows in the pools, and papyrus at their edges. From a tomb at Thebes.* c *1300 B.C*

Such methods provide an intermittent flow. An improvement, used from very ancient times, is the swipe or shaduf (figure 344). Two pillars about 5 ft high, of wood or rushes daubed with mud, are set up less than a yard apart. A horizontal beam is fixed across, over which pivots a long slender pole. To one end of the

[1] Assyrian pulley-wheels of mulberry wood, similar to those used around Mosul today, were found at Nimrud. The word for 'pulley', which has survived in modern Arabic, is found in a tablet of the fifteenth century B.C. from Alalakh. The earliest pulley-wheel discovered in Egypt is of the Roman period.

[2] Harnessing animals to the task of drawing may have been conceived early, but no ancient representations are known of a beast pulling up the bucket.

pole a bucket is suspended, while at the other a large lump of clay acts as a counterpoise. A man stands on a platform at the river's edge to work this device. He pulls down the bucket to fill it from the river or canal, and the counterpoise lifts it to the height of his waist. At the top of the upward swing, he empties the bucket into an irrigation trough, whence the water flows away to the land. The shaduf is shown in various forms on ancient Egyptian tomb-paintings of the New Kingdom (i.e. from *c* 1580 B.C.). It can lift water 6 ft or more. Nowadays several are sometimes used in conjunction, one above the other, each taking water from the trough of the one below. There is, however, no evidence that the ancient Egyptians used more than a single shaduf at a time. Large wooden hooks found at Tarkhan, of Dynasty III, have been thought to be shaduf hooks, but the device is not pictured for us until the New Kingdom,

FIGURE 346—*An early shaduf. From a cylinder seal of the Akkadian period. Third millennium* B.C.

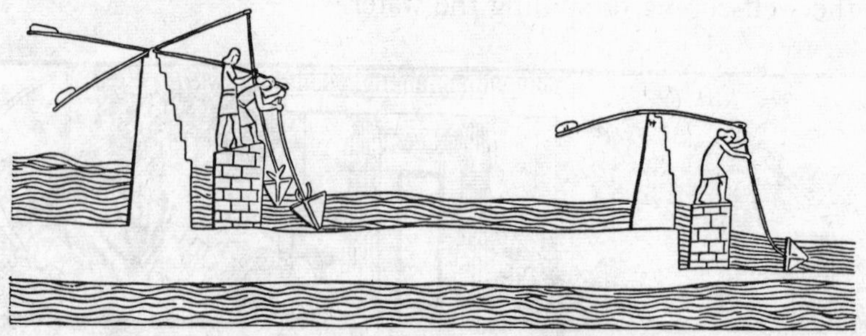

FIGURE 347 A—*Assyrians raising water from the river by shaduf. Three men operate a double lift. The shadufs, on mud uprights, stand at two levels on the river bank, and in front of each a brick platform is built out into the river for the men who fill and empty the buckets. From the palace of Sennacherib at Nineveh, Mesopotamia. Seventh century* B.C.

when this type of irrigation was generally employed in gardens, groves, orchards, and other plots which needed perennial watering (figure 345).

In Babylonia its use is attested as early as the third millennium B.C., for it appears on a cylinder-seal of the Akkadian period (*c* 2400–*c* 2200) in connexion with the cultivation of a tree or garden (figure 346) [3]. A riverine scene of the reign of Sennacherib (705–681 B.C.) shows a double shaduf, that on the upper level having two buckets (figure 347 A). This relief seems to show peasants at work in the fields, but Sennacherib, who was interested in every sort of engineering device, erected a more elaborate machine for watering his palace garden: 'That daily there might be an abundant flow of water-of-buckets, I had made copper cables (?) and pails, and in place of mud-brick pillars I set up great posts and cross-beams over the well.' The shaduf with its rhythm of rise and fall, dip and empty, to which the ancient labourer must have sung as does his modern descendant, can raise an average of about 600 gallons per man-day, much more than any non-mechanical type of water-lift. There is slight archaeological evidence for the use of a hand-wheel or continuous chain of buckets in the Neo-Babylonian period (*c* 600 B.C.) (see p 551); the ox-driven water-wheel, whose continuous flow irrigates up to half an acre per day, is not shown on the reliefs and may not have been used until classical times, though its introduction by the Achaemenides is possible [4].

III. SPRINGS AND WELLS

In areas of scant rainfall where perennial streams are lacking, irrigation and indeed human existence must depend on wells and springs, and devices for the storage of water; and human settlement must be concentrated in a few miles of green oasis bordered by the barren desert.

Water may be found where a permeable rock, resting upon impermeable strata, retains sufficient rain and is near enough to the surface. In any depression in such an area, the impermeable rock is liable to crop out at the surface and a spring will emerge at the edge as long as there is enough rainfall to maintain the water-table. The quantity of the subsoil water also may in some cases give rise to surface springs on level ground, or maintain a level of water in a well sunk in the permeable layer.

The method followed by early man in digging for water must have been similar to that now used in Arabia by nomadic Bedouin. A spot is chosen where digging promises success—likely places are the beds of wadis, or any patch of unexpected vegetation. A hole is there made with hoes or digging-sticks. The loosened earth is piled up around the hole to form a parapet, to prevent animals from coming too close and falling in or fouling the well, and at the same time to shield it from being choked by wind-blown sand. The digger goes down till he finds water. But if such simple temporary water-holes are to be made more lasting, their sides and rim must be protected and some kind of lifting tackle erected over them (p 523). The lining of a well can be of rough stones, ashlar masonry, burnt brick, or wood; if cut in solid rock no such strengthening is needed, but the initial sinking is much more laborious. Heating the rock and then pouring cold water on it to split it is an ancient practice (p 565), but it demands an adequate supply of both fuel and water.

A round pictograph denoting 'well' or 'cistern' occurs on archaic Sumerian tablets. Ea, the patron god of Eridu near the Persian Gulf, was 'lord of the sweet waters that flow under the earth'. But in the alluvial valleys, the rivers supplied general needs. When asked for a definition of Egypt, the oracle of Amen was said to have answered, 'The entire tract which the Nile overspreads and irrigates; and the Egyptians are those who live below Elephantine, and drink the waters of that river'. Once outside the Nile valley, the ancient Egyptians were frequently obliged to dig wells to supply miners or quarrymen in remote places, or travellers on the frequented routes across the eastern desert to the Red Sea, and on the commercial and military route from the eastern branch of the Nile delta across the desert of Sinai to southern Palestine. It is probable that the Old and Middle Kingdom workmen who quarried diorite in Nubia, 55 miles from the Nile, had their needs supplied from wells, for rectangular pits about 27 yd square have been found not far from the quarries [5]. The digging of wells and cisterns is sometimes mentioned in inscriptions. An officer of Dynasty XI (*c* 2000 B.C.), on his expedition through the Wadi Hammamat to equip and dispatch a ship on the Red Sea incense-route and to quarry stone, dug fifteen wells. 'I went forth', he says, 'with a force of 3000 men. I made the road a river, the desert a meadow, and I gave to each a leather bottle and a carrying-pole and two jars of water and twenty loaves daily.' The dimensions given in three cases—30, 20, 20 cubits square—indicate cisterns rather than wells; they may have been intended to store rainwater.

The gold-workings far up Wadi Alaki in Nubia, a little south of the tropic of Cancer, presented so serious a problem of water-supply that, according to Rameses II (1292–1225 B.C.), 'if a few of the gold-washers went thither, it was only the half of them that arrived, for they died of thirst on the road together with their asses. There could not be found for them their necessary supply of drink in going up and coming down [the wadi] from water of the water-skins.' Many previous kings had made vain attempts to dig a well in the valley—even the predecessor of Rameses, Seti I (1313–1292 B.C.), had 'caused to be dug a well of a depth of 120 cubits (200 ft) in his time. Yet it lies abandoned in the road, for no water came out of it.' In spite of the scepticism of the local inhabitants, however, Rameses decided to dig a new well, and with the aid of Hapi, the Nile-god, he struck water at only 20 ft. Seti I had himself been successful on the road to the Gebel Zabara mines (latitude of Asmara), and found the spot for a gushing well.

Caravan-routes which were also regularly used as military roads by the Egyptian and Assyrian armies were provided with fortified wells at intervals. We have formalized representations of a series of such wells built or repaired by Seti I on his march to Palestine along the nine days' desert route. Some are shown as irregular water-pools, others have a round parapet of masonry.

Herodotus (fifth century B.C.) [6] gives a curious account of the preparations made by the Persian Cambyses to supply his army with water on their way to invade Egypt in 525 B.C. He states that the Persians kept water stored in wine-jars along the desert road. These supplemented the supply, arranged by treaty with the paramount shaikh of the region, from camels laden with water-skins.

Digging wells by armies on the march was a necessary feature of campaigns in desert or arid territory. The Assyrian Tukulti Ninurta II in 885 B.C. records the digging of 470 wells or water-holes in the dry bed of the Tartara river; Ashur-bani-pal (669–626 B.C.) during his Arabian campaign found a walled camping-place with cisterns. The water of these cisterns being insufficient, his soldiers 'dug for water to quench their thirst' before attempting the crossing of a waterless tract. Seizure of wells was part of the strategy of desert warfare, and, when Ashur-bani-pal was harrying the Arabs near Damascus, 'in every place where there were springs or wells of water, I set guards over them, depriving them of the water to keep them alive. I made drink costly to their mouths; through thirst and deprivation they perished.'

Most ancient wells uncovered by modern excavation are in the cities of the ancient Near East, where water was needed for domestic purposes rather than for irrigation. Such wells, though of fundamentally the same construction as those in fields and gardens, probably had a rather different superstructure and were more carefully kept in repair. The walls were usually of burnt brick, and as the level of the city rose through the centuries, by accumulation of debris, the top of the well was continually being added to.

In the palace of Ashur-nasir-pal II (884–859 B.C.) at Nimrud, three excellently constructed wells were found [7]. One, round in plan, was more than 330 brick-courses deep, and still held water. Near it stood a stone storage-tank with a capacity of at least 100 gallons. Another and later well was used for watering animals, since tethering-blocks for horses and mules stood nearby; brick steps, waterproofed with bitumen, led up to a platform on the level of the well-head, upon which stood a perforated brick ramp supporting a wooden derrick, and a drip-stone for catching the waste water. When not in use, the well was covered by a shaped capstone. Wells were sunk also in the courtyards of temples for cult purposes. The deep rectangular well in the courtyard of a temple in the city Ashur, re-dug and stone-lined by Sennacherib (705–681 B.C.), supplied water for a piscina of basalt decorated with figures of Ea the water-god and his fish-clad priests.

Artesian wells. Few wells in the Near East are very deep. In the wadis, water can usually be reached at between 12 and 15 ft. The shallow wells of the Libyan oases, sunk in the sub-surface sandstone, may yield up to 8 gallons a minute, though the water is apt to be brackish. When greater quantities are needed, for irrigation or for a large population, it is sometimes necessary to dig much deeper through rock, to tap water-bearing strata beneath. The holy well of Zemzem at Mecca is 120 ft deep, and wells in Palmyra are as much as 250 ft. In oases such as Kharga and Dakhla, the hydrostatic pressure may make the waters rise to the top of a deep borehole; such artesian wells may provide hundreds of gallons a minute. It was probably due to ancient Egyptian efforts to exploit the oases that the artesian principle was discovered and deep wells were first dug. Shallow wells and springs at first provided enough for the agricultural needs of the rather sparse, semi-nomadic population of oasis-dwellers, but Egyptian control, intermittent in the Middle Kingdom (2050–1785 B.C.), was completed in the New, when a 'controller of the oasis regions' was appointed. The oases then enjoyed great development, and became famous for their vineyards and gardens. The technique of deep well-digging can hardly have been learned in Egypt; it may have evolved in the oasis of Dakhla, where artesian water is rather nearer the surface (100 ft) than in Kharga, where one must bore for 240–260 ft before reaching the deep-seated porous sandstone.

The ancient method of digging artesian wells probably continued unchanged till modern well-boring machinery was introduced [8]. The well was started as an open shaft. A pit about 6 ft square was dug as deep as surface-water would allow, and its sides were shored with timber. In the centre a wooden tube was placed upright. This was the lining of the well's upper section, and might consist of hollowed tree-trunks fitted end to end, with watertight joints, or be built of acacia-wood in curved sections. The space between the shaft and the sides of the pit was filled in and packed tightly. Within the shaft, drilling was then started, probably by metal rods driven into the rock by percussion. By this slow and laborious process, a well takes many months to bore, and if the lining collapses it must be dug afresh.

IV. WATER CONSERVATION

In arid areas, the idea must early have occurred of storing the water of a wadi during the spate of spring rains, against the dry months to come. Stones and earth might be piled up to form a dam across the wadi bed, behind which water would accumulate to form a reservoir. In the eastern desert of Egypt, across the narrow ravine of the Wadi Gerrawi, 7 miles from Helwan, remains of such a dam, probably of Old Kingdom date, may still be seen. Possibly the most ancient dam in existence, it is of rough masonry 270 ft thick and 370 ft long, and is faced on the water side with limestone. Water coming down in spate during the brief but violent winter rain-storms was thereby stored for a settlement of some 200 workmen in the nearby alabaster quarries, where stand the ruins of their huts [9]. Later in date, but far surpassing it in length, is the great barrage

FIGURE 347 B—*Assyrian dam of rough masonry and mortared rubble, curved to withstand the flow of the river Khosr above Nineveh*

which stretches across the Orontes valley in Syria to create the Lake of Homs, about 50 sq km (20 sq miles) in area. The date of this stone dyke is uncertain; if it be the 'Egyptian wall' of Strabo it may originally have been the work of the engineers of Seti I (1313–1292 B.C.) of Dynasty XIX, or even of some earlier Pharaoh. It was many times repaired and altered; today it is some 2 km ($1\frac{1}{4}$ miles) long, and its sluices still supply the irrigation canals around Homs [10]. A double dam of Assyrian masonry (figure 347 B), built diagonally across the Khosr river above Nineveh where it passes through a defile, is preserved in part to a height of nearly 10 ft [11]. Sennacherib mentions the damming of this river to create a pool or reservoir above the city. In the time of Herodotus, a dyke ran across the Nile valley to protect the Memphis region from total inundation. Tradition ascribed its construction to Menes, the legendary first king of united Egypt. So great an undertaking would have needed technical resources far in advance of those of the protodynastic Egyptians, but some kind of dyke to conserve water and protect the city from flood may well have been built at the time of the foundation of Memphis.

In Arabia are many ancient dams; the largest and most remarkable is that near Marib in the Yemen, the ancient Sabaean capital. It extends for some 600 yd across the valley, and is of fine masonry with copper fastenings; rectangular sluices in the dam controlled the outflow, which led to a fanlike irrigation-system in the valley, where the water was admitted to strips of cultivable land, broadening downstream and separated by radiating walls. It may go back to the time of Sabaean expansion, 600 B.C. or a little earlier. There are traces of similar systems elsewhere in Arabia; it is a method peculiarly suited to great wadis in desert regions.

In most areas of Arabia, remains of ancient cement-lined tanks and stone cisterns abound. At Aden there is a remarkable series of fifty great cisterns, with a capacity of over 30 million gallons, assigned by tradition to remote antiquity. The majority probably date only from the Persian occupation of *c* A.D. 600, but they may represent an enlargement of a more ancient system.

In Palestine stone cisterns, hewn from a block of stone or merely hollowed in the surface of the rock, have pitted the hillsides since time immemorial. These hold 'the former and the latter rains', which in the Judaean hills fall heavily for some 56 days and hardly at all for the rest of the year. Larger cisterns, or reservoirs fed by springs, served the needs of agriculture and the domestic consumption of cities. One of the ancient tanks above Jericho, which contributed to the remarkable fertility of the district in ancient times, is 6 acres in area. The great rock-cut cisterns known as the Pools of Solomon, which supplied the city of Jerusalem 11 miles away with water, are of great size; one is Herodian, but the others may be considerably older. Unless such pools or reservoirs are very large, evaporation soon leaves only a small brackish remnant. In Palestine and Arabia this difficulty was often solved by hollowing underground cisterns in the rock with a sloping or stepped passage descending to water-level. Occasionally, such subterranean reservoirs were of natural origin, as in the volcanic district of the Hauran, and in the fissured basalts of Transjordan.

In ancient Palestine, the favourite site for a new settlement was on a hill for security, and near a spring for water-supply. The hill would be encircled with fortifications, but the spring or well generally had to be situated outside the walls, since the water would normally issue at the base of the hillside. For safety in war, the ancient Canaanites were accustomed to cut a stepped passage down through the solid rock from the citadel to the spring outside the walls. The source was enclosed, so that it supplied only the dwellers within. Some of these tunnels are of very considerable length; there are well preserved examples at Megiddo and Lachish [12], and the best known is the tunnel by which Hezekiah,

King of Judah (?740–692 B.C.), made the waters of a spring in the side of the hill Ophel at Jerusalem available to the garrison besieged by the Assyrians (*c* 700 B.C.). An inscription marks the spot where two gangs, burrowing from either end, met—a remarkable achievement, since the passage twists and is 1760 ft long [13] (figure 559).

The early inhabitants of the cities of Mycenaean Greece had a similar problem of water-supply in time of siege, and solved it in a similar way. One of the best-preserved examples is the underground conduit constructed in the thirteenth century B.C., to bring the waters of the spring of Perseia within the reach of those defending the citadel of Mycenae. A stepped passage descends obliquely through the thickness of the Cyclopean rampart and continues down through rock, with several changes of direction, till it reaches an underground cistern whither the waters of the spring were conveyed through terracotta pipes [14].

V. WATER CONDUCTION

Water had frequently to be conducted for considerable distances from the source. Ancient irrigation-engineers showed great ingenuity and boldness in this task. Remains of aqueducts near the Syrian coast show how the Phoenicians, reputed by the Greeks to be masters of irrigation, led water long distances over uneven ground by channels and embankments. The gardens, fields, and orchards of their narrow but very fertile coastal plain had a perpetual supply from the mountain streams of Lebanon.

One of the great ancient aqueducts was built by Sennacherib in 691 B.C. to bring the waters of a canal from a tributary of the Greater Zab to augment the supply of his capital Nineveh, 50 miles away (p 469). Wide as an arterial road, and paved with masonry, it must have been one of the most impressive works of hydraulic engineering until Roman times (plate 20 A). Its stone came from a quarry in the foothills near the beginning of the canal, the blocks being transported on wheels down the dry channel itself, which was carefully smoothed and graded. On the wall of the gorge above the weir which directed the river into the canal-head were gigantic figures of the king and gods, with an inscription that records that the king finished the whole work in a year and three months.[1] A dam with sluice-gates regulated the flow and enabled water to be stored. At the junction of other streams on its course, further sluices were built. At one point it was led across a valley over a limestone aqueduct 300 yd long, with 5 corbelled arches in the centre (plate 20 A). Just before the canal entered Nineveh, a

[1] It is estimated that this work involved transporting over 2 million blocks of heavy limestone a distance of no less than 10 miles.

dam deflected part of the water into subsidiary canals and the irrigation-channels of orchards and gardens outside the city walls (cf figure 367).

An elaborate canal-system, bringing water from the surrounding hills, was constructed by these Assyrian monarchs. Traces of cisterns cut in outcrops of rock in the plain indicate further storage, while wells tapped the brackish subsoil-water. In the upland plateau of northern Iraq, normal rainfall generally suffices for cereals and vegetables. Canals and cisterns were needed only for cities, for perpetual irrigation of gardens and orchards, for intensive cultivation in thickly populated areas, and to safeguard supply in times of drought.

Assyrian irrigation laws distinguished between rain-water and water from natural springs, wells, or cisterns. Regulations dealt with the rights and duties of landowners whose properties were irrigated from a common source; they provided for co-operation in maintaining supply, keeping canals free from silt and pollution, and ensuring that those farthest from the source received a fair share. In case of flooding by rain-storms co-operation was urgent, both to prevent damage, and to conserve surplus water. Each must do necessary labour in proportion to his holding, and there was a special court to deal with the recalcitrant farmer [15].

As one travels eastward in Syria beyond Lebanon, the zone of precipitation, the need for irrigation grows ever greater. Damascus stands in an oasis of 20 sq miles of gardens and orchards, between the desert and the sterile slopes of Anti-Lebanon. This fertile area depends entirely on a network of channels from its famous river, the Barada. Many of the canals still in use there are survivors from antiquity [16]. There is a similar but smaller oasis in the Syrian desert, where again an ancient channel is still in use. But the ruined aqueducts at Palmyra, 135 miles north-east of Damascus, tell of that city's vanished fields and gardens, and traces of canals may be seen in other parts of what is now desert.

In southern Arabia also there were ancient canal-systems in areas now barren. These are often attributed to the Nabataeans, one of the pre-Islamic peoples of Arabia, but they may be still older. A network of channels covering 7 sq km (3 sq miles) near the moon-temple in the Wadi ʿAmd (Hadhramaut) in the Aden Protectorate may be fourth to sixth century B.C. or earlier [17]; the banks were mostly of mud, the junctions strengthened with masonry.

When a small volume of water had to be conducted some distance, loss by evaporation was serious. In hilly country, too, it was not always possible to maintain a constant downward gradient. Underground conduits or *qanaats* solved both problems, and kept the water cool and free from pollution. These ancient devices are still extensively employed in Persia, north Syria, and north Africa, areas with an arid summer and seasonal rainfall, in places where there are springs in the hills but no adequate supply of water in the valley. The *qanaat* is a long sloping tunnel driven from a spring, or from the water-bearing stratum of a mountain side, in a gentle incline to the valley site. If the surface at the receiving end of the conduit is too level for its water to emerge as a spring, it may terminate in a well (figure 348). Vertical shafts to the surface every 50 yd or so are made

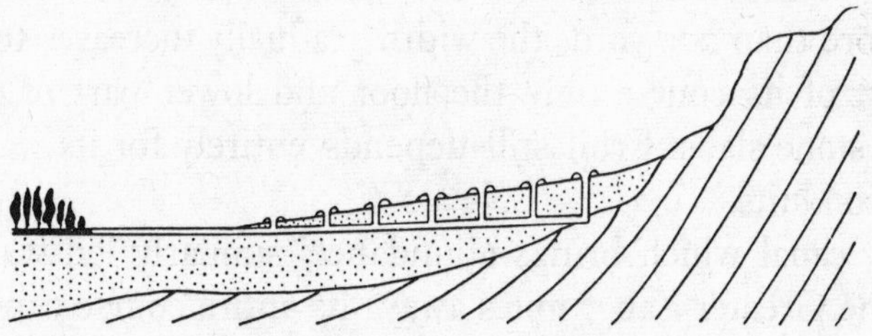

FIGURE 348 A—*A modern* qanaat *in Persia (simplified longitudinal section). These conduits are often some miles in length and have vertical shafts, which may be 300 ft deep, at intervals of about 50 yd.*

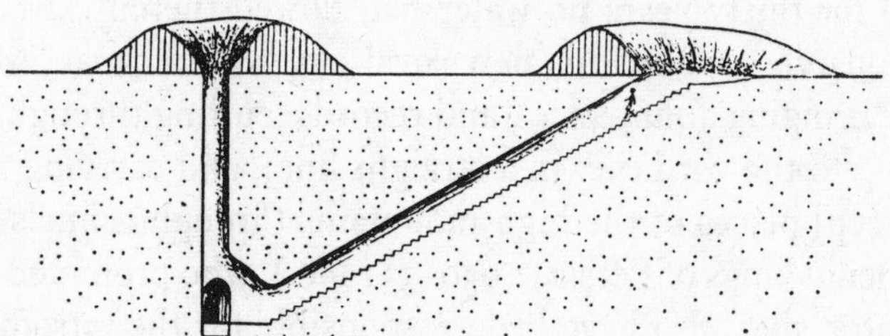

FIGURE 348 B—*Transverse section at a point where an inspection-shaft, used also for drawing water, reaches the conduit.*

to provide air for the tunneller, and to dispose of the excavated debris. Thus the course is marked on the surface by a line of small cones of rubble. These channels may have a flow of several gallons of water per second, and are sometimes many miles long. The enormous labour involved in their construction and upkeep is justified only where water is very greatly needed. An ancient conduit still supplies Aleppo and the gardens around it from a spring 12 km (over 7 miles) away [18].

Most Assyrian cities, even those on a great river, probably relied for some of their fresh water upon this system, since Tigris water is unsuitable for drinking. Sennacherib's engineers carried out a project for supplying Erbil with water by an underground conduit 20 km (12 miles) long [19]. At the entrance, his inscription reads: 'I, Sennacherib, King of Assyria, dug [the beds of] three rivers in the Khani mountains, which are above the city Erbil, the abode of the exalted lady, the goddess Ishtar, and I made their courses straight.' The line of the conduit is marked by remains of wells at intervals of about 46 yards. As it approached Erbil, the water was conducted along an open cutting, whence it could be drawn off to the irrigation-ditches around the city. The entrance to the tunnel, in the river-bed, is faced with ashlar masonry on floor, walls, and ceiling. It is relatively narrow, to regulate the flow of water into the canal. Holes in the sides were doubtless to accommodate the ties which held wooden sluices in place. After rather more than 200 yards the width gradually increases to 270 cm (9 ft), and for the rest of its course only the floor and lower part of the canal-walls are faced with stone slabs. Erbil still depends entirely for its water upon great underground conduits.

The famous 'canal which brings abundance' similarly led water to Nimrud (Calah) from the Greater Zab 7 miles away; its entire course can still be traced. It was in use for centuries and was constantly repaired. Frequently a conduit had to be recut where the rock-tunnel had got hopelessly blocked. Adadnirari II (911–889 B.C.) says that he re-excavated a canal, the head of which 'had fallen into ruins, and for thirty years no water had flowed therein'. About 1240 B.C., an Assyrian monarch supplied his new royal city with a canal 'establishing the life of the land, bringing abundance', and records 'cutting through the low-lying places according to the cord [i.e. in a straight line], and carrying it through the difficult [i.e. steep] places of the high mountains through tunnels of rock'.

The Achaemenid kings of Persia (*c* 650–331 B.C.), who promoted agriculture in their own country, may also have been responsible for the introduction of subterranean water-tunnels elsewhere. The elaborate system of underground reservoirs in the oases of Kharga and Dakhla is probably to be attributed to them; their especial interest in these areas is attested by the temples they built, and is a clear indication of an increasing population with increasing agricultural needs. Similarly the system of vaulted conduits found throughout the Sahara from Tripolitania to Morocco, and generally regarded as Roman in origin, may be due to the Persians. The Greek traveller Megasthenes reported covered cisterns and aqueducts in north India about 300 B.C. [20].

In rocky, mountainous terrain, such as the Lebanon or Judaea, denudation or the scouring-off of humus by torrential rains raises a special problem. This has been met from highest antiquity by terracing. A series of retaining walls is built horizontally across the mountainside at different contours. Each levelled terrace is irrigated by ditches or channels leading from the main stream. The narrow coastal plain of Phoenicia was backed by orchards, olive-groves, and vineyards rising as high as 2500 ft. Wine from the slopes of Anti-Lebanon was exported to

Assyria and Persia. The hills of Samaria and Gilboa were also once famous for their productivity.

The planning of a piped water-supply within towns is linked with domestic drainage, and is discussed elsewhere (p 466). Elaborate systems for supplying water, carrying away rain-water, and removing sewage are found in the cities of the ancient East (figure 349).

FIGURE 349—*Pottery water-pipes from the palace at Knossos in Crete. Each pipe is tapered and fits with a collar into the mouth of the next, where it is cemented to ensure a watertight joint. Ropes threaded through lugs held the pipes yet more firmly together.*

VI. BASIN-IRRIGATION IN EGYPT

The Nile valley is unique as a rainless area which is also one of extreme fertility. Egypt, as Herodotus said and the Egyptians well realized, is truly 'the gift of the Nile'. Its alluvium is in continuous formation. 'Thou dost create the Nile in the underworld', chanted King Akhenaten (*c* 1375–1358 B.C.) to the Sun-god, 'and bringest it, according to thy will, to give life to the people of Egypt.' In the Pyramid Texts, the vegetation god Osiris is identified with Nile water. The Nile-god, 'Father of the gods', is early portrayed as a fat. swollen-breasted being, crowned with aquatic plants; vestiges of his worship still remain in Upper Egypt [21].

'Of all rivers, the Nile is the most gentlemanly.' It rises and falls with almost calendrical precision. The rise is perceptible in Egypt by the beginning of July. At first the river is greenish with vegetable scum from equatorial waters. About a fortnight later, muddy silt begins to arrive, and the river takes on a reddish tinge that was associated with the blood of Osiris, from whom new life would presently spring. As the flood swells and reaches the level of the surrounding fields, the dykes are breached and water covers the land to a depth of 6 ft or more. By September each village, protected by its dykes, stands like an island, and the shining expanse of water with archipelagos of trees and houses stretches from desert edge to desert edge (plate 20 B). The waters then begin to subside, and by the end of October the river is again between its banks. In the mild winter, when evaporation is slight, wheat germinates easily and the land is soon covered with lush green vegetation. The crops ripen, and the harvest is gathered by mid-April or early May. By the end of May the river is a shrunken stream, kept alive only by the more constant flow of the White Nile. The earth is now dry, and cracks in the fierce sun. Then, one magic night, the cycle begins once more. The 'Night of the Drop', when the celestial tear fell and caused the Nile to rise, is still celebrated on 17 June [22].

But Egypt was not always thus. In Palaeolithic times rainfall was heavier, and most of north Africa, now desert, was covered with vegetation. Decreasing rainfall drove men into the valley in search of food. Each year, as the flood spread over the land, they retreated to its edge; when the waters subsided, they gathered their small harvest of wild grasses or, when the lesson of agriculture had been learned, of plants raised from seed.

It may have been on the desert's edge, or in the alluvial soil of the mouth of a small wadi, that the first attempt was made to retain the flood by a barrier of stones and mud. A small gap was made in this dam, through which the flood might enter, and the hole closed with mud; when the ground was saturated, the water could be run off. The next step would be to run a dyke around an area not directly contiguous to the Nile banks, and then to add more dykes. Thus arose the Pharaonic system of basin-irrigation, whereby earthen banks parallel to the river were intersected by cross-banks dividing the whole valley into a checkerboard of dyke-enclosed areas of between 1000 and 40 000 acres each. Canals led the water to areas otherwise difficult to inundate. The system, still in operation in Upper Egypt, enables the flood-water to be run through regulated sluices into each basin in turn, flooding the land to a depth of from 3 to 6 ft. The water may be held for a month or more till the parched mud is thoroughly saturated. The surplus water is then drained to a lower level and returns to the Nile or to canals, and ploughing and sowing can begin.

Basin-irrigation has many advantages. No further watering is needed for a winter crop of wheat, barley, or flax; manuring is unnecessary, for the silt is rich in decomposed vegetable matter and phosphates; and artificial drainage is not needed, for the surplus is drawn off.

We do not know how much of Pharaonic Egypt was under cultivation. The first experiments in basin-irrigation may have been made to the east of the Nile, where the desert hills closely approach the river. A small bay at the foot of the hills could have been shut off by a bank parallel to the river; the attempt to enclose larger bays, farther from the river, would then lead to the construction of cross-banks as well, and as ever-greater areas were cleared of reeds and enclosed more arable land would become available for the growing population. A prince of Siut describes, for instance, how by digging 'a canal of 10 cubits' he 'made a water-supply for this city . . . which had never seen water, and made the high land a swamp'.

The tradition that Menes, the legendary first of the Pharaohs, dammed the

Nile to control the flood-waters reflects the care of the early monarchs for the building of dykes and the digging of canals. One of the earliest known historical reliefs is the ceremonial mace-head of the protodynastic 'King Scorpion'. He is cutting a dyke to inaugurate the inundation (figure 29), a ceremony still performed in the last century at the festival of the 'day of breaking the river' [22]. At all times, Pharaoh was the patron and promoter of irrigation and of agriculture. King Amenemhet I of Dynasty XII (*c* 2000 B.C.), claimed: 'I grew corn, I loved Neper the grain god; in every valley the Nile greeted me; none hungered, none thirsted during my reign.'

The early district-governors of the Old Kingdom had as their chief title 'Digger of Canals'. They were responsible for the upkeep of canals and dykes, for patrolling the banks when the waters reached their height, and for organizing aid when disaster threatened. For there were bad years, when too little or too much water came down. Failure of the Nile was rare but could be disastrous; the resulting famine would be long remembered. On the wall of the temple-causeway of King Unas of Dynasty V at Saqqara, a group of starving peasants is depicted; some are so weak that they are supported by relatives.

Efficient administration and husbandry might minimize the effects of a low Nile. From the correspondence of a man who held land both in Thebes and in the Memphis area, we hear of a famine in Dynasty XI which affected Lower Egypt, as was to be expected, more than the area round Thebes. He writes from Memphis giving instructions that the grain stored at Thebes against just such an emergency shall be rationed among his family. The duty of a prudent householder and of a wise chancellor was to hoard surplus grain against a lean year. The story of Joseph reflects an age-old problem. An inscription from Sehel (near Aswan), probably a Ptolemaic forgery, but purporting to be of the time of Zoser in Dynasty III, tells of a series of seven low Niles causing famine, after which the king, instructed by his magician-vizier Imhotep, sacrificed to the god of the cataract with satisfactory results.

An excessive inundation, when the contributions of the Blue Nile and the Sobat were larger than usual, spelt even greater danger. A state of emergency had to be declared, and every available man was called out to strengthen the dykes. Patrols watched for any dangerous cracks or seepage, for, once saturated, the banks of soil were liable to break up, and the flood, out of control, might drown land and even villages and cities. Exceptional floods in A.D. 1874 caused appalling loss of life, crops, and animals. In the third year of the reign of Osorkon II, about 867 B.C., the height of an abnormal Nile was recorded; a mark on the inner wall of the Luxor temple shows that the water lay 62 cm (2 ft) deep on the temple pavement itself. An inscription tells that: 'The flood [the word is the name of the god of the primeval waters] rose in this whole land; it invaded the two banks as at the beginning. The entire valley was like the sea, there was no dyke which could withstand its fury. All people were as water-birds or swimmers in a torrent . . . all the temples of Thebes were like marshes.' The god Amen was then brought out in his sacred bark and a high priest prayed to him to abate the flood.[1]

Though in theory the gods could control the annual inundation and bring blessing or disaster, it was not left to priestly petitions and royal intercessions to provide for what might come. A highly developed system of measuring the height of the Nile in various parts of the country enabled the daily rise to be compared with the records of past years. Thus the high watermark could be forecast with some accuracy. The 'nilometer' was usually a scale marked in cubits and fractions of a cubit on the walls of a quay, or on the outer wall of a temple flanking the river. There were at least twenty nilometers at intervals along the river valley. The earliest was perhaps that on the island of Rodah, a few miles south of modern Cairo. The nilometer must have been almost as old as the invention of writing and the ability to keep records, for Nile heights are recorded on the Palermo stone, but most of the extant nilometers are of the Persian, Ptolemaic, or Roman periods [23]. In these relatively late times, every considerable Egyptian temple had as an annexe its own nilometer, with a staircase sometimes leading straight down and sometimes, as at Edfu, descending spirally into a well. A scale was marked either on the steps themselves or on the wall beside them. Some were in direct communication with the Nile; others, farther from the river, received only infiltration water and were less reliable.

The maximum height of the inundation was noted annually in the archives of palace and temple. In official annals of the Egyptian kings there survive many records of heights reached by the Nile. Some, of Dynasty XII, are preserved on the rocks at Nubian Semna, by the Second Cataract, the farthest boundary of Egypt's southern possessions. Information from so far upstream could be sent post-haste to Egypt and preparations made in advance. The Semna station performed a function similar to that of the present-day nilometers at Khartoum and on the upper Nile, though telecommunication gives the engineer at the Aswan dam far longer to calculate the adjustment of his sluices. Apart from other inducements, the value of advance knowledge of the height of the inunda-

[1] An even higher flood in the reign of Taharqa (683 B.C.) was recorded by the Nubian king not as a disaster to Egypt—though the land became 'a primordial ocean, an inert expanse'—but as a blessing to Nubia where the unwonted rainfall brought an abundant harvest.

tion made the conquest of Nubia desirable, and led the Pharaohs to push even farther south. A series of Nile-levels of New Kingdom date is engraved on the quay of the great temple of Karnak. An almost unbroken series of Nile records for the 1300 years from the Arab conquest to the present shows that the silt deposited in the Nile valley has raised the land some 8 ft. On this reckoning, the level in Pharaonic times would have been about 20 ft lower than today. A favourable inundation in ancient times measured 28 cubits at Elephantine, 24 at Edfu, 16 at Memphis, and only 6 in the Delta. Pliny said that in his time 12 ells meant hunger, 13 suffering, 14 happiness, 15 security, and 16 abundance, but if the height exceeded 18 disaster followed.[1]

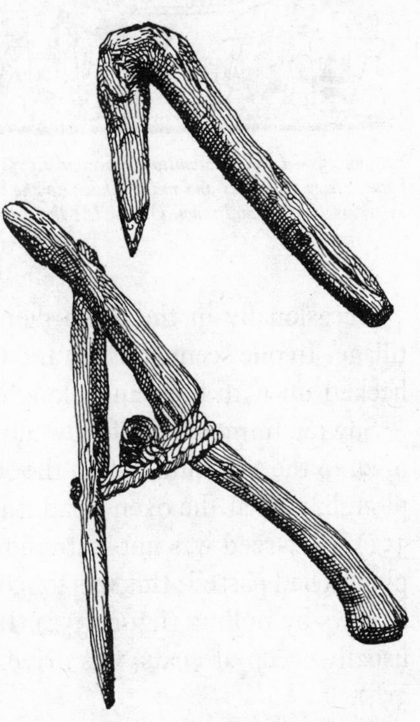

FIGURE 350—(Above) *A primitive Egyptian hoe cut from a forked branch, and* (below) *a more developed form with hafted wooden blade. Both Middle Kingdom.*

VII. PLOUGHING, SOWING, AND HARVESTING

As the flood subsided at the end of October, the deposit on the fields dried and the soil was immediately prepared for sowing. Originally, the ground was merely hacked up with a piece of wood with a projecting branch roughly lopped (figure 350). From this crude implement developed the typical Egyptian hoe, which is portrayed in the protodynastic period and underwent little change throughout Egyptian history (figure 350). The early plough was no more than a hoe drawn through the ground, perhaps first by a man with a rope, but already in the Old Kingdom by a pair of oxen. A man walked behind, driving the point of the plough into the ground (figure 43). Later a metal ploughshare was added, and the plough became a more solid affair. In the New Kingdom the handles were lashed by ladder-like cross-pieces, and the shaft was bound to a double yoke over the horns of the oxen, and attached to the base of the convergent handles. To lighten the ploughman's work, clods of earth were broken up by hoes or by long-handled mallets (figure 351).

[1] The well known Hellenistic statue of the Nile god in the Vatican holds a horn of abundance and is surrounded by sixteen children, each one cubit high.

FIGURE 351—*Land reclamation in ancient Egypt. On uneven ground watered by a pool a man is cutting down trees and bushes. Men with hoes and mallets hack up the rough ground and break the clods. The prepared soil is then ploughed by teams of oxen and sown. On the left the men's food stands ready and a thirsty labourer drinks from a waterskin. From a tomb at Thebes.* c *1420* B.C.

Occasionally in the tomb-paintings we see the reclamation of new land for tillage. In one scene, bushes and trees are cut down on uneven soil which is then hacked up with hoes and ploughed by oxen (figure 351).

Sowing immediately followed ploughing, for the furrows did not long remain open in the soft mud. Often the sower is shown scattering his seed in front of the plough, so that the oxen tread it in and the ploughshare drives it deeper (figure 351). Flax-seed was not scattered but shaken carefully into the furrows after the plough had passed; this was for convenience in gathering, since flax was harvested in rows by pulling (figure 352). Instead of the harrow, a small herd of animals, usually sheep or goats, was driven over the cornfield to tread in the seed (figure 353).

As the ears began to ripen, tax-inspectors came round to measure the fields for the annual assessment. Many New Kingdom scenes show high officials, their inconveniently long robes tucked up round their knees, inspecting a surveying-rope stretched between boundary stones (figure 354). A check was thereby kept on the position of boundaries, since the inundation often removed landmarks, and the ensuing litigation could be settled only by cadastral survey. The wealthy landowner could choose the time of ripening to inspect his crops. The shifting of a boundary stone was a misdemeanour especially condemned by moral teachings such as the text-book maxims attributed to the Egyptian sage Amenophis: 'Remove not the landmark on the boundaries of the sown, nor shift the position of the measuring-cord. Covet not a cubit of land, nor throw

FIGURE 352—*Pulling flax and binding it into sheaves. From the tomb of Hetepet, Old Kingdom.*

FIGURE 353—*Treading in the seed. Sheep are driven across the field to tread in the seed scattered before them by the sower, who here offers them a handful of corn to lure them on. From a tomb at Saqqara, Egypt.* c *2400* B.C.

down the boundaries of the widow. . . . Better a bushel that God giveth thee, than five thousand obtained by force' [24] (figure 355). With this teaching the reader may compare the Biblical passages in Deut. XIX. 14 and XXVII. 17, and Prov. XXII. 28 and XXIII. 10.

Then came the harvest. Sickles used to cut the corn had flint teeth set in a wooden or bone haft. From the simple straight reaping-stick of the Neolithic peoples of the Fayum, with which may be compared the bone and flint sickles of the Natufian agriculturists, evolved the curved sickles with a short hand-grip characteristic of the Dynastic period (figures 329 A, 356).

Metal sickles of rounder shape were common in the New Kingdom, when a new reaping technique was used. Instead of grasping the stalks and hacking through them farther down, the ears were cut off short by the stroke of a much sharper sickle, leaving longer straw. Instead of being bound in sheaves, and later tied on donkey-back, they were now gathered on their short stalks and thrown

FIGURE 354—*Surveyors measuring a field. From a tomb at Thebes.* c *1400* B.C.

FIGURE 355—*Taking the oath on a boundary stone. To surveyors inspecting the fields, the peasant says: 'I swear by the great god that is in heaven that the right boundary stone has been set up' (i.e. that it is still where it should be).* c *1400 B.C.*

loose into baskets or nets, to be carried on poles to the threshing-floor (figures 357–9).

VIII. PERENNIAL IRRIGATION IN EGYPT

Besides the staple field-crops grown on the land, a great variety of vegetables, flowers, vines, and fruit-trees were grown near the river, by the banks of canals, and in the gardens which the Egyptians loved. This vegetation needed constant and controlled watering during the drought of spring and summer. In early times the irrigation was done with pots dipped in the river, by means of a criss-cross of channels into which the water was poured (figure 360). Simple mechanical contrivances for raising water were devised. The shaduf (p 523) became in the New Kingdom the usual irrigating mechanism for gardens, and was used for flower-beds and vines as well as for date-palms, acacias, *Persea*, tamarisk, and other trees, standing each in its ring of banked earth (figure 344). The method was ideal for the cultivation of vegetables of which the Egyptians ate a variety (ch 11). They were fond of flowers, and garlands of lotus and other flowers were worn at parties. Nearly 200 species of flowering and sweet-smelling plants have been found in tombs.

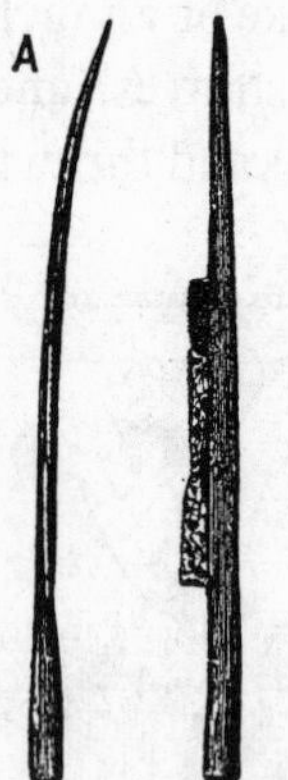

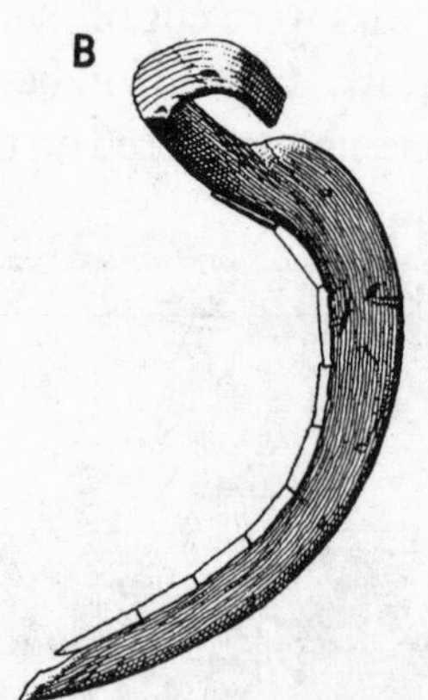

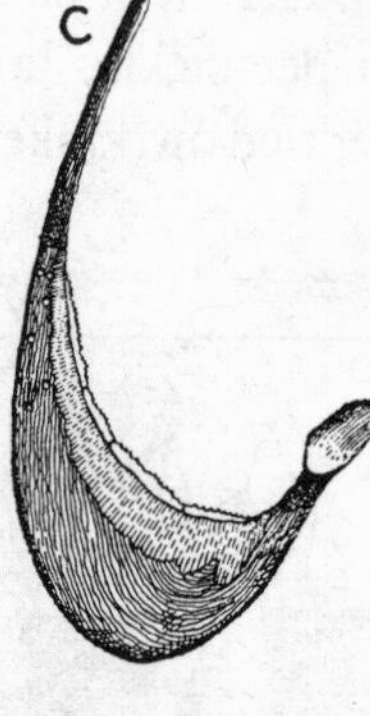

FIGURE 356—*Egyptian sickles.* (A) *Neolithic from the Fayum.* (B) *Dynasty I* (c *3000 B.C.*) *from a Saqqara mastaba.* (C) *Dynasty XII* (c *1900 B.C.*) *from Kahun. All are of wood and have serrated flint blades inset. Note the changing angle of grip. Scale 1/10.*

Pleasure-gardens along the river-front, formally laid out, had generally as a centre-piece a stone-edged pool in which fish swam and water-lilies floated. It was connected by a channel with the Nile. A small summerhouse usually faced the pool, and on either side were avenues of trees or arbours of vines which provided shady walks (figure 361). Country estates had larger gardens, in which fruit and vegetables were combined with more ornamental flowers and shrubs, while avenues of pomegranate and fig-trees (figure 362) led to palm-groves, vineyards, and orchards. The Pharaohs were horticultural connoisseurs. From their foreign campaigns they brought back exotic trees and plants to grow in their palace gardens or in the temples. For his new capital in the Delta, Rameses III (*c* 1200 B.C.) made 'great vineyards; walks shaded by all kinds of sweet fruit trees, a sacred way splendid with flowers from all countries, with lotus and papyrus as numerous as the sand'. The artists of Thothmes III carved the curious plants he had brought from Syria upon the

FIGURE 357—*Reaping corn in the New Kingdom. The harvesters cut the ears off short, leaving a long stubble, and throw them loose into a large net which they will carry on poles to the threshing-floor. From a tomb at Thebes.* c *1420* B.C.

FIGURE 358—*Winnowing and measuring the grain. The master watches in a pavilion while eight men on the threshing-floor toss the grain into the air with wooden scoops. Below, the husked grain is measured in bushels before being stored in the granary. From a tomb at Thebes.* c *1420* B.C.

FIGURE 359—*Harvesting corn in the Old Kingdom. After reaping, the ears are bound into sheaves and loaded on to donkeys. From a tomb at Saqqara.* c *2400* B.C.

FIGURE 360—*A garden of root vegetables. The gardeners carry pots slung across their shoulders from which they pour water into a checker-board of small runnels which irrigate the plot. Another ties onions (?) into bundles. From an early reproduction of a scene in a tomb at Beni Hasan, Egypt.* c *1900* B.C.

walls of the temple of Amen in Karnak, in whose garden he planted them (figure 363), while his aunt Hatshepsut, referring to a ship-load of living myrrh-trees from Punt, which she had planted for 'her father Amen' on the terrace gardens of her temple at Deir el-Bahri (figure 32), claimed: 'That which my fathers did not, I have done . . . I have made for him a Punt in his garden, just as he commanded me for Thebes. It is large for him; he may walk abroad in it.'

The irrigation and land-reclamation scheme carried out by Dynasty XII Pharaohs in the Fayum enabled perennial irrigation to be practised on a far larger scale, and presumably turned the depression into a market-garden where

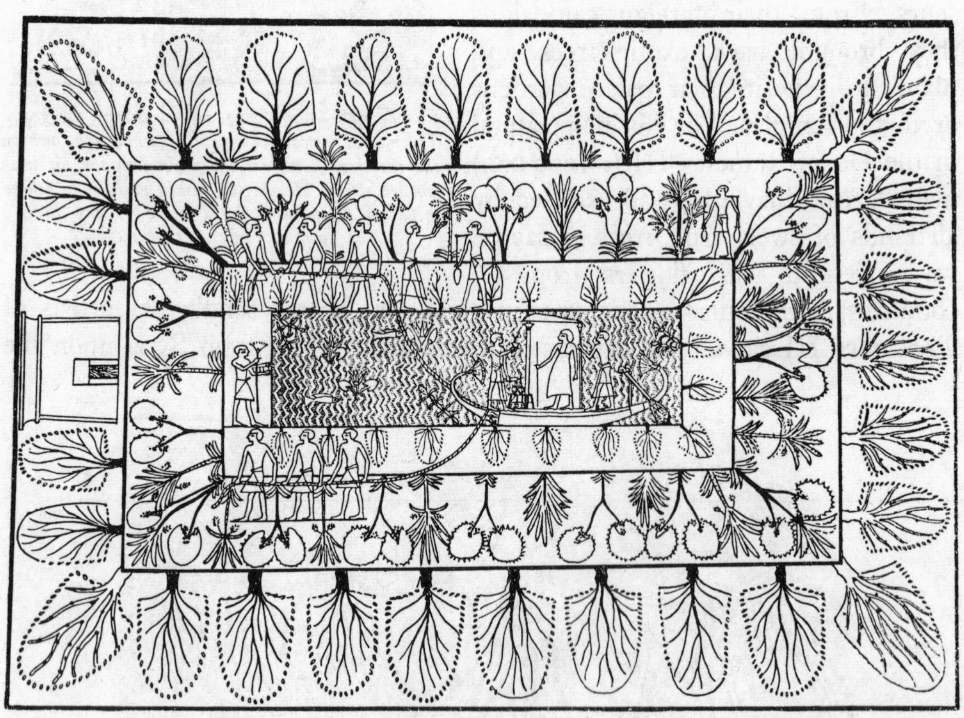

FIGURE 361—*A formal Egyptian garden. The lotus pool, on which the statue of the vizier Rekhmire is being towed in a boat, is faced at one end by a pavilion or summerhouse. Around the pool grow doum palms, date palms, acacias, and other trees and shrubs. From the tomb of Rekhmire at Thebes.* c *1450* B.C.

FIGURE 362—*Picking figs. Fig-gatherers collect the fruit in shallow baskets, helped or perhaps hindered by baboons in the fig-tree. From a tomb at Beni Hasan, Egypt. c 1900 B.C.*

cereal crops, as well as fruit and vegetables, may have been grown. Details are unknown, but the project apparently depended on a barrage with sluices which retained part of the inundation and returned surplus water to the Nile [25].

IX. PERENNIAL IRRIGATION IN MESOPOTAMIA

In the great alluvial river-valley of Sumer and Akkad temperatures are more extreme than in Egypt, varying between 30° F in winter and 120° F in summer. Rainfall is scarce, but less so than in Egypt, and, even in the south, January rains may afford a catch-crop of cereals. A greater difference lies in the régime of the rivers. The Nile is predictable almost to a day: not so the Tigris or Euphrates. They rise without warning, and on variable dates, the Tigris generally first at the beginning of March, and the Euphrates a week or so later. If the two floods coincide, or the snows in the highlands melt over-rapidly,

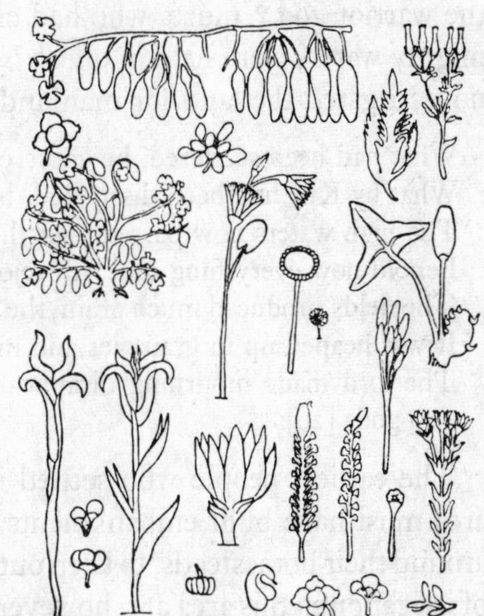

FIGURE 363—*An early botanical collection. Strange plants and seeds brought back from Syria by Thothmes III, as they were carved on the walls of the temple of Karnak, Egypt. c 1450 B.C.*

a huge volume of water sweeps down, and there is danger of floods; the rivers may burst their banks and inundate large tracts. Moreover these rivers carry five times the sediment of the Nile per gallon, so that canals tend to become choked and landmarks buried. They contain a considerable amount of salt in solution, necessitating constant drainage. The annual flood is in early summer, too late for the gentler spring warmth, and the waters recede in June, at the beginning of the hot season when the burning sun parches the ground, just when water is most needed; one prolonged saturation of the ground does not meet agricultural needs. The problem of irrigation in ancient Babylonia was therefore twofold—to retain and regulate flood-waters and to avert their dangers. Both had to be solved to ensure a constant supply to the fields during the burning days of summer and autumn and the intermittent rains of winter and spring; both called for a high degree of skill and organization.

Fear of flood was ever present with the Sumerians and their successors the Babylonians. Legend preserved the story of that greatest of floods which destroyed all but one of mankind, the Sumerian story from which the story of Noah derives. In the memory of every old man this story could be paralleled by some local disaster to lives and crops. Traces of ancient floods have been found on the sites of several ancient cities of Sumer. Kur, the dragon of the primeval waters, the fearful enemy of mankind, had, the story went, been conquered by the warrior god Ninurta who had created the world and made it habitable. The mighty waters were held in check by a great dam of stones, and the tamed flood now irrigated the land for mankind:

> What had been scattered, he gathered,
> What by Kur had been dissipated, he guided and hurled into the Tigris.
> The high waters now passed over the farmland.
> Behold now everything on earth rejoiced again at Ninurta, king of the land,
> The fields produced much grain, the harvest of palm-grove and vineyard was fruitful,
> It was heaped up in granaries and mounds.
> The lord made mourning disappear from the land, he made good the river of the gods [26].

The earliest people who settled in the lower valley of the Tigris–Euphrates area must have built embankments along the river near their homes, and dykes around their homesteads, to keep out the threatening waters. The ultimate origins of irrigation in this area are, however, still obscure. Canal-digging was among the most frequent activities of the rulers of the Sumerian city-states, and irrigation disputes were a constant cause of wars. The Euphrates, slower and more manageable than the Tigris, carries only half its volume of water and recedes more slowly into its bed, which, moreover, lies a little higher than that of the Tigris. This enables surplus water to be drained off into the lower river. It is in this south-western part of Iraq, this flat plain of mud and marshland, with its superabundant water, that the oldest city-sites of Sumer are found. The Euphrates has often changed its course during the centuries, sometimes through natural causes, occasionally by deliberate action, and often through neglect. Many once busy riverine ports with quays and wharves fronting river or branch-canal are now in the barren desert many miles from water.

The Sumerians from the beginning probably practised a simple form of perennial irrigation which entailed keeping the soil covered with a few inches of water from the sowing in November to the harvest in April or May. The success of such a scheme depends on a carefully regulated network of water-channels, with the land divided into fields, and the fields into small plots bounded by little parallel ridges forming the walls of temporary ditches. The permanent irrigation-ditches derive their water from feeder-canals, which in turn are supplied from main canals leading from the river itself or one of its branches. Water is allowed on to the plots in turn; a man with a hoe breaks a gap in the ridge-wall of the irrigation-ditch, allowing the water to cover the plot, or, in the case of root-vegetables, to fill the runnels between the ridges in which the crop is to be sown. When the irrigation of the plot is complete, it is drained, the mud put back to close the gap, and water admitted to the next plot, then to the next, and so on. Since by this method only a few inches of water are allowed on to the field at a time, very careful control of the supply is needed. This entails a system of regulator-sluices in the feeder-canals, and also some method of storing the surplus water which comes down in flood-time.

Little definite is known of the elaborate canal-system of Babylonia before Sassanian times (i.e. before the third century A.D.). Countless ruined canals, marked by great parallel lines of mounds, bear witness to a widespread ancient irrigation-system. There are many mentions of canal-building from the third millennium B.C. onwards in the records of the rulers of Sumer and Akkad, and later of the united country called Babylonia. Arab geographers of the ninth to fourteenth centuries A.D. describe the canals that in their day intersected the country, but many of these must have been built in Sassanian (A.D. 226–641) and even ʿAbbasid (A.D. 750–1258) times. We have no means of telling what area of Mesopotamia was under cultivation even under the Neo-Babylonian dynasty of the sixth century B.C., who left so rich a legacy to their Achaemenid conquerors (*c* 550–331 B.C.). Possibly the area brought under cultivation during Babylonian and pre-Babylonian times has been over-estimated. Yet we know that a series of great waterways intersected the area between the lower Tigris and the Euphrates, and that each city was surrounded by a network of canals which watered the surrounding district and brought prosperity to its people and dues to the local temple. Of the history of the most famous of all the ancient canals, the Nahrwan, which left the Tigris between Tekrit and Samarra, ran parallel to it, and irrigated the land along the left bank to a little above Kut, we know strangely little. This greatest canal of antiquity was 400 ft wide and over 200 miles long. Its construction must have involved extensive engineering works, including a great weir across the Tigris and numerous regulators, and perhaps some method of carrying the canal over two torrential rivers, though this is uncertain. We are ignorant also of the extent and position of the reservoir areas, of the construction of the regulating sluices on barrages, and of the extent to which levels and discharges were measured. There was no official annual record comparable to that of the nilometer readings, nor, because of the erratic behaviour of these rivers, could there be any but uncertain prediction of floods.

A canal-system for a large area demands careful design. At all points the working level of the water must be determined by hydrographic conditions, the nature of the soil, and the general conformation and contour of the land. To secure a flow, canals must run down a slight incline, and the surface of the banked water must be a little above the level of the land. If the slope is too steep, the fast flow will erode the banks; if too gradual, weeds and silt will choke the channels. Surplus water must be stored, and parcelled out in turn to the various holdings. The regulating sluices and embankments must be kept in repair, and the canals freed from silt throughout, for silting in one branch could cause rapid deterioration of a whole section. Once the flow is retarded, the channels become blocked, and the rejected water overflows its banks and floods the country-side, rendering the land useless. Neglect of the canal-banks produces a similar result. This happened during the Mongol invasions of the fourteenth century A.D., from which the country has not yet recovered. It may have happened, on a much smaller scale, in the Gutian period (*c* 2100 B.C.), when hillmen from the Zagros, unaccustomed to the techniques of irrigation in a river-valley, and only imperfectly in control of the country, brought temporary chaos to south Babylonia [27].

The conquest by Hammurabi (*c* 1760 B.C.) of the entire Tigris valley, and that of the Euphrates as far as Mari above ʿAnah, led to strong centralized control of irrigation and resultant prosperity. Several of the laws in his Code deal with irrigation: each man must keep his own part of the dyke- and ditch-system in repair, and in default must recompense the neighbouring farmers whose land has suffered by flooding. Royal letters to local governors show that each district was responsible for the upkeep of its own canals. To the governor of Larsa the king writes: 'Summon the people who hold fields on this side of the Damanu canal, that they may scour it. Within this present month let them finish

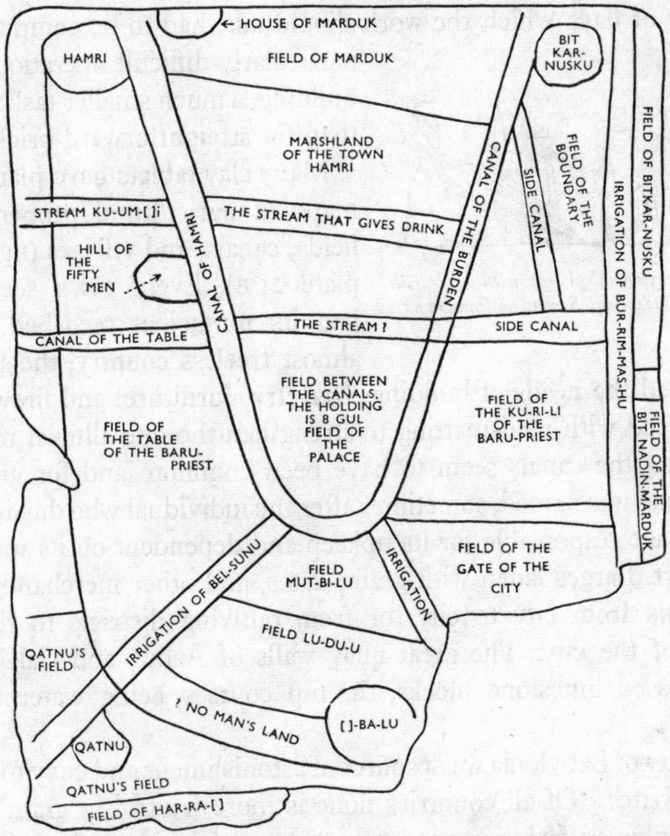

FIGURE 364—*Map of fields and canals near Nippur. This plan was probably made to show the position of the central field, part of the royal estate of a Cassite king. The cuneiform captions have here been translated. The main canal encloses the field in a parabola. Into it run other waterways. Six townships are shown. Note the 'Marshland of the town Hamri', where cane-reed would be cultivated. The unnamed spaces were perhaps common land for grazing. From a cuneiform tablet found at Nippur, Mesopotamia.* c 1300 B.C. (*The original is shown in plate 21 B.*)

it.' In another letter he complains that the bed of a canal has been imperfectly cleared, so that boats cannot enter the city of Erech. The governor must have the necessary work done within three days, with the men at his disposal [28]. The archives of the kings of Mari on the Euphrates, of about the same date, contain many letters dealing with the construction of canals and dykes, and the maintenance of the water-system throughout their kingdom.

Canal-digging and barrage-building employed large numbers of men. Practical mathematical problems were often set in which, given the dimensions of a canal and the 'task' of each man (that is, the volume of earth which he can shift in a day), the length of canal to be allotted to each, the number of men needed, or the number of days which the work should take had to be computed. For the particularly difficult operation of barrage-building, a much smaller task was assigned than for straightforward bricklaying.

FIGURE 365—*Babylonian plough with seed-drill. From a Cassite cylinder-seal. Second millennium* B.C.

Many clay tablets have plans or sketch-maps of agricultural property, showing fields, canals, and villages (figure 364 and plate 21 B). Every town seems to have had its municipal reed-bed, for, in an almost treeless country, the stout, pliable reeds supplied the needs of building, basketry, furniture, and firewood. Dykes were reinforced with reed-matting to strengthen the fine alluvial mud. Certain areas between the canals seem to have been common land for grazing. Each irrigation canal was named, sometimes after the individual who dug it, sometimes after the village responsible for its upkeep and dependent on its water for food and transport. Barges laden with grain, dates, and other merchandise travelled on the canals from city to city, or from outlying districts to the quays in the centre of the city. The great quay walls of Ashur and Calah [29] were built of dressed limestone blocks, the top courses being waterproofed with bitumen.

The fertility of Babylonia was a source of astonishment and envy to the Greeks. Herodotus writes: 'Of all countries none is more fruitful in grain', and states that the Babylonian farmer reaped two- or sometimes even three-hundredfold. Theophrastus (died *c* 287 B.C.) says that the harvest of Babylonia yielded up to a hundredfold, but sometimes more. The Babylonians sowed their seed-corn thickly, allowing $\frac{4}{5}$ bushel to an acre, so that a return of 30 bushels was not unlikely [30], and perennial irrigation allows two or even three harvests a year. Besides several varieties of barley, wheat, emmer, sesame, and flax were staple crops. The seed-plough was early in use (figure 365), and the making and repair of ploughs is frequently mentioned as a care of the rulers of Mesopotamia.

Gardens in Babylonia were usually planted with fruit-trees and flowering shrubs (figure 366). Vineyards are often mentioned, and must often have been large; in one case the number of vines is given as 2400 (p 282). Among the vegetables and herbs listed as growing in Babylonian and Assyrian gardens, or as used for culinary or medicinal purposes, are the beetroot, turnip, leek, garlic, onion, cress, mustard, radish, lettuce, aubergine, colocynth, cucumber, fennel, fenugreek, coriander, marjoram, rue, mint, rosemary, turmeric, ginger, and saffron (ch 14). Most gardens were designed to provide fragrance and coolness, with shrubs or trees like the mulberry, pomegranate, fig, quince, and lemon providing welcome shade from the burning sun, and couches set by running water channels. The so-called 'hanging gardens' of the royal palace of Nebuchadrezzar at Babylon, famous in antiquity as one of the wonders of the world, have been described by several classical writers, and remains of them have perhaps been found in the form of a vaulted building in the palace. If the identification be right, the garden 'hung' only in the sense that it was built over an arched cellar in which was a well, worked possibly by a chain of buckets or water-wheel which irrigated the garden. The cellar-roof was heavily waterproofed by layers of reed and asphalt, stone slabs, brick and mortar, and sheet lead. Over this was piled a deep layer of earth in which trees were planted. The whole building seems to have been roofed over and the garden was possibly surrounded by a two-storeyed cloister providing rooms in which the palace officials could work in a cool green shade, delightful in the heat and dust of a crowded city.[1]

FIGURE 366—*An Assyrian garden. A lioness lies asleep in a garden of date-palms and cypresses. Vines climb the trees, and lilies and sunflowers grow between. From a relief in the palace at Nineveh. Seventh century* B.C.

The most important tree in south Iraq, then as now, was the date-palm, said to have 360 different uses [31]. The wood served in building, the ribs for furniture, the leaves for basketry, and the fibres for ropes and nets, while the delicate green date-spathe provided a salad. The fruit is a staple diet—the Bedouin say 'Seven dates make a meal'. Dates, the poor man's food, were cheaper than bread. A Babylonian educational text contains an instructive dialogue between the tamarisk and the date-palm, in which the latter asks: 'The orphan, the widow, the poor man, what do they eat, when my sweet dates are scarce?' Their rich sugar-content preserves them well and makes them exportable. By-products of the date included a kind of treacle—still called by its ancient Babylonian name—and a jam. The stones provided charcoal or were pounded and eaten as flour and, in very arid regions, used as cattle-fodder; they are still fed

[1] From other evidence, the building may have been the palace granary.

to cattle around the Persian Gulf. A beverage is made by pouring water on macerated dates, which when fermented makes a wine (p 276).

Though the date-palm can be cultivated with a minimum of water, it thrives best with great heat and ample irrigation. The tree likes to grow, as the modern saying goes, 'with her head in hell-fire and her feet in the river'. Today the land around the Shatt al-'Arab, from Qurnah to the Persian Gulf, is ideal territory for it; the tidal waters, flowing up innumerable creeks, lap the roots of the trees. In such conditions, a young tree may bear dates three years after planting. The trees, being unisexual, were artificially fertilized from early times, the method of reaching the flower-heads by rope-sling being the same as today. A ruler of Mari on the Middle Euphrates records (seventh century B.C.) that he planted date-palms in his kingdom, possibly in an attempt at acclimatization, and Ashur-nasir-pal II (883–859 B.C.) grew them in his garden at Calah [32]. Date-gardens were mostly along the rivers; other fruit-trees such as pomegranates could be grown between the palms.

The Assyrians in the north of Mesopotamia, though their problems were somewhat different from those of their more anciently civilized neighbours in the alluvial south, must have learnt from them much about irrigation technique. The kings of Assyria, claiming each to be 'the shepherd of his people', to whom the gods have granted a 'favourable reign, years of justice, fertile rain, a mighty floodstream, and a good market price,' prided themselves, like the Babylonians, on the cutting of canals, and the encouragement of agriculture. Ashur-bani-pal (669–626 B.C.) boasted that in his reign 'Adad [the storm god] sent his rains, Ea [the water god] opened his fountains, the grain grew 5 cubits [i.e. 8 ft] on the stalk, the ear was $\frac{5}{6}$ of a cubit long; heavy crops and a plenteous yield made the fields constantly luxuriant, the orchards yielded a rich harvest, the cattle successfully brought forth their young.' In fact, so unusually heavy had the rainfall been that during his reign the reed thickets, planted by his grandfather Sennacherib (705–681 B.C.) to arrest the flow of his new canal below Nineveh and to provide building material, grew so tall and thick that countless lions now lurked in them and terrorized the country-side: 'Shepherds and herdsmen weep because of the lions, villages are in mourning day and night.'

Ambitious land-reclamation schemes, the creation of reservoirs in the mountains, the blotting out of a city by diverting the course of a river, or addition of land to a city by similar means are commonplaces in the annals of these capable and ingenious kings. They delighted in agricultural experiments. Perennial irrigation, unfamiliar in Assyria, was encouraged by the cutting of new canals. 'I had all the orchards watered in the hot season', says Sennacherib, 'and in winter, a thousand fields of alluvium around and below the city [of Nineveh] I had men water every year.' The Jerwan aqueduct mentioned above (p 531) was one of 18 canals constructed to bring water to his renovated capital. Perennial irrigation produced two crops a year, and since the population of Assyria increased

FIGURE 367—*An Assyrian park, watered by streams from an arched aqueduct. In the centre a path leads up the hillside to a royal pavilion and altar. From a relief in the palace at Nineveh. Seventh century* B.C.

enormously during the period of the Sargonids (722–612 B.C.) such a scheme greatly benefited the national economy.

When recording the cutting of a canal, an Assyrian king nearly always mentions the exotic plants which could thereby be acclimatized in his palace garden, or the orchards and vineyards planted for his own use or that of the gods. Tiglath-pileser I (1115–1102 B.C.), who extended his power to the Mediterranean, is one of the earliest to describe such an experiment. He says: 'I brought cedars, box-wood, and oak (?) trees from the countries which I have conquered, trees the like of which none of the kings my forefathers had ever planted, and I planted them in the gardens of my land. I took rare garden fruits, not found in my own land, and caused them to flourish in the gardens of Assyria.' The reconstruction of the Calah conduit enabled Ashur-nasir-pal to create a beautiful and fragrant garden in which he planted seedlings or shrubs collected during his campaigns in the Lebanon and Amanus mountains. Forty-two varieties of fruit-trees and sweet-smelling shrubs are enumerated: they include mulberry, pistachio, willow, tamarisk, pomegranate, medlar, pear, quince, plum, lilac, sycamore, fig, and frankincense. Besides his personal garden, 'the meadow-land by the Tigris

I irrigated abundantly and planted gardens in its area; I planted all kinds of fruits and vines and the best of them I offered to Ashur my lord and to the temples of my land' [33].

Sargon II (722–705 B.C.), made in his capital 'a park like to Mount Amanus, in which were set out every tree of the Hittite land, and the fruit-trees of every mountain', while Sennacherib's park, as well as containing 'trees such as grow on the mountains and in Chaldea', was experimentally planted with 'wool-bearing trees'—the first mention of cotton in antiquity. The Achaemenid kings of Persia had the same passion for creating royal parks. The 'paradise'—an ancient Persian word that comes to us by way of Hebrew and Greek and meant an enclosed park—was a feature of their royal residences.

In the book of Ecclesiasticus, Wisdom is made to say: 'I came out as a stream from a river, and as a conduit into a garden. I said, I will water my garden, I will water abundantly the soil of my garden. And lo, my stream became a river, and my river a sea.' Wisdom taught the peoples of the Near East the techniques of irrigation, and by long experience they perfected their skill; under their hand, the desert blossomed as the rose, and the hillsides became hanging gardens.

Postscript. The specialized knowledge of flood-control which the irrigation-engineers of Babylonia and Assyria had acquired by age-long experience could be turned to warlike purposes. The systematic ruin of an irrigation-system was one of the Assyrian methods of punishing a defeated enemy. Sargon II describes the fine irrigation-works of a city in Armenia, which he wrecked by damming the main canal and flooding the country. When Sennacherib of Assyria in his fury destroyed the hated Babylon, which had been responsible for his son's death, he pulled down temples and palaces and dumped the debris into the canals. 'Through the midst of that city I dug canals, I flooded the site with water, and the structure of its very foundations I destroyed. . . . So that in days to come, the site of that city and its temples and gods might not be remembered, I completely blotted it out with water-floods and made it like a meadow.' So wholesale was the destruction of the city, according to his son, Esarhaddon (681–669 B.C.), that 'the reeds and cane-brakes throve mightily in the midst [of the city] . . . the birds of heaven and the fish of the sea in countless numbers were found in it.' The task of repairing the damage, twelve years after, which fell to Esarhaddon, involved extensive land-reclamation before rebuilding could be attempted: 'I mobilized all the artisans of Babylonia. . . . Trees and reeds of the brakes they cut down with axes, they pulled up by the roots. The waters of the Euphrates I dammed, from [the city's] midst I shut them off, and into their former channels I directed them.'

The diversion of a river formed part of the great system of defences devised by the Neo-Babylonian kings (early sixth century B.C.) for their threatened capital. As well as massive multiple ramparts around the city itself, an artificial lake was constructed. Herodotus' description [34] of the long detour necessitated by windings of the river may reflect the complexity of the network of canals by which a stranger might travel to Babylon, but the flooding was deliberate engineering, and King Nebuchadrezzar's own words stress its defensive purpose:

'To strengthen the defences of Babylon, I had a mighty dyke of earth thrown up, above the other, from the bank of the Tigris to that of the Euphrates 5 *beru* [16 miles] long, and I surrounded the city with a great expanse of water, with waves on it like the sea, for an extent of 20 *beru*. That the pressure of water should not damage this dyke of earth, I fashioned its slope with bitumen and burnt brick.'

REFERENCES

[1] GARROD, D. and BATE, D. M. 'The Stone Age of Mount Carmel.' Brit. Sch. Archaeol. in Jerusalem, London. 1937.

[2] PIGGOTT, S. 'Prehistoric India', pp. 153 ff. Penguin Books, Harmondsworth. 1950.

[3] DELAPORTE, L. J. 'Catalogue des cylindres de style oriental', Vol. 2. 'Acquisitions', no. 156. Musée du Louvre, Paris. 1923.

[4] TREMAYNE, A. 'Records from Erech.' Yale Oriental Series, Babylonian Texts, Vol. 7. New Haven, London. 1925.
CONTENAU, G. (Ed.) 'Contrats N o-Babyloniens', Vol. 2, no. 182. Mus. du Louvre, Dép. Antiq. orient. 'Textes cunéiformes', Vol. 13. Geuthner, Paris. 1929.

[5] MURRAY, G. W. *Geogr. J.*, **94,** 97, 1939.

[6] HERODOTUS III, 5–9. (Loeb ed. Vol. 2, pp. 7 ff., 1921.)

[7] MALLOWAN, M. E. L. *Ill. Lond. News*, 20 July 1951, figs. 15, 16.
Idem. Iraq, **14,** 13, 1952; **15,** 19, 1953.

[8] BEADNELL, H. J. L. 'An Egyptian Oasis: An Account of the Oasis of Kharga in the Libyan Desert', pp. 186 ff. Murray, London. 1909.

[9] PETRIE, SIR (WILLIAM MATTHEW) FLINDERS and MACKAY, E. J. H. 'Heliopolis, Kafr Ammar and Shurafa', pp. 39 ff. and Pl. XLVI. Egypt. Res. Acc. and Brit. Sch. Archaeol. Egypt, Publ. 24. London. 1915.

[10] DUSSAUD, R. *Monum. Piot*, **25,** 133, 1921–2.
BROSSÉ, L. *Syria*, **4,** 234, 1923.

[11] THOMPSON, R. CAMPBELL. *Archaeologia*, **79,** 114, 1929.

[12] LAMON, R. S. 'The Megiddo Water System.' Univ. of Chicago, Orient. Inst.: Publ. 32. Chicago. 1935.
BARROIS, A. *Syria*, **18,** 237, 1937.

[13] *Idem.* 'Manuel d'archéologie biblique', Vol. 1, pp. 228 ff. Picard, Paris. 1939.

[14] WACE, A. J. B. 'Mycenae; An Archaeological History and Guide', pp. 47, 98, 104, and fig. 35. Princeton University Press, Princeton. 1949.

[15] DRIVER, G. R. and MILES, J. C. 'The Assyrian Laws', pp. 309 ff. Clarendon Press, Oxford. 1935.

[16] THOUMIN, R. *Bull. Étud. orient.*, **4**, 1, 1934.
[17] CATON-THOMPSON, G. *Geogr. J.*, **93**, 18, 1939.
[18] MAZLOUM, S. 'L'ancienne canalisation d'eau d'Alep.' Documents d'Études orientales de l'Institut français de Damas, Vol. 5. [Damascus. 1936].
[19] SAFAR, F. *Sumer*, **3**, 23, 1947.
[20] STRABO XV, C.707. (Loeb ed. Vol. 7, p. 82, 1930).
[21] DARESSY, G. *Rev. égyptologique*, Paris, **9**, 364, 1912.
[22] LANE, E. W. 'Manners and Customs of the Modern Egyptians', chap. 14. Ed. E. RHYS. Everyman's Library, Dent, London. 1908.
[23] BORCHARDT, L. 'Nilmesser u. Nilstandsmarken.' *Preuss. Akad. Wiss., phil.-hist. Abh. nicht zur Akad. gehör. Gelehrter*, no. 1. Berlin. 1906.
[24] GRIFFITH, F. LL. *J. Egypt. Archaeol.*, **12**, 204, 1926.
[25] CATON-THOMPSON, G. and GARDNER, E. W. *Geogr. J.*, **73**, 20, 1929.
[26] KRAMER, S. *Mem. Amer. philos. Soc.*, **21**, 80, 1944.
[27] SMITH, SIDNEY. *J. R. Asiat. Soc.*, 296, 1932.
[28] KING, L. W. 'The Letters and Inscriptions of Hammurabi', nos. 71 and 5. Semitic text and translation series, Vols. 2–4. Luzac, London. 1898–1900.
[29] ANDRAE, W. 'Das wiedererstandene Assur', p. 119. Deutsche Orientgesellschaft, Neunte Sendschrift. Hinrichs, Leipzig. 1938.
MALLOWAN, M. E. L. *Iraq*, **15**, 38, 1953.
[30] CAVAIGNAC, E. 'Population et capital dans le monde méditerranéen antique.' Publ. de la Fac. des Lettres de l'Univ. de Strasbourg, fasc. 18, p. 23. Strasbourg–Paris. 1923.
[31] POPENOE, P. B. 'Date growing in the Old World and the New.' West India Gardens, Altadena, California. 1913.
DOWSON, V. H. W. 'Dates and Date Cultivation in Iraq.' Agricultural Directorate of Mesopotamia, Memoir no. 3. Cambridge. 1921.
[32] WISEMAN, D. J. *Iraq*, **14**, 30, 1952.
[33] *Idem. Ibid.*, **14**, 24, 1952.
[34] HERODOTUS I, 185. (Loeb ed. Vol. 1, p. 230, 1920.)

BIBLIOGRAPHY

BRÄUNLICH, E. 'The Well in Ancient Arabia.' Asia Major, Leipzig. 1925.
BREASTED, J. H. 'Ancient Records of Egypt' (4 Vols and Index). University of Chicago Press, Chicago. 1907.
BROMEHEAD, C. E. N. "The Early History of Water Supply." *Geogr. J.*, **99**, 142, 183, 1942.
BROWN, SIR (ROBERT) HANBURY. 'Irrigation, its Principles and Practice as a Branch of Engineering' (3rd ed.). Constable, London. 1920.
CATON-THOMPSON, G. 'Kharga Oasis in Prehistory.' Athlone Press, University of London. 1952.
CLARK, J. G. D. "Water in Antiquity." *Antiquity*, **18**, 1, 1944.
DARESSY, G. "L'eau dans l'Égypte ancienne." *Mém. Inst. égypt.*, **8**, 201, 1915.
FISH, T. "Aspects of Sumerian Civilisation during the Third Dynasty of Ur, iii, Rivers and Canals." *Bull. of the John Rylands Library*, Manchester, **19**, 90, 1935.
FORBES, R. J. "Overbevloeiing in de Oudheid." *Ex Oriente Lux, Jaarber.* **1**, v, 431, 1937–8.
HARTMANN, F. 'L'agriculture dans l'ancienne Égypte.' Imprin. réunie [Geuthner], Paris. 1923.
IONIDES, M. G. 'The Regime of the Rivers Euphrates and Tigris.' Spon, London; Chemical Publishing Company of New York, New York. 1937.

JACOBSON, T. and LLOYD, SETON. 'Sennacherib's Aqueduct at Jerwan.' Univ. of Chicago, Orient. Inst.: Publ. 24. Chicago. 1935.

LANE, W. H. 'Babylonian Problems'. Murray, London. 1923.

LEIBOVITCH, M. J. "Gods of Agriculture and Welfare in Ancient Egypt." *J. Near East. Stud.*, **12**, 73, 1953.

LUCKENBILL, D. D. 'Ancient Records of Assyria and Babylonia'. University of Chicago Press, Chicago. 1927.

MACKAY, E. J. H. 'Early Indus Civilizations' (2nd ed. of 'The Indus Civilization' revised and enlarged by DOROTHY MACKAY). Luzac. London. 1948.

SOUSA, A. 'Iraq Irrigation Handbook—Part I, The Euphrates.' Ministry of Works, Directorate of Irrigation, Baghdad. 1944.

THOMPSON, R. CAMPBELL. 'A Dictionary of Assyrian Botany.' British Academy, London. 1949.

WILLCOCKS, SIR WILLIAM and CRAIG, J. J. 'Egyptian Irrigation.' Spon, London; Spon and Chamberlain, New York. 1913.

WILLCOCKS, SIR WILLIAM. 'The Irrigation of Mesopotamia' (2nd ed.). Spon, London; Spon and Chamberlain, New York. 1917.

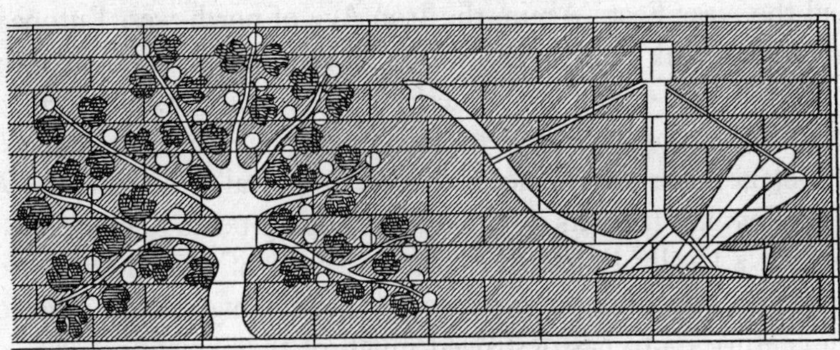

Assyrian seed-plough and fig-tree. Khorsabad. c 700 B.C.

20

MINING AND QUARRYING

C. N. BROMEHEAD

I. THE STONE AGE

As with all the technical accompaniments and results of civilization, no classification by dates can be of any scientific value: reference must be to culture-stages. In the north and west of Europe everything considered in this section is prehistoric, and referable to the Stone, Bronze, and Early Iron Ages; but even Middle Bronze Age technique there (say about 1400 B.C.) may be contemporary with work that already has centuries of written history behind it in Egypt and the Near East. Again, the Iron Age of north-west Europe was later than that of the Greek and Roman world. As an extreme example of this necessary convention, coal-mining by American Indians has been described both as 'prehistoric' and as 'of the seventeenth century A.D.'. Fortunately, classification by culture-stages nearly coincides with a geographical arrangement: 'Westward the course of empire takes its way', and in so doing tends to obliterate the early work on such a locally restricted object as a vein of metallic ore. So, too, at Laurion, near Cape Sunium in Greece, zinc-mining in the nineteenth and twentieth centuries A.D. has destroyed much of the ancient work of the silver mines of the sixth century B.C., though happily not before records of the facts had been made.

Stone Age mining for flint is well exemplified at several localities in England, of which, perhaps, the most famous is Grimes Graves on the Norfolk–Suffolk boundary. The object of all such mining was to obtain nodules of flint of the type most suitable for making implements—axe-heads, knives, borers, arrow- or spear-heads, and the like. At Grimes Graves, the bed of flint sought for is known as the floor-stone. In the side of a glacially cut valley the beds have been distorted, and the floor-stone has been brought from a depth of about $1\frac{1}{2}$ metres to within a few centimetres of the surface. From this outcrop it was followed by mining (figures 368–9).

The earliest pits were shallow, with no galleries. They were cut with bone picks, constructed mostly from the long bones of the ox, though one is from a human femur. The marks found on the sides of the pits fit the picks, many of

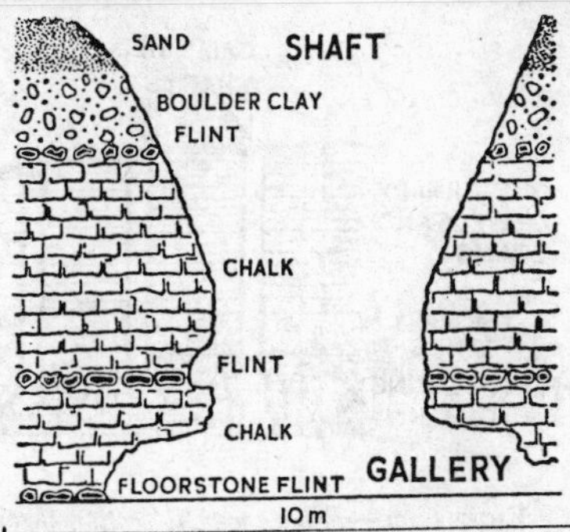

FIGURE 368—*Section through pit no. 1, Grimes Graves flint-mines, East Anglia.*

which have been found *in situ*. These workings are attributed to Late Palaeolithic times. The subsequent shafts of Neolithic man reach as much as 10 m in depth, and are provided with galleries which follow the floor-stone. Layers of inferior flint in these shafts were ignored by the ancient miners who cut through them.

At Spiennes, in Belgium, similar shafts occur over an area of 2–3 hectares; they are mostly from 9 to 12 m deep and 60 to 80 cm in diameter. The chalk here contains several layers of flint, of which the sixth from the surface is the most desirable. When the fifth seam is reached in the shaft, a chamber is excavated 1·8 to 3 m in diameter and 1·2 to 1·5 m in height, the desired bed serving as a floor. Thus there is formed a typical bell-pit resembling those dug for coal in the north of England as late as the nineteenth century. From this chamber, radiating galleries are driven, which sometimes connect with those from neighbouring shafts (figure 370).

At Cissbury in Sussex, and at Champigneulles in France on the left bank of the Moselle, sump-holes to collect rain-water have been recognized near the foot

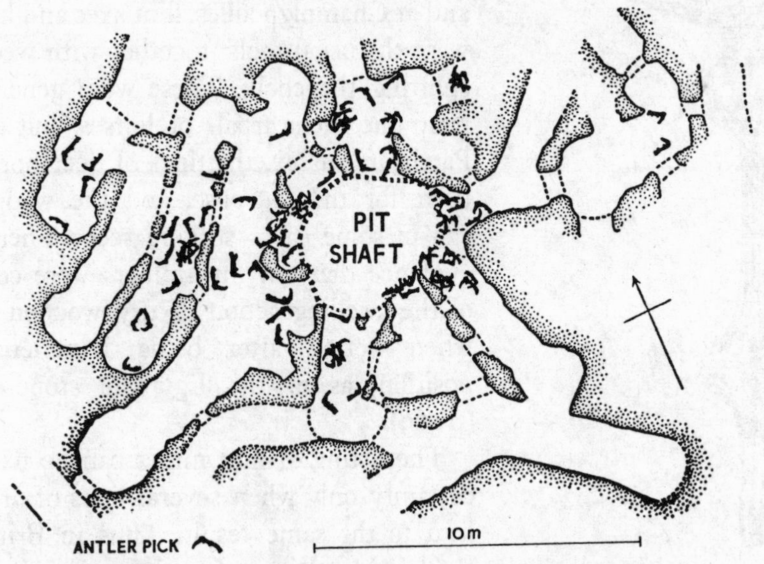

FIGURE 369—*Galleries radiating from pit no. 2, Grimes Graves. The floor of the shaft is about 9 m below ground-level.*

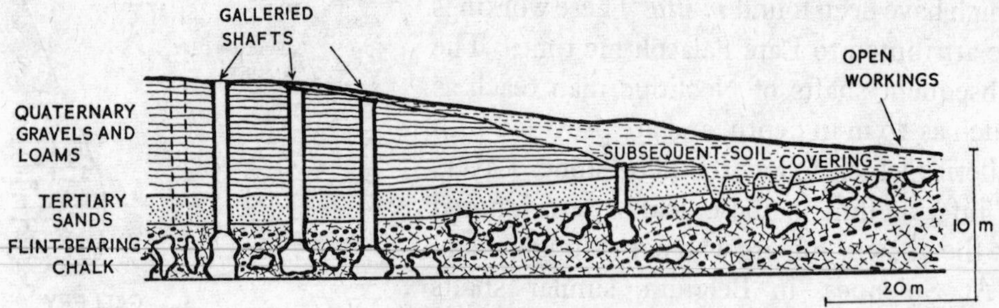

FIGURE 370—*Diagrammatic section through the flint-mines at Spiennes, Belgium, showing the earlier open workings and the later shafts and galleries.*

of some Neolithic mining shafts. Thus the principle of mine-drainage was already followed.

In making the shafts and galleries, a variety of tools was used (figures 371–2). At Obourg, in Belgium, only horn picks occur; the skeleton of a miner buried by a fall of roof held such a single-handed pick (figure 373). The works here were mostly opencast, with occasional tunnels from one trench to the next. The flint is of a quality suitable for making long knives and scrapers, but not axes. One polished axe-head has been found, but the material has been identified as coming from Spiennes. There, and at Champigneulles, flint axes and hammers were the usual tools, together with wedges for splitting the chalk. These were generally cut from the metacarpals of horses, but at Black Patch, in Sussex, the tines of deer-horns were used for this purpose, and the wedge-holes can in some cases still be seen. There is no evidence that any flint-miners were cognizant of the swelling action of dry wooden wedges when wetted after being hammered into position, as in the Egyptian stone-quarries (p 569).

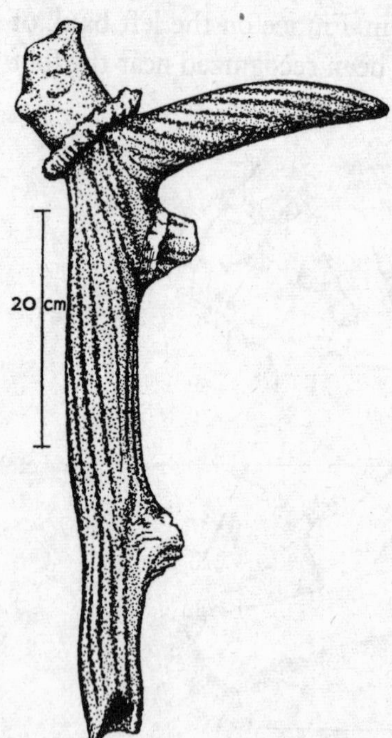

FIGURE 371—*Deer-antler pick from Grimes Graves.*

The dating of flint-mines can be fixed with certainty only when several lines of argument lead to the same result. Thus in Britain the shells of molluscs, found in the shafts and galleries, indicate a climate damper than at present, and datable, in geological terms, as the earliest Holocene (Post-glacial).

On the technological aspect some warnings are necessary. It is certain that form alone is by no means always a safe guide to the age of flint implements. At Spiennes, for instance, were it not for geological considerations, the artifacts from the lower levels might be supposed to represent an Early Palaeolithic culture. In fact they were not made before the Neolithic, although this backward group then passed rapidly through typical stages corresponding to Chellean, Acheulian, and Mesolithic (*tranchet* technique) stages. Finally, in the upper levels, they took to polishing their implements. It is only natural that, in chipping tools out of such material as flint, the same form may be produced repeatedly at different epochs, so that, in dating such implements, form cannot be relied on without full considerations of geological conditions. At Black Patch, the flint tools include types comparable to Acheulian ovates, Mousterian tortoise-cores, Thames picks, etc., yet all are certainly Neolithic.

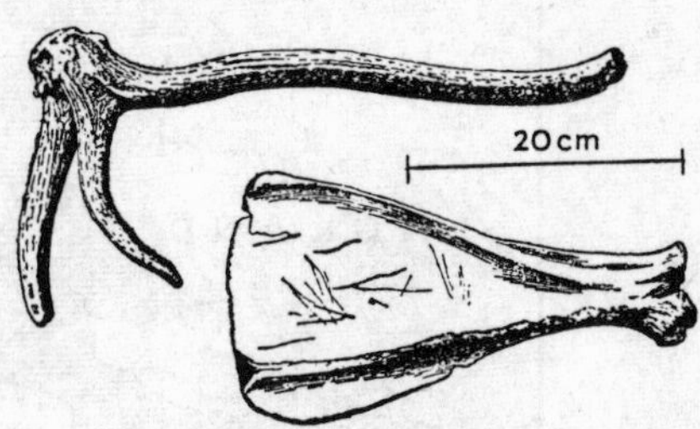

FIGURE 372—*Antler rake, and shovel made from the shoulder-blade of an ox. Harrow Hill flint mines, near Worthing, Sussex.*

At Grimes Graves certain of the shafts were sunk through working-sites on which much earlier (Mousterian) man had chipped his tools. Thus some Palaeolithic tools and chips found their way to the bottom of the shafts. This gave rise to the false idea that such remains were contemporary with the actual mining. However, the mining here had in fact ceased before the Bronze Age, though

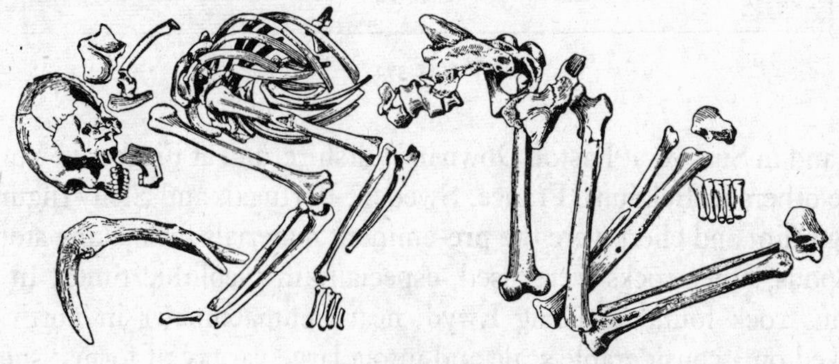

FIGURE 373—*Skeleton of a flint-miner crushed by the collapse of a gallery as he worked with his antler pick. Obourg, Belgium.*

nearby was an Iron Age settlement, the inhabitants of which had actually collected and used Palaeolithic implements.

Besides those mentioned above, flint-mines are known in Britain at other sites in

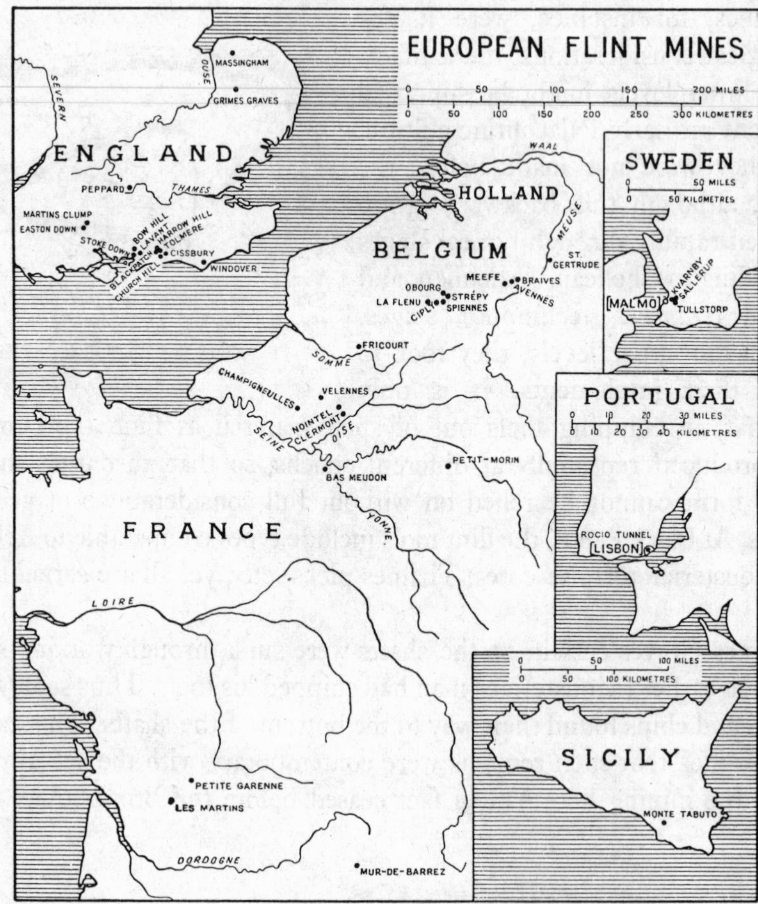

FIGURE 374

Norfolk and in Sussex, at Easton Down in Wiltshire, and at Fimber in Yorkshire; there are others in Belgium, France, Sweden, Portugal, and Sicily (figure 374).

Though flint and chert were the pre-eminent materials for making stone tools and weapons, other rocks were used, especially in Neolithic times. In Britain an igneous rock found at Craig Lwyd, near Penmaenmawr in north Wales, was worked on a considerable scale and into a large variety of forms; specimens have been found as far away as Wiltshire and the coast of Essex. In the south of

England some polished stone celts can be recognized as made from rocks found in Brittany. In the volcanic regions of the Mediterranean, obsidian, a natural glass, was used, just as modern bottle-glass is used by Pacific Islanders and Tierra del Fuegians, whose culture is still in some respects in the Stone Age.

II. EARLY MINING FOR COPPER

The earliest metal worked by man was undoubtedly gold, followed closely by native copper and tin.[1] The earliest method of obtaining supplies was by washing alluvial deposits. Such workings are preserved only in exceptional circumstances. The tools occasionally found in them cannot as a rule be more than roughly datable. They would mostly be of wood, and an oaken shovel used in, say, 1500 B.C. differs but little from one used in A.D. 1500.

Gold and tin from Britain were reaching the eastern Mediterranean early in the Middle Bronze Age. At Carnon, in Cornwall, in a tin-bearing stratum in the river deposits, a horn pick was discovered. It was in two parts: the beam had been pierced just above the burr and a dressed tine inserted, presumably fastened by a thong or sinew. A similar tool from Nointel in France can be dated to the Early Bronze Age. The Carnon pick was accompanied by a human skull, a wooden shovel, and horns. These objects lay far below present sea-level, and also below a layer of oyster-shells *in situ*. In stream-works at Pentuan, in south Cornwall, relics of human occupation were found some 12 m below the surface, and also below a stratum yielding the remains of an extinct whale (*Eschrichtius robustus*). Carey, in his 'Survey of Cornwall' (1598), says that in his time picks of holm (holly), boxwood, or hartshorn were found daily among the refuse of old workings. In nearly all the old tin-streamings blocks of stone, with cup-like hollows caused by their use in pounding the larger lumps of ore, have been found at varying depths. Many bronze axes have also been found.

No doubt many centuries elapsed between the first working of alluvial ores and the development of underground mining to extract these ores from their original position in lodes. However, even within the limits of the Bronze Age, great advances were made.

There is evidence that copper was in use among the Sumerians of southern Mesopotamia as early as 3500 B.C., and that it had become common by 3000 B.C. The metal was obtained from Asia Minor (where certain ores contain the same impurities as are found in the metal objects), from Armenia, and from Elam. Much later, similar sources supplied the Assyrians. Assyrian traders, who had their agencies in Asia Minor early in the second millennium, bought 'bad' (black)

[1] For another opinion, see p. 597.

copper and 'good' (refined) copper, the former being about half the price of the latter. The ingots were in the shape of ox-hides. The peaks of production in this region fall between 2400–2000 B.C. and 1500–1200 B.C. The Assyrians also derived copper from Urartu (Ararat), the metal frequently figuring in the booty recovered from the campaigns waged in this turbulent mountain district; for instance, Sargon II lists 126 tons of crude copper and hundreds of daggers, lance-heads, and vessels among the spoils of war. The miners of the more remote Caucasus supplied the tribes of the Caspian steppes, and for a time even traded with the Danube valley.

Copper was worked in many parts of Egyptian territory from Dynasty III (*c* 2600 B.C.) onwards, the Egyptian knowledge of the metal being later than, and almost certainly derived from, that of Sumeria. It is estimated that something like 10 000 tons were produced over about 1500 years. Some copper-mines are known in the Eastern Desert of Egypt, but by far the greatest quantity came from those of the Sinai peninsula, which are often mentioned in inscriptions and texts. Although these mines were first worked for turquoise to be used as an ornament, crucibles, slag, and copper objects prove that smelting of the ore was already practised in predynastic times. In the historic period, copper was won from Sinai by state expeditions, with soldiers to guard against the desert-dwellers. Production at the oldest mines in the Wadi Maghara continued (with a break between Dynasties V and XI) to *c* 1750 B.C. From 1600 B.C. onwards, mining was concentrated in the neighbouring region of Serabit el-Khadim, until it ceased about 1200 B.C., by which time Egypt had come to depend upon imports from Cyprus and Armenia.

Most of the shafts in these mines are horizontal, and follow the veins some 40–50 m into the rock. Miners' huts, temples, fortified camps, and heaps of waste mark the sites. The miners mainly used stone tools, as copper ones were probably too soft. Smelting was carried out on the spot, but the refining of the metal took place in Egypt.

Another important copper-mining centre is known in the Arabah between the Dead Sea and the Gulf of Aqaba. The mines were worked from the Early to the Middle Bronze Age, and again between the eighteenth and the thirteenth centuries B.C. by the Edomites. Later still, they supplied Solomon and other kings of Israel, and continued to be worked intermittently up to Arab times. Mining here was by the pillar-and-stall method; some of the pillars still show thin veins of ore.

A magnificent description of all the methods used in Bronze Age mining is preserved in Job XXVIII. This poem is considered to be based on the copper-mines just mentioned, and on the neighbouring Egyptian mines in Sinai. It is now dated about 400 B.C. Most translators, in ignorance that fire-setting was a normal mining technique for some 3000 years, insert the words 'as it were' in the statement that 'underneath it [the earth] is turned up by fire'. As amended according to our knowledge of ancient mining technique the passage may be read thus:

Surely there is a mine for silver | And a place for gold which they refine.
Iron is taken out of the earth, | And bronze is molten out of the stone.
Man setteth an end to darkness | And searcheth out to the furthest bound
The stones of thick darkness and of the shadow of death. | He breaketh open a shaft away from where men sojourn;
They are forgotten of the foot that passeth by; | They hang afar from men, they swing to and fro.
As for the earth, out of it cometh bread; | And underneath it is turned up by fire.
The stones thereof are the place of sapphire | And it hath dust of gold.
That path no bird of prey knoweth | Neither hath the falcon's eye seen it.
The proud beasts have not trodden it | Nor hath the fierce lion passed thereby.
He putteth forth his hand upon the flinty rock; | He overturneth the mountains by the roots.
He cutteth out passages among the rocks, | And his eye seeth every precious thing.
He bindeth the streams that they trickle not | And the thing that is hid bringeth he forth to light.

In Cyprus, copper-mining began in the second half of the third millennium B.C. Both the oxide and the sulphide ores found here were in full use and supplying Egypt during Dynasty XVIII (*c* 1580–1350 B.C.). A large tribute was sent from Cyprus to Thothmes III. The mines, which also supplied Troy, Crete, and Greece, were still famous in Homeric times (*c* 1000–800 B.C.). They show huge mounds of mining debris and slag.

In Europe, copper-mines belonging to the Bronze Age are known in Austria, Germany, France, Spain, Portugal, Greece, southern Russia and, above all, in the Tirol. There, the mines of Mitterberg seem to have been worked from about 1600 B.C., in the Bronze Age, to the Hallstatt period of the Iron Age, about 800 B.C. The occurrence of native copper in the valley of the Tisa, in north-eastern Hungary, may have led to the recognition of the ores. Many relics have been found there. Both shafts and adits were driven, and ventilation was provided by two or more shafts connecting with a single level; these shafts were 1–2 m in diameter. Access was gained by tree-stems with notches cut to form a ladder (figure 375). Similar tree-ladders were used well into the seventeenth century A.D. in Europe, and much later at the Sado gold-mine in Japan. At

Mitterberg there was also timbering in the galleries, which were up to 100 m in length. Where the walls were soft, they were revetted with moss and clay squeezed between the boards, exactly as in the more primitive of the gem-stone mines in Burma today. In one or two cases, horizontal passages have been cut in the rock in search of a lost vein. Fire-setting was used to split the hard rock, water being sometimes poured on the heated surface to hasten the action. Water was introduced, if necessary, by launders (troughs) of hollowed half tree-stems and by buckets. The tools were mostly of cast bronze. Illumination was by torches—not yet by the typical miners' lamps of classical times. Bronze hammers were used to crush the ore in the mine. This was graded or sieved in wooden riddles, with hazel-twigs to form the meshes, and brought up in leather bags and wooden troughs. A windlass with three spokes has been found. On the surface, the ore was pounded with small hammer-stones but not, apparently, ground. It was then panned in two-handled vans (shovels).

FIGURE 375—*Reconstruction of a copper-mine at Mitterberg in the Tirol. Fire-setting is being used to break up the rock face.* c *1600–800* B.C.

III. MINING IN THE IRON AGE

For the Early Iron Age, we have a group of mines which have been fully explored at the type-locality for their period, Hallstatt. They are salt-mines; we may note that much salt from this district was later used in the cementation of metallic ores, as described by Pliny. The salt occurs in beds in Triassic rocks and is still worked. There are also masses of exceedingly tough anhydrite (calcium sulphate), which are now dynamited; the early miners were forced to work round them.

Sloping shafts were driven, entering the ground at angles from 25° to 60° to the horizontal. Timbering was used, but the climate was drier than today and the danger from flooding less. When a rich mass of salt was encountered, galleries were driven in various directions according to the yield. The greatest distances worked were 390 m horizontally from adit-mouth, and 100 m below the surface. Large chambers were opened in the salt; one of them, 12 m broad and averaging over 1 m in height, had been carefully timbered.

The tools found were bronze picks and chisels, some of which still had their wooden hafts (figure 376). Wooden mallets were used for pounding the salt, which was then shovelled into leather sacks to be taken out of the mine and carried to the valley. Lamps have not been found, but bundles of twigs were used

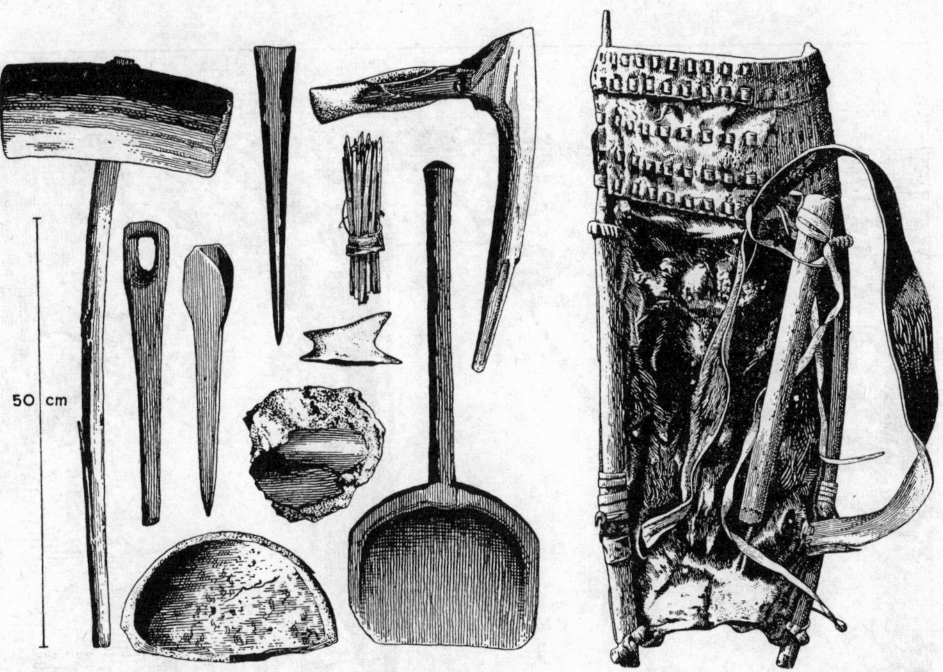

FIGURE 376—*Mining tools and a rucksack from the Early Iron Age salt-mines at Hallstatt, Upper Austria.*

for torches. A platter of maple wood shows that the men had meals below-ground. There are also miners' clothing, caps, and shoes with laces. The skeleton of a miner crushed by a fall of roof was found *in situ*.

At Hallstatt nothing has been revealed of any system of ventilation, which seems essential, and the waste material has mostly vanished. The wastage of tools must have been enormous, for even nowadays a miner may use ten steel picks in an eight-hour shift. The foundries where the bronze picks were cast or recast have not been found.

Copper-mines of the Iron Age, of the La Tène period at Burgas in Bulgaria, include an opencast 50 m long by 40 m deep, and rows of shafts 8 to 15 m apart. A vein of malachite (basic cupric carbonate), which yields over 9 per cent of copper, was completely worked by fire-setting.

Iron ores are so widely distributed and so often available at the surface that it was seldom necessary to mine them. Thus the story of the development of iron is mainly metallurgical (ch 21). An exception is at Velem St Vid in Hungary, a well-known Bronze Age site. Here ores of copper and antimony had long been worked opencast, to make antimony-bronze. At a considerable depth, chalybite

FIGURE 377—*The unfinished obelisk at Aswan, Egypt.*

(siderite, iron carbonate) was mined. Furnaces near by, datable to the Hallstatt period of the Iron Age, were used to smelt this ore.

Great advances in mining technique were made by the Greeks and Romans, but the early methods long survived, as they do even today among primitive tribes. Moreover, the object of technical improvements is to produce the desired results with less labour, and in some countries, and some periods (not excluding the present), labour by condemned criminals or prisoners of war has been available at no expense beyond the minimum sustenance. In such circumstances a reversion to the old techniques has often taken place.

IV. QUARRYING

Methods of quarrying stone are closely allied to those of mining; indeed, some stone is mined from well beneath the surface, so as to produce blocks of uniform shape and large size. Evidence of the technique used in the past, is, however, rare. Even where quarry faces have not been removed by working in subsequent ages, natural weathering has usually destroyed the tool-marks. For direct evidence we are almost confined to Egyptian work in the desert. Though many of the building stones used in ancient Egypt were worked intensively in Ptolemaic and Roman times, there are a number of quarries which have remained untouched for more than 3000 years. Even before actual quarrying began, round about 2800 B.C., natural boulders had been dressed to suitable shapes; the tools used were mostly of chert, a substance closely allied to flint. The extraction of blocks from the solid rock required the use of metal tools, first of copper, then of bronze, and finally of iron.

On the methods of quarrying we have learnt much from the study of the incompletely quarried obelisk at Aswan (figure 377). This granite block, 42 m long, if successfully extracted would have weighed about 1 200 000 kg. Cleopatra's Needle is about 22 m and weighs 190 000 kg, but two obelisks of the Roman period preserved in Rome are estimated to weigh 1 160 000 kg. The Aswan block had been abandoned because of cracks, found when the sides were cut. A much smaller obelisk was marked out on the surface to avoid the cracks; the outline can be seen in a suitable light, but it also had to be abandoned. The upper surface has been dressed flat by pounding with balls of dolerite, 12 to 30 cm in diameter and of average weight 5·5 kg. It was on this surface that the form of the obelisk was marked. The guide-lines can still be seen, as can also a trench nearly a metre wide all round which was then sunk. There are no marks of chisels or of wedges in the trench, though both were in constant use in the same quarry. Wedging and chiselling can be seen where a corner has been cut to allow the top of the obelisk to pass, when the time should come to move it. Chisel-dressing is better shown on an unfinished sarcophagus near by. The wedges were probably of metal, with thin plates now known as 'feathers' hammered in between the wedge and the stone. Dry wooden wedges may have been used elsewhere, but here the holes have a wide splay: if wooden wedges had been used and then wetted in order that their expansion might split the stone, some would certainly have jumped out, and it was important with such huge blocks to avoid irregular strains.

The trench round the obelisk was made by pounding the stone with the dolerite balls, almost certainly shod on rammers. Experiments with this method have been made, and estimates reached of the number of men that could be spaced to work on it simultaneously, and of the rate of progress. It was thus possible to calculate the minimum time required for cutting out an obelisk of this size. The results agree closely with that recorded for an obelisk at Karnak, namely 8·8 months against 8 months, the dimensions being: total height 30 m, base 3 m square, weight about 330 000 kg. Close behind the incomplete obelisk at Aswan is the place from which another has been removed. After the trench was completed it was undercut by the same method, but cracked loose just before work from the two sides met. Investigations at Aswan were carried out by R. Engelbach (1888–1946), who set an example for archaeologists by taking with him an experienced foreman from the Italian marble quarries and consulting him on all practical points.

The Egyptians sometimes worked limestone blocks in the same way as the granite obelisk, by trenching round. They took out stone in regular lifts, and made galleries in those of the best quality. Cracks were not followed, but a layer of stone was left on each side of a crack; these now stand up as walls with fissures along them. Saws were used—copper blades fed with sand or set with emery teeth. Faced stones were dressed with marvellous accuracy; a granite sarcophagus of 3350 B.C. has a surface like ground glass, and the parallelism of the sides is true to a very high degree of exactitude. Dolerite, quartzite, schist, and green breccia are among the other rocks used. Roof-slabs of limestone go back to at least 3000 B.C.

BIBLIOGRAPHY

ANDREE, J. 'Bergbau in der Vorzeit' in HAHNE, H. 'Vorzeit', Vol. 2. Kabitzsch, Leipzig. 1922. (Bibliography).

BROMEHEAD, C. E. N. "The Evidence for Ancient Mining." *Geogr. J.*, **96**, 101, 1940. (Does not include mining in Britain).

Idem. "Geology in Embryo." *Proc. Geol. Ass., Lond.*, **56**, 89, 1945. (Bibliography, but the work does not include mining in Britain.)

Idem. "Practical Geology in Ancient Britain." *Ibid.*, **58**, 345, 1947; **59**, 65, 1948. (Bibliography.)

CLARK, G. and PIGGOTT, S. "The Age of the British Flint Mines." *Antiquity*, **7**, 166, 1933. (Good bibliography for all Europe.)

DAVEY, J. G. "Turquoise in the Sinai Peninsula." *Trans. R. geol. Soc. Cornwall*, **16**, 42, 1928.

DAVIES, O. "Bronze Age Mining round the Aegean." *Nature*, **130**, 985, 1932.

EDWARDS, I. E. S. 'The Pyramids of Egypt.' Penguin Books, Harmondsworth. 1950.

ENGELBACH, R. 'The Problem of the Obelisks.' Fisher Unwin, London. 1923.

GLUECK, N. "King Solomon's Copper Mines." *Ill. Lond. News*, 7 July 1934.

HAWKES, C. F. C. 'The Prehistoric Foundations of Europe to the Mycenean Age.' Methuen, London. 1940.

LUCAS, A. 'Ancient Egyptian Materials and Industries' (3rd ed.). Arnold, London. 1948.

MAHR, A. 'Das vorgeschichtliche Hallstatt' (Führer durch die Hallstatt Sammlung des naturhistorischen Museums in Wien). Vienna. 1925.

PETRIE, SIR (WILLIAM MATTHEW) FLINDERS. 'Researches in Sinai.' Murray, London. 1906.

RICHARDSON, H. C. "Iron Prehistoric and Ancient." *Amer. J. Archaeol.*, **38**, 555, 1934. (Good general summary.)

SANDERS, H. "The Use of the Deer-horn Pick in the Mining Operations of the Ancients." *Archaeologia*, **62**, 101, 1910. (Bibliography covering Europe and the Stone, Bronze, and Iron Ages.)

TAYLOR, J. DU PLAT. "Mines where the Mycenaeans got their Copper, discovered in Cyprus." *Ill. Lond. News*, 24 February 1940.

WARREN, S. H. "The Neolithic Axes of Graig Lwyd, Penmaenmawr." *Archaeologia Cambrensis*, **77**, seventh series **2**, 1, 1922.

Wooden water-trough used in the copper-mines of Mitterberg. c 1600–800 B.C. Diameter 47 cm.

21

EXTRACTING, SMELTING, AND ALLOYING

R. J. FORBES

I. BEGINNINGS OF METAL-WORKING

THE discovery of the extraction of metals gradually brought the Neolithic culture to an end. For many centuries while men still relied on stone, bone, and wood as the materials for their tools, they made some use of native metal (gold, silver, copper, and meteoric iron) for decorative purposes and for small objects such as pins or fish-hooks. The vast possibilities of metal-working were as yet unrecognized; metallurgy proper began only when it was realized that, by smelting, heating, and casting, metal could be given new and controlled forms beyond the scope of the older techniques of chipping, splitting, cutting, and so forth. Only with advancing knowledge could the distinctive plastic properties of metals be exploited, and a critical stage was reached when the connexion between metals and ores, some of which had previously been collected as semi-precious stones, was clearly established.[1] This occurred late in the fourth millennium B.C. Native metal—except gold—is rare in the Near East, so that it was only after processes of extraction had been developed there that metals came to have any important effect upon technology [1].

Within about a thousand years of the discovery of extraction-processes, the simple metallurgy of gold, silver, lead, copper, antimony, tin, and the alloy bronze was mastered, and casting techniques had been established. It is very doubtful whether a true Copper Age preceded a Bronze Age (p 588). It is more probable that, from the first, the pure metal and the alloy were used indiscriminately and without clear distinction. The Iron Age began only after a long series of experiments had established a new set of processes and tools. The slagging of iron ore, the handling of the hot metal, and the techniques of carburizing, quenching, and tempering, all had to be acquired before steel—which alone is more useful than the metals previously known—could be produced. Archaeological evidence indicates that these discoveries had been accomplished by *c* 1400 B.C. (p 592).

In the first use of native metals the material was shaped by cutting, bending,

[1] Compare the Greek *metallao*, to search; thence *metalleia*, searching for metals, prospecting, mining; and *metallon*, place of searching, mine, quarry.

and hammering with a stone hammer on a stone anvil. In the second stage, extraction-methods were used to produce the metal from its ore, but the same methods of working were used. The first makers of any considerable metallic object must have made one of the most important observations in metallurgy: that a metal mass as it is worked up to the desired shape grows hard under continued hammering, but may be restored to its original condition by reheating.

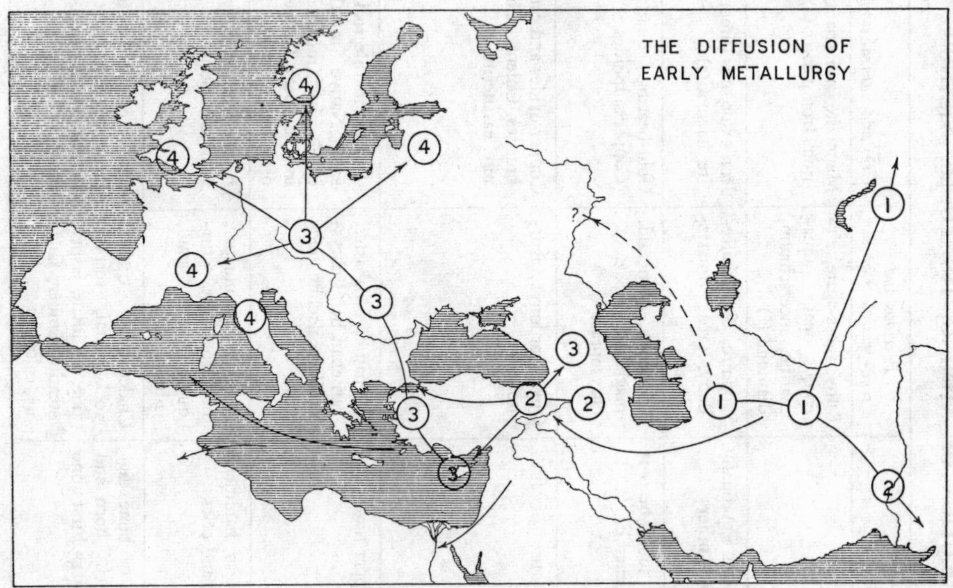

FIGURE 378—*A time-sequence showing the spread of metal technology from central Asia to Europe in four stages.*

This process of annealing must be repeated at frequent intervals if the working is prolonged. When moulds were used to cast implements in a roughly finished state, the necessity for prolonged forging was removed, and implements could be made more cheaply and quickly. But, whether made by cold-working or by casting, the physical properties of the metallic object were mainly determined by the composition—accidental or controlled—of the alloy used, rather than by its treatment.

With the addition of iron to the useful metals a more complex situation arose. Before the introduction of the blast-furnace in the Middle Ages the product of iron smelting was simply wrought-iron, which, though very tough, is too soft to give a better edge than copper or bronze. With prolonged heating in contact with charcoal, however, the surface of a wrought-iron object is converted into steel by diffusion of carbon. The properties of steel (iron containing 0·15–1·5

Table III. Outline of the Evolution of Mining, its Tools, Methods, and Products

Period	*Mining methods*	*Mining tools*	*Precious and semi-precious stones*	*Ores and natural stone*	*Metallurgical methods*
Late Iron Age (500–50 B.C.)	Mechanical drainage, transport, and ventilation	..	Ruby, moss-agate, zircon, opal, aquamarine, meerschaum, diamond (?)	Magnetite and spathic iron. Iron pyrites (?)	Brass from copper and calamine. Higher shaft-furnaces
Early Iron Age (1200–500 B.C.)	Drainage adits. Large quarries	Iron tools gradually supersede others	Sapphire, blue chalcedony, rose quartz, spinels	Iron oxide ores (limonite, haematite)	Wrought iron 'steeled'. Quenching and tempering
Metal Age II (2200–1200 B.C.)	Shafts timbered. Drainage by pails, etc. Wider galleries	Copper tools become more general	Bloodstone, emerald, magnesite, topaz, chrysoprase	Gold-bearing quartz. Copper sulphides	Short shaft-furnaces. Bellows. More general roasting of sulphide ores
Metal Age I (3000–2200 B.C.)	Systematic stripping of outcrops. Shafts with steps (?). Old galleries filled with gangue	General use of fire-setting	Onyx, sardonyx, azurite	Copper oxides and carbonates. Galena, stibnite, cassiterite	Silver from galena. Oxidation and reduction by natural blast. First wrought iron from magnetite. Copper alloyed with lead, antimony, and tin
Egyptian Predynastic (3500–3000 B.C.)	Developments of square and round shafts with galleries. Ventilation. Propping	First copper tools	Haematite, alabaster, carnelian, beryl, chrysocolla, malachite, feldspar	Alabaster, marble, rock-salt. Native metals (gold, silver, meteoric iron, copper). Copper ores from outcrops	Hammering, melting, casting. First reduction of copper oxides
Neolithic (to 3500 B.C.)	Quarries, stone slabs. Open workings, sloping shafts. Later, galleries	Stone picks, hammers, chisels, and celts	Amethyst, fluorspar, nephrite, jet, turquoise, lapis lazuli, jade, agate	Granite, diorite, limestone, sandstone	..
Palaeolithic	Search for boulders, etc. Open workings, conical pits	Wooden or bone digging-sticks, horn and antler picks. First stone tools	Chalcedony, quartz, rock-crystal, serpentine, obsidian, jasper, steatite, amber, jadeite, calcite	Flint and obsidian. Later, ochre and other natural pigments, emery	..

Table IV. Chronological Chart of Early Metallurgy

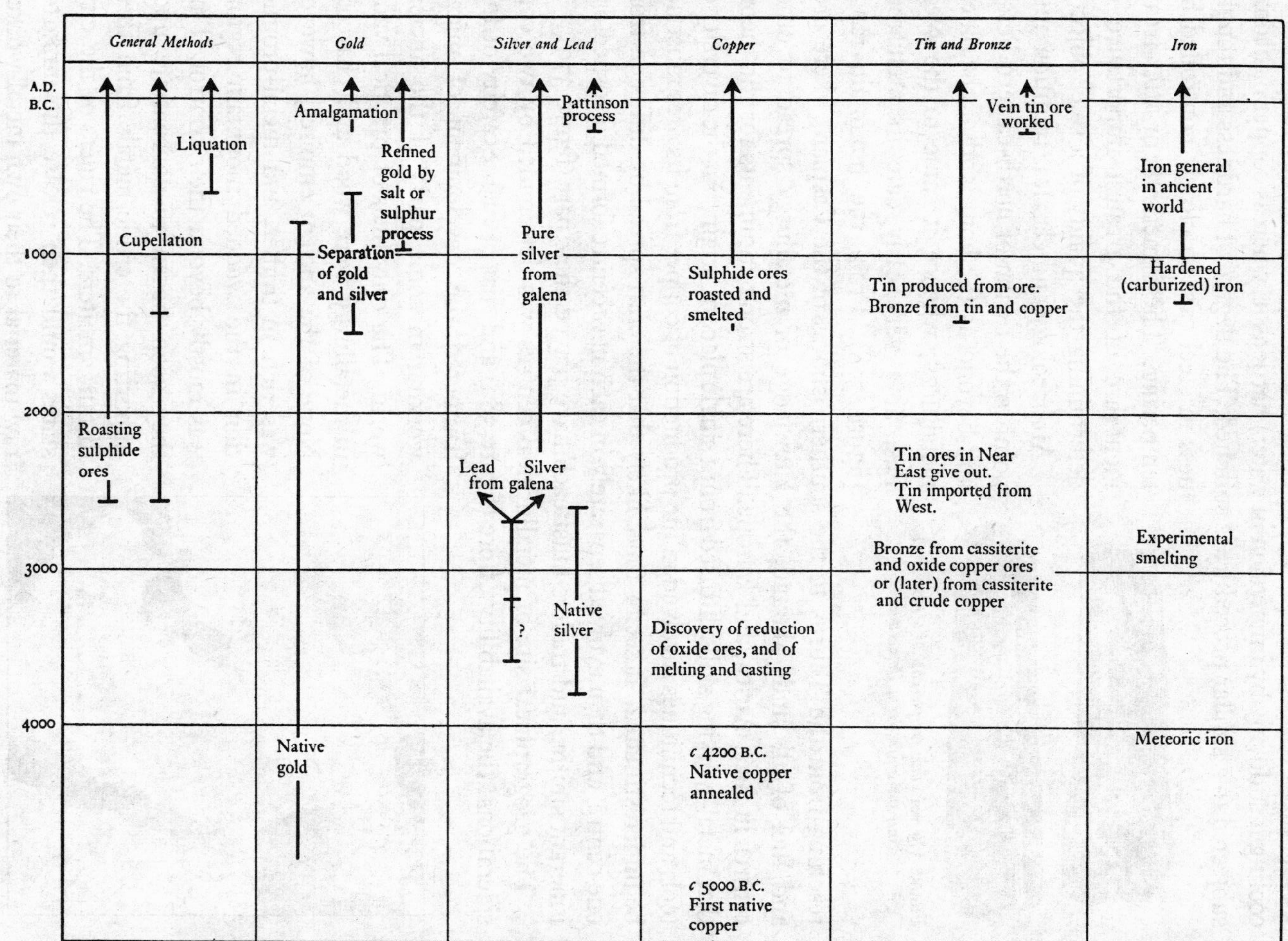

per cent of carbon) are very different from those of the non-ferrous metals. Thus, quenching steel (that is, raising it to a suitably high temperature and cooling it suddenly by immersion in water) hardens it, whereas copper or bronze subjected to a similar procedure is softened. The degree of hardness and toughness in steel can be closely controlled by tempering. These methods of after-treatment are of the greatest importance in determining the quality of a steel object.

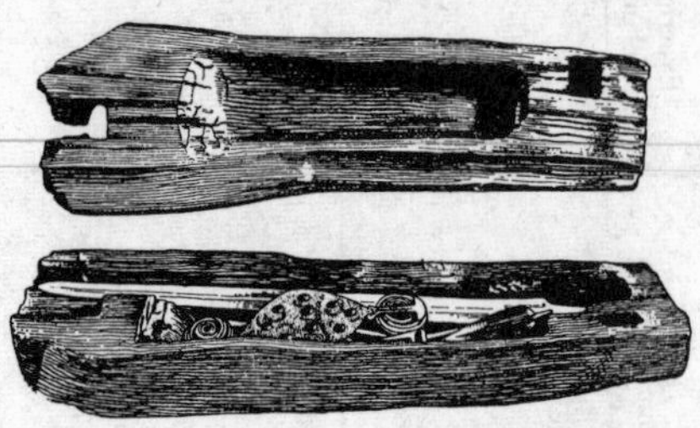

FIGURE 379—*An oak sample-case of a Bronze Age itinerant smith, from Pomerania.*

Archaeology and classical tradition alike point to the region of north-eastern Persia and beyond as the homeland of the oldest metallurgy, whence it came to the Near East at a very early date in prehistory (figure 378). From the mountain range reaching from the Taurus to the southern shores of the Caspian, where ores and fuel of all kinds abound, the knowledge of metallurgy spread to other centres in Asia, Africa, and Europe. There are strong arguments for the theory that metal-working skills diffused from a single place of origin, but the diversity of tools and techniques involved in the production of copper from its ores must not be underestimated. It seems more likely that the craft spread by diffusion from one centre, and then evolved separately in each new centre formed. Prospectors, itinerant smiths, and traders must each have played their part (figure 379).

The geographical site of metallurgical centres was determined by two considerations: the availability of ore (figure 380) and that of fuel. Scarcity of fuel hampered the development of metal-working in some parts of the ancient world. The only fuels of practical value in metallurgy were wood and charcoal. None of the ancient empires, however, was rich in timber, and metal-production in the wooded mountain regions was mostly beyond their control. Thus they soon began to concentrate upon importing the crude metals from these distant smelters. The rulers of the city-states would then release the imported raw material to their own metal-workers for finishing.

FIGURE 380

For the efficient extraction of metals from their ores some form of furnace is needed and, for certain purposes, the fire must be forced by draught. In the simplest operations of smelting, the pieces of ore are mixed in layers with the fuel, and the metal is afterwards collected in a lump from the hearth. An ancient form of the simplest type of furnace, still used by primitive peoples, consisted of a clay-lined or stone-lined hollow in the ground. Later, this bowl-furnace was used mainly for the first roasting, while smelting proper was done in a more elaborate structure. To conserve heat, the upper lip of the bowl might be curved inward, holes being bored at the base for tapping metal and admitting draught. This pot-furnace was still completely buried in the earth. By erecting stone walls around the bowl, and converging them into a chimney, a shaft-furnace was evolved; the bowl became its hearth.

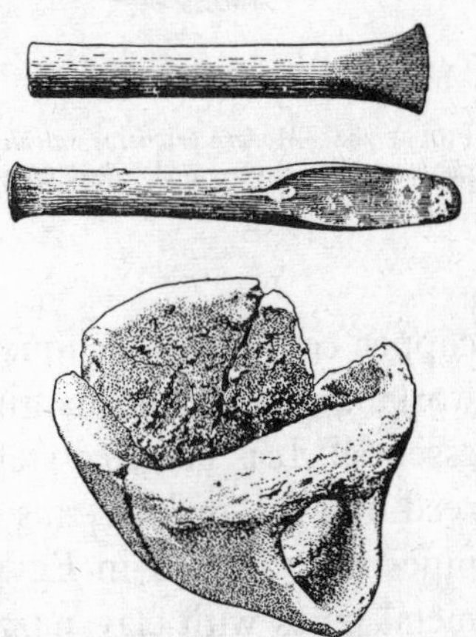

FIGURE 381—*Egyptian copper chisels and pottery crucible.* c *1300 B.C.*

The art of building shaft-furnaces of stone, lined with refractory clay, came into Europe from the eastern Mediterranean toward the end of the Bronze Age. Other types of furnace had long been used in the Near East for baking and glazing pottery (pp 391 ff), baking bread, glass-making, and so on, and doubtless there were evolutionary relationships between the different types. Among them, the metal furnace was a late arrival; indeed, it has been suggested that the first observation of the reduction of copper ore was made while vitrifying cupreous glazing-pigments in a pottery-kiln. Copper ore can be smelted at *c* 800° C, and copper metal melted at 1083° C, temperatures which were certainly attainable in the ancient pottery furnaces.

In larger furnaces, especially with a forced draught, non-ferrous metals could not only be smelted from their ores, but prepared in a molten state suitable for casting. For such purposes as refining the precious metals or making fine castings, it is undesirable that metal and fuel should be in contact. To avoid this, the metal was melted in a crucible of refractory clay, or a mixture of clay and sand (figures 381–3). A pottery-furnace or a bowl-furnace would yield the required temperature. The next stage would be to build the crucible into the structure of the furnace itself, but furnaces designed to protect the melt entirely from the action of the fuel and the products of combustion seem to be unknown in antiquity.

The history of forced draught is obscure. Without it, metals such as gold and

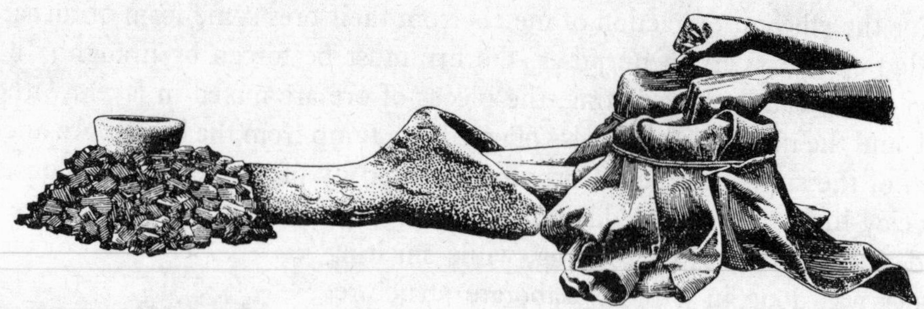

FIGURE 382—*Modern primitive valveless bellows as used for smelting iron in the Sudan. The position of the nozzles in the hood of the* tuyère *allows fresh air to be drawn in at this point and forced forward to the glowing charcoal. The ore is placed in the crucible.*

copper could not be liquefied, nor could iron be worked easily, if at all. For working with small quantities of material, as in jeweller's work, a blow-pipe is essential. It is no great step from blowing with the mouth to the use of a hollow reed. For fire-making, this device must be very ancient, even Palaeolithic. Blow-pipes were figured in Egypt at least as early as 2500 B.C. The Egyptians used metal pipes with clay nozzles or *tuyères* (figure 384) leading into the furnace, and possibly also reeds, like the Sumerians and Babylonians. To give a sufficient volume of air for a furnace-blast some sort of pump is needed; the oldest form is an animal's skin, with the pipe attached to one of the creature's legs. Such bags were perhaps used in series. A more convenient device is the dish-bellows. Two or more rigid vessels are covered with a loose skin diaphragm, the pipes from them are inserted into the *tuyère*, loosely so as to allow air-intake, and the bellows are used alternately (figure 382). As late as Dynasty XVIII (*c* 1500 B.C.)

FIGURE 383—*Casting a bronze door. The bronze is melted in a crucible on an open fire with forced draught from four foot bellows. Bent pieces of wood serve to lift the crucible to the mould in the centre, which has a series of funnels. One of the men on the right carries an ox-hide ingot. From a tomb at Thebes.* c *1500 B.C.*

FIGURE 384—*Egyptian gold workers. Blow-pipes tipped with clay are used at the fire. The man pouring from a crucible probably protects his hands with small stones. Those on the right beat out the gold with stone hammers. From a tomb at Saqqara.* c 2400 B.C.

it is still not clear whether any form of valve was yet in use (figure 383). Remains of *tuyères* have been found in very ancient Sumerian and Assyrian furnaces. There are other forms of bellows still used by primitive peoples, but such types have not been traced in the ancient East.

For the handling of hot metals, native African smiths still employ bent pieces of green wood (figure 386, p 588), such as are shown in Egyptian reliefs of the New Kingdom (figure 383). These were later displaced, first by forceps formed from a piece of springy bent metal, and later by hinged tongs.

Metal-workers were among the earliest specialists in craftsmanship. Neolithic farmers or their women had woven and spun, made their own shoes and pots, and dug their own flint, but the advent of the smith ushered in a new era, in which the urban civilizations of the great river valleys rapidly developed. Thence itinerant smiths ventured into the barbarian fringe to seek ores, and thus spread knowledge of the working of these coloured stones. The awe in which smiths were held is reflected in innumerable legends.

II. GOLD

Despite the general opinion of archaeologists, it is by no means certain that the use of gold preceded that of native copper in the Near East. In Egypt in particular, the evidence suggests that copper came first. However, since the metallurgy of gold is much the simplest, and because gold holds a special place among metals, it is here discussed first.

Deposits of gold were widely distributed throughout the ancient world. They were worked in Arabia, India, Persia, Caucasia, Asia Minor, and the Balkans, but the production of these regions was neither large nor continuous. In Egypt, however, the mining of gold was so extensive as to establish almost a monopoly of its production in ancient times. In the Nubian desert are the remains of more than a hundred gold-mines, and many of them still contain the remains of the washing-tables and querns mentioned by Diodorus Siculus. The yearly yield of

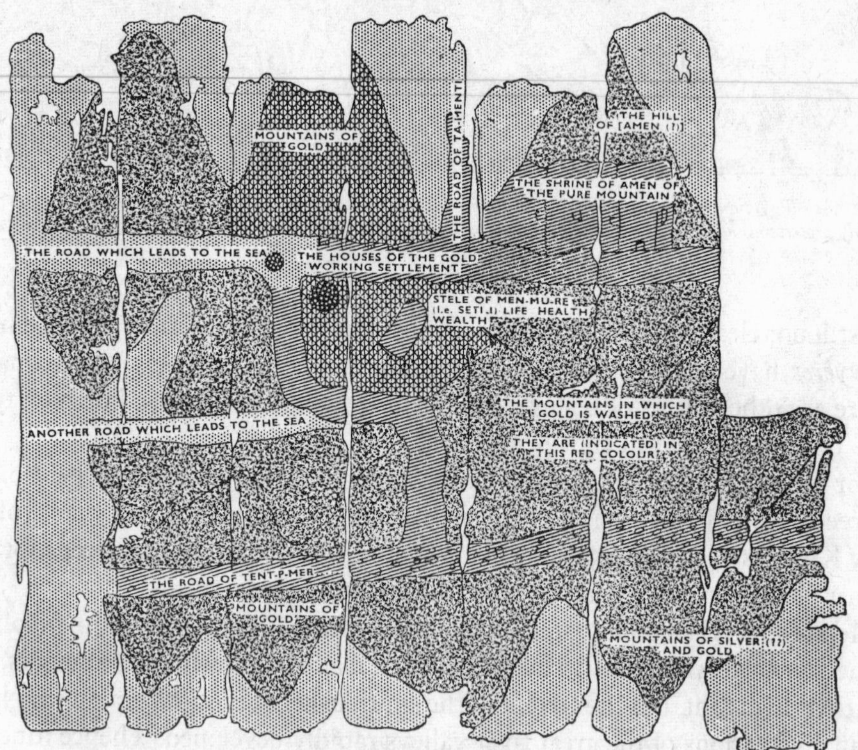

FIGURE 385—*Egyptian map on papyrus of the route used for the transport of a statue through gold mines in the Wadi Hammamat, Eastern Desert, with translations of the hieroglyphs. c 1300 B.C.*

gold from Nubia has been calculated to be of the order of 30 kg; far greater than that of any other region. Indeed, 'Nubia' means 'the land of gold' (from the Egyptian *nub*).

Gold occurs native as a rule, either as reef gold in irregular masses in quartz veins or lodes, or as alluvial or placer (Spanish *placer*, alluvial deposit) gold, formed by erosion of this matrix and subsequent concentration by the action of water. The process of extraction consists merely in the separation of the metal from the detritus of alluvium or crushed rock. Such panning and reef-mining were practised at least as early as the fourth millennium B.C. Diodorus, following a writer of the second century B.C., described the mining and extraction of gold from veins in quartz deposits in Egypt. The fragments of rock were hammered into pieces, pounded in mortars to the size of a pea, and then ground to powder in querns. The powder was washed on wooden tables under a gentle flow of water, which carried off the lighter particles while the heavier bits of gold remained and were collected on sponges. Strabo and others report that, in the Caucasus, alluvial deposits were worked by washing over a layer of fleeces. The gold particles would adhere to the grease in the wool—hence the basis of the legend of the Golden Fleece.

An early Egyptian map of gold-mines shows wells, roads, and temporary houses (figure 385). The gold was mainly collected by expeditions of experts and miners into the desert. The miners were criminals or captives, and were guarded by soldiers. Gold-mining was a state affair, and the goldsmiths either bought their material from the state or worked in the temples under priestly supervision.

Analyses of early gold objects show that the metal nearly always contained impurities such as silver, copper, and iron; refining came later. Native gold is coloured as a result of the presence of these impurities, and the Egyptian metalworkers greatly appreciated the variety of tint, which they skilfully exploited in their designs. Moreover, in both Egypt and Mesopotamia gold alloys were artificially prepared. It would seem that the ancients conceived these differently coloured alloys as separate entities, which the goldsmith could transform one into the other. His skill is sufficiently demonstrated by the fine work described elsewhere (ch 23).

Gold-refining processes, probably adopted from silver metallurgy, in which they had been used many centuries earlier, depended on cupellation, which separates noble from base metals. In cupellation, lead is added to the crude gold, and the metals are fused together in a porous clay crucible or cupel. The lead and other base metals are oxidized by a current of air. The resulting molten litharge, containing all the base-metal oxides, is partly blown off by a blast of air, and partly absorbed by the walls of the cupel, leaving a button of refined gold or, if silver was originally present in the ore, of gold alloyed with silver.

Agatharchides (second century B.C.) is quoted by Diodorus (III, 14, 3–4) as describing the removal of silver as well as the base metals by a modification of the cupellation process:

> 'The workers place the crude gold in a clay vessel, and add a mass of lead, a little salt and tin, and barley husks. Then it is closed with a tight-fitting lid, sealed with lute, and heated for five days and nights in a furnace. After a suitable interval for cooling, nothing is found of the other materials in the vessel, but only pure gold'. [Abbreviated.]

Evidently, at any rate in the first stage of this operation, while the access of air is prevented, the carbonaceous barley husks would act as a reducing agent. In this period, the metals would be fused and the silver converted to silver chloride by the salt. Later, we must suppose that air is admitted, perhaps through cracks; the barley husks would then burn away, and the base metals would be oxidized and absorbed by the crucible. Perhaps the lid is finally removed, and the heating continued for a short while longer to bring about the cupellation.

In another method the silver was removed by conversion to silver sulphide. The gold-silver alloy was heated with sulphur compounds, such as stibnite (Sb_2S_3), and charcoal. Stibnite was a compound well known to the ancients and its use might account for the antimony content of some gold objects. The silver, converted into sulphide, could be recovered by cupellation. Amalgamation, that is, the solution of the gold in mercury, followed by evaporation of the mercury, was practised by the Romans. It was probably unknown in remoter antiquity—unless mercury is the 'water of separation' mentioned in the Bible (Num. xxxi. 23).

Refining methods could be used on a small scale to test gold by loss of weight. Pure gold remains bright when fused in contact with air—the trial by fire of the Bible (Zech. xiii. 9). A rapid, rough assay could be made by streaking the sample of gold on a touchstone (Lydian stone or *basanos*), and comparing the streak with the colour of that made by gold of a known degree of purity. The Amarna Letters of *c* 1500 B.C. refer to the purity of gold and its refining and assaying.

Gold, being relatively soft and plastic, has little practical application, but has always been valued highly for aesthetic and magical reasons. Being produced and worked in small quantities, it never suffered from the general limitation of Near Eastern metallurgy, namely lack of fuel. The gold objects of Ur and of the Pyramid age have perhaps never been excelled for craftsmanship (ch 23).

III. SILVER AND LEAD

Though native silver occurs in the Near East, and was used by the ancients, it could never have been an adequate source of supply. It is significant that silver and lead first appear in excavations at the same time. In Egypt this is in the pre-dynastic period (before 3000 B.C.), in Mesopotamia from the Uruk III period (3000 B.C.). Beautiful silver work has been found at Ur and Lagash. Silver and lead are found in Crete in Middle Minoan strata (*c* 2000–1600 B.C.), but in other regions, such as Palestine, they become common only after 1400 B.C. In pre-historic Europe, generally speaking, silver and lead do not antedate the La Tène period (*c* 300 B.C.).

Silver and lead were closely associated because both were obtained from the same mineral, galena. This is predominantly lead sulphide, but usually has a small proportion of silver. Its occurrence is widespread, and it is often associated with copper ores. Its brilliant metallic appearance may have attracted the attention of the early copper-smelters. The few galena deposits of ancient Egypt were worked for eye-paint only, and in any case the lead produced later from these ores contained little silver. Arabia, Palestine, and Syria are notably poor in workable galena deposits; hence lead and silver, being imported, appear late in these regions. It is doubtful whether the rich deposits of India, Afghanistan, and Persia played a part in the ancient Near East, where much more importance must be attached to the many galena deposits rich in silver in the Armenian mountains, and in the central part of western Asia Minor. Classical tradition and archaeological evidence both point to north-eastern Asia Minor as the birthplace of silver. The 'land of the Chalybes', so important an early centre of metallurgy, was the mining district of the Hittites, whose very capital bears a name written with the ideogram for silver. Asia Minor held an almost complete monopoly of silver production, and Sumerian and Assyrian cities sent their merchants to the Hittites to acquire the silver and lead produced in that country. Earlier potentates like Sargon the Great and Gudea, ruler of Lagash, dispatched expeditions to acquire these metals in the 'silver mountains' of Armenia. The Cappadocian tablets (*c* 2000 B.C.), however, show that there were at that time permanent settlements of Mesopotamian merchants in the land of the Hittites, buying crude and refined silver, pure lead, and pigs of lead, all in sealed containers to prevent pilfering during transport. From the accounts, it is evident that several qualities were produced. The silver was usually sold in bars, and about four times as much silver as lead was sent to the home country.

After its introduction in the early third millennium B.C., production of silver and lead gradually spread west to the Aegean, Crete, and Europe; and to the east, where first the mines north of Mesopotamia (in the land then called Urartu) and in Elam and Carmania, and finally those in Bactria, were exploited. By the first millennium B.C., silver and lead were common metals all over the Near East, except in Egypt, where this phase of metallurgy was delayed for another 400 years. The amounts of these metals taken in tribute and booty by the Assyrian king Tukulti Ninurta II (889–884 B.C.) afford evidence of extensive production. Between 400 and 1000 kg of lead and 100 kg of silver were captured during hi expedition into the northern mountains, which shows that the region between Lake Van and Lake Urmia was already producing them in large quantities. In Egypt, on the other hand, though importation had begun, the comparative value of silver to gold was still as high as 1 : 2 at the time of the Persian occupation. The Persian viceroy of Egypt took advantage of this strange situation, and enriched himself by introducing a silver coinage into the country [2]. Supplies of silver became plentiful in Egypt only in Hellenistic times, when the price of silver dropped to only one-thirteenth of that of gold (see also p 585).

The production of silver and lead was responsible for the introduction into general metallurgy of the methods of working sulphide ores and of cupellation. The working of galena entails partial desulphurization by roasting, followed by reduction of the product, litharge (lead oxide). A simple hearth-furnace or a sloping trench sufficed. The fuel and ore were either thoroughly mixed together, or built up in alternate layers. Natural or artificial blast supplied the necessary air. A proportion of the sulphur escaped as sulphur dioxide, but some remained as unchanged galena and as lead sulphate. When the correct stage of desulphurization was reached, the temperature was raised, and the litharge, lead sulphate, and galena interacted to form lead, which collected at the bottom of the furnace, while the remaining sulphur escaped as sulphur dioxide. The charcoal added as fuel would prevent re-oxidation. The product was a lead-silver alloy harder than pure lead; it contained many impurities, such as antimony, copper, tin, and arsenic. This ancient process combined the two modern stages of roasting and reduction. Though the technique was comparatively simple, the chemical reactions were correspondingly complex, and the ancient metallurgist had not yet sufficient knowledge to control them fully. The inevitable result was a small yield. A main source of the wealth of Athens was its mines at Laurion, but it has been calculated that the slag-heaps there retained more than a third of the silver originally contained in the ore. These mines have more than once been profitably reworked in later times.

However wasteful these methods, a silver-bearing lead was certainly produced fairly free from other base metals, and silver was obtained from it by cupellation. The litharge slag could be used as such, or reduced with charcoal to lead. Finds of pure silver at Ur, at Troy (six bars of very pure silver), and at other places, as well as historical data, lead us to conclude that cupellation was invented in north-eastern Asia Minor in the first half of the third millennium B.C. The fining-pot and the drossing of base metals are frequently mentioned in the Bible (Prov. xvii. 3; Jer. vi. 29–30; Ps. xii. 6). By about 600 B.C. cupellation was well known.

Liquation, a method for extracting gold and silver from other sources such as certain crude coppers, was perhaps also known at this time in the Near East. It involved alloying the crude metal with lead and slowly melting it. The lead flowed away with the precious metals in solution, leaving a porous mixture of the remaining base metals. Liquation was followed by cupellation.

Copper and lead weights, rings, and bars constituted the most primitive form of coinage in the ancient Near East, but they were soon displaced by silver and gold—which, however, more often served as standards only, actual payments being made in copper and lead. The silver : gold value-ratio gives an interesting indication of the supply of silver. It was comparatively high in the earlier periods in Mesopotamia (1:8), and rose still higher, to 1:6, in the reign of Hammurabi, perhaps because of disorder in Asia Minor and Armenia. It fell soon afterwards to 1:10, and remained at that level for a very long period. In Neo-Babylonian and Persian times the ratio varied between 1:12 and 1:13.

IV. COPPER

The technology of copper, the earliest useful metal, is far more important than that of gold or silver. All the important stages of metallurgy before the discovery of iron are outlined in its history.

Native copper occurs in a great many places as small particles, occasionally as nuggets, and very rarely indeed in large masses. In the beds of the mountain streams where gold is often found, purplish-green and greenish-black nodules sometimes occur which, when scratched, show a kernel of native copper. They are hard to work, but the native metal also occurs in thin plates and arborescent forms, which are much more workable. With the discovery of annealing, which removes the brittleness caused by cold-working, the harder nodules became usable, and larger objects could be manufactured. The characteristic microstructure of native copper has been found in several objects of great antiquity in Egypt, Asia Minor, Mesopotamia, Palestine, and the Danube valley.

In the ancient Near East the supply of native copper was quickly exhausted, and the miner had to turn to ores.[1] The first class of copper ores (e.g. cuprite, malachite, azurite) embraces carbonates and oxides. They can easily be reduced to the metal by heating with charcoal. The second class of ores (e.g. chalcocite, chalcopyrite, bornite, covellite) consists of sulphur compounds of copper, sometimes mixed or combined with other metals or metalloids such as iron, antimony, and arsenic. It is commoner than the first class, and is generally found in deeper strata. The most important copper-ore deposits of remoter antiquity were in Sinai, Syria, Baluchistan and Afghanistan, Caucasia and Transcaucasia, the Taurus region, Cyprus, Macedonia, Iberia, and central Europe. The chrono-

[1] Cuprite—Cu_2O; malachite—$CuCO_3,Cu(OH)_2$; azurite—$2CuCO_3,Cu(OH)_2$; chalcocite—Cu_2S; chalcopyrite—$CuFeS_2$; bornite—Cu_3FeS_3; covellite—CuS.

logical chart (Table IV, p 575) shows approximately when the different sources of copper first came to be used.

The simple reduction of oxide and carbonate ores, together with the melting and casting of copper, depended on the introduction into metallurgy of furnaces and crucibles. This was the beginning of a true metal age. At first, furnaces were quite small—sufficient to yield enough metal to make small implements such as arrow-heads. Only gradually were furnaces developed in which alternate layers of charcoal and ore were heaped. Even then the spongy masses of incompletely fused metal mixed with slag and cinders, which were the first products of primitive smelting, could not have looked very encouraging. From the size of prehistoric ingots (20–25 cm in diameter, 4 cm thick) it may be concluded that the first established metallurgical furnaces were about 30 cm in diameter.

The treatment of sulphide ores is more intricate, as they generally contain iron and other impurities. For instance, chalcopyrite, one of the commonest copper sulphide ores, has the formula $CuFeS_2$, and usually contains traces of arsenic, antimony, and bismuth. The modern process aims at first obtaining a pure molten cuprous sulphide or 'matte', and then partially oxidizing it in the molten state, when the cuprous sulphide and cuprous oxide react together to form copper and sulphur dioxide. The ore is first roasted to remove surplus sulphur, and largely the arsenic, antimony, and bismuth, as volatile oxides. Next, the ore is smelted with coke and siliceous fluxes. This separates a fusible copper matte consisting mainly of cuprous sulphide, but containing iron compounds; most of the iron originally present, however, passes into the slag as ferrous silicate. In the third stage, a blast of air is introduced into the molten matte. Iron, having a greater affinity for oxygen than has copper, is the first to be oxidized, and is absorbed by the slag. The blast is continued until the correct proportion of the cuprous sulphide is converted to oxide; the sulphide and oxide then react together to give a copper of about 98 per cent purity.

This is a modern expression of the process, and things were of course not so clearly formulated for the ancient metallurgist. To achieve anything approaching a complete extraction from sulphide ores he must have used many successive stages of roasting, smelting with charcoal, and smelting with blast-air. Alternatively, he could have simplified the process, though with loss of efficiency, by extracting only a small percentage of the copper. Apart from the study of modern primitive methods, considerable light is thrown on these methods by the remains and slag-heaps of the Bronze Age copper-smelting sites in the eastern Alps. Production in these regions may have started as early as 1700 B.C. (the Hyksos age of Egypt), and it has been estimated that some 20 000 tons of copper were produced between 1300 and 800 B.C. For the roasting, which was quite distinct from the other operations, piles of ore and fuel were made. There followed three stages of smelting, which resulted in a copper of about 95 per cent purity. None of the ingots found has a higher purity than this, so that presumably the copper was not refined on the spot but traded in its crude state.

Mild oxidation is the simplest method for refining copper. If air is blown through the molten metal, all remaining impurities, apart from the noble metals, are oxidized and rise to the surface; but the process is a delicate one, for, if it goes too far, the copper itself starts to oxidize as well, and consequently becomes brittle. In the earliest ages, refining was certainly conducted by melting the crude copper with charcoal in a crucible or in a charcoal fire and using blast air for oxidation. The extension of this process known as poling[1] seems not to have been practised before Roman times.

The varying compositions of early copper objects were due to crude methods of smelting and refining, and they sometimes give us an indication of the ores used. As the skill of the metallurgists grew, these differences disappeared. A characteristic puckered appearance indicates that the copper ingots were produced from sulphide smelting. The earlier ingots of black copper were usually broken up into pieces of a typical, columnar, crystal structure. Later, in western and central Europe, they took the form of round cakes, possibly collected from the fore-hearth of the smelting-furnace. In the eastern Mediterranean they were shaped like ox-hides, and weighed about 2 talents (70 kg). These probably served as money, in place of the real ox-hides formerly used. They have been found in Egypt, Crete, Cyprus, Anatolia, and Syria (figure 383).

Copper and its alloys can be hardened only by cold-hammering along the cutting edges. Treated thus, such tools may approach the hardness, but not the tensile strength, of mild steel. It is impossible to harden copper by heating and quenching, like steel; indeed, such treatment softens the metal (p 576). Copper tools were often re-heated and re-hammered, and sometimes careless overheating caused the formation of copper oxide. Because of the resulting brittleness, the tool had then to be either discarded or used for scrap.

The rarity of finds from the earliest stages of copper metallurgy may be partly accounted for by the fact that worn and broken tools were used as scrap for recasting. Hoards of such scrap copper have been found in Asia and in Europe. The discovery of casting probably belongs to the Ubaid-Uruk period of Mesopotamia (*c* 3500 B.C.). Casting was first performed in open moulds (figure 386), in which small flat objects could be rapidly produced. Casting in the round was

[1] Because it involved stirring the molten copper with poles of green wood.

FIGURE 386—*Casting a copper axe-head in an open mould. The crucible is held with a bent withy.*

facilitated by making the mould in two or more parts. The more advanced techniques of core-casting and *cire-perdue* were also known, and were practised with great skill (ch 23).

V. COPPER ALLOYS

Soon after the dawn of the metal age, copper alloys begin to appear in the archaeological record. As knowledge advances, it becomes less and less likely that any true Copper Age preceded that of Bronze anywhere except in Egypt, where bronze became common only about 2000 B.C. Now the copper alloys made in the Near East contain not only tin but frequently lead, antimony, arsenic, and zinc, and this is true also for prehistoric Europe. Generally, tin-bronzes prevailed, though there was a preference in some regions for the antimony or arsenic alloys. In most of the ancient bronzes, however, the presence of antimony is accidental, and the small percentage has hardly any effect on the quality of the bronze. In Mesopotamia, a few objects have been found of pure antimony. The metal doubtless came from the Caucasus region, where antimony and antimony-bronze are fairly frequent—especially from the tenth century B.C.—around Tiflis and the Kuban.

Antimony and arsenic ores were used as eye-paints, pigments, and drugs. There is a constant confusion in ancient texts between stibnite (antimony sulphide), antimony itself, and lead compounds. It is certain that metallic antimony and its sulphur compound were in use, but the early eye-paint known as stibium was most commonly galena (p 293).

In Hungary, finds of pure antimony, and also of bronzes with up to 20 per cent of antimony, are common. It is believed that these were produced in the region of Velem St Vid, where mixed antimony and copper ores occur. Their manufacture may have originated unintentionally, but later, when antimony was isolated, artificial bronzes of this type were made, and even traded to the Swiss lake-dwellings. Antimony can be very readily prepared from stibnite by smelting, and a knowledge of it was soon widely spread. Its nature was unrecognized both in preclassical and in classical texts. Pliny and Dioscorides warn their readers not to carry certain reactions on antimony compounds too far 'lest the residue be turned into lead' [3].

Many ancient bronzes contain appreciable quantities of arsenic, including some from Egypt, the Caucasus, the Indus valley, Hungary, and central Europe. Only in the latter case does there seem to have been a successful intentional working of mixed ores [4]. In most other cases, a high arsenic content has made the bronzes too hard and brittle, though eminently castable.

Tin-bronze with its superior tensile strength, hardness, and casting properties was very much more useful than unalloyed copper. Unfortunately, tin is seldom mentioned in the texts, and the earliest specimens found in excavations date from some thousand years after the first tin-bronzes were used. The only tin ore of any importance is cassiterite or tin-stone (SnO_2), which occurs as stream-tin and as a vein ore. The alluvial stream-tin is often closely associated with gold, as miners have affirmed since the time of Pliny [5]. The recovery of gold from such deposits by panning or placer-mining would yield black heavy cassiterite nodules, besides the shining gold nuggets and dust. In fact, the Romans produced tin ore in Spain by the same method of hydraulic mining as they applied to gold-mining there.

In view of the thorough depletion of the tin deposits in the ancient Near East, it is difficult to find exact indications of where they were. There was a considerable amount of tin-mining in Caucasia, and it occurred in a few places in Asia Minor, Persia, and other countries; Egypt, however, is wholly devoid of tin ore, and this is probably why bronze was introduced so late into that country. The modern deposits in Africa and Asia were beyond the range of the Mediterranean races, but in Europe several important deposits were known and worked in antiquity: in Spain (Cantabria), France (Brittany), Britain (Cornwall), and central Germany.

The mines of Spain were in operation from the beginning of the Bronze Age, and were worked continuously up to Roman times. Tin was mined, and exported to France and the Mediterranean, before the beginning of the Iron Age. The deposits of southern Brittany were worked about 500 B.C., but they must have been abandoned later because of Spanish competition. Cornish tin production entered international trade about 500 B.C.—though local production may have started earlier—and continued until the days of Julius Caesar. Central European tin had a great influence on local bronze production; it also, with Spanish tin, played a part in the supply of the ancient Near East. Unfortunately, we have no textual or archaeological evidence on this line of supply.

As the local tin deposits of the Near East became exhausted, supplies must have come from farther afield, as from Spain, central Europe, and Cornwall.

We have no reliable information on the extent of the tin-supply from the Caucasus.

The extraction of tin from cassiterite was fairly simple. For impure ore which could not be hand-picked, like the stream-tin, some preliminary washing and roasting would be necessary, but these were well-known operations. The ore was then powdered, and charged into the furnace with alternating layers of charcoal. As with most ancient refining-methods, a metal of surprisingly high purity was won, but with heavy loss of metal in the slag, and, in the case of tin, by volatilization. It is strange that no metallic tin has been found in early hoards.[1] It was probably not produced separately on a large scale before 1500 B.C., but was smelted together with copper ore or crude copper to make bronze.

In considering the addition of tin to copper, it is well to remember the close association of vein tin ore and copper ores in a few localities such as Tillek (Turkey), Cornwall, Bohemia, and parts of China.

It has often been argued that the accidental smelting of mixed copper and tin ores led to the discovery of bronze. It may have been that such ores were smelted together and that the less viscous bronze, far more suitable for castings than copper, was thus obtained. Yet it is hard to see how the impurity in the copper ore came to be identified with the stream-tin which is always found mixed with earthy lumps and sand. There is no trace of early exploitation of vein cassiterite, and it would seem that all tin before Roman times was produced from stream-tin. It is difficult to assess the importance of naturally mixed copper and tin ores in the general history of bronze in antiquity. Recent investigations of central European prehistoric bronzes seem to prove, however, that bronze manufacture started with treatment of natural mixed ores, and that, in time, the tin ore component was recognized and artificial mixtures were smelted; or that crude copper was smelted with tin ore.

In the ancient Near East, the story seems to have been slightly different. When working gold by streaming, nodules of cassiterite were found. This cassiterite was reduced by workers already proficient in the production of gold, silver, and lead. The metal obtained was held to be a kind of lead. Lead and antimony were already used to increase the ease with which copper could be cast, but neither of them improved its other qualities, notably the tensile strength. From trials with the new kind of 'lead', it would be learnt that this mixture was now improved in tensile strength as well as in ease of casting. Nor was it necessary

[1] A possible explanation is that, at low temperatures, ordinary tin passes into a powdery modification called grey tin: a fact apparently known to Aristotle.

to produce this new metal first; unrefined copper had only to be smelted with charcoal and stream-tin to produce a new kind of 'copper', namely bronze, with superior qualities for tools and weapons. At the same time, certain naturally mixed ores were also worked, and were found to give the better kind of 'copper' directly. We have no proof that the tin compound of these mixed ores was ever isolated or recognized. Furthermore, at this early stage the tin content of the bronze could not be adequately controlled, and therefore varied between fairly wide limits.

FIGURE 387—*A typical Bronze Age hoard of metal objects, probably belonging to a smith. Brandenburg.*

Gradually, the stream-tin deposits in the Near East began to fail. We find inferior hammered axes of unalloyed copper in the Sargonid era in Mesopotamia, after the excellent bronzes of Ur. Prospectors and traders now began to make for the west, in the hope of finding sources of tin. Without involving direct contact, this pioneering explains the gradual introduction of Sumerian metal types into the Danube regions, and finally into middle Europe, where further tin supplies were found in Bohemia and Saxony. Similarly, overseas trade brought Spanish tin to the eastern Mediterranean. These various imports relieved the scarcity.

At a later stage—about 1500 B.C.—it was realized that a bronze of more constant composition and quality could be obtained if the stream-tin ore were reduced with charcoal, and the resulting tin mixed separately with the copper. Then began a production of alloys with different tin-content, specially adapted to the manufacture of weapons, mirrors, statues, bells, and other objects.

The tin probably still came mostly from central Europe (figure 387). Early tin exports from Spain or Gaul cannot have been very important, in view of the striking poverty of the early Bronze Age remains in those countries. Perhaps the Spanish tin trade did not grow quickly until the late Bronze Age, then ousting Bohemian tin from the front rank. From Hittite sources we hear that bronze was brought from Cyprus, where there is no tin ore; it must therefore have been imported. The strange composition of some of the bronzes in this period may indicate that used bronze was re-melted because of the high cost of tin. This process holds many dangers, such as a partial oxidation of the tin and a consequent lowering of its percentage. The archives of the period show that tin was probably traded as crude bronze, tin being worked only in the copper-producing centres where it was imported from the west. At one time, it was held that the Cretans brought tin directly to Egypt. In the latter country bronze became common only about 1500 B.C., after its introduction some 400 years earlier. The supposed 'Cretans' depicted on certain Egyptian monuments seem, however, to be Syrians or Anatolians bringing ingots of lead. The first bar of tin in an Egyptian grave can be dated at about 600 B.C., and in the fifth century B.C. tin supplies at last became abundant. The Hellenistic civilization brought direct contact between Egypt and such tin-producing regions as Spain and Cornwall.

In Anatolia, tin was for long scarce, for, though the early bronzes there date from at least 3000 B.C., pure copper was still used, and the percentage of tin remained very low until 2200 B.C., when bronze became plentiful. In Caucasia, bronzes are of the same age as in Anatolia, and local tin sources ensured that the metal was never scarce. In Mesopotamia, many types of lead and antimony bronzes preceded the true bronzes. The first clear reference to tin occurs in Assyrian annals, which mention 'white bronze' taken from conquered cities in the northern mountains. Of sources of the tin used by the Indus civilization we have no information. It probably came from the western and north-western mountains.

The zinc sometimes found in ancient bronzes was never added to the copper as such, for zinc was quite unknown throughout antiquity. The so-called brasses found in some excavations are bronzes with a zinc content due solely to contamination of the particular ore used. The story of brass belongs to later metallurgy, and there is no evidence that the ancient metallurgists understood how to make it.

VI. IRON

That iron was brought into use late in the history of metal-working is shown in the myths and ritual practices of many peoples, by whom it was regarded with suspicion. The true Iron Age was hardly inaugurated before 1200 B.C., its development being associated with a great migration of peoples which disturbed almost all the ancient Near East, and with a temporary rise in the prices of many commodities, especially corn. But the effect of the introduction of iron was gradually to extend and cheapen production. Iron ores are widely distributed and readily available; iron tools were cheaper and more efficient than those made of bronze. They rendered possible the clearing of forests, the drainage of marshes, and the improvement of cultivation upon a very much wider scale. Thus iron was the democratic metal, and it greatly reinforced man's equipment for dealing with the forces of nature.

Iron occurs as meteoric iron (with an appreciable nickel content) and in the form of many ores such as magnetite (Fe_3O_4), haematite (Fe_2O_3), ochres (Fe_2O_3, hydrated), and siderite ($FeCO_3$). These ores were known long before the advent of iron. None of the many iron deposits of Egypt and Nubia is known to have been worked in remote antiquity. Ores east of the Jordan and those of Edom were used locally, as well as those of northern Syria. Crete never had any iron-mining of importance, but the deposits there were certainly worked in very early times. The most important iron-mines were those of Asia Minor, the Taurus, and the Armenian and Caucasian ranges, which, with those of northern Persia, contributed most of the iron supplies of the Near East. In Europe, there were deposits in the eastern Alpine provinces (the later Roman province of Noricum), Etruria, Elba, Gaul, Britain, and Spain, and many of them were exploited before Roman times.

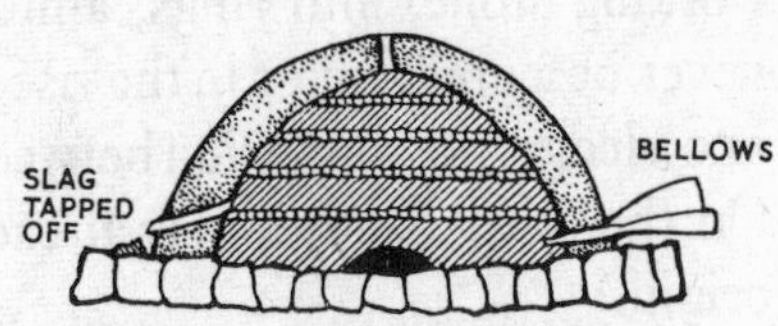

FIGURE 388—*Diagram of a primitive bloomery hearth for the production of wrought iron. It consists of alternate layers of charcoal and ore, heaped on a circular stone platform and covered with clay. Bellows inserted in the clay dome are kept in blast for many hours. The iron concentrates as a spongy mass at the bottom.*

It may seem strange that iron came into general use so much later than copper, for the reduction-temperature of iron oxides is not very different from that of copper oxides. However, a study of the techniques of iron-smelting will demonstrate the difficulties. For more than two millennia, the smelting of certain kinds of coloured stones in a furnace with charcoal had produced a flow of metal. Experiments with other kinds of stones, including iron ores, must have been made; but they would not produce this pattern of events, so well fixed in the mind of the bronze-smelter. From his point of view, the smelting of iron ore would result in a 'bloom', a spongy mass of fused stone full of air-holes, as apparently unmetallic as can be imagined. The small pasty globules of iron which solidify shortly after the reduction, owing to the high melting-point of iron (1535° C), would be concealed in a mass of slag and cinders. Only frequent heatings and hammerings would eject the slag and mould the iron particles together into a lump of wrought-iron (figure 388).

The great centres of bronze-working in the ancient Near East, with their specialized smelting and smithery methods, offered neither good chances for lucky accidents with iron ore nor conditions for deliberate experiment. The rarity of early iron objects, and the fact that they are not tools but ornaments, indicate clearly that there was not yet any established technique for smelting the abundant ores of iron.

The meteoric origin of most of the early finds of iron has been established beyond doubt. Owing to its content of nickel, meteoric iron has properties rather similar to those of steel; it could hardly be worked in large masses by copper and bronze metallurgists who had no high-temperature furnaces. Most of the objects found are small lumps fashioned laboriously, by the methods used in working stone, into rings, amulets, images, and the like. Meteoric iron could never be a great factor in the rise of iron metallurgy, for, in the absence of chemical knowledge, the connexion between it and iron ores must have remained unknown. On the other hand, it was already clearly realized that this iron was of celestial origin.[1]

As early as the first half of the third millennium B.C., pieces of man-made iron appear in Mesopotamia at Tell Asmar, Chagar Bazar, and Mari; in Asia Minor at Alaca; and probably also in Egypt. Perhaps such brilliant ores as magnetite and haematite, which were used as stones for seals, first attracted the attention of primitive smelters. Ochres were also well known as pigments. Some fragments of iron may have been produced in the refining of gold, for very pure magnetite occurs along with gold dust in the gold gravels of Nubia. If smelted in the ancient Egyptian way, in a crucible together with chaff and straw, a slag rich in iron would collect on the top of the mass in the crucible, and directly above the gold a layer of pasty iron would be formed, which could have been forged into small objects. But this can hardly be called a real method of working iron ores.

No doubt the early smelter tested iron ores for metal, but the discovery that a lump of wrought-iron was produced by hammering a red-hot bloom must have been slow in coming. At first, the new metal represented no improvement over the copper and bronze already available. It was less easy to work, it required more fuel, and the cutting-edge made by hammering blunted more readily. Then it was discovered that repeated hammering and heating (which brought the metal into contact with charcoal), followed by plunging into cold water (quenching), gave iron a hardness superior to bronze. The discovery of this process was doubtless obscured by the fact that it could in no way be inferred from the knowledge of the properties of metals already acquired by the smith. The heating and hammering before quenching had transformed the surface of the wrought-iron into steel by diffusion of carbon (cementation), and only with this carburized iron, created by the inhabitants of the mountains of Armenia, does the Iron Age

[1] The Sumerian word for iron means heaven-metal; the Egyptian, black copper from heaven.

properly begin. During the period *c* 1900–1400 B.C., the use of smelted iron ornaments and ceremonial weapons became gradually more common.

The properties of iron depend greatly on its carbon content. Wrought-iron contains little or no carbon, and is soft and malleable. Cast-iron contains between 1·5 and 5 per cent of carbon, is hard and brittle, and has a lower melting-point than wrought-iron. Steel is intermediate in these respects. Its carbon content may vary between 0·15 and 1·5 per cent and its properties vary accordingly.

By the early part of the second millennium, the connexion between man-made iron and the celestial meteoric iron was finally grasped. The 'steeling' of wrought-iron was the invention of the Chalybes, so popular in classical tradition; they were subjects of Hittite kings, who for some 200 years (*c* 1400–1200 B.C.) held the monopoly of its manufacture. Slowly the new steeled iron objects began to spread through the ancient Near East. By 1200 B.C., the knowledge of producing iron from its ores had penetrated to southern Italy, the metal itself becoming more frequent even in Egypt. Yet letters exchanged between the Hittite king Hattušiliš III (1281–1260 B.C.) and his viceroy in the mountain region of Kizzuwadna show that, even then, iron was still prepared in small quantities, and solely in the Armenian mountains.

The incursion of Thraco-Phrygian peoples into Asia Minor, and the subsequent downfall of the Hittite empire, had an enormous influence on the spread of iron-working. Many tribes, including smelters from the Armenian mountains, were driven east or south. The iron-working Philistines settled in the coastlands of Canaan, the Midianites or Kenites near the iron deposits of Edom and Midian. The knowledge of iron-smelting and the cementation process was brought to many peoples. Between 1200 and 1000 B.C. there was a rapid growth of native iron-working in Iran, Transcaucasia, Syria, and Palestine; and Cyprus, Caucasia, and Crete followed closely. The new processes which made steel a material equal, and even superior, to bronze found their way prepared in all these countries by earlier attempts at iron-smelting. This explains why the smelting of iron spread so much more quickly than that of bronze.

In Europe, iron-smelting was brought from southern Italy to the Umbrians round Bologna. The contact of the invaders of Asia Minor with the iron-smelters also provided a passage for the transmission of the new techniques through Greece and the Balkans to the region of the eastern Alps (Noricum). There the working of spathic iron ores, which contain no obnoxious contaminations such as sulphur and phosphorus, but which contain appreciable quantities of manganese, would yield a good malleable alloy in the primitive bloomeries and furnaces. Both the Celts and Romans appreciated this fact, and Noricum became the Sheffield of antiquity. Centuries earlier (*c* 600 B.C.), however, the Iron Age had started here, in the Hallstatt period of prehistory. In the next few centuries, the German tribes of central Europe learned to smelt iron, and the Celts of Gaul acquired the knowledge from their brethren of Noricum.

The smelting of iron ores on a large scale depended on the invention and acquisition of a series of new techniques, tools, and processes. First, there was the correct slagging of the ore, for the flux used had to vary with the gangue in the ore, lime being used for siliceous gangue. In some cases the ancient smelters sacrificed part of their yield by smelting without a flux and losing much of the iron in the slag, which was then often reworked by later generations. Next, there was the handling of the bloom, which had to be reheated in special furnaces and repeatedly hammered, to get rid of the enclosed slag and cinders and to consolidate the iron globules. This required the development of tongs and hammers to manipulate such heavy and red-hot masses. Finally, there was the conversion of the wrought-iron into the more useful steel. The techniques of carburizing, quenching, and tempering were evolved one after the other. The first discovery was of carburization or cementation by repeated heating, in contact with charcoal, and hammering of the wrought-iron ingot. Then quenching, that is the preservation of the red-heat structure of the steel by sudden cooling, was grasped. Finally, the art of tempering the hardness of the steel by heating for some time at a moderate temperature and slowly cooling enabled the ancient smith to sacrifice some of the hardness of his steel to obtain a tougher and less brittle tool. The regulation and interplay of these three techniques determined the success of the ancient smith, and as he did not have at his disposal modern methods of controlling temperature we need not wonder that he often failed.

However, it will be clear that the combination of these three techniques could alone herald the Iron Age. It was a new metallurgical stage, a technical revolution of its own. In the earlier age of metals the stress lay on the composition of the alloy (or on the impurities in the metal); the properties of the iron, on the other hand, are much less dependent upon its natural impurities and far more upon its handling, the temperature to which it has been heated, the manner and speed of quenching, and the time and temperature of tempering. The Iron Age is the true age of the smith as we know him, swinging his hammer and working his bellows.

We learn from analyses that, in Egypt from 1200 B.C. onwards, iron objects were carburized only; between 900 and 700 B.C. quenching was mastered, and in Roman times tempering was understood [6]. The Iron Age proper does not begin before 600 B.C. in Egypt, though blue-coloured metal implements, which suggest iron, are depicted from 2000 B.C. onwards. Comparable dates would be somewhat earlier in other regions.

By 700 B.C., iron-smelting started in the Egyptian province of Meroë in Nubia, slowly penetrating southwards to the Sudan and the rest of Africa. The first set of iron tools in Egypt dates from the Assyrian domination of that country (*c* 670 B.C.). Egypt, therefore, never played a major part in the early history of iron.[1]

In Palestine, iron was introduced by the Philistines, and the Old Testament reflects the superiority they owed to this new metal until the reign of Saul. There was a great metallurgical centre at Gerar, near the Egyptian border; the earliest tools and furnaces are of about 1180 B.C. Blooms or bars of iron imported from the north were here used to produce tools and weapons.

India and Persia later became famous for crucible steel, but it is hard to establish when and where this process was invented. The 'Seric' steel of the classical authors was, in reality, not Chinese but Indian steel; probably the invention was made in India towards the end of the period we are discussing. Persian or Parthian steel was still a rarity at this time.

Mesopotamia entered the Iron Age with the reign of the Assyrian king Tukulti Ninurta II (889–884 B.C.). From then onward we have many records of iron from the northern regions. Sargon II (722–705) used iron on a lavish scale, and nearly 150 000 kg of unworked bars were found in his palace. The documents of this period always speak of 'users of bellows', not of smelters, and thus confirm our suspicion that the Assyrians did not smelt ores but manufactured their tools and weapons from imported iron. The state bought iron, and supplied it to the smiths from the central storehouse in each town for the manufacture of objects specified in contracts. This iron came from northern Syria and Asia Minor. The records speak of quantities of 4000 kg and more being bought or captured

[1] Discoveries of early iron in Egypt include the following specimens: (*a*) A piece from the Great Pyramid of Giza, supposed to belong to Dynasty IV (*c* 2500 B.C.). (*b*) Various pieces of chisels from Saqqara, ascribed to Dynasty V (*c* 2400 B.C.). (*c*) Several pieces of a pickaxe from Abusir of Dynasty VI (*c* 2200 B.C.). (*d*) Some broken tools from Dahshur of Dynasty VI. (*e*) A lump of rust, perhaps a wedge, from Abydos, of Dynasty VI. (*f*) A large spearhead from Nubia of Dynasty XII (*c* 1900 B.C.).

The genuineness of date of all members of this list is under suspicion; (*a*) is of smelted origin, but there is the possibility that it may have belonged to one of the excavator's own workmen; (*b*), (*c*), and (*d*) were all reported long ago by Maspero (1846–1916). To the modern archaeologist the evidence does not suffice to warrant the proposed dating. The iron rust (*e*) found by Petrie (1853–1942) at Abydos was not meteoric, but there is no proof that it formed part of a tool or weapon, and its position in a temple foundation is a mystery. It is difficult to accept the Nubian spearhead (*f*); though the finding and dating seem in order, it appears to be of modern type, and it is unwise to accept this single specimen as evidence for iron in Dynasty XII.

Of more importance is an iron deposit found on a flint wand in the valley-temple of Mycerinus at Giza, Dynasty IV. The iron is not of meteoric origin, and it is suggested that it had magical significance.

during raids. Once, 18 000 kg were sent by the town of Mari, which imported it from Damascus.

In Asia Minor, iron is mentioned in documents and has been found in excavations from the early second millennium B.C.; its Akkadian name seems to go back to a non-Semitic word, the origin of which is to be sought in one of the many languages spoken in the Hittite empire. The earliest iron objects imitated bronze types; then bronze was used for the ornamentation of iron objects, and iron to repair bronze objects. Finally, by 1000 B.C., the smiths discovered the techniques proper to this metal. The peak of ancient iron metallurgy was reached by 800 B.C. In northern Syria, iron-smelting on a large scale was centred round the later town of Doliche, where according to some classical authors 'iron was born'. The iron industry of Cyprus was not of great importance, and documents show clearly that the metal was imported from the Anatolian mainland. Nor does Crete play a large part in iron metallurgy. The legends of gods and demons located by the classical authors in Crete seem to find their origin in the iron metallurgy near the Phrygian Mount Ida rather than in the Cretan Mount Ida.

Greece and Macedonia had many early bloomeries, which were of local importance only, the larger part of European prehistoric iron coming from Noricum, where production started with the Hallstatt period (p 617), and continued through the La Tène period into historic times. On all other European iron deposits, work never assumed more than local importance before about 300 B.C.

Little can be said on the evolution of the bloomeries and the shaft-furnaces used. Reports are both scarce and divergent, and further detailed studies are necessary. However, we may be certain that cast-iron was hardly ever made by early iron metallurgists, their furnaces were too small and the temperatures they employed too low. Cast-iron, if produced, was thrown away as a product that did not yet fit into the technical pattern.

REFERENCES

[1] FORBES, R. J. 'Metallurgy in Antiquity.' Brill, Leiden. 1950.
COGHLAN, H. H. 'Notes on the Prehistoric Metallurgy of Copper and Bronze in the Old World.' *Occ. Pap. Tech. Pitt Rivers Mus.*, no. 4. 1951.
COZZO, G. 'Le origine della metallurgia: I metalli e gli dei.' Bardi, Rome. 1945.
OLDEBERG, A. E. 'Metallteknik under Förhistorisk Tid.' Harrassowitz, Leipzig. 1942–3.
[2] HERODOTUS IV, 166. (Loeb ed. Vol. 2, p. 370, 1920).
[3] PLINY XXXIII, xxxiv, 103–4. (Loeb ed. Vol. 9, pp. 78 ff., 1952).
DIOSCORIDES V, 99.

[4] WITTER, W. 'Die Kenntnisse von Bronze und Kupfer in der alten Welt.' Mannus-Bücherei 63, Kabitzsch, Leipzig. 1938.
Idem. Forsch. Fortschr. dtsch. Wiss., **13**, 39, 1937.
[5] PLINY XXXIV, xlvii, 156–7. (Loeb ed. Vol. 9, p. 240, 1952.)
[6] CARPENTER, SIR (H. C.) HAROLD and ROBERTSON, J. M. *J. Iron St. Inst.*, **121**, no. 1, 417, 1930.

BIBLIOGRAPHY

FORBES, R. J. 'Bibliographia Antiqua, Philosophia Naturalis', Part II "Metallurgy". Nederlandsch Instituut vor het nabije Oosten, Leiden. 1940–50.

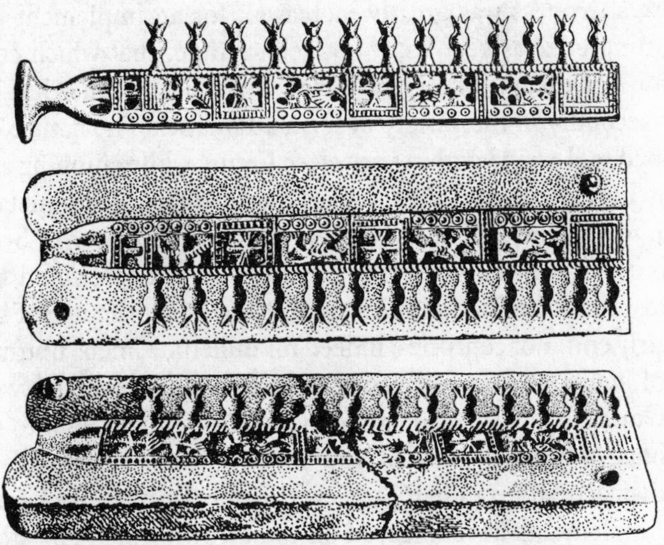

Double mould of a Syrian goldsmith and a cast made from it. Ugarit (Ras Shamra). c 1300 B.C.

METAL IMPLEMENTS AND WEAPONS

H. H. COGHLAN

I. NATIVE COPPER

THE introduction of metals for implements and weapons is so important that it may be said to mark the dawn of a new era. It was not so much that mere sharpness was greatly increased, for an implement of flint may be given a cutting-edge as keen as, if not keener than, that which could then be imparted to one of metal. The great advance lay first in the durability of the material, and secondly in the variety of form attainable. The nature of stone and flint conditioned tool-shape within very close limits, while chipping and breaking of implements in service was a very serious disadvantage. With metal, it became more possible to suit the tool to its work, and the old bugbear of brittleness did not arise. Moreover, a metal implement, even when broken, could be reshaped.

Nevertheless, the introduction of metal did not bring the use of stone implements to an early end. For centuries, indeed for millennia, men continued to make implements of stone, and for centuries after the value of metal was generally accepted they made metal types in stone media. Not until well into our era, and then only among advanced peoples, did metal become sufficiently cheap and plentiful to displace stone. There are even some cultural back-waters where certain stone implements have lingered on to our own time. The stone hammer is a particularly persistent type.

Native copper [1] was in use before the discovery of smelting, but by far the greater proportion of prehistoric copper was obtained, not from the native metal, but from its ores. Ancient copper is often of high purity: 99 per cent or more [2]. As cast, the pure metal is very soft and, although easily worked, would be almost useless for implements. Fortunately for the primitive technician, the hardness of copper may be greatly increased by any form of cold-working, such as hammering. This property, shared by many other metals, is known as work-hardening. Such additional hardness is removed by heating the metal to above about 500° C and cooling—the process of annealing. With a working cycle of hammering followed by annealing, a very considerable range of implements and weapons could be produced. The final operation would be a careful hammering to harden the cutting-edge.

In the earliest copper cultures as, for example, at Badari in Upper Egypt about 4000 B.C., the very small size and very simple form of the implements indicate that much of the work was carried out by forging. This is the stage often called by archaeologists the hammered-copper culture. But an obvious advantage of copper is that it may be cast, and this method was adopted as early as the fourth millennium B.C. in Egypt, for making substantial flat celts. These first castings were of extremely simple form; all that was needed was a shallow depression cut into the surface of a block of stone or baked clay, and shaped to represent the form of the desired casting. The molten copper was poured into it (figure 386). Perfectly sound castings were made thus, the limitation being that the object had to be more or less flat, as with a celt.

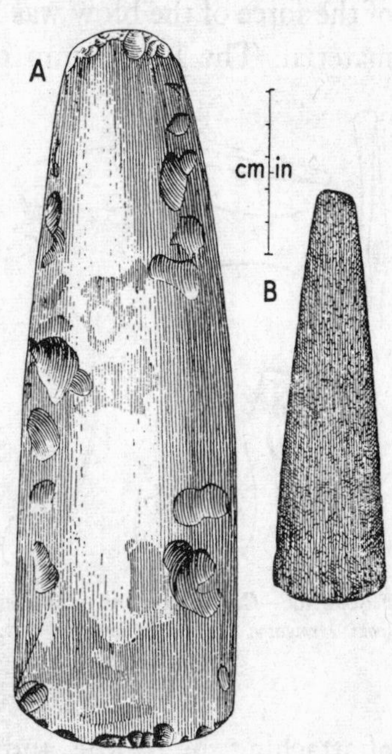

FIGURE 389—(A) *Neolithic polished stone celt from Botesdale, Suffolk.* (B) *Copper celt from Cyprus.*

For more complex forms, a closed or two-part mould was required. Unalloyed copper, however, is not easily cast in a closed mould, because of its tendency to absorb gases, blow-holes from which produce defects in the castings. It has indeed been thought that pure copper could not be cast in closed moulds, but experiment has shown that, with sufficient head of metal and adequate venting of the mould, even very pure copper may be successfully cast [3]. In view of the difficulty of the technique it is not at all surprising that prehistoric castings of complex form from unalloyed copper are very rare.

II. COPPER TOOLS

Except for small and primitive objects like awls and pins, the first implements that demand any considerable volume of unalloyed copper are the well-known flat celts (figure 389). Mounted with the edge transverse to the shaft, the celt becomes an adze; parallel to it, an axe. To function as a true adze, the blade must have its cutting-edge of chisel-form, as distinct from the equi-angled cutting-edge of an axe-blade. In their original form, these celts were no doubt copies of the very widely distributed Neolithic ground and polished stone axes and adzes. The copper axe or adze had certain marked advantages which offset its relative softness.

The use of metal automatically led to improvement in the cross-sectional form of the tool, which could be made thinner. In Neolithic cultures, the most usual polished stone celt was of a rather plump oval cross-section, which gave the maximum strength consistent with the properties of stone. But its cutting-power was relatively small, owing to the wide terminal angle, for much of the force of the blow was lost when the nose of the axe became wedged in the material. The less plump copper tool marked a great advance in efficiency, though in some developed Neolithic stone celts from the Fayum in Egypt the cross-section closely approaches that of a metal celt.

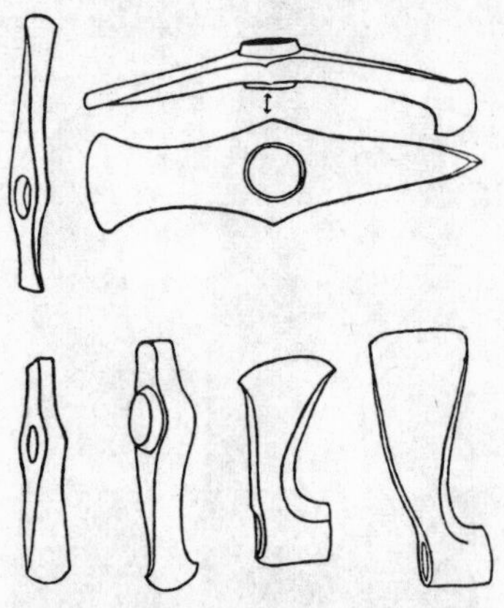

FIGURE 390—*Copper axes and adze-axes from Hungary. Second millennium B.C. Scale 1/7.*

Metal is in general much less brittle than stone. If the maker of a stone celt made his tool strong enough to avoid continual breakage, it became inefficient as an axe. On the other hand, if he made a slender body with an efficient terminal angle and cutting-edge, breakage would be a constant risk. The metal celt might bend, but it did not break, and could easily be sharpened.

A greatly improved form of axe was that with a shaft-hole to take a handle. This device, universal today, is far superior to the method of hafting with thongs. It offers an efficient means of attaching the handle, and through the better balance of the whole implement gives much greater cutting-power. From very early times the shaft-hole idea was applied to bone and stone (figure 325 B, C). The same design was later carried out in metal, and copper shaft-hole axes are not uncommon in certain cultures. The general ancestry of the shaft-hole axe may be traced back to Mesolithic times in the forest cultures of northern Europe.

Metal-workers early adopted the shaft-hole principle, notably in the hatchets of Sumeria and the adzes of Susa. Though a shaft-hole in stone is definitely a weak spot, perforated stone implements continued to be made for many centuries even after metal implements had become well established. Some stone axes, indeed, were made in imitation of metal prototypes (figure 337). Metallic features, such as casting-seams and the collars surrounding shaft-holes, were sometimes reproduced, though they have little or no purpose when rendered in stone. From the ancient centres of metallurgy, copper shaft-hole axes and adzes became widely distributed and, in later times, there appears in Hungary a series marked by fine design and skilful metallurgical technique (figure 390).

The *chisel* is of very great antiquity. It may be traced among the bone and stone tools of Upper Palaeolithic times, and is found in some of the earliest copper cultures. The first copper chisels were very small, and were probably used without handles (figure 391). Later, when the chisel had increased in size, it was provided with a tang to enable it to be fitted into a wooden haft, as with the modern carpenter's tool. In the east, chisels appear before 3000 B.C., but the copper chisel certainly did not fully replace that of stone. Though serviceable for woodworking, a copper chisel is useless against stone. Well into the Bronze Age of Europe we find stone chisels ground to the style of metal ones. Not until the introduction of iron did the metal chisel come into its own.

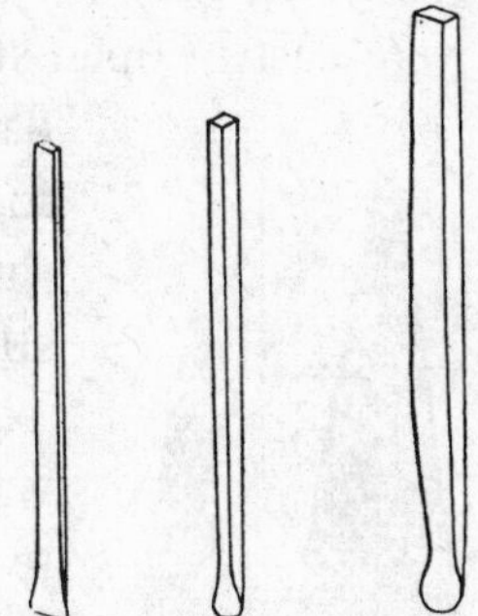

FIGURE 391 — *Predynastic Egyptian copper chisels. Scale 1/4.*

Another tool of great antiquity which was copied in metal was the *saw*. For its origin we must go back to the flint saws with serrated teeth, for cutting wood and bone, of the Magdalenian culture of the Upper Palaeolithic in southern France. Such flint saws were still in use in the Bronze Age (figure 392 A). They had the same disadvantage as the stone celts, for they were so thick that they became wedged in the grooves that they were cutting. The copper saw had a thin blade, and the teeth could be set to give the blade a working clearance. The earliest copper saws followed those of flint, in simply having notched teeth. The modern technique of raking the teeth all in one direction did not appear in Europe until the Iron Age.

III. COPPER WEAPONS

In considering weapons we are faced with a great range and variety, particularly in the later prehistoric periods. Even before 3000 B.C. Egyptian, Sumerian,

FIGURE 392—(A) *Flint saw from Sweden. Scale 1/3.* (B) *Egyptian bronze saw. Scale 1/5.*

and Indian metallurgical methods were distinct, and simple implements had distinctive forms in each of these regions. We shall refer here to only a few principal types.

The *dagger* was one of the earliest copper weapons, and, like the celt, it had behind it a long tradition in stone. As early as the Merimdean culture of Egypt, of about 4000 B.C., we find flint blades that may well have served as daggers. By early predynastic times (*c* 3500 B.C.), beautifully executed flint daggers appear (figure 393). The first metal daggers are flat and triangular; technologically they have much in common with the copper celt, for they too were cast in open stone moulds. The triangular form of the primitive copper dagger may, in some specimens, appear exaggerated, making for ugliness and inefficiency; but the open-cast dagger was thin, and the triangular form was necessary to provide lateral strength (figure 394 A).

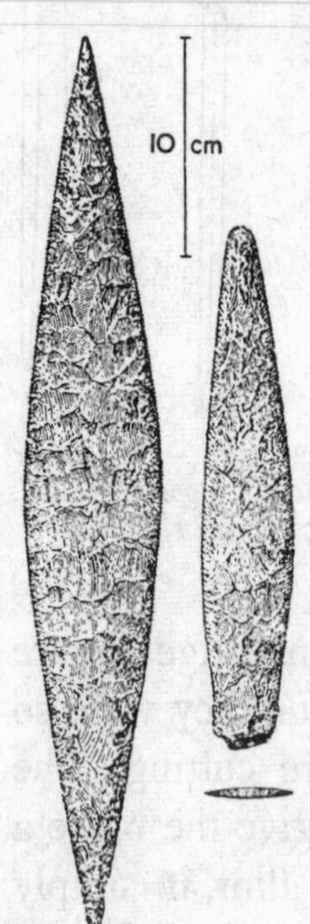

FIGURE 393—*Predynastic Egyptian flint daggers.*

The next mechanical advance in the making of the dagger was the provision of a midrib, to increase lateral rigidity and to permit the blade to be finer. In Egypt, even before Dynasty III, some copper daggers were strengthened by a stout midrib.

In later types and with the introduction of bronze, the midrib became a regular feature of the casting itself, as in examples of Sumerian origin. Early copper daggers were often hafted with a hilt which enclosed the butt of the blade on each side. The attachment was completed by rivets passing through both hilt and blade. Later, the fixing of the hilt was often very elaborate, as in the famous Brigmilston dagger from a Wiltshire barrow, in which the wooden handle was secured by no fewer than thirty bronze rivets (figure 394 B).

Another kind of dagger, associated with the Beaker people, has a wide tang to which the hilt was not secured by rivets (figure 395). This form may be compared with a striking flint dagger of similar shape from Silesia. Both copper daggers of this kind and their flint copies have been recorded as late as the Bronze Age in upper Italy [4]. With a well-proportioned blade having a midrib on both sides and an adequately designed hilt, little more could be done to improve the copper dagger until the coming of bronze.

The *battle-axe* was early in common use, for considerable numbers are recorded, both in stone and in metal. One common form of battle-axe has a rounded body with a splayed blade, and a cylindrical butt behind the shaft-hole; it is thus an axe-hammer. It would seem that the first battle-axe cultures were formally Neolithic but involved some acquaintance with metal. Technologically, the copper battle-axe had the same advantage as the shaft-hole axe. It combined an effective distribution of the metal with a simple but efficient hafting. These shaft-hole weapons and tools mark an important technical achievement. Many were cast, and this operation carried out on unalloyed copper was no mean test of skill (p 601).

The *spear-head* was presumably evolved from a dagger mounted on a long shaft. Doubt has been expressed as to whether the true spear preceded metal, but there is no reason why Stone Age man should not have formed a spear by letting a thin flint blade into the split end of a shaft. Since the javelin, a light form of throwing-spear, was in use in Upper Palaeolithic times, a very respectable antiquity can be claimed for the true spear. In the early Egyptian dynasties, copper spears had a flat tang which fitted into the split end of the shaft, and sometimes a copper ferrule was used to secure the spear-head.

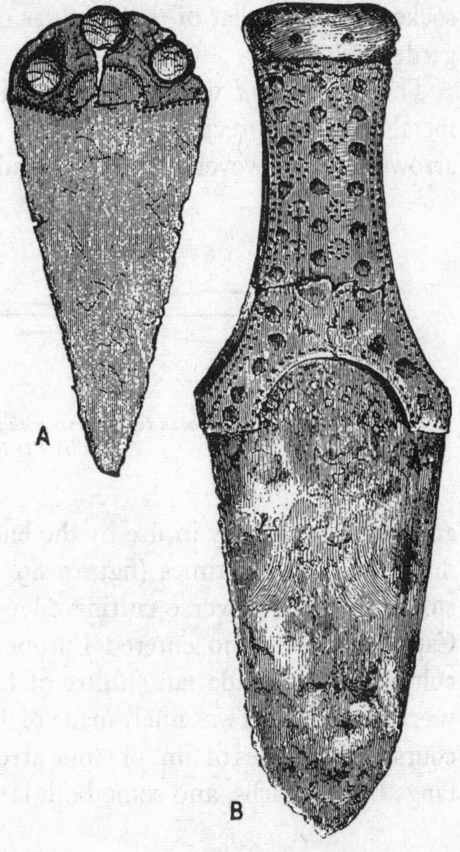

FIGURE 394—(A) *Triangular copper dagger from Cleigh, Argyllshire.* (B) *Dagger with bronze-riveted wooden handle from Brigmilston, Wiltshire. Scale 1/2.*

Concerning the use of copper for spear-heads, the same conditions apply as for the dagger. Since core casting was unusual with copper, the typical copper spear has a tang for its attachment to the shaft. Sockets were also made by folding a wide flat tang into the form of a conical tube. The classical Minoan spear-head (Middle Minoan III) had such a folded socket (figure 396) [5]. This ancient technique for forming a

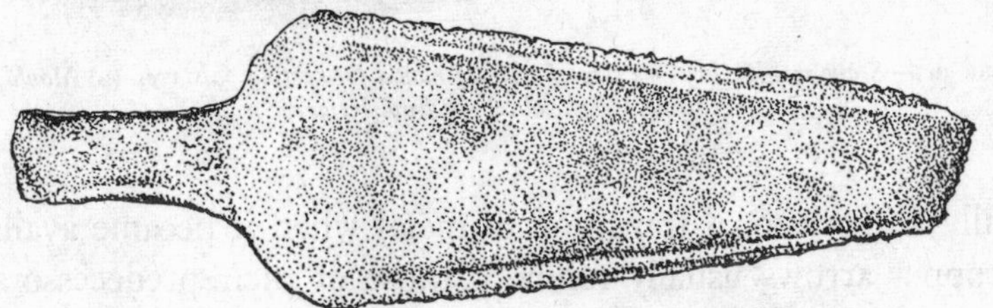

FIGURE 395—*'West European' tanged dagger from Suffolk. Scale 1/2.*

socket, which is that of the smith as opposed to the founder, is still in use for gardeners' tools.

The *arrow-head* was also rendered in metal, but specimens are rare, since metal was too precious for objects which would frequently be lost. Metal arrow-heads, however, had a long tradition in stone behind them. The bow and

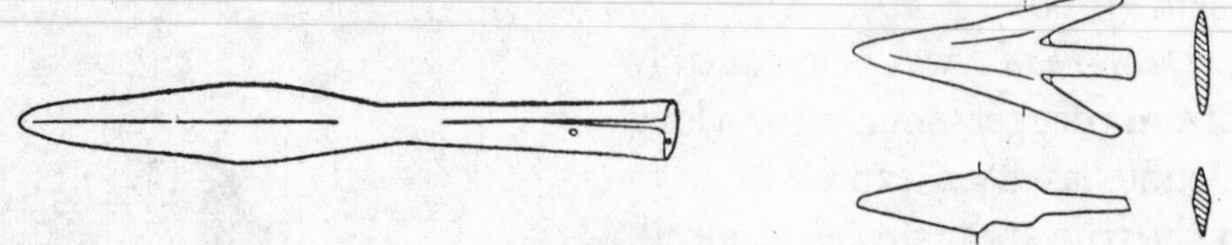

FIGURE 396—*Middle Minoan copper spear with folded socket, and two copper arrow-heads from Lesbos. (Not to the same scale.)*

arrow were probably in use by the end of the Upper Palaeolithic and certainly during Mesolithic times (figures 89, 90). A primitive form of arrow-head in stone, with a transverse cutting-edge instead of a point, was used by the final Capsian people who entered Europe from north Africa bearing a Mesolithic culture. In the Badarian culture of Egypt, a more normal type of arrow-head was adopted. This was finely made of flint, and had long barbs but no tang. In due course, other types of flint or stone arrows appeared, some leaf-shaped, some with tangs but no barbs, and some both tanged and barbed (figure 335). Later, there

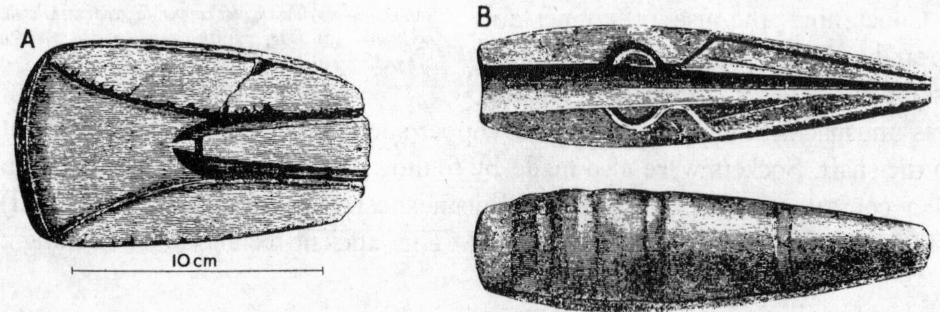

FIGURE 397—*Stone moulds.* (A) *One side of a closed mould for casting palstaves.* (B) *Mould for casting spearheads. Both from Ireland.*

was naturally an occasional transition to metal when it became available. The forms of copper arrows usually followed those of their predecessors in stone (figure 396).

IV. TRANSITION TO BRONZE

Because of the superior physical and casting properties of bronze, the discovery of the manufacture of tin-bronze ranks second in importance only to that of copper-smelting.

By prehistoric tin-bronze we mean a copper-tin alloy which may vary in composition from a mild bronze with 5 per cent of tin to a hard bronze of 15 per cent or more. Bronzes with less than 3 per cent of tin may be called accidental bronzes, since in these cases the tin almost certainly had its origin in an impurity of the copper ore used. When bronze metallurgy had become well established, and the founder had acquired control over his mixtures, he aimed at an alloy with 10 per cent of tin to obtain the best all-round results. Such an alloy may be work-hardened like copper, but is very much harder than the latter metal in a comparable condition [6]. It has about twice the tensile strength of pure copper. Another very important point of superiority is its eminent suitability for casting. Without bronze, complex casting in closed moulds would not have become an important industry.

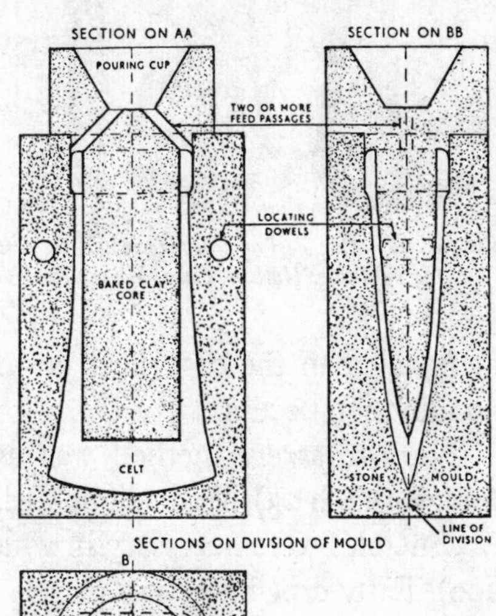

FIGURE 398—*Casting a socketed celt. Diagrammatic sections of a stone mould with baked clay core.*

Three methods of casting were employed: open mould, closed mould, and *cire perdue*. Flat celts continued to be used well into the Bronze Age, and, like those of copper, they were cast in open moulds (figure 386). When this method was unsuitable the closed mould, containing a cavity shaped to the form of the desired implement, was used (figure 397). To allow the casting to be withdrawn without breaking the mould, a closed mould had to be in at least two parts, and the parts had to register accurately. A further development for casting socketed objects was to use a core. This was usually of baked clay; it was arranged within the mould to represent the hollow socket (figure 398). Extreme care and accuracy were essential, and, considering the equipment available, the accuracy and high finish of the best Bronze Age works are most remarkable technological achievements.

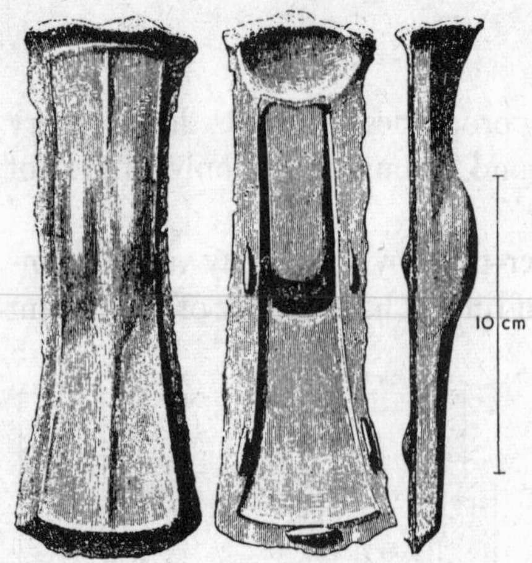

FIGURE 399—*One half of a bronze mould for casting palstaves. Hotham Carr, Yorkshire.*

Moulds made of bronze have been recorded from Mesopotamia, Anatolia, and Europe. Such moulds are not common, although several, used mostly for casting palstaves and socketed celts, have been found in Britain. They must have been costly and difficult to make, and their use would have been justified only when a large number of highly finished and accurately made tools were required (figure 399). It might be supposed that a bronze mould used for casting bronze would suffer considerable damage and have only a short life; however, if the mould contains a much greater weight of metal than the cast, heat is quickly conducted from its inner surface and no adhesion occurs.

The *cire perdue* method was used mainly for casting ornaments and other fine work (ch 23). With slight variations it remains in use to this day.

Crucibles were necessary in which to melt the bronze for casting (figures 381, 400). Early crucibles were merely small shallow dishes made of coarse pottery. Later, when metal was more plentiful, the size of the crucible was enlarged, and the deep cylindrical form, which exposes less metal to atmospheric influences, made its appearance.

V. BRONZE AGE TOOLS

The introduction of bronze led to great increases in the quantity and quality of tools. Many of our present-day craft-tools may be traced to a Bronze Age origin. Evolution of craft-tools, however, has not progressed in an orderly sequence: archaeological stages cannot be rigidly defined, nor can technological tool-stages. Just as stone implements continued into the Bronze Age, and bronze into the Iron Age, so some tool-types persisted long. Even at the close of the last century certain prehistoric tools were being used in Ireland.

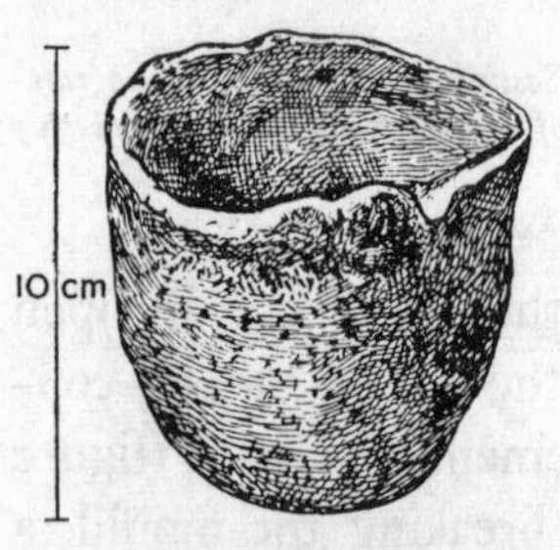

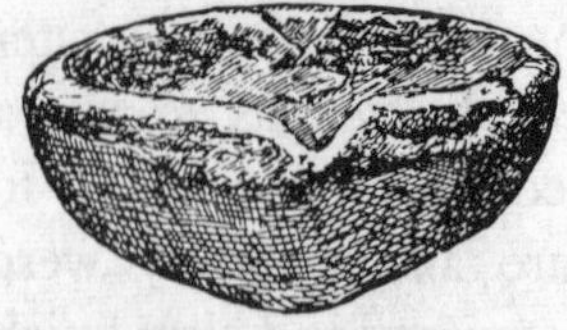

FIGURE 400—*Predynastic Egyptian earthenware crucibles.*

The *hammer* is the oldest tool of all—indeed, it is as old as man himself. Hundreds of thousands of years were required to develop it from the rude hammer-stone, or from club-like implements of bone, to the perforated, handled hammer of the third millennium B.C. The Bronze Age smith still used the hammer-stone, but employed also heavy perforated hammers (figure 401 A). It is remarkable that, in Egypt, a smooth hammer-stone held in the hand was used until iron became general (figure 309 C). The hammer-stone has also been favoured by many

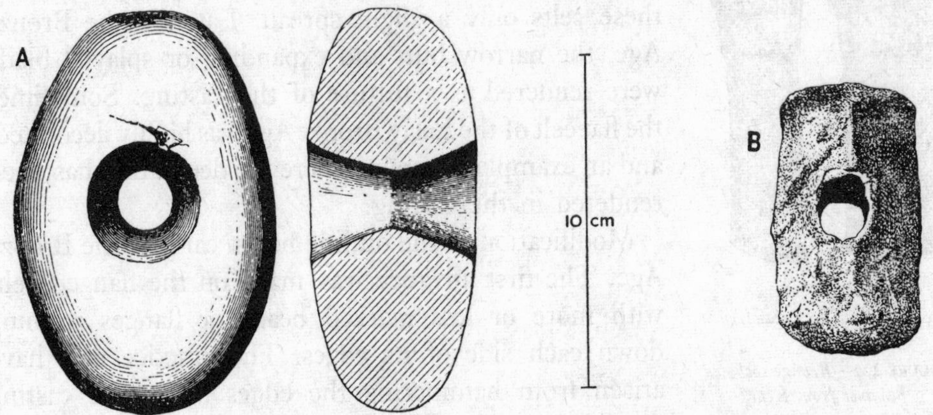

FIGURE 401—(A) *Neolithic perforated stone hammer from Redgrave Park, Suffolk.* (B) *Perforated bronze sledge-hammer from Mitterberg, Salzburg, Austria.*

modern primitive metal-workers. About 1500 B.C. a heavy bronze sledge-hammer of essentially modern form appeared (figure 401 B). In the Late Bronze Age, when socketed tools became popular, hammers of this nature were introduced into Europe (figure 402).

An *anvil* is necessary in every smithy. In the Bronze Age, the working anvil must have been a heavy stone block dressed to a level surface—metal was far too costly for the purpose. In the developed Bronze Age, when work of a fine nature was executed, small bronze anvils appear (figure 403). Sometimes on the surface of a stone anvil a number of semi-circular grooves of various sizes were cut, to serve as dies for forming pins or wire. In a small bronze anvil from Fresné-la-Mère, near Falaise, in northern France, there are many such grooves. Most small anvils had spikes which could be driven into the top of a workbench, or into the ground in the way that field anvils were fixed, till quite recently, by some European continental peasants.

The *celt*. The facility with which bronze may be cast permitted a wide range in the form of axes during the Bronze Age. The following sequence [7] covers the important types: (1) flat celt; (2) flanged celt; (3) winged celts; (4) palstave; (5) constricted celts (Bohemian palstaves); (6) socketed celt.

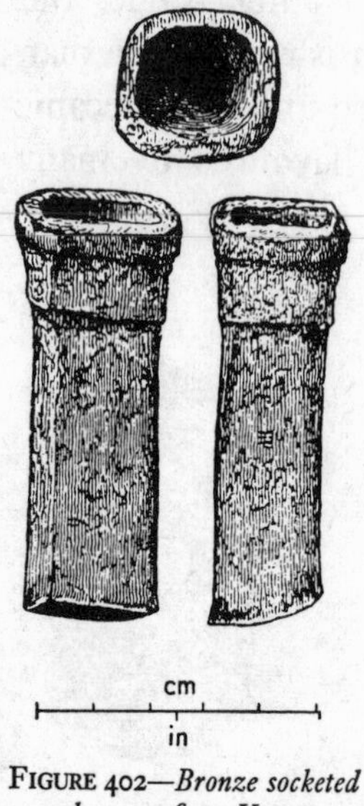

FIGURE 402—*Bronze socketed hammer from Kent.*

It is often difficult to distinguish between a flat copper celt and a bronze celt, except by chemical analysis. The sides of Early Bronze Age celts are nearly parallel and, since hammer-hardening does not splay the blade as much as with soft copper, we find in these celts only a slight spread. Later in the Bronze Age, the narrow butt and expanding or splayed blade were rendered as a feature of the casting. Sometimes the flat celt of the Early Bronze Age was highly decorated, and an example is known where the decoration has been rendered in the casting.

Modification of the outline began early in the Bronze Age. The first advance was made on the flanged celt, with more or less marked beads or flanges running down each side of its edges. The practice may have arisen from hammering the edges of a poor casting to eliminate pores in the metal. However, when the flanges were of reasonable size, the technique had two advantages. First, by raising the edges of a thin celt it increased longitudinal rigidity; secondly, when the celt was mounted in a split knee-shaft, the flanges helped to secure the celt in the haft.

From the flanged celt, it was a natural step to improve the hafting. Until shaft-hole tools became general, the fastening of the axe in its haft was a weakness and must have been a continual trouble. With increased skill in moulding, it became possible to cast deep flanges, or wings, which could be hammered over the prongs of the wooden haft. With conventional methods of moulding, the wings would not have been cast in their curved position, but were hammered over after the tool had been cast. In the Late Bronze Age, a loop was cast on one side of the celt through which a binding was passed to prevent it from slipping out of the haft. With this addition, a thoroughly sound attachment of the tool became possible.

FIGURE 403—*Bronze anvil from Laumes, Côte d'Or, France.*

The *palstave* is the next step in technical development. While the winged celt lent itself to excellent fastening if its butt was thin, a series of severe blows would drive it back in the haft, loosening the grip or even splitting the wood. To overcome this difficulty, the flanges of the celt were left straight and a stop-ridge was cast between them. The force of a blow was now taken by the haft prongs bearing against the stop-ridges. Such stop-ridges between the flanges of palstaves did not appear suddenly. In Europe there are rudimentary stop-ridges on flanged celts of the Early Bronze Age, while the developed palstave with clearly defined stop-ridges seems to be a feature of the Middle Bronze Age. The palstave was a graceful, well balanced, and powerful tool, and had sufficient weight to make its blow effective. It was a more efficient cutting-tool than the socketed celt that succeeded it.

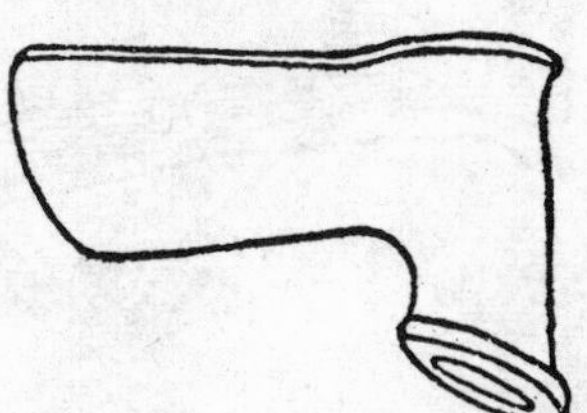

FIGURE 404—*Shaft-hole chopper-axe. Syria. 2300–2000* B.C.

The *socketed celt* or *axe*, introduced in the Late Bronze Age, was an exceedingly abundant type. In earlier axes, the cross-section of the socket was round or oval; later, a square or rectangular socket was used. For hafting, the socket had considerable advantages: the knee-shaft had no longer to be split, it was easy to fit the shaft in the socket, and side and longitudinal slip were avoided. For serious work, the socketed celt does not compare with the heavy palstave, and is technologically a degeneration.

In mechanical efficiency, the terminal development of the socketed celt or axe is the shaft-hole tool represented by the modern felling-axe, the prototype of which is some 5000 years old. In the Near East, the flat celt led to shaft-hole types rather than the flanged and socketed forms of Europe. From approximately 3000 B.C., we find shaft-hole chopper-axes of Sumerian form brought to the Kuban, and soon afterwards spreading to the Aegean (figure 404). Later comes the oval shaft-hole, designed to prevent the axe-head turning upon its handle, and the tool is by now highly efficient and essentially modern in appearance (figure 405 A). Also, even before Sumerian times, the shaft-hole principle was applied to the transverse axe or adze (figure 405 B).

The *chisel* became a widely used and important tool in the Bronze Age. A bronze chisel is primarily a wood-working tool, but an exceptionally well-hardened specimen could perform light work on annealed copper, and might even be used for working soft stone. A number of forms were evolved during the Bronze Age (figure 406). Except in material, there is little difference between our present-day engineers' cold chisels and the simple bar of bronze sharpened at one end and struck with a hammer at the other. In Europe, the tanged chisel appeared rather late in the Bronze Age. An early form had a flat blade continued upwards to form the tang; two lugs about half-way up the blade prevented the tang from being driven too far into its handle. Later, a circular collar between blade and tang (as in the modern carpenter's chisel) served the same purpose. The mortise-and-tenon joint was very early used in carpentry, and for such joints bronze mortise-chisels, socketed for strength as in modern examples, were

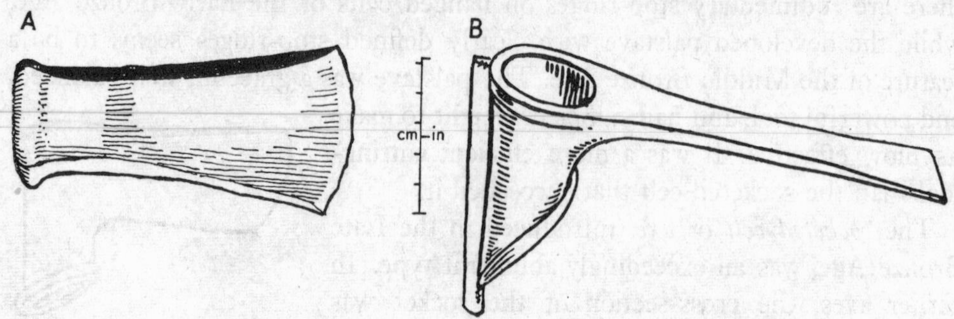

FIGURE 405—(A) *Bronze shaft-hole axe.* (B) *Sumerian transverse axe.*

developed. Another useful tool, the socketed gouge, also became widely distributed during the Late Bronze Age in Europe.

The *drill.* Holes in soft material, such as wood and leather, were first made with flint points in Upper Palaeolithic times (p 188). Awls and points are common in early copper cultures, and continue throughout the Bronze Age, but, like the carpenter's awl, they perforate mainly by crushing and pressure, and thus technically are not drills. The bow-drill, on the other hand, is a true drill; it was in use by the end of the third millennium B.C. (figures 112–13, 487 A). In it we may see the idea for the carpenter's brace, which, however, did not come into general use till the Middle Ages. For drilling holes in hard stone, another method

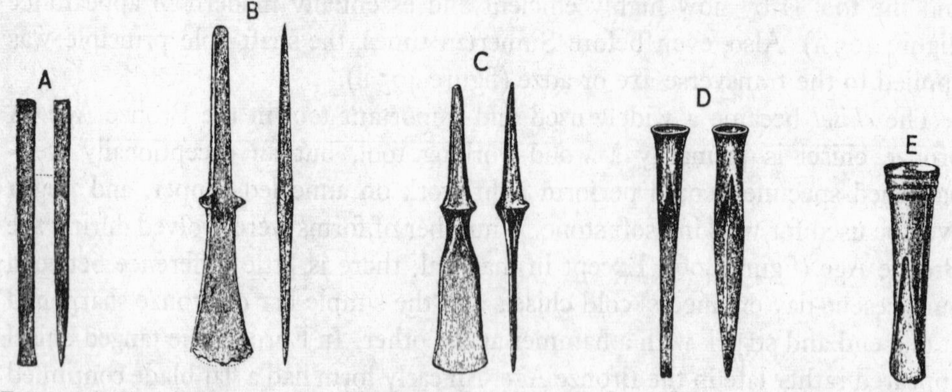

FIGURE 406—*Tanged and socketed Bronze Age chisels.* (A) *Chisel formed from square bar, from Plymstock, Devon;* (B) *from Yattendon, Berkshire;* (C) *from Carleton Rode, Norfolk;* (D) *mortise-chisel from Carleton Rode;* (E) *gouge from Harty, Kent. Scale 1/3.*

was practised by many early prehistoric people. A cylinder of wood or metal was rotated upon the stone to be drilled, while downward pressure was applied to the drill, which was fed with sand or emery. The process was slow, but very good results were often obtained. Small tubular metal drills have been found in the Harappa culture in India, and these are perhaps the earliest example of metal used for drilling (ch 9).

An important step was the invention—possibly in the Bronze Age, for wood-working—of the arrow-headed drill, a type which, in steel, did not lose its popularity until the end of the last century. In the Bronze Age, drilling of metal was avoided, for even a hardened bronze drill would be of little use against a like metal. Much riveted work is known from the Bronze Age, but the rivets were usually small and the rivet-holes were made with a punch.

FIGURE 407—*Hallstatt bronze file.*

Saws were known in the Stone Age, but during the Bronze Age their use as wood-working tools was considerably extended. The saw, however, remained an abrading instrument, without distinction in the direction of the teeth. In Egypt, the saw assumed a modern appearance (figures 392 B, 487–9), and by Dynasty XII even the pistol-grip handle appears. Bronze saws attained what we should regard as normal dimensions. Even large saws were made; a remarkable example, over 5 ft long, comes from Middle Minoan III in Crete.

Files are essential to the metal-worker under modern conditions. They are also used by carpenters, in the form of rasps. The file was known during the Bronze Age, but was probably used for carpentry only. Some files may have been used on material harder than wood, as indicated by a tin percentage of 18 to 31 in some Egyptian files, but the true file for metal had to await the coming of iron. In central Europe the file appears late in the Bronze Age. Flat and round bronze files have been found, especially in the Hallstatt region (figure 407). Bronze files have also been discovered in the great *fonderia* deposit at Bologna.

VI. BRONZE AGE WEAPONS

The *dagger* in the Bronze Age advanced from its primitive triangular form to a slender and shapely one (figure 408). The cast midrib gave longitudinal rigidity against buckling, and the greater strength of bronze as compared with copper permitted a more effective shape. The dagger may be with or without tangs, the tanged form being favoured in Asia. In Europe, the butt of the blade was recessed into the hilt, to which it was secured by rivets (figure 408 D). This gave a more secure and rigid attachment for the hilt. For a satisfactory pitch of the

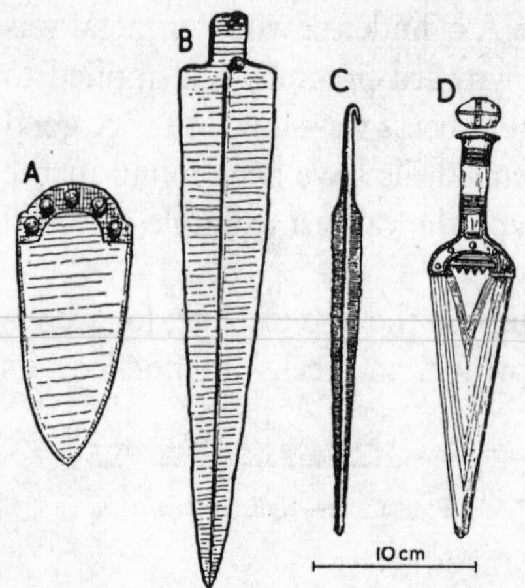

FIGURE 408—*Bronze Age daggers.* (A) *Round-heeled, from England.* (B) *Asiatic tanged form, from Ur, Mesopotamia.* (C) *Cypriot type, from Hungary.* (D) *Bronze-hilted, from Bohemia.*

rivets, the blade had to be broad-butted. Plain working weapons of this class are common, others are highly ornate and may be ceremonial. The attachment of the hilt by a tang had the advantage that the blade could be kept as slender as desired throughout its length. Sometimes the tang resembled that of a modern file, and was a backward prolongation of the midrib (figure 408 C). There were also flat tangs through which rivets were passed to prevent the hilt slipping off, or to attach the hilt-plates (figure 408 B).

The *halberd* was made in the first instance by fixing a dagger at right-angles to the end of a shaft. Occasionally this also was of bronze (figure 409). Early in the Bronze Age of western Europe the halberd was developed in the Spanish peninsula, spreading later along the Atlantic coast. It is well represented in Ireland, where copper specimens are known.

The *sword*, in a varied series of forms, developed from the dagger at the beginning of the Bronze Age. A frequent and early form was triangular, with a hilt attached by rivets. With the advent of bronze, and of the midrib technique, it was natural that the blade should become longer and the hilt proportionately narrower. Such long bronze daggers or dirks (sometimes called rapiers) increased in length to become, in effect, swords (figure 410). Though the weapon was primarily for thrusting, the length and weight imposed an undue strain on the riveted connexion between hilt and blade: the solution was to cast the hilt in one piece with the blade. On either side of the tang were flanges between which grip-plates, often of wood or bone, were secured. This strong and efficient construction permitted the use of stout heavy blades. Thus was evolved something like the well-known cavalry sabre (figure 411).

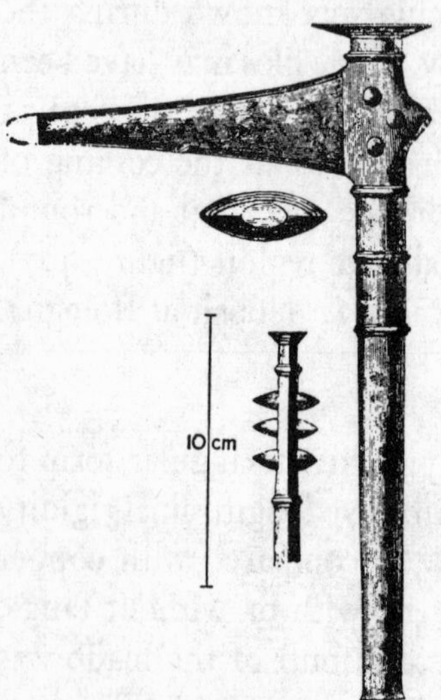

FIGURE 409—*Halberd from Skåne, Sweden.*

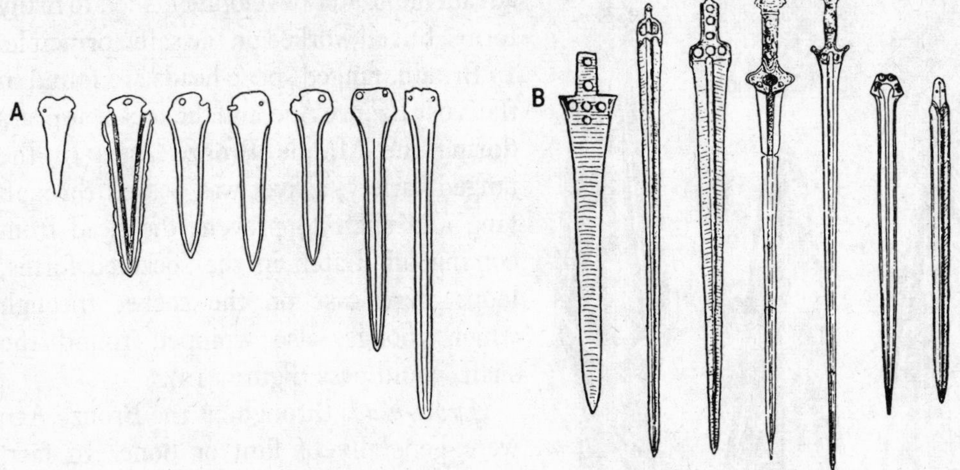

FIGURE 410—(A) *Evolution of the dirk.* (B) *Bronze rapiers from the Mediterranean.*

Such heavy bronze swords lasted into the Hallstatt phase of the Early Iron Age of western Europe, when they gradually gave way before iron weapons.

Technologically, the Bronze Age sword is interesting both for material and for mode of casting. For a sword to be serviceable, the material must be of good quality and free from non-metallic inclusions or flaws, and a balance must be struck between a soft sword liable to bend, and one hard but brittle. For these conditions, the tin content should not be appreciably below 10 per cent, and the blade must be carefully work-hardened. Considerable technical experience was needed in the design of the moulds, particularly in arranging the vents and pouring the metal to ensure soundness of casting. Archaeological evidence indicates that wooden patterns were sometimes used, while the moulds were usually of baked clay, strongly heated before the actual casting.

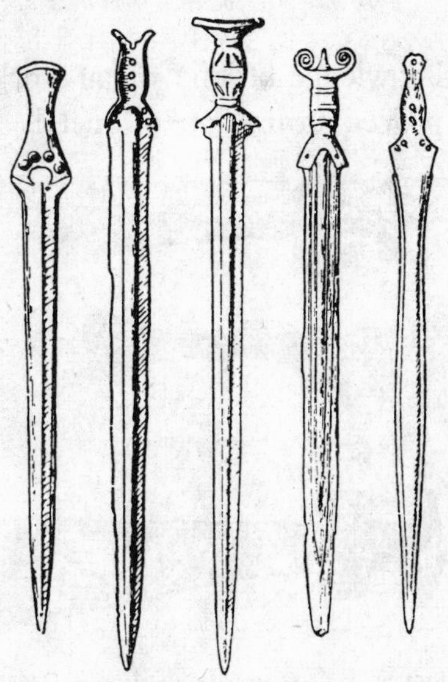

FIGURE 411—*Bronze swords.*

Spear-heads in their early copper form were tanged, but the advent of bronze, and the discovery of core-casting, led to the introduction of socketed types. The socket is mechanically sound, and utilizes the metal to the best

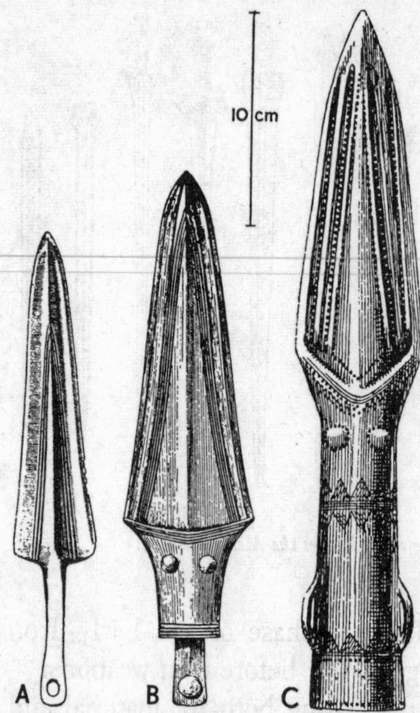

FIGURE 412—*Bronze spearheads.* (A) *Early Bronze Age, tanged, from Hintlesham, Suffolk.* (B) *Early Middle Bronze Age, tanged with ferrule, from Snowshill, Gloucestershire.* (C) *Middle Bronze Age, socketed, from Ireland.*

advantage. Later developments led to many forms, but all worked on the same principle. In Britain, tanged spear-heads are found in the Early Bronze Age, and the socket appears during the Middle Bronze Age. In the tanged variety, a rivet was passed through tang and shaft to prevent the head from coming off. Later, in the socketed forms, loops were cast on the socket through which thongs, also wrapped round the shaft, could pass (figure 412).

Arrow-heads throughout the Bronze Age were generally of flint or bone. In fact, some of the finest tanged and barbed flint arrow-heads belong to this period. During the Middle and Late Bronze Ages, however, tanged and barbed metal arrows were in limited use in Egypt, the Mediterranean, and central Europe. In Europe, the tang gradually gave way to the socket.

Battle-axes of copper and stone, equipped with a shaft-hole, were in use before the Bronze Age. Advance in casting, and the knowledge of fine metal-work, led rather to more ornate forms than to improved utilization of metal. Notably in Hungary, the ceremonial battle-axe was beautifully proportioned and elaborately decorated (figure 413), while some of the axes from Luristan became so elaborate and complex in design that they must have been cast by the *cire perdue* process (figure 414).

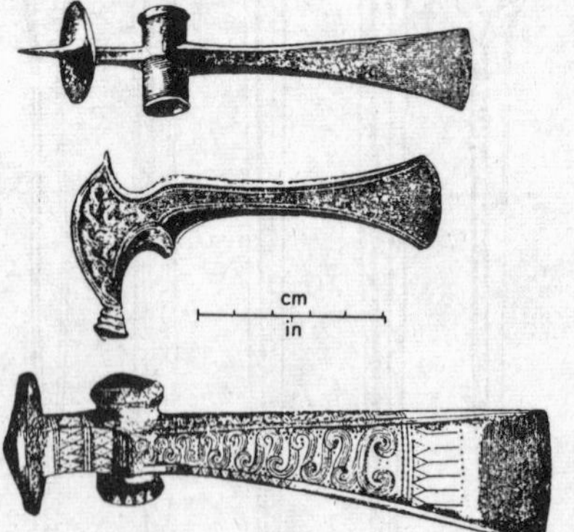

FIGURE 413—*Hungarian battle-axes. Middle Bronze Age.*

VII. IRON WEAPONS

Native iron of meteoric origin has occasionally been found shaped into beads and amulets in excavations of the eastern Mediterranean. The source of the iron can be recognized because of its high nickel content.

Ancient smelting produced wrought-iron, which, though excellent for working and welding, has not the hardness necessary for a sword or cutting-tool. Once the implement was shaped, hardness could be induced by carburizing (case-hardening). Carburizing involved heating the metal in contact with carbon; this in effect converted its surface into steel. By quenching and tempering, the smith could finally impart the best combination of hardness and toughness. Some of the earliest iron implements examined had been carburized. Iron of an intermediate period had been carburized and quenched, while iron of the Roman period had been carburized, quenched, and finally tempered (p 596).

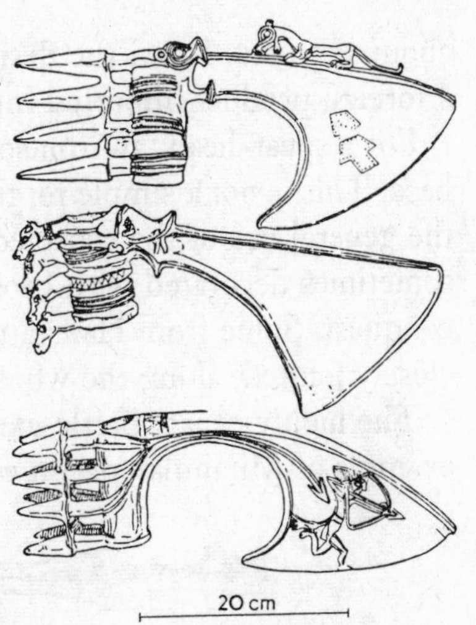

FIGURE 414—*Luristan battle-axes. Persia. 1500–1200 B.C.*

The first uses of iron were very limited. Its scarcity and cost confined it to magical and ornamental objects. Later, when more iron became available, though still rare, it was sometimes incorporated as part of a weapon; thus a dagger might have the blade of iron and the hilt of bronze. When it came into more general use, the whole tool or weapon would be made of iron, and the design became conditioned to its properties.

The sword was the weapon which profited most from the discovery of iron. During the Late Bronze Age it had developed in efficiency, but its power was limited by the strength of the blade: the introduction of iron transferred this limitation to the strength of the human arm. The change from bronze to iron was gradual, involving little alteration in the form of the sword. Early in the Iron Age in Britain, native smiths were making bronze copies of iron Hallstatt swords. Sometimes hilt and pommel were of bronze, the hilt-plate of the iron blade being flat and secured by rivets, as in the traditional bronze sword. Decoration was frequently applied to the hilt, a fine iron sword from Hallstatt even having a hilt and pommel of ivory inlaid with amber.

The widespread Hallstatt culture, named from the famous Early Iron Age cemeteries in that Austrian town, illustrates the transition of the sword from bronze to iron. Bronze antennae swords (figure 415) were succeeded by swords of iron (figure 416). Scabbards were of bronze, iron, wood, and leather. Decoration of scabbards and mounts became very rich during the late La Tène culture in

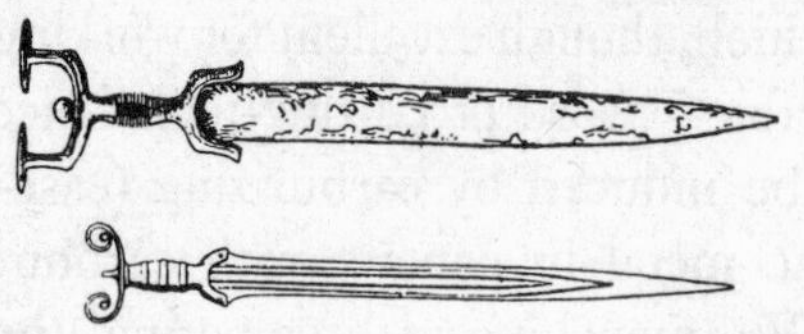

FIGURE 415—*Bronze antennae swords from Hallstatt.*

Europe, while decoration of the blade itself by pattern-welding may also date from the late La Tène cultures.

The dagger, like the sword, changed from bronze to iron, the transition beginning early in the Iron Age—as is shown by a fine iron dagger in Tutankhamen's tomb of about 1350 B.C. From the design and workmanship, this dagger was evidently a foreign product imported into Egypt (figure 417).

For a spear-head, an iron socket had to be made by leaving a flat plate at the base. This is not a simple forging operation, and the difficulty no doubt delayed the general use of the socketed iron spear. Nevertheless, fine iron spear-heads, sometimes decorated with bronze, were produced in Britain before the Roman conquest. Some from Hallstatt resemble those of bronze, being welded, or very closely jointed, along the whole length of the socket.

The highly ornate battle-axe of iron is not common. A magnificent very early example of Mitannian origin comes from Ras Shamra, Syria. It is of about 1300 B.C. and is remarkable as being wrought from three metals, copper and gold for the socket, and iron with a very high percentage of nickel for the blade. This treatment demands considerable metallurgical knowledge and very great technical skill. The copper socket, produced by the *cire perdue* method, has been cast round the blade, the contraction of the copper on cooling being sufficient to hold the blade firmly without rivets (figure 418).

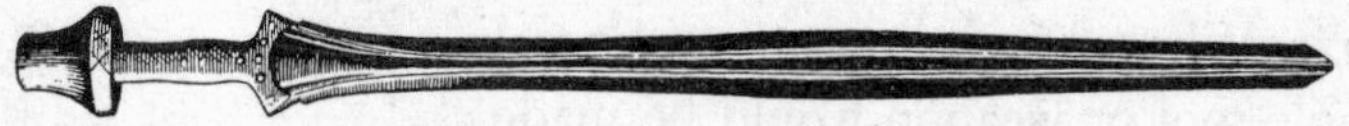

FIGURE 416—*Iron sword from Hallstatt.*

VIII. IRON TOOLS

For the technology of tools, the advent of iron was an event of the greatest importance. New tools appear early in the Iron Age. They include hinged tongs, frame saws, anvils for making nails, and blocks for drawing wire. Later, when it was discovered how to raise the carbon-content of the iron so that tempering and hardening became possible, axes, adzes, chisels, and gouges were much improved. New drills, bits, and augers were made, as well as a range of specialized hammers to suit the various trades. Most of our modern small hand-tools had come into evidence by the Late Iron Age, and certainly by early Roman times.

Early in the first millennium B.C. the more simple and efficient bronze axes and axe-adzes were translated into iron, and a heavy axe with a wide expanding blade was evolved. A socket, while an admirable device in a cast-bronze tool, is not well suited for an iron axe. The socket is also more difficult to forge than a shaft-hole. Nevertheless, socketed iron axes were used north of the Alps until about 400 B.C. At Hallstatt, two socketed axes of iron have been found, one resembling the old winged axe of bronze. From Traprain Law, in Scotland, comes an interesting socketed iron axe of Bronze Age shape, of a type suited to bronze casting but unsuited to forging in iron (figure 419). Design changed slowly in these prehistoric communities, and several examples of socketed iron axes have been found in Britain. Late survivals are known in Ireland, where they may well have continued into the early Christian period.

The chisel, tanged and socketed, was in use, as we have seen, in the Bronze Age. Iron improved the quality of this tool, but its design was not changed. Chisels of tempered semi-steel could be used against metal, like the cold chisel of today.

The drill has a very different history. Its cutting-edges, as distinct from awl-like points, appeared as an essential of a drilling-instrument during the Iron Age. Among the tools from Thebes in Upper Egypt is an S-section drill designed in the modern manner so that both edges cut forward when rotated. At the same time appeared the idea of the centre-pin, devised to prevent the drill from wandering. The large auger, turned by a cross-bar, is another form of drill which may be ascribed to the Late Iron Age.

The Iron Age witnessed marked improvements in the saw. The frame-saw

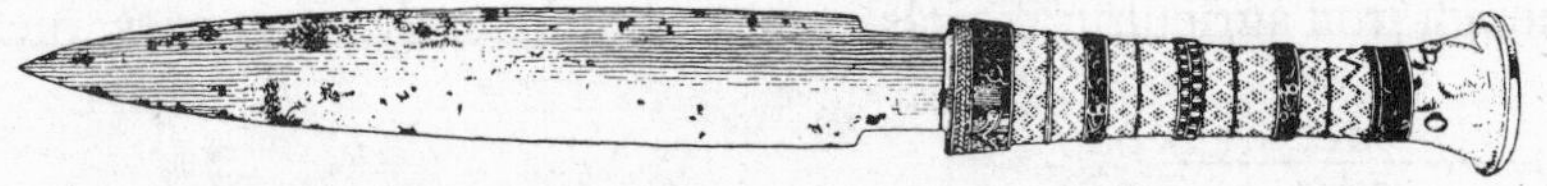

FIGURE 417—*Iron dagger from the tomb of Tutankhamen. Handle of rock-crystal and gold-decorated ivory. c 1350 B.C.*

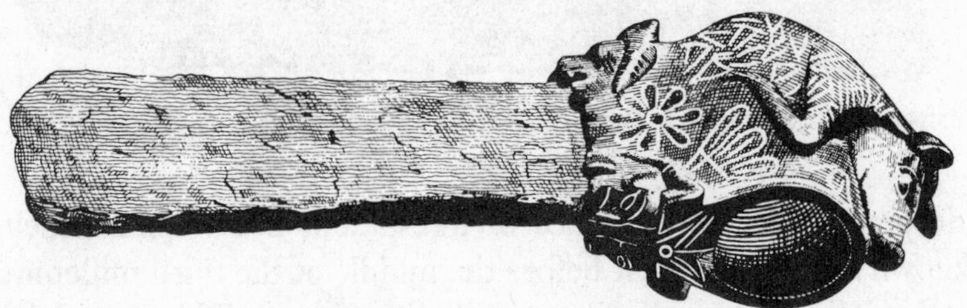

FIGURE 418—*Battle-axe from Ras Shamra, Syria. The blade is of iron, and the socket of copper with gold inlays. c 1300 B.C. Length 19·5 cm.*

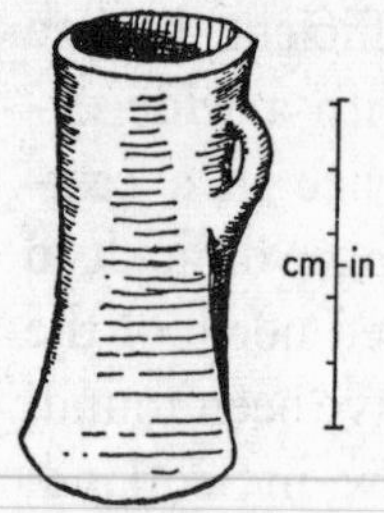

FIGURE 419—*Iron axe of Bronze Age type. Traprain Law, Scotland.*

(figure 420) was introduced in a form almost identical with that of the modern hacksaw. Except in cross-cut saws, the teeth were usually correctly raked in one direction. Examples are also known of Iron Age saws in which a correct set was given, to allow the saw a working clearance in its cut.

For the file, iron opened an entirely new field of use. It was no longer limited to wood and soft materials, but became one of the chief tools of the metal-worker. Following the La Tène phase of the Iron Age, iron files are relatively frequent in Europe, and in the Roman period they become common. Late Iron Age tool-smiths had grasped the true principle of the file. Indeed, instances are known of the teeth being cut obliquely across the working face of the tool, as in modern practice. A further refinement for filing the harder metals is the cutting of two sets of teeth intersecting each other, giving what we term the double-cut file. It is possible that this advanced technique was known by the close of the Iron Age.

Hinged tongs are essential to the smith who forges at red heat. They must have been invented soon after the dawn of the Iron Age, and are represented in very modern form in a Greek smithy of about 500 B.C. By the end of the Iron Age the craftsman's kit of tools was almost complete.

It will be seen that in pre-Roman times the great importance of iron was not so much that it led to a completely new series of tools and weapons, but rather that it resulted in an advance in the working properties of existing types of tools and weapons. During the Early Iron Age, when iron was relatively scarce and costly, the armament industry was probably the chief consumer of the new metal, though iron agricultural tools appeared quite early. Iron axes, picks, and

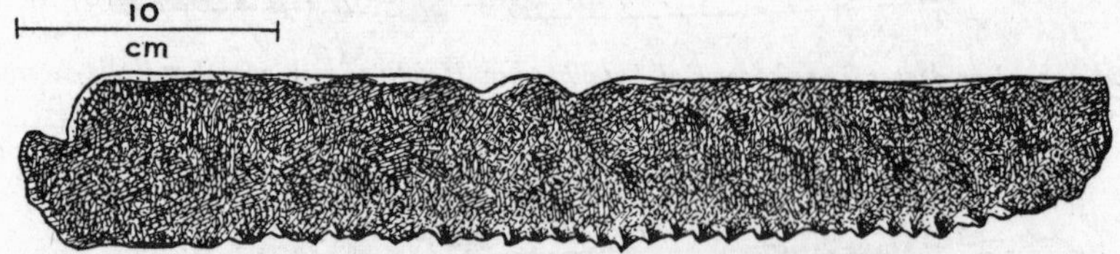

FIGURE 420—*Fragment of the blade of an iron saw from Rhenish Bavaria. Roman period.*

hoes made practicable the clearance of forests and heavy land. Smelted iron became known in the Near East before the middle of the third millennium B.C., but a true Iron Age did not begin until about 1200 B.C. This long delay in the establishment of the industry must be due to the fact that soft iron was no better a material for tools and weapons than tin-bronze, and often not as good. The fully developed Iron Age had to await the discovery of hardening and tempering.

REFERENCES

[1] COGHLAN, H. H. *Man*, **51,** art. 156, 1951.

[2] Proc. of the Ancient Mining and Metallurgy Group of the R. Anthrop. Inst. *Man*, **48,** arts. 3 and 17, 1948. (Reports on recent analyses of native copper.)

[3] COGHLAN, H. H. 'Notes on the Prehistoric Metallurgy of Copper and Bronze in the Old World.' *Occ. Pap. Tech. Pitt Rivers Mus.*, no. 4, p. 56, 1951.

FRANKFORT, H. *et al.* 'Tell Asmar and Khafaje.' Univ. of Chicago, Orient. Inst.: Commun. no. 13, pp. 76–78. Chicago. 1932.

[4] CHILDE, V. GORDON. 'The Dawn of European Civilization' (5th ed. rev.), pp. 239 ff. and fig. 116. Routledge and Kegan Paul, London. 1950.

[5] *Idem. Ibid.*, p. 32.

[6] COGHLAN, H. H. See ref. [3], p. 44.

[7] CHILDE, V. GORDON. 'The Bronze Age.' University Press, Cambridge. 1930.

BIBLIOGRAPHY

CARPENTER, SIR (HENRY CORT) HAROLD and ROBERTSON, J. M. "The Metallography of some Ancient Egyptian Implements". *J. Iron St. Inst.*, **121,** no. 1, 417, 1930.

CHILDE, V. GORDON. 'The Bronze Age.' University Press, Cambridge. 1930.

Idem. 'The Danube in Prehistory.' Clarendon Press, Oxford. 1929.

Idem. 'The Dawn of European Civilization' (5th ed. rev.). Routledge and Kegan Paul, London. 1950.

Idem. 'New Light on the Most Ancient East' (4th ed.). Routledge and Kegan Paul, London. 1952.

Idem. 'Prehistoric Communities of the British Isles' (3rd ed.). Chambers, Edinburgh, London. 1949.

Idem. 'The Story of Tools.' Cobbett, London. 1944.

COGHLAN, H. H. "The Evolution of the Axe from Prehistoric to Roman Times." *J. R. Anthrop. Inst.*, **73,** 27, 1943.

COWEN, J. D. "The Earliest Bronze Swords in Britain." *Proc. Prehist. Soc.*, new series **17,** 195, 1951.

EVANS, SIR JOHN. 'Ancient Bronze Implements.' Longmans, Green & Co., London. 1881.

Idem. 'Ancient Stone Implements.' Longmans, Green & Co., London. 1897.

FORBES, R. J. 'Metallurgy in Antiquity.' Brill, Leiden. 1950.

FRIEND, J. A. N. 'Iron in Antiquity.' Griffin & Co., London. 1926.

GARLAND, H. and BANNISTER, C. O. 'Ancient Egyptian Metallurgy.' Griffin & Co., London. 1927.

GOMPERTZ, M. 'The Master Craftsmen.' Nelson, London. 1933.

GRIMES, W. F. 'The Prehistory of Wales.' National Museum of Wales, Cardiff. 1951.

HUTCHINSON, R. W. "Battle-axes in the Aegean." *Proc. Prehist. Soc.*, new series **16,** 52, 1950.

LUCAS, A. 'Ancient Egyptian Materials and Industries' (3rd ed.). Arnold, London. 1948.

MARYON, H. "Technical Methods of the Irish Smiths." *Proc. R. Irish Acad.*, **44,** section C, vii, 1938.

MEGAW, B. R. S. and HARDY, E. M. "British Decorated Axes and their Diffusion during the Earlier Part of the Bronze Age." *Proc. Prehist. Soc.*, new series **4**, 272, 1938.

OLDEBERG, A. E. 'Metallteknik under Förhistorisk Tid' (2 Vols). Harrassowitz, Leipzig. 1943.

Ó'RÍORDÁIN, S. P. "The Halberd in Bronze Age Europe." *Archaeologia*, **86**, 195, 1937.

OTTO, H. and WITTER, W. 'Handbuch der ältesten vorgeschichtlichen Metallurgie in Mitteleuropa.' Barth, Leipzig. 1952.

PEAKE, H. J. E. 'The Bronze Age and the Celtic World.' Benn, London. 1922.

Idem. 'Early Steps in Human Progress.' Sampson Low, London. 1933.

PEAKE, H. J. E. and FLEURE, H. J. 'Corridors of Time Series.' Vol. 7: 'Merchant Venturers in Bronze.' 1931. Vol. 8: 'The Horse and the Sword.' 1933. Vol. 9: 'The Law and the Prophets.' 1936. The Clarendon Press, Oxford.

PETRIE, SIR (WILLIAM MATTHEW) FLINDERS. 'Tools and Weapons.' Egypt Res. Acc. and Brit. Sch. Archaeol. Egypt, Publ. 30. London. 1917.

PIGGOTT, S. "Swords and Scabbards of the British Early Iron Age." *Proc. Prehist. Soc.*, new series **16**, 1, 1950.

PRZEWORSKI, S. "Die Metallindustrie Anatoliens in der Zeit von 1500–700 vor Chr." *Int. Arch. Ethnogr.*, **36**, supplement. 1939.

RAFTERY, J. 'Prehistoric Ireland.' Batsford, London. 1951.

RICKARD, T. A. 'Man and Metal' (2 Vols). McGraw-Hill, New York, London. 1932.

SCHAEFFER, C. F. A. 'Stratigraphie comparée et chronologie de l'Asie occidentale.' University of Oxford, Griffith Institute. Oxford University Press, London. 1948.

SMITH, R. A. "The Perforated Axe-hammers of Britain." *Archaeologia*, **75**, 77, 1926.

WALKER, W. F. 'The Bronze Axe.' Hull Museum Aids. 1939.

Phalanx of Sumerian soldiers armed with copper-tipped spears. Relief on a stele from Tello, Mesopotamia. Third millennium B.C.

23

FINE METAL-WORK

HERBERT MARYON AND H. J. PLENDERLEITH

I. THE CRAFTSMAN AND HIS MATERIALS

THE term 'fine metal-work' conveniently describes a type of craftsmanship well recognized but difficult to define. It falls within the province of technology as well as that of art. We shall consider metal objects which display both taste and mastery of technique as satisfying our definition, irrespective of use or function. Weapons as such are not dealt with here, but specimens of great technical or artistic merit come within our scope.

The metals available to the ancient craftsman were gold and silver (frequently as the natural gold-silver alloy electrum), copper, tin, lead, and iron. Association for decorative purposes of the two precious metals in a single work is rare in later times, but such combinations were earlier regarded with pleasure. Thus from Ur comes a silver bowl decorated by ribbons of electrum, simulating basketry, and a plaque—perhaps part of a buckle—decorated with electrum bosses resting on silver filigree. Again, Irish craftsmen of the Late Bronze Age made thick penannular gold rings, about an inch in diameter and perhaps used as hair-rings or as a convenient medium of exchange, which have round them a spiral inlaid band of a grey colour, probably silver or niello.[1] From Mycenaean and Cypriote sites—also of the Bronze Age—come works of great interest. Notable are silver cups decorated with bulls' heads between flowers, inlaid in gold and silver, with niello very skilfully employed to strengthen the design (figure 421).

When knowledge of the working of the more refractory metals was attained, iron and bronze were sometimes coupled together in decorative work. At Nimrud, in Assyria, about the eighth century B.C., iron was a new and interesting material, sometimes used as an embellishment for bronze fittings, as in some bronze feet for chairs with a purely ornamental iron collar (figure 422). By contrast, there are iron grilles with a cast-bronze decorative link at each of the crossings of the square bars. This method may indicate that the welding of such an iron grille was then impracticable in Assyria.

[1] Niello (Latin *nigellus*, blackish) is a mixture of metallic sulphides, fused as an inlay into gold- or silver-work. It is generally blue-black or grey-black in colour.

FIGURE 421—*Silver bowl with inlays of gold and niello. Enkomi, Cyprus. c 1400 B.C. Scale 1/2.*

Many of the earliest examples of fine metal-work are from the riverine civilizations of Mesopotamia and Egypt. Technologically, the most important single find was that made in 1926–32, in the royal cemetery of Ur. When the cemetery was in use (before 2500 B.C.), most technical processes employed during the long history of metal-working had already been invented. The exceptions are enamelling, niello, wire-drawing, making of beaded wire, spinning, and, of course, electro-chemical processes.

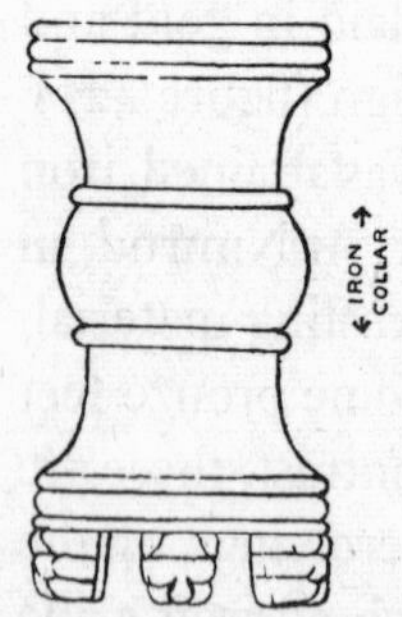

FIGURE 422 — *Bronze chair-foot with iron collar, from Nimrud, Mesopotamia. Eighth century B.C.*

II. ANNEALING

The skill demonstrated in the finds suggests that the discovery of these processes was much more ancient, and was made in the fourth millennium B.C. The settled Neolithic way of life had by then given the craftsman time and opportunity to discover that the bright yellow substance, gold, from some river-beds could be hammered into pin, hook, or thin flat plate. The craftsman had also found that hammering made the somewhat similar 'stone', copper, stiffer and harder to work. If he tried to fashion a bowl from a much-hammered plate he found that it became too hard to shape further. Perhaps he pleated the edges a little to make a vessel in which to boil water; it proved specially useful, for it did not break as did pots of clay. It boiled dry on one occasion and became red-hot; he drew it from the fire with his lifting-sticks and found, to his surprise, that it was now soft and pliable. The bowl could be hammered again to a better shape. It hardened with the renewed blows, and he remembered the fire and found that whenever the metal became hard under his hammer he could soften it again by fire. He had discovered annealing.

Copper and other metals which have become hard and strained as a result of hammering or bending may be softened by heat. The effect of hammering or bending a metal is that the crystals of which it is composed become distorted and strained and, as a rule, if the cold-working is continued for long, cracks may develop. However, under the influence of heat, though the external shape is not changed, the crystals rearrange themselves so that they are no longer under strain, the metal becomes soft again, and the hammering or other work may proceed.

III. MOULDING AND CASTING

Another stage was reached when a craftsman, having placed a piece of gold on the fire to anneal it, saw it melt suddenly and run down among the ashes. The precious pieces were recovered, but he determined not to give himself such a task again. He would put the nugget, on which he was working, into a cooking-pot. This time, on giving it a good firing, he was surprised to find his plate running into a button. He had melted instead of annealing it. Beginning to form his plate afresh, he was careful not to overheat it when it became hard. To make a bigger bowl, he tried running small pieces of native gold into a large lump. Now, becoming familiar with molten metal, he could pass on to make moulds in which it could be cast into convenient shapes. Casting involves pouring liquefied metal into a mould where it can cool and solidify. Such metal has a characteristic micro-crystalline structure, which may be changed by mechanical treatment.

In many parts of the ancient world, the earliest axes and other objects in metal were cast in open moulds of stone or baked clay. Later, two-piece moulds came into use, with core-pieces for sockets when required. From many Bronze and Early Iron Age sites in Europe piece-moulds of stone, burnt clay, and bronze have been recovered, and fine examples of bronze-casting abound. We have but to look at the splendid bronze implements and weapons from Hungary, Scandinavia, and some other parts of Europe to realize that these founders were complete masters of their craft, and could design and execute works which would hold their own in any company. By the time of the early cemetery at Ur, foundry-work had reached a high level of efficiency. Three- or four-pieced moulds were in regular use. Examination of a little gold monkey surmounting a bronze pin, of the electrum onager on Queen Shub-ad's rein-ring (figure 219), and of the silver bull on a king's rein-ring (figure 423) suggests that they were probably first modelled in wax, but then, like the axes, cast in piece-moulds. The monkey and the onager, as their surfaces indicate, were thoroughly 'chased' (p 642) after casting, to remove all casting-webs and rough surfaces. The silver bull, however, was not smoothed, and the original cast surface can be seen. Surviving parts of the webs outline a piece of the mould which covered most of the right side of the bull's body. There would be other pieces also. Enough evidence is available to show that the wax or clay in which the bull was modelled could have been removed piece-meal when the side piece was lifted away from the rest of the mould. The craftsmen were able to cast bulls' heads in copper or silver up to 4 or 5 inches in length, besides many smaller works; the cast heads are solidly made and weighty. On some of them, between the horns, down the front of the head, and under the lower jaw there remain traces of the casting webs. The ears and horns were cast in one piece with the head.

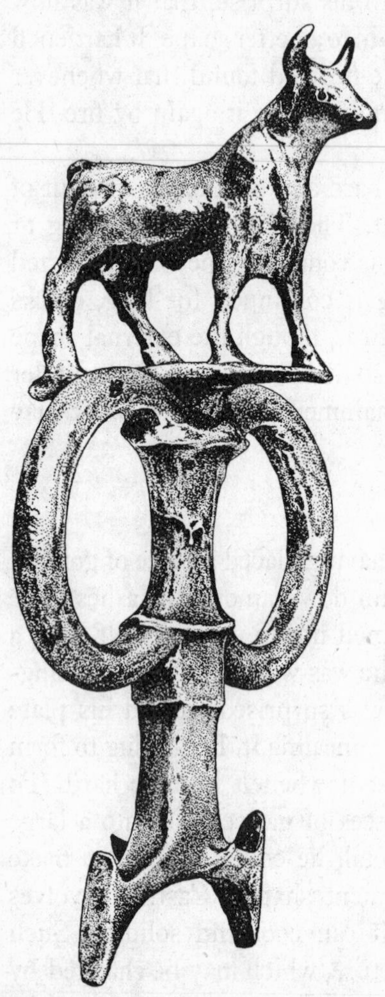

FIGURE 423—*Silver bull on a rein-ring from Ur, Mesopotamia. Before 2500 B.C. Height about 8½ in.*

Cored castings. The early craftsman found that the casting of a figure of a god or a spear-head consumed much of his precious metal, and it was an obvious saving to make the castings hollow. For this he needed some means of fixing a solid mass of material inside his mould to occupy all the space except the gap to be filled with metal. The making of such a core provided problems. It had to be kept in place, for should it touch the inner surface of the mould, the casting would show an unwelcome hole. Sometimes it was easy to keep the core in position; thus the core of a figure with drapery reaching to the ground could be attached firmly to the base of the mould. Another method was to fasten stout projecting spikes of bronze and, at a later period, of iron, into the surface of the core. This could be laid inside the mould, but kept from touching it by the spikes. Bronze spear-heads and sword-chapes from the Late Bronze and Early Iron Ages provided with such 'chaplets' are known. Gradually the founder became skilled in making cores so accurately shaped that the space left for the metal was of even thickness.

FIGURE 424—*Bronze head of Sargon the Great of Akkad. Nineveh, Mesopotamia.* c *2250* B.C.

The founder had other difficulties. When molten metal was poured into a mould the heat expanded any air in its substance; so, to permit the air to escape, the mould was made of porous material. But the craftsman soon realized that he must find a way to ventilate the core also, for, if totally enclosed by molten metal, the expanding air would leave the cast full of bubbles. He had to provide in the core a passage or vent through which air might escape.

A fine head from Nineveh, of Sargon, King of Akkad, is probably the earliest surviving life-sized portrait-head in cast bronze. The founder had mastered all his technical problems, though his cast is rather heavy. He chased the whole surface, and inserted the eyes, probably in shell or stone (figure 424).

On the walls of the tomb of Rekhmire, prefect of Upper Egypt in the reign of Amenhetep II (*c* 1440 B.C.), there are paintings showing the casting of copper doors for a temple (figure 383). Workers bring charcoal in a sack, tend the fire, and work the leather bellows with their feet. The crucible is lifted off the fire with lifting-sticks and the metal poured into the mould through a series of seventeen funnels. Of the mould itself, only a rectangular outline is shown. It was probably of slabs of baked clay, like the ordinary Egyptian brick, but burnt to terracotta hardness to make it strong enough to withstand the great pressure of the liquid metal. In many hollow-cast statues from Egypt there are cores of sandy material containing blackened organic matter, which bound it and gave it porosity.

In spite of statements to the contrary, moulds constructed of sand packed tightly within a pair of linked casting-flasks or moulding-boxes were nowhere

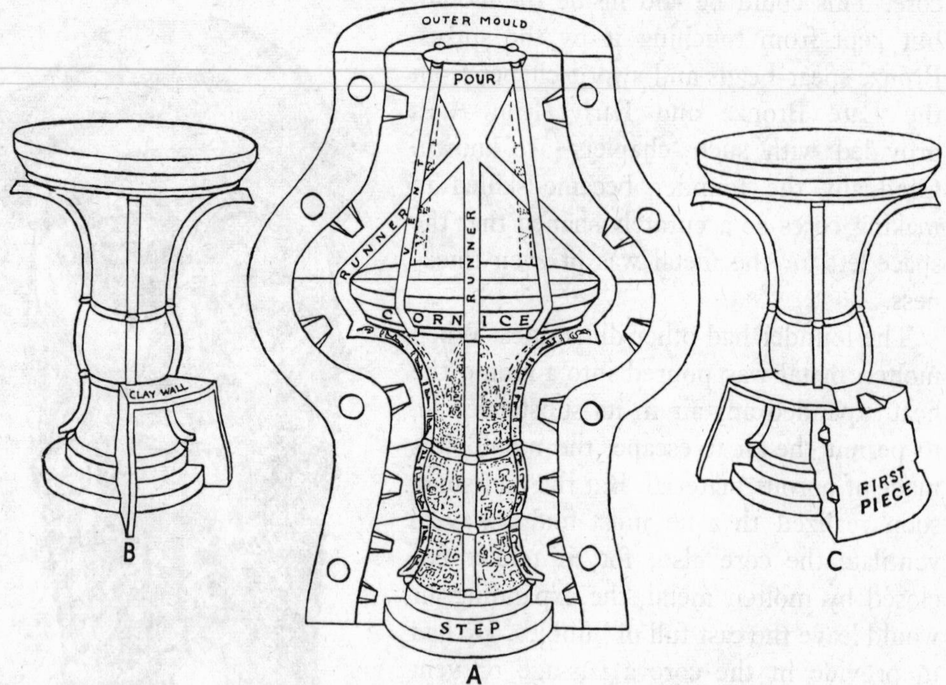

FIGURE 425—*Piece-moulding a Chinese* tsun *(wine vessel).* (A) *General view of interior of mould.* (B) *Wax-model with walls for first part of piece-mould in position.* (C) *First part of piece-mould completed with mortises cut; boundaries of second part in position. Note: the modelled ornament has been omitted in* (B) *and* (C). *Vessel hollow-based up to level of first piece of mould in* (C).

employed before the later Middle Ages. Moulding in clay was the principal process for casting in antiquity, stone or metal being less frequently employed. Actual piece-moulds in which bronze vessels have been cast, of the Shang-Yin Dynasty (*c* 1766–1122 B.C.), have recently been discovered in China [1]. Made of burnt clay, they retain upon their inner surface original ornamental designs characteristic of contemporary bronze-work.

We may reconstruct the process of a simple casting, viz. of a *tsun* or wine-vessel. A mass of clay was prepared, incorporating sand, powdered brick, and sawdust or bonedust to make it porous on firing. From this, a core for the lowest section of the vessel, up to the septum, was thrown on a potter's wheel. It had a stepped-out foundation-member (figure 425 A), which would subsequently form a support for other pieces of the mould. The core was dried, and a layer of wax, of the thickness desired for the bronze, spread over its surface, including the septum, or bottom of the vessel. The wax was rolled out and fitted round the core, and its edges were joined by heating. The fashioning of the upper part of the core and the wax layer for it was now undertaken. On the upper edge of the core, a stepped-out member, a kind of cornice, similar to the step on the lowest section, was formed. Against this cornice, when the wax layer had been completed, the third row of pieces of the mould would rest. They, in their turn, would support the core by its cornice when the wax septum, which had temporarily supported the upper part of the core, had been removed. The four projecting fins, the eyes, and other strongly projecting parts of the ornament would be added in wax, and the remainder of the ornament modelled. Before the pieces were formed, the craftsman made provision for the construction of the pour, the runners, and the vents, by means of which the molten metal might enter the mould and the air escape.

It is probable that the four projecting fins which ran from the top to the bottom of the vessel would be recognized as conveniently placed 'runners' for the entry of the metal. The usual breaks in their length would be temporarily filled by pads of wax. The model for the pour was a funnel-shaped mass of wax connected with the tops of the fins by rods of wax, or runners, to form passages through which the molten metal might pass into the mould. A further series of wax rods leading upwards from the rim of the vessel formed vents for the escape of the air when the metal entered the mould.

The piece-mould was constructed as follows. A strip of clay about $\frac{3}{4}$-in wide and $\frac{1}{4}$-in thick was fitted against each of the two vertical fins which outlined one-quarter of the lowest section of the vessel (figure 425 B). A third, horizontal, strip joined them, in line with the septum, and the stepped-out foot of the core formed part of the fourth side of the wall, or boundary, within which the first part of the piece-mould was to be made. The surface of the clay bands and of the step was oiled to prevent adhesion. Some of the prepared clay was ground finely, and painted over the wax and against the adjacent clay bands and step. Care was taken to ensure that every part of the pattern was completely covered, and that there were no air-bubbles. When this layer had dried, several additional layers of clay were painted over the first, the later layers containing more of the roughage employed to induce porosity. When the 'piece' had been built up to about an inch thick, and had dried sufficiently, the clay bands were removed, and the piece was carefully lifted from the model. It was replaced after a series of wedge-shaped mortises had been cut along its edges, so that the adjoining pieces, about to be made, might register accurately. Temporary walls of clay were now fitted to outline the next piece; one edge of the first-made piece and part of the stepped-out core forming two of them (figure 425 C). After the walls had been oiled, the second piece of the mould was prepared in the same way as the first. When sufficiently dry, the second piece was lifted away and its mortises were cut. The remaining pieces of all three tiers were formed in a similar manner. The original wax model of the *tsun* had now been invested inside and out by the core and the mould. After the third tier of pieces had been completed, a fourth tier was made embracing the vents, the pour, and the runners. When the last-made pieces were dry enough to be handled, the mould was opened, and every part of the wax removed. Any defect in the face of the mould might now be made good; accessibility to the modelled surface of the mould is one of the virtues of a piece-mould. The pieces were next replaced on the core and a thick layer of coarse moulding-material (the outer mould) was spread over the whole mould, binding all the parts together and leaving exposed only the tops of the pour and the air-vents. The mould was allowed to dry slowly, then baked to terracotta hardness, and filled with metal before it cooled.

Some Chinese bronze vessels of the Shang-Yin period are provided with loose ring handles. In several examples, their staples were cast separately from the vessels which they were to adorn, and were fitted into their places and fused there by running molten metal into the gap between them. In some specimens, the mould required for this operation had shrunk back a little on drying, and a thin web of bronze shows where some of the metal escaped. In a few cases, the tang of a pre-cast handle projects within the vessel, and, in the centre of the tang, the characteristic hollow may be observed where the molten metal at the head of the casting had contracted on cooling.

The Chinese moulds mentioned above provide additional evidence that they had at some time been used in the foundry, and had held molten metal within them. Originally they were fired to a red colour, but their inner surface, against which the molten bronze flowed, has changed to a grey colour. Such a change is a characteristic phenomenon, well known to bronze-founders. That these moulds were piece-moulds demonstrates also that the founder wished to lift them from the model and to remove the wax by hand. Had he wished to employ the *cire perdue* process (p 634) there would have been no need for the piece-mould—the mould could have been made as a whole.

It may be noted that in many examples the background or depressed portion of the ornament was once filled with black lacquer.

Sometimes the Chinese craftsman wished to set an inscription in a place that could not be easily reached, say at the bottom of a narrow-mouthed vessel. He incised the inscription on a slab of wax, then beat up some clay to a fine slip and painted it over the work. Several fine coats were laid on until all the hollows were completely filled. Then, while the last coat was plastic, the inscribed clay slip, still supported by the wax slab, was stuck on to the core. The

FIGURE 426—*Bronze lion-gryphon from Bactria. About third century* B.C. *Height 9·8 in.*

edges of the inscribed slab were then carefully joined to the rest of the wax model, and the inscription was thus embodied as part of the mould.

A raised grid pattern was formed on the floor of a bronze vessel in a similar manner. The slab of wax was rolled out on a board in which a grid pattern had been incised. The raised pattern in wax would be filled with the slip before it was affixed to the core. There is evidence that on some Chinese caskets a clay mould was formed over the original model, which itself may have been of clay suitably prepared against adhesion. The model was removed, probably piecemeal, and the mould was then lined with slabs of wax before the core was formed within it. That this was the method employed is demonstrated by the rows of tool-marks, visible within the completed bronze vessel, which show that the wax slabs were joined up and tooled from the inside of the vessel.

The great headless statue of Queen Napir-aṣu, consort of Ountash-gal, a Cassite king of *c* 1300 B.C., is an example of fine metal-work, and is of considerable internal interest. The statue is entirely covered with inscriptions and ornaments worked with the tracer, and weighs nearly 2 tons. The external layer of the casting is about an inch thick, rising to 3 in at the hands. Within, there is a mass of metal apparently formed by many successive pourings from small crucibles. Since the metal cooled a little between each pouring, this mass is less compact than the outer shell of the statue. Perhaps the additional metal was added to strengthen a crack that formed in the casting when it cooled. It is to avoid this mischance that modern bell-founders rake out the core of a large bell as soon as the metal has set, and before it has had time to contract strongly.

The pair of bronze *barrières* in the Louvre, inscribed with the name of Shilk-hak-in-shushinak, King of Susa, demonstrate the skill of the founders of the eleventh century B.C. They are tubular, about 20 ft long, 8 inches in diameter, and about ½-in thick. They are squared for about 2 ft at each end. The metal for each casting was probably poured simultaneously from crucibles through many funnels.

The fierce, threatening attitude of a lion-gryphon from Bactria (figure 426) may be compared with that of the better known chimera from Arezzo. The detailed modelling of the gryphon is not carried so far as that on the Etruscan beast, but it has considerable power and dignity. Its aesthetic tradition is that of the Persian armlet discussed below. The figure stands nearly 10 in high and is of cast bronze. It dates from about the third century B.C.

Moulds provided with heavy wooden supports are suggested by the description given by Sennacherib, King of Assyria (705–681 B.C.), of the figures decorating his palace at Nineveh:

> 'Eight lions, open at the knee, advancing, constructed out of 11 400 talents of shining bronze . . . together with two colossal pillars the copper-work for which came to 6000 talents'; and again 'I, Sennacherib, first among all princes, wise in all craftsmanship [wrought] great pillars of bronze, colossal lions, open at the knees, which no king before my time had fashioned, through the clever understanding which the noble [god] Nin-igi-kug had given me [and] in my own wisdom. I pondered deeply the matter of carrying out the task. . . . Over great posts and crossbars of wood, 12 fierce lion colossi, together with 12 mighty bull colossi . . . clothed with exuberant strength and with abundance and splendour heaped upon them. . . . I built a forme of clay and poured bronze into it, as in making half shekel pieces, and finished their construction' [2].

From this description it is clear that the legs of these figures were in the round, and sufficiently strong in themselves to support the body. Sennacherib's moulds were of clay; they would be piece-moulds, built up individually against the original models. When removed from the model they would be fitted with a core, and the necessary jets and vents for casting would be provided. Next, the core and mould would be set up near the furnace and fired to enable them to withstand the pressure of the molten metal. Then brick walls would be built round them, strengthened by the 'great posts and crossbars of wood'. These could not have been placed within the moulds themselves, for the heat of the molten metal might have set them alight, with disastrous results; nor could the mould have been baked if they were within.

We need not take at its face value Sennacherib's claim that this method of working was his own invention, for 250 years earlier Hiram of Tyre was making even greater works for the temple which Solomon built at Jerusalem. Among them were the two brazen (that is, bronze) pillars, 23 cubits high, and the great 'sea', or basin,

'ten cubits from brim to brim, round in compass, and the height thereof was five cubits: and a line of thirty cubits compassed it round about.... It stood upon twelve oxen ... the Sea was set upon them above, and all their hinderparts were inward. It was a handbreadth thick: and the brim thereof was wrought like the brim of a cup, like the flower of a lily.... In the Plain of Jordan did the king cast them, in the clay ground between Succoth and Zarethan [or Zeredah].' (2 Chron. IV. 2, 4, 5, 17; cf. 1 Kings VII. 23, 25, 26, 46.)

It has been estimated that the 'brazen sea' alone weighed 200 tons. The oxen would have been cast separately.

In the Jordan valley the prevailing winds blow from the north, and smelting-ovens for copper, e.g. near Elath, were oriented accordingly. The soil is a marl, with patches of clay. It is clear that the moulds were actually excavated in one of these patches—there is no indication in the Hebrew text that any special clays were used. Such vast moulds could hardly have been constructed in any other way. This was only a small step beyond the method, already being used in Egypt, and commonly elsewhere, of supporting clay moulds by burying them in the ground before the furnace. The furnaces for this work would also have been placed so as to make use of the prevailing winds.[1] The way of fashioning the mould for the great bowl may be reconstructed. In front of the furnaces a pit was dug. To an arm pivoted at its centre a template was attached, the outer edge being curved to the profile of the basin, so that when the arm swung round the pivot the template described the desired shape. Ropes, probably of straw, were laid on the floor and up the sides of the pit, and then covered with well beaten clay mixed with broken pots. The ropes provided vents for the escape of gases evolved

[1] The authors wish to acknowledge information kindly given them by Professors A. Reifenberg and L. Picard of the Hebrew University, Jerusalem; and by Dr S. Yeivin, Director of Antiquities for the State of Israel.

when the molten metal was poured into the mould. The space between the walls and floor of the pit and the edge of the template was gradually filled up with more clay and broken bricks or pots, the template being moved round as required. The outermost $\frac{1}{4}$-in or so of the filling was of more finely textured clay, suitable for modelling the decorative borders of the bowl, 'like the brim of a cup, like the flower of a lily'. The clay surface was allowed to dry slowly, cracks being stopped with clay. The construction of the core for the inner surface of the basin was now considered. This core would be suspended within the mould, and only a hand-breadth above it. A framework of metal supports would be placed to keep it in position. After drying, the mould and channels leading into it from the furnaces would be well baked, and heated with charcoal so that the metal would not become chilled. When the glowing coals had been swept out, the sections of the inner mould were firmly secured in register, lest it should float upon the molten metal. The mould was now ready for the metal. The method of casting the oxen was probably similar to that described above for the work executed for Sennacherib (p 632).

Nearly 400 years after these works had been completed for Solomon, Nebuchadrezzar, King of Babylon, twice conquered Jerusalem (597, 586 B.C.) and his Chaldean warriors broke up all the bronze work which Solomon had caused to be made for the temple, and carried it away to Babylon.

From this time onwards there are many cast-bronze fittings for interior decoration and furniture from Mesopotamian and Egyptian sites. These show that the craftsmen had complete control over the design and use of their material. It was the great experience in the modelling of such works, in the preparation of moulds, and in the handling of large masses of molten metal—the prerogative of the bronze founders of the Near East for perhaps a thousand years—which made technically possible that renaissance of fine sculpture and craftsmanship in bronze, so characteristic a feature of Dynasty XXVI in Egypt, and of the sixth and later centuries B.C. in Greece.

The *cire perdue* or *waste-wax process* is a method of casting in metal by means of an external mould in one piece, from which the wax of the model can be removed only by melting. (A casting made in a mould which might have been opened for the removal of the wax is not a *cire perdue* casting.) A model, if small, may be cast solid, but for a hollow cast a core, or mould for the internal surface of the metal, must be provided. The model may be constructed in wax over a previously prepared core. Failing that, a complete piece-mould in plaster or some flexible material, such as gelatine, is made, into which a layer of wax of the thickness required for the metal is painted or poured. Inside this wax layer, the core of clay and pounded brick or other infusible material is formed. It should be provided with suitable vents. The temporary mould is removed, and then a complete system of runners, through which the metal may flow from the pour to all parts of the mould, and of vents by which the air may escape, is built up of rods of wax. They are all arranged to incline in one general direction, for each piece of wax must be so placed that it will drain out of the mould on melting. The wax system being completed, a thin layer of fine clay is painted over it, and further layers, now mixed with powdered brick or other material to afford porosity, are added until the mould is of sufficient thickness. Iron wires may be bound round it if necessary. The complete external mould is thus built up in one piece. It is placed in the oven in such a position that all the wax may escape when heated. The mould is then baked and is ready for the metal. When this has been cast, the mould is broken off, all runners and vents (now in metal) are cut away, and the rough surfaces are chased. In work cast by the piece-moulding process, a little metal may escape into gaps between individual pieces of the mould, and these webs must be removed when the surface is chased. With *cire perdue* work there are no such webs, though of course the scars left by the runners and vents must be removed. Generally it is the form of any individual model which guides the founder in his choice between the two processes.

IV. WORKING IN SHEET METAL

The early craftsman developed the technique of forging native copper. The question whether the hot-forging or cold-working process was used by ancient smiths can be answered only from knowledge of their tools. Hot-forging implies efficient tools for holding the work during hammering. A modern blacksmith's tongs are about 20 in long, the jaws extending some 3 in beyond the hinge. His grip when holding them equals a pressure of at least 40 lb. Suppose this pressure to be applied 16 in from the hinge of the tongs, and the grip on the work to be centred about 2 in beyond the hinge, then the grip on the work will be $40 \times 8 = 320$ lb. With this ample hold the work does not slip, but it will be held about 18 in from where the hammer-blows fall. No metal-worker would attempt to raise or sink a bowl with so distant a grip. Moreover, so far as Egypt is concerned, the use of hinged tongs seems to have been unknown even as late as the fifteenth century B.C. In paintings of that period, the tongs of founders casting a door are only crossed strips of wood or metal (figure 383).[1] When hot metal is being worked the hand must be kept a reasonable distance from it —say 8 in. The grip on the work itself would be correspondingly reduced, and

[1] The earliest representations of tongs of the modern type are Greek of the fifth century B.C.

insufficient for a safe hold. Alternatively, the metal could have been held on the anvil by pressing with a rod, but to form a bowl thus, from a hot sheet, would be difficult. Thus beaten work, such as that from Ur, must have been done mostly by cold-forging, a process still employed wherever hand-working is practised. To the craftsman, it has the immense advantage that by holding the work in his hand he has complete control over it.

Consider the fabrication of a vessel, of a single original piece, or of a number of pieces soldered or riveted together after each had been given its particular form. The metal disk from which the vessel was to be constructed had first to be prepared. One example of such a blank is a circular cake of bronze about 4 inches in diameter and $\frac{1}{8}$-in thick, from Ringstead, Norfolk. It shows how the ancient worker prepared a flat sheet from the rounded button of bronze he had cast. He first flattened it with a heavy hammer and annealed it. Then he beat it with a convex-faced hammer, the face in this case measuring $\frac{1}{2}$ in by about $\frac{1}{8}$ in. Blows from such a hammer stretch the metal at right-angles to the longer side of the hammer face. Without rotating it, the smith worked all over one surface of the cake. He then turned the cake over and gave it a series of blows, this time in a direction at right-angles to the first series. Thus he stretched the metal evenly in two directions at right-angles, so that the thinning proceeded regularly. He would anneal it at intervals when it hardened. Finally, if a smooth sheet was required, he would beat it with a flat-faced hammer to remove the dents. A cake of bronze so treated with deep hammer-marks in sets of parallel grooves on both faces was found at Clough, County Antrim, Ireland. It would not be always necessary to hammer such a piece of metal very smooth.

If the smith wished to produce a bowl, he had a choice between two ways of working. He might sink it from a small, comparatively thick disk by continued hammering on the inside of the bowl; or raise it from a thinner, larger disk by hammering the outside of the bowl while it was supported locally by a suitably-shaped 'stake' or anvil. Stakes are made in a great variety of forms, so that a work of any profile may be shaped upon them. Small stakes are held in a 'horse'—an iron bar with a socket for the tang of the stake.

To sink a bowl, the smith would hold the disk on an anvil of metal or stone and, with a convex-faced hammer, beat it at or near the centre. Each blow would thin the metal a little as the rounded-face of the hammer compressed the metal and drove some of it laterally all around the surface of contact. He would strike a series of blows in a long spiral from the centre of the disk, but would stop hammering before he reached the edge. This hammering would produce a shallow dish which would require annealing. The smith would repeat his hammering again and again, always beginning near the centre and stopping before he reached the edge, and annealing the work before proceeding further.[1]

When the smith had produced a bowl of the general dimensions desired, he would employ a suitable stake, conveniently curved, on which to planish it. Planishing is a general, all-over hammering to bring the surface to a smooth, even finish. It is carried out with a flat-faced hammer. A certain amount of final shaping proceeds simultaneously. It should be remembered that whenever a piece of metal is planished, the blows must stretch it a little. Continued hammering on any supported area of the bowl will cause an expansion of the work at that spot, and if long continued will produce a bump there.

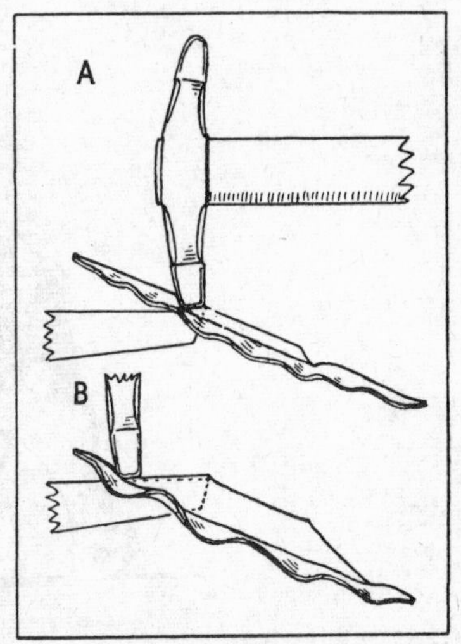

FIGURE 427—*Raising a bowl.*

Should the craftsman decide to raise the bowl instead of sinking it he would find it convenient to use a raising-hammer. In its most useful form, this tool has two faces, each measuring about $1\frac{1}{4}$ in by rather less than $\frac{1}{4}$ inch in thickness (figure 427). The face in general use is flat, but its front corners and all its edges are rounded away so that they cannot cut the metal. The second face, though as wide as the other, is convex instead of being flat. Its edges to right and left are ground off like those of the other face. It is employed to thin the metal, should the bowl become too thick-walled rather than tall enough. A thinner hammer, as wide as the other and similarly shaped, but only $\frac{1}{8}$ inch in thickness, may be employed to raise a bowl from unusually thin metal. Here it may be noted that the raising or the sinking in sheet copper of the bowl-like cranium, or of the face and neck, of the statue of Pepi I (figures 429–30) would have been a perfectly practicable proposition. It would have been possible even though the metal was of the same thickness as that of the arm and hand, about $\frac{1}{5}$ inch in parts. It would have meant heavy work, but it could have been done. In order to understand the technical achievement in the execution of such a work we must consider what is involved in making even a simple bowl.

To raise a bowl, say 6 in high, 5 in across the mouth and 3 in at the base, with

[1] In England there used to be made a silver five-shilling-piece with an inscription in relief round the edge. From these coins little bowls have been sunk, without injury to the inscription.

either straight or curved sides, one may take a disk of metal $\frac{1}{20}$ in thick, and about 10 inches in diameter (i.e. the height plus the average diameter of the bowl which is to be made). The stake on which the raising is to be done may be a straight bar of iron or brass, or even of hard wood, say 2 inches in diameter, fixed horizontally; or a T-shaped stake with one arm of about that size. The end of the stake is generally undercut by about 20°, so that it shall not impede the free movement

FIGURE 428—*Copper bull. El-Ubaid, Mesopotamia. Before 3000 B.C. Height 2 ft.*

of the bowl while it is being raised. One could raise this bowl on a stake or bar only an inch in diameter, but the small radius of such a bar would make the work more difficult. A circle about the size of the base of the bowl is scratched lightly round the centre of the disk. The sheet of metal is held against the end of the stake, with the scratched circle in line with the corner of the stake, and the farther edge of the metal is tilted up about an inch above the top of the stake, as shown in figure 427 A. A sharp blow from the hammer $\frac{1}{4}$ in beyond the scratched line will drive all the metal touched by it into close contact with the top of the stake. The blow must be heavy enough to bend the metal sharply at an angle to its original direction, and the displaced metal must be driven downwards as far as it will go. The disk is now rotated a little, and a second blow is delivered alongside the first. The metal is again rotated and struck, and the hammering is repeated right round the circle and continued in a long spiral till it reaches the edge. By now, the metal will have taken a saucer shape (figure 427 B) and have become hard. It must be annealed before the hammering is resumed, and again at the conclusion of each subsequent course. The work proceeds until the mouth of the bowl is of a little less than the required diameter, and the desired height has been reached.

The utmost care must be taken to avoid the formation of a sharp fold, for it usually becomes a crack. Should a pleat or fold seem to be developing, the point of the pleat, after annealing, should be carefully tapped until it is possible to flatten out the incipient defect. If at any time the metal seems to be wearing too thin at the angle where it rests against the corner of the stake, the raising should be continued from another circle at a little distance above the original line. If the shape of a bowl seems to require it, the latter part of the raising may be done from an entirely new circle, perhaps half-way up the profile of the bowl. A certain amount of angularity is inevitable in raising, but it causes no inconvenience, for, when the mouth of the bowl has attained approximately correct dimensions, the angularity may be obliterated in the final shaping and planishing. During the shaping, all irregularities in the profiles of the bowl which may have developed during the raising are hammered out, while the bowl rests temporarily on any stake which fits that particular part of its curve. The planishing which follows eliminates any remaining blemish.

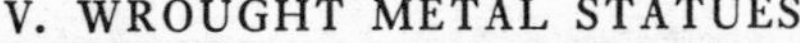

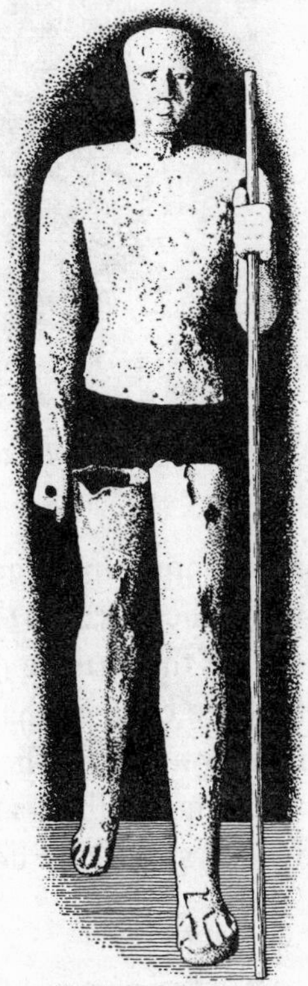

V. WROUGHT METAL STATUES

FIGURE 429—*Life-size copper statue of Pepi I from Hierakonpolis, Egypt.* c 2300 B.C.

When the early craftsman attempted to construct figures of sheet metal, he was faced with new technical problems. A large statue could not be hammered out of a single sheet of metal, nor would thin plates have adequate mechanical strength to stand alone; they must be supported on a substantial framework.

Several figures of standing bulls in copper from El-Ubaid (before 3000 B.C.) are fashioned on different lines. They are in the round, and measure a little over 2 ft in height and length (figure 428). With the copper statues of Pepi I (figures 429–30) and his son (*c* 2300 B.C.) at Cairo, they are believed to be the oldest metal statues. Their method of construction is worthy of consideration. A piece of wood, measuring about $18 \times 6 \times 3$ in, was roughly shaped with the axe to the

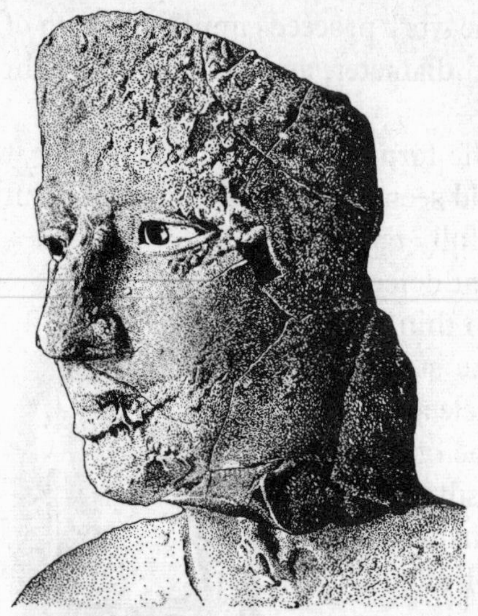
FIGURE 430—*Detail of the statue of Pepi.*

general form of the bull's body. To it were fitted, by mortise and tenon joints, further pieces for the head and legs. The whole wooden core was then covered with sheets of thin copper: head and legs first, then body, horns, etc., each piece being fixed in place by large-headed nails. Each leg was constructed from one piece of metal. Now, though a piece of copper could be bent round the core to form a kind of leg, much work would be needed before it assumed its final shape. Thus the formation of the concave anterior border of a hind leg would entail much hammering near the back edges of the folded sheet to stretch the metal over the hock, and this demanded frequent annealings. Then the smith, after a final annealing, tacked the long edge on to a bitumen-covered core. He would warm the metal, so that the bitumen would flow closely against it to form a support during the chasing of the surface modelling. The last task would be to fold over the free edge so that it overlapped that already nailed to the core, and to drive in a row of large-headed nails, which held all together.

From El-Ubaid also comes the large copper panel of Im-Dugud (figure 431). It shows the large lion-headed eagle of the god Ningursu of Lagash between two

FIGURE 431—*Copper panel of Im-Dugud. El-Ubaid, Mesopotamia. Before 3000 B.C. Height 3½ ft.*

stags, in a heavy copper-covered wooden frame. The heads and antlers of the stags, and the head of the eagle, are in the round. Their bodies are in high relief and the bird's wings in low. The workmanship resembles that of the figure of the El-Ubaid bull (figure 428).

The life-sized statue of the Egyptian King Pepi I of Dynasty VI (figures 429–30), and the smaller figure of his son already mentioned, once parts of a group, are

FIGURE 432—*Gold hawk's head from Hierakonpolis, Egypt.* c 2400 B.C. *Height 4 in.*

of sheet copper, the technique used being similar to that of the smiths of El-Ubaid [3]. The figures were built up of sheets of copper wrought by the hammer and finished by chasing exactly as were the El-Ubaid figures. The joints and nails can be seen even from the outside. Nails on the top edge of the forehead suggest that this was fastened to the wooden core before the missing portion which formed the top of the head was fixed.

From the temple in which these statues were found, and probably of like date (*c* 2400 B.C.), came a magnificent hawk (figure 432). The head, nearly 4 inches in height, was made from one piece of gold and varies in thickness from $\frac{1}{50}$ in near the edge to $\frac{1}{12}$ in near the beak. It was raised from a thick sheet, and finished by repoussé and chasing. Round its base is a row of nails, by which it was attached to the core. The eyes are the polished ends of a rod of obsidian which passes right through the head. The outer surface of the gold is smoothly polished, but the inside is covered with rounded hammer or punch marks. The alert expression and the technical skill displayed in this splendid work match the fine craftsmanship of the heads of Pepi and his son, and are in accord with the deservedly famous portraiture of the day.

VI. REPOUSSÉ, STAMPING, AND ENGRAVING

Repoussé is work in relief executed with hand-controlled punches from the back of sheet metal. In modern practice, the use of the term repoussé has been extended to cover also that work done on the face of the metal to which the term chasing strictly belongs.

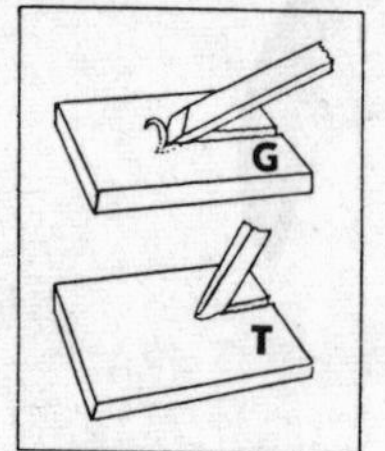

FIGURE 433—*Use of the graver* (G) *and tracer* (T).

One of the oldest ways of decorating a piece of metal is to raise a pattern in relief, by blows on its underside while its decorated side rests on a yielding bed of wood, lead, or pitch. Much depends upon the character of relief. If there is to be an all-over pattern having no relief, it is simplest to fix the metal on a bed of pitch by pressure or slight heat, and work over the whole pattern from the front with a tracer; this is a small chisel with a blunt edge. The grip of the pitch keeps the surface flat, and prevents any disturbance of it by the concentrated local pressure from the hammer through the tool. If we consider the groove produced by the tracer, we shall find that the metal at the bottom of the groove has been compressed, and that some of the material which once filled its site has been driven up as a slight ridge on either side. Naturally, these small ridges disappear rapidly under polishing or wear, so they may not be visible on an object that has been in use. If the metal is thin, a ridge may be driven up on the underside, but if it is thick there will be no evidence of the line there. Traces of the intermittent advance of the tool under the hammer-blows may be left as 'stitches' along the line (figure 433).

Chasing is the term used to describe surface decoration carried out on the front or outer surface of a piece of cast or wrought metal by means of tools, either 'tracers' or 'punches'. These are of simple shape and hand-directed. In general, they are employed to outline, or to complete the modelling of, the forms.

To produce a pattern with relief of not more than, say, $\frac{1}{16}$ in, take a smooth, evenly grained board, rather larger than the metal, and fasten the sheet of metal down all round by nails with flattened heads, placing them about $\frac{1}{4}$ in beyond the edges of the metal. Bend over the heads of the nails to hold down the metal all round without injuring its surface. With a flat-ended punch of hard wood, say $\frac{1}{2}$ in square and 4 in long, drive down into close contact with the board that part of the metal upon which work is to be begun. Then work the pattern with the tracer. When the metal shows signs of rising off the board from hammering, it may be tapped back again with the wooden punch. The design having been outlined, the background is driven down with chasing tools, matted if desired. Thus the pattern stands up in a very low relief.

If a higher relief is required, another method may be adopted. Consider a relief of which the highest part is about as far above the background as its own

FIGURE 434—*Gold figurines from the Royal Cemetery at Ur, Mesopotamia. Before 2500 B.C. Actual size.*

diameter, say a head or a figure almost in the round. The surface of a sphere, from which we could work the head, has four times the area of a flat disk of the same diameter, so that the part of the original plate from which the head is to be formed would be stretched to a quarter of its original thickness when punched into the roughly spherical head. If with a round-headed punch we drive up from the back a hemispherical boss on a flat metal sheet, the greatest stretching will take place near the top, and if the hammering is continued the boss will eventually crack there. To avoid this mishap, the metal must be annealed at intervals. It is important, moreover, that the hammering and consequent thinning should be distributed all over the worked area. As the upper part of the boss becomes thinner, its sides will have suffered little stretching, being merely bent from the horizontal to the vertical. These parts must then be thinned to provide material for the sides and back of the head. Therefore, after driving upwards sufficient material for the front of the head, the background and the sides of the boss are driven downward and inward by work from the front. This work is continued, using any conveniently shaped tools, until the ball-like projection is of approximately even thickness. From it, the head may then be formed. By working in this way, a figure in high relief, say 2 in long, and almost in the round, may be hammered from a sheet of silver $\frac{1}{100}$ in thick.

From the royal cemetery at Ur (before 2500 B.C.) come many gold figurines of animals, of which we illustrate three examples (figure 434). They are of sheet gold only a few thousandths of an inch thick. Gold of this thickness can be bent or folded as easily as paper. But to form such figurines the metal must be worked, by repoussé technique, into very high relief. To attain such a departure from the original flat sheet, much beating, burnishing, and annealing were needed. For

FIGURE 435—*Gold and lapis calf's head, and electrum helmet of Mes-kalam-dug. Ur, Mesopotamia. Before 2500 B.C. Scale c 1/3.*

this reason, among others, the figures could not have been formed over carved wooden models, which would have to be removed for every annealing. Moreover, the position and shape of the heads of the animals would have made this withdrawal impossible. Nor would the craftsman have carved such figures in wood, to be covered up at once with gold. In the calf's head from a harp found in the tomb of Queen Shub-ad (before 2500 B.C.) at Ur (figure 435), the neck and ears are from separate pieces, simplifying the making of the principal part. A piece of thin gold, large enough to form the forehead, nose, and lower jaw was hammered into an irregular bowl shape. When the material for the more difficult parts, the muzzle and chin, had been sunk deeply enough, the craftsman took a suitably formed stake and hammered the work to shape, striking it inside or out at need. This rough shaping having gone far enough, he annealed the work and filled it with bitumen, and, perhaps, a wooden core. Then he drew on the gold the forms of the nostrils, mouth, and eyes, and gave them their final form with chasing tools. When the gold got hard he warmed it to remove the bitumen, then annealed, replaced the bitumen, and so on till the chasing was completed.

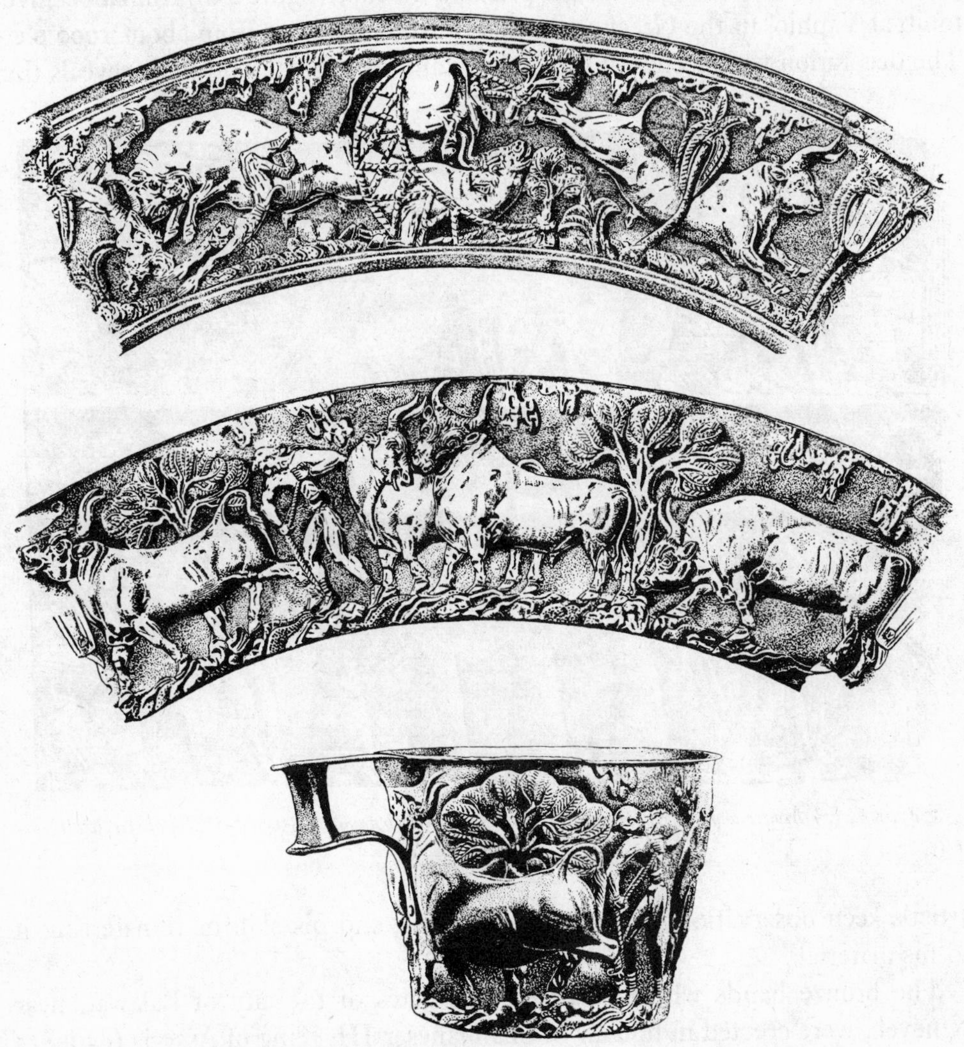

FIGURE 436—(Above) *Repoussé decorations on two gold cups from Vaphio, Greece. c 1600 B.C.* (Below) *The cup with the lower relief; height 3·1 in.*

An impressive example of early repoussé work is the helmet of Mes-kalam-dug from the early cemetery at Ur (figure 435). It was hammered up from a sheet of electrum, and its ornamental details were worked in repoussé with chasing tools.

Repoussé technique, besides being used in modelling figures, was applied to embellishing sheet-metal objects with scenes, bas-reliefs, and ornament. Masterpieces of Minoan technique are the pair of gold cups (figure 436) from a beehive tomb at Vaphio, in the Greek peninsula of Morea, dating from about 1600 B.C. The decoration with scenes of the hunting and capture of wild bulls reveals the

FIGURE 437—*Bronze doors of Shalmaneser III. Balawat, Mesopotamia.* c 850 B.C. *Width of this detail* $6\frac{1}{4}$ *in.*

artist's keen observation of life and movement, and his skill in transferring it to his material.

The bronze bands which decorated the gates of the city of Balawat, near Nineveh, were erected in honour of Shalmaneser III, King of Assyria (859–825 B.C.), and of his father, Ashur-nasir-pal II. Reliefs on the bands show the king in Armenia, Syria, and Mesopotamia, with a trail of burning cities and dead men. The bands were in repoussé, worked mainly from the front, where the tilting downwards of the background toward the outlines of the figures, and the marks of chasing tools and tracers, are clearly visible in the original (figure 437).

Among later works, the deer from Kul Oba, near Kerch in south Russia, (figure 438) is worth special notice as indicating the wide extension, both in

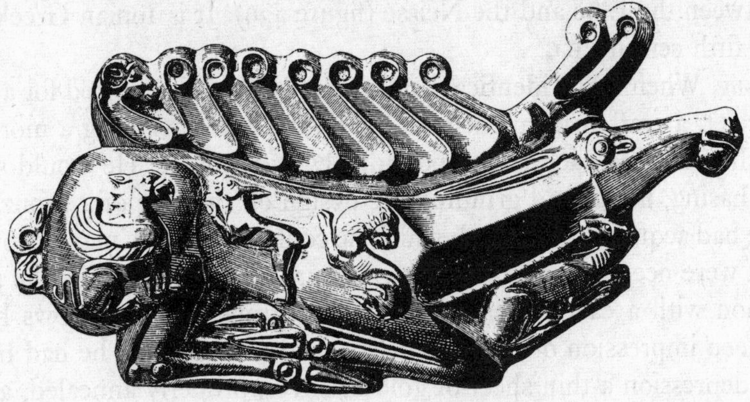

FIGURE 438—*Scythian gold deer. Kerch, Crimea. Sixth to fifth century* B.C. *Length* $12\frac{1}{4}$ *in.*

space and time and in a totally different art-tradition, of the goldsmith's craft that originated in the Near East. The deer was probably the central ornament for a shield, and is in relief of rather more than 1 in. It was formed from a single plate of gold by repoussé work. Traces from the tools employed are freely visible on both sides. The object exhibits a common feature of Scythian art: the development of some characteristic quality of an animal as a decorative pattern on plain surfaces. Note the serrated pattern of the antlers, produced by multiplied tines; the animals' figures and heads which fill the available spaces on the body; and the row of facets for coloured stones (now lost) in the tines and tail. An interesting touch is the strong ridge driven up along the side of the neck to emphasize the form. In a similar art tradition is the great golden fish from Vetters-

FIGURE 439—*Gold fish from Vettersfelde, Brandenburg, Germany. Fifth century* B.C. *Length 16 in.*

felde, between the Elbe and the Neisse (figure 439). It is Ionian Greek work of the early fifth century B.C.

Stamping. When many identical patterns in relief were required for a necklace or a bracelet, a craftsman might turn his thoughts to inventing a more speedy method than making each panel individually by repoussé. He would soon find that by chasing, filing, and grinding the design on the face of a bronze or iron punch he had acquired a tool with which he could produce as many copies of the design as were needed, without further labour. He would employ the punch in conjunction with a cake of lead. With a few strong hammer-blows he would make a deep impression of the punch-face in the lead. Then he had but to lay over the depression a thin sheet of gold or silver, properly annealed, and drive it in with a few steady blows. The relief thus produced would be an exact copy of the pattern on his punch. To finish the work he had but to trim the metal round, and file it true.

Occasionally the craftsman set to work in another way. With steel tools he would carve the design in intaglio[1] in a piece of bronze. During carving he would take an impression in wax from time to time, to see how the work progressed. When the die was complete, he would take a piece of thin sheet metal, properly annealed, and lay it on the die with a piece of thick sheet lead above it. A few blows with the hammer would give a complete reproduction of the design, which he could trim and finish at leisure.

Engraving. Confusion has resulted from indiscriminate use of the term engraving. From Palaeolithic times, flint points were used for cutting patterns on bone, ivory, and soft stone. Such works may properly be described as engraved. Later, marks were occasionally scratched on metal with flints, but at no time were regularly cut patterns on metal effected with flint tools. There was no art of engraving on metal in the Bronze Age, or indeed until steel tools became available.

Experimental attempts with bronze tools, variously hardened, to engrave upon gold, copper, and bronze objects prove that no regular engraved work can thus be done. The edges of the tool splinter almost at once [4]. In Syria, with improved furnaces and greater experience in working metal, the use of iron and steel for agricultural implements and weapons showed a marked increase from about the eleventh century B.C. onwards.

The Urartu (people of Ararat) and the Assyrians seem to have been the first to arm their warriors with iron. To this equipment was partly due the great

[1] I.e. the parts of the design which are to appear raised in relief on the surface of the sheet-metal object are cut as corresponding depressions in the die.

extension of Assyrian power, even to the highlands of Armenia in the north and the borders of Nubia in the south, under Ashur-nasir-pal II (884–859 B.C.) and his successors. The bronze gates of his son Shalmaneser III (859–825 B.C.) are monuments to this dominion and its technical revolution. With the exception of a single example from Egypt, the inscriptions on them are probably the earliest examples of true engraving on metal, the technique of cutting inscriptions on stone with steel tools having been transferred to a new material—bronze. The exception referred to is that of a little ornament of Dynasty XII (*c* 1950 B.C.). It is a vulture in gold with outstretched wings. The feathers are outlined with a graver, the little peck in the metal at the end of each cut being clearly visible.

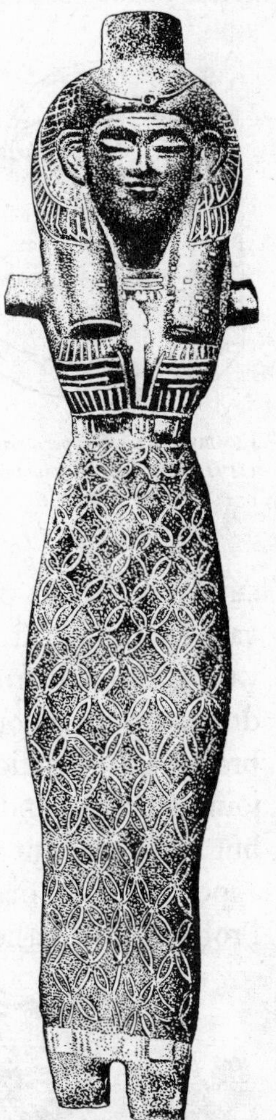

FIGURE 440—*Bronze goddess, inlaid. Egypt.* c *750 B.C. Scale* c *3/5.*

The difference between the line on the metal produced by a steel graver, and that made by the much older chasing- or tracing-tool, is easy to define but not always easy to recognize. In engraving, the metal which filled the site of the groove is removed, coming away as a little curl as the tool is pushed along (figure 433). The line is sharp and angular. In tracing, no metal is removed.

In Cairo there is a set of steel tools of about 600 B.C., showing signs of wear, left at El-Amarna by an Assyrian smith. Other evidence for the use of steel tools in Egypt at about this time is provided by a small bronze standing figure of a queen or goddess (*c* 750 B.C.) of which the hair and dress are elaborately inlaid with lines and plates of a copper alloy, electrum, and gold. The extreme sharpness of the angles in some of the rectilinear patterns indicates that the recesses for these inlays were prepared with steel tools (figure 440).

VII. SOLDERING AND WELDING

An insistent problem for the early metal-workers was the joining of separate pieces of gold or copper. They could be fastened with pins or rivets, which were indeed commonly used at Ur for fixing a handle to a dagger or knife, or for sheet-metal work, as in a type of vessel the body of which was built up of separate pieces (figure 441). In Ireland, the goldsmiths fastened plates by folding the edges together, or by sewing them with a wire. Such methods, however, did not properly solve the problem.

In the Near East, an observant craftsman, melting together nuggets of gold from various sources, noticed that some fused earlier than others and, spreading over the rest, bonded them together. Moreover, he found that it was always the nuggets from a particular source that melted first. Of course, he could not know —as we do—that native gold is always alloyed with some other metal, and that gold with a proportion of copper or silver melts at a lower temperature than purer gold. Nevertheless, such easily fusible gold was, in fact, the earliest solder, and long preceded any conscious attempt to make solder by adding copper or silver to gold.

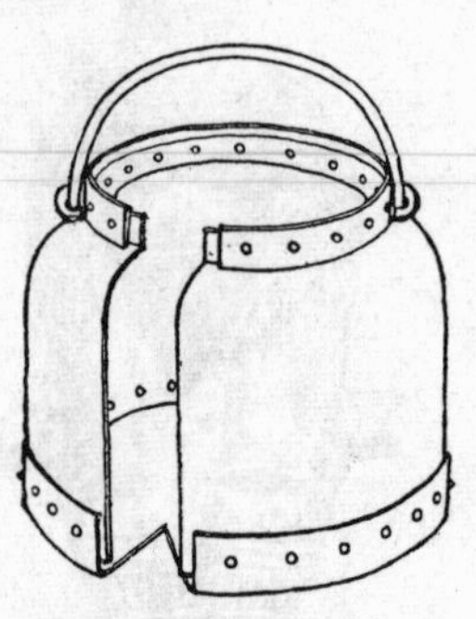

FIGURE 441—*Copper riveted vessel from Ur, Mesopotamia. Before 2500 B.C. (Section removed.)*

After this discovery, search was naturally made for a similar material by which copper or bronze might be joined. A few ancient specimens of such work have survived, for the problem had been solved before 1000 B.C. In the Louvre is a vase from Susa, from which the heads and shoulders of eight oxen project. The vase was raised from sheet copper or bronze, and the bodies of the oxen were driven up by repoussé. Their heads and shoulders were made separately, and brazed into position (figure 442). Modern brazing materials (i.e. materials for joining copper and its alloys) are usually composed of alloys of copper and zinc, but in the ancient world there was no definite knowledge of zinc; the Romans appear to have made brass by smelting copper ores with calamine ($ZnCO_3$). Probably the earliest example of essentially pure zinc is a coin of Yung Lo (A.D. 1402–24), Ming dynasty, China. Brazing materials, like all other hard solders, require a high working temperature, and form much stronger joints than soft solders.

FIGURE 442—*Brazing. Copper vase with brazed-on bulls' heads, from Susa, Persia. Before 1000 B.C.*

Solder. A solder is a metal or alloy which, having a lower melting-point than the pieces to be joined, may be caused to flow between those pieces and, on cooling, bond them. There is a clear distinction between hard soldering (including brazing) which needs a temperature of 550°–900° C or higher, employed for jewelry, silver-work, and better class copper and bronze work; and soft soldering, for joining tin-plate, lead, etc., which may need only 183° C or less. Copper and gold melt at nearly the same temperature (1083° C as against 1063° C), but if 10 parts by weight of copper be added to 90 of gold the melting-point of the alloy falls to 940° C, which suffices

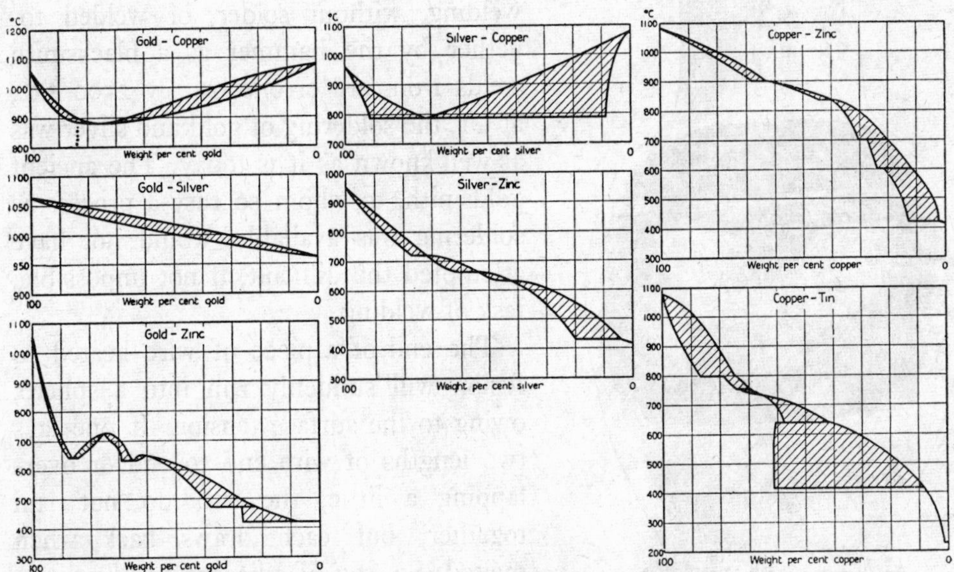

FIGURE 443—*Simplified equilibrium diagrams of some alloys useful as solders. The area between solidus and liquidus lines is shaded. An alloy of a given composition gradually solidifies as its temperature falls through this region.*

to make it a safe solder for pure gold. If 18 parts of copper be added to 82 of gold, the alloy will melt at 878° C, the lowest melting-point of any gold-copper alloy. If a yet lower melting-point be required, a proportion of another metal, such as zinc (m-p 419° C), must be added.

Ancient works of art are rarely of pure gold; many contain a high proportion of other metals, such as silver or copper. For soldering such material a careful choice of solder is needed. The point can be seen demonstrated in the equilibrium diagrams (figure 443) in which the melting-points of many alloys useful as solders are expressed. A solder for silver (m-p 961° C) may be prepared, like that for gold, by adding a proportion of copper to the metal. Zinc may be used to lower the melting-point still further. Hard solders used in brazing commonly consist of alloys of copper and zinc. With soft solders (alloys of lead, tin, bismuth, etc.) it is possible to join pieces of metal at the comparatively low temperature of 120° C, or even less.

There has been confusion in technical literature as to the methods actually employed by the early craftsmen in joining pieces of gold, electrum, silver, bronze, or copper. Statements that they were either fused together by autogenous welding, without solder, or welded together by the hammer as a blacksmith welds iron, are erroneous. By 2500 B.C., at Ur, the soldering of gold and silver was as well known as it is today. The ancient goldsmith, to whom so easy a process as soldering was available, would not have attempted the difficult, if not impossible, task of welding.

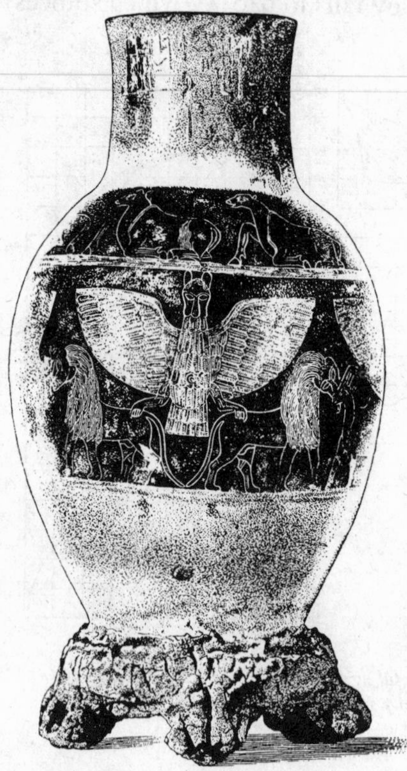

FIGURE 444—*Silver vase of Entemena. Tello, Mesopotamia. c 2800 B.C. Height 14 in.*

The end of a piece of wire heated to fusion will suddenly run into a sphere, owing to the surface tension. If one lays two lengths of wire end to end or overlapping a little, the two do not run together, but each draws back when melted. So, too, if adjacent edges of two plates of metal are fused they will draw back from one another. When, however, a more fusible material is present, it forms a bridge between the two, alloying itself with each, running through the joint, and fastening the parts together.

When copper or any of its alloys is heated, as in the charcoal furnace—the only one available in antiquity—a film of copper oxides forms on the surface. This keeps a heated sheet of copper from direct metallic contact with another. Neither a flux nor hammering will unite the surfaces. Copper surfaces, unlike those of iron, could not be welded together by heat or hammering. Early metal-workers could not weld bronze, silver, or indeed gold in the ordinary sense. Of soldering they had a good knowledge and employed it widely.

Gold behaves in a rather exceptional manner. An Early Iron Age Irish craftsman was making some little boxes, perhaps $1\frac{1}{2}$ inches in diameter [5]. He beat out some almost pure gold into strips from which to form the sides. He allowed their ends to overlap perhaps a quarter of an inch, and burnished each extremity down to that part of the strip against which it rested, with the result that it adhered firmly. In the interval between the two burnished (welded) joints a double thickness of gold may be seen. Apart from such adhesion by burnishing, no other welded joint in gold is known from the ancient world. Hard-soldered joints for goldwork were the rule at Ur. From Tello, in Mesopotamia, is the silver vase of Entemena (*c* 2800 B.C.) (figure 444). It was raised from sheet metal, and is supported by a corroded base of copper or bronze. On its shoulder is a row of seated bulls and, below them, lions seize stags. There is a lion-headed eagle above each pair of lions. All the decoration is executed with the tracer. The neck of the vase is lined with a plain, deep collar, silver-soldered in position. A blow has cracked the joints in one place, making its structure clear. An early example of the use of silver solder in Egypt is on the canopy from the tomb of Queen Hetep-heres (Dynasty IV, *c* 2500 B.C.). This canopy is supported by copper poles, retained in their sockets by silver solder (figure 502) [6].

Fluxes are used with nearly all solders. A surface of heated metal exposed to the air is liable to become oxidized, and the film thus produced will interfere with the flow and adhesion of the solder. It is therefore usual to employ a flux which, running through the joint, excludes the air and keeps the surface clean. Borax is employed as a flux for many hard solders, and zinc chloride for soft.

Soft solder has a very long history, and one of the earliest examples of its use must be that of the Im-Dugud relief already noted (figure 431). It is decorated with two stags, with a lion-headed eagle above them. The stags' antlers are of square copper bars, and the joints between the main stem and the tines are made with soft solder.

Sweating. When the contiguous surfaces of two or more pieces of metal have been separately coated with some more fusible material, such as a solder, and the temperature is raised high enough to melt this coating, a joint is formed which may be described as sweated. For example, a joint may be sweated between two pieces of a tin canister (made from tinned iron) without the aid of any additional solder.

Burning together was practised from the Bronze Age onwards. By it, a joint can be made on a bronze tool or weapon without the aid of solder. A bronze sword, broken at the hilt, might be thus repaired. The smith fitted the pieces together and formed a mould in clay round them. He left a passage all round the joint, and provided the mould with a funnel-shaped pour for the introduction of the metal, and an overflow hole. Then he poured into and through the mould several pounds of molten bronze. The metal flowed between, and heated up, the broken parts of the sword, partly melting them. Most of the molten metal escaped through the overflow hole, but enough remained to make the joint strong. Superfluous metal could be cut away later. Similarly, a new part could be cast on to an existing metal object. Care was always needed that sufficient molten metal passed through the mould to fuse the old work; the oxides rise to the surface as a scum.

Welding is the art of joining separate pieces of metal by heat or mechanical treatment without solder. For wrought-iron it requires a temperature of about 1350° C. At this temperature, scales of iron oxide flake off continually from the incandescent surfaces, leaving them clean. The metal is in a pasty state, and the surfaces to be united can come into intimate contact. The crystals at the surface break up under the hammer-blows, and the fragments grow into new crystals interlocking across the joint.

The welding of iron has been practised from early times in Asia Minor, as, for example, on the iron headrest of Tutankhamen (*c* 1350 B.C.), when as yet iron was practically unknown in Egypt [7]. This headrest was probably a gift from some ruler in Syria, where iron-working was more advanced. Not until welding and the making and hardening of steel became well understood, which in Syria was between the eleventh and ninth centuries B.C., can a true Iron Age be said to have begun.

FIGURE 445—(A) *Gold dagger sheath.* (B) *Gold cosmetic case. Ur, Mesopotamia. Before 2500 B.C. Scale c 4/5.*

VIII. FILIGREE AND GRANULATION

Early in the third millennium B.C., goldsmiths of the Near East realized that they might decorate a metallic surface by the addition of wires or grains in patterns, or they might leave the filigree pattern *à jour* (open). This was rendered possible by their success in making fine wires from sheet metal, and by their early acquired skill in soldering.

The craftsman of those days had no easy mechanical means of making wire. To obtain a wire he cut a narrow strip from the edge of a sheet of gold, or, if he wanted a considerable length, he could cut round and round a circular plate in a long spiral. Illustrations of such a spiral, probably for producing a leather thong, are known from a sixteenth-century B.C. Egyptian tomb (figure 284); and ribbons of gold, flattened from such a strip and measuring more than 5 ft in length, were found in one of the royal tombs at Ur. The strip of metal, as cut off by the flint chisel, was necessarily angular in section and somewhat irregular in thickness, but it could be hammered true.

Swaging is the employment of dies to shape a length of moulding or wire. A plain moulding or wire of almost any section may be drawn between dies, and an ornamented moulding or a beaded wire may be formed by pressure between dies of suitable profile. A wire square in section is not difficult to make, and twisting gives it a rich quality of its own. Examples of the use of such wires were found in the royal cemetery at Ur before 2500 B.C., and at Ałalakh, Syria, of *c* 1450 B.C. The craftsman could bend a wire with his tweezers to form many interesting shapes—loops, coils, rings, spirals, or wave patterns. He could also twist two wires together, with either a dextral or a sinistral turn, to make a more attractive compound wire motif.

The goldsmith found that he could make a number of equal-sized rings by coiling a wire round a cylindrical rod of suitable size, and cutting off each ring in succession with his chisel. The Sumerian as well as the Egyptian craftsman needed little disks, or domes, or balls in his jewelry to contrast with the wires. Such small domes, as on the gold dagger-sheath from Ur (figure 445 A), he could easily make from a piece of thin gold, by driving a little round boss on it with a punch, or he might stamp out sequins for the decoration of drapery. The metal might need to be trimmed to shape with the chisel, and then trued-up with an abrasive stone file. For very small domes this method would be too slow, so he used solid grains instead. These could be made without difficulty from a scrap of gold, which when heated would melt into a tiny ball or grain. This could be used as it was, or flattened with the hammer into a disk, and domed to form a boss. Such disks and grains formed convenient units of design. For example, there is a necklace from Egypt almost entirely composed of grains. It consists of ten pendants, each of a hollow cylinder with an arched loop above and a hemisphere below. The cylinder is about $\frac{1}{4}$ inch in diameter and $\frac{3}{4}$ inch long (figure 446).

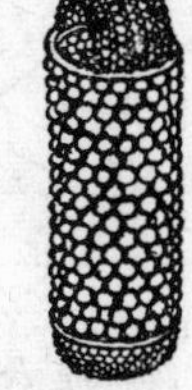

FIGURE 446.

FIGURE 447—*Gold ear-ring. Ur, Mesopotamia. Before 2000 B.C. Actual size.*

The goldsmiths sometimes built up little pyramids of grains, or coiled wire into cones and flat spirals, for the embellishment of their work. The small golden cosmetic case from a royal grave at Ur (figure 445 B) is decorated with coils and spirals and applied bands of twisted wires, soldered in position. Close beside it lay the golden dagger (figure 445 A), the outer side of whose sheath is entirely covered with panels of filigree work composed of twisted wires and rows of little bosses of sheet gold. All are soldered to the backplate—an operation of extreme delicacy. Indeed, such technical skill is not surpassed by any other work of the third millennium B.C.

The goldsmiths of Ur occasionally decorated the outer side of an ear-ring with a series of spikes, each about $\frac{1}{16}$ in high and placed as close together as possible. The projections were repoussé, a conical-ended punch being employed. The thin sheet gold of the ear-ring was supported on a yielding bed—perhaps of pitch—while the work was being done. A fine ear-ring of this type comes from the Larsa period of about 2000 B.C. (figure 447).

Beaded wire was used on late Egyptian jewelry, and was sometimes made with beads measuring not more than $\frac{1}{70}$ inch in diameter. It may have been made by punching or swaging the plain wire between two dies (figure 448) constructed of two superimposed bars, kept in registration by pins. Along each of the adjacent faces of such a die is a groove which expands into a series of hemispherical hollows. A piece of annealed wire of the correct size is pushed through the groove between the dies; being larger than the groove it lifts the uppermost die slightly. The die is then struck with a hammer while the wire is slowly rotated. When one section of the plain wire has been shaped it is moved forward to bring the next into the die.

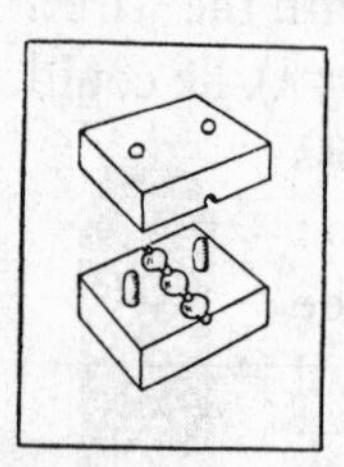

FIGURE 448—*Swage for forming beaded wire.*

Chains formed from rings, each folded in half and tucked through the open ends of the next link, are known from the early cemetery at Ur. They have a heavy four-sided appearance. Chains formed from S-shaped links are known from Nimrud from the eighth century B.C. onward, and there are heavy cast-bronze chains from the same place and date. Chains formed from plain, round links seem to have been unknown in early times in Sumeria and Egypt. Some of uncertain date come from Syria and Phoenicia.

Strands of square-sectioned twisted wires have been found at Ur and other early sites. Beaded wire seems to have been unknown at Ur, but little spherical

FIGURE 449 A—*Etruscan gold bowl with granular decoration (actual size).* c 600 B.C.

beads, soldered together in lines, or grouped in geometric shapes, e.g. to form a triangular pattern of 6, 5, 4, 3, 2, 1 beads soldered together, are found as spacers in a necklace.

The formation of patterns composed exclusively of grains soldered to a background ('granulation') does not seem to have been practised at Ur. In a tomb of Dynasty XII at Dahshur, Egypt, a necklace was found from which hung a golden butterfly and some five-pointed stars, in which the whole ground of the ornament is covered with fine gold grains. This necklace was made for the Princess Khnumet in the reign of Amenemhet II (*c* 1920 B.C.). In the tomb of another princess, about a century later, there was a tubular ornament of gold, decorated with a series of zigzag bands of gold grains. Similar tubular

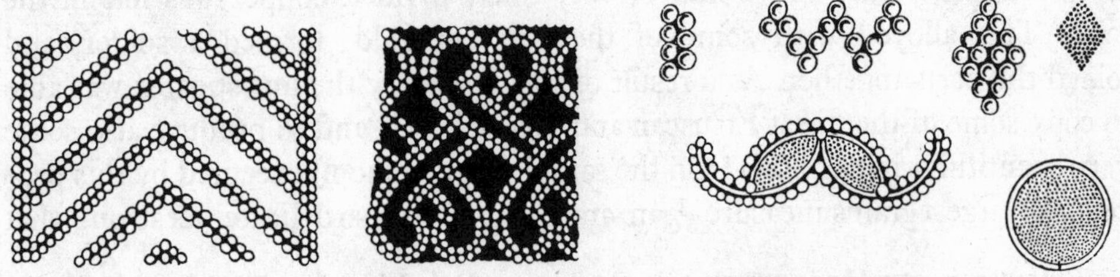

FIGURE 449 B—(Left) *Details of the bowl.* (Right) *Samples of the technique by the author.*

pendants have been found at Alalakh, in Syria, dating from the fifteenth century B.C. In these pendants, the grains are $\frac{1}{60}$ inch in diameter. Very delicate granular ornamentation is found on a number of objects in the tomb of Tutankhamen (*c* 1350 B.C.).

Even finer work was done by the Etruscan and Greek goldsmiths of the eighth to the second centuries B.C. In some of this jewelry, the grains are of $\frac{1}{100}$ in or less in diameter; the very finest grains measure only $\frac{1}{180}$ in. They were arranged in regular patterns, or sprinkled so closely over the background that they look like a bloom on the surface of the gold. This and some of the wire-work, done without a background, are more delicate than the finest lace. No finer work is known from any part of the world, at any time. One of the richest examples of Etruscan granular decoration is a golden bowl about 4 inches in diameter (figure 449 A). The grains are not so small as those used on other works from Etruscan and Greek sites, but the whole pattern is worked in double rows of grains, each grain measuring $\frac{1}{80}$ inch in diameter. There are more than 860 linear inches in the pattern, and over 137 000 grains were used on this beautiful little bowl: an unsurpassed effort. A glance at a piece of modern jewelry will indicate the distance that separates us from such works as this technical triumph. The arrangement of the grains and the soldering of such small masses, without flooding or clogging them with solder, required very skilful manipulation.

After Roman times the art of granulation was lost. Many efforts to recover it were made during the late nineteenth century, but this work did not possess the delicacy and freedom of the old. The solder, however finely cut or filed, tended to flood the grains or wires, and the flux employed in the soldering was liable to boil up and displace the grains. The first difficulty was overcome by dividing the solder into even more minute particles—chemically rather than mechanically—and the second by omitting the flux altogether. A copper compound, say copper hydroxide, $Cu(OH)_2$, was used with glue to fasten the grains or wires in place. When heated, the glue carbonized and the copper compound turned into copper oxide. The carbon then reduced the copper oxide to copper and disappeared as carbon monoxide, and a film of very finely divided copper was left in the joint. This alloyed with some of the adjacent gold, formed a solder, and joined the parts together. As a result of this discovery the investigator was able to copy some of the finest Etruscan and Greek jewels and to produce also some very beautiful original work.[1] On the sample (figure 449 B) executed by this process, the largest grains measure $\frac{1}{50}$ in, and the process is so delicate, yet strong, that

[1] This method is covered by a patent granted to the discoverer, H. A. P. Littledale. British Patent No. 415181. March, 1933.

'daylight' may be seen beneath each grain. The smaller grains are less than $\frac{1}{200}$ inch in diameter.

FIGURE 450—*Gold rings with* cloisonné *inlays. Ur, Mesopotamia. Before 2500* B.C. *Actual size.*

IX. INLAYS AND ENAMELS

An inlay is a piece of material fitted or moulded into a recess in another body. The Sumerians were not content to display their abundant gold unadorned. In their necklaces and pendants, patterned beads of gold were in juxtaposition with others of lapis lazuli and carnelian, agate and jasper, marble and silver, glazed frit or shell. They sought also for a means of bringing colour to their finger-rings and belt-ornaments. Curiously enough, they seem to have had no great interest in bracelets. Realizing that stones in a finger-ring might meet with considerable wear, and thus needed careful setting, they put a band of metal round each stone. They made their settings by soldering on to the back-plate a series of narrow strips of gold to form little cells. A stone was then cut to fit into each cell, and fastened in with cement. From the early cemetery at Ur there are examples of such work: patterns of lapis lazuli and shell set in gold (figure 450). This *cloisonné* setting, devised by the Sumerian craftsmen nearly 5000 years ago, has proved its worth in every quarter of the globe.[1] The figure of the sun god Shamash, carved on the stele of Hammurabi, King of Babylon about 1780 B.C., wears a wristlet with roundels which would be filled with coloured stones. The kings of Assyria, as shown on their monuments from the ninth century B.C. onwards, wore necklaces and bracelets similarly decorated, and arranged in star or floral patterns.

In no part of the ancient world was *cloisonné* carried to a higher level than in Egypt. Some of the pectorals are the finest of their period. The pendant jewel illustrated (figure 451) is of gold openwork, and its *cloisonné* decoration contains nearly 400 pieces of semi-precious stones: turquoise, lapis lazuli, carnelian, and garnet. The back is a carefully chased repoussé plate to which the *cloisons* in front are soldered. The beauty of such work was

FIGURE 451—*Inlaid gold pectoral of Rameses II, from Memphis, Egypt.* c *1300* B.C. *Width 3¼ in.*

[1] *Cloisonné* work consists of open-fronted cells made of metal strip, forming settings to be filled with precious stones, enamel, niello, glass, or other material.

unrivalled until, in 1926, the opening of the tomb of Tutankhamen, with its magnificent treasures of fine craftsmanship and design, revealed the achievements of the Egyptian goldsmiths of Dynasty XVIII. Pride of place must undoubtedly be accorded to the coffin of the king. The innermost coffin is of solid gold, about $\frac{1}{8}$ in ($2\frac{1}{3}$–$3\frac{1}{2}$ mm) thick, and its weight is about 243 lb (110·4 kg) (frontispiece and plate 22). The lid was raised from a large sheet of gold, and wrought by direct hammering and repoussé into a finely modelled portrait in high relief. The figure wears the *Nemes* head-dress, with the vulture and uraeus insignia on the brow. The hands hold the Osiride emblems. The face, neck, and hands are burnished, the feet draped. The large conventional collarette is adorned with bands of *cloisonné* set with semi-precious stones. The lower part of the body, and the arms, of the king are enfolded by the protective figures of two goddesses in the form of vultures with outstretched wings, emblematic of Upper and Lower Egypt. These are wrought in rich *cloisonné* with inlays of opaque polychrome glass, lapis lazuli, carnelian, green felspar, and other semi-precious stones. The remainder of the figure is covered with a feathered design and inscribed texts, worked with the tracer.

FIGURE 452—*Inlaid gold armlet, Median or Persian. Oxus treasure, British Museum. Fifth to fourth century* B.C. *Height 5 in.*

The decoration of early Hellenic metal-work is pictured by Homer in his description of Achilles' shield, made for him by the god Hephaestus.

'Also he set therein a vineyard teeming plenteously with clusters, wrought in fine gold, black were the grapes, but the vines hung throughout on silver poles. And around it he ran a ditch of cyanus, and round that a fence of tin. . . .

'Also he wrought a herd of kine with upright horns, and the kine were fashioned of gold and tin. . . .

'Fair wreaths had the maidens, and the youths daggers of gold hanging from silver baldrics.' *Iliad* XVIII.

No work from Hellenic lands at all resembling that on this shield was known until 1876, when Schliemann excavated the shaft-graves at Mycenae, in southern

Greece, dating from the sixteenth century B.C. Among the treasures found there were bronze daggers with inlays of various metals. On one, there are lions in relief, and in the background are rocks inlaid with gold, electrum, and silver. Another dagger has an inlaid strip of silver, with cats pursuing birds by a flower-bordered river full of fish. The inlays are of gold, silver, and copper with a background of niello, then a newly discovered material, black in colour. On other daggers are scenes of lion-hunts in gold, silver, and niello, flower panels in niello, and bronze griffins in relief.

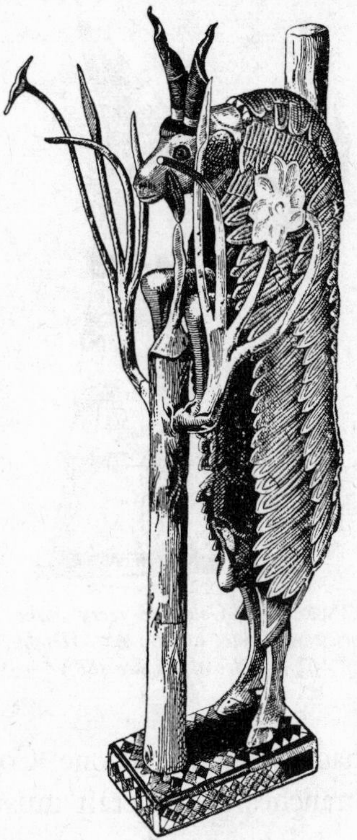

FIGURE 453—*'Ram' made of gold, electrum, shell, and lapis. The gold and electrum are mounted on a wooden core for head and belly; the fleece is made up of overlapping pieces of shell and lapis; the base is inlaid. From Ur, Mesopotamia. Before 2500 B.C. Height 20 in.*

A Median or Persian gold armlet of the fifth–fourth century B.C. shows another type of inlaid work. It was once decorated with polychrome stone inlays. Some of the recesses for the jewels were chiselled out of the mass of the armlet, but others were built up by soldering *cloisons* to the background. Horned monsters of the kind here presented are characteristic of Persian art (figure 452).

The cementing of pieces of coloured glass, together with lapis lazuli, carnelian, or other stones, in a *cloisonné* setting is quite distinct from true enamelling, though it might be difficult to decide whether the glass was cemented or fused in position. The essential quality of an enamel is that it is a vitreous material fused to a base. When the base is metal, it is usually gold, silver, copper, or bronze and (in recent times) iron.

A work which almost anticipated the chryselephantine work of the Greeks is the 'Ram caught in a Thicket' from Ur. It is of gold, electrum, lapis lazuli, and carved shell (figure 453).

The association of goldsmiths' work with ivory—chryselephantine work—is a somewhat rare combination in modern art, but it was much favoured in the ancient world. We recall the throne of Solomon in Jerusalem about the year 950 B.C., of ivory 'overlaid with gold'. About 500 years later, the massive chryselephantine statues, some 40 ft high, of Athena at Athens and of Zeus at Olympia, were the work of the sculptor Phidias. They were made from pieces of

FIGURE 454—*Gold and ivory snake priestess. Crete.* c *1500 B.C. Height 6½ in. (See also figure 468.)*

carved ivory, mounted upon a wooden framework, with draperies of beaten gold. These great works have perished, but from Minoan times in Crete we have the little ivory figure of a snake priestess, her dress decorated with bands of gold, standing upright with a golden snake in either hand. She may help us to realize something of the power and beauty of those vanished statues, of which it was felt that their presence filled the temple, and that they added something to the revealed religion (figures 454, 468).

From the above brief survey of fine metal-working from the earliest times to about 500 B.C. it may be observed that the work of some of the pioneers and discoverers reached so high a standard aesthetically and technically that it has scarcely been equalled in the long history of metal-working. However, there yet remained for later craftsmen other fields for exploitation, though in some cases, as in the making of coins, and the development of niello, of engraving, and of enamelling the pioneer work had already been done. Consideration of the finest flowering of these and other branches of the craft must be reserved for subsequent volumes of this work.

REFERENCES

[1] KARLBECK, O. 'Yin and Chou Researches.' Museum of Eastern Antiquities, Stockholm. 1936.

[2] LUCKENBILL, D. D. 'Ancient Records of Assyria and Babylonia', Vol. 2, pp. 162–169. University of Chicago Press, Chicago. 1927.

[3] QUIBELL, J. E. and GREEN, F. W. 'Hierakonpolis II', pp. 46 ff. Egypt. Res. Acc. and Brit. Sch. Archaeol. Egypt, Publ. 5. London. 1902.

[4] MARYON, H. *Amer. J. Archaeol.*, **53**, ii, 117, 1949.

[5] ARMSTRONG, E. C. R. 'Catal. of Irish Gold Ornaments in the Coll. of the Royal Irish Academy' (2nd ed.), frontispiece, figs 485–488. Guide to the Collections of Irish Antiquities. Nat. Mus. of Science and Art, Dublin. 1933.

[6] LUCAS, A. 'Ancient Egyptian Materials and Industries' (3rd ed.), p. 248. Arnold, London. 1948.

[7] *Idem. Ibid.*, p. 272.

24

FINE IVORY-WORK

R. D. BARNETT

I. SOURCES OF SUPPLY AND GENERAL UTILIZATION

THE qualities that make ivory precious as a material are fine grain, soft colour, a cool and pleasant surface and, in figures, a suggestion of the texture of the human flesh. All these, which commend it to us, rendered it equally precious in antiquity. Moreover, in some quarters, such as archaic Greece, where the elephant had not been seen before Aristotle, it was also considered a somewhat mysterious substance.[1]

The use of ivory of mammoth and elephant goes back to Palaeolithic times. Startlingly skilful carving in it was executed in the Magdalenian period (figure 223). The real exploitation, however, begins with the chalcolithic and Early Bronze periods (figure 458). With the improvement in the efficiency of weapons that came with metals, ivory became more accessible, and as the fashioning of metal tools improved it became easier to carve and shape it.

The technique of ivory-carving as a craft doubtless originated in the Near East, where plentiful supplies of elephant ivory were available.[2] In Egypt the elephant was well known in predynastic times. By the early dynastic period it had retreated to the First Cataract, where the city of Elephantine was named after it. Elephants even today are found in the Nilotic Sudan and in parts of Abyssinia as far as Uganda. In Eritrea, though elephants are now extinct, there were thousands until Roman times [1]. We have good records from Dynasty XVIII of an Egyptian naval expedition to Punt (?Somaliland) (figure 32) *c* 1500 B.C. [2], which brought back ivory of elephant and hippopotamus, amongst other precious merchandise. Farther west, elephant herds were then plentiful in Libya and Mauretania. From these sources Egypt obtained supplies throughout antiquity.

Another source of supply of elephants was Syria, where lived a separate sub-species now long extinct and seldom mentioned by naturalists. It haunted the marshes of the upper Euphrates, which were very much richer in vegetation then

[1] See R. D. Barnett, *J. Hell. Stud.* **48**, 2, 1948.

[2] This statement may require limitation when more is known about early Indian and Chinese civilizations, but for the present it holds good.

than now. This species was known to the Egyptians in the fifteenth century B.C. (figure 455), but appears to have been exterminated by Assyrian kings in the eighth century B.C. It may have been hunted much earlier by the Sumerians who, however, do not seem to have employed ivory extensively. Their small needs were perhaps met from the Indus valley, with which we know they were in touch [3]. Carved ivory fragments have been found at Bahrain in the Persian Gulf, associated with vases of about 2000 B.C. [4]; this suggests a stage on the road between India and Sumer.

FIGURE 455—*Part of a fresco from the tomb of Rekhmire at Thebes, showing Syrians bringing an elephant, tusks of ivory, etc., as gifts. Fifteenth century B.C.*

By the tenth century B.C. the chief exploiters of the ivory trade were the Phoenicians and certain peoples of north Syria who, it would seem, sought for fresh sources as the Syrian supplies dwindled. Thus Hiram, King of Tyre (*c* 950 B.C.), entered into partnership with Solomon to send an expedition to Ophir—apparently Suppara, near Bombay. 'King Solomon made a navy of ships in Ezion-Geber on the shore of the Red Sea. And Hiram sent in his navy his servants, shipmen that had knowledge of the sea, with the servants of Solomon (1 Kings ix. 27). . . . Once every three years came the navy bringing gold, *almug* (i.e. sandalwood), ivory, and monkeys and peacocks' (1 Kings x. 22). It is interesting that the Hebrew words used for all these objects of merchandise in the Biblical account are of Indian origin. The Tyrians kept their supremacy in the ivory trade until the sixth century B.C., drawing on both India and Africa. 'Many isles were the merchandise of thine hand,' wrote the prophet Ezekiel about 586 B.C.; 'they brought thee for a present horns of ivory and ebony' (Ezek. xxvii. 15). A piece of an ivory throne from Nimrud, in Assyria, is part of a tusk which, when whole, must have measured 19 cm in diameter; of such a size, it could have come only from an African beast and may well have been brought by a Tyrian trader.

II. ORGANIZATION OF ARTISANS

As the ancient economies developed surplus wealth, they found the means to support specialist artisans (p 44). Craftsmen were early organized into fraternities and guilds,[1] and came to form a recognized part of ancient city and temple life. Sometimes the organized guild faded into a social group of kindred, or a caste with special rites and privileges.

Guilds of ivory-workers, however, are not mentioned in ancient Oriental sources, except in India. Their existence is doubtless masked under a more

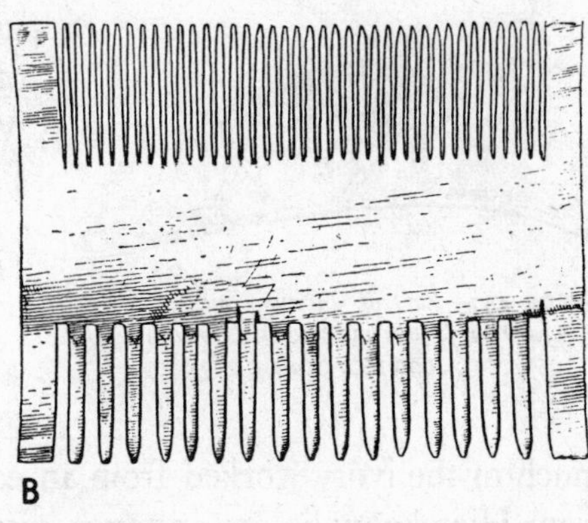

FIGURE 456—(A) *Ivory two-sided comb from Megiddo, Palestine.* c *1200 B.C.* (B) *Modern Syrian comb.*

general heading, such as carpenters, but we can trace them by their works. Often itinerant, they spread their products and cultural traditions far and wide. Transmitting technical traditions from father to son, they imparted to their craft features which were incredibly long-lived. Some of their traditions are still alive in the Near East. Thus ivory combs are now made in Aleppo by Armenian workmen of exactly the shape of those of north Syrian craftsmen 3000 years ago (figure 456). Furniture and trinket boxes are to this day inlaid at Damascus with ivory, mother-of-pearl, and coloured woods in a tradition that may have descended from Phoenician times. Nearer home we find long-standing traditions of ivory-work and ivory-workers. In the fourteenth century, mariners of Dieppe began to visit the Guinea and Ivory Coasts. Thus Dieppe started a local industry

[1] A clay tablet from Ra's Shamra of the fourteenth century B.C. (C. VIROLLEAUD, *Syria*, **21**, 138, 1940) is a list of the guilds in that city. They are sometimes called 'sons of' such and such craftsmen e.g. 'sons of the carpenters'. See also J. MENDELSOHN, *J. Amer. orient. Soc.*, **60**, 68, 1940. Of their cults, two examples suffice: in Egypt, Horus was patron of the smiths of Edfu; at Lagash in Sumer, Nintukalamma was god of metal-workers. (A. BOISSIER, *Orientalische Literaturzeitung*, Leipzig, **2**, 236, 1908.)

of ivory-carving, which flourished with ever greater skill until the late nineteenth century, but then declined [5]. There were carvers of this school belonging to families which had practised the art for centuries. Much the same situation ruled in antiquity.

The most useful approach to ancient ivory-working is to consider it as the product of a long-lived craft. The natural limitation of size of the work has restricted it largely to ornamentation. Small-scale ivory sculpture, however, must also be considered, for it has a tradition of work at once delicate, detailed, and usually freer and more naturalistic than other arts. This was notably the case in Minoan Crete, but is true also of Egypt, Phoenicia, and archaic Greece.

FIGURE 457—*Part of an ivory magical 'knife' with fabulous figures and amuletic symbols. Egypt.* c *2000* B.C. *Scale* c *1/3.*

III. EGYPT[1]

In dynastic times, the hippopotamus was still common in the marshlands of Egypt, and its canines and incisors supplied much of the ivory worked from an early period. Certain predynastic figurines from Hierakonpolis, for instance, were of this substance, which is dense, hard, and difficult to work.

The hippopotamus was revered as a sacred animal by the Egyptians, and there is evidence that artifacts made from its teeth received peculiar respect. Thus at Qau, not far from Badari, toilet-objects of hippopotamus-ivory had been carefully collected and interred in a special pit along with hippopotamus bones. This custom may account for the relative paucity of ivory objects in human burial sites [6]. In the Middle Kingdom (Dynasties XI–XII, *c* 2050–1790 B.C.), curved magical objects (known as knives), engraved with symbols to protect the owner from bites of venomous creatures, were fashioned from hippopotamus incisors [7] (figure 457). Among these symbols, the most commonly recurring device is that of Thoeris, the hippopotamus goddess [8]. Some of these knives display consummate skill in the engraving and carving of a very hard substance [9]. As graver, the artist probably used an instrument of flint or chert, for a copper tool would hardly scratch the surface.

Elephant-ivory, on the other hand, the Egyptians merely regarded without special respect as a hard, fine-grained, white substance, the counterpart of dark ebony, with which they often combined it in contrasting veneers and inlays. The association was the closer since both materials were imported from the Sudan.

[1] This section is contributed by Mr Cyril Aldred.

There are good grounds for thinking that carving in elephant-ivory had a long tradition in Egypt, distinct from that of other crafts. Unlike wood, ivory may be

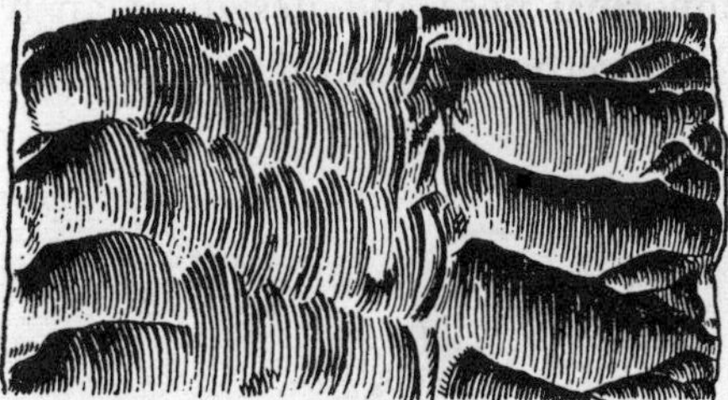

FIGURE 458—*Predynastic flint knife with carved ivory handle, showing scenes of animal life on one side and a battle, with boats below, on the other.* (Below, right) *A detail of the very skilfully flaked blade. From Gebel-el-Arak, Egypt. Length of knife 25 cm.*

carved without regard to its grain, thus making possible a freer and more naturalistic treatment of form. Predynastic ivory figures, such as those on various knife-handles, of which that of Gebel-el-Arak is the most celebrated (figure 458), as well as certain figurines of women [10] and toilet spoons [11], reveal remarkable facility in use of the medium. An exquisite figure of a king of one of the first dynasties, wearing a robe and taking part in a ceremony (figure 459), illustrates

FIGURE 459—*Ivory figure of an early dynastic Egyptian king wearing a cloak, perhaps for a jubilee celebration.* c *3000 B.C. Height 8·8 cm.*

the degree of skill and sensibility achieved even in the earliest historical times. It may be that ivory was a royal monopoly reserved for the master craftsmen of the court, since most of the Old Kingdom ivories represent Pharaohs. Statuettes of Cheops, builder of the Great Pyramid [12], and of Mycerinus, his successor [13], are other examples from this period of fine sculpture on a miniature scale. That of Ka-wer is also evidently the work of a court craftsman, and perhaps a gift of the king [14].

In the Middle Kingdom, with an intensive exploitation of the Sudan, supplies of elephant-ivory doubtless became more plentiful, and the medium ceased to be confined to objects for the court. It may, indeed, have been exported in worked forms as well as in the tusk, since two ivory figures of the period in Crete strongly suggest an Egyptian origin (figure 460 A) [15]. Similar squatting figures as handles of seals [16] show the persistence of a tradition from royal sculpture of the Old Kingdom (figure 460 C). A certain number of pieces show features not usually thought characteristic of the Egyptian style; such are a figure of a dwarf carrying a calf on his back [17] and a remarkable toy of dancing dwarfs from Lisht, 45 miles south of Cairo (figure 461). Their naturalistic proportions, unusual poses, free carving, and fineness of detail, all suggest a school of ivory-carving having its own ideals. Even as late as the end of the second intermediate period, i.e. between the Middle Kingdom and the New (*c* 1788–1580 B.C.), the influence of this style can be seen in the abnormal pose and design of an ivory handle from Abydos, in the form of the forepart of a royal sphinx seizing a human enemy (figure 460 B).

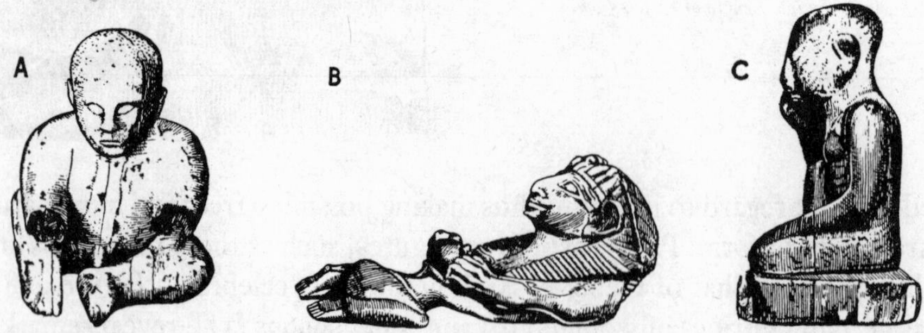

FIGURE 460—(A) *Figure of a boy, from Palaikastro, Crete (Minoan art).* c *2000 B.C.* (B) *Forepart of a royal sphinx, with non-Egyptian features, from Abydos, Egypt.* c *1700 B.C.* (C) *Seal with handle in form of squatting man, from Abydos.* c *2000 B.C. All ivory. Scale 4/5.*

In the New Kingdom (1580–1090 B.C.), as one would expect in a wealthy and sophisticated age, ivory objects, especially toilet apparatus, become more common. Moreover, ivory was now imported also from Asia [18]. Thus Thothmes III hunted a herd of 120 elephants near the Euphrates in Syria 'for the sake of their tusks'. With these foreign supplies, there naturally came foreign ideas, and we detect Syrian influence in the greater emphasis on the carving of scenes in low relief. This technique had hitherto been very seldom employed for ivory,

FIGURE 461—*Egyptian ivory mechanical toy with figures of dancing dwarfs—perhaps central African pygmies. Strings were inserted through holes in the bases of the figures and in the stand, so that the dwarfs turned when the strings were pulled.* c *1900 B.C. Scale* c *2/3.*

apart from such things as name-panels. The handles of very early flint or chert knives, such as that of Gebel-el-Arak (figure 458) are, it is true, carved in relief, but these are from a time when influences from Mesopotamia were particularly strong. The archer's brace of Thothmes IV (*c* 1420 B.C.) from El-Amarna is the first notable example of an ivory artifact in relief from this period, and its design is wholly Egyptian [19].

More remarkable examples are the panels on a wooden casket from the tomb of Tutankhamen (*c* 1350 B.C.), which show king and queen in the domestic settings typical of the Amarna style. The various plaques of ivory making up each complete panel of this work have been fastened to the wooden base by ivory pegs. These are left as frank protuberances. Each panel was probably carved in position in a coin-like relief, and stained in simple tones ranging from pale red to deep brown (plate 23, tail piece, p. 352). From the wealth of ivory objects found in this tomb, such as scribes' palettes, fan-stocks, toilet-boxes, bracelets, and gaming-boards and pieces, we illustrate here only a casket of ivory treated as wood (figure 490, p 691), and a head-rest carved from two large pieces of tusk (plate 24 A).

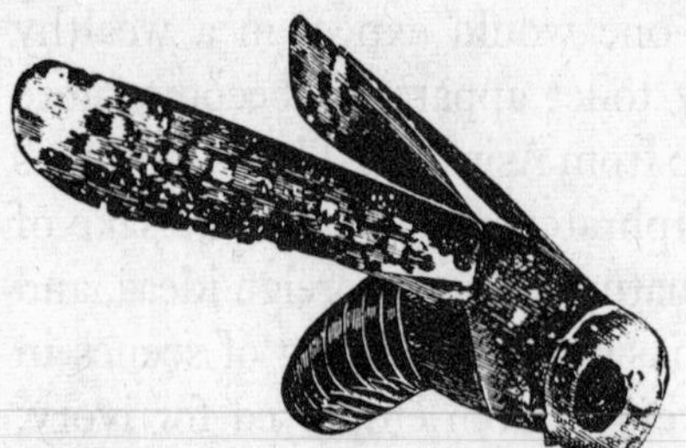

FIGURE 462—*Egyptian painted ivory unguent-vessel in the form of a grasshopper, with movable wings.* c *1350 B.C. Length 8·8 cm.*

Among many other fine pieces of the same period are a toilet-vase in the form of a grasshopper (figure 462), and an engraved gazelle upon a hillock with desert plants.[1] All were stained in bright colours and represent the court tradition of ivory-carving at its most exquisite.

From later times come a number of notable pieces. A mirror-case found in the coffin of Queen Henut-tawi (Dynasty XXI, *c* 1050 B.C.) is of wood veneered with ivory, charmingly engraved and stained in red, ochre, and green. It shows much of the old skill in its manufacture and in the ingenious arrangement of the various pieces that make up the design of the lid [20]. From the yet later Saite period (Dynasty XXVI, *c* 660–525 B.C.) are panels from a casket, expertly carved in delicate low relief with certain details enhanced with pale green (figure 463). Each part is marked on the back with signs indicating its position in the final assembly. These, and others like them, show that even at this late period the tradition of fine ivory-work was still strong.

FIGURE 463—*Two panels of ivory from a casket, with marsh scenes. The panels were held by tenons. Egypt.* c *660–525 B.C. Height 16·5 cm.*

IV. MESOPOTAMIA AND SYRIA

Ivory was well known to the Sumerians but was rare, and its use shows little art. Doors and a throne of ivory were, however, made for the temple in Eshnunna (Tell Asmar) in 2100 B.C. or earlier. In Mesopotamia proper, the first known technique for treating ivory ornamentally seems to be derived from an earlier technique, that of inlays in shell, mother-of-pearl, or bone. The art of cutting flat human or other figures in thin slips of white shell or bone was both economical and easy. The Sumerians used them in this way to achieve an effective contrast against a darker background. Details of the figures, instead of being carved in relief, were incised with deep lines which could be filled in with dark material, giving a clear and striking contrast. An excellent example of

[1] Now at New York. See H. RANKE, 'Masterpieces of Egyptian Art', Pl. xxxvi. Holbein-Verlag, Basel. 1951.

FIGURE 464—*Ivory inlay pieces from a panel, showing a god with sacred streams, trees, and a winged bull. From Ashur, Mesopotamia. Probably thirteenth century* B.C. *Scale* c 1/2.

this technique in shell is the royal standard from Ur, of before 2500 B.C. (figure 517). A similar splendid mosaic inlaid with figures, also in shell, was found at Mari on the Euphrates, on the western fringe of Sumer [21]. Others occur on ivory.

The taste for this inlay work of flat figures with details incised became so deeply established that it is reflected in Mesopotamian work several centuries later, when ivory became more easily available (figure 464). In Assyria, exquisite work in very low relief was practised [22]. Open-work in ivory is also known [23], and figures in the round were carved with considerable success [24]. The incised line, however, was still preferred in Assyrian art for rectangular panels. Such panels often bear vigorous representations of the king and his courtiers, or of military scenes, and recall the Assyrian royal sculptures. They formed the decora-

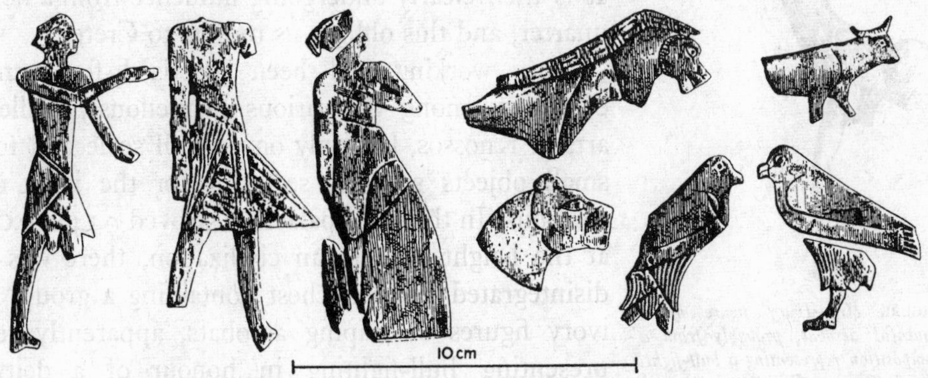

FIGURE 465—*Ivory figures for inlaying, from El-Jisr, Palestine.* c 1500 B.C.

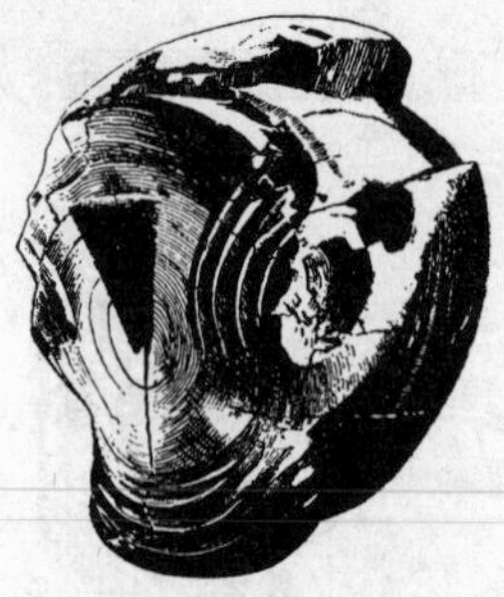

FIGURE 466—*Ivory bull's head, from Jericho. A triangular blaze was inlaid in the forehead.* c 2000 B.C. *Height 4·75 cm.*

tion of boxes, to which they were attached by copper nails [25]. From Assyria, this incised-line technique passed to Greece in the sixth century B.C.

From Palestine, where Mesopotamian and Egyptian influences met, we have interesting examples both of inlay figures and of incised panels. One of the former, *c* 1500 B.C., from El-Jisr (figure 465), though carved in the Sumerian way, actually shows figures in Egyptian style [26]. Incised-line technique on panels is shown in a scene of Egyptian character of the thirteenth century B.C. from Tell Fara [27]. This technique also spread to the Phoenicians, and found acceptance in their colonies in Spain [28].

V. CRETE AND SYRIA

Carving in the round was early and fully assimilated by Syrian, Phoenician, and even Palestinian craftsmen. The Gebel-el-Arak knife (figure 458) shows Egyptian contact with Syria and Mesopotamia at a very early date; its conception of a hero subduing two lions is purely Asiatic. A highly stylized bull's head carved in the round, from Jericho, belongs to the beginning of the second millennium B.C. (figure 466) [29]. However, excavations in Syria have been few and restricted. In some Syrian ivories Hittite influence is strong, but we can form no detailed picture of the culture of the coastal region of Syria until about 1400 B.C. It is then clearly undergoing influence from a new quarter, and this obliges us to look to Crete.

FIGURE 467—*Ivory figure of a youthful acrobat, probably from a composition representing a bull-fight. From Knossos, Crete.* c 1400 B.C. *Height 28·7 cm.*

Ivory working had been practised for many centuries among the various marvellously skilled arts of Knossos, but only on a small scale and for small objects such as seals, or for the inlay of weapons. In the great palace, destroyed *c* 1400 B.C., at the height of Minoan civilization, there was a disintegrated wooden chest containing a group of ivory figures of leaping acrobats, apparently representing bull-fighting in honour of a deity. They show a mastery of the technique of carving, and an extraordinary grace and vigour nowhere recaptured in antiquity (figure 467).

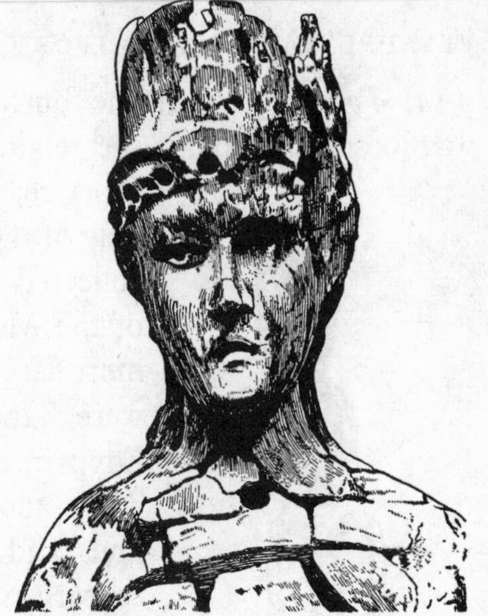

FIGURE 468—*Head of an ivory figure of a goddess or priestess. Crete.* c *1500–1400* B.C. *Scale 2/1. (See also figure 454.)*

A technical detail in Minoan ivory-carving is that, for locks of hair, spirals of plaited bronze wire were inserted into holes drilled in the heads, which were themselves mortised to the trunks. A well known object illustrating this is the famous snake priestess (figures 454, 468). For a brief moment, the Cretan ivory-workers raised this rendering of minute objects naturalistically to the level of a major art. The feat is the more notable in that the Minoan Cretans seem hardly to have practised sculpture on the large scale.

To return to the Syrian coast. Ra's Shamra (ancient Ugarit) was a busy port (*c* 1400 B.C.) where goods of Syria and of the Hittite realm were exchanged with those of Knossos, Mycenae, Cyprus, and Egypt. A similar picture, though on a smaller scale, has been furnished by the excavations at Atshana (ancient Alalakh) on the north Syrian coast near Alexandretta. After the fall of the empire of the Hyksos Pharaohs (*c* 1580 B.C.), who ruled the Syrian coast, a vigorous mixed culture had grown up on Syrian soil, where the lifelike art of Crete and Mycenae infused the technical traditions of the older cultures of the mainland. Though low relief had long been known, the art of carving groups or figures in low relief combined with open work was now borrowed from New Kingdom Egypt. The loan was influential, and some excellent examples of the new technique are from Megiddo, where in 1479 B.C. Thothmes III had defeated a Syrian army (figure 469).

FIGURE 469—*Ivory openwork panel from a piece of furniture, showing the winged figure of the Egyptian god Bes. From Megiddo, Palestine.* c *1200* B.C. *Height 4 cm.*

VI. APPLICATIONS OF IVORY

(*a*) *Toilet objects.* In the fourteenth century B.C., Egypt's hold on north Syria was loosened, though she retained partial control of Phoenicia and Palestine. Ivory may have been regarded in some way as a monopoly of the Pharaoh during his rule over Syria, and thus collected as tribute. This perhaps explains the extent of the Megiddo find [30]. In any event, ivory was now more largely used, and workers of Syria and Phoenicia were expanding their craft rapidly, borrowing from Egypt many subjects and motifs, mostly for the toilet. They adopted a variety of styles: open work, incised line, and in the round. These set the fashion for centuries to come. Greatly influenced by Egyptian art and symbolism, and equally influencing them, the Syrian and Phoenician workers invented shapes for ointment-vases and combs, and were ingenious and skilful in decorating furniture. The commonest type of vase became that in the form of a woman, with a spoon shaped like a hand on the stopper (figure 470). This curious device was also used with plain horn-shaped vessels for anointing. A prettier form, probably a Phoenician idea, is the playful swimming maiden catching a duck, a design also represented in wood (figure 504). All these types were still in use in Phoenicia in the seventh century B.C.—a further illustration of the long continuance of these craftsmen's traditions.

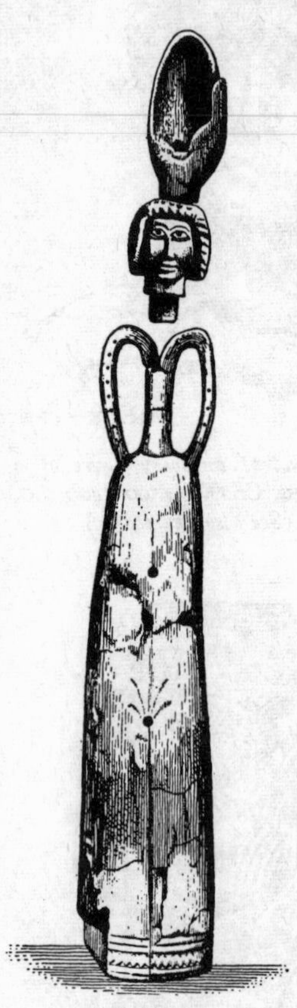

FIGURE 470—*Ivory unguent-vase in the form of a woman with head as stopper. From Lachish, Palestine. Fourteenth century* B.C. *Height 24 cm.*

(*b*) *Pyxides.* In the fourteenth–thirteenth centuries B.C. the half-Syrian craftsmen explored markets in mainland Greece, where ivory-work of Minoan masters was already familiar. There are several examples from Greece of carved circular boxes cut from sections of the tusk, doubtless used for precious ointments. They are known by the ancient name of pyxis, a word connected with *pyxos*, boxwood, of which such boxes had formerly been made. This emphasizes the link in craftsmanship between the ivory-carver and the worker in hard woods, such as box or cedar, for which Phoenicia was famous because of the forested mountains of Lebanon. A fine pyxis of the fourteenth century B.C. was found at Athens below the

Areopagus, seat of the high judicial court. This specimen is strongly Oriental in its motif (figure 471). Similar pyxides of the thirteenth century B.C. have been recovered from Palestine, and were still being made by Phoenician craftsmen in the eighth century B.C.

FIGURE 471—*Mycenaean ivory pyxis. From a grave on the Areopagus, Athens.* c *1350 B.C. Diameter 11 cm.*

(*c*) *Furniture.* Ivory-carvers of Syria and Phoenicia in the second millennium B.C. made immense progress in the ornamentation of furniture. Their achievement is often mentioned in the Bible, and in the annals of the Egyptian kings [31]. In the ninth and eighth centuries B.C. there is evidence that their craftsmanship was still holding its own in Syria and Phoenicia. From Zinjirli in the extreme north of Syria comes a sculptured stone slab which shows a stool inlaid with a row of what we now know to be extremely stylized palm-trees (figure 472) [32]. The form of the stool can be restored. Panels showing this type of palm-tree have been found at several other sites, Samaria and Carchemish among them [33].

Furniture entirely made of ivory was naturally very unusual. Thrones of ivory, apparently of Phoenician workmanship, and probably depicted in figure 473, are described in the Bible as owned by Solomon, 'The king [Solomon, *c* 950 B.C.] made a great throne of ivory, and overlaid it with gold. And there was . . . a footstool of gold fastened to the throne and stays on either side by the place of the seat' (2 Chron. ix. 17–18) (figure 473). (See also 1 Kings x. 18.) In the time of Ahab (*c* 876 B.C.) the prophet Amos uses 'beds of ivory' as a symbol of reckless luxury, but the ivory houses of certain other Biblical books (1 Kings xxii. 39 and Psalm xlv. 8; Amos iii. 15) may be mere hyperbole expressing the amount of ivory used for their ornamentation. A whole series of panels of Phoenician workmanship found at several sites in Syria and adjacent areas, in some cases in Assyrian palaces as at Khorsabad and Nimrud (figure 474), can be regarded as belonging to beds of this kind.

FIGURE 472—*Fragment of a basalt slab, representing a stool with inlays. From Zinjirli, north Syria.* c *Ninth century B.C.*

The precise and frequent repetition of motifs suggests that the Phoenician workman had pattern-books comparable to those

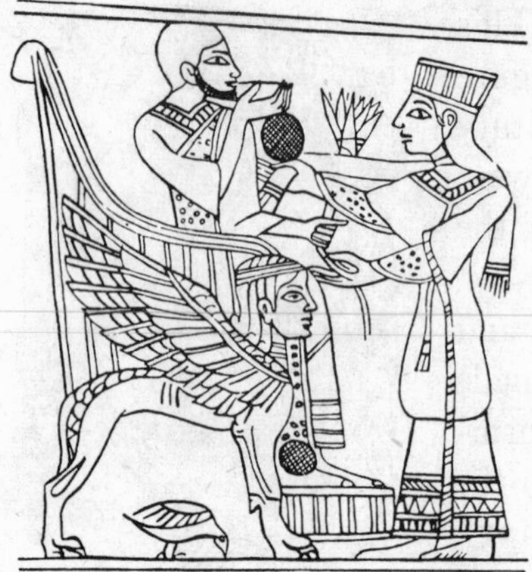

FIGURE 473—*Part of an incised ivory panel showing a king on his throne receiving wine. From Megiddo, Palestine.* c *1200* B.C. *Height 6 cm.*

generally used in the Middle Ages, the Renaissance, and later. The panels are ornamented in relief with Phoenician mythological subjects in a quasi-Egyptian style, arranged somewhat monotonously in rows. The projecting tenons above and below each panel show that they were fitted into a wooden frame. It seems likely that certain of these frames were ritual marriage-beds for the worship of Astarte (Ishtar or Ashtaroth of the Bible), the Phoenician goddess of fertility. Such objects were admired as works of luxury and elegance. Ashur-banipal (669–626 B.C.) of Assyria, who as Sardanapalus went down to Greek legend as the embodiment of luxurious living, is depicted on a sculpture from Nineveh at a ritual banquet, reclining on a divan apparently of Phoenician manufacture (figure 475). The Phoenician ivory-workers early invented and applied original motifs and did not merely copy Egyptian art. This is perhaps the place to mention a gaming-board of Phoenician workmanship found in Cyprus. It is in the form of a small chest, the sides being of thin sheets of ivory, delicately carved with scenes of the chase (figure 476).

FIGURE 474—*Ivory panel, probably from a ritual bed, showing a goddess or votaress looking out of a window. Phoenician art.* c *725* B.C. *Height 10·8 cm.*

(*d*) *Wall-panels* inlaid with ivory were used in decorating temples and palaces. Such panel-work, though not necessarily of ivory, is described as in the temple of Solomon (1 Kings vi. 29), and in the temple as envisaged by Ezekiel (Ezek. xli. 18–25). Ahab had an 'ivory house' (1 Kings xxii. 39). The doors of Assyrian palaces are also sometimes described as ornamented with ivory. The assembling of such panels on a comprehensive scale would present no great difficulties to Phoenician craftsmen. Entire screens of ivory panels, combined with others of boxwood, were regularly made in the ninth and tenth centuries A.D. for the Coptic Christian churches in Old Cairo, by

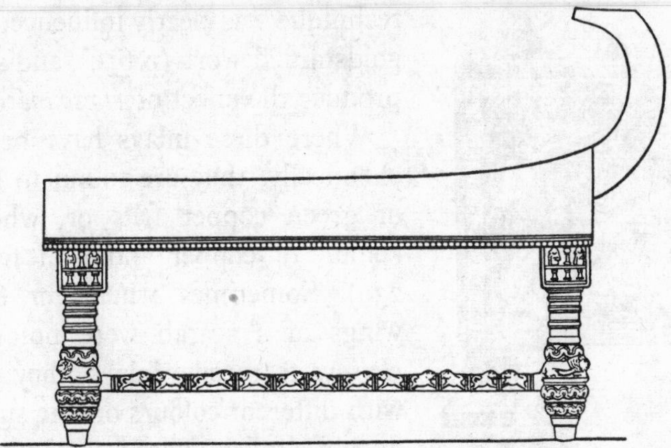

FIGURE 475—*Bed of Ashur-bani-pal, probably Phoenician work, with panels roughly of the type of figure 474. Bas-relief from Nineveh, Mesopotamia.* c 650 B.C.

craftsmen inheriting perhaps the same traditions. These screens were assembled without the use of metal pins.

VII. WESTERN ASIATIC TECHNIQUES

(*a*) *Decoration* of ivories was in itself a matter of much skill. Often they were overlaid with gold-leaf, an enrichment which caused their savage destruction in times of upheaval, but usually they were embellished with gay colours, by staining or with inlays. Homer in a famous simile compares the blood on a wounded hero's thigh to the red-purple dye with which a Lydian girl stains an ivory blinker of a horse [34]. Some Assyrian ivories are stained black, perhaps by smoking [35]. Inlay techniques involved filling small raised partitions with coloured paste, or sometimes glass of different colours, inlaid cold. This

FIGURE 476 A—*Ivory gaming-board in the form of a chest. From Enkomi, Cyprus.* c 1200 B.C. *Height 7·2 cm.*

FIGURE 476 B—*End view of the chest, with gaming pieces in position.*

technique was clearly influenced by Egyptian goldsmiths' work (p 659), and sought to reproduce the effect of *cloisonné* or *champlevé*.

Where these inlays have been examined chemically, they are found to be either red or green copper frits or, when of bluish colour, of copper and iron frits mixed (p 239). Sometimes when, for example, the wings of a scarab were not excavated in *cloisons* to receive inlays, they were painted with different colours on the surface to produce a similar effect [36]. In certain cases, as at Nimrud and Samaria, instead of glass, actual shapes of lapis lazuli were inserted, and on a magnificent Phoenician ivory from Nimrud recently examined it was established that the lapis lazuli was bedded on a thin layer of calcium carbonate and blue powdered frit, which acted as mortar [37]. The gold-leaf was attached by some sort of gum.

Sometimes the surface beneath the gold on pieces from Nimrud is stained purple. In a small group of ivories from Samaria the whole polychrome effect is produced by cells inlaid flush with the surface, without any additional raised modelling of the ivory. This technique seems to be that called *tamlu* (filling) by the Assyrians as opposed to *ihzu* (gripping), i.e. raised *cloisons*.[1] These pieces when complete must have presented a very striking appearance, as the new piece from Nimrud shows. Such polychromy was familiar enough to the eye in the ancient world, where sculpture of all kinds was regularly painted. For some reason, however, the *tamlu* technique was not widely followed, perhaps because it was too difficult.

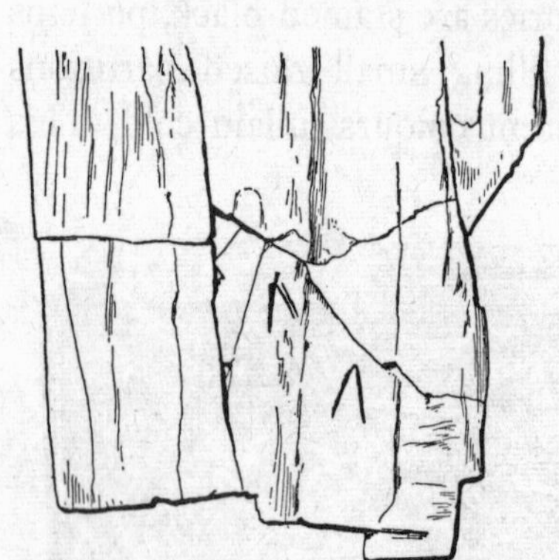

FIGURE 477—*Back view of the ivory panel seen in figure 474, showing carpenter's marks.*

(*b*) *Methods of attachment*. Phoenician panels are usually attached to their background by small tenons secured in a mortise with a pin, probably of ivory. To avoid confusion in assembly they were marked on the back with a letter of the Phoenician alphabet

[1] F. THUREAU-DANGIN ('Arslan Tash', p. 139. Geuthner, Paris. 1931) interprets the terms differently. He takes *ihzu* to mean 'overlaid', *sc* with gold, and *tamlu* as '*cloisonné*'.

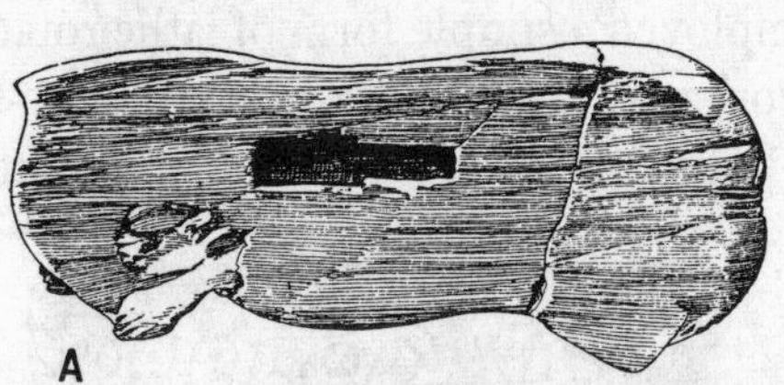

FIGURE 478—(A) *Back view of ivory figure of a cow, showing the 'bottle-necked slot' by which it was attached to a background. Phoenician art. Late eighth century* B.C. (B), (C) *Ivory wedges with tenons to fit into 'bottle-necked slots' for attachment. Phoenician art. Ninth century* B.C. *Scale 3/4.*

or other sign to indicate their appropriate place (figure 477). Sometimes there are no tenons or pinholes, and they must then have been attached with glue or bitumen.

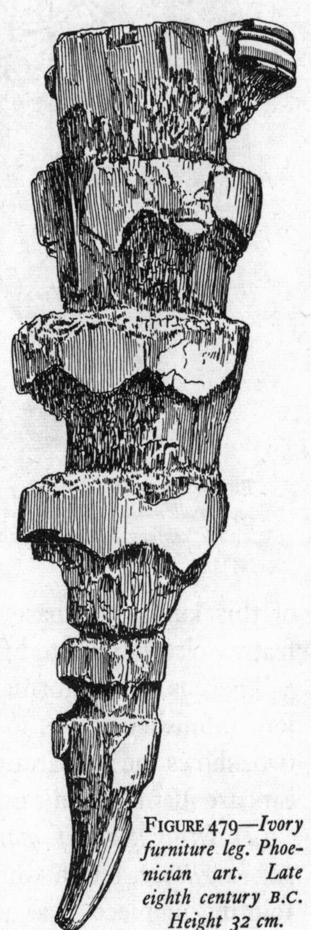

FIGURE 479—*Ivory furniture leg. Phoenician art. Late eighth century* B.C. *Height 32 cm.*

Another method used in Syria and Phoenicia to attach ornamental figures was an ingenious invention, of Egyptian origin. It may be described as a bottle-neck mortise (figures 478 A, 492 B). A terracotta figure from Atshana shows that this device was known by the fourteenth century B.C. In the ninth century it was in regular use in Phoenicia (figure 478 B, C). The tenon fitting into the mortise was often made as a separate piece and secured with an ivory pin. Such ivory pins are still used in ivory work, and are preferable to metal, which may rust or stain.

(*c*) *Tools.* Except for Egypt, we are dependent on examination of the objects themselves for knowledge concerning the tools used. There are traces of small saws, drills, and chisels. Occasionally pieces, instead of being sawn, were broken along a line of small drilled holes. An example from Nimrud is prepared for such breaking. A core of ivory remaining in one of the holes shows that the drill-bits were semi-tubular and of metal.[1] Abrasives were no

[1] Bits of this type, operated by a bow-drill, are still used in the pianoforte trade, to place the pegs for the piano-strings.

doubt employed for smoothing and polishing, and in Roman times were made of shark-skin [38]. Files are unknown before Roman times, but there is reason to suppose that the ivory-carver in Asia employed a simple form of lathe rotated by a bow-drill, such as is used today by workmen in the Near East. A chair-leg (figure 479) and a small model of a vase (figure 480) were made on some lathe

FIGURE 480—*Model of ivory vase (neck and handle missing). Phoenician art. Ninth century* B.C. *Height 10 cm.*

FIGURE 481—*A piece of an ivory pyxis, showing an ivory plug used to replace a defect. From Nimrud, Mesopotamia. Height 6·5 cm.*

of this kind. The base of the handle of the vase is masked by a palmette, a feature clearly imitated from a metal original.

There is little information on the way a carver set to work, for there are very few unfinished pieces to give indications. A head from Nimrud, now broken in two, shows the preparation of a bust wearing an Egyptian ritual head-cloth. The ears are just blocked out, and the cloth is marked in red lines for carving.

(*d*) *Utilization of material.* The Phoenician craftsmen were ivory-workers *par excellence*, and a word must be said as to their general use of the material. Jointing of pieces was understood. Little was wasted from the valuable tusk. A flaw was cut out and plugged (figure 481). From the broad hollow end near the base of the tusk, a section would be cut to form a circular pyxis. The narrower tips might be used for statuettes. Strips cut from the length served to make panels both for relief and for engraving, though only sections cut across the tusk could be properly used for panels in relief. These should be worked on the grain end, since otherwise the cut is less clear and the fibres 'pick up' in the cutting [39]. The end grain was kept for specially fine work, such as seals. There are cases, however, where the ivory might have been used more economically.

The last department in which the ancient ivory-carvers developed special skill was in combining ivory with other substances to form statuettes. In these cases, the flesh was of ivory while the dress was of some other precious substance. The pieces were joined by tenons and pegs (figure 482). This technique was known in Mesopotamia from early times, and became highly developed. Eventually it passed into Greek hands, and was the medium for what is said to have been the greatest sculpture by the greatest sculptor of antiquity—the Zeus of Phidias at Olympia. The carving of ivory had become once more, as in Phoenicia, a major art.

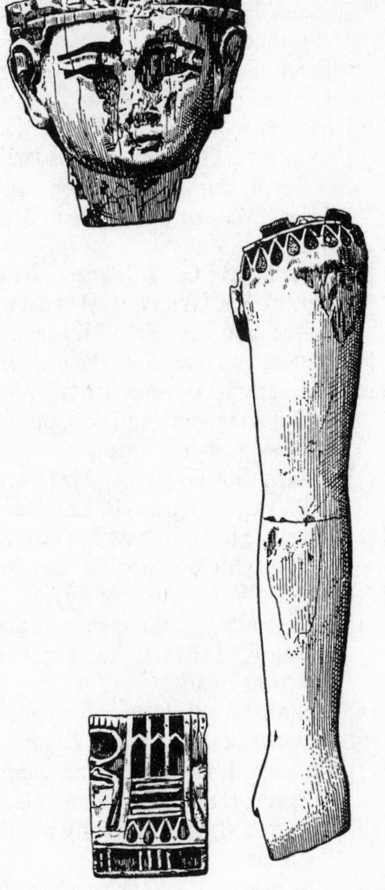

FIGURE 482—*Ivory fragments from composite figures. Phoenician art from Nimrud. Late eighth century B.C. Scale 3/4.*

REFERENCES

[1] PLINY, Nat. Hist. V, i, 15. (Loeb ed. Vol. 2, p. 228, 1942.)

[2] NAVILLE, E. 'The Temple of Deir el Bahari', Vol. 3. Egypt Explor. Fund. Kegan Paul, London. 1898.

[3] GADD, C. J. *Proc. Brit. Acad.*, **18**, 191, 1932.
LEGRAIN, L. 'Seal Cylinders', pp. 624–32. Ur Excavations. Reports. Vol. 10. Publ. of Joint Exped. Brit. Mus. and Mus. of Univ. of Pennsylvania. 1951. (A curious cylinder-seal found at Khafaje, and apparently of Indus Valley origin, admirably depicts an elephant of Indian type, a rhino, and an alligator.)

[4] MACKAY, E. J. H., HARDING, L., and PETRIE, SIR (WILLIAM MATTHEW) FLINDERS. 'Bahrein and Hemamieh', Pl. I. Egypt. Res. Acc. and Brit. Sch. Archaeol. Egypt, Publ. 47. London. 1929.

BENT, T. and BENT, M. V. A. 'Southern Arabia', p. 26. Smith, Elder and Co., London. 1900.

[5] MILET, A. 'Ivoires et Ivoiriers de Dieppe.' Libr. de l'Art. Moreau, Paris. 1906.

[6] BRUNTON, G. 'Qau and Badari III', p. 20. Egypt. Res. Acc. and Brit. Sch. Archaeol. Egypt, Publ. 50. London. 1930.

Idem. 'Matmar', p. 65. Brit. Mus. Exped. to Middle Egypt 1929–31. Quaritch, London. 1948.

[7] STEINDORFF, G. *J. Walters Art Gallery*, **9**, 41, 1946.

[8] PETRIE, SIR (WILLIAM MATTHEW) FLINDERS. 'Objects of Daily Use', p. 41. Egypt. Res. Acc. and Brit. Sch. Archaeol. Egypt, Publ. 42. London. 1927.

[9] LEGGE, F. *Proc. Soc. Biblical Archaeol.*, **27**, 138, 139, 1905.

[10] For early ivories see SMITH, W. S. 'A History of Egyptian Sculpture and Painting in the Old Kingdom' (2nd ed.), pp. 1–7. Boston Mass., Mus. of Fine Arts. Oxford University Press, London. 1949.

[11] PETRIE, SIR (WILLIAM MATTHEW) FLINDERS and QUIBELL, J. E. 'Naqada and Ballas', Pl. LXI, 2. Quaritch, London. 1896.

[12] PETRIE, SIR (WILLIAM MATTHEW) FLINDERS. 'Abydos II', Pl. XIII, XIV. Egypt Explor. Fund, Memoir no. 24. London. 1903.

[13] SMITH, W. S. 'Ancient Egypt', fig. 22. Mus. of Fine Arts, Boston, Mass. 1942.

[14] BORCHARDT, L. 'Statuen und Statuetten von Königen und Privatleuten im Museum von Kairo', Teil III, no. 815. Catal. gén. antiq. égypt. Mus. Caire. Reichsdruckerei, Berlin. 1930.

[15] PENDLEBURY, J. D. S. 'Aegyptiaca', p. 34. University Press, Cambridge. 1930.

[16] GLANVILLE, S. R. K. *J. Egypt. Archaeol.*, **17**, 98, 1931.

[17] QUIBELL, J. E. 'The Ramesseum', Pl. II, 1, 2. Egypt. Res. Acc. and Brit. Sch. Archaeol. Egypt, Publ. 2. London. 1898.

[18] BREASTED, J. H. 'Ancient Records of Egypt', Vol. 2, p. 588. University of Chicago Press, Chicago. 1907.

[19] BORCHARDT, L. *Rep. Smithson. Instn. for 1915*, 455, Pl. X, 1916.

CAPART, J. 'L'Art égyptien', Part II, Vol. 4: 'Les arts mineurs', Planche 675. Vromant, Brussels, Paris. 1951.

[20] BÉNÉDITE, G. 'Miroirs', Pl. XXIII. Catal. gén. antiq. égypt. Mus. Caire. Imprim. Inst. franç. Archéol. orient. Cairo. 1907.

[21] PARROT, A. *Syria*, **16**, 117, and Pl. XXVIII, 1935.

[22] e.g. Panel with figure of Ashur-nasir-pal, MALLOWAN, M. E. L. *Iraq*, **14**, 1, and Pl. I, 1952.

[23] e.g. From Toprak Kale (Urartu), BARNETT, R. D. *Ibid.*, **12**, 1, and Pl. XV, 1950.

[24] *Idem. Ibid.*, Pl. XIV. For a fine figure from Susa in the Louvre see JÉQUIER, J. *Mém. Délég. Perse*, **7**, Pl. IV, 1909.

[25] e.g. On an unpublished piece from Nineveh in the British Museum. No. 118122.

[26] ORY, J. *Quart. Dept. Antiq. Palest.*, **12**, Pl. XIV, 1946.

[27] PETRIE, SIR (WILLIAM MATTHEW) FLINDERS. 'Bethpelet (Tel Fara) I', Pl. LV. Egypt. Res. Acc. and Brit. Sch. Archaeol. Egypt, Publ. 48. London. 1930.

[28] See the incised ivories from Carmona in Spain, BONSOR, G. *Rev. archéol.*, third series, **35**, 126 ff., 232 ff., 1899.

[29] GARSTANG, J. *Ann. Archaeol. Anthrop.*, **19**, 18, 1932.
[30] LOUD, G. 'The Megiddo Ivories.' Univ. of Chicago, Orient. Inst.: Publ. 52. Chicago. 1939.
[31] BREASTED, J. H. 'Ancient Records of Egypt', Vol. 2, pp. 436, 509. University of Chicago Press, Chicago. 1907.
[32] LUSCHAN, F. VON. 'Die Kleinfunde von Sendschirli', ed. by W. ANDRAE, Pl. LXII. Staatl. Mus., Mitt. aus den orient. Sammlungen, Heft 15. De Gruyter, Berlin. 1943.
[33] CROWFOOT, J. W. and CROWFOOT, GRACE M. 'Early Ivories from Samaria', fig. 5. Palest. Explor. Fund. Samaria–Sebaste Reports 1931–3, 1935, no. 2. London. 1938.
[34] ILIAD, 4, 141. (Loeb. ed. Vol. 1, p. 162, 1924.)
[35] From Toprak Kale. BARNETT, R. D. *Iraq*, **12**, Pl. XV, 1950.
[36] On an unpublished piece from Abu Habbah in the British Museum (Brit. Mus. no. 118161).
[37] MALLOWAN, M. E. L. *Ill. Lond. News*, 16 August 1952, [colour] suppl. p. I, foll. p. 256.
[38] PLINY, XIX, xxvi, 87; IX, xiv, 40. (Loeb ed. Vol. 3, pp. 190 ff., 1940.)
[39] WRIGHT, T. H. 'Small Carvings.' Dryad Handicrafts, Leaflet no. 35, London. No year.

BIBLIOGRAPHY

BARNETT, R. D. "The Nimrud Ivories and the Art of the Phoenicians." *Iraq*, **2**, 179, 1935.
Idem. "Phoenician and Syrian Ivory Carving." *Palest. Explor. Quart.*, **71**, 4, 1939.
Idem. "Early Greek and Oriental Ivories." *J. Hell. Stud.*, **48**, 1, 1948.
CROWFOOT, J. W. and CROWFOOT, GRACE M. 'Early Ivories from Samaria.' Palest. Explor. Fund. Samaria-Sebaste Reports 1931–3, 1935, no. 2. London. 1938.
FRÉDÉRICQ, M. "The Ointment Spoons in the Egyptian Section of the British Museum." *J. Egypt. Archaeol.*, **13**, 7, 1927.
KLEBS, L. 'Die Reliefs und Malereien des Mittleren Reiches', pp. 26, 115. *Abh. heidelberg. Akad. Wiss., phil.-hist. Kl.*, no. 6, 1922.
Idem. 'Die Reliefs und Malereien des Neuen Reiches', p. 125. *Abh. heidelberg. Akad. Wiss., phil.-hist. Kl.*, no. 9, 1934.
KUNZ, G. F. 'Ivory and the Elephant in Art, in Archaeology and in Science.' Doubleday, Page and Co., Garden City, New York. 1926.
LOUD, G. 'The Megiddo Ivories.' Univ. of Chicago, Orient. Inst.: Publ. 52. Chicago. 1952.
LUCAS, A. 'Ancient Egyptian Materials and Industries' (3rd ed.), chap. 2. Arnold, London. 1948.
MÜLLER, V. C. "Das phönizische Kunstgewerbe" in 'Geschichte des Kunstgewerbes', ed. by H. TH. BOSSERT, Vol. 4. Wasmuth, Berlin–Zürich. 1930.
PENNIMAN, T. K. 'Pictures of Ivory and Other Animal Teeth, Bone and Antler'. *Occ. Pap. Tech. Pitt-Rivers Mus.*, no. 5. Oxford. 1952.
THUREAU-DANGIN, F. *et al.* 'Arslan-Tash.' Haut Commissariat de la Républ. Franç. en Syrie et au Liban. Service des Antiq., etc. Biblioth. archéol. et hist. Vol. 16. Geuthner, Paris. 1941.
WOLF, W. "Das ägyptische Kunstgewerbe: Holz und Elfenbein" in 'Geschichte des Kunstgewerbes', ed. by H. TH. BOSSERT, Vol. 4, pp. 142–56. Wasmuth, Berlin–Zürich. 1930.

25

FINE WOOD-WORK

CYRIL ALDRED

I. TIMBER SUPPLIES

WOOD was worked very early: no elaborate tools were needed. In recent times, Australian natives have made good implements of wood using casual blocks of stone, while natives of Oceania have produced wooden objects of beauty as well as utility with stone adzes and gouges. The craftsmanship, in fact, has often depended more on the character of the wood than on the tools for working it, though joinery, as distinct from carving, can hardly develop without metal implements.[1] Even so, accurate work is not possible unless suitable timbers are available. In modern Europe, fine joinery became common only when oak was replaced by close-grained walnut, mahogany, and similar woods.

In the ancient Near East, timber of high quality was not available except from certain restricted areas. In the valley region of Mesopotamia such woods did not grow, but they were imported, especially from the richly forested areas of Syria, Armenia, and Anatolia. Many types were known, and their qualities were appreciated by the Sumerians and Babylonians. There are cuneiform documents which give long lists of many kinds of wooden objects. Hittite hieroglyphic inscriptions were sometimes carved on wooden tablets. In the climate of western Asia wooden objects have, however, seldom survived.

Of these survivors we may mention those at the royal cemetery at Ur (*c* 2500 B.C.), whence come sledges, harps, and dagger-handles of wood. These have disintegrated, but have been accurately restored and their inlays replaced. From Armenia (Karmir Blur) are fragments of woodwork of the seventh century B.C., inlaid with large pieces of bone, which exhibit a similar technique to that used at Ur nearly 2000 years earlier; there is also a small wooden vase (figure 483) similar to the Phoenician ivory vase mentioned above (figure 480) and, like it, made on the lathe. From Jericho come some interesting wooden objects of unknown date (figure 484).[2]

Most ancient fine woodwork, however, has been recovered from the dry sands

[1] Natives of Micronesia have produced accurate joinery, but their tools of bone and shell are copies of metal originals.

[2] The information on Asiatic wood-work is contributed by Mr Barnett.

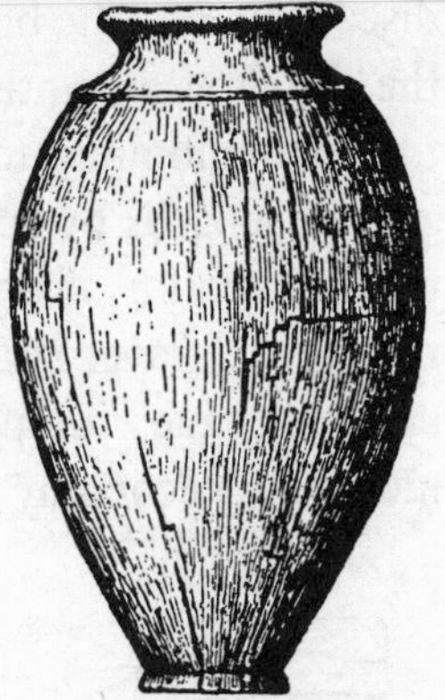

FIGURE 483—*Wooden vase from Karmir Blur, near Erivan, Armenia. End of seventh century B.C.*

of Egypt, though there, too, home-grown trees, such as the acacia, sycamore-fig, sidder (*Zizyphus spina Christi*), and tamarisk were too fibrous, knotty, and small for good craftsmanship. For this reason, much Egyptian woodwork was made only for concealment beneath a layer of plaster, paint, or gold-leaf. This practice naturally does not call for a high standard of accuracy or finish on the underlying wood.

To exploit the special qualities and appearance of wood, higher grades and larger logs had to be imported. There was a regular sea-borne timber trade from early times, cedar, cypress, juniper, pine, and yew of Syria and the Lebanon being exchanged for the products of Egypt. Ebony was imported as tribute from Punt and the Sudan, and even re-exported in the form of logs and finished products.[1] Ebony was in fact the wood *par excellence* of ancient Egyptian joinery, its very name being ultimately derived from the Egyptian *hbny*; other woods were sometimes painted and grained to imitate it. Ivory is intimately associated with ebony for veneers and inlays. Like ebony it was used in early dynastic times as thin plates for inscribed dockets, and it resembles ebony in having a close hard grain which does not easily split.

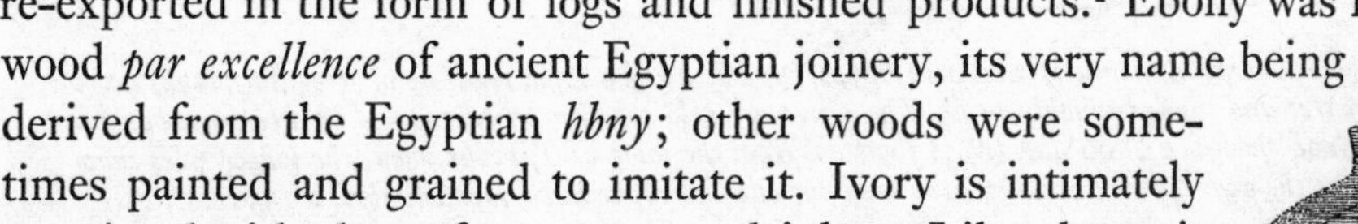

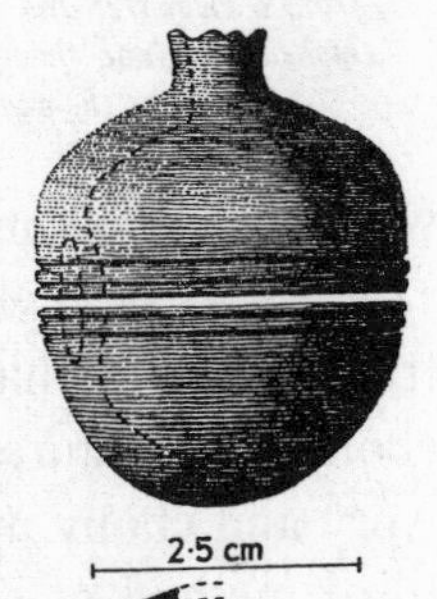

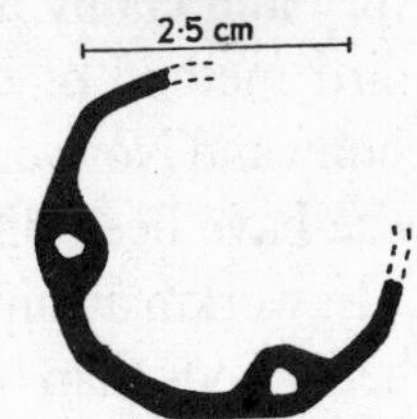

FIGURE 484—*Miniature wooden vase, perhaps for the toilet, in the form of a pomegranate. The upper half pivots upon the lower by means of a peg concealed in a thickening of the wall. From a tomb at Jericho. About sixteenth to fifteenth century B.C.*

Wooden furniture must have been rare before dynastic times, when copper tools became more plentiful. Until then, reed and rush were used for making stools, stands, tables, boxes, and similar objects. Such light-weight furniture continued into later times for everyday use, and influenced the design of certain wooden stools and caskets, which are translations into a firmer material of flimsy rush or reed archetypes (plate 25 B).

Scarcity of timber involved economy. Planks cut from the same trunk were placed side by side, so that the convex edge of one fitted the concave edge of its neighbour. The internal edges were trimmed to make the fit closer; in the best examples the join is barely perceptible. Only the outside edges were sawn straight (figure 485 A). Knotty pieces were not

[1] Amenhetep III, for example, sent thirteen ebony chairs and one hundred pieces of ebony to the King of Arzawa in Asia Minor. J. A. KNUDTZON, 'Die El-Amarna Tafeln' No. 31, lines 36–38. Cf. also no. 5, lines 20–25. Vorderasiatische Bibliothek, Hinrichs, Leipzig. 1915.

discarded, but the blemishes were cut out and replaced by patches or plugs, and the filling was painted to match. Even the royal workshops sometimes adopted this parsimonious technique (figure 485 B). Smaller pieces were united into greater lengths by scarf-joints or other devices (figure 492 A). A fragment of a plywood coffin of Dynasty III (*c* 2700 B.C.) is of six pegged layers of pieces of wood, each layer so tongued together that the grain of the different woods—cypress, pine, juniper, and sidder—ran alternately crosswise [1]. A second method of economy was to use an inferior wood as a foundation, and cover it

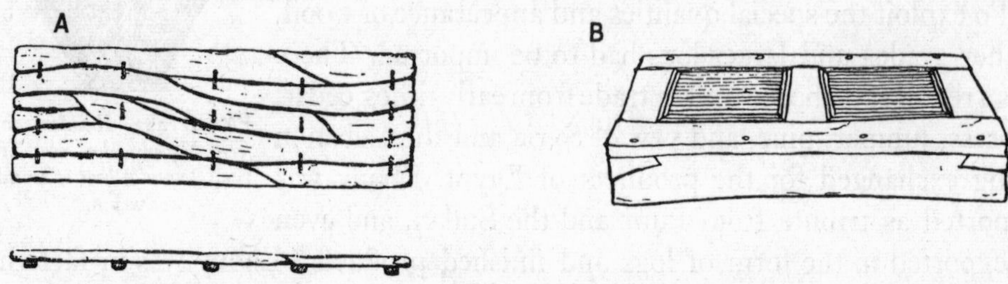

FIGURE 485—*Economy in the use of timber in Egypt.* (A) *The lid of a coffin made up of irregular planks sawn from a local tree and shaped roughly to fit. The pieces are held together by tenons and by five cross-battens lashed with hide thongs.* c 2000 B.C. (B) *A footstool from the tomb of Tutankhamen; the longer sides show insets at the ends where blemishes have been cut out and replaced by sound timber.* c 1350 B.C.

with a veneer of one more precious. Thus a toilet-casket of Amenhetep II (1447–1420 B.C.) has a cylindrical body of cedar, veneered with thin slips of ebony cut from wood in which small knot-holes have been drilled clean and plugged with ebony pegs (figure 486). Much of the furniture of Tutankhamen is of veneered ivory and ebony upon inferior wooden grounds, and there are many parallels. A third method of economizing was to veneer with marquetry slips, usually of ebony and ivory or of red wood, employing very small pieces which might otherwise have been discarded (figure 494).

In workmanship, the Egyptians were much less trammelled by the character of their woods than by preconceived ideas of form. In the New Kingdom (Dynasties XVIII-XX, *c* 1580–1090 B.C.) there was, it is true, some regard to the natural shape of timber in making curved chair- and bed-frames, but we can seldom be sure that this is not due to foreign influences, or to a more developed taste for comfort, especially as the surviving examples date from the atypical Amarna period (*c* 1370 B.C.) (plates 24 B, 25). There are specimens, however, which appear to be but chance exploitation of freak forms. Thus the striding statue of King Hor (*c* 1800 B.C.) has the torso and right leg cut from a single tree-trunk and its diverging limb, but the final appearance of the statue does not differ from that achieved by a more orthodox construction [2]. On the other hand, the wooden angle-pieces for strengthening the joints of furniture appear to have been cut from trees grown espalier-wise, with branches at right angles to the stem. According to Petrie, three-legged stools in Dynasty I were formed by a similar means [3].

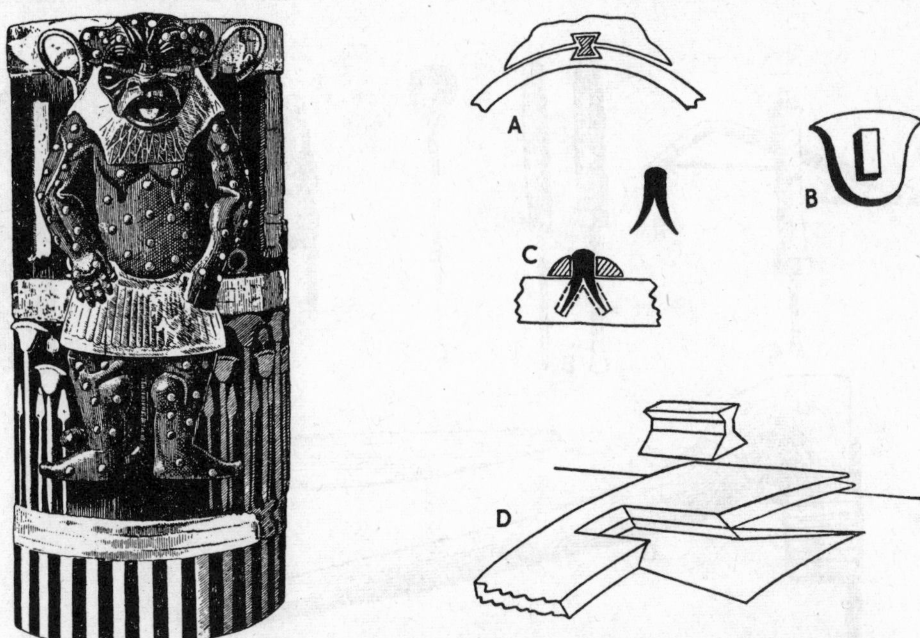

FIGURE 486—*Toilet casket of King Amenhetep II. The cylindrical body of the casket has probably been hollowed from a cedar log. Its exterior is covered with thin slips of ebony, and ornamentation is applied in ivory. The three raised bands are covered with gesso, and gilded. The figure of Bes is of ebony with collar and kilt of gilded gesso; the spots are gilded copper nails. It is mortised to the body by means of cramps sliding in under-cut channels* (A). *The casket was fixed to a second body, now missing, by means of a cramp sliding in a tapering channel, which had the effect of bringing the two parts into very firm and intimate contact* (D). *The tail of Bes is fixed to the body of the casket by tiny split pegs* (C). *The ivory umbels of the papyrus plants are fixed by means of small raised tongues on their backs* (B). *Egypt.* c *1420* B.C. *Height of casket 21·5 cm.*

II. TOOLS AND CRAFTSMEN

The introduction of copper tools towards the end of the fifth millennium B.C. did much for the technique of joining timber (figure 487). Chisels suitable for cutting mortises, dovetails, and sockets were devised in the early dynasties, and axes and adzes for hewing and trimming timber were refined. Shaping, planing, and smoothing were done with a small adze, which in the hands of an experienced workman can be a very versatile and accurate instrument (figure 488). Pull-saws exist from the early dynasties. They were probably used on the harder timbers, with an abrasive such as quartz sand. The work was lashed firmly to an upright post and sawn downwards, with the force concentrated on the pulling stroke (figure 489). Bow-drills had long been known, and could now be fitted with metal points and fed with abrasive (see also figure 112). To obtain greater pressure, the drill-cap could be pressed by one man while another worked the bow [4]. There were also metal awls, doubtless used for making small holes in

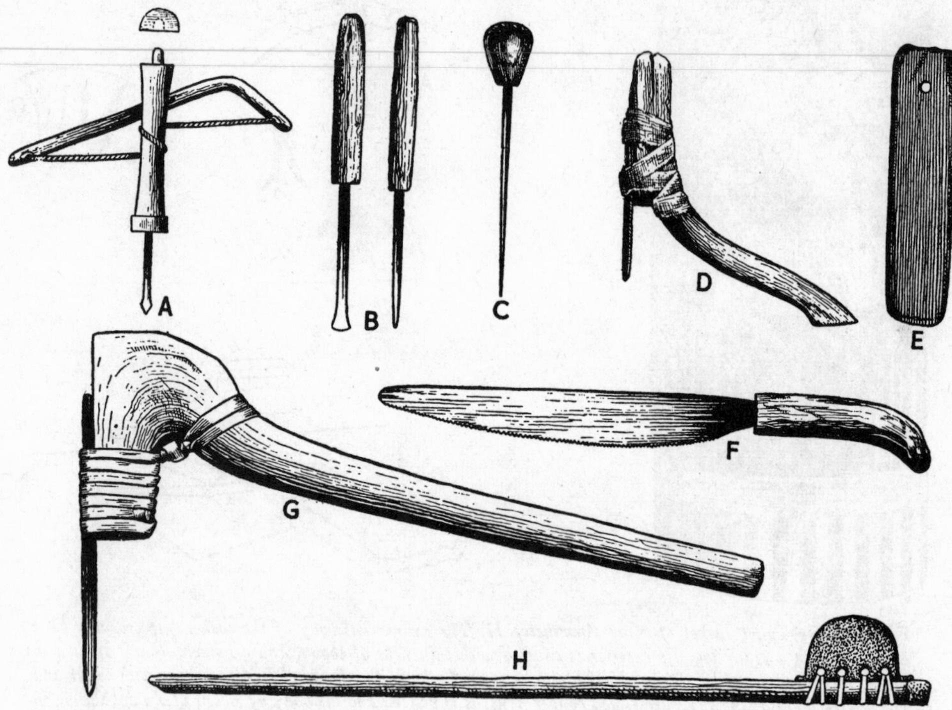

FIGURE 487—*Egyptian wood-working tools.* (A) *Bow-drill with copper bit.* (B) *Copper chisel for cutting mortises (front and side elevations).* (C) *Copper awl with hardwood handle.* (D) *Small adze; copper blade lashed with rawhide to wooden handle.* (E) *Whetstone.* (F) *Small hand-saw with serrated copper blade.* (G) *Large adze.* (H) *Large axe with copper blade lashed into a channel on the shaft, which is strengthened by a copper ferrule.* c *1200 B.C.*

finer work. Mallets and hammers of various types and weights were used. A heavy mallet was made from a section of tree-trunk trimmed to shape, with a limb as a long handle [5]. The final smoothing and finishing were done with sandstone rubbers of different degrees of fineness.

There is doubt whether the lathe proper was known in ancient Egypt. Wood-turning was common there in Greco-Roman times, but positive evidence for the true lathe is lacking earlier. On the other hand, bow-drills and the method of shaping and grinding-out stone vases (figure 117), to say nothing of the potter's wheel, all involve the principle of turning. A Dynasty XIX (*c* 1300 B.C.) stool

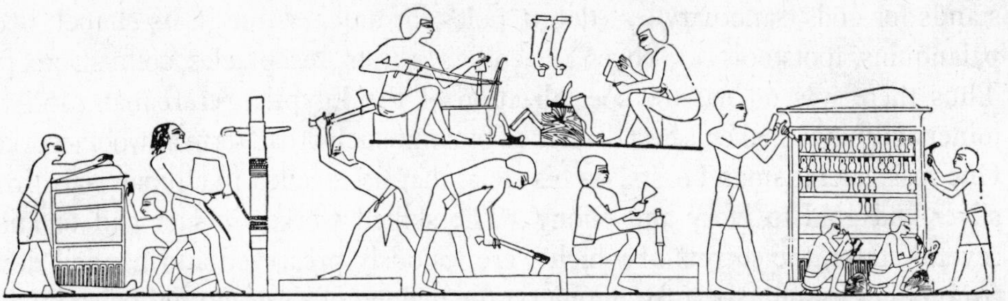

FIGURE 488—*Furniture-makers at work. On the left two men are rubbing down a completed shrine. Next to them a sawyer re-lashes a plank higher up the sawing-post (the Egyptian equivalent of the vice) while his saw remains jammed in the work. Two men split planks with heavy axes and a joiner uses a chisel and a mason's wooden mallet of modern type (see figure 314). In the background a workman is drilling holes in a chair to take the woven seat, while another smooths down the four legs of a chair he is making; near the chopping-block before him are two adzes and a square. On the right two men with adze and chisel are fitting the openwork elements, carved by two squatting men, into the panels of a shrine. From a tomb at Thebes.* c *1440* B.C.

has waisted, circular legs decorated with a series of rings, but there is no trace of a pivot-hole on the underpart. These rings may have been made by some such technique as a bowstring coated with abrasive, and it seems probable that they were not so much turned as filed or ground into shape. The maker may well have been imitating a foreign lathe-turned effect [6].

It cannot be said that the Egyptian joiner was appreciably restricted in the use of wood by the nature of his tools. No doubt he found sawing with copper and bronze implements laborious and uncertain, but he could always subsequently adze or rasp the work to the desired degree of finish.

The Egyptians distinguished terminologically between the carpenter, the carver, and the portrait sculptor, all of whom might work in wood. A writing-board enumerates the products of the carver thus: 'chapel, divine boat, carrying-

FIGURE 489—*Joiners at work. On the left a workman is sawing with a heavy pull-saw a plank lashed to an upright post by a tourniquet. Next to him a man chisels a block of wood, using a club-shaped mallet. Another saws a lighter piece of timber. Two men are smoothing a finished bed with sandstone rubbers; a completed neck-rest and a casket are shown beneath the bed. The man on the right uses a bow-drill. From a tomb at Saqqara, Egypt.* c *2500* B.C.

stands for gods, sanctuary . . . doors, poles for uraei, statue in its chapel, beds, palanquins, footstools . . . boxes . . . coffers, chests, receptacles, coffins', etc. [7]. Thus there was no narrow specialization of the Egyptian craftsman, and the joiner or cabinet-maker is best described by some such broad term as wood-worker. One master-craftsman boasts, on his stela, that he excelled in all materials 'from silver and gold to ivory and ebony'. The skilled worker in fact had to know several crafts, the secrets of which were jealously preserved and handed down from father to son. Apart from joinery, the making of a casket might also involve covering surfaces with plaster moulded in relief, painting, or gilding, or inlaying with ivory or faience or hard stones, or any combination of these processes, so that the scope of the work was very varied.

Memphis, in the Old Kingdom at least (*c* 2800 B.C.), was a traditional centre of handicrafts. Ptah, creator-god of the place, was the patron of craftsmen, and his high priests bore the title 'Greatest of the Craftsmen'. It is probable that they were the chief designers of all the important works of art executed under their supervision. In later ages, it would appear that similar offices were held by scribes or priests, that is educated men, attached to the more important temples or to the court. The court jeweller to Akhenaten, for instance, was also a chamberlain. Two craftsmen responsible for the statue of a high Theban dignitary, who have taken the rare step of signing their work, were both priests and outline-draughtsmen in the treasury of the god Amen at Thebes [8]. For the most part, however, craftsmen worked anonymously in their workshops; joiners, jewellers, goldsmiths, and sculptors are depicted cheek by jowl.[1]

III. TECHNIQUES

Fine work in wood—apart from sculpture and other objects carved from the solid such as dishes, ointment spoons, gaming-pieces, and staves—is scarcely possible without the ability to make firm and accurate joints. In Europe, cabinet-making displayed no great craftsmanship until framed and panelled structures replaced the plank construction of the carpenter. In Egypt, fine wood-work is based upon a similar technique. Boards were joined by independent tongues of hard wood, inserted at intervals in mortises cut in the thickness of each board. Where such panels were not to be covered with plaster, and in superior work, the edges were sawn parallel and the fit was made as close as possible, sometimes by the insertion of flat butterfly-cramps. Such cramps were inserted in a coffin of Queen Meryet-Amen (Dynasty XVIII, *c* 1440 B.C.) when, during the making, an unseasoned plank showed signs of splitting.

[1] e.g. in tombs of Rekhmire and Nebamen and Ipuky at Thebes.

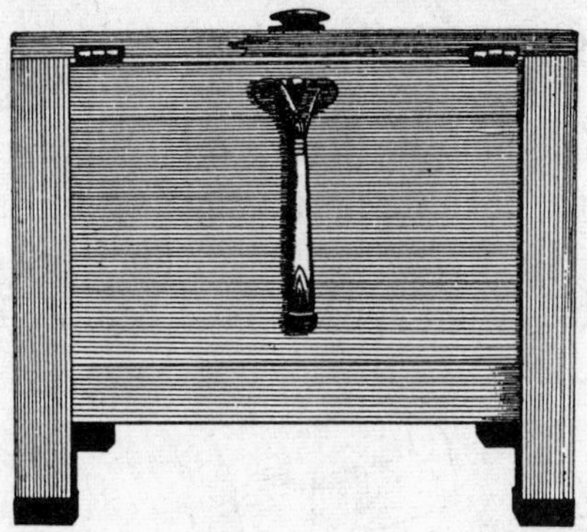

FIGURE 490—*Back of an ivory casket of Tutankhamen. Hinges, knobs, and feet-casings are of gold. The tonguing and grooving of the two sheets of ivory that make up the lid should be noted.* c 1350 B.C. *Scale* 1/3.

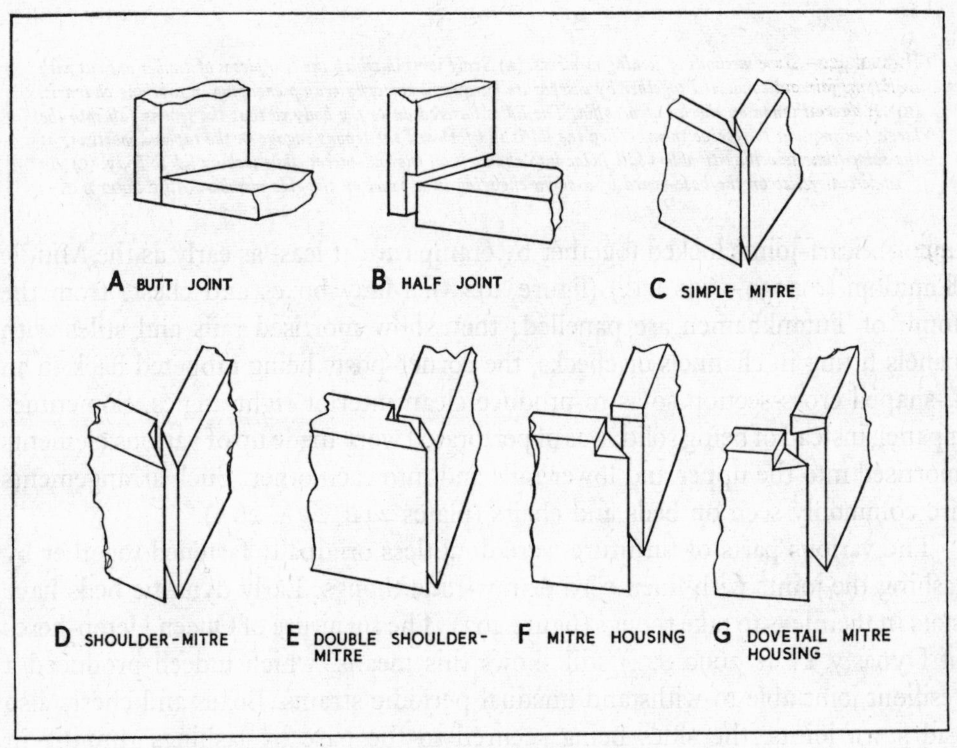

FIGURE 491—*Joints from Old Kingdom Egyptian coffins.* c 2500 B.C.

An ivory casket from the tomb of Tutankhamen (*c* 1350 B.C.) provides an example of tonguing and grooving (figure 490). Corners were united by various means—halving-joints, mitres, shoulder-mitres, double shoulder-mitres, mitre-housing and dovetail mitre-housing (figure 491). Mortise-and-tenon joints were common, even on simple furniture, and dovetailing is certainly as early as Dynasty IV (*c* 2690 B.C.) [9]—it may have existed in ivory even earlier. What may be described as a dovetail tenon appears on a Middle Kingdom coffin (figure

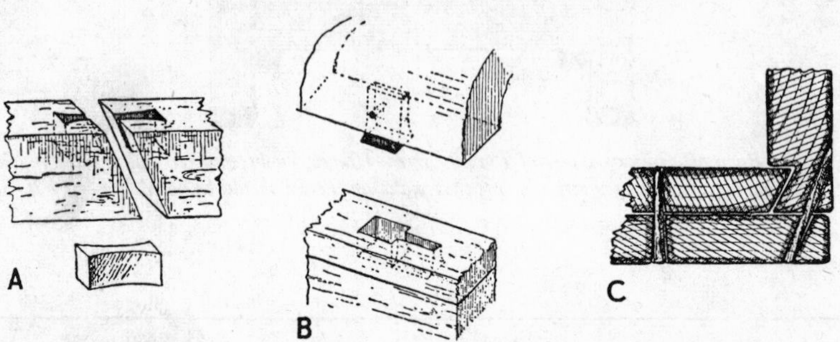

FIGURE 492—*Some methods of joining members.* (A) *Scarf joint in which the two pieces of timber are cut with a sloping join and connected together by a separate hardwood butterfly cramp engaging in tapering channels.* (B) *A dovetail tenon on the lid of a coffin. The lid is lowered on to the body so that the tenons fall into the large housings cut to receive them. When the lid is slid forward the tenons engage in the tapered mortises; at the same time swivelling tumblers fall home into channels on the end-pieces, thus locking lid to body.* (C) *An undercut rebate on the base-board of a coffin engaging in a bevel on the side member. All* c *2000 B.C.*

492 B). Scarf-joints locked together by cramps are at least as early as the Middle Kingdom (*c* 2050–1790 B.C.) (figure 492 A). Many boxes and chests from the tomb of Tutankhamen are panelled; they show mortised rails and stiles with panels fitting in channels or checks, the corner-posts being rabbeted back to an L-shaped cross-section so as to produce clean interior right-angles. Sometimes a panel, instead of being solid, was of perforated work made up of various elements mortised into the upper and lower rails and into each other. Such arrangements are commonly seen on beds and chairs (plates 24 B, 25 A, 26 A).

The various parts of furniture were doubtless originally fastened together by lashing the joints with linen cord or raw-hide thongs. Early dynastic beds have slots in their legs to take thongs (figure 493). The furniture of Queen Hetep-heres of Dynasty IV (*c* 2690 B.C.) still shows this means, which indeed produced a resilient joint able to withstand unequal periodic strains. Boxes and chests also had sewn joints, the sides being secured to the base by lashings running in specially cut channels. Large wooden coffins were similarly held together by stout copper bands. Hardwood dowels, driven in at various angles, were employed to fix sides to base-boards and to each other, and to keep tongues in position (figure 492 c). Such pegs were normally cut flush with the exterior surface and subsequently covered with plaster or paint.

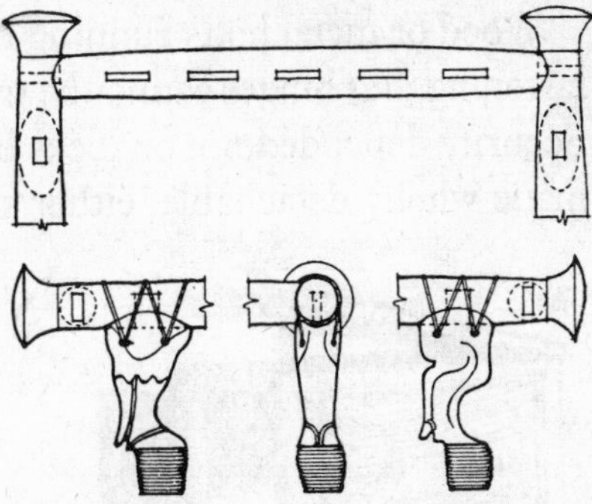

FIGURE 493—*Details of a Dynasty I bed. The members of the frame are mortised together, and the bull-leg supports secured by raw-hide lashings. The slots in the frame are to take thongs from the mattress.* c *3000 B.C.*

Bronze pins or nails are used on a chair from a tomb of Dynasty XVIII.[1] The casket of Amenhetep II (*c* 1447–1420 B.C.) shows several ingenious methods of fastening the various parts together (figure 486). The figure of the god Bes is attached to the casket by separate cramp-shaped tenons sliding in undercut grooves, both on the figure and in the casket itself. The ivory veneers have small rectangular tenons at the back, cemented into slots cut to receive them in the ebony veneer of the casket. An ingenious method of securing small members to larger parts was by a tapering peg, split for part of its length and driven into two holes drilled with a common orifice but at divergent angles. In furniture of the New Kingdom, and indeed earlier, the pegs that keep the tenons fixed in their mortises are frankly revealed and made a decorative feature. The Tutankhamen furniture (*c* 1350 B.C.) often shows such pegs capped with gold buttons, sometimes of elaborate granular work (figure 494).

FIGURE 494—*Marquetry casket of Tutankhamen. The marquetry panels are composed of thin slips of embony and ivory arranged as in the detail below. The pegs securing the ivory veneer are capped with granulated gold buttons.* c *1350 B.C. Scale 1/7.*

[1] Small nails were used to fix copper or gold foil to wood at least as early as the Old Kingdom.

Wood or metal bolts running in staples appear from earliest times as a form of fastening, but hinges cannot be traced before late in Dynasty XVIII (*c* 1360 B.C.). Security depended not on locks but upon unbroken seals. Covers of caskets were made wholly detachable, either sliding in grooves as a flush-fitting lid, or with a

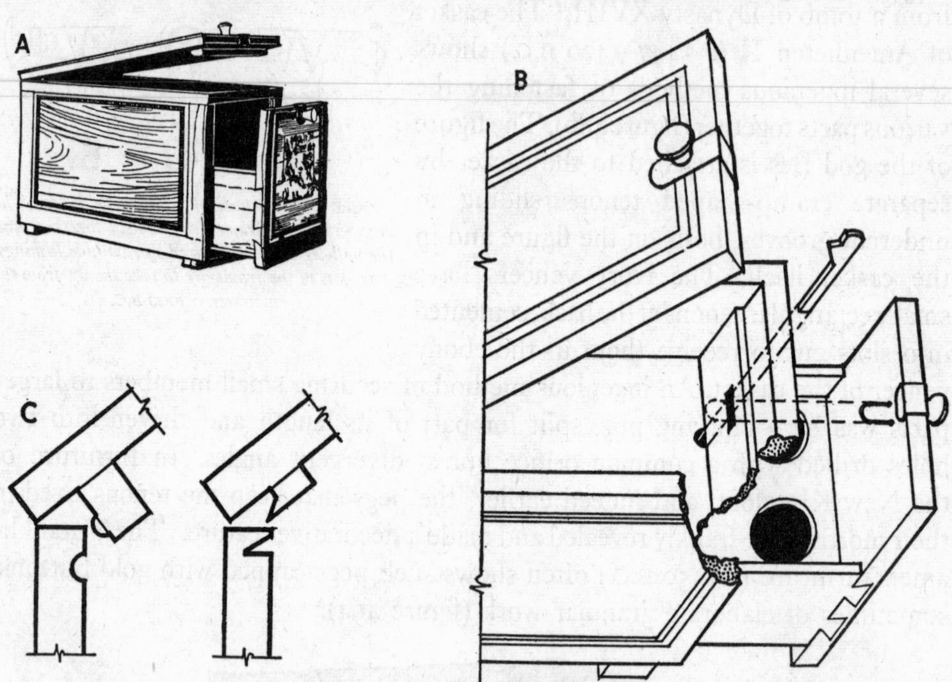

FIGURE 495—*Toilet casket from Thebes.* (A) *The box is made of cedar-wood; the front, two sides, end, and lid are veneered with large plates of ivory bordered by ebony and ivory slips. One side, engraved with a scene representing the owner offering to his king, forms the end of a shallow drawer with a perforated shelf for holding cosmetic iars; note the dovetailing.* (B) *Access to the upper tray which held a mirror may be had by removing the detachable lid. When the drawer is shut a metal peg may be inserted in a staple projecting through a slot in the upper tray and pushed home in a hole in the floor of the tray. The lid is secured by inserting a tongued fillet at one end in a corresponding channel in the end wall of the box* (*as at* C), *closing the lid, and lashing the two silver knobs together. Egypt.* c *1800* B.C. *Height 20 cm.*

projecting batten on the underside near the rear edge, engaging in a channel in the interior of the casket (figure 495 C). When the cover was slid into position and secured by a sealed lashing around the projecting knot-handles, it could not be raised except by breaking the seal. From Sedment (70 miles south of Cairo) have come boxes with lids turning on pivots in holes in the side-pieces. From the same site are simple trinket-boxes with lids sliding on overlapping rails formed by decorative bone or hard-wood slips (figure 496 A) [10]. A similar device seems to have been employed for the sliding lids of the various compartments of the toy-chest of Tutankhamen.

Other caskets and boxes of Tutankhamen have copper and gold hinges of modern type, but with the leaves inserted into narrow mortises on lid and body, and retained in position by metal rivets (figures 490, 497). A folding camp-bed has four substantial copper hinges, with two subsidiary hinges at right-angles to

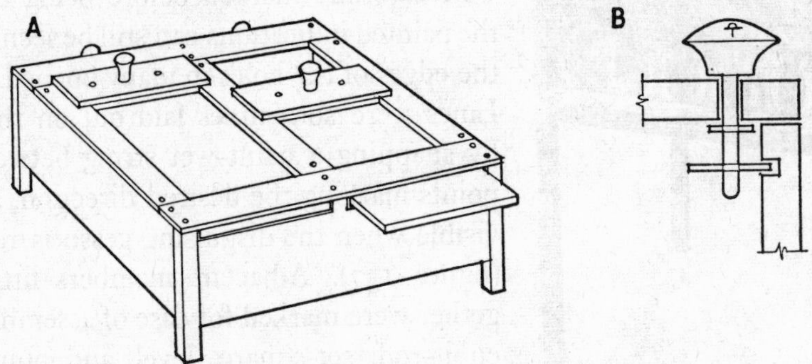

FIGURE 496—(A) *Trinket box from Sedment. The box is divided into two compartments. The lids slide under slips projecting from the edges of sides and partition; they are secured by lashing their knobs to corresponding knobs on the farther side of the box. Egypt.* c *1300 B.C.* (B) *Automatic fastening on the hinged lid of the 'play-box' of Tutankhamen. The metal knob and spindle rotate so that a cross-bar engages in a slot cut in the side of the box. An* ankh-*sign on the knob shows by its position when the box is locked.* c *1350 B.C.*

take supporting legs folded down when the bed was extended. Two boxes from the same find have simple locks operated by rotating a knob, the earliest known examples of automatic fastening (figure 496 B). Ingenious locking devices, depending upon the fall of weighted tumblers, had been common on the coffins of the Middle Kingdom, but, once locked, such coffins could not be reopened except illicitly (figure 492 B) [11].

In early times glue does not appear to have been widely used for wood, pegs, for instance, being used to keep together the various layers of the plywood fragment mentioned previously. Glue, however, must have been used to secure the various inlays of the boxes found in a tomb of Dynasty I (*c* 3000 B.C.). Though evidently used sparingly in the tomb furniture of Queen Hetep-heres of Dynasty IV (*c* 2690 B.C.) it may be supposed that thereafter it was employed on an increasing scale as an essential element of the plaster on coffins, cartonnages, and other funerary equipment. The ebony and ivory inlays on a casket dating from Dynasty XII (*c* 1800 B.C.), found by Carter at Thebes, were said by him to be glued upon a cedar-wood foundation (figure 495). A substantial mass left in a Dynasty XVII coffin (*c* 1600 B.C.) resembles present-day glue.

Essentials of modern methods of working are very closely foreshadowed in early Egyptian practice. Working-plans might be drawn on board, papyrus, or

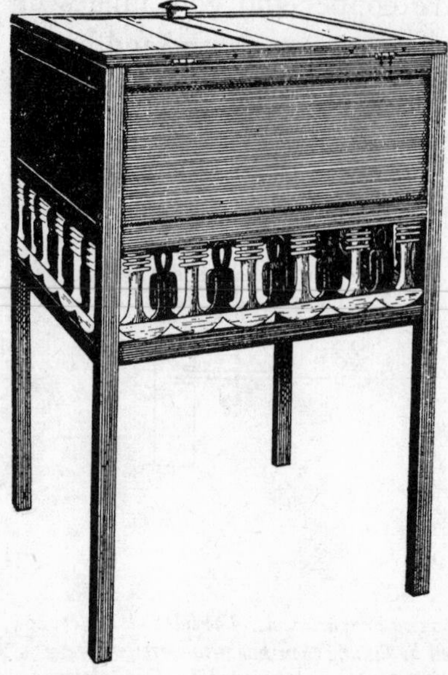

FIGURE 497—*Back of linen chest of Tutankhamen. A later version of a form that had existed in Egypt from the earliest times (compare figure 498). It is of panelled construction, the legs, rails, and stiles being of ebony and the rest of a coniferous wood. The lid pivots on bronze hinges. The dado is of gilded wood and ebony.* c *1350* B.C. *Scale 1/10.*

leather, or even on a flake of limestone. Thus there is a papyrus squared off in red, on which the side and front elevations of a shrine are drawn in strong black outline [12]. Mortises were carefully marked before being cut, and the painted indications can still be seen around the edges of the holes in many opened coffins. Lines were sometimes laid out on the work by snapping a paint-wet string between two points marking the desired direction, and are visible when the disguising gesso is removed (figure 157). Adjacent members fitting together were marked for ease of assembly. The cubit-rod, set-square, level, and plumb-line were used (figure 314), but it is clear, too, that the Egyptians primarily depended on a free-hand style of construction, rather than a final assembly of parts made to some predetermined standard of accuracy. Any miscalculation in one part might be compensated for in another; making and fitting, in fact, were carried on concurrently.

The Egyptian joiner adopted certain methods to reduce errors to a minimum or mitigate their effects. Thus he would cut out the side of a small box to the required length and height but twice its proper thickness, and then saw the piece longitudinally into two of identical shape. Errors would be in the thickness, where they would matter less—especially if the corners were mitred. Again, by mixing a filler such as plaster with his glue he could manœuvre a badly cut and loose-fitting tenon into its mortise while the adhesive was still plastic, so that when it dried the joint would be firm and in its correct position.

IV. DEVELOPMENT OF WOOD-WORK

It is probable that, apart from statuary, the first articles for which wood was used with more than usual care were coffers and chests. Chairs and other furniture, shrines, houses, and even small river-craft could be made from reeds (p 731), but a strong-box for keeping precious possessions could be made most conveniently of wood. An example is a circular box from the Dynasty I tomb of Hemaka at Saqqara. It shows a checker-board pattern of veneers of various woods. Even thus early, the craftsman was clearly following an established tradition. The form of this box was obtained by hollowing a single block of wood. The bottom is a separate disk and, like the narrow inlays of ebony, was secured in position by some adhesive. The circular lid had a flange.[1] The cylindrical shape is against most of the later instincts of the Egyptian, and suggests imitation in wood of a basketry prototype. Contemporary fragments of wood and ivory from Abydos, carved in imitation of woven surfaces, reinforce this view.

FIGURE 498—*Furniture represented in the tomb of Hesi-Re. Left to right: casket with dado in ebony; casket with framing of ebony and panels of softwood; chair with back-rest, the seat strengthened by bent wood supports, in hard- and soft-woods; chair with animal feet lashed with thongs, and a panelled back; light stool with bent wood reinforcement; stool with animal feet and laced hide seat. Egypt.* c *2800* B.C.

The skill of the joiner was early called on for strong wooden chair- and bed-frames to take the strain of a mattress or seat woven separately and lashed in position, not woven *in situ* as was the later practice (figure 493) [13]. The mastaba tomb of Hesi-Re at Saqqara (*c* 2800 B.C.) provides the earliest evidence for the scope and design of Old Kingdom furniture. Eleven wooden panels from this tomb give a most favourable impression of the great skill and artistry with which the Egyptian wood-carver could work on both a large and a small scale (plate 26 B). The wall-paintings give valuable information on the furniture of the period, which is not only executed in ebony and other fine-grained imported woods but has achieved the square, framed, and accurate construction which persists thereafter (figure 498). Chests and coffers have reached a definitive form, with their hieroglyphic motifs duly worked in open-work or applied to a contrasting background. Representations of such boxes should be compared with later examples, to show the persistence of a classic design severely constructed from rails and stiles at right-angles to each other (figure 497). Stools and chairs, on the other hand, are in a transitional stage from a reinforced bent-wood construction, probably adapted from rush-work, to a plainer, less organic type, depending for its appeal on clean lines and good proportions. The traditional pattern of the chair-legs, the fore and hind quarters of the bull, soon to be generally replaced by the lion, is here preserved—though, with the Egyptian urge towards cubic treat-

[1] Information supplied by Professor W. B. Emery.

FIGURE 499—*An armchair of Queen Kawit depicted on a relief on her sarcophagus. The design owes little to tradition or to comparable furniture in rush-work; it shows in fact a joiner's conception with its severely rectangular construction. A thick cloth or mat is thrown over the back and seat to act as a cushion. Egypt.* c *2000 B.C.*

ment, a stark rectangular leg doubtless already existed. Certainly its representation appears by Dynasty XI on the sarcophagus of Queen Kawit (*c* 2000 B.C.) (figure 499).

Early coopering is to be seen in the representation of corn-measures of Hesi-Re, built up from separate planks with bevelled edges and held together by bent-wood hoops (figure 500), if the later example preserved in Cairo is any guide [14]. In both of these, and in the ebony furniture, the craftsman has come to accept the beauty of choice timber undisguised by paint or gold-leaf. An appreciation of the quality of fine wood for its own sake becomes apparent from now on. A later proof of this taste is to be seen in a beautiful model sickle in yellow wood, which has been stained in parts, not to disguise the material but to emphasize the quality of an implement made from woods of contrasting appearance [15].

The tomb of Queen Hetep-heres of Dynasty IV (*c* 2690 B.C.) has preserved actual furniture of the Old Kingdom. Though we must largely depend on its gold plating for our information—since the wooden core has mostly decayed—it yielded reliable data about construction. The carrying-chair was panelled with a framework of rails and stiles carved in a rush-mat pattern, mortised into each other and covered with gold foil before the final assembly: the cedar-wood panels were left perfectly plain. Raw-hide lashings and wooden pegs fastened the various members together, the peg-ends frankly exposed as ornament. The severity of the design was relieved by ebony rails inlaid with gold hieroglyphs, and by gold palm-leaf finials at the ends of the carrying-poles (figure 501).

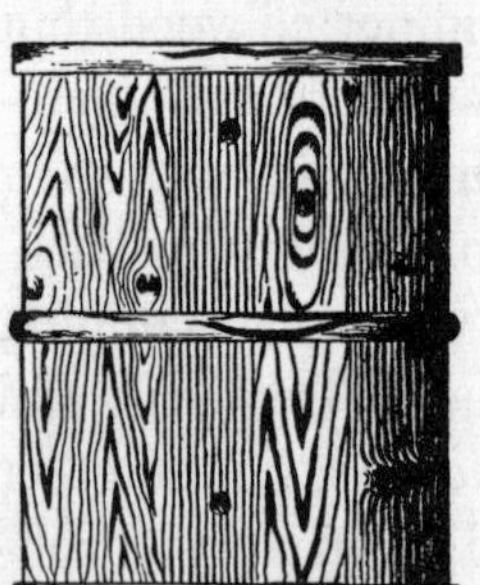

FIGURE 500—*Corn-measure represented in the tomb of Hesi-Re. This early example of coopering is built up of bevelled softwood planks held in position by three hoops of bent wood. Egypt.* c *2800 B.C.*

The chair follows the same design and construction, though its austere angularity is relaxed by the motif of the lotus flowers tied together to form open-work side-panels (figure 502).

The bed of Queen Hetep-heres is a simple development of earlier forms, having lions' in place of bulls' legs, and a detachable foot-board of an inlaid panel within a tenoned frame, fitting by two projecting tongues into copper-bordered slots. The portable canopy for suspending linen (mosquito?) curtains over the the bed-space suggests in its matting-decoration a rush prototype, yet its construction is fine joinery of a framework of three floor-beams carrying four corner-posts supporting the cornice, as well as subsidiary tent-poles. The canopy could be dismantled for transport, and the various members fitting into each other were copper-sheathed. The corner-posts were ingeniously stapled into each other by slotted bolts tightened by metal wedges (figure 503). The furniture of Hetep-heres shows that by the early part of the third millennium B.C. accurate joinery had already a long tradition. Its simple

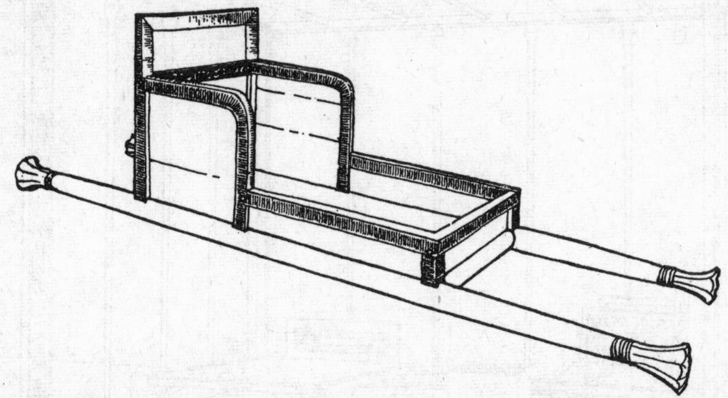

FIGURE 501—*Palanquin of Queen Hetep-heres. The woodwork is of cedar finished smooth and left quite plain. Decoration is restricted to the gold-encased rails and stiles, carved in a rush-mat pattern, and the gold palm-leaf finials. The inscribed rail (lower back) shown in this view was of ebony inlaid with exquisite gold hieroglyphs. Other stiles at the rear of the back panel were similarly embellished. Egypt.* c *2690* B.C.

and elegant proportions accord with the restrained taste of this classic period of Egyptian art.

Most surviving wood-work of the Old Kingdom is sculpture, in some of which craftsmanship of the very highest achievement is apparent, for wood allowed realistic forms to be carved with free-standing limbs and active poses. The work of mortising the forearms to the upper arms and the limbs to the torso is generally as accomplished as is the actual carving. But only in examples such as the masterpiece known as the 'Shaikh el-Beled', which has lost its thickly painted plaster, can the wood-carver's triumphant command over his material be fully appreciated [16]. A style of large, even life-sized, sculpture in wood persisted for centuries in Egypt. The larger statuettes from the Meket-Re groups [17], the statues of Senusret I from Lisht, of King Hor from Dahshur [18], and a Dynasty XIII king from Kerma in Nubia [19] maintain the tradition during the Middle Kingdom. Of the New Kingdom there are several damaged statues from the tombs of the kings at Thebes. Two life-sized specimens from the tomb of Tutankhamen are intact, but the workmanship is obscured by a coat of black resin [20].

The joinery of the Middle Kingdom is best studied in the large box-coffins with their many ingenious devices for joining planks and corners. Much of this material is crude, but in the best examples, such as the coffins from El-Bersheh, notably the outer coffin of Djehuti-nakht, the construction is skilful and refined, and the finish careful and conscientious. The wood is not covered with the usual

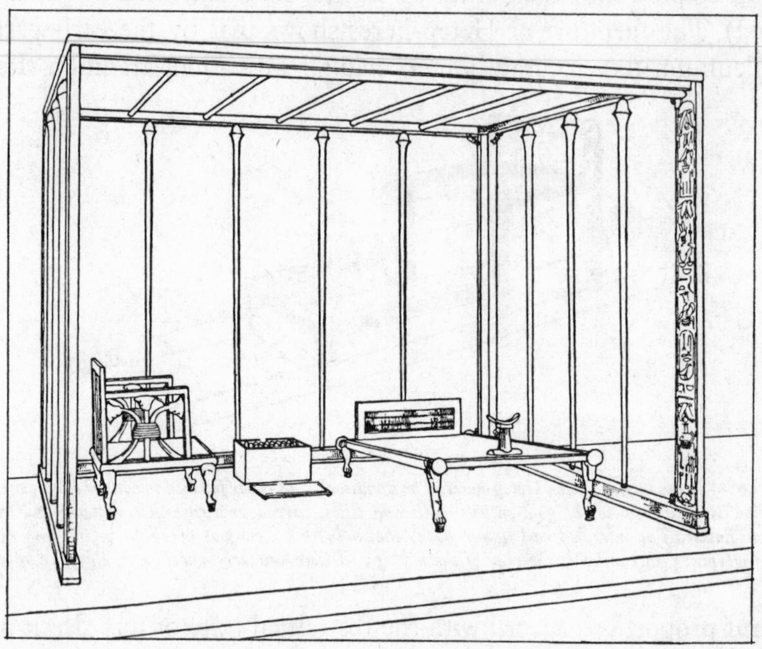

FIGURE 502—*Bedroom furniture of Queen Hetep-heres. The illustration shows the gold-covered canopy for suspending curtains around the bed space; the bed with its gold-sheathed frame, inlaid ebony foot-board, and neck-rest; a bracelet-box covered with heavy rilled foil; and an armchair of gold-sheathed wood. Egypt. c 2690 B.C.*

coat of plaster, but the painted scenes and inscriptions are applied direct to the warm brown wood in bright enamel-like pigments.

From the early New Kingdom has come an embarrassing wealth of material which, by comparison with earlier and later ages, is apt to give an unbalanced impression. The design of wood-work during this period differs from that of the earlier in being less severe and more elaborate. It reflects the spirit of imperial Egypt to which flowed tribute from Asian and African conquests. Novel influences in design may derive from a more general contact with other cultures. The new horse-drawn chariot, for example, with its light yet strong construction and its exploitation of different woods for special purposes, may have encouraged the Egyptian wood-worker to explore the possibilities of a bent-wood construction, as well as to use such decorative devices as veneers of different coloured barks, and ivory panels elaborately carved in relief. One of the most remarkable joinery efforts of antiquity is to be seen in Egyptian chariot-wheels (figure 132).

The material from the tomb of Tutankhamen, which has yielded us new conceptions of furniture design and manufacture in the ancient world, still awaits expert detailed report, but it is clear that it differs from earlier work in its predilection for the curve rather than the uncompromising right-angle (plate 25 A). The beds of Yuaa and Tutankhamen, and thrones and faldstools of the latter, have frames and stretchers deeply curved by some process of bending the wood, or by cutting it on a curve, or by the use of specially grown timber (plates 24 B, 25 B). On the other hand, cylindrical boxes, such as the casket of Amenhetep II (figure 486) and a box of Hemaka, were probably made by hollowing a section of log on the same principles as those followed in grinding stone vases.

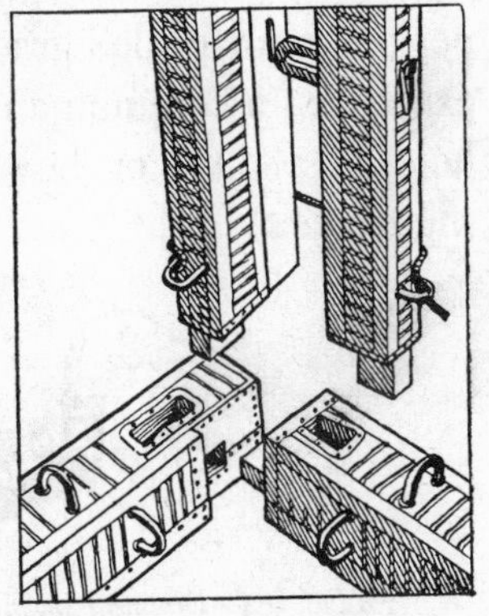

FIGURE 503—*Jointing of the canopy shown in figure 502. Mortises are sheathed in copper, and the parts secured together by lashings through copper staples. The corner-posts are held firmly together by slotted copper tongues tightened by wedges.*

All this furniture—beds, chairs, stools, and caskets, with their rigid construction in fine woods, their elegance, their gilding and inlays of ivory, glazes, and semi-precious stones—bears testimony to the skill and ingenuity of the Egyptian craftsman, even when the taste is florid. In the larger constructions from the tomb of Tutankhamen, such as the heavy shrines that rested around the sarcophagus, where a traditional design was rigidly imposed by ritual, the joiner showed the old skill in the making of massive structures carved in relief and covered with painted plaster and gold-leaf. Parts of an ebony naos (sanctuary) made earlier in the dynasty for Queen Hatshepsut for her temple at Deir el-Bahri show with what precision and skill the wood-worker could carve the inner and outer surfaces of such shrines in a shallow coin-relief before the gold foil was applied [21]. The Tutankhamen specimens show greater elegance but no more skill [22].

A clear idea of the joiner's achievement can also be gained from the immense coffins of Queen Meryet-Amen of Dynasty XVIII (*c* 1500 B.C.), which in their stripped and plundered state show the basic wood-work in all its superb carving and finish. These coffins, representing the human form, were made of thick cedar planks, hewn roughly to shape and then carved to a uniform thickness of about 4 cm. The outside modelling was followed consistently, while, inside, every contour was faithfully reflected in reverse, even to details of wig and face.

Despite the relative thinness of this wooden shell, the many hidden tongues joining the separate planks had been exposed in only one or two places.

In contrast to such massive pieces, we have a profusion of smaller work of equal importance and accomplishment. The wooden statuette achieves in this period an unrivalled grace and a very high technical excellence. There are many examples: a common and very pleasing conceit is that of a girl swimming, and holding a duck or bowl—one example among a profusion of elegant forms (figure 504) [23].

FIGURE 504—*Ointment spoon of wood and ivory in the form of a swimming girl supporting a duck whose hollowed body beneath the pivoted wings held the unguent. Egypt.* c *1400* B.C. *Scale 1/2.*

We may pass very rapidly over the late period of Egyptian history. A cupboard [24] and a shrine [25], and representations upon temple reliefs, suggest that the furniture of the age still differed little in style from traditional forms. During the Saite period (*c* 660–525 B.C.), however, there appears on the private reliefs an elegantly fantastic furniture which must be regarded as idealistic rather than practical [26]. There was no radical change until turnery was widely adopted in Roman times.

In wood-work on both a large and a minute scale the ancient Egyptian with his simple copper implements reached a technical standard not equalled in Europe until the Renaissance. For some thousands of years his craftsmanship at its best was extraordinarily accurate and accomplished.

REFERENCES

[1] LUCAS, A. *Ann. Serv. Antiq. Égypte*, **36**, 1–4, 1936.

[2] MORGAN, J. J. M. DE. 'Fouilles à Dahchour, 1894–5', p. 92. Holzhausen, Vienna. 1903.

[3] PETRIE, SIR (WILLIAM MATTHEW) FLINDERS. 'Wisdom of the Egyptians', p. 120. Brit. Sch. Archaeol. Egypt, Publ. 63. London. 1940.

[4] DAVIES, NORMAN DE G. 'The Tombs of Menkheperrasonb, Amenmose and another', Pl. XXX, F. Egypt Explor. Soc., Theban Tombs series, 5th Memoir. London. 1933.

[5] PETRIE, SIR (WILLIAM MATTHEW) FLINDERS. 'Deshasheh', p. 33. Egypt Explor. Fund, Memoirs no. 15. London. 1898.

[6] WAINWRIGHT, G. A. *Ann. Serv. Antiq. Égypte*, **25**, 113, 1925.

[7] GARDINER, SIR ALAN H. 'Ancient Egyptian Onomastica', Vol. 1, p. 65. Oxford University Press, London. 1947.

[8] LEGRAIN, G. 'Statues et statuettes de rois et de particuliers', Vol. 1, no. 42126. Catal. gén. antiq. égypt. Mus. Caire. Imprim. Inst. franç. Archéol. orient., Cairo. 1906.
[9] REISNER, G. *Bull. Boston Mus.*, **25,** (Suppl.), 30, 1927.
[10] PETRIE, SIR (WILLIAM MATTHEW) FLINDERS. 'Sedment II', Pls. XLVIII, 6; LV, 20; LVII, 30, 31. Egypt. Res. Acc. and Brit. Sch. Archaeol. Egypt, Publ. 35. London. 1924.
[11] MACE, A. C. and WINLOCK, H. E. 'Tomb of Senebtisi', fig. 24. Publ. of the Metr. Mus. of Art Egypt. Exped., New York. 1916.
[12] CLARKE, S. and ENGELBACH, R. 'Ancient Egyptian Masonry', p. 46. Oxford University Press, London. 1930.
[13] DAVIES, NORMAN DE G. See ref. [4].
[14] LUCAS, A. and ROWE, A. *Ann. Serv. Antiq. Égypte*, **40,** 77, 1940.
[15] COONEY, J. D. *Bull. Brooklyn Mus.*, **12,** ii, 1, 1951.
[16] CAPART, J. *J. Egypt. Archaeol.*, **6,** 225, 1920.
[17] ALDRED, C. 'Middle Kingdom Art in Ancient Egypt', fig. 7. Tiranti, London. 1950.
[18] *Idem. Ibid.*, figs. 20, 79.
[19] SMITH, W. S. 'Ancient Egypt', fig. 52. Mus. of Fine Arts, Boston, Mass. 1942.
[20] CARTER, H. and MACE, A. C. 'The Tomb of Tut-ankh-Amen', Vol. 1, Pl. XLI. Cassell, London. 1923.
[21] ROEDER, G. 'Naos', Pls. I–III. Catal. gén. antiq. égypt. Mus. Caire, Vol. 75. Breitkopf und Härtel, Leipzig. 1914.
[22] FOX, PENELOPE. 'Tutankhamun's Treasure', Pls. XVIII, XXI. Oxford University Press, London. 1951.
[23] FRÉDÉRICQ, M. *J. Egypt. Archaeol.*, **13,** 7, 1927.
[24] CAPART, J. 'L'Art égyptien', Part II, Vol. 4: 'Les Arts mineurs', Planche 797. Vromant, Brussels, Paris. 1951.
[25] ROEDER, G. See ref. [21], Pl. XLIV.
[26] COONEY, J. D. *J. Near East Stud.*, **9,** 195, 1950.

BIBLIOGRAPHY

CARTER, H. and MACE, A. C. 'The Tomb of Tut-ankh-Amen', Vols. 1–3. Cassell, London. 1923–33.
LACAU, P. 'Sarcophagues antérieurs au Nouvel Empire', Vols. 1 and 2. Catal. gén. antiq. égypt. Mus. Caire, Vols. 11, 12. Imprim. Inst. franç. Archéol. orient., Cairo. 1904–6.
LUCAS, A. 'Ancient Egyptian Materials and Industries' (3rd ed.). Arnold, London. 1948.
MACE, A. C. and WINLOCK, H. E. 'The Tomb of Senebtisi at Lisht.' Publ. of the Metr. Mus. of Art Egypt. Exped., New York. 1916.
PETRIE, SIR (WILLIAM MATTHEW) FLINDERS. 'Tools and Weapons.' Egypt. Res. Acc. and Brit. Sch. Archaeol. Egypt, Publ. 30. London. 1917.
PETRIE, SIR (WILLIAM MATTHEW) FLINDERS and MACKAY, E. J. H. 'Heliopolis, Kafr Ammar and Shurafa.' Egypt. Res. Acc. and Brit. Sch. Archaeol. Egypt, Publ. 24. London. 1915.
WINLOCK, H. E. 'The Tomb of Queen Meryet-Amūn at Thebes.' Metr. Mus. of Art, Publ. 6. New York. 1932.

26

LAND TRANSPORT WITHOUT WHEELS

ROADS AND BRIDGES

S. M. COLE

IT was not until man had learned to trade peacefully with his neighbours that he ventured on long journeys along well defined routes. Primarily, the hunter made expeditions to kill and collect food, and devices (whether animal or mechanical) to aid him in transport were unnecessary; he had few possessions, and the very nature of his occupation made it essential that he should be unhampered. With the start of agriculture it became necessary to gather in the harvest, and, when stock was domesticated, fodder for winter use had to be carted, so primitive devices were evolved to make these tasks less arduous. Judging by the distribution of materials used in the making of implements, such as flint and obsidian, trade in these commodities must have started in very early times, and thus the first man-made tracks were formed. The nature of the environment, including drainage, relief, soil, and vegetation would determine the routes chosen to overcome obstacles, and would later influence the kinds of animals domesticated and the type of vehicle used.

Man's increased mobility after the domestication of animals, and the invention of boats and land-vehicles, had a profound effect on the divergence and intermingling of races which took place after the end of the Ice Age. Great strides were made in cultural achievements as a result of the interchange of ideas, and it is to the opening-up of communications that must be attributed the spread of inventions and even the growth of language.

The stage at which wheeled vehicles came into use can be defined in broad terms, although for the earliest of these vehicles the archaeological record is scanty. For the transport devices which preceded the cart, wagon, and chariot it offers still less evidence. In exceptional circumstances, fragments of very early wooden vehicles have survived, such as sledge-runners in Scandinavian bogs. Other evidence may be obtained from various sources, such as rock-paintings and engravings, reliefs, models, and seals, and, with necessary reservations, deductions can be made from the practices of modern technologically backward peoples. It is only to be expected, however, that there should be vast gaps in our knowledge of the evolution of transport, since the earliest vehicles were almost certainly made of perishable materials and their form was but seldom recorded in paint or stone.

FIGURE 505—(Above) *Load-carrying with supporting thongs over the forehead; from the mosaic 'standard' of Ur, Mesopotamia.* c 2500 B.C. (Below) *Large vessel carried on a pole between two bearers; relief from Khafaje, Mesopotamia. Early third millennium* B.C.

I. PACK TRANSPORT

Man's oldest beast of burden was woman—on the more or less justifiable plea that the male had to be unencumbered, to protect his family. Gradually, simple contrivances were evolved to distribute the weight of the load fairly evenly over the body, and to leave the hands as free as possible. Babies, or a load of firewood, could be carried in a skin on the back, with supporting thongs over the forehead, a method that is widely used today by African women. Men carrying bundles in this way are depicted on the 'standard' of Ur, which dates from *c* 2500 B.C. (figure 505). Among the Chinese and other Far Eastern peoples loads still are, and probably always were, carried on the end of a stick over the shoulder—the single yoke —or on either end of a yoke across both shoulders—the double yoke. A dead animal, with legs slotted through one another, could easily be borne on a pole between two men; an alabaster relief from Khafaje in Sumer dating from the beginning of the third millennium B.C. shows a large vessel thus carried on a pole between two bearers (figure 505).

Probably some form of litter was used for well-to-do travellers in early times, and for transporting the aged and infirm. An interesting clay model of a kind of palanquin comes from the miniature sanctuary of the Palace of Minos in Crete of about 1600 B.C. (figure 506).

Although the domestication of animals may have taken place somewhere in Asia as early as 5000 B.C. (ch 13) it is impossible to tell how long it was before their potentiality as bearers of burdens was grasped. The ass, a native of north-east Africa, was almost certainly the oldest pack-animal. It was used as such long before its relative, the onager, was harnessed to a vehicle, which we know to have occurred in Mesopotamia before 3000 B.C.

FIGURE 506—*Model of a palanquin from Crete.* c *1600* B.C.

In Upper Egypt the ass may have been used as a pack-animal as early as the Amratian period (*c* 3500 B.C.), and its employment in that capacity is certainly attested at the beginning of the early dynastic period (*c* 3000 B.C.). The surviving business-letters of a colony of Assyrian merchants, established at the court of a Hittite prince in central Asia Minor about 2000 B.C., give a lively picture of caravans of pack-asses regularly crossing the Syrian steppes and the

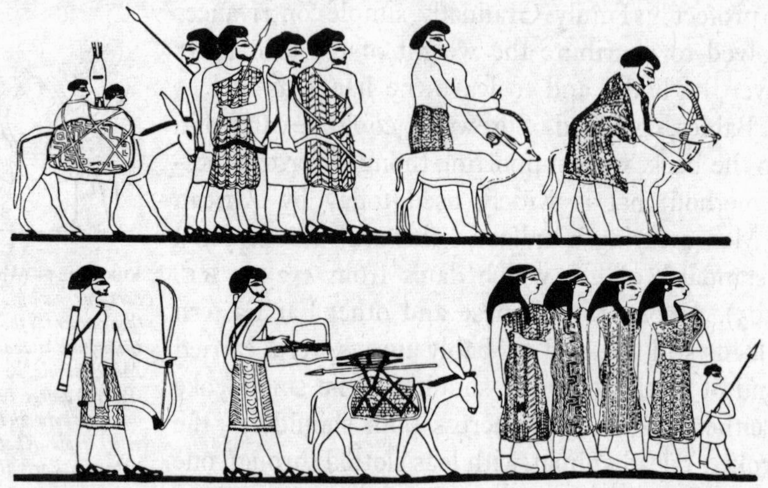

FIGURE 507—*Pack-asses among a group of tribute carriers. From a tomb at Beni Hasan, Egypt. c 1900 B.C.*

Taurus mountains. An Egyptian relief from Beni Hasan, *c* 1900 B.C., depicts the arrival of the Canaanites with their pack-asses laden with children and tribute (figure 507).

Though oxen were primarily used for pulling the plough and cart, they may be seen bearing packs on their backs in early rock-engravings from the Sahara. In that region they were used as beasts of burden long before the arrival of the horse and, later still, the domesticated camel. The Sahara during the first millennium B.C. was not the formidable obstacle that it is today. The greater rainfall of the time made water more easily obtainable, and oxen and asses could traverse it without difficulty. Judging by rock-paintings and -engravings, the camel was not known in the western desert in its domesticated form before about 100 B.C. It is a native of Asia, and the period when it was first used there as a beast of burden is still unknown. However, a two-humped camel is depicted on an Egyptian tomb of Dynasty I (*c* 3000 B.C.), and the one-humped camel appears as a pack-animal in Mesopotamia by 1000 B.C.

In early times, the horse was probably little used for pack-transport and was regarded as an aristocrat of war, as appears repeatedly in the Bible. It was probably ridden by the Turco-Tatar peoples before being harnessed to a vehicle, though it is held that in other parts of the world, such as western Asia, Mediterranean Europe, and China, horses were used to pull vehicles before they were ridden. In Europe, indeed, it is not until the La Tène period (second stage of the Iron Age) that the wooden frame of a horse-pack is found, although it is assumed that pack-horses were used very much earlier. In Britain, no animal porterage of any kind is known before the Late Bronze Age.

II. WHEEL-LESS VEHICLES

Long before the wheel was invented, sledges slid over the coniferous forest

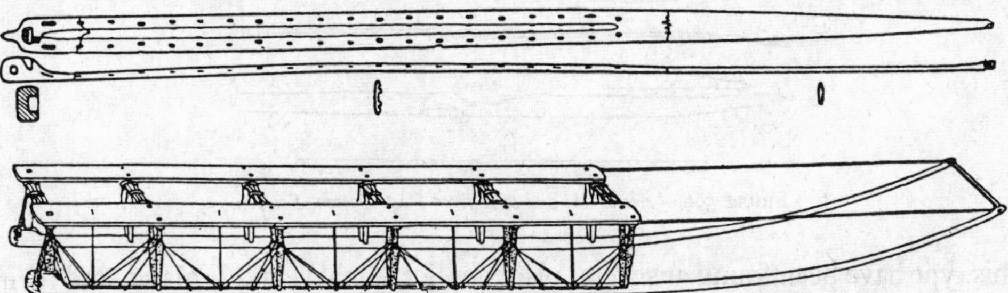

FIGURE 508—*Runner from Kuortane, Finland, with a reconstruction of the sledge. Length 3·17 m.*

zone of northern Europe. The most primitive sledge was probably made out of raw hide or bark, and was used to drag slaughtered animals back to the shelter or dwelling-place. These simple sledges could be dragged equally well over grass, clay, marsh, or snow; they are used to this day in Lapland, northern Asia, and British Columbia. Dug-out sledges with rounded bottom and no runners, such as those used by the Ostyaks (figure 512 A), were probably chiselled out of tree-trunks by Neolithic man, using stone axes and adzes.

The idea of adding runners to a sledge may have originated in placing an animal's horns or, in the north, perhaps the curved jawbone of a whale, under a load to reduce friction. In Scandinavia remains of runners were found, which were virtually skis on which a load was balanced and pushed from behind. Several sledge-runners found embedded in Scandinavian bogs have been dated accurately by pollen analysis; the earliest are of Mesolithic age. The superstructure of the sledges must remain conjectural, but it is possible to deduce the number of uprights, for instance, by the holes in the runners (figure 508). Sledge-runners found so far may be divided into three groups:

(*a*) The earliest group includes heavy runners from Finland, hollowed out along the length and with the sides perforated at intervals in opposite pairs. They may be the keels of single-runner boat-sledges, but more probably they belong to double-runner sledges with raised platforms. It is obvious that if the sledge floor had no clearance above the ground, it must have stuck in soft snow and got caught in every snag in the ground, and the replacement of a single keel (if such existed) by a pair of runners would make for greater stability.

(*b*) A second group is represented by many finds in which the runners have medial grooves, and a complex series of holes in the upper surface to hold the wooden uprights through which lashings were passed (figure 508). Runners of

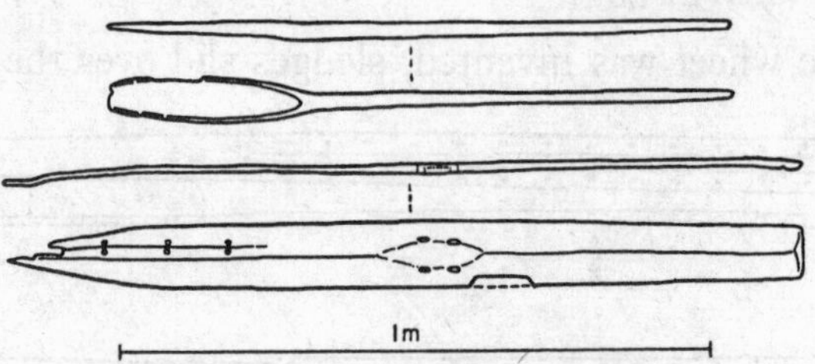

FIGURE 509—*'Arctic' ski and stick from Västerbotten, Sweden.*

this type have been found at several places in Scandinavia and Finland, and their range extends as far as the Urals, where they are associated with pottery of the beginning of the local Bronze Age. Many of the finds from Scandinavia can be referred to the Arctic Stone Age by pollen analysis. The runners were heavy and long (especially the example from Kuortane, which was 3 m in length) and the sledges were probably drawn by dogs, for there is no evidence that the reindeer had then been domesticated. The probable appearance of these sledges has been reconstructed (figure 508).

(*c*) The third group includes the Swedish Morjärv type, the runners of which are lighter than those of the other groups; the sledges may have been drawn by men on skis. The vertical side-posts are few and unimportant, and the runners are narrow and convex on the under surface. This type was first used during the transition period between the Late Bronze and Early Iron Ages.

Finds from Scandinavian bogs also indicate that skis were used as early as the Late Neolithic. One of the earliest of such finds is a pair of runners (one fragmentary) and a stick with a spatulate end from Kalvträsk, Västerbotten, north Sweden (figure 509). This kind of ski is known as the 'Arctic' type; in it the foot is secured by thongs passed through the thickness of the runner itself. The Arctic type is short and broad, and the under-surface of the runner was often covered by a skin. The southern type of ski is represented by a find from Riihimaki in Finland. The foot rests in a hollow between two raised side-pieces, and the thongs were passed through these flanges.

The provision of a raised foot-rest marked a considerable advance in ski-design; this type is known from the most northerly provinces of Sweden and

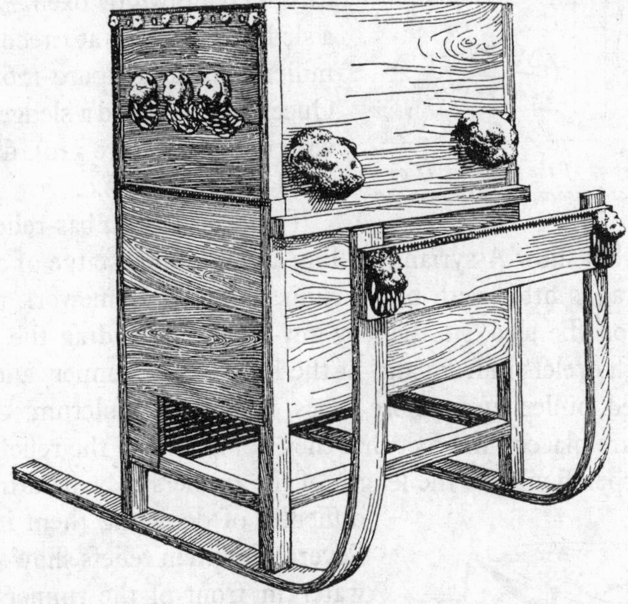

FIGURE 510—*Reconstruction of the sledge-chariot of Queen Shub-ad. No trace of the runners was found, but in front of the car was a horizontal strip of wood which must have been the cross-piece between the front ends of the runners. Ur, Mesopotamia.* c *2500* B.C.

Finland. It came into use at a period contemporary with the Neolithic of southern Sweden, and continued throughout the Nordic Bronze Age. Farther south, the Scandic type had emerged by the Bronze Age; it was characterized by grooves and lists on either edge of the sliding surface. A single specimen of the medially grooved type, which is commonly used at the present time, comes from Ovrebö, south-west Norway, and has been assigned to the Late Bronze Age by pollen analysis. It is of oak, and is the only example made from any wood other than pine. Men on skis are depicted on rock-engravings at Zalavrouga on the river Vyg (which flows into the White Sea) and possibly again at Rödöy in Norway (though some authorities believe that the 'skis' are in fact a boat).

Sliding vehicles were by no means confined to the northern countries, and sledges were used in many parts of the east before wheeled vehicles were invented, and survived for a long time after. Runners were commonly used in

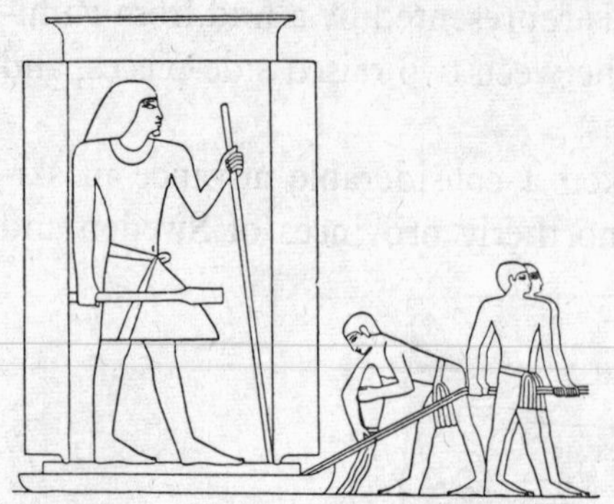

FIGURE 511—*Transport of the statue of Ti on a sledge. From a tomb at Saqqara, Egypt. c 2400 B.C.*

Egypt, Assyria, and Sumer to shift colossal statues, even after the adoption of the wheel for war-chariots and funerary wagons. In Mesopotamia, from the Jemdet Nasr phase onwards, both sledges and carts were drawn by oxen. A pictograph of a sledge was found at Erech, of the fourth millennium B.C. (figure 126), and, at Ur, Queen Shub-ad had a sledge-chariot fitted with runners (figure 510), dating from the third millennium B.C.

Two well-known bas-reliefs from Kuyunjik (figure 283) show Assyrians hauling an enormous statue of a winged bull; the sled or drag is fitted with heavy runners, and a framework to support the statue stands on the sled, steadied by guy-ropes. Men drag the sled by ropes slotted through eyelets in front and at the back of the runner, and a large lever behind the sled, pulled up by more ropes, is used on a fulcrum. Under the sled small rollers are placed; the fact that they are shown in the relief lying parallel instead of perpendicular to the length of the runners may be attributed to the difficulty of depicting them in perspective. Several Egyptian reliefs show slaves pouring water in front of the runners, to facilitate gliding when rollers were not used (figure 511). Apart from their common use for shifting monuments and for funerary purposes, smaller Egyptian sledges are known to have been used for the transport of corn-sacks.

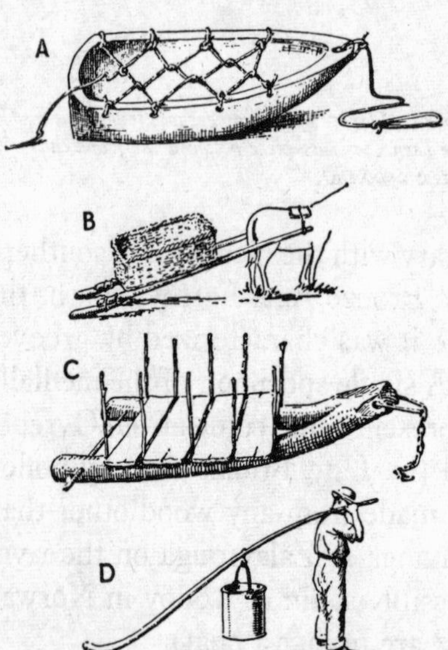

FIGURE 512—*Primitive draught vehicles.* (A) *Dug-out sledge from Siberia.* (B) *Irish slide-car.* (C) *Y-sledge.* (D) *Single beam travois or draught pole.*

Evidence of the use of sledges in southern Europe is lacking, with the possible exception of a figure which may represent a sledge on some Spanish rock-engravings of chalcolithic or Bronze Age date.

The function of sledges and skis is to present a smooth surface to the ground so that friction is reduced; this function is repeated in other forms of wheel-less vehicles such as the travois, slide-car, and Y-sledge, all of which have survived to recent times.

Certainly some such primitive construction must have been invented even before sledges, although archaeological evidence is lacking.

When dairy-farmers first started to transport hay to feed their cattle, they probably shifted a haycock on the forked branch of a tree. From this, there could easily have arisen the Y-sledge (figure 512 C), which is actually cut from the fork of a tree, the arms forming the runners. In later times, oxen were attached to the stump by a rope or chain. Struts were passed horizontally between the two branches to form the floor, and the superstructure was built on it. The Y-sledge was widely distributed in northern Europe up to recent times, and was used throughout the cattle regions of Africa.

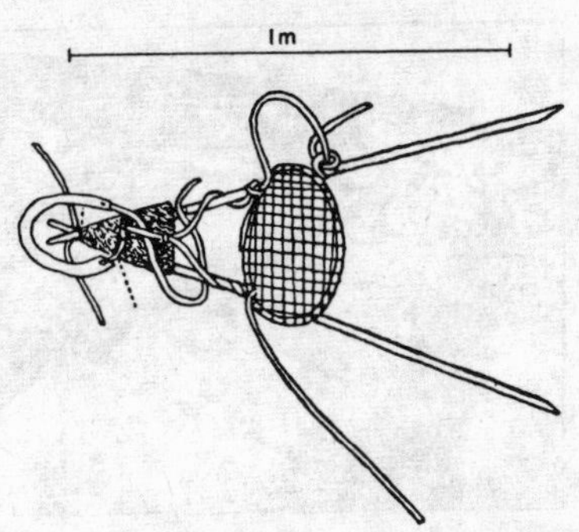

FIGURE 513—*Dog-travois of the Hidatsa Indians, Missouri.*

In North America, the Indians used to fasten their tents into bundles when they moved, with the poles dragged by a dog, one on each side of it. This practice no doubt suggested the travois, which consists simply of two poles tied together, with the inverted V resting on the dog's back (figure 513). Between the poles is slung a wooden or net frame upon which a load can be placed. The small dog-travois was enlarged and adapted for the horse after the introduction of this animal into North America by Europeans.

The travois is made and unmade as required, but the slide-car (figure 512 B) is a more lasting vehicle. Two shafts are harnessed to a horse and their ends drag along the ground; the shafts are kept apart by cross-bars, which form the floor of the carrier. The very wide distribution of the slide-car is evidence of its high antiquity. It held its own in mountainous districts of various parts of Europe until recent times. One authority holds that the single-horse cart arose from the slide-car, as is indicated by the custom of riding the draught-horse of both the slide-car and the cart in ancient times. There is a similarity that appears to be more than accidental in the harnessing of the slide-car and the single-horse cart.

BIBLIOGRAPHY

BERG, G. 'Sledges and Wheeled Vehicles.' *Nord. Mus. Handl.*, no. 4. Stockholm, Copenhagen. 1935.

CHILDE, V. GORDON. 'Man Makes Himself.' Watts, London. 1951.

Idem. 'What Happened in History.' Pelican Books, Harmondsworth. 1946.

CLARK, J. G. D. 'Prehistoric Europe.' Methuen, London. 1952.

Goodwin, A. J. H. 'Communication has been Established.' Methuen, London. 1937.
Woolley, Sir (Charles) Leonard. 'The Royal Cemetery.' Ur Excavations. Reports Vol. 2. Publ. of Joint Exped. Brit. Mus. and Mus. of Univ. of Pennsylvania. 1934.

ROADS AND BRIDGES

Roads with prepared surfaces did not appear until wheeled transport came into general use. In the Stone Age, man must have utilized tracks made by wild animals, and during the Neolithic he followed paths trodden by his cattle and sheep. These ridgeways, which can still be traced in Britain and elsewhere, followed the downs and open country, avoiding the swampy floors and forest-covered sides of valleys. As settlements developed on alluvial land, however, the high ridgeways became less important than tracks on lower slopes which were sufficiently above the valley floors for drainage, yet low enough to avoid unnecessary climbing. These tracks, dating from Late Neolithic and Early Bronze Age times, are known as hollow-ways, since they have been worn down into deep grooves after thousands of years of use. The Harroway in Hampshire and Wiltshire may mean *hearg-weg*, the Old English for 'shrine-way': it leads to Stonehenge.

Figure 514—*Ancient cart tracks in Malta.*

It is often stated that Roman roads followed the course of pre-existing, prehistoric tracks; but the straight alignments show that, on the contrary, they ignored them, as they also ignored natural features. Prehistoric tracts, on the other hand, follow a sinuous course, avoiding wet ground and the needless crossing of valleys. The names given to some of the chief Roman roads all originated in later times. The Icknield Way, from Norfolk to Salisbury Plain, may be of Neolithic origin, for it passes by the flint-mines of Grimes' Graves. There was another prehistoric track called (in modern times) the Jurassic Way, leading from Lincolnshire to Somerset.

In forest regions where soft ground had to be crossed, timber or brushwood trackways were sometimes laid down; several of them have been dated by pollen analysis to the Late Bronze Age, e.g. those in the Cambridgeshire and Somerset fens and moors, and in north-west and south Germany. They crossed river valleys to fords or ferries, and linked islands of habitable ground in low-lying areas with surrounding dry land; the trackway joining Stuntney with the Isle of Ely provides an example. 'Corduroy' tracks were used in the Bronze Age to pave the streets of some settlements; layers of osiers and twigs with logs laid parallel were found in some of the Swiss lake-villages. Later the timber was held down by mortised stakes.

In Malta, V-shaped ruts over a foot deep run parallel over long distances (figure 514). They are usually 10 to 20 in wide at the top and 4 in wide at the bottom, the distance between the ruts being about 4 ft 6 in. Possibly in places they were first cut by hand and then deepened by Neolithic carts carrying soil and water for crops up the bare limestone hillsides. Since the stone between the ruts is not hollowed by the impact of hooves, it is assumed that human beings did the haulage.

Rivers were more important than roads in the ancient valley civilizations, and one of the chief functions of war-chariots was to protect river traffic. While chariots could operate on open grassland, the heavier wagons needed roads, and were therefore little used in early times except for funerary purposes. Military roads usually followed the old caravan trade routes. The first organized road-building was in the Assyrian Empire. Inscriptions mention that a king's army engineers 'hewed a way with bronze pickaxes and made passable a passage for my chariot and my troops'. Watch-houses were set along such roads. But although monarchs such as Esarhaddon (681–668 B.C.) encouraged their Babylonian subjects 'to open their roads throughout the land so that they could resume traffic with all neighbouring countries', they had no centralized cultural policy like their Persian conquerors (figure 160 B).

The Persian kings, ruling the entire Near East, anticipated the policy of Alexander and his Hellenistic successors and tried to build a national empire out of the conquered inhabitants of the Near East. Their hierarchy of civil servants had to be directed by a swift postal service, which involved a system of roads. These levelled and partly paved tracks were policed by guards posted at rest-houses about every 15 miles. A continuous line of stations linked Sardis on the Aegean to the capital Susa, 1600 miles away. Special messengers could cover the distance from Susa to Babylon at an average speed of 100 miles a day. The Persian Empire fell too soon, however, for these tracks to be transformed into paved roads.

China developed what is perhaps the oldest system of roads for everyday use, with post-stages comparable with the magnificent organization of the Incas in later times. Even before the Chow dynasty (*c* 1100–255 B.C.), communications were controlled and roads maintained by a highways commissioner. During the Chow dynasty the traffic necessitated the prescription of a uniform scale of size for wheeled vehicles, prohibition of furious driving, and traffic regulations at crowded crossings. Roads were classified into five grades: (*a*) pathways for men and pack-animals; (*b*) roads taking a vehicle of narrow gauge; (*c*) roads with room for a wider wagon; (*d*) roads wide enough for wagons to pass one another; (*e*) highroads taking three wagons abreast.

Evidence of grooved tracks in early Sumer and India is fragmentary, but the builders of Mesopotamia and Chaldea must have had roads for the transport of their material over the soft ground. A stone-paved road or ramp was made by Cheops in Egypt for the conveyance of the huge limestone blocks of which he built the Great Pyramid about 2500 B.C. Herodotus says: 'It took ten years' oppression of the people to make the causeway for the conveyance of the stones, a work not much inferior, in my judgement, to the pyramid itself. The causeway is five furlongs long, ten fathoms wide, and in height at the highest part, eight fathoms. It is built of polished stone and covered with carvings of animals.' The limestone and granite blocks were quarried at Tura, on the eastern bank of the Nile, and were floated downstream on reed boats to Giza. They were then dragged up the ramp on sledges, 100 ft above the level of the river. The Egyptians also had tracks to gold-mines, turquoise-mines, and quarries, but little is known of their surfacing.

Short lengths of paved roads were discovered at the Palace of Knossos in Crete, dating from about 2000 B.C., and a road of Cyclopean blocks was laid in the island of Skyros. The remains of a road paved with stones leading to Nineveh have been found, and Rameses II had a road tunnelled into rock along the coast of Syria. There were, in fact, short lengths of well made roads in several parts of the Old World long before the Romans.

Bridges. In early days, when a stream had to be crossed fords were sought, and, later, settlements grew up around these crossing-places. The idea of a bridge presumably developed from a tree-trunk laid across a narrow part of a stream. Where the stream was broader, many tree-trunks could be laid end to end to connect the two banks, junctions being effected by erecting supports at shallow points. This seems the simplest explanation of the origin of the bridge.

The oldest known bridges in Britain were of wood. Remains of one of these have been found in the Fens, but they indicate that the bridge dated only from the period of the Roman occupation. The famous clapper bridges of Devon are all of medieval or even later date.

The pygmies of central Africa know how to swing a man over a river on cables of lianas, and presumably this idea, too, has an ancient origin. Very few remains of bridges of remoter antiquity have been traced, but the architects of the Jerwan aqueduct (p 469), for instance, would have had no difficulty in bridging a river.

Herodotus tells of a boat-bridge across the Struma made by the Persian king Xerxes, and describes the construction of a later one:

'That they might lighten the strain of the cables, they laid fifty-oared ships and triremes alongside each other, 360 to bear the bridge that was nearest to the Euxine Sea and 314 to bear the other; all lay obliquely to the line of the Pontus and parallel with the current of the Hellespont. They stretched cables from the land, twisting them taut with wooden windlasses. For each bridge two cables of flax and four of papyrus were used. When the strait was bridged, they sawed balks of wood to a length equal to the breadth of the floating supports and laid them in order on taut cables, and having set them alongside they then made them fast. They then heaped brushwood on the bridge, and heaped earth and stamped on it. They made a fence on either side lest the beasts of burden should be affrighted by the sight of the sea below them.'

Boat-bridges were much favoured in ancient times, since they were easy to construct and demolish, and thus were very suitable for military purposes.

The oldest bridge of technical importance was constructed over the Euphrates and connected the two parts of the ancient city of Babylon; it is supposed to have been built by Nebuchadrezzar. The river is 1000 yd wide at that point, and more than 100 stone piers were erected in it. On them, the platform of the bridge was placed; it was 30 ft wide, made of beams cut from palm-trees, and was roofed. There were several technical weaknesses; in the first place the space between the stone piers, whose width is unknown, was very small, perhaps 17 to 20 ft. Narrow gaps and a large number of piers would be a great hindrance to the flow of the river, causing blockages and flooding at high water. The method of building under water was not known, and the river had to be diverted during the construction of the bridge. The piers were pointed upstream, so that the water broke easily on them, and were blunt on the downstream side. Later, in Mesopotamia, bridge-construction was improved by adopting arched openings built on the principle of the vault. The bridge at the Palace of Minos in Crete was 36 ft wide, and the culvert bridges of the viaduct were 15 to 20 ft wide.

BIBLIOGRAPHY

CLARK, J. G. D. 'Prehistoric Europe.' Methuen, London. 1952.

EVANS, SIR ARTHUR J. 'The Palace of Minos at Knossos', Vol. 2. Macmillan, London. 1935.

FORBES, R. J. *Chem. & Ind.* (*Rev.*), 70, 1953.

GOODWIN, A. J. H. 'Communication has been Established.' Methuen, London. 1937.

GREGORY, J. W. 'The Story of the Road.' Maclehose, London. 1931 (2nd ed. rev. and enl. by C. J. GREGORY. Black, London, 1938).

ZAMMIT, T. "Prehistoric Cart Tracks in Malta." *Antiquity*, **2**, 18, 1928.

27

WHEELED VEHICLES

V. GORDON CHILDE

I. CARTS AND WAGONS[1]

THE invention of the wheel (ch 9) transformed transport and communications by land. The sledge, the slide-car, and even the travois are efficient enough, but only seasonally or under peculiar local conditions. Mounted on wheels, the sledge can travel in summer as well, and the slide-car can transcend the narrow limits imposed by the landscape; efficiency is everywhere enormously augmented.

The curious structure of the earliest known wheels has already been described (p 204), and reasons have been advanced for thinking that the device was invented not far from the Tigris–Euphrates valley a little before 3000 B.C. and diffused thence. Though the oldest known wheels everywhere, from the Indus to the Severn, from the North Sea to the Persian Gulf, conform to the same curious pattern, no such uniformity can be detected in the vehicles mounted on them. It is true that vehicular chassis and bodies are even less often preserved than the wheels that carried them, and are less faithfully reproduced in toys and models. Yet from the meagre data available it appears that all early vehicles shared one other peculiarity besides solid wheels—namely paired draught. A central pole on either side of which the draught-animals were yoked is attested for all vehicles of which we have any knowledge down to 1000 B.C. Even in China, where shafts were already normal by the beginning of our era, the earliest pictographic characters (1300–1000 B.C.) plainly represent the standard form known from the west (figure 515 A), while on the Kalmuk steppes, just west of the Volga, a clay model of a covered cart of the same age has provision for a central pole (figure 515 B). Shafts and a single draught animal or a team of three must have been adopted in the Far East and central Asia after the period covered by this volume.

It has been suggested (p 210) that the cart is 'a sledge on wheels... attached in place of share and beam to the pole of an ox-drawn plough'. On this theory, the under-carriage should be just the frame of the sledge—or slide-car—thus drawn.

[1] The important distinction made here is that carts have two wheels, wagons four.

Since such devices are much older than wheels, the observed diversity of vehicle-bodies would be due to pre-existing local differences in the type previously in use. There is, of course, no evidence to support or refute this plausible theory, for very little indeed survives of the chassis of early carts, and nothing at all, beyond a couple of runners, of the postulated older sledges. It is not even clear whether the pole was normally attached direct to the axle-tree or rather to the under-carriage.

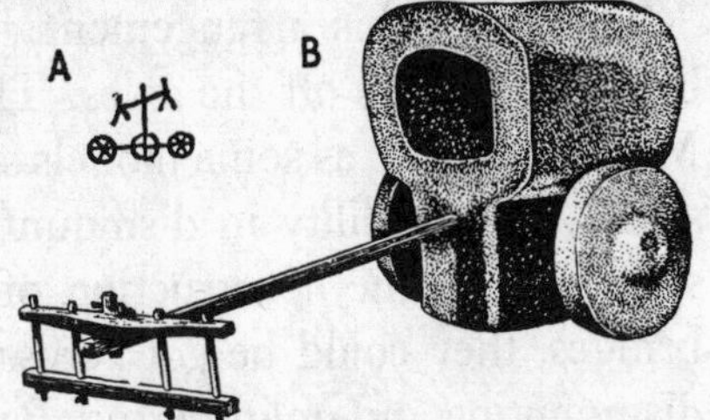

FIGURE 515—*Carts with paired draught.* (A) *Early Chinese pictograph.* (B) *Clay model (yoke, pole, and wheels reconstructed) from the Kalmuk steppe, U.S.S.R. Both second millennium* B.C.

In Mesopotamia, the under-carriage consisted (to judge from those of the hearses found at Kish and Ur) of a single plank, 45 to 56 cm wide, which may have served at the same time as the floor of the vehicle. It may have been attached to the axle-tree by straps, in which case the axle could have turned with the wheels; but most authorities believe that the wheels turned freely on the axles. In the case of four-wheeled wagons there is no evidence at all that the front axle was an independent pivoted bogie. In the Indus valley, numerous models illustrate the under-carriages of the carts of the Harappa civilization, which were constructed in just the same way as the contemporary village carts of Sindh, whose axle turns with the wheels. The frame consisted of two curved beams set parallel, and joined by two to six cross-bars. The pole might run under the cross-bars or be mortised into the foremost (figure 516). Two or three corresponding holes in each of the side-beams must have held upright poles to contain the box of the vehicle, presumably of wickerwork. A pair of holes at the centre of each side-beam would have held pegs projecting downwards to fit on either side of the axle.

FIGURE 516—*Clay model of a cart (pole, posts, and axle reconstructed), with a top view of the chassis. Chanhu-Daro, Indus Valley. Before 2000* B.C.

Thanks to this arrangement, it is easy to dismantle the vehicle by simply lifting the frame off the axles. The operation would have been equally easy in Mesopotamia if, as some models suggest, the frame were attached to the axles by straps. Such facility in dismounting must indeed have been a governing consideration in the construction of early vehicles. In the absence of roads and bridges, they could be got across streams, gullies, or swampy patches only by dismounting and unlimbering. Bas-reliefs of the Assyrian kings Ashur-nasir-pal and Sennacherib depict wheels, yokes, and other chariot-parts being carried

FIGURE 517—*Four-wheeled war-chariots illustrated on the mosaic 'standard.' Ur, Mesopotamia. c 2500 B.C.*

separately across rivers by swimming soldiers as late as 750 B.C. The simplicity of dismemberment must be borne in mind in estimating the utility of wheeled vehicles for transport and communications in the long ages when made-up roads were non-existent or badly maintained.

Dismounting and unlimbering were wasteful of labour and time, but the only effective alternative method of inland transport was exposed to precisely the same kind of troubles and delays. On unregulated rivers, frequent portages are required to convey both vessel and load over rapids and shallows, and for their transfer across the watersheds between river systems. Thus, save in very rugged or heavily wooded country, the wheeled cart or wagon offered a definitely economical method for the transport of heavy or bulky articles, though for the conveyance of able-bodied persons and light packages the ox-cart could hardly compete with the pack- or saddle-ass—to say nothing of camels or horses when, at a later date, these animals had been tamed and trained for the task. Right down to the present day, carts have been traversing the steppes and deserts of central Asia, including the Gobi, where roads are still no better than they were in Hither Asia 5000 years ago. Even the lofty Tien Shan can be crossed by wheeled traffic at three passes.

Models and pictures from the Orient in the Bronze Age show us carts and wagons, open or covered, passenger-cars, and war-chariots, mounted on these various chassis. In all cases the superstructure must have been light—generally wickerwork, sometimes thin planks. Wagons are represented in Mesopotamia, Syria, Crete, and the Anatolian plateau, but only exceptionally in Turkmenia and the Indus valley (figures 127, 517, 129, 518 A). In the last two areas, however, carts were preferred, and the earliest vehicles known from Georgia and the south Russian steppes (*c* 1250 B.C.) are exclusively two-wheeled. Covered wagons with an arched roof of wickerwork, open at both ends, are represented already in the third millennium B.C. by models from Assyria and Syria. Carts, similarly roofed,

FIGURE 518—(A) *Model wagon from Crete.* (B) *Copper model of a cart from Chanhu-Daro, Indus Valley. Both third millennium B.C.*

are illustrated by the model from a tomb on the Kalmuk steppe about 1250 B.C. (figure 515 B), and were used to carry their wives and children by migrants who invaded Egypt from the north in the reign of Rameses III. These covered carts appear to agree precisely with the *arabas* still used throughout upper Eurasia, save that the latter are equipped with shafts and can thus be drawn by a single animal. In the Indus valley, three copper models from Harappan cities represent passenger cars, unfortunately without draught animals (figure 518 B). A chassis of the usual type supports a light body covered with a gabled roof. The passengers sit back to back, and in one case the driver sits on the front cross-bar of the frame. Similar vehicles can still be seen in India. In fact, the various types of vehicle devised during the third millennium B.C. were so efficient for commercial and domestic transport that, apart from the introduction of spoked wheels, they underwent no fundamental change during the period covered in this volume, and have indeed survived to the present day. The significant improvements affected motive power and military engines.

II. TRACTION

The first draught animals were oxen, which continued to be used exclusively for heavy transport to about 1000 B.C. The beasts always worked in pairs yoked on either side of a single shaft—the pole. Tractive power was transmitted to the wheels by the pole, and to the pole by the wooden yoke. At its centre, the latter was pegged to the pole; it sat comfortably on the shoulders of the oxen, which pressed against the yoke and so pushed the pole and the vehicle forward. Collars of metal or perishable material, slipped over the animals' heads, ensured the security of the yoke. Control was effected by reins attached to a copper ring passed through the upper lip of each member of the team.

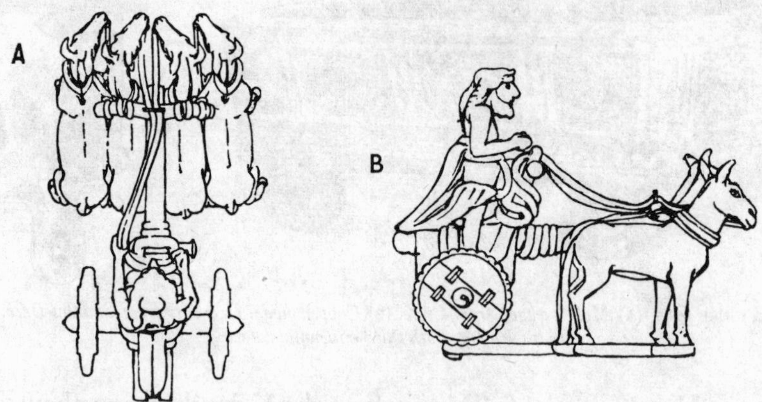

FIGURE 519—*Copper model of a chariot with four onagers harnessed abreast, from Tell Agrab, Mesopotamia. Third millennium* B.C. *(The stand has been removed in* A.*)*

For drawing war chariots and passenger vehicles the Sumerians in the third millennium B.C. employed the onager (*Equus onager* Pallas), yoked in the manner of oxen. But equids do not possess shoulders prominent enough to push against a yoke and, to secure a pull, it was necessary to attach to the yoke a breast-band. This was a broad strip of hide or other supple material crossing the animal's chest, and held in place by a strap passing between its legs and fixed to a girth-strap encircling the body behind them immediately below the yoke. The breast-band was liable to press on the animal's wind-pipe to a degree which must have incommoded the beast seriously and reduced the effective tractive power exerted. Only by arching the neck could the pressure on the wind-pipe be relieved and transferred to the extended muscles, and this was not the best attitude for pulling. Partly to compensate for the loss of power, and partly owing to the small size and strength of onagers, the Sumerians often used four, instead of two, of these animals. They were still yoked abreast, two on either side of the pole, but in such a way that the outspanners pulled on their neighbours' collars rather than on the pole itself (figure 519).

Thus, down to 2000 B.C. oxen and onagers are the only draught animals directly attested anywhere. Shortly afterwards, horses yoked to war chariots appear rather abruptly in Hither Asia, regularly associated with a new type of wheel—the spoked wheel. It is most unlikely that horses were first domesticated or yoked to chariots in Mesopotamia, for the wild equid to be expected in that area was the onager, which had in fact been tamed there by 3000 B.C. It is true that a single pictographic tablet of about that date contains the sign, compounded of 'ass' and 'mountain', that a thousand years later was to be the regular cuneiform ideogram for 'horse'. But this early occurrence is isolated, and its historical meaning, 'ass of the mountains' (or 'of foreign lands'), implies that the beast was not at home in Mesopotamia, and perhaps that it came from the mountainous north-east.

Wild horses (*Equus caballus*)—essentially steppe dwellers—have existed in northern Eurasia: the Przewalski horse still roams wild in Mongolia; the tarpan lived recently on the Aralo-Pontic steppes; in western Europe there were plenty of horses, at least in Pleistocene times when much of the continent was open steppe. It now seems likely that, even after the end of the Ice Age, some wild horses survived in the Iberian Peninsula and in parts of the temperate forest zone; horses' bones have been found in Mesolithic kitchen-refuse in the Peninsula and in Early Neolithic sites there, and occasionally also north of the Pyrenees. Of course, no expert can tell from a few scraps of bones whether they belonged to wild horses or to tame ones. It is only after 2000 B.C. that horse-bones occur in such quantities on some domestic sites in Denmark, Germany, Austria, Hungary, and the Ukraine as to provoke a strong suspicion that they belonged to domestic animals. For that matter, no more plausible evidence for domestication at an earlier date is available in Asia. A few horse-bones from Anau in Turkmenia do not suffice for proof; other bones from Shah-tepe on the Turkoman steppe, from Sialk II in Iran, and from Rana-Ghundai in Baluchistan may not belong to horses at all.

However, the likely parts of upper Asia are archaeologically so nearly blank that the absence of positive evidence for early domestication in this region is no disproof that it happened there, which remains *a priori* plausible. The earliest convincing representations of equids drawing cars with spoked wheels occur on cylinder-seals from Hissar in north-east Persia (2000±200 B.C.) and from Cappadocia (1950–1850 B.C.). There are written references to horse-breeding at Chagar Bazar on the Khabur by 1800 B.C. Within the next five centuries horse-drawn chariots had come to play a decisive role in warfare from the Hoang-Ho to the Nile and the Rhine; they were familiar in Egypt, Crete, and Mycenaean Greece even before 1550 B.C., and in China and Sweden about 1300 B.C.

For the control of spirited chariot-horses—normally stallions, judging by Egyptian pictures—the nose-ring, as applied to oxen and onagers, proved less suitable than the bit, though horses can be controlled perfectly well by reins attached to a nose rope. Indeed, Arabs are today content with such a bridle, and no bits have been found with the chariots buried in the tombs of Thothmes IV, Tutankhamen, and other Egyptian notables, or in the chariot graves of Yin (Anyang) in China. It should be said that Egyptologists today attribute their absence to tomb-robberies, and in any case bits can be made of perishable material; a wooden bar or a strand of rope and twisted thong between the teeth would be quite effective, though not very durable.

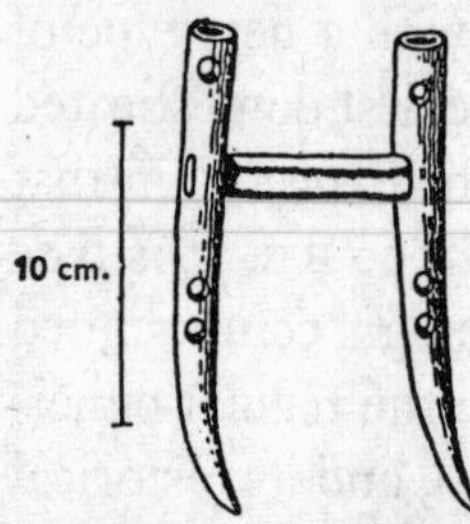

FIGURE 520—*Bit made of bone and antler. Switzerland. Late Bronze Age.*

Be that as it may, a bit in the horse's mouth has proved the most satisfactory instrument of control, and, save in China, bits appear in the archaeological record almost, but never quite, as soon as horse-drawn chariots are attested in any region. A primitive-looking bit is represented in the Late Bronze Age lake-dwelling of Corcelettes in Switzerland (figure 520). It consists of a sheep's marrow-bone fixed between two sawn-off antler-tines, each of which is pierced with holes at both ends, in addition to the central socket-hole for the bone mouthpiece. It is, however, far from certain that this representation illustrates a really original type. The earliest extant bits are made of metal. The simplest type (type O) consists of a light metal bar with loops for the reins at each end; just inside the loops metal plates (generally small openwork wheels) are threaded on the bar, presumably to keep it from slipping out of the horse's mouth. Spikes projecting from the inner side of the metal plates are thought to have served for the attachment of some leather insertion on the nose-strap, rather than to cause the animal pain (figure 521 A). Bits of this type are known from north Syria, Palestine, and Egypt, and are dated to the centuries round about 1400 B.C.

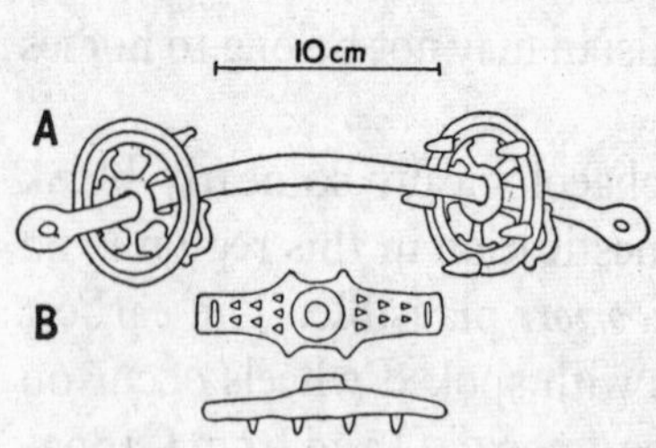

FIGURE 521—(A) *Bronze bit with cheek-pieces, and* (B) *cheek-piece. Egyptian. c 1500 B.C.*

By that time, however, bits with jointed mouthpieces are already known from Greece (Mycenae), Asia Minor (Miletus), Palestine, and Egypt (figure 522). In type I bits, the little metal wheels of type O have been replaced by flat cheek-pieces of metal some 12 cm long attached to each branch of the mouthpiece. Each is perforated at both ends with slots at right-angles to its length, and has a circular aperture at the centre through which the branch is threaded. Judging by Egyptian and Assyrian pictures, the ends of a forked cheek-strap were held by the slot, which may also have held straps joining the two cheek-pieces above the muzzle and under the chin; spikes on the inner sides of the cheek-pieces may have engaged these cross-straps. The pictures leave us in some doubt as to whether the reins were attached to the projecting ends of the mouthpiece or to the lower slots of the cheek-pieces (figures 521 B, 523).

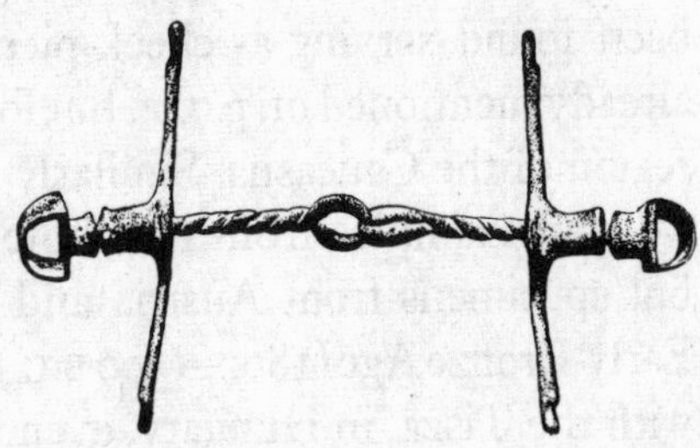

FIGURE 522—*Jointed Egyptian bit. c 1200 B.C.*

Type I bits, in use in Hither Asia, Egypt, and Greece by 1400 B.C., were still fashionable in Assyria down to 850 B.C., and form the immediate starting-point for a series of more ornate devices in Iran and Italy. Indeed, they illustrate the main principle of all bridling-devices applied to horses down to 400 B.C., and surviving today in the 'branks' still used for tethering ponies and cattle in Orkney and Shetland. The branks are two pieces of wood curved to fit the profile of the muzzle and pierced by three holes. Lengths of rope passing through the terminal holes join the two branks above and below the muzzle, one end of the lower rope being continued to serve as the tether. But no bar passing through the mouth fits into the central holes, which merely hold a rope looped over the beast's head behind its ears.

After 800 B.C. a modified version appears on Assyrian monuments. The flat cheek-piece of type I is replaced by a crescent-shaped one; the forked cheek-straps are still attached to the terminal holes of the cheek-pieces, but the opposite ends are joined together by ornamental metal studs, instead of the simple knots shown on Ashur-nasir-pal's sculptures, and the continuations of the cheek-strap are joined to the head-strap in the same way. The arrangement accordingly required four metal studs, together

FIGURE 523—*Relief showing Assyrian bit with flat cheek-piece. From the palace at Nimrud, Mesopotamia. Ninth century B.C.*

with one larger one for the frontlet; they have often survived where the leather has vanished.

The crescentic cheek-pieces depicted on Assyrian sculptures certainly look like sections of antler-tine, and such tines, pierced with three holes, have in fact been found serving as cheek-pieces for bits, and that not only for the bone-bit already mentioned on p 722, but for jointed metal mouthpieces, particularly in the region of the Caucasus. Similarly perforated tines occur much earlier in Europe. Alleged examples from Neolithic sites in Germany are now generally rejected, but specimens from Austria and Silesia have been plausibly attributed to the Early Bronze Age (1800–1500 B.C.) and one found near the junction of the Maros with the Tisza, in Hungary, even to the so-called Copper Age (2000–1600 B.C.). The dates given for these European objects are highly speculative. All the objects are certainly older than their analogues in Assyrian sculptures, and at least as old as the actual type I bits from the Near East, though certainly no older than the first archaeological and literary evidence for horse-traction in Hither Asia. If really used with mouthpieces of perishable material, and not as mere branks for tethering cattle, they would provide evidence for the domestication for traction of horses—perhaps survivors from the Pleistocene—in Europe as well, towards 2000 B.C. On the other hand, antler cheek-pieces were also used much later—in England, for instance, at least until the Roman conquest—while characteristic bone cheek-pieces (*psalia*) were favoured by the Scythians and central Asian horse-nomads of the Iron Age.

Bits with curved metal cheek-pieces that might be translations of the antler ones occur very widely about, or soon after, 800 B.C. not only in Assyria but in temperate Europe, on both sides of the Caucasus, in Iran, and in central Asia. They exhibit a bewildering variety of shapes, though all preserve some reminiscence of the curve presumably derived from an antler model. For instance, in the Achaemenid Persian type cheek-pieces and mouthpiece were cast as one; in the Maiemeric period of the Altai the central hole through the cheek-piece is replaced by a projecting hook, on to which the looped end of the mouthpiece was hung; and among the Scythian nomads in south Russia, and right across central Asia to China, the cheek-piece, often of bone, is passed through a large ring at the outer end of the mouthpiece. As all the essential principles of bridling illustrated in type I bits are preserved, it is superfluous here to examine the variations in great detail.

III. CHARIOTS IN WAR AND PEACE

As early as 3000 B.C., vehicles drawn by onagers had been used in Mesopotamia for passenger transport and as engines of war. Both two- and four-wheeled vehicles are depicted, but the former are the better known and eventually replaced the less manœuvrable four-wheelers. The simplest form, represented by a copper model from Tell Agrab, carried only one person (figure 519). The body was little more than 'a kind of centre-board continuing the line of the pole. Astride this stood the driver, his feet supported on a small ledge suspended in front of the axle'. The type most usually depicted on the monuments, however, carried a warrior as well as the driver. The body was a light affair, probably of wickerwork, open at the back but protected in front by a very high dash-board, to which was attached a sort of basket charged with weapons—spears and an axe—and presumably a whip. The floor was apparently a plank set over the axle. The pole seems to have run level across this low floor and then curved up to a height appropriate for the yoke. The wood was no doubt heat-bent, as among the Egyptians a thousand years later. In several representations after 2500 B.C. there seems to have been some additional bond between the rim of the dash-board and the upper segment of the pole.

Chariots of this kind are known from extant texts to have been attached to the several temples, and were doubtless used by the higher officials and clergy for civil visitations and in religious ceremonies. Perhaps, too, they helped to maintain communications between the various parts of the far-flung but ephemeral empires established by the kings of Agade (2350–2250 B.C.) and of Ur (2130–2030 B.C.). It is their use in war that is emphasized most strongly on the figured monuments, and the Sumerian onager-chariot must have been a formidable military engine. As such, its use was adopted by the various minor states that arose on the fringe of the Sumerian province during the third millennium B.C. Yet with its small, heavy wheels it was cumbersome to manœuvre, and slow even when drawn by four onagers.

The replacement of onagers by horses, and the substitution of spoked for solid wheels, evidently revolutionized warfare in the Near East. The results were catastrophic. By the eighteenth century B.C., the new weapon of offence had provoked new means of defence that reacted on town-planning; in Palestine, for instance, huge glacis at Jericho and other cities replaced the nearly vertical ramparts that had provided adequate security for over 2000 years. In the seventeenth century B.C., wielders of the new arm burst through the natural defences of Egypt and, for the first time since the union of the Two Lands (*c* 3000 B.C.), imposed a foreign dominion on part of the Nile valley.

It has been plausibly suggested that with the might of this new arm the Indo-European-speaking Hittites imposed their sway on the Anatolian plateau (*c* 1850 B.C.), the Hellenic Achaeans made themselves masters of mainland Greece (? 1750 B.C.), and the Aryans conquered the Indus valley. In any case, chariotry was the decisive factor in the great wars of empire that ravaged Hither Asia in the sixteenth and following centuries B.C., and it was the rapid communications maintainable by horse-drawn chariots that enabled the Egyptians, the Hittites, and the Assyrians to organize and administer empires vastly larger and more durable than the domains conquered by the kings of Agade and Ur less than a millennium earlier. The establishment of the first Celestial Empire by the Shangs, in the valley of the Hoang-Ho, may be attributed to a like cause. It is at least certain that the Shang dynasts employed horse-drawn chariots with spoked wheels and paired draught-animals by 1300 B.C. And at most a couple of centuries later, a horse-drawn chariot with spoked wheels was being carved on a chieftain's tomb at Kivik in Sweden (figure 524).

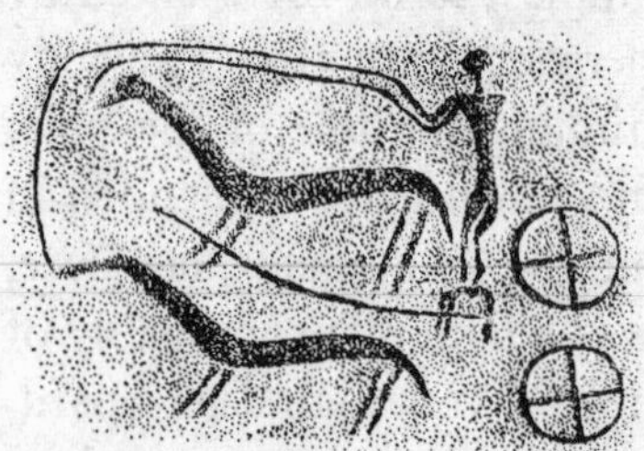

FIGURE 524—*Engraving depicting a chariot with paired draught and spoked wheels. From Kivik, Sweden. Northern Bronze Age.*

The origin of the new means of communication and offence is still a matter for speculation, even if it be admitted that the subjugation of the horse as a draught-animal and the invention of the spoked wheel are connected. It may well be merely an accident of the record that both innovations can first be discerned in a datable context in and around the Tigris–Euphrates basin. Both seem to appear rather abruptly in Mesopotamia, as if introduced ready-made from abroad, but this appearance may be due to a similar accident. Still, it must be admitted that upper Asia offers both a native land for wild horses and a theatre for the operation of wheeled vehicles over far wider areas than can be found anywhere south

FIGURE 525—*Egyptian chariot from Thebes. Fifteenth century* B.C.

FIGURE 526—*The Assyrian hunting chariot. Relief from the palace of Ashur-nasir-pal, Nimrud, Mesopotamia. Ninth century B.C.*

of the mountain spine. The difficulty is to find north of it a centre of Bronze Age culture possessing both the capital and the technical equipment requisite for perfecting the chariot. As long as such a centre remains a mere hypothesis, it would be premature to assume that the horse-drawn war chariot was introduced into the old established centres of historical civilization in the Near East by intruders from the north.

The oldest wheeled vehicles that have survived complete are the chariots from Egyptian tombs of the fifteenth and fourteenth centuries B.C. (figure 525). They are marvels of ingenuity and masterpieces of the wheelwright's art, composed of

FIGURE 527—*Chariot of Thothmes IV. From a stucco relief which forms part of the decoration of the actual chariot. c 1420 B.C.*

many pieces of various selected woods fitted together with incredible deftness and accuracy. They afford the first concrete evidence for the technique of heat-bending applied to pole and felloes, a technique attested also for Bronze Age India by a simile in the Rig-Veda. Apart from this feature, it cannot be said that they or any Egyptian and Assyrian sculptures (figure 526) illustrate fundamental improvements on designs that can be inferred as existing in the previous millennium. In Thothmes IV's chariot the pole was strapped to the axle-tree and dovetailed into the back of the socket. The body was of canvas overlaid with stucco on a light wooden frame (figure 527). The floor of Tutankhamen's chariot was made of interlaced leather thongs. The yoke, pegged to the pole, rested on a saddle on the horse's back. The saddle itself was held in place by a girth-strap to which the breast-harness also was attached, and which carried a loop for the reins. The axle-tree was pear-shaped, but tapered beyond the body to a round working axle which projected 5 cm beyond the hub. The linchpin fitted into a hole through this projection, so as to leave a play of about 1 cm for the wheel. The reins were fixed to a nose-strap which, together with a forehead-strap, three cheek-straps, and a neck-strap, constituted the bridle. No bits survived in any tombs—they may have been removed by robbers—but Tutankhamen's steeds were already furnished with blinkers. Though such late Bronze Age Egyptian and Asiatic chariots illustrate no revolutionary advance from the Sumerian, changes are observable in chariots of the Iron Age and classical times, to be considered later.

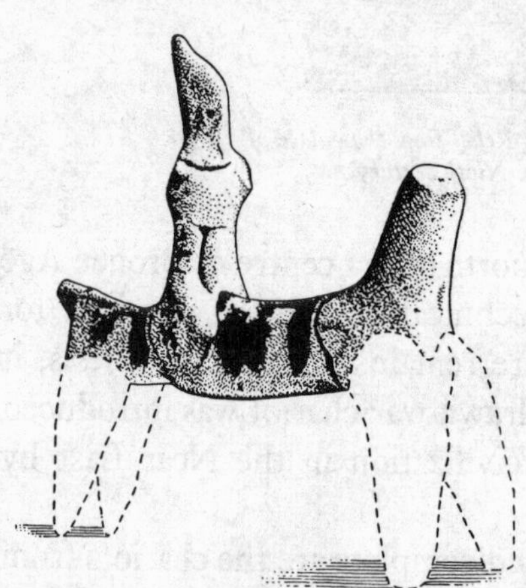

FIGURE 528—*Fragment of a clay toy which may represent a mounted warrior. From Mycenae, Greece. Thirteenth century B.C.*

IV. RIDING AND CAVALRY

Asses had almost certainly been used as pack-animals in Egypt before 3000 B.C., and were doubtless ridden as well. Throughout the Bronze Age in the Orient, as down to the present day, donkeys were regularly used as pack-animals and to carry riders. The horse too, as soon as domesticated, was used for both purposes. Riders are occasionally depicted in Egyptian tomb-paintings. A thirteenth century B.C. model from Mycenae seems to represent a mounted warrior (figure 528), but the earliest conclusive evidence for cavalry is the representation of a mounted warrior on a sub-Mycenean burial-urn from Muliana in Crete. About the same time, hacks are mentioned in Babylonian documents. The subject is further treated in the next volume.

BIBLIOGRAPHY

BERG, G. 'Sledges and Wheeled Vehicles.' *Nord. Mus. Handl.*, no. 4. Stockholm, Copenhagen, 1935.

CARTER, H. and NEWBERRY, P. E. 'The Tomb of Thoutmôsis IV.' Catal. gén. antiq. égypt. Mus. Caire. Constable, London. 1904.

CHILDE, V. GORDON. "The First Waggons and Carts—from the Tigris to the Severn." *Proc. Prehist. Soc.*, new series **17**, 177, 1951.

EVANS, SIR ARTHUR J. 'The Palace of Minos', Vol. 4, Part II, pp. 807–32. Macmillan, London. 1935.

HERMES, G. "Das gezähmte Pferd im neolithischen und frühbronzezeitlichen Europa." *Anthropos*, **31**, 115, 1936.

Idem. "Das gezähmte Pferd im alten Orient." *Ibid.*, **31**, 364, 1936.

Idem. "Der Zug des gezähmten Pferdes durch Europa." *Ibid.*, **32**, 105, 1937.

LEFEBVRE DES NOËTTES, R. J. E. C. 'La force animale à travers les âges.' Berger Lerrault, Nancy, Paris. 1924.

POTRATZ, H. A. "Die Pferdegebisse des Zweistromländischen Raums." *Arch. Orientforsch.*, **14**, 1, 1941.

QUIBBELL, M. J. E. 'The Tomb of Yuaa and Thuiu.' Catal. gén. antiq. égypt. Mus. Caire, Vol. 32. Imprim. Inst. franç. Archéol. orient. du Caire. Cairo. 1908.

UNGER, E. "Trense", in EBERT, M. 'Reallexikon der Vorgeschichte', Vol. 13, p. 424. De Gruyter, Berlin. 1929.

Idem. "Wagen." *Ibid.*, Vol. 14, p. 231.

WIESNER, J. 'Fahren und Reiten in Alteuropa und im alten Orient.' Der alte Orient, Vol. 38, Heft 2–4. Hinrichs, Leipzig. 1939.

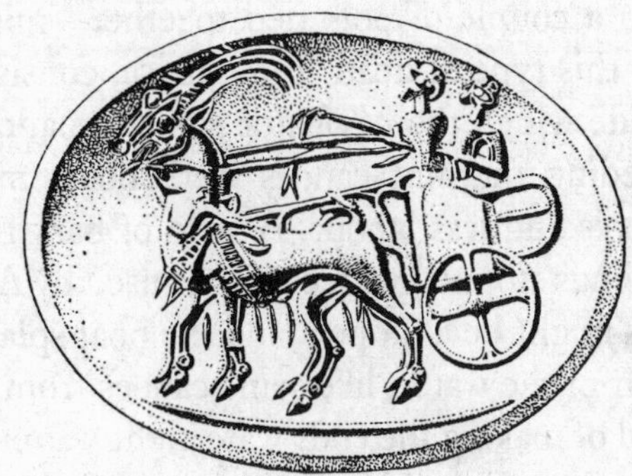

Cretan chariot drawn by wild goats. Design on a signet-ring from a site near Knossos. Fifteenth century B.C.

28

BOATS AND SHIPS

ADRIAN DIGBY

I. DUG-OUTS; BARK CANOES; REED BOATS; SKIN FLOATS

BEFORE ships or even boats there must have been a long succession of floats and rafts used as aids to swimming. These devices, being perishable, are lost, but we can draw analogies from later peoples in a relatively primitive technological stage, and can obtain information concerning early craft from drawings, carvings, and models of Egyptian, Greek, Assyrian, and Minoan times, and even from the work of Scandinavian Neolithic artists.

Early man merely seized floating objects when he was floundering in the water: the choice of material was environmental. In Egypt, where the Nile was formerly flanked by thickets of papyrus, bundles of these rushes were the first floats. In the forests of the Amazon, where dug-out canoes are the rule, their ancestors were wooden logs. In our own forested islands also, the earliest craft were dug-out canoes. Even earlier, fishermen must have floated down the rivers supported by baulks of wood, plying their nets as they went—a custom still to be seen on the rivers of southern India. Where neither logs nor reeds were available, inflated skins were used, or skins stretched over simple wicker frames like the modern coracles on the Teifi, Wye, and other Welsh rivers (figure 529). Any buoyant objects—even a couple of pots tied together—might have been used. A modern example of this type of float, from Africa, consists of two petrol tins joined by a rope, astride which the navigator sits and paddles with his hands.

Perhaps even preceding dug-out canoes were boats made of bark, which demand far simpler tools and less labour. A strip of bark removed from a tree, allowed to curl and its ends stopped with clay, was used by Australian aborigines. Alternatively, the ends might be left open, and the boat splayed amidships to lift the two open ends clear of the water, like some canoes from Tierra del Fuego. A more advanced method of making the ends watertight was either to tie them or to fold and peg them together. Examples of this type of canoe were also used on Australian rivers. Later developments would be the addition of stiffeners along the gunwale, and the insertion of curved ribs to keep the sides from bending in. Craft of this kind have been used in all forested regions.

Each of these aids to flotation may be regarded as the remote ancestor of a type of craft which ultimately developed into a ship. The papyrus raft was the model for the curious frameless Nile sailing-ship; the wicker coracle evolved into the large *quffa* or lighter of the Euphrates; the skin float was the forerunner of large rafts; the log, by way of the dug-out, was the ancestor of the early Mediterranean sailing-ship and the war-galley of antiquity; while an ultimate origin in the bark canoe can be traced in details of various later vessels.

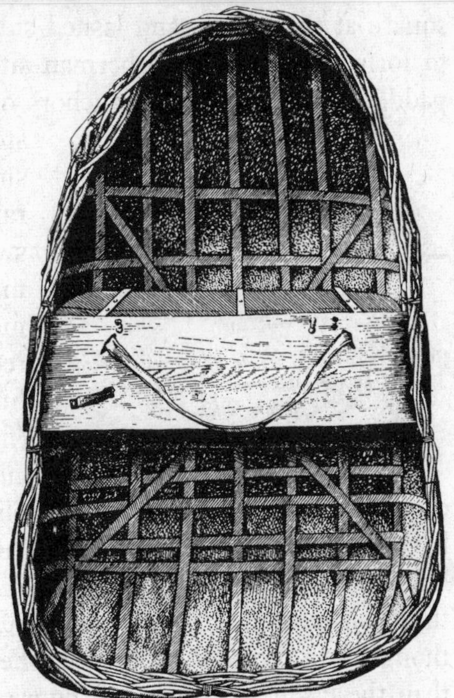

FIGURE 529—*Coracle from the river Towy, south Wales.*

We can distinguish four main phases in the early development of boats. First is the simple float. Secondly, this is modified into a number of floats joined together for stability and greater carrying capacity. Thirdly, the craft is shaped for greater ease of manœuvre; sometimes stages two and three are simultaneous. Fourthly, there emerges the true boat, in which hollowness increases buoyancy and gives better protection to passengers.

In Egypt, where all habitable and cultivated land was irrigated by the Nile, we should expect a very early start in navigation. The environment suggested the papyrus raft; indeed, little models of reed rafts or canoes, with painted bands to represent the lashing of the bundles, have been attributed to the Neolithic and predynastic Badarian civilizations. Details of these models do not suffice to indicate their construction, but we can form a picture of the early reed canoe if we turn our eyes to Peru. There the coastal fishermen use reed rafts, known as *caballitos* ('little horses'). Basically, the *caballito* consists of two conical bundles of reeds, cut off

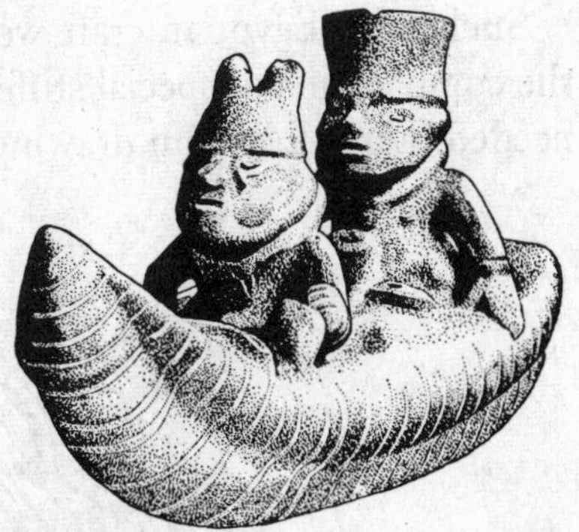

FIGURE 530—*Pottery vase made in the form of a boat consisting of three bundles of reeds. Chimu culture, Peru.* c *1200* B.C.

square at their bases and lashed side by side, with the pointed end curved up to form a prow. The fisherman sits astride this craft and propels it with a paddle. When fishing, he anchors outside the breakers, and turns facing the stern to ply his line. The fish are put into a small well cut in the bundle of reeds. The raised prow, facing seawards, rides to the swell and breaks the force of the sea, which might otherwise sweep the fisherman off his mount. A slightly more advanced form of reed boat was made by lashing a third bundle below and between the other two (figure 530).

FIGURE 531—*Boat made of ambatch reeds, used by the Dinka and Shilluk of the White Nile.*

Similar but bigger and double-ended craft, the so-called *balsas*, are used to carry cargo on Lake Titicaca in Bolivia. They are not only double-ended but have extra bundles of reeds lashed along each side as bulwarks. On the White Nile, in the region of Kodok, the Dinka and Shilluk tribesmen use little boats of the local ambatch (*Herminiera elaphroxylon*) reeds, shaped almost like a *caballito*, though with prow less upturned: the smooth Nile waters are easier to navigate than the Pacific coastal swell (figure 531). If we assume a like development in Egypt, the larger craft there would have been very similar to the *balsas*. With three, or perhaps five, cigar-shaped bundles lashed together they would have been roughly spoon-shaped, and the narrow tapering ends, instead of curving upwards, would, when lashed together, form the long overhangs so characteristic of Egyptian pictures of Dynasty V (figure 532).

II. EARLY SAILS

Such early Egyptian craft would have been paddled rather than rowed, and the complication of special stiffening to take the strain of rowlocks would not be needed. Early Egyptian drawings show some of these craft equipped to carry a

FIGURE 532—*Egyptian papyrus canoe under construction. From a tomb at Saqqara, Egypt. c. 2500 B.C.*

square sail, spread from a short yard made from a single spar hoisted on a bipod mast. This was supported by a single forestay. The ropes used to hoist the sail (halyards) were led aft from the masthead. No shrouds were needed, since the spread of the mast-legs gave lateral stability. A precisely similar rig is used on the reed boats of Lake Titicaca, except that the sail is hoisted on the aft side of the mast and stiffened by battens.

Some type of bipod mast is inevitable with a reed-built vessel, because the stresses caused by a one-pole mast on such a craft would pull it apart through tension on the shrouds. The two legs of the mast also spread the weight better, a process carried further in a reed sailing-boat of Dynasty VI, in which each of the two legs is forked, giving four points of support (figure 533). Steering was apparently effected by two long paddles lashed to the side, or on a crutch attached to the side of the hull near the stern.

FIGURE 533—*Reed sailing boat with bipod mast, legs forked. From a tomb at Deir el-Gebrawi, Egypt.* c *2400* B.C.

Conditions of navigation on the Nile were peculiar. The prevailing wind blows steadily from the north, so that a voyage upstream merely involved hoisting mast and sail, which were lowered again when drifting downstream. This explains why the mast was stepped forward in Nile craft, in contrast to the later Egyptian and other sea-going ships of the eastern Mediterranean, where, as drawings and models show, it was stepped amidships (cf figures 533, 536). A sail near the bows tends to keep the head of the ship before the wind, but, in any attempt to sail across the wind, the forward position would pull the head away to leeward, and this could be counteracted only by keeping the helm hard down to leeward, with no margin for emergencies. At sea, where it would be necessary to sail as much into the wind as possible, the mast would have to be set nearly amidships and a more efficient steering mechanism provided. These differences are evident in the later sea-going craft, yet even with these refinements it is doubtful whether they would have been able to do better than sail across the wind.

We must not regard reed-built ships as being confined to the calm waters of the Nile. The prophet Isaiah (XVIII. 2), writing about 740 B.C., speaks of Egypt 'that sendeth ambassadors by the sea, even in vessels of bulrushes upon the waters'. Some authorities consider that Egyptian reed boats were sometimes rendered seaworthy by being given a waterproofing of pitch.

III. EGYPTIAN WOODEN SHIPS

It is impossible to say when the first wooden ships were built in Egypt; it may have been in predynastic times, but there were certainly wooden boats in Dynasty IV (*c* 2600–2500 B.C.). Naturally, they followed the same external lines as the reed craft. Egyptian shipwrights were essentially builders and carpenters, and had none of the traditions of the dug-out, or of the bark canoes with framing. Applying their usual methods, and with little knowledge of nautical problems, they produced a wooden hull reminiscent of the reed boat. Short lengths of timber were joined edge-to-edge, and kept in place by wooden pins and dove-tails. There was no true keel or interior frame, and the finished structure could best be described as a spoon-shaped wooden shell. Transverse deck beams were laid across the shell, and passed through the top planking to provide extra strength. This design has been likened to an arch. It is strong against pressure from without, but weak against pressure from within. Passengers and cargo were therefore carried on the deck. In form and convenience there was little change from the reed boat, and one delightful picture shows such a river boat rowed in a lady-like manner by men seated on stools on the deck (figure 534).

FIGURE 534—*Egyptian plank-built river boat. From a tomb at Beni Hasan.* c *1900 B.C.*

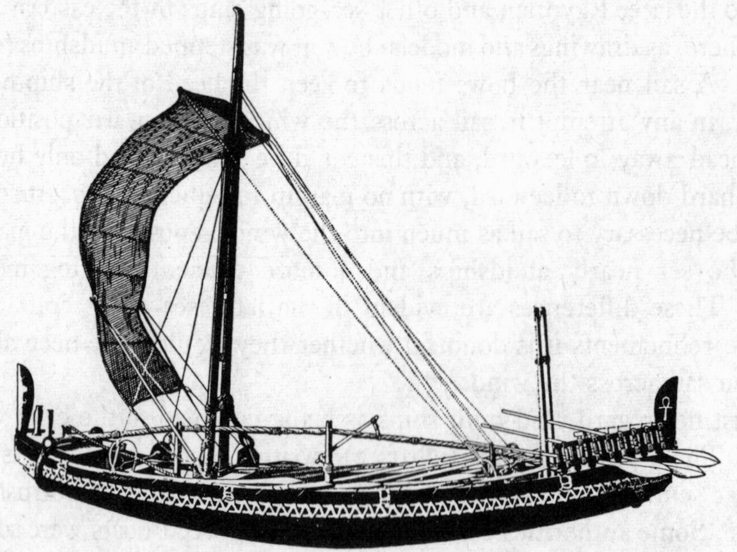

FIGURE 535—*Model of an Egyptian seagoing ship of Dynasty V.* c *2500 B.C.*

The weakest feature of this constructional type was the lack of a keel to give longitudinal strength. Stiffness was provided by a hogging truss, that is, a cable running from bow to stern, and supported on crutched poles to prevent the ends from sagging. It was tightened by a 'Spanish windlass', i.e. a bar inserted through a bight of the rope and twisted (figure 535). Ships of this type from Dynasty V (*c* 2500 B.C.) had already reached a length of 115 ft. We have no pictures of big ships of the Middle Kingdom (2160–1788 B.C.), but from literary sources we learn of really large ships with a length of 120 cubits (180 ft), a beam of 40 cubits

FIGURE 536—*Model of an Egyptian seagoing ship of the time of Queen Hatshepsut.* c *1500 B.C.* (*See also figure 32.*)

(60 ft), and carrying a crew of 120; the measurements give a fineness-ratio of three to one, about the same as that of medieval merchant shipping. Models and pictures of smaller ships, however, show various graded refinements, especially in rigging. The sail is much wider, and is extended from a very long yard made of two spars joined together in the middle; a similar spar serves as a boom, the weight of which is taken by rope supports running from boom to masthead (topping lifts). A single-pole mast without stays now replaces the clumsy bipod. This implies adequate internal framing to take and distribute the strain. Steering is improved by lashing one rudder on each quarter to a post and again to the gunwale, and providing a tiller set at right angles to the loom of the oar. Probably only the lee rudder was actually used, but the helmsman could exert far more force by twisting the blade through the action of the tiller than could be applied by the older method of using three paddles without the tiller.

Minor improvements of this sort accumulated steadily. They reached their highest point in the ships of Queen Hatshepsut's expedition to the land of Punt (figure 32); here all the improvements mentioned are included, together with other refinements. The hogging truss is now tautened by being hauled down towards the deck instead of being twisted. The mast is dead amidships, almost over the centre of lateral resistance, which would make tacking easier, though it is hard to see how such ships could avoid making considerable leeway. Oars are still carried for moving to windward. The lacing round the top strake has disappeared, and all the deck beams pass right through the hull.

IV. MESOPOTAMIAN SKIN FLOATS AND THEIR CONGENERS

In Mesopotamia, Assyria, and the eastern Mediterranean development proceeded on different lines. On the Tigris and Euphrates, where papyrus was lacking, early floats were skins inflated with air, upon which a man could lie and kick his way across a river. The device is widespread; it was known until recent times in the Balkans, and a double variant appears in America. The best-known ancient illustration of this type of float is a bas-relief from the palace of Ashur-nasir-pal (ninth century B.C.) at Nimrud, where, supported by skin floats, remnants of a defeated army are escaping across a river.

Assembling a number of skin floats and attaching them to a wooden framework produced a serviceable raft capable of carrying a heavy load. Such rafts were generally known as *kelek*s; their history goes back almost to the beginning of civilization. One of the earliest pictorial records of them in this region is from Nineveh (figure 283). Similar rafts were used until recently for downstream journeys. At their destination the timbers were sold, and the skins were placed on the backs of pack animals for the upstream journey. It may be that the animals themselves were carried downstream on the rafts.

Closely allied to the skin float, which is kept expanded by air pressure, is the skin boat in which a flexible leather or hide cover is stretched over an internal frame. Such craft still survive today in the kayaks and the large open women's boats or *umiak*s of the Eskimo, as well as the curraghs of the west coast of Ireland, the Welsh coracles, the modern canvas canoe, and their counterparts spread widely over Asia and America. Indeed, the steel-plated ships of today, though not directly descended from such craft, have a strong structural resemblance to them, for the plating of a modern ship bears much the same relationship to the forces acting upon it as the skin of a coracle, and both are prevented by the frame from collapsing inwards.

All the evidence points to the coracle type having been first developed in Asia, probably on the Tigris and Euphrates, where such boats were in common use. They were used for general cargo in the reigns of Ashur-nasir-pal and Ashur-bani-pal (ninth and seventh centuries B.C.). An impression of them can be obtained from the sculptured panels from Nimrud and Nineveh (figure 283). These boats show an analogy to the modern *quffa*, still at work on the Tigris (figure 537). Two stout staves are crossed at right-angles, and bent to form a frame to the

FIGURE 537—*Modern* quffas *on the Tigris. Construction: bent wood and interlaced rope frame covered with bitumen.*

sloping sides. The quadrants thus formed are filled with radial members bent to the same contour, and woven into place by interlacing of ropes. A stout ring of sticks lashed together forms the gunwale, while the skin of the *quffa*'s ancient progenitor is replaced by a thick coating of bitumen. The oars have been replaced by paddles. Normal cargo-carrying *quffa*s have a mouth-diameter of 13 ft and a depth of $7\frac{1}{2}$ ft, and these dimensions seem to fit the proportions of the Nimrud sculpture. Such boats would be simple to construct, very stable, and capable of carrying heavy loads. Though slow and unwieldy, the *quffa* is well adapted to ferrying downstream in a placid river.

Circular boats are widespread. Examples with slight local variations are described from China and Tibet. In India, the Duke of Wellington ordered his engineer-officer to construct twenty basket boats with a diameter of 10 ft and a depth of 3 ft, and with double skins. The Welsh coracles, at the other end of the scale, are light one-man affairs in which the fisherman drifts downstream, paddles ashore, and then carries his vessel upstream for another journey. This emphasizes the disadvantage of the circular or nearly circular boat, which can hardly be paddled upstream.

Strange craft of this sort are not directly in that line of evolution which developed into the two standard types of ship, the round tub-like merchant ship, and the long narrow war galley. Both of these were keeled and ribbed, and both derive ultimately from the dug-out canoe, which may in some circumstances be derived from bark vessels. As previously mentioned, the bark vessel is probably the earlier, because less labour is required to strip off the bark than to hollow out a tree-trunk.

V. EVOLUTIONARY DEVELOPMENT FROM THE DUG-OUT

As the Palaeolithic passed into the Neolithic stage, and better tools became available and experience in woodwork accumulated, dug-outs superseded bark canoes, though more or less specialized bark canoes have survived to our time.

FIGURE 538—*Dug-out canoe. Bronze Age Britain. Length* c *35 ft.*

Dug-out canoes have been found wherever there are suitable forests. They vary in shape according to local requirements and to the material available. The limiting factor is tree-diameter. Enormous seagoing dug-outs were built from the giant trees of British Columbia. Other dug-outs, notably in Africa, may have a beam of no more than 18 in. Maximum beam was often increased during manufacture by filling the hull with wet sand, the weight of which forced the sides apart. Prehistoric canoes must have been constructed by similar means, and had similar limitations. An ancient British canoe of the Bronze Age is about 35 ft

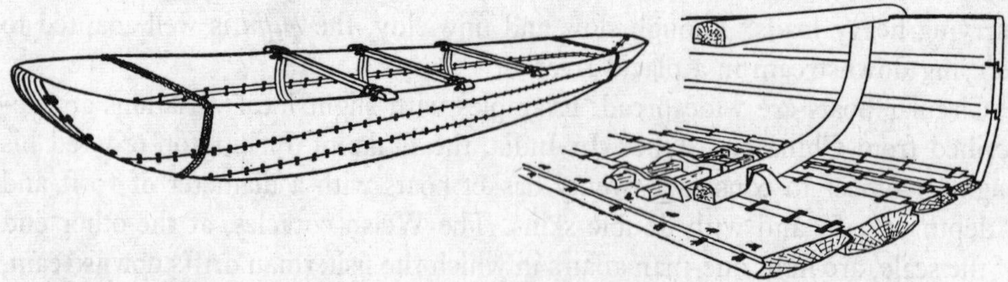

FIGURE 539—*Plank-built boat excavated at Ferriby, Yorkshire. Probably Iron Age. Estimated length 52 ft.*

long, with a depth of 2 ft and a beam of nearly 5 ft (figure 538). For a simple dug-out, these dimensions are near the limits possible in most localities. Inside this canoe are several transverse ribs cut from the solid, and integral with the hull. It is tempting to believe that these are vestigial memories of ribs in the flimsier bark canoes which must have preceded them.

Larger craft would necessarily be of more composite construction. One possible line of advance is seen in the remains of the two boats, probably of the Iron Age, discovered at Ferriby, on the Humber (figure 539). The hull was roughly pontoon-shaped, with five thick floor-planks bevelled and grooved to fit each other, and sewn together with withies. A very interesting feature was a series of perforated cleats through which stout wooden rods were driven to provide rigidity. These were supplemented by a number of open cleats to which ribs were attached to support the side-planking, in a manner allied to that used in joining the floor-planking. The underlying conception in the design of these vessels was obviously that of a craft like a dug-out, but built of a number of shaped timbers fitted and sewn together. This idea is analogous in conception to the Egyptian dovetailed construction, and is not in the evolutionary line of normal shipping.

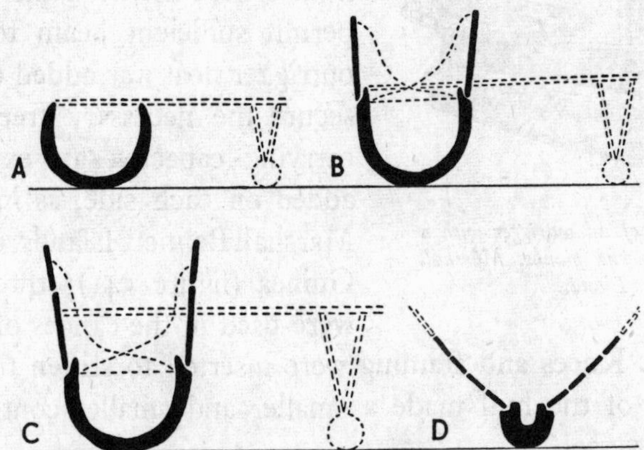

FIGURE 540—*Diagrammatic sections illustrating the development of the keel from the dug-out hull.* (A) *Trobriand Islands* kewou, *a dug-out with no wash strakes.* (B) *Trobriand Islands* kalipoulo, *dug-out hull with one row of wash strakes.* (C) *Trobriand Islands* masawa, *with two rows of wash strakes.* (D) *Singhalese* yathra dhoni (*lower portion only*). *In the three examples from the Trobriand Islands outriggers and frames are indicated by dotted lines, but in the case of the* yathra dhoni *frames have been omitted for simplicity.*

A far more likely line of development can be inferred from various types of canoe hulls in the Pacific (figure 540). The Maori canoe represents the first stage (plate 27). Large single trunks were cut out, and additional freeboard was

FIGURE 541—*Model of an outrigger with a dug-out keel built up with planks. Marshall Bennett Islands.*

provided by lashing beams along each side, thus raising bulwarks which did not quite reach bow and stern. In the bows, a board was inserted athwartships, and an ornamental figure-head was placed on the projecting portion of the dug-out hull. Where the available timber did not permit sufficient beam for stability, an outrigger float was added on one side. To secure the necessary freeboard for any carrying capacity, an extra plank was added on each side, as in canoes of the Marshall Bennett Islands, off eastern New Guinea (figure 541); three such planks were used in the canoes of Rossel Island in the same area. Knees and framing were inserted to stiffen the planks. The dug-out portion of the hull made a smaller and smaller contribution to the buoyancy of the vessel.

Until the early years of the present century, the *yathra dhoni*, a type of vessel used by the traders of Colombo, was built of sewn planks, flared out to give a beam equal to about one-third the length of the ship (figure 542). These vessels, with somewhat similar types from Madagascar, and some other south Indian ships, were the last survivors of a type once widespread in the Indian Ocean. They resembled craft used by the Hindus who invaded Java in the ninth century A.D.

Many vessels of this kind, and indeed all canoes in Melanesia and Polynesia, attained stability either by carrying an outrigger float supported on beams or by being built as twin hulls. Almost the only exception was the Maori canoe; this was made of such enormous trees that the extra stability given by the outrigger was unnecessary. The outrigger produced its own navigational problems because, treated as a counterpoise rather than a float, it had to be kept to windward. If on the lee side, it would be driven under water and broken off. Tacking as we understand it was therefore impossible,

FIGURE 542—*Singhalese* yathra dhoni. *A vestige of the dug-out is retained in the hollowing of the keel.* (*See also figure* 540D.)

unless a balancing platform was provided on the other side of the hull. Some canoes, especially those of the Marshall Islands and Gilbert Islands (west-central Pacific), were tacked by reversing.

VI. ORIGIN OF THE AEGEAN GALLEY

As we have seen, the main types of Mediterranean ships were derived from dug-outs. It seems probable that, before their builders had learned to flare the

FIGURE 543—*War galley with ram depicted in the palace of Kuyunjik, Mesopotamia. Seventh century* B.C.

planking sufficiently, an outrigger was used, although there is no direct evidence of this. But if we examine the *yathra dhoni*, which incidentally still used an outrigger, we find that the dug-out log has shrunk to a mere keel, and that more and more planks have been added, and splayed out farther. Thus a type has been evolved of which the section is that of a normal plank-built vessel (figure 540 D). A curious but important survival in these craft is the hollowed keel. Its excavation can serve no useful function, for it is too small to provide additional buoyancy. It is a survival of the dug-out hull, which the conservative boat-builders have continued to incorporate, possibly for magical reasons.

The profile of a *yathra dhoni* is strikingly similar to drawings of merchant ships on early Greek vases (Volume II), and it seems reasonable to postulate a similar development for them. These merchant vessels of early traders of the Aegean, forerunners of the *naves rotundae* of classical antiquity, had a length-to-beam ratio very similar to that of the *yathra dhoni*. It may seem fanciful, on the strength of profile and proportions alone, to assume a similar method of construction, and therefore a similar descent from the dug-out. We may remember, however, that even earlier Mediterranean craft, namely Phoenician war-galleys, also have features similar to those of dug-out canoes (figure 543). Since, then, each of the two main types of craft in the Mediterranean resembles one of two lines of evolution of the dug-out canoe, it seems likely that they have had a similar evolution, especially when the ancestors of their builders must have come from areas where large timber was available, whether 'cedars of Lebanon' or other timber.

It might be objected that these Mediterranean galleys were rowed with oars, while the canoes were propelled by paddles; but the transition from a paddle to an oar is not very revolutionary or obscure. As the value of a fulcrum for the steering-paddle came to be appreciated, it was simple to apply it to the propulsive paddle and so convert it into an oar. Before accepting this reasoning, the case should be substantiated by comparison of the earliest known war-galley with the dug-out canoes most like it, namely those of the Maori of New Zealand and of the Trobriand Islanders (figures 541, 543, plate 27). The galley has a sharp pointed ram low down on the water, obviously a continuation of the keel, and behind the ram is a bulkhead. Abaft of this, two rows of oars protrude from the sides of the galley, and above them are seen the heads of the upper bank of rowers. The oar-ports and the thwarts were staggered, so that the lower rowers sat between the spaces occupied by the upper row. In the Trobriand Islands canoe and the Maori canoe, the place of the ram is taken by the projecting end of the dug-out hull. A bulkhead or wash-board is placed across the hull in the same position as the bulkhead on the Assyrian galley, while planking along the side corresponds to that of the galley. In making these comparisons, it is to be remembered that the Assyrian represents a higher stage of evolution than the Trobriand craft, and that the planking had been flared out and built up far more. With these allowances, the comparison is close enough. The Assyrian galley, however, is far less developed than the *yathra dhoni*. Both can be regarded as evolved from the dug-out, though the galley, which becomes the prototype of all galleys down to the sixteenth century, here branches off from the main line of evolution.

The further development of the galley is obscure, because our only evidence is on Minoan coins, where the drawing of the ships is so conventionalized that we can reach no firm conclusions about their construction. Almost the only information to be gleaned from them is that most had no more than five oars a side. No doubt, as the need arose for bigger and faster galleys, more oars were added and extra rows incorporated. The larger ships of a later age, and the literary references to triremes, quinqueremes, and such fantastic craft as ships alleged to mount sixteen banks of oars, will be discussed in a later volume.

BIBLIOGRAPHY

BELL, C. D. J. "Ancient Egyptian Ship Design." *Ancient Egypt*, 101, 1933.

BOREAUX, CHARLES. 'Études de nautique égyptienne.' Mém. de l'Inst. franç. Archéol. orient. du Caire, Vol. 50. Cairo. 1925.

CLOWES, G. S. L. 'Sailing Ships, their History and Development. Part I—Historical Notes.' Science Museum, London. 1930.

EDGERTON, W. F. "Ancient Egyptian Ships and Shipping." *Amer. J. Semitic Lang. and Lit.*, **39**, 109, 1922–3.

FAULKNER, R. O. "Egyptian Seagoing Ships." *J. Egypt. Archaeol.*, **26**, 3, 1940.

HORNELL, J. 'Water Transport.' University Press, Cambridge. 1946.

MARINATOS, S. P. "La marine créto-mycénienne." *Bull. Corr. Hell.*, **57**, 170, 1933.

PETRIE, SIR (WILLIAM MATTHEW) FLINDERS. "Egyptian Shipping." *Ancient Egypt*, 1 and 63, 1933.

POUJADE, J. 'La route des Indes et ses navires.' Payot, Paris. 1946.

TORR, C. 'Ancient Ships.' University Press, Cambridge. 1894.

WRIGHT, E. V. and WRIGHT, C. W. "Prehistoric Boat from North Ferriby, East Yorkshire." *Proc. Prehist. Soc.*, new series **13**, 114, 1947.

Reed boat on Lake Titicaca, Bolivia.

29

RECORDING AND WRITING

S. H. HOOKE

I. THE EARLIEST WRITING

Of all the discoveries and inventions by which man has created what we call civilization, the most decisive has been the instrument which enabled him to make a permanent record of his own achievements and history. Such an instrument is the art of writing.

Some Late Palaeolithic paintings show an extraordinary technical skill, which obviously involves a long tradition as well as some formal training. These works are held to contain magical elements, usually designed to bring the hunted within the hunter's power. Occasionally, however, they record events or supposed events. Thus one group of figures on the walls of the caves at Lascaux (Dordogne) records an attack on a buffalo with a javelin that has pierced its viscera, and a fatal stroke by the dying buffalo on the hunter. Across some 20 000 years the artist's work tells that which he wished it to tell (figure 544).

Men so artistically capable could well convey to their fellows pictographic messages relating to their day-to-day life. None such is known from Palaeolithic times, but it must be remembered that pictographs intended to transmit a message would have very little chance of surviving. They would naturally stand in the open, and there would be no motive to engrave or model them laboriously on durable stone. Nevertheless, plenty of perishable pictographs are known from living peoples in the Neolithic stage. For rapid delineation the figures of men, of animals, or of objects are often reduced to simple diagrammatic forms. In this process we have the dawn of ideographs, a method of recording still in use in the Chinese script. Very early pictographs have survived both from predynastic Egypt and from the earliest civilization of Mesopotamia. These represent the beginnings of true hieroglyphic writing.

Archaeological evidence shows that between 5000 and 4000 B.C. there settled in the delta of the twin rivers of Mesopotamia a people known as the Sumerians. Their culture forms the basis of all the subsequent development of civilizations in that area. A most important legacy of the Sumerians was their system of recording, which rapidly passed out of the realm of mere pictographs. The earliest known examples that can be called writing come to us in the form of clay tablets from the temple of Inanna at Erech. On these tablets are inscribed signs, assumed to be numerals, and pictures of objects, such as heads of animals, birds, fishes, plants, domestic utensils, and parts of the human body (figure 545). Hence it is safe to conclude that in Sumer, as in Egypt, writing began with, and developed from, pictures. In both countries, men had discovered how to make pictures represent sounds as well as objects. That point once reached, writing had begun.

The motive which brought about this invention of writing was economic. By

FIGURE 544—*Rhinoceros, buffalo, and hunter. Cave painting at Lascaux. Upper Palaeolithic.*

the middle of the fourth millennium B.C., men in lower Mesopotamia had passed beyond Neolithic barbarism. The region of Sumer and the neighbouring region of Akkad were already divided into many small city-states. Each of the cities contained one or more temples with a large staff of priests. The city god was regarded as the owner of all the state lands. Dues were payable to the temple in the form of products of the soil. Hence arose the need for a system of accounts, or records of dues owing or paid. It is generally agreed that these earliest tablets from Erech, Jemdet Nasr, and other Sumerian cities are records, kept by the priests, of the temple incomes. A tablet containing a picture of a cow's head, an ear of corn, or a fish, together with circular impressions taken to be numerals, would be a memorandum of so many head of cattle, so much grain, or so much fish, due to the temple from some individual or village community. A similar tablet with a hole pierced through the centre perhaps records dues paid; it is, in other terms, a receipted bill.

We believe that such tablets represent the true beginnings of writing. Their purpose is clearly to record. Those from Erech, stored in the temple archives, were made to communicate economic information. Some of the signs on these early tablets are compound, and show the first attempts to express verbal notions or actions. For example, the pictures of a man's head and mouth, combined with the picture of bread or food, serve to express the action of eating. It is also possible that some of these compound signs represent proper names. If

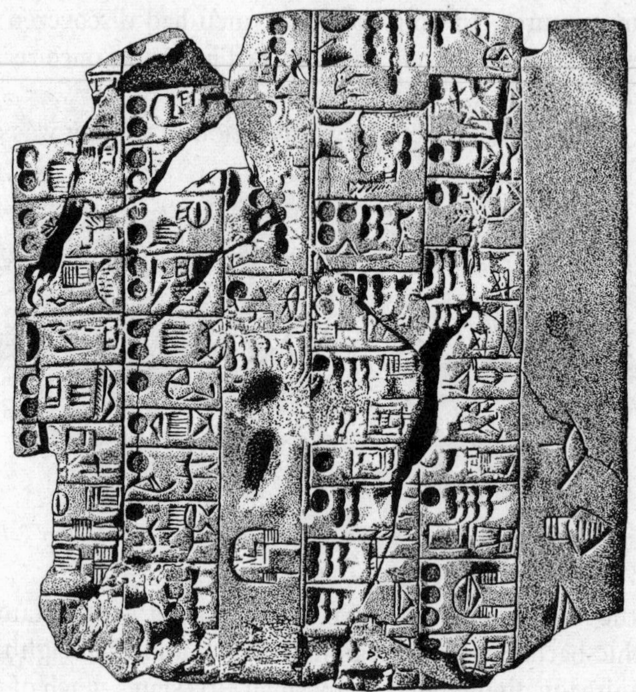

FIGURE 545—*Pictographic tablet from Erech, probably a statement of temple accounts.* c 3500 B.C.

so, we have in them the beginnings of the use of pictographic signs to represent sounds.

Obviously word-signs, as these early pictograms are now generally called, cannot by themselves fulfil the essential functions of a developed system of recording, namely, the representation in visible form of intelligible discourse, the movement of thought. For example, in attempting to write such a simple sentence as 'This is the king's house', the juxtaposition of the picture signs for 'king' and 'house' would fail to yield that meaning unambiguously. It might be read in several ways such as 'The king goes to a house' or 'The house is for the king' and so on. The history of writing, both in Sumer and in Egypt, shows that the solution of this difficulty was sought along different lines in the two countries.

The first solution was to increase the detail of the picture-sign, in other words to make the picture do more work. Thus, in the Egyptian hieroglyphic system, the basic picture of a man is used in many different ways. In the list of Egyptian word-signs collected by Sir Alan Gardiner, no less than 53 represent a man in different states or activities. The Sumerian scribes, however, devised another plan. They marked the picture-sign with what are called *gunu*-lines; these were indications of some modification of its original meaning. Thus lines under the chin in the picture of a man's head indicated that only the mouth was referred to, and the sign *SAG*, head, was thereby transformed into the sign *KA*, mouth. Such a tendency greatly increased the number of pictorial signs employed. Gardiner's sign-list, representing Egyptian usage of the Middle Kingdom, contains 732 signs, while the number of signs used in the early documents from Erech in Sumer is estimated at about 2000. Apart from its cumbrous nature, the great limitation of the system is that, however details were increased in number, they could not represent all possible extensions of meaning in a picture-sign, nor could they ever succeed in denoting all the relations of the words in a sentence.

II. THE SYLLABARY

An alternative solution, along what proved to be the line of development for writing, was to make the picture-signs represent sounds without regard to meaning. This process was possibly first suggested by the existence, both in Egyptian and in Sumerian, of homonyms, that is of words with the same sounds but different meanings, as for example 'Pole' and 'pole'; the man Pole might be represented by the symbol pole. The earliest known example of this method of extending the range of pictorial signs is perhaps in tablets found at Jemdet Nasr, on the Tigris a little north of Babylon, of about 3000 B.C. In them occurs the personal name En-lil-ti, meaning in Sumerian 'Enlil [the god] causes to live'. The word-sign *TI* pictures an arrow, but the sound *ti* was Sumerian both for an arrow and also for life—which would be difficult to represent pictorially. Similarly, in Egyptian we find the familiar sign for the scarab (*hpr*) transferred to the homonym *hpr* meaning to be, to exist.

This device increases the range of expression of the pictorial signs. Unfortunately it also increases their ambiguity, and moreover its use is limited by the comparatively small number of homonyms. Nevertheless, this use of homonyms to increase the range of utility of a single sign points to the main line of development along which early writing was destined to progress, namely, the divorce of sound from meaning. The fact that the Sumerian vocabulary was mainly monosyllabic aided the process. Early in the third millennium B.C. we find three well-developed tendencies:

(*a*) Use of the same word-sign for words similar in sound but not in meaning, and the closely related development of syllabic signs.
(*b*) Introduction of determinatives.
(*c*) Arrangement of the signs within a compartment of the tablet in the order in which the words would be read or spoken.

The effect of the development of syllabic signs was to reduce the number of signs in current use. Thus at one stage of the late Uruk (Erech) period in Mesopotamia (Uruk IVb, *c* 3600 B.C.) 2000 signs were in use; tablets found at the site of Fara of a date perhaps about 300 to 400 years later indicate that their number had dwindled to about 800. By the time of King Urukagina of Lagash (*c* 2900 B.C.) another 200 of the signs used in the Fara texts have disappeared.

An interesting example of this process is afforded by the story of the sign *UDU*, Sumerian for 'sheep'. These early tablets are mainly lists of offerings in temple accounts, so that it is not surprising that the sign for sheep should occur frequently. Now in the material from Erech at stratum IVb there are no fewer than 31 variations of the sign *UDU*, corresponding no doubt to the many different kinds and conditions of sheep and goats used for ritual purposes in the temples. But in the next main level only three signs for sheep remain, and in the top stratum only two. Here, then, is a deliberate rejection of an almost unrestricted tendency to differentiation.

The use of determinatives is a device to remove ambiguities which appears early in the development of both the Sumerian and the Egyptian systems of writing. Determinatives are certain signs used to denote classes of persons or things, and are placed before or after the sign to be determined. Probably the earliest of such signs is the Sumerian *DINGIR*, god, prefixed to the names of gods. The Sumerian sign *GIS*, wood, is placed before the names of things made wholly or partly of wood. Thus the word-sign for plough, originally the picture of a plough, and capable of meaning either a plough or a ploughman, by the use of determinative signs can have its meaning limited. With the sign *GIS* prefixed it means plough, but with the sign *LU*, man, prefixed it can mean only ploughman. Two other very common determinatives are the signs *KUR* and *KI*, used respectively to mark the names of countries and cities, *KUR* coming before, and *KI* after, the sign which it determines. The traditional rules governing the use and position of determinatives were established very early.

In the course of the development of this divorce of sound from meaning, the word-signs were not used to express simple sounds, as an alphabet does, but syllables. The syllabary which thus came into existence contained more than

300 signs. These were in addition to such signs as continued to be used as word-signs without having a syllabic value. The development of syllabic signs made it possible to express in writing those grammatical elements of speech, such as case-endings, pronominal affixes and suffixes, prepositions, adverbs, and conjunctions, which by their nature cannot be expressed pictorially.

Another important use of syllabic signs as an aid toward clearness of meaning is their use as phonetic complements. This is found early in both the Egyptian and the Sumerian systems of writing. It can best be explained by an example. An ambiguity which had to be overcome by those who shaped the Sumerian script was that many Sumerian word-signs were polyphons, that is, they could be pronounced in two or more ways, carrying two or more meanings. This difficulty itself arose from the pictorial origin of the script. For example, the Sumerian sign *DU*, whose original form was the human foot, might stand for the various activities connected with the feet, and the words describing such activities would naturally be represented by quite different sounds. Thus the sign *DU* came to stand for the words *gin*, to go, *gub*, to stand, and *tum*, to bring. By writing the syllabic signs *-NA*, *-BA*, and *-MA*, respectively, after the sign *DU*, the scribe indicated which value was to be given to it. Thus the sign *DU* with the syllabic sign *NA* written after it would be read *gin-na*, going, and similarly with the other words named.

The third tendency mentioned above, namely arrangement of signs within a compartment of a tablet in their spoken order, completed the early stage of the internal development of Sumerian writing. On the earliest tablets no compartments are marked, and the few signs which each of such tablets contain are arranged quite arbitrarily. When compartments begin to appear, the signs which they contain show no traces of arrangement. This is no doubt because these early documents were memoranda of merely temporary importance relating to passing temple business. They were quite intelligible to those who wrote them, but were not intended as permanent records. When, however, it became of interest to the rulers of cities, such as Lagash, to preserve records of their achievements, this rough-and-ready way of making occasional notes gave place to an orderly arrangement of the signs in successive lines within the compartments of the tablet. This process seems to have been complete by the time of King Eannatum (*c* 3000 B.C.).

Thus by the end of the fourth millennium B.C., the Sumerian system of writing consisted of a syllabary or sign-list containing about 500–600 signs. About 100 were phonetic, representing the vowels *a*, *e*, *i*, *o*, *u*, and the various combinations of these vowels with the consonantal sounds. Unlike the Egyptians, however, the

Sumerians had devised no method of representing simple consonantal sounds, that is, they had not reached, nor did they ever reach, the final stage in the development of writing, the creation of an alphabet. But it is interesting that, though the Egyptians had early discovered the alphabetic principle of writing, they never took the logical step of discarding the cumbersome machinery of word-signs, determinatives, and phonetic complements. To the end of their civilization, the Egyptians continued to use the alphabetic method of writing simply as an adjunct to the rest of their ancient traditional system.

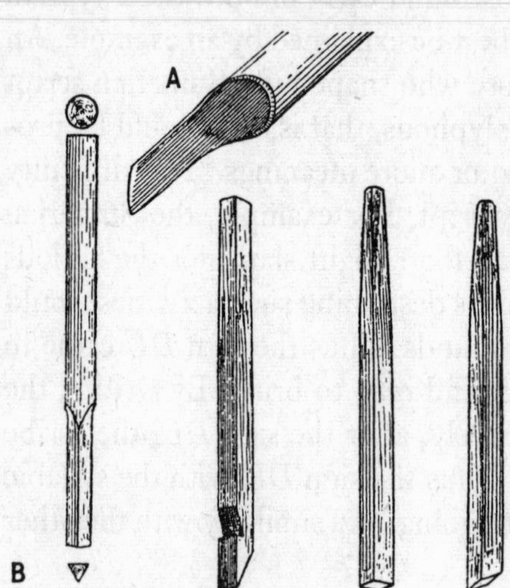

FIGURE 546—*Reconstruction of the cuneiform stylus.* (A) *Early form of reed-pen used before* c 3000 B.C. (B) *Possible shapes of the later stylus after* c 3000 B.C.

III. DEVELOPMENT OF CUNEIFORM

Side by side with this internal development of Sumerian writing, a process of external change was also proceeding. The Tigris–Euphrates delta had no reeds suitable as a source of writing-material comparable to the papyrus of Egypt. There was, however, an inexhaustible supply of clay. From the earliest times to the end of the Seleucid era (first century B.C.), the Mesopotamian peoples continued to use clay tablets, cylinders, or prisms for all forms of recording except monumental ones. For the latter alone, stone or occasionally metal was used. On the earliest tablets the outlines of the pictorial signs were drawn in the soft clay with a reed stylus. At first the fineness of the lines in the tablets shows that an almost knife-sharp reed was used; but it must have been difficult to draw correctly curved lines on wet clay, and by the time of the Fara tablets the scribes had begun to cut the ends of their reed-pens in a fairly wide-angled wedge. Instead of drawing their pictures in lines, curved or straight, they were beginning to make them by pressing the wedge-shaped end of the stylus into the clay, and forming the required design by a group of wedges of different sizes and thicknesses (figure 546, plate 30 A).

The process is best illustrated by observing the change in such a characteristic sign as *SAG*, representing the head of a man (figure 547). At first, the head is fully drawn, with eye, nose, and mouth; later it is still drawn, but in a greatly simplified form; in the Fara tablets it has degenerated into a design of seven wedges, in which it would be hard to recognize a human head; finally we have the sign in the compact form which it received from the Assyrian scribes. It is from the appearance which the script presents in this stage of its development that it has received its name cuneiform, i.e. wedge-shape (Latin *cuneus*, a wedge).

There is another curious phenomenon in the external development of the Sumerian script. It too may be seen in the sign *SAG*, head. When we first meet the sign, it is drawn in its normal position, i.e. upright and facing to the right.

FIGURE 547—*Development of the sign SAG.*

Later, however, it is lying on its back, with the face pointing upward. All the other signs have suffered the same change. The reason for this curious alteration seems to be that the early tablets were small enough to be grasped comfortably in the left palm and were held by the scribe at an angle of about 45° (figure 548). The signs were then written on the tablet as if it were horizontal, being read vertically, and written from right to left. With an increase in the conventional size of the tablets this position became inconvenient and the tablet was laid on a table and turned in a counter-clockwise direction till it was perpendicular. But as the turn was only one of 45°, the signs were written in the same way as before; hence, when the tablet was read in the perpendicular position, the signs would appear to be lying in a horizontal position face upward, and would read from left to right. By the time the change took place, the form of the signs had changed from their pictorial character and were no longer felt to be in an unnatural position. This explanation is supported by the fact that with inscriptions on monuments of stone or metal, where such a change of position was not practicable, the old position of the signs was still maintained. For example, on the stele of Hammurabi (*c* 1750 B.C.), the signs are engraved in the old position. But shortly after Hammurabi's time, i.e. about the end of the eighteenth century B.C., the method of inscribing monumental inscriptions was brought into line with that long used for clay tablets.

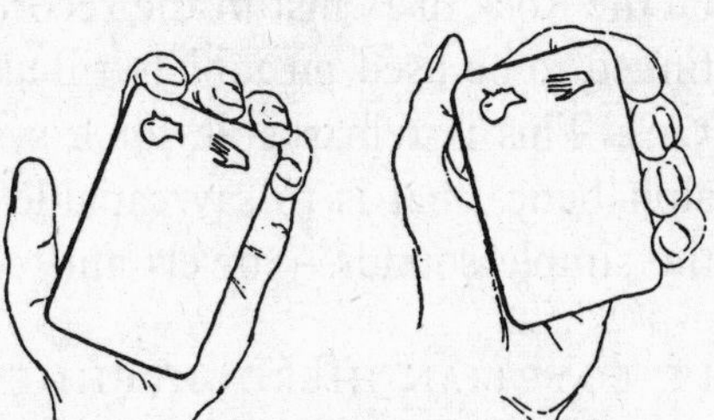

FIGURE 548—*Diagram showing the change of position of the tablet in the hand.*

An important event in the history of the Sumerian system of writing is associated with the conquest of Mesopotamia by Semites. The Semitic invaders adapted

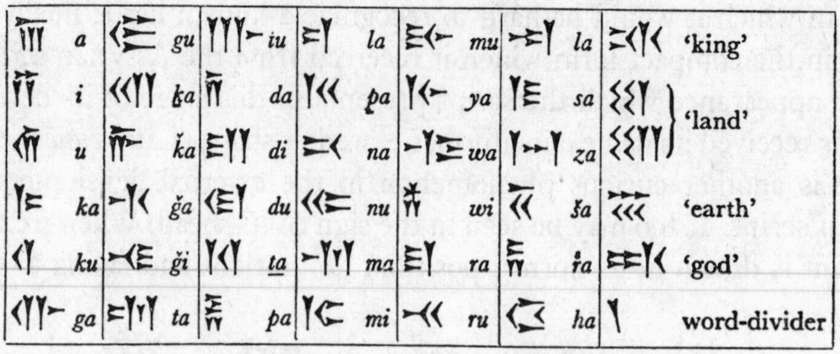

a	*gu*	*iu*	*la*	*mu*	*la*	'king'
i	*ḳa*	*da*	*pa*	*ya*	*sa*	'land'
u	*ǩa*	*di*	*na*	*wa*	*za*	
ka	*ǧa*	*du*	*nu*	*wi*	*ša*	'earth'
ku	*ǧi*	*t̲a*	*ma*	*ra*	*ṙa*	'god'
ga	*ta*	*pa*	*mi*	*ru*	*ha*	word-divider

FIGURE 549—*Early Persian syllabary. Fifth century* B.C.

the Sumerian script to the writing of a language of which the sounds and vocabulary were totally different from those for which the script was invented. While this change had no effect on the nature of the script itself, it had very disturbing effects on its use, since, to the values which any Sumerian sign possessed as a word-sign or a syllabic sign, there were now added Semitic values. Moreover, Sumerian continued to be used as the language of religion, for ritual purposes, much as Latin is today. Hence it had to be studied by the priests. The large number of lexical and bi-lingual tablets discovered shows that the difficulties which these ancient texts present to the modern scholar also existed in some measure for the Babylonian and Assyrian scribes (plate 29 B).

In spite of these difficulties, the cuneiform script acquired a place in the ancient Near East which its most important rival, the Egyptian hieroglyphic, never attained. The El-Amarna letters show that cuneiform was used in diplomatic correspondence between Egyptian Pharaohs, Hittite kings, Mitannite princes, and Canaanite chiefs, in the middle of the second millennium B.C. It was used at an even earlier date as a means of writing the Hittite, Hurrian, and other kindred languages, which were totally different from either Sumerian or Akkadian. It was used at the time of Darius the Great (died 485 B.C.) to inscribe in Susian on the Rock of Behistun the record of his victories (plates 28, 29 A), and it continued to be used on tablets till about the end of the pre-Christian era (figure 549). This is remarkable for a system of writing which never became purely alphabetic, that is to say capable of representing by a separate sign each of the simple sounds—vowels and consonants—used in any speech.

IV. EGYPTIAN HIEROGLYPHIC

In Egypt, as in Mesopotamia, the earliest elements of written speech were pictures of recognizable objects. It is but right to remind the reader that an alternative origin of writing in Egypt has been suggested. Sir Flinders Petrie, who collected a body of linear signs or marks on predynastic pottery, wrote of them: 'The body of signs belongs to the early age, when drawing was of the rudest, and only mechanical abilities were developed in the art. Hence . . . it is impossible to presuppose a pictorial source for them. They start at an age when rude marks satisfy the mind by symbolizing the intended meaning, and long before more exact copies of forms were thought needful.' It is difficult, in view of the archaeological evidence, to accept this suggestion that linear signs arise in a stage of culture when the power of pictorial representation is still rudimentary. The earliest appearance of anything resembling linear signs occurs in the pebbles of Mas d'Azil (France) painted in Palaeolithic times. But whether these were a script or not, they are certainly contemporary with a highly developed power of pictorial representation both in the flat and in the round. At a very much later period a form of script composed of linear signs did develop in Egypt, but its evolution from the hieroglyphic script is clear and has no connexion with Petrie's signary. Hence the theory of a dual origin of Egyptian writing is hardly tenable.

But did the early Egyptians invent their system of writing or borrow it? On the Kish tablet several of the pictorial signs show a remarkable resemblance to Egyptian hieroglyphs. This resemblance may be accidental or the result of dependence or of imitation. According to one exponent of the latter view: 'The writing which appeared without antecedents at the beginning of the First Dynasty was by no means primitive. It has, in fact, a complex structure. It includes three different classes of signs: ideograms, phonetic signs, and determinatives. This is precisely the same state of complexity which had been reached in Mesopotamia at an advanced stage of the Protoliterate period. There, however, a more primitive stage is known in the earliest tablets, which used only ideograms. To deny, therefore, that Egyptian and Mesopotamian systems of writing are related amounts to maintaining that Egypt invented independently a complex and not very consistent system at the very moment of being influenced in its art and architecture by Mesopotamia where a precisely similar system had just been developed from a more primitive stage'.[1] Present evidence suggests rather dependence of the Egyptian system upon the Sumerian. Nevertheless, there are important differences in the way in which the two systems developed. Of these we may consider three:

(*a*) The Egyptian hieroglyphs, unlike the Mesopotamian, remained pictures to the end. This was due in part to the difference in writing-material. The

[1] H. Frankfort. 'The Birth of Civilization in the Near East', pp. 106–7. Williams and Norgate, London. 1951.

development of cuneiform was entirely due to the practical difficulty of drawing pictures on soft clay, but in Egypt the early discovery that the papyrus reed (*Cyperus papyrus*) provided an unlimited source of excellent writing-material enabled the scribe to perfect a graphic art involving representations of an immense variety of objects. That art survived practically unchanged for occasional use till Roman times, but the employment of a system of word-signs (or ideograms), syllabic signs, and determinatives was common to the Sumerian and Egyptian systems.

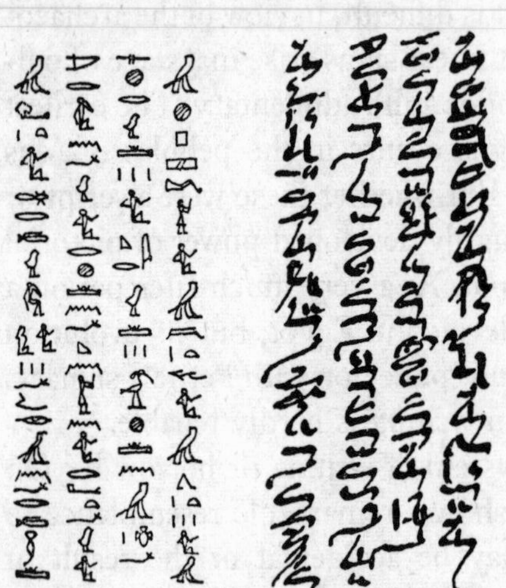

FIGURE 550—*The same passage in hieroglyphic and hieratic scripts. Egypt.*

(*b*) At a very early period, at least as early as the time of the fourth king of Dynasty I, a cursive form of the hieroglyphic script, called hieratic, was developed in Egypt and displaced the hieroglyphic for day-to-day needs (figure 550). It was used for documentary purposes, while the pictorial hieroglyphs were retained for monumental and ceremonial uses. Gardiner remarks concerning hieratic that it 'was nothing more, in the beginning, than hieroglyphic in the summary and rounded forms resulting from the rapid manipulation of a reed-pen as contrasted with the angular and precise shapes arising from the use of the chisel'. A still more rapid form of writing, called demotic, was developed about the eighth century B.C. (plate 36). It was the usual form of script during the Ptolemaic and Roman periods, and is found on the famous Rosetta Stone.

(*c*) While it is clear that Sumerian writing developed to meet economic and administrative needs, in Egypt writing seems to occur first as an element in monumental art, supplying names and titles to make clear the identity of figures on reliefs. Hence, in view of the sacred or magical character attached to such figures, it might be inferred that the earliest use of writing in Egypt had a religious as well as a utilitarian purpose underlying it.

The moment in Egyptian history when we can observe the emergence of writing as distinct from pictorial representation coincides with the beginnings of the united monarchy in Egypt. It is on the famous slate palette of a king (figure 551) that we can observe the birth of hieroglyphs, as it were taking place under our eyes. The king, whose Horus-name is usually read as Narmer, was possibly the second king of Dynasty I of the Old Kingdom. On his palette, as on so many other pictorial representations of the Pharaohs, the military achievements of the monarch are commemorated. Most of the palette is filled with a vigorous representation of Narmer striking down a vanquished foe with his mace. At the top are two hieroglyphs enclosed in an early form of the conventional cartouche which usually frames the Horus-name of a Pharaoh. In the use of these two hieroglyphs we find the beginning of that separation between sound and meaning which marks the development of word-signs into phonetic symbols. The first sign symbolizes a kind of fish, the *n'r*-fish, and its phonetic value is *nar*; the second sign represents a chisel (?), and its phonetic value is *mer*. Hence the name of the king, Nar-mer, is expressed by ignoring the pictorial value of the two signs and using their sound value only.

FIGURE 551—*King Narmer's palette. Hierakonpolis, Egypt.* c 3100 B.C.

The top right corner of the palette offers a further example of the same process in its earliest stage. The god Horus in the form of a falcon is shown grasping with a human hand a cord attached to the nose of a head protruding out of an oblong with rounded ends. From this oblong grow six plants, probably lotus buds. Here is a mixture of pictorial and phonetic elements. Pictorial and easily recognizable are the Horus-falcon, the head of an Asiatic depicted as a captive, and the oblong which is the word-sign *ta*, country. But the phonetic element which turns the group of signs into written speech is to be found in the six lotus buds growing out of the oblong. The word-sign *kha* means 'lotus', but a sign with the same sound-value, *kha*, means 1000, so that the six lotus buds mean 6000, and the whole group means, according to Gardiner's interpretation: 'Horus brings to the Pharaoh six thousand foreigners captured within their land.' Here then we find the point at which the symbolic expression of ideas, which is writing, begins to diverge from the realistic representation of persons, things, and actions.

It is important to note that this vitally significant advance is directly connected with a stage of social development. At a certain low level of society there is no adequate motive for the rise of such a complicated social mechanism as written speech. It is possible, as we can see from a survey of present-day savage societies, for a language to reach a high degree of flexibility and a large vocabulary without any development of writing. But among the ancient Egyptians, at the beginning of the Old Kingdom, certain elements in the social situation combined to produce a need which only the invention of writing could satisfy.

We have seen that in the first place the art of pictorial representation arose as a

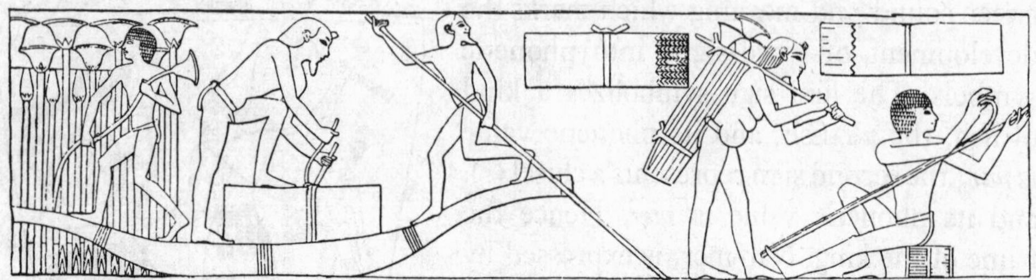

FIGURE 552—*Collecting and preparing the papyrus plant for making papyrus. From a tomb at Thebes, Egypt.* c *1500 B.C.*

way of exercising a magical control over the food-supply. Early in the Old Kingdom a new and urgent social motive appeared. The disposal of the dead assumed an importance which it has never possessed in any other civilization. The elaborate system of mummification began to develop (ch 11). Among the many arts which it carried in its train was that of pictorial representation, with a magical significance, which became an essential feature of funerary ritual. The primary object in recording the words of the spells and incantations which formed part of the ritual of mummification was similarly magical. Preserved in the tomb, or about the person of the dead, the efficacy of the spoken word was perpetuated in the written word.

Furthermore, these funerary beliefs and practices centred on the person of the king, and the achievement of a united monarchy produced a social situation of which the invention of writing was a natural product. The palette of Narmer shows the rising need for a written record to supplement the pictorial representation of the king's exploits. It is possible that even here the pictured scene and the written word had a magical value. On the reverse of the palette a bull is goring a fallen enemy. In 1 Kings xxii. 10–12 is an account of how the chief of the court prophets assumes a bull-mask and dramatically enacts in a similar fashion the coming victory of the Israelite king over the Syrians. He is engaged in making victory, not merely in predicting it. So too it may be conjectured that the palette of Narmer served not only as a record of victory achieved, but also as a magical means of ensuring it.

We have already observed that paper made from the papyrus-reed was the common writing-material in Egypt from the Old Kingdom onwards (figure 552). The part of the plant used was the pith. Paper was made by cutting the pith into slices, laying the slices crosswise, vertically and horizontally, pressing them, and drying them in the sun. The prepared sheets were then smoothed, and glued or gummed together intc a long strip which was cut to the lengths required for the scribe's rolls. Leather and parchment were also used in Egypt. There is evidence for the use of leather as early as Dynasty IV of the Old Kingdom. The British Museum possesses a parchment roll of *c* 1288 B.C. said to have come from Thebes. For occasional purposes, potsherds were often used as writing-material. The characters might be painted in colour with a brush, or written with a reed-pen dipped in ink. A relief from Saqqara shows Egyptian scribes at work. Two carry pens or brushes behind their ears. They have the usual scribe's outfit: a bottle for ink or colour, a container for brushes or pens, and a palette with hollows for mixing ink or colour (plate 32).

V. HITTITE WRITING

There are two systems of writing to which the name Hittite is applied, a cuneiform and a hieroglyphic script. The decipherment of the former has been placed on a secure basis, and numerous cuneiform Hittite texts have now been transcribed and translated, but the latter has not yet been adequately read.

(*a*) *Cuneiform Hittite* is the language and script of a people who entered Asia Minor about 2000 B.C., and built a powerful empire which lasted for about 750 years. Excavation of their capital, at Boghazköy, at the beginning of this century, brought to light the royal archives of the Hittite kings. From them we learn that the Hittites had adapted to their own language the Babylonian cuneiform script —just as the Babylonians had done with the Sumerian script. Hittite has proved to belong to the Indo-European group of languages (ch 4), and is an early relative of Latin. In adopting the cuneiform system, the Hittites retained its most characteristic elements: the word-signs or ideograms, the syllabic signs, the determinatives, and the phonetic complements. The Hittite syllabary was, however, much smaller than the Babylonian, comprising only about 130 signs. In general, the word-signs and phonetic signs which the Hittites borrowed retained their Akkadian values. They used clay tablets of varying sizes, and their technique of writing was probably the same as that of the Babylonians.

(*b*) *Hieroglyphic Hittite*. This remarkable system of writing has been found mainly in the form of monumental inscriptions (figure 553), but examples of a cursive form, comparable to Egyptian hieratic or demotic, also occur. It was known to the people of the imperial period. The relation between the two scripts is still obscure, and it is possible that the name Hittite is wrongly applied to the hieroglyphic script and language. The signs are true pictorial hieroglyphs, like those of Egypt. There are about 220 signs, of which 56 are phonetic and the rest

FIGURE 553—*Hittite hieroglyphs from Carchemish, on the Euphrates. Ninth to eighth century* B.C.

purely ideographic. A remarkable feature of the Hittite hieroglyphic system is that it occasionally presents a *boustrophedon* arrangement of the lines, i.e. the lines are read from right to left and left to right alternately, a feature also found in very early Greek inscriptions. Forty of the Hittite hieroglyphs show a striking resemblance to signs in the Cretan writing, which has not yet been definitely deciphered.

VI. MINOAN

The late Sir Arthur Evans, excavator of Knossos, and discoverer of the brilliant civilization of what he called the Minoan Empire in Crete, divided the various types of script which came to light in the course of his excavations into pictographic and linear scripts, the latter being divided into linear A and linear B (figure 554 A). According to a recent interpretation, the language which they express seems to be allied to Greek (see note on p 773).

The earliest pictographic signs, of about the beginning of the third millennium B.C., are engraved on seals. It is not certain that they represent true writing. Later, more developed, pictographs appear about 2000 B.C. These are found not only on seals, but on tablets and bars. The signs resemble both the Hittite signary and Egyptian hieroglyphs.

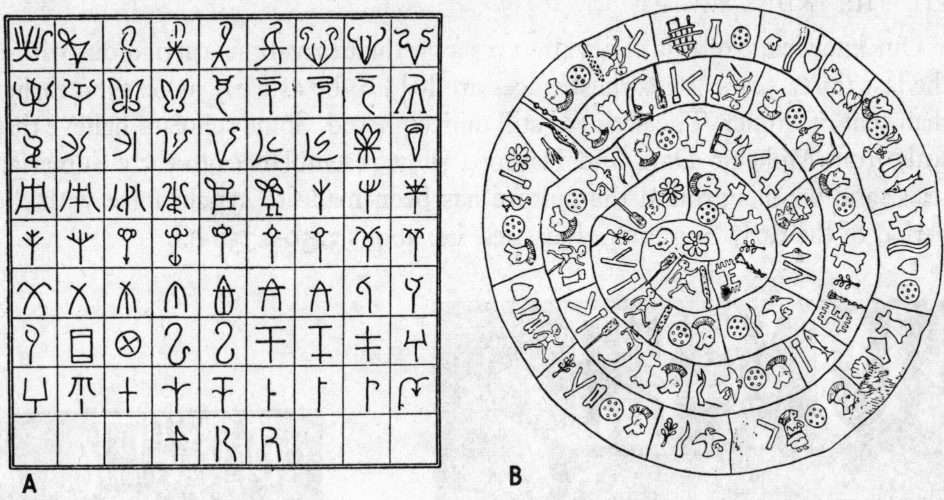

FIGURE 554—(A) *Linear Minoan Script B. 1400 B.C.* (B) *One side of the Phaistos disk. Crete. 1700 B.C.*

About the middle of the seventeenth century B.C., linear script A begins to appear; linear B appears about 1400 B.C. Both are cursive, but it is impossible to say whether they developed from pictorial signs, as did the Egyptian hieratic and demotic. The pictorial signs continue to be used until the end of the Minoan civilization. Some examples of the linear script have been found outside Crete, e.g. on a vase from Orchomenos in Boeotia.

The numbers of both types of signs, pictorial and linear, make it clear that neither can be alphabetic. Evans numbered the pictorial signs at about 135, and believed the script to be partly ideographic, partly phonetic, and partly determinative. The direction of the script is sometimes from left to right, and sometimes *boustrophedon*. There are about 90 signs in linear A, and about 64 in linear B. The latter type was found only in the palace at Knossos, and would seem to consist mostly of lists and accounts.

The famous Phaistos disk, discovered in Crete in 1908, is a roughly circular tablet of terracotta 6½ inches in diameter, inscribed on both sides with a spiral inscription of pictorial signs stamped by means of separate dies (figure 554 B). There are 241 signs representing human and animal figures, parts of the body, and objects of various kinds. There are several figures of ships, and the most frequent sign represents a human head with a plumed head-dress, resembling those of Philistines in the Egyptian pictures on the Ramesseum. No other collection of signs offers any close parallels, and the date and place of origin of the disk still remain undetermined.

VII. THE INDUS SCRIPT

Our knowledge of this civilization rests on the excavations carried out within the last thirty years. Its earliest traces are held to be as early as or even earlier than that of Sumer. The script is still undeciphered. Some scholars believe that seals from Mohenjo-Daro and Harappa show resemblances to early Sumerian seals, and on this ground the culture has been made to synchronize with the period of the early Sumerian dynasties, i.e. about 3250–2750 B.C.

FIGURE 555—*Pictographic seal impressions from the Indus valley showing script above the figures.* c *2500* B.C.

The specimens of the script hitherto discovered are almost entirely on seals, and therefore probably represent proper names (figure 555). The signs are pictorial, but show a tendency to become linear. The number of characters has been placed at about 400 and hence they cannot be alphabetic. As it is possible on ethnographic grounds that the first settlement in the Indus valley may have been due to racial movements from Mesopotamia and Elam, there may be some connexion between the Indus valley script and the early Elamite script.

VIII. EARLY ELAMITE SCRIPT

The ancient kingdom of Elam, frequently mentioned in the Bible and in Babylonian and Assyrian documents, lay to the north of the Persian Gulf and east of the Tigris in what is now Khuzistan. The specimens of early Elamite writing that we possess are found on some hundreds of clay tablets. The signs are still in recognizable pictorial form, but show the beginning of the change into cuneiform writing. Diringer regards the proto-Elamite script as indigenous, and offers two alternative suggestions as to its possible origin: (*a*) that both early Elamite and Sumerian script are derived from some more primitive writing, or (*b*) that one of them was invented earlier, while the other 'is an artificial creation impelled by the *idea-diffusion* or *stimulus-diffusion*'. This term seems to imply the borrowing of an idea, which in the case of writing is hard to distinguish from the borrowing of the system. In any case, the relation of proto-Elamite to Sumerian remains obscure. The partial decipherment of proto-Elamite suggests that the language underlying it was not Sumerian.

IX. CYPRIOTE SCRIPT

Cyprus, lying as it does between Crete on the west and the sea-board of the Levant on the north and east, was open to a variety of cultural influences, and some have seen in the Cypriote syllabary resemblances to the Hittite hieroglyphic on the one hand, and to the Cretan linear scripts on the other. Like the Hittite system, the Cypriote syllabary represents only open syllables, i.e. those composed of a consonant followed by a vowel. Since in the majority of inscriptions the Greek language is written in the Cypriote script, it is possible to discover the phonetic values of the Cypriote syllabic signs; but it also appears from earlier forms of Cypriote script, generally called Cypro-Minoan, that the Cypriote script was invented to express an indigenous language which, like the Cretan, still remains unknown. The syllabary, so far as it has been deciphered, contains 88 signs, entirely linear, although some of the signs in the Cypro-Minoan script are clearly pictographic. The inscriptions are mostly written from right to left, but occasionally they are written *boustrophedon*.

Before leaving the subject of the pre-alphabetic forms of writing, some of which continued to be used long after the discovery of the alphabet, mention may be made of the inscriptions from Byblos recently discovered and published.[1] They consist of ten whole or fragmentary inscriptions, in a 'pseudo-hieroglyphic' script. They contain 114 signs, many of which are clearly pictographic, but some are linear. They may be of about 1375 B.C., in the Amarna period. The script is syllabic, and the number of signs is about 100. There is said to be no connexion between the pictorial and the phonetic value of the signs, and it is claimed that they are in Phoenician, a Semitic language allied to Hebrew.

[1] M. Dunand. 'Byblia grammata', ch. 4. République Libanaise, Ministère de l'éducation nationale . . . Études et documents d'archéol. Vol. 2. Beyruth. 1945.

X. ORIGIN OF THE ALPHABET

Before the invention of alphabetic writing, the art of writing was largely the possession of priests and professional scribes. The Egyptians of the Old Kingdom had discovered the principle of expressing a single sound, whether consonant or vowel, by a single sign. Owing to their intense conservatism, they did not fully use it. Diringer therefore does not regard their method of writing single sounds as alphabetic, since if they had realized the alphabetic principle they would have abandoned their cumbrous hieroglyphic system in its favour. Gardiner, on the other hand, does not hesitate to call the list of signs which each express a single sound 'an alphabet'. It cannot be denied that the Egyptians employed this device, though they never recognized the full potentialities of expressing single sounds by single signs. Egypt cannot rightly be regarded as the true place of origin of the alphabet, even if, as some hold, early forms of alphabetical letters are derived from Egyptian script. Among the various theories of the origin of the alphabet, the most likely seems to be that the discovery was made among one of the Semitic peoples in contact with the Egyptians about the beginning of the second millennium B.C., and that it was developed in Palestine and probably carried to completion by the Phoenicians.

FIGURE 556—*Sinaitic script. c 1400 B.C.*

Certain inscriptions have been found in the Sinai peninsula, and in recent excavations in Palestine, which have been regarded as precursors of the alphabet. Those in Sinai consist of rather crudely executed linear signs, many of which are clearly borrowed from or based on Egyptian hieroglyphic signs (figure 556). It is generally admitted that the signs are alphabetic, and various attempts have been made to translate them. The most recent and perhaps the most successful is that of Albright. He regards it as normal alphabetic Canaanite from the early fifteenth century B.C., and the language is what he calls 'vulgar' Canaanite, with dialectical peculiarities which distinguish it from the language of the contemporary inscriptions from Byblos. The latter, together with some short inscriptions from Gezer, Lachish, and Shechem, may be regarded as other precursors of the earliest true alphabets.

We have now to consider the two earliest representatives of a true alphabetic script, the Ugaritic and the Phoenician, of which the latter was to prevail and to provide the fertile root of later alphabets.

Ugaritic. In 1928 a French expedition under the leadership of Claude Schaeffer began the excavation of the ancient city of Ugarit, modern Ras Shamra, on the north coast of Syria, opposite the eastern end of Cyprus. This port had a continuous history from the time of man's earliest settlement in Syria, but its period of greatest prosperity was between 1800 and 1200 B.C. The population spoke a dialect closely resembling Phoenician and Hebrew, but with certain phonetic peculiarities. In the library of one of the temples a large number of tablets were discovered. Many were in ordinary cuneiform and easily read, but some 600 were in a script different from any known system of cuneiform (plate 30 B). The limited number of signs in them suggested that the script was alphabetic. Soon it was discovered that they were in an alphabet composed of cuneiform signs specially invented to express the phonemes (p 87) peculiar to the Semitic dialect of Ugarit. In 1949, Schaeffer discovered at Ugarit a tablet containing the Ugaritic alphabet in the order of its letters, as we may now call its signs. It was at once observed that this order corresponded to that of the Hebrew and Phoenician alphabets, except that there were inserted the eight additional letters of the Ugaritic alphabet. These represent sound-values which were either absent or unexpressed in Phoenician and Hebrew. The Ugaritic alphabet evidently approximated also to the Arabic, in its differentiation between shades of guttural, dental, and sibilant sounds.

Scholars have sought to find the origin of the Ugaritic alphabet in various directions. Connexions with cuneiform, Egyptian, proto-Sinaitic, and south-Semitic sign-lists have been considered without offering a satisfactory solution to the problem. Between the middle and end of the second millennium B.C. experiments were being made in the direction of an alphabet, but the Ugaritic experiment was doomed to failure, mainly because the Phoenician was already in the field, but also because clay was not a natural writing-material in Palestine. Moreover, the destruction of the Ugaritic civilization by the invasion of the sea-peoples in the thirteenth century B.C. would help to bring about the disappearance of their characteristic script.

Phoenician. The earliest evidence of a linear alphabet of the type generally known as Phoenician is in a group of inscriptions belonging to kings of Byblos. The first of these, Shaphatbaal, is placed between the seventeenth and the fifteenth centuries B.C. The next, and best known, is Ahiram (plate 31 A), whose sarcophagus is assigned to an indefinite point between the thirteenth century B.C. (Diringer) and the tenth (Albright). It shows a crudely cut group of linear signs clearly related to those of the Sinaitic and proto-Semitic inscriptions on the one hand, and to the later and more finished inscriptions on the Mesha Stele and the Siloam tunnel on the other. The alphabet which these north-Semitic inscriptions present is of 22 letters, written from right to left. They express consonants only, though, as in Hebrew, necessity led to some of them being used as vowels. The restriction of the various Semitic alphabets to consonants is difficult to explain, but it must be remembered that the structure of all the Semitic languages rests on the basis of consonantal bi-literal or tri-literal roots. These give the essential conception of the word, the vowels only providing the relations, case, tense, mood, and so forth.

XI. DEVELOPMENT AND SPREAD OF THE PHOENICIAN SCRIPT

That the Phoenician alphabet spread through Palestine, Syria, and Arabia is an established fact. The earliest Palestinian example of the definitive form of the Phoenician alphabet is the so-called Gezer farmer's calendar (figure 557). It is a limestone tablet giving a list of farming activities for each month of the year. It is in an archaic form of Phoenician script, and might be contemporary with David. The next and most important example is the famous Mesha stele or Moabite Stone (figure 558), a monument set up by Mesha, King of Moab, in 850 B.C., to commemorate the successful revolt of Moab from the overlordship of the Omri dynasty (1 Kings xvi). This stone shows a great development of the script, for an inscription cut in stone necessarily exhibits greater clearness and definition in lettering than the more cursive style of occasional writings on potsherds. The Moabite Stone is the earliest inscription to show division of words and clauses by points and strokes.

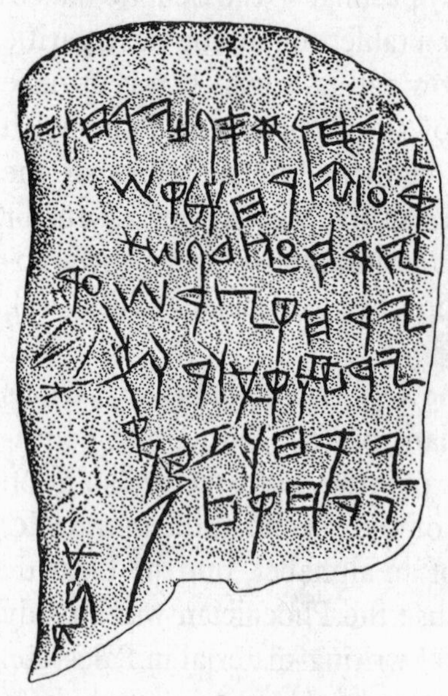

FIGURE 557—*A farmer's calendar in Hebrew from Gezer, Palestine. c 900 B.C.*

From Samaria come many inscribed potsherds of the eighth century B.C., not much later than the Moabite Stone. There is also a number of inscribed seals from various excavated sites, ranging in date from 1000 to 600 B.C. The next long inscription from Palestine is the Siloam inscription (figure 559), commemorating the completion of the Siloam tunnel made in the reign of Hezekiah, to whom there is ample reference in several Biblical books. This tunnel linked the waters of the Virgin's Spring with the Pool of Siloam. The inscription is slightly more cursive than that of the Moabite Stone, and changes have taken place in the forms of some letters. Its language is good Biblical Hebrew.

FIGURE 558—*Moabitic inscription on the stele of King Mesha of Moab. 850 B.C.*

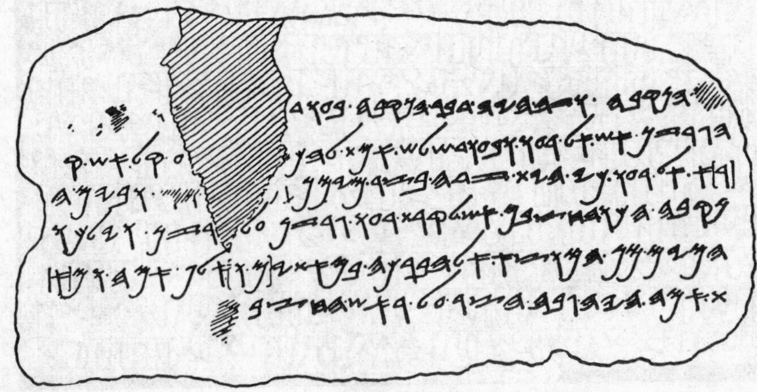

FIGURE 559—*Hebrew inscription in the Siloam tunnel. Palestine. Reign of Hezekiah, King of Judah. Eighth century B.C.*

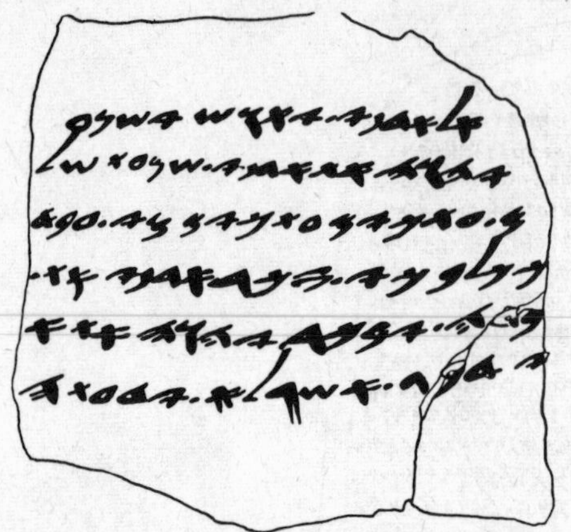

FIGURE 560—*Inscribed sherd (ostracon) in Hebrew from Lachish (Tell ed-Duweir), Palestine. 586 B.C.*

A century later we have the ostraca discovered by Starkey in his excavation of Tell ed-Duweir, the biblical Lachish (figure 560). They consist of some twenty letters between the military governor of Lachish and the commander of an unnamed town threatened by the advance of Nebuchadrezzar's army in 586 B.C. They are inscribed in ink, and show a considerable development in cursive Hebrew style.

The latest discovery of early Palestinian script is that of scrolls, found in 1948 by some Bedouin in a cave near the Dead Sea. Among them are a complete book of Isaiah and some fragments of Leviticus. As their date is still a matter of dispute, it is difficult to estimate their bearing on the development of Hebrew script. Albright assigns the Isaiah scroll to the second century B.C. Its script, and that of certain other scrolls in the same hoard, is an early form of the familiar 'square' script, ancestor of that of the printed Hebrew Bible. The script of the Leviticus fragments, however, is an example of the Hebrew book-hand, a more careful and stylized form of the cursive writing used for everyday purposes.

In Syria, the development of the Phoenician script began to follow a somewhat divergent line after the ninth century B.C. Early Aramaic inscriptions show much

FIGURE 561—*Nabataean inscription. From El-Hejra, north Arabia. A.D. 26.*

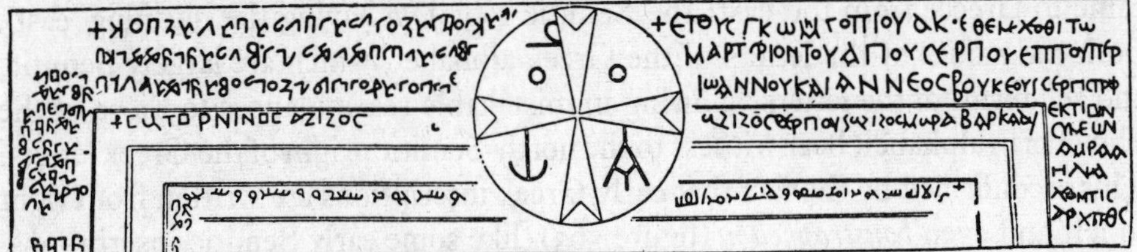

FIGURE 562—*The earliest extant written Arabic. Trilingual inscription from Zabad, near Aleppo, in Greek, Syriac, and Arabic.* A.D. *512.*

the same character as those from Palestine during the same period, but in the next century begin to develop a cursive form.

Before turning to the westward spread of the Phoenician alphabet, something must be said about the south-Semitic scripts. These are descended from the same archetype as the Phoenician or north-Semitic alphabet, but show a considerable divergence. The south-Semitic scripts are historically important because a development from one of them, the Nabataean alphabet, coming from a small south-Semitic Arabian kingdom with inscriptions between the last century B.C. to the first century A.D., can be traced with some certainty as the ancestor of the Arabic alphabet (figure 561). While the general tendency of Phoenician and Aramaic scripts is towards a sloping cursive style, the south-Semitic scripts tend to assume an upright and lapidary form preserved to some extent in the early Arabic Kufic characters, although Arabic itself ultimately becomes the most cursive of all Semitic scripts (figure 562).

Westward Spread of the Phoenician Alphabet

In the development of their maritime enterprises, the Phoenicians established many colonies on the Mediterranean coasts. Inscriptions in their alphabet from the fifth to the first century B.C. have been found in Cyprus, Malta, Sardinia, and Marseilles, while Carthage has yielded many. But the aspect of the westward spread of the Phoenician alphabet which most concerns us is the fabled carrying of the 'Cadmean letters' to the Aegean and Hellas, by which the Phoenician alphabet gave birth to the earliest Greek alphabets and so became the ancestor of all the western alphabets.

FIGURE 563—*Earliest treaty known in the Greek language. The lines run* boustrophedon. *Sixth to fifth century* B.C.

The name Cadmus, in the Greek legend, simply reflects the fact that the art of writing came to Greece from the east, the Semitic root *qdm* having the meaning 'east'. Both the names of the letters of the Greek alphabet, which are largely Semitic, and the forms of the letters, showing unmistakable resemblances to those of the Phoenician alphabet, bear witness to the north-Semitic origin of the Greek letters. This is confirmed by the fact that early Greek inscriptions are written from right to left and even *boustrophedon* (figure 563), like some early Semitic inscriptions.

While the origin of the Greek letters is thus certain, the date of their transmission is less clear. Driver's careful comparison of the forms of the letters in the earliest Greek inscriptions with those in the early Phoenician led him to suggest that the Greek alphabet is based on forms of the Phoenician letters current about the middle of the ninth century B.C. Thus the Greek *delta* never has a tail, while the corresponding Phoenician *daleth* has no tail before the Zinjirli inscription (*c* 850 B.C.). Hence the Greek *delta* is likely to have been borrowed before that date. A mid-ninth-century transmission accords with the general archaeological and historical evidence. During the next two centuries the alphabet underwent a process of adaptation to the Greek language. By the middle of the seventh century it had come into use for public purposes.

The most important changes in the Greek alphabet were (*a*) the adaptation of certain Phoenician letters expressing sounds non-existent in Greek to serve as vowel-letters; (*b*) the addition of signs to express the double consonants *ph*, *ch*, and *ps*; (*c*) the use of the Phoenician *waw* to express the vowel *u* and the half-vowel *w* or *v*, and *digamma* and two other signs representing Phoenician *ṣadde* and *qoph*, all of which soon became obsolete and have disappeared from classical Greek. Finally (*d*), to distinguish aspirated from non-aspirated vowels, the Greeks divided the Phoenician guttural *heth* into halves to form the rough and smooth breathings, placed above initial vowel letters. The order of the Greek alphabet continued mainly that of the Phoenician.

Like all the alphabetic as well as the pictographic and syllabic scripts considered, the Greek developed a cursive form at a later stage of its history. The earlier forms, without ligatures, later known as uncials, are found in the early New Testament codices. From the uncial there developed a cursive hand about the third century B.C. From the cursive a special book-hand called minuscule was developed much later for scribal purposes.

Since Hellas was divided into many small city-states during the early period of its history, the alphabet assumed a considerable diversity of forms. By the middle of the fourth century B.C., however, the Ionic alphabet of 24 letters had become standardized. It was the most perfect instrument for recording and preserving human speech that had come into existence.

XII. EARLY OFFSHOOTS OF THE GREEK ALPHABET

The Etruscans, a people whose origin, language, and racial affinities are unsolved problems, were the dominant power in Italy during the first half of the first millennium B.C. They ruled in Rome from the end of the seventh to the end of the sixth century B.C. Inscriptions in their script are numerous (figure 564). Most are from the ancient Etruria, roughly corresponding to the modern Tuscany, but many have been found in other parts of Italy. The Etruscan alphabet is certainly derived from the Greek, but there is some divergence of opinion concerning its transmission to Italy, and therefore on the particular type of Greek alphabet from which it originated. The Etruscans entered Italy before the standardization of the Ionic alphabet, and it is suggested that they possessed an alphabet before they left the mainland of Greece. This assumes the Grecian origin of the Etruscans, a view which has obtained no general assent. Diringer places the date of origin of the Etruscan alphabet in the eighth century B.C., and regards it as being of mixed parentage, i.e. as having taken or adapted forms from various types of early Greek alphabet.

FIGURE 564—*The* cippus *of Perugia. Etruscan inscription. After fifth century* B.C.

An important source for the study of the Etruscan alphabet is an ivory tablet from Marsiliana d'Albegna, now in the Archaeological Museum of Florence. It is of the end of the eighth or the beginning of the seventh century B.C., and contains the whole Etruscan alphabet of 26 letters written from right to left. They are in their Semitic order, with the addition of the four extra Greek letters already mentioned in the section on the Greek alphabet. In the course of time the early Etruscan alphabet changed. It dropped several letters, until its standard form contained 20 letters, namely, the four vowels, *a*, *e*, *i*, *u*, and 16 consonants, including the *digamma* and the *san* that became obsolete in Greek.

The group of scripts called Italic were offshoots of the Etruscan. The Oscans inhabiting southern Italy (*c* 500 B.C.) used an alphabet written, like the Etruscan, from right to left, but differing from it in having special letters for *b* and *g*. The non-Etruscan people who inhabited what is now the modern Italian district of Umbria used a script very close to the Etruscan. In the history of writing, the term Siculan (after the people who, according to tradition, gave their name to Sicily) is used to denote the script of the few non-Greek documents found in Sicily. The most important is a long inscription assigned to the fifth century B.C., written *boustrophedon*. Its alphabet is derived from an early Etruscan form.

FIGURE 565—*The 'fibula' of Praeneste with the earliest-known Latin inscription. Seventh century* B.C.

The Faliscans were closely related to the Romans and inhabited a small district north of Rome. Their inscriptions go back to the sixth century B.C., and their alphabet too is derived from the early Etruscan. In speech and script they were nearest to the Romans.

XIII. EARLY LATIN SCRIPTS

The Latin letters are obviously of Greek origin. It seems that the script was not derived direct but was an offshoot of the early Etruscan. Latin is by far the most important descendant of the ancestral Phoenician alphabet, having become the parent of all the European alphabets, and of the 'roman' and 'italic' of typography.

The earliest Latin inscription is on the Praeneste 'fibula' (figure 565). It is commonly attributed to the seventh century B.C. It is written from right to left, and shows clear signs of its relation to early Etruscan in its use of the *digamma* and *h* together, to represent the sound *f* which was in common use in Latin, and also by the use of the letters *d* and *o*, which are not found in the later form of the Etruscan alphabet. Early Latin inscriptions are rare, but by the beginning of the first century they become too numerous to record.

The principal changes which the Latin alphabet underwent in the course of its development are the following: (*a*) The *digamma*, dropped by the later Greek alphabets, became the Latin *F*, while Greek *Υ* (*upsilon*) was made to serve both for the consonant *v* and vowel *u*. (*b*) The Greek *gamma*, which in the Etruscan alphabet had become *C*, with the sound *k*, was kept in the Latin alphabet, and did duty for both the sounds *k* and *g*. Moreover, Latin also retained the two other letters which the Greek had for the sound *k*, namely, *K* and *Q*, using the *Q* when a *u* followed. Later the *K* was dropped out of general use, being kept for official words like *Kalends*, and a bar was added to the lower side of the *C*, making it into a *G*. (*c*) The three Greek letters *theta*, *phi*, and *khi*, were dropped, as the Romans had no sounds corresponding to them, but they were used to represent numbers. (*d*) Of the three Etruscan *s* letters, the Latin alphabet kept the one corresponding to the Greek *sigma*. (*e*) The Etruscan symbol for the aspirate assumed the form *H*. (*f*) The letter *I* became the sign for both the vowel *i* and the consonant *y*. (*g*) The letter *X* was added to represent the sound *ks*, and was placed at the end of the alphabet. (*h*) The shapes of some of the letters were modified; the Greek *delta* became *D*, the Greek uncial *sigma* became *S*, a stroke was added to the *P* which in Greek had the value *r*, and so the letter *R* came into being. Later the seventh letter, the Greek *zeta*, was dropped, and replaced by the new letter *G*. Finally, after the conquest of Greece, when it became necessary to transliterate Greek words, the letters *Y* and *Z* were adopted and placed at the end of the alphabet.

At the end of this process, about the first century B.C., the Latin alphabet had come to consist of 23 letters whose forms were substantially the same as at the present time. The only subsequent changes, which added the three further letters of our English alphabet, were the development of *U* and *W* from *V* to represent the vowel *u* and the consonant *w*, and the development of *J* from *I* for the soft *g* sound.

XIV. FAR EASTERN SCRIPTS

Something has been said about the Indus valley script. It is impossible at present to suggest any relation between it and the various later Indian scripts. The migration of Aryan tribes into India, and the great body of Vedic literature which they probably brought with them, may be assigned to about 1500 B.C., but there is no evidence of a knowledge of writing at that period. There is historical evidence, however, of a great expansion and organization of civilization in India from the eighth to the sixth centuries B.C., and it is most likely that writing developed about this time. The rise in the sixth century B.C. of the two great religions, Jainism and Buddhism, may have helped to spread the knowledge of writing.

Scholars are divided concerning the origin of the Brahmi script, the earliest recognized script in India. Some regard it as an independent Indian invention, while others hold that it had either a Greek or a Semitic origin. The latter view seems to be better supported by the evidence, and the second alternative, namely a Semitic origin, is also the more probable, since Greek influence came too late into India to have had any considerable effect on the development of writing there. Among the varieties of Semitic script which may have been the source of the Brahmi, the Aramaic seems the most probable. The earliest Brahmi inscriptions are from right to left, and occasionally *boustrophedon*. The writing is not alphabetic but semi-syllabic. The various forms of script which sprang from the Brahmi prototype are too numerous to describe, but two main forms should be mentioned, namely Sanskrit and Prakrit. The latter was the form of writing familiar to the common people, and the famous edicts of Asoka (*c* 274–237 B.C.) were written in Prakrit, because he intended them to be read by all. Sanskrit represents the language of the Brahmin civilization. As the script of the learned it did not come into general use until the middle of the second century A.D.; to Indian culture it was the language and script of religion and learning.

The spread of writing from India to central Asia occurred in the early centuries of the Christian era. India was to some of the countries south-east of her what Greece was to the western world, the ultimate parent of their vast variety of scripts. With the coming of Islam, Arabic has supplanted most of the native scripts in Malaysia.

Theories concerning the influence of Sumerian cuneiform signs, or of Egyptian hieroglyphs, are untenable in relation to the invention of writing in China. The earliest extant Chinese inscriptions go no farther back than the fourteenth century B.C. It seems most probable that Chinese writing is an independent development from a pictographic stage, in the course of which the original pictographs gradually lost their resemblance to the objects depicted. The earliest Chinese inscriptions were discovered in 1899, in the province of Honan (north China). These famous 'Honan bones', consisting of several thousand fragments of bone and tortoise-shell, are inscribed with ancient Chinese characters, over 3000 in number. Only about 600 of them have yet been identified. In the early stages of Chinese writing many different forms of script developed, and there were considerable changes in sign-forms. Chinese scholars early sought to systematize and classify the enormous mass of their signs, and compiled lexicons and phonetic dictionaries, somewhat as did Babylonian and Assyrian scribes. But the Chinese have never developed their script on the alphabetic principle, mainly because of the nature of their language.

Owing to the extremely complicated nature of the Chinese writing it was not adopted by most of the neighbouring peoples, the Japanese and the Annamese being the principal exceptions. The Chinese script seems to have reached Japan by way of Korea, about the third or fourth century A.D. The adaptation of the script to the Japanese language, which unlike Chinese is agglutinative, presented great difficulties. It developed a very large number of ideograms or word-signs, and also syllabaries, and a group of syllabic signs which might be used as determinatives and phonetic complements. Thus the development of Japanese writing presents a parallel to the development of the Sumerian and Egyptian systems.

Note: While this book was in the press, the decipherment of Minoan Linear B (p 758) was achieved by Ventris and Chadwick.

BIBLIOGRAPHY

DIRINGER, D. 'The Alphabet' (2nd ed.). Hutchinson, London. 1949.

DRIVER, G. R. 'Semitic Writing.' The Schweich Lectures, British Academy, London. 1948.

FORRER, E. 'Die Hethitische Bilderschrift.' Univ. of Chicago, Orient. Inst.: Stud. ancient Orient. Civiliz., no. 3. Chicago. 1932.

GARDINER, SIR ALAN H. 'Egyptian Grammar' (2nd ed.). University of Oxford, Griffith Institute, London. 1950.

HOOKE, S. H. "The Early History of Writing." *Antiquity*, 11, 261, 1937.

PETRIE, SIR (WILLIAM MATTHEW) FLINDERS. 'The Formation of the Alphabet.' Brit. Sch. Archaeol. Egypt: Studies, Vol. 3. Macmillan, Quaritch, London. 1912.

Impression of a pictographic seal from the Indus valley. c 2500 B.C.
See also figure 555.

30

MEASURES AND WEIGHTS

F. G. SKINNER

I. ORIGINS OF STANDARDIZATION

BEFORE the general introduction of the metric system in Europe, in the course of the nineteenth century, not only did every nation have its own standards of weights and measures, more or less unrelated to those of any other nation, but the principal cities in any one country often had standards of their own, quite different from those of other cities of their own people. It was quite usual for a city to possess a standard of commercial weight for bulky merchandise, and another of troy weight for gold and silver—sometimes, indeed, two troy standards, one for gold and one for silver. Then in linear measures there would be a foot unit for building and for land-measure, another and larger measure for woollen and linen cloths, and still another measure for silk fabrics, the two latter measures being known by such names as ell, aune, braccio, etc., and being the direct lineal descendants of one or other of the cubits of the most ancient civilizations of the Middle East.

The ancient civilizations to which Europe is most indebted for its metrological heritage arose in Egypt, in Mesopotamia, and around the eastern sea-board of the Mediterranean. From about 8000 B.C., the village communities in these fertile lands began the cultivation of the grain-bearing grasses (p 362). As life became more settled, trade developed at first by barter without requiring standards of weight. With the rise of the city states and, later, of the early empires, weighing and measuring began to develop into an applied science. The necessity to preserve specimen weights and measures as national reference-standards of primary authority, inscribed with the king's name and deposited in the principal temples, was recognized at least as early as 3000 B.C.

Measures of length must have been the first to be developed, though for this assumption there is only inferential evidence. With man's emergence from the cave-dwelling stage to that of building huts and houses in open country, some form of linear measure would be required. Notches cut on a straight young sapling would have served an occasional purpose earlier, and would have fed the family fire afterwards. With building, however, there arose the need for some more permanent standard of reference. This was supplied quite naturally by the proportions of man's own limbs, using as the primary unit the length of the forearm from the point of the elbow to the tip of the middle finger. This length is very easily and rapidly laid down for marking off units along a rod or pole. Subdivisions of it came naturally from the great span, i.e. the length from outstretched thumb-tip to that of the little finger, roughly equal to half the forearm length, or the little span, i.e. the length from the outstretched forefinger tip to little finger tip, equal to one-third of the forearm. Other subdivisions were the foot length, varying from three-fifths to two-thirds of the forearm; the palm, varying from 6 to 7 palms to the forearm, according to whether the measure were taken at the base of the fingers or the base of the finger-nails; and the finger-widths, 4 to a palm. The foot was also reckoned equal to 4 palms or 16 finger-widths. Finally, the height of a man, equal to the length across his arms outstretched horizontally each side of him, was reckoned equal to 4 forearms or 6 foot lengths.

The forearm length became the cubit, and 4 cubits made the fathom. All these terms for linear measures with their subdivisions still persist under various names in all languages, including Latin.

II. EGYPTIAN LINEAR MEASUREMENTS

The ancient Egyptian hieroglyphic sign for the cubit was a forearm, and upon various Egyptian cubit-rods of stone or wood now preserved in various museums all the subsidiary divisions of digits or fingers, palms, great and little spans, and the foot are found marked (figure 566). The Egyptian royal cubit was divided into 7 palms and 28 digits, these awkward divisions having perhaps some mystical significance in connexion with the 28 days of the lunar month by which the passage of time was reckoned. The ratio of 4 digits to a palm is a fairly obvious additional subdivision Other ancient cubits were generally divided into 2 feet, each of 3 or 4 palms, and the palms again into 4 digits. The Roman foot, itself derived from the Egyptian royal cubit, was invariably divided into 4 palms and 16 digits, as well as into 12 uncial divisions or inches.

Since the cubit arose as a forearm length, and men vary in height and arm-length, one would expect there to be a variety of cubit standards in the ancient world, and there were at least 6 principal cubits, besides subsidiary ones. Each people, as it rose to national importance, standardized one customary length for its particular cubit, and these lengths were maintained to within $\pm$ 2 per cent of the mean from about 3000 B.C. to the mid-nineteenth century. Later European measures were derived from them in the course of time by early migrations from

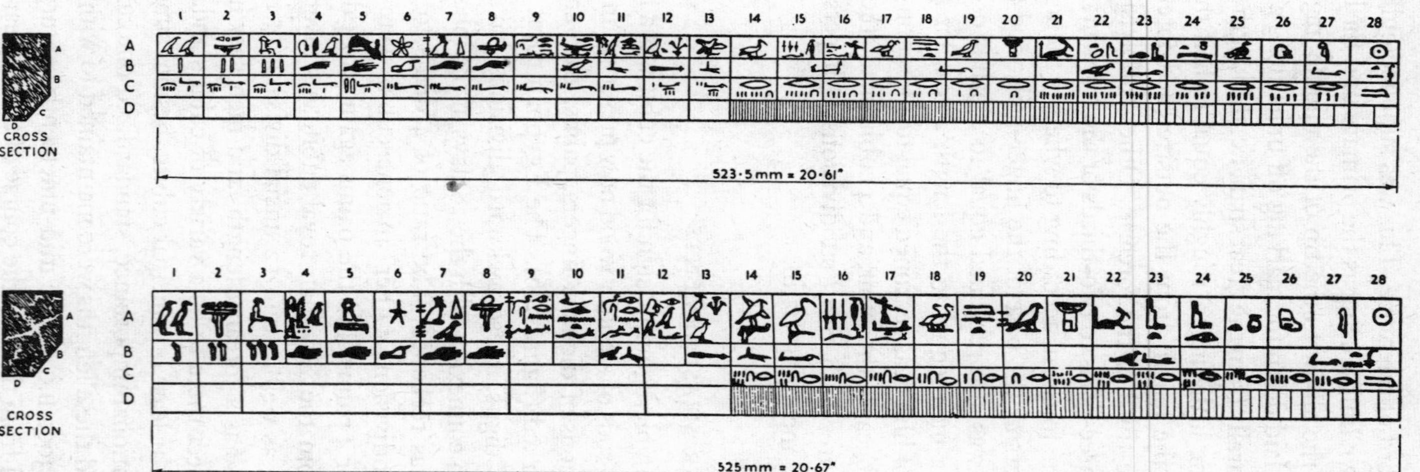

FIGURE 566—*Egyptian royal cubits of Amenhetep I* (above) *and of his vizier.* c *1550* B.C.

east to west across Europe, and later by trade, both overland and by sea through the Mediterranean.

The Egyptian royal cubit of 20·63″±0·2″ (524 mm±5 mm) was divided into 7 palms of 2·95″ (74·9 mm) and 28 digits of 0·74″ (18·7 mm). From this cubit was formed the double remen, the length of the diagonal of a square with sides equal to the royal cubit (p 111). Thus the double remen $= \sqrt{2} \times 20{\cdot}63'' = 29{\cdot}16''$ (740·7 mm). This was the basis of the ancient Egyptian land-measure; and by having the two systems, one the diagonal of the square on the other, it was possible to denote areas in squares equal to one-half, or twice, the area of another—the theorem of Pythagoras in an early form. The double remen was divided into 40 digits of 0·73″ (18·5 mm).

The Egyptian short cubit of 6 palms and 24 digits (17·68″ or 449 mm) was also the early Jewish cubit, at 17·60″ (447 mm). The common Greek foot of 12·45″ (316·25 mm), formed from $\frac{3}{5}$ of a cubit of 20·75″ (527 mm), is found at Athens as 12·44″ (316 mm); at Aegina as 12·40″ (315 mm); in Etruria as 12·45″ (316 mm); and in medieval England up to the twelfth century as 12·47″ (316·75 mm). In the medieval Germanic states, $\frac{3}{5}$ of a cubit of 20·60″ (523 mm) was taken as the Rhineland foot of 12·36″ (314 mm); this also became the unit of the Prussian system until metric measures were adopted throughout Germany.

Measures derived from the double remen 29·16″ (740·70 mm) and its digit 0·73″ (18·5 mm) were:

(*a*) the Greek Olympic cubit = 25 digits = 18·23″ (463 mm);

(*b*) the Greek Olympic foot = $\frac{2}{3}$ Greek Olympic cubit = 12·15″ (309 mm). This foot was not so common in Greece as the 12·45″ (316·25 mm) foot; it was itself divided into 16 digits of 0·76″ (19·5 mm). It was used for agriculture.

(*c*) The Roman foot = 16 digits = 11·66″ (296·25 mm); it was later slightly reduced. Two Roman bronze foot-measures in the British Museum are 292 mm (11·50″) and 294 mm (11·60″); each shows subdivisions of 16 digits, as well as 12 uncial divisions and 4 palms.

The Egyptian royal cubit and remen series of linear measures formed the general Mediterranean standard.

III. THE NORTHERN, THE SUMERIAN, AND THE ROYAL PERSIAN CUBITS

The Northern cubit, including its half or foot (the 'foot of Drusus', see below), is the most interesting of the known ancient standards of linear measurement, on account of its long history, its wide diffusion, and its remarkable tenacity wherever Teutonic peoples migrated. It can be traced in full use from about 3000 B.C. to the mid-nineteenth century A.D., since when it has been displaced almost completely by the metric system. Originating in the Orient, it was in use in ancient Egypt, north Africa, Syria, India, and China, and passed to central Europe, England, Scotland, and Ireland.

As a foot-unit it became the basis of one of the great systems of land measurement in Europe, while as a cubit it was particularly associated in Europe from the thirteenth to nineteenth centuries A.D. with woollen and cloth measures. The cubit had a median value of 26·6″ (676 mm), with a few extreme variations (generally in later times) from 26 to 27″ (660–686 mm). The most usual value for the foot, used independently, was 13·1 to 13·2″ (333–335 mm), with a few extreme variations up to 13·48″ (343 mm).

The Sumerian cubit, 19·5″ (495 mm) and its foot, $\frac{2}{3}$ of the cubit (13″ or 330 mm), was first found inscribed as a measure on the basalt statue of Gudea of Lagash, *c* 2300 B.C., now in the Louvre (figure 567). It was $\frac{3}{4}$ of the Northern cubit's lower limit, with the foot-measures of the two cubits nearly equal.

The Northern cubit and foot are found:

(*a*) 3000–100 B.C. As ancient independent measures (26·4 to 26·8″, or 671 to 681 mm) cut on wooden rods or stone slabs in Egypt, and (2500–1700 B.C.) in the pre-Aryan civilization of northern India.

(*b*) 1550–250 B.C. Specially marked on five ancient Egyptian wood and stone cubit-rods (now at Turin, Florence, Leiden, Alexandria, and Cairo) made as reference standards showing the Egyptian royal cubit of 20·63″ (524 mm) with its subdivisions, and also marking the lengths of a number of other known linear standards and noting them in hieroglyphic characters; the Northern foot was generally marked at or near the 18th Egyptian digit (18×0·737″ = 13·3″ = 338 mm).

(*c*) 12 B.C. As the standard for land-measurement among the Tungri in lower Germany, where the Northern foot was so firmly established that the Romans under Drusus (38 B.C.–9 B.C.), a very capable general and administrator, adopted it for use in Roman northern border-settlements outside Italy. Thus it became known as the Drusian foot. Its length is recorded as 2 *digiti* longer than the Roman foot of 16 *digiti* (11·65″+2×0·73″ = 13·12″, or 296 mm+2×18·5 mm = 333 mm).

(*d*) Seventh to thirteenth centuries A.D. As the rod or perch of 15 feet and furlong of 600 ft (the foot = 13·2″ or 335 mm), the basis of customary roods (quarter-acres) of the Middle Saxon kingdoms of England, for land-measurement. This rod later became the basis of the English statute acre, as defined in a statute of the realm in 1305, when also the English yard (then called an ulna) is first found properly defined, and equated as '$5\frac{1}{2}$ ulne make 1 perch' (or rod).

The royal Persian cubit was instituted by the Persian king Darius the Great (521–485 B.C.), whose dominions included Persia, Assyria, Babylonia, Asia Minor, Palestine, Egypt, and, in south-east Europe, Macedonia and Thrace. The metrology of this great empire was to have a lasting effect on that of later centuries.

The royal Persian cubit was derived from the addition of one-sixth to the older Assyrian cubit of 21·6″ (549 mm), which was divided into 6 palms of 3·6″ (91 mm). Thus 21·6″+3·6″ = 25·2″ (640 mm), as found by Oppert in 1842. Later, Flinders Petrie traced this cubit in ancient buildings in Persia as 25·34″ (643·5 mm), in Palestine as 25·28″ (642 mm), and as a reference-cubit cut on a masonry wall at Abydos in Egypt, of 25·13″ (638·5 mm).

In the Islamic empire, from the seventh century A.D., the royal Persian cubit became the Hashimi cubit, slightly increased in length to 25·56″ (649 mm). As such, it is traditionally the standard of linear measure which, together with a set of weights for Arabic gold coinage, was presented to the western emperor Charlemagne in A.D. 789 by the ambassador of the 'Abbasid Caliph Harun al-Rashid, the caliph of 'The Thousand and One Nights'.

IV. STANDARDS OF WEIGHT

Weights and balances were first used for weighing gold-dust and not, as might be supposed, for commercial transactions. The earliest commercial use of weighing was about 2500 B.C., in the pre-Aryan Indus civilization of northern India and perhaps to a limited extent in the Sumerian cities of Mesopotamia. In Egypt, all the early evidence shows commerce by barter only, the first indication of the use of the balance in ordinary trade being as late as 1350 B.C.

The earliest pictorial evidence of weighing in Egypt, dating back to the period of Dynasty V (about 2500 B.C.), shows the balance in use only by goldsmiths and jewellers, or for weighing gold ingots of one of the temple treasuries. So far, no evidence has been found anywhere of the use of weighing until there is also evidence that gold was in use. The oldest weights at present known are some limestone specimens that came, together with a small balance-beam also of limestone and of primitive design, from prehistoric graves at Naqada in Egypt (plate 31 B). Petrie, who collected thousands of specimens of ancient weights, found that they belong to a standard later known as the *beqa*, which has the longest history of any weight-standard, and has always been associated with the weighing of gold.

All weights until about 1450 B.C. were of stone, generally highly polished—a

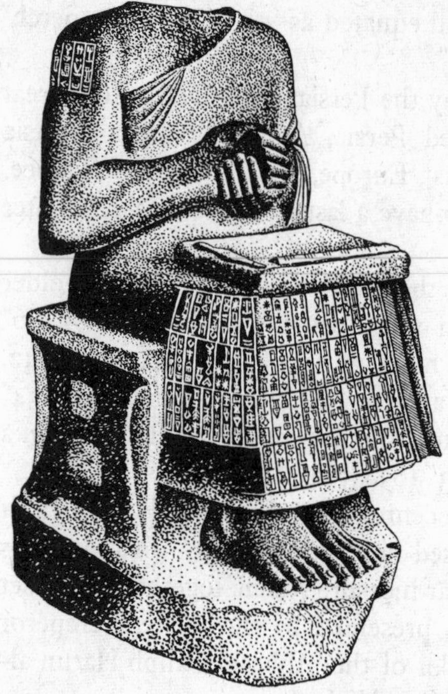

FIGURE 567—*Statue of Gudea, ruler of Lagash, bearing on his knee a tablet with a graduated rule. Mesopotamia. Third millennium B.C.*

fortunate circumstance since they do not deteriorate as do bronze weights. The various nations had weights of characteristic forms, e.g. the 'sleeping duck' of the Sumerians and Babylonians (figure 568), and the crouching lion of the Assyrians. The Indus people, and the earlier Egyptian dynasties down to 1500 B.C., had more utilitarian forms; they used mainly polished blocks of hard stone, cubical in northern India, and flat rectangular with rounded edges and corners in Egypt, where more artistic forms arose from 1450 B.C. onwards (figure 569).

Eight principal standards of weight were in use among the ancient civilizations of the Middle East; they are tabulated below. All these standards arose in the first instance from small units known generally as shekels, the standards of which varied from 120 grains (7·78 g) to 218 grains (14·13 g). The larger units which came later, known generally as minas, were 25, 50, or 60 shekels—except in Egypt, where decimal multiplication was used. Only small units were required in the earliest times, there being no commercial use for weighing. The heaviest later unit was the talent of 60 minas, the earliest specimen of which is a Sumerian weight of the 'sleeping duck' form, of dark grey basalt inscribed 'Ur-Nin-gir-su, two talents correct weight', i.e. 120 minas. It is of 2350 B.C., and weighs 1 cwt $21\frac{1}{2}$ lb, i.e. 60·55 kg.

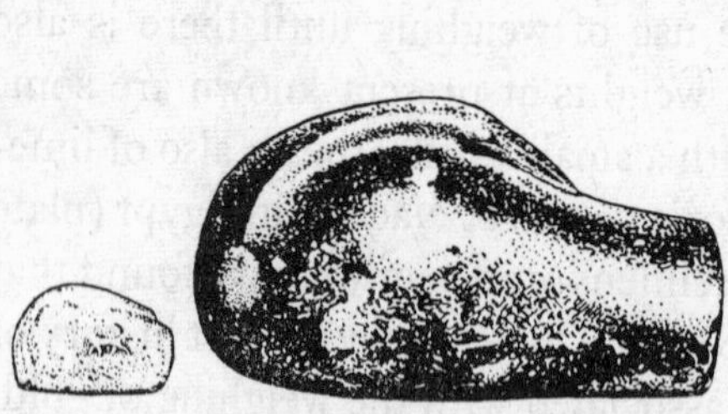

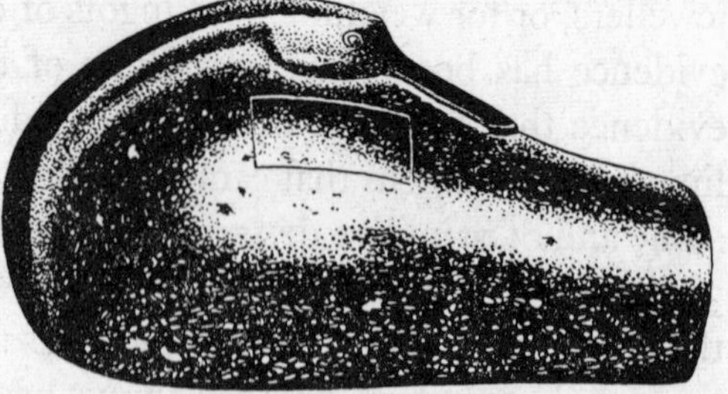

FIGURE 568—*Babylonian 'sleeping duck' weights. As a result of the conquest of Babylonia by Sargon II of Assyria (eighth century B.C.) the smallest weight has his lion mark inscribed on it. Scale c 1/7.*

THE PRINCIPAL ANCIENT STANDARDS OF WEIGHT OF THE MIDDLE EAST, 5000 B.C.–A.D. 1

(arranged in ascending value of units)

System	Unit Shekel			Mina		Origin
	Grains	Grams	Factor	Grains	Grams	
Peyem	120	7·78	×50	6000	389	Palestine (Israel).
Daric	129	8·36	×60	7740	502	Sumeria, Babylonia, Assyria.
Stater	135	8·75	×50	6750	437	Aryan, Achaean, and Babylonian.
Qedet	144	9·33	×100	14 400	933	Egyptian national standard.
Necef	160	10·37	×50	8000	518	Syrian.
Khoirine	178	11·53	×50	8900	577	Persian silver standard.
Beqa	200	12·96	×50	10 000	648	Egyptian gold standard.
Sela	218	14·13	×25	5450	353	Phoenician.

It should be noted that the terms shekel and mina were common to all the systems except the Egyptian *qedet*, where the terms were: *qedet* (unit) or *kedet*, *deben* (10 *qedet*), and *sep* (100 *qedet*).

All unit weights above are median[1] values, subject to ±5 per cent variation. In each system, this spread of 5 per cent on either side of the median was due to (*a*) limitations of the balance in use; (*b*) errors in copying; (*c*) the tendency to local sub-standards within each main standard, higher and lower than the median; (*d*) the time-factor of some 5000 years.

The *beqa*, *stater*, and *daric* systems have had the most far-reaching effect upon subsequent centuries. The *khoirine* and *sela* had a more limited, though long-lasting, effect. The *qedet* and *necef* have had little effect beyond Egypt and Syria, and the *peyem* none at all.

From 5000 to 1500 B.C. the sensitivity of balances ranged from 2 grains (0·13 g) with 100 grains (6·48 g) in each pan, to 30 grains (1·94 g) with 2000 grains (130 g) in each pan. From 1500 B.C. to the fourth century A.D., the sensitivity of the improved balance was: 1 grain (0·065 g) with 100 grains in each pan, and 5 grains (0·324 g) with 2000 grains in each pan.

V. MEASURES OF CAPACITY

(*a*) The Egyptian *hon* or *hin* was 29·1 cu in ± 2 cu in = 477 cc ± 33 cc = 0·84 imperial pint. The *hon* (plural, *hennu*) was divided binarily down to $\frac{1}{32}$, and there was also $\frac{1}{3}$ *hon* known as the *khay*—thirds being an Egyptian peculiarity occurring also in the subdivision of the *qedet*. The multiples of the *hon* were decimal,

[1] As used in this context, the median is a measure of central tendency in which individual values are given an arbitrary amount of emphasis according to their reliability. It is not to be taken in its usual statistical meaning.

as in the weight system: 10 *hennu* = 1 *hekat* = 291 cu in (about half-a-pint more than an imperial gallon) = 4·77 litres.

The weight of water contained in the *hon* was 50 *qedet* of 147 grains (9·5 g), the median value between the main standard of the *qedet* of 144 grains (9·3 g) and the sub-standard of 151 grains (9·8 g) that existed for Lower and Upper Egypt respectively during the period of Dynasties XVIII–XXV (1573–663 B.C.).

(*b*) The Syrian-Phoenician *kotyle* was 21·4 cu in ± 2 cu in = 350 cc ± 33 cc = 0·62 imperial pint. It was divided binarily, and 36 *kotyle* = 1 *saton* = 770 cu in = 2·78 gallons or 12·6 litres. The Syrian *kotyle*—the word appears to be Indo-European, not Semitic—was actually the commonest capacity-measure in Egypt, especially during the early part of Dynasty XVIII from Thothmes I to Amenhetep III (1539–1376 B.C.), owing partly to the conquest of Syria by Egypt, but mainly to trade in wine and olive-oil in return for Egyptian wheat, gold, and linen.

(*c*) The Syrian-Babylonian *log*, 33 cu in ± 2 cu in = 541 cc ± 33 cc = 0·95 imperial pint, was divided binarily down to ⅛ and had various multiples, the general scale being:

log	*log* × 4 = *kab* or *kapitha*	*kab* × 6 = *saton* or *seah* (24 *log*)	*saton* × 3 = *ephah* (72 *log*)
33 cu in	132 cu in	792 cu in	2376 cu in
541 cc	2·165 litre	12·99 litre	38·97 litre

The *log* was also used by the Phoenicians at a standard of 31 cu in (508 cc); by the Israelites and Judaeans at a standard of 32 cu in (525 cc); and by the Egyptians at about the Syrian-Babylonian standard, the inscribed copper *log* measure of Amenhetep III (1412–1376 B.C.) (figure 570) being 33·26 cu in (545 cc).

There were also various larger national capacities, e.g.:

Phoenician *kor*	= 720 *log*	= 22 320 cu in	= 10·05 imperial bushels or 365·8 litres.
Jewish *homer*	= ”	= 23 040 ”	= 10·4 imperial bushels or 378 litres.
Syro-Babylonian *homer*	= ”	= 23 760 ”	= 10·7 imperial bushels or 389·6 litres.
Babylonian *akhane*	= 4320 *log* or 6 *homer*	= 142 560 ”	= 64·25 imperial bushels or 2338 litres.

(*d*) The Persian *kapetis*, 74·5 cu in ± 1 cu in = 1221 cc ± 16·4 cc = 2·21 imperial pints, was divided binarily and had two main multiples: the *artaba* = 48 *kapetis* = 3576 cu in = 1·61 imperial bushels or 58·61 litres. The *akhane* = 1920

FIGURE 569—*Egyptian wooden balance from El-Amarna, with bronze animal and bird weights typical of this period.* c *1350* B.C. *Length of beam 30 cm.*

kapetis = 143 040 cu in = 64·40 imperial bushels or 2344 litres. (Cf Babylonian *akhane* = 142 560 cu in.) The value of the *kapeti* was obtained by Petrie from gauging Persian bronze bowls of the sixth century B.C. The modern Persian *artaba* is of no help, because, unlike the system of weights, measures of capacity have been very indifferently kept; but Herodotus (484–425 B.C.) records the proportions of the Syro-Babylonian *log* to the Persian *kapetis* as 4 : 9. With the *log* at 33 cu in (541 cc) this gives exactly 74·25 cu in (1217 cc), agreeing so closely with Petrie's value that the difference amounts to no more than a teaspoonful.

VI. CONNEXIONS BETWEEN THE ANCIENT STANDARDS OF LENGTH, WEIGHT, AND CAPACITY

There is no substantial basis for the general derivations of the ancient standards of mass from the weight of water contained in vessels made to the various standards of linear measure; or for a view that all ancient capacity-standards were based on their water-content weighed to the standards of mass (weight). If any such connexion existed in their origins, one would expect the basis to have been wheat instead of water, but of this also there is no proof. Such connexions did arise, but much later. Only in ancient China was there any original connexion between their standards, which were all based on red millet seed, but Chinese weights and measures were evolved independently and have had no evolutionary effects outside that area.

With the decline of the great ancient empires of the Middle East, their standards of weights and measures, which had already passed in the course of international trade to the Greeks and Romans, became the basis of new systems built up by these two rising nations. From the seventh century B.C. until the rise of the Islamic empire in the seventh century A.D., it was the Greek and Roman systems of metrology and coinage that formed the basis of all trade.

FIGURE 570—*Egyptian copper capacity measure of one Syrian–Babylonian* log. *Inscribed with the cartouche of Amenhetep III.* c *1400 B.C.*

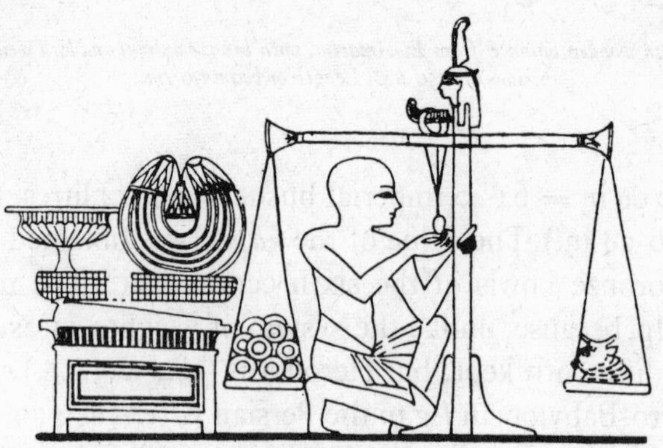

A jeweller's balance of Dynasty XVIII. From a tomb at Thebes. c *1350 B.C.*

31

ANCIENT MATHEMATICS AND ASTRONOMY

O. NEUGEBAUER

I. INTRODUCTION

THE development of the two leading civilizations of early antiquity, in Egypt and in Mesopotamia, shows many close parallels but also marked differences. In both regions the art of writing arose—whether independently or not is a moot question—around 3000 B.C., perhaps slightly earlier in Mesopotamia than in Egypt. In both regions, writing was based on the pictorial representation of ideas. This pictographic character of the script was never forgotten as long as the Egyptian language was written with its own hieroglyphics, but Mesopotamian scribes, writing on clay tablets, soon stylized their original signs to such a degree that no picture could be recognized. Furthermore, the position of the signs suffered a shift of 90°, thus changing from an arrangement in vertical columns to one in horizontal lines, written from left to right (figures 547–8). This process was undoubtedly accelerated by the shift of language from non-Semitic Sumerian to the Semitic dialects that prevailed in the subsequent Babylonian and Assyrian cultures.

Similar phenomena can be observed in the development of number-signs. Small numbers are denoted everywhere by a corresponding number of strokes, which appear as wedges on the clay tablets of Mesopotamia, arranged, when necessary, in easily recognizable groups. In both civilizations, new symbols are used for tens and for hundreds, and larger numbers are expressed in a fashion familiar to us from the Roman numerals. Some special fractions, like 'half' or 'quarter', are denoted by special characters (for example, + or ×); the rest are given names like 'the 5th part' or 'four out of five'. At an early stage, however, a new notation originated in Mesopotamia. In contrast to what happened in Egypt, the material civilization of Mesopotamia was far advanced when writing was invented. Economic life made rapid use of the new tool, and tens of thousands of tablets were inscribed in the administrative offices of large estates and governmental centres. A monetary system based on the weight of silver came into existence, and it so happened that the two major units, the shekel and the mina (to use the borrowed Biblical terms) had the convenient ratio of 1 to 60 (p 781).

Thus prices were expressed in a form according to which the lower units never exceeded 59, and a notation was developed which omitted the explicit mention of the single units. Exactly as £1. 10. 6 is today understood without further ado, so would 1,23 denote 1 mina 23 shekels (or 83 shekels).

For some time, the symbols for the higher numbers were written in larger size, but a uniform size for all symbols was finally adopted. The result was a place-value system based on the step 60. This system is still alive in our present reckoning of time, where 1.23 p.m. corresponds to the writing of the Old Babylonian period. The similarity would be still closer if we wrote I XXIII p.m., because cuneiform writing on clay tablets uses one wedge for the initial I (of 60 units) followed by two ten-wedges and three unit-wedges).[1] As a matter of convenience for the modern reader, however, we shall henceforth use the notation 1,23—which exactly follows the ancient principle, except that one must keep in mind that all the tens up to 50 are written by special signs.

This very convenient form of writing numbers soon expanded beyond the original monetary *milieu* to apply to numbers in general. It is now called the sexagesimal system. This name lays undue weight on the ratio 1:60 of the fundamental step, ignoring the most essential feature, namely, the fact that the position of a number-symbol, its place, determines its value such that 1,23 and 23,1 represent totally different numbers: 83 and 1381 units, respectively. This second feature, too, is in use today, not only in its original form in our reckoning of time and our measurement of degrees but, in a modified form, in our ordinary numbers. In distinguishing 83 from 38 we use the same place-value principle, substituting the basic step 10 for the Babylonian step of 60. This modification has a long history, which is connected with the transmission of late Babylonian astronomy to the Greeks and thence to the Hindus. It took many innovations, some accidental, some conscious, to transform the 'natural' method of recording numbers by marks to the 'simple' decimal system of our day.

Before describing the earlier phases of this process in greater detail, a few general remarks must be made. We shall often have occasion to refer to the different periods to which our source-material belongs. Such statements cannot be properly demonstrated within a short article. Considerations of sign-forms, language, and archaeological evidence constitute the often very complex basis for our datings. We must also underline the frequently accidental character of our knowledge. Babylonian mathematics, for instance, is known to us only from tablets written between 1800 to 1500 B.C., and between 300 B.C. and the beginning

[1] For the actual appearance of these numerals see plate 34 and compare it with the transcription on the opposite page.

of our era. We have no possibility of following its initial development, nor do we know in what form Mesopotamian science was made available to Greek scientists in Hellenistic and Roman Egypt. The survival of the documents of early history is largely a matter of chance, and much of the primary material is irrevocably destroyed or inaccessibly buried under tons of ruins, or lies still unexplored in the basements of museums.

II. BABYLONIAN MATHEMATICS

Our present knowledge of Babylonian mathematics is based on several hundred tablets and fragments of tablets found in the ruins of cities situated in the southern part of Iraq, and in Susa across the Persian border. The vast majority of the tablets were written in the Old Babylonian period (about 1800 to 1500 B.C.); the remainder belong to the period of Greek and Parthian rule over Mesopotamia after 300 B.C. The extant material suffices to establish the continuity of tradition through this millennium and a half.

These texts can be classified into two major groups: table texts and problem texts. There can be little doubt that the table texts answered practical needs. Many of them contain lists of measures used for the conversion of larger units to smaller, and *vice versa*. Another group comprises tables for multiplication or division, based on the sexagesimal system. Many of these table texts were written in scribal schools, for we have not only tablets which repeat tables written in different hands, but tablets which, in addition to tables, contain word-lists and sign-lists to be memorized by the professional scribes.

It must be emphasized, however, that practical needs alone do not suffice as an explanation for the contents of these table texts. In addition to the simple tables for measures, multiplication, and division, we find also tables for squares and cubes (or square roots and cube roots), tables for the sums of squares and cubes, tables of a^n and its inverse, and so on. The explanation for the use of this class of tables is found in the second major category of mathematical texts, the problem texts, which we will now describe.

Problem texts are tablets which contain mathematical exercises, with or without an indication of their solution. Most of these problems would today be called elementary algebra. This can best be illustrated by quoting one example, inscribed as one of eight problems on a clay prism of the Old Babylonian period. The text begins as follows:

'Length and width. I multiplied length and width and thus formed an area. Furthermore, I added the excess of the length over the width to the area, the result being

3,3 [= 183]. Finally, the sum of length and width is 27. What are the length, the width, and the area?'

Using modern symbols, and denoting the length by x and the width by y, we have here the problem of determining x and y from

$$\begin{aligned} xy+x-y &= 3{,}3 \\ x+y &= 27 \end{aligned}$$

The text proceeds to give, step by step, the procedure for solving this problem. Describing it in modern symbols, we can say that the first step consists in introducing $y' = y+2$ as an auxiliary unknown quantity, obviously because we then obtain two simpler equations, namely,

$$\begin{aligned} xy' &= 3{,}30 \\ x+y' &= 29. \end{aligned}$$

This is the standard type of quadratic equation in Babylonian mathematics: the product and the sum (or difference) of the unknowns are given. From this, the solution follows directly as

$$\begin{aligned} x &= \tfrac{1}{2}29+\surd(\tfrac{1}{4}29^2-3{,}30) = 15 \\ y' &= \tfrac{1}{2}29-\surd(\tfrac{1}{4}29^2-3{,}30) = 14 \end{aligned}$$

and thus $y = 12$. As a check, the text adds:

$$xy+x-y = 3{,}0+3 = 3{,}3$$

which shows that the initial condition has been satisfied.

This example is in many ways typical. It not only illustrates complete mastery in solving quadratic equations, but demonstrates that the geometrical formulation is only a convenient form of expression; calling xy an 'area' corresponds exactly to our calling n times n 'n-squared'. Obviously, no geometrical interpretation is connected with $xy+x-y$, nor is the method of solution anywhere motivated by geometric construction.

This purely algebraic character of the majority of the Old Babylonian mathematical problems can be demonstrated in many ways. Similar quadratic equations can be formed with the number of workmen and their wages as unknown quantities. Equations were formed whose algebraic equivalents are equations of order 4, 6, or 8 in the special case where x^2 or x^3 or the square of x^2 satisfies a quadratic equation. Everywhere the trick of the solving-process consists in a proper reduction to a quadratic equation of the above-mentioned fundamental type:

$$xy = a \qquad x \pm y = b$$

which can easily be reduced to a pair of two linear equations:

$$x+y = c$$
$$x-y = d$$

from which follows the general formula whose application in a numerical example we have quoted above.

The solution of algebraic equations—linear, quadratic, or reducible to quadratic—was evidently the central goal of Babylonian mathematical education. Plate 33 shows a tablet which contains a collection of nearly 200 examples inscribed on a surface measuring about 5 by 6 in. We know that at least 14 such tablets formed a connected set of problems, all purely algebraic in character despite a generally geometric terminology. This type of terminology, however, is by no means the absolute rule. We know, for instance, of examples in which a ratio takes the place of an unknown quantity such as length or width. Similarly, there are numerous problems concerned with numbers of men or the weights of precious stones, etc.

It would be wrong to assume, however, that only algebraic procedures were considered legitimate means for solving equations. The tables for n^2+n^3 mentioned above (p 787) were computed in order to solve cubic equations of the form $x^2+x^3 = a$. Indeed, if we have a table for n^2+n^3 we need only look for the occurrence of the given value a. If a itself does not happen to occur in the table, interpolation between the nearest values b and c ($b < a < c$) will give at least an approximate solution. Numerical methods were undoubtedly fully permissible for the solution of problems whenever a general algebraic procedure was not at hand.

Purely geometrical relations were also fully understood. We find many quadratic equations which concern the division of a field shaped like a trapezoid into subsections which must satisfy certain conditions. The procedure followed in the solution reveals the use of such geometric relations as the similarity between triangles with parallel sides, the Pythagorean theorem for the sides of a right triangle, and the triangle inscribed in a semicircle.

Here too we find the same flexibility of methods. If possible, geometric problems were solved algebraically. On the other hand, very accurate numerical approximations were used when the application of the Pythagorean theorem led to square roots like $\sqrt{2}$ or $\sqrt{3}$. In many cases a crude approximation, like 3 for π, sufficed for a numerical example. In other cases, $\pi \approx 3\frac{1}{8}$ had to be used.

Elementary volumes were determined either accurately or approximately. A great variety of linear, area, and capacity measures forced the ancient pupil to face the same difficulties which theoretical physicists experience when confronted with the jungle of engineering units. But, apart from such practical problems, we find purely geometric investigations, such as the determination of the areas of regular polygons or patterns of polygons, circles, and circle segments.

A large group of problems is taken from, if not directly concerned with, practical engineering. Huge irrigation systems played a vital part in Mesopotamian economic life (ch 19). Consequently we find many texts concerned with the requirements for the construction and maintenance of irrigation canals. We learn about different work-quotas per man for light work on the surface of canals, and for digging in deeper and deeper levels. The food requirements, primarily barley, of the workers had to be calculated. We learn about the transport and manufacture of bricks. No less than seven standard types of bricks are mentioned in mathematical texts. The man-power necessary to complete dams, wells (circular or prismatic), and foundations of buildings in a given time, the volume of earth to be removed, the bricks needed, etc., had to be computed.

We can also see that, even in Old Babylonian scribal schools, there was no protection against educational artificiality which fancies it is making simple geometrical problems more appealing by using practical examples containing unreal assumptions. Thus we read of a city surrounded by a circular wall having a trapezoidal cross section. Another problem concerns the area to be inundated with water from a cistern of a given volume; the solution shows that a square of about three miles wide would be covered to a depth of one finger-breadth. It is consoling to see from a very old text [1] that a teacher, to gain 'a seat of honour' at the table in his pupil's home, as well as substantial gifts, was willing to promote his much 'caned' pupil to be 'the leader of his brothers, their chief, and to let him rank highest among all schoolboys'.

In view of the highly developed economic life of ancient Mesopotamia it is not surprising to find mathematical texts concerned with weaving, with sheep, with grain measures, and with the value of silver and precious stones. One example mentions, for instance, a mixture of gold and copper in a vessel in the ratio 1:9. Additional conditions about the weights lead to two linear equations for the determination of the weight of the single substances.

Undoubtedly of real practical interest are many problems of inheritance-division among 'brothers' according to given ratios, a type of question which was later to be popular in Islamic mathematics. Here also we find the use of the tables mentioned above for an exponential function (p 787) and its inverse. We know that compound interest was computed exactly as it is in schools today. The rate of interest fortunately no longer follows Mesopotamian standards, which required one-fifth as annual interest, the business year being counted as twelve months of 30 days each. This high rate doubtless reflected the high risk encountered in an economic system which depended to a large degree on the vicissitudes of a river system surrounded by desert.

Despite the sparsity of the sources so rapidly reviewed, it will be clear that these texts reveal a great deal about one of the most important civilizations of early antiquity. Here the tools of mathematical procedures were successfully formed for the first time, foremost of all being numerical methods which were fully adequate for computation on any scale required. General rules of procedure, whose generality was fully understood, were built up, although couched in the form of numerical examples. Economic life and practical needs undoubtedly were a great stimulus in this development. We can, however, be equally sure that a pure mathematical interest existed when we come across algebraic problems of the fourth or sixth degree, formulae for the areas of regular polygons, or the formation of Pythagorean triplets of integers which satisfy the relation

$$a^2+b^2 = c^2$$

of which we need quote only one example from one of our earliest texts:

$$57{,}36^2+56{,}7^2 = 1{,}20{,}25^2$$

whose decimal equivalent is

$$3456^2+3367^2 = 4825^2.$$

III. EGYPTIAN MATHEMATICS

Very little need be said about Egyptian mathematics. Its interest for the history of civilization lies in the fact that it provides a test case for the impossibility of predicting historical developments. In spite of closely similar conditions in Egypt and Mesopotamia, the level of mathematical achievement was totally different in the two countries.

However, to a certain extent there does exist a parallelism with regard to the content of some of the problems. In both countries, areas of triangular, rectangular, and trapezoidal fields were computed. In Egypt, as in Mesopotamia, the curse of a great variety of measures of area and capacity made things more complicated than was necessary. A computation of the amount of material required to fill the inner core of a ramp illustrates the scope of practical geometry in early

Egypt. The ramp was needed for transporting stones up to the higher levels of a pyramid under construction. The slope of the planes of hewn stones was denoted by a special term, and the volume of a truncated pyramid was determined correctly.

The largest part of our sources is devoted to problems dealing with bread and beer rather than to geometrical problems. From a certain amount of grain a certain number of loaves of bread can be baked, or a certain number of jars of beer brewed. This equivalence is at the basis of a great variety of examples, however trivial their mathematical contents may be. The significance of these problems in daily life is known to us from economic texts which record the delivery of beer of different strengths to temple staffs and workers (p 279).

It would be deceptive, however, to leave the reader with this enumeration of subjects which, though much less numerous than their Babylonian counterparts, are nevertheless comparable in scope. The profound difference between the two regions becomes evident only if one examines the numerical execution of these problems. The best the Egyptians could perform in algebraical problems were of the type 'If a scribe says to you: "10 is two-thirds and one-tenth of what?"—let him hear . . .', followed by a long computation with unit fractions arranged in steps of successive duplications. This procedure was typical of all Egyptian computation. Multiplication was reduced to a series of duplications, e.g. a factor 13 would be replaced by the sum of the partial products with 1, 4, and 8. Fractions occurred only as unit fractions, such that, for example, twice one-fifth would appear as $\frac{1}{3}$ and $\frac{1}{15}$. The Egyptian methods of operating with unit fractions can still be found in the economic papyri of the Greco-Roman period, and even in Latin writings on surveying. These methods originated, however, in very early periods when the handling of fractions appeared to be a real problem. Some symbols for fractional units, such as those for 'half', 'third', and 'two-thirds', are found in the earliest hieroglyphic writings. When expanding economic life made it necessary to carry out more complex computations, attempts were made to express the repetition of fractions, as they would necessarily occur in the course of a multiplication, as the result of 'natural fractions' of fractions. The 'natural fractions' are the well known common fractions which are even distinguished in language (for example, our 'half' or 'quarter' instead of '2th', '4th'). Thus the double of one-fifth is expressed as a third of a fifth (that is, $\frac{1}{15}$) plus one and two-thirds of a fifth (that is, $\frac{1}{3}$). In similar fashion a long list of equivalent expressions for the double of unit fractions was composed, and had constantly to be used in operations with fractions.

Here is the point where the difference in procedure was most marked. A

Babylonian scribe would replace $\frac{1}{5}$ by its sexagesimal equivalent 12, because $\frac{1}{5}$ of one unit is 12 of the next lower units (just as 12 minutes are $\frac{1}{5}$ of one degree). Thus it is obvious that $\frac{2}{5}$ of the larger unit is the same as twice 12 of the smaller, and multiplication by a fraction does not require techniques different from those used in ordinary multiplication. We can now see the enormous advantage of the Babylonian place-value notation over the 'natural' but exceedingly clumsy procedure of the Egyptians. It cannot be doubted that this advantage made possible the high development of Babylonian mathematics (and, a millennium later, of astronomy). Egyptian engineering achievements—such as the construction of the pyramids, the erection of enormous monolithic obelisks, and the construction of temple walls and ceilings—by far surpassed Mesopotamian technology. However primitive or advanced, no ancient or medieval mathematician could solve the problems of statics or strength of materials; such problems were settled empirically by the ancient architects. Questions of food-supply or transport of material could be answered by simple arithmetic, whether it involved a mere glance at a table or slow figuring on a papyrus or potsherd. The really remarkable feature lies in the fact that the Mesopotamian scribal schools developed a general background of intellectual interest such that they were conscious of purely mathematical difficulties and successfully solved them. After these mathematical tools had been fashioned, many centuries were to elapse before they were used for the solution of astronomical problems in the last three centuries before our era. And for more than a millennium thereafter, theoretical astronomy remained the only field in which the power of mathematical methods for the understanding and description of natural phenomena was utilized. It was astronomy that shaped the problems which found their final solution in Newton's *Principia*, the starting-point of modern science.

IV. PRE-SCIENTIFIC ASTRONOMY

The naming of streams and rivers and the worshipping of storm-gods is not the beginning of hydrodynamics. Similarly, astronomy does not originate with the recognition of irregular configurations of stars or the invention of celestial or astral deities. Scientific astronomy does not begin until an attempt is made to predict, however crudely, astronomical phenomena such as the phases of the Moon.

A preliminary step in the direction of actual prediction can be found in the creation of a calendar, though one must realize that none of the early calendars makes any attempt to predict lunar or solar phenomena for any great length of time (ch 5). Both Egypt and Mesopotamia originally had strictly lunar calendars;

that is to say, the beginning of a new month was determined by the actual observation of the waning or waxing Moon. In Egypt, a lunar month began with the morning of invisibility of the waning Moon, in Mesopotamia with the evening of the reappearing crescent. Consequently, calendarial days began in Egypt with sunrise, in Mesopotamia with sunset. These lunar months had a length of either 29 or 30 days, but the succession of 'hollow' and 'full' months depends, in a very complicated fashion, on solar and lunar motion. It was not before about 300 B.C. that Babylonian astronomers succeeded in predicting the lengths of lunar months. Until then, either actual observation or a crude scheme determined the distribution of hollow and full months. This state of affairs prevailed in Egypt to the latest (Roman) period of its history as an independent civilization.

Many religious festivals were by their nature associated with the phases of the Moon and therefore fixed in the lunar calendar, which thus acquired a deeper significance. The time of our Easter holiday, which is related to the time of the new Moon, is a witness to this fact. Economic life, however, could not operate effectively with months whose exact length it was impossible to foresee for even a relatively short interval of time. Thus both in Egypt and in Mesopotamia civil months of fixed length, 30 days, were used whenever economic estimates or agreements had to be made. We have seen (p 791) that the computation of interest in Old Babylonian mathematical texts was based on these civil months, and on a business year of 12 times 30 days. This is confirmed by economic texts, whose terms have to be interpreted not in actual lunar months, but in the simpler scheme of formal months.

Another element supported this tendency. The strongly agricultural character of both civilizations emphasized the importance of the seasons of the solar year. Consequently it was natural to try to associate the lunar months in a more or less fixed fashion with the agricultural seasons. A month called 'barley-harvest' could not be permitted to stray far from the proper time of the year. This necessity was satisfied in Babylonia by adding, whenever needed, an intercalary 13th lunar month to the 12 regular months. For many centuries, these intercalations were handled in a purely arbitrary manner whenever deemed necessary in view of the actual agricultural situation. Cities only a few miles apart could decree different intercalations, and it was solely as a result of the centralizing political pressure that local variations tended to disappear in the course of history. In Egypt, unification of the country was achieved earlier and to a higher degree than in Mesopotamia. Thus the civil calendar of 12 civil months of 30 days each was universally used in Egypt at an early date, despite the co-existence of a religious lunar calendar based on actual observation. The country was completely dependent upon the inundation by the Nile, with its annual deposit of fertile silt. There exist early records of annual flood-levels, marked on specially constructed nilometers in wells connected with the river. A few years or decades of noting these data must have shown that the calendar of 12 civil months fell short of recording the sequence of inundations correctly, however large the fluctuations of their individual dates may have been. It turned out that 5 additional days appeared to be the proper correction for keeping in step with this all-important phenomenon of the flood. This 'Nile year' of $(12\times30)+5$ days remained the civil year of Egypt throughout its history, even though it became obvious after the passing of a few centuries that the Nile no longer accurately followed this simple scheme. But, being so convenient in practical use, it was by that time a well established convention. The resulting shift in seasons was so slow that it was not perceivable in the span of a man's life. Today we call it a 'wandering' year, because it moves through all the seasons in 1460 years. Its constant length, however, was not merely of administrative advantage: it became the ideal year for astronomical computations, and was used as such from Ptolemy to Copernicus.

It was only through a small difference in emphasis that the development in Babylonia proceeded in a totally different direction. In spite of the existence of schematic months and years, the real lunar calendar remained the calendar of daily life. The Assyrians for centuries did not even try to intercalate an occasional thirteenth month, but used a lunar year of twelve lunar months only—a method of time-reckoning which, again, is used by Islamic nations up to the present day. But the Babylonian practice of intercalation produced finally—probably around 380 B.C.—a step of great consequence, namely the invention of a fixed intercalation rule consisting of a 'cycle' of 19 years, 7 of which contained 13 months, the rest 12. Because in 432 B.C. the same cycle was proposed by Meton in Athens and was officially adopted there (though never put into actual use), this cycle is now known as the Metonic cycle. It remained the most important cycle in the calendars of the Near East in antiquity and the Middle Ages, because of its relation to the computation of the date of Easter.

It is not its practical use which makes the Babylonian cyclical regulation of a lunar calendar a step of great importance, but rather a shift in emphasis from mere observation to systematic prediction of lunar phenomena. The invention of periodic cycles proved to be the corner-stone in the development of theoretical astronomy. It was the first step towards astronomy proper.

Before describing this latest phase of Babylonian science, we must complete our discussion of the pre-scientific phase by mentioning some other features of early time-reckoning.

As we have seen, the Egyptian civil year was originally an agricultural year, based on schematic lunar months and on the periodic recurrence of the inundation of the Nile. But we also know that all primitive civilizations recognized the fact that different constellations are visible at different seasons of the year. Greeks and Romans as well as Egyptians and Babylonians related their agricultural work to the first appearance of conspicuous stars or groups of stars in the region of the Sun after they had been invisible for a time. These heliacal risings of stars were found to be reliable guides for the proper time of sowing, etc. In Egypt, the rise of the Nile coincided with the reappearance of the brightest fixed star, Sirius, which thus became 'the bringer of the Nile' and the harbinger of the agricultural seasons.

The appearances of other stars were similarly associated with the civil calendar. In the Mesopotamian lunar calendar, the intercalations prevented the months from deviating too far from their proper season. One could therefore schematically associate the months with the risings of stars, and rules of this type are actually preserved in early calendarial texts. Furthermore, in Egypt the well established civil calendar permitted the association of constellations with the 10-day intervals, or 'decades', three of which formed a civil month. If a certain star, e.g. Sirius, appeared in the morning just before sunrise at the beginning of the first decade, it would rise at the beginning of the next decade about 40 minutes earlier. By that time, another star would appear just before sunrise and thus mark the end of night. At intervals of ten days this process was repeated, so that each decade came to be represented by some specific star. The intervals elapsing between the risings of these stars during one night were called *wnwt*, a term conventionally translated as 'hours'. The stars themselves were called 'decans', to use the Greek term. The consecutive risings of the decans were used by about 2500 B.C. as a star-clock to indicate the 'hours of night'. Approximately twelve of these decans covered the interval of darkness between dusk and dawn.

In Egyptian belief there existed a strict symmetry between our world and the nether world, where the Sun shines after it has set for us; thus the 12 hours of the night of the nether world ought to correspond to 12 hours of daylight for us. In this way the division of the day into 24 hours evidently originated in Egypt. When Egypt became part of the Hellenistic (and, later, of the Roman) Empire, this division was maintained as 'seasonal hours', 12 from sunset to sunrise, 12 from sunrise to sunset. When Babylonian astronomy finally reached Egypt, the sexagesimal division of the Babylonian units was combined with the Egyptian 24-hour system. For astronomical purposes, 'hours' of equal length called 'equinoctial hours' were used, because only at the equinoxes are the 12 hours of night of the same length as the 12 hours of day. These equinoctial hours and their sexagesimal minutes and seconds were kept in use during the Middle Ages for theoretical astronomy, especially by Islamic scholars. After the invention of mechanical clocks they eventually became our fundamental units of time-reckoning. Thus we are using today the end-product of a Hellenistic combination of primitive Egyptian star-clocks with Babylonian numerical methods.

Babylonian astronomers never used these hours. In their own computations the day was divided into six parts which were in turn divided sexagesimally. The six-division itself was originally based on terrestrial distance-measurements, which were transferred to the sky in such a way that a whole circle contained six parts. In modern terminology, this is the division of the circle into degrees which still survives, both as degrees and in the time-measurements of the astronomers known as right-ascension.

Time-reckoning by decans did not remain the only one in Egypt. It was in fact replaced after some centuries by an improved method of observing transits of stars, which entailed looking in a general north-south direction at a sitting person, the upper part of whose body (centre of head, ears, and shoulders) served as a system of reference. By this time, water-clocks also were used; but, here too, poor accuracy was achieved, as preserved samples demonstrate. During the day, simple shadow-clocks permitted a similarly rough estimate of the passage of time (figures 44–5, 48). Equally crude devices existed in Babylonia. Nowhere is there evidence of high observational accuracy—a favourite misconception found in many modern books on the history of science. Accuracy in the modern sense of the word enters astronomy no earlier than the application of mathematical methods, that is, not before about 300 B.C.

In Egypt this step was never reached, and one can understand why this was so by remembering how very primitive were the Egyptian mathematical tools. In one point, nevertheless, the Egyptians almost came to grips with a theoretical problem. The co-existence of a religious lunar calendar with the 365-day civil year in Egypt called for some concordance between the two systems. Some years, the 'small' years, contained 12 lunar months; others, the 'great' ones, contained 13. It was found that after 25 civil years the same pattern was repeated, such that 9 'great' years occurred in this interval. This rule was cast into the form of a simple scheme, which is preserved in an Egyptian papyrus written in the period of the Roman Empire but undoubtedly based on older sources. This text, known as Papyrus Carlsberg 9, is reproduced as plate 36. It simply lists the $(12\times 25)+9$, i.e. 309, months in an even distribution over the dates of the civil calendar. This 25-year-cycle was well known to Greek astronomers—Ptolemy in A.D. 150 for instance—and was used as a convenient basis for the tabulation of lunar phenomena, computed in Egyptian years. Thus Egyptian astronomy ends at the same point, the invention of a cycle, at which Babylonian astronomy began its development toward a real scientific approach.

V. BABYLONIAN ASTRONOMY

The texts from which we gather our knowledge of Old Babylonian mathematics do not vouchsafe us any glimpses into its prehistory. In the oldest available sources, Babylonian mathematics stands before us like an adult who has no memory of his childhood. Perhaps we must assume a long prehistory; perhaps—and this seems more likely—a relatively short period sufficed to develop the basic ideas and to draw consequences. We face the same situation once more in the third century B.C. Several hundred astronomical tables and fragments of treatises are preserved, densely covering the period from about 240 B.C. to 40 B.C. These texts reflect a highly theoretical level without any reference to preliminary stages. Whatever prehistory we reconstruct is therefore of a very conjectural character.

Nevertheless, at least two major steps must be reconstructed in order to make the mere existence of the texts intelligible. The first consists in the empirical establishment of relations between the important periodic phenomena of the type of the 19-year cycle, which is based on the fact that 19 solar years contain $(19\times 12)+7$, i.e. 235 lunar months. Similar rules must have been abstracted for the finer details of lunar and solar motion from the counting and comparison of lunar eclipses. The number of appearances and disappearances of the planets within fixed periods of years also had to be determined. The centuries, let us say, between 500 B.C. and 300 B.C. might have been needed to establish these facts with the rather high degree of accuracy in which they are utilized in the extant texts.

The second prerequisite is the establishment of a definite system of reference on the celestial sphere. The ancient method of referring lunar or planetary positions to nearby stars in known constellations is not only inaccurate but cannot be used for numerical computation. It is therefore a step of far-reaching significance that the apparent orbit of the Sun in its yearly course through the fixed stars, the ecliptic, was introduced as an ideal line of reference for all lunar and planetary motion. Any attempt to explain the historical details of this step must remain mere speculation, in the present state of our information, but the time when it happened can again be estimated as around 500 B.C.—perhaps even somewhat later.

More clear to us are the motivating forces of this whole development. From our texts it is evident that the lunar theory was developed to a much higher level of refinement than the theory of the planets. It is furthermore clear that it was the goal of the lunar theory to determine in advance the length of the lunar month, that is, to be able to establish ahead of time whether the new crescent would be visible after 29 or after 30 days, counting from the previous reappearance. Thus it is the accurate theory of the lunar calendar that forms the nucleus of the new theory. Hence it is scarcely accidental that at the beginning of this new epoch of Babylonian science the invention of the 19-year lunisolar cycle appears.

The problems answered in the planetary texts are closely related to the problem of the visibility of the new crescent. Exactly as the Moon remains invisible when too close to conjunction with the Sun, so do the planets disappear for a time in the rays of the Sun. To predict last and first visibility of the planets forms an essential problem in the Babylonian theory. With the development of methods to compute dates and positions for these phenomena, other problems, such as the prediction of lunar eclipses and the determination of planetary retrogradations, were almost automatically solved. We shall now present a short, and of necessity very simplified, description of the methods used in this earliest, truly remarkable, mathematical theory of astronomical appearances.

To begin with, the reader must realize that when we speak about lunar or planetary 'theory' we refer only to strictly numerical methods of predicting dates and positions of the phenomena in question. We have no indication of the underlying ideas concerning the mechanism which was thought to bring about these phenomena: we merely have hundreds of thousands of numbers, written in strictly sexagesimal notation, and some often fragmentary rules telling how to compute them. We can be fairly certain that it is not the incompleteness of our source-material which prevents us from knowing the physical assumption upon which the theory is based. A careful analysis of the assumptions which must be made in order to compute our texts shows nowhere the need for specific mechanical concepts such as are familiar to us from the Greek theory of eccentrics or epicycles, or from the corresponding planetary models of Tycho Brahe or Kepler. All that we need to know is the fundamental relation between periods, and the rate of change and amplitudes of the observable motions. Numerical data are given, and numerical results are desired. At no point can we detect the introduction of an hypothesis of a general character. This is an attitude which is so strikingly modern that it would have appeared rather strange to scientists of the past century.

The arithmetical methods employed in Babylonian astronomy are best illustrated by an example. Plate 34 shows the original text, in which the arrangement of numbers in parallel columns is clearly visible. Plate 35 offers the transcription of the same text, restored numbers being enclosed in square brackets. We are interested only in the first four columns, the remaining columns being merely a continuation which follows the same scheme. Column I gives the days: line 12 represents the last, 29th, day of month XI; line 13 gives the first day of month XII, called 'barley [-harvest]'. Thus we are dealing here with the day-by-day motion of a planet, which can be shown to be Jupiter. The second column contains numbers increasing by 6, as is easily recognizable; e.g., reading from line 5 downwards, 8 (that is 8,0) is followed by 8,6 8,12 8,18, etc. The first units are seconds of arc, the second ones are sixtieths of seconds. The numbers in the third column decrease by the amount indicated in the second column, as is seen, for example, in lines 4 and 5: 7,16,0 is 8,0 seconds smaller than 7,24,0, the first unit being minutes of arc. Similarly, in lines 5 and 6, 7,7,54 minutes is 8,6 seconds smaller than 7,16,0, etc. Column III represents the velocity of Jupiter measured in minutes and fractions of minutes per day. Column IV gives the place of Jupiter in the zodiac. In line 5 we find 13,25,44,0 where 13 is the number of degrees, 25 the minutes, etc. From line 6 in column III we know that at that time (month XI, day 23) the daily velocity was 7,7,54 minutes. Thus the next position will be 13,25,44,0+7,7,54 = 13,32,51,54 as is indicated in line 6. Now the whole scheme can be described very simply: column I gives the dates, column III the velocity, column II the acceleration (which is negative in this case), and column IV the corresponding positions of the planet.

It is essentially this procedure which we find employed everywhere in Babylonian astronomy. In the lunar tables the motions of the Sun and Moon are tabulated in this fashion. The variable velocity is assumed to increase linearly up to a certain maximum, and then to decrease at the same rate until the proper minimum is reached. We may call such numerical sequences linear zigzag functions. Similar sequences are used to tabulate the periodic variations in the Moon's distance from the ecliptic, the so-called latitude. Only when the latitude is very small, that is to say, when the Moon is in or close to the ecliptic, are eclipses possible. From the velocities can be found the moments and places when Sun and Moon are seen in the same or opposite direction from the earth, that is, the new and full Moons. The moments of first visibility require additional columns which take into account the variable inclination of the ecliptic to the horizon. The combination of all these columns, between ten and twenty in number, answers the question when the Moon will again be visible after conjunction, or, in other words, when the new lunar month will begin.

The planetary theory is much less elaborate, but it uses one new idea. Instead of an attempt at the direct prediction of the positions of a planet day by day, all the moments and positions of one typical phenomenon are computed, e.g. the first appearance of a planet or the moment when it apparently stands still before reversing the direction of its motion. Each such phenomenon is treated separately from year to year. After such positions have been found, the intermediate positions are determined by interpolation. The table discussed above (p 800) gives the results of interpolations of this sort, describing the motion of Jupiter from the previously found moment of appearance to the stationary point, the position of which has also been found previously. This illustrates our statement that the motion is determined by means of arithmetical methods, namely, proper interpolations, without reference to mechanical concepts about the actual motion in space.

These few remarks will suffice to give the reader an impression of the predominantly mathematical character of late Babylonian astronomy. Detailed investigation confirms this impression everywhere. As an example, it may be mentioned that the computation of eclipses is based on tables which give eclipse magnitudes from month to month, despite the fact that eclipses can occur only at intervals of not less than 5 (ordinarily 6) months. But it is mathematically more convenient to introduce negative eclipse magnitudes for the intermediate months, such that the occasional shift to positive values indicates the possibility of a real eclipse. Similarly, invisible as well as visible 'appearances' of Mercury were computed, because greater consistency of mathematical procedure was obtained in this way. One can also demonstrate that tables for the phenomena of Jupiter, computed ahead for several decades, were based on a single observational element, the rest being derived therefrom in strictly mathematical fashion.

This conforms to a conscious tendency of ancient astronomers to reduce the empirical data to the barest minimum, because they were well aware of the great insecurity of direct observation, especially for such major problems as the date of the first visible crescent or the reappearance of planets. All these phenomena are located near the horizon, where climatic and optical disturbances exercise a most pernicious influence. The 'natural' definition of a month as the time from one first visibility of the moon to the next led to most difficult mathematical problems. Many generations of astronomers had passed before meridian observations were introduced and the basic concepts simplified in such a way that they were easier to compute and easier to check empirically. Nevertheless, the arithmetical methods which were developed by the Babylonian astronomers to force a solution of the problems handed down to them proved to be of the greatest value for all future progress.

VI. THE IMPACT OF ANCIENT NEAR EASTERN SCIENCE ON HELLENISTIC SCIENCE

The profound influence of Babylonian astronomy upon Greek science was historically possible because this development took place when the Near East and the entire eastern Mediterranean basin were unified as a result of Alexander's conquests. In the resulting new Hellenistic civilization, knowledge could spread rapidly. By the time of Hipparchus (about 150 B.C.), the Babylonian arithmetical methods had been assimilated by the Greeks. The methods of computing sexagesimally and the place-value notation, including a symbol for zero, were adopted. At the same time, new geometrical concepts were introduced into astronomical theory. The discovery of the sphericity of the earth (probably in the fifth century B.C.) may have suggested the hypothesis of the sphericity of the heavens and, finally, the explanation of celestial phenomena by circular motions.

Arithmetical schemes were then slowly replaced by trigonometrical methods, which culminated, in the neighbourhood of A.D. 100, in the invention of spherical trigonometry. New numerical and graphical methods were developed by the Greeks and utilized for instruments like the astrolabe, which is based on the stereographic projection of the celestial sphere. Nevertheless, the arithmetical methods survived side by side with the improved trigonometrical methods. They can be found in medieval treatises of western Europe as well as in Hindu works of the sixth century A.D. They were kept alive especially in astrological works, which represent more closely the level of the Hipparchic period, when astrology was rapidly expanding from Alexandria over the whole Hellenistic world and far into India. Because this new astrological science was totally dependent upon the possibility of astronomical computation, the transmission of the new creed also contributed much to the spread of astronomical knowledge. For active astronomical research, astrology had virtually no importance, because its own development is directed only to the enlargement of its framework of prediction rather than to a refinement in the description of the celestial movements. As a typical example may be mentioned the *Almagest* and the *Tetrabiblos*, both written by one of the greatest astronomers of antiquity, Claudius Ptolemaeus (about A.D. 150). The *Almagest* develops, in a strictly scientific fashion, the empirical foundations and the mathematical theory of lunar and planetary motions. In the astrological *Tetrabiblos*, however, the same author is satisfied with the much cruder arithmetical methods, to answer the same astronomical questions which he had formerly treated with full rigour in the *Almagest*.

Both the development and the spread of Babylonian and Hellenistic astronomy proceeded at a rapid pace. Much less spectacular, but equally visible, was the expansion of mathematical knowledge into the Hellenistic and Roman world. Since the decipherment of the Babylonian mathematical texts, it has become evident that much of the material presented by Heron of Alexandria (end of first century A.D.) or by Diophantus (date unknown, possibly third century A.D.) does not represent a degenerate state of Greek mathematics but a reflex of methods and problems well known for fifteen centuries in the Orient. We know today that 'Greek' mathematics is a much more complex structure than we were accustomed to assume in the light of the purely Euclidean tradition. At the same time, we are better equipped to understand the great manifold of influences and accidents which determined the origin of the exact sciences upon which our modern development rests.

REFERENCE

[1] KRAMER, S. N. *J. Amer. orient. Soc.*, **69**, 199, 1949.

BIBLIOGRAPHY

NEUGEBAUER, O. 'The Exact Sciences in Antiquity.' Munksgaard, Copenhagen; Oxford; Princeton. 1951. This gives a more detailed summary and bibliography.

Mathematical cuneiform texts were edited and translated into German by the present author in 1935–38. For additional texts, translated into English, see:

NEUGEBAUER, O. and SACHS, A. 'Mathematical Cuneiform Texts.' American Oriental Society, New Haven. 1945.

Egyptian mathematics:

PEET, T. E. 'The Rhind Mathematical Papyrus.' The University Press, Liverpool. 1923.

No modern work on *Egyptian astronomy* exists. The current presentations are utterly antiquated and based on secondary material. An edition with translations and commentary of the Egyptian astronomical texts is in preparation by R. A. PARKER and O. NEUGEBAUER.

Egyptian calendars:

PARKER, R. A. 'The Calendars of Egypt.' Univ. of Chicago, Orient. Inst.: Stud. ancient Orient. Civiliz., no. 26. Chicago. 1950.

Babylonian astronomy:

The pioneer work was done by F. X. KUGLER, and published in Germany between 1900 and 1924. The present author has prepared an edition of all available texts, now (1954) in the press. Lund Humphries, London.

Finally the reader may consult a work, written in the year A.D. 1000, by the great Islamic scholar AL-BĪRŪNĪ, on the origin and survival of ancient time-reckoning: 'The Chronology of Ancient Nations', translated by C. E. SACHAU. Allan, London. 1879.

I. INDEX OF PERSONAL NAMES

Adadnirari II, Assyrian king, 534.
Agatharchides, Greek historian, 581.
Agricola, Georgius, German metallurgist, 252.
Ahiram, king of Byblos, 763.
Akhenaten, Egyptian king, 690.
Albright, W. F., 762, 763, 766.
Alexander the Great, 371, 713, tables E, F.
Amasis II, Egyptian king, 262.
Amenemhet I, Egyptian king, 537, table F.
Amenemhet II, Egyptian king, 657.
Amenhetep I, Egyptian king, 776, table F.
Amenhetep II, Egyptian king, 440, 627, 686, 687, 693, 701.
Amenhetep III, Egyptian king, 283, 286, 483, 685 n., 782, 784, table F.
Amenhotep, *see* Amenhetep.
Amenophis, Egyptian sage, 540.
Aristotle, 590 n., table F.
Ashur-bani-pal, Assyrian king, 282, 527, 552, 676, 677, 736–7, table F.
Ashur-nasir-pal II, Assyrian king, 247, 282, 527, 552, 553, 646, 649, 718, 723, 727, 736, table F.
Asoka, Indian emperor, 772.
Athenaeus, Greek author, 266.

Brahe, Tycho, Danish astronomer, 799.
Breuil, Abbé, 152.

Caesar, Gaius Julius, 378, 410 (6), 589, 712.
de Candolle, A. P., 355.
Carter, H., 695.
Caton-Thompson, G., 511.
Celsius, O., 450.
Charlemagne, emperor, 779.
Cheops, Egyptian king, 356, 668, 714.
Childe, V. Gordon, 80, 302, 322, 374, 378, 411, 445, 490, 513, 621, 711.
Clark, J. G. D., 516.
Ctesias, Greek physician and historian, 246.

Daga, Egyptian vizier, 437–8.
Dagan (Dagon), fishgod, 253.
Darius the Great, Persian king, 752, 779.
Diodorus Siculus, Greek historian, 266, 267, 280, 288, 473, 580, 581.
Diophantus, mathematician, 803.
Dioscorides, Greek physician, 247, 588.
Diringer, D., 761, 762, 763, 769.
Driver, G. R., 768.
Drusus, Roman administrator, 778.

Eannatum, Sumerian king, 749.
Engelbach, R., 570.
Entemena, king of Lagash, 652, 653.
Esarhaddon, Assyrian king, 554, 713.
Evans, Sir Arthur, 758.

Fisher, Edna, 5.
Franchet, L., 409.
Franklin, Benjamin, 1.

Gardiner, Sir Alan H., 747, 754–5, 762.
Gudea, king of Lagash, 194, 252, 282, 583, 778, 780, table F.

Hammurabi, Assyrian king, 548, 585, 659, 751, tables E, F.
Hatshepsut, Egyptian queen, 55, 422, 544, 701, 735, table F.
Hattušiliš III, Hittite king, 595.
Hemaka, 696, 701.
Henut-tawi, Egyptian queen, 670.
Herodotus, Greek historian, 105, 247, 257, 262, 263, 264, 266–8, 288, 373, 449, 468, 482, 484 n., 527, 529, 550, 555, 714, 715, 783.
Heron of Alexandria, 803.
Hesiod, Greek poet, 116.
Hesi-Re, Egyptian noble, 697–8, plate 26 B.
Hetep-heres, Egyptian queen, 268, 653, 692, 695, 698–9, 700.
Hezekiah, king of Judah, 530–1, 764, 765.
Hipparchus of Rhodes, Greek astronomer, 264, 802.
Hiram, king of Tyre, 633, 664.
Homer, Greek poet, 660, 677.
Hor, Egyptian king, 686, 699.

Im-Dugud, divine eagle, 640, 653.
Imhotep, Egyptian vizier, 537.
Isocrates, Greek rhetorician, 408.

Jones, F. Wood, 10, 12.

Kawit, Egyptian queen, 698.
Keller, Helen, 18.
Kelso, J. L., 409.
Kenyon, Dr Kathleen, 372.
Kepler, J., German astronomer, 799.
Kha, Egyptian king, 440.
Khnumet, Egyptian princess, 657.
Köhler, W., 14.
Kohts, Mme, 14.
Ktesibios of Alexandria, 113.

Leach, B., 409.
Littledale, H. A. P., 658 n.

Lucas, A., 373, 409.
Lucretius, Roman poet, 216.

Marais, Eugène, 5.
Martial, Roman poet, 284.
Maspero, H., 597 n.
Menes, legendary Egyptian king, 267, 529, 536.
Meryet-Amen, Egyptian queen, 422, 690, 701.
Mesha, Moabite king, 764, 765.
Mes-kalam-dug, noble of Ur, 644, 645.
Meton, Greek astronomer, 795.
Mycerinus, Egyptian king, 668.

Nabonidus, Assyrian king, 282.
Nabopalassar, Assyrian king, 256.
Napir-asu, Cassite queen, 631.
Narmer, Egyptian king, 754–5, table F.
Nearchos, Macedonian admiral and author, 371.
Neb-Hepet-Re, Egyptian king, 435.
Nebuchadrezzar, Assyrian king, 256, 282, 551, 555, 634, 715, 766, table F.

Oppert, J., 779.
Osorkon II, Egyptian king, 537.
Ountash-gal, Cassite king, 631.

Paracelsus, Swiss alchemist, 293.
Pepi I, Egyptian king, 637, 639–40, 641, 642, table F.
Perabsen, Egyptian king, 283.
Petrie, Sir W. M. Flinders, 127, 305, 411, 446, 447, 489, 597 n., 622, 682, 687, 702–3, 753, 779, 783.
Phidias, sculptor, 661, 681.
Picard, L., 633 n.
Piggott, S., 492, 494.
Pitt-Rivers, A., 313.
Pliny, Roman writer, 238, 240, 243, 247, 251, 254, 257, 260, 262, 288, 356, 449, 539, 588, 589.
Ptolemaeus, Claudius, astronomer, 802.

Rameses II, Egyptian king, 284, 526, 659, 714, table F.
Rameses III, Egyptian king, 286, 441, 543.
Reifenberg, A., 633 n.
Rekhmire, vizier of Upper Egypt, 453, 544, 627, 690 n.
Richter, Gisela M. A., 409.
Rosenthal, E., 409.

Sahure, Egyptian king, 482, table F.
Sardanapalus, *see* Ashur-bani-pal.
Sargon I the Great, Assyrian king, 56–7, 253, 371, 583, 627, table F.
Sargon II, Assyrian king, 239, 282, 469, 554, 564, 597, 780, table F.
Schaeffer, C., 762–3.
Schliemann, H., 660.
'Scorpion King', protodynastic Egyptian king, 51, 537, table F.
Seneferu, Egyptian king, 283, 482, table F.
Senmut, Egyptian official, 122, 124, 441, plate 13 B.
Sennacherib, Assyrian king, 282, 452, 469, 524, 527, 529, 531, 533, 552, 554, 632–3, 718, table F.
Senusret I, Egyptian king, 699.
Senusret III, Egyptian king, 49.
Seti I, Egyptian king, 286, 526, 529.
Shalmaneser III, Assyrian king, 646, 649, table F.
Shaphatbaal, king of Byblos, 763.
Shilkhak-in-shushinak, king of Susa, 632.
Shub-ad, queen of Ur, 340, 626, 644, 709, 710.
Smith, E. Baldwin, 305.
Solomon, 633, 661, 664, 675, 676, table F.
Sprengel, C. K., 450.
Stone, E. H., 494.
Strabo, Greek geographer, 246, 252–3, 254, 256, 257, 260, 284, 288, 529, 581.

Tacitus, Roman historian, 253.
Taharqa, Nubian king, 538 n.
Thales of Miletus, 105.
Theophrastus, Greek philosopher, 240, 355, 356, 358, 371, 550.
Thorley, J. P., 409.
Thothmes I, Egyptian king, 782, table F.
Thothmes III, Egyptian king, 112, 439, 480, 543, 545, 565, 669, 673, plate 14 A, table F.
Thothmes IV, Egyptian king, 439, 440, 669, 722, 727, plate 14 A.
Thotnefer, Egyptian official, 439.
Tiglath-pileser I, Assyrian king, 246, 553, table F.
Tiglath-pileser III, Assyrian king, 54, table F.
Tracy, N., 4.
Tukulti Ninurta II, Assyrian king, 251, 527, 583, 597.
Tutankhamen, *see* Index of Subjects.

Unas, Egyptian king, 434, 537.
Ur-nammu, Sumerian king, 467.
Urukagina, Sumerian king, 280, 282, 748.

Valerius Maximus, Roman historian, 264.
Vavilov, N. I., 368.
Vitruvius, Roman architect, 113, 216, 217, 240.

Weidenreich, F., 35.
Woolley, Sir Leonard, 199, 200, 396, 446, 469, 489, 490, 712.

Wu, G. P., 409.

Xanthudides, S., 199, 202, 411.
Xerxes, Persian king, 715, table F.

Yeivin, S., 633 n.
Yuaa, official of Dynasty XVIII, 270.

Zer, Egyptian king, 434.
Zoser, Egyptian king, 283, 475–8, 482, 537, plate 19, table F.
Zosimos, Greek alchemist, 280.

II. INDEX OF PLACE NAMES

This index includes the names of ancient sites such as tombs, burial-grounds, temples, and caves. It also includes names of countries and provinces which do not appear in the Index of Subjects.

Abu Ghalep, Egypt, 362.
Abusir, Egypt, 482, 597 n., map 6.
Abydos, Egypt, 165, 305, 434, 597 n., 668, 779, map 6.
Afghanistan, 359, 367, 368.
Agade, Mesopotamia, 725.
Aggtelek, Hungary, 359, 370.
Aichbühl, Württemberg, 310–11, map 3.
Alaca, Cappadocia, 594, map 4.
Alalakh (Atshana), Syria, 523 n., 655, 658, 673, 679, map 4.
Alcalá, Spain, 511.
Aleppo, Syria, 665, map 4.
Alexandria, Egypt, 113, map 6.
Algeria, 72.
Alishar, Cappadocia, 373, 518, map 4.
Altamira, Spain, 147, 148, 151, plate 2.
El-Amarna, Egypt, 240, 242, 306, 422, 433, 473–4, 649, 669, 783, map 6, table F.
Amphlett Islands, 44, 406, 407.
El-Amrah, Egypt, 304, map 6.
Anau, Turkestan, 367, 501, 502, 721, map 5, table F.
Anyang, China, 722.
Aqar Quf, Mesopotamia, 468, map 7.
Aradac, Yugoslavia, 421.
Araña, Cueva de la, Bicorp, Valencia, 275.
Ararat, *see* Urartu.
Arezzo, Italy, 390, 632.
Arminghall, Norfolk, 314.
Arpachiyah, Mesopotamia, 365, 484 n., map 7.
Aswan, Egypt, 238, 568–70, map 6.
Ashur, Mesopotamia, 255, 362, 550, 671, map 7.
Athens, Greece, 401, 406, 408–9, 584, 661, 674–5, 777, map 4.
Atshana, *see* Alalakh.
Avebury, Wiltshire, 491.
Azerbaijan, Iran, 261.

Babylon, 56, 251 (map), 457, 468, 471, 554–5, 713, 715, map 7, plate 18.
Bactria, 631, 632, map 5.
Badakhshan, Russia, 55, map 5.
Badari, Egypt, 304, 387, 418–19, 420, 431, 432, 456, 473, 511, 514, 516, 518, 601, map 6, table E.
Bahrain, Persian Gulf, 664.
Baikal, Lake, 301.
Balawat, Mesopotamia, 646, map 7.
Balreji, Sind, 406.
Baluchistan, 359, 385, map 5.
Baradello (lake-village), 357.
Barkaer, Denmark, 312.
Barvas, Lewis, 391.
Battersea, London, 512.
Bavian, Mesopotamia, 469–70, map 7.
Beaulieu Heath, Hampshire, 313.
Beit el-Wali, Egypt, 483, map 6.
Belgian Congo, 506.
Belt cave, Caspian Sea, 351.
Beni Hasan, Egypt, 43, 73, 241, 263, 265, 291, 330, 331, 388, 437, 438, 477, 544, 545, 706, 734, map 6.
Benoajan, Malaga, Spain, 148.
El-Bersheh, Egypt, 200, 437, 700, map 6.
Beth-Asbea, 'town of Byssos', Palestine, 249.
Bienne, Lake, 361, 369, 370, map 3.
Birs-Nimrod (Borsippa), Mesopotamia, 468, map 7.
Biskupin, Poland, 323.
Black Patch, Sussex, 560, 561, 562 (map).
Bleasdale, Lancashire, 313.
Böckingen, Heilbronn, 355, 357.
Bockum, Hanover, 303.
Bodman (lake-village), 357, map 3.
Boghazköy (Hittite Hattusas), 457, 489, 757, map 4.
Bolivia, 223.
Bologna, Italy, 595, 613.
Borneo, 226, 227.
Bornholm, Denmark, 369.
Borum Eshoj, Denmark, 442.
Botel-Tobago Island, 118.
Botesdale, Suffolk, 601.
Le Bourget (lake-village), Savoy, 359, 361, 369.
Brandenburg, 591.
Brandon, Suffolk, 134–5.

Brazil, 160.
Brigmilston, Wiltshire, 604, 605.
British Columbia, 160, 176, 177, 178, 179, 184, 312, 318, 707, 738.
Brittany, 388, 389, 407.
Bubastis (Zagazig), Egypt, 484 n., map 6.
Buchau, Württemberg, 316, 355, map 3.
Burma, 218, 226.
Buryet, Siberia, 301.
Byblos (Jbail), Lebanon, 762, map 8, plate 31 A.

Caballos, Cueva de los, Albocácer, Castellón, Spain, 161.
Cadiz, Spain, 257.
Cairnpapple, West Lothian, 491.
Cairo, Egypt, 420, 427, 477, 676, 778, map 6.
Calah, *see* Nimrud.
California, 69, 174, 176.
Cambridge, England, 232, 511, 517.
Cappadocia, Turkey, 212, map 4.
Carchemish, Mesopotamia, 395–6, 675, 758, map 4.
Carmel, Mount, Palestine, 31, 503, 520, maps 1 A, 8.
Carnon, Cornwall, 563.
Chagar Bazar, Mesopotamia, 212, 213, 594, 721, map 7.
Champigneulles, France, 559, 560, 562 (map).
Chanhu-Daro, Indus valley, 717, 719, map 5.
Charlton Rode, Norfolk, 612.
Chelles, France, 131, map 2.
Chicama valley, Peru, 421, 436.
Chiu Chen, Indo-China, 393.
Choukoutien, China, 23–5, 30, 37 (map).
Cissbury, Sussex, 559, 562 (map).
Clacton-on-Sea, Essex, 28, 29, 141.
Cleigh, Argyllshire, 605.
Clough, County Antrim, Ireland, 636.
Clwyd, Vale of, Wales, 32.
Constance, Lake, 517, map 3.
Copan, Honduras, 125.
Corcelettes, Switzerland, 722, map 3.
Corinth, Greece, 392, 401, 406, 409, map 4, table F.
Cornete, Italy, 518.
Cortaillod (lake-village), 508, 512.
Les Cottes, Vienne, 147.
Craig Lwyd, Penmaenmawr, N. Wales, 44, 562.

Dahshur, Egypt, 368, 597 n., 657, 699, map 6.
Dakhla oasis, Egypt, 239, 262, 528, 534, map 6.
Dalsland, Sweden, 513.
Damascus, Syria, 598, 665, map 8.
Deir el-Bahri, Egypt, 55, 295, 422, 423, 435, 544, 701, map 6, plates 12 A, 13.
Deir el-Gebrawi, Egypt, 733, map 6.
Delphi (Mount Parnassus), Greece, 262.
Dieppe, France, 665.
Dira Abu'n-Nega, Thebes, Egypt, 370, map 6.
Doliche, Syria, 598, map 4.
Dorchester, Dorset, 491.
Down, Co., Ireland, 400.
Duddul, *see* Hit.
Dümmer, Oldenburg, 364.
Durnberg, Austria, 443.
Dystrup Mose, Denmark, 209.

Edfu, Egypt, 538, 539, 665 n., map 6.
Egtved, Denmark, 442, 518, plate 17 A.
Eilean an Tighe, North Uist, 390, 397, plate 8.
Elath, Jordan valley, 633.
Elburz, Iran, 261.
Elephantine, Egypt, 539, 663, map 6.
Enkomi, Cyprus, 624, 677, map 4.
Epirus, Greece, 359, map 4.
Erbil, Mesopotamia, 533–4, map 7.
Erech (Uruk; mod. Warka), Mesopotamia, 199, 200, 205, 206, 461, 462, 463, 496, 510, 512, 549, 582, 710, 745–6, 747, 748, map 7, tables E, F.
Erfurt, Thuringia, 359.
Eridu, Mesopotamia, 461, 462, 463–4, 526, map 7.
Erösd, 309, map 4.
Ertebølle, Denmark, 303, 495–6, 499, 507.
Eshnunna (Tell Asmar), Mesopotamia, 466–7, 670, map 7.
Esna, Egypt, 477, map 6.
Estonia, 166.
Les Eyzies, Dordogne, 26.
Ezinge, Holland, 322.

Faeroe Islands, 442.
Fara, Mesopotamia, 748, 750, map 7.
Farnham, Surrey, 303, 394, 497.
Fayum (Neolithic sites), Egypt, 241, 304, 354, 365, 367–8, 373, 376, 377, 387, 418–19, 423, 431, 448, 501, 506, 511–12, 514, 516, 541, 542, 602, map 6, table E.
Federsee, Württemberg, 303, 310, 316, 355, 359, map 3.
Ferguson Island, 406.
Ferriby, Yorkshire, 738, 739.
Finavon, Scotland, 322.
Finland, 166, 452.
Font-de-Gaume, Dordogne, France, 151, 300.
Fontéchavade, Charente, 22, 29, 34, 37 (map), table C.
Fresné la Mère, Falaise, France, 609.

Gagarino, Russia, 301.
Galapagos Islands, 3.
Gaza, Palestine, 410 (22), maps 6, 8.
Gebel-el-Arak, Egypt, 516, 667, 669, 672, map 6.

Gebel Zabara, Egypt, 526..
Gerar, Palestine, 597.
Gerumsberg, Sweden, 442, 443.
Gerzeh, Egypt, 431, map 6, table E.
Gezer, Palestine, 201, 239, 248–9, 274, 762, 764, map 8.
Ghassul, Palestine, 419, 432, 433, map 8.
Girsu, 253; *see also* Lagash.
Giza, Egypt, 241, 482, 597 n., 714, map 6.
Gjeithus, Norway, 150.
Glastonbury, Somerset, 318–21, 322, 323, 404–5, plate 4.
Glencrutchery, Isle of Man, 410 (18).
Goldberg, Neresheim, Württemberg, 311, 322.
Götland, Sweden, 369.
Gournia, Crete, 387, map 4.
Granada, Spain, 359.
Grand Pressigny, France, 500–1, 505, 509.
Grange, Limerick, 195.
Grimaldi caves, Italy, 168, map 2.
Grimes Graves, East Anglia, 44, 235, 515, 558–61, 562 (map).
Guiana, 164, 166.
Gurob, Fayum, Egypt, 419, 420, 422, 433, map 6.

Haida, British Columbia, 178.
Halaf, Mesopotamia, 201, 365, 367, 460, maps 4, 7, table E.
Haldon Hill, Exeter, 312.
Hallstatt, Austria, 567, 617–18, 619, map 3; *see also under* Cultures *in* Index of Subjects.
Hama, Syria, 201, map 4.
Hamairan, Persia, 262.
Harappa, Indus valley, 52, 194, 195, 202, 207, 360 n., 366, 385, 512, 613, 717, 719, 760, map 5.
Harran, Mesopotamia, 282, 371, map 4.
Harrow Hill, Worthing, Sussex, 561, 562 (map).
Harty, Kent, 612.
Hassuna, Mesopotamia, 193, 306, 456, 459, 502, 507, 512, map 7, table E.
Hat-Nub, Egypt, 477, map 6.
Hebrides, 376, 381, 382, 391, 392, 397, 406, 407–8.
Heidelberg, Germany, 23, table C.
El-Hejra, Arabia, 766.
Helbon, Damascus, Syria, 282, map 8.
Heliopolis, Egypt, 359, map 6.
Hierakonpolis, Egypt, 51, 305, 639, 641, 666, 755, map 6.
Hintlesham, Surrey, 616.
Hissar, Persia, 212, 721, map 5.
Hit, Mesopotamia, 251 (map), 252–3, 258, map 7.
Holbaek, Zealand, 167.
Holderness, Yorkshire, 315.
Holmegaard, Denmark, 161–2, 499.
Holt, Denbighshire, 394.
Homs, Syria, 529, maps 4, 8.
Honan, China, 772.
Hooge Mierde, Holland, 314.
Hotham Carr, Yorkshire, 608.
Hudson Bay, 498.
Hunsbury, Northamptonshire, 322.

Indre, France, 149.
Iraq, 160, 198, 306.
Irgenhausen, Switzerland, 436, map 3, plate 12 B.

Jarmo, Iraq, 306, 365, 367, 368, 376, 418, 502, map 7, table E.
Java, 226.
Jemdet Nasr, Mesopotamia, 745, 747, map 7, tables E, F.
Jericho, Palestine, 201, 306, 372, 376, 387, 388, 391, 419, 501, 502, 530, 672, 684, 685, 725, map 8, table F.
Jerusalem, Palestine, 259, 292, 661, map 8, table F.
El-Jisr, Palestine, 671–2, map 8.
Jutland, Denmark, 156, 496, 514, 518.

El-Kab, Egypt, 260, map 6.
Kafr Ammar, Egypt, 434, map 6.
Kahun, Egypt, 433, 542, map 6.
Kalmuk steppes, 716, 717, 719.
Kalvträsk, Sweden, 708.
Kanam, Kenya, 22, 25, 37 (map).
Kara Hissar, Armenia, 262, map 4.
Karhof Cave, Westphalia, 367.
Karmir Blur, Armenia, 684, 685.
Karnak, Egypt, 457–8, 479–80, 483, 539, 544, 545, 570, map 6.
Kerma, Nubia, 422, 435, 699.
Khafaje, Mesopotamia, 205, 242, 354, 362, 372–3, 681 (3), 705, map 7.
Kharga oasis, Egypt, 262, 528, 534, map 6.
Khartoum, Sudan, 501.
Khorsabad, Mesopotamia, 469, 470, 472, 675, map 7.
Kirjath Sepher, Palestine, 248.
Kish, Mesopotamia, 206, 208, 209, 717, 753, map 7.
Kivik, Sweden, 213, 726.
Kizzuwadna, Armenia, 595, map 4.
Knidos, Asia Minor, 237, map 4.
Knockadoon, Limerick, 312.
Knossos, Crete, 212, 214, 361, 387, 388, 398, 400, 403, 485–8, 535, 672, 673, 714, 758, map 4.
Kodok (Fashoda), Sudan, 732.
Köln-Lindenthal, Neolithic village, 308, 309.
Korpilahti, Finland, 413.
Kostenki, Russia, 302.
Kostromskaya Stanitsa, Russia, 324–5.

Kouphonisi island, 247, map 4.
Kreimbach, Rhenish Bavaria, 620.
Kuban, R., 588, 611, map 4.
Kul Oba, Kerch, Russia, 646–7, map 4.
Kuortane, Finland, 707, 708.
Kurdistan, 520, map 7.
Kuyunjik, Mesopotamia, 452–3, 710, 741, map 7; *see also* Nineveh.

Lachish (Tell ed-Duweir), Palestine, 201, 385, 388, 390, 530, 674, 762, 766, map 8.
Lagash, Mesopotamia (Tello), 582, 583, 640, 665 n., 748, 749, 778, 780, map 7; *see also* Girsu.
Lagonza, Italy, 359.
Lapland, 413, 436.
Lascaux, France, 147, 331, 744, 745.
Laumes, Côte d'Or, France, 610.
Laurion, Greece, 558, 584, map 4.
Laussel, Dordogne, France, 152, 153.
Lehringen, Germany, 30.
Leicestershire, 382.
Lengyel, Hungary, 369.
Leubingen, Saxony, 314.
Levallois-Perret, France, 133, map 2.
Libya, 150.
Lisht, Egypt, 668, 699, map 6.
Little Woodbury, Wiltshire, 317–18.
London, England, 27.
Loose Howe, Yorkshire, 313.
Luristan, Persia, 616, 617, map 7.
Lusatia (Lausitz), Germany, 359.
Luxor, Egypt, 283, 537, map 6.
Luz, Shechem, 249.

Maadi, Egypt, 365, 368, map 6.
Machairus, Peraea, 263, map 8.
La Madeleine, France, 134.
Madras, India, 27.
'Magdala of the dyers', 248, 259, map 8.
Maiden Castle, Dorset, 321–2.
Makapan cave, Transvaal, 20, 28, 37 (map).
Malay Peninsula, 164, 219, 221, 226, 234.
Malta, 712, 713, 767.
Mal'ta, Siberia, 413.
Mareotis, Lake, 257, map 6.
Mari, Mesopotamia, 549, 552, 594, 598, 671, map 7.
Marib, Yemen, 530.
Marmariani, Greece, 370, map 4.
Marseilles, France, 767.
Marshall Bennett Islands, Oceania, 740, 741.
Marsiliana de'Albegna, Italy, 769.
Mas d'Azil, Ariège, France, 157, 347, 358, 753, map 2.
Matarrah, Mesopotamia, 367, 502, map 7.
Matmar, Egypt, 431.
Matto Grosso, South America, 171.
Meare, Somerset, 318, 320.
Medinet Habu, Egypt, 209, map 6.
Megiddo, Palestine, 201, 433, 434, 435, 530, 665, 673–4, 676, map 8.
Melos, island, 423, map 4.
Memphis, Egypt, 283, 529, 537, 539, 659, 690, map 6.
Mercurago, N. Italy, 209, 213, 214, map 3.
Merimde, Egypt, 304, 360, 362, 365, 376, 473, 509, 511, 512, 514, 516, map 6.
Meroë, Nubia, 597.
Mersin, Cilicia, 456, 502, 509, 513, map 4.
Meydum, Egypt, 434, 482, map 6.
Michelsberg, Germany, 399.
Midlothian, Scotland, 402.
Miletus, Asia Minor, 722, map 4.
Los Millares, Almeria, Spain, 511.
Mistelbach, Austria, 359.
Mitterberg, Salzburg, Austria, 566, 609, map 3.
Moeris, Lake, Egypt, 418, 545, map 6.
Mohenjo-Daro, Indus valley, 202, 246, 251 (map), 374, 381, 406, 420, 432, 466, 760, map 5.
Mondsee (lake-village), 357, map 3.
Montélier (lake-village), 369.
Montespan, France, 152.
Mörigen (lake-village), 369, 370, map 3.
Mostagedda, Tasa, Egypt, 368, 431.
La Motte d'Apremont, Haute Saône, France, 443.
Le Moustier, Dordogne, 31, maps 1 A, 2.
La Mouthe, Dordogne, France, 235.
Muliana, Crete, 729.
Murciélagos, Cueva de los, Andalusia, 421, 436, 450, plate 9.
Mycenae, Greece, 213, 214, 359, 403, 459, 486–8, 531, 623, 660–1, 673, 722, 728, map 4, table F.

Naga-ed-Der, Egypt, 434, map 6.
Naqada, Egypt, 433, 434, 779, map 6, plate 31 B.
Naucratis, Egypt, 260, map 6.
Neuchâtel, Lake, 357, 361, 508, map 3.
New Caledonia, 71.
New Guinea, 44, 119, 158, 221.
Nias, Indonesia, 191.
Nicobar Islands, 406.
Nigeria, 407.
Nimrud (Calah), Mesopotamia, 54, 470, 523 n., 527, 534, 550, 552, 553, 623, 624, 656, 664, 675, 678, 679–80, 723, 727, 736–7, map 7.
Nineveh, Mesopotamia, 167, 243, 251 (map), 452, 469, 470, 471–2, 524, 531–2, 551, 552–3, 627, 632, 676, 677, 714, 736–7, map 7, table F.
Nippur, Mesopotamia, 549, map 7.
Nointol, France, 562 (map), 563.

Noricum, Roman province, 595–6.
Northdale, Yorkshire, 511.
Northern Massim Islands, 119.

Obourg, Belgium, 560, 561, 562 (map).
Oedenburg (Sopron), Hungary, 443.
Öhringen, Germany, 355.
Olduvai, Tanganyika, 25, 37 (map).
Olympia, Greece, 661, 681, map 4.
Olynthus, Macedonia, 395, map 4.
El-Omari, Helwan, Egypt, 366.
Ophir (Suppara), India, 664.
Orkney, 382, 408, 421.
Oseberg, Norway, 356.
Öster-Götland, Sweden, 362.
Ostrakina, Palestine, 259.
Ovrebö, Norway, 709.

Palmyra, Syria, 528, 532, map 8.
Palmyrene salt-oases, 257.
Pech-Merle, Lot, France, 144, 145.
Pelusium, Egypt, 257, 259, map 6.
Pentuan, Cornwall, 563.
Per-Amen, Egypt, 284.
Perugia, Italy, 769.
Petersinsel (lake-village), 369, map 3.
Petsofa, Palaikastro, Crete, 403, map 4.
Phaistos, Crete, 403, 486, map 4.
Philippine Islands, 165, 219, 226.
Phylakopi, Melos, 423.
Piltdown, Sussex, 141.
Plymstock, Devon, 612.
Pomerania, 576.
Pompeii, 231.
Popudnia, Ukraine, 307, 309.
Praeneste, Italy, 770.
Punjab, India, 202.
Punt, 55, 243, 293, 295, 544, 663, 685, 735.
Pushkari, Ukraine, 301, 302.

Qau, Egypt, 368, 477, 666, map 6.
La Quina, Charente, 31.

Radley, Berkshire, plate 8.
Rana-Ghundai, Baluchistan, 721.
Ras Shamra, Syria, 247, 618, 619, 665 n., 673, map 4; *see also* Ugarit.
Redgrave Park, Suffolk, 609.
Remedello, Italy, 505, 508, 510, 511.
Riihimaki, Finland, 709.
Ringstead, Norfolk, 636.
Ripac, Bosnia, 370.
Robenhausen (lake-village), 356, 357, 359, map 3.
Rödöy, Norway, 709.
Rossel Island, Oceania, 740.
Rudstone, Yorkshire, 218.
Ruhestetten, Hohenzollern, 357.

Sadu, Japan, 565.
St Acheul, France, 131, map 2.
St Blaise (lake-village), 357, map 3.
St Catherine's Hill, Winchester, 313.
Samaria, Palestine, 675, 678, map 8.
Sangiran, Java, 23, 37 (map).
Saqqara, Egypt, 193, 241, 265, 273, 291, 341, 343, 368, 395, 475–8, 481–2, 483, 537, 541, 542, 543, 579, 597 n., 689, 696, 697, 710, 732, 757, map 6, plate 19.
Sardis, Lydia, 713.
Schaffhausen, Switzerland, 443, map 3.
Schussenthal, Ravensburg, 356, map 3.
Scilly Isles, 421.
Seamer, Yorkshire, 303.
Sedment, Egypt, 422, 694, 695, map 6.
Sehel, Egypt, 537.
Semna, Nubia, 538.
Serabit el-Khadim, Egypt, 564.
Sergeac, Dordogne, 32.
Shaheinab, Sudan, 501, 506, 515–16.
Shah-tepe, Turkoman steppe, 721, table F.
Shatt al-'Arab, 552, map 7.
Shechem, Palestine, 762, map 8.
Sialk, Persia, 306, 394, 396, 432, 502, 507, 721, map 5.
Sicily, 770.
Silesia, 359.
Siloam, Pool of, 764.
Silsila, Egypt, 477, 478, 483, map 6.
Sindh, 202, 206, 207, 213, 381, 385, 386, 396, 406, 717.
Singara, Mesopotamia, 282.
Sipplingen (lake-village), 355, 356, 357, 359, map 3.
Sirgenstein Cave, Württemberg, 369.
Skåne, Sweden, 497, 614.
Skara Brae, Orkney, 312, 500, 516.
Skendleby, Lincolnshire, 313.
Skrydstrup, Denmark, 442.
Snowshill, Gloucestershire, 616.
Soay, Hebrides, 344, 345.
Sodom, Palestine, 259.
Solothurn, Switzerland, 443, map 3.
Somaliland, 196.
Spiennes, Belgium, 559, 560, 562 (map).
Star Carr, Yorkshire, 499.
Stenild, Jutland, Denmark, 514.
Sterkfontein, South Africa, 23, 37 (map).
Stonehenge, 81, 195, 315, 490–4, 712, plate 21 A.
Sudan, 140.
Sumatra, 226.
Susa, Persia, 205, 206, 207, 208, 209, 396, 398, 432, 489, 511, 602, 632, 650, 713, 787, maps 5, 6.
Swanscombe, Kent, 22, 28, 29, 34, 68, table C.

Takla Makan desert, Sinkiang, 72.

Tapper, N. Germany, 209.
Tarkhan, Egypt, 420, 434, 524, map 6, plates 9, 11.
Tasa, Egypt, 387, map 6, table E.
Tasmania, 161, 222.
Taungs, Bechuanaland, 20, 22, 37 (map).
Tel El-Yahudiya, Egypt, 237, map 6.
Tell Agrab, Mesopotamia, 720, 725, map 7.
Tell Asmar, Mesopotamia, 594, map 7; *see also* Eshnunna.
Tell Beit Mirsim, Palestine, 381, 383, 409, map 8.
Tell ed-Duweir, Palestine, 390, map 8; *see also* Lachish.
Tell Fara, Palestine, 672, map 8.
Tello, Mesopotamia, 652, 653, map 7; *see also* Lagash.
Tepe Gawra, Mesopotamia, 205, 460, 461, 462, 504, 512, map 7, table E.
La Terrière, Charente-Inférieure, 391.
Thebes, Egypt, 122, 156, 189, 213, 232, 239, 242, 251 (map), 264, 266, 273, 274, 277, 278, 290, 292, 329, 389, 437, 439, 440, 453, 454, 481, 522–3, 537, 540, 541, 543–4, 578, 619, 664, 689, 690, 694, 699, 726, 757, map 6, plate 10.
Thorny Down, Winterbourne Gunner, Wiltshire, 316.
Thrapsanos, Crete, 406.
Tiberias, Lake, 259, map 8.
Tibet, 362, 367.
Tierra del Fuego, 160, 165, 178.
Tiflis, Russia, 588.
Timonovka, Russia, 302.
Tiryns, Greece, 359, 457, 488, map 4.
Titicaca, Lake, Bolivia, 732, 733.
Tollund, Denmark, 355, 359, 370, plate 6 B.
Torquay, England, 188.
Traprain Law, Scotland, 619, 620.
Trialeti, Georgia, 209.
Trinil, Java, 23, 37 (map).
Tripolye, Ukraine, 370.
Trois-Frères, Ariége, France, 151.
Troldebjerg, Denmark, 311.
Troy, 362, 364, 365, 398, 402, 403, 427, 433, 435, 488, 504, 565, 584, map 4.
Trundholm, Denmark, 213.
Tuc D'Audoubert, Ariége, France, 144, 151, 152.
Tura, Egypt, 453, 714.
Tuz Khurmatli, Mesopotamia, 262, map 7.
Tyre, Lebanon, 247–8, map 8.

El-Ubaid, Mesopotamia, 306, 456, 465, 638, 639–40, 641, map 7, table E.
Uganda, 384.
Ugarit, Syria, 201, 247, 762–3, map 4, plate 30 B.
Uqair, Mesopotamia, 462–3, map 7.
Ur, Mesopotamia, 56, 199, 200, 205, 206, 208, 209, 236, 247, 253, 254, 261, 278, 306, 340, 465–6, 467, 468–9, 582, 584, 591, 614, 626, 636, 643, 644, 649–50, 652–7, 659, 661, 684, 705, 709, 717, 718, 725, map 7, tables E, F.
Urartu (Ararat), Mesopotamia, 564, 583, map 7.
Uruk (Warka), *see* Erech.
Utoquai (lake-village), 356, 517.

Valle, Sweden, 150.
Valley of Kings, Egypt, 440.
Van, Lake, Armenia, 282, maps 4, 7.
Vaphio, Greece, 400, 645, 646, map 4.
Västerbotten, Sweden, 708.
Velem St Vid, Hungary, 568, 588.
Věstonice, Moravia, 147, 152, 376.
Vettersfelde, Brandenburg, Germany, 647–8.
Victoria West, South Africa, 133.
Vogtland, Germany, 508.
Vounous, Cyprus, 403, 420, 433, 435, map 4.
Vučedol, Yugoslavia, 311.

Wadi Alaki, Nubia, 526.
Wadi ‘Amd (Hadhramaut), Arabia, 532.
Wadi Ghazzeh, Palestine, 232, 420, map 8.
Wadi Gerrawi, Egypt, 528, map 6.
Wadi Halfa, Egypt, 477, map 6.
Wadi Hammamat, Egypt, 477, map 6.
Wadi Maghara, Palestine, 564, map 8.
Wadi Natrum oasis, 260, map 6.
Wangen, Baden, 357, 358, 367, map 3.
Warka, *see* Erech.
White Leaf Hill, Buckinghamshire, 313.
Willendorf, Lower Austria, 152, 153.
Windmill Hill, Wiltshire, 510, 515.
Wolvercote, Oxfordshire, 26.
Woodhenge, 314–15, 493.
Wor Barrow, Dorset, 313.
Württemberg, 366, 369.

Yang Shao, China, 419.
Yattendon, Berkshire, 612.
Yelista, S. Russia, 209.
Yucatan, 83.

Zabad, Aleppo, Syria, 767.
Zagazig, Egypt, 484 n., map 6.
Zalavrouga, 709.
Zemzem, Mecca, 528.
Zinjirli, Syria, 675, 768, map 4.
Zug, Lake, 361, map 3.
Zuni, U.S.A., 406.
Zürich, Lake, 355, 356, 360, 366, 421, map 3.
Zwierzyniec, Poland, 342.

III. INDEX OF PLANT NAMES

More general information about plants will be found in the Index of Subjects under Agriculture; Food; Gardens; and Plants.

Abies cilicica, 288.
Acacia arabica, 243.
Acacia nilotica, 244–5, 288.
Acorus calamus, 285, 288.
Aegilops, 366–7.
Antiaris toxicaria, 169.
Artemisia absinthia, 282.
Arundo donax, 371.
Astralagus, 244.
Atriplex hortensis, 355.
Avena, 369.

Balanites aegyptica, 288.
Bambus wrayi, 164.
Boehmeria nivea, 431, 449.
Brassica, 354–5, 360, 370.

Camelina, 354, 359, 370.
Canarium strictum, 245.
Cannabis sativa, 373.
Capsella bursa-pastoris, 370.
Carex, 450.
Carthamus tinctorius, 246, 288, 441.
Caryota mens, 372.
Cassia tora, 288.
Cedrus libanotica, 288.
Ceratonia siliqua, 289.
Chenopodiaceae, 261.
Chenopodium album, 355, 370.
Cinnamomum malabrathrum, 288.
Citrullus colocynthis, 288.
Citrus medica, 288.
Cocos nucifera, 372.
Convolvulus scammonia, 249.
Corchorus, 450.
Crocus sativus, 246.
Cruciferae, 360.
Curcuma, 247.
Cymbopogon schoenanthus, 288.
Cyperus esculentus, 288.
Cyperus papyrus, 285, 754.
Cyperus rotundus, 288.

Daucus, 356.
Durio, 169.

Echinochloa, 369.
Erysimum cheiranthoides, 370.
Euphorbia, 172.

Ficus sycomorus, 371.

Galeopsis, 370.
Glycine max, 361.
Gossypium, 373, 432, 449.

Heliotropaeum europaeum, 288.
Herminiera elaphroxylon, 732.
Hibiscus cannabinus, 373.
Hordeum, 367–8, plate 7.
Hyphaene thebaica, 271, 423, 450.

Indigofera tinctoria, 247, 249.
Isatis tinctoria, 247.

Juglans regia, 358.
Juncus acutus, 420, 450.
Juncus maritimus, 245.

Lactuca sativa, 288, 355.
Lactuca serriola, 355.
Lagenaria siceraria, 372.
Lansium, 169.
Lathyrus, 362.
Laurus cinnamomum, 288.
Lawsonia inermis, 246, 294.
Lecanora, 246.
Lens, 362.
Lepidium sativum, 356.
Linum usitatissimum, 288, 358, 372–3, 431, 448.
Lygeum spartum, 423, 450.

Malus, 357.
Mentha piperita, 288.
Moringa oleifera, 288.

Olea europaea, 288, 359.
Opuntia coccinellifera, 245.

Panicum, 369.
Papaver somniferum, 358.
Pennisetum, 369.
Persea, 542.
Phaseolus, 361.
Phoenix dactylifera, 371, 450.
Phragmites communis, 450.
Pimpinella anisum, 288.
Pisum, 361–2.
Plantago lanceolata, 370.
Polygonum lapathifolium, 370.
Prunus, 288, 357–8.
Punica granatum, 372.
Pyrus, 357.

Quercus coccifera, 245.

Raphanus sativus, 288, 356.
Raphia vinifera, 277.
Rhus, 247.
Ricinus communis, 288.
Roccella, 246.
Rosa sancta, 288.
Rosmarinus officinalis, 288.
Rubia tinctorum, 246.
Rubus, 353.
Rumex acetosella, 370.

Saccharum officinarum, 370–1.
Salsola kali, 261.
Santalum album, 288.
Saponaria officinalis, 249.
Scirpus, 420, 421, 450.
Secale, 368.
Sesamum indicum, 288.
Sesamum orientale, 288.
Setaria, 369.
Setaria pumila, 370.
Sinapis, 370.
Sorghum, 369.
Sphagnum, 370.
Spergula arvensis, 370.
Spinacia oleracea, 355.
Stellaria media, 370.
Stipa tenacissima, 421, 450.

Thlaspi arvense, 370.
Trigonella, 248.
Triticum, 363–6, 520, plate 7.
Typha angustata, 420.

Urtica, 355–6, 449.

Vaccinium, 353.
Vicia, 361, 362.
Viola arvensis, 370.
Vitis silvestris, 281.
Vitis vinifera, 281.

Zingiber officinale, 288.
Zizyphus lotus, 271.
Zizyphus spina, 685.

IV. INDEX OF SUBJECTS

Acheulian, *see* Cultures.
Adzes:
  differentiated from axes, 505–6, 601.
  metal, 504, 601–2, 687, 688.
  stone, 497–8, 502, 507.
Agriculture and stockbreeding:
  cultivation: of cereals, 362–70, 522, 550, plate 7; of fruit, 357–8, 551–4; of green vegetables, 354–6; of mustard and sugar, 370–1; of nuts and oil-seeds, 358–60; of pulses, 360–2; of root vegetables, 356; of trees, 371, 450.
  and the lunar calendar, 794–5.
  Neolithic, 42–5, 46–7, 79, 340–1, 349–50, 353–4, 362–3, 374, 501–2.
  in the Nile valley, 539–42, 795.
  in the Tigris and Euphrates valleys, 547–54.
  see also Animals, domestication of; Irrigation.
Ahrensburgians, 160, 161, table E.
Akkadians, 246, 262, 464–9, 524, 545; *see also* Mesopotamia.
Alcohol, 275–85; etymology of, 293.
Algonkin peoples, 176.
Alkali, natural, 260–1.
Alpenquai lake-dwellers, 355, 360, 369.
Alphabet, *see under* Writing, alphabetic.
Alum, 262–3.
Amratians, 509, table E.
Andamanese, 61, 160, 162, 170, 217.
Animals, communication among, 88–9, 91.
Animals, domestication of, 43, 44–5, 75, 79, 175, 501, 704.
  and decoy-hunting, 336, 337–8, 350, plate 6 A.
  development of taming, 338–40.
  draught animals, 719–24.
  experiments in, 340–1.
  morphological effects, 343–50.
  pack-animals, 705–6, 728.
  scavengers and social parasites, 332–7, 351.
  sequence of domestication among animals, 351–2.
  stages in the process of, 341–2.
  symbiosis of species, 328–32.
  theories of the origins of, 327–8, 331, 332, 337, 350.
Antimony, 588, 590; *see also* Stibnite.
Antler, *see* Bone and antler.
Ants, 328–9, 333–5, 338–9.
Anvils, 130–1, 609, 618.
Apes:
  development of the hand, 9–10, 11.
  intelligence, 12–13.
Apes (*cont.*).
  as users of tools, 13; as makers of tools, 14–15.
  visual powers, 12.
Aqueducts, 469, 531–2, 553, 715, plate 20 A.
Arabia, Arabs, 355, 525, 530, 532.
Architecture, *see* Building; Houses.
Arrow-heads, 33, 169, 171, 496, 499, 510–12, 606, 616.
Art, early Celtic, 82.
Art, Egyptian, 209.
  painting grounds, 240–3.
  pigments, 238–40.
Art, Palaeolithic, plate 2.
  artistic impulse in early man, 27–8, 144–5.
    cave drawings and paintings, 33–4, 235, 300, 451, 499, 710, 744, 745; methods of dating, 146–7; techniques, 147–9.
    Cro-Magnon, 32.
  engraving, 149–51.
  plastic: in relief, 151; in the round, 151–3.
  sculpture, 153.
Artesian wells, 528.
Assyrians, 358, 360, 371, 374, 469–73, 532, 552–4, 671; *see also* Mesopotamia.
Astrology, 121, 802.
Astronomy, plates, 34–6.
  and calendar systems, 123–4, 793–5.
  eclipses, computation of, 800, 801.
  'harmony of the spheres', 126.
  planetary theory, 798–801.
  primitive observations, 112–13, 115, 116–20.
  scientific development, 802–3.
Athabaskan peoples, 176.
Aurignacians, *see* Cultures.
Australian aborigines, 35, 138, 157, 730.
  fire-making, 220–1.
  as food-gatherers, 42, 155, 158, 184.
  language, 94, 98–100.
  pet-keeping among, 330.
Australopithecine, 11.
Australopithecus, 20, 22, table C.
Awls, 188, 416, 516, 688.
Axes of bone and antler, 516.
Axes of metal:
  bronze, 609–11; battle-axes, 616; palstaves, 610–11.
  copper, 588, 601–2, 688; battle-axes, 604–5.
  iron, 619; battle-axes, 618, 619.
Axes of stone:
  battle-axes, 512–13, 604.
  differentiated from adzes, 505–6.
  hafted, 70, 307, 497–8, 502; historical survey, 506–8.

Axes of stone (*cont.*).
hand, 25–31, 68, 131–3, 188.
with shaft-hole, 602.

Baboons, 8, 13, 19–20.
Babylonia, 457, 550–1, 787–91, 798–801, table. F; *see also* Mesopotamia.
Badarians, 502, 606; *see also under* Badari *in* Index of Place Names.
Bag-press, 290–1.
Bamboo:
fire kindled with, 219, 220–1, 227.
tools made of, 164, 169, 233.
Bark, objects made of, 518.
Basalt, 477, 506, 675.
Baskets, basketry, 154–5, 173, 174, 304, 448, 449–50, plates, 9, 10.
origins, 413–15; chronological development, 418–24.
bituminous mastic shaped by, 254.
as coffins, 419, 420.
coloured, 422–3.
influence on shapes of pottery, 376–7, 398.
as sieves, 275, 422.
techniques, 415–18.
traps of, 167, 168.
travois of, 175.
Beakers, 401–2.
Beavers, 4–5.
Bedouin, 438, 551.
Beer, 277–81.
Bees, domestication of, 276.
Bellows, 233, 578, 597.
Bible, 157, 230, 243, 248, 249, 252, 253, 258–61, 264, 275, 277, 282, 285, 286–7, 289–90, 292, 359, 365, 448, 451, 541, 554, 564–5, 582, 584, 633, 664, 676–7, 707, 733, 756, 764; Dead Sea scrolls, 766.
Birds, instinctive behaviour of, 2–4.
Bits, *see* Harness.
Bitumen, 250–6, 460, 466, 468, 470, 471, 502, 737.
Blow-gun, 163–6, 170.
Boats and ships, 255.
early development, 731–2; evolution of design and techniques, 738–41.
British, 738, 739.
Egyptian, 734–6.
Mesopotamian coracles and skin floats, 256, 736–8.
sails, 733.
war galleys, 741–3.
see also Canoes.
Bolas, 166, 175.
Bone and antler:
cheek-pieces and bits, 724.
early techniques for working in, 140–1, 188–9.
sculpturing of, 153.
Bone and antler (*cont.*).
tools and weapons of, 31, 32–3, 62, 141, 172, 432–3, 435, 497–8, 506, 514–17, 561.
used in building, 516.
Boomerang, *see* Throwing-stick.
Bow and arrow, 61, 161–3, 172, 178, 499.
arrow-heads, 33, 169, 171, 496, 499, 510–12, 606, 616.
compound bow, 163, 173, 182.
Brachiation, 9, 10, 11–12.
Brain:
in early man, 27, 35.
size, 3, 7, 10, 12, 16, 34–5.
see also Intelligence.
Bridges, 256, 316, 714–15; *see also* Aqueducts.
Britain:
basketry and matting, 421.
boats, 738–9.
Bronze Age burial structures, 312–13; dwellings, 315–16.
cultivation of food plants, 355, 358, 359, 365–6, 369.
culture of Neolithic revolution, 80–2, 195, 510–11.
fire-making, 219, 220, 226.
Iron Age dwellings, 317–22.
linear measurement, 778–9.
Mesolithic and Neolithic dwellings, 303–4, 312.
mining: flint, 558–61; tin, 563, 589–90.
pottery, 377–8, 385–6; carinated bowls, 400; kilns, 393, 396–7.
roads, 712–13.
saltworks, 257.
solid wheel, 203, 206, 211.
weapons, metal, 604, 605, 616, 618.
see also Language; Stonehenge; Woodhenge.
British Columbia, 160, 176, 177, 178, 179, 184, 312, 318, 707, 738.
Bronze, 81–2, 213, 399, 414.
braziers of, 231.
casting, 607–8.
copper alloys, 588–92.
fine metal-work in, 646.
pillars of, in temple of Solomon, 633.
tools and weapons of, 504–5, 510, 608–16.
see also Metal.
Building in brick and stone, plates 18–21 A.
geological and regional influences on, 456–9.
religious architecture, 457–8, 460–1, 462–4, 482–4.
roofing, 472–3, 476, 484.
techniques: in Crete, 484–7; in Egypt, 473–84; in Greece, 485; in Mesopotamia, 459–73.
ziggurats, 467–9.
see also Houses; Stonehenge.
Building in wood, 143, 241, plates 4, 5 A.
bitumen used in, 250, 253, 255–6.

Building in wood (*cont.*).
  Bronze Age burial structures, 312–15; dwellings, 315–17.
  constructional methods: in early Egypt, 304–6, 371–2; in Neolithic Europe, 306–12.
  Iron Age techniques: in Britain, 317–22; in Europe, 322–4.
  see also Houses; Wood; Woodhenge.
Burial mounds, burial structures, megaliths, and tombs:
  beehive tombs at Mycenae, 403, 486, 488.
  in Britain, 81, 195, 312–13, 314–15, 490–4.
  in France, 510–11.
  in Germany, Holland, and Denmark, 314.
  Minoan tholos tombs, 484.
  in Russia, 324–5.
  see also Mummification; Pyramids.
Burrowing wasp (*Ammophila*), 1–2.

'Cadmean letters', 767–8.
Camargue cattle, 344.
Canals:
  from Bavian to Nineveh, 469–70, 531–2.
  irrigation systems, 521, 531–5, 536–7, 546–50, 552–3.
  Nahrwan canal, 548.
  Siloam tunnel, 764.
Candles, 234–5.
Canoes, 313.
  coastal fishing in, 176–7.
  dug-out canoes, 143, 730–1, 738–40, plate 27.
  Egyptian, 731, 732.
  Indonesian, 170.
  whaling canoes, 176–7.
Canopic jars, 268–70, plate 3.
Capsian culture, *see* Cultures.
Casting, *see under* Metal.
Cereals, *see* Plants, cultivation of.
Chains, 656.
Charcoal, 229, 231, 240, 392, 551, 573, 576, 586, 594.
Chariots, 209–10, 700–1, 713, 718, 720, 724–8.
Chelleo-Acheulian culture, *see* Cultures.
Chemical arts and processes:
  bitumen production, 250–6.
  fermentation techniques, 275–7, 284.
  organic dyes, 245–8; craft of dyeing, 248–50, 441, 677–8.
  painting grounds, 240–3.
  painting media, varnishes, and inks, 243–5, 248.
  pigments, 238–40, 244, 502, 514.
  preservative substances, 256–70.
  refining: of gold, 581–2; of galena, 584; of copper ores, 585–7.
  see also Cosmetic arts.
Chileans, 179.
China, 35.
  basketry and matting, 419.
  coin of pure zinc, 650.
  cultivation: of barley, 368; of hemp, 373.
  language, nature of, 88, 94, 97, 772.
  measurement, standards of, 111–12, 783–4.
  metallurgy, 590, 628–31.
  pack transport, 705.
  Pekin man, 23–5.
  porcelain, 78.
  pottery, 385, 401; decoration of, 402, 405; kilns, 393.
  roads, 713–14.
  textiles, 415, 445.
  wheel: potter's, 198, 200; spoked, 213.
  wheeled vehicles, 716; chariots, 722, 726; pictograph, 717.
Chisels:
  bronze, 611–12.
  copper, 603, 687, 688.
  iron, 619.
Chuckchi of Siberia, 225.
Cinerary urns, 324, 378, 401.
Civilizations, *see* Cultures and civilizations.
Clactonian culture, *see* Cultures.
Clay, potter's, 379–80, 405–6, 407.
Cleopatra's Needle, 569.
Clocks:
  sand-clocks, 126.
  shadow-clocks, 112, 113, 797; *see also* Sundials.
  water-clocks, 113, 122, 123, 126, 797.
Clothes, plates 16, 17.
  of fur, 413.
  of hemp, 373.
  sandals of matting, 422.
  of wool, 442.
Cochineal, 245–6.
Coffins of basketry and matting, 419, 420.
Coins, coinage, 584, 585, 637 n., 648, 650.
Combs, 515, 516, 665.
Copper, 64, 66, 399.
  alloys of, 588–92.
  brazing materials, 650–1; soldering of, 652.
  bulls of, on temple at El-Ubaid, 465, 638, 639–40.
  casting techniques: core-casting, 601, 627–8; *cire-perdue*, 588, 607, 608, 634–5.
  mining for, 563–6, 567, 574.
  sheet copper-work, 641.
  smelting and refining, 585–8, 633–4.
  tools and weapons made of, 46, 59–60, 73, 207–8, 509, 513, 600–7, 687.
  tyres of, on primitive wheels, 208.
  see also Metal.
Cosmetic arts:
  alabaster cosmetic jar, plate 3.
  gold cosmetic case from Ur, 654, 656.

Cosmetic arts (*cont.*)
nature and significance of ancient cosmetics, 285–7.
oils and fats used in, 287–9.
preparation of perfumes, 289–91; of ointments, 291–2; of eye-paints, 292–4; of face-paints, 294.
see also Incense.
Cotton:
early history, 373–4.
use of, in textiles, 449.
Crete, Minoan civilization in, 199–200, 202, 204, 212, map 4, table F.
building techniques, 484–7.
chryselephantine work, 662.
dyes, 246–7.
fresco paintings, 242–3.
ivory work, 672–3.
Palace of Minos, 232, 235, 486–7, 672, 714, 715.
pottery, 397, 398, 399, 401 n. 1, 403, 404, 406–7.
roads, 714.
writing, 758–9.
Cro-Magnons, 32, 35.
Cultures and civilizations:
Abbevillian, *see* Chellean.
Acheulian, 25–8, 68, 131–2, table D.
American (Aztec, Inca, Maya), 82–4, 124–6.
Aurignacian, 33, 190, 497, table D.
Capsian, 501, 509, 511, 606.
Chellean, 27, 131, table D.
Chelleo-Acheulian, 25–9, 131–2.
Clactonian, 28–30, 188, table D.
Cortaillod, 373.
Danubian, 309–11, 354, 355, 357, 359, 361, 362, 364–5, 366, 368, 372, 373, 387, 502, 507.
Early Egyptian, 46, 49–55, 80, 102–3, 111, 139, 161; *see further under* Egypt.
Eskimo, 180–3; *see further under* Eskimo.
Greek, 104–5; *see further under* Greece.
Hallstatt, 362, 367, 369, 370, 399, 400, 443, 451, 518, 565, 566–7, 613, 617–18, table E.
Indus valley, 46, 50, 80, 194, 202, table F.
Levalloisian, 29–30, 31, 35, 132–4, table D.
Lower (Early) Palaeolithic, 22, 27, 30, 31, 68.
Magdalenian, 32, 134, 136, 157, 158, 160, 161, 188, 497, table D.
Maglemosian, 175, 190, 498–9, table E.
Mesolithic, 34, 100, 156–7, 161–2, 495 ff., tables D, E.
Middle Palaeolithic, 32.
Minoan, 199–200, 202, 204; *see further under* Crete.
Mousterian, 30–2; map 1 A, table D.
Natufian, 496, 501, 502, 503, 511, 513, 515 520, 542, table E.
Cultures and civilizations (*cont.*)
Neolithic, 42–5, 79, 80–4, 192, 304, 306–12, 349–51, 353, 376–7, 418, 499–503, 561, table E; *see also* Agriculture.
Roman, 82.
Solutrean, 32, table D.
Sumerian, 46, 48–9, 50, 52, 54–7, 80, 101–2, 194, 199–200.
La Tène, 514, 567, 617, 618, table E.
Upper (Late) Palaeolithic, 32–4, 101, 134, 136–9, 300, 413, 495, 559, 745, table D; *see also* Art; Tools and weapons.
see also Diffusion.
Cyprus, map 4.
alum production, 263.
copper mines, 565.
iron industry, 598.
ivory-work, 676, 677.
metal-work, 623–4.
pottery, 403.
script, 761.

Daggers:
bronze, 510, 613–14, 661.
copper, 603–4, 605.
flint, 509–10.
gold dagger sheath from Ur, 654, 656.
iron, 618, 619.
wood, 517.
Danubian culture, *see* Cultures.
Denmark, 168, 192, 314, 355.
food-gatherers, 495–6.
Mesolithic and Neolithic building, 302–3, 311–12.
textiles, 442–3, plate 17 A.
the wheel, 206, 207, 209, 210, 213.
Diffusion, 45, 64.
between the Old World and the New 'not proven', 82–4, 166.
effects of, on Britain, 80–2.
of fire-drills, 226.
a fundamental factor in technological progress, 77–80, 84.
of metal-working skills, 573, 576.
of microliths, 496.
of primitive writing, 761.
of the wheel, 203–4, 207, 209–11, 716.
see also Invention, independent.
Digging-sticks, 59, 502, 510.
Discovery:
definition, 58–9; example, 59–60.
for further entries see under Invention.
Door-sockets, 193–4, 306, 472.
Drills:
arrow-headed drill, 613.
bow-drill, 182, 187, 189–90, 224–5, 612–13, 679–80, 688, 689.
fire-drill, 198, 220, 222–4.
hand-drill, 189.

Drills (*cont.*)
  pump-drill, 190, 191, 225–6.
  S-section iron drill, 619.
  strap-drill, 197.
  thong-drill, 220, 221, 224–5.
  tubular drill, 191–2.
Dyaks of Borneo, 117.
Dyes, dyeing, *see* Chemical arts.

Economic organization, *see* Society, forms of.
Egypt, map 6, tables E, F.
  art, 209, 238; painting grounds, 240–3; painting media, varnishes, and inks, 243–5; pigments, 238–40.
  basketry and matting, 418–19, 420, 422–4, plates 9, 10.
  boats and ships, 731, 732–6.
  boring and drilling, 190, 192, 193.
  building construction, 304–6, 371–2, 473–84, plate 19.
  calendar systems, 121–4, 793–8.
  copper production, 564–5.
  cosmetic arts, 286–95.
  domestication of animals, 340–1.
  dyes and dyeing, 246–50, 441.
  early civilization, 49–55, 139, 161, 168, 496, 509.
  fire-making, 224–5; lighting, 234, 237.
  food: culinary arts, 271–85; cultivation of food plants, 355–6, 359, 360, 361–2, 365–6, 367–8, 371, 501–2, 514, 539–42; preservation of, 263–5.
  gold-mining, 579–81.
  iron production, 594, 596–7.
  irrigation, 46; cisterns and wells, 526, 528; dams, 529; Nile flood, 535–42, 795, plate 20 B; water-lifting devices, 523–4, 542.
  ivory work, 663–4, 666–70, 674, 679.
  language and writing, 102–3, 287, plate 32; alphabetic signs, 762; hieroglyphics, 80, 192, 222, 223, 237, 263, 281, 439–40, 747, 752–7; syllabic signs, 747–50.
  mathematics, 791–3.
  measurement, 111, 775–7, 778; standards of capacity, 781–2; of weight, 779–81, 783, plate 31 B.
  metallurgy, 578–9; fine metal-work, 627–8, 641–2, 649, 655–8, 659–60; tools and weapons, 504, 604, 606.
  mummification, 266–70, 277, 756.
  pleasure-gardens, 523, 543–4.
  pottery, 377, 387, 388, 389; kilns, 394, 395.
  religion, 123–4.
  rope-making, 452–4.
  salt production, 257–60; alum, 262.
  silver and lead production, 583–4.
  stone quarrying, 477–9, 526, 568–70.

Egypt (*cont.*)
  textiles, 414, 431–2, 434–5, 436–41, 449; looms, 427; plates 11, 12 A, 13–16.
  transport, 706, 710, 714; draught animals, 722–3; chariots, 725–8.
  viticulture, 282–4.
  wheel, potter's, 199, 200; wheeled vehicles, 209, 211–12.
  wood-work, 685–7, 688–702.
  for numerous references to specific sites and localities, see Index of Place Names.
Electrum, 623.
Embalming, *see* Mummification.
Ertebølle people, Denmark, 303, 495–6, 499, table E.
Eskimo, 62, 63, 69, 94, 156, 163, 190, 413, 736.
  as food-gatherers and hunters, 41, 42, 158–61, 166, 180–3, 184–5, 336.
  use of fire, 219, 222–3, 224–5, 226, 229; heating and lighting, 235–6.
Esparto-grass (halfa), 450.
Etruscans, 518.
  gold bowl with granular decoration, 657, 658.
  inscriptions, 769–70.

Falcon clan, rulers of Egypt, 49–50.
Fat, use of, in ancient cosmetics, 289, 290.
Fermentation techniques, *see* Chemical arts.
Fezzan sheep, 345.
Fibre plants, 355–6.
  cultivation of, 372–4, 522.
  preparation for spinning, 424.
  use of, in ancient textiles, 447–51; in rope-making, 453–4.
Files, 613, 620.
Fire:
  discovery of, 25, 28, 58, 216–18.
  instruments for making: bow-drill, 224–5; fire-drill, 198, 220, 222–4, 226; fire-piston, 226–8; fire-plough, 221–2; fire-saw, 220–2; pump-drill, 225–6; thong-drill, 220, 221, 224–5.
  methods of making: by percussion, 218–20; by wood-friction, 229–30.
  transfer and transport of, 229–30.
  use of, in metallurgy, 65, 576–9, 594, 624–5, 627, 633–4; in mining, 565–6, 567; in pottery-making, 376, 382–3, 391–7.
  see also Fuel; Heating and lighting.
Fish-hooks, 166–8, 176–7, 498–9, 515–16.
Fishing:
  with blow-gun, 164.
  by flares, 119.
  with harpoon, 158, 160, 176–7.
  with line and hook, 166–8, 176–7, 516, 732.
  with nets, 166, 176–7, 180, 265.
  with poison, 173.
  with traps, 168, 177.

Flails, 70.
Flax, 288, 358, 540.
early history, 372–3.
use of, in textiles, 448–9.
Food:
beginnings of agriculture and stockbreeding, 42–4, 46–7, 79, 340–1, 349–50, 353–4, 362–3, 374.
cultivation of cereals, 362–70, 522, 550; of fruit, 357–8, 551–4; of mustard and sugar, 370–1; of nuts and oil-seeds, 358–60; of pulses, 360–2; of vegetables, 353–6.
growth in variety of, 270–2.
man's progress in the quest of, 64.
in the organization of primitive societies, 40–4.
Food, cooking of:
in primitive societies, 31, 41, 231, 270–1.
methods and equipment, 271–5, 401.
Food, preservation of:
contributes to the settlement of peoples, 184–5.
by drying, 263–4.
food stores in early civilizations, 42, 43, 47, 50, 52, 263, 537.
methods of Paiute Indians, 173; of Patagonian Indians, 175.
by salting, 258, 259, 264–6.
by smoking, 263.
Food-gatherers:
characteristics of economies and social organization, 184–6.
diversity of techniques among, 183–4.
honey-collectors, 275.
primitive economies of, 40–2, 154, 495–6.
techniques in specific habitats: Arctic regions, 179–83; continental scrub and desert, 172–3; high latitude grasslands, 174–5; 'Mediterranean' regions, 173–4; northern forest lands, 175–9; tropical grassland and scrub, 171–2; tropical rain forests, 168–71.
tools and techniques used in foraging, 154–5; in hunting and fishing, 155–68, 336–8, 350, 498–9, 510–12, 515–16, 518.
variations in economic reward, 184.
beginnings of cultivation, 353–4, table E.
Fruit, *see* Plants, cultivation of.
Fuegians, 184, 219, 300, 563, 730.
harpoon of, 158, 159, 178.
method of transporting fire, 230.
Fuel, 228–30, 277, 382, 391–2.
influence on development of metal-working, 576.
Furniture, 685, 686, 689, 692–3, 696–702, plates 23–5.

Galena (lead sulphide), 293, 583, 584.
Gardens:
Babylonian, 550–4; hanging gardens at Babylon, 551.
Egyptian, 523, 543–4.
Geoponica, 405–6, 412 (59).
Gerzeans, 509, 512, 516, table E; *see also under* Gerzeh *in* Index of Place Names.
Gesture, systems of, to supplement speech, 94–5.
Glass:
bottles of, 286.
obsidian, 563, 642.
recipes, 260, 261, 262.
Glazing, 471, 485.
Glue, 695, 696.
Gold, 64, 66, 243.
filigree and granulation, 654–8.
gold-leaf, 677–8, 698–9, 700, 701.
jewellery, 656, 659.
mining and refining, 526, 563, 572, 574, 579–82, 589, 594.
objects of: Etruscan bowl, 657, 658; figurines and objects from Ur, 643–5, 654; hawk's head from Hierakonpolis, 641–2; Russian and German objects, 646–8; Tutankhamen's coffin, 660, frontispiece, plate 22.
as solder, 650–1, 652–3.
value-ratio with silver, 585.
weighed by balance, 779.
Granite, 477, 478, 569–70, 574.
Grasses, *see* Reeds.
Gravettians, 190.
Greece, Greeks, 234, map 4, table F.
astronomical knowledge, 802–3.
building techniques, 485, 487–8.
fine metal-work, 645–6, 658, 660–1; chryselephantine work (Zeus of Phidias), 661–2, 681.
food plants cultivated, 355, 356.
iron production, 598.
ivory work, 674–5.
language, 104–5; writing, 767–8, 769–71.
measurement: linear, 777; of time, 121, 126.
pottery, 386, 390; decoration of, 403; kilns, 393, 395; trade in, 401.
textiles, 443–5.
water conservation, 531.
Gypsum, 469, 482 n.

Hadendoa people, 427.
Halberds, 614.
Hallstatt culture, *see* Cultures.
Hammers, 129–32, 608–9, 610, 618, 688.
Hammurabi, Code of, 256, 280, 548–9.
Hands:
of apes, 9–10, 11; of man, 10–12.
communication by gesture, 18.

Hands (*cont.*)
finger-tip painting by primitive man, 146, 148.
left hand/right hand, 19, 24–5, 31.
Harness and yoke, 719–22.
bits, 722–4.
Harpoons, 158–61, 176–7, 178, 498, 516.
of the Eskimo, 181–2.
Heating and lighting:
by primitive man, 230–1.
development of the indoor fire, 231–3.
hearth accessories, 232–3, plate 5 B.
oil-lamps, 235–7.
tapers and candles, 234–5.
torches, 233–4, 566, 567.
Helwanians of Egypt, 496.
Hemp, 373.
Henna, 246, 289, 294, 441.
Hoes, 502, 507, 539–40, 620.
Hominidae, 12–13, 18, 20, 22, 34.
Homo:
neanderthalensis, 22; *see also* Man, Neanderthal.
sapiens, 22–5, 27–30, 32, table C.
Houses, 177, 178.
bitumen used in building, 250, 253, 255–6, 460, 466.
Bronze Age, 315–17.
Cretan, 484–5.
drainage systems, 466.
early stone door-sockets, 193–4, 306, 472.
Egyptian, 304–6, 473–5.
influence of environment on structure-type, 299, 307, 456–7, 459.
Iron Age, 317–24.
Mesopotamian, 306, 459–60, 469, 472.
Neolithic, 306–12.
Palaeolithic and Mesolithic, 299–304.
Hungary, metal tools and weapons from, 602, 614, 616, 625.

Incense, 55, 260, 289.
preparation of, 294–5.
India:
Brahmi, Sanskrit, and Prakrit scripts, 771–2.
fire-making, 220, 224, 229.
iron production, 597.
potter's wheel, 198, 202.
sugar cultivation, 370–1.
textiles, 432, 449.
see also Indus valley civilization.
Indigo, 247, 249, 441.
Indus valley civilization, 46, 50, 80, 194, 246, map 5.
irrigation, 521–2.
script, 760.
wheeled vehicles, 717, 719.
see also Harappa *and* Mohenjo-Daro *in* Index of Place Names.
Ink, *see* Chemical arts.
Inscriptions, 57, 102, 453, 459, 531, 537–8, 713, plates 28–31.
boustrophedon arrangement of lines, 758, 761, 767–8, 770, 772.
from Byblos, 761, 762, 763, plate 31 A.
Chinese oracle bones, 772.
Etruscan, 769–70.
on fine metal-work, 630–1, 637 n., 649.
Greek, 104.
Latin, 770.
on the Moabite Stone, 764–5.
of Sennacherib, 533–4.
in Sinaitic script, 762.
on stone door-socket, 194.
on wood, 684.
Insects:
instinctive behaviour of, 1–2.
as scavengers, 333–5.
as slave-holders, 338–9.
symbiosis among, 328–9.
Instinctive behaviour patterns, 1–6.
Intelligence:
of apes and monkeys, 7–8, 12–13.
and the capacity for invention, 60–2.
in primitive racial groups, 34–6.
related to development of the cortex of the brain in man, 13, 15–17, 19, 35.
Invention:
definition, 59, 60.
analysis of the factors contributing to: mutation and variation, 66–74, 83–4; mental states in man, 75; directional research, 75–7.
extreme slowness of man's progress in, 60–2, 128–9.
independent, 133, 166, 226, 227–8.
limited by environment and material resources, 62–6.
Iron, 73, 219–20, 243.
in fine metal-work, 623.
meteoric iron, 593–4, 616.
opencast working and mining, 568, 574, 593.
smelting and 'steeling', 573, 576–9, 593–8, 617.
spread of iron-working, 595–6, 597, 654.
tools and weapons, 82, 321, 322, 504, 616–21.
welding of, 654.
see also Metal.
Iroquois Indians, 36, 225.
Irrigation:
beginnings, 520–2.
mathematics of, 790.
in the Nile valley, 535–9, plate 20 B.
perennial: in Egypt, 542–5; in Mesopotamia, 545–54, plates 20 A, 21 B.
and warfare, 554–5.

Irrigation (*cont.*)
water conservation, 528–31; conduction by canals and *qanaats*, 531–5.
water-lifting devices, 522–5, 542.
wells and water-holes, 525–8.
see also Canals.
Israel, *see* Palestine.
Italy, 211, 213–14.
dwellings: Bronze Age, 317; Iron Age, 324.
Ivory, plates 23–5.
chryselephantine work, 661–2, 681.
colouring of, 243, 669–70, 677–8.
fine ivory work: in Egypt, 666–70, 685, 691–2; in Mesopotamia, 670–2; in Crete and Syria, 672–3.
furniture, 675–6.
panels, 671, 673, 676–7, 678.
pyxides, 674–5, 680.
sculpturing of, 153, 666, 668–9, 673, 681.
sources of supply, 663–4.
techniques for working in, 677–81.
toilet objects, 665, 670, 674.
tools and weapons of, 32–3, 62, 435, 514–17, 665.

Japan, 234.
language and writing, 96, 772–3.
pottery, 384; potter's wheel, 197.
Javelins, 156, 157, 158, 605.
and blow-gun, 163–6.
Jewellery, 655–9.
Jute, 450–1.

Kalahari Bushmen, 162.
economy of, 171–2, 184.
Kilns, potters', 392–7.
Knives, 508–9, 513.
carved handles, 516–17, 667, 669.

Lake-villages, 310, 311, 312, 318–21, 323, 414, 588, 713, map 3.
basketry and matting from, 420–1, plate 9 D.
cultivation of plants at, 355, 357, 358, 360, 361, 362, 369, 370, 372, 373.
textiles from, 435–6, 445, 448, plate 12 B.
weapons and tools from, 508, 510.
Lamps, 33, 147, 235–7, 259.
Language:
defined in relation to speech, 89.
facilitates development of tool-making, 17–19, 27.
a fundamental factor in the development of social groups, 89–92, 101–3, 104–6.
grammatical systems, 96–8, 102, 746–7.
Indo-European group, 103–5, 757.
linguae francae, 97–8.
a primitive language examined, 98–100.
sound values in relation to words and forms, 85–8, 89–90, 93, 95–6, 104, 106, 755; syllabic signs, 747–50.

Language (*cont.*)
specific languages: Arabic, 86, 97, 98; Arunta, 94, 98–100; Bantu, 95; Chinese, 88, 94, 97, 772; Egyptian, 102–3, 287, 755–6; English, 85–8, 90, 97–8, 99, 104; Finno-Ugric, 98; French, 93; German, 86, 93; Greek, 97, 102, 104–5, 761, 767–8; Hebrew, 97, 761, 764–6; Hittite, 752, 757–8; Hottentot, 90, 95–6; Japanese, 96, 772–3; Korean, 96; Latin, 97, 104–5; Polish, 93; Russian, 99; Sanskrit, 104; Sumerian, 101–2, 748–50, 751–2; Syriac, 767.
spread of, in Stone Age, 100–1.
see also Speech.
Lasso, 166.
Lathes, 192–3, 518, 680, 688.
Lead, 581, 582–5, 590.
Leather, 398, 399, 453, 454, 728, 757.
Levalloisian culture, *see* Cultures.
Lighting, *see* Heating and lighting.
Locking devices, 692, 695.
Looms, 414, 417, 425–8, 432, 435–6.
backstrap loom, 445.
horizontal ground-loom, 426, 427, 437–8.
vertical, 426, 427, 438–40.
warp-weighted loom, 426, 427–8, 442, 443–5.
Lubrication, 198.
'Lyngby' culture, 497, table E.

Mace-heads as weapons, 510, 512, 517.
Madder (*Rubia tinctorum*), 246, 249, 441.
Magdalenian culture, *see* Cultures.
Magic, *see* Superstition and magic.
Maglemosian culture, *see* Cultures.
Malachite (copper carbonate), 293.
Man, primitive:
carnivorous habits, 19–21.
development of the cortex of the brain, 13, 15–17, 19, 35.
evolution of, 9–10, tables B, C.
hand of, 10–12.
intelligence, 34–6.
Neanderthal, 29–31, 35, table C.
Pekin, 21, 23–5, 31, 218.
skill, 22–34, 60–1.
speech and language, 18–19, 89–92.
visual power, 12, 35–6.
for Swanscombe, etc., *see* Index of Place Names.
Manipuris, 407.
Maoris, 318, plate 27.
Mathematics, plates 33–6.
astronomical calculations, 798–803.
early number-symbols, 785–7.
and economic problems, 790–1, 792.
fractions, 792–3.
geometrical problems, 789–90, 791–2.
linear and quadratic equations, 787–9.

Mats, 413, 414.
bed-matting, 420.
reed and rush mats, 419, 420, 423, 468, 550.
Maya civilization, 82–3.
calendar system, 121, 124–6.
use of hand-drills, 189.
Measurement:
linear measurement: Egyptian, 775–7, 778; Greek, 777; Northern cubit, 777–8.
primitive scales of, 110–13, 775.
standardization, 110, 774–5.
of time, 112–13; by primitive peoples, 115–20; by early civilized peoples, 120–7.
see also Weights and measures.
Medicine, 287.
salt as an emetic, 258, 260.
Megaliths, *see* Burial grounds.
Melanesians, 406, 407.
Mercurago, spoked wheel from, 213–14.
Mesolithic culture, *see* Cultures.
Mesopotamia, maps 4, 7, tables E, F.
astronomical observations and calculations, 798–801; calendar systems, 793–4, 795; plates 33–5.
boats and ships, 256, 731, 736–8.
bridge over the Euphrates, 256, 715.
building construction: beginnings, 306, 459; early use of brick and stone, 459–64; improved techniques in Akkadian period, 464–9; in Assyrian period, 469–73; plates 18, 20.
chemical arts, 239–40, 241–3, 244, 245, 247; bitumen industry, 250–6; brewing techniques, 279–80; salt production, 258; soap and detergents, 261–2.
copper production, 563–4.
cosmetic arts, 286–95.
food preservation, 264–5; culinary arts, 272–82; cultivation of food plants, 360, 362, 364, 365, 367, 547–54.
gardens, 550–4.
iron production, 594, 597–8.
irrigation: canals, 469–70, 531–2; dams, 529; perennial irrigation, 545–55; *qanaats*, 532–4; water-lifting devices, 524–5; wells, 526–7.
ivory work, 664, 670–2, 675, 677–8.
language and writing, 80, 101–2, 205, 206, 252, 280, 745–7; cuneiform script, 750–2; syllabic signs, 747–50.
mathematics: algebraic and geometrical problems, 787–91; number symbols, 785–7.
measurement: linear, 778; of capacity, 782; of weight, 780–1.
metal-work, 623–4, 626, 627, 632–3, 638–41, 643–6, 648–9, 654–6, 659, 661.
pottery, 378, 405; kilns, 395; potter's wheel, 199–200, 202–3.
Mesopotamia (*cont.*)
silver and lead trade, 583.
social organization of Sumerian civilization, 46, 48–9, 50, 52, 54–7.
textiles, 432.
transport, 705–6, 710, 713; draught animals, 720–1, 723; wheeled vehicles, 207–8, 209–10, 717–18, 725–7.
wood-work, 684.
woollen industry, 248–9.
for numerous references to specific sites and localities, see Index of Place Names.
Metal, Metallurgy:
annealing, 624–5, 636–7.
casting and moulding, 625–35; of bronze, 607–8; *cire-perdue* process, 588, 607, 608, 634–5; of copper, 588, 601, 606, 627–8; cored castings, 625–7.
colouring of, 243.
discovery, 46–7, 59–60; early use, 64–5, 73, 503–5, 572–9, 600–1.
engraving, 648–9.
extraction of silver and lead, 582–5.
filigree and granulation, 654–9.
gold refining, 580–2, 594.
inlays and enamels, 659–62.
repoussé and chasing, 642–8.
rivets, 649–50.
sheet metal-work (sinking and raising a bowl), 636–9.
smelting, 564, 573; of copper ores, 585–8, 633–4; of iron ores, 576–9, 593–8, 617.
soldering and welding, 649–54.
stamping, 648.
wrought metal statues, 639–42.
see also Mining; Tools; *and names of individual metals.*
Mills, 274.
Mining:
copper, 563–6, 567.
evolution of techniques (chart), 574.
flint, 514–15, 558–63.
gold, 526, 563, 579–81, 589.
iron, 568, 574, 593.
salt, 566–7.
tin, 563, 589–90.
Minoan civilization, *see* Crete.
Moabite Stone, 764–5.
Mosaic decoration, 462, 464, 465.
mosaic 'standard' from Ur, 705, 718.
'town mosaic' from Knossos, 485.
Mother-of-pearl, 465, 665, 670.
Mousterian culture, *see* Cultures.
Mummification, 260, 266–70, 277, 756.
Murex purple, 247–8.

Nagas, pottery made by, 406, 407.
Natron (sodium carbonate), 257, 259–60, 268–70.

Natufians of Palestine, *see* Cultures.
Nazarites, 285.
Needle-shuttles, 432–4.
Neolithic, *see* Agriculture; Cultures.
Nets used in hunting and fishing, 166, 167, 170, 176–7, 178.
Nettles as fibre-plants, 355–6, 449.
Nicobar Islanders, 170.
Niello, 623–4.
Nitre (potassium nitrate), 261–2.
Noose, 166.
Nootka peoples, 168, 176, 177.
Nuts and oil-seeds, *see* Plants, cultivation of.

Odyssey, 444.
Oil as a cosmetic, 286, 287–9, 290–2.
Olive, 359–60.
Opium, 358–9.
Ovens, 272–3.

Painting:
  by early man, 33–4, 146–9, 235, 451, 744, 745, plate 2.
  on frescoes in Crete, 486; in Mesopotamia, 462–3, 470–1.
  grounds for, 240–3.
  media for, 243–4.
  pigments, 238–40, 244, 502, 514.
  on pottery, 241, 383–4, 408.
  see also Art.
Paiute Indians, 172–3, 183, 184, 300.
Palace of Minos, Knossos, 486–7, 672, 714, 715.
Palanquins, 705.
Palestine, maps 4, 8, table F.
  agriculture, primitive, 520.
  basketry and matting, 419–20.
  copper production, 564.
  cosmetic arts, 289, 292.
  dyeing, 250.
  earthenware lamps, 236–7.
  food preservation, 265; culinary arts, 271–2, 274, 277, 281–2, 285.
  fuller's soap, 261.
  iron production, 597.
  ivory work, 672, 675.
  metal-work, 633–4.
  Phoenician alphabet, spread of, 764–6.
  pottery, 387, 390; potter's wheel, 200–2, 204.
  salt production, 258–9; alum, 263.
  textiles, 432, 434.
  water conservation, 530–1.
  see also Cultures, Natufian; Phoenicians.
Paper, 450, 756, 757.
Parchment, 757.
Patagonian Indians, 175.
Paviotso seed-gatherers, 154–5.
Pekin man, *see* Man.
Perfumes, *see* Cosmetic arts.
Persia, map 5.
  early syllabary, 752.
  measurement: linear, 779; of capacity, 782–3.
  metal-work, 660, 661.
  potter's wheel, 203.
  roads, 713.
  wheeled vehicles, 204–9.
Peru:
  basketry, 414, 415, 421–2.
  early cultures, 82–4.
  reed rafts, 731–2.
  textiles, 424, 436, 445, 449.
Pestle and mortar, 273, 502, 514.
Petroleum products:
  bitumen, 250–6.
  crude oil, 251.
Phaistos disk, 759.
Phoenicians:
  alphabetic script, 104, 763–8.
  dyeing, 247.
  irrigation, 531.
  ivory work, 672, 674–6, 678–81.
  measurement, 782.
  as traders, 56, 664.
  weapons, 512.
Picks, 514–15, 558, 561, 563, 620.
Pigment, *see* Chemical arts.
Piston, 226–8.
Pithecanthropus, 22–3, table C; *see also* Man, Pekin.
Pitjendadjara tribe, 23.
Plants, cultivation of:
  origins, 353–4.
  cereals, 362–70, 522, 550, plate 7.
  fibre plants (flax, hemp, cotton, etc.), 372–4, 424, 447–51, 522.
  fruit, 357–8.
  gourds, 372.
  green vegetables, 354–6.
  mustard and sugar, 370–1.
  nuts and oil-seeds, 358–60.
  pulses, 360–2.
  reeds, 371–2, 449–50.
  root vegetables, 356.
  trees, 371, 450, 551–4.
  see also Agriculture and stockbreeding; Gardens.
Plaster of Paris, 482 n.
Ploughs, 74, 210, 504, 539–40.
  seed-plough, 550.
Poison used in hunting, 158, 163, 166, 169, 172, 173.
Potter's wheel, 65, 71–2, 80, 83, 187, 194–5, 377.
  archaeological evidence for, in early civilizations, 198–202.
  function and operation of, 195–7, 378, 388–90.

Potter's wheel (*cont.*)
origin and diffusion of, 202–4, 404–5.
varieties of the simple wheel, 197–8.
Pottery, 65, 73, 78, 174, 372, 501–2, plate 8.
origins and early history, 376–9.
basic processes of manufacture, 379–84.
cinerary urns, 324, 378, 401.
decoration of, 241, 383–4, 400–5, 408.
firing, 382–3, 391–7, 410, 411.
industry, methods of organization, 405–9.
shaping, 384–91; influence of magic on, 400–1; imitation in pottery shapes, 397–400.
wine-jars of, 283, 406.
Proconsul (Miocene ape), 9, table C.
Prosimians, 6–10.
Przewalski horse of Mongolia, 342, 346–7, 721.
Pulses, *see* Plants, cultivation of.
Punan people of Borneo, 164.
Pygmies, 170–1.
Pyramids, 473, 475–6, 714, 792, 793.
method of construction, 481–2.

Qanaats, 532–4.
Quarrying, 477–9, 526, 560, 569–70.

Ramie (China grass), 449.
Reeds, rushes, sedges, grasses, 371–2, 449–50, 468, 473, 550.
Religion, religious practices, 114.
animal sacrifice, 327.
and cosmetics, 286–7, 289.
of early Egyptians, 123–4; rites connected with mummification, 266, 267.
and the lunar calendar, 794.
primitive temples, 47–9.
taboos, 241, 331.
see also Burial grounds; Stonehenge; *for* Religious architecture *see under* Temples.
Rig-Veda, 449, 728.
Roads, 712–14.
Rock asphalt, *see* Bitumen.
Romans, 82, 219, 231, 770.
food plants cultivated by, 355, 356, 362.
linear measurement, 778.
pottery, 378; kilns, 393, 394.
torches and candles, 234, 235; lamps, 237.
Rope-making, 451–4.
Rosetta Stone, 754.
Rotary motion, 71, 187, 274.
partial: boring, 187–9; drilling, 189–93; spinning, 194.
true or continuous: potters' wheels, 194–204; wheeled vehicles, 204–14.
Russia:
Iron Age burial structures, 324–5.
metal-work, 646–7.
Palaeolithic and Neolithic settlements, 301–2, 307, 309.

Russia (*cont.*)
wheeled vehicles, 716, 717, 719.
Yukaghir peoples, 179.

Saddle-querns, 273–4, 502, 514.
Safflower, saffron, turmeric, 246–7, 249, 259, 441.
Sakai people of Malaya, 164–5, 169–70.
Sal ammoniac (ammonium chloride), 262.
Salt (sodium chloride), 256–9, 264–6.
mining for, 566–7.
Saws:
bronze, 613.
copper, 207–8, 570, 603, 688.
fire-saw, 220–2.
flint, 603.
iron, 619–20.
Sculpture, 153.
in ivory, 153, 661–2, 666, 668–9, 673, 681.
in stone, 469, 470.
in wood, 689–70, 699, 702.
Scythes, 514.
Scythians, 373.
Semang people of Malaya, 162, 168–70, 183, 184.
Sheep, 344, 345, 451.
Shells:
as burnishing tools, 390.
as currency, 174.
as decoration in ivory work, 670–1; in metal-work, 661.
as lamps, 236.
Ships, *see* Boats and ships.
Shoe-last celts, 507.
Sickles, 502, 503, 513–14, 520, 541–2, 698.
Sieves, 275, 422, 566.
Siloam tunnel, 764–5.
Silver, 581, 582–5.
vase of Entemena, 652, 653.
Skill:
evolution of, in lower animals, 1–6; in primates, 6–19; in man, 22–34.
hereditary influences on, 35–6.
related to power of conceptual thought, 14, 17.
Skis, 708–9.
Sledges, 205, 206, 210, 479, 481, 516, 707–11.
types of runner, 708.
Sleeve and socket, 71.
Slings, 156, 157, 502, 512.
Smiths, advent of, 579, 591, 596.
Soap, 260, 261.
Soay (Hebrides) sheep, 344, 345.
Society, forms of:
and domestication of animals, 327–8.
economic classes, emergence of, 53.
economic imperialism, 56–7.
food-gatherers, 40–2, 184–6.

Society, forms of (*cont.*)
language and writing, role of, in development of social groups, 89–92, 102–3, 104–6, 745–6, 755–7.
of the Neolithic revolution, 42–5, 46–7, 79, 340–1, 349–50.
organization of ivory workers, 664–6.
tribute state, 50–5.
of the urban revolution, 45, 49–50, 52–3, 80, 101–2, 377.
Solder, *see under* Metal.
Solutreans, 500.
Spain, tin mines of, 589, 591–2.
Spears, 73.
all-wooden, 30, 141.
hafted, 32–3, 142.
heads: bronze, 615–16; copper, 605; iron, 618; multiple-point, 160–1, 173, 498.
widely used by food-gatherers, 157–61.
see also Harpoon; Javelin.
Spear-thrower, 157–60.
Speech:
in children and aphasiacs, 92–4.
'clicks' of Bushmen and Hottentots, 90, 95–6.
defined in relation to language, 89.
distinguished from sounds made by animals, 88–9.
earliest forms of communication, 18–19.
and sound-values in language: consonants, 86–8, 93; onomatopoeia, 89–90, 91–2; vowels, 85–6, 93.
supplemented by gesture, 94–5.
see also Language.
Spindles, 70, 187, 194, 424–5, 433, 437–8.
Spindle-whorls, 433, 434, 435, 438.
Spinning, 424–5, 434, 437–8, 453, plates 14–17; *see also* Textiles.
Spinning wheel, 72, 83.
Steel, *see under* Iron.
Stibnite (antimony trisulphide), 293, 582, 588.
Stone:
beads, 139–40.
building in, 469–70, 475–84, 491.
door-sockets, 193–4, 306, 472.
lamps, 33, 147, 235–6.
microliths, 496, 502.
quarrying in Egypt, 477–9, 526, 560, 569–70, 714.
roads of, 714.
sculpture in, 469, 470.
techniques for working in: anvil, 130–1; blade-flake, 134–6; cylinder-hammer, 131–2; hammerstone, 129–30; with metal tools, 504; polishing and grinding, 139–40, 506; prepared-core (tortoise-core), 132–4; pressure-flaking, 137–9; secondary flaking, 136–7; *tranchet*, 496–7; plates 1, 21 A.
Stone (*cont.*)
tools and weapons of, 19–32, 67–9, 73, 128–9, 503, 601.
vessels, 398–9.
see also under names of specific tools and weapons.
Stonehenge, 81, 195, 315, 490–4, 712, plate 21 A.
Stones as missiles, 157, 512.
Stones, precious, 574.
Stones, semi-precious, 243, 572, 574, 659, 661.
Sumer, 48–9, 101–2, 203, 464–9, 545, 670, 745–52, 777; *see also* Mesopotamia.
Sundials, 113, 123, 126.
Superstition and magic, 47, 114, 125, 251, 504, 592.
and cosmetics, 286–7, 289.
influence on pottery shapes, 400–1.
magical 'knife', 666.
magical powers of salt, 257, 259, 260; of alum, 262.
and mummification, 266, 267, 270, 756.
primitive art as sympathetic magic, 144, 146.
Swiss lake-villages, *see* Lake-villages.
Swords:
bronze, 614–15.
iron, 617–18.
Syria, map 8.
ivory work, 672–3, 675–6.
spread of alphabetic script, 766–7.

Tapers, 234.
Tasmanians, 183, 184, 185.
Technology, progress of:
and accident, 60–2.
and the cooking of food, 270–1, 272–5.
and the cultivation of plants, 374.
and diffusion, 77–80.
environmental factors, 62–6.
and the individual, 38–40.
see also Invention.
Teeth, evolution of, in man, 20–1.
Temples, architectural features of, 457–8, 460–1, 462–4, 482–4.
Painted Temple, Uqair, 462–3.
Red Temple, Erech, 463.
White Temple, Erech, 462.
La Tène culture, *see* Cultures.
Textiles, plates 11–17.
origins, 413–15.
chronological development, 431–45.
techniques of spinning, 424–5; of weaving, 428–31.
see also Fibre plants; Looms.
Thracians, 373.
Throwing-sticks (boomerangs), 155–7, 499, 517, 518.

Time, measurement of, 110.
  calendar systems, 123–4, 793–5.
  by early civilized peoples, 120–7.
  by primitive peoples, 115–20.
  temporal and equinoctial hours, 113, 796–7.
  time-dimension, different aspects of, 114–15, 126–7.
  zodiacal hours and degrees, 112–13, 797.
  see also Astronomy; Clocks; Sundials.
Tin, 563, 588–92.
Tollund (Iron Age) Man, 355, 359, 370, plate 6 B.
Tomb:
  of Agamemnon, 486, 488.
  of Baqt, 437–8.
  of Hetepet, 540.
  of Khety, 437–8.
  of Khnemhetep, 437, 438.
  of Mereruka, 341.
  of Tehutihetep, 438.
  of Tutankhamen, *see* Tutankhamen's tomb.
  see also Burial mounds.
Tongs, 233, 620, 635.
Tool-making:
  analysis of factors in the discovery of, 67–74.
  distinguished from tool-using, 14, 128.
  encouraged by growth of carnivorous habits, 19–21.
  facilitated by development of language, 17–19, 27.
  growth of specialists in, 46–7, 49, 52, 53.
  intermittent in early man, 23.
  mechanical principles applied to, 33.
  techniques for working in bone and ivory, 140–1, 188–9; in copper, 600–1; in stone, 129–40.
Tools and weapons:
  core-tools and flake-tools, 23, 28–30, 132–9.
  first standardized implements, 25, 27, 29, 68, 79, 188.
  hafting of, 31, 33, 69, 70.
  materials used for: bamboo, 164, 169, 233; bone, 31, 32–3, 62, 141, 172, 432–3; bronze, 81–2, 504–5, 608–16; copper, 46, 59–60, 600–7; iron, 82, 321, 322, 618–21.
  Neolithic trade in, 500–1.
  primitive stone artifacts, 23–5, 128–9, 496.
  tools to make other tools, 15.
  used by: apes and monkeys, 13–15; early man, 15, 19–34; early primates, 10–13; food-gatherers, 154–68; lower animals, 1–6.
  used for: boring, 188–9; carpentry and fine woodwork, 307, 311–12, 517–18, 611–12, 613, 685, 687–90, 696; drilling, 189–93, 612–13, 679; engraving, 642, 648–9; farming, 513–14, 620; iron smelting, 596; ivory work, 679–80; masonry, 481; mining, 514–15, 560–3,

Tools and weapons (*cont.*)
    567, 574; quarrying, 478, 479; rope-making, 454; smoothing pottery, 390.
  see also under specific names of tools and weapons.
Torches, 233–4, 566, 567.
Tortoise-core technique, 29–30, 31, 35, 132–4.
Trade and commerce:
  beginnings, 44, 52, 54–7, 500–1, 704.
  assisted by invention of writing, 102–3.
  a factor in the diffusion of culture, 78–9.
  in copper, 563–4.
  in incense, 295.
  in ivory, 664.
  in pottery, 401, 406, 408–9.
  in radishes, 356.
  in silver and lead, 583.
  in timber, 685.
  in tin, 589, 591.
  in tools, 500–1.
  see also Weights and measures.
Transport:
  beginnings, 704–5.
  bridges, 256, 714–15.
  pack transport, 705–7, 728.
  roads, 712–14.
  sledges, 205, 206, 210, 479, 481, 516, 707–11.
  see also Wheeled vehicles.
Tread-traps, 518.
Trees, cultivation of, 371, 372, 450, 551–4.
  for Timber *see under* Wood.
Trobriand Islanders, 119–20, 739, 742.
Tutankhamen's tomb, 658, table F.
  objects from: baskets, 422, 450, plate 10 B; bow-drill, 224; chariot, 722, 728; coffin of gold, 660, frontispiece, plate 22; cosmetic jar, plate 3; dagger of iron, 618, 619; furniture, 686, 691–6, 699, 701, plates 23–5; headrest of iron, 654; natron, 269; pigment, 239; pottery wine-jar, 283; textiles, 440, 448, plate 16; writing materials, plate 32.

Upper Palaeolithic culture, *see* Cultures.
Urali Kurumbars of Wynad, India, 410 (14).

Varnish, *see* Chemical arts.
Vegetables, *see* Plants, cultivation of.
Vinegar, 285.
Vision, Visual faculty:
  co-ordinated with touch in higher primates, 8.
  man's capacity for sustained visual attention, 12.
  power of, related to skilled behaviour, 6, 7–8, 33.
  in racial groups, 35–6.
Viticulture, 282–4.

Warfare:
cavalry, 728–9.
chariots in, 209–10, 713, 718, 724–8.
development of the galley, 741–3.
water-supply problems in desert campaigns, 526–7; destruction of irrigation systems, 554–5.
Water-supply, *see* Irrigation.
Weapons, *see* Tools and weapons, *and under specific names*.
Weaving, 414, 415, 417, 422, plates 13, 16, 17.
in the girdle of Rameses III, 441, plates 14, 15.
techniques, 428–31, 437; 'sprang', 442.
twill weaves, 430, 443, 445.
see also Textiles.
Weights and measures:
balance, use of the, 779, plate 31 B.
of capacity, 781–3.
standardization, 110, 774–5, 783–4.
weight standards, 779–81.
see also Measurement.
Welding, *see* Metal, soldering and welding.
Wheat, 363–7, 522, plate 7.
Wheel:
diffusion of, 203–4, 207, 209–11, 716.
dimensions of early wheels, 209.
evolution of, 71–2, 80, 187, 194–5, 206–7, 716.
spoked wheel, development of, 211–14, 721.
see also Potter's wheel; Spinning wheel; Wheeled vehicles.
Wheeled vehicles:
origins, 209–11, 704.
carts and wagons, 716–19.
chariots, 209–10, 700–1, 713, 718, 720, 724–8.
draught animals, 719–24.
with solid wheels and paired draught, 204–9, 716.
with spoked wheels, 211–14.
Windlass, 214, 566, 735.
Wine, 275–7, 281–5, 782.
Wire, 655–7.
Woad, 247, 249.
Women:
as basket-makers, 173, 413–14.
as beasts of burden, 705.
as food-gatherers, 154–5, 177.
as potters, 49, 407, 408.
as spinners and weavers, 437, 438, 443–4.
Wood:
fine woodwork: craftsmanship and techniques, 685, 687–96; growth and development, 696–702.
Wood (*cont.*)
fire produced by wood-friction, 220–6.
as fuel, 229, 230, 576.
furniture, 685, 686, 689, 692–3, 696–702.
sculpturing of, 689–90, 699, 702.
sources of timber, 684–7.
structures of, 143, 300–24, 371–2, 469, 472, plate 4.
tools and weapons, 30, 32–3, 70, 141–3, 517–18; *see also* Bamboo.
torches, 233–4.
vessels of, 517–18, 685.
wheels: potters', 196; vehicle, 204, 206, 207–8.
Woodhenge, 314–15, 493.
Wool:
composition of, 451.
industry in Mesopotamia and Syria, 248–9.
Scandinavian textiles of, 442.
Writing, alphabetic:
origin of the alphabet, 762.
Brahmi, Sanskrit, Prakrit, 771–2.
early Latin, 770–1.
Etruscan, 769–70.
Greek, 767–8, 769–71.
Nabataean, 766, 767.
Phoenician, 763–8.
Ugaritic, 762–3.
Writing, pre-alphabetic:
Chinese, 772.
cuneiform script, 83, 103, 750–2, 757, 763, plates 29 B, 30 B.
Cypriote, 761.
Elamite, 760–1.
hieratic script, 754, 759.
hieroglyphs: of the Egyptians, 80, 192, 222, 223, 237, 263, 281, 439–40, 747, 752–7, 785; of the Hittites, 757–8, 761; of the Mayas, 83; of the Sumerians, 80, 101–2, 205, 206, 252, 280, 745–7, 761.
Indus, 760.
invention, 49, 53–4, 80, 101–2, 744–7, 785; social consequences of, 102–3.
materials for: in Egypt, 245, 753–4, 757, plate 32; in Mesopotamia, 750–1.
Minoan, 758–9.
of numbers, 785–6.
syllabic signs, 747–50.
see also Inscriptions.

Yami of Botel-Tobago Island, 118–19.
Yokuts of central California, 173–4.
Yukaghir peoples of Siberia, 179.

Ziggurats, 467–9.

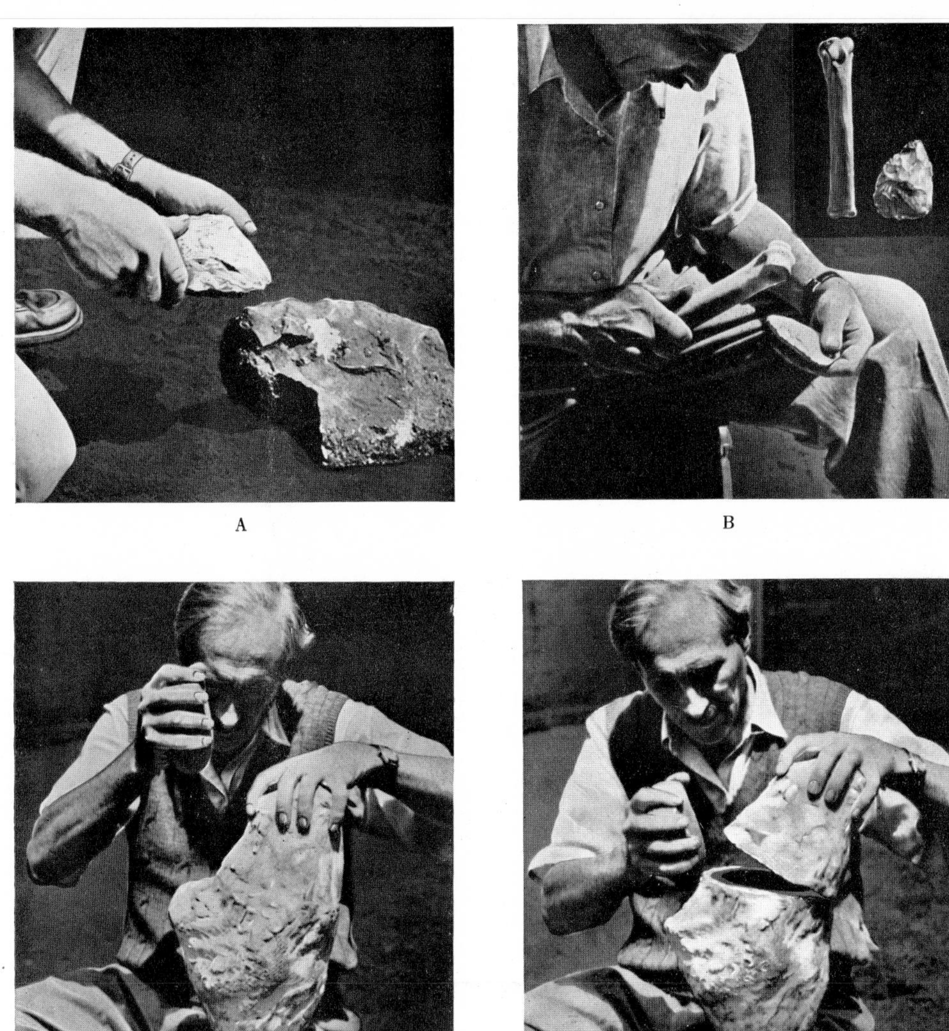

A B

C D

Flint-working techniques

A. *Removal of flakes by the* anvil technique. *The stone from which flakes are to be struck is held in both hands and so swung against a projection on the anvil, with the correct angle of impact, that a flake is removed from the upper part. The scar of the first flake so removed can be seen.* (p 130) B. *Making an Acheulian-type hand-axe with a bone* cylinder-hammer, *here the metacarpal of a horse. The action is from the wrist, only light blows are struck, and the hammer is never more than 6 to 8 inches from the work. A finger held beneath the flint controls the pressure where the flakes are to be struck off.* (Inset) *Hammer and finished axe.* (p 131) C *and* D. Quartering technique. *Note the direction of the blow upon a projection of the flint nodule. As the hammer-stone strikes the projection the nodule is split along a plane more or less at right angles to the direction of the blow. This fracture has no bulb of percussion. The projection which was struck will be useless because of cracks, but the main upper and lower parts of the block will serve as cores for blades.* (p 134)
Demonstrations by L. S. B. Leakey

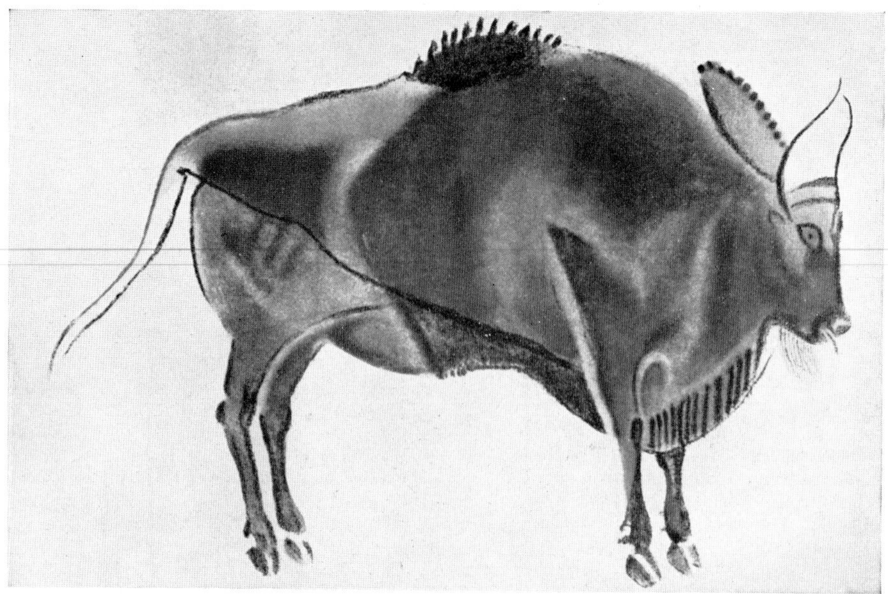

A. *Bison, outlined with a brush and daubed, from Altamira, Spain. Length about 1·7 m.* (p 148)

B. *Horse, depicted by 'dotting', from the Covalanas cave, Cantabria mountains, Spain. Length about 1·2 m.* (p 149)

Late Palaeolithic representations of animals

A. *Cosmetic jar, carved in calcite, from the tomb of Tutankhamen.* c 1350 B.C.

(p 286)

B. *Canopic jars of Dynasty XXI. Egypt.* c 1000 B.C.

(p 268)

PLATE 4

Worked oak timbers and wattle-work in the foundations of mound LVI, Glastonbury lake-village, Somerset. Iron Age
(See also figure 206)
(p 320)

A. *Italian Neolithic fragments of wall-daub showing impressions of wattle-work*

Scale in inches and cm

(ch 12)

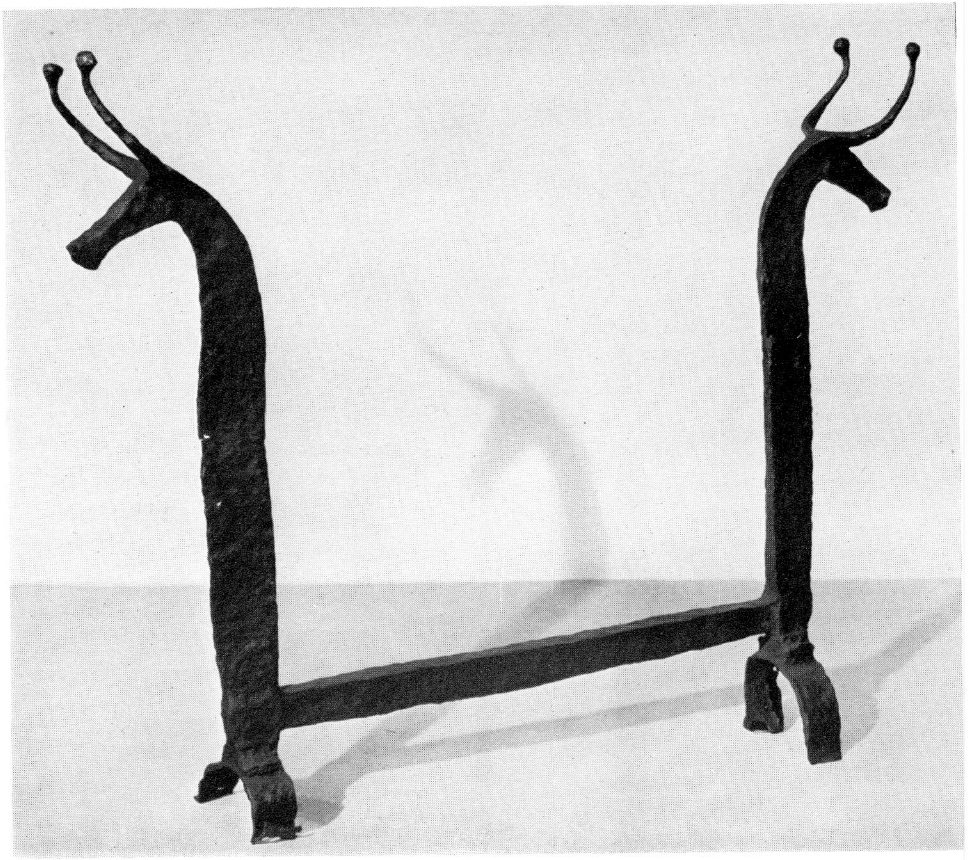

B. *One of a pair of Iron Age fire-dogs from Cambridgeshire. Logs were laid upon the horizontal bar, and another bar was laid across between the horns for the suspension of cooking-pots, etc.*

(p 232)

A. *Deer-shooting with a decoy. From a mosaic found at Lillebonne, Normandy. Second century* A.D.

(p 337)

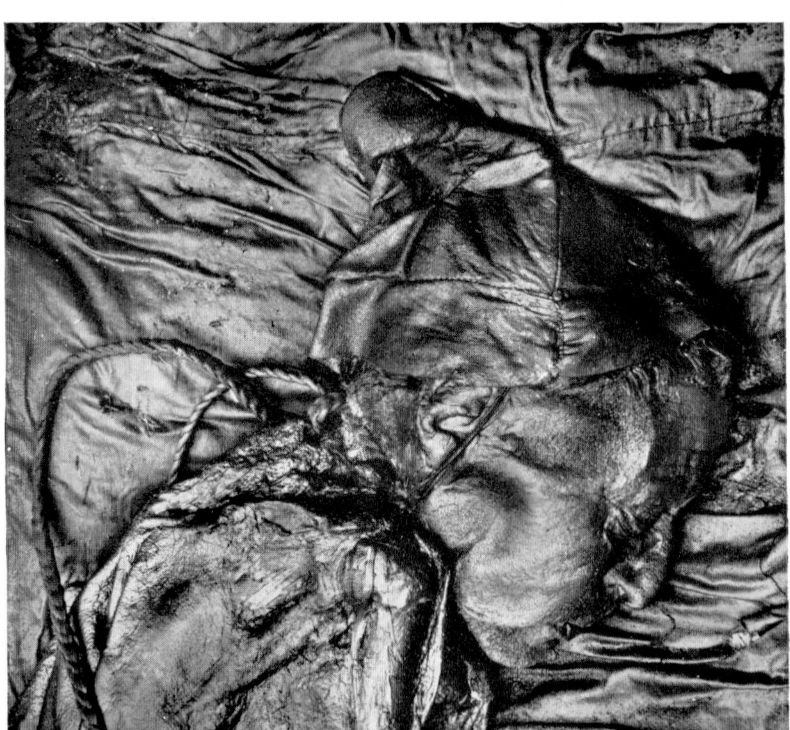

B. *Head of an Iron Age man whose body remained preserved in a peat bog for 2000 years near Tollund, Denmark. The leather noose by which he was hanged, probably sacrificially, was left round his neck*

(pp 355, 359)

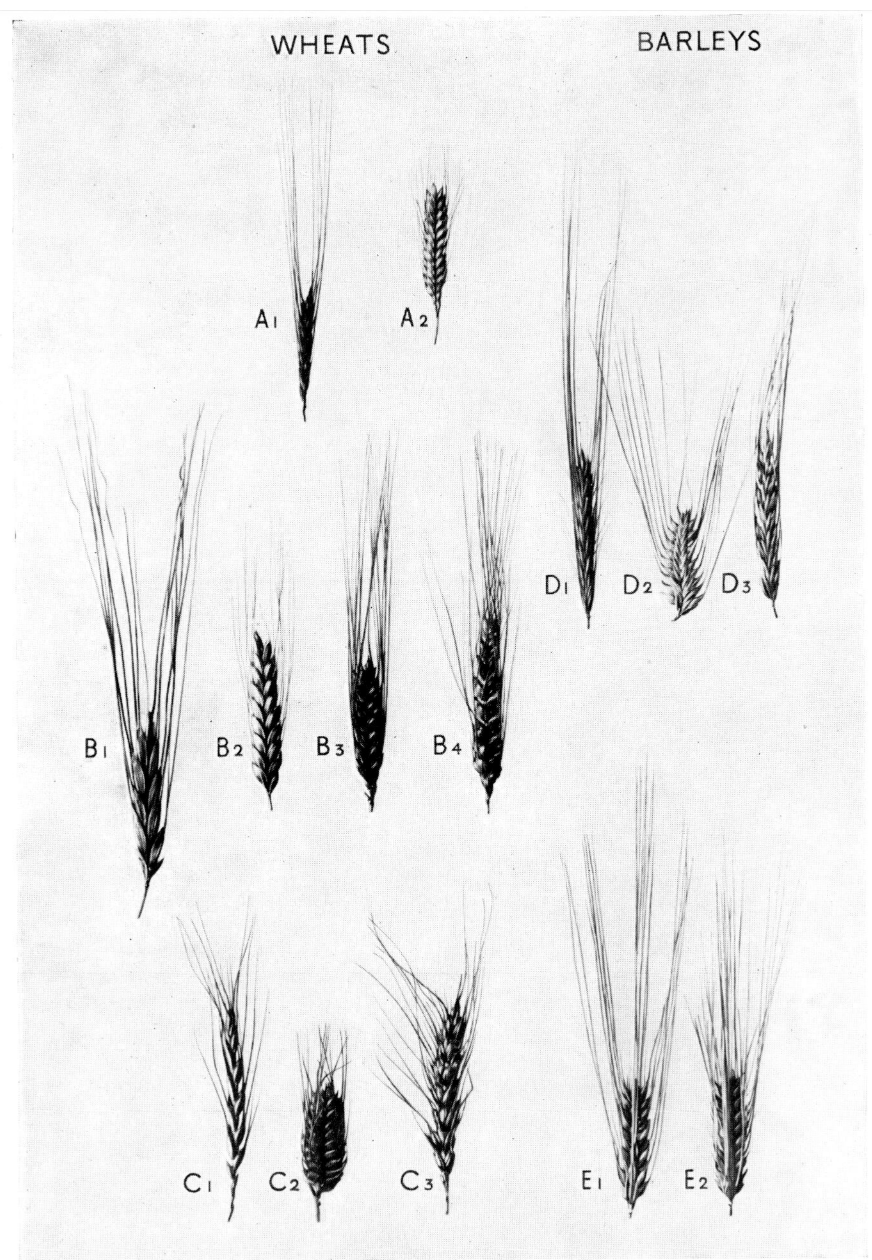

Ears of wheat, genus Triticum

A. *Einkorn group*: (1) *wild*, T. aegilopoides; (2) *cultivated*, T. monococcum. B. *Emmer group*: (1) *wild*, T. dicoccoides; (2) *cultivated*, T. dicoccum; (3) *macaroni-wheat*, T. durum; (4) *rivet-wheat*, T. turgidum. C. *Bread-wheat group*: (1) *spelt*, T. spelta; (2) *club-wheat*, T. compactum; (3) *bread-wheat*, T. vulgare. (p 363)

Ears of barley, genus Hordeum

D. *Two-row*, H. distichum: (1) *wild*, H. spontaneum; (2) *dense-eared*, H. zeocriton; (3) *lax-eared*, H. nutans. E. *Six-row*, H. polystichum: (1) *lax-eared*, H. tetrastichum; (2) *dense-eared*, H. hexastichum. (p 367)

A

B

C

D

Some Western Neolithic pottery types

A. 'Unstan' *bowl, showing a sharp carination where the moulded base joins the nearly vertical rim, which was perhaps made on a turn-table. These thin flat bowls may have been used for cheese-making. From Eilean an Tighe, North Uist.* (pp 385, 387) B. *Bell-beaker with everted lip and zoned decoration, from Radley, Berks.* (p 404) C. *Jar, the upper part of which is ridged externally, providing horizontal zones with deeply incised decoration. From Eilean an Tighe.* (pp 384, 404) D. *Bowl* (*restored*), *showing a carination to produce a sharp change in the direction of the wall of the vessel. From Eilean an Tighe.* (pp 384, 387, 402). *Scale 1/4*

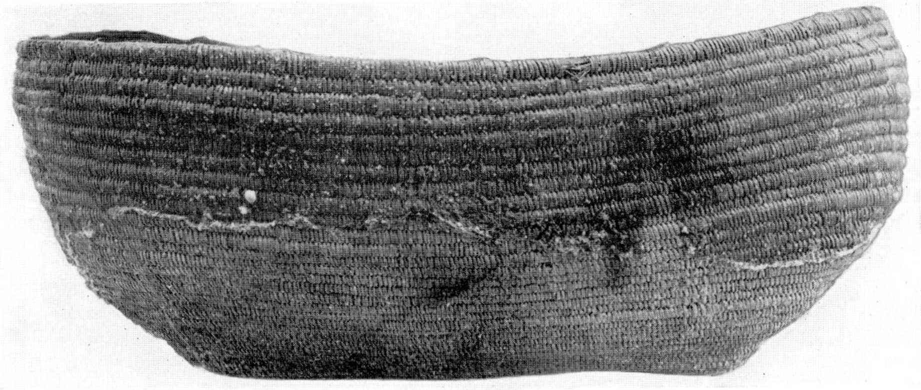

A. *Egyptian Neolithic boat-shaped basket*
Fayum A; c 4500 *B.C. Length 41 cm.* (p 418)

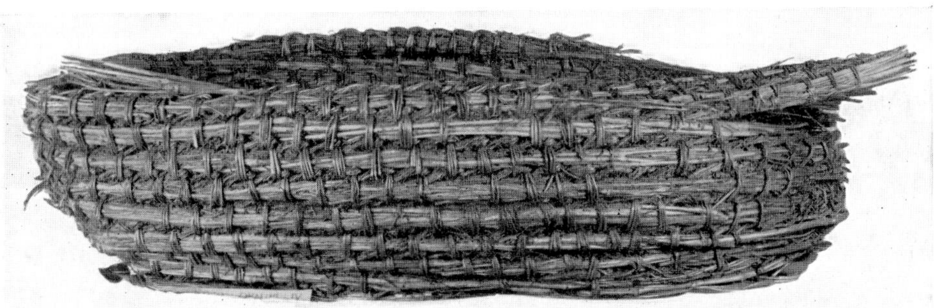

B. *Hamper coffin of woven rushes from Tarkhan, Egypt*
c 3400 *B.C. Length 117 cm.* (p 420)

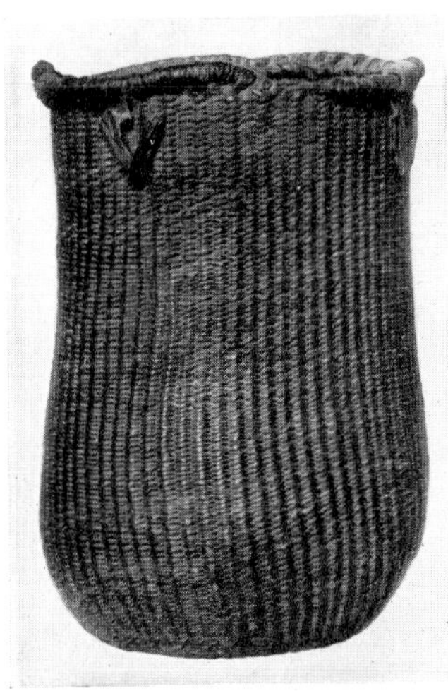

C. *Basket of woven esparto-grass, from Cueva de los Murcielagos, Andalusia. Height 14 cm.* (p 421)

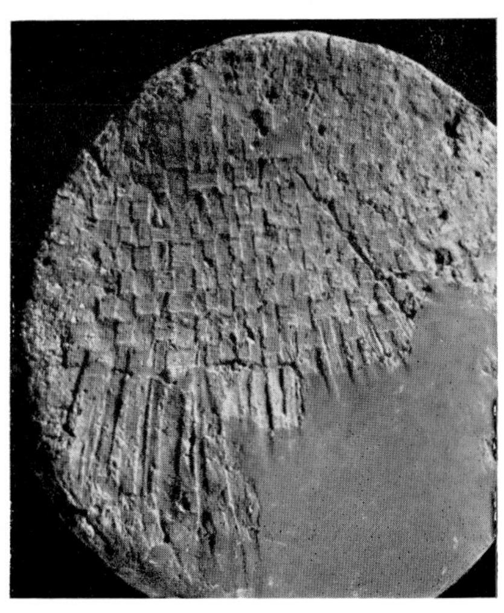

D. *Impression on a clay plate of a plain-weave rush mat, Swiss lake-villages.* c 2500 *B.C. Diameter* c *15 cm.* (p 421)

Basket-work

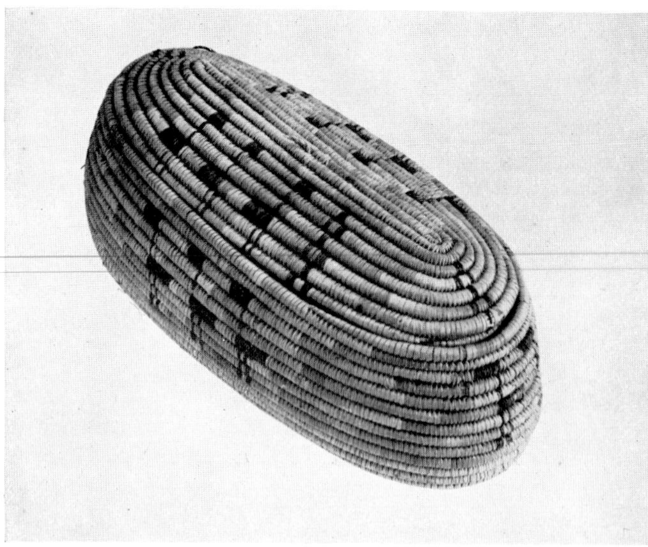

A. *Oval basket from the tomb of Meryet-Amen, Thebes.* c *1440* B.C. (p 422)

B. *Basket-work bottle* (*height 26 cm*), *and round basket with lid* (*diameter 19 cm*), *from the tomb of Tutankhamen, Thebes.* c *1350* B.C. (p 423)

Basket-work

A. *Fragment of linen from Fayum A*; c 4500 B.C. *Actual size.* (p 431)

B. *Front and back of the selvedge fringe on a fabric from Tarkhan.* c 2700 B.C. *Scale 3/2.* (p 434)

Early Egyptian textiles

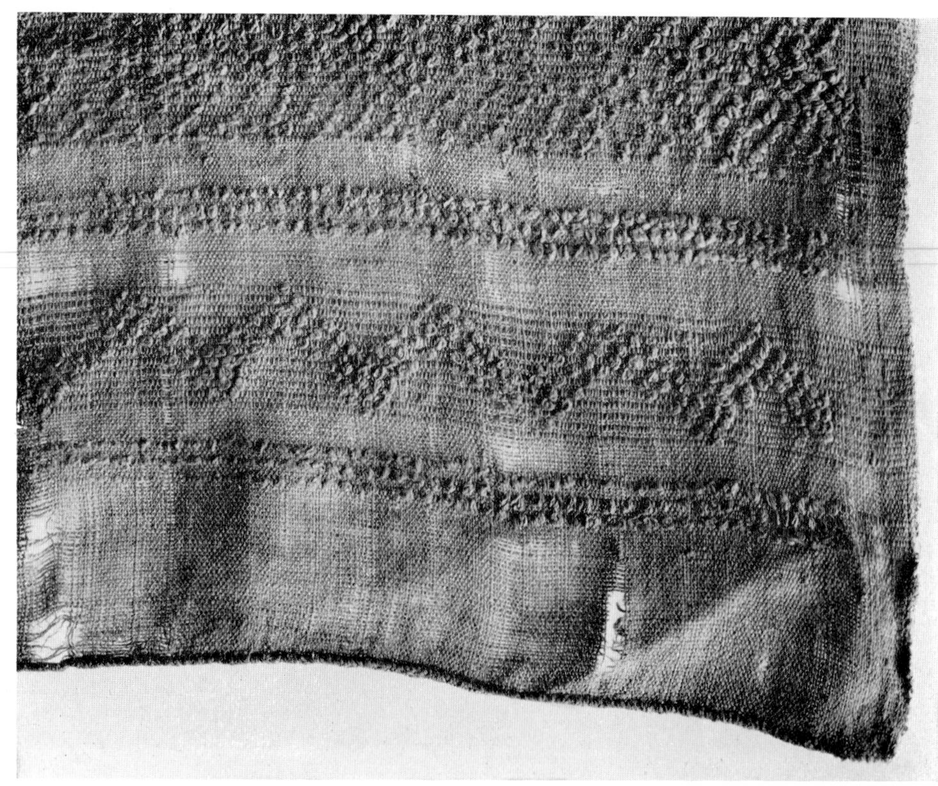

A. *Part of a towel, with loops arranged in a pattern, from Deir el-Bahri, Egypt.* c *2160* B.C. *Average size of these towels 52×45 cm*

(p 435)

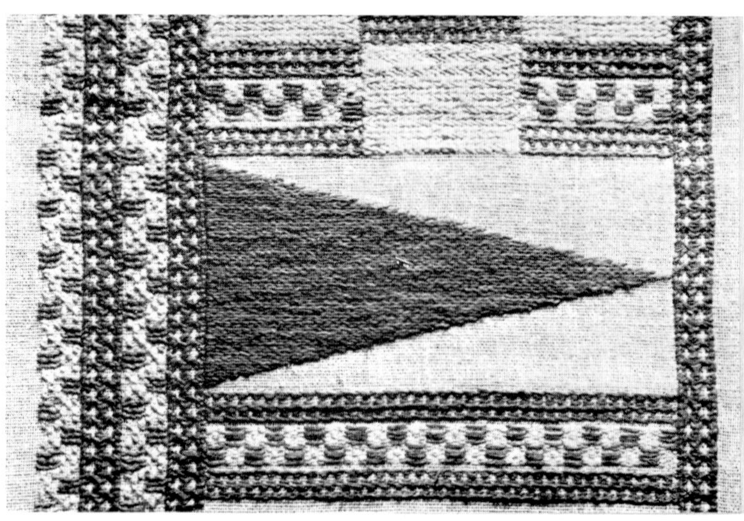

B. *Part of a reconstruction of a fabric in a patterned Soumak weave, found at Irgenhausen lake-village, Zürich.* c *2000* B.C. *Scale ½*

(p 436)

A. *Model of a spinning- and weaving-room, from the tomb of Meketre, Deir el-Bahri, Egypt.* c *1800* B.C.

(pp 427, 437)

B. *Braid on a linen saddle-cloth from the tomb of Senmut, Deir el-Bahri.* c *1500* B.C. *Actual size*

(p 441)

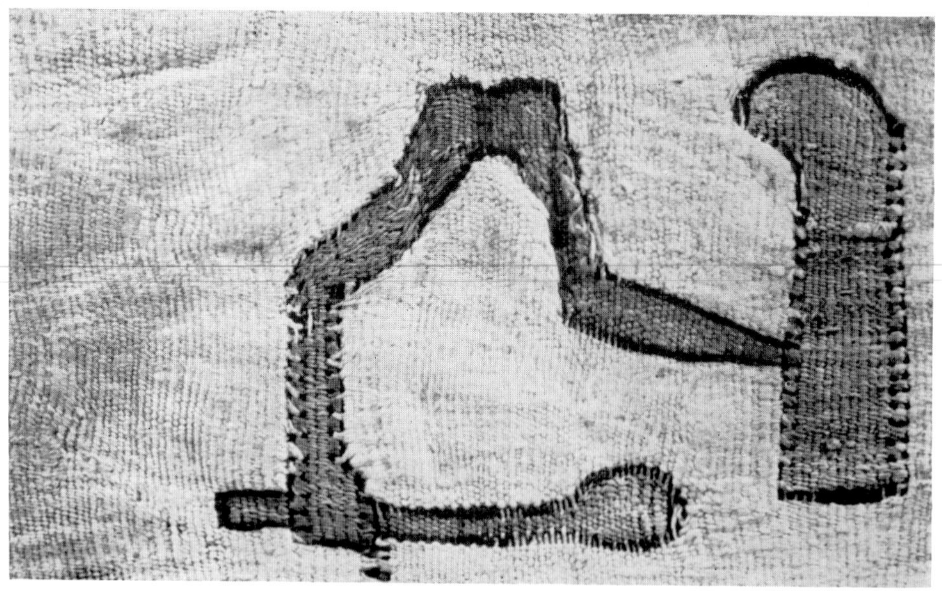

A. *Detail of a tapestry from the tomb of Thothmes IV, showing the* 'ka-*name*' *of Thothmes III* (×2)
(p 439)

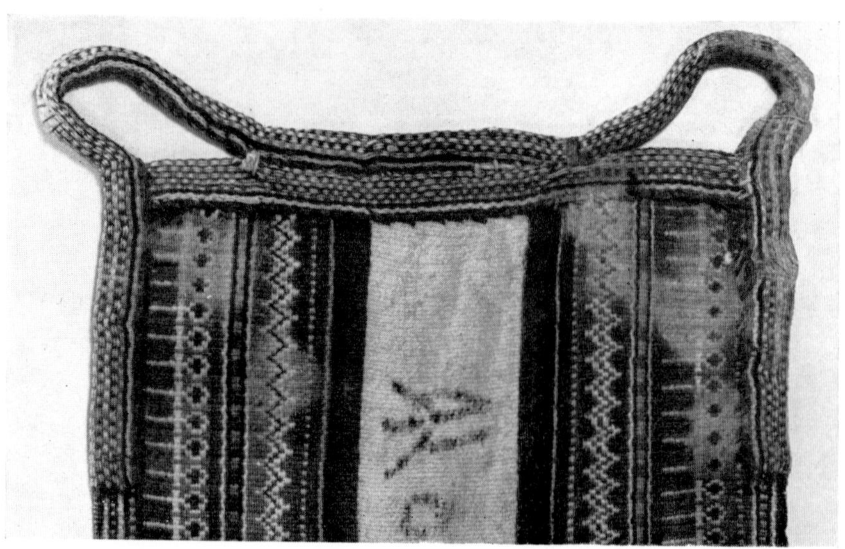

B. *Front of one end of the girdle of Rameses III.* c 1170 B.C.
(p 441)

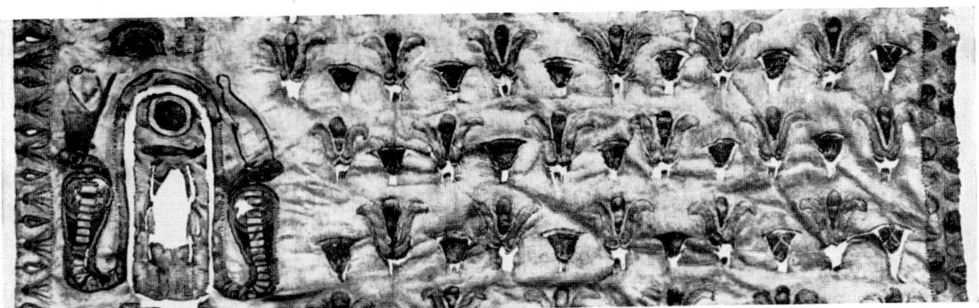

A. *Part of another tapestry from the tomb of Thothmes IV, with the name of Amenhetep II. From Thebes, Egypt.* c *1400* B.C. *Width 42 cm*

(p 439)

B. *Back of the girdle of Rameses III. Scale in cm*

(p 441)

PLATE 16

Embroidered linen tunic and sleeves, with braids of warp-face weave, from the tomb of Tutankhamen. c *1350 B.C. 113·5×95 cm*

(p 440)

A. *Girl's dress (woollen top, belt, and corded skirt), found at Egtved, Denmark, Bronze Age*

(p 442)

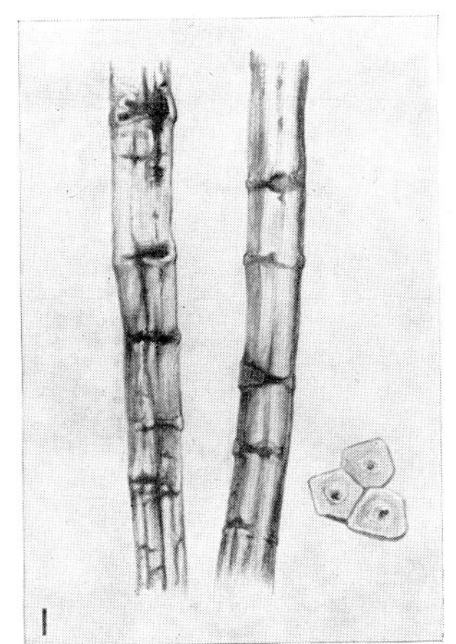

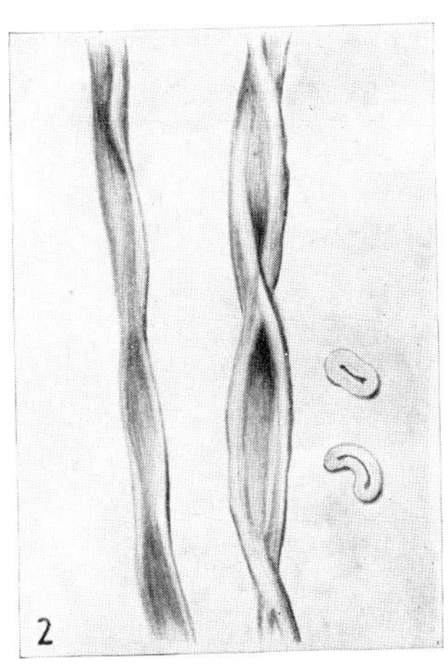

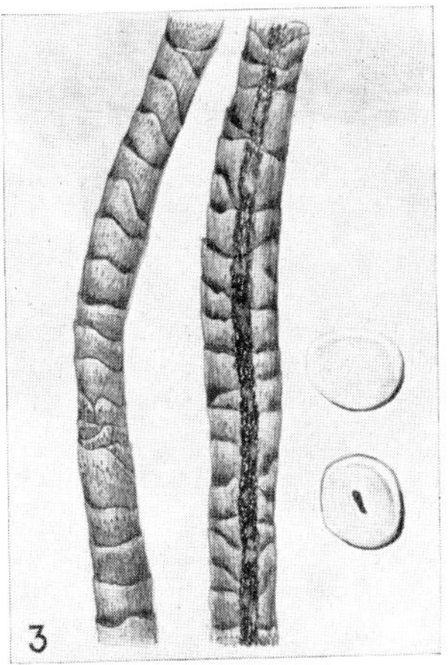

B. *Drawings of textile fibres.* (1) *Flax,* (2) *cotton,* (3) *wool.* (×250).

(pp 424, 448–51)

Reconstruction of Babylon viewed over the Ishtar Gate. To the right on the horizon is the 'Tower of Babel'. (See also figure 286.)

(p 471)

Reconstruction of an entrance colonnade. Masonry of King Zoser, Saqqara, Egypt. c 2600 B.C.
(p 476)

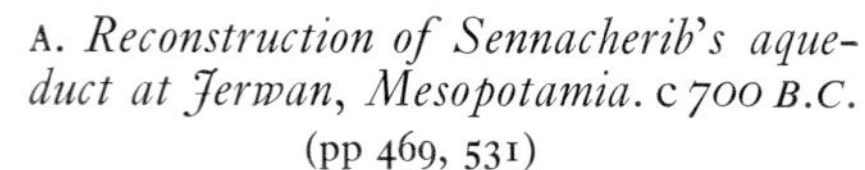

A. *Reconstruction of Sennacherib's aqueduct at Jerwan, Mesopotamia.* c *700 B.C.*
(pp 469, 531)

B. *Egypt: the Nile in flood*
(p 535)

A. *Marks of dressing on a trilithon upright at Stonehenge, showing grooves formed by pounding*

(p 493)

B. *Map of fields and irrigation canals near Nippur, Mesopotamia.* c *1300* B.C. *(For a transcription see figure 364.)*

(p 550)

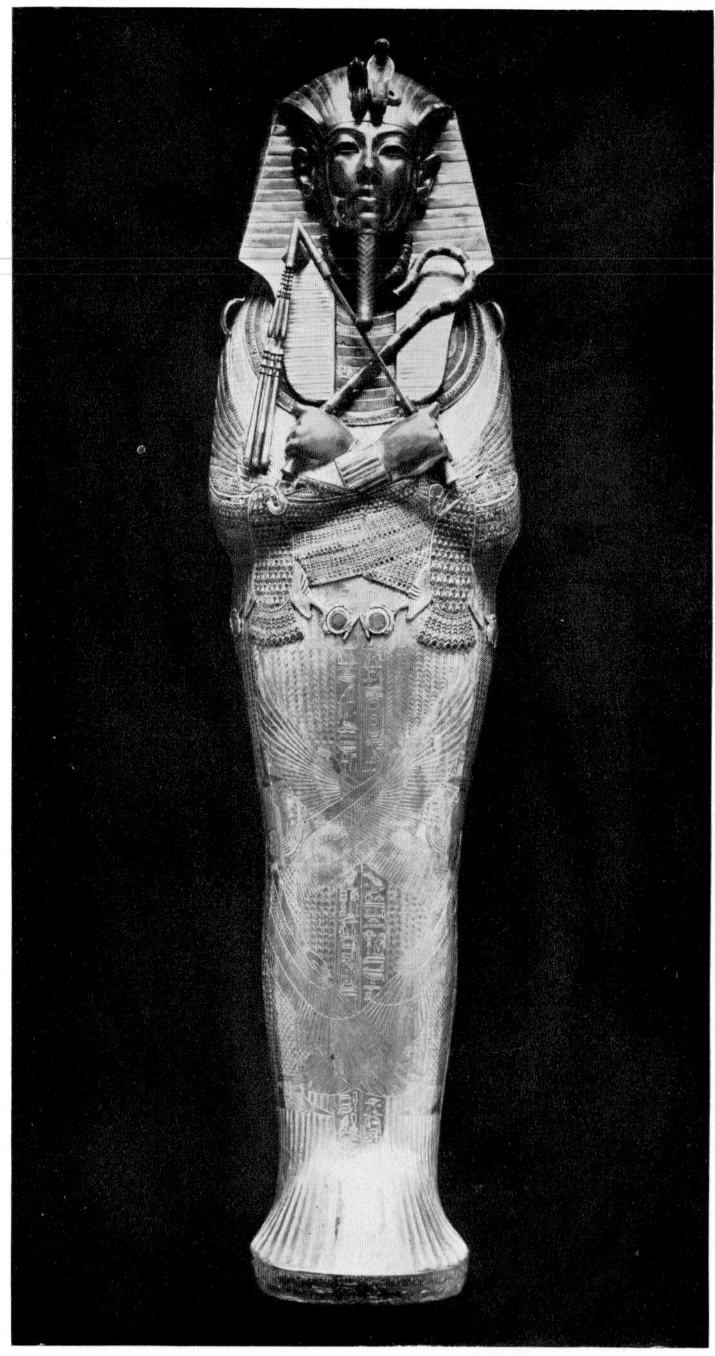

The gold inner coffin of Tutankhamen
(*A painting of the upper part of this coffin is reproduced as the frontispiece.*) c 1350 B.C.

(p 660)

Carved and stained panel, made in sections of ivory. From a casket found in the tomb of Tutankhamen. The scene shows the Pharaoh, Queen, and maidens in a garden. Height 31 cm

(p 669)

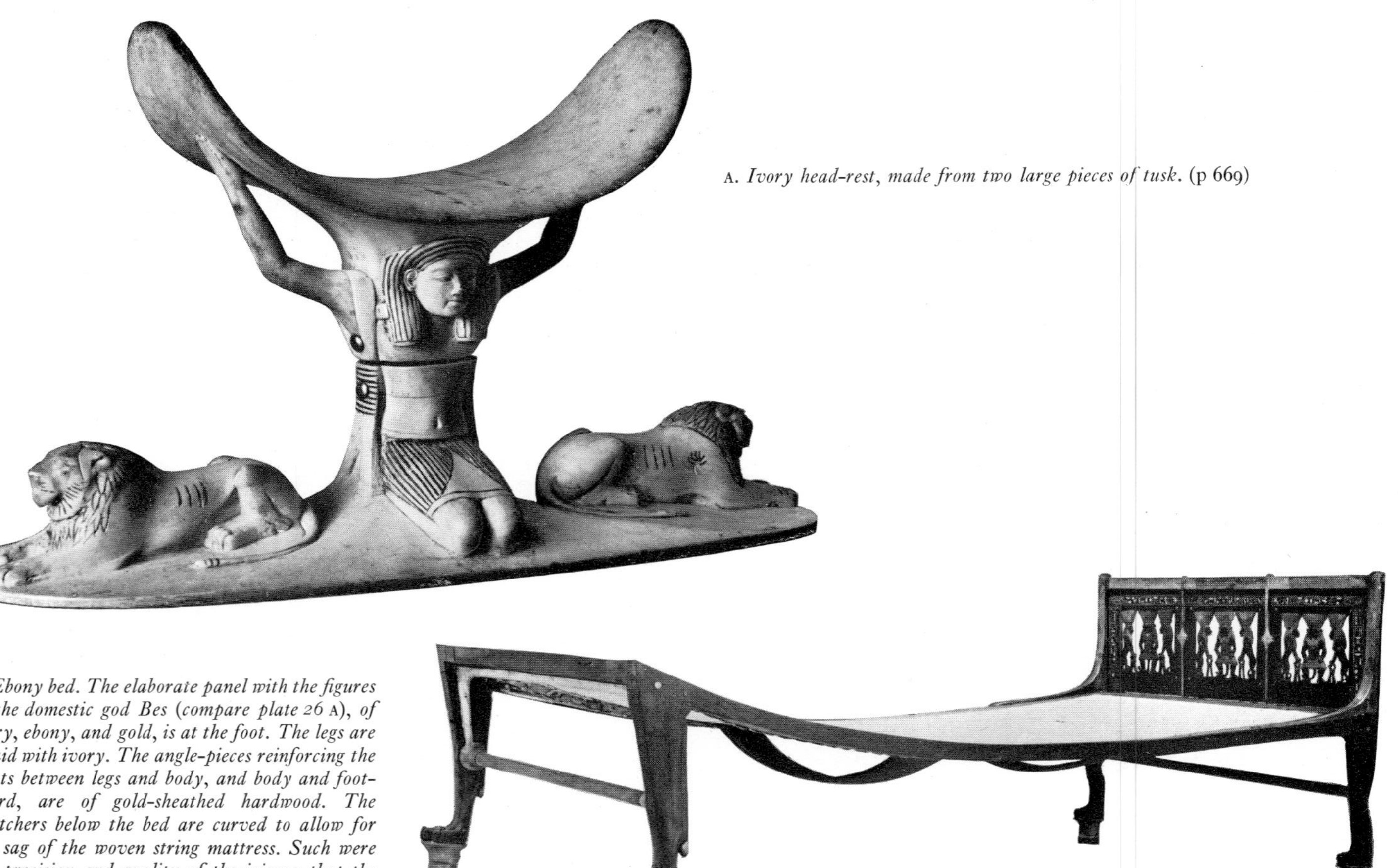

A. *Ivory head-rest, made from two large pieces of tusk.* (p 669)

B. *Ebony bed. The elaborate panel with the figures of the domestic god Bes (compare plate 26 A), of ivory, ebony, and gold, is at the foot. The legs are inlaid with ivory. The angle-pieces reinforcing the joints between legs and body, and body and foot-board, are of gold-sheathed hardwood. The stretchers below the bed are curved to allow for the sag of the woven string mattress. Such were the precision and quality of the joinery that the ebony has not warped appreciably since the bed was made.* (pp 686, 692, 701)

Furniture from Tutankhamen's tomb

A. *Chair of state, of cedar-wood left plain. The claws of the animal feet are of ivory, all other embellishments of leaf gold. The sloping back supported by upright struts was usual at this period. The openwork panel is carved with a figure of Eternity supporting the names of the king. A gold-plated openwork decoration was torn from the lower rails by plunderers.* (pp 692, 701)

B. *Stool, of a coniferous wood inlaid with ivory and ebony. The design, with its reinforcing styles and diagonal members, copies light constructions in rush-work. The mortises of the side-rails are cut higher than those of the front rails in order not to weaken the legs unduly. The pegs are left exposed and capped with ivory bosses.* (pp 685, 701)

Furniture from Tutankhamen's tomb

PLATE 26

B. *Detail of one of the panels of Hesi-Re* (c 2750 B.C.). *Eleven large panels of cedar-wood were found in the tomb of this official. Here skilful carving in high relief shows Hesi-Re wearing a curled wig and cloak, with a scribe's outfit hanging over his right shoulder, seated before an offering-table.* (p 697)

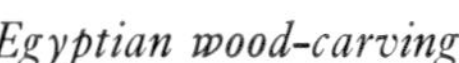

A. *Stile in the form of a figure of the god Bes. This carving formed an upright element in an openwork panel similar to that shown in plate* 24 B. *The kilt and the shawl tied round the shoulders were originally inlaid with ivory, of which one fragment remains in place. Other incisions were inlaid with yellow paste. Tongues for fitting into the rails may be seen at the top of the headdress and below the right foot.* (p 692)

Egyptian wood-carving

A Maori war-canoe as drawn by a member of Captain Cook's expedition. The dug-out hull has wash-strakes lashed along each bulwark to give additional freeboard

(p 739)

Inscription of Darius on the Rock of Behistun, Persia. The slab to the left of the sculpture shows the Babylonian version. Three columns below this version are inscribed in Susian. The Persian version is below the sculpture. c 500 B.C.

(p 752)

A. *Detail of the Rock of Behistun. Darius and his prisoners, the chiefs of subdued provinces. The inscriptions above the heads are partly in Susian, partly in Persian. They describe the persons represented in the sculpture. The figure of Darius is 5 ft 8 in high.*
(p 752)

B. *Babylonian syllabary inscribed with names, pronunciations, and meanings of cuneiform characters. 442* B.C. (p 752)

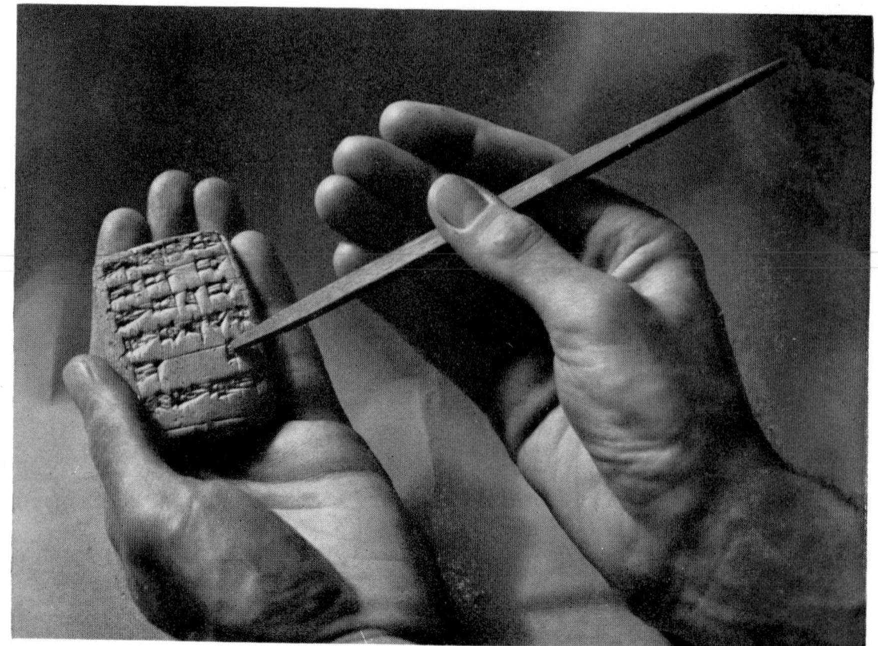

A. *Method of writing on a clay tablet*
(p 750)

B. *Tablet from Ugarit, Syria, written in alphabetic cuneiform.* c 1300 B.C.
(p 763)

A. *Inscription from the tomb of Ahiram at Jebail (ancient Gebal, Byblos), Lebanon. Eleventh century* B.C.

(p 763)

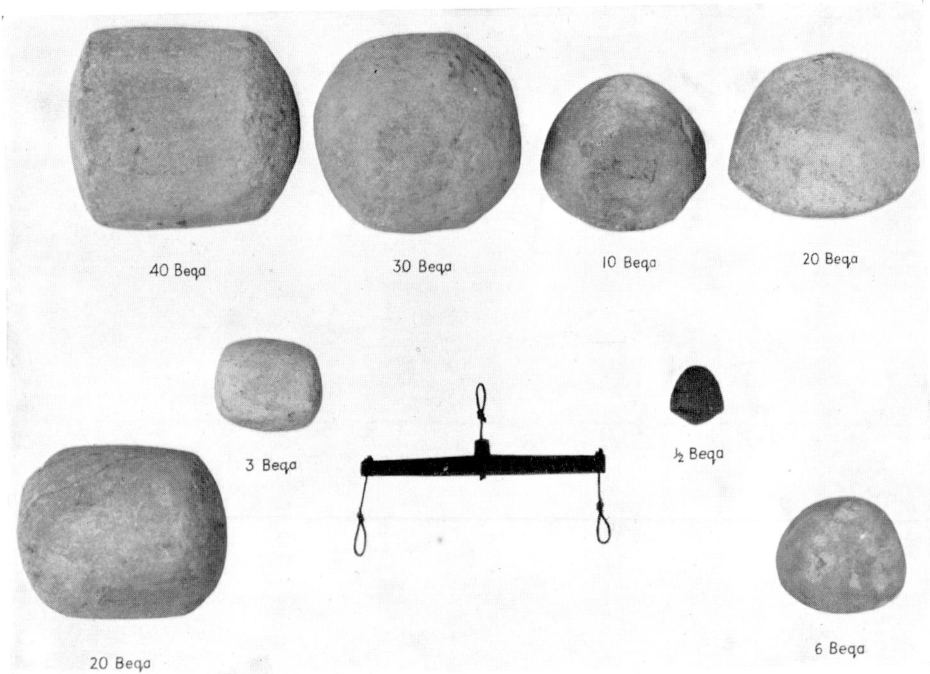

B. *Prehistoric Egyptian balance and weights. The balance is of red limestone, length 8·5 cm. The weights are of limestone; those on the left (Amratian period) being in the form of cylinders, while those on the right (Gerzean period) are cones with convex bases. All are from Naqada, Egypt, and probably fifth millennium* B.C. *1* beqa = *200 grains = 12·95 g*

(p 779)

Late Babylonian table for the motions of the planet Jupiter
Scale in cm (pp 786, 800)

Rev.	I	II	III	IV		V	VI	VII
	[17]	[7,30]	[7,55]	[12,48, 5	pa kur-ád]	[7]	[7,42]	[4,30,46]
	[18]	[7,36]	[7,47,24]	[12,55,52,2]4	pa kur-ád	[8]	[7,52]	[4,22,54]
	[19]	[7,4]2	7,39,[42]	13,[3,32,]6	pa kur-ád	9	[8, 2]	[4,14,52]
	[20]	[7,]48	7,31,54	13,1[1,4	pa] kur-ád	10	8,12	4, 6,40
	[21]	7,54	7,24	13,[18,28	pa kur]-ád	11	8,22	3,58,18
	[22]	8	7,16	13,[25,44	pa kur]-ád	12	8,32	3,49,[4]6
	[23]	8, 6	7, 7,54	13,32,51,[54	pa kur]-ád	13	8,42	3,41, 4
	[2]4	8,12	6,59,42	13,39,51,36	[pa kur]-ád	14	8,52	3,3[2],12
	25	8,18	6,51,24	13,46,43	pa kur-ád	15	9, 2	3,23,10
	26	8,24	6,43	13,53,26	pa kur-ád	16	9,12	3,13,58
	27	8,30	6,3[4,30]	14, ., .,30	[pa kur]-ád	17	9,22	3, 4,36
	28	8,36	6,2[5,54]	14, 6,26,24	[pa kur]-ád	18	9,32	2,55, 4
	29	8,42	6,17,[12]	14,12,43,[36]	pa kur-ád	19	9,42	2,45,2[2]
	še 1	8,48	[6,]8,24	14,18,52	pa kur-ád	20	9,52	2,35,30
	2	8,54	5,59,30	14,24,51,30	pa kur-ád	21	10, 2	2,25,28
	3	9	5,50,30	14,30,42	pa kur[-ád]	22	10,12	2,15,16
	4	9, 6	5,41,24	14,36,23,24	pa kur [-ád]	23	10,22	2, 4,[5]4
	5	9,12	5,32,12	14,41,55,36	pa kur-ád	[24]	10,32	1,54,[22]
	6	9,18	5,22,54	14,47,18,30	pa kur-ád	25	10,42	1,43,40
	[7]	9,24	5,13,30	14,52,32	pa kur-ád	26	10,52	1,3[2],4[8]
	[8]	[9],30	5, 4	14,57,36	pa kur-ád	27	11, 2	1,2[1,46]
	[9]	[9],36	4,54,24	15, 2,30,24	pa kur-ád	28	11,12	1,1[0,34]
	[10]	[9,4]2	4,44,42	15, 7,15, 6	pa kur-ád	29	11,22	5[9,12]
	[11]	[9,48]	4,34,54	15,11,50	pa kur-ád	30	11,32	[47,40]
	[12]	[9,54]	[4,]25	15,16,15	pa kur-ád	i[zi] 1	11,42	[35,58]
	[13]	[10]	[4,]15	15,20,30	pa kur-ád	2	11,52	[24, 6]
	[14]	[10, 6]	[4, 4,]54	15,24,34,54	pa kur-ád	3	12, 2	[12, 4]
	[15]	[10,12]	[3,54,4]2	15,28,29,36	pa kur-ád	4	12,12	[///]
	[16]	[10,18]	[3,44,24]	15,32,14	pa kur-ád	5	12, 6	[///]
	[17]	[10,24]	[3,34]	[15,3]5,48	pa kur-ád	6	12, 1	[///]
	[18]	[10,30]	[3,23,30]	[15],39,11,30	pa kur-ád	7	11[///]	[///]
	[19]	[10,36]	[3,12,54]	[15],42,24,24	pa kur-ád	8	11[///]	[///]
	[20]	[10,42]	[3, 2,12]	[15,4]5,26,36	pa kur-ád	9	11[///]	[///]
	[21]	[10,48]	[2,51,24]	[15,48,18]	pa kur-ád	10	[///]	[///]
	[22]	[10,54]	[2,40,30]	[15,50,58,30	pa] kur-ád	11	[///]	[///]
	[23]	[11]	[2,29,30]	[15,53,28	pa kur-ád]	12	[///]	[///]

Transcription of plate 34

The commas between different numbers have no counterpart in the text and are used only to make a clear separation between sexagesimal places. Final zeros are not expressed in the text, and are shown above as empty spaces, e.g. in column II lines 5 and 15, or column III lines 4 and 5. Internal zeros, however, are denoted by a special sign, here transcribed as a period; thus in column IV line 10 we have 14, ., .,30 for 14° 0′ 0″ 30‴.

PLATE 36

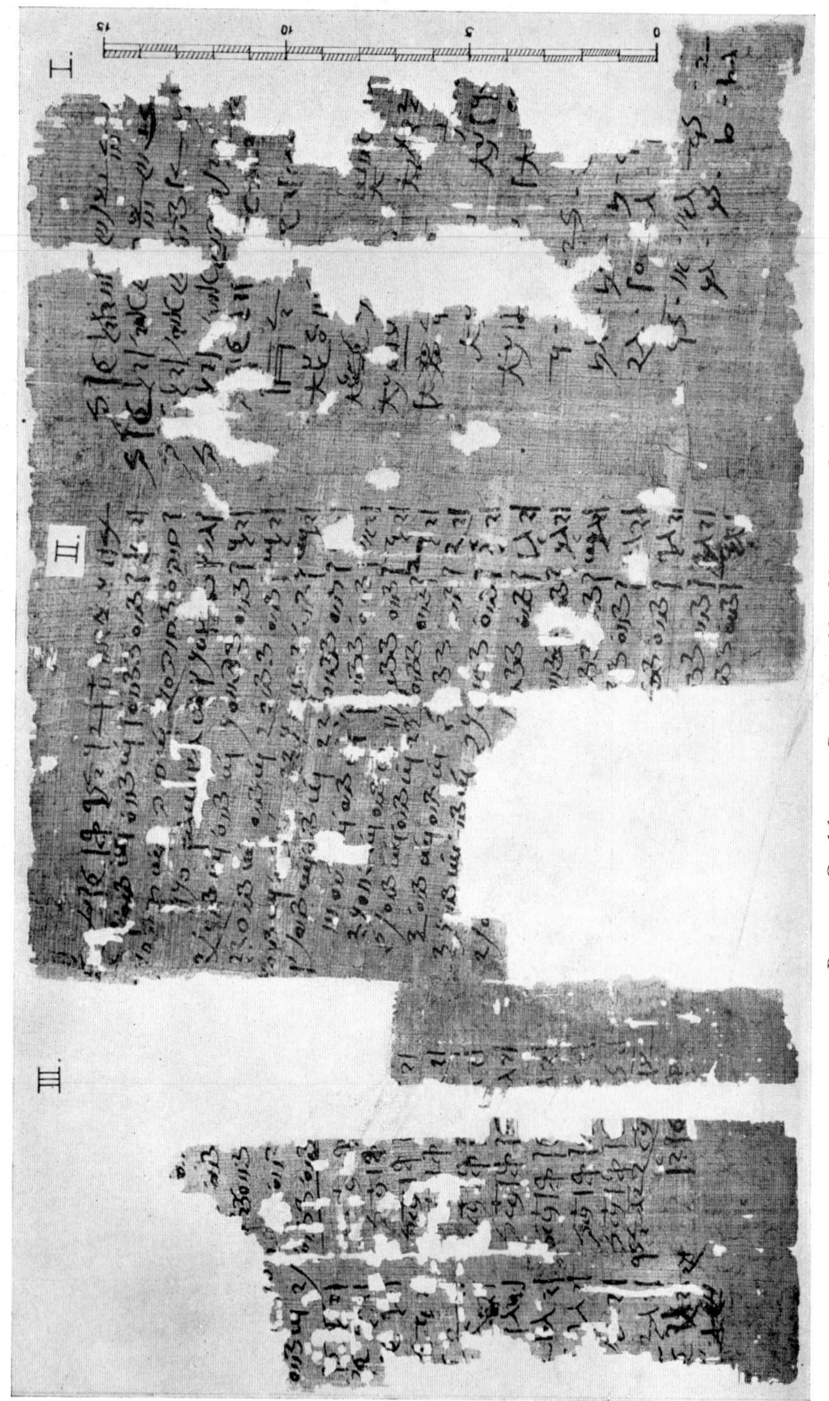

Papyrus Carlsberg 9. Demotic table of lunar months

Scale in cm (pp 754, 797)